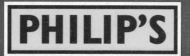

STREET ATLAS Essex

Chelmsford, Colchester, Harlow, Southend-on-Sea

www.philips-maps.co.uk

First published in 2003 by

Philip's, a division of
Octopus Publishing Group Ltd
www.octopusbooks.co.uk
2-4 Heron Quays, London E14 4JP
An Hachette Livre UK Company

Second edition 2008
First impression 2008
ESXBA

ISBN-13 978-0-540-09195-9 (spiral)

© Philip's 2008

This product includes mapping data licensed from Ordnance Survey® with the permission of the Controller of Her Majesty's Stationery Office. © Crown copyright 2008. All rights reserved. Licence number 100011710.

No part of this publication may be reproduced, stored in a retrieval system or transmitted in any form or by any means, electronic, mechanical, photocopying, recording or otherwise, without the permission of the Publishers and the copyright owner.

To the best of the Publishers' knowledge, the information in this atlas was correct at the time of going to press. No responsibility can be accepted for any errors or their consequences.

The representation in this atlas of a road, track or path is no evidence of the existence of a right of way.

Data for the speed cameras provided by PocketGPSWorld.com Ltd.

Ordnance Survey and the OS Symbol are registered trademarks of Ordnance Survey, the national mapping agency of Great Britain.

Printed and bound in Spain
by Cayfosa-Quebecor

Contents

II **List of mobile speed cameras**

III **Key to map symbols**

IV **Key to map pages**

VI **Route planning**

X **Administrative and Postcode boundaries**

1 **Street maps** at 3½ inches to 1 mile

384 **Index** of towns, villages, streets, hospitals, industrial estates, railway stations, schools, shopping centres, universities and places of interest

Digital Data

The exceptionally high-quality mapping found in this atlas is available as digital data in TIFF format, which is easily convertible to other bitmapped (raster) image formats.

The index is also available in digital form as a standard database table. It contains all the details found in the printed index together with the National Grid reference for the map square in which each entry is named.

For further information and to discuss your require… co.uk

Mobile speed cameras

The vast majority of speed cameras used on Britain's roads are operated by safety camera partnerships. These comprise local authorities, the police, Her Majesty's Court Service (HMCS) and the Highways Agency.

This table lists the sites where each safety camera partnership may enforce speed limits through the use of mobile cameras or detectors. These are usually set up on the roadside or a bridge spanning the road and operated by a police or civilian enforcement officer. The speed limit at each site (if available) is shown in red type, followed by the approximate location in black type.

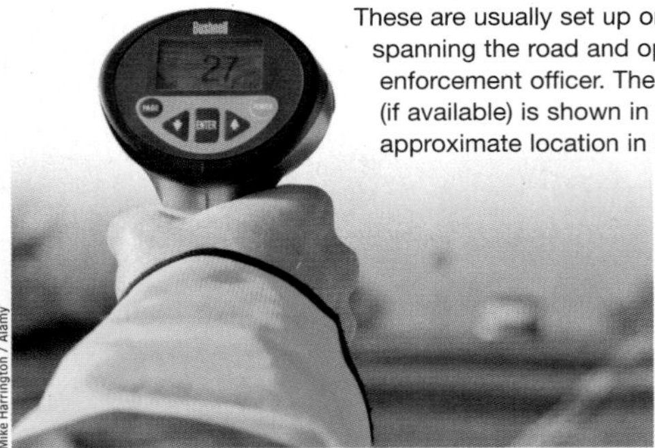

Mike Harrington / Alamy

A12
Braintree, Overbridge nr Kelvedon Interchange

A13
30 Castle Point, High St (Hadleigh twds London)
30 Leigh on Sea, London Rd
Southend, Bournes Green Chase
Southend, North Shoebury
Southend, Southchurch Boulevard

A1016
30 Chelmsford, Waterhouse Lane

A1017
30 Sible Hedingham, Swan St
30 Witham / Braintree, Rickstone Rd

A1023
30 Brentwood, Chelmsford Rd
30 Brentwood, London Rd
30 Brentwood, Shenfield Rd

A1025
40 Harlow, Second Avenue
40 Harlow, Third Avenue

A1060
Little Hallingbury, Lower Rd

A1090
30 Purfleet, London Rd
30 Purfleet, Tank Hill Rd

A1124
30 Colchester, Lexden Rd

A113
30 Epping, High Rd

A1158
30 Westcliff on Sea, Southbourne Grove

A1168
30 Loughton, Rectory Lane

A1169
40 Harlow, Southern Way

A120
Little Bentley, Pellens Corner
Wix, Harwich Rd nr Colchester Rd

A1205
40 Harlow, Second Avenue

A121
30 Epping, High Rd
30 Loughton, Goldings Hill (j/w Monkchester Close)
Loughton, High Rd
Waltham Abbey, Farm Hill Rd
Waltham Abbey, Sewardstine Rd

A126
30 Grays, London Rd
30 Tilbury, Montreal Rd

A128
Chipping Ongar, High St
30 Ingrave/Herongate, Brentwood Rd
40 Kelvedon Hatch, Ongar Rd

A129
30 Basildon, Crays Hill
Billericay, Southend Rd
Rayleigh, London Rd
30 Wickford, London Rd
Wickford, Southend Rd

A130
30 Canvey Island, Long Rd
South Benfleet, Canvey Way

A133
30 Elmstead Market, Clacton Rd
Little Bentley, Colchester Rd

A134
40 Great Horkesley, Nayland Rd

A137
30 Lawford, Wignall St

B170
Chigwell, Chigwell Rise
Loughton, Roding Lane

B172
Theydon Bois, Coppice Row

B173
Chigwell, Lambourne Rd

B184
40 Great Easton, Snow Hill

B186
30 South Ockendon, South Rd

B1002
30 Ingatestone, High St

B1007
30 Billericay, Laindon Rd
30 Billericay, Stock Rd
40 Chelmsford, Stock Rd

B1008
30 Chelmsford, Broomfield Rd

B1013
30 Hawkwell, High Rd
30 Hawkwell, Main Rd
30 Hockley/Hawkwell, Southend Rd
Rayleigh, High Rd

B1014
30 South Benfleet, Benfleet Rd

B1018
30 Latchingdon, The St
30 Maldon, The Causeway

B1019
30 Hatfield Peveral, Maldon Rd
30 Witham, Powers Hall End

B1021
Burnham on Crouch, Church Rd

B1022
30 Colchester, Maldon Rd
30 Heckfordbridge, Maldon Rd
30 Maldon, Colchester Rd
30 Tiptree Heath, Maldon Rd

B1027
30 Clacton-on-Sea, Valley Rd/Old Rd
30 St Osyth, Pump Hill
40 Wivenhoe, Brightlingsea Rd

B1028
30 Wivenhoe, Colchester Rd
30 Wivenhoe, The Avenue

B1033
30 Kirby Cross, Frinton Rd

B1335
40 South Ockendon, Stifford Rd

B1352
Harwich, Main Rd

B1383
30 Newport, London Rd
Stansted Mountfitchet, Cambridge Rd

B1389
30 Witham, Colchester Rd
30 Witham, Hatfield Rd

B1393
30 Epping, Palmers Hill

B1441
30 Clacton-on-Sea, London Rd
Tendring, Clacton Rd

B1442
30 Clacton-on-Sea, Thorpe Rd

B1464
30 Bowers Gifford, London Rd

UNCLASSIFIED
40 Alresford, St Osyth Rd
30 Aveley, Purfleet Rd
Aveley, Romford Rd
30 Barstable, Sandon Rd
30 Basildon, Ashlyns
Basildon, Clay Hill Rd
40 Basildon, Cranes Farm Rd (j/w Honywood Rd)
30 Basildon, Felmores
Basildon, London Rd, Wickford
30 Basildon, Vange Hill Drive
30 Basildon, Whitmore Way
30 Basildon, Wickford Avenue
30 Billericay, Mountnessing Rd
30 Bowers Gifford, London Rd
30 Braintree, Coldnailhurst Avenue
30 Brentwood, Eagle Way (nr j/w Clive Rd twds Warley Rd)
30 Brentwood, Eagle Way
30 Buckhurst Hill, Buckhurst Way/Albert Rd
30 Canvey Island, Dovervelt Rd
30 Canvey Island, Link Rd
30 Canvey Island, Thorney Bay Rd
Chadwell St Mary, Brentwood Rd
30 Chadwell St Mary, Linford Rd
30 Chadwell St Mary, Riverview
30 Chelmsford, Baddow Rd
30 Chelmsford, Chignall Rd
30 Chelmsford, Copperfield Rd
Chelmsford, Galleywood Rd
30 Chelmsford, Longstomps Avenue
30 Clacton-on-Sea, St Johns Rd
30 Clacton, Kings Parade
30 Clacton, Marine Parade East
30 Colchester, Abbots Rd
30 Colchester, Avon Way
30 Colchester, Bromley Rd
Colchester, Ipswich Rd
30 Colchester, Old Heath Rd
30 Colchester, Shrub End Rd
30 Corringham, Southend Rd
30 Corringham, Springhouse Rd
Danbury, Maldon Rd
30 Daws Heath, Daws Heath Rd
30 Eastwood, Green Lane j/w Kendal Way
30 Eastwood, Western Approaches j/w Rockall
30 Grays, Blackshots Lane
30 Grays, Lodge Lane
Grays, London Rd (nr Angel Rd)
Grays, London Rd (nr Bransons Way)
30 Hainault, Fencepiece Rd
40 Harlow, Abercrombie Way, twds Southern Way
40 Harlow, Howard Way
30 Hawkwell, Rectory Rd
30 Hockley, High Rd
30 Hullbridge, Coventry Hill
30 Laindon, Durham Rd

30 Laindon, High Rd
30 Laindon, Nightingales
30 Laindon, Wash Rd
Langdon Hills, High Rd
30 Leigh on Sea, Belton Way East
30 Leigh on Sea, Belton Way West
30 Leigh on Sea, Blenhelm Chase
30 Leigh on Sea, Grand Parade/Cliff Parade
30 Leigh on Sea, Hadleigh Rd
30 Leigh on Sea, Highlands Boulevard
30 Leigh on Sea, Manchester Drive
30 Leigh on Sea, Mountdale Gardens
30 Leigh on Sea, Western Rd
30 Loughton, Alderton Hill
30 Loughton, Loughton Way
Loughton, Valley Hill
30 Maldon, Fambridge Rd
30 Maldon, Holloway Rd
30 Maldon, Mundon Rd
30 Pitsea, Rectory Rd
30 Prittlewell, Kenilworth Gardens
30 Prittlewell, Prittlewell Chase
30 Rayleigh, Bull Lane
Rayleigh, Downhall Rd
30 Rayleigh, Trinity Rd, nr Church Rd
30 Rochford, Ashingdon Rd
30 Rochford, Rectory Rd
Rush Green, St Osyth Rd
30 Shoeburyness, Ness Rd
30 South Woodham Ferrers, Hullbridge Rd
30 South Woodham Ferrers, Inchbonnie Rd
30 Southend on Sea, Lifstan Way
Southend, Bournemouth Park Rd
30 Southend, Hamstel Rd
Southend on Sea, Bournemouth Park Rd
Southend, Western Esplanade/Westcliff on Sea
30 Springfield, New Bowers Way
30 Stanford le Hope, London Rd
30 Tendring, Burrs Rd, Clacton
30 Tendring, Frinton Rd, Frinton
Tendring, Harwich Rd, Wix Arch Cottages to Cansey Lane
30 Tendring, Osyth Rd, Rush Green
Theydon Bois, Piercing Hill
30 Thorpe Bay, Barnstaple Rd
30 Thorpe Bay, Thorpe Hall Avenue
Waltham Abbey, Paternoster Hill
Weeley Heath, Clacton Rd
Weeley Heath, Clacton Rd
30 West Thurrock, London Rd
30 Westcliff on Sea, Chalkwell Avenue
30 Westcliff on Sea, Kings Rd
30 Wickford, London Rd
30 Wickford, Radwinter Avenue
30 Witham, Powers Hall End
30 Witham, Rickstones Rd

Key to map symbols

Motorway with junction number	**Ambulance station**
Primary route – dual/single carriageway	**Coastguard station**
A road – dual/single carriageway	**Fire station**
B road – dual/single carriageway	**Police station**
Minor road – dual/single carriageway	**Accident and Emergency entrance to hospital**
Other minor road – dual/single carriageway	**Hospital**
Road under construction	**Place of worship**
Tunnel, covered road	**Information Centre** (open all year)
Speed cameras - single, multiple	**Shopping Centre**
Rural track, private road or narrow road in urban area	**Parking**
Gate or obstruction to traffic (restrictions may not apply at all times or to all vehicles)	**Park and Ride**
	Post Office
Path, bridleway, byway open to all traffic, road used as a public path	**Camping site**
Pedestrianised area	**Caravan site**
Postcode boundaries DY7	**Golf course**
County and unitary authority boundaries	**Picnic site**
Railway, tunnel, railway under construction	**Important buildings, schools, colleges, universities and hospitals** Prim Sch
Tramway, tramway under construction	**Built up area**
Miniature railway	**Woods**
Railway station Walsall	**Water name** River Medway
Private railway station	**River, weir, stream**
London Underground station	**Canal, lock, tunnel**
Tram stop, tram stop under construction	**Water**
Bus, coach station	**Tidal water**
	Non-Roman antiquity Church
	Roman antiquity ROMAN FORT
	Adjoining page indicators 87 58

Acad	**Academy**	Inst	**Institute**	Recn Gd	**Recreation Ground**
Allot Gdns	**Allotments**	Ct	**Law Court**		
Cemy	**Cemetery**	L Ctr	**Leisure Centre**	Resr	**Reservoir**
C Ctr	**Civic Centre**	LC	**Level Crossing**	Ret Pk	**Retail Park**
CH	**Club House**	Liby	**Library**	Sch	**School**
Coll	**College**	Mkt	**Market**	Sh Ctr	**Shopping Centre**
Crem	**Crematorium**	Meml	**Memorial**	TH	**Town Hall/House**
Ent	**Enterprise**	Mon	**Monument**	Trad Est	**Trading Estate**
Ex H	**Exhibition Hall**	Mus	**Museum**	Univ	**University**
Ind Est	**Industrial Estate**	Obsy	**Observatory**	W Twr	**Water Tower**
IRB Sta	**Inshore Rescue Boat Station**	Pal	**Royal Palace**	Wks	**Works**
		PH	**Public House**	YH	**Youth Hostel**

■ The small numbers around the edges of the maps identify the 1 kilometre National Grid lines

■ The dark grey border on the inside edge of some pages indicates that the mapping does not continue onto the adjacent page

The scale of the maps on the pages numbered in blue is 5.52 cm to 1 km • 3½ inches to 1 mile • 1: 18103	0 ¼ ½ ¾ 1 mile
	0 250 m 500 m 750 m 1 kilometre

Cambridgeshire STREET ATLAS

Hertfordshire STREET ATLAS

London STREET ATLAS

Kent STREET ATLAS

Great Shelford
Sawston
Cavendish
Hinxton
Ickleton
Great Chesterford
Hadstock
Shudy Camps
Haverhill
Boyton End
Clare
Pentlow
Ashdon
Sturmer
Stoke by Clare
Drapers Green
Birdbrook
Ridgewell
Belchamp Walter
Gestingthorpe
Heydon
Chrishall
Elmdon
Littlebury
Little Walden
Saffron Walden
Helions Bumpstead
Hempstead
Steeple Bumpstead
Royston
Duddenhoe End
Wendens Ambo
Radwinter
Cornish Hall End
Toppesfield
Audley End
Nuthampstead
Langley
Arkesden
Newport
Elder Street
Great Sampford
Gainsford End
Sible Hedingham
Baldock
Wicken Bonhunt
Debden
Little Sampford
Finchingfield
Southey Green
Brent Pelham
Clavering
Widdington
Quendon
Cutlers Green
Thaxted
Great Bardfield
Wethersfield
Blackmore End
Halstead
Buntingford
Rickling Green
Manuden
Henham
Broxted
Elsenham
Richmond's Green
Duton Hill
Shalford
Bardfield Saling
Lindsell
Beazley End
High Garrett
Gosfield
Stevenage
Stansted Mountfitchet
Birchanger
Molehill Green
Stansted Airport
Great Easton
Church End
Stebbing
Stebbing Green
Panfield
Rayne
Braintree
Bradwell
Stisted
Ware
Bishop's Stortford
Takeley Street
Great Hallingbury
Takeley
Great Canfield
Great Dunmow
Barnston
Felsted
Willows Green
Great Notley
White Notley
Cressing
Silver End
Hertford
Little Hallingbury
Sawbridgeworth
Taverners Green
Hatfield Heath
High Easter
Ford End
Pleshey
Howe Street
Great Leighs
Church End
Terling
Witham
Hunsdonbury
Gilston
Sheering
White Roding
Leaden Roding
Great Waltham
Mashbury
Little Waltham
Broomfield
Hatfield Peverel
Stanstead Abbotts
Roydon
Harlow
Matching Green
Abbess Roding
Hoddesdon
Tye Green
Roydon Hamlet
Lower Nazeing
Tilegate Green
Hastingwood
High Laver
Fyfield
Moreton
Willingale
Roxwell
Writtle
Chelmsford
Boreham
Little Baddow
Woodham Walter
Cheshunt
Aimes Green
Waltham Abbey
Holdbrook
Bumble's Green
North Weald Bassett
Epping
Bobbingworth
Chipping Ongar
Norton Heath
Loves Green
Widford
Great Baddow
Danbury
Cock Clarks
Cuffley
Potters Bar
Enfield
Ivy Chimneys
Theydon Bois
Fiddlers Hamlet
Stapleford Tawney
Stanford Rivers
Kelvedon Hatch
Doddinghurst
Blackmore
Mill Green
Margaretting
Ingatestone
West Hanningfield
East Hanningfield
Woodham Ferrers
High Beach
Loughton
Abridge
Stapleford Abbotts
Navestock Heath
Bentley
Pilgrims Hatch
Shenfield
Mountnessing
Ramsden Heath
Runwell
South Woodham Ferrers
Hullbridge
East Barnet
Southgate
Chingford
Chigwell
Chigwell Row
South Weald
Brentwood
Ingrave
Great Warley
South Green
Dunton Wayletts
Nevendon
Wickford
Rawreth
Shotgate
Rayleigh
Friern Barnet
Wood Green
Edmonton
Chingford Hatch
Tottenham
Woodford
Harold Hill
West Horndon
Cranham
Laindon
Basildon
Thundersley
Hadleigh
Golders Green
Stoke Newington
Walthamstow
Barkingside
Wanstead
Ilford
Romford
Goodmayes
Upminster
Langdon Hills
Vange
Camden Town
Islington
Hackney
Stratford
Bow
West Ham
Becontree
Barking
Elm Park
Dagenham
Rainham
Corbets Tey
North Ockendon
Bulphan
Horndon on the Hill
Stanford-le-Hope
Fobbing
Winter Gardens
Canvey Island
Paddington
Finsbury
Shoreditch
City of London
Poplar
London City
Wennington
Aveley
South Ockendon
Little Thurrock
Orsett
Chadwell St Mary
Linford
Westminster
Chelsea
Battersea
Clapham
Camberwell
Bermondsey
Deptford
Greenwich
Woolwich
Erith
Purfleet
Grays
Tilbury
Northfleet
East Tilbury
Gravesend
Wimbledon
Mitcham
Streatham
Brixton
Lewisham
Eltham
Bexley
Crayford
Dartford
Swanscombe
Strood
Rochester
Penge
Catford
Bromley
Chislehurst
Sidcup
Swanley

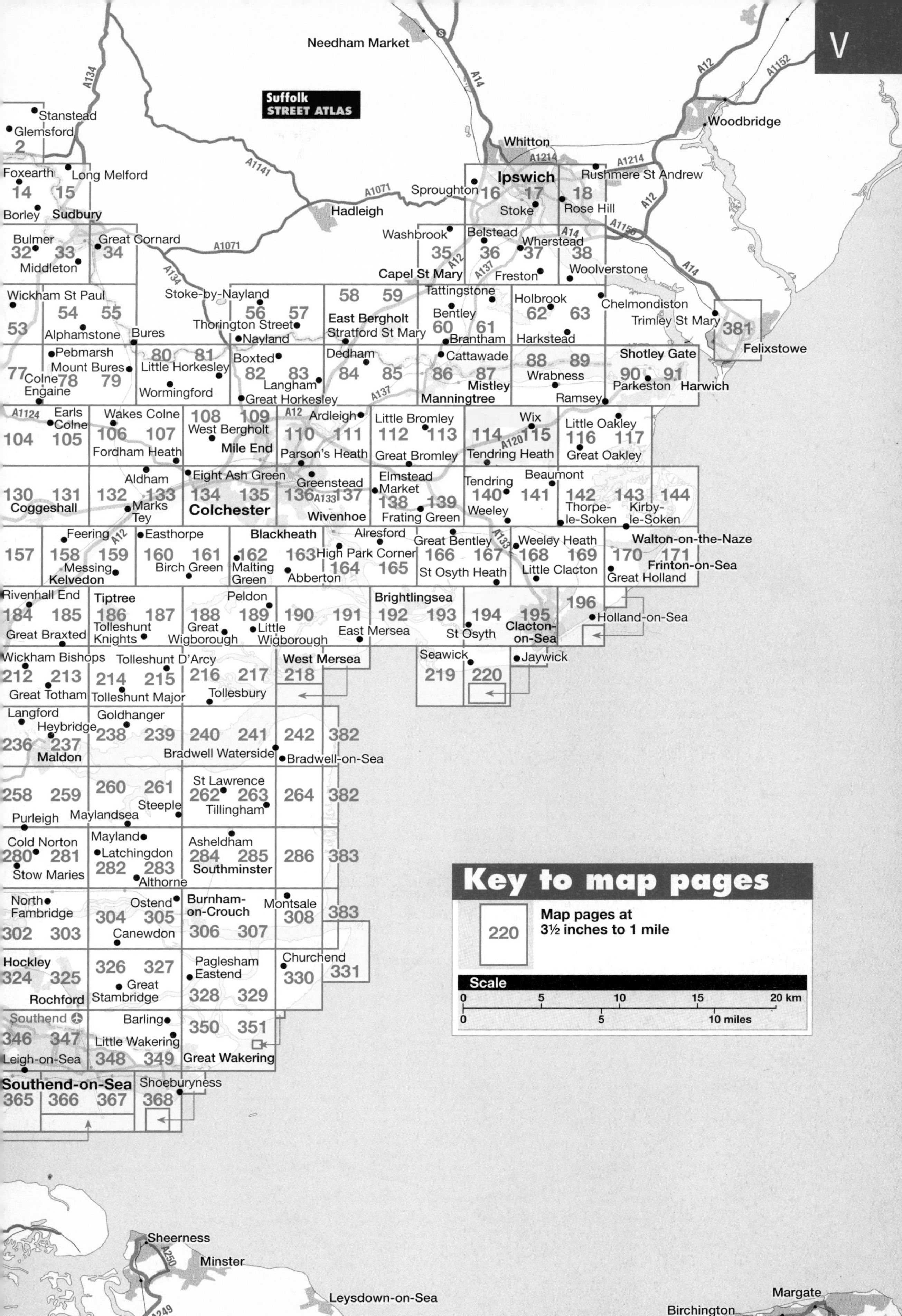
Key to map pages
220
Map pages at 3½ inches to 1 mile
Scale
0 5 10 15 20 km
0 5 10 miles
Suffolk STREET ATLAS
Needham Market
A14
A12
A1152
Woodbridge
Whitton
A1214
Ipswich
Rushmere St Andrew
Sproughton 16 17 18
Stoke
Rose Hill
A1071
Hadleigh
A1141
A134
Stanstead
Glemsford
2
Foxearth
Long Melford
14 15
Borley
Sudbury
Bulmer
32 33 34
Great Cornard
Middleton
A1071
Washbrook
Belstead
Wherstead
35 36 37 38
A1156
Capel St Mary
Freston
Woolverstone
A137
Tattingstone
Holbrook
Chelmondiston
Trimley St Mary
381
Felixstowe
Wickham St Paul
54 55
53
Alphamstone
Bures
Stoke-by-Nayland
56 57
Thorington Street
Nayland
58 59
East Bergholt
Stratford St Mary
Bentley
60 61
Brantham
62 63
Harkstead
Pebmarsh
Mount Bures
77 Colne Engaine 78 79
80 81
Little Horkesley
Wormingford
Boxted
82 83
Langham
Great Horkesley
Dedham
84 85
Cattawade
86 87
Mistley
Manningtree
88 89
Wrabness
Ramsey
Shotley Gate
90 91
Parkeston
Harwich
A1124
Earls Colne
104 105
Wakes Colne
106 107
Fordham Heath
108 109
West Bergholt
Mile End
A12
Ardleigh
110 111
Parson's Heath
Little Bromley
112 113
Great Bromley
Wix
114 115
A120
Tendring Heath
Little Oakley
116 117
Great Oakley
Aldham
130 131
Coggeshall
132 133
Marks Tey
Eight Ash Green
134 135
Colchester
Greenstead
136 137
A133
Wivenhoe
Elmstead Market
138 139
Frating Green
Tendring
140 141
Weeley
Beaumont
142 143 144
Thorpe-le-Soken
Kirby-le-Soken
Feering
157 158 159
Messing
Kelvedon
Easthorpe
160 161
Birch Green
Blackheath
162 163
Malting Green
Abberton
Alresford
High Park Corner
164 165
Great Bentley
166 167
St Osyth Heath
A133
Weeley Heath
168 169
Little Clacton
Walton-on-the-Naze
170 171
Frinton-on-Sea
Great Holland
Rivenhall End
184 185
Great Braxted
Tiptree
186 187
Tolleshunt Knights
Peldon
188 189
Great Wigborough
Little Wigborough
190 191
East Mersea
Brightlingsea
192 193
194 195
St Osyth
Clacton-on-Sea
196
Holland-on-Sea
Wickham Bishops
212 213
Great Totham
Tolleshunt D'Arcy
214 215
Tolleshunt Major
216 217
Tollesbury
West Mersea
218
Seawick
219 220
Jaywick
Langford
Heybridge
236 237
Maldon
Goldhanger
238 239
240 241
Bradwell Waterside
242 382
Bradwell-on-Sea
258 259
Purleigh
260 261
Maylandsea
Steeple
St Lawrence
262 263
Tillingham
264 382
Cold Norton
280 281
Stow Maries
Mayland
Latchingdon
282 283
Althorne
Asheldham
284 285
Southminster
286 383
North Fambridge
302 303
Ostend
304 305
Canewdon
Burnham-on-Crouch
306 307
Montsale
308 383
Hockley
324 325
Rochford
326 327
Great Stambridge
Paglesham Eastend
328 329
Churchend
330 331
Southend
346 347
Leigh-on-Sea
Barling
Little Wakering
348 349
350 351
Great Wakering
Southend-on-Sea
365 366 367
Shoeburyness
368
Sheerness
A250
Minster
A249
Leysdown-on-Sea
Birchington
Margate

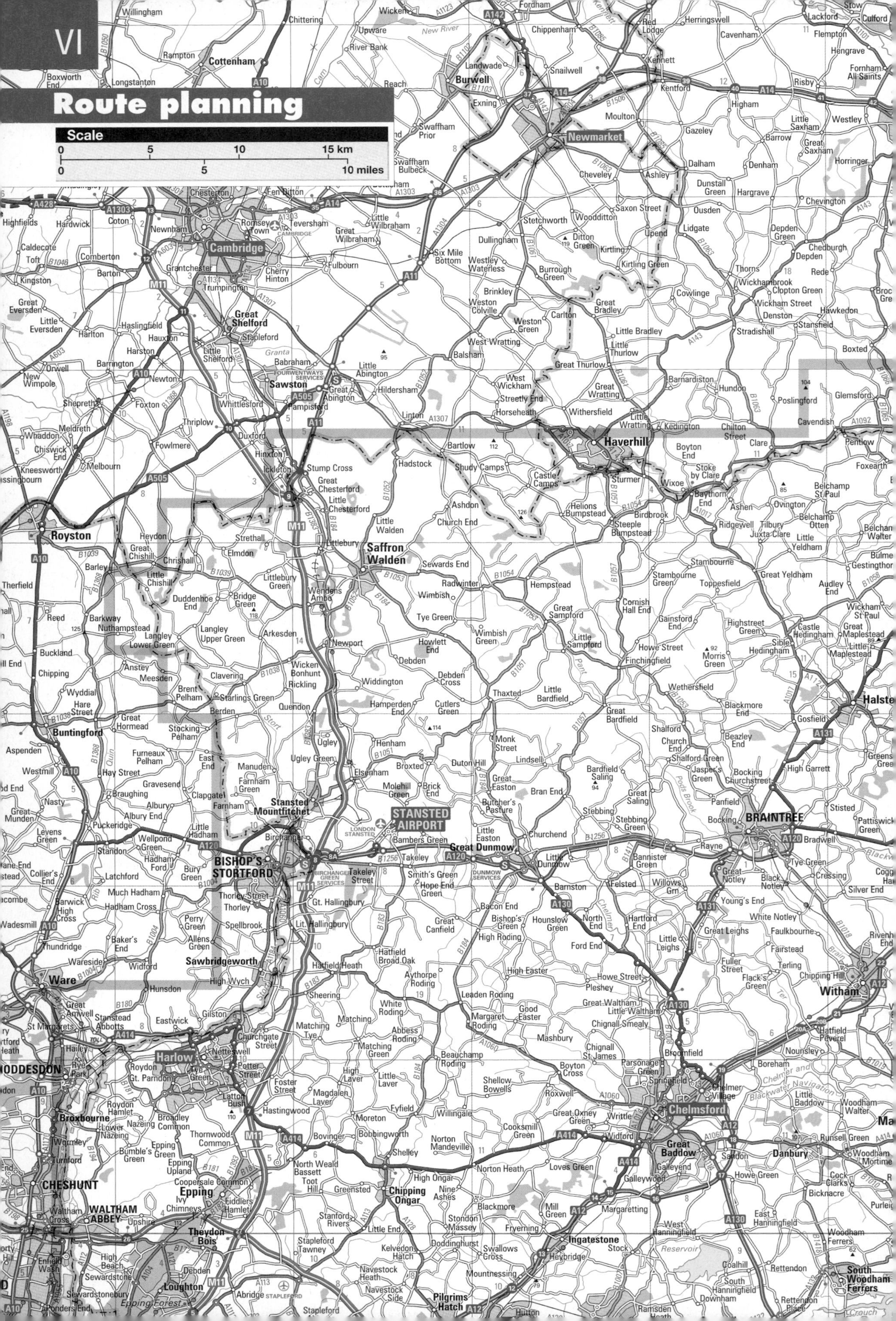
VI
Route planning
Scale
0
5
10
15 km
0
5
10 miles
Cambridge
Newmarket
Haverhill
Royston
Saffron Walden
Buntingford
Stansted Mountfitchet
STANSTED AIRPORT
BISHOP'S STORTFORD
Great Dunmow
BRAINTREE
Sawbridgeworth
Ware
Harlow
HODDESDON
Chelmsford
Witham
Epping
Chipping Ongar
CHESHUNT
WALTHAM ABBEY
Loughton
Ingatestone
Halstead
South Woodham Ferrers

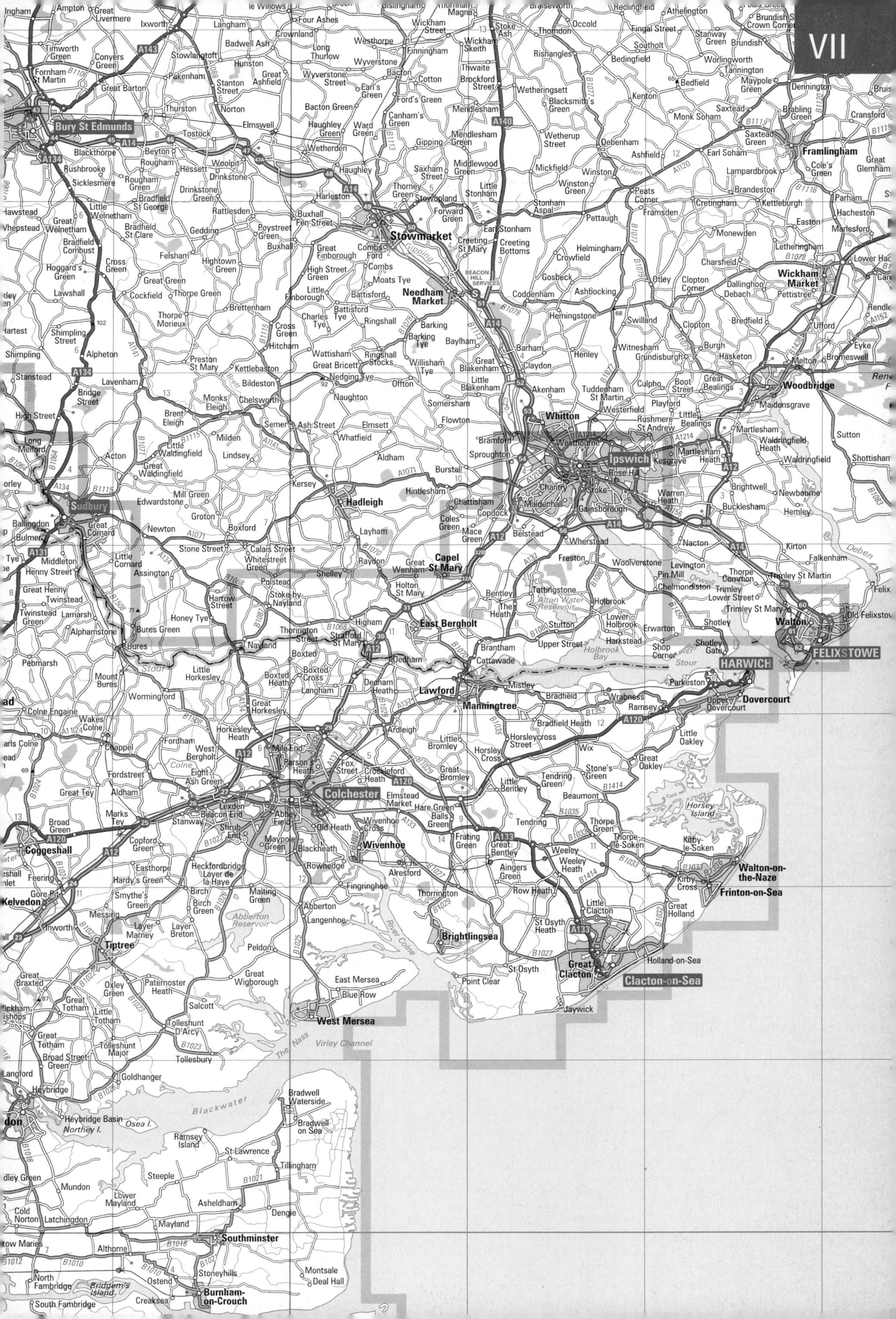
Ingham
Ampton
Great Livermere
Ixworth
Langham
Four Ashes
Crownland
Wickham Street
Stoke Ash
Thorndon
Occold
Athelington
Fingal Street
Stanway Green
Brundish
Brundish Street
Crown Corner
Timworth Green
Conyers Green
Badwell Ash
Long Thurlow
Westhorpe
Finningham
Wickham Skeith
Rishangles
Southolt
Bedingfield
Worlingworth
Tannington
Fornham St Martin
Stowlangtoft
Pakenham
Hunston
Great Ashfield
Wyverstone
Wyverstone Street
Bacton
Cotton
Thwaite
Brockford Street
Wetheringsett
Blacksmith's Green
Kenton
Bedfield
Maypole Green
Dennington
Great Barton
Stanton Street
Norton
Earl's Green
Ford's Green
Bacton Green
Mendlesham
Saxtead
Brabling Green
Cransford
Thurston
Elmswell
Haughley Green
Ward Green
Canham's Green
Monk Soham
Bury St Edmunds
Tostock
Wetherden
Gipping
Mendlesham Green
Wetherup Street
Debenham
Saxtead Green
Framlingham
Blackthorpe
Beyton
Rougham
Hessett
Woolpit
Drinkstone
Haughley
Saxham Street
Middlewood Green
Mickfield
Ashfield
Earl Soham
Cole's Green
Great Glemham
Rushbrooke
Sicklesmere
Rougham Green
Drinkstone Green
Harleston
Thorney Green
Stowupland
Little Stonham
Winston
Winston Green
Lampardbrook
Brandeston
Bradfield St George
Rattlesden
Forward Green
Stonham Aspal
Peats Corner
Framsden
Cretingham
Kettleburgh
Parham
Hawstead
Little Welnetham
Great Welnetham
Bradfield St Clare
Bradfield Combust
Gedding
Poystreet Green
Buxhall Fen Street
Stowmarket
Earl Stonham
Pettaugh
Monewden
Easton
Hacheston
Marlesford
Whepstead
Buxhall
Great Finborough
Combs Ford
Creeting St Mary
Creeting Bottoms
Helmingham
Crowfield
Letheringham
Charsfield
Wickham Market
Lower Hacheston
Hoggard's Green
Cross Green
Felsham
Hightown Green
High Street Green
Combs
Moats Tye
Beacon Hill Services
Gosbeck
Ashbocking
Otley
Clopton Corner
Dallinghoo
Debach
Pettistree
Lawshall
Great Green
Cockfield
Thorpe Green
Little Finborough
Battisford
Needham Market
Coddenham
Hemingstone
Swilland
Clopton
Bredfield
Ufford
Rendlesham
Hartest
Shimpling Street
Thorpe Morieux
Brettenham
Cross Green
Charles Tye
Battisford Tye
Ringshall
Barking
Barking Tye
Baylham
Barham
Witnesham
Grundisburgh
Burgh
Hasketon
Melton
Bromeswell
Eyke
Shimpling
Alpheton
Hitcham
Wattisham
Great Bricett
Ringshall Stocks
Willisham Tye
Great Blakenham
Claydon
Henley
Stanstead
Preston St Mary
Kettlebaston
Nedging Tye
Naughton
Offton
Little Blakenham
Akenham
Tuddenham St Martin
Culpho
Boot Street
Great Bealings
Woodbridge
Maidensgrave
Lavenham
Bridge Street
Bildeston
Brent Eleigh
Monks Eleigh
Chelsworth
Somersham
Whitton
Westerfield
Playford
Little Bealings
Rushmere St Andrew
Martlesham
Sutton
High Street
Semer
Ash Street
Elmsett
Flowton
Long Melford
Milden
Little Waldingfield
Lindsey
Whatfield
Aldham
Bramford
Westbourne
Ipswich
Kesgrave
Martlesham Heath
Waldringfield Heath
Waldringfield
Shottisham
Acton
Great Waldingfield
Sproughton
Burstall
Rose Hill
Chantry
Stoke
Maidenhall
Gainsborough
Warren Heath
Brightwell
Newbourne
Bucklesham
Hemley
Sudbury
Edwardstone
Mill Green
Groton
Kersey
Hadleigh
Hintlesham
Chattisham
Copdock
Coles Green
Mace Green
Belstead
Wherstead
Nacton
Kirton
Falkenham
Ballingdon
Bulmer
Great Cornard
Newton
Boxford
Stone Street
Calais Street
Whitestreet Green
Layham
Raydon
Capel St Mary
Great Wenham
Freston
Woolverstone
Levington
Pin Mill
Chelmondiston
Thorpe Common
Trimley
Trimley St Martin
Trimley St Mary
Lower Street
Middleton
Little Cornard
Henny Street
Assington
Polstead
Shelley
Holton St Mary
Bentley
Tattingstone
Alton Water Reservoir
Holbrook
Lower Holbrook
Erwarton
Shotley
Walton
Old Felixstowe
Felixstowe
Great Henny
Twinstead
Twinstead Green
Lamarsh
Alphamstone
Hartow Street
Honey Tye
Stoke-by-Nayland
Thorington Street
Stratford St Mary
Higham
East Bergholt
The Heath
Stutton
Harkstead
Upper Street
Shop Corner
Shotley Gate
Holbrook Bay
Stour
Harwich
Bures Green
Bures
Nayland
Boxted
Boxted Cross
Dedham
Brantham
Cattawade
Pebmarsh
Mount Bures
Little Horkesley
Boxted Heath
Langham
Dedham Heath
Lawford
Manningtree
Mistley
Bradfield
Wrabness
Ramsey
Parkeston
Dovercourt
Upper Dovercourt
Wormingford
Great Horkesley
Ardleigh
Bradfield Heath
Little Oakley
Colne Engaine
Wakes Colne
Chappel
Earls Colne
Fordham
West Bergholt
Horkesley Heath
Mile End
Parson's Heath
Fox Street
Crockleford Heath
Little Bromley
Horsley Cross
Horsleycross Street
Wix
Great Oakley
Fordstreet
Eight Ash Green
Colne
Great Tey
Aldham
Colchester
Elmstead Market
Great Bromley
Stone's Green
Tendring Green
Little Bentley
Beaumont
Horsey Island
Broad Green
Marks Tey
Stanway
Lexden
Beacon End
Abbey Field
Old Heath
Hare Green
Balls Green
Tendring
Thorpe Green
Thorpe-le-Soken
Kirby-le-Soken
Coggeshall
Copford Green
Shrub End
Maypole Green
Wivenhoe Cross
Wivenhoe
Frating Green
Great Bentley
Weeley
Weeley Heath
Walton-on-the-Naze
Easthorpe
Heckfordbridge
Layer de la Haye
Blackheath
Rowhedge
Alresford
Aingers Green
Kirby Cross
Frinton-on-Sea
Feering
Hardy's Green
Birch
Fingringhoe
Row Heath
Gore Pit
Kelvedon
Smythe's Green
Birch Green
Malting Green
Thorrington
Little Clacton
Great Holland
Messing
Abberton
Abberton Reservoir
Brightlingsea
St Osyth Heath
Inworth
Layer Marney
Layer Breton
Langenhoe
Tiptree
Peldon
River Colne
Holland-on-Sea
Great Braxted
Oxley Green
Paternoster Heath
Great Wigborough
East Mersea
St Osyth
Great Clacton
Point Clear
Clacton-on-Sea
Great Totham
Little Totham
Salcott
Blue Row
Jaywick
Wickham Bishops
Tolleshunt D'Arcy
West Mersea
Great Totham
Tolleshunt Major
The Nass
Virley Channel
Broad Street Green
Tollesbury
Langford
Goldhanger
Heybridge
Bradwell Waterside
Blackwater
Heybridge Basin
Osea I.
Northey I.
Bradwell on Sea
Ramsey Island
St Lawrence
Tillingham
Steeple
Mundon
Lower Mayland
Asheldham
Dengie
Cold Norton
Latchingdon
Mayland
Southminster
Althorne
Montsale
Deal Hall
North Fambridge
Ostend
Stoneyhills
Bridgemarsh Island
Burnham-on-Crouch
Creeksea
South Fambridge
A14
A134
A143
A140
A120
A12
A133
A1071
A1214
A137
A131
A1141
A1120
A1156
B1115
B1113
B1078
B1077
B1079
B1070
B1068
B1029
B1027
B1032
B1033
B1414
B1035
B1352
B1018
B1021
B1010
B1023
B1026
B1025

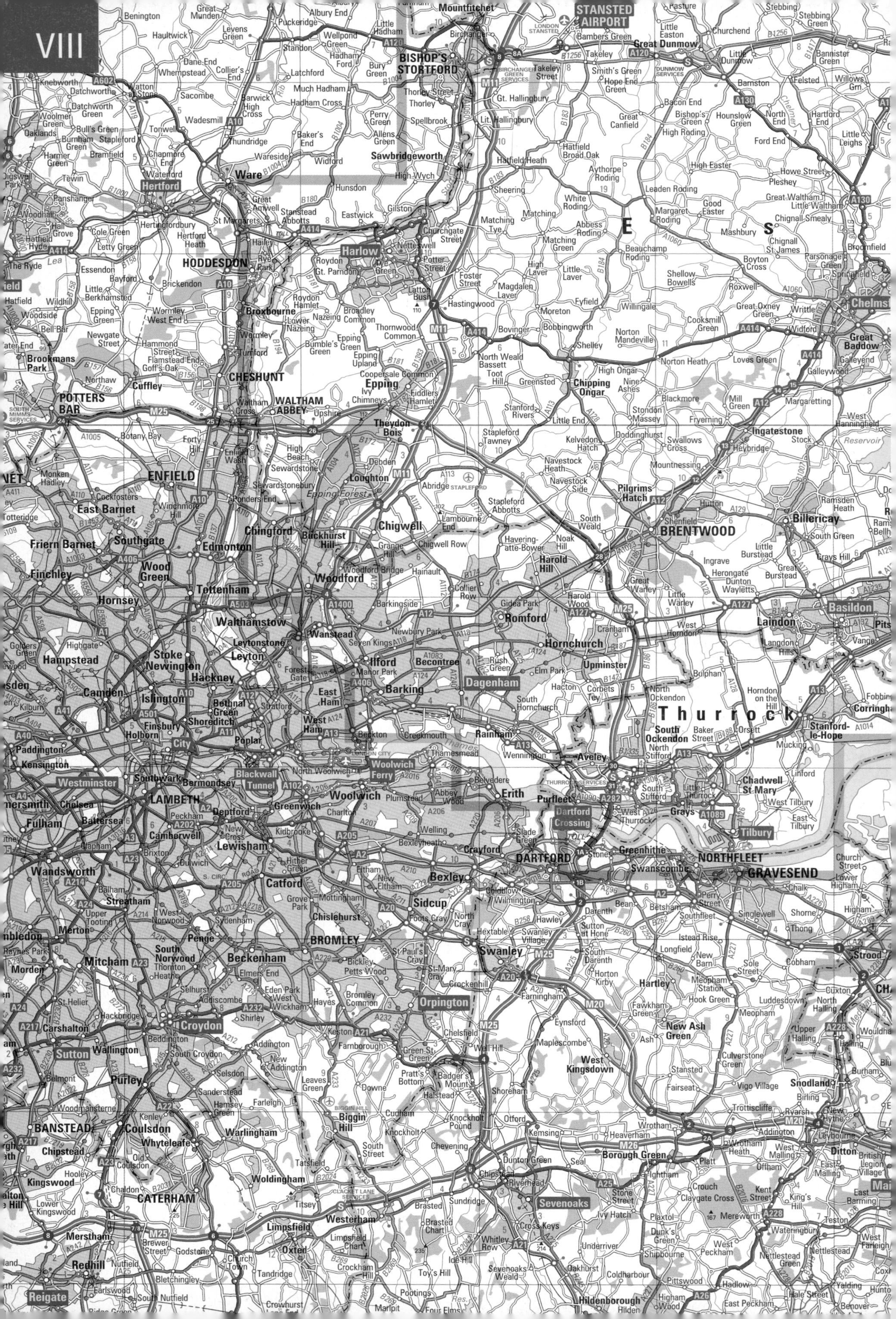

Benington
Great Munden
Albury End
Mountfitchet
STANSTED AIRPORT
Pasture
Stebbing
Haultwick
Levens Green
Puckeridge
Little Hadham
Standon
Wellpond Green
Hadham Ford
Bury Green
BISHOP'S STORTFORD
Birchanger
Bambers Green
Little Easton
Great Dunmow
Churchend
Takeley
Little Dunmow
Bannister Green
Dane End
Collier's End
Whempstead
Latchford
Much Hadham
Thorley Street
Thorley
Smith's Green
Hope End Green
Felsted
Knebworth
Datchworth
Watton at Stone
Sacombe
Barwick
Hadham Cross
Barnston
Willows Grn
Datchworth Green
Woolmer Green
High Cross
Wadesmill
Perry Green
Spellbrook
Gt. Hallingbury
Bacon End
Bishop's Green
Hounslow Green
North End
Hartford End
Oaklands
Bull's Green
Burnham Green
Stapleford
Tonwell
Thundridge
Baker's End
Allens Green
Lit. Hallingbury
Great Canfield
High Roding
Ford End
Little Leighs
Bramfield
Chapmore End
Wareside
Sawbridgeworth
Hatfield Heath
Hatfield Broad Oak
Harmer Green
Tewin
Waterford
Widford
High Wych
High Easter
Howe Street
Pleshey
Hertford
Ware
Hunsdon
Aythorpe Roding
Sheering
Leaden Roding
Great Waltham
Little Waltham
Panshanger
Great Amwell
Stanstead Abbotts
Eastwick
Gilston
White Roding
Good Easter
Margaret Roding
Chignall Smealy
Woodhall
Hertingfordbury
St Margarets
Matching
Matching Tye
Abbess Roding
Mashbury
Chignall St James
Hatfield Hyde
Cole Green
Letty Green
Hertford Heath
Hailey
Churchgate Street
Harlow
Netteswell
E
S
Broomfield
The Ryde
Essendon
HODDESDON
Rye Park
Roydon
Gt. Parndon
Potter Street
Matching Green
Beauchamp Roding
Boyton Cross
Parsonage Green
Springfield
Bayford
Brickendon
Foster Street
High Laver
Little Laver
Shellow Bowells
Roxwell
Chelmsford
Hatfield
Little Berkhamsted
Wildhill
Broxbourne
Roydon Hamlet
Latton Bush
Magdalen Laver
Fyfield
Willingale
Woodside
Epping Green
Wormley West End
Nazeing
Broadley Common
Hastingwood
Moreton
Cooksmill Green
Great Oxney Green
Writtle
Bell Bar
Newgate Street
Lower Nazeing
Thornwood Common
Bovinger
Bobbingworth
Norton Mandeville
Widford
Great Baddow
Brookmans Park
Hammond Street
Flamstead End
Goff's Oak
Wormley
Turnford
Bumble's Green
Epping Green
Epping Upland
North Weald Bassett
Toot Hill
Shelley
Norton Heath
Loves Green
Galleyend
Galleywood
Northaw
Cuffley
CHESHUNT
Coopersale Common
Epping
Ivy Chimneys
Fiddlers Hamlet
Greensted
Chipping Ongar
High Ongar
Nine Ashes
Blackmore
Mill Green
Margaretting
POTTERS BAR
Waltham Cross
WALTHAM ABBEY
Upshire
Theydon Bois
Stanford Rivers
Little End
Stondon Massey
Fryerning
Ingatestone
West Hanningfield
Botany Bay
Forty Hill
Enfield Wash
High Beach
Stapleford Tawney
Kelvedon Hatch
Doddinghurst
Swallows Cross
Stock
Heybridge
Reservoir
Monken Hadley
ENFIELD
Sewardstone
Debden
Loughton
Abridge
Navestock Heath
Navestock Side
Mountnessing
Sewardstonebury
Ponders End
Epping Forest
Cockfosters
East Barnet
Winchmore Hill
Chigwell
Lambourne End
Stapleford Abbotts
Pilgrims Hatch
Hutton
Ramsden Heath
Billericay
Totteridge
Chingford
Buckhurst Hill
Grange Hill
Chigwell Row
Havering-atte-Bower
Noak Hill
South Weald
Shenfield
BRENTWOOD
South Green
Friern Barnet
Southgate
Edmonton
Woodford
Woodford Bridge
Hainault
Harold Hill
Ingrave
Little Burstead
Grays Hill
Finchley
Wood Green
Tottenham
Collier Row
Great Warley
Herongate
Dunton Wayletts
Great Burstead
Hornsey
Walthamstow
Barkingside
Gidea Park
Romford
Harold Wood
Little Warley
Laindon
Basildon
Highgate
Wanstead
Newbury Park
Cranham
West Horndon
Golders Green
Hampstead
Stoke Newington
Leytonstone
Leyton
Seven Kings
Ilford
Becontree
Rush Green
Hornchurch
Upminster
Langdon Hills
Vange
Hackney
Forest Gate
Manor Park
Elm Park
Bulphan
Camden
Islington
Bethnal Green
Stratford
East Ham
Barking
Dagenham
South Hornchurch
Hacton
Corbets Tey
North Ockendon
Horndon on the Hill
Fobbing
Corringham
Kilburn
Finsbury
Shoreditch
West Ham
Thurrock
Paddington
Holborn
City
Poplar
Beckton
Creekmouth
Rainham
South Ockendon
Baker Street
Orsett
Stanford-le-Hope
Kensington
Wennington
Aveley
North Stifford
Mucking
Thames
Thamesmead
Westminster
Southwark
Bermondsey
Blackwall Tunnel
North Woolwich
Woolwich Ferry
Belvedere
Purfleet
South Stifford
Little Thurrock
Chadwell St Mary
Linford
Chelsea
LAMBETH
Deptford
Greenwich
Woolwich
Plumstead
Abbey Wood
Erith
Dartford Crossing
West Thurrock
Grays
West Tilbury
East Tilbury
Fulham
Battersea
Peckham
Camberwell
New Cross
Kidbrooke
Charlton
Welling
Slade Green
Tilbury
Brixton
Lewisham
Bexleyheath
Crayford
DARTFORD
Stone
Greenhithe
NORTHFLEET
Church Street
Wandsworth
Clapham
Dulwich
Hither Green
Eltham
New Eltham
Bexley
Swanscombe
GRAVESEND
Lower Higham
Balham
Catford
Grove Park
Mottingham
Sidcup
Wilmington
Bean
Betsham
Perry Street
Chalk
Streatham
Upper Tooting
West Norwood
Sydenham
Chislehurst
Foots Cray
North Cray
Hawley
Darenth
Southfleet
Singlewell
Shorne
Higham
Wimbledon
Merton
Penge
BROMLEY
Hextable
Swanley Village
Sutton at Hone
Istead Rise
Thong
Raynes Park
South Norwood
Thornton Heath
St Paul's Cray
Swanley
Longfield
New Barn
Sole Street
Cobham
Strood
Morden
Mitcham
Beckenham
Elmers End
Bickley
Petts Wood
St Mary Cray
Crockenhill
South Darenth
Horton Kirby
Hartley
Meopham Station
Cuxton
St Helier
Selhurst
Addiscombe
Eden Park
West Wickham
Hayes
Bromley Common
Farningham
Hook Green
Luddesdown
North Halling
Hackbridge
Croydon
Shirley
Orpington
Fawkham Green
Meopham
Carshalton
Keston
Chelsfield
Eynsford
New Ash Green
Upper Halling
Sutton
Wallington
Beddington
Addington
Farnborough
Green St Green
Well Hill
Maplescombe
Ash
Halling
Belmont
South Croydon
New Addington
Pratt's Bottom
Badger's Mount
West Kingsdown
Culverstone Green
Burham
Purley
Selsdon
Leaves Green
Downe
Halstead
Stansted
Fairseat
Vigo Village
Snodland
Sanderstead
Shoreham
Birling
Woodmansterne
Farleigh
Hamsey Green
Biggin Hill
Cudham
Knockholt Pound
Knockholt
Otford
Kemsing
Trottiscliffe
Ryarsh
New Hythe
BANSTEAD
Coulsdon
Kenley
Whyteleafe
Warlingham
Wrotham
Heaverham
Addington
Leybourne
Chipstead
Old Coulsdon
Chevening
Tatsfield
South Street
Dunton Green
Seal
Borough Green
Wrotham Heath
West Malling
Ditton
Hooley
Woldingham
Chipstead
Riverhead
Ightham
Platt
Offham
East Malling
British Legion Village
Kingswood
Chaldon
CATERHAM
Titsey
Sundridge
Brasted
Sevenoaks
Stone Street
Crouch
Claygate Cross
Kent Street
King's Hill
East Barming
Lower Kingswood
Westerham
Brasted Chart
Ivy Hatch
Plaxtol
Mereworth
Teston
Merstham
Limpsfield
Limpsfield Chart
Cross Keys
Dunk's Green
Wateringbury
Brewer Street
Godstone
Oxted
Whitley Row
Underriver
Shipbourne
West Peckham
Nettlestead
West Farleigh
Redhill
Nutfield
Church Town
Tandridge
Crockham Hill
Ide Hill
Sevenoaks Weald
Oakhurst
Coldharbour
Nettlestead Green
Bletchingley
Toy's Hill
Pittswood
Hadlow
Yalding
Reigate
Earlswood
South Nutfield
Crowhurst
Marlpit
Four Elms
Hildenborough
Higham Wood
East Peckham
Hale Street
Benover
M25
M11
M20
M26
A10
A12
A13
A120
A414
A130
A127
A2
A20
A21
A23
A25
A26
A228

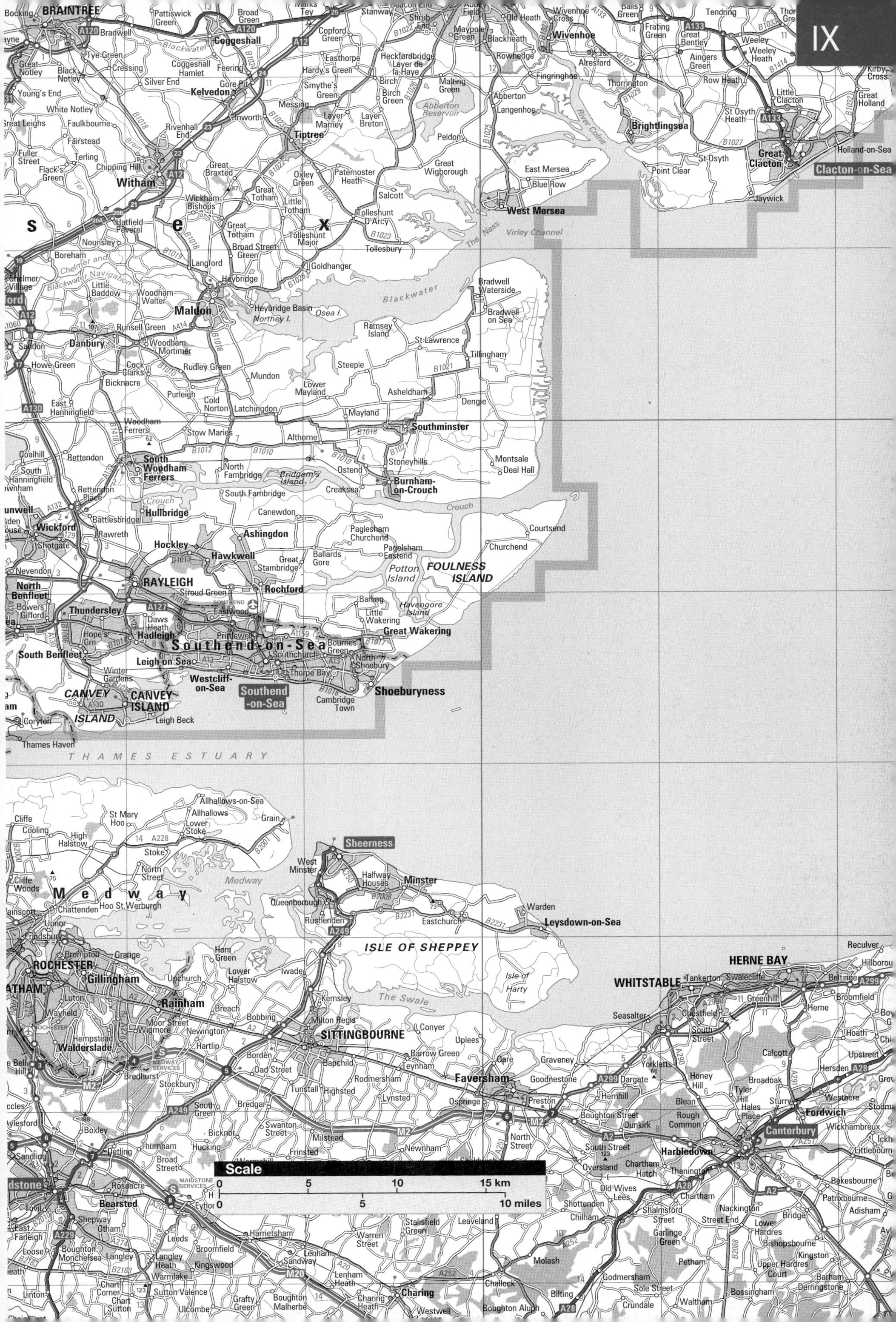
BRAINTREE
Bocking
Pattiswick Green
Broad Green
Coggeshall
Blackwater
Bradwell
Great Notley
Black Notley
Tye Green
Cressing
Coggeshall Hamlet
Feering
Silver End
Kelvedon
Young's End
White Notley
Faulkbourne
Great Leighs
Fairstead
Rivenhall End
Inworth
Fuller Street
Terling
Flack's Green
Chipping Hill
Witham
Great Braxted
Messing
Tiptree
Copford Green
Easthorpe
Hardy's Green
Smythe's Green
Layer Marney
Layer Breton
Heckfordbridge
Layer de la Haye
Birch
Birch Green
Shrub End
Stanway
Tey
Maypole Green
Blackheath
Rowhedge
Old Heath
Malting Green
Abberton Reservoir
Abberton
Langenhoe
Fingringhoe
Peldon
Great Wigborough
Wivenhoe Cross
Wivenhoe
Alresford
Thorrington
Brightlingsea
River Colne
Frating Green
Great Bentley
Aingers Green
Row Heath
Tendring
Weeley
Weeley Heath
Little Clacton
St Osyth Heath
St Osyth
Point Clear
Great Clacton
Great Holland
Kirby Cross
Holland-on-Sea
Clacton-on-Sea
Jaywick
East Mersea
Blue Row
West Mersea
The Nass
Virley Channel
Paternoster Heath
Salcott
Oxley Green
Great Totham
Little Totham
Tolleshunt D'Arcy
Tolleshunt Major
Tollesbury
Wickham Bishops
Hatfield Peverel
Nounsley
Boreham
Chelmer and Blackwater Navigation
Broad Street Green
Langford
Heybridge
Goldhanger
Heybridge Basin
Northey I.
Osea I.
Blackwater
Chelmer Village
Little Baddow
Woodham Walter
Maldon
Runsell Green
Danbury
Sandon
Woodham Mortimer
Howe Green
Cock Clarks
Rudley Green
Bicknacre
Purleigh
Mundon
Cold Norton
Latchingdon
East Hanningfield
Woodham Ferrers
Stow Maries
Bradwell Waterside
Bradwell on Sea
Ramsey Island
St Lawrence
Tillingham
Steeple
Lower Mayland
Asheldham
Dengie
Mayland
Southminster
Althorne
Coalhill
Rettendon
South Woodham Ferrers
South Hanningfield
North Fambridge
Bridgemarsh Island
Ostend
Stoneyhills
Montsale
Deal Hall
Burnham-on-Crouch
Creeksea
Rettendon Place
South Fambridge
Crouch
Hullbridge
Battlesbridge
Canewdon
Courtsend
Churchend
Wickford
Rawreth
Hockley
Ashingdon
Hawkwell
Paglesham Churchend
Paglesham Eastend
Ballards Gore
Great Stambridge
Potton Island
FOULNESS ISLAND
Shotgate
Nevendon
North Benfleet
RAYLEIGH
Rochford
Stroud Green
Eastwood
Barling
Little Wakering
Havengore Island
Great Wakering
Bowers Gifford
Thundersley
Daws Heath
Hadleigh
Hope's Grn
Prittlewell
Southend-on-Sea
Bournes Green
Southchurch
North Shoebury
South Benfleet
Leigh on Sea
Thorpe Bay
Winter Gardens
Westcliff-on-Sea
Shoeburyness
Cambridge Town
CANVEY ISLAND
Coryton
Leigh Beck
Thames Haven
THAMES ESTUARY
Allhallows-on-Sea
Allhallows
St Mary Hoo
Grain
Cliffe
Cooling
Lower Stoke
High Halstow
Stoke
North Street
Cliffe Woods
Medway
Hoo St.Werburgh
Chattenden
Upnor
Frindsbury
Sheerness
West Minster
Halfway Houses
Minster
Queenborough
Rushenden
Eastchurch
Warden
Leysdown-on-Sea
ISLE OF SHEPPEY
Isle of Harty
The Swale
Brompton
Grange
ROCHESTER
Gillingham
Ham Green
Lower Halstow
Upchurch
Iwade
Kemsley
Rainham
Breach
Luton
Wayfield
Hempstead
Walderslade
Moor Street
Wigmore
Bobbing
Newington
Milton Regis
SITTINGBOURNE
Conyer
Uplees
Hartlip
Borden
Barrow Green
Bapchild
Teynham
Oare
Faversham
Graveney
Goodnestone
Bredhurst
Oad Street
Stockbury
Rodmersham
Tunstall
Highsted
Lynsted
Ospringe
Preston
Boughton Street
Dunkirk
Dargate
Hernhill
Yorkletts
Seasalter
WHITSTABLE
Tankerton
Swalecliffe
HERNE BAY
Greenhill
Chestfield
South Street
Herne
Reculver
Hillborough
Beltinge
Broomfield
Hoath
Calcott
Upstreet
Hersden
Broad Oak
Tyler Hill
Honey Hill
Blean
Rough Common
Hales Place
Sturry
Westbere
Fordwich
Canterbury
Wickhambreux
Littlebourne
Harbledown
Thanington
Chartham Hatch
Oversland
South Street
North Street
Bredgar
South Green
Swanton Street
Milstead
Newnham
Frinsted
Boxley
Bicknor
Hucking
Thurnham
Detling
Broad Street
Sandling
Maidstone
Roseacre
Bearsted
Eyhorne Street
Tovil
Shepway
Otham
East Farleigh
Loose
Boughton Monchelsea
Langley
Langley Heath
Leeds
Broomfield
Kingswood
Harrietsham
Lenham
Sandway
Lenham Heath
Warren Street
Stalisfield Green
Leaveland
Old Wives Lees
Shottenden
Chilham
Chartham
Shalmsford Street
Garlinge Green
Nackington
Street End
Lower Hardres
Bishopsbourne
Bekesbourne
Patrixbourne
Adisham
Bridge
Kingston
Upper Hardres Court
Petham
Barham
Derringstone
Molash
Challock
Godmersham
Sole Street
Crundale
Bilting
Waltham
Bossingham
Charing
Charing Heath
Westwell
Boughton Aluph
Warmlake
Chart Corner
Chart Sutton
Sutton Valence
Linton
Grafty Green
Boughton Malherbe
Ulcombe
Scale
0 5 10 15 km
0 5 10 miles

Major administrative and Postcode boundaries

- County and unitary authority boundaries
- District boundaries
- Postcode boundaries
- Area covered by this atlas

Scale

0 5 10 15 km

0 5 10 miles

Cambridgeshire
Suffolk
Hertfordshire
London
Medway
Kent
Essex
Uttlesford
Braintree
Colchester
Tendring
Harlow
Epping Forest
Chelmsford
Maldon
Brentwood
Basildon
Rochford
Castle Point
Southend-on-Sea

TL TM TQ TR

Glemsford
Haverhill
Clare
Belchamp St Paul
Sudbury
Ipswich
Holbrook
Felixstowe
East Bergholt
Manningtree
Harwich
Great Chesterford
Steeple Bumpstead
Saffron Walden
Castle Hedingham
Bures
Newport
Great Sampford
Great Bardfield
Clavering
Thaxted
Halstead
Earls Colne
Ardleigh
Great Oakley
Stansted Mountfitchet
Elsenham
Stebbing
Braintree
Coggeshall
Colchester
Wivenhoe
Walton-on-the-Naze
Frinton-on- Sea
Great Dunmow
Tye Green
Bishop's Stortford
Layer-de-la- Haye
Brightlingsea
St Osyth
Clacton-on-Sea
Great Leighs
Tiptree
Witham
Sawbridgeworth
Hatfield Heath
West Mersea
Hatfield Peverel
Tollesbury
Harlow
Broomfield
Chelmsford
Maldon
Chipping Ongar
Danbury
Tillingham
Waltham Abbey
Epping
East Hanningfield
Cold Norton
Southminster
Stock
Loughton
Abridge
Burnham-on-Crouch
Canewdon
Billericay
Brentwood
Wickford
Chingford
Rayleigh
Ingrave
Romford
Basildon
Great Wakering
Upminster
Southend-on-Sea
Barking
Stanford-le-Hope
Canvey Island
Tilbury

IP29 IP1 IP2 IP3 IP4 IP5 IP7 IP8 IP9 IP10 IP11
CB1 CB9 CB11 CO1 CO2 CO3 CO4 CO5 CO6 CO7 CO8 CO9 CO10 CO11 CO12 CO13 CO14 CO15 CO16
SG8 SG9 SG12
CM0 CM1 CM2 CM3 CM4 CM5 CM6 CM7 CM8 CM9 CM10 CM11 CM12 CM13 CM14 CM15 CM16 CM17 CM18 CM19 CM20 CM21 CM22 CM23 CM24 CM77
EN3 EN8 EN9 EN10 EN11
E4 E6 E7 E11 E12 E17 E18
IG1 IG2 IG3 IG4 IG5 IG6 IG7 IG8 IG9 IG10 IG11
RM1 RM2 RM3 RM4 RM5 RM6 RM7 RM8 RM9 RM10 RM11 RM12 RM13 RM14 RM15 RM16 RM17 RM18 RM19 RM20
SS0 SS1 SS2 SS3 SS4 SS5 SS6 SS7 SS8 SS9 SS11 SS12 SS13 SS14 SS15 SS16 SS17
DA1 DA2 DA8 DA9 DA10 DA11 DA12 DA17 DA18

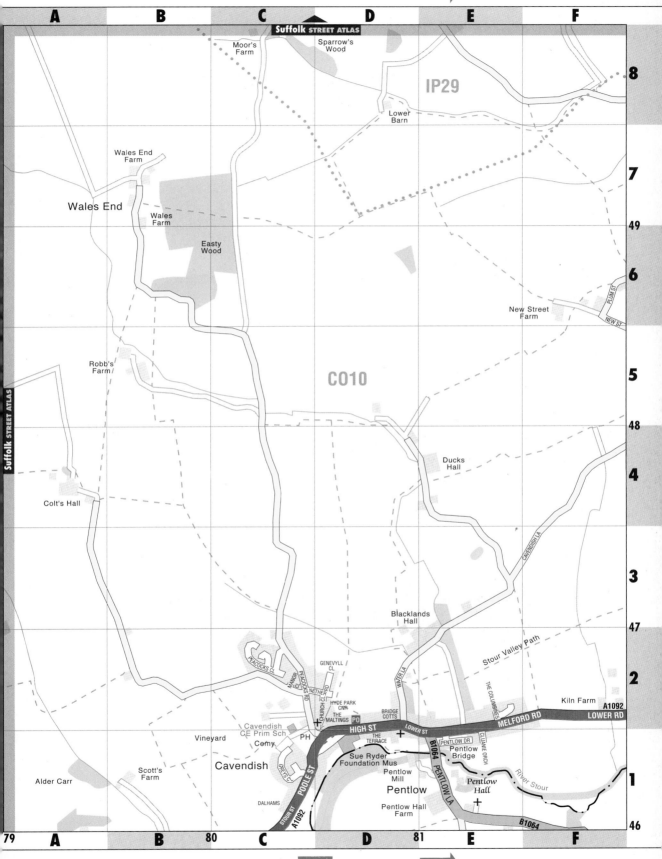

2

A
B
C
D
E
F
Suffolk STREET ATLAS
Moor's Farm
Sparrow's Wood
IP29
Lower Barn
Wales End Farm
Wales End
Wales Farm
Easty Wood
8
7
49
6
New Street Farm
PLUM ST
NEW ST
Robb's Farm
CO10
5
48
Ducks Hall
Colt's Hall
4
CAVENDISH LA
3
Blacklands Hall
47
Stour Valley Path
PEACOCKS CL
MANOR CL
PEACOCKS RD
GENEVYLL CL
NETHER RD
CHURCH CL
HYDE PARK CNR
THE MALTINGS
PO
BRIDGE COTTS
WATER LA
THE COLUMBINES
Kiln Farm
A1092
MELFORD RD
LOWER RD
2
HIGH ST
LOWER ST
Cavendish CE Prim Sch
PH
Vineyard
Cemy
THE TERRACE
PENTLOW DR
CLUANIE ORCH
Pentlow Bridge
B1064
Sue Ryder Foundation Mus
Cavendish
GREYS CL
POOLE ST
Scott's Farm
Alder Carr
Pentlow Mill
Pentlow
PENTLOW LA
Pentlow Hall
River Stour
1
DALHAMS
STOUR ST
A1092
Pentlow Hall Farm
B1064
46
79
A
B
80
C
D
81
E
F

13

2

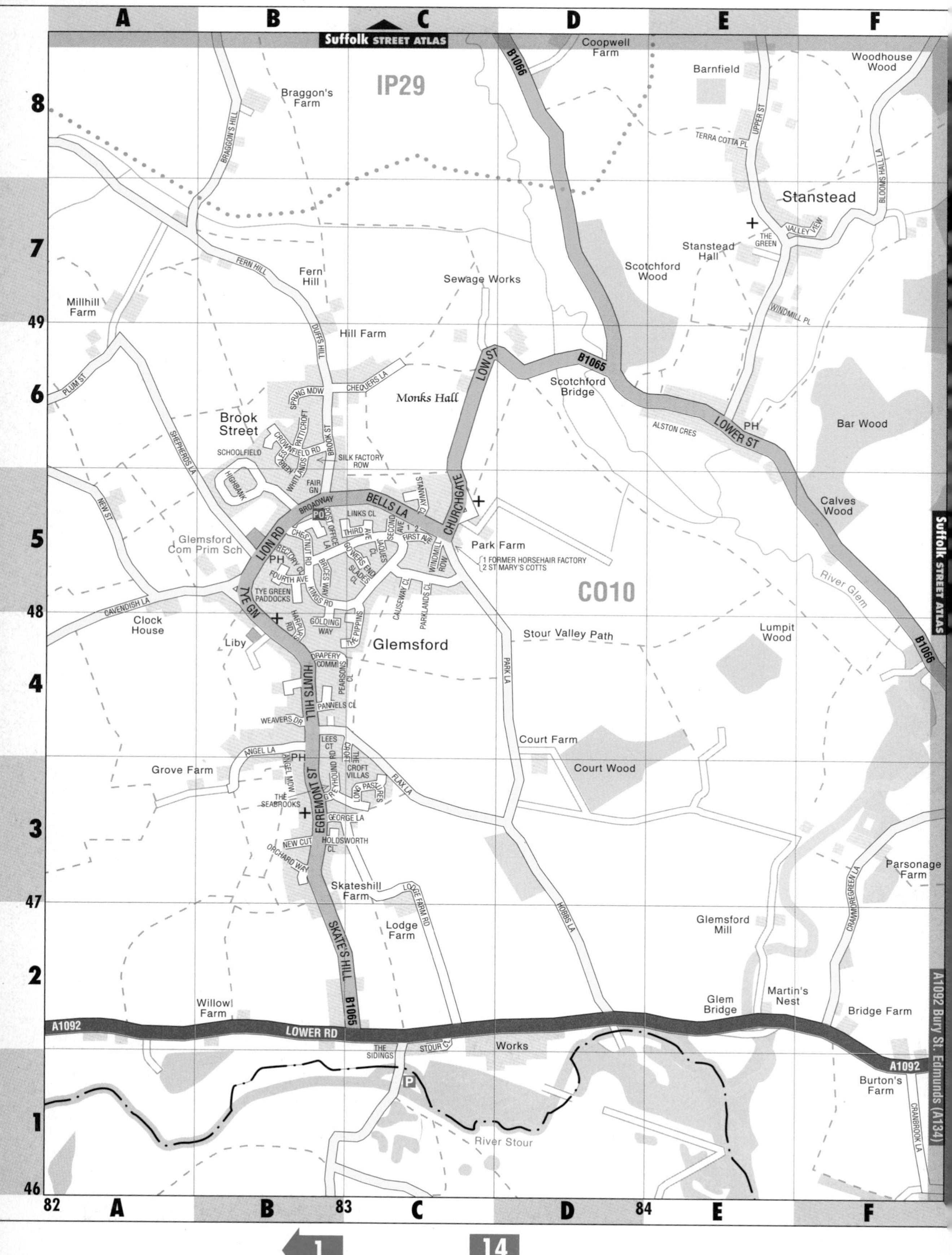

Suffolk STREET ATLAS

IP29

Coopwell Farm

Barnfield

Woodhouse Wood

Braggon's Farm

UPPER ST

BLOOMS HALL LA

TERRA COTTA PL

Stanstead

BRAGGON'S HILL

8

FERN HILL

Fern Hill

Stanstead Hall

THE GREEN

VALLEY VIEW

7

Sewage Works

Scotchford Wood

WINDMILL PL

Millhill Farm

PLUM ST

DUFFS HILL

Hill Farm

49

LOW ST

B1065

Scotchford Bridge

SHEPHERDS LA

SPRING MDW

CHEQUERS LA

Monks Hall

ALSTON CRES

LOWER ST

PH

Bar Wood

6

Brook Street

PATTICROFT

WHITLANDS RD

CROWNFIELD RD

BOOTH ST

SILK FACTORY ROW

SCHOOLFIELD

FAIR GN

HIGHBANK

Glemsford Com Prim Sch

Calves Wood

NEW ST

LION RD

PH

BROADWAY

REGENT ST

RECTORY CL

CHESTNUT RD

POST OFFICE

LINKS CL

THIRD AVE

SECOND AVE 1 2

STANWAY CL

BELLS LA

FIRST AVE

CHURCHGATE

Park Farm

River Glem

B1066

5

CAVENDISH LA

THE GN

FOURTH AVE

BRACES WAY

KINGS RD

TYE GREEN PADDOCKS

JACQUES CL

BOWERS END

SLADE CL

WINDMILL ROW

CAUSEWAY CL

PARKLANDS CL

1 FORMER HORSEHAIR FACTORY 2 ST MARY'S COTTS

CO10

Clock House

48

Liby

GOLDING WAY

HARGRAVE CL

ST PIPPINS

DRAPERY COMM

PEARSON WAY

Glemsford

Stour Valley Path

PARK LA

Lumpit Wood

4

HUNTS HILL

WEAVERS DR

ANGEL LA

PANNELLS CL

LEES CT

NEW CUT

PH

ANGEL MDW

THE SEABROOKS

CROFT VILLAS

THE CROFT

PASS

FLAX LA

Court Farm

Court Wood

Grove Farm

EGREMONT ST

GEORGE LA

HOLDSWORTH CL

HOBBS LA

Parsonage Farm

3

ORCHARD WAY

Skateshill Farm

Lodge Farm

LODGE FARM RD

CRAMMREGREEN LA

Glemsford Mill

47

SKATE'S HILL

Willow Farm

B1065

2

Glem Bridge

Martin's Nest

Bridge Farm

A1092

LOWER RD

THE SIDINGS

STOUR CL

Works

Glem Bridge

A1092

A1092 Bury St. Edmunds (A134)

P

Burton's Farm

River Stour

CRABBROOK LA

1

46

Suffolk STREET ATLAS

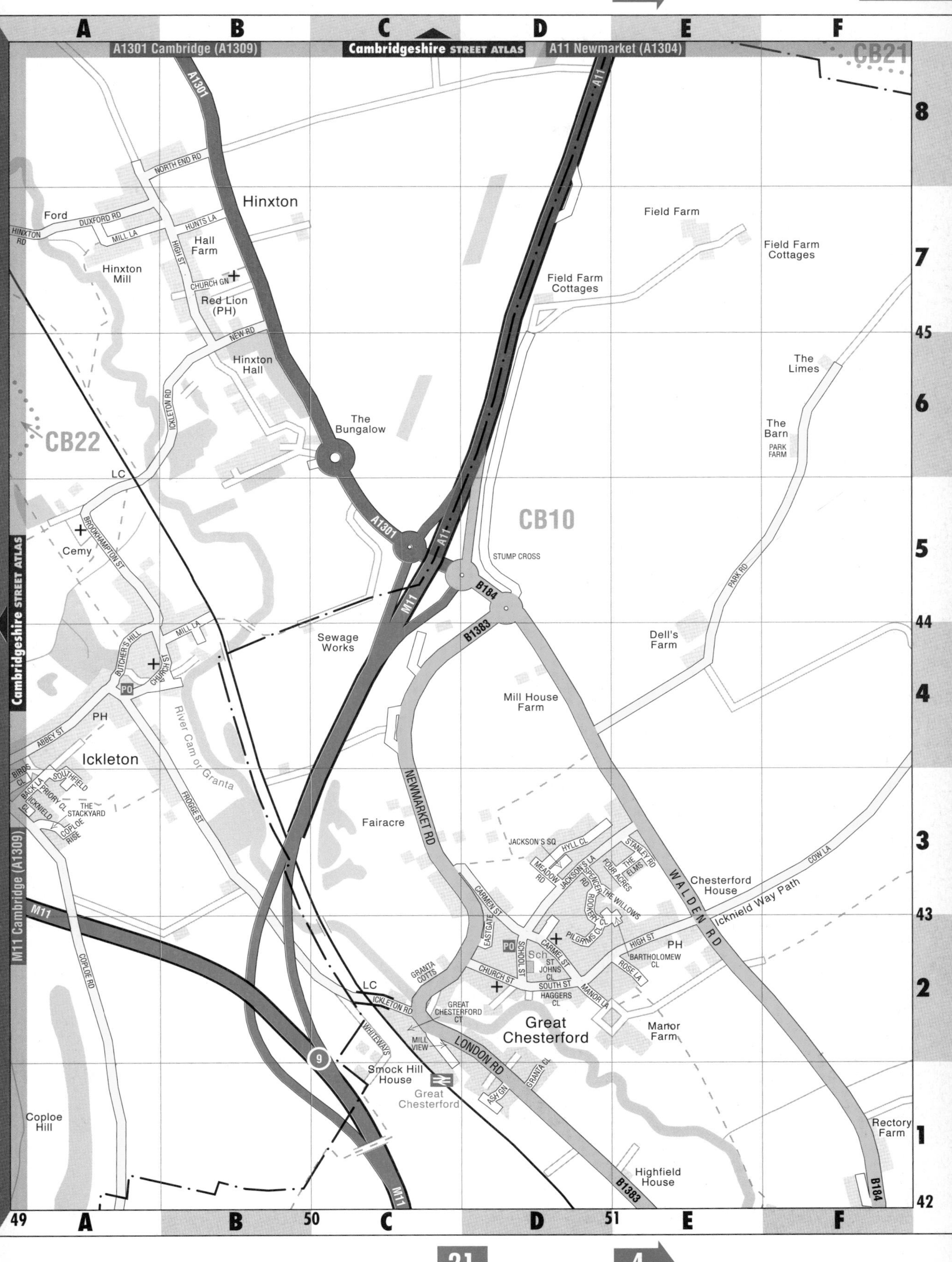

A1301 Cambridge (A1309)

A11 Newmarket (A1304)

CB21

CB22

Hinxton

Ford

DUXFORD RD

HINXTON RD

NORTH END RD

MILL LA

HUNTS LA

HIGH ST

Hinxton Mill

Hall Farm

CHURCH GN

Red Lion (PH)

NEW RD

Hinxton Hall

ICKLETON RD

The Bungalow

LC

BROOKHAMPTON ST

Cemy

BUTCHER'S HILL

CHURCH ST

MILL LA

PO

PH

Ickleton

ABBEY ST

BIRDS CL

SOUTHFIELD

BACK LA

PRIORY CL

ICKNIELD

COPLOE RIDE

THE STACKYARD

FROGGE ST

River Cam or Granta

Sewage Works

Stump Cross

CB10

A1301

A11

M11

B184

B1383

Dell's Farm

Mill House Farm

Fairacre

NEWMARKET RD

Field Farm

Field Farm Cottages

Field Farm Cottages

The Limes

The Barn

PARK FARM

PARK RD

Chesterford House

WALDEN RD

Icknield Way Path

COW LA

STANLEY RD

HYLL CL

JACKSON'S SQ

JACKSON'S LA

MEADOW RD

FOUR ACRES

THE ELMS

TANNERS-THE-WILLOWS

ROOKERY RD

CARMEL ST

PILGRIMS CL

EASTGATE

SCHOOL ST

PO

Sch

ST JOHNS CL

CARMEL ST

CHURCH ST

SOUTH ST

HAGGERS CL

HIGH ST

ROSE LA

BARTHOLOMEW CL

PH

MANOR LA

GRANTA COTTS

LC

ICKLETON RD

GREAT CHESTERFORD CT

WHITEWAYS

MILL VIEW

Smock Hill House

9

LONDON RD

ASH GN

GRANTA CL

Great Chesterford

Great Chesterford

Manor Farm

B1383

Highfield House

Rectory Farm

B184

Coploe Hill

M11 Cambridge (A1309)

M11

COPLOE RD

8
7
45
6
5
44
4
43
3
2
1
42

49   A   B   50   C   D   51   E   F

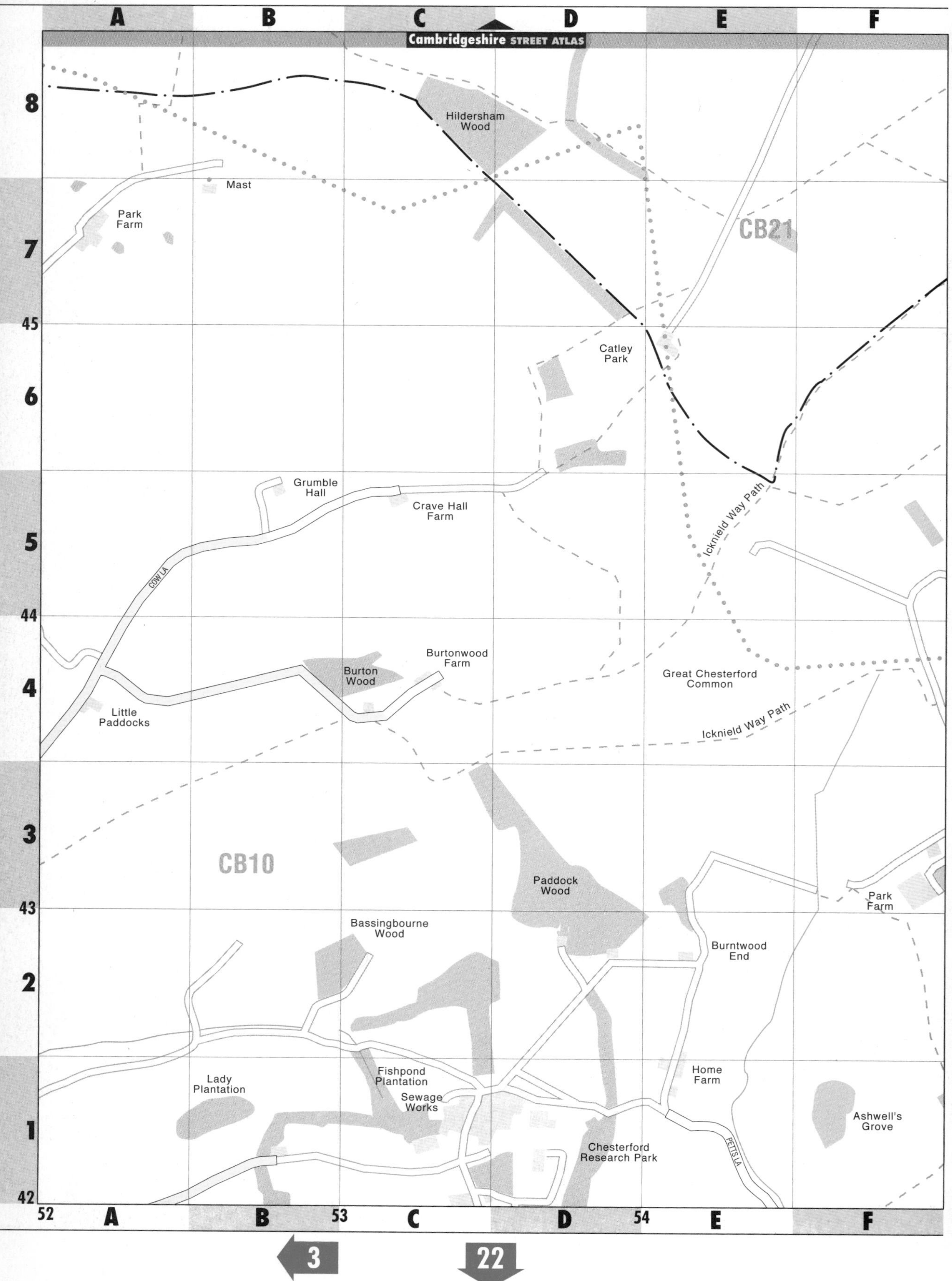

Cambridgeshire STREET ATLAS

A   B   C   D   E   F

8

Hildersham
Wood

Mast

7

Park
Farm

CB21

45

Catley
Park

6

Grumble
Hall

Crave Hall
Farm

5

COW LA

Icknield Way Path

44

Burtonwood
Farm

4

Burton
Wood

Great Chesterford
Common

Little
Paddocks

Icknield Way Path

3

CB10

Paddock
Wood

Park
Farm

43

Bassingbourne
Wood

Burntwood
End

2

Lady
Plantation

Fishpond
Plantation

Home
Farm

Ashwell's
Grove

Sewage
Works

1

PETTS LA

Chesterford
Research Park

42

52   A   B   53   C   D   54   E   F

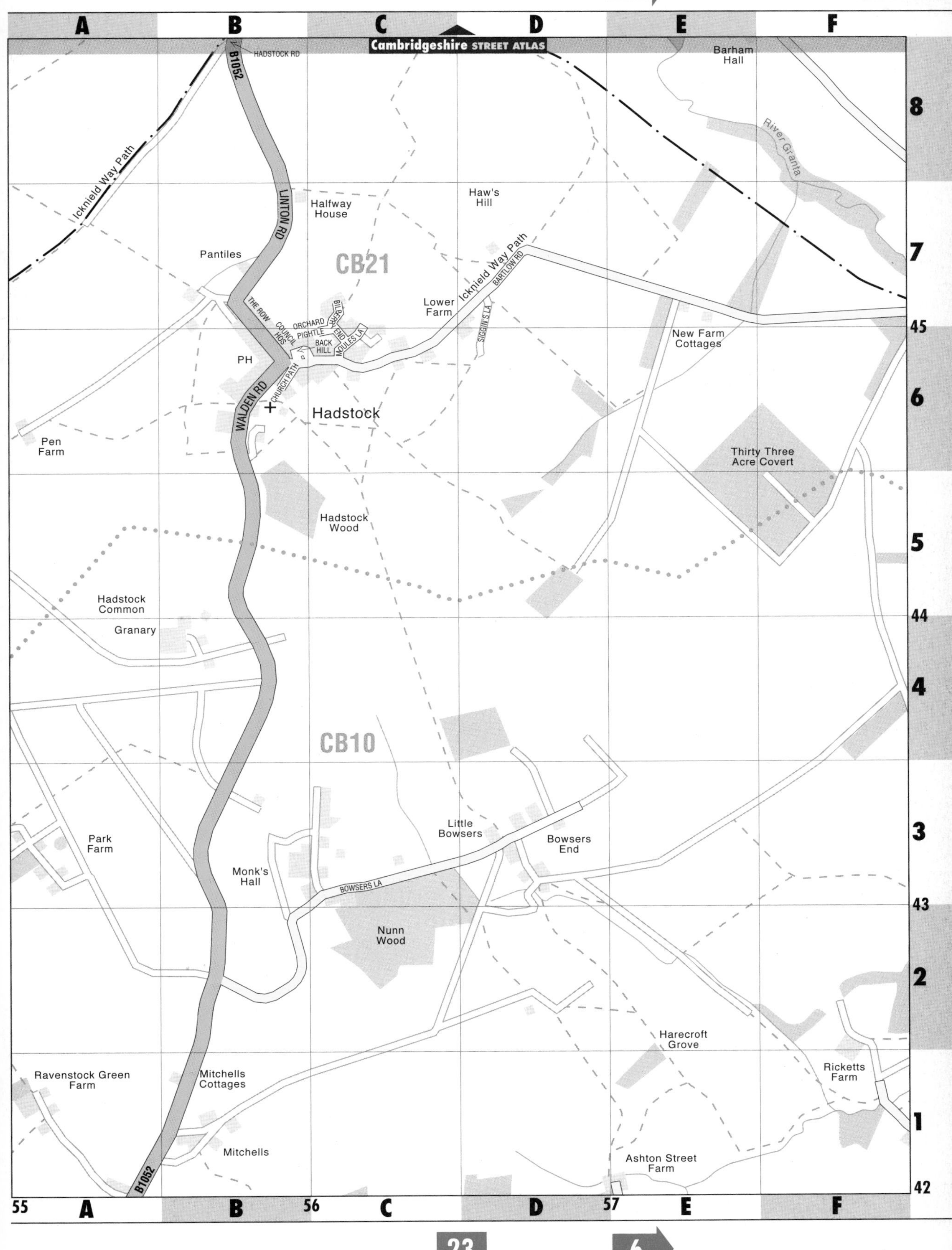

Cambridgeshire STREET ATLAS

Barham Hall

River Granta

Haw's Hill

Halfway House

CB21

Pantiles

Icknield Way Path

B1052

HADSTOCK RD

LINTON RD

THE ROW

COUNCIL HSES

ORCHARD
PIGHTLE
BILL'S END
MOULES LA
BACK HILL

PH

WALDEN RD

CHURCH PATH

+

Hadstock

Pen Farm

Lower Farm

SUGGIN'S LA

BARTLOW RD

Icknield Way Path

New Farm Cottages

Thirty Three Acre Covert

Hadstock Wood

Hadstock Common

Granary

CB10

Park Farm

Monk's Hall

BOWSERS LA

Little Bowsers

Bowsers End

Nunn Wood

Harecroft Grove

Ricketts Farm

Ravenstock Green Farm

Mitchells Cottages

Mitchells

B1052

Ashton Street Farm

5

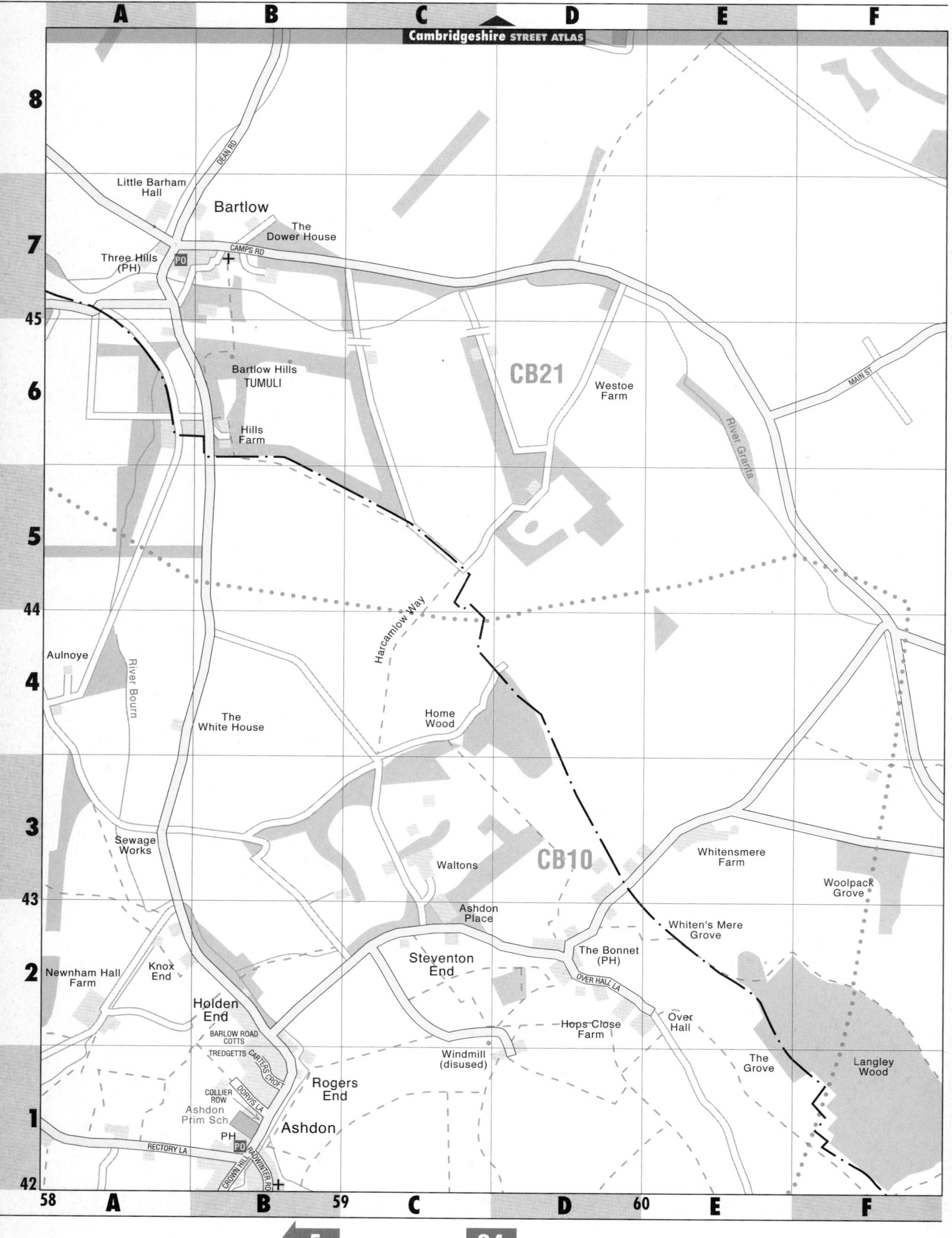

Cambridgeshire STREET ATLAS

Little Barham Hall

Bartlow

The Dower House

Three Hills (PH)

PO

CAMPS RD

DEAN RD

Bartlow Hills TUMULI

Hills Farm

CB21

Westoe Farm

River Granta

MAIN ST

Harcamlow Way

Aulnoye

River Bourn

The White House

Home Wood

Sewage Works

Waltons

CB10

Whitensmere Farm

Woolpack Grove

Ashdon Place

Whiten's Mere Grove

Newnham Hall Farm

Knox End

Steventon End

The Bonnet (PH)

OVER HALL LA

Over Hall

Holden End

BARLOW ROAD COTTS

TREDGETTS CARTERS CROFT

Hops Close Farm

Windmill (disused)

The Grove

Langley Wood

COLLIER ROW

DOBYS LA

Ashdon Prim Sch

PH

PO

RADWINTER RD

Rogers End

Ashdon

RECTORY LA

CROWN HILL

5 24

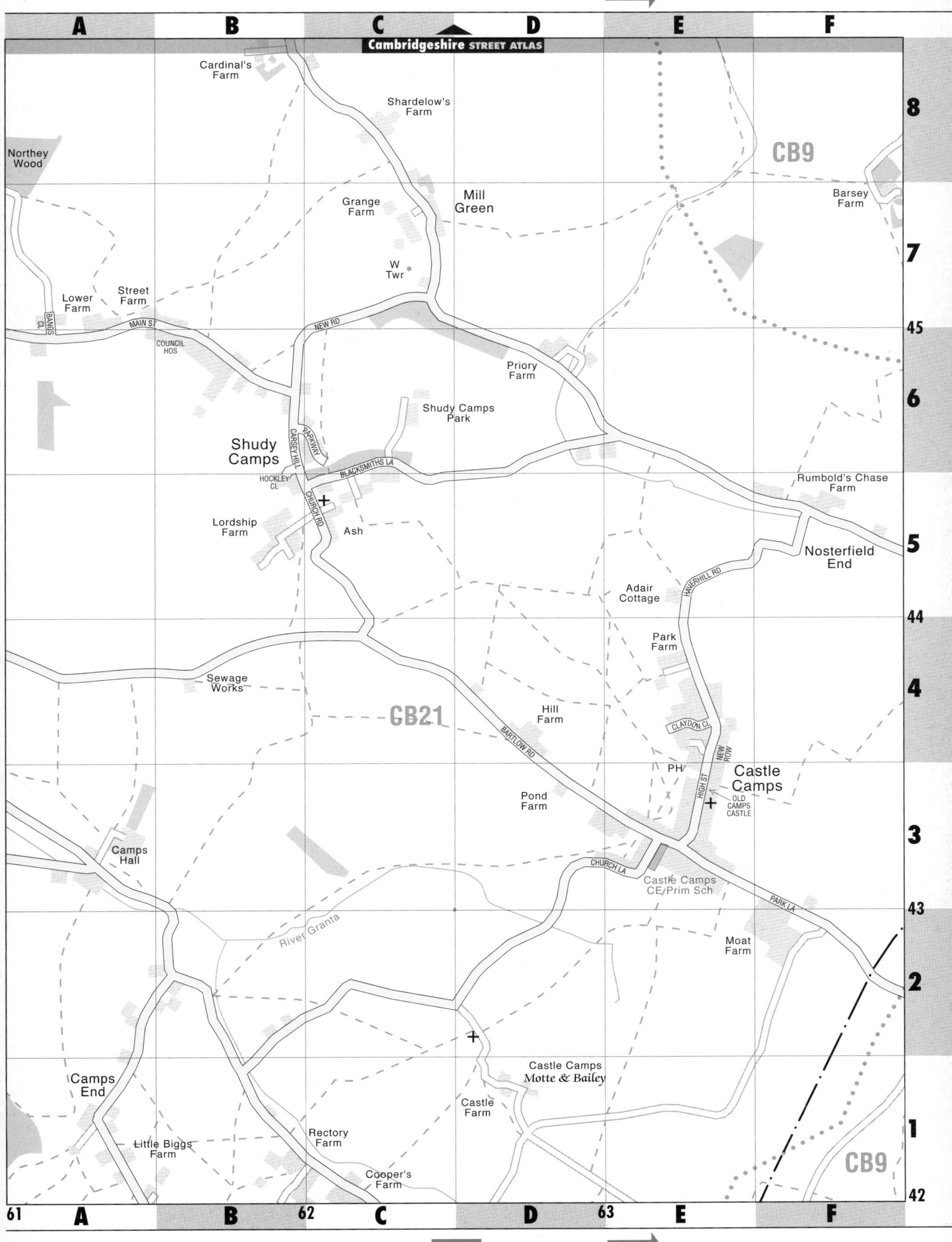

Cambridgeshire STREET ATLAS

CB9

8

8

Northey Wood

Cardinal's Farm

Shardelow's Farm

Mill Green

Barsey Farm

7

Grange Farm

W Twr

Lower Farm

Street Farm

BANKS CL

MAIN ST

NEW RD

45

COUNCIL HOS

Priory Farm

6

Shudy Camps Park

Shudy Camps

CARSEY HILL

PARKWAY

BLACKSMITHS LA

Rumbold's Chase Farm

HOCKLEY CL

Nosterfield End

5

CHURCH RD

Lordship Farm

Ash

Adair Cottage

HAVERHILL RD

44

Park Farm

GB21

Sewage Works

Hill Farm

BARTLOW RD

CLAYDON CL

4

NEW ROW

PH

Castle Camps

Pond Farm

HIGH ST

OLD CAMPS CASTLE

3

Camps Hall

CHURCH LA

Castle Camps CE/Prim Sch

PARK LA

43

River Granta

Moat Farm

2

Camps End

Castle Camps Motte & Bailey

Little Biggs Farm

Rectory Farm

Castle Farm

CB9

1

Cooper's Farm

42

61

62

63

25

8

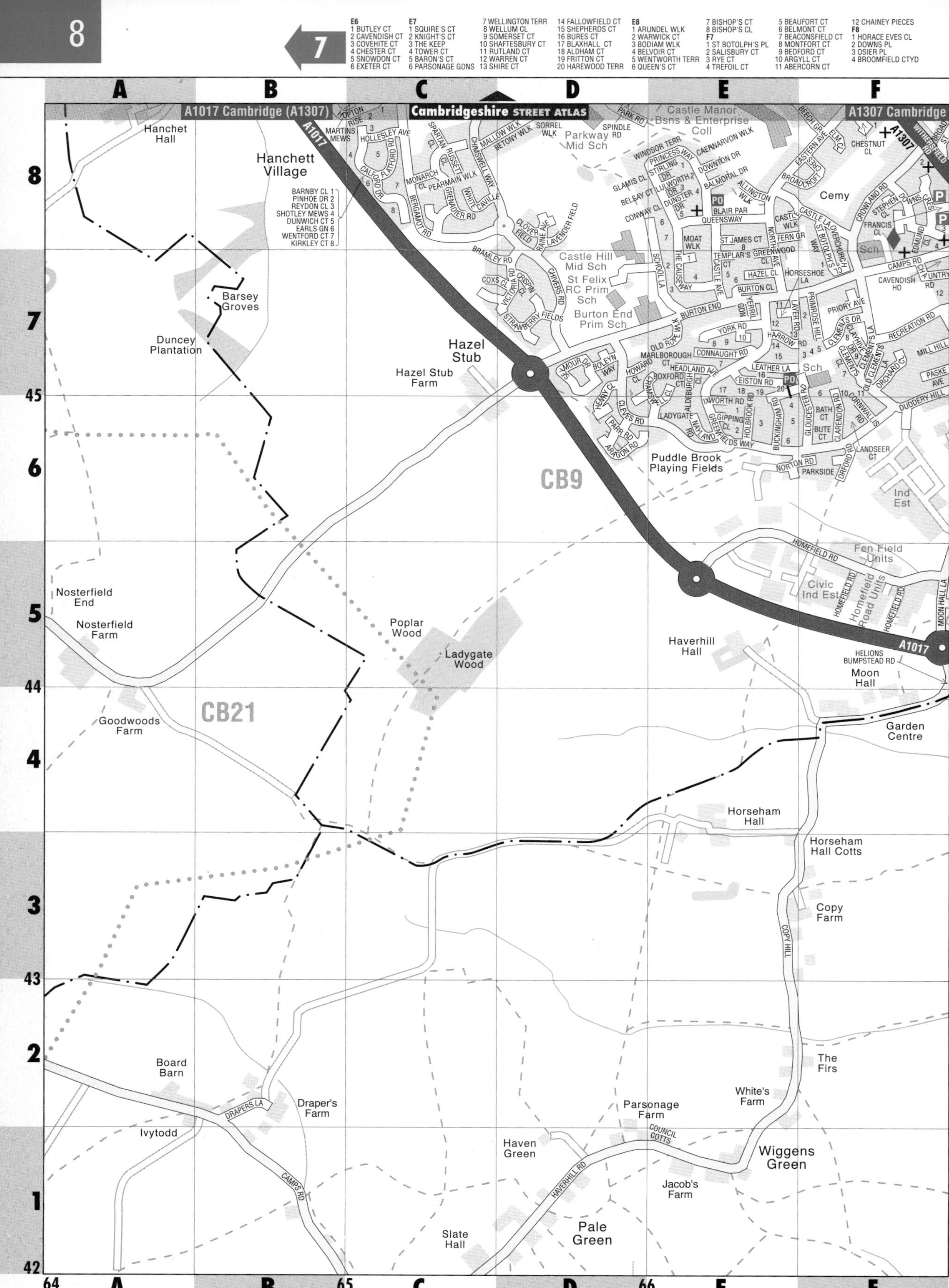

7

E6
1 BUTLEY CT
2 CAVENDISH CT
3 COVEHITE CT
4 CHESTER CT
5 SNOWDON CT
6 EXETER CT

E7
1 SQUIRE'S CT
2 KNIGHT'S CT
3 THE KEEP
4 TOWER CT
5 BARON'S CT
6 PARSONAGE GDNS

7 WELLINGTON TERR
8 WELLUM CL
9 SOMERSET CT
10 SHAFTESBURY CT
11 RUTLAND CT
12 WARREN CT
13 SHIRE CT

14 FALLOWFIELD CT
15 SHEPHERDS CT
16 BURES CT
17 BLAXHALL CT
18 ALDHAM CT
19 FRITTON CT
20 HAREWOOD TERR

E8
1 ARUNDEL WLK
2 WARWICK CT
3 BODIAM WLK
4 BELVOIR CT
5 WENTWORTH TERR
6 QUEEN'S CT

7 BISHOP'S CT
8 BISHOP'S CL
F7
1 ST BOTOLPH'S PL
2 SALISBURY CT
3 RYE CT
4 TREFOIL CT

5 BEAUFORT CT
6 BELMONT CT
7 BEACONSFIELD CT
8 BEDFORD CT
10 ARGYLL CT
11 ABERCORN CT

12 CHAINEY PIECES
F8
1 HORACE EVES CL
2 DOWNS PL
3 OSIER PL
4 BROOMFIELD CTYD

Cambridgeshire STREET ATLAS

A1017 Cambridge (A1307)

A1307 Cambridge

Hanchet Hall

Hanchett Village

BARNBY CL 1
PINHOE DR 2
REYDON CL 3
SHOTLEY MEWS 4
DUNWICH CT 5
EARLS GN 6
WENTFORD CT 7
KIRKLEY CT 8

Barsey Groves

Duncey Plantation

Hazel Stub

Hazel Stub Farm

CB9

Puddle Brook Playing Fields

Nosterfield End

Nosterfield Farm

Poplar Wood

Ladygate Wood

Haverhill Hall

Helions Bumpstead Rd

Moon Hall

CB21

Goodwoods Farm

Garden Centre

Horseham Hall

Horseham Hall Cotts

Copy Farm

Board Barn

Draper's Farm

DRAPERS LA

The Firs

White's Farm

Parsonage Farm

COUNCIL COTTS

Wiggens Green

Ivytodd

CAMPS RD

Haven Green

Jacob's Farm

HAVERHILL RD

Slate Hall

Pale Green

64   A   65   B   C   D   66   E   F

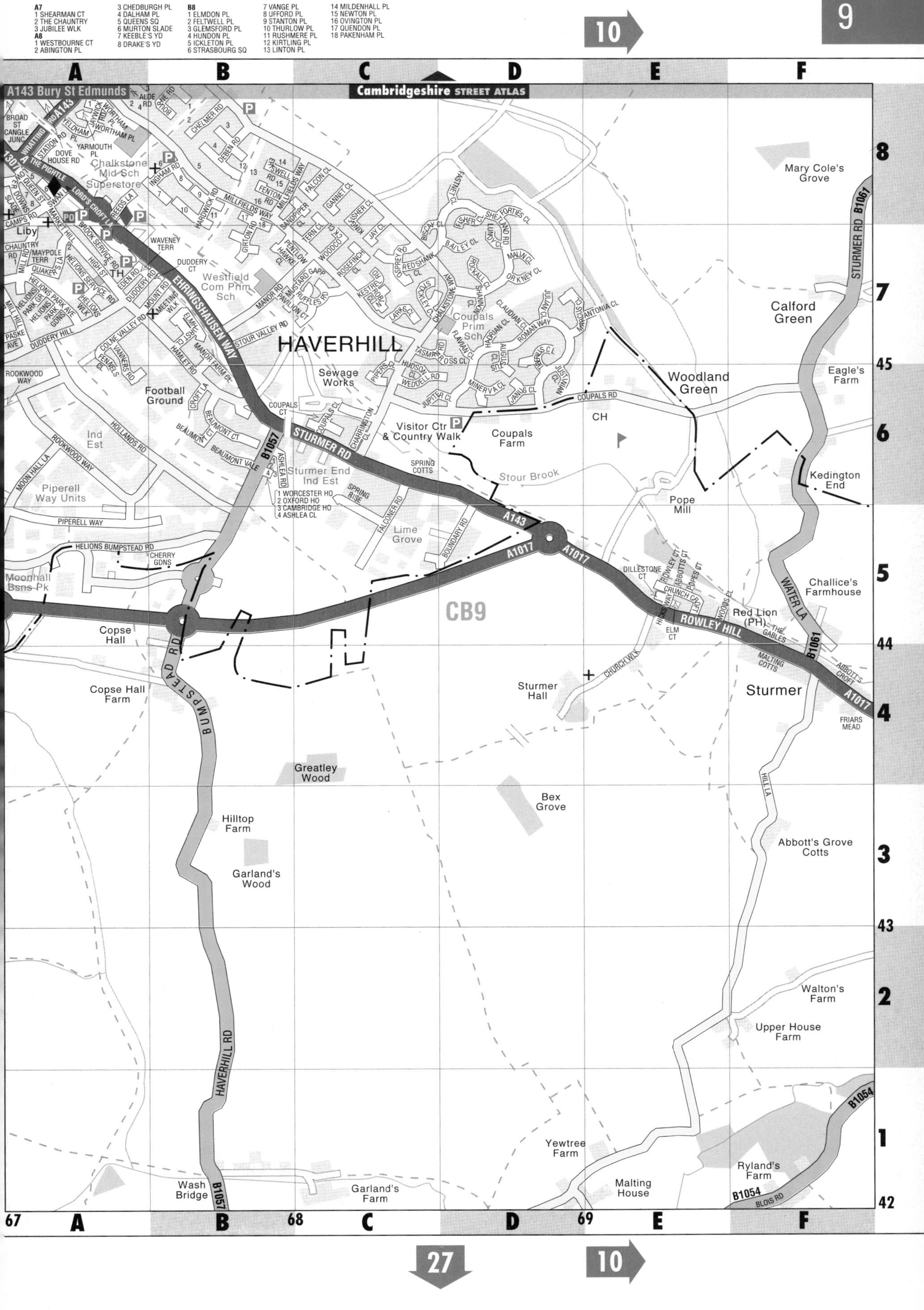

A7
1 SHEARMAN CT
2 THE CHAUNTRY
3 JUBILEE WLK

A8
1 WESTBOURNE CT
2 ABINGTON PL

3 CHEDBURGH PL
4 DALHAM PL
5 QUEENS SQ
6 MURTON SLADE
7 KEEBLE'S YD
8 DRAKE'S YD

B8
1 ELMDON PL
2 FELTWELL PL
3 GLEMSFORD PL
4 HUNDON PL
5 ICKLETON PL
6 STRASBOURG SQ

7 VANGE PL
8 UFFORD PL
9 STANTON PL
10 THURLOW PL
11 RUSHMERE PL
12 KIRTLING PL
13 LINTON PL

14 MILDENHALL PL
15 NEWTON PL
16 OVINGTON PL
17 QUENDON PL
18 PAKENHAM PL

A143 Bury St Edmunds

Cambridgeshire STREET ATLAS

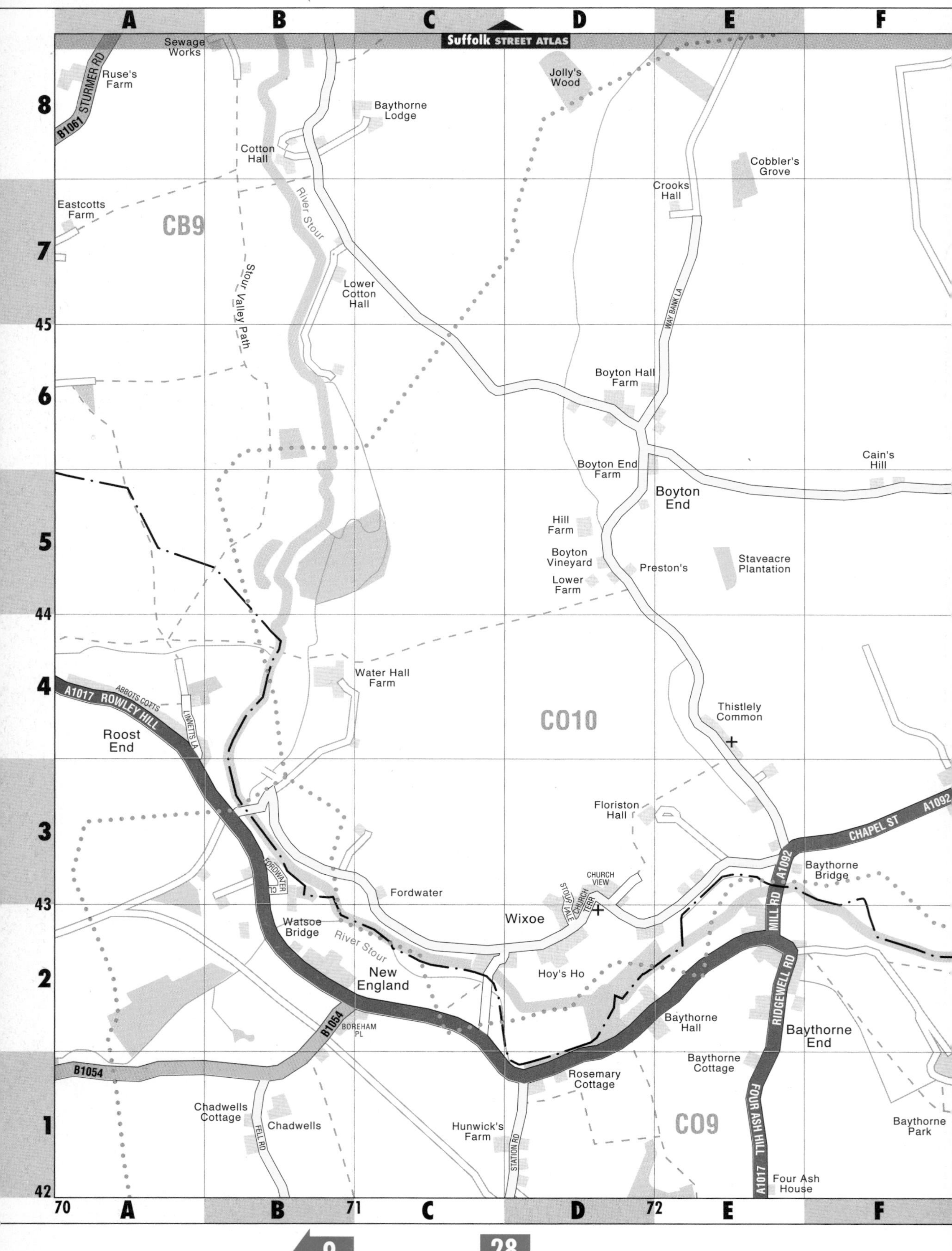

Suffolk STREET ATLAS

STURMER RD
B1061

Sewage Works

Ruse's Farm

Jolly's Wood

Baythorne Lodge

Cotton Hall

Cobbler's Grove

Crooks Hall

River Stour

Eastcotts Farm

CB9

Stour Valley Path

Lower Cotton Hall

WAY BANK LA

Boyton Hall Farm

Cain's Hill

Boyton End Farm

Boyton End

Hill Farm

Boyton Vineyard

Staveacre Plantation

Preston's

Lower Farm

CO10

Thistlely Common

Water Hall Farm

ABBOTS COTTS

A1017 ROWLEY HILL

LINNETTS LA

Roost End

Floriston Hall

CHAPEL ST

A1092

A1092

Baythorne Bridge

MILL RD

CHURCH VIEW

STOUR VALE

CHURCH TERR

Fordwater

Wixoe

Watsoe Bridge

River Stour

New England

Hoy's Ho

Baythorne Hall

RIDGEWELL RD

Baythorne End

Baythorne Cottage

B1054

BOREHAM PL

Rosemary Cottage

Baythorne Cottage

CO9

FOUR ASH HILL

A1017

Baythorne Park

B1054

Chadwells Cottage

FELL RD

Chadwells

Hunwick's Farm

STATION RD

Four Ash House

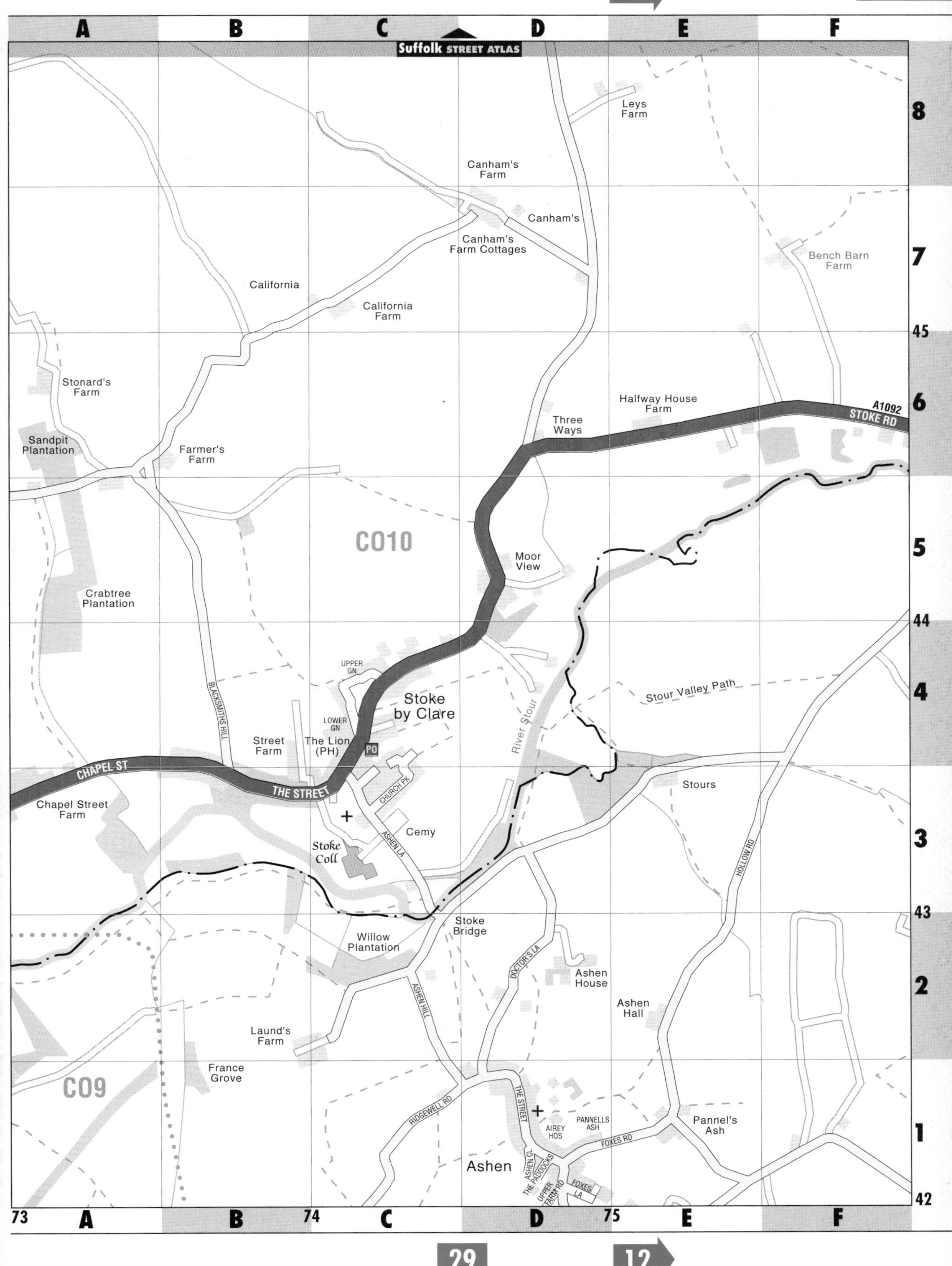

Suffolk STREET ATLAS

A1092 STOKE RD

CO10

CO9

Leys Farm

Canham's Farm

Canham's

Canham's Farm Cottages

California

California Farm

Bench Barn Farm

Stonard's Farm

Sandpit Plantation

Farmer's Farm

Crabtree Plantation

Halfway House Farm

Three Ways

Moor View

Stour Valley Path

River Stour

BLACKSMITHS HILL

UPPER GN

LOWER GN

Stoke by Clare

Street Farm

The Lion (PH)

PO

CHURCH PK

CHAPEL ST

THE STREET

Chapel Street Farm

Cemy

Stoke Coll

ASHEN LA

Stours

HOLLOW RD

Willow Plantation

Stoke Bridge

ASHEN HILL

DIXTOR'S LA

Ashen House

Ashen Hall

Laund's Farm

France Grove

RIDGEWELL RD

THE STREET

Ashen

AIREY HOS

PANNELLS ASH

Pannel's Ash

FOXES RD

THE PADDOCKS

ASHEN CL

UPPER PARM RD

FOXES LA

73 A B 74 C D 75 E F

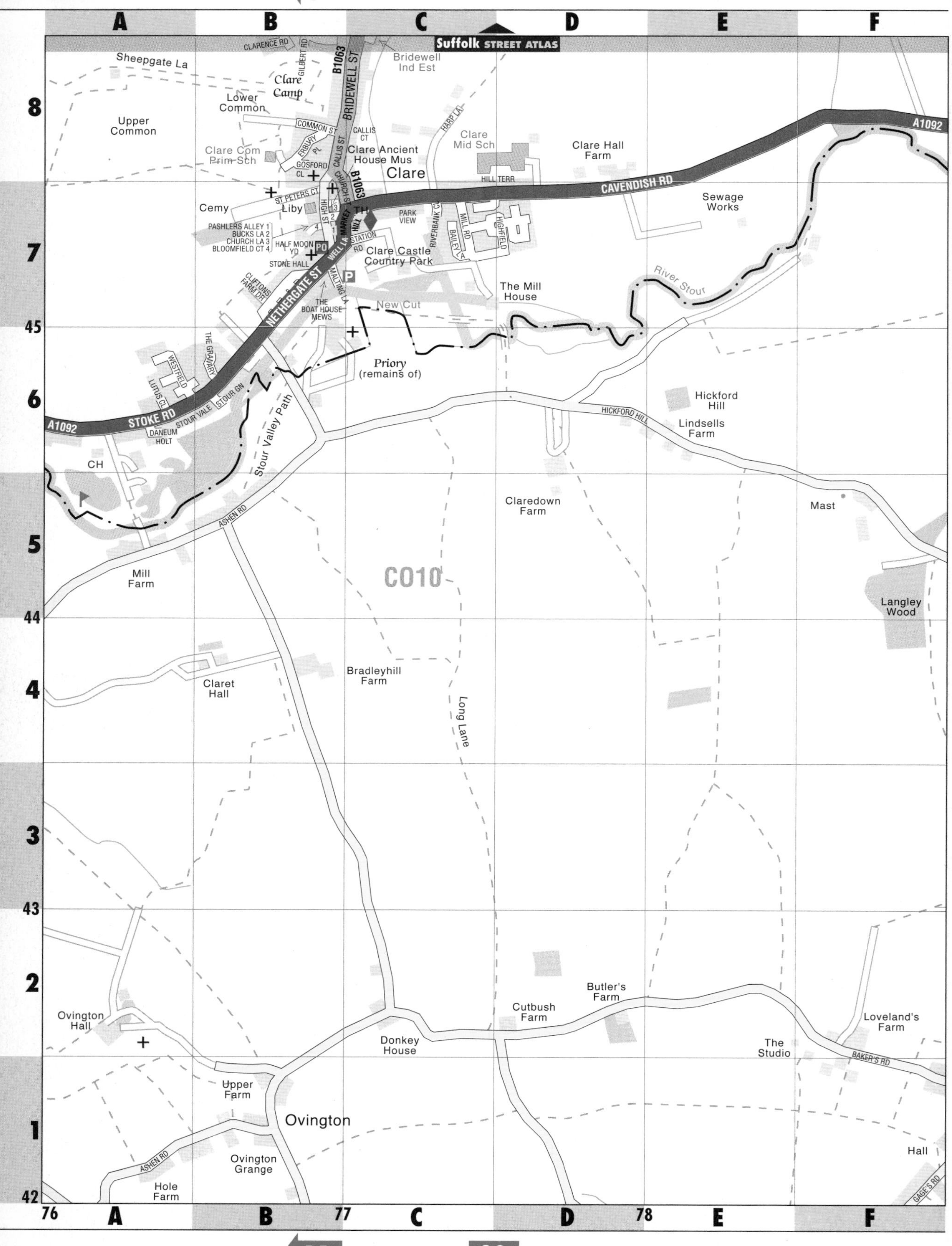

Suffolk STREET ATLAS

A B C D E F

8

7

45

6

5

44

4

3

43

2

1

42

76 A B 77 C D 78 E F

Sheepgate La

CLARENCE RD

GILBERT RD

Clare Camp

BRIDEWELL ST

B1063

Bridewell Ind Est

Upper Common

Lower Common

COMMON ST

Clare Com Prim Sch

FERBURY PL

GOSFORD CL

CALLIS CT

Clare Ancient House Mus

HARP LA

Clare Mid Sch

Clare Hall Farm

A1092

CAVENDISH RD

Sewage Works

HILL TERR

Clare

Cemy

ST PETERS CT

Liby

PASHLERS ALLEY 1
BUCKS LA 2
CHURCH LA 3
BLOOMFIELD CT 4

HALF MOON YD

HIGH ST

CHURCH ST

B1063

TH

WELL LA

MARKET

PO

STATION

PARK VIEW

RIVERBANK CL

MILL RD

BAILEY'S

HIGHFIELD

CLIFTONS FARM

STONE HALL

NETHERGATE ST

MALTING LA

P

Clare Castle Country Park

The Mill House

River Stour

THE BOAT HOUSE MEWS

New Cut

THE GRANARY

WESTFIELD

LOTUS CL

STOUR VALE

STOUR GN

DANEUM HOLT

STOKE RD

A1092

Priory (remains of)

Stour Valley Path

Hickford Hill

HICKFORD HILL

Lindsells Farm

CH

ASHEN RD

Mill Farm

Claredown Farm

Mast

CO10

Langley Wood

Claret Hall

Bradleyhill Farm

Long Lane

Ovington Hall

Cutbush Farm

Butler's Farm

Loveland's Farm

The Studio

BAKER'S RD

Upper Farm

Donkey House

Ovington

ASHEN RD

Ovington Grange

Hole Farm

Hall

GAGE'S RD

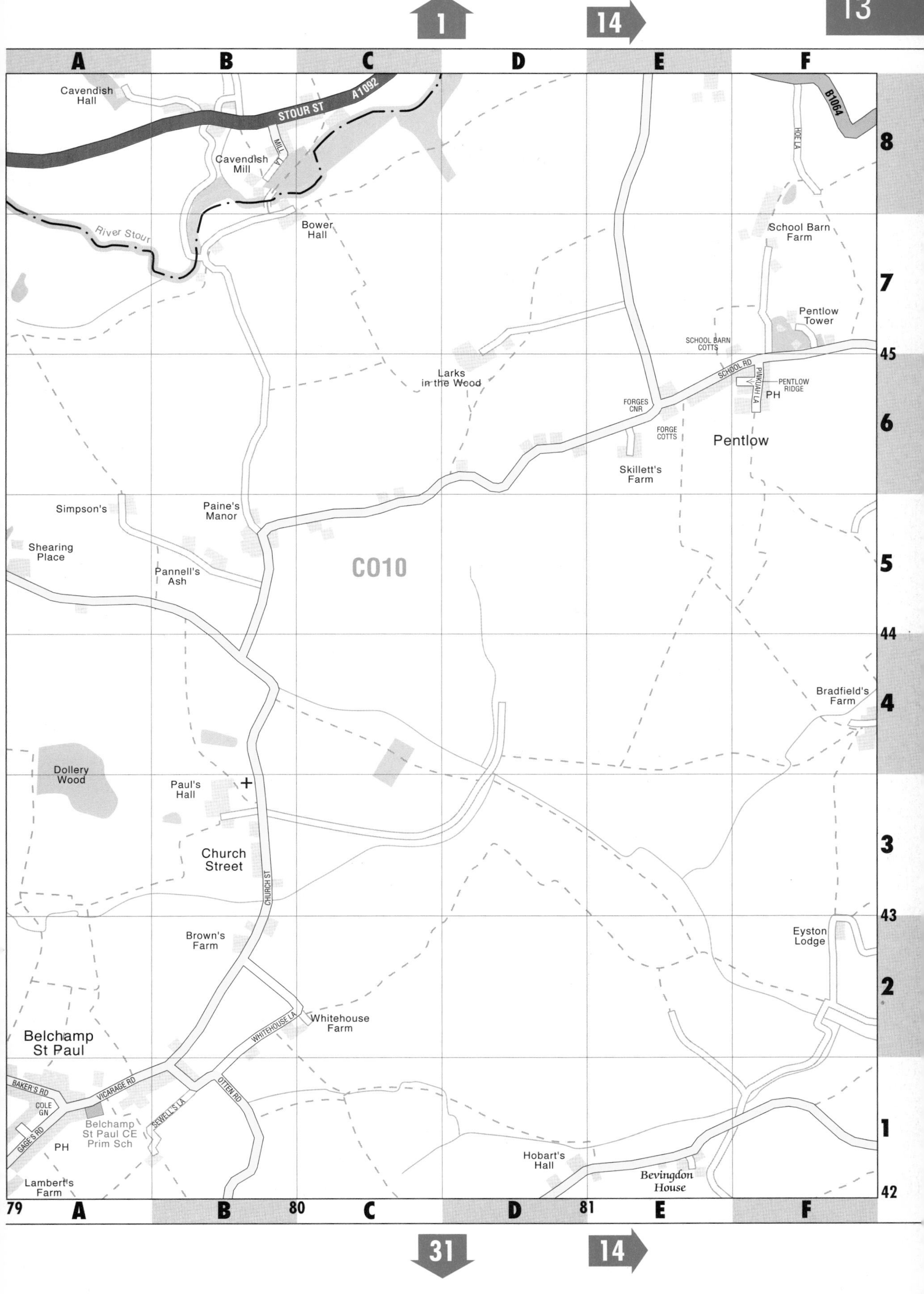

A B C D E F

8
7
45
6
5
44
4
43
3
2
1
42

Cavendish
Hall

STOUR ST A1092

MILL

Cavendish
Mill

Bower
Hall

River Stour

B1064

HOE LA

School Barn
Farm

Pentlow
Tower

SCHOOL BARN
COTTS

SCHOOL RD

PINKUAH LA

Larks
in the Wood

FORGES
CNR

FORGE
COTTS

Pentlow
Ridge

PH

Pentlow

Skillett's
Farm

Simpson's

Paine's
Manor

Shearing
Place

Pannell's
Ash

CO10

Bradfield's
Farm

Dollery
Wood

Paul's
Hall

+

Church
Street

CHURCH ST

Eyston
Lodge

Brown's
Farm

WHITEHOUSE LA

Whitehouse
Farm

Belchamp
St Paul

BAKER'S RD

VICARAGE RD

SEWELL'S LA

OTTEN RD

COLE
GN

GAGE'S RD

PH

Belchamp
St Paul CE
Prim Sch

Lambert's
Farm

Hobart's
Hall

Bevingdon
House

79 A B 80 C D 81 E F

13
2

A B C D E F

8

Pentlow Street

B1064

THE STREET

PENTLOW HILL

Constable's Farm

Liston Gardens

Works

7

Hartsbuckle Farm

Park Farm

45

Roper's Farm

Bunting's Farm

Weston Hall

Cardinal's Farm

Liston Hall

6

Foxearth Hall

THE STREET

Foxearth

THE CHASE

SCHOOL ST

Hawk's Farm

The Plantation

CLAPPIS LA

5

Huntsman's Farm

MILL RD

Mill Cottage

Red Cottages

B1064

44

Bellybones

Claypit Hall

CO10

Brook Hall

4

Temple End

3

Hubbard's Farm

Borley Place

Borley

HALL RD

43

Eyston Smyth's Farm

Purkis Farm

2

Borleylodge Farm

Borley Green

1

Eyston Hall

42

Bardfield Bridge

13
32

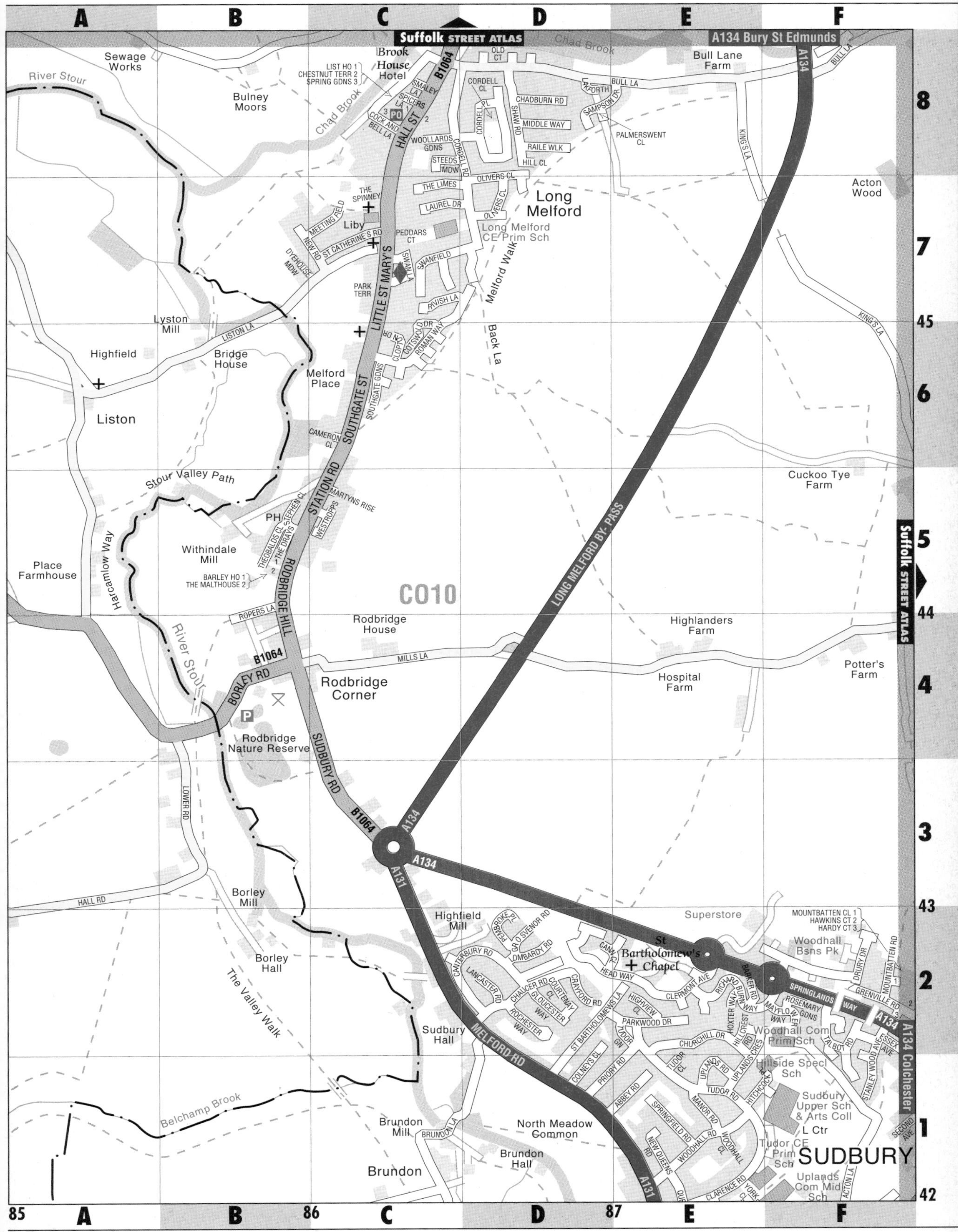

A134 Bury St Edmunds

Suffolk STREET ATLAS

Long Melford

CO10

Sewage Works

River Stour

Bulney Moors

Chad Brook

Chad Brook

Brook House Hotel

LIST HO 1
CHESTNUT TERR 2
SPRING GDNS 3

B1064

OLD 1

CORDELL CL

CHADBURN RD

SHAW RD

MIDDLE WAY

RAILE WLK

HILL CL

OLIVERS CL

SAMPSON CL

PALMERSWENT CL

Bull Lane Farm

Bull La

A134

KING'S LA

Acton Wood

SMALLEY LA 1
SPICERS LA 2

HALL ST

WOOLLARDS GDNS

STEEDS MDW

THE LIMES

LAUREL DR

THE SPINNEY

Liby

MEETING FIELD

NEW RD

ST CATHERINE'S RD

DYDHOUSE MDW

PEDDARS CT

SHANFIELD

Long Melford CE Prim Sch

KING'S LA

PARK TERR

RIVISH LA

Melford Walk

Back La

Highfield

Lyston Mill

LISTON LA

Bridge House

Melford Place

Liston

Place Farmhouse

Stour Valley Path

Hacamlow Way

CAMERON CL

SOUTHGATE GDNS

SOUTHGATE ST

LITTLE ST MARY'S

STATION RD

RODBRIDGE HILL

MARTYNS RISE

WESTROPS

PH

THEOBALDS CL
ST STEPHEN'S CL
THE TURNS

Withindale Mill

BARLEY HO 1
THE MALTHOUSE 2

ROPERS LA

Cuckoo Tye Farm

Long Melford By-Pass

Rodbridge House

MILLS LA

Highlanders Farm

Potter's Farm

River Stour

B1064

BORLEY RD

P

Rodbridge Nature Reserve

LOWER RD

Rodbridge Corner

SUDBURY RD

Hospital Farm

B1064

A134

A131

A134

Superstore

MOUNTBATTEN CL 1
HAWKINS CT 2
HARDY CT 3

Woodhall Bsns Pk

HALL RD

Borley Mill

The Valley Walk

Borley Hall

Highfield Mill

PEMBROKE RD

GROSVENOR RD

LOMBARDY RD

CANTERBURY RD

LANCASTER RD

CHAUCER RD

COTTENHAM WAY

CRAXFORD RD

GLOUCESTER WAY

ROCHESTER WAY

St Bartholomew's Chapel

CAM CL

HEAD WAY

CLERMONT AVE

HIGHVIEW CL

RICKARD

BARKER RD

HOXTER WAY

DRURY DR

SPRINGLANDS WAY

ROSEMARY GDNS

MAYFLOR GDNS

GRENVILLE CL

MOUNTBATTEN RD

A134 Colchester

Woodhall Com Prim Sch

Belchamp Brook

Sudbury Hall

MELFORD RD

Brundon Mill

BRUNDON LA

North Meadow Common

ST BARTHOLOMEW'S LA

COLNEYS CL

PRIORY RD

PARKWOOD DR

CHURCHILL RD

UPLANDS RD

UPLANDS RD

TUDOR RD

HITCHCOCK

TALBOT

ESSEX

STANLEY WOOD AVE

Hillside Specl Sch

Sudbury Upper Sch & Arts Coll

L Ctr

Brundon

Brundon Hall

A131

NEW QUEENS RD

QUEENS RD

WOODHALL RD

WOODHALL RD

MANOR RD

ABBEY RD

SPRINGFIELD RD

CLARENCE RD

YORK RD

SECOND AVE

Tudor CE Prim Sch

SUDBURY

Uplands Com Mid Sch

85   A   B   86   C   D   87   E   F

33

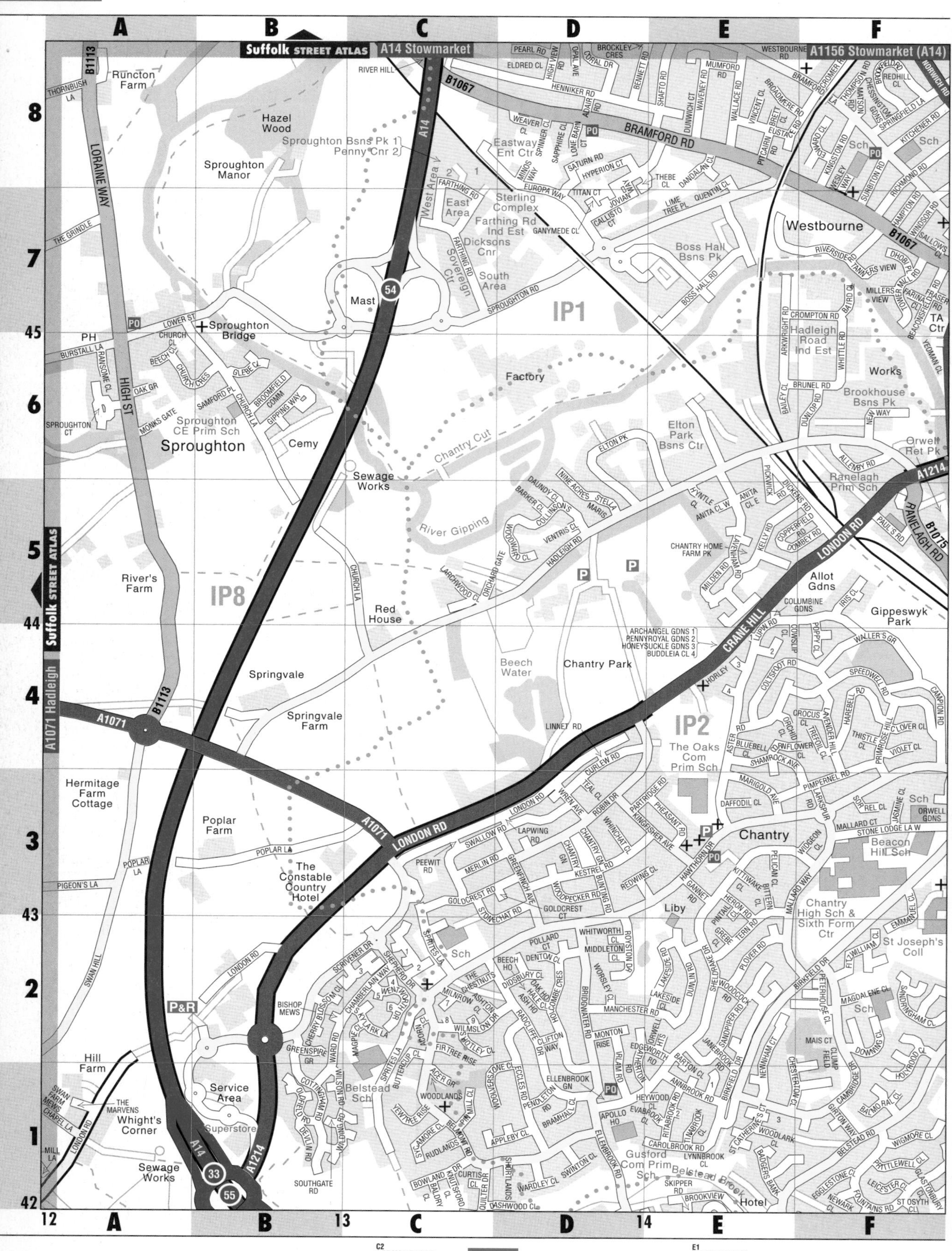

A14 Stowmarket

A1156 Stowmarket (A14)

36

C2
1 BRAMBLEWOOD
2 LABURNUM CL
3 BROAD MEADOW
4 INNES END
5 PEACOCK CL
6 HALFORD CT
7 MERRION CL
8 MATLOCK CL
9 MOTTRAM CL

E1
1 DAWNBROOK CL
2 HILDABROOK CL
3 VINNICOMBE CT

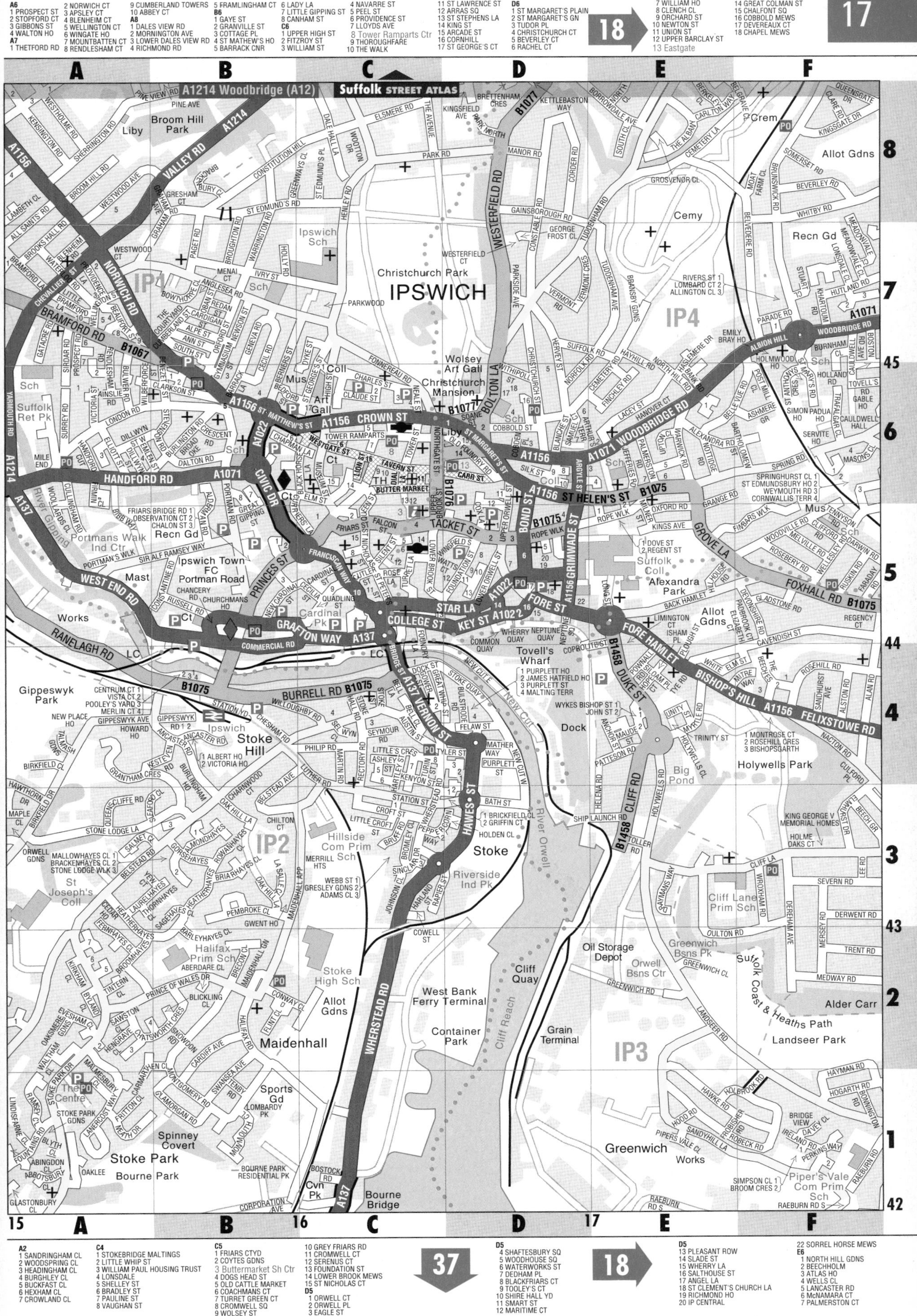
17
A6
1 PROSPECT ST
2 STOPFORD CT
3 GIBBONS ST
4 WALTON HO
A7
1 THETFORD RD
2 NORWICH CT
3 APSLEY CT
4 BLENHEIM CT
5 WELLINGTON CT
6 WINGATE HO
7 MOUNTBATTEN CT
8 RENDLESHAM CT
9 CUMBERLAND TOWERS
10 ABBEY CT
A8
1 DALES VIEW RD
2 MORNINGTON AVE
3 LOWER DALES VIEW RD
4 RICHMOND RD
5 FRAMLINGHAM CT
B6
1 GAYE ST
2 GRANVILLE ST
3 COTTAGE PL
4 ST MATHEW'S HO
5 BARRACK CNR
6 LADY LA
7 LITTLE GIPPING ST
8 CANHAM ST
C6
1 UPPER HIGH ST
2 FITZROY ST
3 WILLIAM ST
4 NAVARRE ST
5 PEEL ST
6 PROVIDENCE ST
7 LLOYDS AVE
8 Tower Ramparts Ctr
9 THOROUGHFARE
10 THE WALK
11 ST LAWRENCE ST
12 ARRAS SQ
13 ST STEPHENS LA
14 KING ST
15 ARCADE ST
16 CORNHILL
17 ST GEORGE'S CT
D6
1 ST MARGARET'S PLAIN
2 ST MARGARET'S GN
3 TUDOR PL
4 CHRISTCHURCH CT
5 BEVERLEY CT
6 RACHEL CT
18
7 WILLIAM HO
8 CLENCH CL
9 ORCHARD ST
10 NEWTON ST
11 UNION ST
12 UPPER BARCLAY ST
13 Eastgate
14 GREAT COLMAN ST
15 CHALFONT SQ
16 COBBOLD MEWS
17 DEVEREAUX CT
18 CHAPEL MEWS
A1214 Woodbridge (A12)
Suffolk STREET ATLAS
IPSWICH
Christchurch Park
IP1
IP2
IP3
IP4
Broom Hill Park
Ipswich Sch
Wolsey Art Gall
Christchurch Mansion
Cemy
Crem
Allot Gdns
Recn Gd
Suffolk Ret Pk
Portmans Walk Ind Ctr
Ipswich Town FC
Portman Road
Cardinal Pk
Tovell's Wharf
Suffolk Coll
Alexandra Park
Gippeswyk Park
Ipswich
Stoke Hill
Dock
Holywells Park
Big Pond
Hillside Com Prim Sch
Stoke
Riverside Ind Pk
St Joseph's Coll
Cliff Lane Prim Sch
Halifax Prim Sch
Stoke High Sch
Oil Storage Depot
Greenwich Bsns Pk
Orwell Bsns Ctr
Cliff Quay
West Bank Ferry Terminal
Container Park
Grain Terminal
Alder Carr
Suffolk Coast & Heaths Path
Landseer Park
Maidenhall
Sports Gd
Spinney Covert
Stoke Park
Bourne Park
The Centre
Greenwich
Works
Piper's Vale Com Prim Sch
Bourne Bridge
Cvn Pk
River Orwell
River Gipping
New Cut
Cliff Reach
A1156 CROWN ST
HANDFORD RD
WEST END RD
GRAFTON WAY
COLLEGE ST
STAR LA
KEY ST
FORE ST
FORE HAMLET
BISHOP'S HILL
FELIXSTOWE RD
WOODBRIDGE RD
ST HELEN'S ST
FOXHALL RD
WHERSTEAD RD
CLIFF RD
DUKE ST
BURRELL RD
NORWICH RD
VALLEY RD
WESTERFIELD RD
BOLTON LA
CIVIC DR
PRINCES ST
TACKET ST
GRIMWADE ST
15
A
B
16
C
D
17
E
F
8
7
45
6
5
44
4
3
43
2
1
42
A2
1 SANDRINGHAM CL
2 WOODSPRING CL
3 HEADINGHAM CL
4 BURGHLEY CL
5 BUCKFAST CL
6 HEXHAM CL
7 CROWLAND CL
C4
1 STOKEBRIDGE MALTINGS
2 LITTLE WHIP ST
3 WILLIAM PAUL HOUSING TRUST
4 LONSDALE
5 SHELLEY ST
6 BRADLEY ST
7 PAULINE ST
8 VAUGHAN ST
C5
1 FRIARS CTYD
2 COYTES GDNS
3 Buttermarket Sh Ctr
4 DOGS HEAD ST
5 OLD CATTLE MARKET
6 COACHMANS CT
7 TURRET GREEN CT
8 CROMWELL SQ
9 WOLSEY ST
10 GREY FRIARS RD
11 CROMWELL CT
12 SERENUS CT
13 FOUNDATION ST
14 LOWER BROOK MEWS
15 ST NICHOLAS CT
D5
1 ORWELL CT
2 ORWELL PL
3 EAGLE ST
37
D5
4 SHAFTESBURY SQ
5 WOODHOUSE SQ
6 WATERWORKS ST
7 DEDHAM PL
8 BLACKFRIARS CT
9 TOOLEY'S CT
10 SHIRE HALL YD
11 SMART ST
12 MARITIME CT
18
D5
13 PLEASANT ROW
14 SLADE ST
15 WHERRY LA
16 SALTHOUSE ST
17 ANGEL LA
18 ST CLEMENT'S CHURCH LA
19 RICHMOND HO
20 IP CENTRAL
22 SORREL HORSE MEWS
E6
1 NORTH HILL GDNS
2 BEECHHOLM
3 ATLAS HO
4 WELLS CL
5 LANCASTER RD
6 McNAMARA CT
7 PALMERSTON CT

17

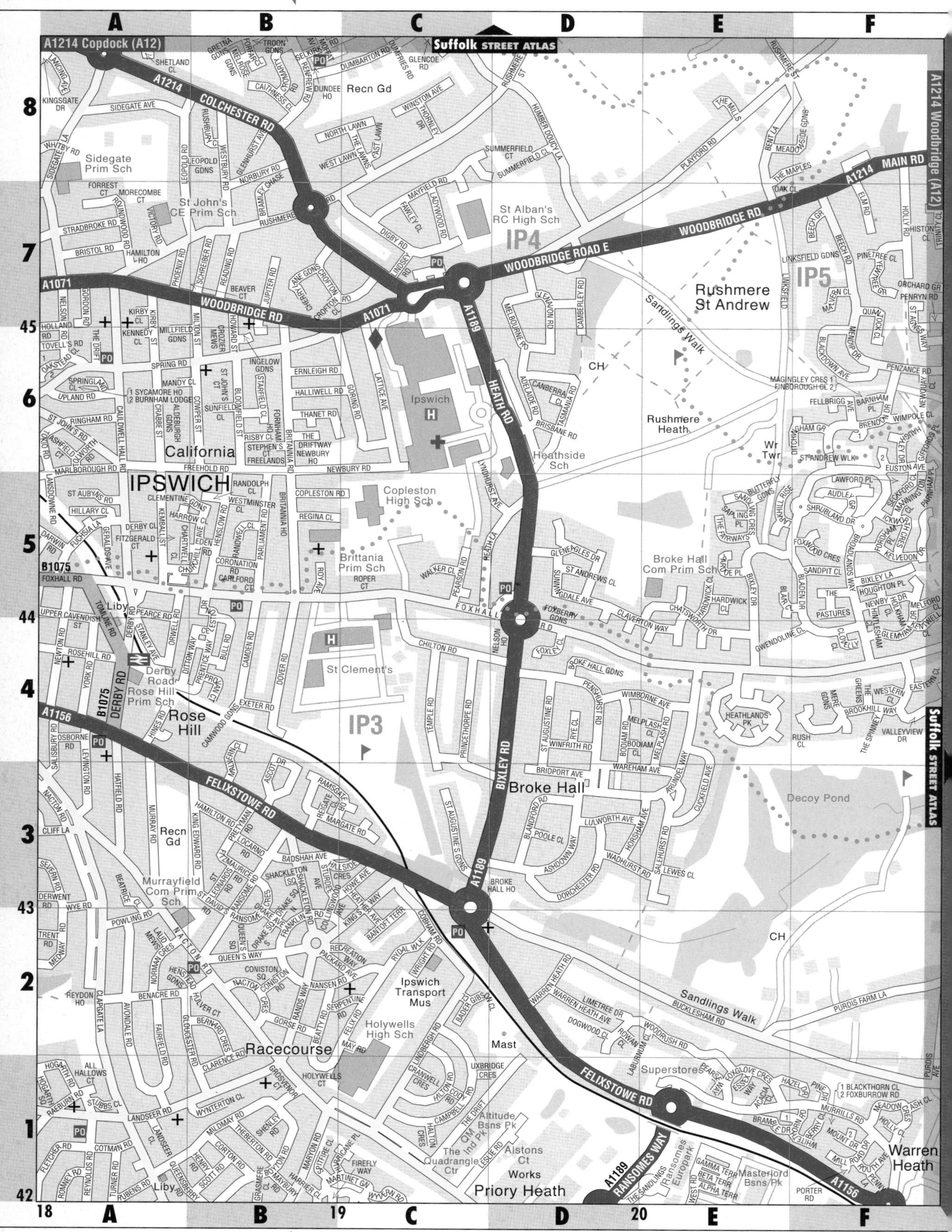
A
B
C
D
E
F
A1214 Copdock (A12)
Suffolk STREET ATLAS
A1214 Woodbridge (A12)
8
7
45
6
5
44
4
3
43
2
1
42
18
19
20
COLCHESTER RD
A1214
SIDEGATE AVE
Sidegate Prim Sch
St John's CE Prim Sch
Recn Gd
St Alban's RC High Sch
IP4
WOODBRIDGE ROAD E
WOODBRIDGE RD
MAIN RD
A1071
WOODBRIDGE RD
Rushmere St Andrew
IP5
Sandlings Walk
CH
Ipswich
H
HEATH RD
A1189
Rushmere Heath
Heathside Sch
Wr Twr
California
IPSWICH
Copleston High Sch
Brittania Prim Sch
Broke Hall Com Prim Sch
B1075
FOXHALL RD
FOXHALL RD
Liby
Derby Road
Rose Hill Prim Sch
Rose Hill
St Clement's
IP3
A1156
FELIXSTOWE RD
BIXLEY RD
Broke Hall
Decoy Pond
Recn Gd
Murrayfield Com Prim Sch
PO
Ipswich Transport Mus
Holywells High Sch
Racecourse
Mast
Sandlings Walk
BUCKLESHAM RD
PURDIS FARM LA
Superstores
FELIXSTOWE RD
A1189
RANSOMES WAY
Ransomes Europark
Masterlord Bsns Pk
Altitude Bsns Pk
QM Ind Pk
The Quadrangle Ctr
Alstons Ct Works
Priory Heath
Warren Heath
A1156

17

38

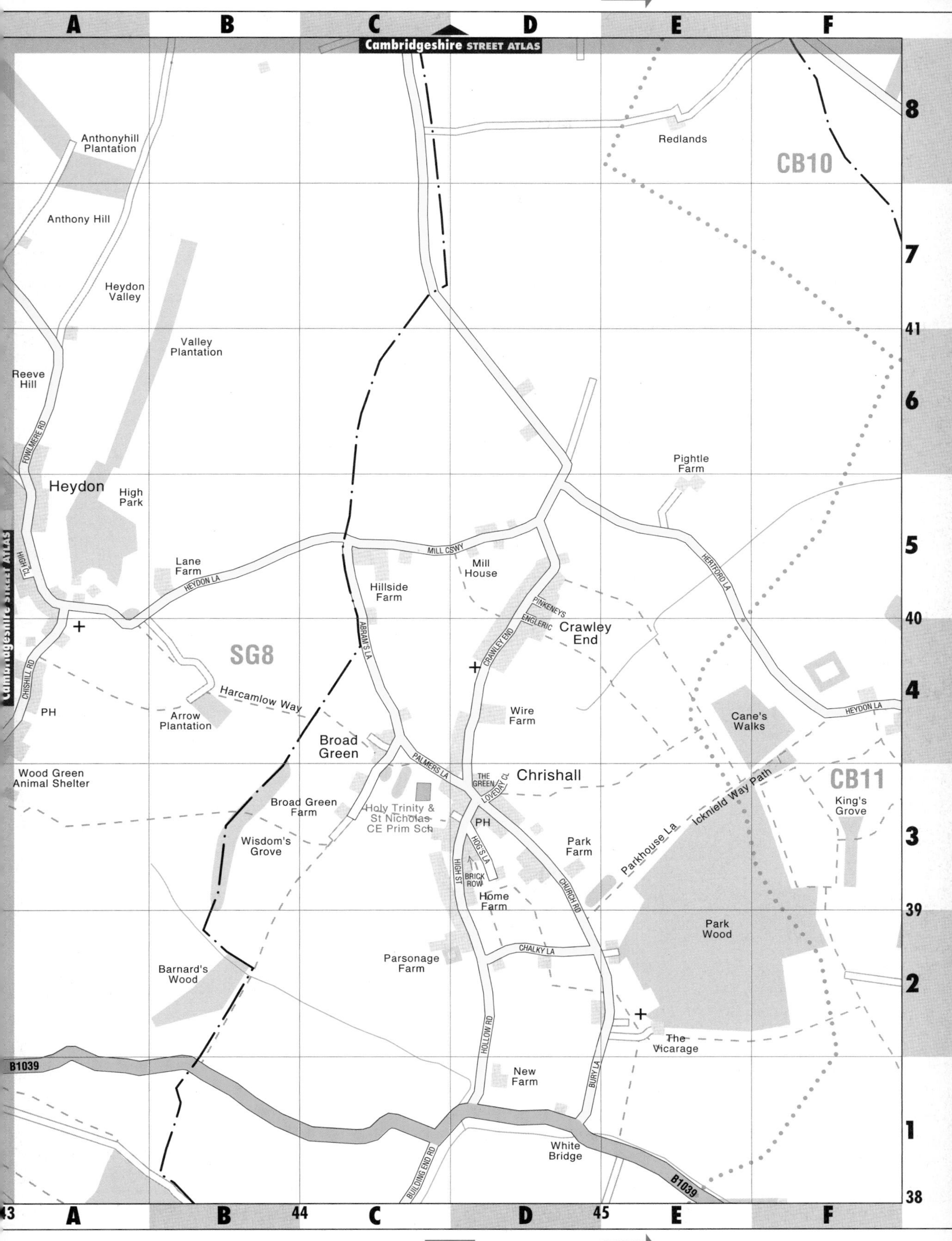

Cambridgeshire STREET ATLAS

Anthonyhill Plantation

Anthony Hill

Heydon Valley

Valley Plantation

Reeve Hill

Redlands

CB10

8

7

41

6

Heydon

High Park

FOWLMERE RD

Pightle Farm

Lane Farm

HEYDON LA

MILL CSWY

Mill House

HERTFORD LA

5

Hillside Farm

CHISHILL RD

PINKENEYS

ENGLERIC

Crawley End

40

SG8

ABRAMS LA

CRAWLEY END

Cane's Walks

HEYDON LA

4

Harcamlow Way

Wire Farm

CB11

PH

Arrow Plantation

Broad Green

PALMERS LA

Chrishall

Parkhouse La

Icknield Way Path

King's Grove

Wood Green Animal Shelter

THE GREEN

LOVEDAY CL

Broad Green Farm

Holy Trinity & St Nicholas CE Prim Sch

PH

Park Farm

CHURCH RD

Park Wood

3

Wisdom's Grove

HIGGS LA

BRICK ROW

HIGH ST

Home Farm

39

Barnard's Wood

Parsonage Farm

CHALKY LA

2

HOLLOW RD

BURY LA

The Vicarage

B1039

New Farm

White Bridge

B1039

1

38

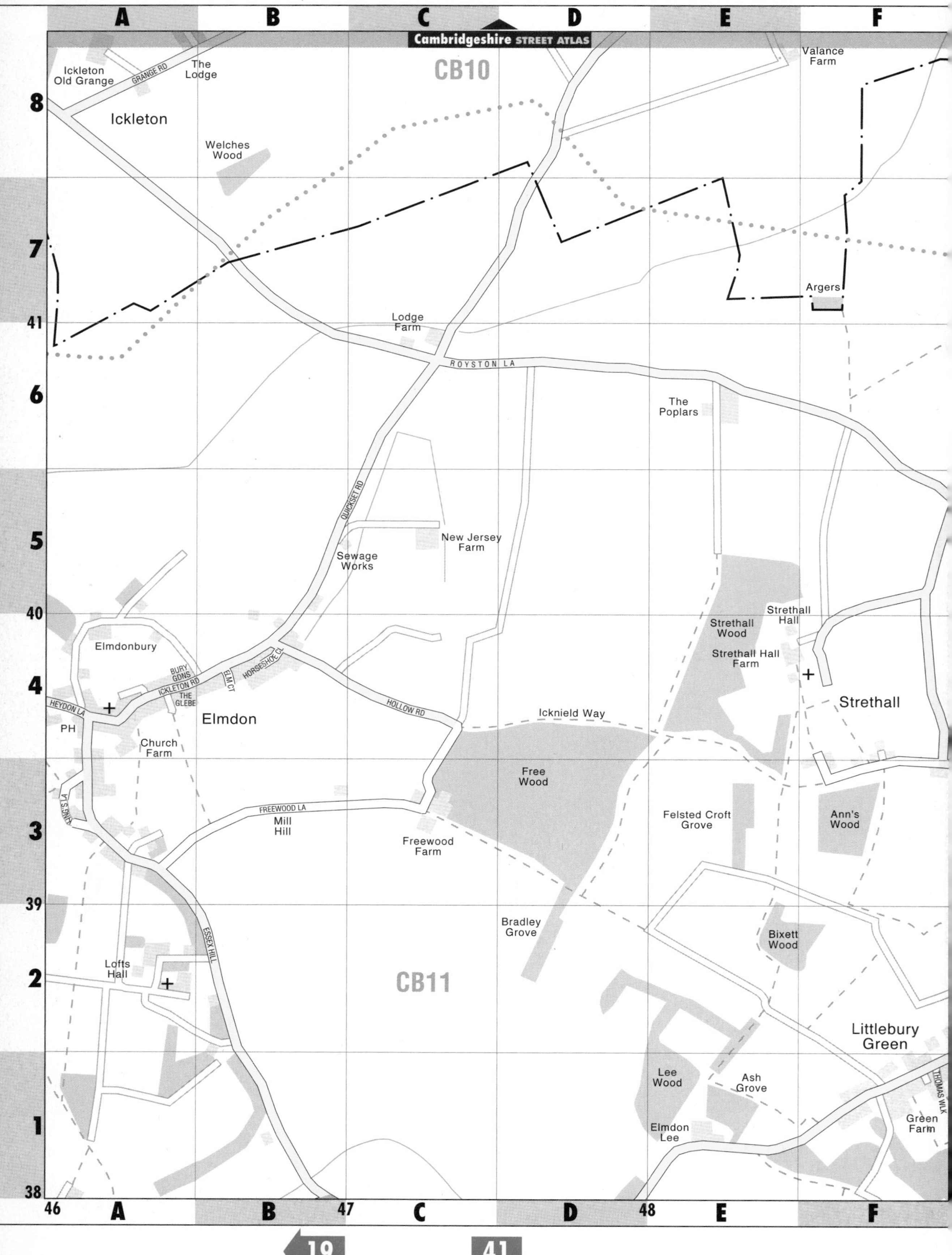

Cambridgeshire STREET ATLAS

CB10

Ickleton
Old Grange

GRANGE RD

The Lodge

Ickleton

Welches Wood

Valance Farm

Argers

Lodge Farm

ROYSTON LA

The Poplars

QUICKSET RD

New Jersey Farm

Sewage Works

Strethall Wood

Strethall Hall

Strethall Hall Farm

Elmdonbury

BURY GDNS

ICKLETON RD

ELM CT

HORSESHOE CL

THE GLEBE

HEYDON LA

HOLLOW RD

Icknield Way

Strethall

PH

Church Farm

Free Wood

Felsted Croft Grove

Ann's Wood

PLASHES

FREEWOOD LA

Mill Hill

Freewood Farm

Elmdon

ESSEX HILL

Bradley Grove

Bixett Wood

Lofts Hall

CB11

Littlebury Green

Lee Wood

Ash Grove

THOMAS WLK

Elmdon Lee

Green Farm

A   B   47   C   D   48   E   F

3
22

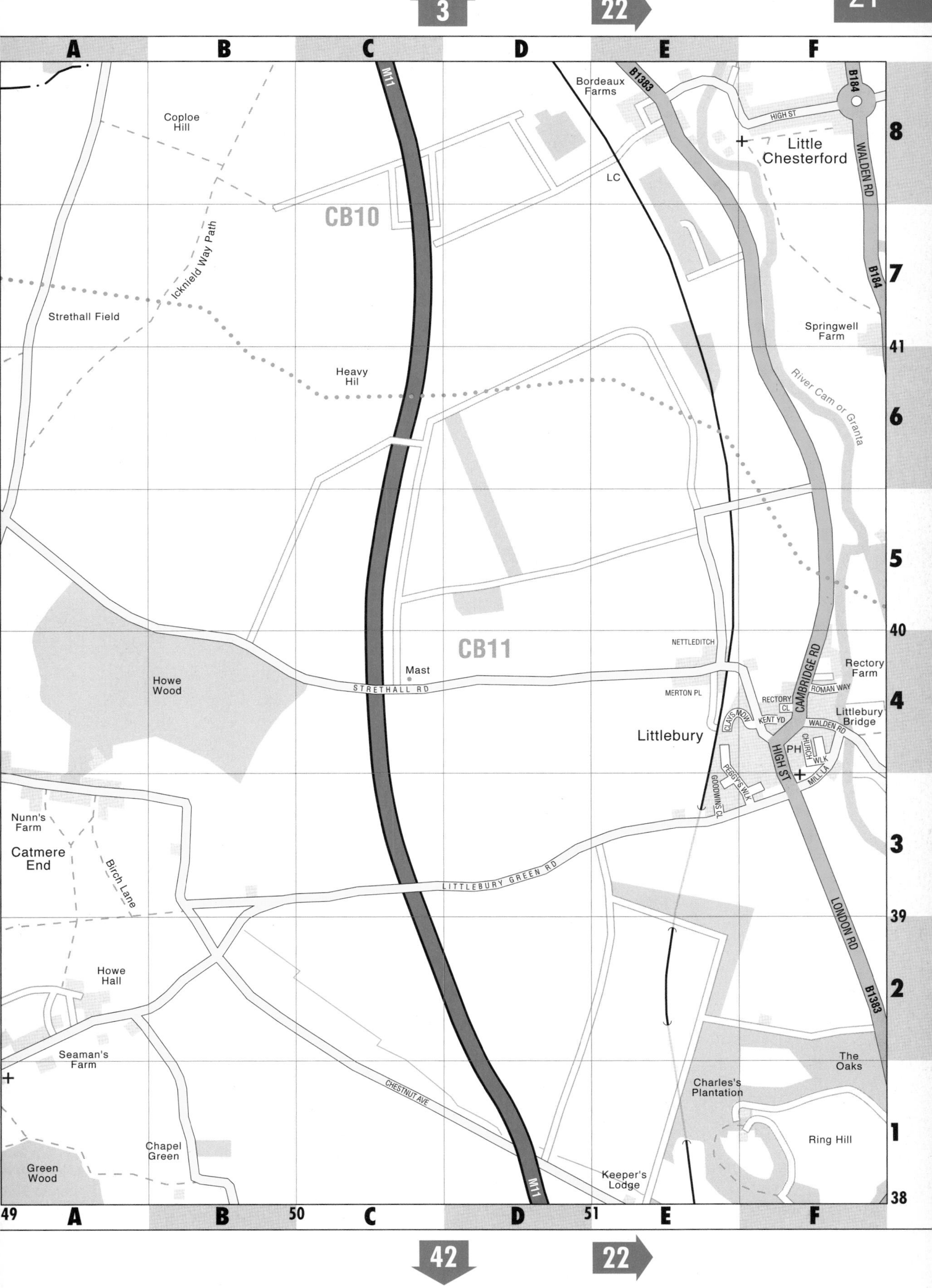
A
B
C
D
E
F
Coploe Hill
Bordeaux Farms
B1383
B184
HIGH ST
Little Chesterford
WALDEN RD
LC
CB10
Icknield Way Path
M11
Strethall Field
Springwell Farm
Heavy Hil
River Cam or Granta
CB11
NETTLEDITCH
Mast
Rectory Farm
Howe Wood
STRETHALL RD
MERTON PL
CAMBRIDGE RD
ROMAN WAY
RECTORY CL
KENT YD
CLAYS MDW
WALDEN RD
Littlebury Bridge
Littlebury
HIGH ST
PH
CHURCH WLK
MILL LA
PEGGY'S WLK
GOODWINS CL
Nunn's Farm
Catmere End
Birch Lane
LITTLEBURY GREEN RD
LONDON RD
Howe Hall
Seaman's Farm
CHESTNUT AVE
Charles's Plantation
The Oaks
Ring Hill
Chapel Green
Green Wood
Keeper's Lodge
8
7
41
6
5
40
4
3
39
2
1
38
49
50
51

42
22

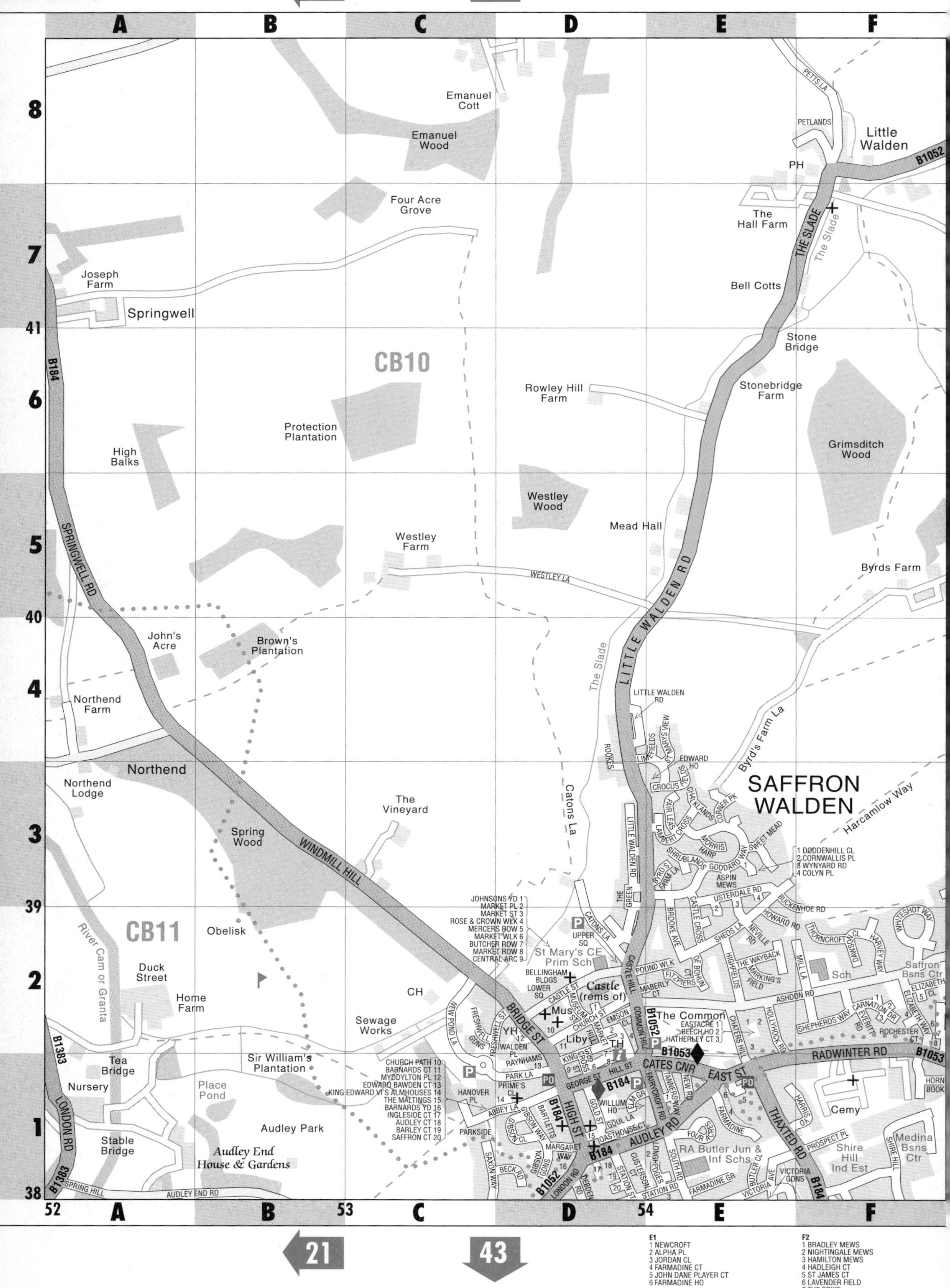

A B C D E F

8

Emanuel Cott

Emanuel Wood

PETTS LA

PETLANDS

Little Walden

B1052

THE SLADE

The Slade

The Hall Farm

Four Acre Grove

7

Joseph Farm

Springwell

Bell Cotts

41

CB10

Stone Bridge

6

Rowley Hill Farm

Stonebridge Farm

Protection Plantation

High Balks

Grimsditch Wood

Westley Wood

Mead Hall

LITTLE WALDEN RD

5

Westley Farm

WESTLEY LA

Byrds Farm

40

John's Acre

Brown's Plantation

The Slade

LITTLE WALDEN RD

4

Northend Farm

Northend

LITTLE WALDEN RD

Byrd's Farm La

SAFFRON WALDEN

Harcamlow Way

Northend Lodge

The Vineyard

Catons La

ROOKES

1 DODDENHILL CL
2 CORNWALLIS PL
3 WYNYARD RD
4 COLYN PL

3

Spring Wood

WINDMILL HILL

USTERDALE RD

BUCKENHOE RD

River Cam or Granta

CB11

Obelisk

39

JOHNSONS YD 1
MARKET PL 2
MARKET ST 3
ROSE & CROWN WLK 4
MERCERS ROW 5
MARKET WLK 6
BUTCHER ROW 7
MARKET ROW 8
CENTRAL ARC 9

UPPER SQ

St Mary's CE Prim Sch

B1052

RADWINTER RD

B1053

2

Duck Street

Home Farm

CH

Sewage Works

BELLINGHAM BLDGS
LOWER SQ

Castle (rems of)

The Common

EASTACHE 1
BEECH HO 2
HATHERLEY CT 3

B1184

P

B1053

Tea Bridge

B1383

Nursery

Sir William's Plantation

CHURCH PATH 10
BARNARDS CT 11
MYDDYLTON PL 12
EDWARD BAWDEN CT 13
KING EDWARD VI'S ALMHOUSES 14
THE MALTINGS 15
BARNARDS YD 16
INGLESIDE CT 17
AUDLEY CT 18
BARLEY CT 19
SAFFRON CT 20

HANOVER PL

PARKSIDE

GATES CNR

EAST ST

PO

Cemy

HORN BOOK

1

Stable Bridge

LONDON RD

B1383

Place Pond

Audley Park

Audley End House & Gardens

B1184

RA Butler Jun & Inf Schs

Shire Hill Ind Est

Medina Bsns Ctr

38

SPRING HILL

AUDLEY END RD

52 A 53 B C 54 D E F

E1
1 NEWCROFT
2 ALPHA PL
3 JORDAN CL
4 FARMADINE CT
5 JOHN DANE PLAYER CT
6 FARMADINE HO

F2
1 BRADLEY MEWS
2 NIGHTINGALE MEWS
3 HAMILTON MEWS
4 HADLEIGH CT
5 ST JAMES CT
6 LAVENDER FIELD
7 THE SPIKE
8 CAVENDISH CT

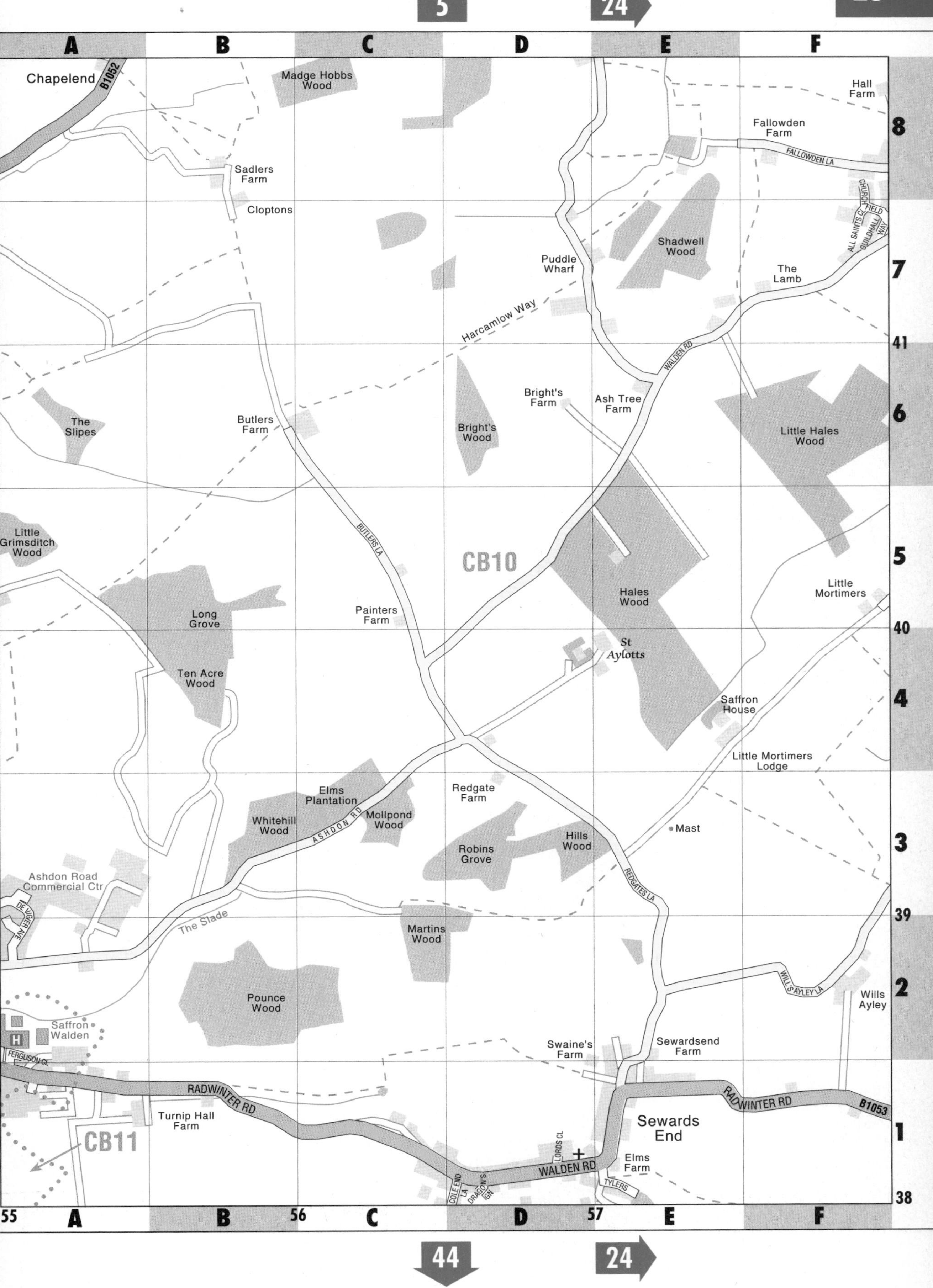

5 **24**

A B C D E F

Chapelend

Madge Hobbs Wood

Hall Farm

Fallowden Farm

8

Sadlers Farm

Cloptons

Shadwell Wood

FALLOWDEN LA

7

Puddle Wharf

The Lamb

ALL SAINTS CHFIELD / CHURCH / CHFIELD WAY

Harcamlow Way

41

Bright's Farm

Ash Tree Farm

WALDEN RD

6

The Slipes

Butlers Farm

Bright's Wood

Little Hales Wood

Little Grimsditch Wood

BUTLERS LA

CB10

Hales Wood

Little Mortimers

5

Long Grove

Painters Farm

40

St Aylotts

Ten Acre Wood

Saffron House

4

Little Mortimers Lodge

Elms Plantation

Redgate Farm

Mast

3

Whitehill Wood

Mollpond Wood

Robins Grove

Hills Wood

REDGATES LA

ASHDON RD

Ashdon Road Commercial Ctr

DE VIGIER AVE

The Slade

Martins Wood

39

Pounce Wood

WILLS AYLEY LA

Wills Ayley

2

Saffron Walden

H

FERGUSON CL

Swaine's Farm

Sewardsend Farm

RADWINTER RD

CB11

Turnip Hall Farm

RADWINTER RD

B1053

Sewards End

1

LORDS CL

WALDEN RD

Elms Farm

COLE END LA

DRAGON'S IGH

TYLERS

38

55 A B 56 C D 57 E F

44 **24**

23
6

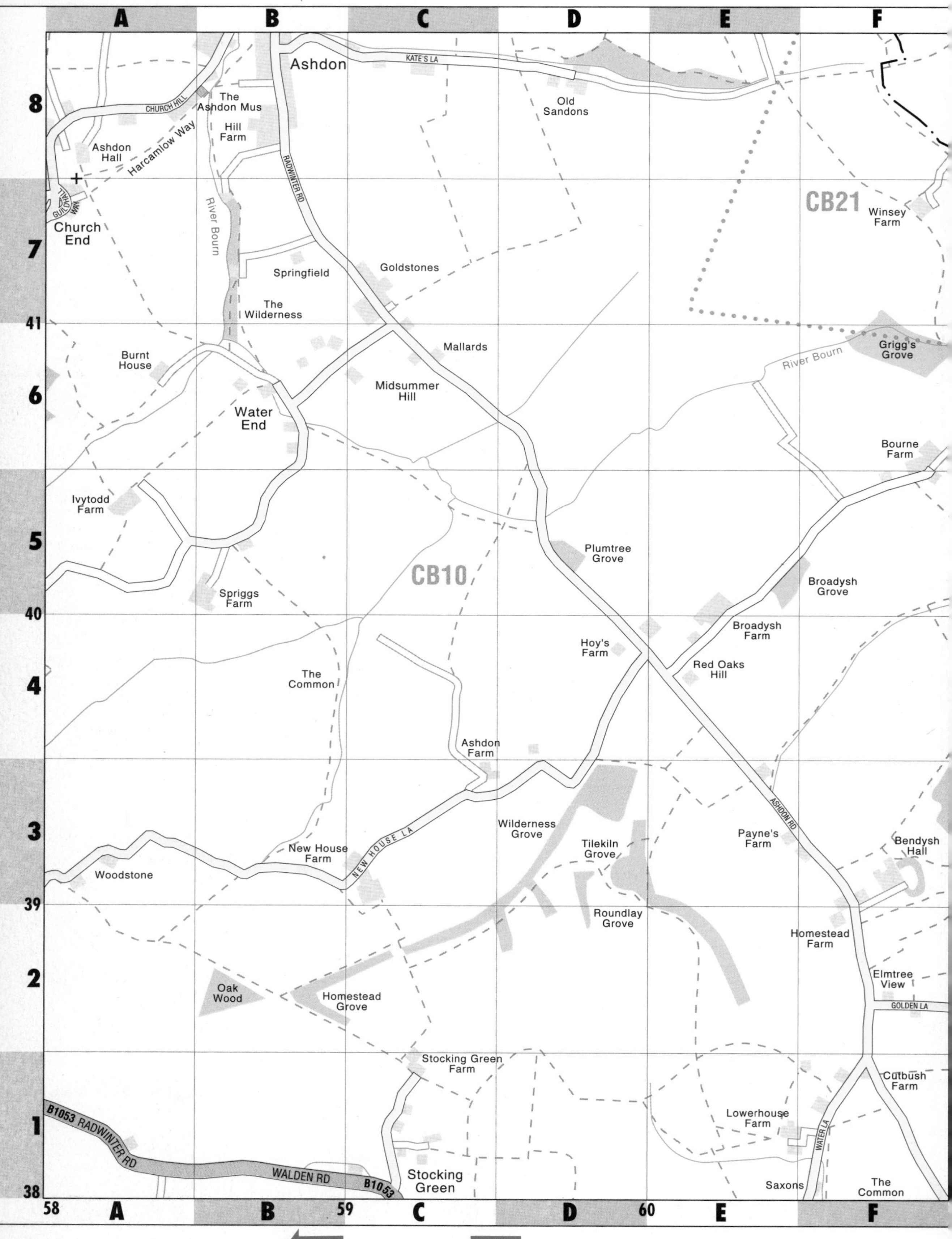
A
B
C
D
E
F
8
7
41
6
5
40
4
3
39
2
1
38
58
59
60
Ashdon
KATE'S LA
The Ashdon Mus
Hill Farm
Old Sandons
CHURCH HILL
Harcamlow Way
Ashdon Hall
RADWINTER RD
GUILDHALL WAY
Church End
River Bourn
CB21
Winsey Farm
Springfield
Goldstones
The Wilderness
Burnt House
Mallards
Grigg's Grove
River Bourn
Midsummer Hill
Water End
Bourne Farm
Ivytodd Farm
Plumtree Grove
CB10
Broadysh Grove
Spriggs Farm
Broadysh Farm
Hoy's Farm
Red Oaks Hill
The Common
Ashdon Farm
ASHDON RD
Wilderness Grove
Payne's Farm
Bendysh Hall
Tilekiln Grove
New House Farm
NEW HOUSE LA
Woodstone
Roundlay Grove
Homestead Farm
Elmtree View
GOLDEN LA
Oak Wood
Homestead Grove
Stocking Green Farm
Cutbush Farm
Lowerhouse Farm
B1053 RADWINTER RD
WATER LA
WALDEN RD
B1053
Stocking Green
Saxons
The Common

23
45

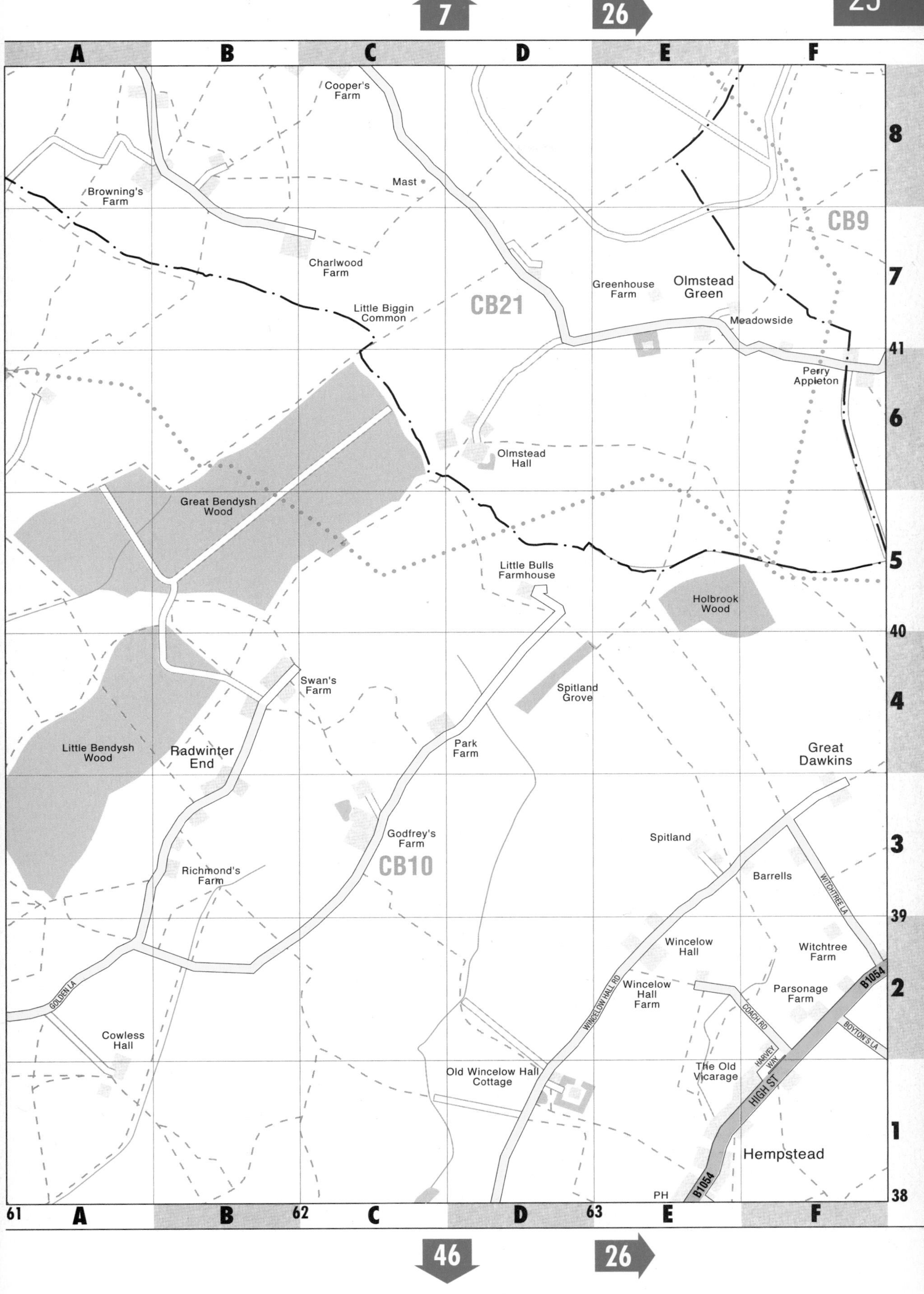

A   B   C   D   E   F

8

CB9

Cooper's Farm

Mast

7

Charlwood Farm

Greenhouse Farm

Olmstead Green

Browning's Farm

Little Biggin Common

CB21

Meadowside

41

Perry Appleton

6

Great Bendysh Wood

Olmstead Hall

Little Bulls Farmhouse

Holbrook Wood

5

40

Swan's Farm

Spitland Grove

4

Little Bendysh Wood

Radwinter End

Park Farm

Great Dawkins

Spitland

3

Godfrey's Farm

CB10

Barrells

WITCHTREE LA

39

Richmond's Farm

Wincelow Hall

Witchtree Farm

B1054

GOLDEN LA

WINCELOW HALL RD

Wincelow Hall Farm

COACH RD

Parsonage Farm

BOYTON'S LA

2

Cowless Hall

The Old Vicarage

HARVEY WAY

HIGH ST

Old Wincelow Hall Cottage

1

Hempstead

PH

B1054

38

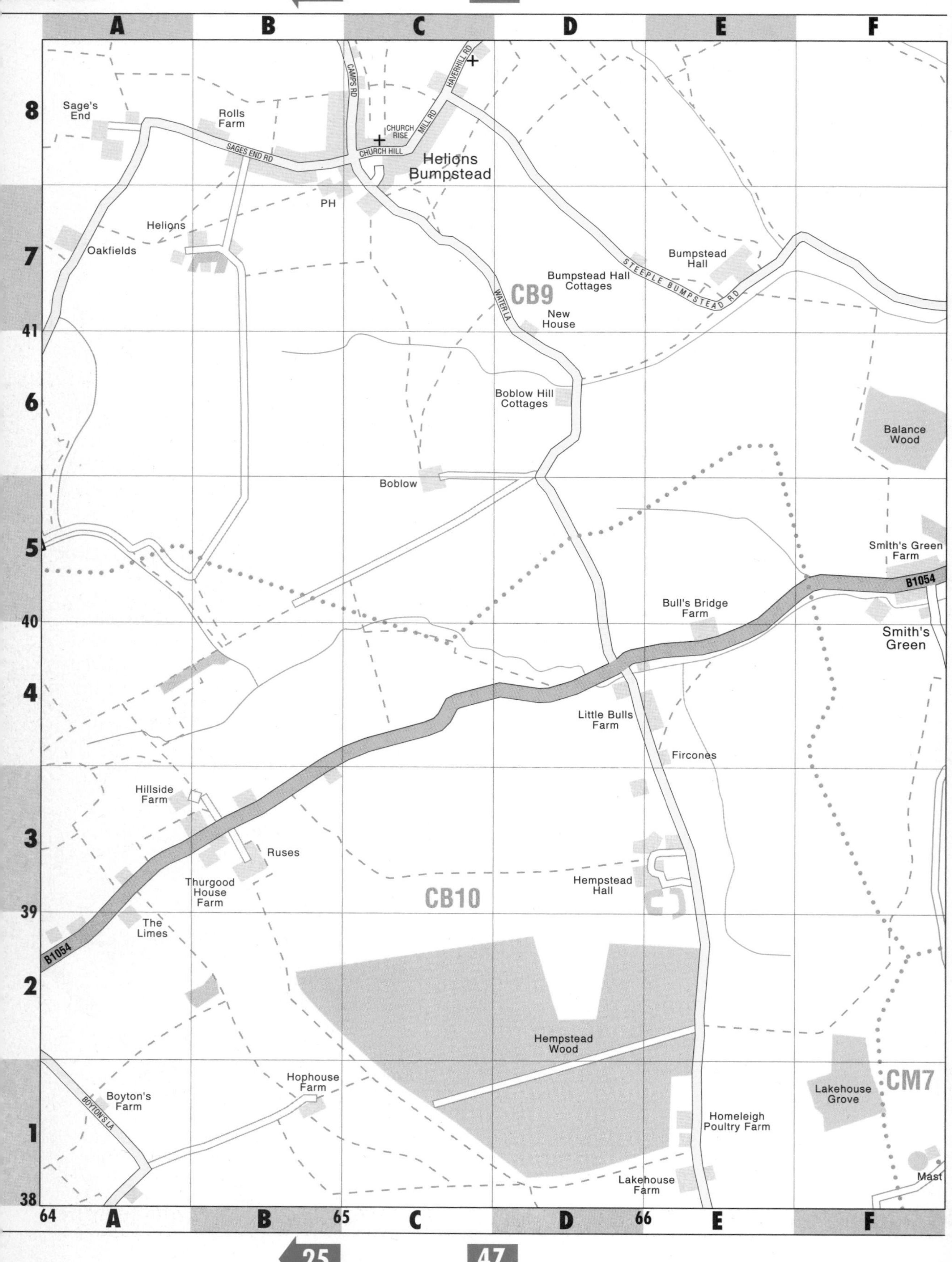

A B C D E F

8 Sage's End | Rolls Farm | CAMPS RD | HAVERHILL RD | MILL RD
CHURCH RISE
CHURCH HILL
SAGES END RD
Helions Bumpstead
PH
Helions
7 Oakfields | Bumpstead Hall | STEEPLE BUMPSTEAD RD
Bumpstead Hall Cottages
CB9
WATER LA
New House
41
6 Boblow Hill Cottages | Balance Wood
Boblow
5 Smith's Green Farm
B1054
40 Bull's Bridge Farm | Smith's Green
4 Little Bulls Farm
Fircones
Hillside Farm
3 Ruses | Hempstead Hall
Thurgood House Farm
CB10
39 The Limes
B1054
2 Hempstead Wood
Hophouse Farm
CM7
Lakehouse Grove
1 Boyton's Farm | Homeleigh Poultry Farm
BOYTON'S LA
Lakehouse Farm
Mast
38 64 A B 65 C D 66 E F

9
28

A
B
C
D
E
F
Monkhams
Sewage Works
Lowerhouse Farm
Ford
Broadgreen Hall
B1057
B1054
HAVERHILL RD
BLOIS RD
Broad Green
Steeple Bumpstead
THE ENDWAY
Blois Meadows Bsns Ctr
Blois Farm
NORTH CRES
CLAYWALL BRIDGE
THE CHASE
PO
NORTH ST
Devil's Grove
CLAYWALL COTTS
LION MDW
CHAPEL ST
OLD HALL CL
HOME CL
SUCKLINGS YD
FREEZES BARNS
Freeze's Farm
THE CRESCENT
PH
CHURCH ST
Ford
STEEPLE BUMPSTEAD RD
HELIONS RD
LILLY CNR
WATER LA
CHURCHFIELDS WLK
CHURCHFIELD
ST MARY'S WLK
BARKERS CL
Recn Gd
Cemy
Hawk's Nest
Rookery Wood
Park Plantation
Moyn's Park
The Wilderness
JOHN TIBAULD CT
QUEEN EDITH DR
BORRADALE CT
ROBERT SUCKLING CT
BOWER HALL DR
EDITH CAVELL WAY
GEORGE GENT CL
ANN COLES CL
WOOLNOUGH CL
Stanley Drapkin Prim Sch
FINCHINGFIELD RD
Stud Farm
Moyn's Park
Dock Plantation
SMITH'S GREEN COTTS
CB9
Bower Hall Farm
Arbour Grove
Maze Plantation
Mill Farm
MILL CHASE
Old Hall
Coote's Farm
Bushel Leys
Latchley's Farm
Whitehouse Farm
Round Wood
Oldhall Wood
Eggshell Cottage
Wilding's Farm
Wakeland's Farm
CO9
EGGSHELL LA
Herkstead Green Farm
CM7
Martin's Farm
Prouds Farm
Messing's Farm
Revels Farm
CORNISH HALL END RD
Herkstead Hall Farm
High Folly Cottages
8
7
41
6
5
40
4
3
39
2
1
38
67
68
69

48
28

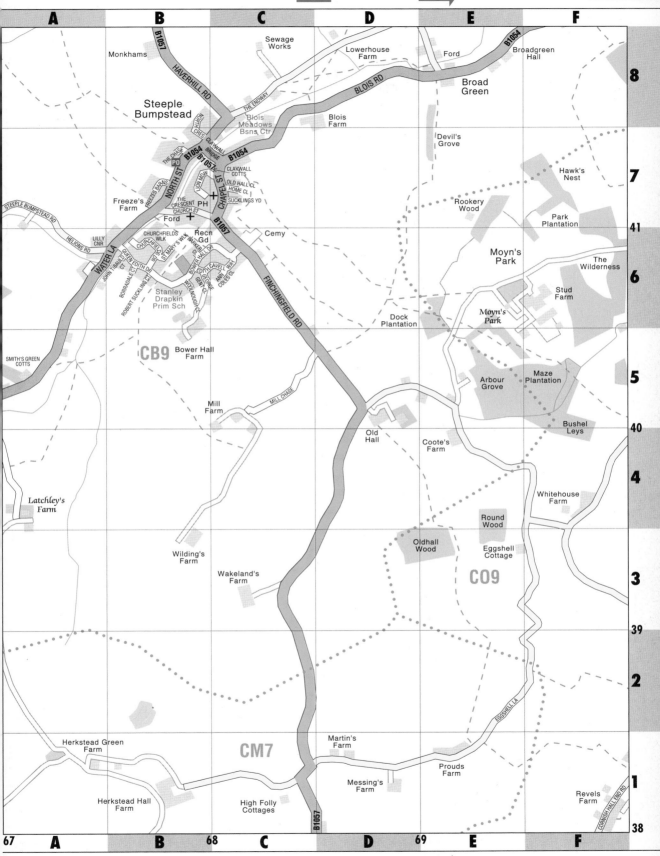

A   B   C   D   E   F

27
10

8

Moyn's Wood

CB9

Birdbrook

7

Birdbrook Hall

41

Churchfield Grove

The Plough (PH)

MOAT FARM

MOAT RD

STATION RD

FELL RD

THE STREET

DAW ST

Whitley House

A1017

FOUR ASH HILL

THE CAUSEWAY

A1017

Causeway Hall

6

Paddock Belt

SCHOOLFIELD

The Rectory

Wash Bridge

Carter's Bridge

Wash Farm

Stubland's Farm

Wash Farm

Highfield Clump

Finkle Green

Bailey Hill Farm

Bailey Hill

CO9

Woodview

Three Chimneys Wood

5

Three Chimneys Farm

Essex Hall

STAMBOURNE RD

Pettyfield La

40

Park Wood

4

Wesley End Rd

Wesley End

3

Warren Farm

BIRDBROOK RD

Little Collin's Farm

MILL RD

Hill Farm

39

Slough Farm

CORNISH HALL END RD

Chapelend Way

PO

CHAPEL END WAY

Oldhouse Farm

Stambourne

CHURCH RD

Stambourne Hall

Mill Farm

2

Moat Hall Farm

Stambourne Grange

DYERS RD

Greenfield's Farm

Dyer's End

1

Stambourne Green

Great Tagley Farm

FINCHINGFIELD RD

Elm's Farm

38

70   A   B   71   C   D   72   E   F

11
30

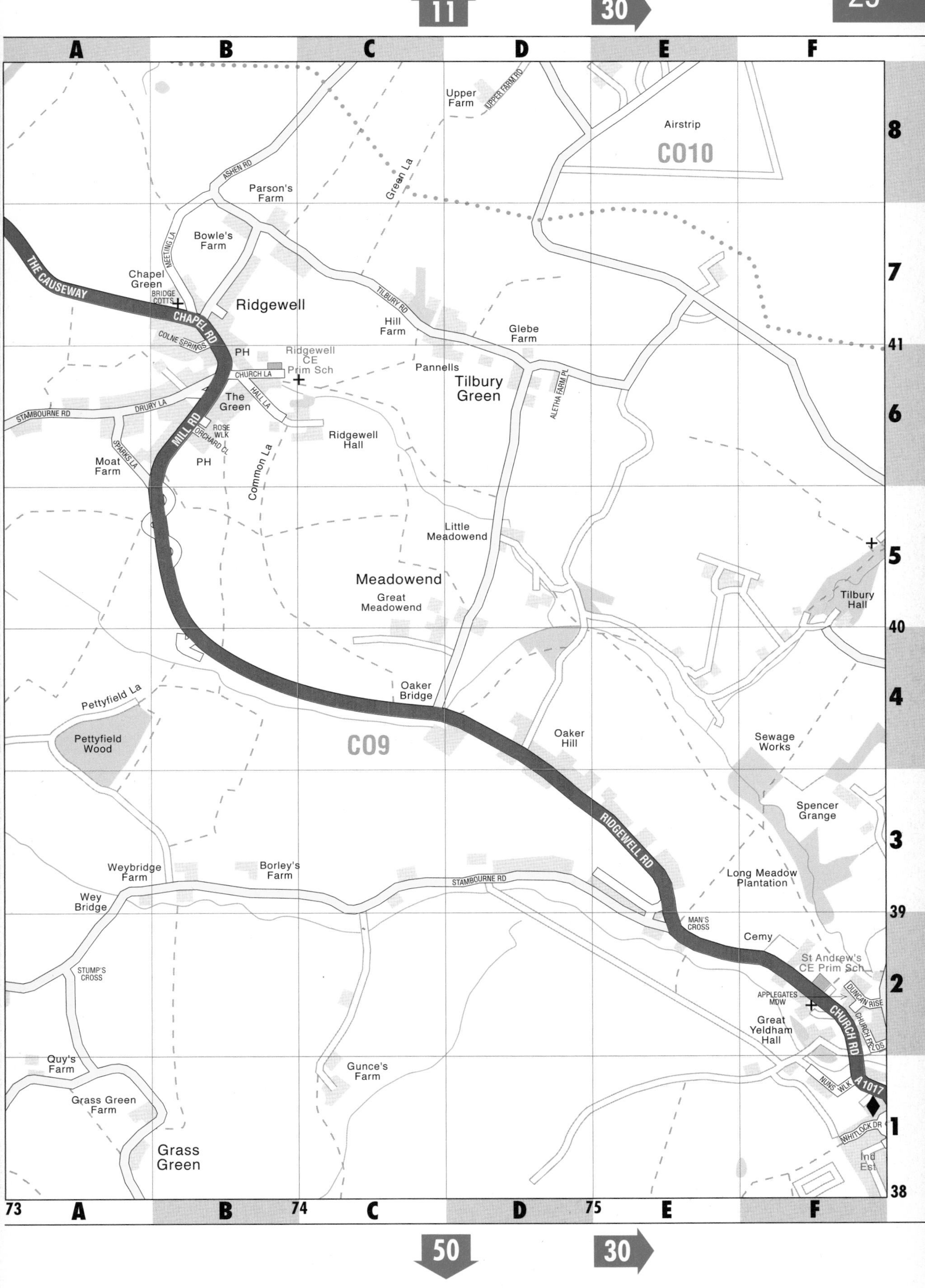
Upper Farm
UPPER FARM RD
Airstrip
CO10
ASHEN RD
Parson's Farm
Green La
Bowle's Farm
MEETING LA
Chapel Green
BRIDGE COTTS
THE CAUSEWAY
Ridgewell
CHAPEL RD
TILBURY RD
Hill Farm
Glebe Farm
COLNE SPRINGS
PH
Ridgewell CE Prim Sch
CHURCH LA
Pannells
Tilbury Green
ALETHA FARM PL
HALL LA
The Green
STAMBOURNE RD
DRURY LA
MILL RD
ROSE WLK
ORCHARD CL
SPARKS LA
Ridgewell Hall
Moat Farm
PH
Common La
Little Meadowend
Meadowend
Great Meadowend
Tilbury Hall
Oaker Bridge
Pettyfield La
Pettyfield Wood
CO9
Oaker Hill
Sewage Works
Spencer Grange
RIDGEWELL RD
Weybridge Farm
Borley's Farm
STAMBOURNE RD
Long Meadow Plantation
Wey Bridge
MAN'S CROSS
Cemy
St Andrew's CE Prim Sch
STUMP'S CROSS
APPLEGATES MDW
DUNCAN RISE
CHURCH RD
CHURCH FLDS
Great Yeldham Hall
Quy's Farm
Gunce's Farm
NUNS WLK
A1017
Grass Green Farm
WHITLOCK DR
Grass Green
Ind Est
A B C D E F
1 2 3 4 5 6 7 8
38 39 40 41
73 74 75

50
30

29
12

ASHEN RD

Silver End

CO10

Gage's House

Rowan Bank House

Knowl Green

Hole Farm

Wakeshall La

Wakeshall Farm

Cherry Tree (PH)

Lodge Farm

Park Farm

Marshy La

Wood Barns Farm

8

7

41

Mashay Farm

Marshy Wood

6

Tilbury Cottage

Twelve Acre Wood

CLARE RD

BELCHAMP RD

Tilbury Juxta Clare

Red Barn

Jay's La

MASHAY RD

Red House

5

40

Tilbury Court

4

Hyde Wood

CO9

Little Yeldham

CHURCH GN

Lodge

HYDEWOOD RD

The Hyde

SCHOOL RD

Bendysh House

TILBURY RD

MILL LA

3

Brook Farm

LITTLE YELDHAM RD

The Hyde Farm

Hall Green

NORTH END RD

North End

39

PH

2

ARMSTRONG WAY

HIGHFIELDS

GOODCHILD WAY

LITTLE HYDE CL

THE CROFT

CARLTON CL

LEATHER LA

BUTLERS WAY

Upper Yeldham Hall

NORTH RD

BRIDGE ST

GREAT OAK CL

PH

Highlands Farm

1

A1017 HIGH ST A1017

WHITLOCK DR

Great Yeldham

Spayne's Hall

POPLAR CL

Hunt's Wood

Priestfields Farm

MARKET GR

38

76   77   78

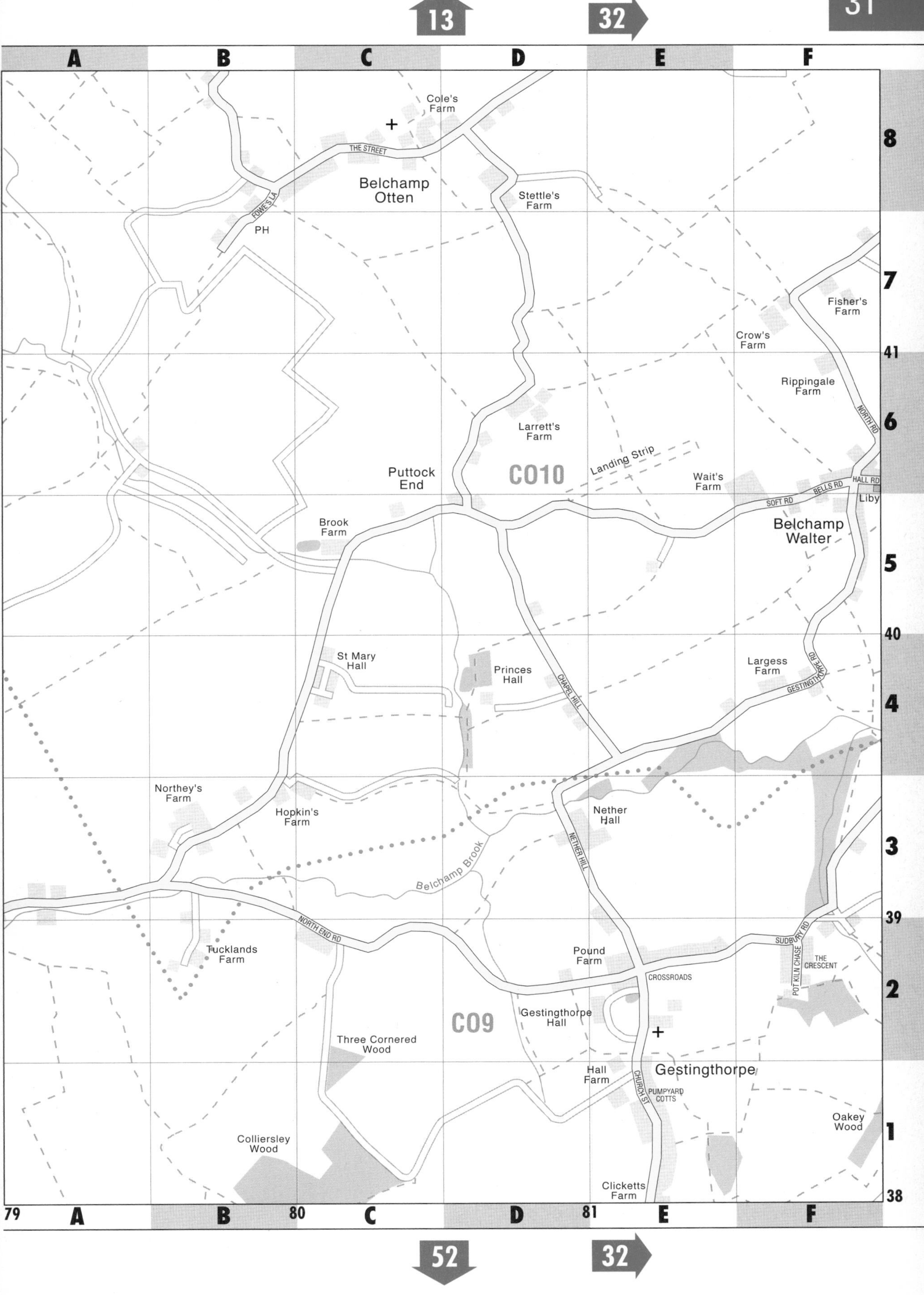
13
32
A
B
C
D
E
F
Cole's Farm
THE STREET
Belchamp Otten
FOWE'S LA
PH
Stettle's Farm
Fisher's Farm
Crow's Farm
Rippingale Farm
NORTH RD
Larrett's Farm
Landing Strip
Puttock End
CO10
Wait's Farm
HALL RD
BELLS RD
SOFT RD
Liby
Brook Farm
Belchamp Walter
St Mary Hall
Princes Hall
CHAPEL HILL
Largess Farm
GESTINGTHORPE RD
Northey's Farm
Hopkin's Farm
Nether Hall
NETHER HILL
Belchamp Brook
NORTH END RD
Tucklands Farm
Pound Farm
SUDBURY RD
POT KILN CHASE
THE CRESCENT
CROSSROADS
CO9
Gestingthorpe Hall
Three Cornered Wood
Hall Farm
CHURCH ST
Gestingthorpe
PUMPYARD COTTS
Oakey Wood
Colliersley Wood
Clicketts Farm
8
7
41
6
5
40
4
3
39
2
1
38
79
80
81
52
32

31
14

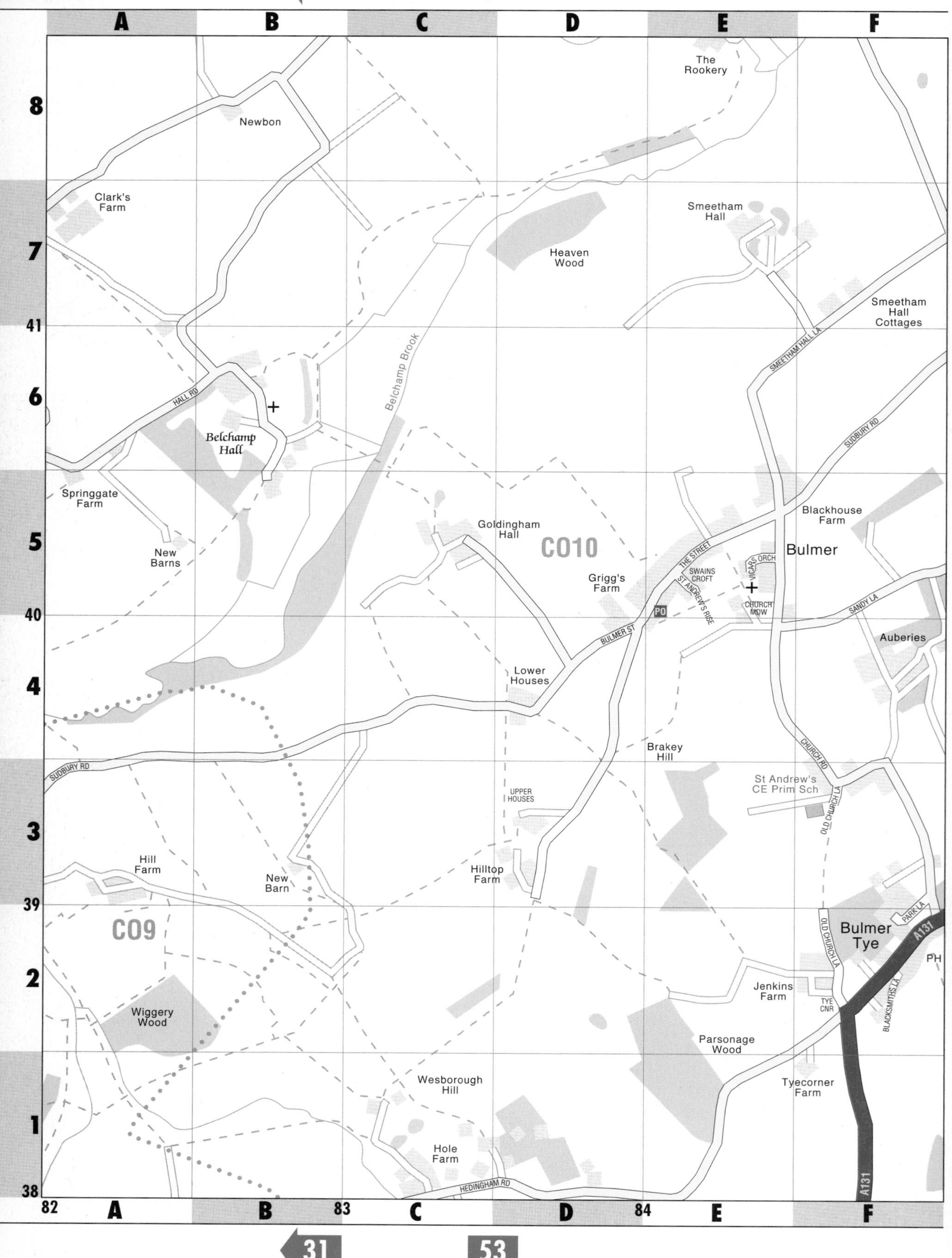

31
53

A   B   C   D   E   F

8

The Rookery

Newbon

Smeetham Hall

7

Clark's Farm

Heaven Wood

Smeetham Hall Cottages

41

SMEETHAM HALL LA

6

HALL RD

Belchamp Hall

Belchamp Brook

SUDBURY RD

Springgate Farm

Goldingham Hall

CO10

Blackhouse Farm

Bulmer

5

New Barns

Grigg's Farm

THE STREET

SWAINS CROFT

VICAR'S ORCH

CHURCH MDW

SANDY LA

Auberies

40

BULMER ST

PO

ST ANDREW'S RISE

4

Lower Houses

CHURCH RD

Brakey Hill

St Andrew's CE Prim Sch

SUDBURY RD

UPPER HOUSES

OLD CHURCH LA

3

Hill Farm

New Barn

Hilltop Farm

39

CO9

Bulmer Tye

PARK LA

A131

OLD CHURCH LA

PH

2

Wiggery Wood

Jenkins Farm

TYE CNR

BLACKSMITHS LA

Parsonage Wood

Tyecorner Farm

1

Wesborough Hill

Hole Farm

HEDINGHAM RD

A131

38

82   A   B   83   C   D   84   E   F

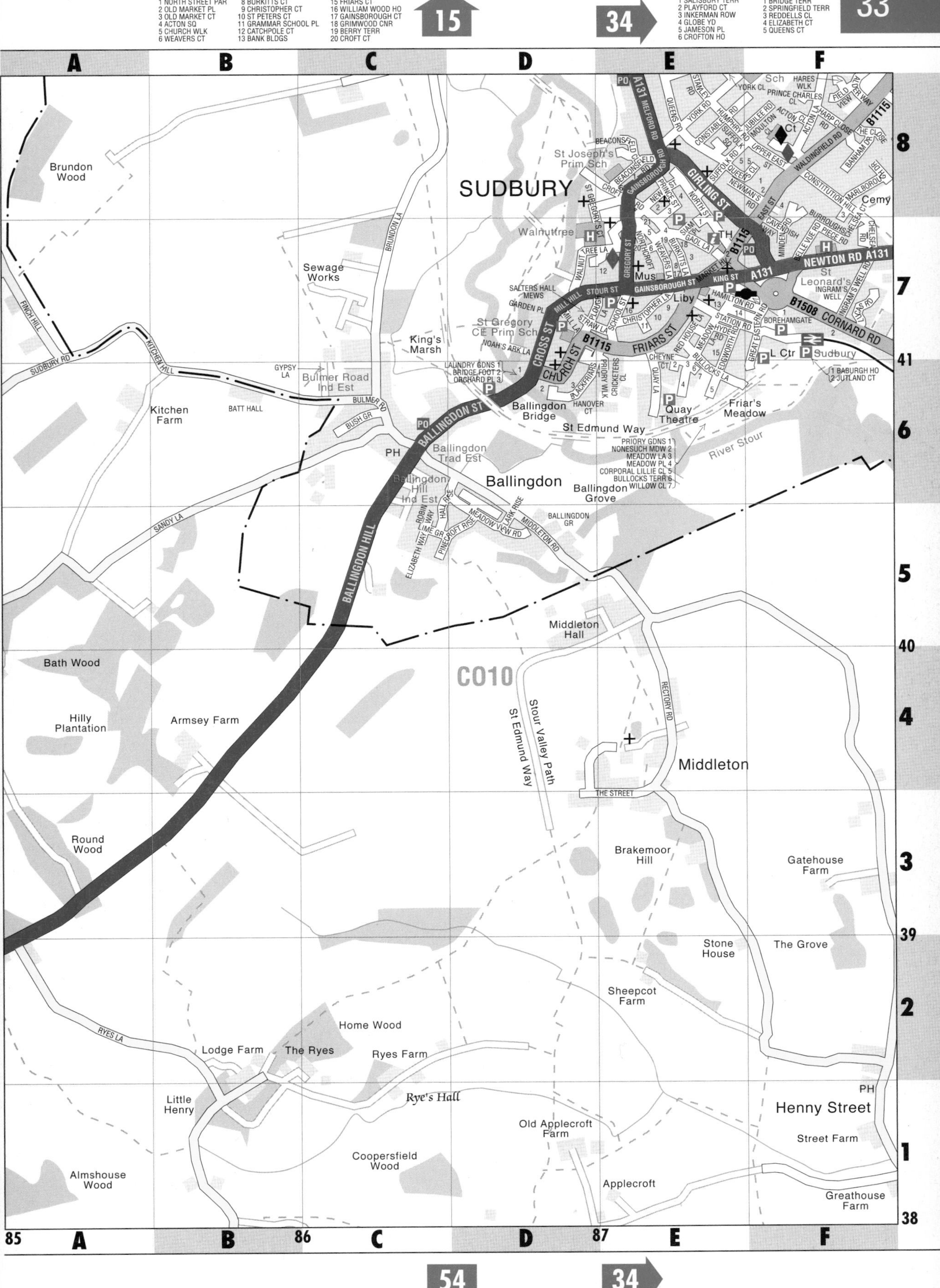

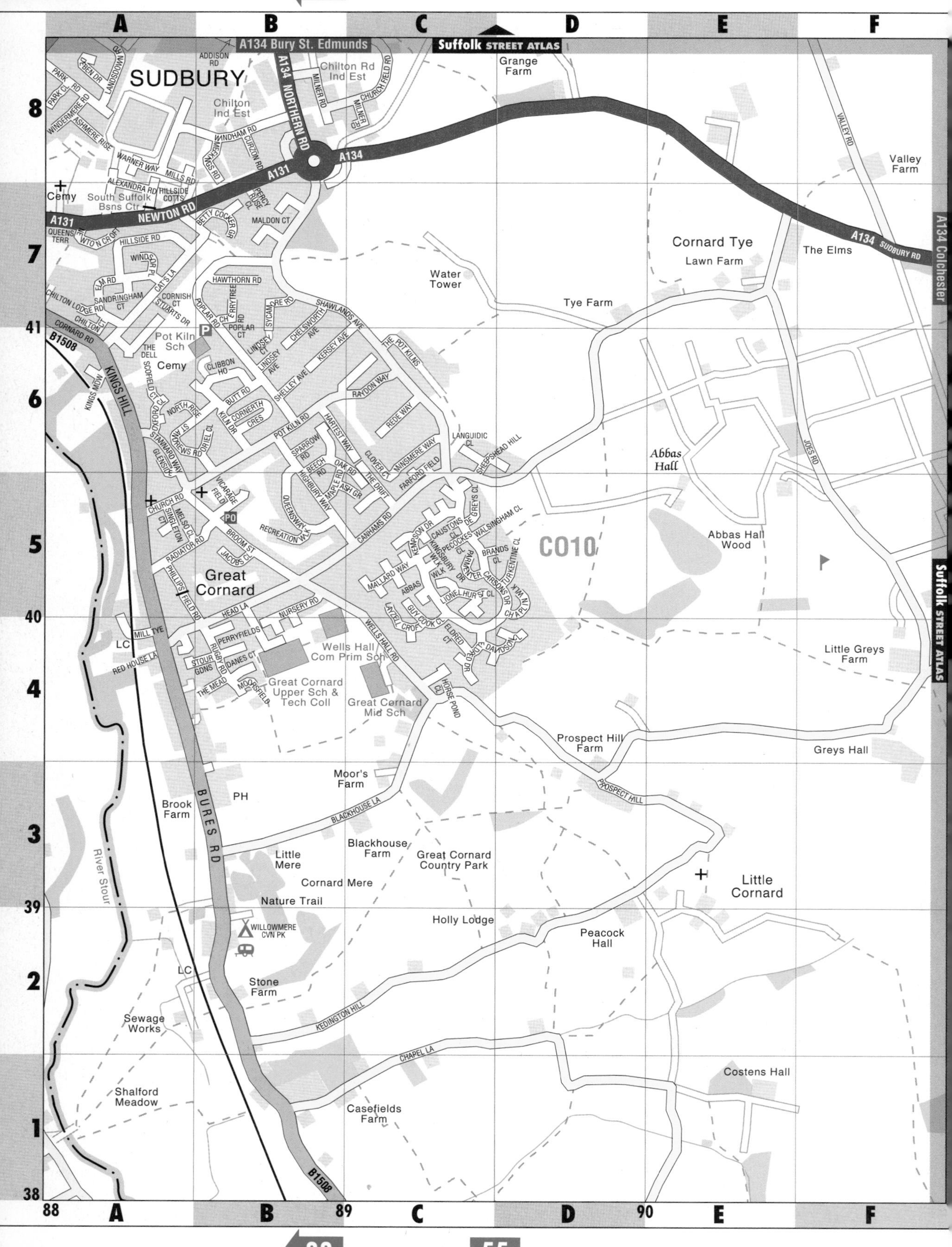

33

A134 Bury St. Edmunds

Suffolk STREET ATLAS

SUDBURY

Grange Farm

ADDISON RD

Chilton Rd Ind Est

Chilton Rd

Chilton Ind Est

A134

A134

Valley Farm

8

Cornard Tye

Lawn Farm

The Elms

A134 SUDBURY RD

A134 Colchester

A131

NEWTON RD

WTO N CROFT

HILLSIDE RD

Water Tower

Tye Farm

7

41

B1508

CORNARD RD

CHILTON LODGE RD

THE DELL

KINGS MDW

Pot Kiln Sch

Cemy

Abbas Hall

6

KINGS HILL

Languidic Cl

Sheepshead Hill

Abbas Hall Wood

5

Great Cornard

CO10

40

LC

MILL TYE

RED HOUSE LA

Recreation Way

Wells Hall Com Prim Sch

Little Greys Farm

4

BURES RD

Great Cornard Upper Sch & Tech Coll

Great Cornard Mid Sch

HORSE POND RD

Prospect Hill Farm

PROSPECT HILL

Greys Hall

Moor's Farm

PH

Brook Farm

BLACKHOUSE LA

3

River Stour

Little Mere

Blackhouse Farm

Great Cornard Country Park

Little Cornard

39

Cornard Mere

Nature Trail

Holly Lodge

Peacock Hall

WILLOWMERE CVN PK

2

LC

Stone Farm

KEDINGTON HILL

Sewage Works

CHAPEL LA

Costens Hall

Shalford Meadow

Casefields Farm

1

B1508

38

88

A

89

B

C

90

D

E

F

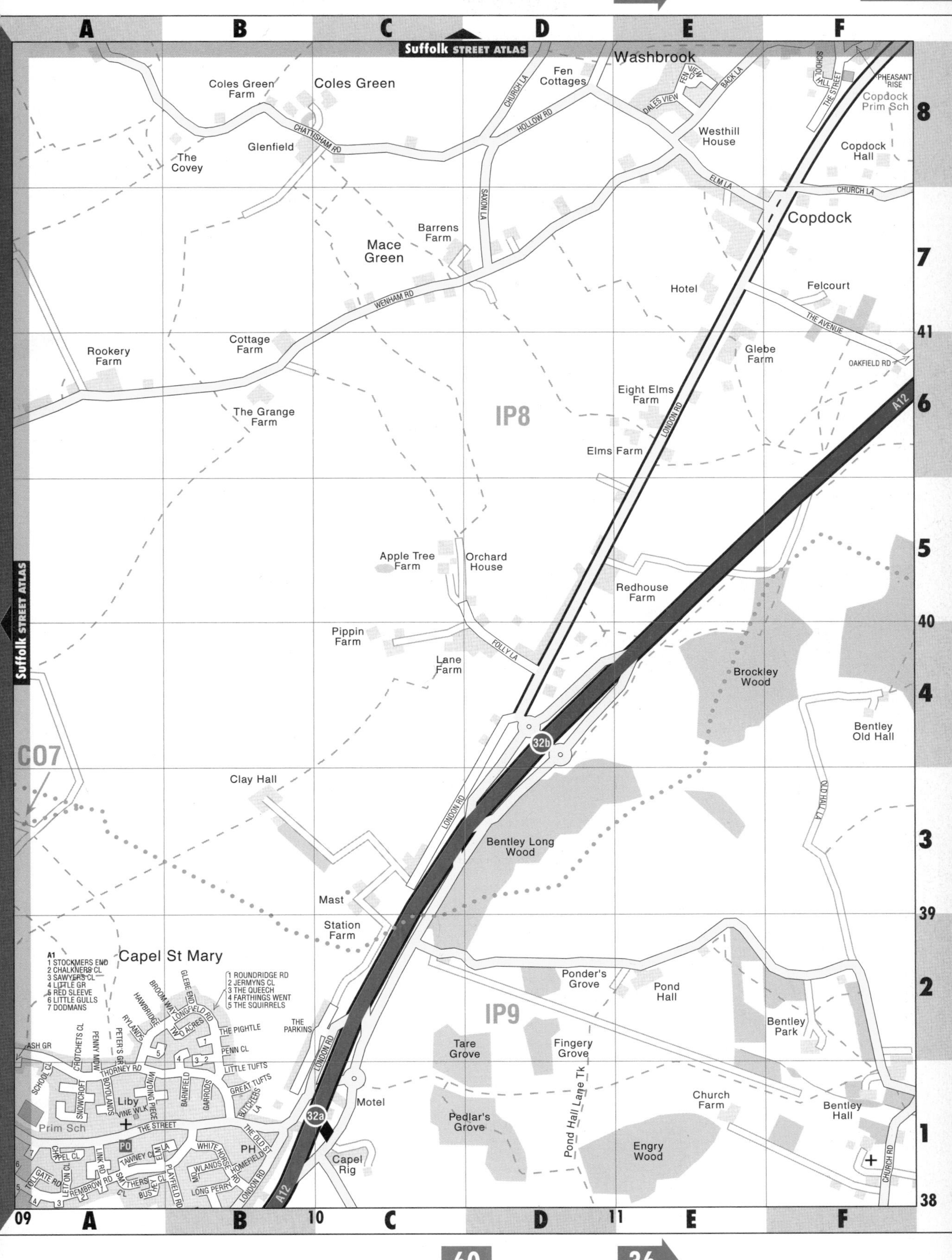

Suffolk STREET ATLAS

Suffolk STREET ATLAS

Coles Green Farm
Coles Green
Fen Cottages
Washbrook
PHEASANT RISE
Copdock Prim Sch
8

The Covey
Glenfield
CHATTISHAM RD
CHURCH LA
HOLLOW RD
DALES VIEW
Westhill House
ELM LA
Copdock Hall
CHURCH LA
Copdock

Mace Green
Barrens Farm
SAXON LA
Hotel
Felcourt
THE AVENUE
7

Rookery Farm
Cottage Farm
WENHAM RD
Glebe Farm
OAKFIELD RD
41

The Grange Farm
IP8
Eight Elms Farm
LONDON RD
6

Elms Farm

Apple Tree Farm
Orchard House
Redhouse Farm
A12
5

Pippin Farm
FOLLY LA
40

Lane Farm
Brockley Wood
4

C07
Clay Hall
32b
Bentley Old Hall

Bentley Long Wood
OLD HALL LA
3

Mast
39

Station Farm
Ponder's Grove
Pond Hall
Bentley Park
2

Capel St Mary
A1
1 STOCKMERS END
2 CHALKNERS CL
3 SAWYERS CL
4 LITTLE GR
5 RED SLEEVE
6 LITTLE GULLS
7 DODMANS
1 ROUNDRIDGE RD
2 JERMYNS CL
3 THE QUEECH
4 FARTHINGS WENT
5 THE SQUIRRELS
IP9
Tare Grove
Fingery Grove
Pond Hall Lane Tk

THE PARKINS
LONDON RD
Motel
Pedlar's Grove
Church Farm
Bentley Hall
1

Liby
Prim Sch
PO
PH
32a
Capel Rig
Engry Wood
A12
38

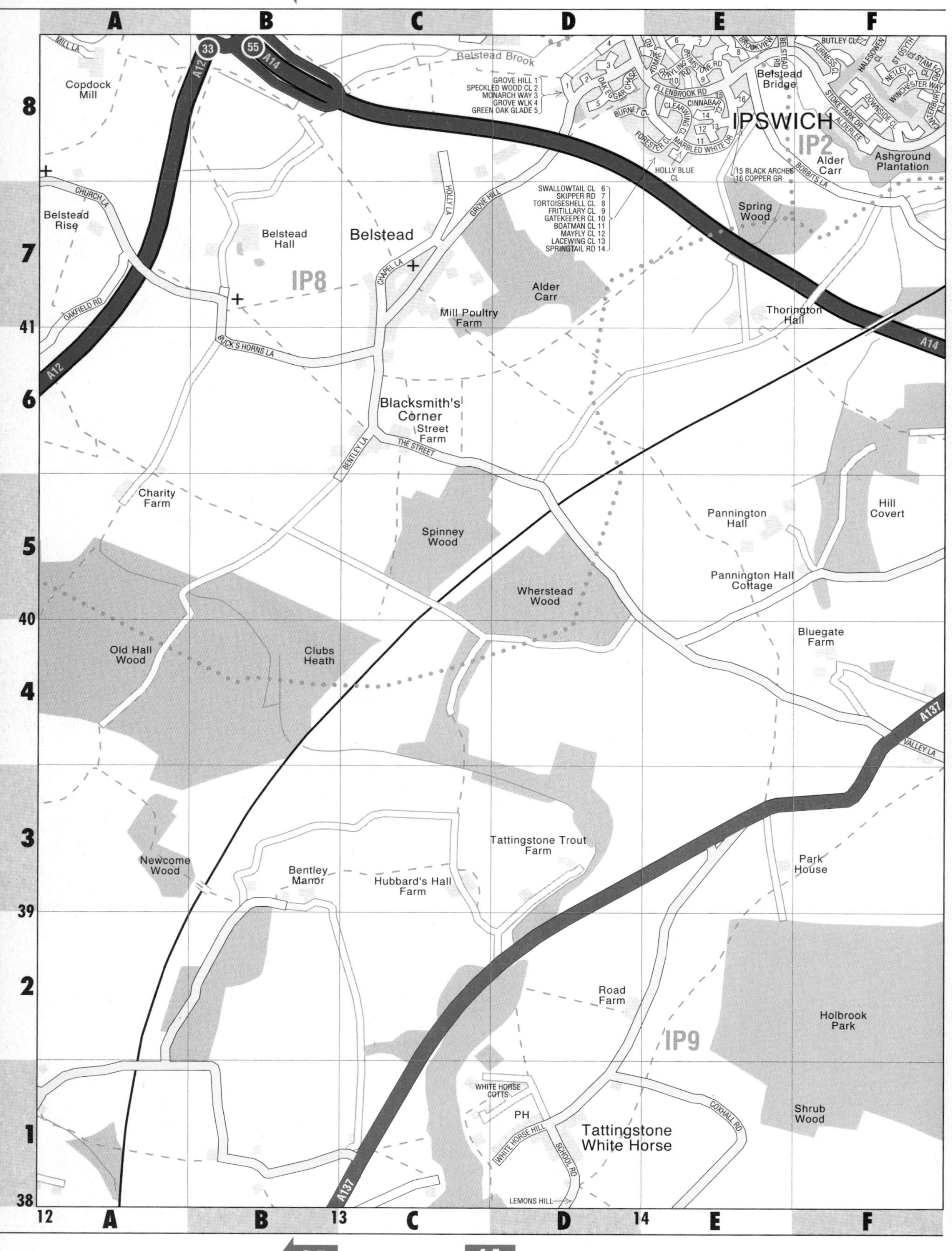

35
16

A B C D E F

8

7

41

6

5

40

4

3

39

2

1

38

Copdock
Mill

Belstead Brook

GROVE HILL 1
SPECKLED WOOD CL 2
MONARCH WAY 3
GROVE WLK 4
GREEN OAK GLADE 5

Belstead
Bridge

IPSWICH
IP2

Alder
Carr

Ashground
Plantation

Belstead
Rise

Belstead
Hall

Belstead

IP8

HOLLY BLUE
CL

Spring
Wood

Thorington
Hall

A14

CHURCH LA

OAKFIELD RD

A12

HOLLY LA

CHAPEL LA

GROVE HILL

SWALLOWTAIL CL 6
SKIPPER RD 7
TORTOISESHELL CL 8
FRITILLARY CL 9
GATEKEEPER CL 10
BOATMAN CL 11
MAYFLY CL 12
LACEWING CL 13
SPRINGTAIL RD 14

Mill Poultry
Farm

Alder
Carr

15 BLACK ARCHES
16 COPPER GR

BUCK'S HORNS LA

Blacksmith's
Corner
Street
Farm

BENTLEY LA

THE STREET

Charity
Farm

Spinney
Wood

Wherstead
Wood

Pannington
Hall

Pannington Hall
Cottage

Hill
Covert

Old Hall
Wood

Clubs
Heath

Bluegate
Farm

A137

VALLEY LA

Newcome
Wood

Bentley
Manor

Hubbard's Hall
Farm

Tattingstone Trout
Farm

Park
House

A137

Road
Farm

IP9

Holbrook
Park

WHITE HORSE
COTTS

PH

WHITE HORSE HILL

SCHOOL RD

Tattingstone
White Horse

COXHALL RD

Shrub
Wood

LEMONS HILL

12 A 13 C 14 E F
B D

17
38

A B C D E F

8
7
41
6
5
40
4
3
39
2
1
38

Corporation Ave
Walsingham Ct
Bourne Park
Stoke Park Dr
Whitland Cl
A137
B1456
Bourne Terr
Braky Wood
Camp Yard
Sewage Works
Suffolk Ski Ctr
Bourne Hill
IP2
Bourne Hall Farm
The Strand
Wharf
Sewage Works
Ash Disposal Area
IP3
Raeburn Rd S
Works
Orwell Country Park
Stour and Orwell Walk
Pipers Vale
Morland Rd
Fletcher Rd
Lely Rd
Gainsborough La
Allot Gdns
New Channel
Wherstead Ooze
Orwell Bridge
A14
Sandpit Covert
Home Covert
Chapman's Grove
Bobbits La
Black Ooze
River Orwell
56
Wherstead Park
Wherstead Hall
Broomhoughton Covert
Mast
The Street
Wherstead
The Peninsula Bsns Ctr
Redgate Farm
Redgate Hard
Pond Ooze
IP10
Masts
Constables Manor
Park Farm
B1456
Freston Reach
Redgate La
Vicarage La
Redgate House
Wharf
Freston Point
Lee's Farm
IP9
Freston Brook
Stour and Orwell Walk
Freston Hill
Hillside Cotts
Freston Wood
Freston Hill
Freston Twr
PH
Freston Park
Stalls Valley
Valley La
Valley Farm
Freston Lodge Farm
Freston Lodge
Tower Plantation
Freston
Toweralder Carr
Broom Knoll
Freston House
Freston St
Home Farm
B1080
Cutler's Wood
Bond Hall
Main Rd
B1456
Bond Hall Farm
Wr Twr
Harkstead La
Turkey Farm
Dench Wood
B1080

15 A B 16 C D 17 E F

62
38

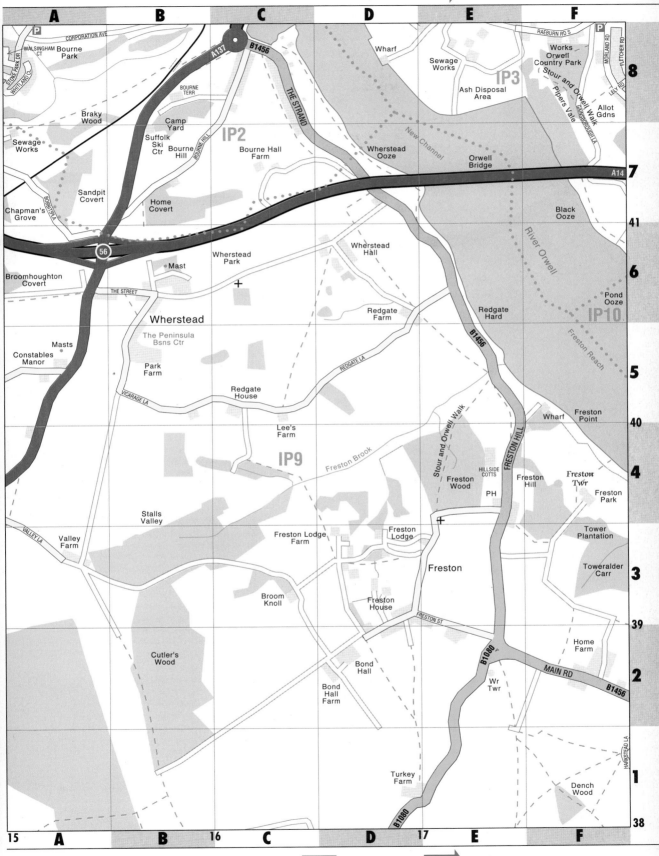

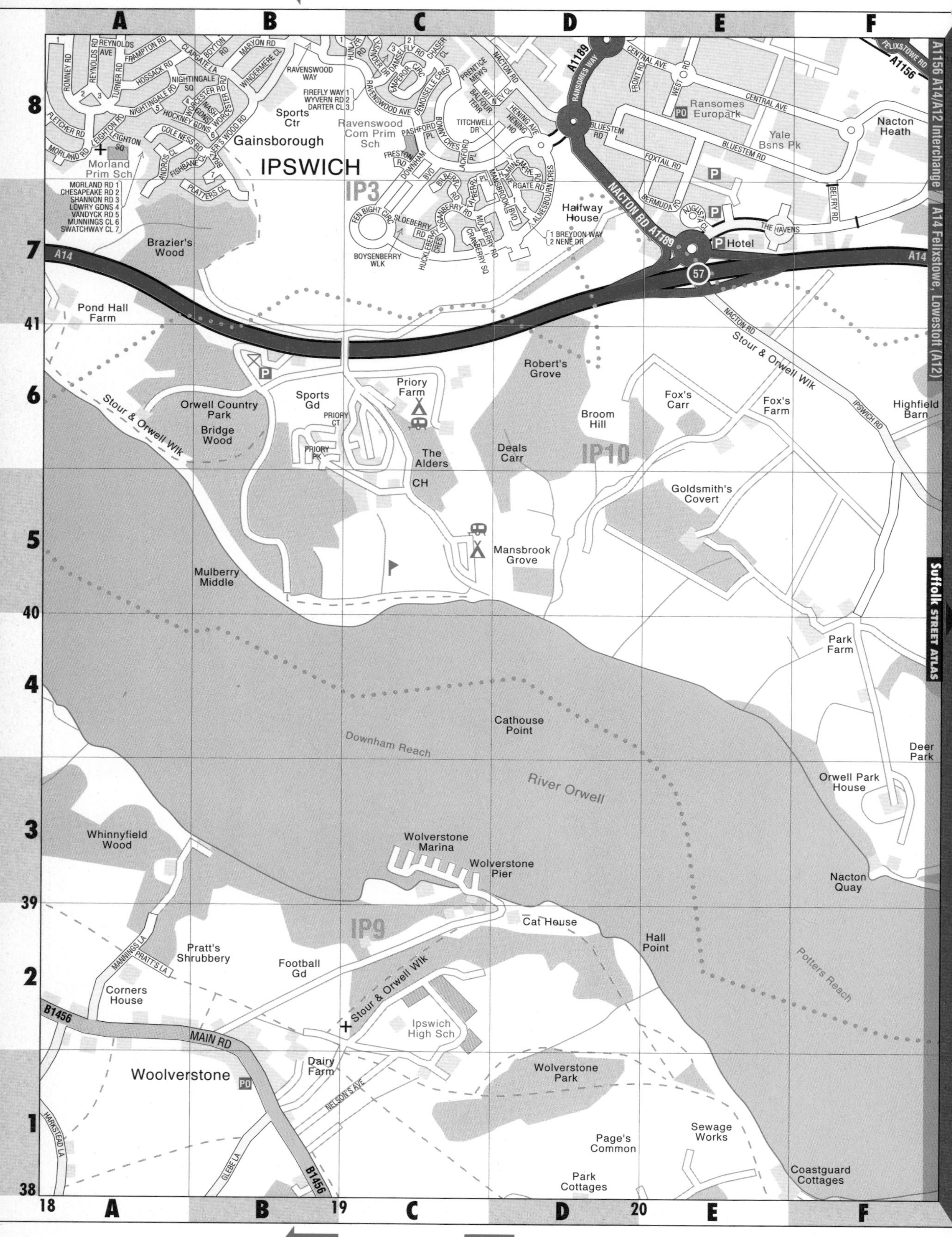

A B C D E F

A1156 A14/A12 Interchange // A14 Felixstowe, Lowestoft (A12)

Suffolk STREET ATLAS

8
7
41
6
5
40
4
3
39
2
1
38

18 A B 19 C D 20 E F

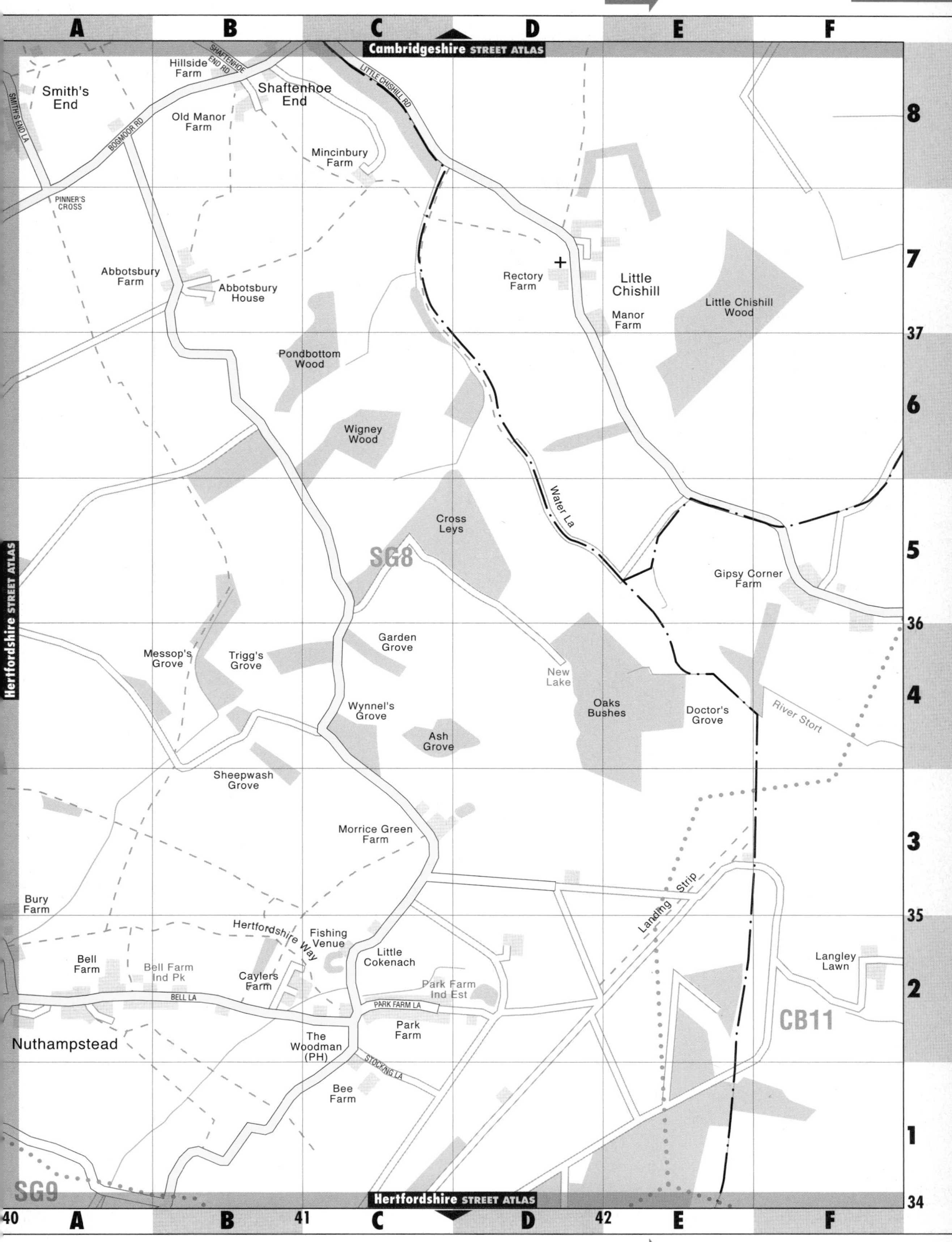

Hertfordshire STREET ATLAS

A **B** **C** **D** **E** **F**

Smith's End

Hillside Farm

Shaftenhoe End

Old Manor Farm

SHAFTENHOE END RD

LITTLE CHISHILL RD

Mincinbury Farm

BOGMOOR RD

SMITH'S END LA

PINNER'S CROSS

8

Rectory Farm

Little Chishill

Little Chishill Wood

7

Abbotsbury Farm

Abbotsbury House

Manor Farm

37

Pondbottom Wood

6

Wigney Wood

Water La

Cross Leys

SG8

Gipsy Corner Farm

5

Garden Grove

36

Messop's Grove

Trigg's Grove

New Lake

Oaks Bushes

Doctor's Grove

River Stort

4

Wynnel's Grove

Ash Grove

Sheepwash Grove

Morrice Green Farm

Landing Strip

3

Bury Farm

35

Hertfordshire Way

Fishing Venue

Little Cokenach

Langley Lawn

Bell Farm

Bell Farm Ind Pk

Caylers Farm

Park Farm Ind Est

CB11

2

BELL LA

PARK FARM LA

Park Farm

Nuthampstead

The Woodman (PH)

STOCKNG LA

Bee Farm

1

SG9

34

39 19

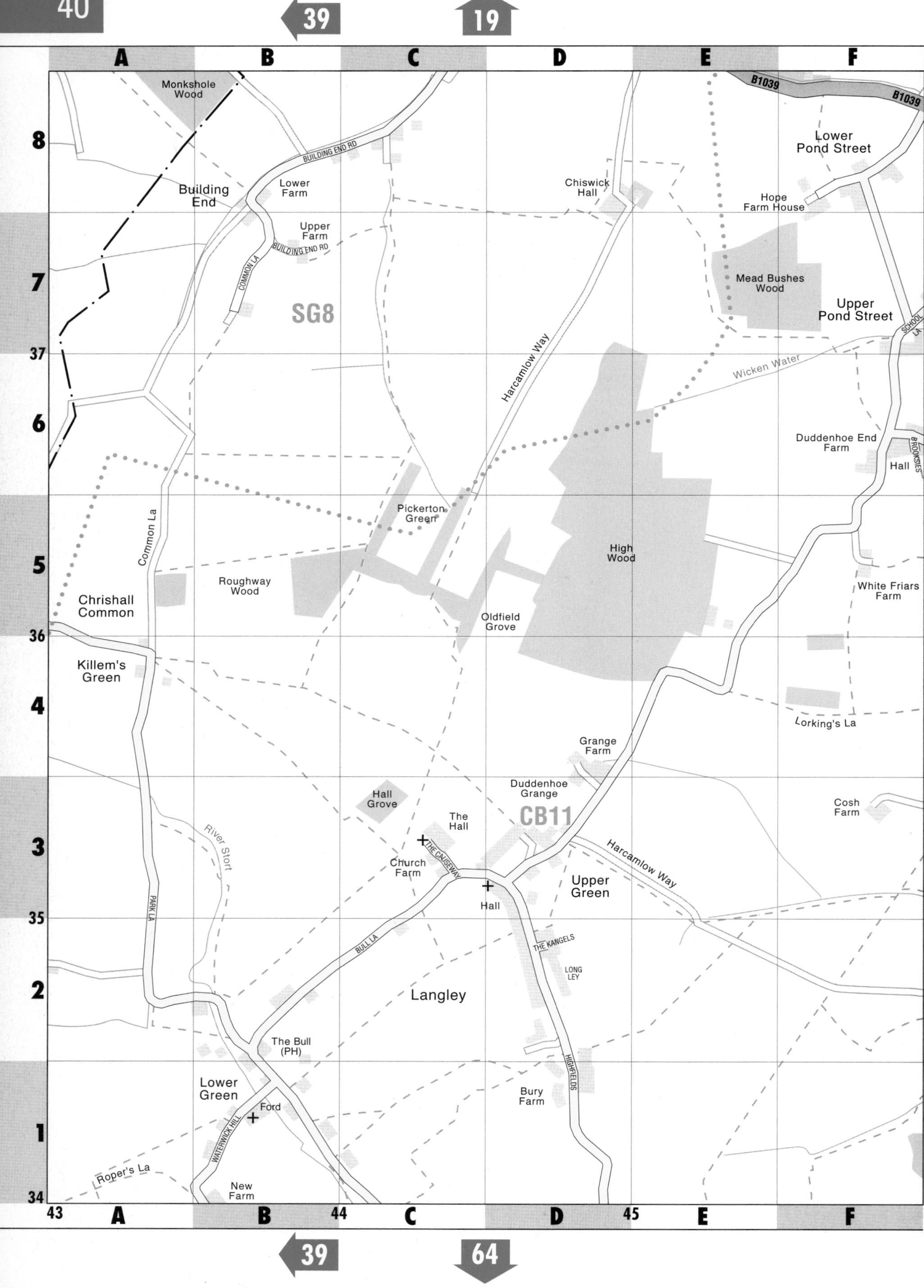

A   B   C   D   E   F

Monkshole Wood

B1039   B1039

8

Lower Pond Street

Building End

BUILDING END RD

Lower Farm

Chiswick Hall

Hope Farm House

Upper Farm

BUILDING END RD

COMMON LA

7

SG8

Mead Bushes Wood

Upper Pond Street

37

Wicken Water

SCHOOL LA

6

Duddenhoe End Farm

Hall

BROOKSIES

Common La

Pickerton Green

High Wood

White Friars Farm

5

Chrishall Common

Roughway Wood

Oldfield Grove

36

Killem's Green

4

Lorking's La

River Stort

Grange Farm

Cosh Farm

PARK LA

Hall Grove

Duddenhoe Grange

CB11

Harcamlow Way

3

The Hall

THE CAUSEWAY

Church Farm

Hall

Upper Green

35

BULL LA

THE KANGELS

LONG LEY

2

Langley

The Bull (PH)

HIGHFIELDS

Lower Green

Bury Farm

Ford

WATERWICK HILL

1

Roper's La

New Farm

34

43   A   B   44   C   D   45   E   F

Harcamlow Way

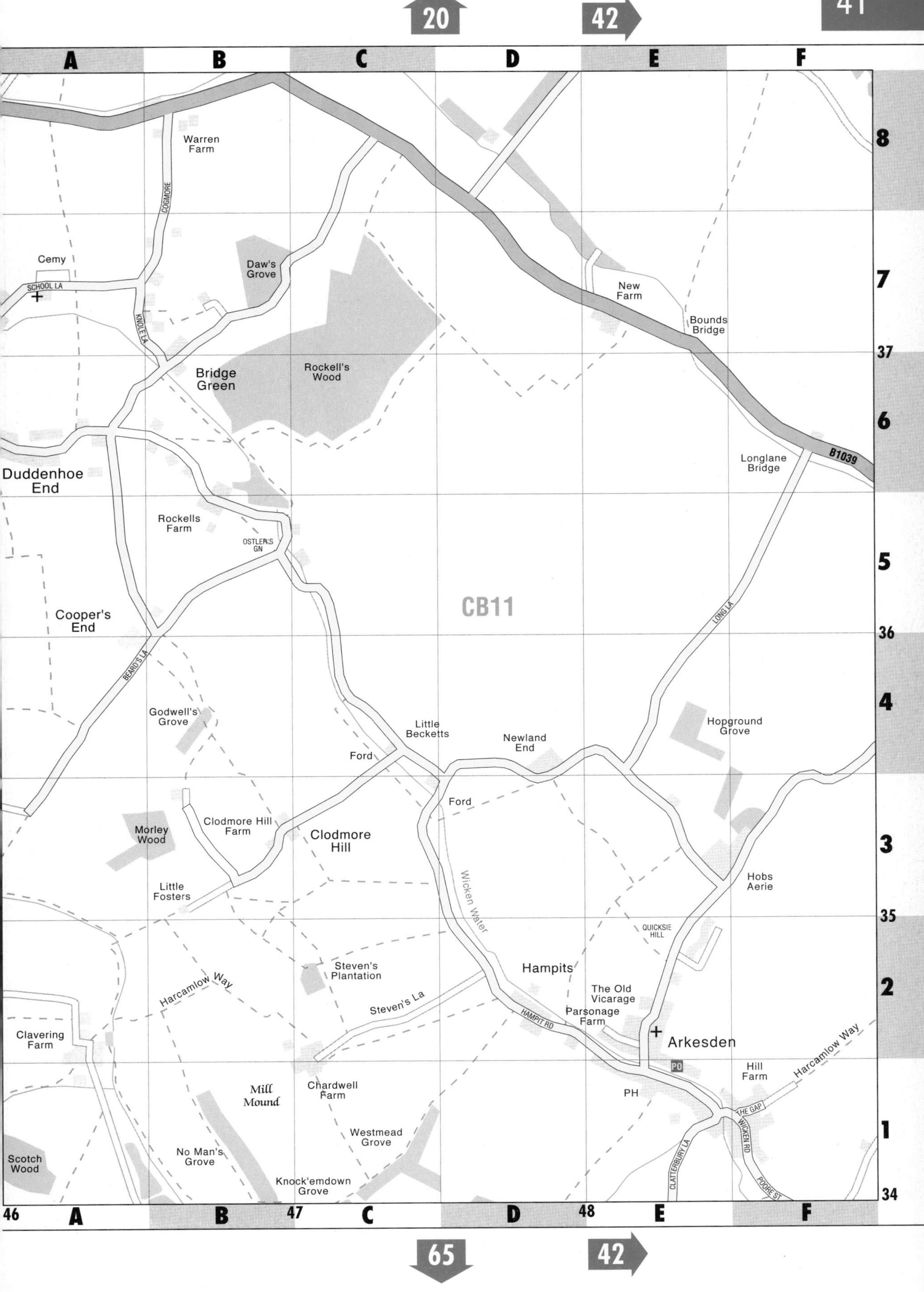

A B C D E F

8

7

37

6

B1039

Warren
Farm

COGMORE

Cemy

SCHOOL LA

KNOX LA

Daw's
Grove

New
Farm

Bounds
Bridge

Bridge
Green

Rockell's
Wood

Longlane
Bridge

Duddenhoe
End

Rockells
Farm

OSTLER'S
GN

LONG LA

5

36

4

CB11

Cooper's
End

BEARD'S LA

Godwell's
Grove

Little
Becketts

Newland
End

Hopground
Grove

Ford

Ford

Morley
Wood

Clodmore Hill
Farm

Clodmore
Hill

Hobs
Aerie

Little
Fosters

Wicken Water

3

35

QUICKSIE
HILL

Harcamlow Way

Steven's
Plantation

Hampits

The Old
Vicarage

2

HAMPIT RD

Parsonage
Farm

Steven's La

Clavering
Farm

Arkesden

Harcamlow Way

Hill
Farm

PO

Chardwell
Farm

PH

THE GAP

WICKEN RD

1

Mill
Mound

Scotch
Wood

No Man's
Grove

Westmead
Grove

Knock'emdown
Grove

CLATTERBURY LA

POORE ST

34

41
21

A **B** **C** **D** **E** **F**

8

Bush Pasture Grove

Cups Grove

The Triangle

Strawberry Close Belt

CHESTNUT AVE

The Willows

B1383

Cornwallis Hill

Mast

7

Neville Hill

LONDON RD

Red Leg Plantation

37

WALDEN RD

6

The Old Vicarage

Wenden Place Farm

NAT LA

THE BEECHES

RAILWAY COTTS

PH

B1039

STATION RD

MUTLOW RD

B1039

CHURCH ST

MUTLOW HILL

SILVER ROW

ROYSTON RD

CB11

PH

Mutlow Farm

Mutlow Hall

5

Wenden Hall

Bearwalden Bsns Pk

Audley End

Clanverend Farm

Clanverend Bridge

DUCK ST

CRISWEL LA

Wendens Ambo

36

Norton End

Rookery Farm

LC

ROOKERY LA

4

Mill Farm

Bulse Farm

Duddenhoe La

Mill Hill

3

35

Whiteditch Farm

Tudhope Farm

2

Harcamlow Way

Long Plantation

WHITEDITCH LA

B1383

Newport Free Gram Sch

BURY WATER LA

Nursery

BURYWATER COTTS

1

Severals Farm

BURY WATER LA

TENTERFIELDS

GACES ACRE

SCHOOL LA

MELDONFORD

GILBEY LH

WICKEN RD

34

B1038

M11

49 **A** 50 **B** **C** 51 **D** **E** **F**

22
44

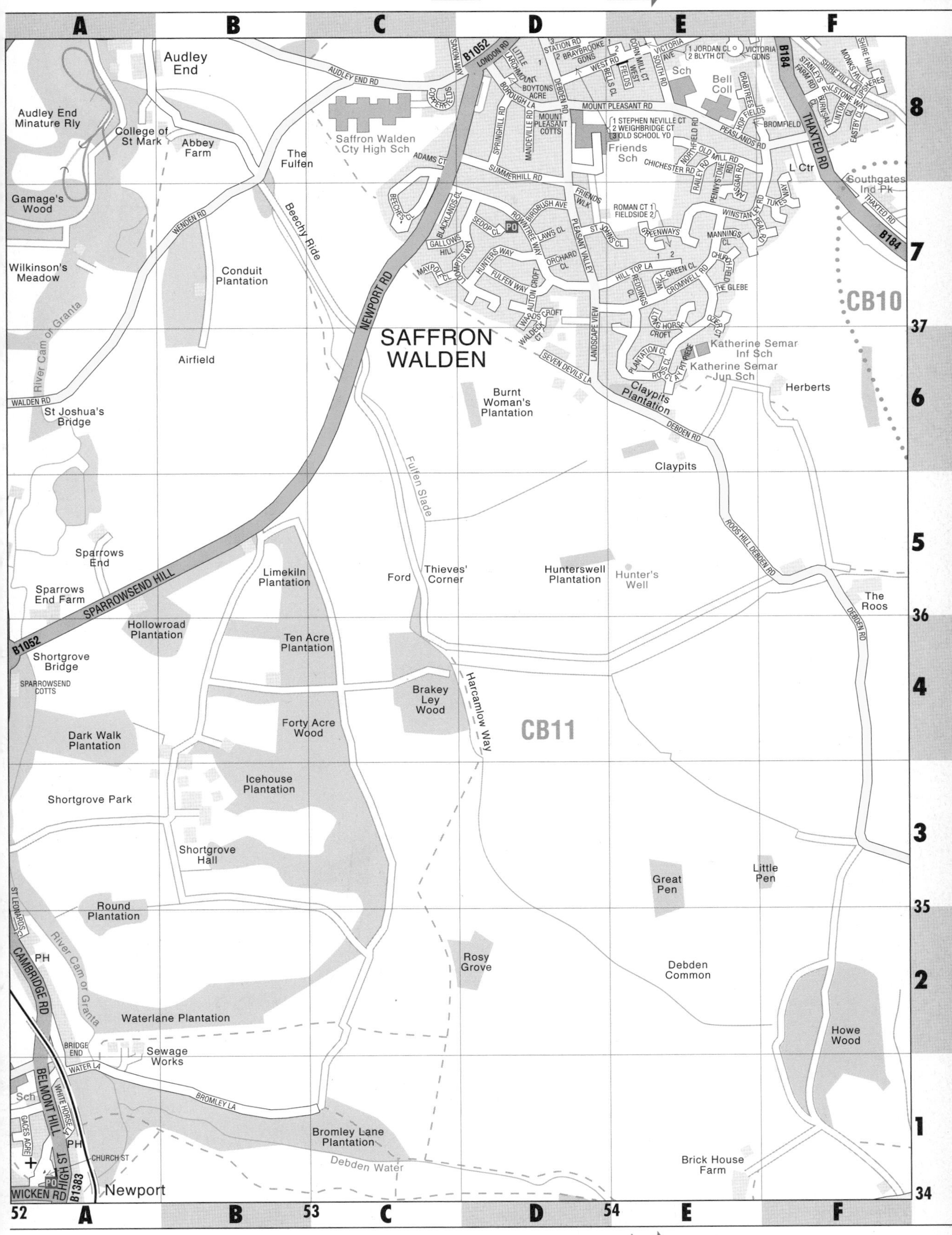
A
B
C
D
E
F
Audley End
Audley End Minature Rly
College of St Mark
Abbey Farm
Saffron Walden Cty High Sch
The Fulfen
Gamage's Wood
Wilkinson's Meadow
Conduit Plantation
Beechy Ride
NEWPORT RD
SAFFRON WALDEN
Airfield
St Joshua's Bridge
WALDEN RD
WENDEN RD
AUDLEY END RD
LONDON RD
B1052
Friends Sch
Bell Coll
Sch
L Ctr
Southgates Ind Pk
THAXTED RD
B184
CB10
Katherine Semar Inf Sch
Katherine Semar Jun Sch
Herberts
Burnt Woman's Plantation
Claypits Plantation
Claypits
DEBDEN RD
Fulfen Slade
Sparrows End
Sparrows End Farm
SPARROWSEND HILL
Limekiln Plantation
Ford
Thieves' Corner
Hunterswell Plantation
Hunter's Well
ROOS HILL DEBDEN RD
The Roos
Hollowroad Plantation
Shortgrove Bridge
SPARROWSEND COTTS
Ten Acre Plantation
Brakey Ley Wood
Harcamlow Way
CB11
Dark Walk Plantation
Forty Acre Wood
Icehouse Plantation
Shortgrove Park
Shortgrove Hall
Great Pen
Little Pen
Round Plantation
River Cam or Granta
PH
CAMBRIDGE RD
Rosy Grove
Debden Common
Waterlane Plantation
Howe Wood
BRIDGE END
Sewage Works
WATER LA
BROMLEY LA
BELMONT HILL
Sch
Bromley Lane Plantation
Brick House Farm
CHURCH ST
Debden Water
HIGH ST
B1383
WICKEN RD
Newport
MOUNT PLEASANT RD
SUMMERHILL RD
SEVEN DEVILS LA
LANDSCAPE VIEW
PLEASANT VALLEY
PEASLANDS RD
8
7
37
6
5
36
4
3
35
2
1
34
52
53
54

67
44

43
23

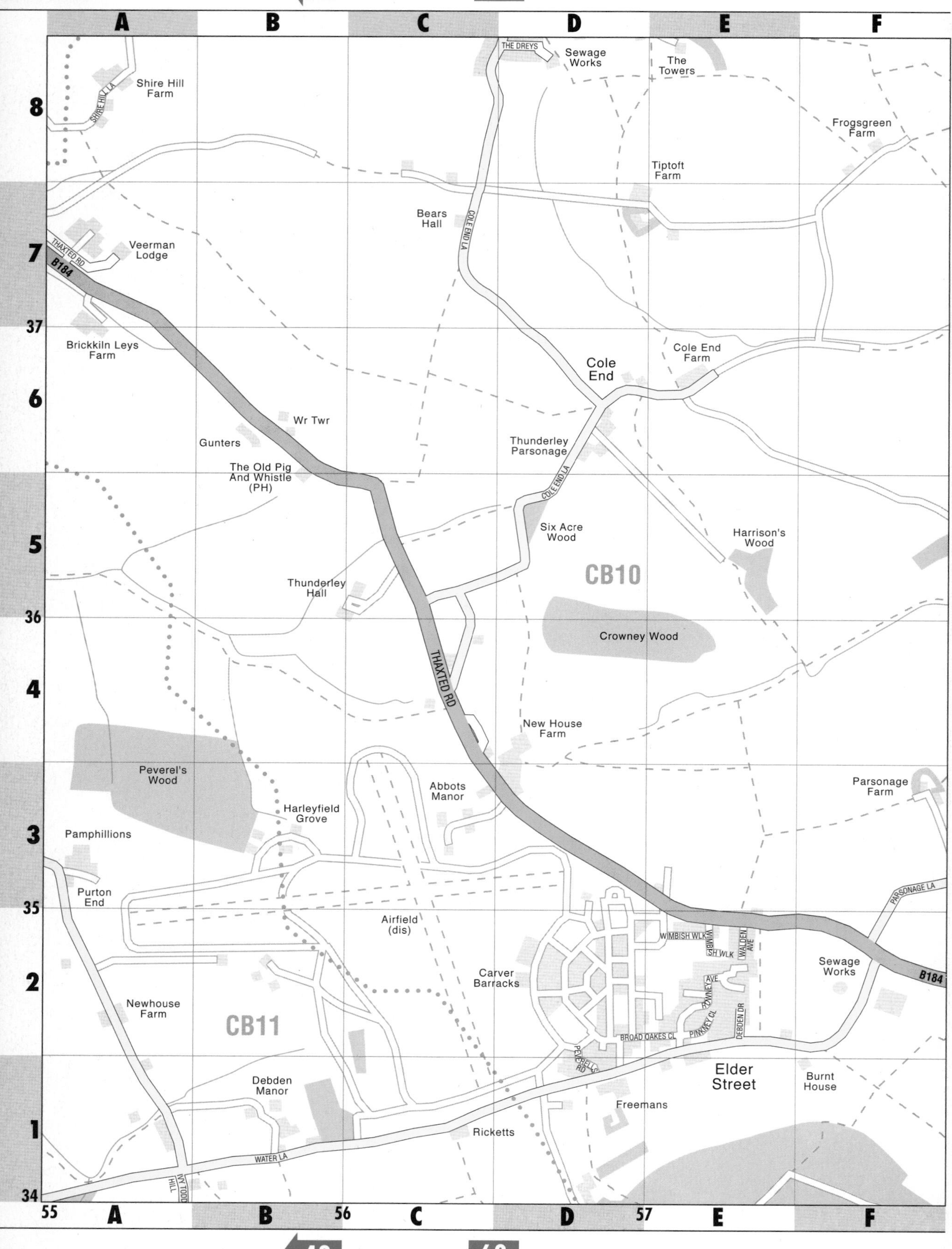
A
B
C
D
E
F
8
7
37
6
5
36
4
3
35
2
1
34
55
56
57
THE DREYS
Sewage Works
The Towers
Shire Hill Farm
SHIRE HILL LA
Frogsgreen Farm
Tiptoft Farm
Bears Hall
COLE END LA
THAXTED RD
B184
Veerman Lodge
Brickkiln Leys Farm
Cole End Farm
Cole End
Wr Twr
Gunters
Thunderley Parsonage
The Old Pig And Whistle (PH)
COLE END LA
Six Acre Wood
Harrison's Wood
CB10
Thunderley Hall
Crowney Wood
THAXTED RD
New House Farm
Peverel's Wood
Abbots Manor
Parsonage Farm
Harleyfield Grove
Pamphillions
Purton End
PARSONAGE LA
Airfield (dis)
WIMBISH WLK
WIMBISH WLK
WALDEN AVE
Sewage Works
B184
Carver Barracks
AVE
ROWNEY
Newhouse Farm
CB11
PINKNEY CL
DEBDEN DR
BROAD OAKES CL
PEVERELLS RD
Elder Street
Debden Manor
Burnt House
Freemans
Ricketts
WATER LA
IVY TODD HILL

43
68

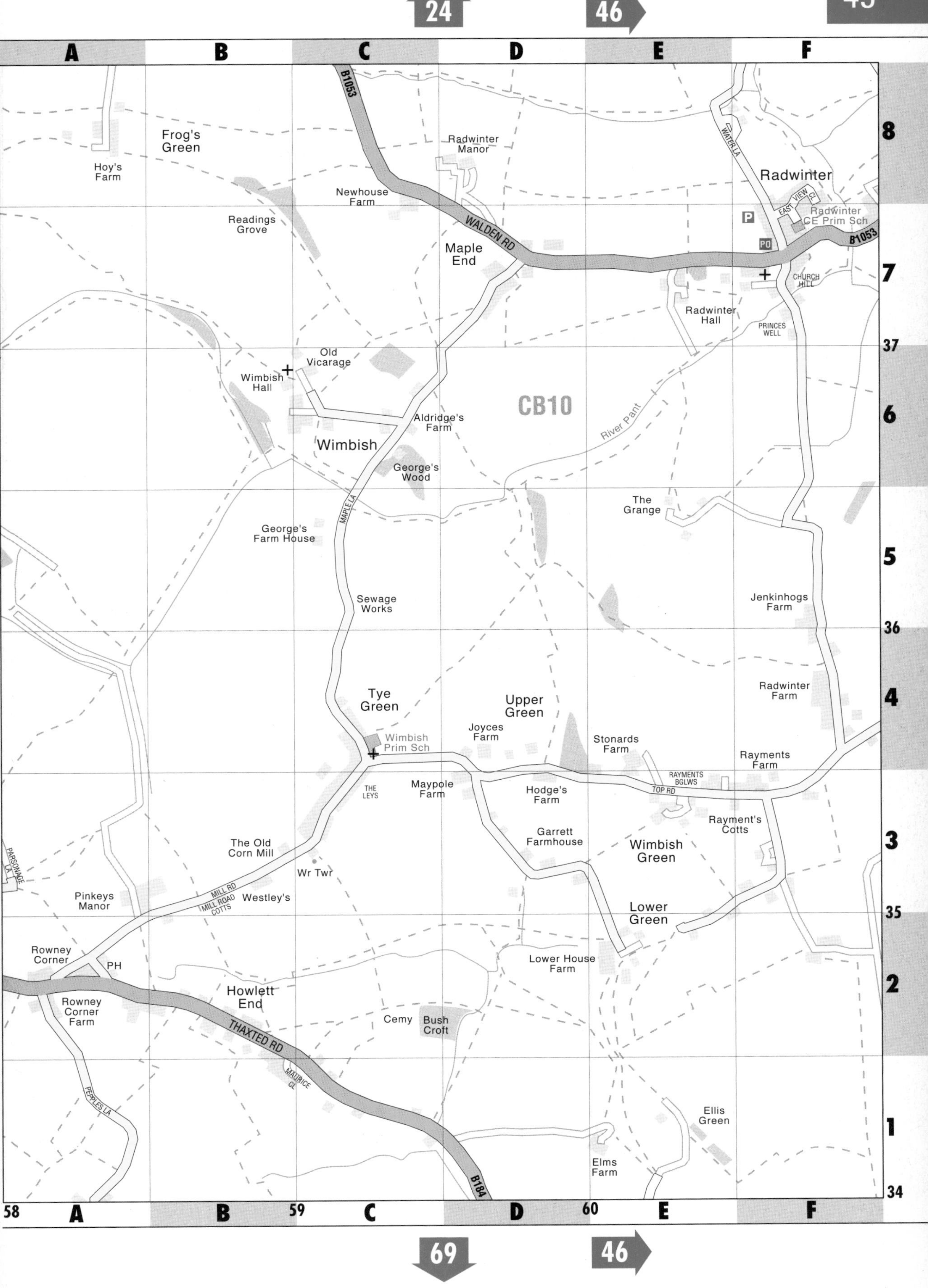
24
46
A
B
C
D
E
F
8
7
37
6
5
36
4
3
35
2
1
34
58
59
60
Frog's Green
Hoy's Farm
Readings Grove
B1053
Newhouse Farm
Radwinter Manor
WALDEN RD
Maple End
WATER LA
Radwinter
EAST VIEW CL
Radwinter CE Prim Sch
P
PO
B1053
CHURCH HILL
Radwinter Hall
PRINCES WELL
Old Vicarage
Wimbish Hall
Aldridge's Farm
CB10
River Pant
Wimbish
George's Wood
MAPLE LA
The Grange
George's Farm House
Sewage Works
Jenkinhogs Farm
Radwinter Farm
Tye Green
Upper Green
Wimbish Prim Sch
Joyces Farm
Stonards Farm
Rayments Farm
RAYMENTS BGLWS
TOP RD
THE LEYS
Maypole Farm
Hodge's Farm
Rayment's Cotts
Garrett Farmhouse
Wimbish Green
The Old Corn Mill
Wr Twr
PARSONAGE LA
MILL RD
MILL ROAD COTTS
Westley's
Pinkeys Manor
Lower Green
Rowney Corner
PH
Lower House Farm
Howlett End
Rowney Corner Farm
Cemy
Bush Croft
THAXTED RD
MAURICE CL
PEPLES LA
Ellis Green
Elms Farm
B184
69
46

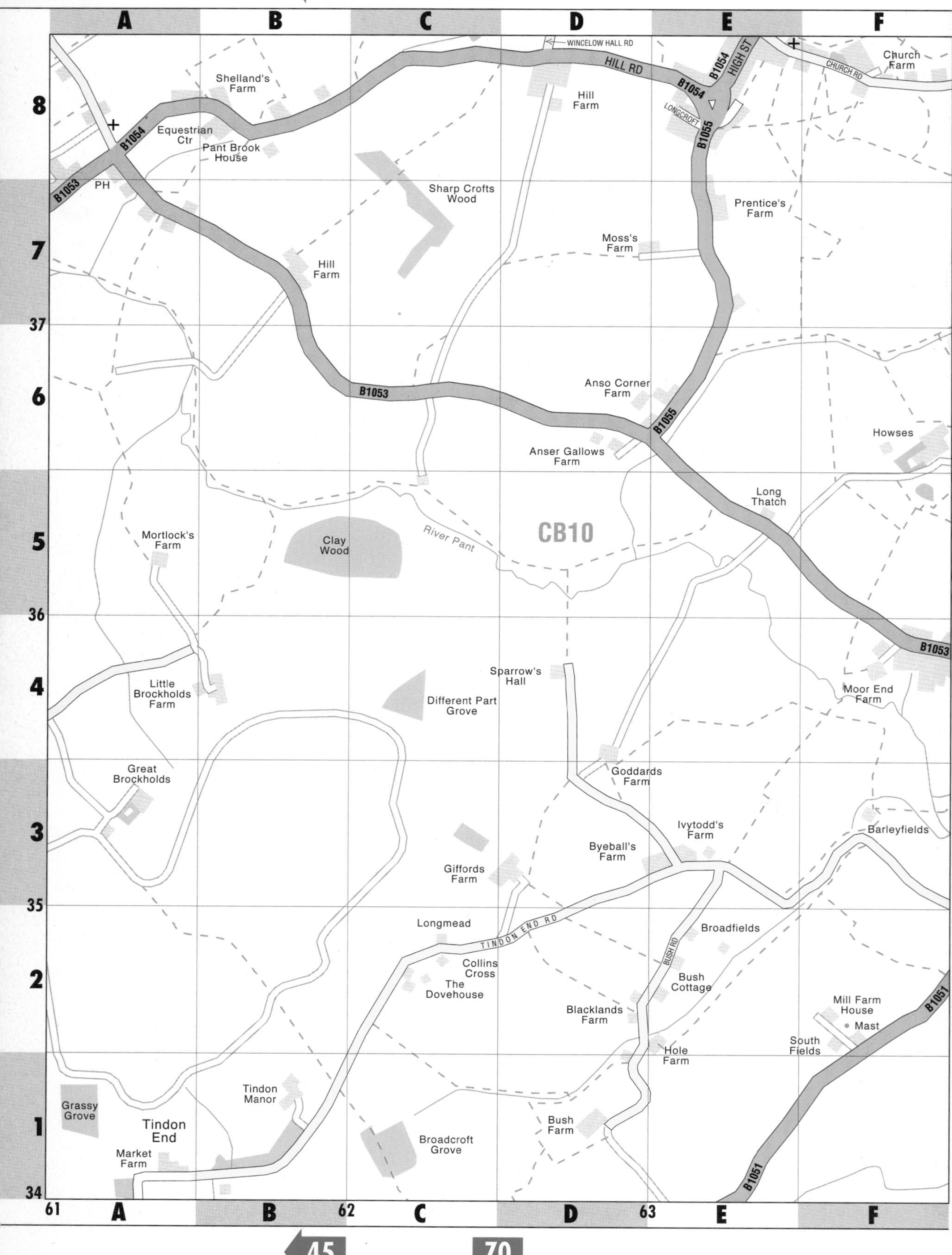

A B C D E F

8

7

37

6

5

36

4

3

35

2

1

34

Shelland's Farm

Equestrian Ctr

Pant Brook House

B1054

PH

B1053

Hill Farm

Sharp Crofts Wood

Hill Farm

Moss's Farm

WINCELOW HALL RD

HILL RD

B1054

B1054

LONGCROFT

HIGH ST

B1055

CHURCH RD

Church Farm

Prentice's Farm

Anso Corner Farm

Anser Gallows Farm

B1053

B1055

River Pant

CB10

Clay Wood

Mortlock's Farm

Little Brockholds Farm

Great Brockholds

Sparrow's Hall

Different Part Grove

Long Thatch

Howses

Moor End Farm

B1053

Goddards Farm

Ivytodd's Farm

Byeball's Farm

Barleyfields

Giffords Farm

Longmead

Collins Cross

The Dovehouse

Blacklands Farm

Broadfields

Bush Cottage

BUSH RD

TINDON END RD

Hole Farm

Mill Farm House

Mast

South Fields

B1051

Grassy Grove

Tindon End

Tindon Manor

Broadcroft Grove

Bush Farm

Market Farm

B1051

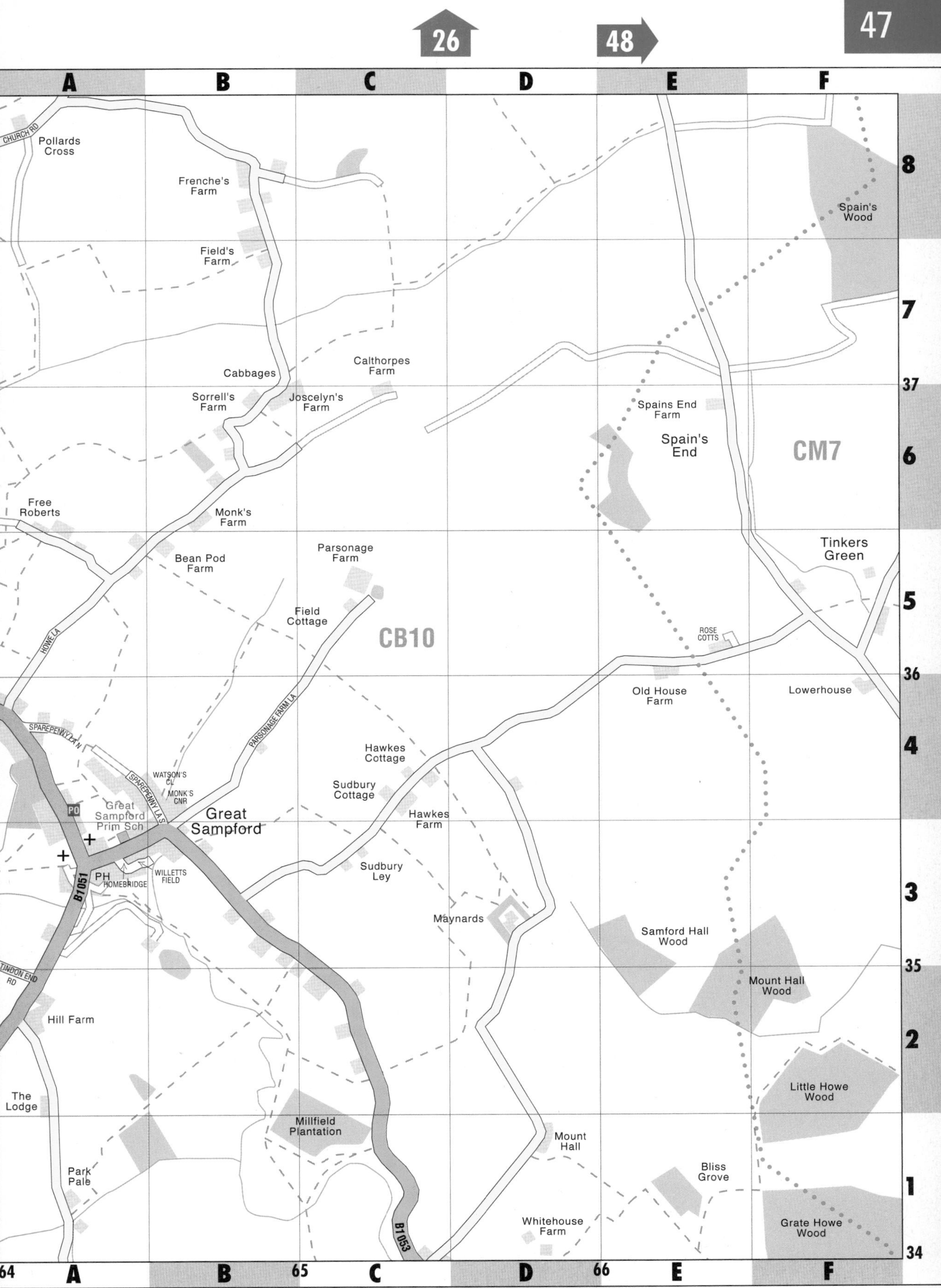

A B C D E F

8
7
37
6
5
36
4
3
35
2
1
34

64 A B 65 C 66 D E F

CHURCH RD
Pollards Cross
Frenche's Farm
Field's Farm
Spain's Wood
Cabbages
Calthorpes Farm
Sorrell's Farm
Joscelyn's Farm
Spains End Farm
Spain's End
CM7
Free Roberts
Monk's Farm
Tinkers Green
Bean Pod Farm
Parsonage Farm
HOWE LA
Field Cottage
CB10
ROSE COTTS
Old House Farm
Lowerhouse
PARSONAGE FARM LA.
SPAREPENNY LA N
Hawkes Cottage
Sudbury Cottage
Hawkes Farm
WATSON'S CL
MONK'S CNR
SPAREPENNY LA S
PO
Great Sampford Prim Sch
Great Sampford
Sudbury Ley
B1051
PH
HOMEBRIDGE
WILLETTS FIELD
Maynards
Samford Hall Wood
TINDON END RD
Hill Farm
Mount Hall Wood
Little Howe Wood
The Lodge
Park Pale
Millfield Plantation
Mount Hall
Bliss Grove
B1053
Whitehouse Farm
Grate Howe Wood

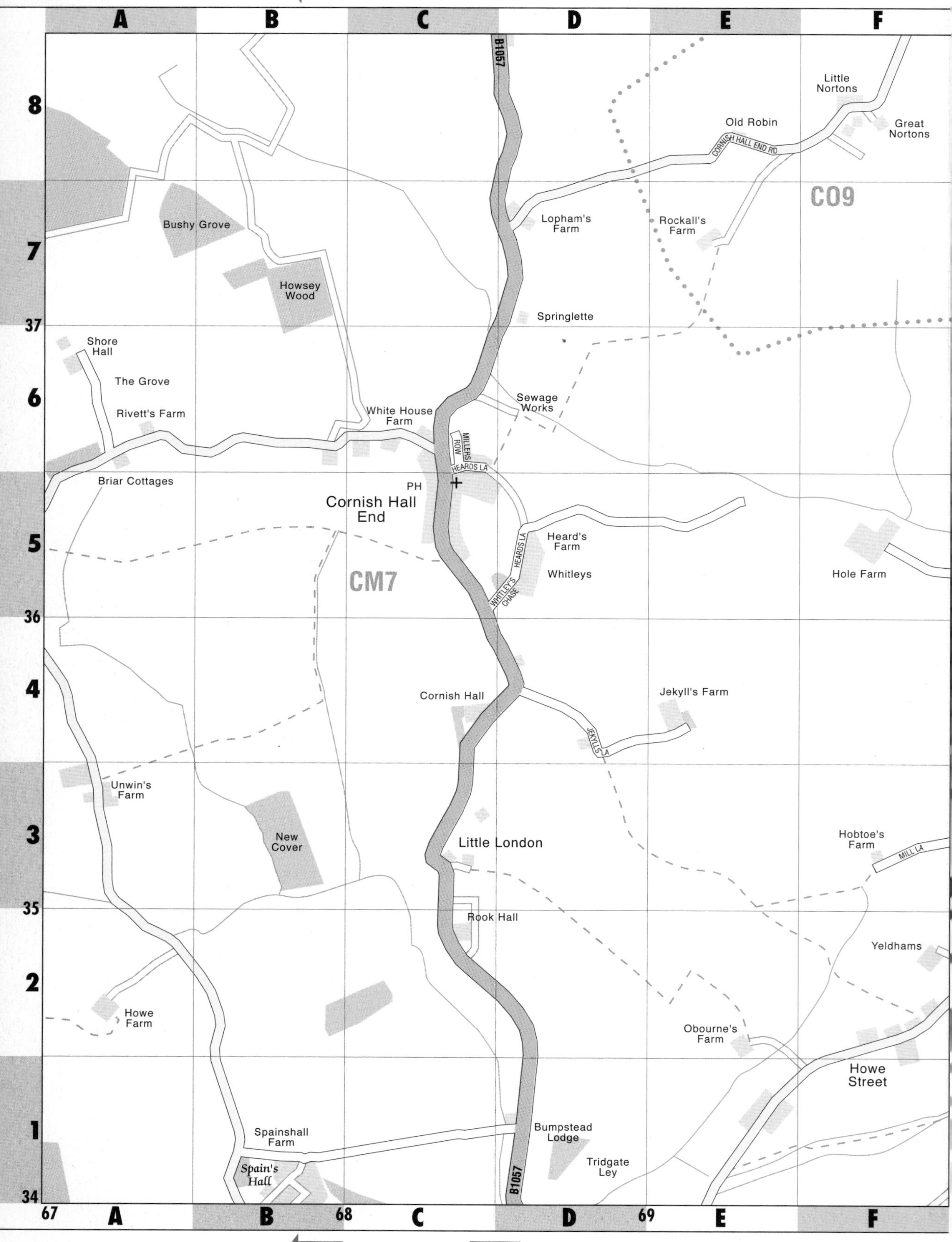

A B C D E F

8

7

37

6

5

36

4

35

3

2

1

34

Little Nortons
Old Robin
Great Nortons
CORNISH HALL END RD
CO9
Lopham's Farm
Rockall's Farm
Bushy Grove
Howsey Wood
Springlette
Shore Hall
The Grove
Rivett's Farm
White House Farm
Sewage Works
MILLERS ROW
HEARDS LA
Briar Cottages
PH
Cornish Hall End
Heard's Farm
WHITLEY'S CHASE
HEARDS LA
Whitleys
Hole Farm
CM7
Cornish Hall
Jekyll's Farm
JEKYLLS LA
Unwin's Farm
New Cover
Little London
Hobtoe's Farm
MILL LA
Rook Hall
Yeldhams
Howe Farm
Obourne's Farm
Howe Street
Spainshall Farm
Spain's Hall
Bumpstead Lodge
Tridgate Ley
B1057

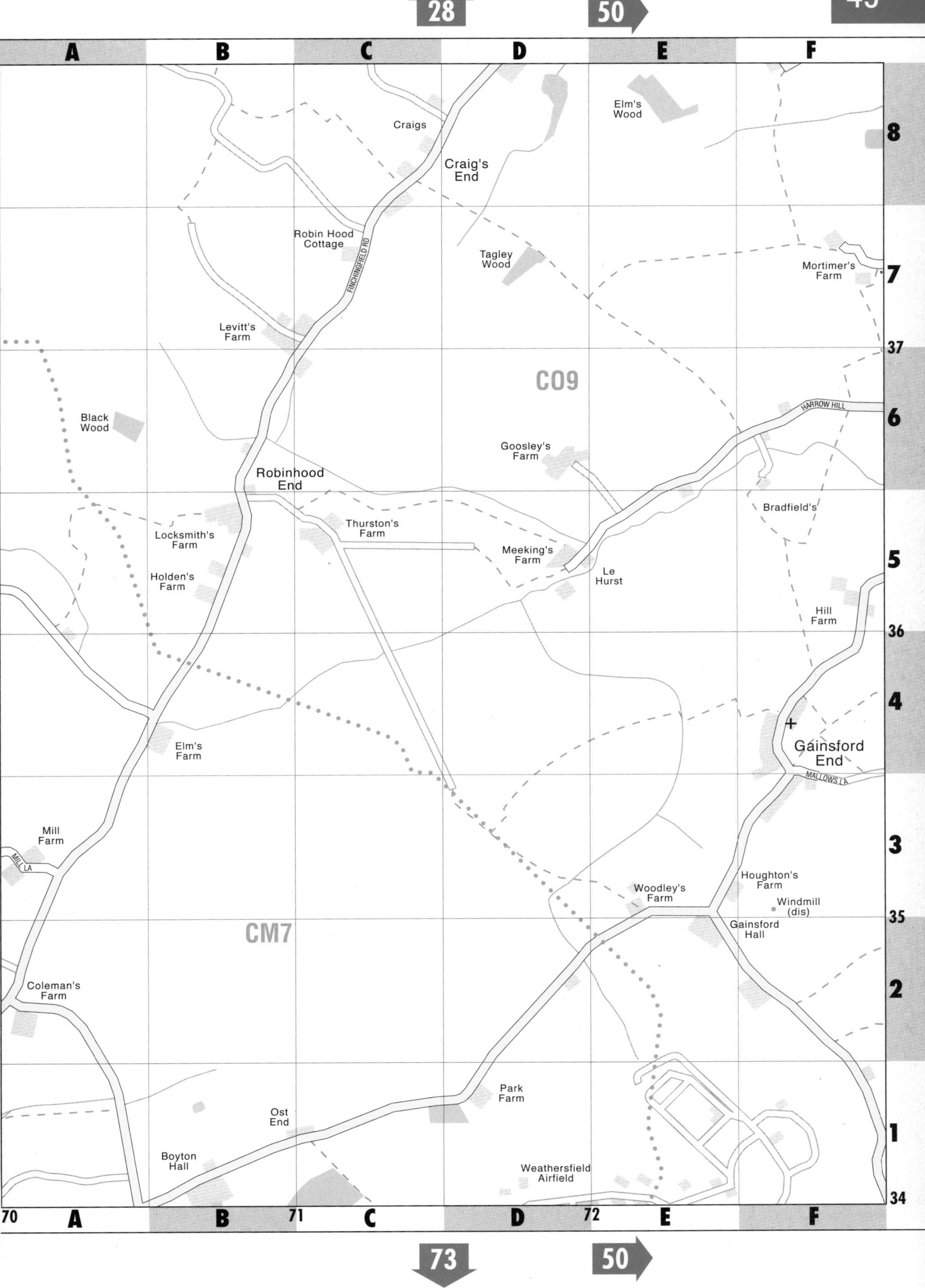

A   B   C   D   E   F

8

Elm's
Wood

Craigs

Craig's
End

7

Robin Hood
Cottage

Tagley
Wood

Mortimer's
Farm

FINCHINGFIELD RD

37

Levitt's
Farm

CO9

HARROW HILL

Black
Wood

6

Goosley's
Farm

Robinhood
End

Bradfield's

Locksmith's
Farm

Thurston's
Farm

Meeking's
Farm

5

Holden's
Farm

Le
Hurst

Hill
Farm

36

Elm's
Farm

4

+

Gainsford
End

MALLOWS LA

Mill
Farm

3

MILL LA

CM7

Woodley's
Farm

Houghton's
Farm

Windmill
(dis)

35

Gainsford
Hall

Coleman's
Farm

2

Park
Farm

Ost
End

1

Boyton
Hall

Weathersfield
Airfield

34

70   A   B   71   C   D   72   E   F

49
29

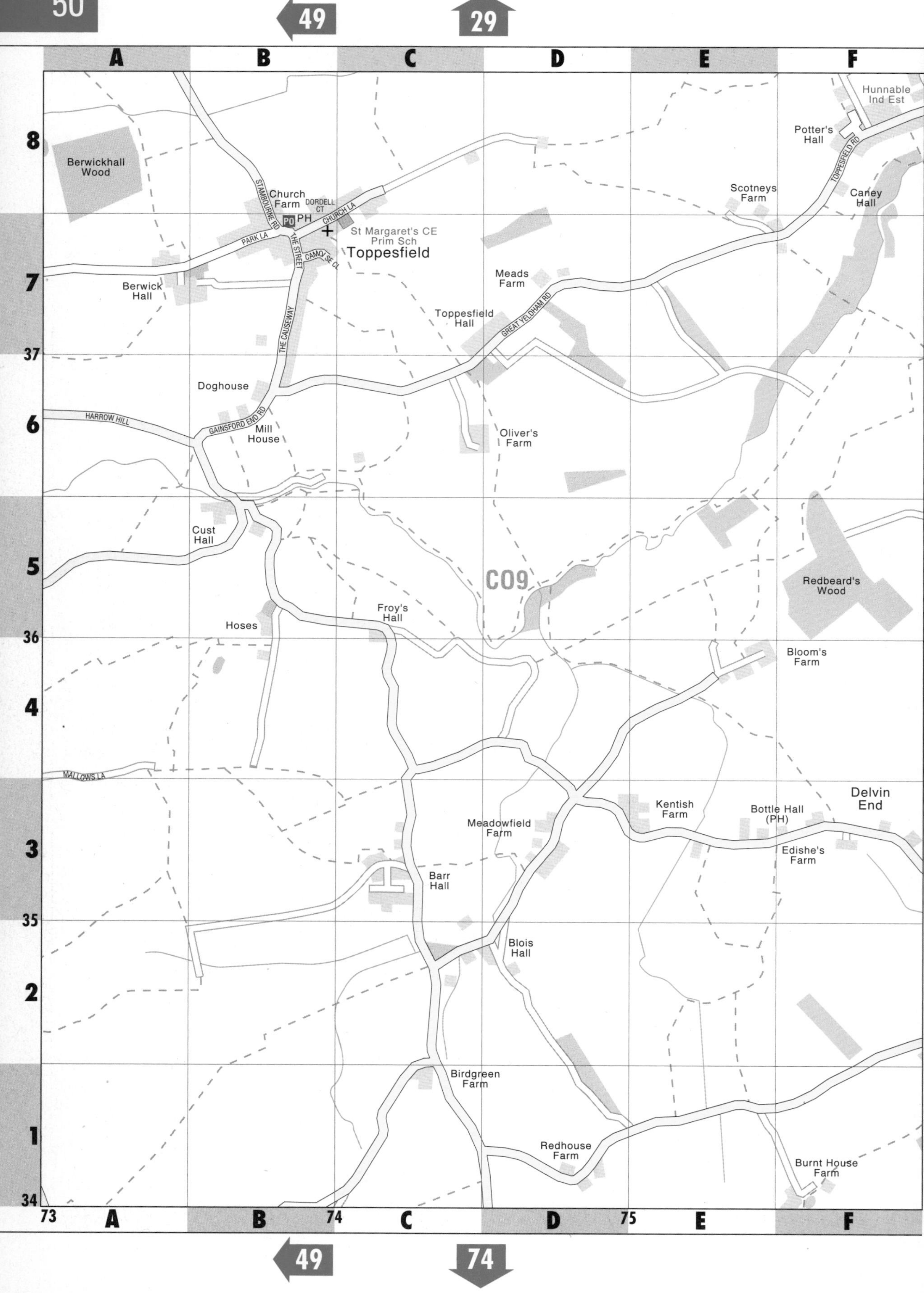
A
B
C
D
E
F
8
7
37
6
5
36
4
3
35
2
1
34
73
74
75
Hunnable Ind Est
Potter's Hall
Berwickhall Wood
Church Farm
DORDELL CT
PO PH
CHURCH LA
STAMBOURNE RD
PARK LA
THE STREET
CAMOYSE CL
St Margaret's CE Prim Sch
Toppesfield
Scotneys Farm
TOPPESFIELD RD
Caney Hall
Berwick Hall
Meads Farm
Toppesfield Hall
GREAT YELDHAM RD
THE CAUSEWAY
Doghouse
HARROW HILL
GAINSFORD END RD
Mill House
Oliver's Farm
Cust Hall
CO9
Redbeard's Wood
Hoses
Froy's Hall
Bloom's Farm
MALLOWS LA
Delvin End
Kentish Farm
Bottle Hall (PH)
Meadowfield Farm
Edishe's Farm
Barr Hall
Blois Hall
Birdgreen Farm
Redhouse Farm
Burnt House Farm

49
74

30
52

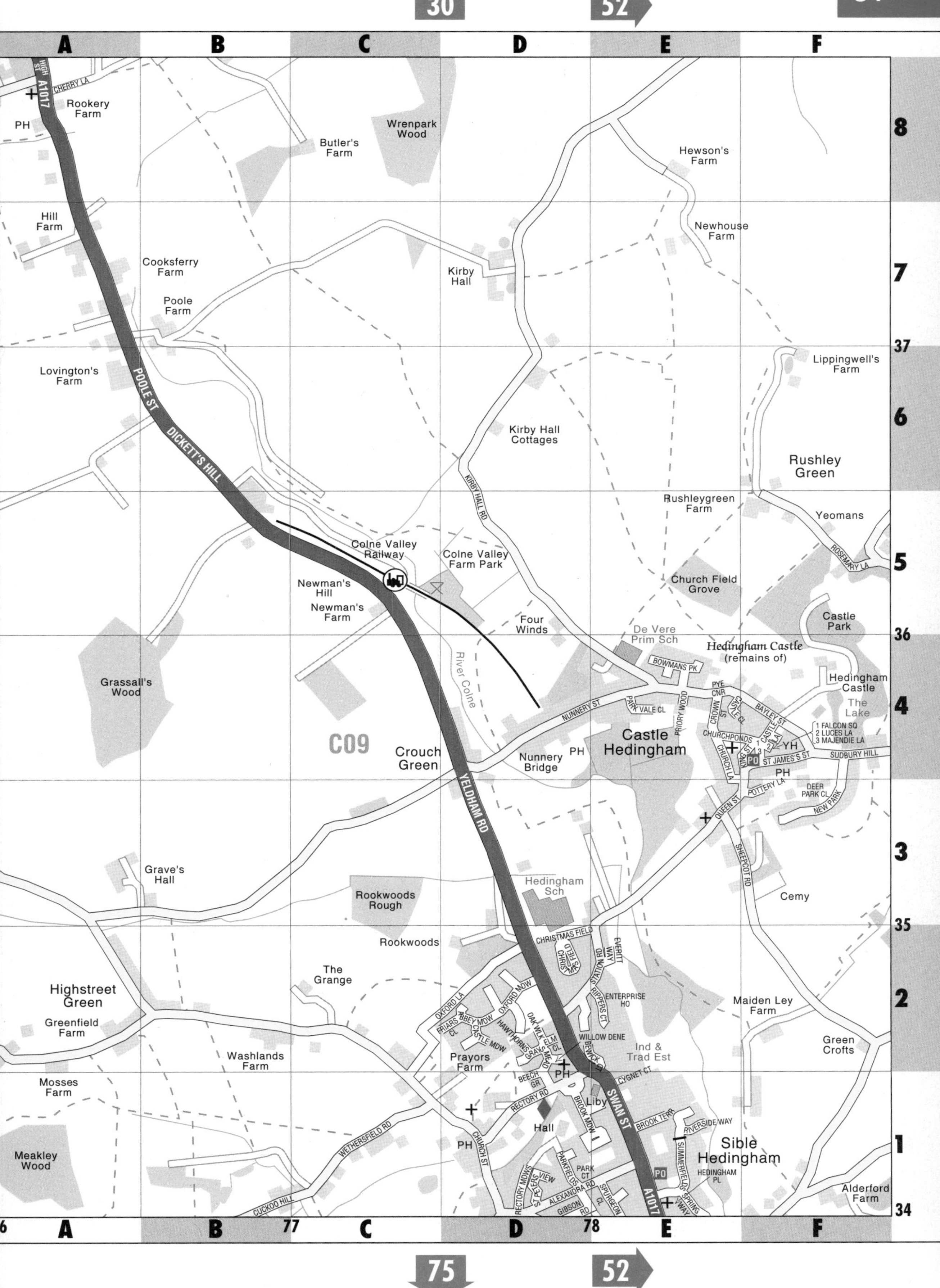
Rookery Farm
PH
Hill Farm
Butler's Farm
Wrenpark Wood
Hewson's Farm
Newhouse Farm
Cooksferry Farm
Poole Farm
Kirby Hall
Lovington's Farm
POOLE ST
DICKETT'S HILL
Kirby Hall Cottages
KIRBY HALL RD
Lippingwell's Farm
Rushley Green
Rushleygreen Farm
Yeomans
ROSEMARY LA
Colne Valley Railway
Colne Valley Farm Park
Newman's Hill
Newman's Farm
Four Winds
Church Field Grove
Castle Park
Grassall's Wood
River Colne
De Vere Prim Sch
Hedingham Castle (remains of)
BOWMANS PK
Hedingham Castle
The Lake
NUNNERY ST
PARK VALE CL
PRIORY WOOD
PYE CNR
CROWN ST
CASTLE CL
BAYLEY ST
1 FALCON SQ
2 LUCES LA
3 MAJENDIE LA
C09
Crouch Green
Nunnery Bridge
Castle Hedingham
CHURCHPONDS
CHURCH LA
YH
PO
ST JAMES'S ST
SUDBURY HILL
POTTERY LA
DEER PARK CL
NEW PARK
QUEEN ST
YELDHAM RD
SHEEPCOT RD
Grave's Hall
Rookwoods Rough
Hedingham Sch
Cemy
Rookwoods
CHRISTMAS FIELD
STATION RD
EVERITT WAY
The Grange
Highstreet Green
Greenfield Farm
OXFORD LA
OXFORD MDW
ABBEY MDW
FRIARS CL
CASTLE MDW
HAWTHORNS
OAK WLK
ELM CL
ENTERPRISE HO
RIPPERS CT
Maiden Ley Farm
WILLOW DENE
BERWICK CT
Washlands Farm
Prayors Farm
Ind & Trad Est
Green Crofts
Mosses Farm
BEECH GR
CYGNET CT
RECTORY RD
BROOK MDW
Liby
SWAN ST
Hall
BROOK TERR
RIVERSIDE WAY
Meakley Wood
WETHERSFIELD RD
CHURCH ST
Sible Hedingham
SUMMERFIELDS
HEDINGHAM PL
PARKFIELDS
PARK CT
ALEXANDRA RD
SPURGEON CL
GIBSON RD
RECTORY MDWS
ST PETERS VIEW
CUCKOO HILL
A1017
SPRING WAY
Alderford Farm
HIGH ST
CHERRY LA
A B C D E F
8 7 37 6 5 36 4 3 35 2 1 34
76 77 78

75
52

	A	B	C	D	E	F

8 Ridley's Wood · Delvyn's Lane · Edeys Farm · CHURCH ST · Delvyn's Farm · Audley End · PH

7 Parkgate Farm · Crouch House

37 Great Lodge Farm · DELVYN'S LA · Branwhite's Grove · The Moat · Rectory Farm

6 Lawrence's Farm · C09

5 Pannells Ash Farm · Odewells

36 Rosemary Farm · ROSEMARY LA · SUDBURY RD · Pantile Cottage · Kendallscroft Grove · Little Chelmshoe House

4 ST JAMES'S ST · Byham Hall

3 Little Lodge Farm · Chelmshoe House Farm · Monks Lodge Farm · New Barn · Monks Lodge

35 Hosden's Farm · MONKS LODGE RD · St Giles CE Prim Sch · Link Hills

2 Hopwell's Farm · ST GILES CL · STONE COTTS · Great Maplestead · Lucking Street · Luckinghouse Farm

1 Purls Cottage · CHURCH ST · Barrett's Hall · Little Lodge Farm

34

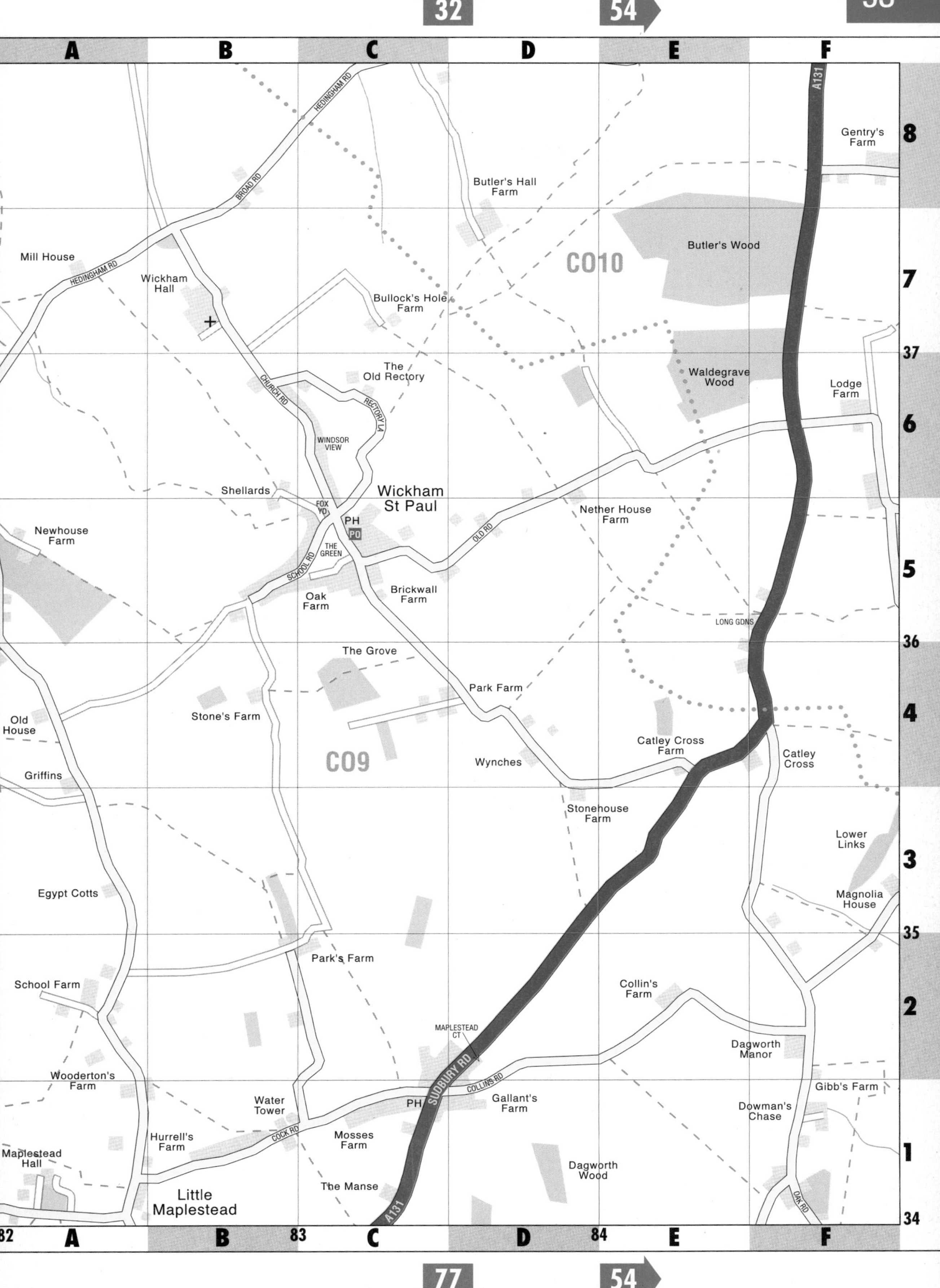

A B C D E F

8
37
7
6
5
36
4
35
3
2
34
1

Gentry's Farm

Butler's Hall Farm

CO10

Butler's Wood

Mill House

HEDINGHAM RD

BROAD RD

Wickham Hall

Bullock's Hole Farm

Waldegrave Wood

Lodge Farm

A131

The Old Rectory

CHURCH RD

RECTORY LA

WINDSOR VIEW

Shellards

FOX YD

Wickham St Paul

PH
PO

Nether House Farm

OLD RD

Newhouse Farm

SCHOOL RD

THE GREEN

Oak Farm

Brickwall Farm

LONG GDNS

The Grove

Park Farm

Stone's Farm

CO9

Wynches

Catley Cross Farm

Catley Cross

Old House

Stonehouse Farm

Griffins

Lower Links

Egypt Cotts

Magnolia House

Park's Farm

School Farm

Collin's Farm

Dagworth Manor

Wooderton's Farm

Water Tower

MAPLESTEAD CT

SUDBURY RD

COLLINS RD

PH

Gallant's Farm

Gibb's Farm

Dowman's Chase

OAK RD

Hurrell's Farm

COCK RD

Mosses Farm

Dagworth Wood

Maplestead Hall

The Manse

A131

Little Maplestead

53
33

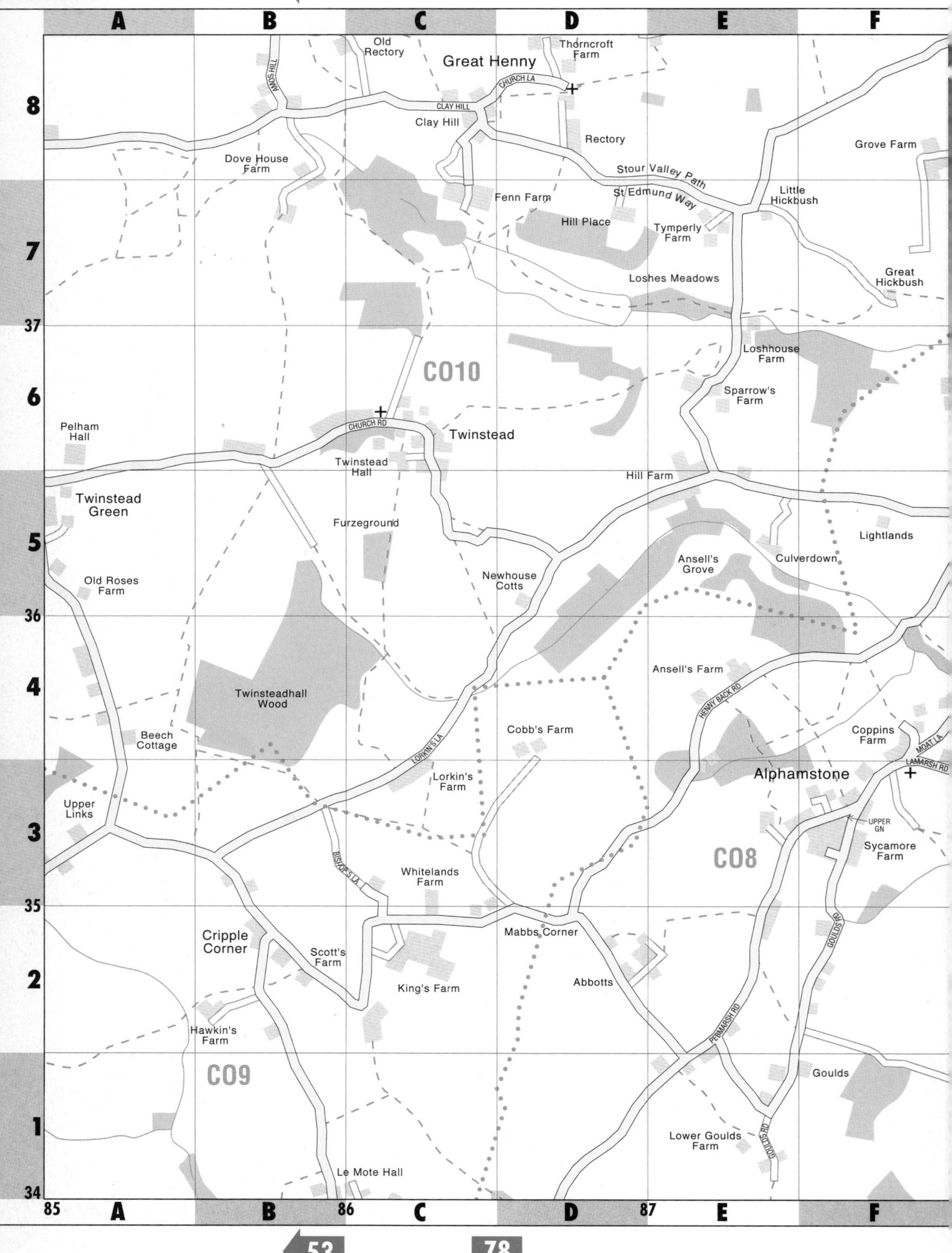
A
B
C
D
E
F
8
7
37
6
5
36
4
3
35
2
1
34
85
86
87
Old Rectory
Great Henny
Thorncroft Farm
AMOS HILL
CHURCH LA
CLAY HILL
Clay Hill
Rectory
Grove Farm
Dove House Farm
Stour Valley Path
St Edmund Way
Little Hickbush
Fenn Farm
Hill Place
Tymperly Farm
Great Hickbush
Loshes Meadows
Loshhouse Farm
CO10
Sparrow's Farm
Pelham Hall
CHURCH RD
Twinstead
Twinstead Hall
Hill Farm
Twinstead Green
Furzeground
Lightlands
Ansell's Grove
Culverdown
Newhouse Cotts
Old Roses Farm
Ansell's Farm
HENNY BACK RD
Twinsteadhall Wood
Cobb's Farm
Coppins Farm
Beech Cottage
MOAT LA
LAMARSH RD
LORKIN'S LA
Lorkin's Farm
Alphamstone
Upper Links
UPPER GN
Sycamore Farm
CO8
BISHOP'S LA
Whitelands Farm
Mabbs Corner
Cripple Corner
Scott's Farm
GOULDS RD
King's Farm
Abbotts
PEBMARSH RD
Hawkin's Farm
CO9
Goulds
Lower Goulds Farm
GOULDS RD
Le Mote Hall

53
78

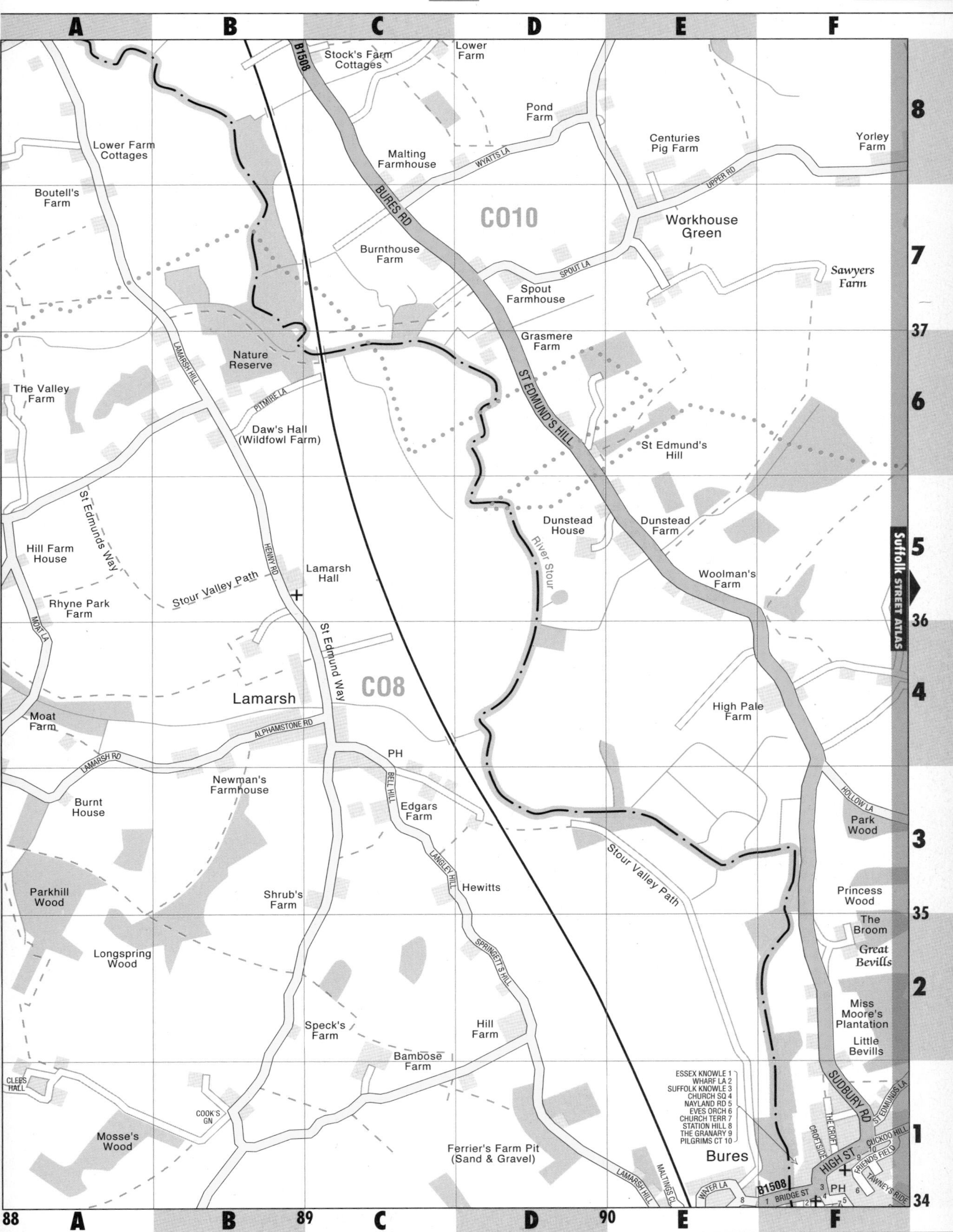

A B C D E F

Stock's Farm
Cottages

Lower
Farm

Pond
Farm

Centuries
Pig Farm

Yorley
Farm

Lower Farm
Cottages

Malting
Farmhouse

WYATTS LA

CO10

Workhouse
Green

Boutell's
Farm

BURES RD

Burnthouse
Farm

SPOUT LA

Sawyers
Farm

Spout
Farmhouse

Grasmere
Farm

St Edmund's
Hill

The Valley
Farm

LAMARSH HILL

Nature
Reserve

PITMIRE LA

Daw's Hall
(Wildfowl Farm)

ST EDMUND'S HILL

Dunstead
Farm

Dunstead
House

Hill Farm
House

ST EDMUNDS WAY

Stour Valley Path

HENNY RD

Lamarsh
Hall

River Stour

Woolman's
Farm

Rhyne Park
Farm

ST EDMUND WAY

CO8

MOAT LA

Lamarsh

ALPHAMSTONE RD

PH

High Pale
Farm

HOLLOW LA

Moat
Farm

LAMARSH RD

Newman's
Farmhouse

BELL HILL

Edgars
Farm

Park
Wood

Burnt
House

Stour Valley Path

Princess
Wood

Parkhill
Wood

Shrub's
Farm

LANGLEY HILL

Hewitts

The
Broom

Great
Bevills

Longspring
Wood

SPRINGETT'S HILL

Miss
Moore's
Plantation

Little
Bevills

Speck's
Farm

Hill
Farm

Bambose
Farm

SUDBURY RD

CLEES
HALL

ESSEX KNOWLE 1
WHARF LA 2
SUFFOLK KNOWLE 3
CHURCH SQ 4
NAYLAND RD 5
EVES ORCH 6
CHURCH TERR 7
STATION HILL 8
THE GRANARY 9
PILGRIMS CT 10

ST EDMUNDS LA

COOK'S
GN

Ferrier's Farm Pit
(Sand & Gravel)

Bures

THE CROFT

CROFTSIDE

CUCKOO HILL

FRIENDS FIELD

TAWNEYS RIDE

Mosse's
Wood

LAMARSH HILL

MALTINGS CL

HIGH ST

WINTER LA

B1508

BRIDGE ST

PH

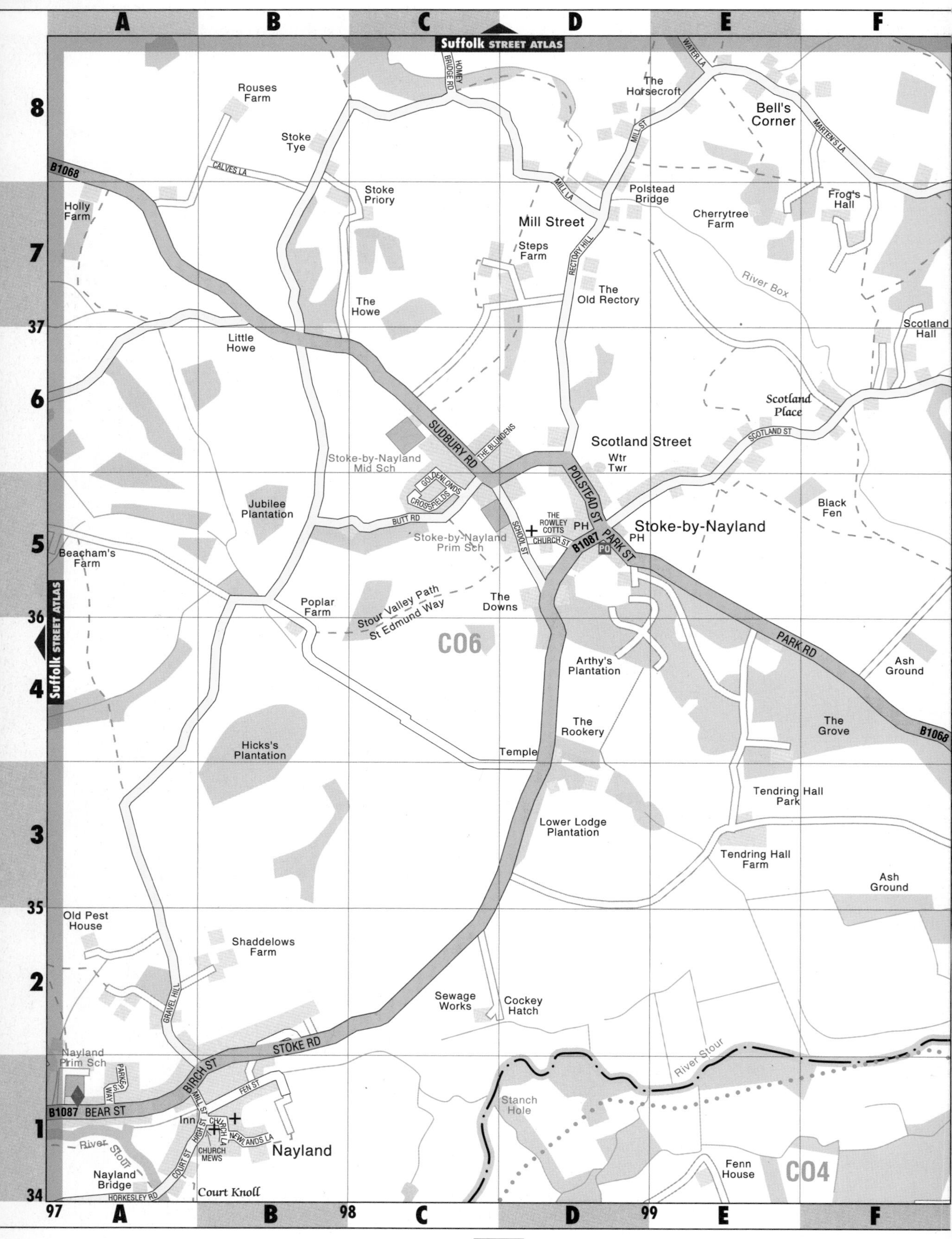

Suffolk STREET ATLAS

8
7
37
6
5
36
4
3
35
2
1
34

A · B · C · D · E · F

97 · 98 · 99

B1068

Rouses Farm

Stoke Tye

Stoke Priory

CALVES LA

Holly Farm

Little Howe

The Howe

SUDBURY RD

Stoke-by-Nayland Mid Sch

THE BLUNDENS

Jubilee Plantation

GOLDENLONDS CROSSFIELDS

BUTT RD

Stoke-by-Nayland Prim Sch

Poplar Farm

Beacham's Farm

Stour Valley Path
St Edmund Way

The Downs

CO6

Hicks's Plantation

Temple

Old Pest House

Shaddelows Farm

GRAVEL HILL

Nayland Prim Sch

PARKERS WAY

B1087 BEAR ST

Inn

BIRCH ST

STOKE RD

FEN ST

HIGH ST
CHURCH LA
COURT ST
NEWLANDS LA

CHURCH MEWS

Nayland

Nayland Bridge

HORKESLEY RD

Court Knoll

River Stour

The Horsecroft

WATER LA

Bell's Corner

MARTEN'S LA

MILL ST

Polstead Bridge

MILL LA

Frog's Hall

Cherrytree Farm

Mill Street

RECTORY HILL

Steps Farm

The Old Rectory

River Box

Scotland Hall

Scotland Place

Scotland Street

SCOTLAND ST

Wtr Twr

POLSTEAD ST

PARK ST

SCHOOL ST

THE ROWLEY COTTS

CHURCH ST

PH

B1087

PO

PH

Stoke-by-Nayland

Black Fen

Arthy's Plantation

PARK RD

Ash Ground

The Grove

B1068

The Rookery

Tendring Hall Park

Lower Lodge Plantation

Tendring Hall Farm

Ash Ground

Sewage Works

Cockey Hatch

River Stour

Stanch Hole

Fenn House

CO4

Suffolk STREET ATLAS

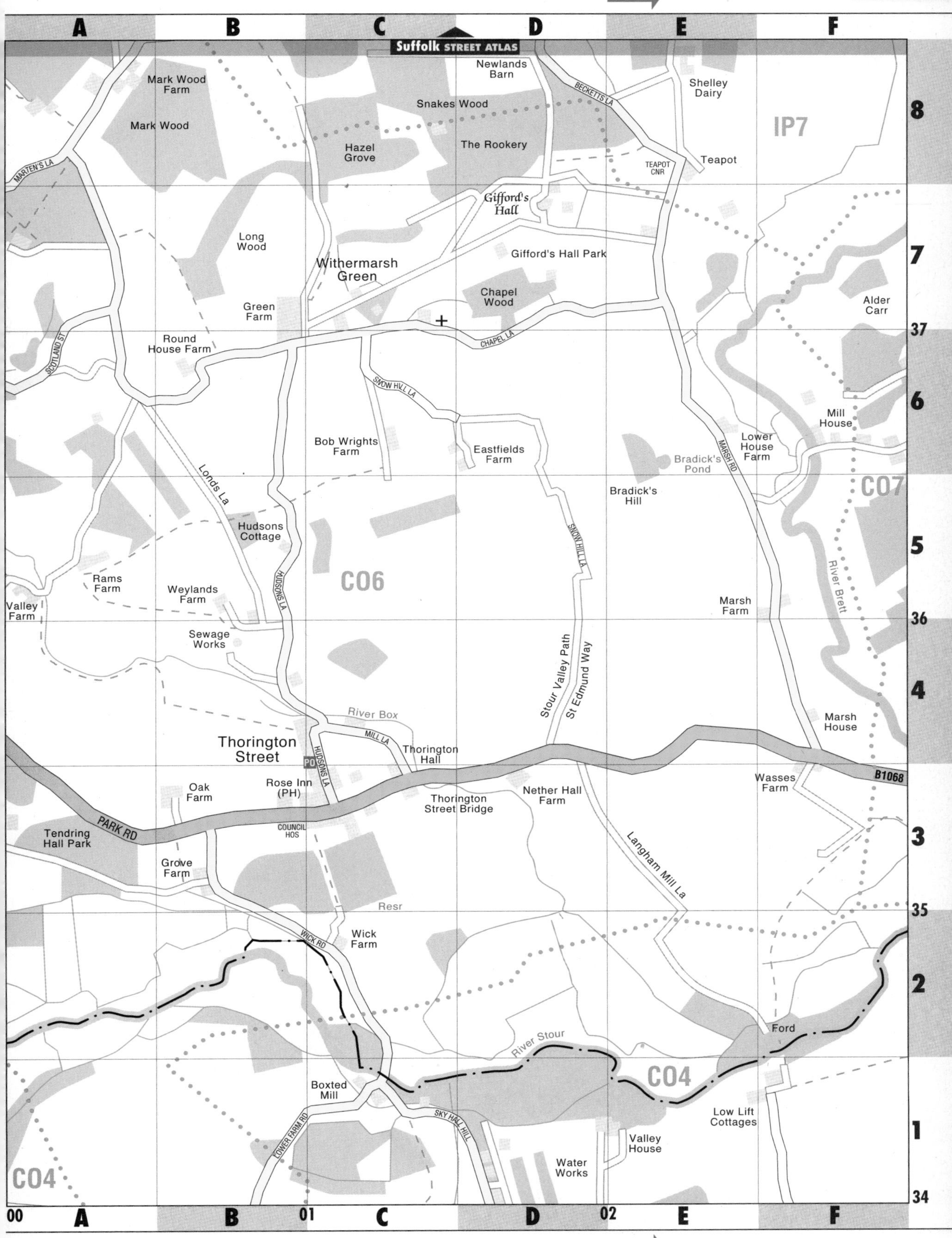

Suffolk STREET ATLAS

A **B** **C** **D** **E** **F**

Mark Wood Farm

Mark Wood

Newlands Barn

Snakes Wood

BECKETTS LA

Shelley Dairy

IP7 8

Hazel Grove

The Rookery

Teapot

TEAPOT CNR

MARTEN'S LA

Gifford's Hall

Long Wood

Gifford's Hall Park

Withermarsh Green

7

Chapel Wood

Alder Carr

Green Farm

+

CHAPEL LA

37

SCOTLAND ST

Round House Farm

SNOW HILL LA

Mill House 6

Bob Wrights Farm

Eastfields Farm

Bradick's Pond

Lower House Farm

CO7

Londs La

Bradick's Hill

River Brett

Hudsons Cottage

SNOW HILL LA

5

Rams Farm

CO6

Marsh Farm

36

Valley Farm

Weylands Farm

HUDSONS LA

Sewage Works

MARSH RD

St Edmund Way

Stour Valley Path

4

River Box

Marsh House

MILL LA

Thorington Hall

Thorington Street

HUDSONS LA

Thorington Street Bridge

Nether Hall Farm

Wasses Farm

B1068

Oak Farm

Rose Inn (PH)

PARK RD

COUNCIL HOS

Langham Mill La

3

Tendring Hall Park

Grove Farm

Resr

35

WICK RD

Wick Farm

2

Ford

LOWER FARM RD

Boxted Mill

SKY HALL HILL

River Stour

CO4

Low Lift Cottages

1

CO4

Water Works

Valley House

34

A **B** **C** **D** **E** **F**

00 01 02

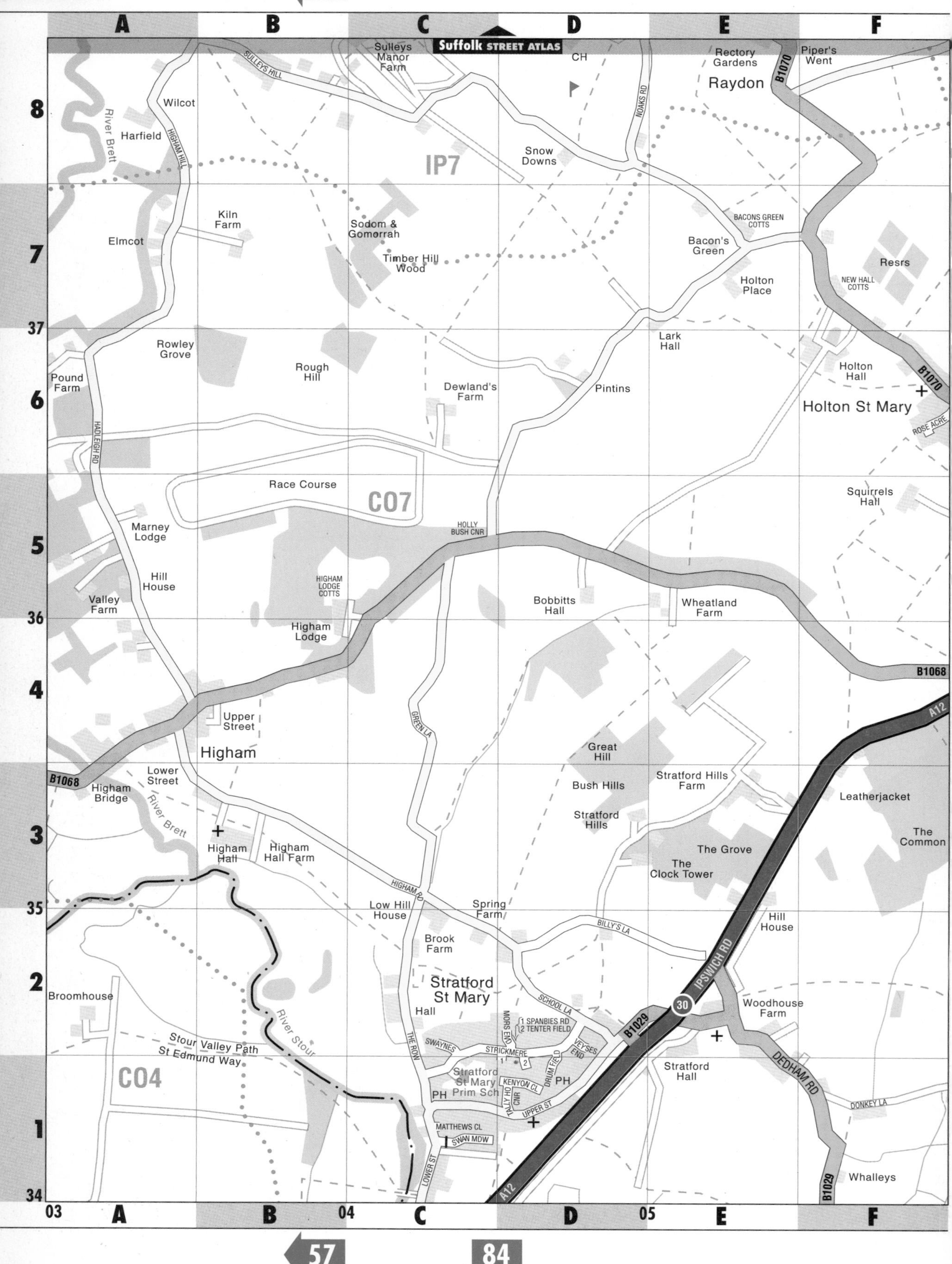

Suffolk STREET ATLAS

A B C D E F

8

7

37

6

5

36

4

35

3

2

1

34

03 A B 04 C D 05 E F

River Brett

SULLEYS HILL

Sulleys Manor Farm

CH

Rectory Gardens

Piper's Went

B1070

Raydon

Wilcot

Harfield

HIGHAM HILL

IP7

Snow Downs

NOAKS RD

BACONS GREEN COTTS

Bacon's Green

Resrs

Kiln Farm

Elmcot

Sodom & Gomorrah

Timber Hill Wood

Holton Place

NEW HALL COTTS

Rowley Grove

Rough Hill

Dewland's Farm

Lark Hall

Pintins

Holton Hall

B1070

Holton St Mary

Pound Farm

HADLEIGH RD

ROSE ACRE

Race Course

CO7

HOLLY BUSH CNR

Squirrels Hall

Marney Lodge

Hill House

HIGHAM LODGE COTTS

Bobbitts Hall

Wheatland Farm

Valley Farm

Higham Lodge

B1068

Upper Street

Higham

A12

GREEN LA

Great Hill

Stratford Hills Farm

Leatherjacket

The Common

Lower Street

Bush Hills

B1068

Higham Bridge

River Brett

Higham Hall

Higham Hall Farm

HIGHAM RD

Stratford Hills

The Grove

The Clock Tower

Hill House

Low Hill House

Spring Farm

BILLY'S LA

IPSWICH RD

Brook Farm

Broomhouse

River Stour

Stour Valley Path St Edmund Way

CO4

Stratford St Mary

Hall

THE ROW

SWAYNES

SCHOOL LA

MORS END

STRICKMERE

1 SPANBIES RD
2 TENTER FIELD

VEYSES END

B1029

30

DEDHAM RD

Woodhouse Farm

Stratford Hall

DONKEY LA

Stratford St Mary Prim Sch

PH

PH

FLATTY LA

DRUM FIELD

KENYON CL

UPPER ST

MATTHEWS CL

SWAN MDW

LOWER ST

B1029

A12

Whalleys

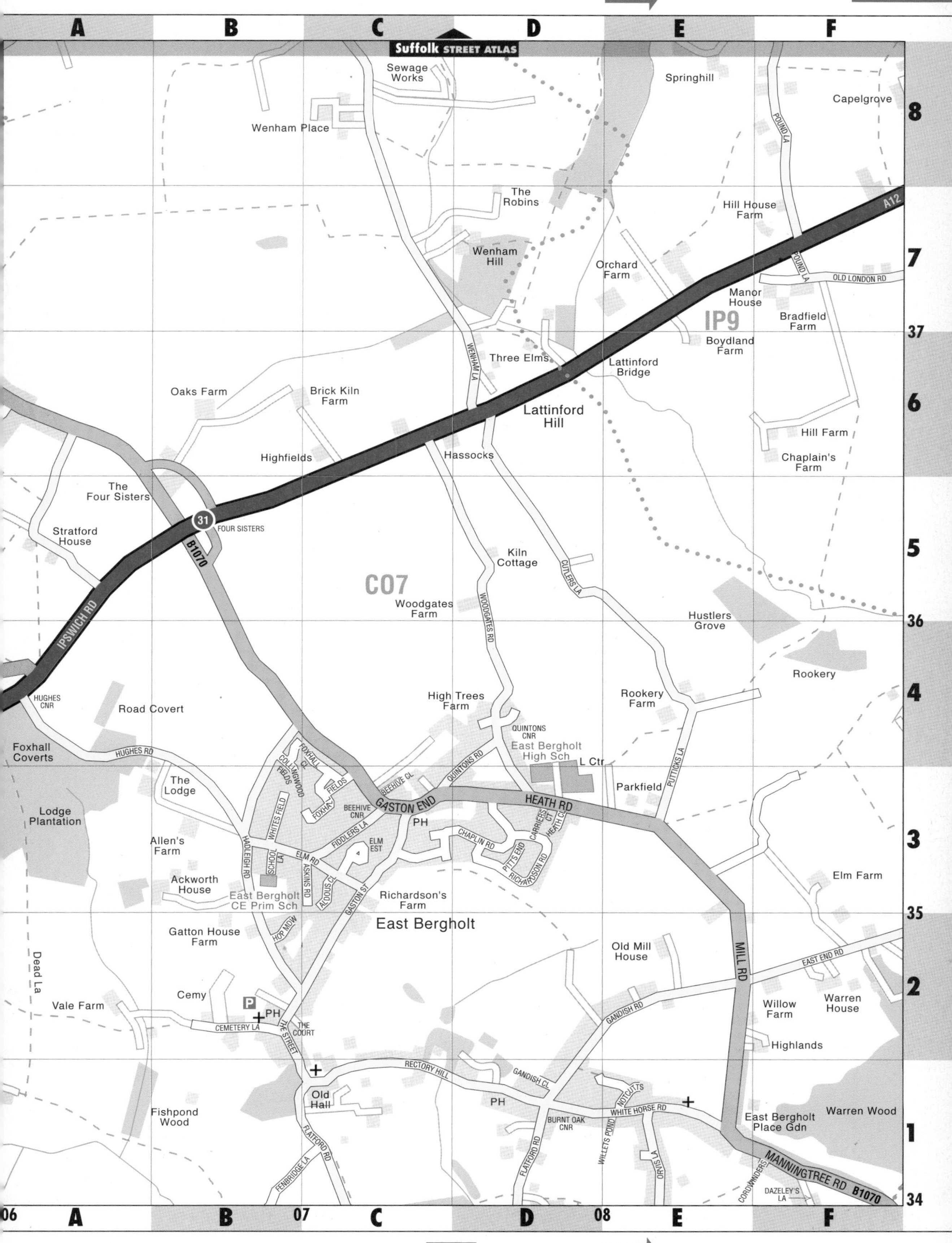

Suffolk STREET ATLAS

A B C D E F

8
7
37
6
5
36
4
3
35
2
1
34

Sewage Works
Springhill
Capelgrove
Wenham Place
The Robins
Hill House Farm
A12
Wenham Hill
Orchard Farm
POUND LA
OLD LONDON RD
Manor House
Bradfield Farm
IP9
Oaks Farm
Brick Kiln Farm
WENHAM LA
Three Elms
Lattinford Bridge
Boydland Farm
Highfields
Lattinford Hill
Hassocks
Hill Farm
Chaplain's Farm
The Four Sisters
31 FOUR SISTERS
B1070
Stratford House
Kiln Cottage
C07
Hustlers Grove
IPSWICH RD
Woodgates Farm
WOODGATES RD
CUTLERS LA
Rookery
HUGHES CNR
Road Covert
High Trees Farm
Rookery Farm
Foxhall Coverts
The Lodge
QUINTONS CNR
East Bergholt High Sch
L Ctr
Parkfield
PUTTICKS LA
Lodge Plantation
HUGHES RD
COLNEWOOD FIELDS
FOXHALL
FOXHALL FIELDS
WHITES FIELD
BEEHIVE CNR
FIDDLERS LA
QUINTONS RD
BEEHIVE CL
GASTON END
HEATH RD
PH
CARRIERS CT
HEATH CL
Allen's Farm
HADLEIGH RD
SCHOOL HOUSE
ELM RD
ELM EST
CHAPLIN RD
PITTS END
RICHARDSON RD
Ackworth House
East Bergholt CE Prim Sch
GASTON ST
ISKINS RD
ACROUS CL
Richardson's Farm
Elm Farm
Gatton House Farm
HOP MDW
East Bergholt
35
Old Mill House
Dead La
Vale Farm
Cemy
P
PH
THE COURT
THE STREET
CEMETERY LA
GANDISH RD
MILL RD
EAST END RD
Willow Farm
Warren House
Highlands
Fishpond Wood
Old Hall
RECTORY HILL
GANDISH CL
PH
NOTCUTTS
WHITE HORSE RD
East Bergholt Place Gdn
Warren Wood
FLATFORD RD
BURNT OAK CNR
WILLET'S POND
ORVIS LA
CORDWINDERS
DAZELEY'S LA
MANNINGTREE RD
B1070
FENBRIDGE LA

59
35

A **B** **C** **D** **E** **F**

8

White Horse Farm

Grove Farm

POTASH LA

FALSTAFF COTTS

Potash

POTASH COTTS

Falstaff Manor

A12

Bush Farm

Great Gilberts Farm

BLUEGATE LA

Windy Farm

CHURCH RD

7

OLD LONDON RD

Tawney's Farm

RED LA

FRIARS RD

LONDON RD

Boynton Hall

Bluegate Farm

Bentley CE Prim Sch

Bentley

37

CASE LA

PH

SOUTH VIEW GN

EAST MILL GN

HIGHFIELDS

THE LINK

WEST MILL GN

STATION RD

SILVER LE'S

PO

LC

6

Woodfield

LINK LA

GROVE RD

Dingle Dell

IP9

Holly Wood

Bentley Grove

Teapot Hill

Martin's Hill Cottage

Kenmure

Hazel Shrub

5

Great Martin's Hill Wood

Martin's Glen

King's Field

Dodnash Wood

Coppey Farm

36

Dodnash Priory Farm

4

Little Dodnash Farm

Little Charles New Plantation

Dobnash Fruit Farm

The Grange

CO7

Manor Farm

Alder Carr

Keeble's Grove

3

Meadow Cottages

PH

MISSION LA

FISHER'S LA

THE ELMS

GRAVEL PIT LA

CO11

EAST END RD

35

Home Farm

Woodlands Farm

East End

HOLLY COTTS

BROOM KNOLL

PARK RD

2

Park House

ALBERT COTTS

EAST END LA

THE DRIFT

SLOUGH RD

THE POPLARS

IPSWICH RD

A137

Brantham

Church Farm

1

Barn Hazel

VALLEY RD

SCHOOL LA

CHURCH LA

RECTORY LA

Brantham Glebe

THE CHASE

JIMMY'S LA

BRANTHAM HILL

A137

ACACIA CT

ELM CL

SYCAMORE WAY

BIRCH DR

QUINCE CL

CEDAR CT

BLENHEIM CL

34

Brookland Farm

09 **A** **B** 10 **C** **D** 11 **E** **F**

59
86

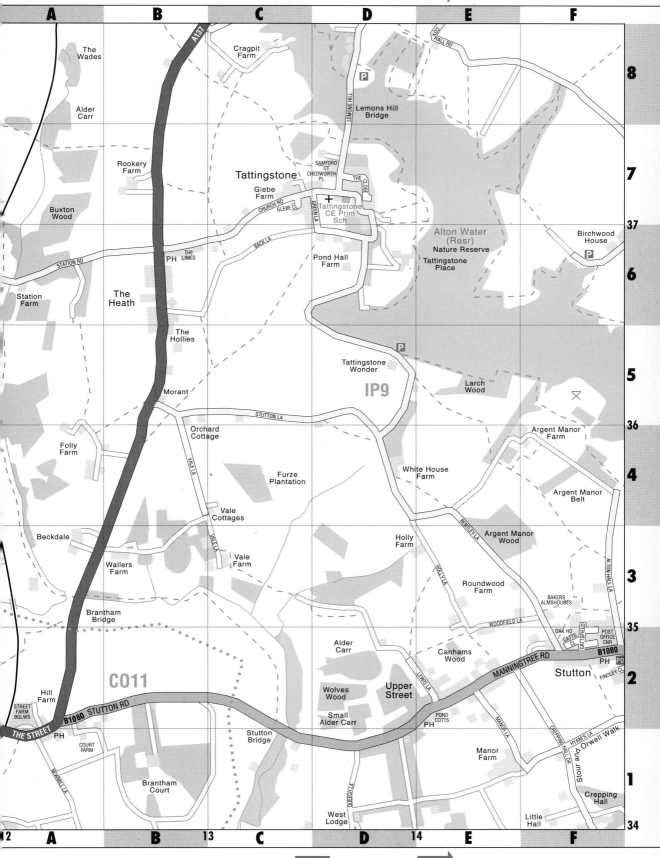
36
62

A
B
C
D
E
F
8
7
37
6
5
36
4
3
35
2
1
34
12
13
14
The Wades
Alder Carr
Cragpit Farm
A137
Lemons Hill Bridge
LEMONS HILL
HALL RD
COX
Rookery Farm
Tattingstone
SAMFORD CT
CHEDWORTH PL
THE CLOSE
Glebe Farm
CHURCH RD
GLEBE CL
GREEN LA
Tattingstone CE Prim Sch
Buxton Wood
Alton Water (Resr)
Nature Reserve
Tattingstone Place
Birchwood House
STATION RD
PH
THE LIMES
BACK LA
Pond Hall Farm
Station Farm
The Heath
The Hollies
Tattingstone Wonder
IP9
Larch Wood
Morant
STUTTON LA
Orchard Cottage
Argent Manor Farm
Folly Farm
VALE LA
Furze Plantation
White House Farm
Argent Manor Belt
Vale Cottages
Beckdale
BENTLEY LA
Argent Manor Wood
Holly Farm
Vale Farm
Wallers Farm
HOLLY LA
Roundwood Farm
ALTON HALL LA
BAKERS ALMSHOUSES
Brantham Bridge
WOODFIELD LA
OAK HO
CATTS CL
CATTSFIELD
POST OFFICE CNR
Alder Carr
Canhams Wood
MANNINGTREE RD
B1080
PH
PO
Stutton
FINDLEY CL
CO11
LEWIS LA
Hill Farm
Wolves Wood
Upper Street
STREET FARM BGLWS
B1080 STUTTON RD
Small Alder Carr
POND COTTS
PH
THE STREET
PH
COURT FARM
Stutton Bridge
MANOR LA
CREPPING HALL DR
HYAM'S LA
Stour and Orwell Walk
Manor Farm
NEWMILL LA
Brantham Court
QUEECH LA
Crepping Hall
West Lodge
Little Hall
87
62

61 37

A B C D E F

8

Great Birch Wood

The Dower House

Potash Farm

B1080

The Woodlands

Woodlands Farm

7

Woodley Wood

Freston Grove

Little Birch Wood

Hale's Grove

Woodlands Rd

Redhouse Farm

Samford Cl

Clench Rd

Council Hos

37

Halesgrove Cottage

Brown's Farm

Holbrook High Sch

Ipswich Rd

6

Brook Farm

The Street

Broomhill Holbrook Prim Sch

Clifton Wood

Holmoak

Denmark Gdns

Pettwood Gdns

Coachman's Paddock

Park House

East Row

Crag Hall Covert

Walkgate Cottages

IP9

Brook Farm La

Giffo Cl

Firebronds Rd

Reade Rd

Ha'penny Dr

PO

Holbrook Gardens

Fish Pond

River View

Heathfield Rd

PH

5

Old Alton Hall Farm

Alton Hall Cottages

Ha'penny La

Hyam's La

Mill Rise

Five Acres

Little Orch

Church Hill

Fishponds La

Holbrook

36

Alton Water (Resr) Nature Reserve

Sewage Works

Back Hill

Fir Tree Hill

New La

4

Chestnut Spinney

Primrose Hill

Holbrook Mill

Brick Cotts

Holbrook Lodge

Water Sports Ctr

Park Covert

Wall Farm

Visitor Ctr

P

P

Royal Hospital Sch

Lower Holbrook

3

Larkfield Rd

Wall Farm Wharf

P

35

Stutton CE Prim Sch

Holbrook Rd

B1080

Findley Cl

Stutton Cl

The Drift

Alton Wharf

The Hermitage

2

Church Rd

Bay Tree Farm

Lower St

Church Field Rd

Hyam's La

Stutton Gn

Markwell's Farm

Stour & Orwell Walk

Crowe Hall La

Lower Street

Stutton House

Holbrook Bay

1

Crowe Hall

Crowe Hall Farm

River Stour

34

15 A B 16 C D 17 E F

61 88

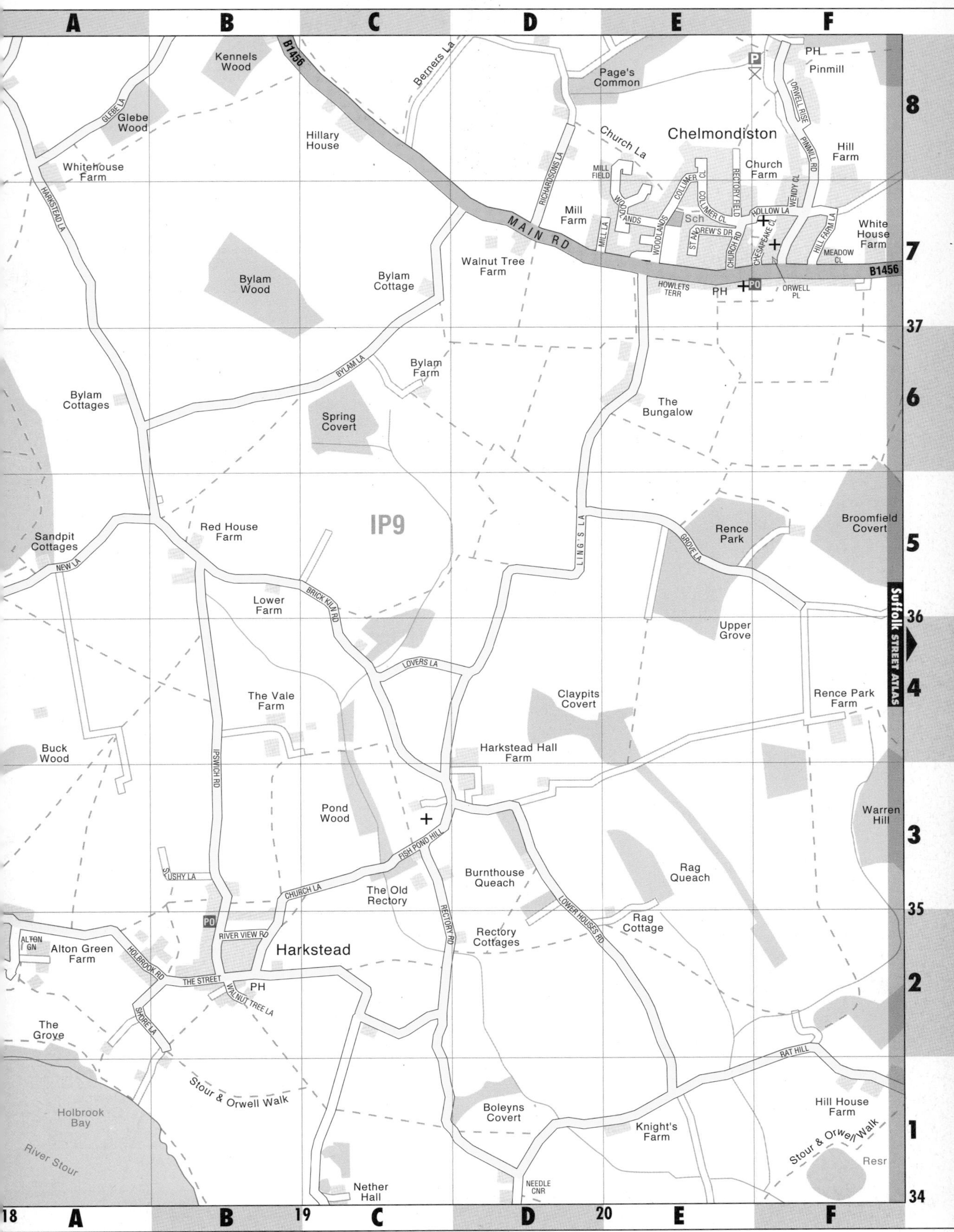

A B C D E F

8

7

37

6

5

36

4

3

35

2

1

34

18 A B 19 C D 20 E F

Chelmondiston

Page's Common

PH
Pinmill

Church La

Mill Field

Church Farm

Hill Farm

White House Farm

B1456

Mill Farm

Walnut Tree Farm

The Bungalow

Rence Park

Broomfield Covert

IP9

Spring Covert

Bylam Farm

Bylam Cottage

Bylam Wood

Kennels Wood

Hillary House

Glebe Wood

Whitehouse Farm

Bylam Cottages

Sandpit Cottages

Red House Farm

Lower Farm

Upper Grove

Rence Park Farm

Warren Hill

The Vale Farm

Buck Wood

Claypits Covert

Harkstead Hall Farm

Pond Wood

Burnthouse Queach

Rag Queach

Rag Cottage

The Old Rectory

Rectory Cottages

Harkstead

Alton Green Farm

PH

The Grove

Stour & Orwell Walk

Boleyns Covert

Knight's Farm

Hill House Farm

Stour & Orwell Walk

Resr

Holbrook Bay

River Stour

Nether Hall

NEEDLE CNR

MAIN RD

B1456

BERNERS LA

RICHARDSONS LA

HARKSTEAD LA

GLEBE LA

BYLAM LA

NEW LA

BRICK KILN RD

LINGS LA

GROVE LA

LOVERS LA

IPSWICH RD

FISH POND HILL

RECTORY RD

CHURCH LA

RIVER VIEW RD

HOLBROOK RD

THE STREET

WALNUT TREE LA

SHORE LA

CUSHY LA

LOWER HOUSES RD

RAT HILL

Suffolk STREET ATLAS

40

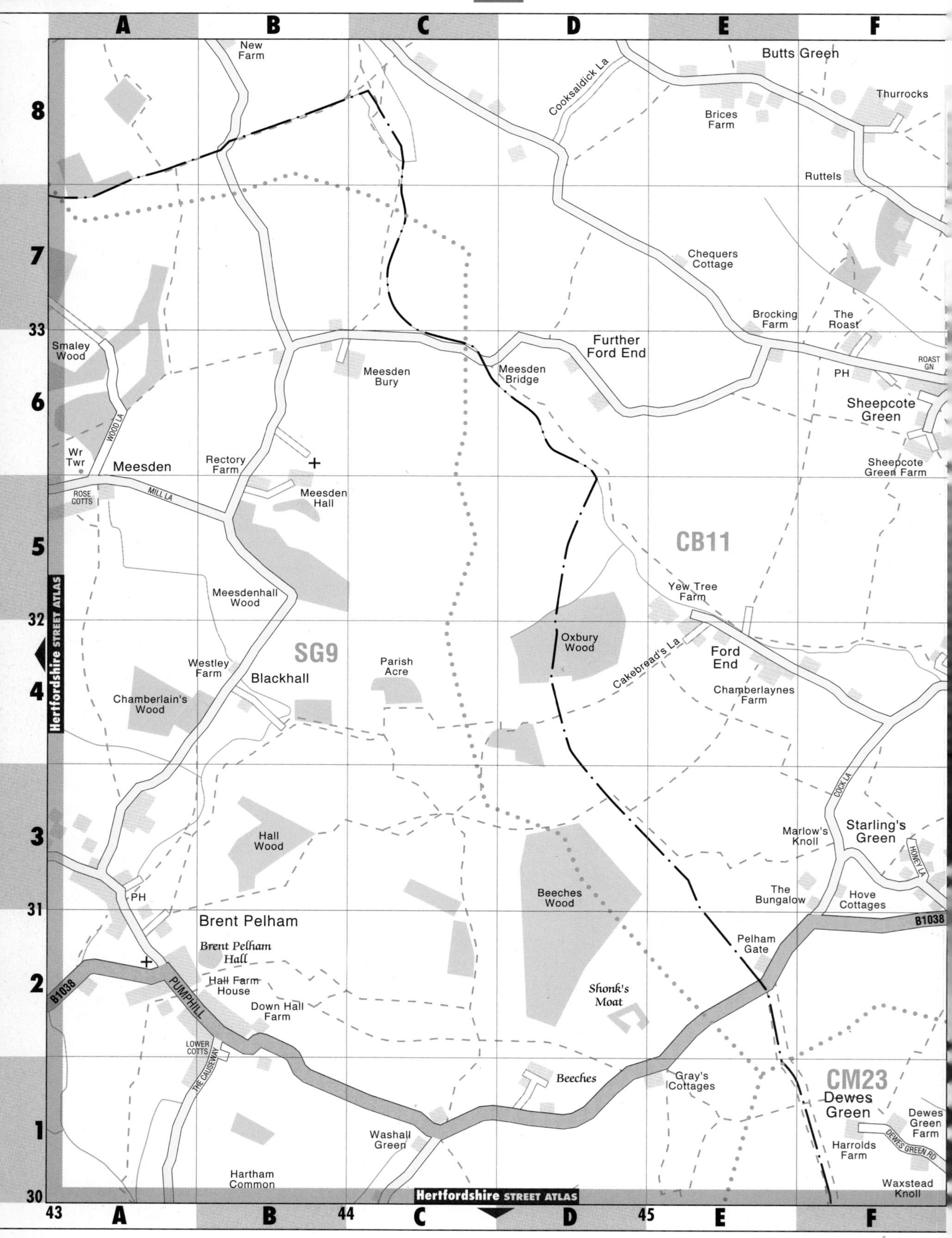
A
B
C
D
E
F
8
7
33
6
5
32
4
3
31
2
1
30
43
44
45
New Farm
Cooksaldick La
Butts Green
Thurrocks
Brices Farm
Ruttels
Chequers Cottage
Brocking Farm
The Roast
ROAST GN
PH
Sheepcote Green
Sheepcote Green Farm
Smaley Wood
Further Ford End
Meesden Bury
Meesden Bridge
WOOD LA
Wr Twr
Meesden
Rectory Farm
Meesden Hall
ROSE COTTS
MILL LA
CB11
Yew Tree Farm
Meesdenhall Wood
SG9
Oxbury Wood
Cakebread's La
Ford End
Westley Farm
Blackhall
Parish Acre
Chamberlaynes Farm
Chamberlain's Wood
Hertfordshire STREET ATLAS
COCK LA
Hall Wood
Marlow's Knoll
Starling's Green
HONEY LA
PH
The Bungalow
Hove Cottages
Beeches Wood
Brent Pelham
B1038
Pelham Gate
Brent Pelham Hall
Hall Farm House
PUMPHILL
Shonk's Moat
Down Hall Farm
B1038
LOWER COTTS
THE CAUSEWAY
Beeches
Gray's Cottages
CM23
Dewes Green
Dewes Green Farm
DEWES GREEN RD
Harrolds Farm
Washall Green
Hartham Common
Waxstead Knoll
Hertfordshire STREET ATLAS

41
66

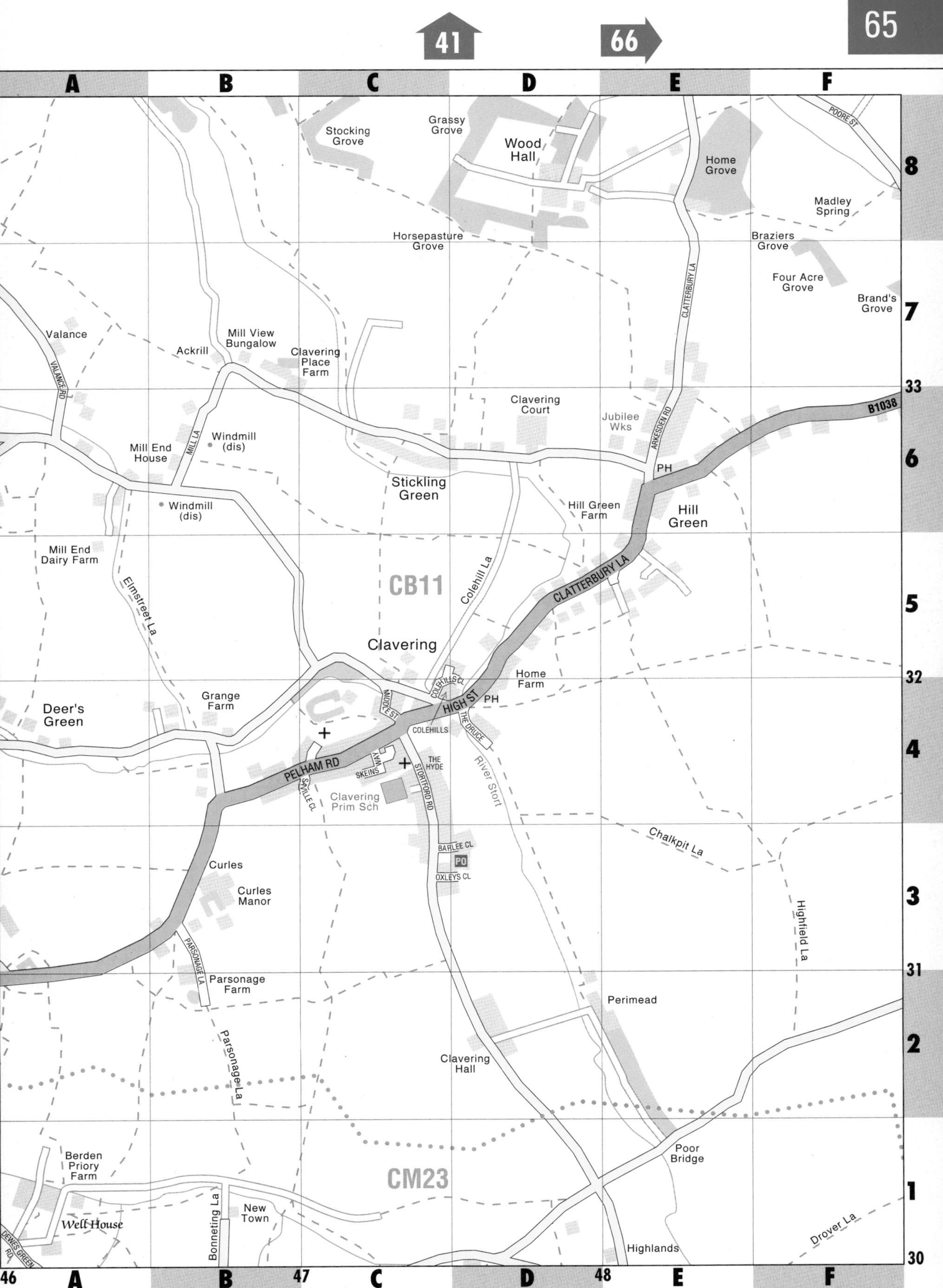
A
B
C
D
E
F
Stocking Grove
Grassy Grove
Wood Hall
Home Grove
POORE ST
Madley Spring
Horsepasture Grove
Braziers Grove
Four Acre Grove
Brand's Grove
CLATTERBURY LA
Valance
VALANCE RD
Ackrill
Mill View Bungalow
Clavering Place Farm
Clavering Court
Jubilee Wks
ARKESDEN RD
B1038
Mill End House
MILL LA
Windmill (dis)
PH
Stickling Green
Windmill (dis)
Hill Green Farm
Hill Green
Mill End Dairy Farm
Elmstreet La
CB11
Colehill La
CLATTERBURY LA
Clavering
Deer's Green
Grange Farm
COLEHILLS CL
HIGH ST
PH
Home Farm
MIDDLE ST
COLEHILLS
THE DRUCE
PELHAM RD
SKEINS WAY
THE HYDE
STORTFORD RD
River Stort
SAVILLE CL
Clavering Prim Sch
Chalkpit La
BARLEE CL
PO
OXLEYS CL
Curles
Curles Manor
Highfield La
PARSONAGE LA
Parsonage Farm
Perimead
Parsonage La
Clavering Hall
Berden Priory Farm
Poor Bridge
CM23
Well House
Bonneting La
New Town
DEWES GREEN RD
Highlands
Drover La
8
7
33
6
5
32
4
3
31
2
1
30
46
47
48

92
66

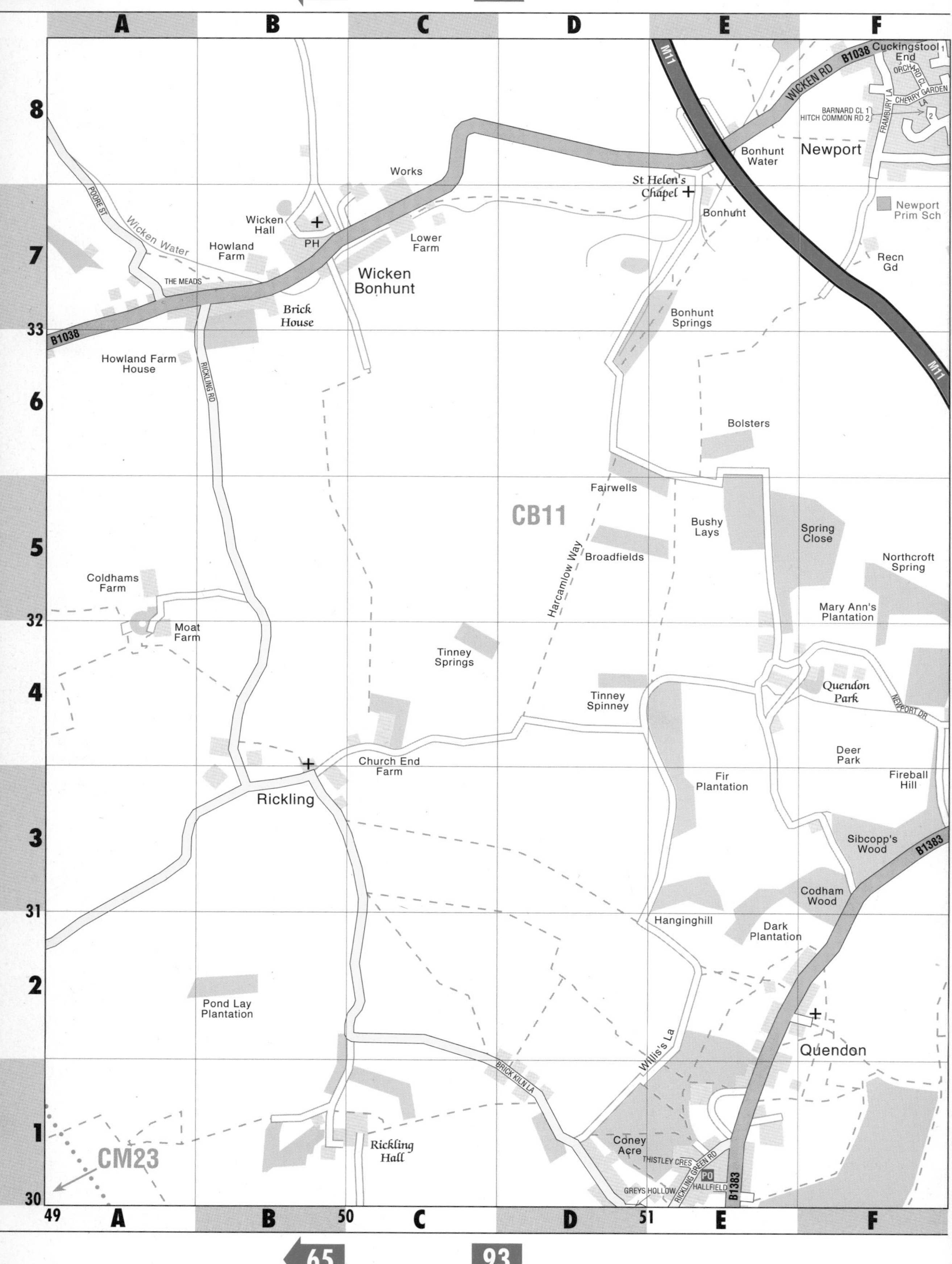

A B C D E F

8

7

33

6

5

4

3

2

1

32

31

30

Newport

Cuckingstool End

B1038 WICKEN RD

M11

ORCHARD CL
CHERRY GARDEN LA
FRAMBURY LA

BARNARD CL 1
HITCH COMMON RD 2

Newport
Prim Sch

Recn
Gd

Bonhunt
Water

St Helen's
Chapel

Bonhunt

Bonhunt
Springs

Works

Wicken
Hall

PH

Howland
Farm

Lower
Farm

THE MEADS

Wicken Water

Wicken
Bonhunt

ROBIE ST

B1038

Howland Farm
House

Brick
House

RICKLING RD

Bolsters

Fairwells

Bushy
Lays

Spring
Close

Northcroft
Spring

CB11

Broadfields

Harcamlow Way

Mary Ann's
Plantation

Coldhams
Farm

Moat
Farm

Tinney
Springs

Tinney
Spinney

Quendon
Park

NEWPORT DR

Deer
Park

Fireball
Hill

Fir
Plantation

Sibcopp's
Wood

B1383

Church End
Farm

Rickling

Codham
Wood

Hanginghill

Dark
Plantation

Pond Lay
Plantation

Quendon

Willis's La

BRICK KILN LA

Rickling
Hall

Coney
Acre

THISTLEY CRES

RICKLING GREEN RD

PO

HALLFIELD

GREYS HOLLOW

B1383

CM23

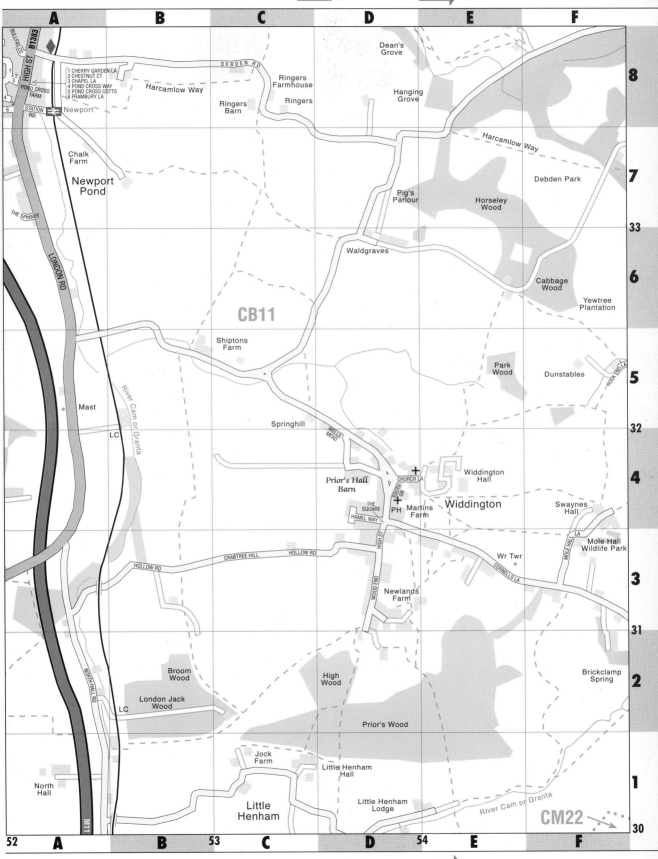

43
68

A B C D E F

1 CHERRY GARDEN LA
2 CHESTNUT CT
3 CHAPEL LA
4 POND CROSS WAY
5 POND CROSS COTTS
6 FRAMBURY LA

BULLFIELDS
B1383
HIGH ST
POND CROSS FARM
STATION RD
Newport
DEBDEN RD
Harcamlow Way
Ringers Barn
Ringers Farmhouse
Ringers
Dean's Grove
Hanging Grove
Harcamlow Way
Chalk Farm
Newport Pond
THE SPINNEY
Pig's Parlour
Horseley Wood
Debden Park
Waldgraves
Cabbage Wood
Yewtree Plantation
LONDON RD
CB11
Shiptons Farm
Park Wood
Dunstables
ROOK END LA
Mast
River Cam or Granta
Springhill
LC
WELLS MEAD
Prior's Hall Barn
CHURCH LA
SOUTH GN
Widdington Hall
THE SQUARE
PH
Martins Farm
Widdington
Swaynes Hall
HAMEL WAY
HIGH ST
LA
MOLE HALL
Mole Hall Wildlife Park
CRABTREE HILL
HOLLOW RD
HOLLOW RD
Wr Twr
CORNELLS LA
WOOD END
Newlands Farm
Broom Wood
High Wood
Brickclamp Spring
NORTH HALL RD
London Jack Wood
LC
Prior's Wood
Jock Farm
Little Henham Hall
North Hall
Little Henham
Little Henham Lodge
River Cam or Granta
CM22
M11

8
7
33
6
5
32
4
3
31
2
1
30

52 A B 53 C D 54 E F

94
68

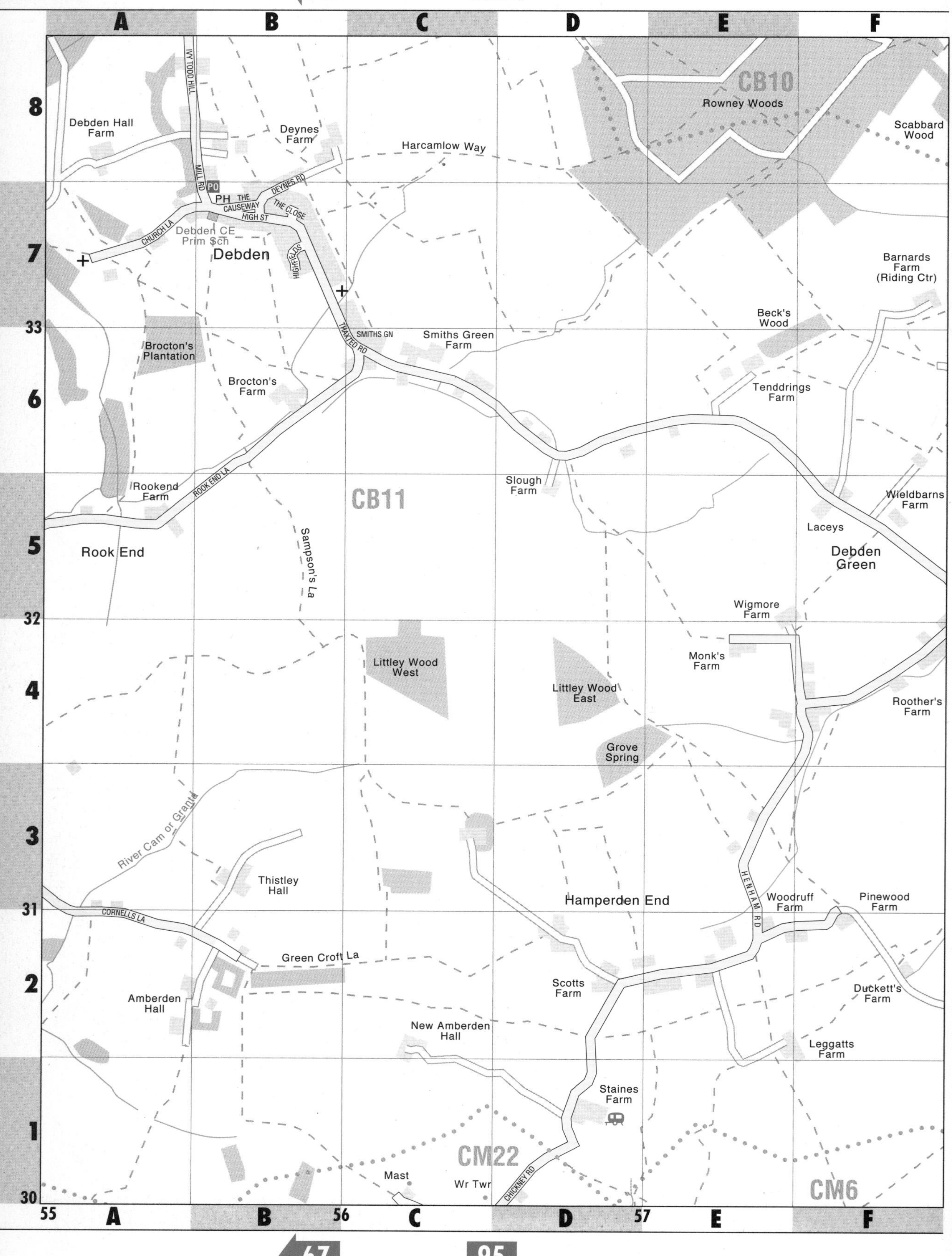

Map Labels

8 Debden Hall Farm · Deynes Farm · Harcamlow Way · Rowney Woods · CB10 · Scabbard Wood

7 IVY TODD HILL · MILL RD · PO · PH · THE CAUSEWAY · DEYNES RD · THE CLOSE · HIGH ST · CHURCH LA · Debden CE Prim Sch · Debden · Barnards Farm (Riding Ctr) · Beck's Wood

33 SMITHS GN · TRAYED RD · Smiths Green Farm

6 Brocton's Plantation · Brocton's Farm · Tenddrings Farm

5 Rookend Farm · ROOK END LA · CB11 · Slough Farm · Wieldbarns Farm · Laceys · Debden Green · Rook End · Sampson's La

32 Wigmore Farm

4 Littley Wood West · Littley Wood East · Monk's Farm · Roother's Farm · Grove Spring

3 River Cam or Granta · Thistley Hall · Hamperden End · HENHAM RD · Woodruff Farm · Pinewood Farm

31 CORNELLS LA · Green Croft La · Scotts Farm · Duckett's Farm

2 Amberden Hall · New Amberden Hall · Leggatts Farm

1 Staines Farm · CM22 · Mast · Wr Twr · CHICKNEY RD · CM6

30

55 · A · B · 56 · C · D · 57 · E · F

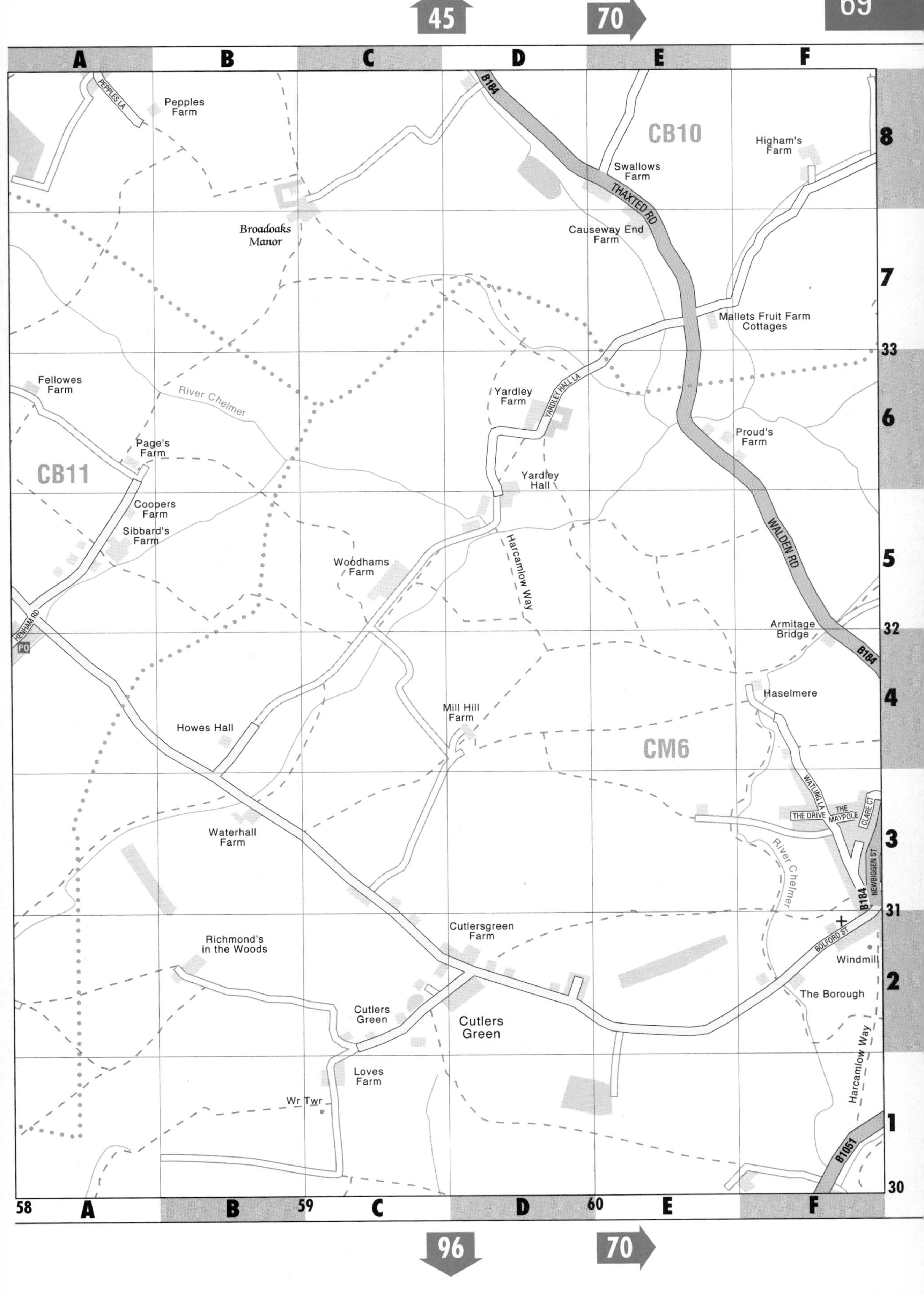
45
70
A
B
C
D
E
F
PEPPLES LA
Pepples Farm
B184
CB10
Higham's Farm
Swallows Farm
THAXTED RD
Broadoaks Manor
Causeway End Farm
Mallets Fruit Farm Cottages
Fellowes Farm
River Chelmer
Yardley Farm
YARDLEY HALL LA
Proud's Farm
Page's Farm
CB11
Yardley Hall
Coopers Farm
Sibbard's Farm
Woodhams Farm
Harcamlow Way
WALDEN RD
HENHAM RD
PO
Armitage Bridge
B184
Haselmere
Howes Hall
Mill Hill Farm
CM6
WATLING LA
THE DRIVE
THE MAYPOLE
CLARE CT
Waterhall Farm
River Chelmer
NEWBIGGEN ST
B184
BOLFORD ST
Richmond's in the Woods
Cutlersgreen Farm
Windmill
The Borough
Cutlers Green
Cutlers Green
Loves Farm
Harcamlow Way
Wr Twr
B1051
8
7
33
6
5
32
4
3
31
2
1
30
58
59
60
96
70

69
46

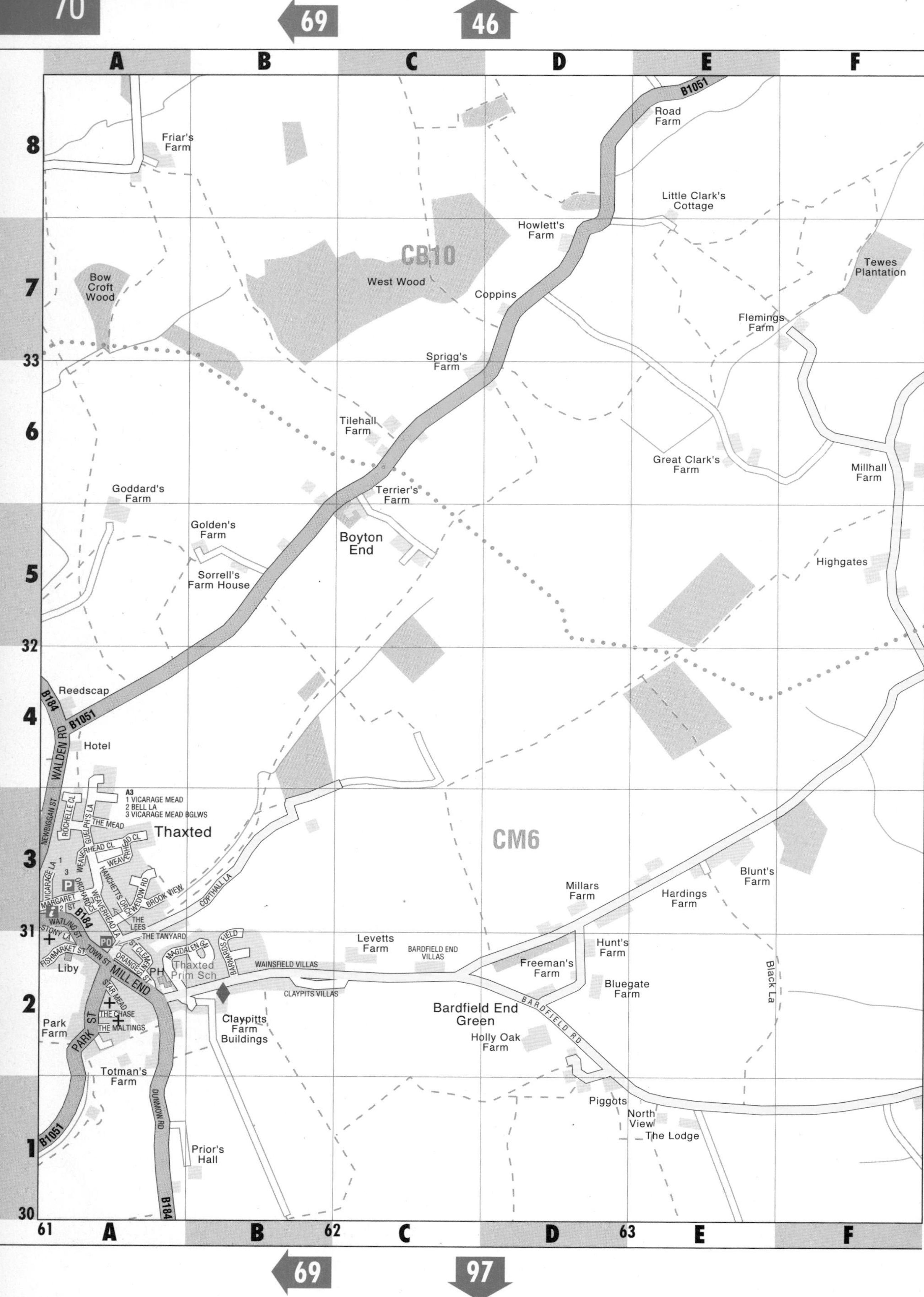

A B C D E F

8

Friar's Farm

Road Farm

B1051

Little Clark's Cottage

Tewes Plantation

7

Bow Croft Wood

West Wood

CB10

Howlett's Farm

Coppins

Flemings Farm

33

Sprigg's Farm

6

Tilehall Farm

Great Clark's Farm

Millhall Farm

Goddard's Farm

Terrier's Farm

Golden's Farm

Boyton End

5

Sorrell's Farm House

Highgates

32

Reedscap

4

B184

B1051

WALDEN RD

Hotel

A3
1 VICARAGE MEAD
2 BELL LA
3 VICARAGE MEAD BGLWS

NEWBIGGIN ST

ROCHELLE CL

BELLFIELDS CL

THE MEAD

Thaxted

CM6

3

VICARAGE LA

WEAVERHEAD CL

MEAD CL

WEAVERS

WEAVERHEAD LA

HANDBETTS GREEN

ORCHARD CL

MEADOW RD

BROOK VIEW

COPTHALL LA

Millars Farm

Hardings Farm

Blunt's Farm

P

31

MARGARET ST

B184

WATLING ST

THE LEES

THE TANYARD

ST CHAD

MAGDALEN GN

SOUTHVIEW

FIELD

Levetts Farm

Bardfield End Villas

Hunt's Farm

STONY LA

PO

PH

Thaxted Prim Sch

Wainsfield Villas

Freeman's Farm

Bluegate Farm

Black La

FISHMARKET ST

TOWN ST

ORANGE ST

MILL END

Liby

CLAYPITS VILLAS

Bardfield End Green

BARDFIELD RD

2

Park Farm

GATE MEAD

THE CHASE

THE MALTINGS

Claypitts Farm Buildings

Holly Oak Farm

PARK ST

Totman's Farm

Piggots

North View

The Lodge

1

B1051

DUNMOW RD

Prior's Hall

30

61 A B 62 C D 63 E F

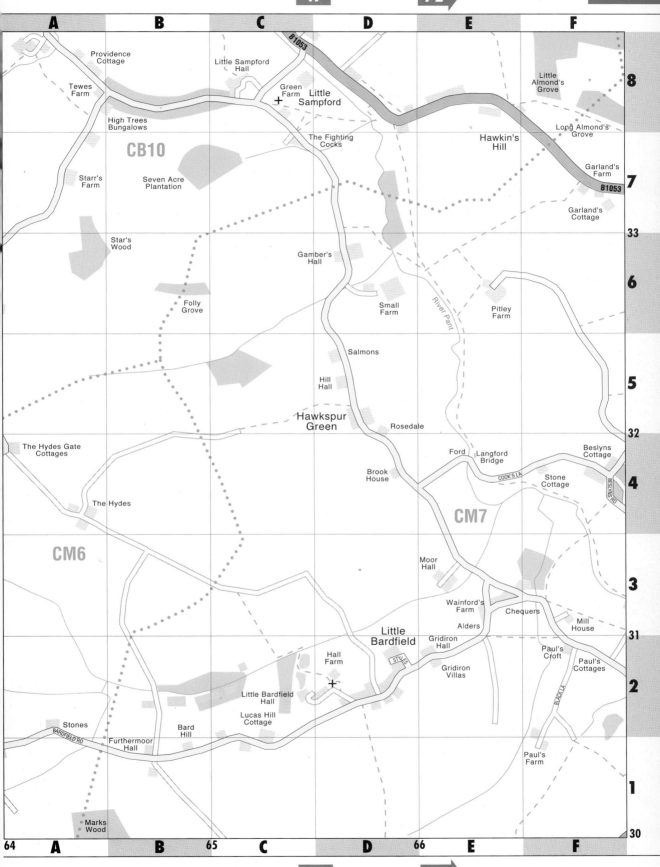

A   B   C   D   E   F

B1053

Providence Cottage

Little Sampford Hall

Little Almond's Grove

8

Tewes Farm

Green Farm

Little Sampford

Long Almond's Grove

High Trees Bungalows

The Fighting Cocks

Hawkin's Hill

Garland's Farm

CB10

Starr's Farm

Seven Acre Plantation

B1053

7

Garland's Cottage

33

Star's Wood

Gamber's Hall

6

Folly Grove

Small Farm

River Pant

Pitley Farm

Salmons

Hill Hall

5

Hawkspur Green

Rosedale

32

The Hydes Gate Cottages

Ford

Langford Bridge

Beslyns Cottage

COOK'S LA

Brook House

Stone Cottage

BESLYNS RD

4

The Hydes

CM7

CM6

Moor Hall

3

Wainford's Farm

Chequers

Mill House

Alders

31

Little Bardfield

Gridiron Hall

Paul's Croft

Paul's Cottages

Hall Farm

STV

Gridiron Villas

2

Little Bardfield Hall

BLACK LA

Stones

Lucas Hill Cottage

BARDFIELD RD

Bard Hill

Furthermoor Hall

Paul's Farm

1

Marks Wood

30

64   A   B   65   C   D   66   E   F

71
48

A B C D E F

8 7 33 6 5 32 4 3 31 2 1 30

Lodge
Darielay Farm
Mill End
Fancy Covert
Howe Hall
B1057
LITTLE LONDON HILL
SPAINS HALL RD
The Thicket
Spinney Lodge
The Moors
The Round House
B1053
Brent Hall
Duck End
BRENT HALL RD
TOM'S LA
COACHMANS MEAD
PH
THE CAUSEWAY
Windmill (dis)
VALLEY VIEW
CHURCH HILL
BRIDGE ST
Mus
THE PIGHTLE
Great Biggins Farm
Highbank
KEMPE RD
VICARAGE RD
PO
WINSEY CHASE
COUNCIL HOS
PARSONAGE TERR
Finchingfield CE Prim Sch
STEPHEN MARSHALL AVE
THE HOPGROUNDS
THE OLD VICARAGE
Justice's Hill
Winsey Chase
Gatward's Farm
Finchingfield
B1053
Finchingfield Brook
BARDFIELD RD
Little Winceys Farm
The Mill House
MILL RD
Dynes Cottage
The Haven
Talavera
CM7
Normans
Daw Street Cottages
DAW ST
Beslyns
Pakes
Daw Street
Petches
Petches Cottages
Littles
BESLYNS RD
Robjohns Farm
Bridge End
The Briars
Bridge Farm
NORTHFIELD
Champions
Brooklands
The Watermill
Sculpin's Bridge
Petches Bridge
BRIDGE ST
MEADOW VIEW
High Chimneys
WEDGEWOOD END
RUTLAND PL
Southcotts
Windmill
Claypit Hall
Whinbush Farm
NORTHAMPTON MDW
ST JOHN'S TERR
School Farm
BELL LA
Gage
MILL CL
MILL RD
Waltham's Cross
PH
PO
VINE ST
HIGH ST
CROWN ST
BROOK ST
Great Bardfield Prim Sch
DURHAM CL
THE CORNICHE
Great Bardfield
Cross Farm Cottage
HIGH ST
Liby
TH
Mus
The Cross Farm
BRAINTREE RD
NEWLAND AVE
BENDLOWES RD
ST MARY'S VILLAS
Lodge Wood
B1057 DUNMOW RD
Bardfield Ctr
WEATHERVANE COTTS
HALL VILLAS
ALIENOR AVE
The Nutshell

67 A B 68 C D 69 E F

71
99

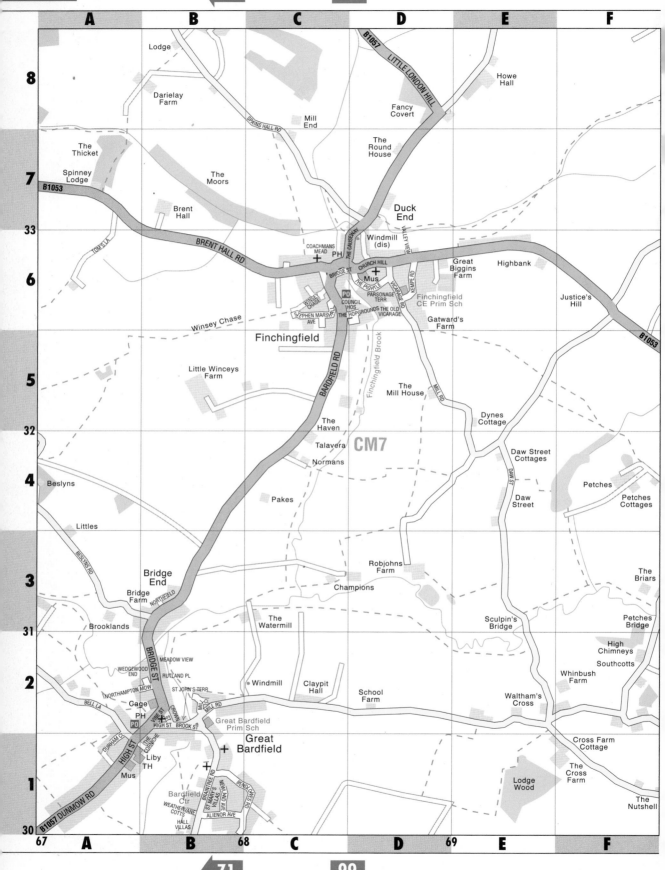

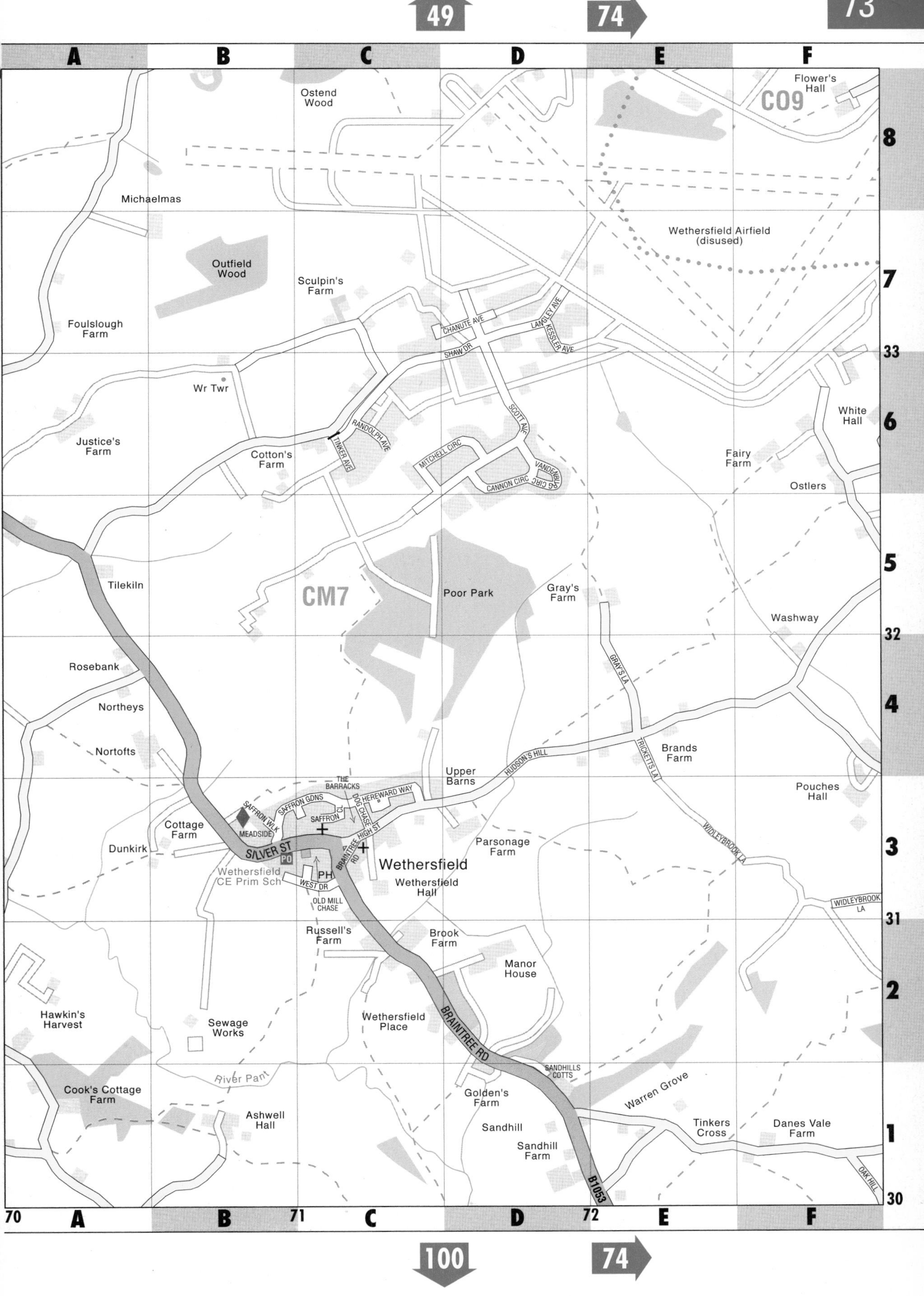

CO9

Flower's Hall

Ostend Wood

Michaelmas

Wethersfield Airfield (disused)

Outfield Wood

Sculpin's Farm

CHANUTE AVE

LANGLEY AVE

KESSLER AVE

SHAW DR

Foulslough Farm

Wr Twr

White Hall

RANDOLPH AVE

SCOTT AVE

TINKER AVE

Fairy Farm

Justice's Farm

Cotton's Farm

MITCHELL CIRC

VANDENBERG

Ostlers

CANNON CIRC

96 CIRC

Tilekiln

CM7

Poor Park

Gray's Farm

Washway

Rosebank

GRAY'S LA

Northeys

Nortofts

TRICKETTS LA

Brands Farm

Pouches Hall

Upper Barns

HUDSON'S HILL

THE BARRACKS

SAFFRON GDNS

HEREWARD WAY

WIDLEYBROOK LA

SAFFRON WALK

DOG CHASE

Parsonage Farm

Cottage Farm

MEADSIDE

SAFFRON

SILVER ST

PO

BRAINTREE HIGH ST

Wethersfield

Dunkirk

Wethersfield CE Prim Sch

PH

WEST DR

Wethersfield Hall

WIDLEYBROOK LA

OLD MILL CHASE

Russell's Farm

Brook Farm

Hawkin's Harvest

Sewage Works

Wethersfield Place

BRAINTREE RD

Manor House

River Pant

Golden's Farm

SANDHILLS COTTS

Warren Grove

Cook's Cottage Farm

Ashwell Hall

Sandhill

Tinkers Cross

Danes Vale Farm

Sandhill Farm

B1053

OAK HILL

8
7
33
6
5
32
4
3
31
2
1
30

A B C D E F

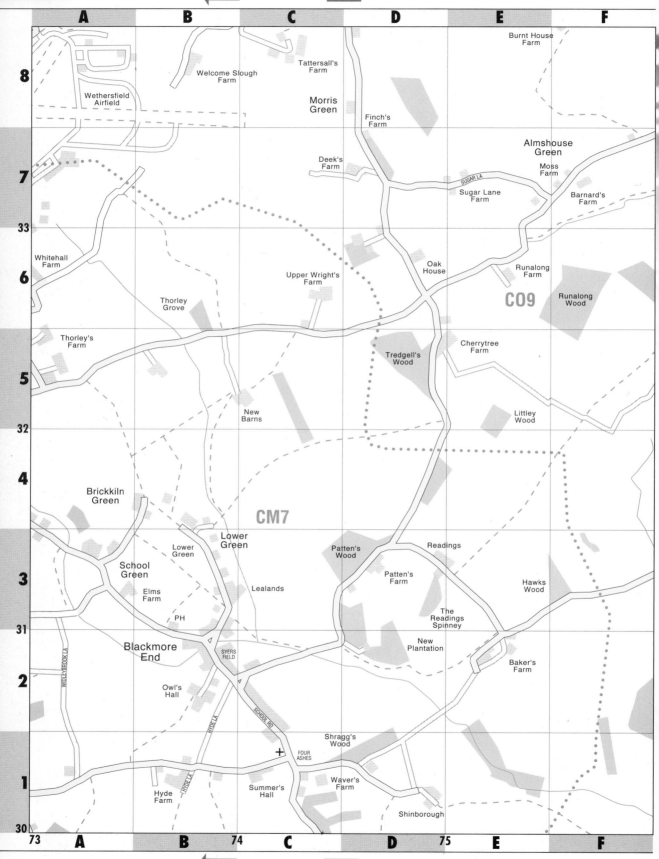

A B C D E F

8
7
33
6
5
32
4
3
31
2
1
30

Wethersfield Airfield

Welcome Slough Farm

Tattersall's Farm

Morris Green

Finch's Farm

Burnt House Farm

Almshouse Green

Deek's Farm

Sugar Lane Farm

SUGAR LA

Moss Farm

Barnard's Farm

Whitehall Farm

Upper Wright's Farm

Oak House

Runalong Farm

CO9

Runalong Wood

Thorley Grove

Thorley's Farm

Tredgell's Wood

Cherrytree Farm

Littley Wood

New Barns

CM7

Brickkiln Green

Lower Green

Patten's Wood

Readings

Hawks Wood

School Green

Lower Green

Lealands

Patten's Farm

The Readings Spinney

Elms Farm

PH

New Plantation

Baker's Farm

Blackmore End

SYERS FIELD

WIDLEY BROOK LA

Owl's Hall

HYDE LA

SCHOOL RD

Shragg's Wood

FOUR ASHES

Hyde Farm

HYDE LA

Summer's Hall

Waver's Farm

Shinborough

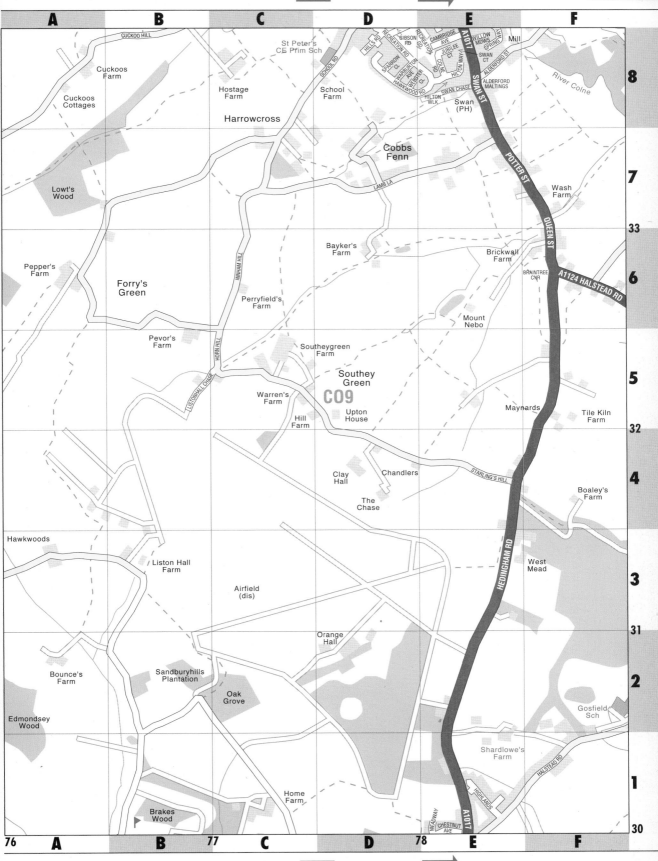

51
76

A
B
C
D
E
F
CUCKOO HILL
Cuckoos Farm
Cuckoos Cottages
Lowt's Wood
Hostage Farm
Harrowcross
St Peter's CE Prim Sch
SCHOOL RD
School Farm
HILLS RD
RECREATION RD
GIBSON RD
RECREATION GD
CAMBRIDGE AVE
SPARROW CL
WARBURTON AVE
WEBSTER CL
HAWKWOOD RD
COLNE RD
JUBILEE CT
HILTON WAY
HILTON WLK
SWAN CHASE
A1017
WILLOW MDWS
SPRING WAY
SWAN CT
ALDERFORD ST
ALDERFORD MALTINGS
Mill
River Colne
SWAN ST
Swan (PH)
Cobbs Fenn
LAMB LA
POTTER ST
Wash Farm
QUEEN ST
Bayker's Farm
Brickwall Farm
BRAINTREE CNR
A1124 HALSTEAD RD
Pepper's Farm
Forry's Green
INNHAM HILL
Perryfield's Farm
Mount Nebo
Pevor's Farm
HORN HILL
Southeygreen Farm
Southey Green
LISTONHALL CHASE
Warren's Farm
CO9
Hill Farm
Upton House
Maynards
Tile Kiln Farm
Clay Hall
Chandlers
STARLING'S HILL
The Chase
Boaley's Farm
Hawkwoods
Liston Hall Farm
HEDINGHAM RD
West Mead
Airfield (dis)
Orange Hall
Bounce's Farm
Sandburyhills Plantation
Oak Grove
Gosfield Sch
Edmondsey Wood
Shardlowe's Farm
HALSTEAD RD
HIGHLANDS
Home Farm
Brakes Wood
MEADWAY
CHESTNUT AVE
A1017
8
7
33
6
5
32
4
3
31
2
1
30
76
77
78

102
76

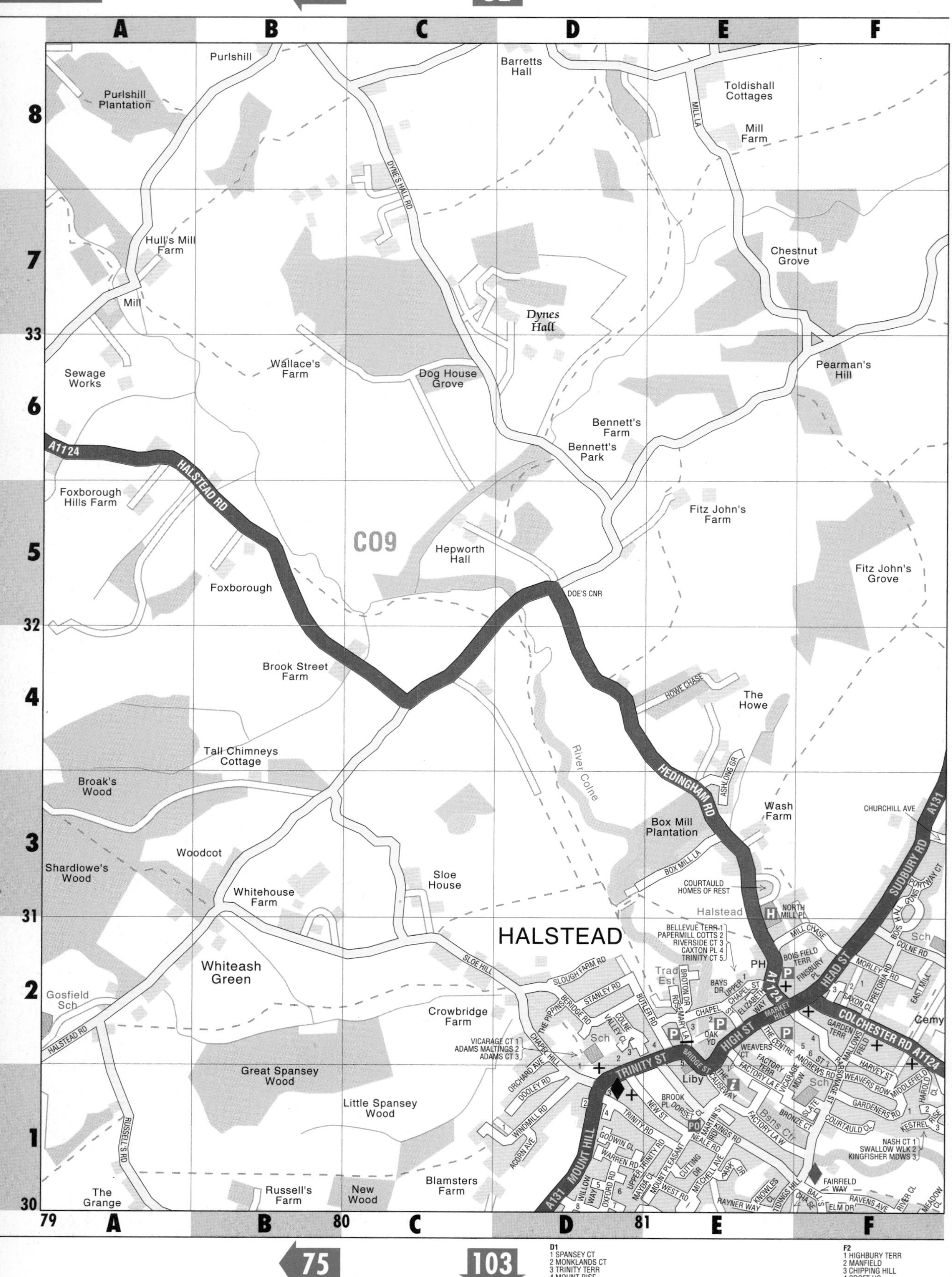

D1
1 SPANSEY CT
2 MONKLANDS CT
3 TRINITY TERR
4 MOUNT RISE
5 CLOVERS
6 TRYON CT
7 DE VERES RD
8 RAMSEY RD

F2
1 HIGHBURY TERR
2 MANFIELD
3 CHIPPING HILL
4 CROFT HO
5 CONGREGATION HO
6 SYMONDS CT
7 PARSONS CT

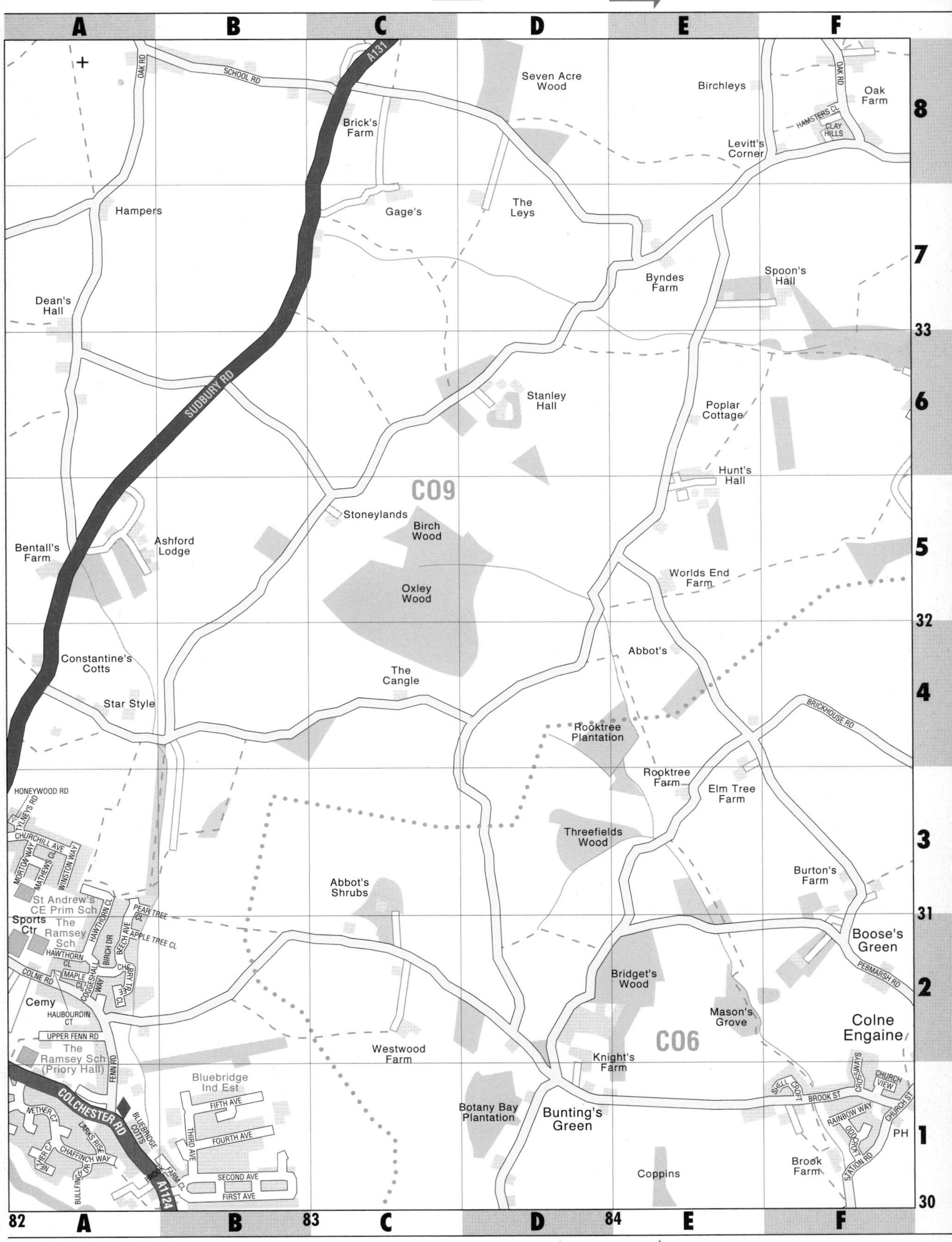

53
78
104
78

A B C D E F

8
7
33
6
5
32
4
3
31
2
1
30

82 A B 83 C D 84 E F

Oak Farm
Birchleys
Seven Acre Wood
Levitt's Corner
Clay Hills
Hamsters Cl
Oak Rd

Hampers
School Rd
Brick's Farm
Gage's
The Leys
Byndes Farm
Spoon's Hall

Dean's Hall
Sudbury Rd
A131

Stanley Hall
Poplar Cottage

Bentall's Farm
Ashford Lodge
Stoneylands
Birch Wood
Hunt's Hall

CO9
Oxley Wood
Worlds End Farm

Constantine's Cotts
The Cangle
Abbot's

Star Style
Rooktree Plantation
Brickhouse Rd

Honeywood Rd
Rooktree Farm
Elm Tree Farm

Threefields Wood
Burton's Farm

Boose's Green
Pebmarsh Rd

St Andrew's CE Prim Sch
The Ramsey Sch
Sports Ctr
Abbot's Shrubs
Bridget's Wood
Mason's Grove

Cemy
Colne Engaine
CO6

The Ramsey Sch (Priory Hall)
Westwood Farm
Knight's Farm
Church View
Brook St

Bluebridge Ind Est
Colchester Rd
A1124

Botany Bay Plantation
Bunting's Green
Coppins
Brook Farm
PH
Station Rd

Fifth Ave
Fourth Ave
Third Ave
Second Ave
First Ave

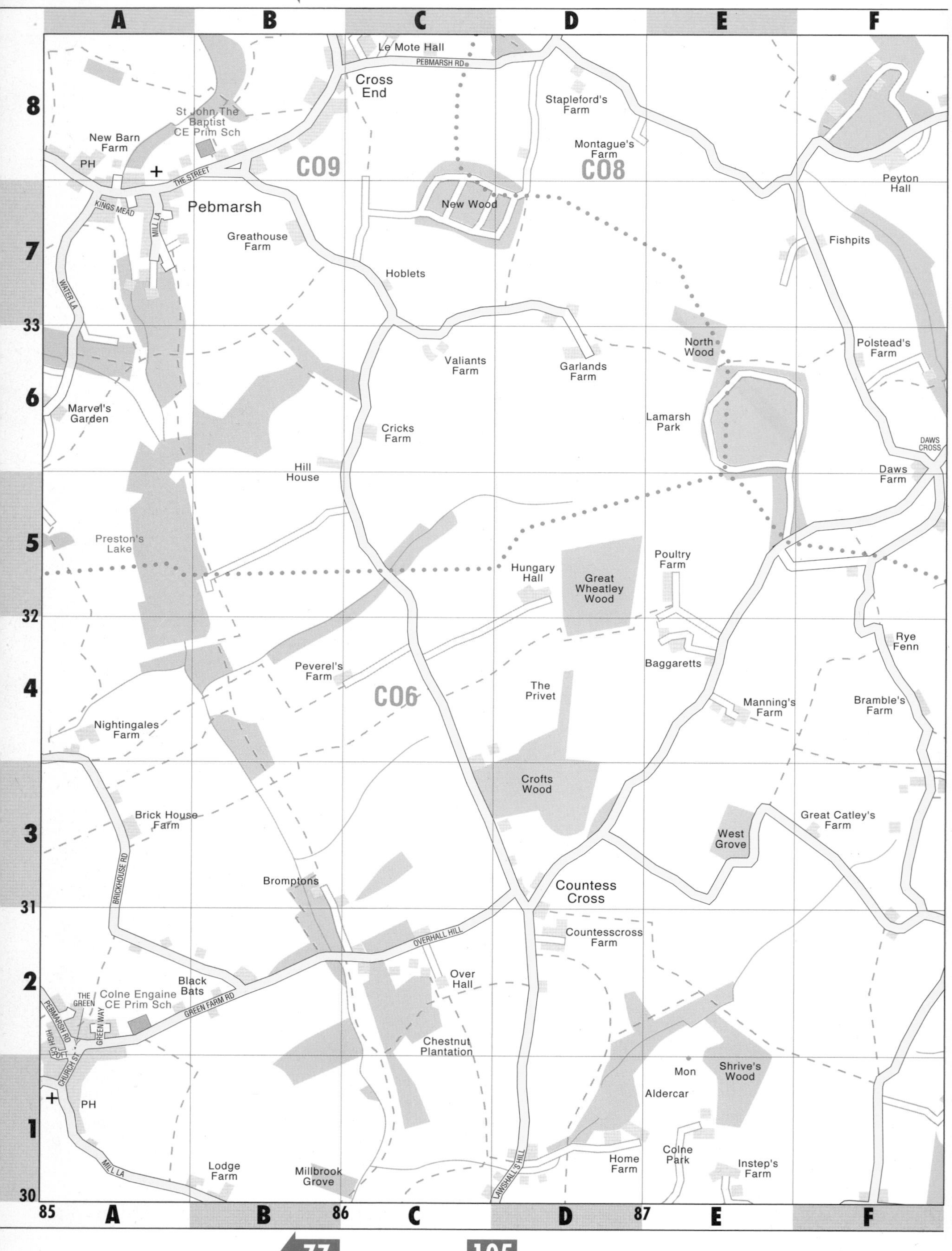

Le Mote Hall
PEBMARSH RD
Cross End
Stapleford's Farm
Montague's Farm
CO9
CO8
St John The Baptist CE Prim Sch
New Barn Farm
PH
THE STREET
Pebmarsh
Peyton Hall
KINGS MEAD
MILL LA
Greathouse Farm
New Wood
Fishpits
WATER LA
Hoblets
Polstead's Farm
North Wood
Valiants Farm
Garlands Farm
Marvel's Garden
Cricks Farm
Lamarsh Park
DAWS CROSS
Hill House
Daws Farm
Preston's Lake
Hungary Hall
Great Wheatley Wood
Poultry Farm
Rye Fenn
Peverel's Farm
CO6
The Privet
Baggaretts
Manning's Farm
Bramble's Farm
Nightingales Farm
Crofts Wood
Brick House Farm
Great Catley's Farm
West Grove
BRICKHOUSE RD
Bromptons
Countess Cross
Countesscross Farm
OVERHALL HILL
Black Bats
Over Hall
THE GREEN
Colne Engaine CE Prim Sch
GREEN FARM RD
PEBMARSH RD
GREEN WAY
Chestnut Plantation
Mon
Shrive's Wood
Aldercar
HIGH ST
CHURCH ST
PH
Colne Park
Home Farm
MILL LA
Lodge Farm
Millbrook Grove
LAWSHALL'S HILL
Instep's Farm

85 A B 86 C D 87 E F

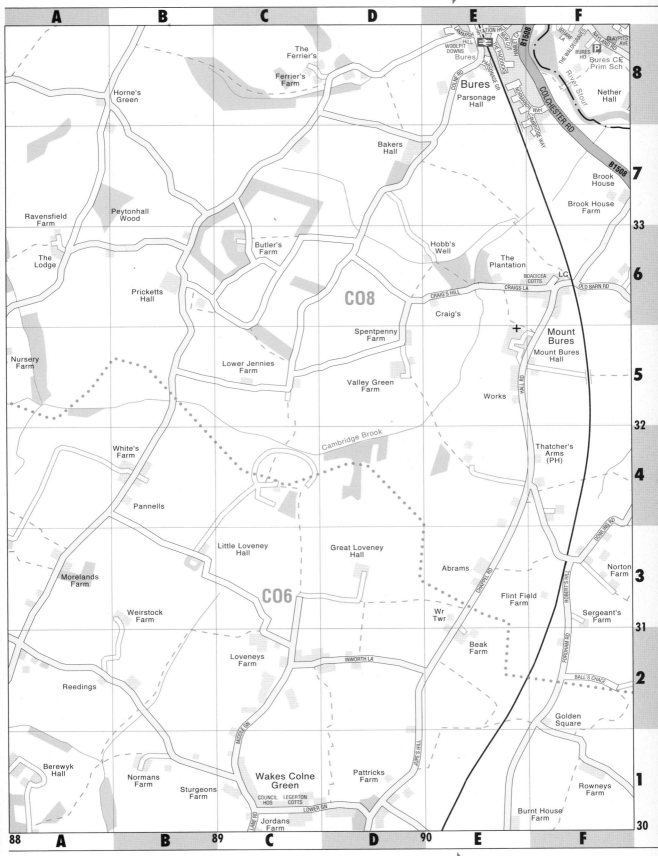

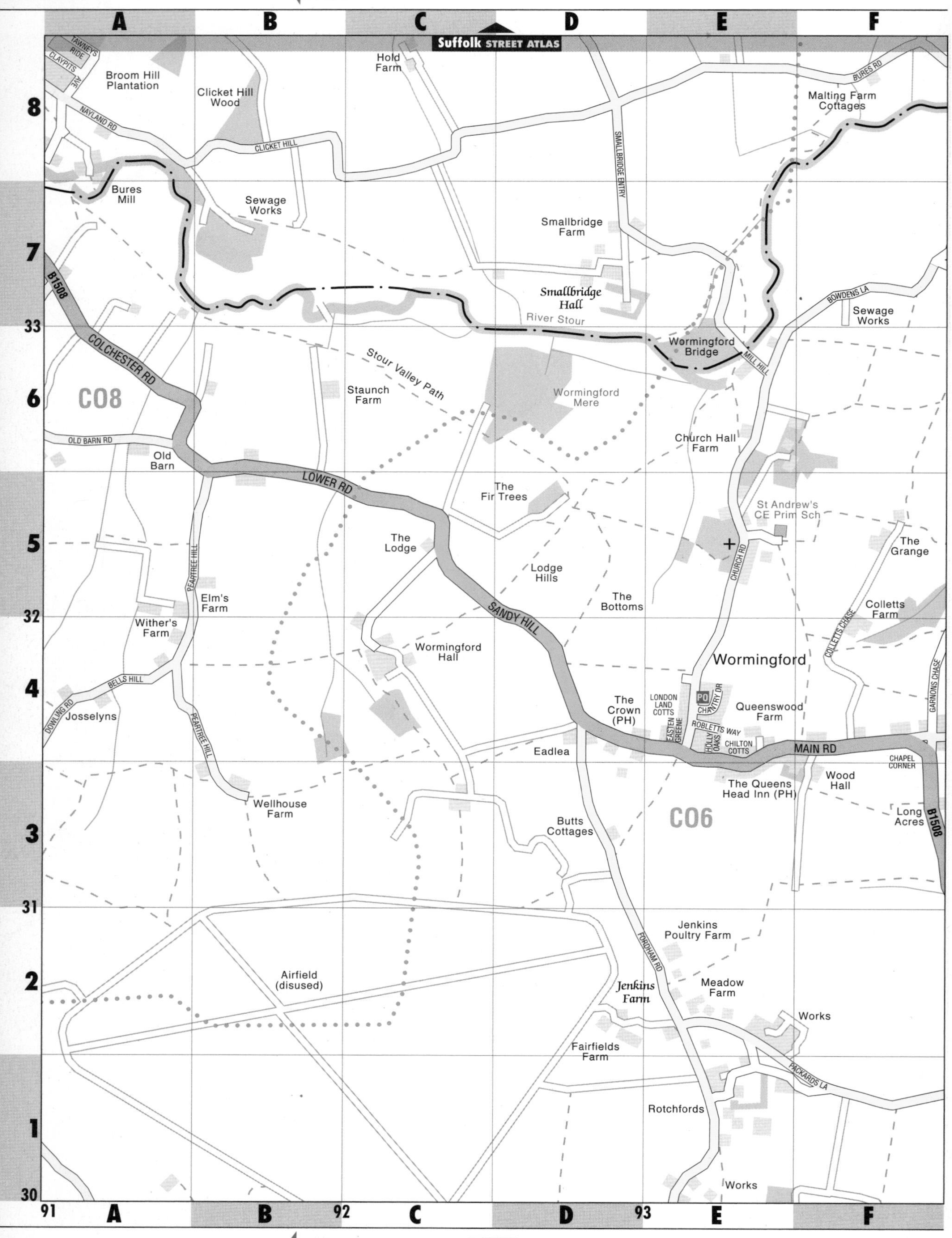

A   B   C   D   E   F

8

7

33

6

CO8

5

32

4

3

31

2

1

30

TAWNEYS RIDE
CLAYPITS AVE
NAYLAND RD

Broom Hill Plantation

Clicket Hill Wood

CLICKET HILL

Hold Farm

SMALLBRIDGE ENTRY

BURES RD

Malting Farm Cottages

Bures Mill

Sewage Works

Smallbridge Farm

Smallbridge Hall

BOWDENS LA

Sewage Works

B1508

River Stour

Wormingford Bridge

MILL HILL

COLCHESTER RD

Stour Valley Path

Staunch Farm

Wormingford Mere

Church Hall Farm

OLD BARN RD

Old Barn

LOWER RD

The Fir Trees

CHURCH RD

St Andrew's CE Prim Sch

The Grange

PEARTREE HILL

The Lodge

Lodge Hills

The Bottoms

Colletts Farm

COLLETTS CHASE

Elm's Farm

Wither's Farm

Wormingford Hall

Wormingford

GARNONS CHASE

BELLS HILL

Josselyns

DOWLING RD

PEARTREE HILL

The Crown (PH)

LONDON LAND COTTS

EASTER GREENE

PO

CHS

ROBLETTS WAY

HOLLY OAKS

CHILTON COTTS

Queenswood Farm

MAIN RD

CHAPEL CORNER

Wood Hall

Wellhouse Farm

Eadlea

The Queens Head Inn (PH)

CO6

Long Acres

B1508

Butts Cottages

FORDHAM RD

Jenkins Poultry Farm

Airfield (disused)

Jenkins Farm

Meadow Farm

Works

Fairfields Farm

PACKARDS LA

Rotchfords

Works

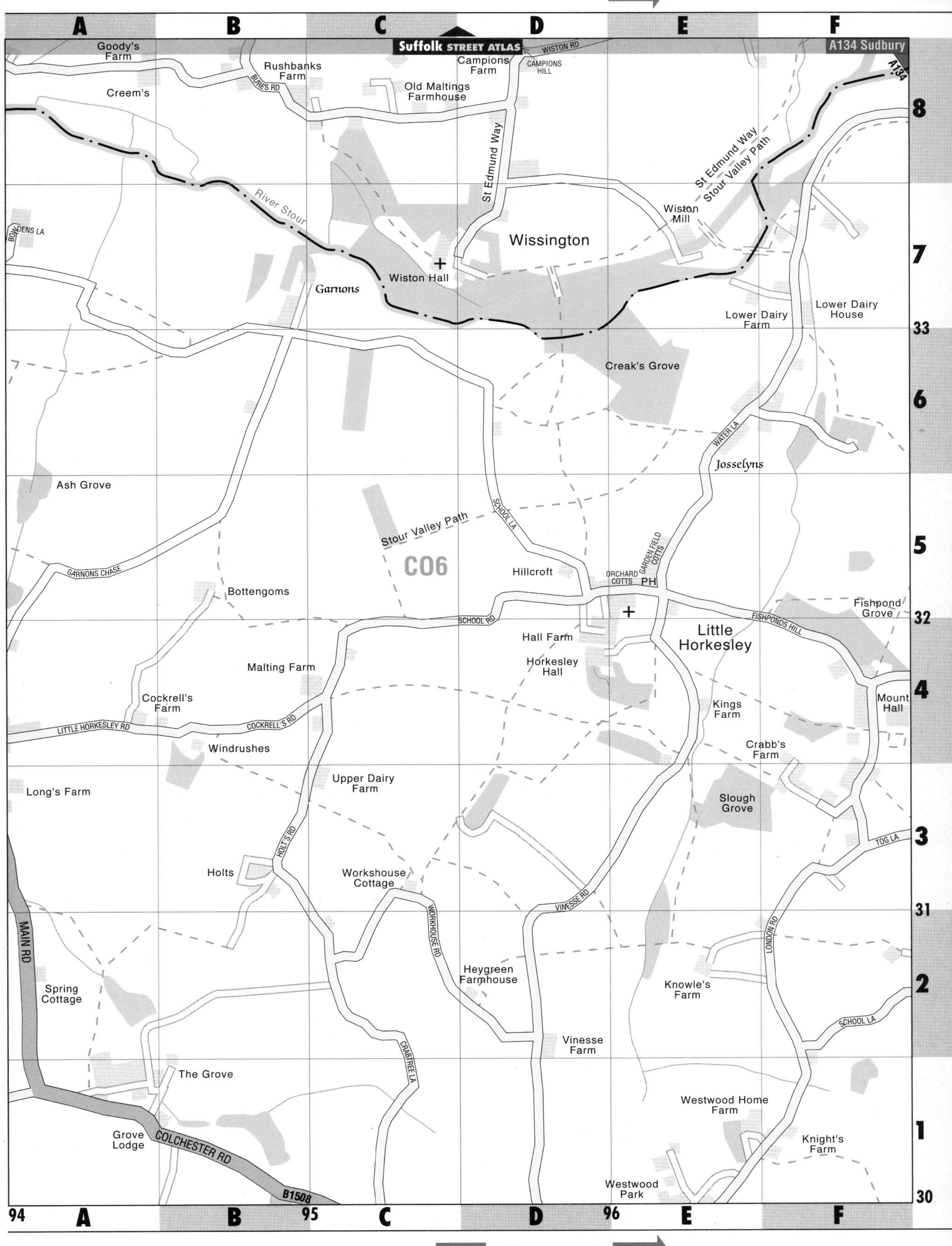

Suffolk STREET ATLAS

A134 Sudbury

Goody's Farm

Creem's

Rushbanks Farm

BURES RD

Old Maltings Farmhouse

Campions Farm

WISTON RD

CAMPIONS HILL

St Edmund Way

St Edmund Way
Stour Valley Path

Wiston Mill

BOWDENS LA

River Stour

Garnons

Wiston Hall

Wissington

Lower Dairy Farm

Lower Dairy House

Creak's Grove

WATER LA

Josselyns

Ash Grove

Stour Valley Path

SCHOOL LA

CO6

Hillcroft

ORCHARD COTTS

GARDEN FIELD COTTS

PH

Fishpond Grove

GARNONS CHASE

Bottengoms

SCHOOL RD

Hall Farm

Horkesley Hall

Little Horkesley

FISHPONDS HILL

Malting Farm

Cockrell's Farm

COCKRELL'S RD

Kings Farm

Crabb's Farm

Mount Hall

LITTLE HORKESLEY RD

Windrushes

Upper Dairy Farm

Slough Grove

TOG LA

Long's Farm

HOLTS RD

Holts

Workshouse Cottage

WORKHOUSE RD

VINESSE RD

LONDON RD

Knowle's Farm

SCHOOL LA

MAIN RD

Spring Cottage

Heygreen Farmhouse

CRABTREE LA

Vinesse Farm

Westwood Home Farm

Knight's Farm

The Grove

Grove Lodge

COLCHESTER RD

B1508

Westwood Park

81
56

A 134
WATER LA
River Stour
PARK RD

Thrift
Farm

HORKESLEY HILL

Horkesley
Park
Littlegarth
Sch

King's Yard
BURNT DICK HILL

Boxtedhall
Great Wood

Gulsons

CHURCH ST

Boxted
Boxted
St Peter's
CE Prim Sch

Valley
Yard

Whitepark
Farm

Little Wood

Boxted Hall

CHURCH RD

Kerseys

Pond House

South Lodge

CO4

GREENFIELD
COTTS

The
Chantry

Ridgnalls

Potter's
Farm

Orchard
Farm

Carters
Vineyard

MELL LA

BOXTED CHURCH RD

Carter's Farm

Brook
Farm

CO6

Martins
PH

Coveneys

Horkesley
Green

GREEN LA

BROOK
COTTS

NAYLAND RD

Boxted Lodge

LONDON RD

Holly Lodge
Farm

Workhouse
Hill

WORKHOUSE HILL

The
Grove

SCARFE'S
CNR

HOLLY LA

Barritts Farm

MILL RD

WINDMILL CT

Nevards
Farm

Enfields Farm

Noakes
Farm

TOG LA

Lodge Farm

Old Ellis
Farmhouse

ELLIS RD

Altyre
House

BOXTED RD

Frost's
Grove

QUEEN'S HEAD RD

THE CAUSEWAY

Harrow
Corner

REDHOUSE LA

Breewood Hall

PO

Essex Way

Priory Hall
Farm

STRAIGHT RD

OLD HOUSE RD

Redhouse
Farm

OLD HOUSE RD

SCHOOL LA

BROAD LA

Great Horkesley

PH

LINCOLN LA

PEPPER'S RD

Horkesley
Plantation

LANGHAM RD

THE CRESCENT

GLENWAY CT
GLEBELANDS
CT
MORLAND
CT
GLENWAY

Spratt's Marsh

A 134

81
109

57
84

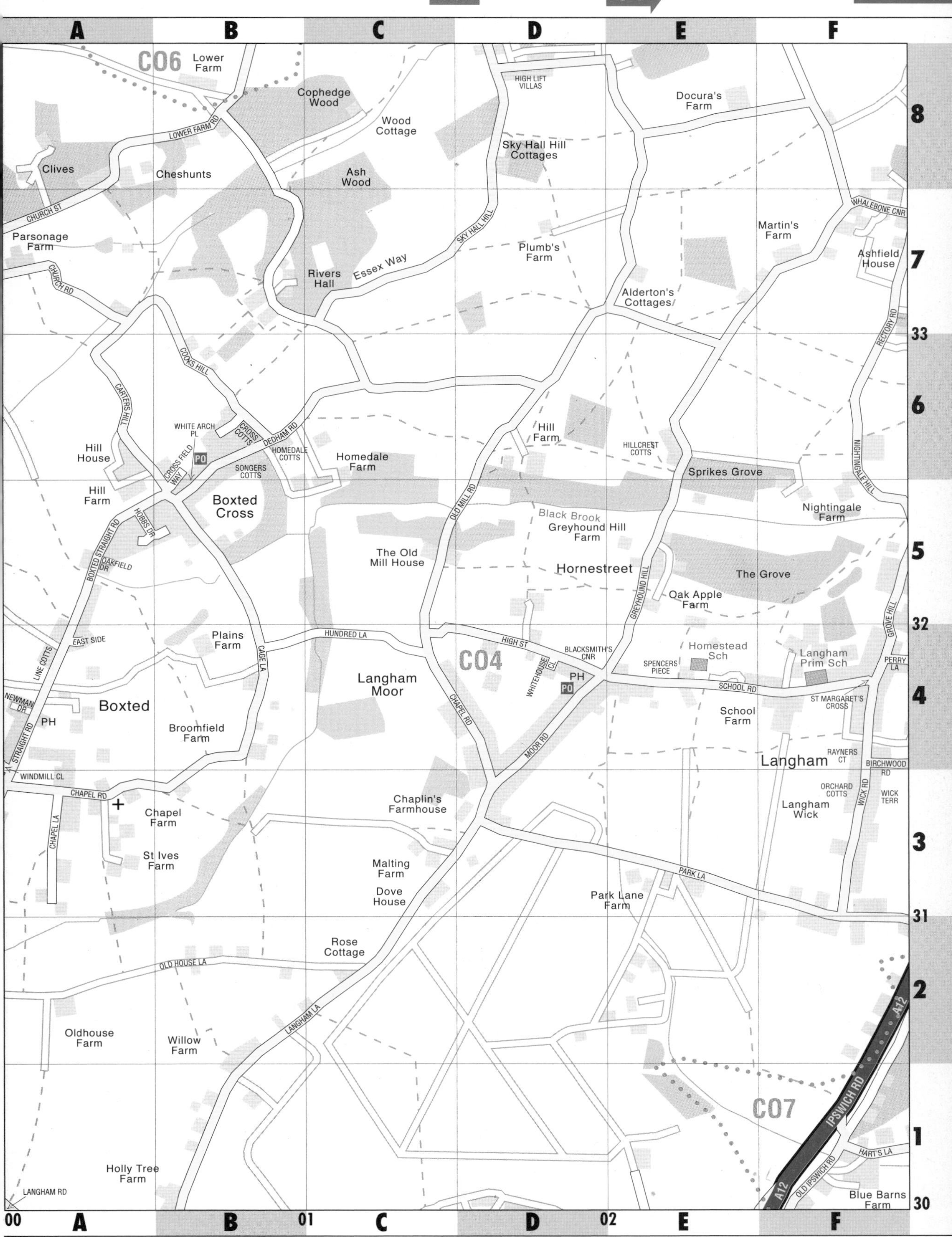
A
B
C
D
E
F
CO6
Lower Farm
Cophedge Wood
Wood Cottage
HIGH LIFT VILLAS
Docura's Farm
Sky Hall Hill Cottages
LOWER FARM RD
Clives
Cheshunts
Ash Wood
CHURCH ST
Parsonage Farm
Rivers Hall
Essex Way
SKY HALL HILL
Plumb's Farm
Martin's Farm
WHALEBONE CNR
Ashfield House
CHURCH RD
Alderton's Cottages
COOKS HILL
CARTERS HILL
RECTORY RD
WHITE ARCH PL
CROSS COTTS
DEDHAM RD
HOMEDALE COTTS
Homedale Farm
Hill Farm
HILLCREST COTTS
Hill House
CROSS FIELD WAY
PO
SONGERS COTTS
Sprikes Grove
NIGHTINGALE HILL
Hill Farm
Boxted Cross
HOBBS DR
OLD MILL RD
Black Brook
Greyhound Hill Farm
Nightingale Farm
BOXTED STRAIGHT RD
OAKFIELD DR
The Old Mill House
Hornestreet
GREYHOUND HILL
The Grove
Oak Apple Farm
Plains Farm
HUNDRED LA
HIGH ST
CO4
BLACKSMITH'S CNR
Homestead Sch
Langham Prim Sch
GROVE HILL
PERRY LA
EAST SIDE
CAGE LA
LINE COTTS
Langham Moor
WHITEHOUSE CL
PH
SPENCERS PIECE
SCHOOL RD
ST MARGARET'S CROSS
NEWMAN DR
Boxted
PH
PO
CHAPEL RD
School Farm
STRAIGHT RD
Broomfield Farm
MOOR RD
Langham
RAYNERS CT
BIRCHWOOD RD
WINDMILL CL
ORCHARD COTTS
WICK RD
WICK TERR
CHAPEL RD
Chapel Farm
Chaplin's Farmhouse
Langham Wick
CHAPEL LA
St Ives Farm
Malting Farm
PARK LA
Dove House
Park Lane Farm
Rose Cottage
OLD HOUSE LA
LANGHAM LA
A12
Oldhouse Farm
Willow Farm
IPSWICH RD
CO7
HART'S LA
OLD IPSWICH RD
Holly Tree Farm
LANGHAM RD
A12
Blue Barns Farm
8
7
33
6
5
32
4
3
31
2
1
30
00
01
02

110
84

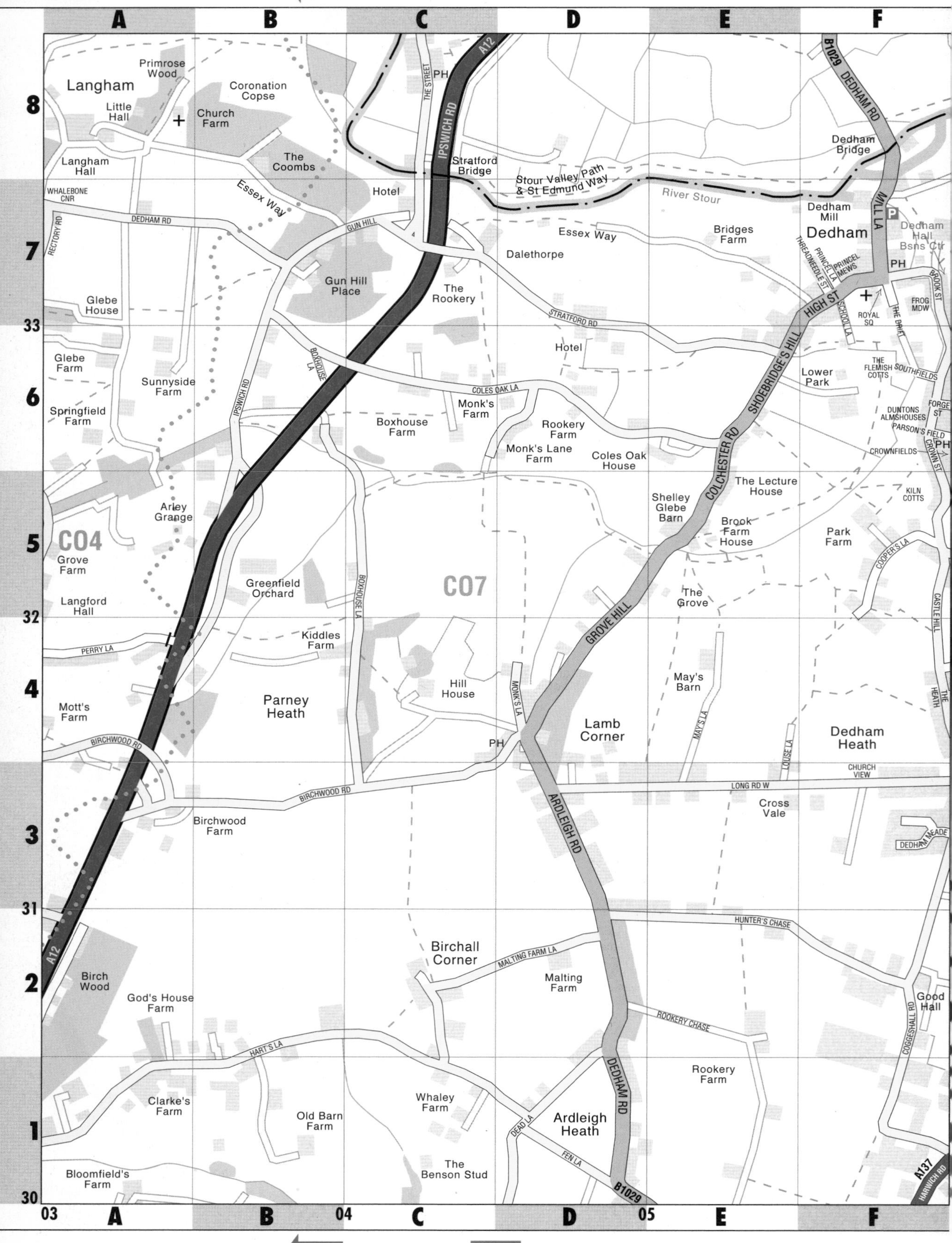

A B C D E F

8

Langham
Primrose Wood
Little Hall
Coronation Copse
Church Farm
The Coombs
Langham Hall
WHALEBONE CNR
Essex Way
RECTORY RD
DEDHAM RD

THE STREET
PH
IPSWICH RD
A12
Stratford Bridge
Hotel
Stour Valley Path & St Edmund Way
River Stour
B1029 DEDHAM RD
Dedham Bridge

7

33

Glebe House
Glebe Farm
GUN HILL
Gun Hill Place
IPSWICH RD
BOXHOUSE LA
The Rookery
Dalethorpe
STRATFORD RD
Essex Way
Hotel
Bridges Farm
Dedham Mill
Dedham
MILL LA
Dedham Hall Bsns Ctr
P
PH
THREADNEEDLE ST
PRINCEL LA
PRINCEL MEWS
HIGH ST
SCHOOL LA
ROYAL SQ
THE DRIFT
BROOK ST
FROG MDW

6

Springfield Farm
Sunnyside Farm
Boxhouse Farm
Monk's Farm
COLES OAK LA
Rookery Farm
Monk's Lane Farm
Coles Oak House
SHOEBRIDGE'S HILL
COLCHESTER RD
The Lecture House
Lower Park
THE FLEMISH COTTS
Southfields
DUNTONS ALMSHOUSES
PARSON'S FIELD
CROWNFIELDS
FORGE ST
CROWN ST
KILN COTTS

5

CO4
Grove Farm
Arley Grange
Greenfield Orchard
CO7
Shelley Glebe Barn
Brook Farm House
The Grove
Park Farm
COOPER'S LA
CASTLE HILL
THE HEATH

32

Langford Hall
PERRY LA
BOXHOUSE LA
Kiddles Farm

4

Mott's Farm
BIRCHWOOD RD
Parney Heath
Hill House
MONK'S LA
PH
Lamb Corner
May's Barn
MAY'S LA
LOUISE LA
Dedham Heath
LONG RD W
CHURCH VIEW

3

Birchwood Farm
BIRCHWOOD RD
ARDLEIGH RD
GROVE HILL
Cross Vale
DEDHAM MEADE
DEDHAM RD

31

A12
HUNTER'S CHASE

2

Birch Wood
God's House Farm
HART'S LA
Birchall Corner
MALTING FARM LA
Malting Farm
ROOKERY CHASE
DEDHAM RD
Rookery Farm
Good Hall
CORBETT'S RD
HARWICH RD

1

Clarke's Farm
Old Barn Farm
Whaley Farm
DEAD LA
FEN LA
Ardleigh Heath
B1029
A137

30

Bloomfield's Farm
The Benson Stud

03 A B 04 C D 05 E F

59
86

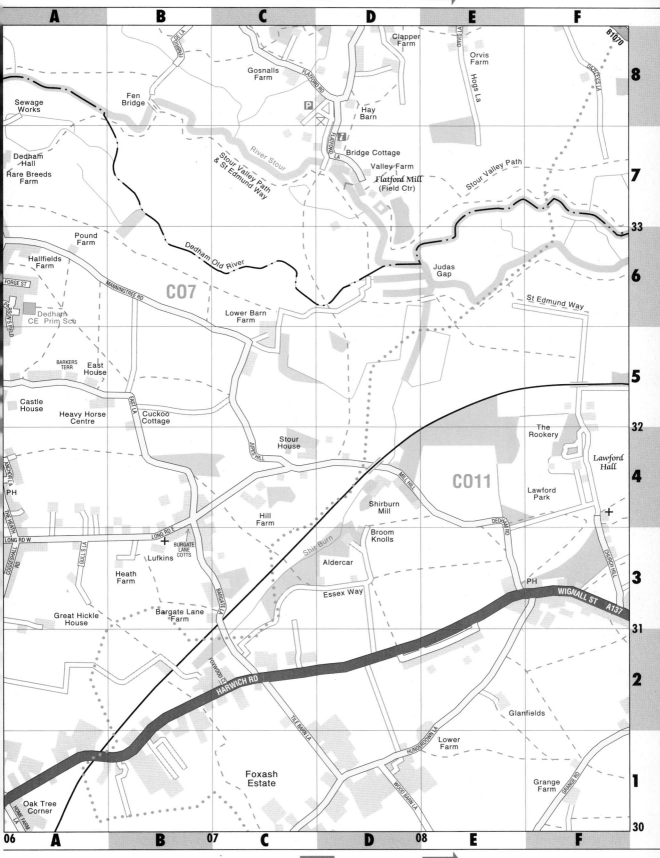
A
B
C
D
E
F
Clapper Farm
Orvis Farm
ORVIS LA
Hogs La
B1070
DAZELEY'S LA
Gosnalls Farm
FLATFORD RD
FENBRIDGE LA
Fen Bridge
Sewage Works
Hay Barn
River Stour
Stour Valley Path & St Edmund Way
Dedham Hall
Rare Breeds Farm
FLATFORD LA
Bridge Cottage
Valley Farm
Flatford Mill
(Field Ctr)
Stour Valley Path
Pound Farm
Hallfields Farm
Dedham Old River
Judas Gap
FORGE ST
MANNINGTREE RD
CO7
St Edmund Way
PARSON'S FIELD
Dedham CE Prim Sch
Lower Barn Farm
BARKERS TERR
East House
Castle House
Heavy Horse Centre
EAST LA
Cuckoo Cottage
Stour House
The Rookery
JUPES HILL
Lawford Hall
ANCHOR LA
PH
MILL HILL
CO11
Lawford Park
Shirburn Mill
THE HEATH
Hill Farm
DEDHAM RD
LONG RD W
LONG RD E
BURGATE LANE COTTS
Broom Knolls
Shir Burn
COGGESHALL RD
GULL'S LA
Lufkins
Aldercar
CHURCH HILL
Heath Farm
PH
Essex Way
BARGATE LA
WIGNALL ST
A137
Great Hickle House
Bargate Lane Farm
FOXWOOD CL
HARWICH RD
Glanfields
TILE BARN LA
HUNGERDOWN LA
Lower Farm
Foxash Estate
WOOD BARN LA
Grange Farm
GRANGE RD
Oak Tree Corner
HOME FARM LA
8
7
33
6
5
32
4
3
31
2
1
30
06
07
08

112
86

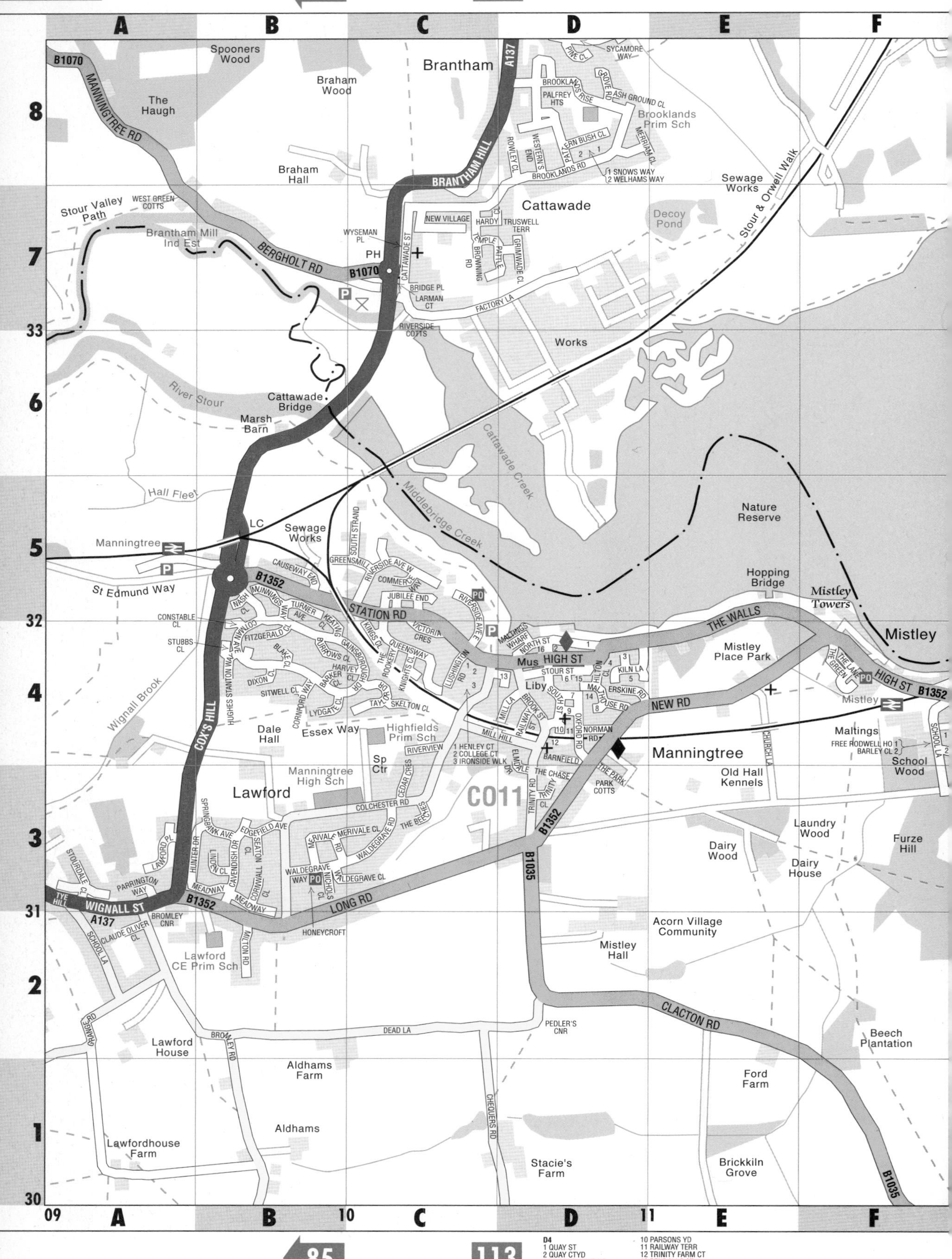

D4
1 QUAY ST
2 QUAY CTYD
3 BROOKS MALTING
4 ALMA SQ
5 THE CENTRAL MAILTINGS
6 ST MICHAELS CT
7 YORK ST
8 FALKLANDS DR
9 REGENT ST
10 PARSONS YD
11 RAILWAY TERR
12 TRINITY FARM CT
13 BENDALLS CT
14 GASFIELD
15 THE OLD LIBRARY
16 COMPASS CT

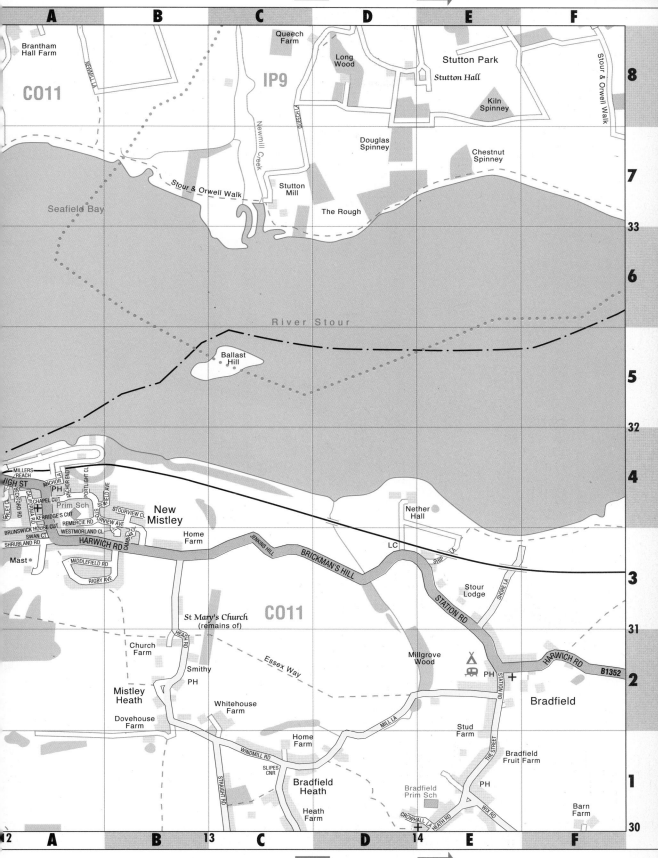
61
88

A B C D E F

Brantham Hall Farm
NEWMILL LA
CO11
Queech Farm
IP9
Long Wood
Stutton Park
Stutton Hall
Kiln Spinney
Stour & Orwell Walk
8
Newmill Creek
QUEECH LA
Douglas Spinney
Chestnut Spinney
7
Stour & Orwell Walk
Stutton Mill
Seafield Bay
The Rough
33
6
River Stour
Ballast Hill
5
32
MILLERS REACH
HIGH ST
ANCHOR LA
ANCHOR END
PORTLIGHT CL
SEAFIELD AVE
PH
CHAPEL CUT
BECKFORD RD
CALIFORNIA RD
Prim Sch
KERRIDGE'S CUT
REMERCIE RD
STOURVIEW CL
STOURVIEW AVE
New Mistley
4
BRUNSWICK HOUSE CUT
SWAN CT
WESTMORLAND CL
CAMBRIA CL
SHRUBLAND RD
HARWICH RD
Home Farm
Nether Hall
JENKINS HILL
BRICKMAN'S HILL
LC
SHIP LA
Mast
MIDDLEFIELD RD
RIGBY AVE
3
Stour Lodge
SHORE LA
STATION RD
St Mary's Church (remains of)
CO11
31
Church Farm
HEATH RD
Essex Way
Millgrove Wood
HARWICH RD
Smithy
PH
PH
B1352
2
Mistley Heath
STATION RD
Bradfield
Whitehouse Farm
Dovehouse Farm
MILL LA
Stud Farm
Home Farm
THE STREET
WINDMILL RD
Bradfield Fruit Farm
SLIPES CNR
Bradfield Heath
PH
1
STRAIGHT RD
Bradfield Prim Sch
Heath Farm
WIX RD
Barn Farm
CROWHALL LA
HEATH RD
30

12 A B 13 C D 14 E F

114
88

A B C D E F

8

IP9

Backhouse
Ley

Holbrook Bay

Stour & Orwell

7

Graham's
Wharf

W/M

33

Stutton
Ness

River Stour

6

5

Stone
Point

Wrabness
Point

Shore
Farm

STONE LA

32

Jacques Bay

Essex Way

Oakfield Wood
Nature Reserve

Wrabness
Hall

4

WALL LA

Lower
Farm

Wrabness

CHURCH RD

P

Wrabness Local
Nature Reserve

P

STATION RD

Ragmarsh
Farm

WHEATSHEAF CL

Dimbols
Farm

3

Brakey
Grove

WHEATSHEAF LA

Jacques
Hall Sch

31

Domine
Farm

Foxes
Farm

COUNCIL
HOS

Gateways

CO11

B1352

2

B1352 HARWICH RD

Lonbarn

COOK'S
CNR

The
Firs

LONBARN HILL

Lonbarn
Bridge

HARWICH RD

Priory
Farm

BUTLER'S LA

SPINNEL'S HILL

Butler's
Farm

Spinnel's
Farm

1

Windmill

SPINNEL'S LA

Pondhall
Wood

Bluehouse
Farm

30

63
90

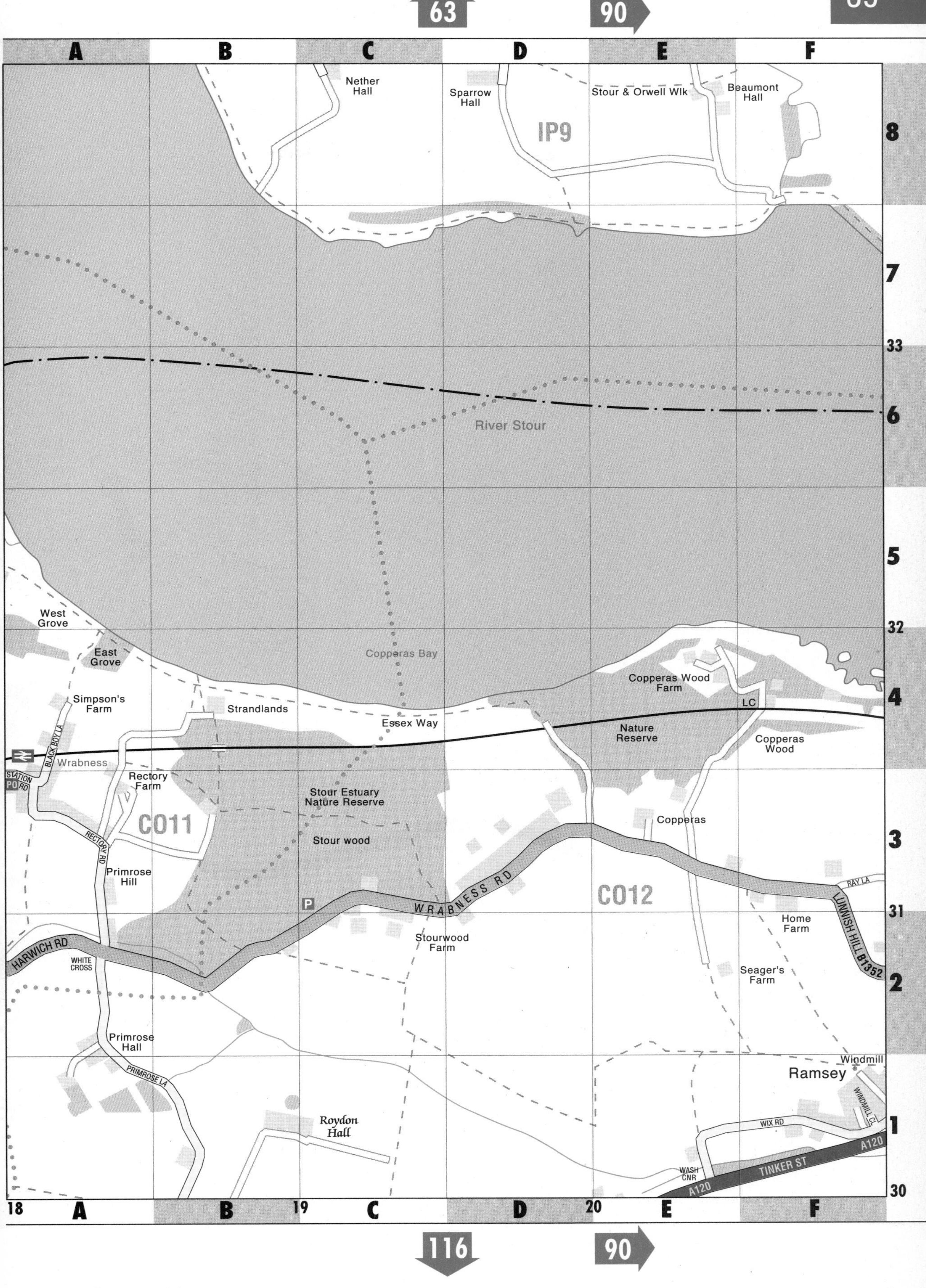
A
B
C
D
E
F
Nether Hall
Sparrow Hall
Stour & Orwell Wlk
Beaumont Hall
IP9
8
7
33
6
River Stour
5
West Grove
East Grove
32
Copperas Bay
Copperas Wood Farm
Simpson's Farm
Strandlands
LC
4
Essex Way
Nature Reserve
Copperas Wood
BLACK BOY LA
Wrabness
STATION RD
PO
Rectory Farm
Stour Estuary Nature Reserve
CO11
Copperas
3
RECTORY RD
Stour wood
Primrose Hill
P
WRABNESS RD
RAY LA
CO12
LUNNISH HILL B1352
31
Home Farm
HARWICH RD
WHITE CROSS
Stourwood Farm
Seager's Farm
2
Primrose Hall
PRIMROSE LA
Windmill
Ramsey
WINDMILL CL
Roydon Hall
WIX RD
1
A120
TINKER ST
WASH CNR
A120
30
18
19
20

116
90

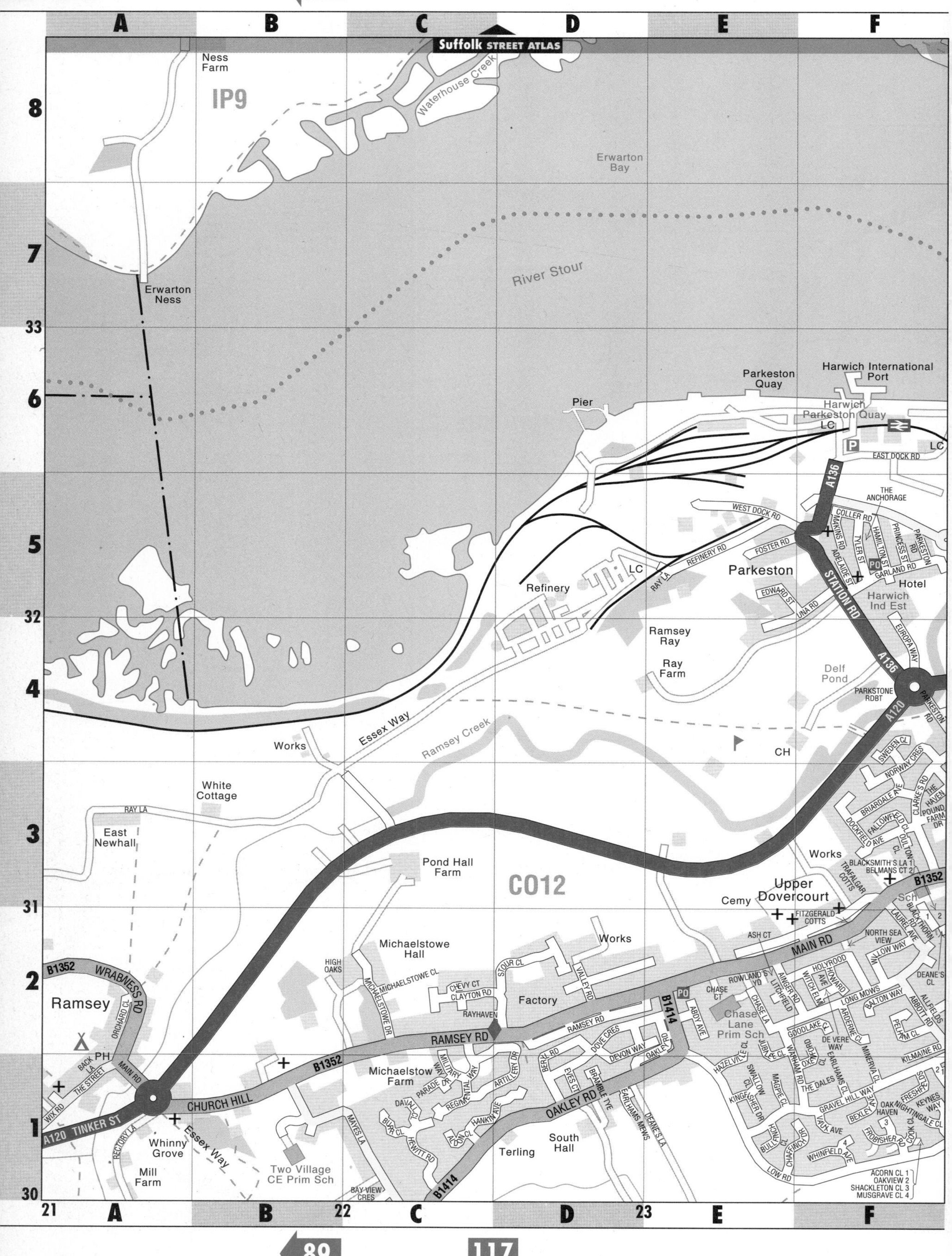

Suffolk STREET ATLAS

A **B** **C** **D** **E** **F**

8

IP9

Ness
Farm

Waterhouse Creek

Erwarton Bay

7

River Stour

Erwarton Ness

33

6

Pier

Parkeston
Quay

Harwich International
Port

Harwich
Parkeston Quay
LC

P

LC

EAST DOCK RD

A136

THE
ANCHORAGE

5

WEST DOCK RD

LC

Refinery

Ray La

REFINERY RD

FOSTER RD

COLLER RD

HAMILTON ST

RAE LADE ST

TYLER ST

PRINCESS
RD

PARKESTON RD

PO

GARLAND RD

Parkeston

Hotel

Harwich
Ind Est

EUROPA WAY

STATION RD

32

Ramsey
Ray

Ray
Farm

EDWARD RD

UNIA RD

Delf
Pond

PARKSTONE
RDBT

A120

PARKESTON RD

A136

4

Works

Essex Way

Ramsey Creek

CH

SWEDEN CL

NORWAY CRES

THE
HAVEN

POUND
FARM
DR

3

RAY LA

White
Cottage

Pond Hall
Farm

CO12

Upper
Dovercourt

Cemy

Works

BRIARDALE AVE

DOCKFIELD AVE

CLARKES RD

OULTON RD

B1352

Sch

East
Newhall

FITZGERALD
COTTS

BLACKSMITH'S LA 1
BELMANS CT 2

TRAFALGAR
RD

31

MAIN RD

NORTH SEA
VIEW

WILLOW WAY

DEANE'S CL

ALLFIELDS

2

B1352

WRABNESS RD

Ramsey

ORCHARD CL

THE STREET

MAIN RD

HIGH
OAKS

Michaelstowe
Hall

MICHAELSTOWE CL

MICHAELSTOWE DR

CHEVY CT

CLAYTON RD

RAYHAVEN

Works

STOUR CL

Y'LEY RD

Factory

RAMSEY RD

DOVE CRES

DEVON WAY

PO

B1414

ASH CT

CHASE
CT

ROWLAND'S YD

Chase
Lane
Prim Sch

HOLYROOD

ANGER RD

LITCHARD

HAZEL VIEW

WOBURN RD

LONG MDWS

HAWTHORN AVE

DE VERE CL

GOODLAKE

EARLHAMS CL

SWALLOW CL

KINGSMERE DR

MAGPIE CL

GRAVEL HILL WAY

THE DALES

PELHAM CL

MC

DEANE'S CL

KILMAINE RD

OAK FRESHFY

KEYNES
CL

TROUSHERS CT

HAVEN

VAUX AVE

1

A120

TINKER ST

CHURCH HILL

Essex Way

Whinny
Grove

RECTORY LA

Mill
Farm

BACK PH
LA

WIX RD

B1352

MILITARY
RD

MAYES LA

REGINAL RD

DAVAL CL

BVR CL

HEWITT RD

HANKYN AVE

ARTILLERY DR

BERS RD

EYES CL

OAKLEY RD

South
Hall

Terling

BRAMBLE TYE

DEANE'S LA

EARLHAMS MEWS

Two Village
CE Prim Sch

BAY VIEW
CRES

B1414

OLD RD

ROSS HAVEN

CHAFFCL

TUDOR CL

BULL

WHINFIELD AVE

LOW RD

ACORN CL 1
OAKVIEW 2
SHACKLETON CL 3
MUSGRAVE CL 4

30

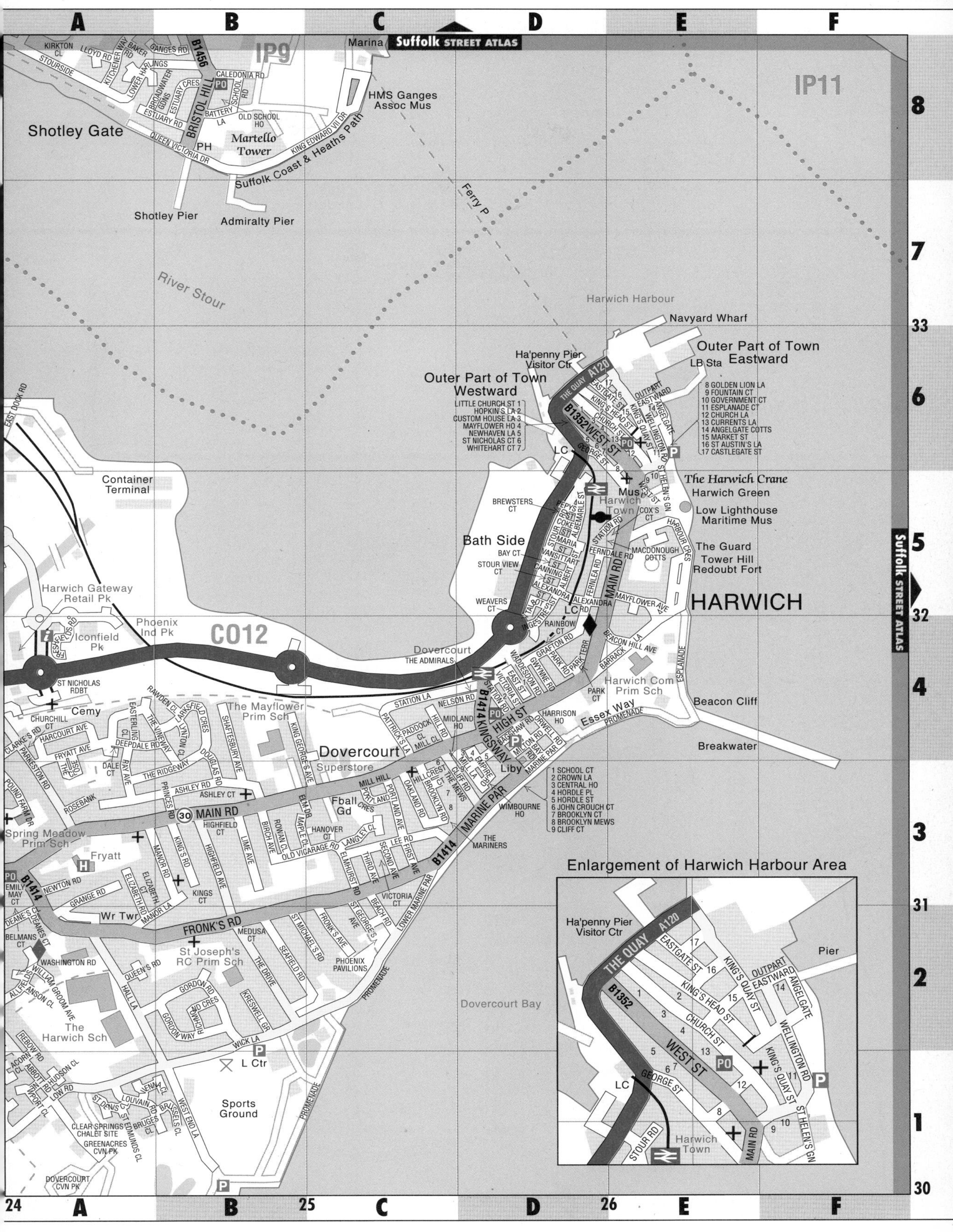
Suffolk STREET ATLAS
Shotley Gate
Martello Tower
Shotley Pier
Admiralty Pier
HMS Ganges Assoc Mus
River Stour
Harwich Harbour
Navyard Wharf
Outer Part of Town Eastward
Outer Part of Town Westward
Ha'penny Pier Visitor Ctr
LITTLE CHURCH ST 1
HOPKIN'S LA 2
CUSTOM HOUSE LA 3
MAYFLOWER HO 4
NEWHAVEN LA 5
ST NICHOLAS CT 6
WHITEHART CT 7
8 GOLDEN LION LA
9 FOUNTAIN CT
10 GOVERNMENT CT
11 ESPLANADE CT
12 CHURCH LA
13 CURRENTS LA
14 ANGELGATE COTTS
15 MARKET ST
16 ST AUSTIN'S LA
17 CASTLEGATE ST
The Harwich Crane
Harwich Green
Low Lighthouse Maritime Mus
The Guard Tower Hill Redoubt Fort
Container Terminal
Bath Side
Harwich Gateway Retail Pk
Phoenix Ind Pk
Iconfield Pk
CO12
HARWICH
Dovercourt
The Mayflower Prim Sch
Harwich Com Prim Sch
Beacon Cliff
Breakwater
1 SCHOOL CT
2 CROWN LA
3 CENTRAL HO
4 HORDLE PL
5 HORDLE ST
6 JOHN CROUCH CT
7 BROOKLYN CT
8 BROOKLYN MEWS
9 CLIFF CT
Spring Meadow Prim Sch
Fryatt
St Joseph's RC Prim Sch
The Harwich Sch
Sports Ground
Dovercourt Bay
Enlargement of Harwich Harbour Area
IP9
IP11
24
25
26
30
31
32
33

65

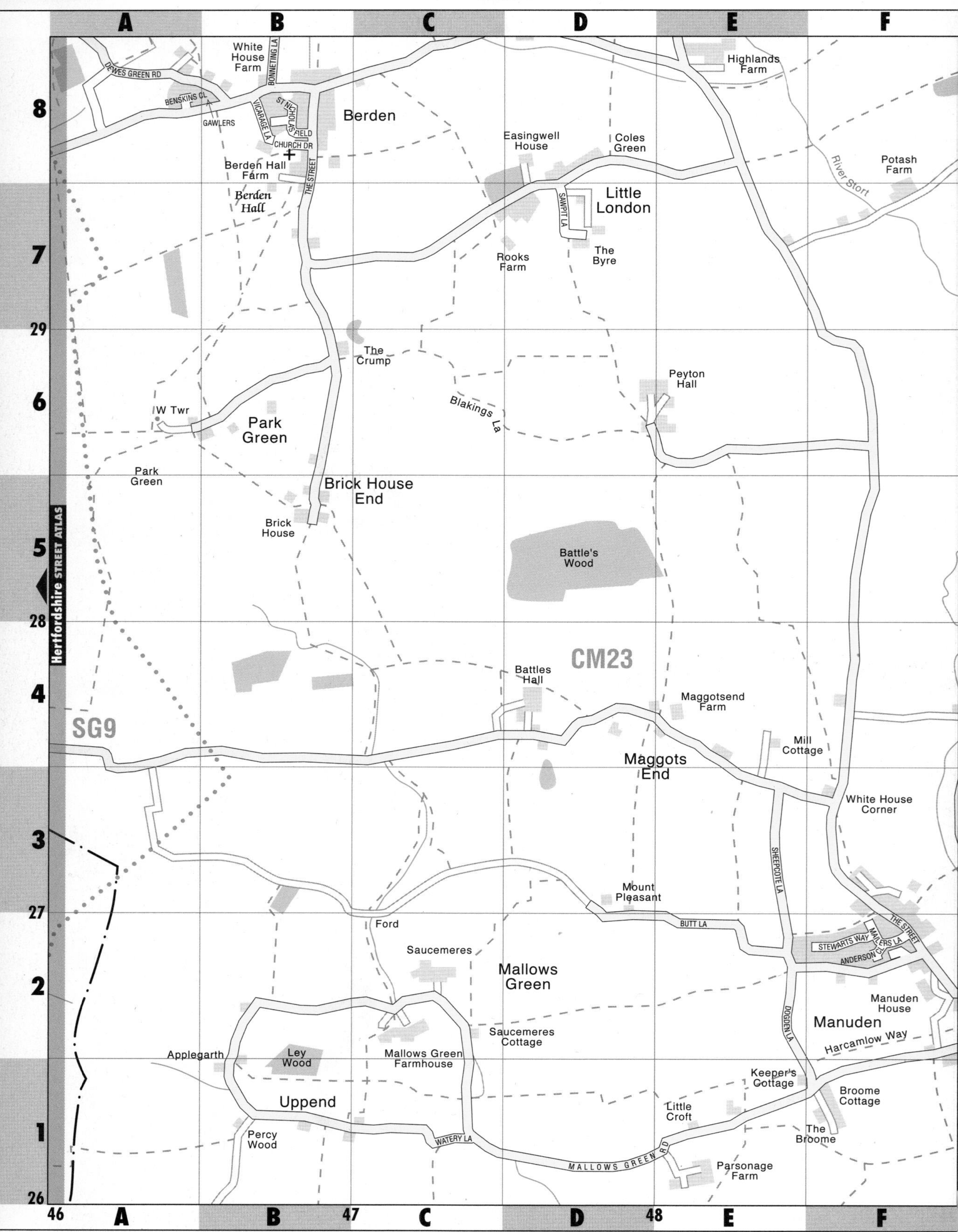

A
B
C
D
E
F
8
7
29
6
5
28
4
3
27
2
1
26
46
47
48
White House Farm
BONNETING LA
DEWES GREEN RD
BENSKINS CL
GAWLERS
VICARAGE LA
ST NICHOLAS FIELD
CHURCH DR
THE STREET
Berden
Berden Hall Farm
Berden Hall
Easingwell House
Coles Green
Highlands Farm
Potash Farm
River Stort
Little London
SAWPIT LA
The Byre
Rooks Farm
The Crump
W Twr
Park Green
Park Green
Blakings La
Peyton Hall
Brick House End
Brick House
Battle's Wood
Hertfordshire STREET ATLAS
CM23
SG9
Battles Hall
Maggotsend Farm
Mill Cottage
Maggots End
White House Corner
SHEEPCOTE LA
Mount Pleasant
BUTT LA
Ford
Saucemeres
Mallows Green
STEWARTS WAY
MAILERS LA
ANDERSON CL
THE STREET
Manuden House
Manuden
Harcamlow Way
DOGDEN LA
Saucemeres Cottage
Applegarth
Ley Wood
Mallows Green Farmhouse
Keeper's Cottage
Broome Cottage
Uppend
Little Croft
Percy Wood
WATERY LA
MALLOWS GREEN RD
The Broome
Parsonage Farm

118

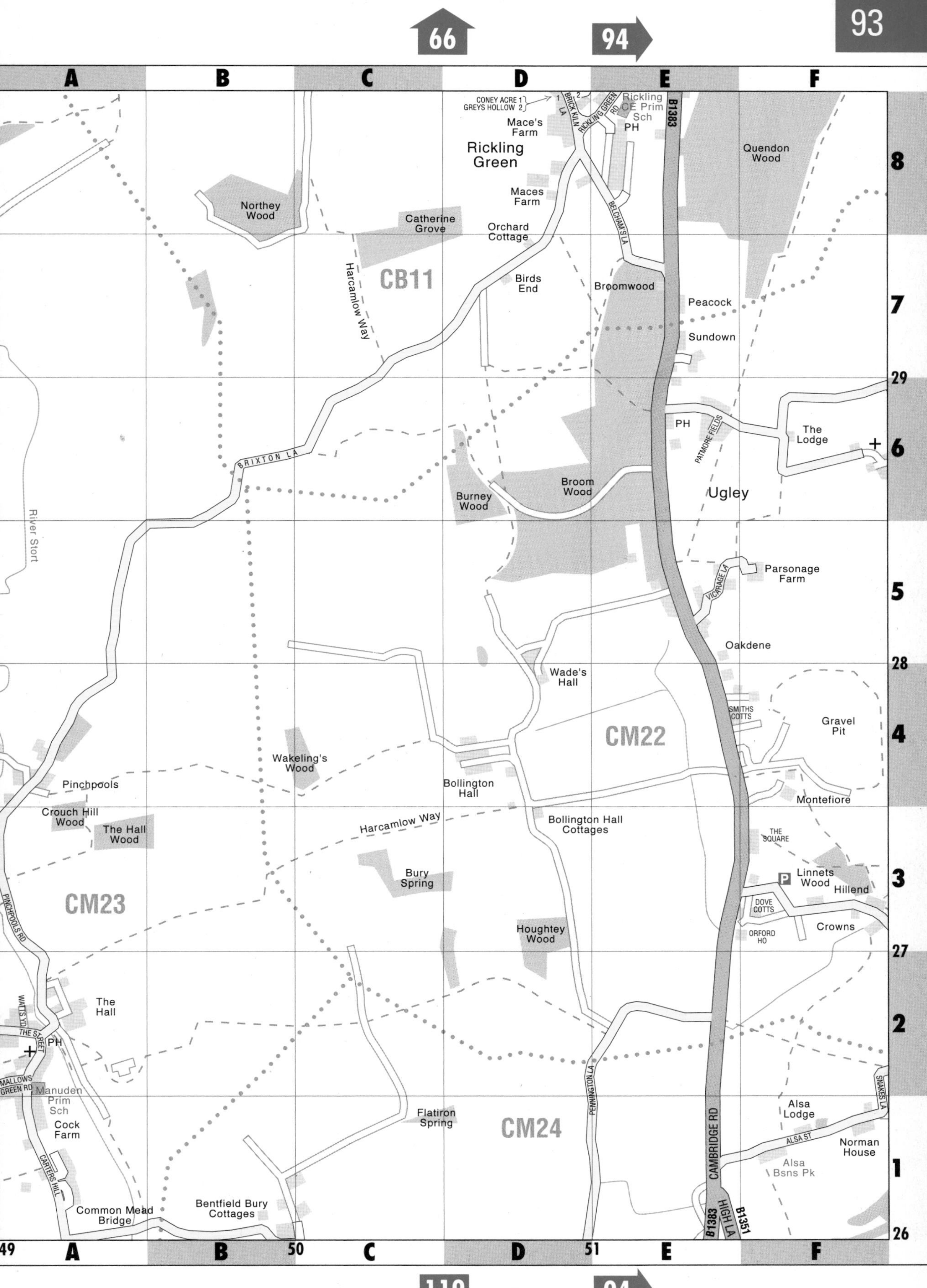

A B C D E F

8
7
29
6
5
28
4
3
27
2
1
26

CONEY ACRE 1
GREYS HOLLOW 2

Rickling
Green

Mace's
Farm

Maces
Farm

Catherine
Grove

Northey
Wood

Orchard
Cottage

Birds
End

CB11

Harcamlow Way

BRIXTON LA

River Stort

Broomwood

Quendon
Wood

Rickling
CE Prim
Sch
PH

BELCHAM'S LA

B1383

Peacock

Sundown

PH

PATMORE FIELDS

The
Lodge

Burney
Wood

Broom
Wood

Ugley

VICARAGE LA

Parsonage
Farm

Oakdene

Wade's
Hall

CM22

SMITHS
COTTS

Gravel
Pit

Wakeling's
Wood

Bollington
Hall

Bollington Hall
Cottages

Montefiore

THE
SQUARE

Pinchpools

Crouch Hill
Wood

The Hall
Wood

Harcamlow Way

CM23

Bury
Spring

Houghtey
Wood

P Linnets
Wood
Hillend

DOVE
COTTS

ORFORD
HO

Crowns

PINCHPOOLS RD

The
Hall

WATTS LN

THE STREET
PH

MALLOWS
GREEN RD

Manuden
Prim
Sch

Cock
Farm

CARTERS HILL

Flatiron
Spring

CM24

PENNINGTON LA

CAMBRIDGE RD

Alsa
Lodge

SNAKES LA

ALSA ST

Alsa
Bsns Pk

Norman
House

Common Mead
Bridge

Bentfield Bury
Cottages

B1383

HIGH LA

B1351

49 A B 50 C D 51 E F

93 67

A B C D E F

8 7 29 6 5 28 4 3 27 2 1 26

CB11

Fivefoot Bridge
M11
NORTH HALL RD
CH
LC
The White House
River Cam or Granta
Sheepcote La
Meadside
Ugley Hall Farm Cottages
Ugley Hall Farm
Down Hall House
Birds Farm
The Cock (PH)
Henham
CHURCH ST
THE CHASE
PO
HIGH ST
STARR RD
HALL CL
HIGHFIELDS
Parsonage Farm
CROW ST
Hazelmoor Common
OLD MEAD RD
CM22
Birch Grove
Bacons Farm
PIMBLETT ROW
CARTERS LA
SAGES
SCHOOL LA
The Vicarage
Henham & Ugley Prim Sch
VERNONS CL
Old Mead
OLD MEAD LA
Playing Field
Church Common
Mast
MILL RD
Works
Byculla
The Mill House
Mill Pond Farm
Fieldgate Farm House
FIELD GATE LA
Ugley Green
Hudsons Farm
Bedwell Common
MILL RD B1051
Ugley Park
The Hermitage
BEDWELL RD
MAYTREE GDNS
SPENCER CL
GOLD CL
JENKINS DR
Golds Nursery Bsns Pk
P
LC
Elsenham
FENMAN CT
NEW RD
HUNTERS CT
ALSA LEYS
ALSA GDNS
CRANMORE CL
DELLOWS LA
SNAKES LA
Sand Pit
Pennington Hall
HENHAM RD
Harewood
BROOM FARM RD
ELM CL
RIDLEY GDNS
STATION RD
DE MANDEVILLE RD
OZIERS
MARKWELLS
CORRIANDER DR
PARK RD
HAILES WOOD
Alsa Wood
Driving Range
CH
Elsenham
THE CROFT
The Crown (PH)
Mast
P
Playing Field
FOURWAYS
PAGET CT
HIGH ST
HAILES WOOD CL
ELSENHAM CROSS
Elsenham Place
Stansted Brook
LEIGH DR
Alsa Wood Cottage
Aubrey Buxton Nature Reserve
STANSTED RD
PO
GLEBE END
THE GLEBE
ROBIN HOOD RD
GILBEY COTTS
MILL CL
Elsenham CE Prim Sch
HALL RD
CM24
MAY WLK
May Tree Farm
Nursery
SAUNDERS CL
RUSH LA
The Old Vicarage
Abbotsford Bridge
B1051
M11

52 A B 53 C D 54 E F

93 120

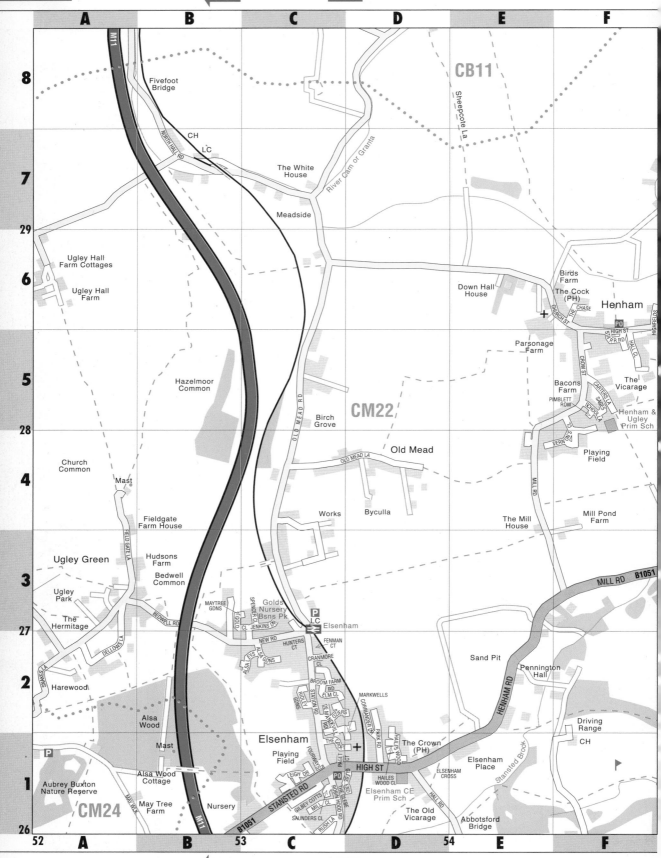

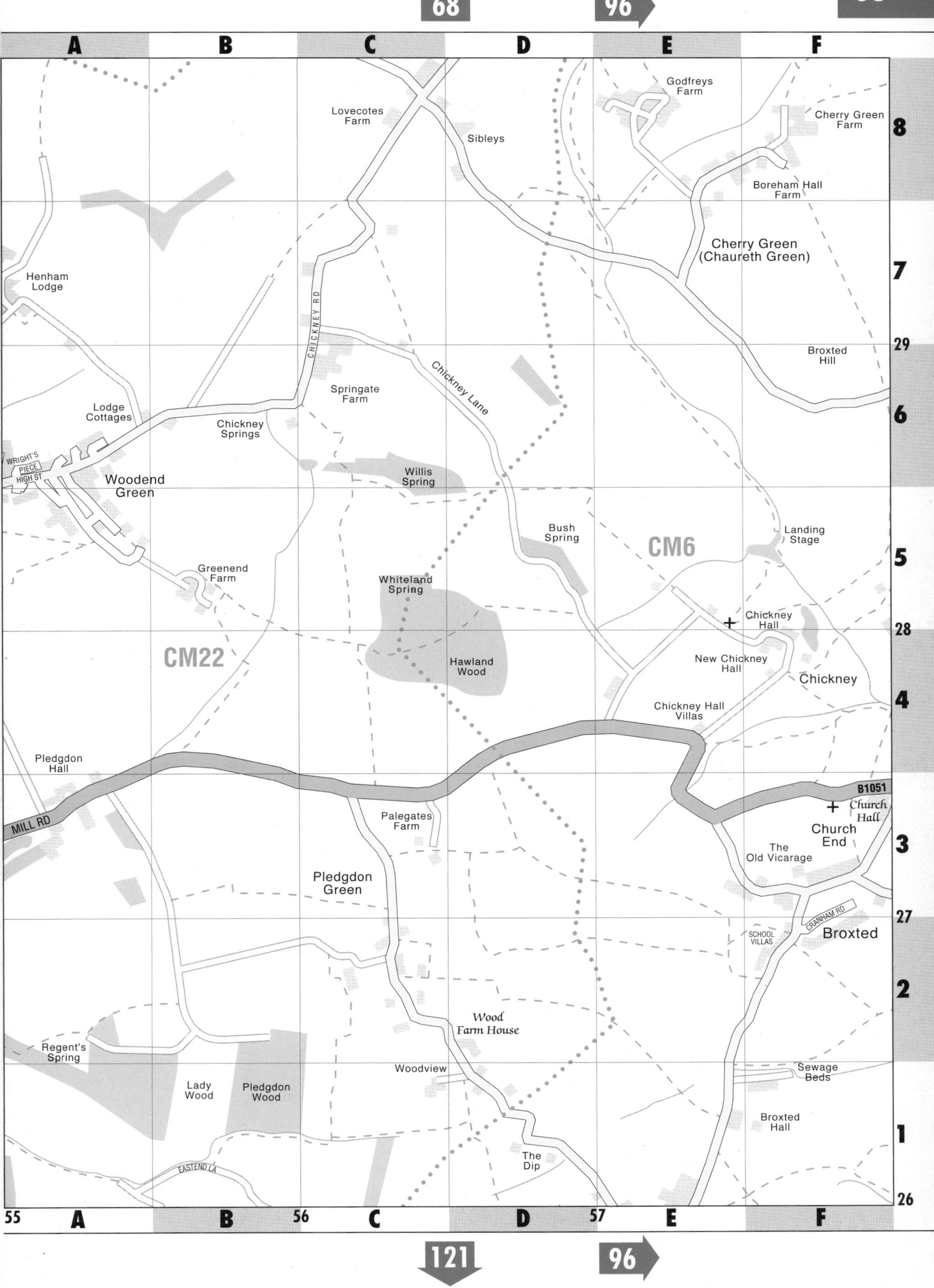

68
96
121
96

A B C D E F

8
7
29
6
5
28
4
3
27
2
1
26

Godfreys Farm
Cherry Green Farm
Lovecotes Farm
Sibleys
Boreham Hall Farm
Cherry Green (Chaureth Green)
Henham Lodge
Broxted Hill
CHICKNEY RD
Chickney Lane
Lodge Cottages
Springate Farm
Chickney Springs
WRIGHT'S PIECE
HIGH ST
Woodend Green
Willis Spring
Bush Spring
CM6
Landing Stage
Greenend Farm
Whiteland Spring
Chickney Hall
CM22
Hawland Wood
New Chickney Hall
Chickney
Chickney Hall Villas
Pledgdon Hall
B1051
MILL RD
Palegates Farm
Church Hall
Church End
The Old Vicarage
Pledgdon Green
SCHOOL VILLAS
CRANHAM RD
Broxted
Wood Farm House
Regent's Spring
Woodview
Sewage Beds
Lady Wood
Pledgdon Wood
Broxted Hall
EASTEND LA
The Dip

55 A B 56 C D 57 E F

A B C D E F

8

Brown's Wood

Home Wood

Stan Brook

Hill Farm

Dairygreen Farm

B1051

Warrens Wood

Brickmead

Buckingham's Farm

Stanbrook

7

Horham Hall

Armigers Farm

29

Armigers

Hammer Hill Farm

Hart's Grove

Sharpes Farm

FOLLY MILL LA

6

Sucksted Green

The Stepps

Follymill

River Chelmer

Delfits La

CM6

Broadfans Farm

Harcamlow Way

5

Chaureth Hall Farm

28

Broadwater Bridge

4

Hill Pasture

B 1051

Walters Cottage

Brick House Farm

Tingates

Wolsey's Farm

Lower Barn

Tilty Hill Farm

3

Coldharbour Farm

Eseley Wood

Duton Hill

27

Coldharbour Villas

Dutonhill Bridge

Duton Hill Farm

PH

ABBEY VIEW

2

The Maltings

Malting Bridge

Home Wood

Mill

Tilty

The Grange

1

Moor End Farm

26

58 A B 59 C D 60 E F

70
98

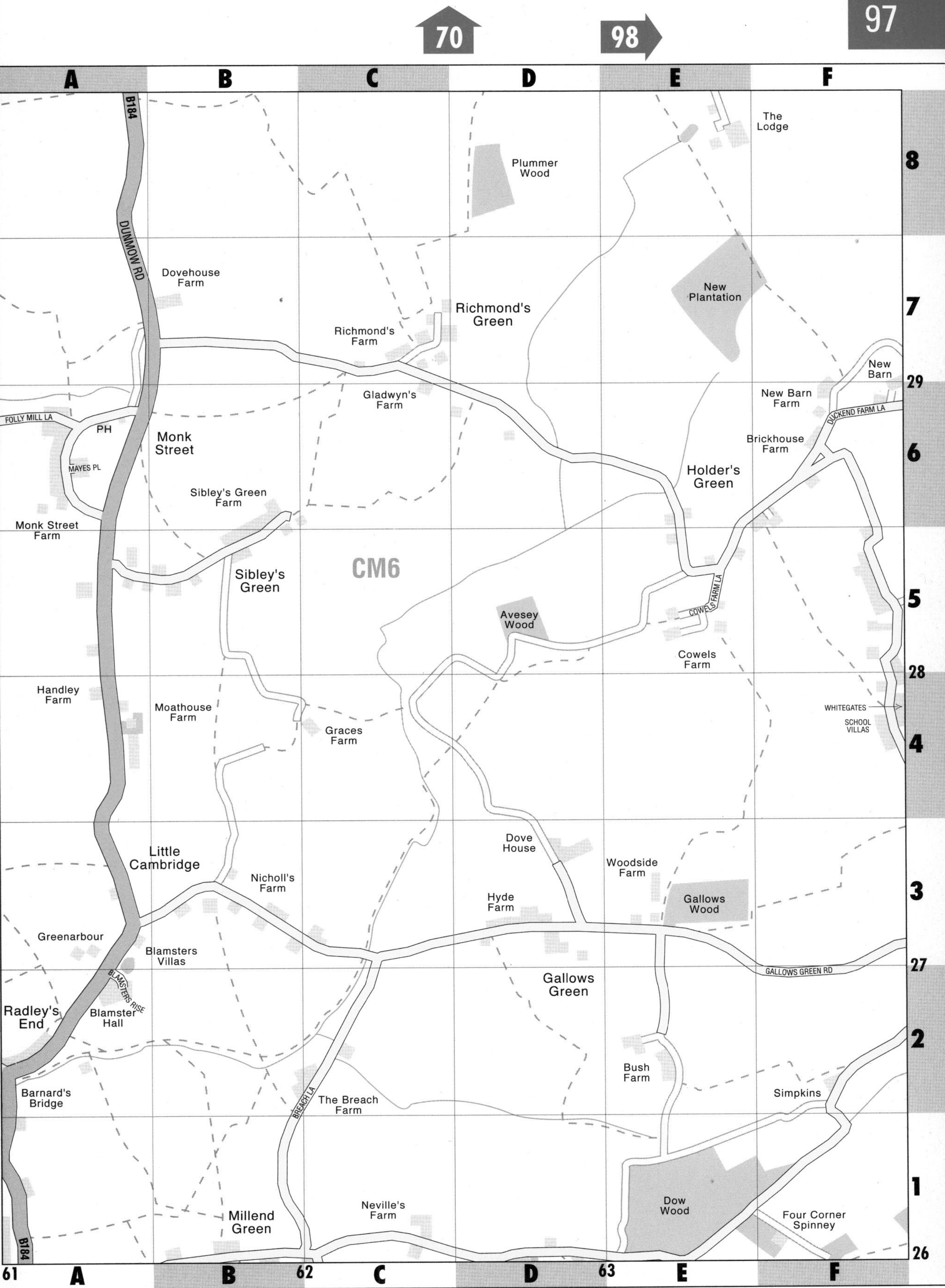
A
B
C
D
E
F
8
7
29
6
5
28
4
3
27
2
1
26
61
62
63
B184
DUNMOW RD
The Lodge
Plummer Wood
Dovehouse Farm
Richmond's Green
Richmond's Farm
New Plantation
New Barn
New Barn Farm
Gladwyn's Farm
FOLLY MILL LA
PH
Monk Street
MAYES PL
DUCKEND FARM LA
Brickhouse Farm
Holder's Green
Sibley's Green Farm
Monk Street Farm
CM6
Sibley's Green
COWELS FARM LA
Avesey Wood
Cowels Farm
Handley Farm
Moathouse Farm
Graces Farm
WHITEGATES
SCHOOL VILLAS
Dove House
Little Cambridge
Nicholl's Farm
Woodside Farm
Hyde Farm
Gallows Wood
Greenarbour
Blamsters Villas
GALLOWS GREEN RD
Gallows Green
BLAMSTERS RISE
Radley's End
Blamster Hall
Bush Farm
Barnard's Bridge
BREACH LA
The Breach Farm
Simpkins
Dow Wood
Neville's Farm
Millend Green
Four Corner Spinney

123
98

97
71

A B C D E F

8

7

CM7

29

Duck End
Farm

6

Bustard Green Lane

Bustard
Green

Charity
Farm

Oxen
End

The Grove

Fann's
Farm

Coft
Hall

Frenches
Farm

5

Porridge
Hall

Templars

28

Daisyley Brook

DAISYLEY RD

Brazenhead
Farm

4

CM6

Page's
Farm

Tolladay's
Farm

Pratt's
Farm

LUBBERHEDGES LA

3

Lindsell

Church
End

GALLOWS GREEN RD

LINDSELL LA

27

Goland's
Bridge

Poplar
Farm

2

Carter's
Farm

Hill
Farm

Stebbing Brook

Holt's
Farm

1

Lashley
Hall

Duck End

B1057

26

64 A B 65 C 66 D E F

Markswood
Farm

DUNMOW RD

B1057

Drakeswell

97
124

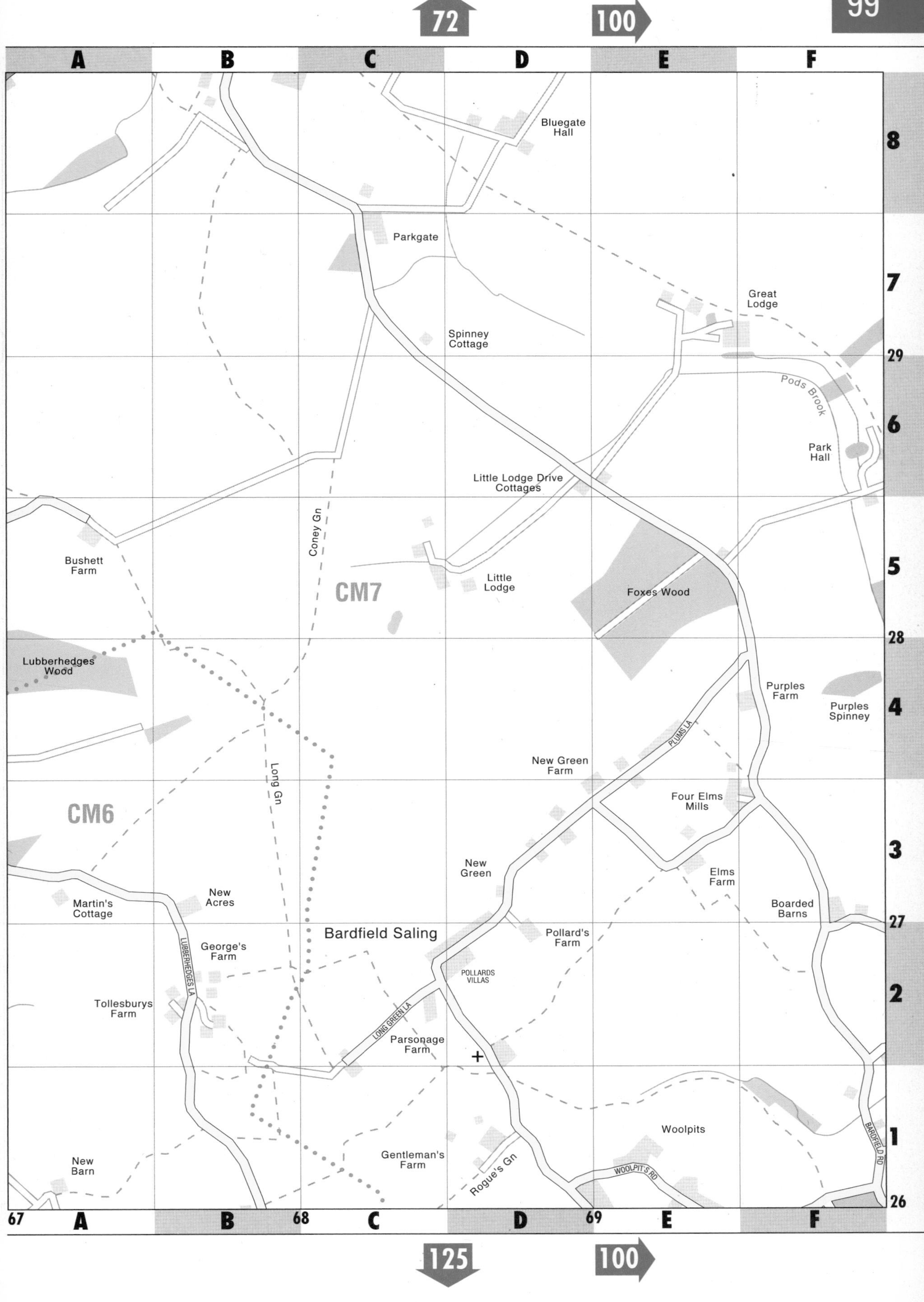

72
100

Bluegate
Hall

Parkgate

Great
Lodge

Spinney
Cottage

29

Pods Brook

Little Lodge Drive
Cottages

Park
Hall

Coney Gn

Bushett
Farm

CM7

Little
Lodge

Foxes Wood

Lubberhedges
Wood

28

Purples
Farm

Purples
Spinney

Long Gn

New Green
Farm

Four Elms
Mills

CM6

New
Green

Elms
Farm

Martin's
Cottage

New
Acres

Boarded
Barns

27

George's
Farm

Bardfield Saling

Pollard's
Farm

LUBBERHEDGES LA

POLLARDS
VILLAS

Tollesburys
Farm

LONG GREEN LA

Parsonage
Farm

+

BARDFIELD RD

Woolpits

New
Barn

Gentleman's
Farm

Rogue's Gn

WOOLPIT'S RD

26

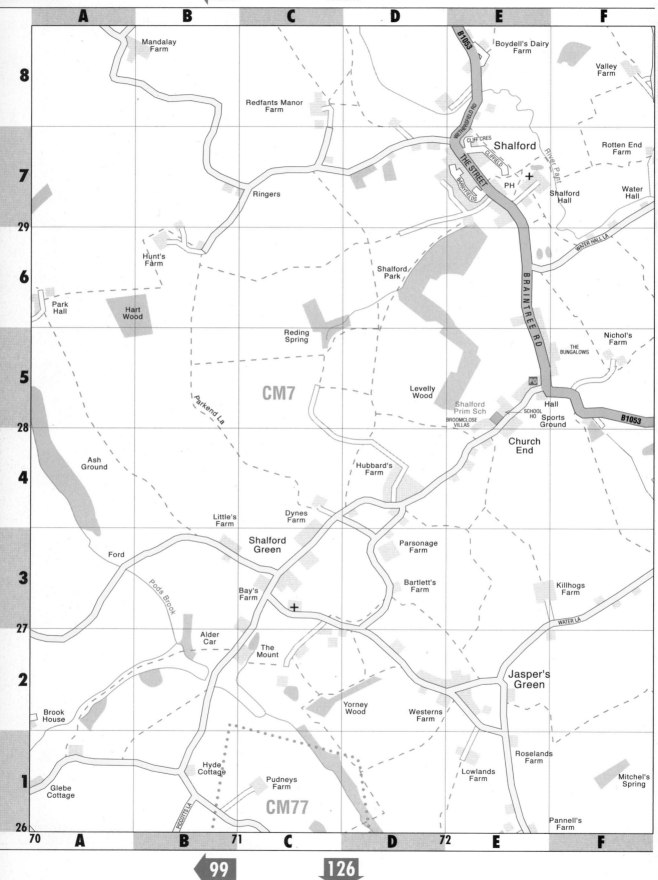

A B C D E F

8

Mandalay Farm

Redfants Manor Farm

B1053

Boydell's Dairy Farm

Valley Farm

WETHERSFIELD RD

CLIFF CRES

CLIFFIELD

Shalford

Rotten End Farm

River Pant

7

Ringers

THE STREET

BRAYFIELDS

PH

Shalford Hall

Water Hall

29

Hunt's Farm

Shalford Park

WATER HALL LA

6

Park Hall

Hart Wood

Reding Spring

Shalford Park

BRAINTREE RD

THE BUNGALOWS

Nichol's Farm

5

CM7

Parkend La

Levelly Wood

Shalford Prim Sch

BROOMCLOSE VILLAS

SCHOOL HO

PO

Hall

Sports Ground

B1053

28

Ash Ground

Church End

4

Hubbard's Farm

Little's Farm

Dynes Farm

Shalford Green

Parsonage Farm

Killhogs Farm

3

Ford

Pods Brook

Bay's Farm

Bartlett's Farm

WATER LA

27

Alder Car

The Mount

Jasper's Green

2

Brook House

Yorney Wood

Westerns Farm

Roselands Farm

1

Glebe Cottage

Hyde Cottage

Pudneys Farm

CM77

Lowlands Farm

Mitchel's Spring

PIGGOTTS LA

Pannell's Farm

26

70 A B 71 C D 72 E F

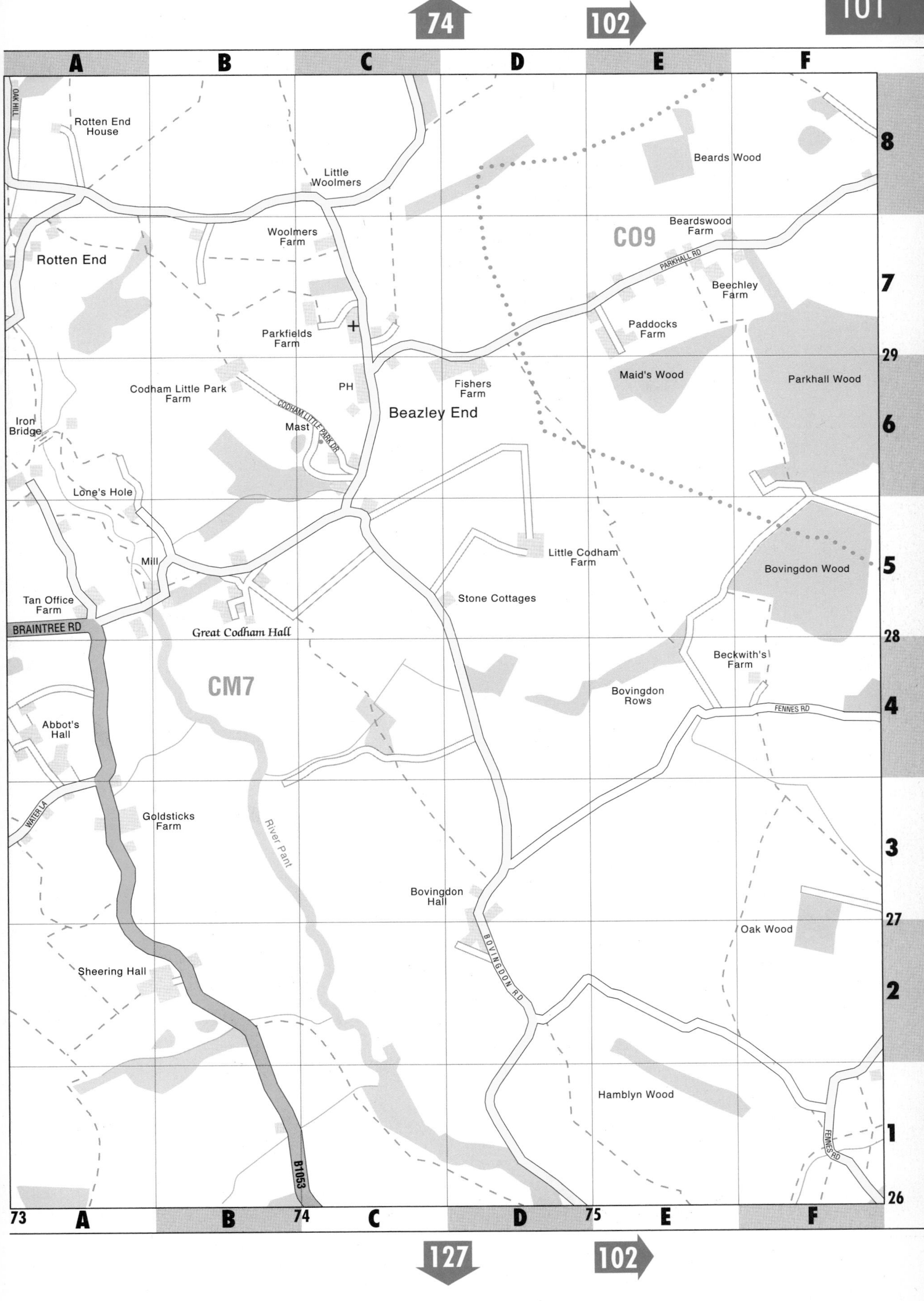

A B C D E F

Oak Hill

Rotten End House

Little Woolmers

Beards Wood

8

Woolmers Farm

CO9

Beardswood Farm

PARKHALL RD

Rotten End

7

Beechley Farm

Parkfields Farm

Paddocks Farm

29

Codham Little Park Farm

PH

Maid's Wood

Parkhall Wood

Mast

Fishers Farm

Beazley End

6

Iron Bridge

CODHAM LITTLE PARK DR

Lone's Hole

Little Codham Farm

Bovingdon Wood

5

Mill

Stone Cottages

28

Tan Office Farm

Great Codham Hall

Beckwith's Farm

BRAINTREE RD

CM7

Bovingdon Rows

FENNES RD

4

Abbot's Hall

WATER LA

Goldsticks Farm

River Pant

3

Oak Wood

27

Bovingdon Hall

BOVINGDON RD

Sheering Hall

2

Hamblyn Wood

FENNES RD

1

B1053

26

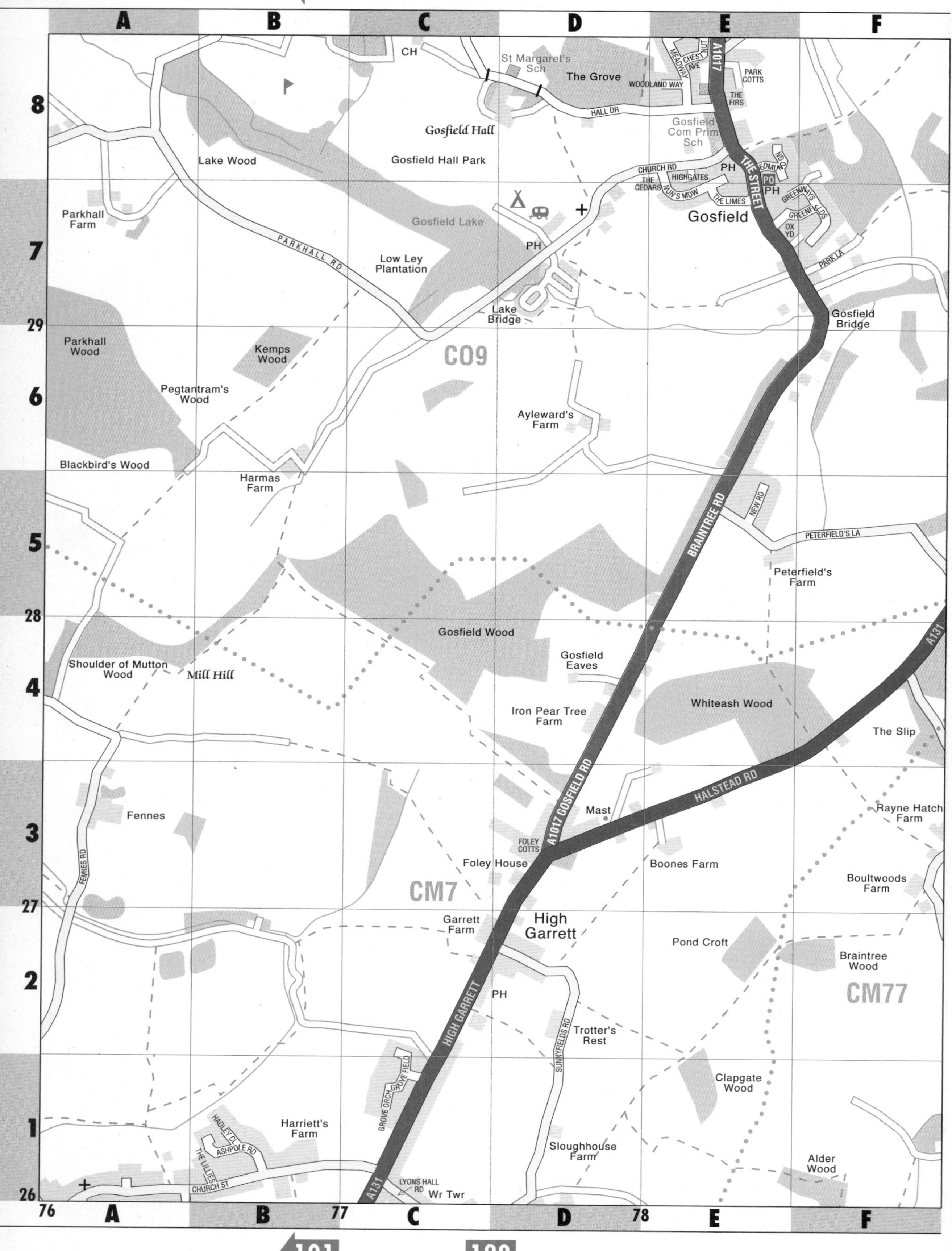

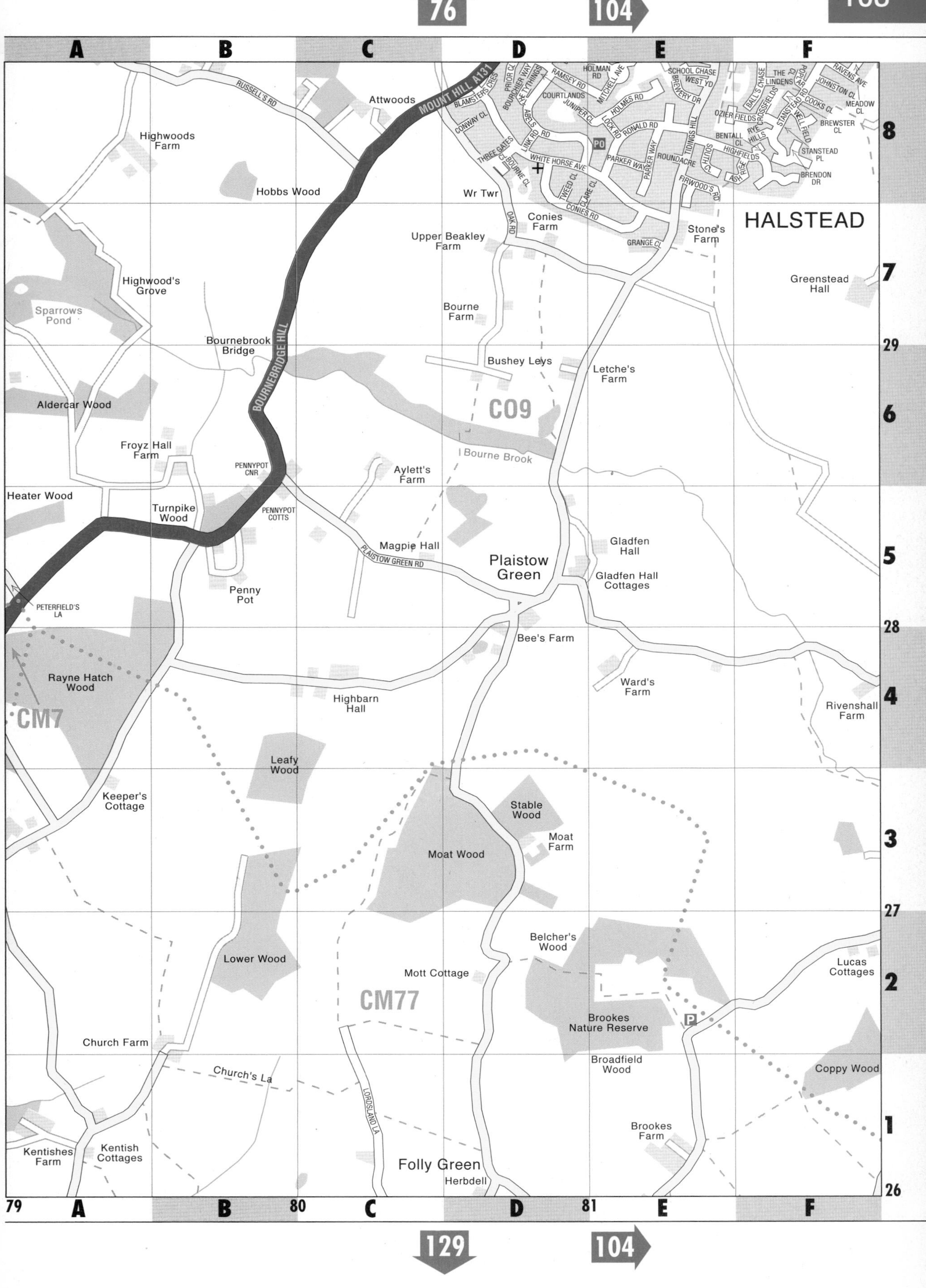

HALSTEAD

CO9

CM7

CM77

Locations and labels:

Russell's Rd
Highwoods Farm
Hobbs Wood
Attwoods
MOUNT HILL A131
Highwood's Grove
Sparrows Pond
Bournebrook Bridge
Aldercar Wood
BOURNEBRIDGE HILL
Froyz Hall Farm
PENNYPOT CNR
Heater Wood
Turnpike Wood
PENNYPOT COTTS
PETERFIELD'S LA
Penny Pot
PLAISTOW GREEN RD
Magpie Hall
Rayne Hatch Wood
Keeper's Cottage
Leafy Wood
Highbarn Hall
Lower Wood
Moat Wood
Mott Cottage
Church Farm
Church's La
LORDSLAND LA
Kentishes Farm
Kentish Cottages
Folly Green
Herbdell

Upper Beakley Farm
Conies Farm
Wr Twr
Bourne Farm
Bushey Leys
Bourne Brook
Aylett's Farm
Plaistow Green
Bee's Farm
Stable Wood
Moat Farm
Belcher's Wood
Brookes Nature Reserve
Broadfield Wood
Brookes Farm

Stone's Farm
GRANGE CL
Letche's Farm
Gladfen Hall
Gladfen Hall Cottages
Ward's Farm

Greenstead Hall
Rivenshall Farm
Lucas Cottages
Coppy Wood

Halstead street names:
PRIOR CL
BOURCHIER WAY
RAMSEY CL
HOLMAN RD
MITCHELL AVE
SCHOOL CHASE
WEST YD
BREWERY DR
THE LINDENS
RAVENS AVE
JOHNSTON CL
MEADOW CL
BLAMSTERS CRES
CONWAY CL
JUNIPER CL
COURTLANDS
HOLMES RD
BALL'S CHASE
COOKS CL
BREWSTER CL
THREE GATES
ABEL'S RD
LIME CL
LOCK RD
RONALD RD
OZIER FIELDS
CRESSELFS
STANSTEAD
WELFIELD
WHITE HORSE AVE
TWEED CL
CLARE CL
PO
PARKER WAY
RYE
HIGHFIELDS
HILLS
STANSTEAD PL
OAK RD
CONIES RD
FIRWOOD'S RD
BENTALL CL
SMITH CL
ASH
BRENDON DR

Grid references (right edge): 8, 7, 29, 6, 5, 28, 4, 3, 27, 2, 1, 26

Grid references (columns): A, B, C, D, E, F

103
77

A   B   C   D   E   F

8

A1124

COLCHESTER RD

Blue Bridge

Bluebridge
Farmhouse

Langley Mill

Elms Hall

ELMS HALL RD

Munn's Farm

Sewage
Works

River Colne

Riverside
Bsns Pk

STATION RD

DE VERE RD

7

Lodge

PARLEY BEAMS
COTTS

STONEBRIDGE HILL

Stonebridge
Hill

Stone Bridge

HALSTEAD RD

A1124

ATLAS RD

GREEN CT

DUDLEY RD

29

Parley Beams
Farm

THE
KENNELS

HUNT RD

6

Stanstead
Hall

Bullock Wood

Don Johns

Ash
Bottom

+

CHURCH RD

Greenstead
Green

STONE
COTTS

Warren
Farm

CO6

Homely Ash
Grounds

5

Nightingale
Hall

28

Greenstead
Green Farm

CROCKLANDS

PO

CO9

BURTON'S GREEN RD

New Wood

Bourne Brook

NEWHOUSE RD

4

The
Grange

Nightingale
Hall Farm

Keepers

3

Perces

Home
Farm

Whitings

Lodge
Farm

Landing
Strip

27

Tyler's
Wood

Long Ley
Grove

CH

2

Clavering's
Farm

Burton's Green

Villa Farm

Riefields

Mann's
Farm

Cleveland
Wood

Markshall Wood

Ind Est

LANCASTER WAY

HALIFAX WAY

1

NUNTY'S LA

Great Nunty's
Farm

Nunty's Wood

Lily Wood

Deer Park

Thrift Wood

CM77

26

82   A   B   83   C   D   84   E   F

103
130

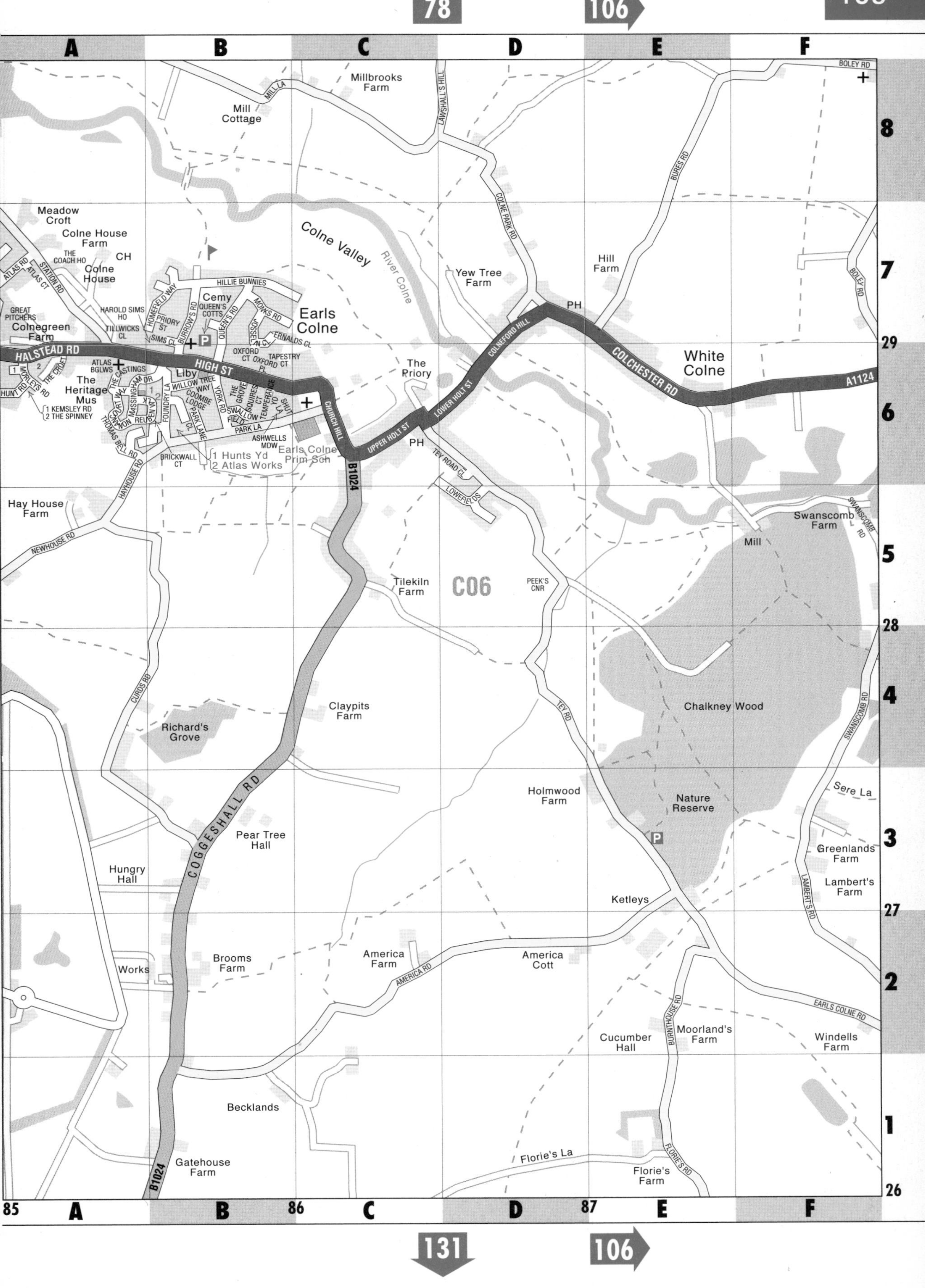

A B C D E F

8

BOLEY RD

Mill Cottage

Millbrooks Farm

LAWSHALL'S HILL

COLNE PARK RD

BURES RD

BOLEY RD

7

Meadow Croft
Colne House Farm
THE COACH HO
CH
Colne House

Yew Tree Farm

Hill Farm

COLNEFORD HILL

PH

Earls Colne

Colne Valley

River Colne

29

Halstead RD
ATLAS BGLWS
HIGH ST
HILLIE BUNNIES
Cemy
Queen's Cotts
MONKS RD

White Colne

COLCHESTER RD

A1124

6

GREAT PITCHERS
Colnegreen Farm
The Heritage Mus
1 KEMSLEY RD
2 THE SPINNEY

The Priory

LOWER HOLT ST

CHURCH HILL

UPPER HOLT ST

PH

TEY ROAD CL

LOWER CL

Earls Colne Prim Sch
1 Hunts Yd
2 Atlas Works

Hay House Farm

NEWHOUSE RD

B1024

Tilekiln Farm

C06

PEEK'S CNR

Swanscomb Farm

SWANSCOMB RD

Mill

5

28

HANTHOUSE RD

CURDS RD

Richard's Grove

Claypits Farm

TEY RD

Chalkney Wood

SWANSCOMB RD

4

Sere La

Pear Tree Hall

Holmwood Farm

Nature Reserve

Greenlands Farm

Lambert's Farm

LAMBERT'S RD

3

COGGESHALL RD

Hungry Hall

Ketleys

27

Works

Brooms Farm

America Farm

AMERICA RD

America Cott

EARLS COLNE RD

2

BURNTHOUSE RD

Moorland's Farm

Cucumber Hall

FLORIE'S RD

Windells Farm

1

Becklands

B1024

Gatehouse Farm

Florie's La

Florie's Farm

26

105
79

A   B   C   D   E   F

8

Bart Hall

Friday's Cottage

Myrtle Villa

Janke's Green

Lane Farm

BURES RD

Thornfield Wood

7

Alder Car

Acorn Wood

Norton Hall Farm

Prales Belt

LANE RD

Iris Plantation

Oldhouse Farm

New Wood

29

Fox & Pheasant Farm

Wakes Hall Farm

East Anglian Rly Mus

BOLEY RD

A1124

TYBURN HILL

Wakes Hall Bsns Ctr

Wakes Colne House

Wakes Colne

Chappel & Wakes Colne

SPRING GARDENS RD

6

Wakes Hall

WAKES ST

NEW COTTS

STATION RD

Pontisbright Cotts

The Claypits

Old Hall Farm

Mills

CHAPPEL CNR

PO

PH

Crepping Hall

CO6

THE STREET

Chappel CE Prim Sch

Rose Green Cotts

VERNONS RD

5

Chappel

CHAPPEL HILL

SWAN GR

ALLEN COTTS

COLCHESTER RD

Rose Green

Vernons

28

Hill House

River Colne

SWANSCOMBE RD

4

Hickmore Fen

POPE'S RD

Pope's Hall

Broom House

A1124

Priory House

PRIORY RD

OAK RD

SWAN ST

Oaklands

Swan Street

Essex Way

3

Croft Cottage

Jenny Barn

BACON'S LA

Bacon's Farm

27

Spendpenny Farm

Pattock's Farm

Wick Grove

2

Woolfney Wood

PATTOCK'S LA

Wick Farm

LAMBERT'S RD

Teycross Farm

Mast

Marshalls Farm House

CHAPPEL RD

Smythers Farm

EARLS COLNE RD

Hoe Wood

1

Newbarn

LANGLEYS

Bett's Farm

Checkley's Farm

NEWBARN RD

LOWER LANGLEY

Great Tey CE Prim Sch

WINDMILLS

MOOR RD

CHR'SMUND WAY

FARMFIELD RD

SCH FIELD WAY

TEY RD

TEY RD

26

88   A   B   89   C   D   90   E   F

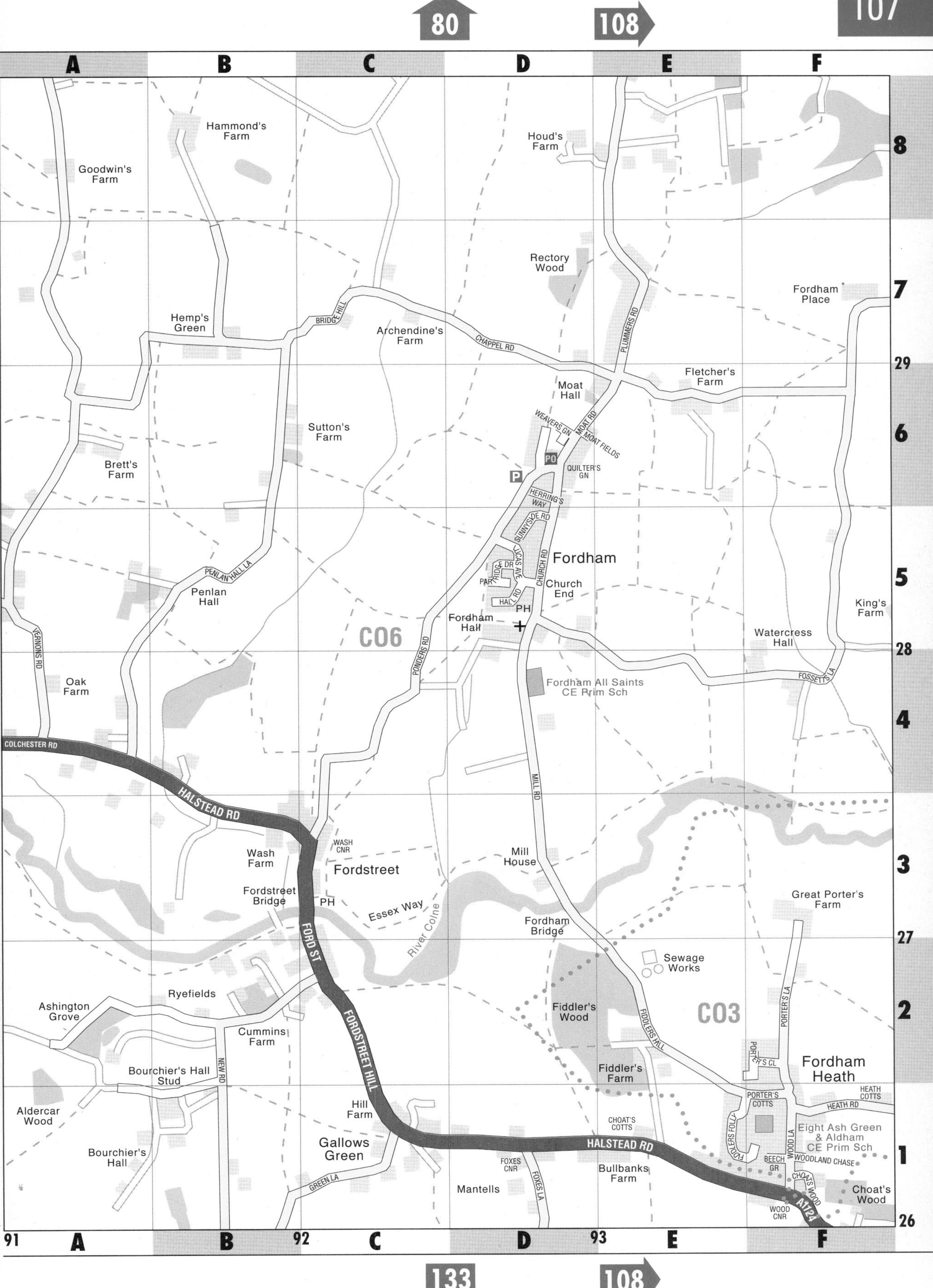

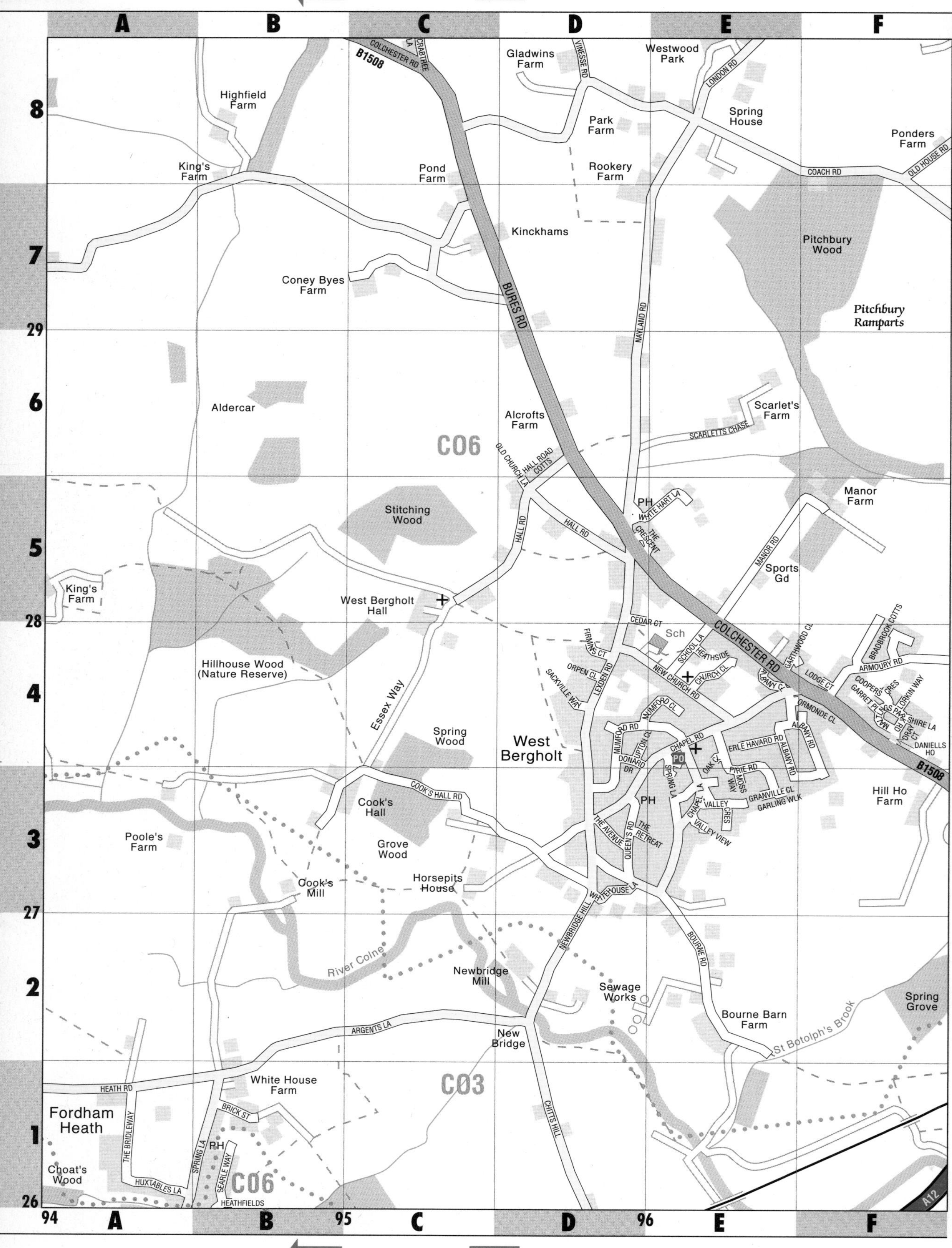

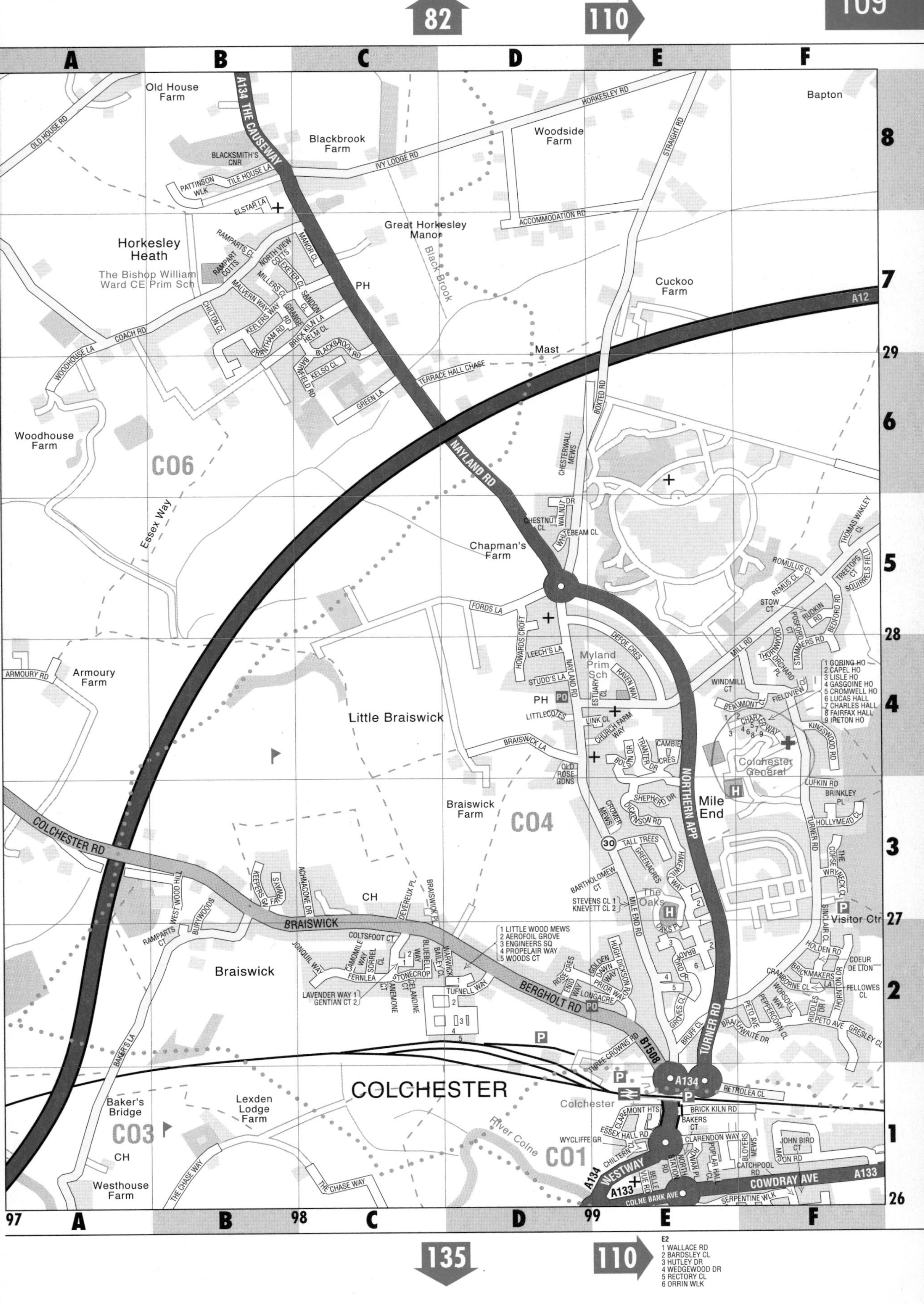

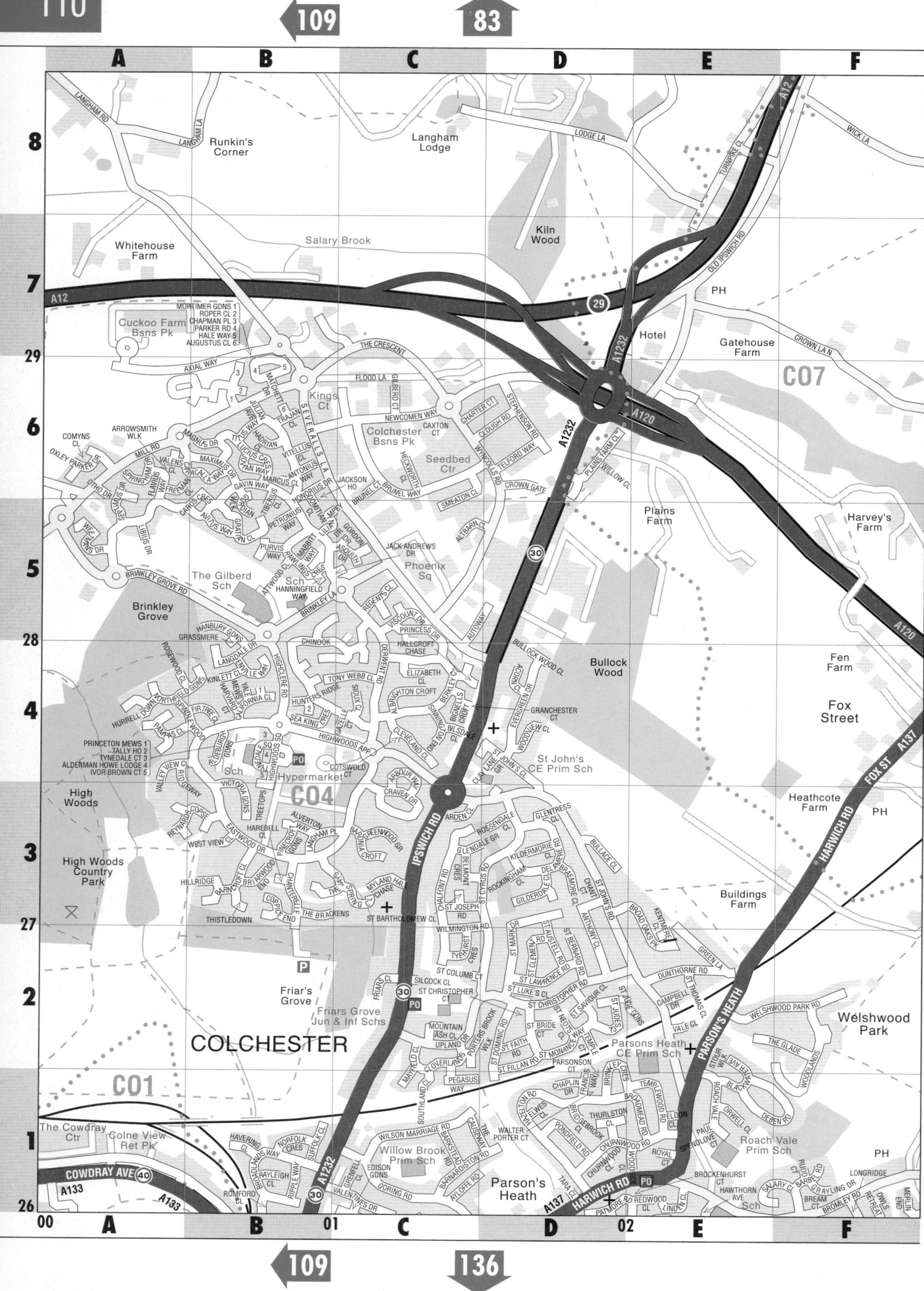

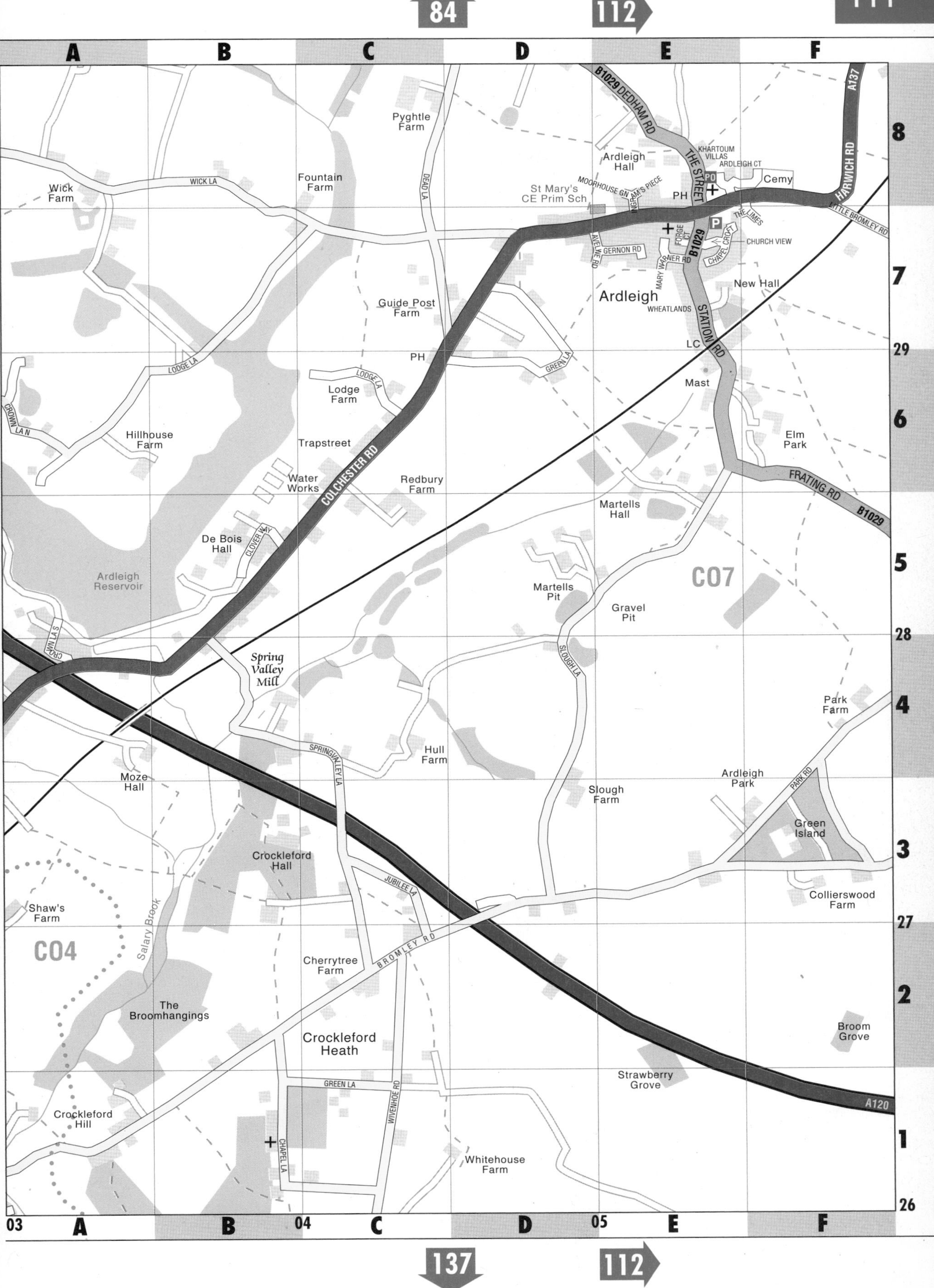

84
112

A B C D E F

8
29
7
6
29
5
28
4
3
27
2
1
26

Wick
Farm

Fountain
Farm

Pyghtle
Farm

WICK LA

DEAD LA

B1029 DEDHAM RD

Ardleigh
Hall

KHARTOUM
VILLAS
ARDLEIGH CT

THE STREET

Cemy

HARWICH RD

A137

St Mary's
CE Prim Sch

MOORHOUSE GN

AM'S PIECE

PO

PH

LITTLE BROMLEY RD

Ardleigh

New Hall

WHEATLANDS

THE LIMES

CHURCH VIEW

GERNON RD

AVELINE RD

MARY WARNER RD

CHAPEL CRESC

B1029

STATION RD

CROWN LA N

LODGE LA

Hillhouse
Farm

Guide Post
Farm

PH

GREEN LA

LC

Mast

CO7

Lodge
Farm

LODGE LA

Trapstreet

Water
Works

Redbury
Farm

COLCHESTER RD

Martells
Hall

Elm
Park

FRATING RD

B1029

De Bois
Hall

CLODER WAY

Ardleigh
Reservoir

Martells
Pit

Gravel
Pit

SLOUGH LA

Park
Farm

CROWN LA N

Spring
Valley
Mill

Hull
Farm

Slough
Farm

Ardleigh
Park

PARK RD

Green
Island

Moze
Hall

SPRINGVALLEY LA

Crockleford
Hall

Col--
Colliers wood
Farm

CO4

Salary Brook

JUBILEE LA

Cherrytree
Farm

Shaw's
Farm

The
Broomhangings

BROMLEY RD

Broom
Grove

Crockleford
Heath

GREEN LA

WIVENHOE RD

Strawberry
Grove

Crockleford
Hill

CHAPEL LA

Whitehouse
Farm

A120

03 A B 04 C D 05 E F

137
112

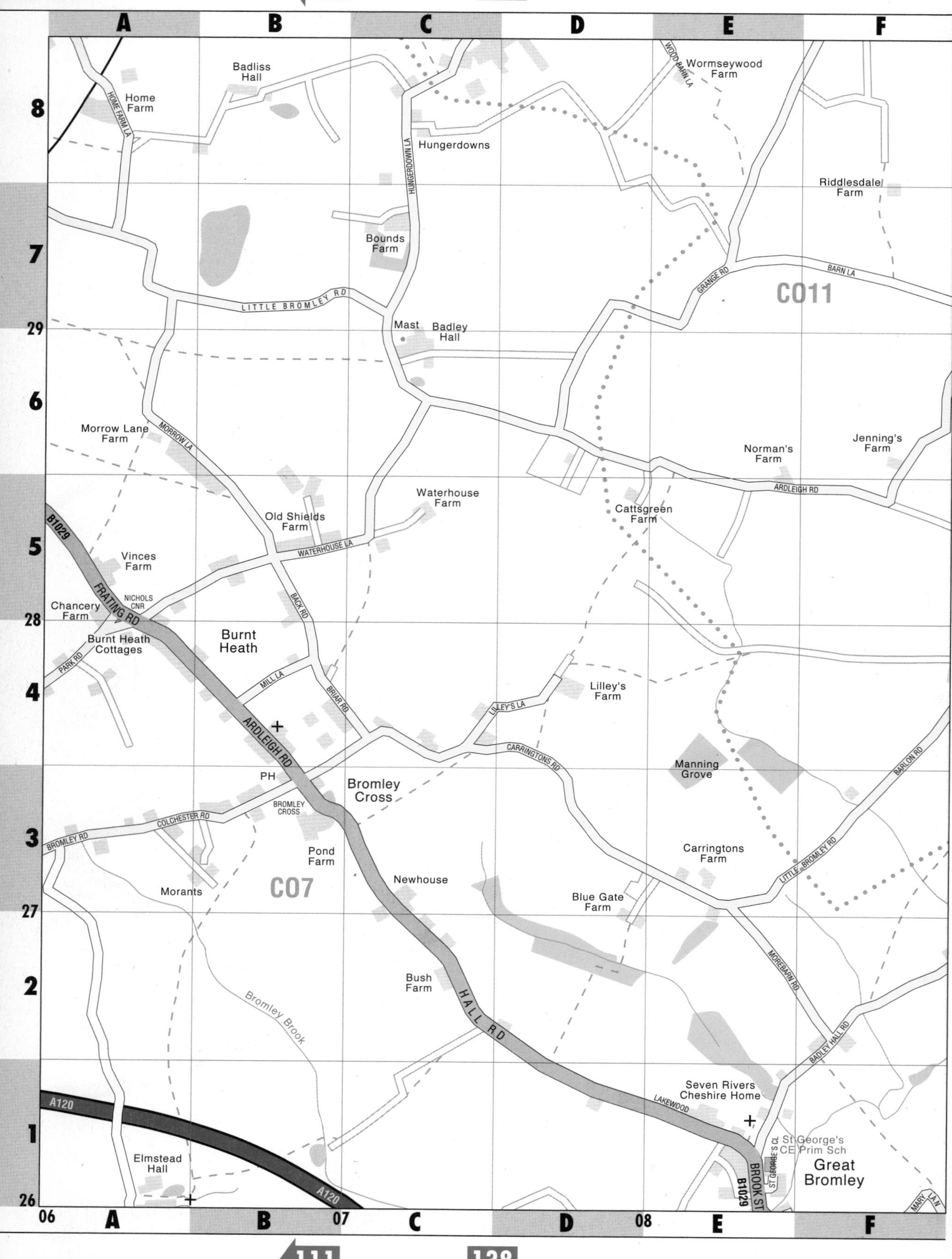

A   B   C   D   E   F

8
7
29
6
5
28
4
3
27
2
1
26

Home Farm
Badliss Hall
Hungerdowns
Bounds Farm
Wormseywood Farm
Riddlesdale Farm
LITTLE BROMLEY RD
Mast
Badley Hall
GRANGE RD
BARN LA
CO11
Morrow Lane Farm
MORROW LA
Jenning's Farm
Norman's Farm
ARDLEIGH RD
Old Shields Farm
Waterhouse Farm
WATERHOUSE LA
Cattsgreen Farm
B1029
Vinces Farm
FRATING RD
NICHOLS CNR
BACK RD
Chancery Farm
Burnt Heath Cottages
PARK RD
Burnt Heath
MILL LA
BRIAR RD
Lilley's Farm
LILLEY'S LA
Manning Grove
BARLON RD
+
PH
ARDLEIGH RD
BROMLEY CROSS
Bromley Cross
CARRINGTONS RD
Carringtons Farm
LITTLE BROMLEY RD
BROMLEY RD
COLCHESTER RD
Pond Farm
CO7
Newhouse
Blue Gate Farm
Morants
Bush Farm
MOREBARN RD
HALL RD
Bromley Brook
BADLEY HALL RD
Seven Rivers Cheshire Home
LAKEWOOD
A120
+
St George's CE Prim Sch
A120
Elmstead Hall
ST GEORGE'S CL
BROOK ST
B1029
Great Bromley
MARY LA

06   A   B   07   C   D   08   E   F

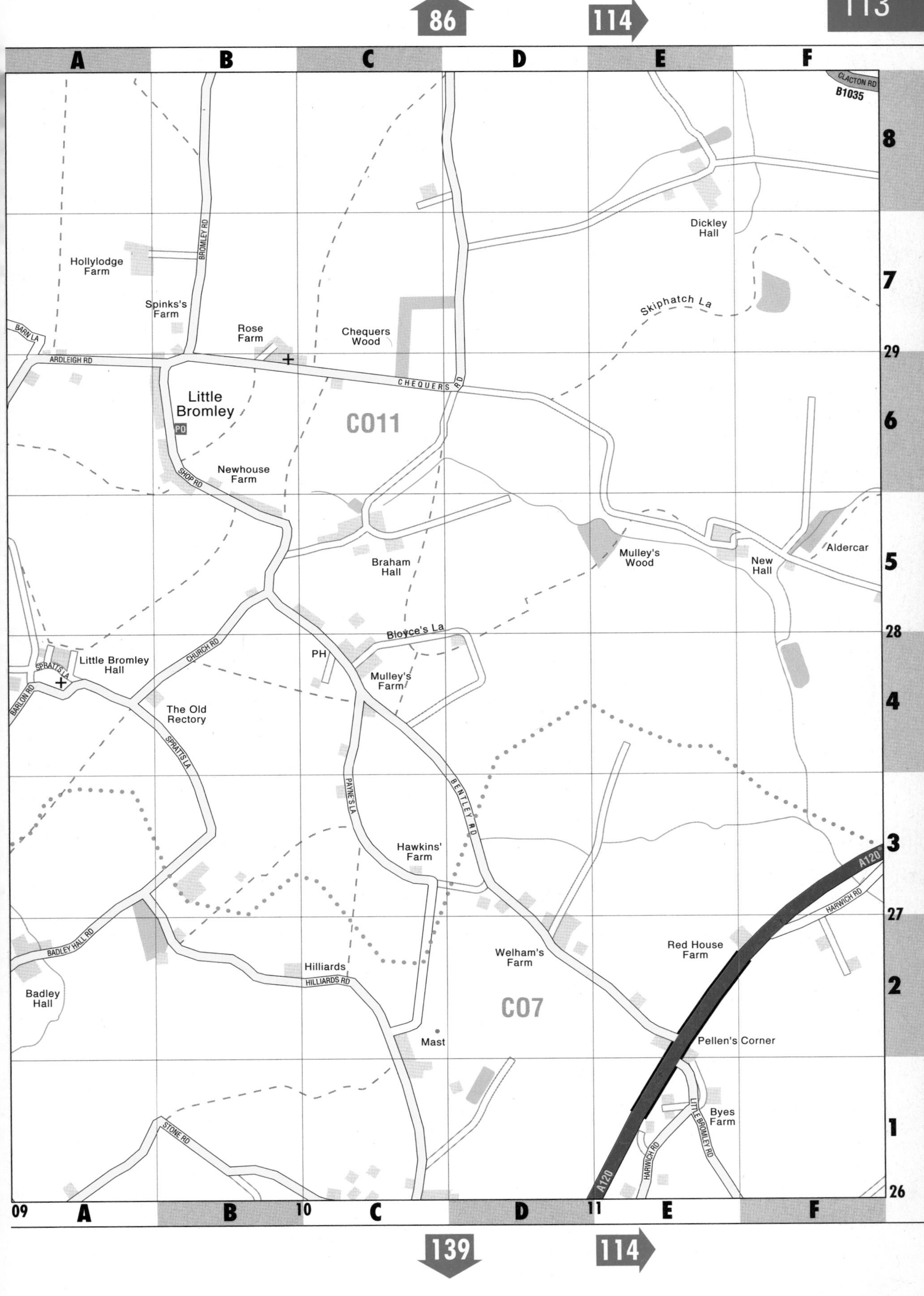

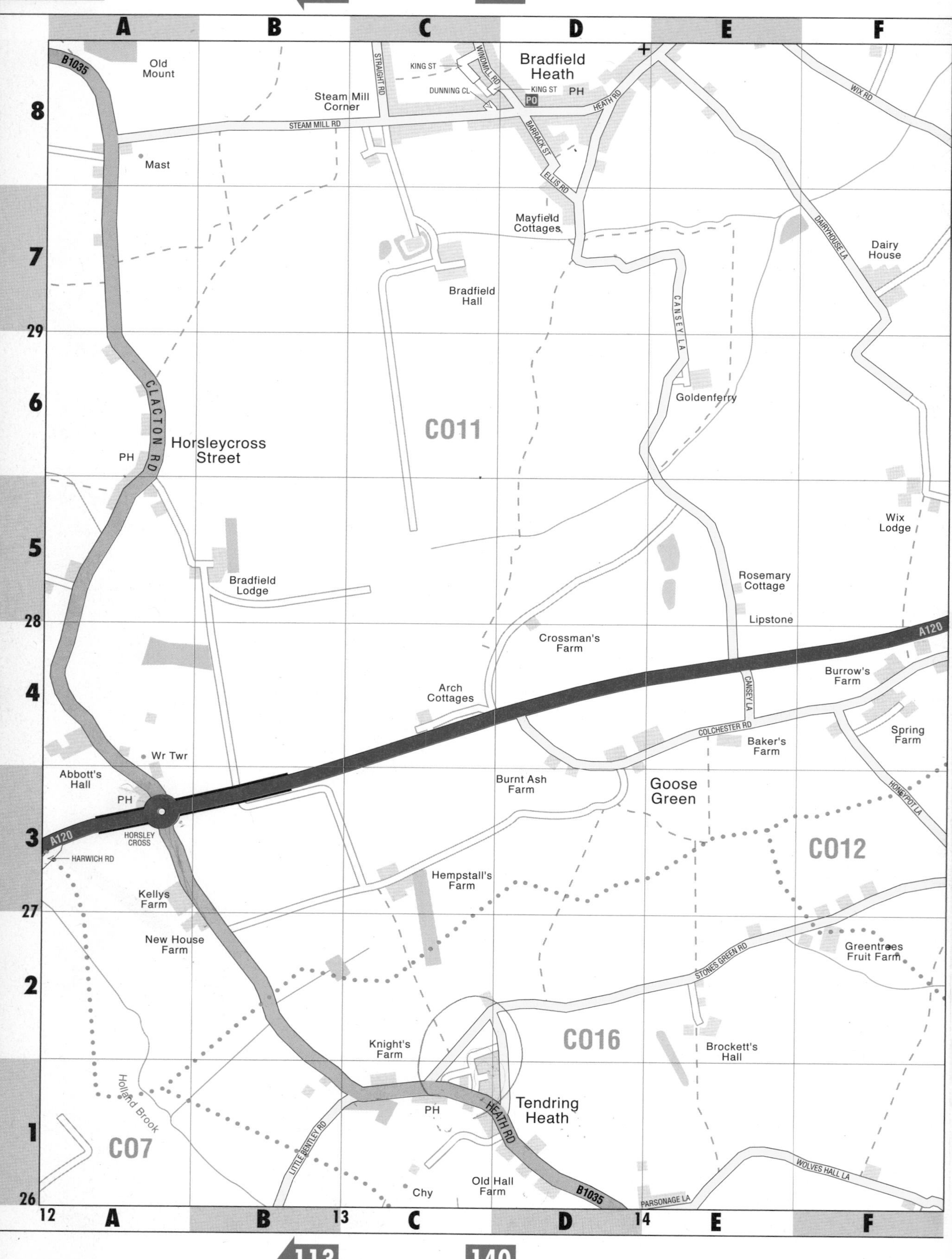

113
87

A B C D E F

8

B1035

Old
Mount

Steam Mill
Corner

STRAIGHT RD

KING ST

WINDMILL RD

DUNNING CL

KING ST

Bradfield
Heath

PO

PH

HEATH RD

WIX RD

BARRACK ST

ELLIS RD

Mast

Mayfield
Cottages

DAIRYHOUSE LA

Dairy
House

7

29

Bradfield
Hall

CANSEY LA

CO11

Goldenferry

6

CLACTON RD

PH

Horsleycross
Street

Rosemary
Cottage

Lipstone

Wix
Lodge

5

28

Bradfield
Lodge

Crossman's
Farm

A120

4

Arch
Cottages

CANSEY LA

Burrow's
Farm

COLCHESTER RD

Baker's
Farm

Spring
Farm

Wr Twr

Burnt Ash
Farm

Goose
Green

HONEYPOT LA

Abbott's
Hall

PH

3

A120

HORSLEY
CROSS

CO12

HARWICH RD

Hempstall's
Farm

27

Kellys
Farm

STONES GREEN RD

Greentrees
Fruit Farm

New House
Farm

2

Knight's
Farm

CO16

Brockett's
Hall

Holland Brook

CO07

1

LITTLE BENTLEY RD

PH

HEATH RD

Tendring
Heath

B1035

WOLVES HALL LA

26

Chy

Old Hall
Farm

PARSONAGE LA

12 A 13 B C 13 D 14 E F

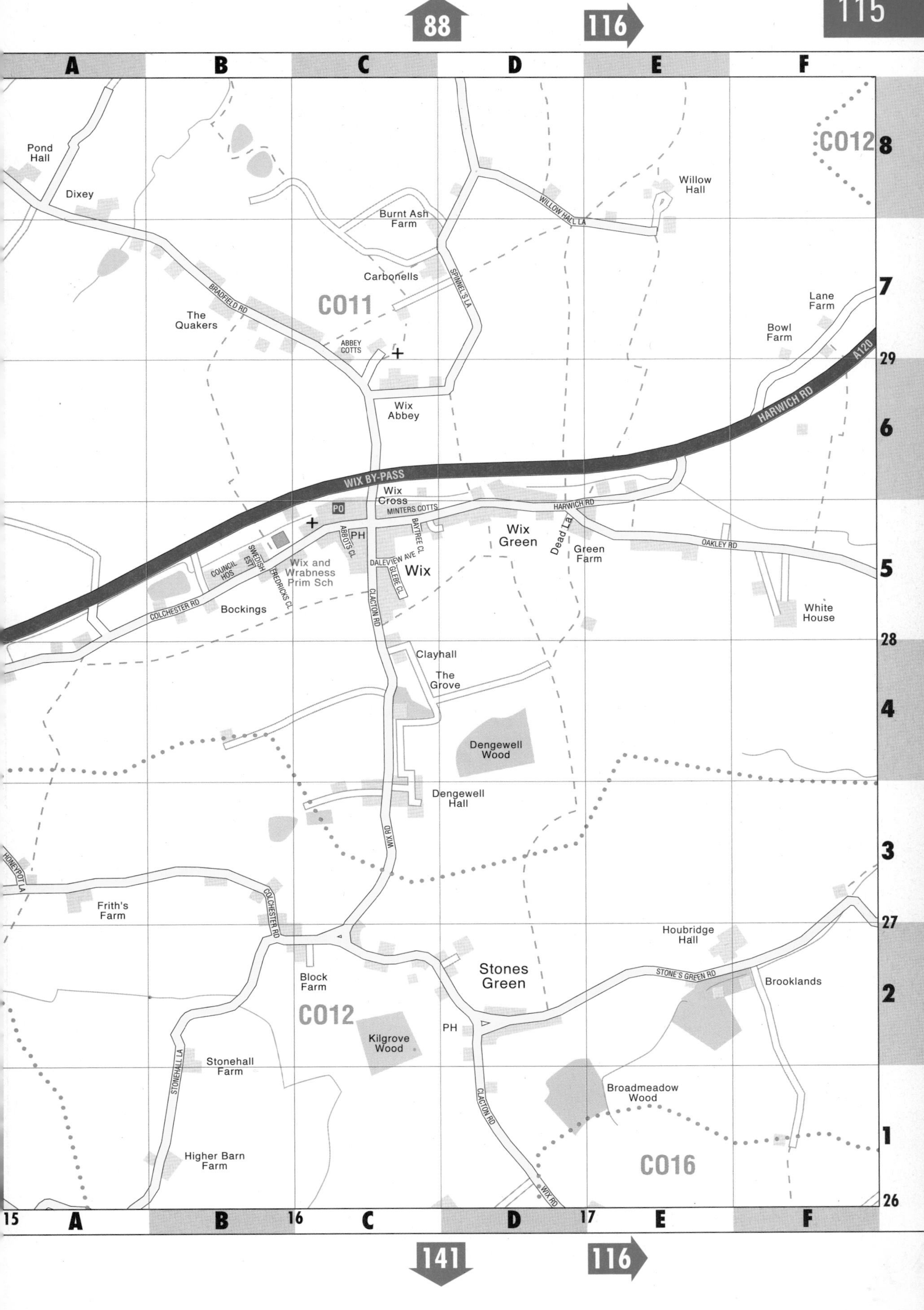

88
116
A
B
C
D
E
F
8
7
29
6
5
28
4
3
27
2
1
26
15
16
17
141
Pond Hall
Dixey
Burnt Ash Farm
Willow Hall
WILLOW HALL LA
Carbonells
SPINNEL'S LA
CO11
CO12
BRADFIELD RD
The Quakers
ABBEY COTTS
Lane Farm
Bowl Farm
A120
HARWICH RD
Wix Abbey
WIX BY-PASS
Wix Cross
PO
MINTERS COTTS
HARWICH RD
PH
ABBOTS CL
BAYTREE CL
Wix Green
Dead La
Green Farm
OAKLEY RD
COUNCIL HOS
SWEDISH EST
Wix and Wrabness Prim Sch
DALEVIEW AVE
GLEBE CL
Wix
FREDRICKS CL
COLCHESTER RD
Bockings
CLACTON RD
White House
Clayhall
The Grove
Dengewell Wood
Dengewell Hall
WIX RD
HONEYPOT LA
Frith's Farm
COLCHESTER RD
Houbridge Hall
Block Farm
Stones Green
STONE'S GREEN RD
Brooklands
CO12
Kilgrove Wood
PH
Stonehall Farm
STONEHALL LA
CLACTON RD
Broadmeadow Wood
Higher Barn Farm
CO16
WIX RD

115
89

A **B** **C** **D** **E** **F**

CO11

CO12
Great Oakley

CO16

Poplar Hall
Ramsey Hall Cottages
Ramsey Hall
Model Cottages
PRIMROSE LA
HARWICH RD
A120
TINKER ST
A120
THE MALTINGS
Hill House
HILL RD
Millpond Farm
RECTORY RD

Brickkiln Farm
Southhouse Farm
Saltwater Bridge
Soils Wood
Soilspond Bridge
THE SOILS

Redhouse Farm
Great Oakley Lodge
Sparrow's Farm
Park Pale Farm
SPARROWS CNR
HARWICH RD
Great Oakley Hall
B1414

Whitehouse Farm
OAKLEY RD
Parkers Farm
Holt Farm
PARTRIDGE CL
DOCK LA

HIGH ST
MILL HOUSE COTTS
PO
QUEEN ST
PH
P
BUCK LA
WIX RD
SCHOOL RD
ORCHARD CL
HAMFORD DR
FARM RD
Mosses Farm

THE AVENUE
All Saints CE Prim Sch
WORKHOUSE CNR
PESTHOUSE LA
BEAUMONT RD

Brook Farm
STONE'S GREEN RD
WOOD LANDS
RED BARN LA
Red Barn Farm
Cabbage Row

Marden's Farm

CROSS HILL
MOZE CROSS
HARWICH RD
Holland's Farm
B1414
Old Moze Hall
Buck's Farm

A **B** **C** **D** **E** **F**

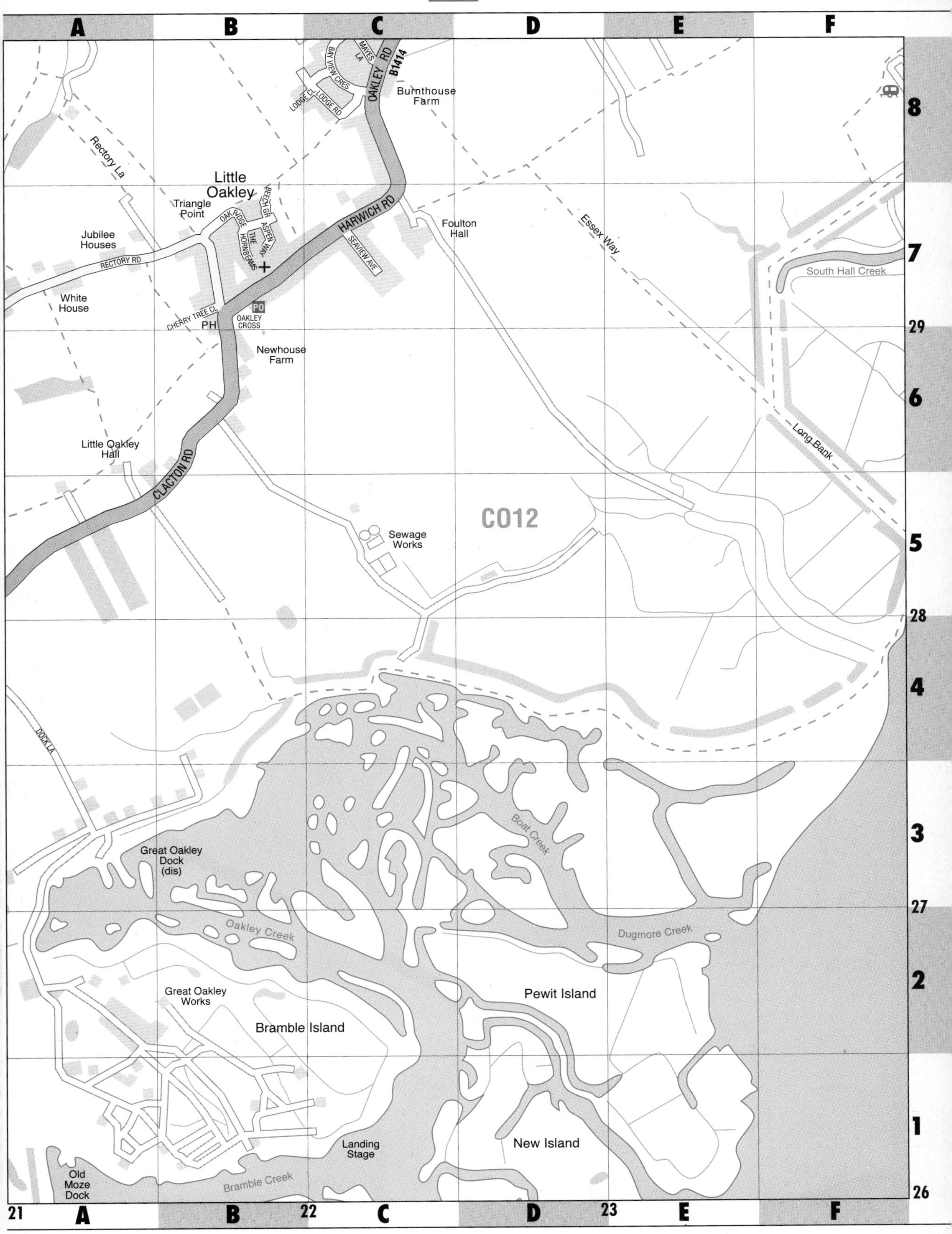

A   B   C   D   E   F

8

Bay View Cres

Mayes La

Oakley Rd

B1414

Lodge Cl

Lodge Rd

Burnthouse
Farm

Little
Oakley

Triangle
Point

Beech Gr

Oak Chase

Aspen Way

The
Hornbeams

HARWICH RD

Seaview Ave

Foulton
Hall

Essex Way

7

South Hall Creek

Jubilee
Houses

RECTORY RD

Rectory La

29

White
House

Cherry Tree Cl

PH

PO

OAKLEY
CROSS

Newhouse
Farm

Long Bank

6

Little Oakley
Hall

CLACTON RD

CO12

Sewage
Works

5

28

DOCK LA

4

Boat Creek

3

Great Oakley
Dock
(dis)

Oakley Creek

Dugmore Creek

27

Great Oakley
Works

Bramble Island

Pewit Island

2

Landing
Stage

New Island

1

Old
Moze
Dock

Bramble Creek

26

92

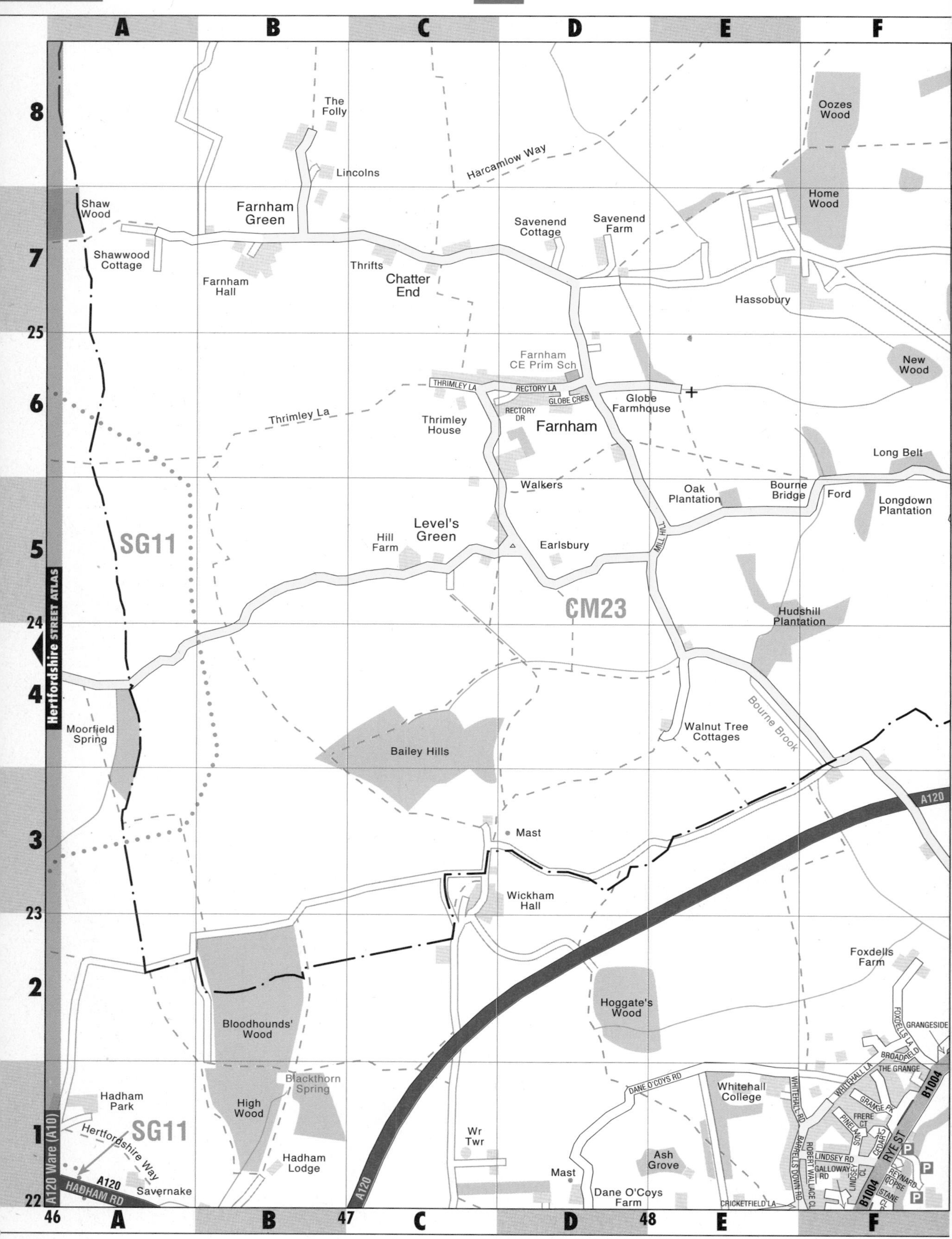
A
B
C
D
E
F
8
7
25
6
5
24
4
3
23
2
1
22
46
47
48
The Folly
Lincolns
Harcamlow Way
Shaw Wood
Farnham Green
Shawwood Cottage
Farnham Hall
Thrifts
Chatter End
Savenend Cottage
Savenend Farm
Oozes Wood
Home Wood
Hassobury
New Wood
Farnham CE Prim Sch
THRIMLEY LA
RECTORY LA
GLOBE CRES
RECTORY DR
Globe Farmhouse
Thrimley La
Thrimley House
Farnham
Long Belt
Walkers
Oak Plantation
Bourne Bridge
Ford
Longdown Plantation
Level's Green
Hill Farm
Earlsbury
MILL HILL
SG11
CM23
Hudshill Plantation
Hertfordshire STREET ATLAS
Moorfield Spring
Bailey Hills
Walnut Tree Cottages
Bourne Brook
A120
Mast
Wickham Hall
Foxdells Farm
Hoggate's Wood
Bloodhounds' Wood
GRANGESIDE
FOXDELLS LA
BROADFIELD
WHITEHALL LA
THE GRANGE
B1004
DANE O'COYS RD
Whitehall College
WHITEHALL RD
GRANGE PK
FRERE CT
PINELANDS
CEDARS
RYE ST
Hadham Park
Blackthorn Spring
High Wood
SG11
Hertfordshire Way
Wr Twr
Ash Grove
LINDSEY RD
GALLOWAY RD
LINDSEY CL
REYNARD COPSE
STANE CL
ROBERT WALLACE CL
BARRELLS DOWN RD
A120 Ware (A10)
HADHAM RD
Savernake
Hadham Lodge
Mast
Dane O'Coys Farm
CRICKETFIELD LA
P

145

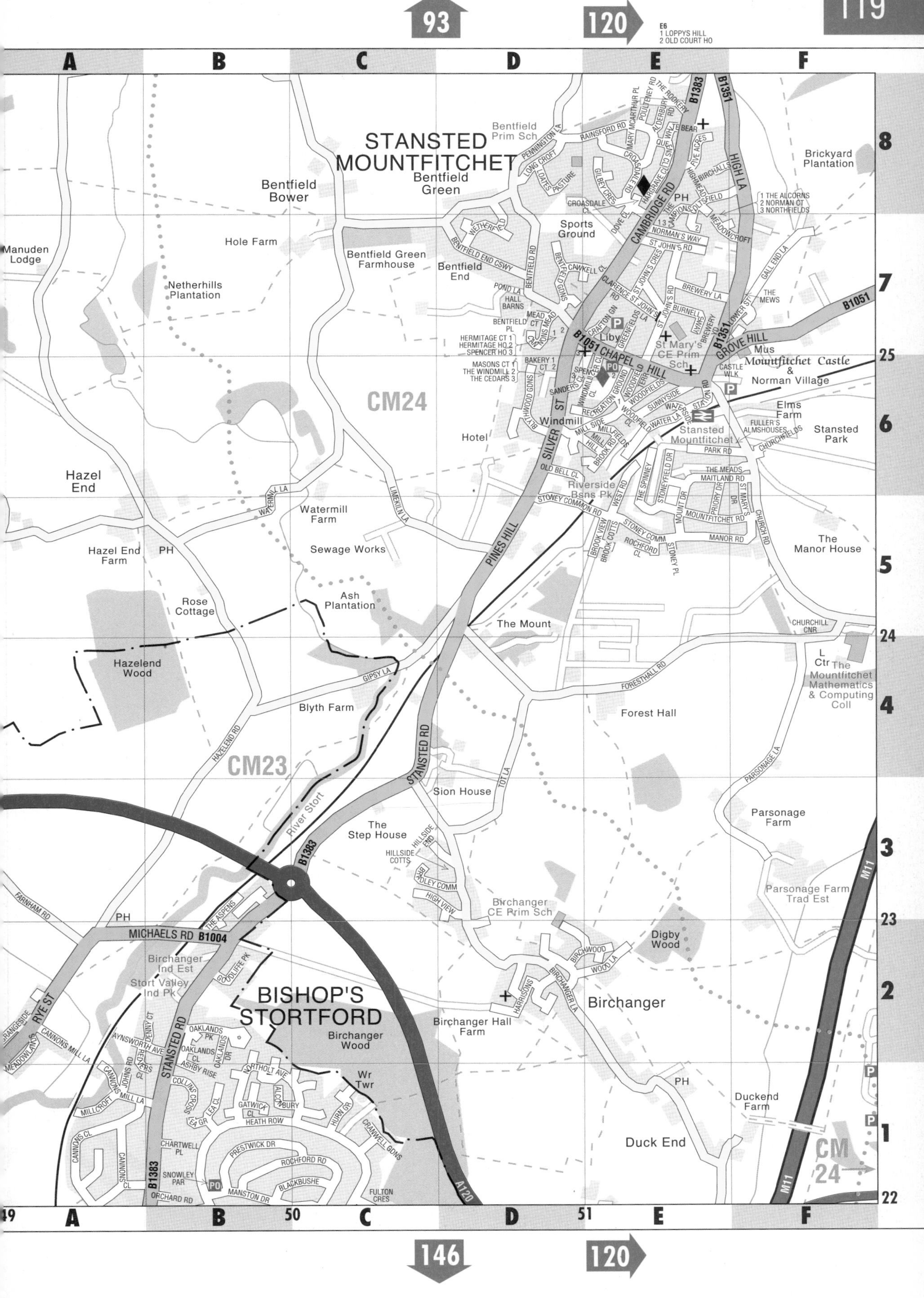

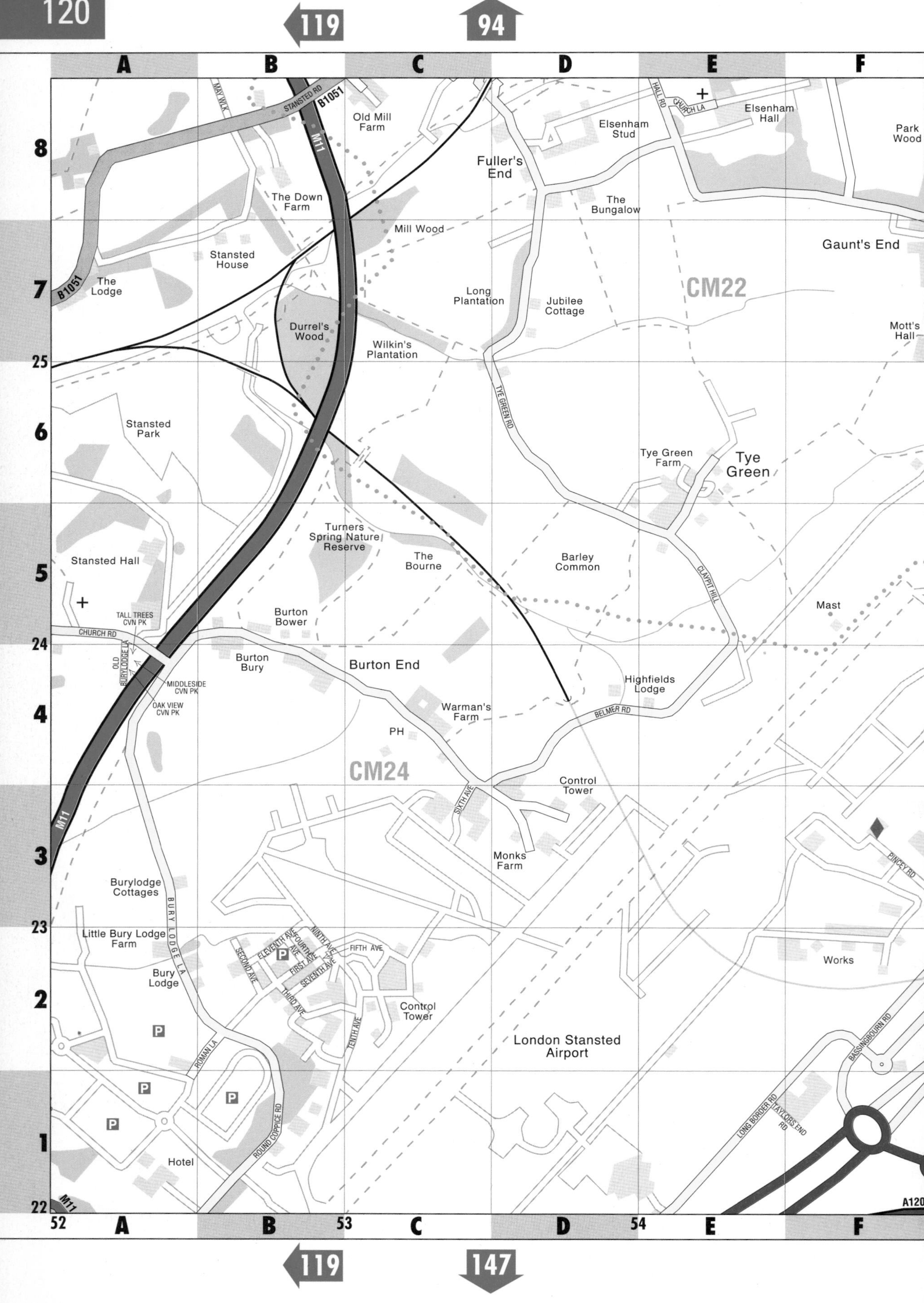

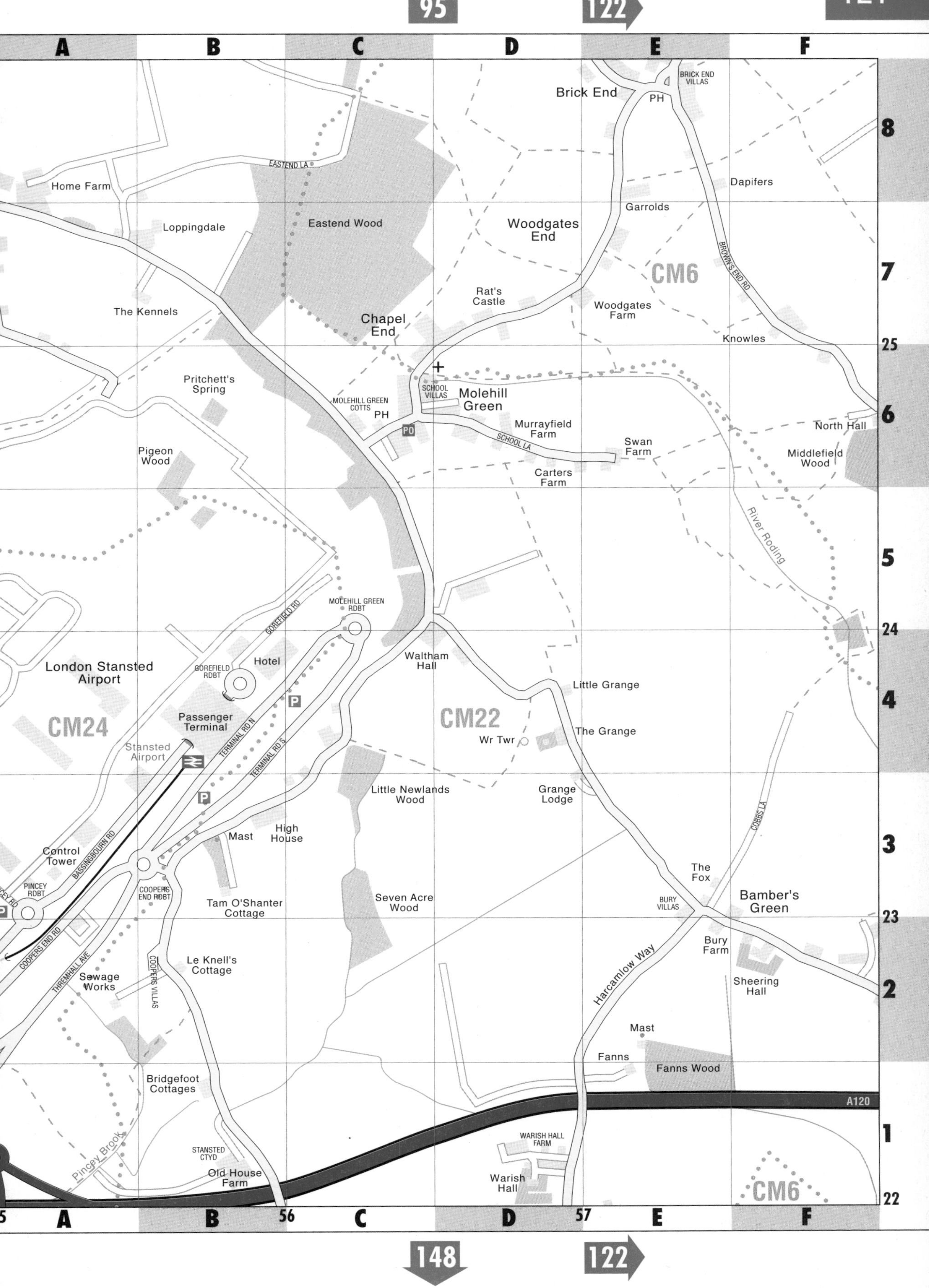

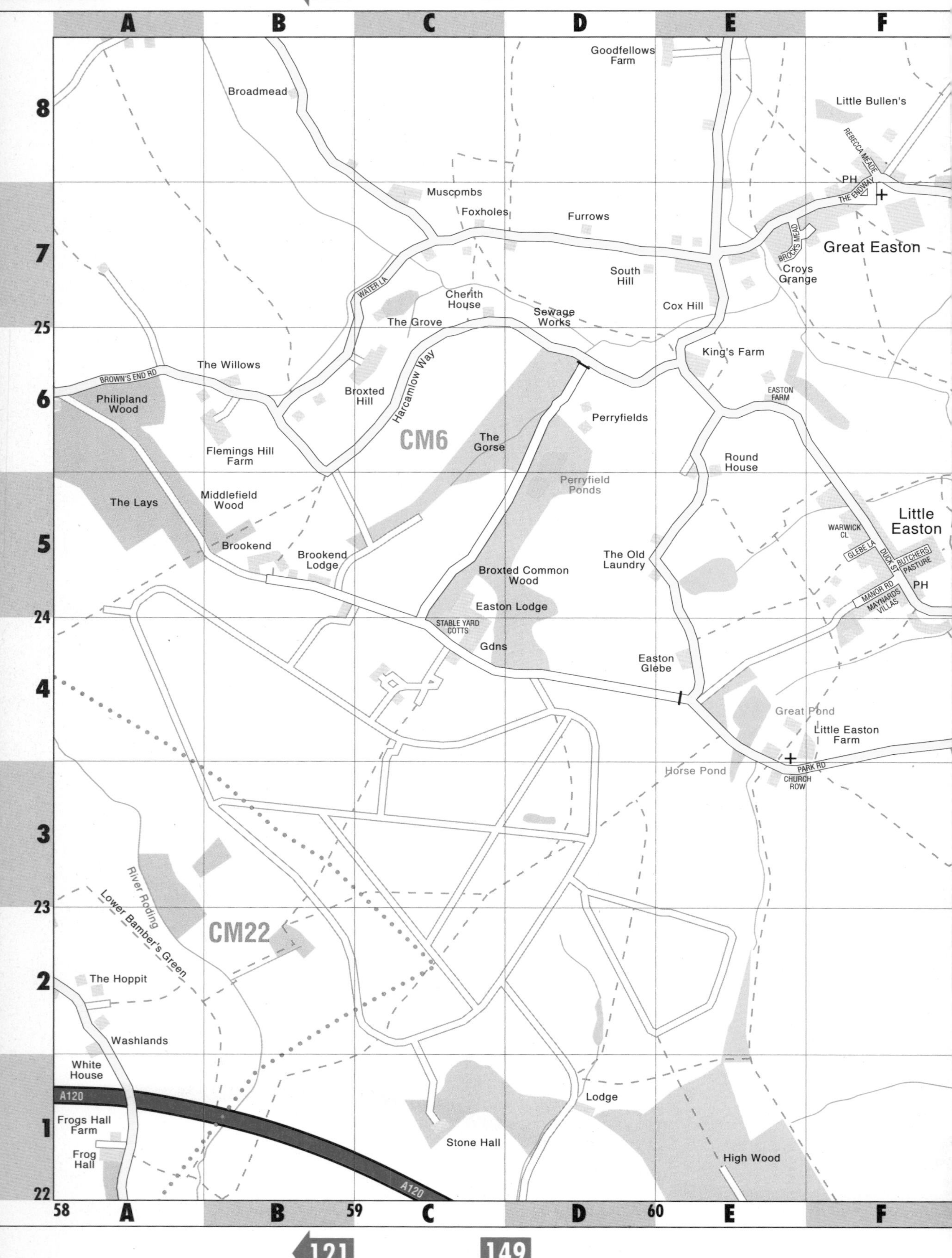

Goodfellows Farm

Broadmead

Little Bullen's

REBECCA MEADE

THE GIDWAY

Muscombs

Foxholes

Furrows

PH

Great Easton

South Hill

WATER LA

Cherith House

Cox Hill

BROOK'S MEAD

Croys Grange

The Grove

Sewage Works

The Willows

King's Farm

BROWN'S END RD

Philipland Wood

Broxted Hill

Perryfields

EASTON FARM

Harcamlow Way

CM6

The Gorse

Flemings Hill Farm

Round House

Perryfield Ponds

WARWICK CL

Little Easton

The Lays

Middlefield Wood

GLEBE LA

BUTCHERS PASTURE

DUCK ST

Brookend

The Old Laundry

Brookend Lodge

Broxted Common Wood

MANOR RD

MAYNARDS VILLAS

PH

Easton Lodge

STABLE YARD COTTS

Gdns

Easton Glebe

Great Pond

Little Easton Farm

River Roding

Horse Pond

PARK RD

CHURCH ROW

CM22

Lower Bamber's Green

The Hoppit

Washlands

White House

A120

Lodge

Frogs Hall Farm

Frog Hall

Stone Hall

High Wood

A120

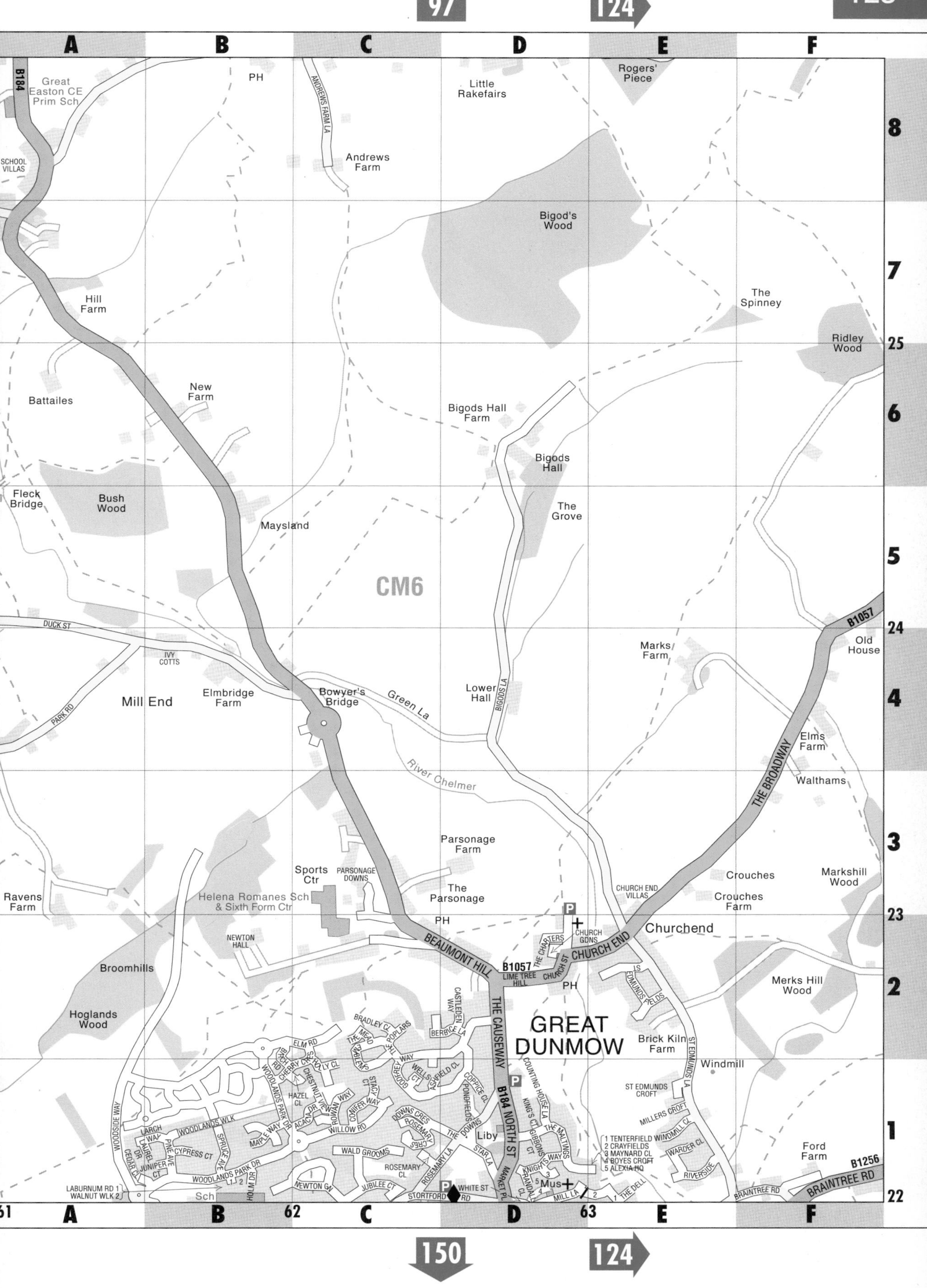

97
124
150
124

A B C D E F

8 7 25 6 5 24 4 3 23 2 1 22

B184
Great Easton CE Prim Sch

SCHOOL VILLAS

PH

ANDREWS FARM LA

Little Rakefairs

Rogers' Piece

Andrews Farm

Bigod's Wood

The Spinney

Hill Farm

Ridley Wood

Battailes

New Farm

Bigods Hall Farm

Bigods Hall

CM6

Fleck Bridge

Bush Wood

Maysland

The Grove

DUCK ST

B1057
Old House

IVY COTTS

Marks Farm

PARK RD

Mill End

Elmbridge Farm

Bowyer's Bridge

Green La

Lower Hall

BIGODS LA

THE BROADWAY

Elms Farm

Walthams

River Chelmer

Parsonage Farm

Crouches

Markshill Wood

Sports Ctr

PARSONAGE DOWNS

The Parsonage

CHURCH END VILLAS

Crouches Farm

Ravens Farm

Helena Romanes Sch & Sixth Form Ctr

PH

THE CHARTERS

Church Gdns

Churchend

NEWTON HALL

BEAUMONT HILL

B1057

CHURCH ST

CHURCH END

PH

Merks Hill Wood

Broomhills

LIME TREE HILL

Hoglands Wood

BRADLEY CL

POPLARS

CASTLEDEN WAY

BERBICE LA

THE MEAD

GREAT DUNMOW

Brick Kiln Farm

ST EDMUNDS LA

Windmill

ELM RD

CHERRY CL

CHESTNUT CL

LILY CL

GODFREY WAY

WELLSFIELD CL

POUNDFIELDS

THE CAUSEWAY

COUNTING HOUSE LA

KING'S CL

GIBBONS WAY

St Edmunds Croft

Millers Croft

WOODSIDE WAY

LARCH WAY

CEDAR DR

PINE AVE

JUNIPER CT

CYPRESS CT

SPRUCE AVE

WOODLANDS WLK

WOODLANDS PARK DR

MAPLE WAY

HAZEL CL

RUWAN CONIFER WAY

ACACIA DR

WILLOW RD

DOWNS CRES

STACEY CL

ROSEMARY CRES

ROSEMARY CL

THE DOWNS

STAR LA

WALD GROOMS

JUBILEE CT

NEWTON GV

HOLM DR

ROSEMARY LA

STORTFORD

WHITE ST

MARKET PL

B184 NORTH ST

THE MALTINGS

KNIGHT'S WAY

Liby

MILL LA

Mus

1 Tenterfield
2 Crayfields
3 Maynard Cl
4 Boyes Croft
5 Alexia Rd

WINDMILL CL

WAAQER CL

RIVERSIDE

THE DELL

Ford Farm

B1256

LABURNUM RD 1
WALNUT WLK 2

Sch

BRAINTREE RD

BRAINTREE RD

61 62 63

A B C D E F

124

123 98

A   B   C   D   E   F

8

Hangman's Wood
Nick's Hole

B1057

Hornsea Farm
Bran End

Tanner's Farm

ROSEMARY LA

HORNSEA MLS

BRAN END FIELDS

PULSFORD PL

Brick Kiln Farm

7

Leaselands Spring

BRICK KILN LA

CLAY LA

25

Nettle Spring

BRONKS FIELDS

DOWNS TERR

6

Hick's Plantation

MARSHALLS PIECE

The Downs

POUND GATE

PARK SIDE

GARDEN FIELDS

Lucas Farm

William's Farm

CM6

Stebbing Park

The Mount

Stebbing Prim Sch

Stebbing

Spike House

THE BROADWAY

Stebbing Brook

PO
PH

LIVERY MEWS

PH

Watch House

5

B1057

Dunmow Farm

MILL LA

HIGH ST

MOTTS YD

WATCH HOUSE RD

WHITEHOUSE RD

24

The Fir Wood

RUFFELS FIELD

WAREHOUSE RD

Church End

4

Dunmow Farm Wood

Church Farm

Haydens

3

Tooley's Farm

23

Merks Hall Farm

Brookend

Brookend Farm

Rookwoods

2

Merks Hall

Homelye Wood

Homelye Farm

HOMELYE CHASE

Throws Farm

B1256

BRAMBLE LA

A120

1

Wr Twr

B1256

BRAINTREE RD

BRAMBLE LA

Blatches

22

A120

64   A   B   65   C   66   D   E   F

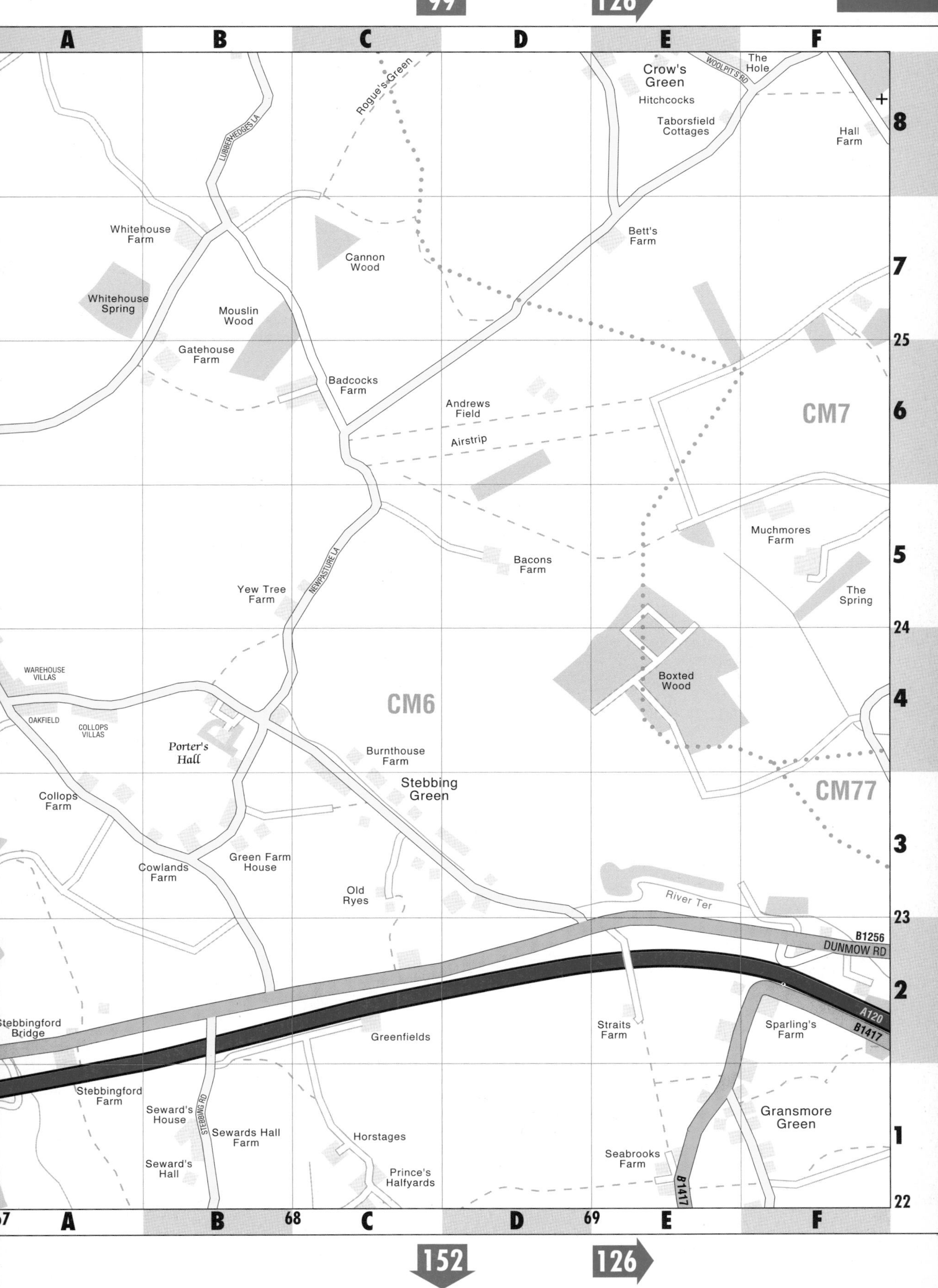

A B C D E F

8

Crow's Green
Hitchcocks
Taborsfield Cottages
The Hole
Hall Farm

WOOLPIT'S RD

Whitehouse Farm
Whitehouse Spring

Bett's Farm

7

Mouslin Wood
Cannon Wood

Gatehouse Farm
Badcocks Farm

25

LUBBERHEDGES LA

Andrews Field
Airstrip

CM7

6

NEWPASTURE LA

Bacons Farm

Muchmores Farm

5

Yew Tree Farm

The Spring

24

WAREHOUSE VILLAS
OAKFIELD
COLLOPS VILLAS

Boxted Wood

CM6

CM77

4

Porter's Hall

Burnthouse Farm
Stebbing Green

Collops Farm

Cowlands Farm
Green Farm House
Old Ryes

River Ter

3

B1256
DUNMOW RD

23

Stebbingford Bridge

A120
B1417

2

Greenfields
Straits Farm
Sparling's Farm

Stebbingford Farm
Seward's House
Sewards Hall Farm

STEBBING RD

Horstages
Prince's Halfyards
Seabrooks Farm

Gransmore Green

B1417

1

Seward's Hall

22

125
100

A **B** **C** **D** **E** **F**

Saling Hall Gardens

Great Saling

GROVE VILLAS

PO

VICARAGE CL

PH

THE MEWS

PICCOTTS LA

Piccotts Farm

Chapel Hill

Cold Hall Farm

Ivy Hall

KYNASTON RD

CM7

8

Saling Grove

Kynaston's Farm

7

New Spinney

Mount's Farm

Lightwaters Farm

HALL RD

25

CM7

Jubilee Spinney

Park's Farm

Perry Childs Farm

6

Onchor's Farm

Golden Grove

Old Hall

Pods Brook

5

Rumley Wood

24

4

Blackbush Wood

Blake House Farm

Craft Ctr

Moor's Farm

Pound Farm

Pound Farmhouse

Gould's Farm

Duckend Green

3

MOORS LA

SHALFORD RD

Moor's Spinney

CM77

Rayne Prim Sch

23

PH

B1256

Rayne

BLYTH'S WAY

CAPEL RD

CAPEL CL

LEYSIDE

BRUNWIN RD

ELM WAY

SMITHS FLD

PHILLIPS RD

PHILIPS CL

2

A120

B1417

B1417

Blake End

DUNMOW RD

Havering's Farm

THE STREET

BARNARDS ORCH

BAYTREE CL

MANOMBRES CL

STATION RD

VAUGHAN CL

HANCE LA

PO

MEDLEY RD

KIDDER RD

WARNER CL

NEW RD

THE NEW ROAD TERR

THE RUSKINS

SYMMONS CL

LEVEREDS

CM6

Broadfield Farm

Hazelmere Farm

DUNMOW RD

B1256

Sorrell's Farm

Gatewoods Farm

SCHOOL RD

Little Paddocks

Fairy Hall

1

Graunt Courts

DRAPERS CHASE

MILL LA

A120

22

A **B** **C** **D** **E** **F**

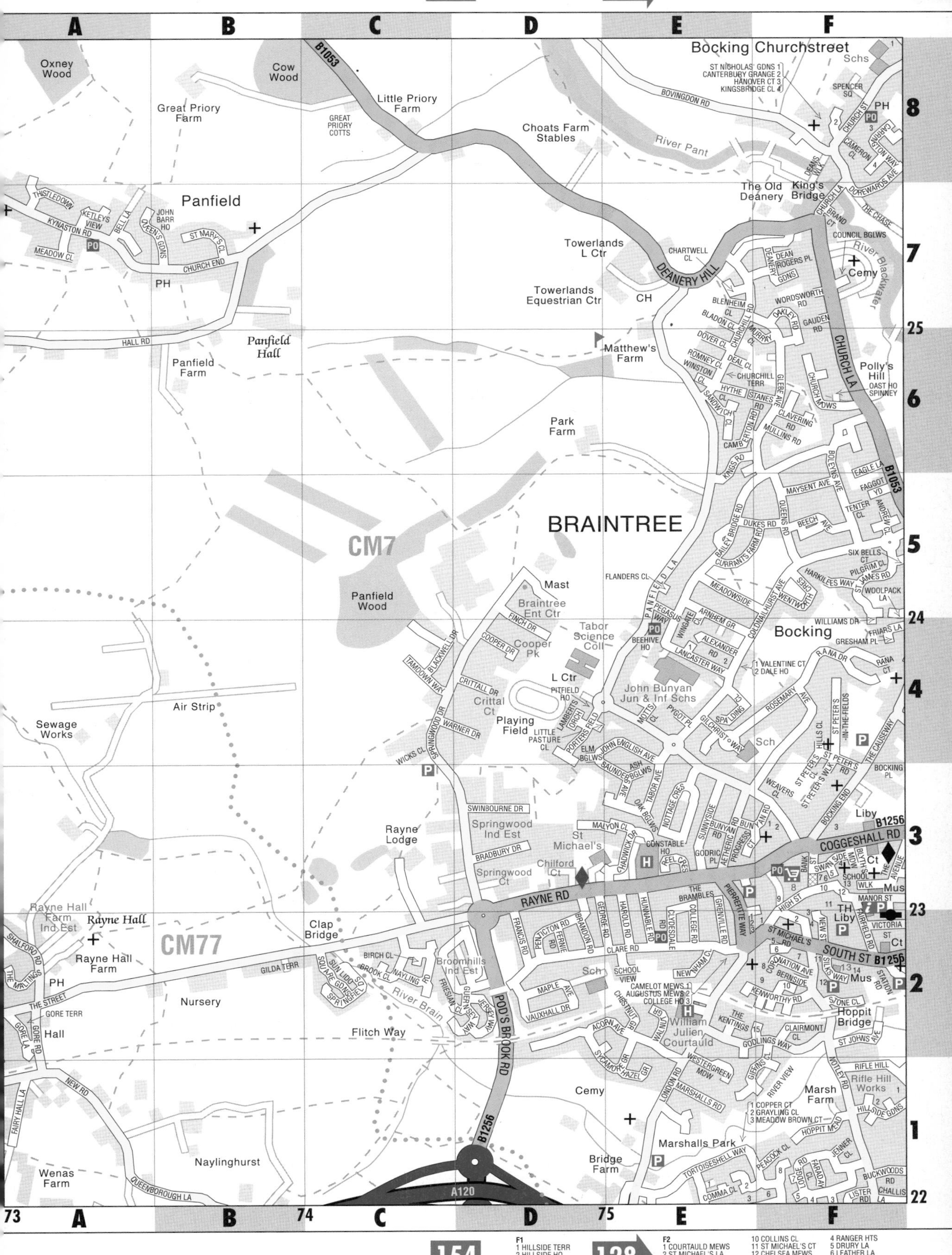

F1
1 HILLSIDE TERR
2 HILLSIDE HO
3 EDISON CL
4 NEWTON CL
5 DARWIN CL
6 WALL CT
7 FLEMING CL
8 GATEKEEPER CL

F2
1 COURTAULD MEWS
2 ST MICHAEL'S LA
3 BELLAMY HO
4 TRAFALGAR HO
5 ST MICHAELS MEWS
6 RUE DE JEUNES
7 THE BRAINTREE FOYER
8 TOM DAVIES HO
9 JAYMAR CT

10 COLLINS CL
11 ST MICHAEL'S CT
12 CHELSEA MEWS
13 WARNERS MILL
14 MAZERS CT
15 STRUDWICK CL

F3
1 CHERRY BGLWS
2 WRIGHT CT
3 ST LAWRENCE CT

4 RANGER HTS
5 DRURY LA
6 LEATHER LA
7 LITTLE SQ
8 George Yd Sh Ctr
9 SANDPIT LA
10 GREAT SQ
11 MARKET ST
12 MARKET PL
13 TOFTS WLK

127 102

BRAINTREE

CM7

CM77

Windmill (dis)
NDMILL GDNS
MILLERS CL
CHURCH ST
Round Wood
MONKEN HADLEY
Willoughbys Farm
WILLOUGHBY'S LA
Bramble Wood
Woolmer Green Farm

Doreward's Hall
THE CHASE
BROAD RD
A131
LYONS HALL RD
Lyons Hall
Lyonshall Wood
Covenbrook Hall

B1053
THISTLEY GREEN RD
Thistley Green
THISTLEY GREEN RD

THE RIDGE
Highfield Stile Farm
HIGHFIELD CL
HIGHFIELD STILE RD
Works
Sewage Works

Braintree Coll
CONVENT HILL
CONVENT LA
B1053
CHURCH LA
CROSS MILL
Mill
NURSERY DR
THE CLOISTERS
DOUBLEDAY GDNS
Jenkin's Farm

River Blackwater

Kingfisher Gate
NORTHUMBERLAND
VICTORY GDNS 1
TRAFALGAR CT 2
FALKLAND CT 3
MOUNTBATTEN CT 4
ST VINCENT
ACH
AJAX CL
EXETER
ALBEM GDNS
BOSCAWEN GDNS
CAVENDISH
NORRIS
RAYLEIGH CL
HEREFORD CL
BOUCHER AVE
Great Bradfords Jun & Inf Schs
1 GEORGIAN HO
2 LITTLE BRADFORDS
3 THE COURTYARD
DRON
WARWICK
BEDFORD
KYM
MOUNTBATTEN GDNS
BLACKWATER
KEYES
LIBERTY WAY
CAVENDISH GDNS
ANSON WAY
SHEER
GUINEA
SOVEREIGN CL
CROWN GDNS
STAFFORD
NORTHAMPTON
DEERLEAP WAY

PO
PHILLIPS CHASE
BRADFORD ST
RIVER
MOLLY BROOK
VALLEY RD
BAWN CL
BRADFORDS
JULIEN COURT RD
COURT RD
Beaufort
GDNS
RUTLAND GDNS
NORFOLK GDNS
DEVONSHIRE GDNS
WARWICK
ESSEX
KENT GDNS
YORK GDNS
CUMBERLAND GDNS
CORNWALL GDNS
CONNAUGHT GDNS
WELLINGTON CL
TRAFALGAR WAY
VANGUARD WAY
BALMORAL GDNS
BEATTY GDNS
NELSON GDNS
WARLEY CL
KINGSMEAD PK
HAWKINS
DRAKE GDNS
ROCHESTER
HARWELL CL
Sch
DUNOW
1 TIDESWELL CL
2 SNOWBERRY CT
Hatches Farm
A131

Recn Gd
1 ALBERT QT
2 TEMPLETON CT
3 FULLERS CT
ALLEN HO
WESTMINSTER
JOHN RAY ST
TURNPIKE
KEBLE
PORTLAND
DALLWOOD
GLOUCESTER GDNS
COGGESHALL RD
30
B1256
CLAY PITS WAY
COGGESHALL RD
A120

B1256
CROFT CL
MOUNT RD
WOODFIELD RD
RAILWAY ST
MANOR ST
ALBERT RD
JOHN ENGLISH AVE
EAST ST
ST MARY'S RD
PO
TROTTERS FIELD
ELLIOTT PL
BADGER GR
HOWARD CL
BELLMONT
CUNNINGTON RD
HAY LAN
WHEATLEY AVE
BARTRAM AVE E
GULLS CROFT
FORE FIELD
CRABS CROFT
LIE FELD CL
CLAY PITS
KITCHEN FIELD
BISNEY
GOLDING CRES

CRAIG HO
THE LAURELS
VICTORIA ST
Ind Est
MANOR PL
BISHOPS AVE
BEDFORD WAY
HANDS LA
THORPE MEAD
PEARL DR
RUSTY CT
FEATHER CL
MOORS
1 WILD BOAR FIELD
2 DE-MARCI CT
3 BLACK BREAD CL

B1256 SOUTH ST
TIMBER YD
ROSE GDNS
ENTERPRISE
THE YARD
LAKES RD
CHAPEL HILL
STUARTS WAY
CLOCKHOUSE WAY
WARREN RD
Ley Wood
P
Templeborder Wood

STATION APP
P
Braintree
DAVIES CT
ALPHA
MILL CT
ANGLIA WAY
Lakes Ind Pk
ANGLIA WAY
Braintree Town FC
IRON VIEW
CRESSING RD
THE CHASEWAY
HAYTOR CL
LETWOOD CL
BICKERS GREEN RD
BRICK KILN WAY
BARN MEAD
Sch
TANNERS MDW

APPLETREE WLK
PEARTREE CL
STRAWBERRY CL
HILLSIDE GDNS
THE RIDGEWAY
LONGACRES
DUGGERS LA
SKITTS HILL
THE LINDENS
CENTURY DR
MILL PARK DR
FREEPORT OFFICE VILLAGE
Freeport Designer Outlet
CHERITOM CT
HUNTER DR
SALT COMBE
RODING WAY
TAPESTRY WLK
MIDDLE KING
PLAINS FIELD
LOWER KING
1 CRESS CROFT
2 PUNDERS FIELD
3 STILEMANS WOOD
4 DEBEN CT
5 STOUR CT
6 FRATING CT
7 GOLDHANGER CT
8 SALCOTT CREEK CT
9 CROUCH CT
10 BOURNE CT

STEPHENSON RD
FORD RD
BRUNEL RD
WORCESTER RD
THE BRISE
ORCHARD DR
BLACKMOORS
BEADON DR
BRAMLEY CT
RUSSET CT
HARRISON DR
RYE GRASS
RUSHMOOR DR
BLU RUSH CL
Skitts Hill Ind Est
CHARTER WAY
Freeport
Chapel Hill Bsns & Ret Pk
B1018
THE SPINNEY
MERSEA
FLEET
COLNE CT
CANT WAY
THAMES CT
CHELMER WAY
LEA CL
SLOUGH HOUSE CL
A120
PH
Cressing Lodge
Lanham Wood

76 77 78

A2
1 CAMULUS CL
2 GRESLEY DR
3 SIDINGS PL
4 VICTORIA CT
5 GROOMSIDE
6 JACQUARD WAY
7 ALEXANDRA MEWS
8 THE MULBERRIES
9 DAMASK MEWS
10 SOUTHVIEW

B2
1 WINDSOR CT
2 STUART CT
3 TUDOR CT
4 YORK CT
5 LANCASTER CT

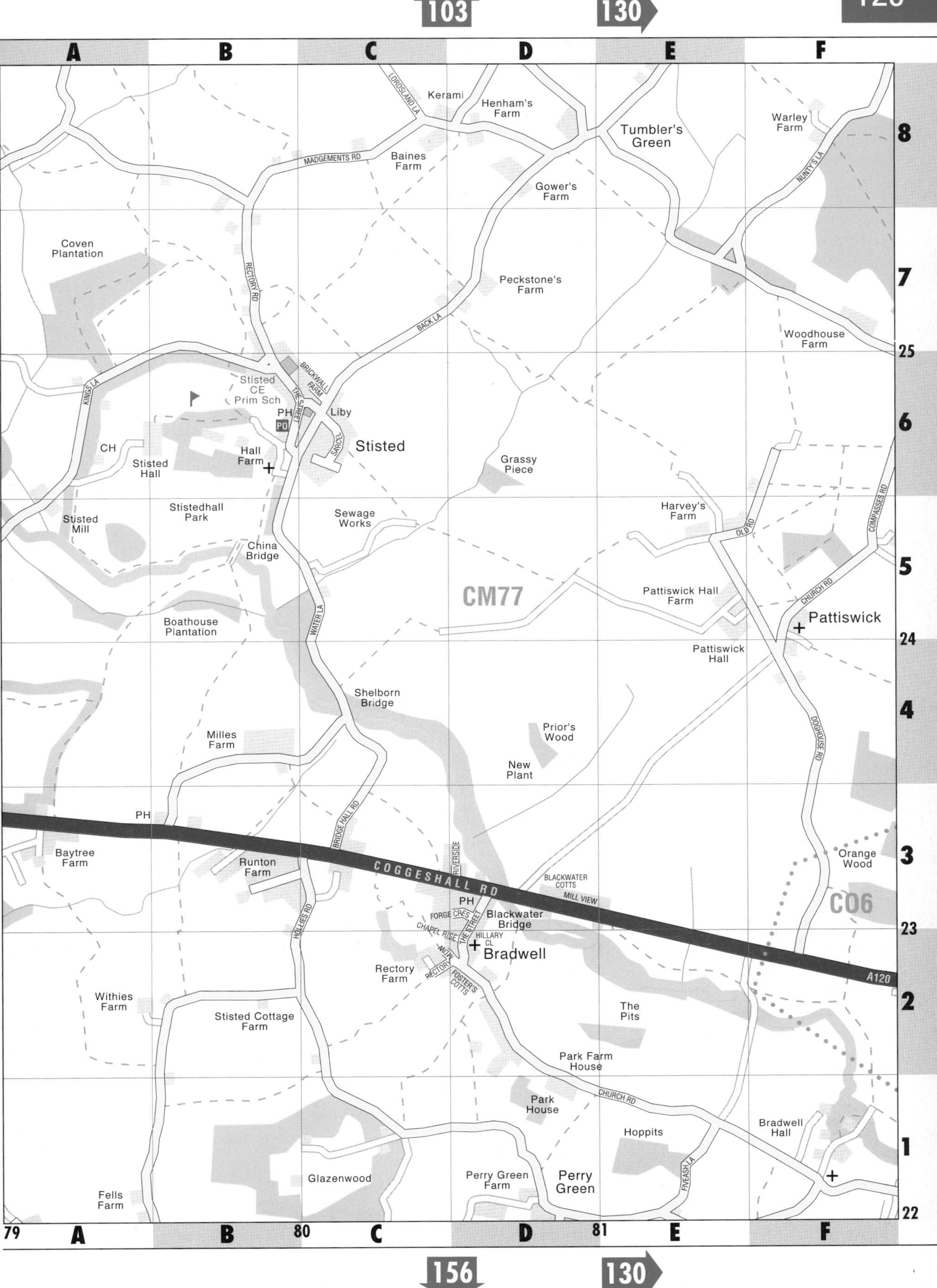

A   B   C   D   E   F

8

7

25

6

5

24

4

3

23

2

1

22

Kerami
Henham's Farm
Baines Farm
Tumbler's Green
Warley Farm
MADGEMENTS RD
LORDSLAND LA
Gower's Farm
NUNTY'S LA
Coven Plantation
RECTORY RD
Peckstone's Farm
BACK LA
Woodhouse Farm
BRICKWALL FARM
Stisted CE Prim Sch
Liby
PH
PO
CH
Stisted
KINGS LA
THE STREET
Hall Farm
Stisted Hall
Grassy Piece
OLD RD
Harvey's Farm
COMPASSES RD
Stistedhall Park
China Bridge
Sewage Works
CM77
Pattiswick Hall Farm
CHURCH RD
Pattiswick
Stisted Mill
WATER LA
Boathouse Plantation
Pattiswick Hall
Shelborn Bridge
Prior's Wood
DOGHOUSE RD
Milles Farm
New Plant
BRIDGE HALL RD
PH
Orange Wood
CO6
Baytree Farm
Runton Farm
RIVERSIDE
COGGESHALL RD
BLACKWATER COTTS
MILL VIEW
PH
FORGE CRES
Blackwater Bridge
CHAPEL RISE
HILLARY CL
Bradwell
A120
Withies Farm
MILLES RD
THE STREET
Rectory Farm
RECTORY
MOLK
FOSTER'S COTTS
The Pits
Stisted Cottage Farm
Park Farm House
CHURCH RD
Fells Farm
Glazenwood
Perry Green Farm
Perry Green
Park House
Hoppits
FIVEASH LA
Bradwell Hall

8

7

25

6

5

24

4

3

23

2

1

22

A B C D E F

CO9

Grange Wood

Crowlands Wood

Markshall Park

Little Monks Wood

Markshall

Great Monks Wood

Little Nunty's Farm

Arboretum

Marks Hall Country Estate

Raynor's Wood

CM77

Iron Bridge

Bouchiers Barn Visitors Ctr

P

Potash Farm

Bungate Wood

New England

Marygolds

PH

Big Joslins

Robin's Brook

Kilnshill Bridge

Crown Plantation

Little Joslins

MARKS HALL RD

KELKAS HILL

MARKS HALL RD

Church Farm

Capels Grove

The Lowes

Rectory

Well Plantation

Hovells Farm

Coggeshall Grove

Rack Meadow

Cradle House

Fen Plantation

Pegs Folly

CO6

A120

The Rookery

Gate House

Pond Piece

Park Lodge

Gate House Spinney

AMBRIDGE RD

Tilkey

Captain's Wood

Holfield Grange

MELLINGS

DAMPIER RD

TILKEY RD

HITCHAM RD

HAWKES RD

Bankfield

Avenue Spinney

BUXTON RD

WINDMILL FIELDS

JAGGARD'S RD

VESTA CL

PRAIL CT

A120

Robin's Bridge

COGGESHALL RD

Stockstreet Farm

Stockstreet

Highfields Farm

HOMEWEAVE HO 1
SCHOOL MEWS 2
DOUBLEDAY CNR 3
GRAVEL CT 4

ROBINSBRIDGE RD

STONEHAM ST

KNIGHT'S

WRIGHTS RD

Liby

Allot Gdns

P

LYONS ACRE

THE GRAVEL

MARKET END

Whiteshill Farm

WAVERLY LA

WEST ST

Griggs Bsns Ctr

WEST ST

Paycocke's House

Grigg's Farm

Garden Ctr

CULVERT CL 1
RIVERSIDE MALTINGS 2
GRANGE MILL 3

BRIDGE ST

GRANGE HILL

GREENACRES

The Slades

CM77

Essex Way

Horseshoe Hole

Grange Barn

Grange Farm

River Blackwater

KELVEDON RD

82 A 83 B C 83 D 84 E F

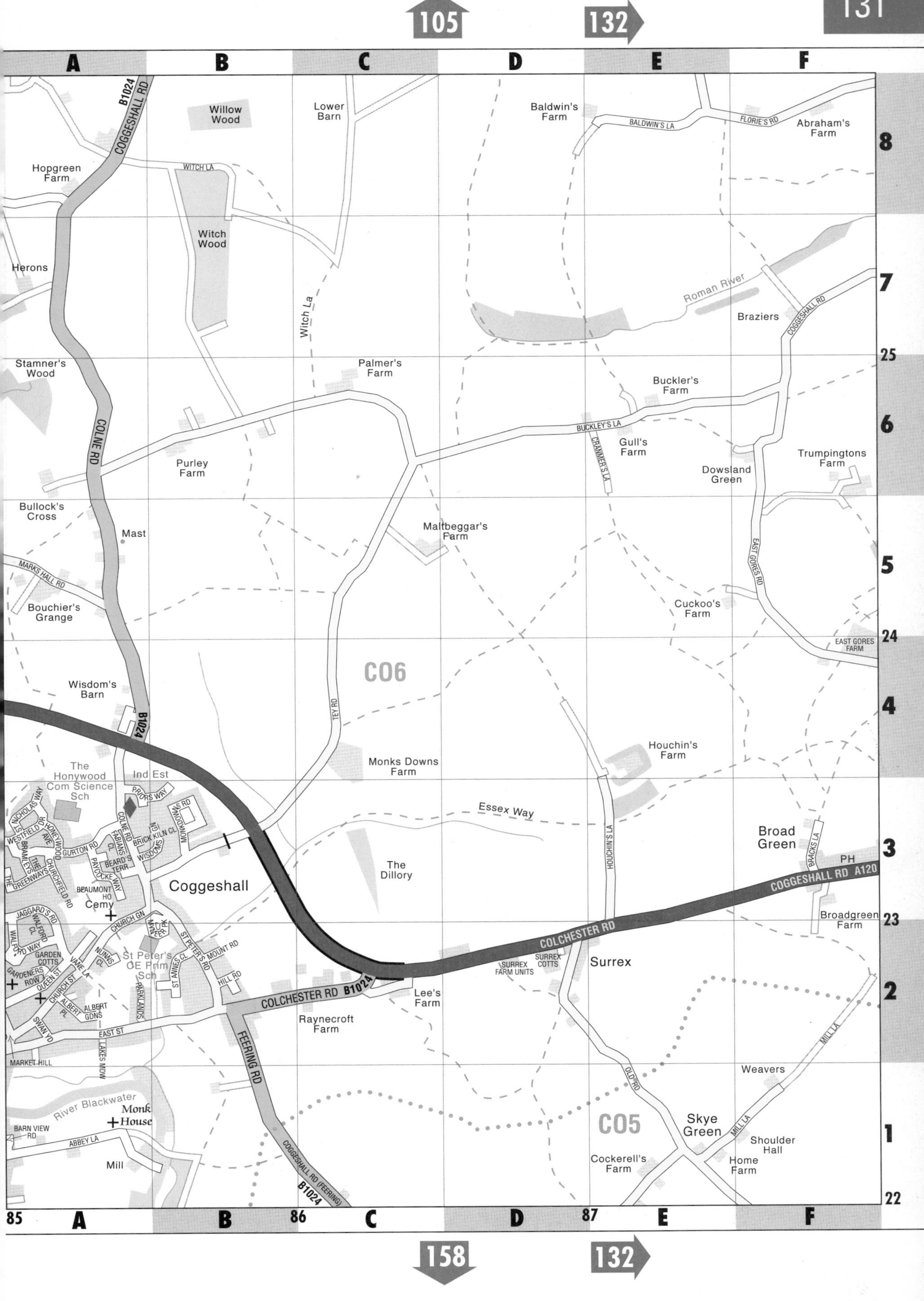

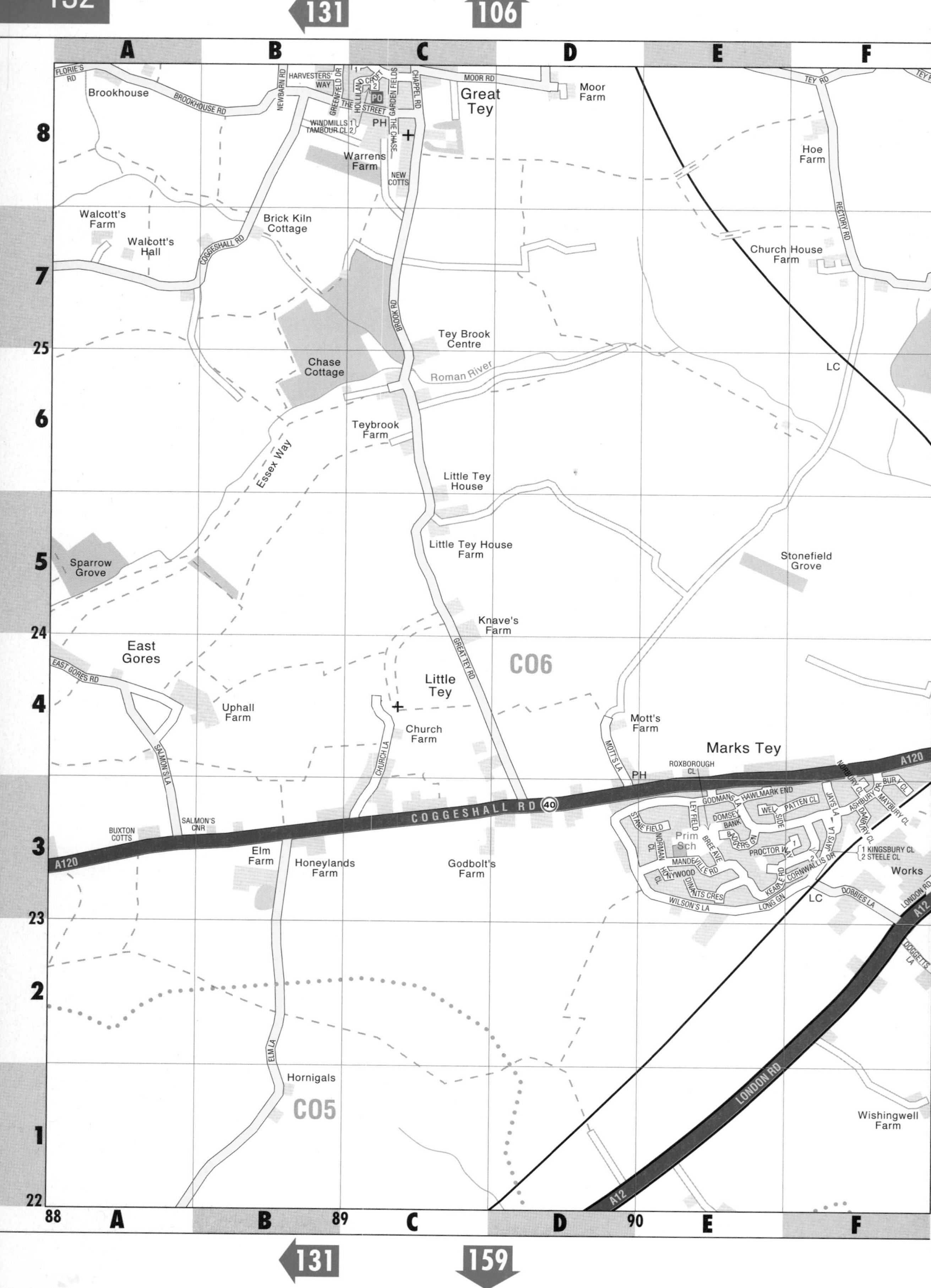

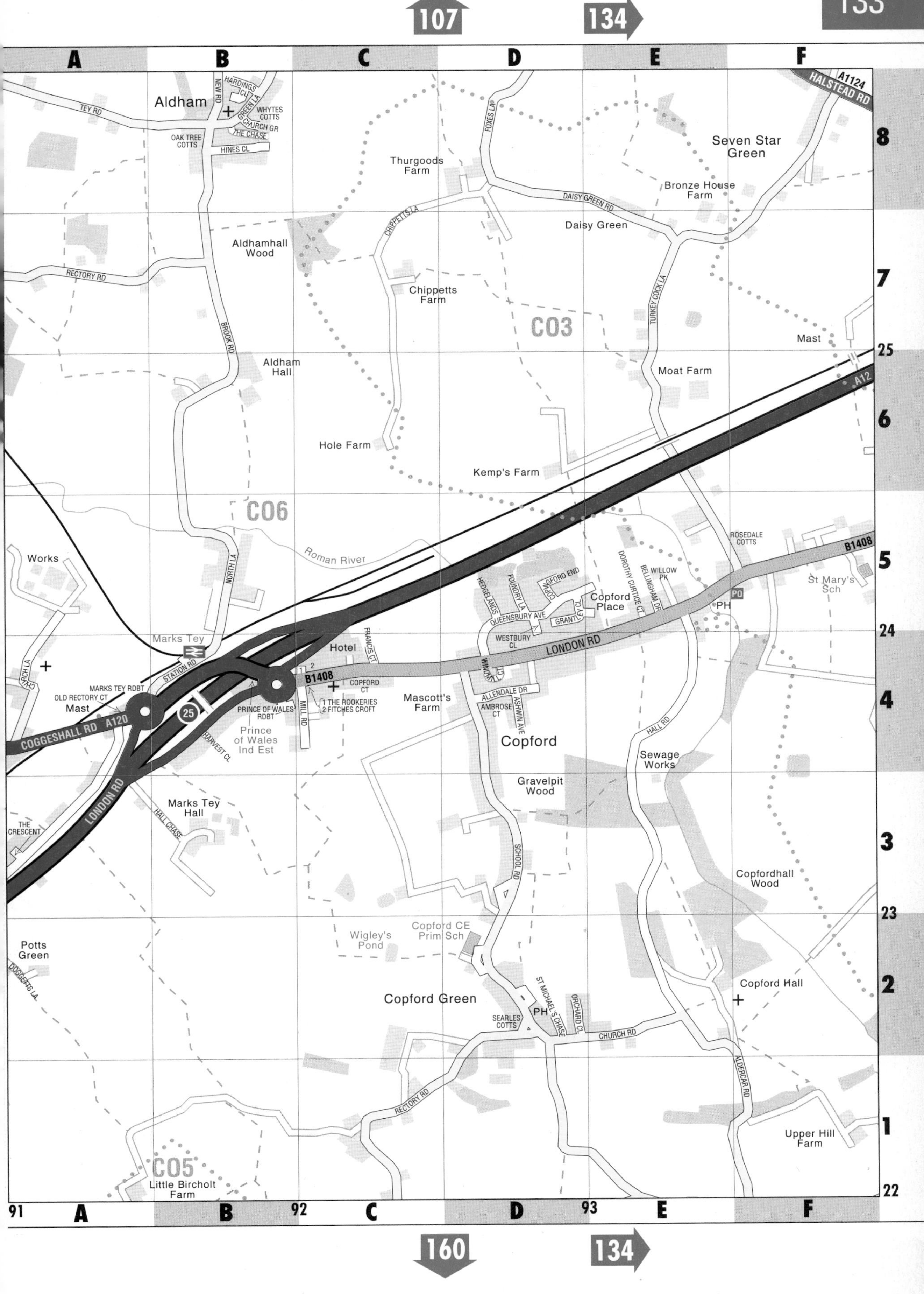

133
108

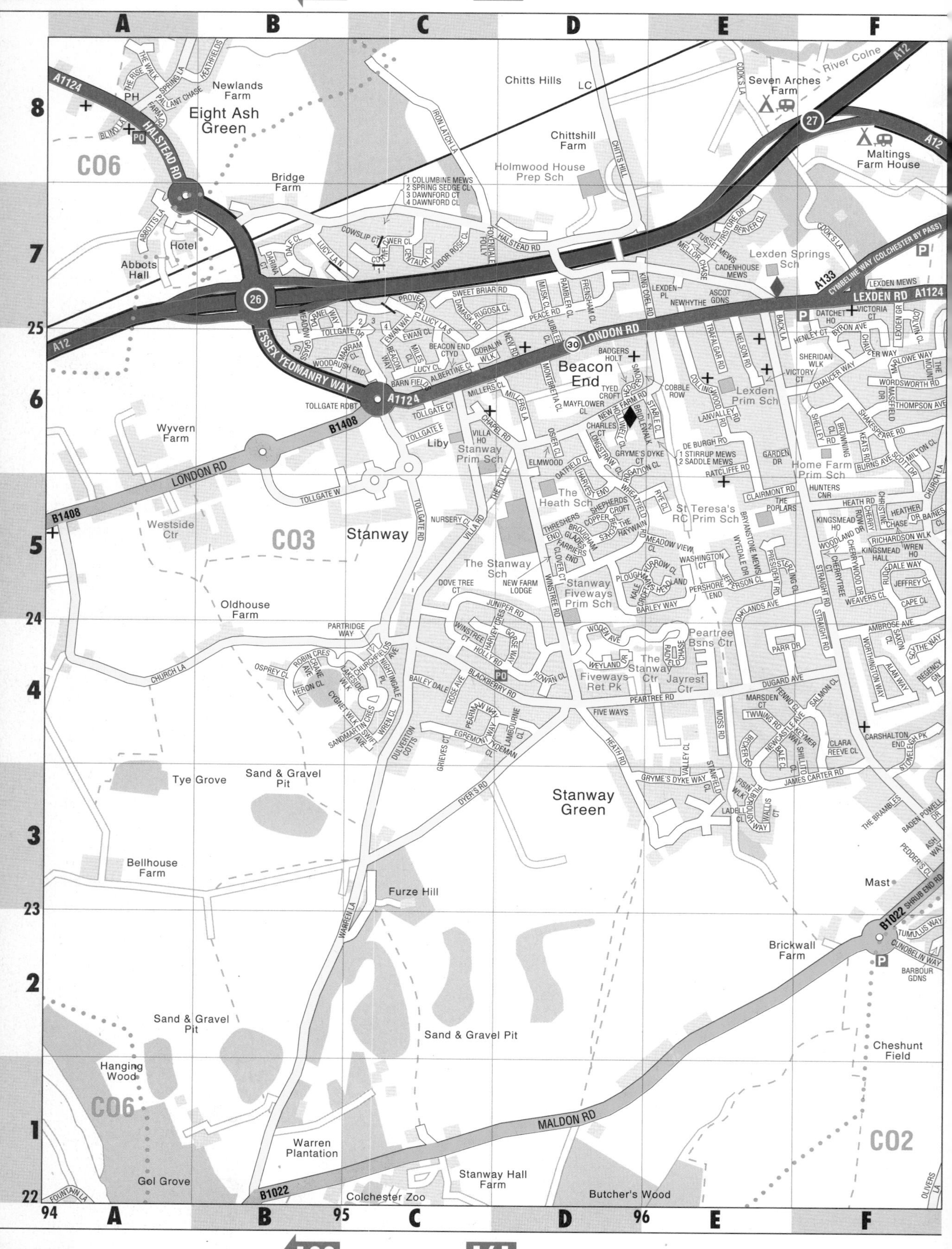
A
B
C
D
E
F
8
7
25
6
5
24
4
3
23
2
1
22
94
95
96
A1124
HALSTEAD RD
PH
PO
CO6
Newlands Farm
Eight Ash Green
Bridge Farm
Hotel
Abbots Hall
ABBOTTS LA
HEATHFIELDS
SPRING LA
THE RISE
THE WALK
PALLANT CHASE
Chitts Hills
LC
Chittshill Farm
Holmwood House Prep Sch
IRON LATCH LA
CHITTS HILL
1 COLUMBINE MEWS
2 SPRING SEDGE CL
3 DAWNFORD CT
4 DAWNFORD CL
COWSLIP CT
LUCY LA N
TUDOR ROSE CL
FOXENDALE FOLLY
HALSTEAD RD
A12
26
ESSEX YEOMANRY WAY
SWEET BRIAR RD
DAMASK RD
RUGOSA CL
PEACE RD
MUSK CL
RAMBLER CL
FRENSHAM CL
KING COEL RD
LEXDEN PL
NEWHYTHE
ASCOT GDNS
MEADOW GRASS
TOLLGATE DR
MARRAM CL
WOODRUSH END
EWAN WAY
EWAN CL
BEACON WAY
MILES CL
LUCY CL
BEACON END CTYD
ALBERTINE CL
CORALIN WLK
NEW RD
JUBILEE CL
30
LONDON RD
BADGERS HOLT
Beacon End
TYED CROFT
BARN FIELDS
TOLLGATE RDBT
A1124
MILLERS CL
MILLERS LA
MONTBRETIA CL
MAYFLOWER CL
NEW FARM RD
HEDGE
CHARLES CT
BRIDLEWALK
STABLE CL
COBBLE ROW
Wyvern Farm
B1408
TOLLGATE CT
TOLLGATE E
Liby
VILLA HO
CHAPEL RD
Stanway Prim Sch
OSIER CL
ELMWOOD
OATFIELD CL
LONGSTRAW CL
HOLLINGWELL CL
GRYME'S DYKE CT
ROGATION CL
1 STIRRUP MEWS
2 SADDLE MEWS
LONDON RD
TOLLGATE W
HARVEST END
The Heath Sch
SHEPHERDS CROFT
WHEATFIELD RD
RYE CL
St Teresa's RC Prim Sch
B1408
Westside Ctr
CO3
Stanway
TOLLGATE RD
NURSERY CL
VILLA RD
THE FOLLEY
THRESHERS END
COPPER BEECHES
THE HAYWAIN
BROUGHAM GLADES
FARRIERS END
CLOVER CT
MEADOW VIEW CL
The Stanway Sch
DOVE TREE CT
NEW FARM LODGE
WINSTREE RD
Stanway Fiveways Prim Sch
PLOUGHMANS HEADLAND
FURROW CL
KALE CROFT
WASHINGTON CT
PERSHORE END
JEFFERSON CL
BARLEY WAY
Oldhouse Farm
JUNIPER RD
PARTRIDGE WAY
WINSTREE CT
HARVEY CRES
GORSE WAY
HOLLY RD
WODEN AVE
Peartree Bsns Ctr
RADFORD CL
CHASE
The Stanway Ctr
WEYLAND DR
Fiveways Ret Pk
Jayrest Ctr
CHURCH LA
OSPREY CL
ROBIN CRES
CRANE AVE
HERON CL
LAKESIDE WLK
CHURCHFIELDS AVE
NIGHTINGALE PL
CYGNET WLK
SANDMARTIN CRES
SWIFT AVE
WREN CL
BAILEY DALE
ROSE AVE
BLACKBERRY RD
PO
ROWAN CL
PEARTREE RD
FIVE WAYS
PEARMAIN WAY
EGREMONT WAY
LAMBOURNE CL
TYDEMAN CL
DULVERTON COTTS
GRIEVES CT
HEATH RD
DYER'S RD
Tye Grove
Sand & Gravel Pit
Stanway Green
Bellhouse Farm
Furze Hill
WARREN LA
Sand & Gravel Pit
Hanging Wood
CO6
Sand & Gravel Pit
Warren Plantation
MALDON RD
Gol Grove
FOUNTAIN LA
B1022
Colchester Zoo
Stanway Hall Farm
Butcher's Wood
River Colne
Seven Arches Farm
COOK'S LA
27
A12
Maltings Farm House
A12
FIRSTORE DR
BEEVER CL
TUSSET MEWS
MELLOR CHASE
CADENHOUSE MEWS
Lexden Springs Sch
COOK'S LA
P
CYMBELINE WAY (COLCHESTER BY PASS)
A133
LEXDEN MEWS
LEXDEN RD
A1124
P
DATCHET HO
VICTORIA CT
BACK LA
HENLEY CT
BYRON AVE
CHAUCER WAY
LEXDEN GR
COLVIN CL
SHERIDAN WLK
VICTORY CT
MARLOWE WAY
THE MOUNT
TRAFALGAR RD
NELSON RD
COLLINGWOOD RD
Lexden Prim Sch
LANVALLEY RD
WORDSWORTH RD
THOMPSON AVE
SHELLEY RD
BROWNING CL
KEATS RD
SHAKESPEARE RD
MASEFIELD DR
DE BURGH RD
RATCLIFFE RD
GARDEN DR
Home Farm Prim Sch
BURNS AVE
SCOTT DR
MILTON CL
CLAIRMONT RD
HUNTERS CNR
THE POPLARS
CHURCH LA
HEATH RD
CHRISTINE CHASE
HEATHER CT
DR BAINES CL
KINGSMEAD HO
BRYANSTONE MEWS
WYEDALE DR
PRESIDENT RD
STERLING CL
STRAIGHT RD
WOODLAND DR
CHERRY ROW
RICHARDSON WLK
KINGSMEAD HALL
WREN HO
CHERRYWOOD DR
CHERRYTREE CT
ROSEDALE WAY
JEFFREY CL
WEAVERS CL
CAPE CL
OAKLANDS AVE
STRAIGHT RD
AMBROSE AVE
SAXON CL
SOUTHWAY
PARR DR
WORTHINGTON WAY
ALAN WAY
REGENCY GN
DUGARD AVE
MARSDEN CT
TENNO CL
SALMON CL
TWINING RD
NEWCASTLE AVE
KEYMER WAY
SHILLITO CL
CLARA REEVE CL
CARSHALTON END
STONELEIGH PK
MOSS RD
VALLEY CL
STANFIELD CL
GRYME'S DYKE WAY
BECKER RD
BALE CL
FISIN WLK
PILBROUGH WAY
WALLIS CT
LADELL CL
JAMES CARTER RD
THE BRAMBLES
BADEN POWELL DR
ASH WAY
PEDDER'S CL
Mast
B1022
SHRUB END RD
TUMULUS WAY
CUNOBELIN WAY
Brickwall Farm
P
BARBOUR GDNS
Cheshunt Field
CO2
OLIVERS LA

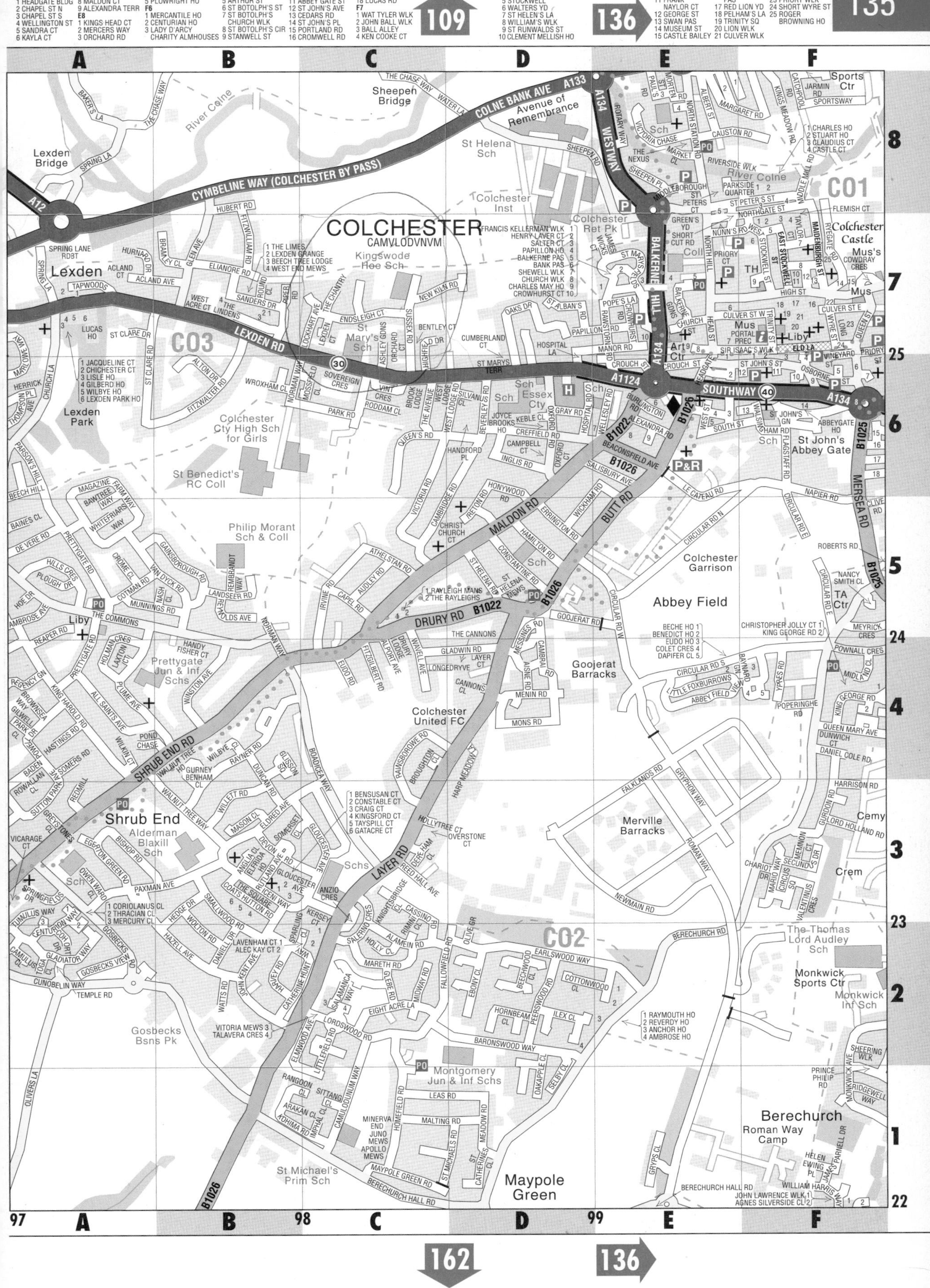

E6
1 HEADGATE BLDG
2 CHAPEL ST N
3 CHAPEL ST S
4 WELLINGTON ST
5 SANDRA CT
6 KAYLA CT
7 WELLESLEY HO
8 MALDON CT
9 ALEXANDRA TERR
E8
1 KINGS HEAD CT
2 MERCERS WAY
3 ORCHARD RD
4 JOHN HARPER ST
5 PLOWRIGHT HO
F6
1 MERCANTILE HO
2 CENTURIAN HO
3 LADY D'ARCY CHARITY ALMHOUSES
4 VINEYARD GATE
5 ARTHUR ST
6 ST BOTOLPH'S ST
7 ST BOTOLPH'S CHURCH WLK
8 ST BOTOLPH'S CIR
9 STANWELL ST
10 WHITEWELL RD
11 ABBEY GATE ST
12 ST JOHN'S AVE
13 CEDARS RD
14 ST JOHN'S PL
15 PORTLAND RD
16 CROMWELL RD
17 FAIRFAX RD
18 LUCAS RD
F7
1 WAT TYLER WLK
2 JOHN BALL WLK
3 BALL ALLEY
4 KEN COOKE CT
109
F7
5 STOCKWELL
6 WALTERS YD
7 ST HELEN'S LA
8 WILLIAM'S WLK
9 ST RUNWALDS ST
10 CLEMENT MELLISH HO
136
F7
11 FRANK NAYLOR CT
12 GEORGE ST
13 SWAN PAS
14 MUSEUM ST
15 CASTLE BAILEY
16 ST NICHOLAS PAS
17 RED LION YD
18 PELHAM'S LA
19 TRINITY SQ
20 LION WLK
21 CULVER WLK
22 ST NICHOLAS ST
23 PRIORY WLK
24 SHORT WYRE ST
25 ROGER BROWNING HO
135
A
B
C
D
E
F
COLCHESTER
CAMVLODVNVM
Lexden
Lexden Bridge
Lexden Park
CO3
CO1
CO2
CYMBELINE WAY (COLCHESTER BY PASS)
COLNE BANK AVE
A12
A133
A134
A1124
B1022
B1026
B1025
WESTWAY
BALKERNE HILL
LEXDEN RD
MALDON RD
BUTT RD
DRURY RD
SHRUB END RD
LAYER RD
SOUTHWAY
MERSEA RD
River Colne
Sheepen Bridge
Avenue of Remembrance
St Helena Sch
Colchester Inst
Colchester Ret Pk
Kingswode Hoe Sch
St Mary's Sch
Colchester Cty High Sch for Girls
St Benedict's RC Coll
Philip Morant Sch & Coll
Prettygate Jun & Inf Schs
Colchester Garrison
Abbey Field
Goojerat Barracks
Merville Barracks
Colchester United FC
Shrub End
Alderman Blaxill Sch
Essex Cty
Colchester Castle
Mus's
St John's Abbey Gate
Colchester Garrison
The Thomas Lord Audley Sch
Monkwick Sports Ctr
Monkwick Inf Sch
Crem
Cemy
Berechurch
Roman Way Camp
Maypole Green
Montgomery Jun & Inf Schs
St Michael's Prim Sch
Gosbecks Bsns Pk
Sports Ctr
TA Ctr
8
7
6
5
4
3
2
1
25
24
23
22
97
98
99
162
136

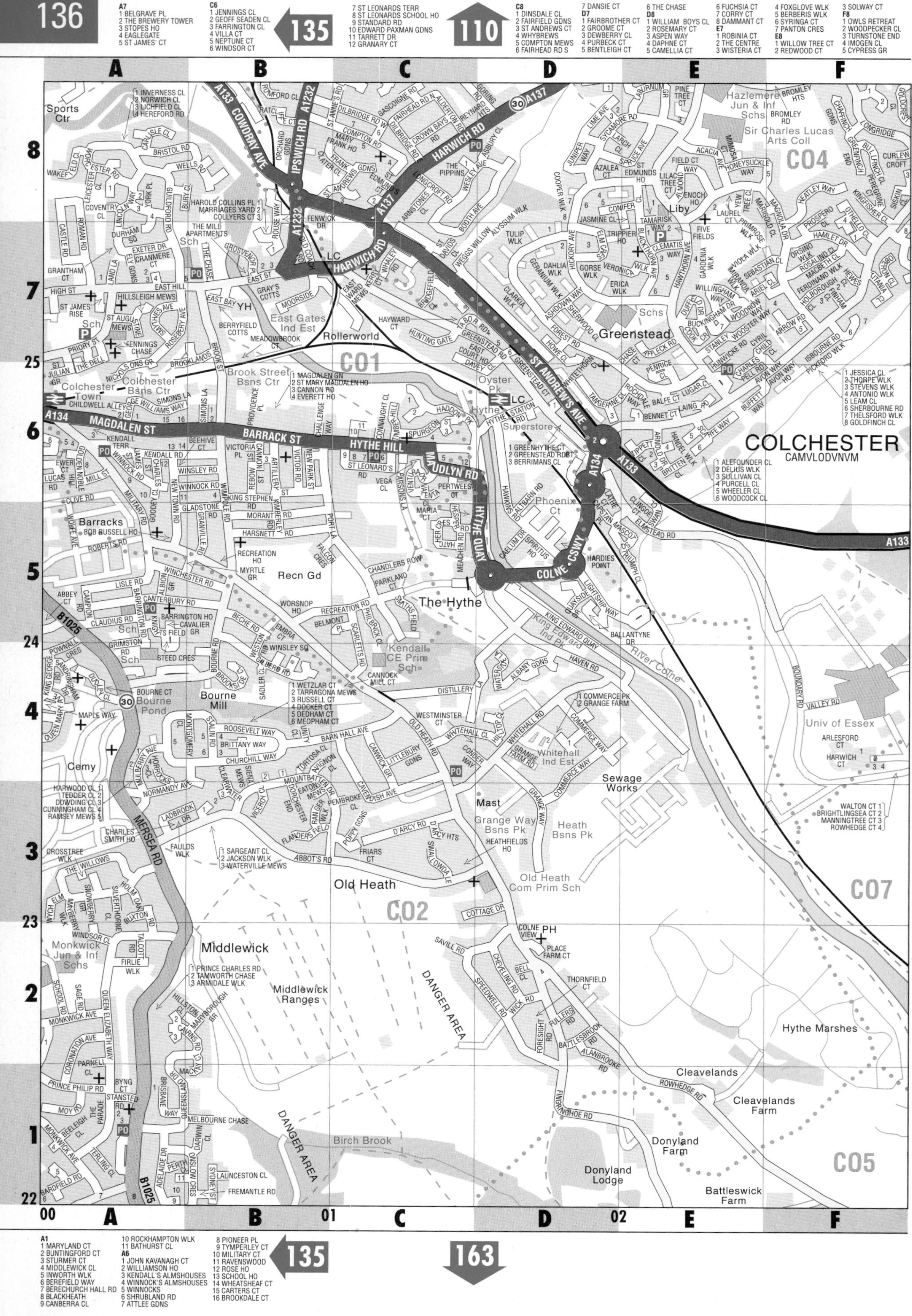
A7
1 BELGRAVE PL
2 THE BREWERY TOWER
3 STOPES HO
4 EAGLEGATE
5 ST JAMES' CT
C6
1 JENNINGS CL
2 GEOFF SEADEN CL
3 FARRINGTON CL
4 VILLA CT
5 NEPTUNE CT
6 WINDSOR CT
135
7 ST LEONARDS TERR
8 ST LEONARDS SCHOOL HO
9 STANDARD RD
10 EDWARD PAXMAN GDNS
11 TARRETT DR
12 GRANARY CT
110
C8
1 DINSDALE CL
2 FAIRFIELD GDNS
3 ST ANDREWS CT
4 WHYBREWS
5 COMPTON MEWS
6 FAIRHEAD RD S
7 DANSIE CT
D7
1 FAIRBROTHER CT
2 GROOME CT
3 DEWBERRY CL
4 PURBECK CT
5 BENTLEIGH CT
6 THE CHASE
D8
1 WILLIAM BOYS CL
2 ROSEMARY CT
3 ASPEN WAY
4 DAPHNE CT
5 CAMELLIA CT
6 FUCHSIA CT
7 CORRY CT
8 DAMMANT CT
E7
1 ROBINIA CT
2 THE CENTRE
3 WISTERIA CT
4 FOXGLOVE WLK
5 BERBERIS WLK
6 SYRINGA CT
7 PANTON CRES
E8
1 WILLOW TREE CT
2 REDWOOD CT
3 SOLWAY CT
F8
1 OWLS RETREAT
2 WOODPECKER CL
3 TURNSTONE END
4 IMOGEN CL
5 CYPRESS GR
A B C D E F
8 7 25 6 5 24 4 3 23 2 1 22
00 01 02
COLCHESTER
CAMVLODVNVM
CO1
CO2
CO4
CO5
CO7
Greenstead
The Hythe
Old Heath
Middlewick
Hythe Marshes
Cleavelands
Donyland Farm
Battleswick Farm
Univ of Essex
A1
1 MARYLAND CT
2 BUNTINGFORD CT
3 STURMER CT
4 MIDDLEWICK CL
5 INWORTH WLK
6 BEREFIELD WAY
7 BERECHURCH HALL RD
8 BLACKHEATH
9 CANBERRA CL
10 ROCKHAMPTON WLK
11 BATHURST CL
A6
1 JOHN KAVANAGH CT
2 WILLIAMSON HO
3 KENDALL'S ALMSHOUSES
4 WINNOCK'S ALMSHOUSES
5 WINNOCKS
6 SHRUBLAND RD
7 ATTLEE GDNS
8 PIONEER PL
9 TYMPERLEY CT
10 MILITARY CT
11 RAVENSWOOD
12 ROSE HO
13 SCHOOL HO
14 WHEATSHEAF CT
15 CARTERS CT
16 BROOKDALE CT
135
163

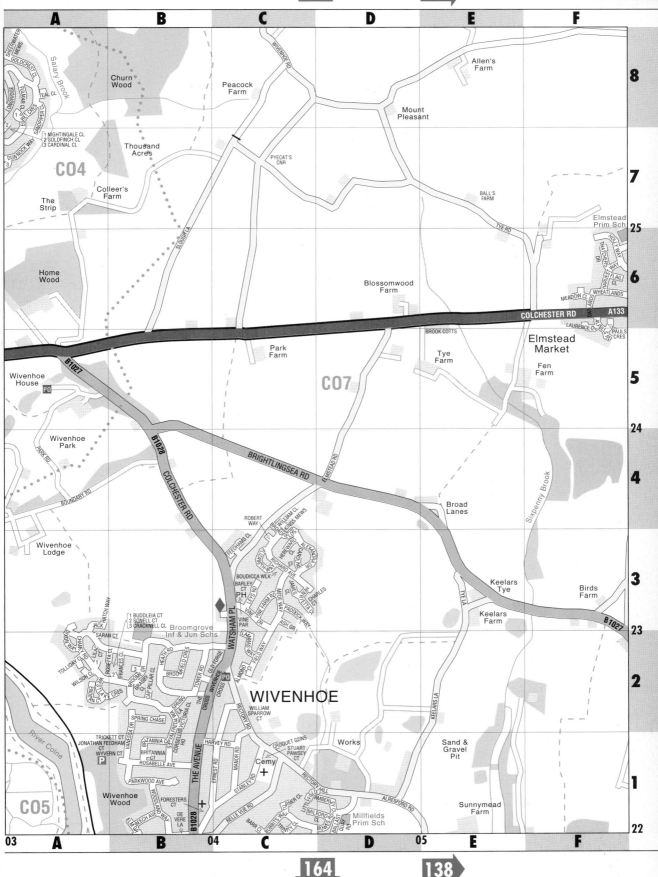

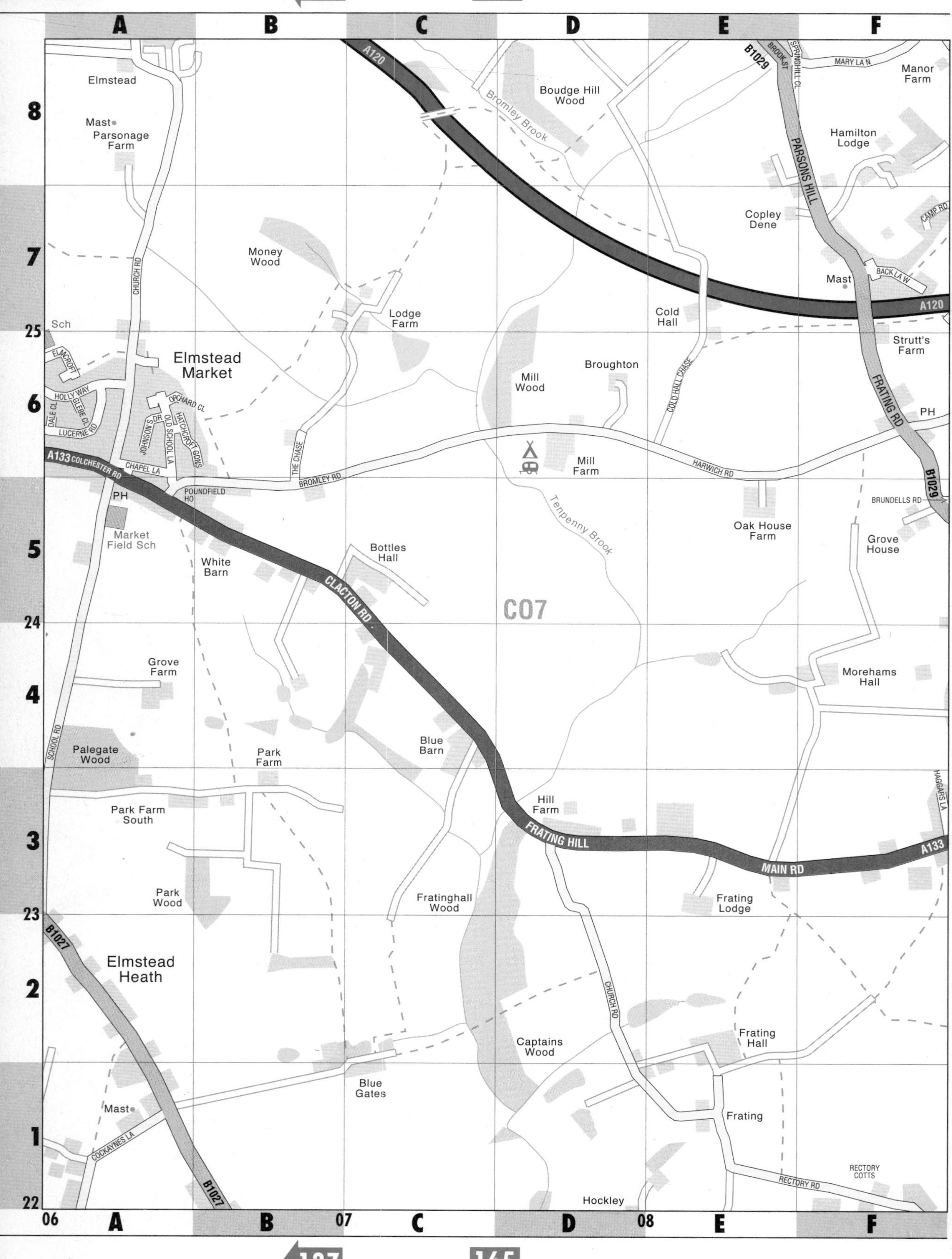

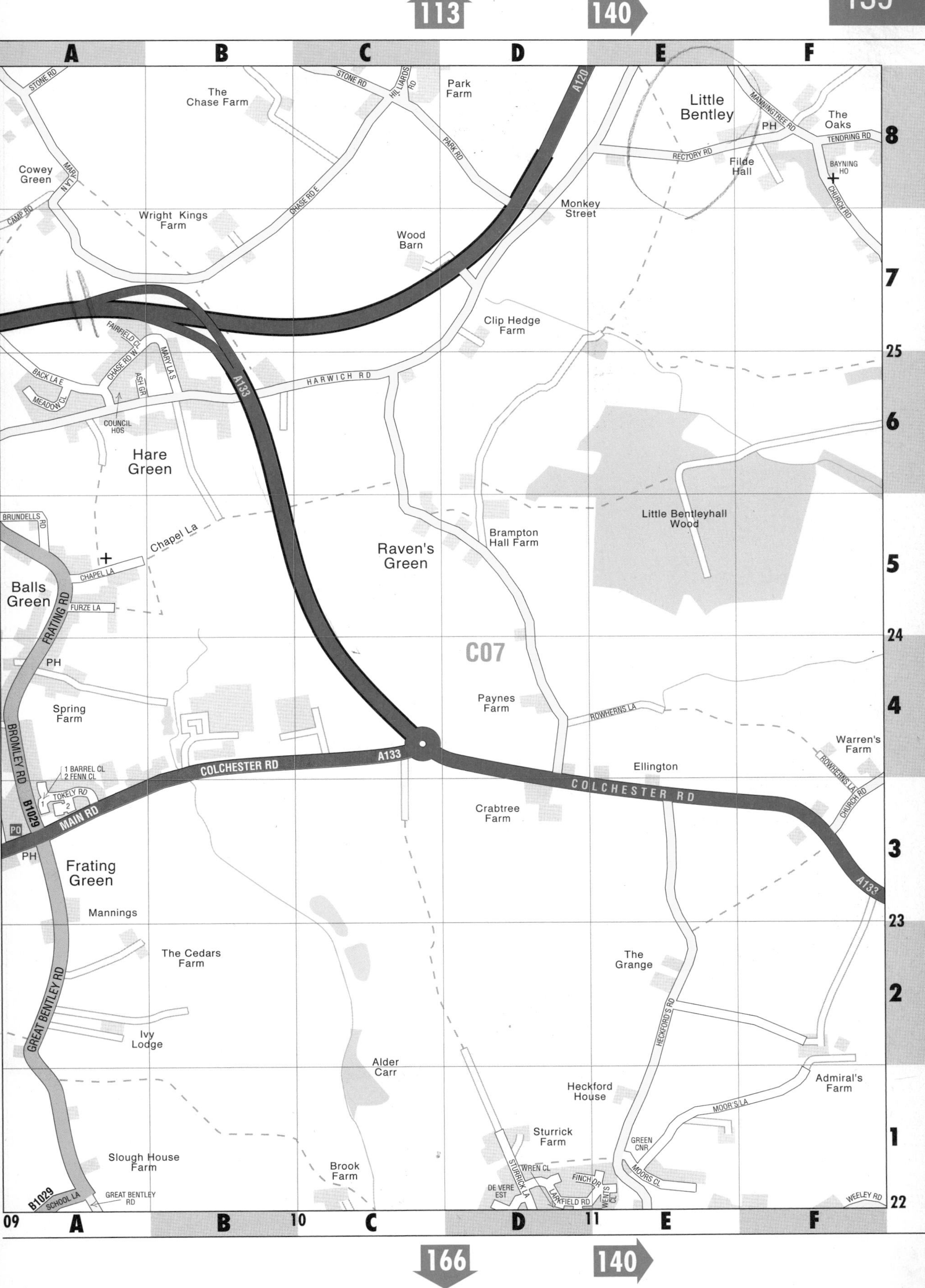

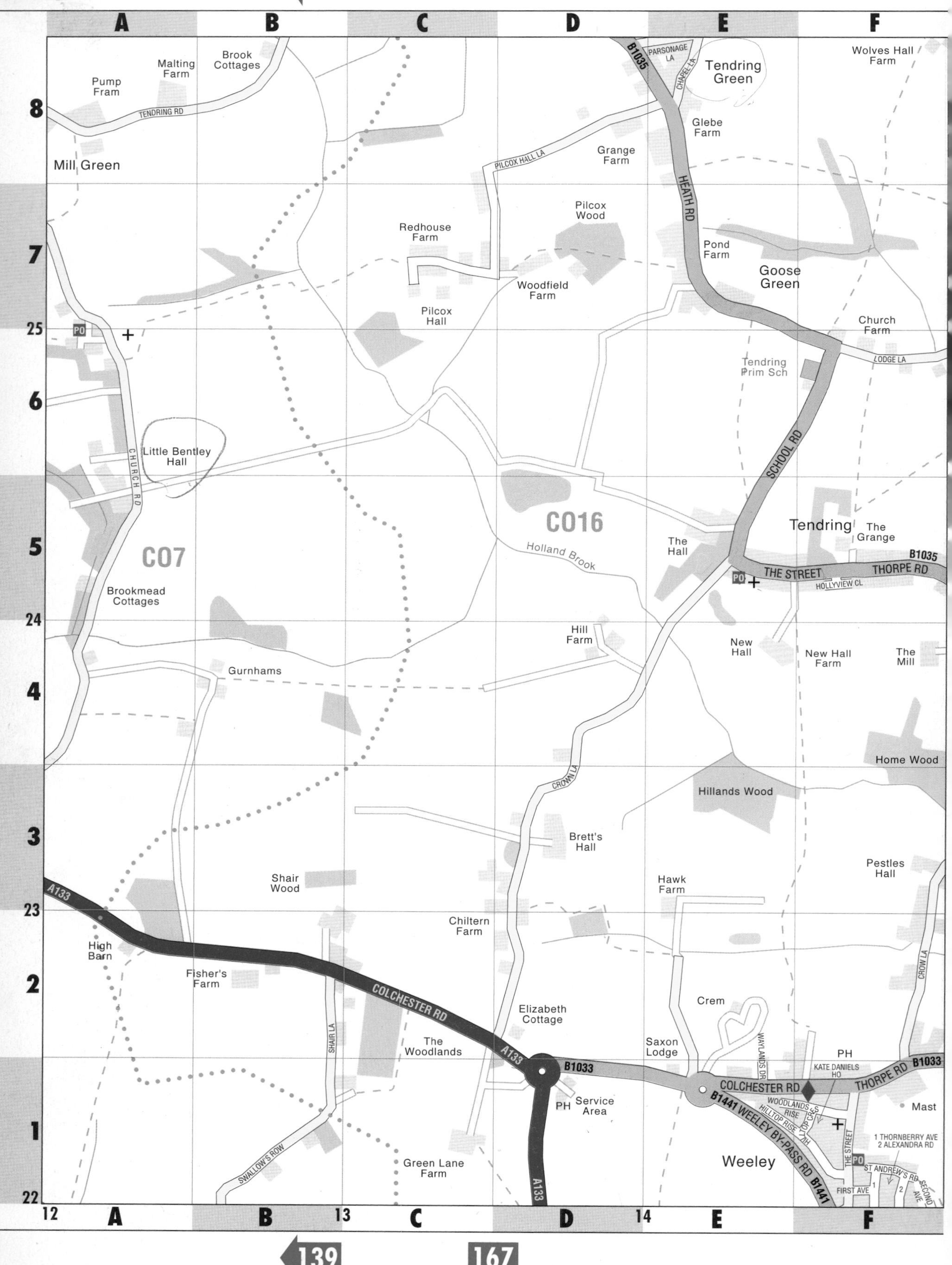

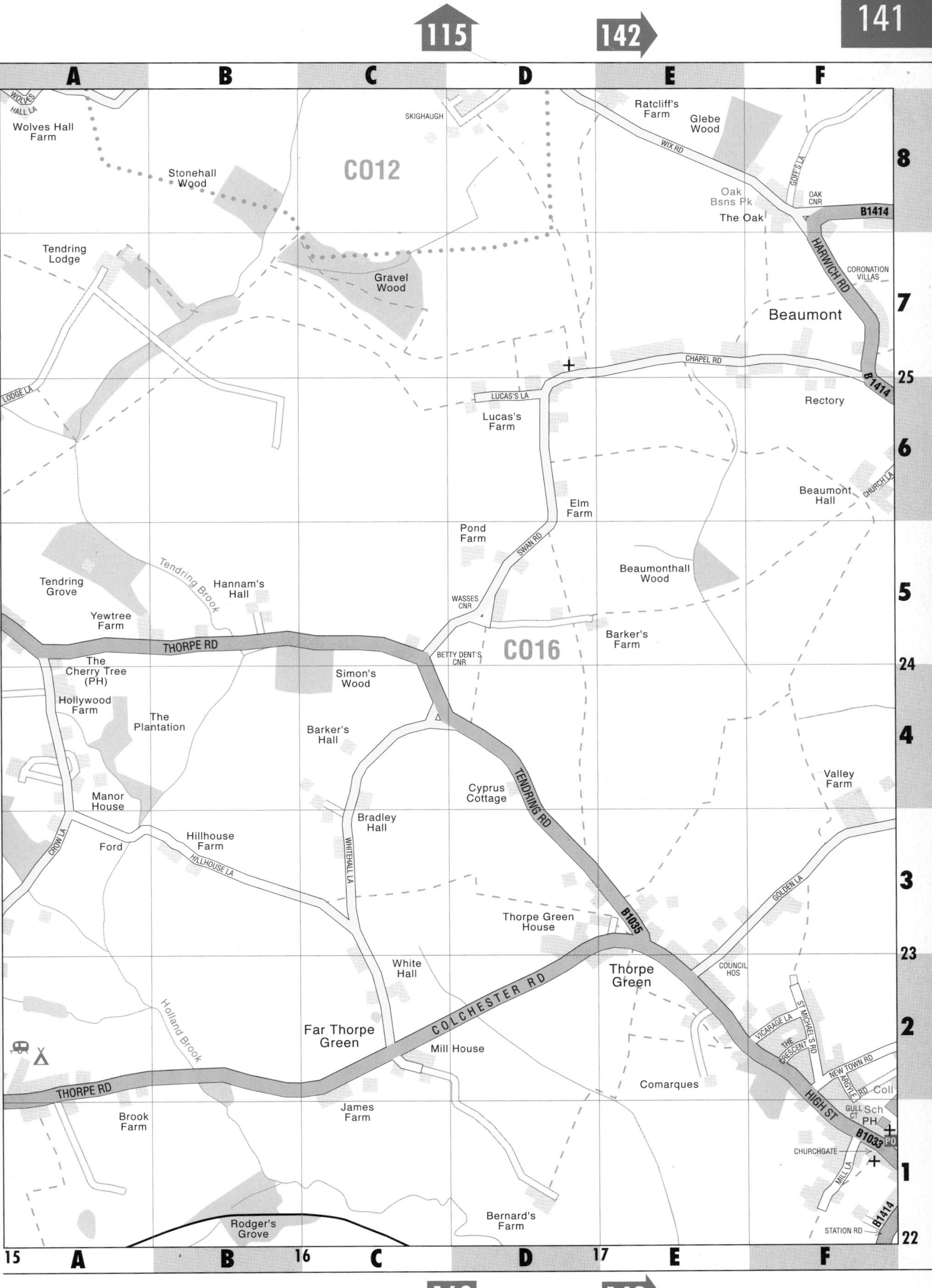

115
142
168
142

A   B   C   D   E   F

8
7
25
6
5
24
4
3
23
2
1
22

WOLVES HALL LA
Wolves Hall Farm

Stonehall Wood

SKIGHAUGH

CO12

Ratcliff's Farm
Glebe Wood
WIX RD
Oak Bsns Pk
The Oak
OAK CNR
GOFE'S LA
B1414
HARWICH RD
CORONATION VILLAS

Beaumont

Tendring Lodge

Gravel Wood

CHAPEL RD
B1414

LODGE LA

LUCAS'S LA
Lucas's Farm

Rectory

Elm Farm

Beaumont Hall
CHURCH LA

Pond Farm
SWAN RD

Tendring Brook
Hannam's Hall

Beaumonthall Wood

Tendring Grove

Yewtree Farm

WASSES CNR

Barker's Farm

CO16

THORPE RD

Simon's Wood

BETTY DENT'S CNR

The Cherry Tree (PH)

Hollywood Farm

The Plantation

Barker's Hall

Cyprus Cottage

Valley Farm

TENDRING RD

Manor House

Bradley Hall

GOLDEN LA

CROW LA

Ford

Hillhouse Farm

HILLHOUSE LA

WHITEHALL LA

Thorpe Green House

B1033

Thorpe Green

COUNCIL HOS

23

White Hall

COLCHESTER RD

VICARAGE LA
ST MICHAEL'S RD
THE CRESCENT

Holland Brook

Far Thorpe Green

Mill House

NEW TOWN RD
ST ARGYLE RD
Coll

THORPE RD

Comarques

HIGH ST
GULL CT
Sch
PH
B1033
PO

Brook Farm

James Farm

CHURCHGATE
MILL LA

Rodger's Grove

Bernard's Farm

STATION RD
B1414

15   A   B   16   C   D   17   E   F

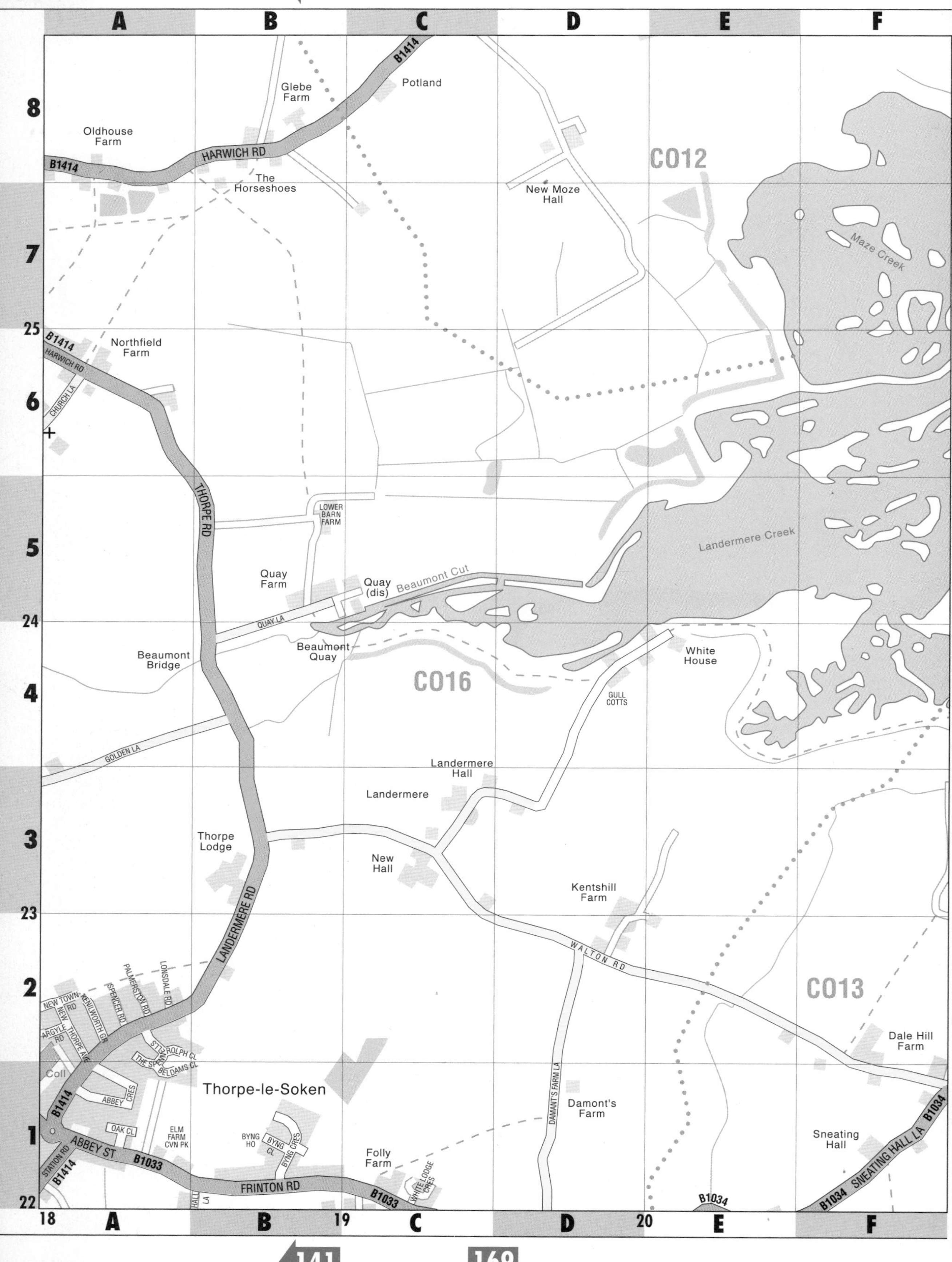

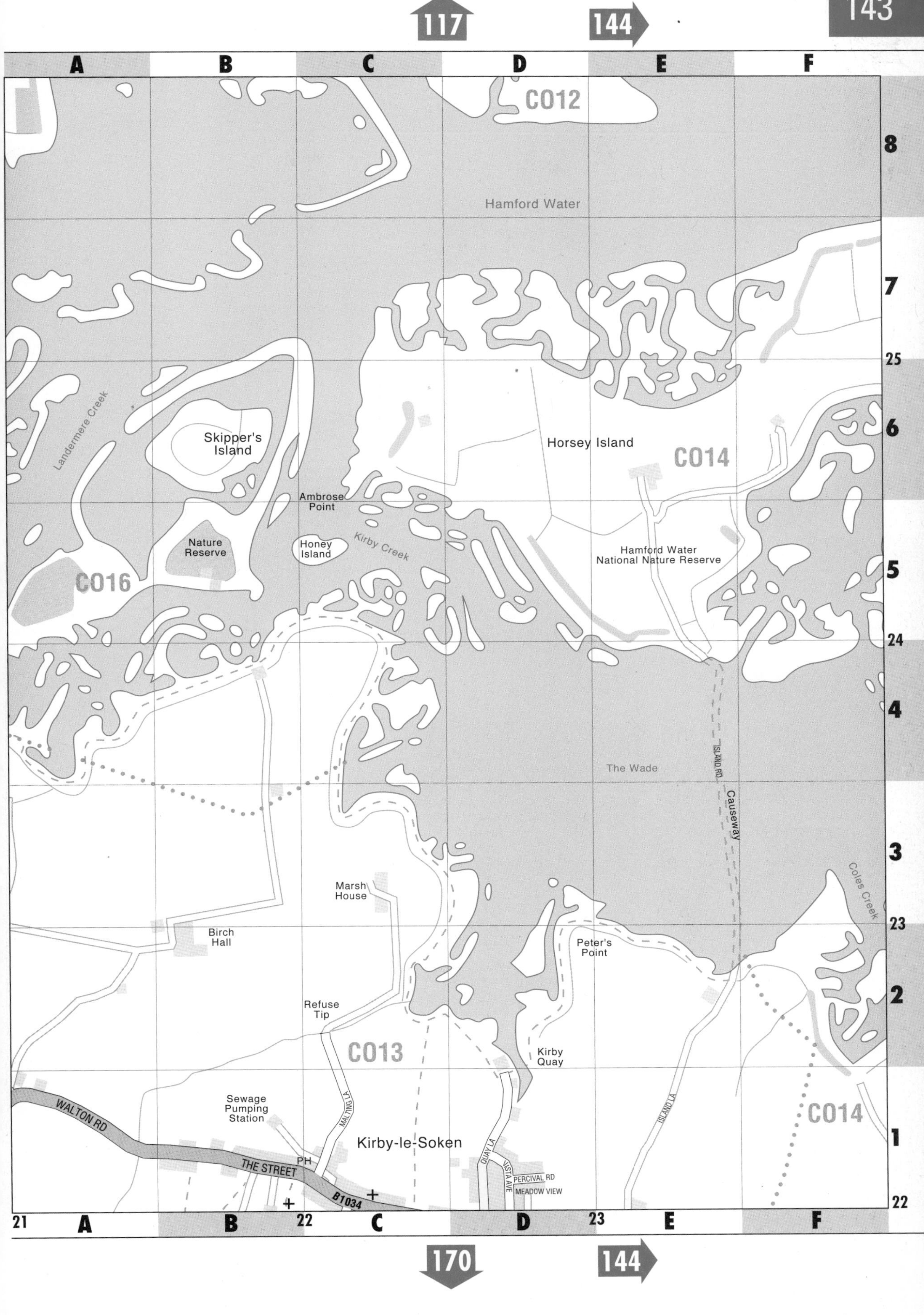

CO12

Hamford Water

Landermere Creek

Skipper's
Island

Horsey Island

CO14

Ambrose
Point

Nature
Reserve

Honey
Island

Kirby Creek

Hamford Water
National Nature Reserve

CO16

The Wade

ISLAND RD
Causeway

Coles Creek

Marsh
House

Peter's
Point

Birch
Hall

Refuse
Tip

CO13

Kirby
Quay

Sewage
Pumping
Station

MALTING LA

ISLAND LA

CO14

WALTON RD

Kirby-le-Soken

QUAY LA

THE STREET

PH

PERCIVAL RD
MEADOW VIEW

VISTA AVE

B1034

143

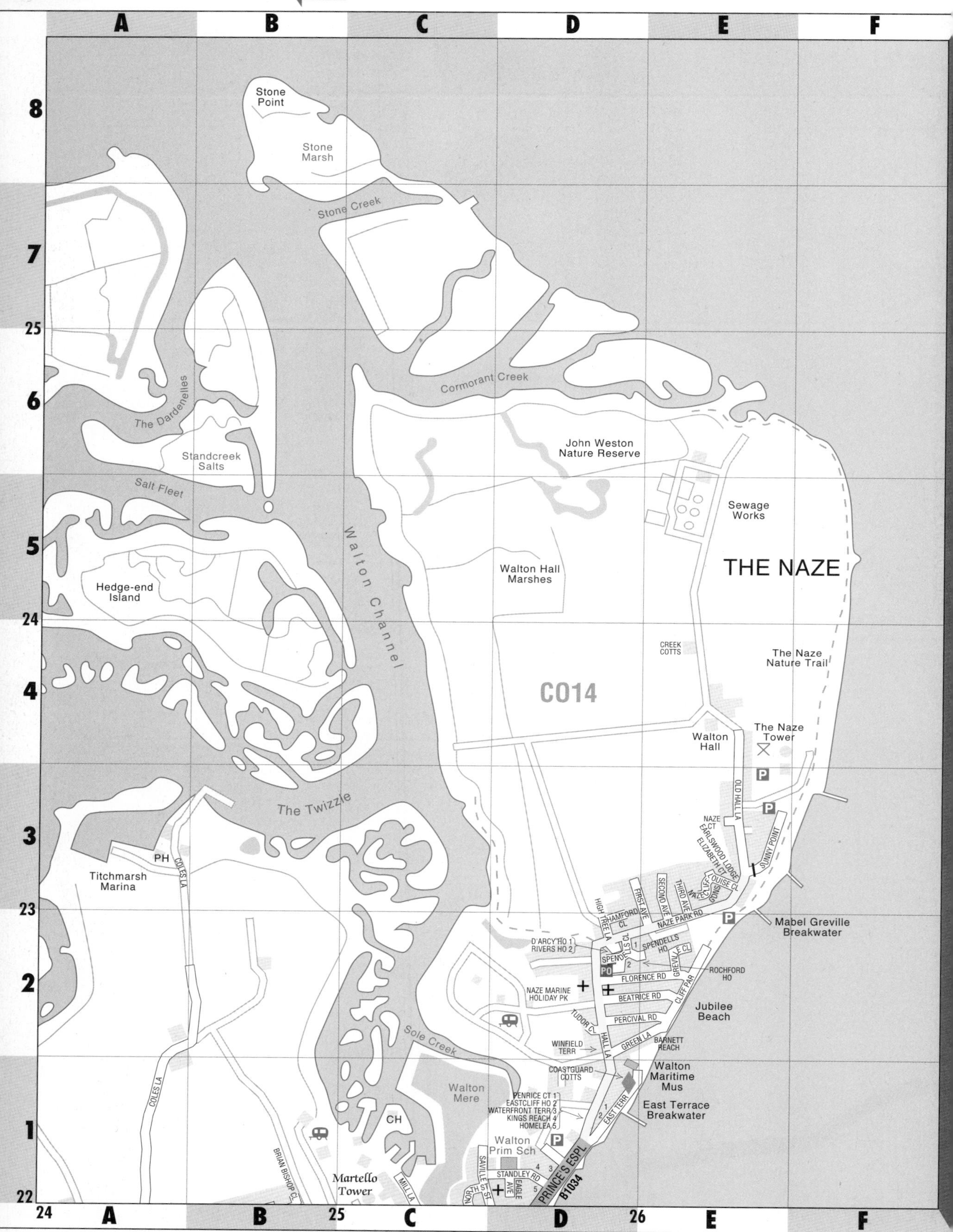
A
B
C
D
E
F
8
7
25
6
5
24
4
3
23
2
1
22
Stone Point
Stone Marsh
Stone Creek
Cormorant Creek
The Dardenelles
Standcreek Salts
Salt Fleet
John Weston Nature Reserve
Sewage Works
Walton Channel
Walton Hall Marshes
THE NAZE
Hedge-end Island
CREEK COTTS
The Naze Nature Trail
CO14
Walton Hall
The Naze Tower
The Twizzle
OLD HALL LA
NAZE CT
EARLSWOOD LODGE
ELIZABETH CT
LOUISE CL
NAZE CLIFF GDNS
SUNNY POINT
PH
COLES LA
Titchmarsh Marina
FIRST AVE
SECOND AVE
THIRD AVE
HIGH TREE LA
HAMFORD CL
NAZE PARK RD
Mabel Greville Breakwater
D'ARCY HO 1
RIVERS HO 2
SPENDELLS CL
SPENDELLS HO
GREVILLE CL
ROCHFORD HO
PO
FLORENCE RD
NAZE MARINE HOLIDAY PK
BEATRICE RD
CLIFF PAR
Jubilee Beach
PERCIVAL RD
TUDOR CL
WINFIELD TERR
HALL LA
GREEN LA
BARNETT REACH
Sole Creek
COASTGUARD COTTS
Walton Maritime Mus
Walton Mere
PENRICE CT 1
EASTCLIFF HO 2
WATERFRONT TERR 3
KINGS REACH 4
HOMELEA 5
EAST TERR
East Terrace Breakwater
CH
Walton Prim Sch
BRIAN BISHOP CL
SAVILLE ST
STANDLEY RD
EAGLE AVE
NORTH ST
PRINCE'S ESPL
B1034
Martello Tower
MILL LA
24
25
26

143
171

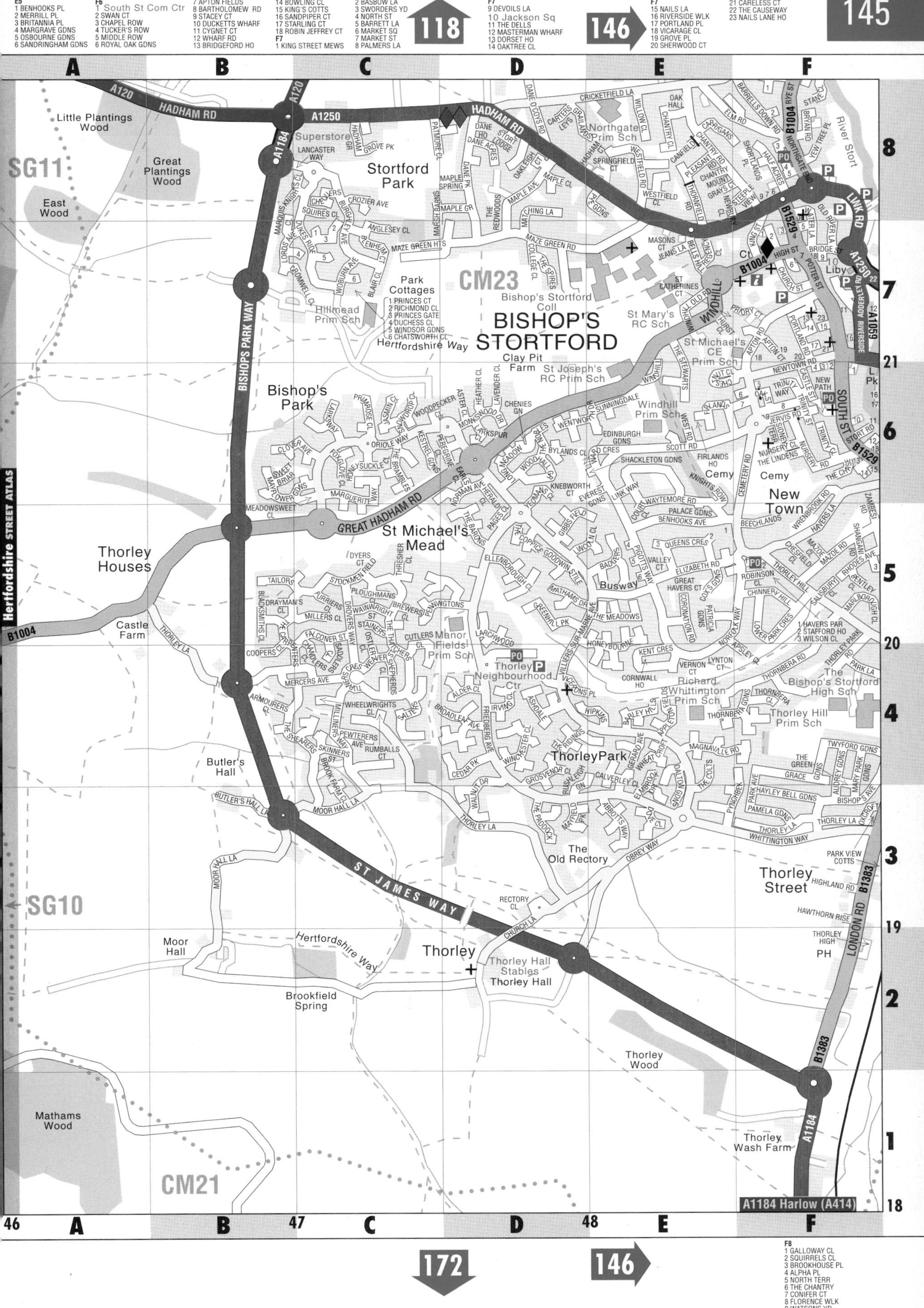

E5
1 BENHOOKS PL
2 MERRILL PL
3 BRITANNIA PL
4 MARGRAVE GDNS
5 OSBOURNE GDNS
6 SANDRINGHAM GDNS

F6
1 SOUTH ST COM CTR
2 SWAN CT
3 CHAPEL ROW
4 TUCKER'S ROW
5 MIDDLE ROW
6 ROYAL OAK GDNS

7 APTON FIELDS
8 BARTHOLOMEW RD
9 STACEY CT
10 DUCKETTS WHARF
11 CYGNET CT
12 WHARF RD
13 BRIDGEFORD HO

F7
1 KING STREET MEWS

14 BOWLING CL
15 KING'S COTTS
16 SANDPIPER CT
17 STARLING CT
18 ROBIN JEFFREY CT

2 BASBOW LA
3 SWORDERS YD
4 NORTH ST
5 BARRETT LA
6 MARKET SQ
7 MARKET ST
8 PALMERS LA

F7
9 DEVOILS LA
10 JACKSON SQ
11 THE DELLS
12 MASTERMAN WHARF
13 DORSET HO
14 OAKTREE CL

F7
15 NAILS LA
16 RIVERSIDE WLK
17 PORTLAND PL
18 VICARAGE CL
19 GROVE PL
20 SHERWOOD CT

21 CARELESS CT
22 THE CAUSEWAY
23 NAILS LANE HO

F8
1 GALLOWAY CL
2 SQUIRRELS CL
3 BROOKHOUSE PL
4 ALPHA PL
5 NORTH TERR
6 THE CHANTRY
7 CONIFER CT
8 FLORENCE WLK
9 WATSONS YD

A7
1 THE CAUSEWAY
2 THE OLD MALTINGS
3 FULLER CT
4 RED LION CT
5 BAKERS CT
6 HOCKERILL CT
7 HARRINGTON CL
8 PRIORS
9 CLIFFORD CT
10 THOMAS HESKIN CT
11 JOSCELYN'S YD
12 JUBILEE COTT
13 THE PUMP HO

B8
1 BOYD CL
2 HEATH ROW
3 STORTFORD HALL RD
4 GROSVENOR HO
5 EATON HO
6 BELGRAVE HO

LEGIONS WAY
GOLDINGS
Collins Cross
CANNONS RD
ELLIOTT CT
DOLPHIN WAY
THE BOURNE
KINGSBRIDGE RD
KINGSMEAD RD
GLEB CT
GLEB GR
CHURCH MANOR
STORTFORD HALL PK
MANSTON DR
PARSONAGE LA
THE COPSE
PLAW HATCH CL
FRIARS
WOODLANDS
CLUFTON CRES

All Saints CE Prim Sch
Birchwood High Sch

A120
BIRCHANGER LA
M11

Waytemore Castle
CASTLE
HERON WAY
KINGFISHER WAY
ALL SAINTS
SONIX
Hockerill Anglo-European Coll
Mast
RAYNHAM RD
RAYNHAM RD
RAYNHAM RD
PEISLEY
NYTON
ELM GR
EDENS CL
URBAN RD
Summercroft Prim Sch
MAYES CL
CECIL CL
WOODSIDE
PLAW HATCH CNR
CH
Hotel
Birchanger Green Services
THREMHALL AVE A120
B1256 DUNMOW RD

A1250
B1383
A1060
A1250
HOCKERILL ST
POST
CROWN TERR
HILLSIDE
GRANGE RD
WALK
A1059
DANE ST
STATION RD
ANCHOR ST
DANE ST
WHARF
EIDER CT
SWALLOW CT
JOHN DYDE CL
MALLARD CT
Southmill Trad Ctr
B1529
Mus
SOUTHMILL
King's Cotts
THE MOORINGS
Mside Ind Est
Island
1 KIMBERLEY CL
2 MILL ST
3 WHITEPOST CT
4 EMMERSON HO
Bishop's Stortford
Hockerill
WARWICK RD
CRESCENT RD
AVENUE RD
PINE GR
PRIORY AVE
THORN GR
PRYORS
THE SYCAMORES
DIMSDALE CRES
GREAT EASTERN RD
BELDAMS LA
The Hertfordshire & Essex High Sch
Herts & Essex Com
FAIRWAY
ROSEBERY
GREENWAY
HAMPCADE RD
HIGHFIELD AVE
LINGSIDE RD
BELDAMS GATE
NEWTON RD
HAYCROFT
PH
BROOKE GDNS
MORRIS CL
DUNMOW RD
MANOR LINKS
MANOR LINKS

BISHOP'S STORTFORD
CM23

Little Beldams
Grate Beldams
Harps Farm

London Rd
B1383
RHODES AVE
WILS CL
MULBERRY CT
HASLEMERE RD
PROCTORS WAY
THORLEY HILL PARK
MITRE GDNS
Thorley
The Twyford Bsns Ctr
Haslemere Ind Est
Twyford Villas Ind Est
TWYFORD MEWS
THE MEWS
TWYFORD MILL
River Stort
Twyfordbury Farmhouse
Hertfordshire Way

Grate Beldams
Great Jehkins
JENKINS LA
Sewage Works
Great Jehkins

COPTHALL CL
THE POPLARS
Long Plantation
THE GROVE

HALLINGBURY RD
LATCHMORE BANK

CM22

Anvil Cross
Captain's Plantation
Hall Farm
The Hall
Great Hallingbury
CHURCH RD
Ladywell Plantation

Howe Green
Howe Green House Sch
Hallingbury Park
Ladywell
Morleys

B1383
BISHOPS AVE
PORT LA
Little Hallingbury
NORMANDALE KENNELS
Normandale Kennels
NEW BARN LA
HALLINGBURY CL
A1060
DELL LA
GEORGE GREEN BGLWS
PH

M11
Woodside Green

49
A
B
50
C
D
51
E
F

8
7
21
6
5
20
4
3
19
2
1
18

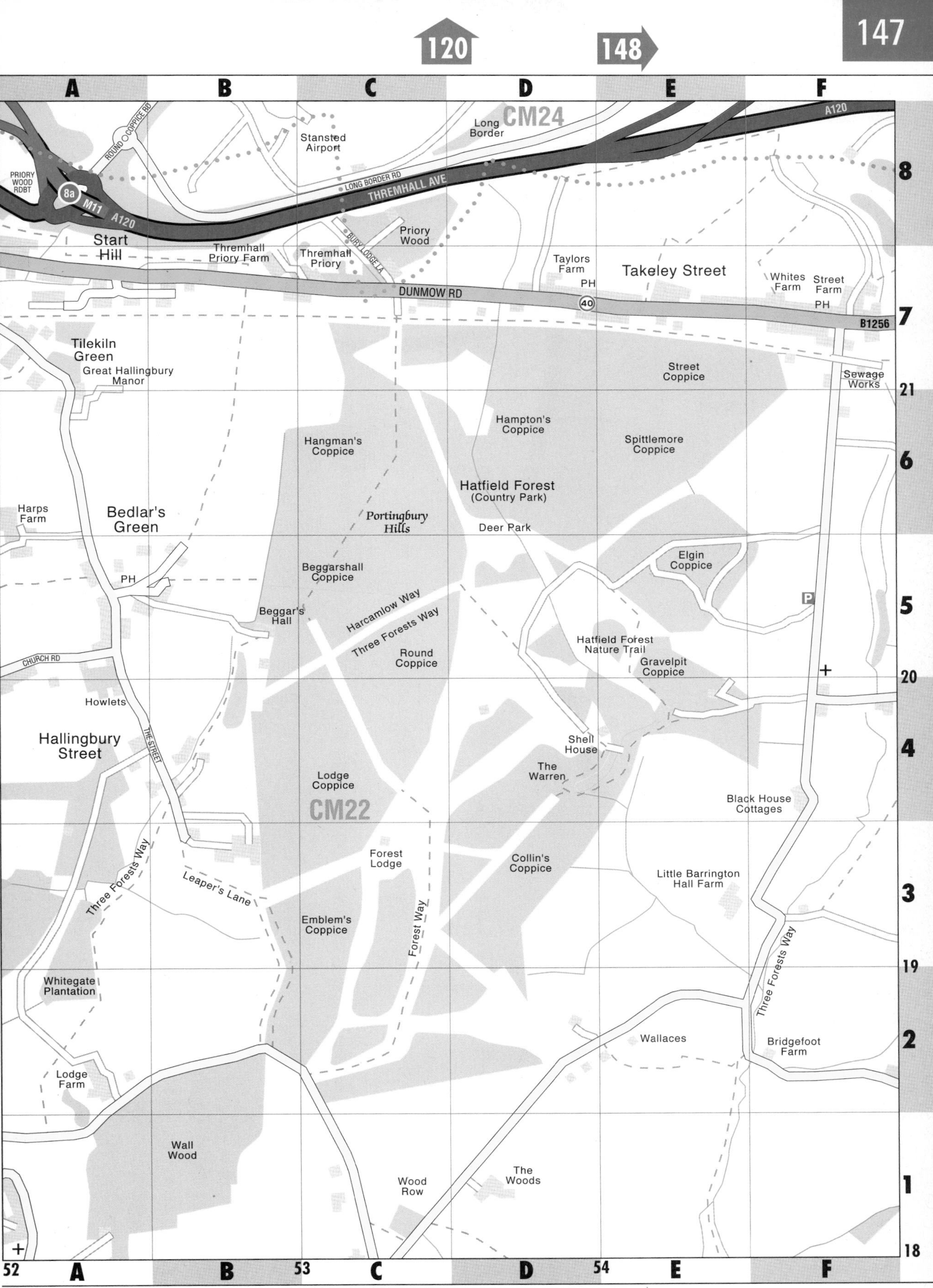

A B C D E F

Stansted Airport

PRIORY WOOD RDBT

ROUND O COPPICE RD

8a M11 A120

Start Hill

Long Border

CM24

Long Border Rd

THREMHALL AVE

Priory Wood

Taylors Farm
PH

Takeley Street

Whites Farm

Street Farm
PH

8

Thremhall Priory Farm

Thremhall Priory

BURY LODGE LA

DUNMOW RD

40

B1256

7

Tilekiln Green

Great Hallingbury Manor

Street Coppice

Sewage Works

21

Harps Farm

Bedlar's Green

Hangman's Coppice

Hampton's Coppice

Hatfield Forest (Country Park)

Portingbury Hills

Deer Park

Spittlemore Coppice

6

Elgin Coppice

P

5

Beggarshall Coppice

CHURCH RD

PH

Beggar's Hall

Harcamlow Way

Three Forests Way

Round Coppice

Hatfield Forest Nature Trail

Gravelpit Coppice

20

Howlets

THE STREET

Hallingbury Street

Shell House

The Warren

Black House Cottages

4

Lodge Coppice

CM22

Forest Lodge

Forest Way

Collin's Coppice

Little Barrington Hall Farm

Three Forests Way

3

Three Forests Way

Leaper's Lane

Emblem's Coppice

19

Whitegate Plantation

Wallaces

Bridgefoot Farm

2

Lodge Farm

Wall Wood

Wood Row

The Woods

1

18

52 A B 53 C D 54 E F

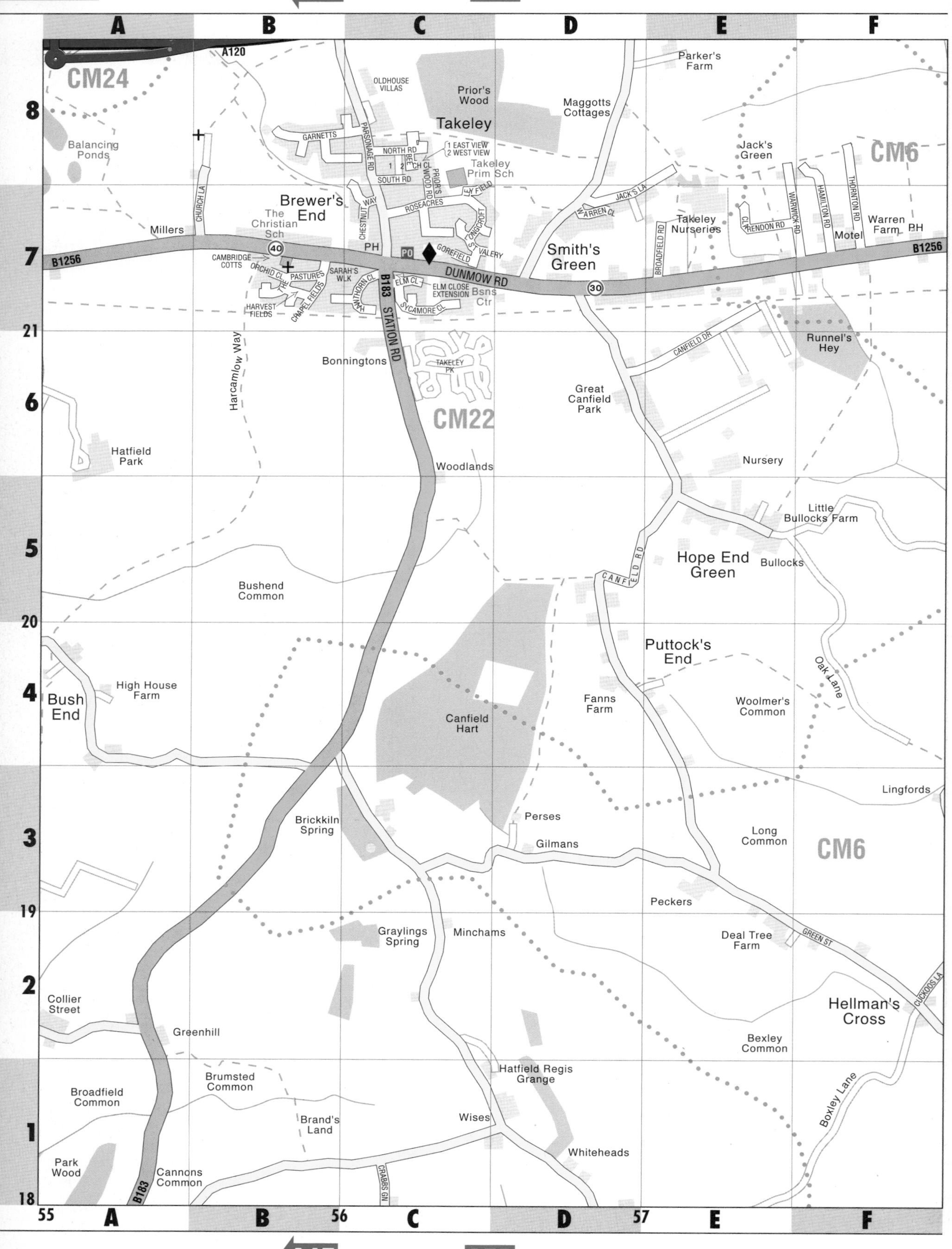

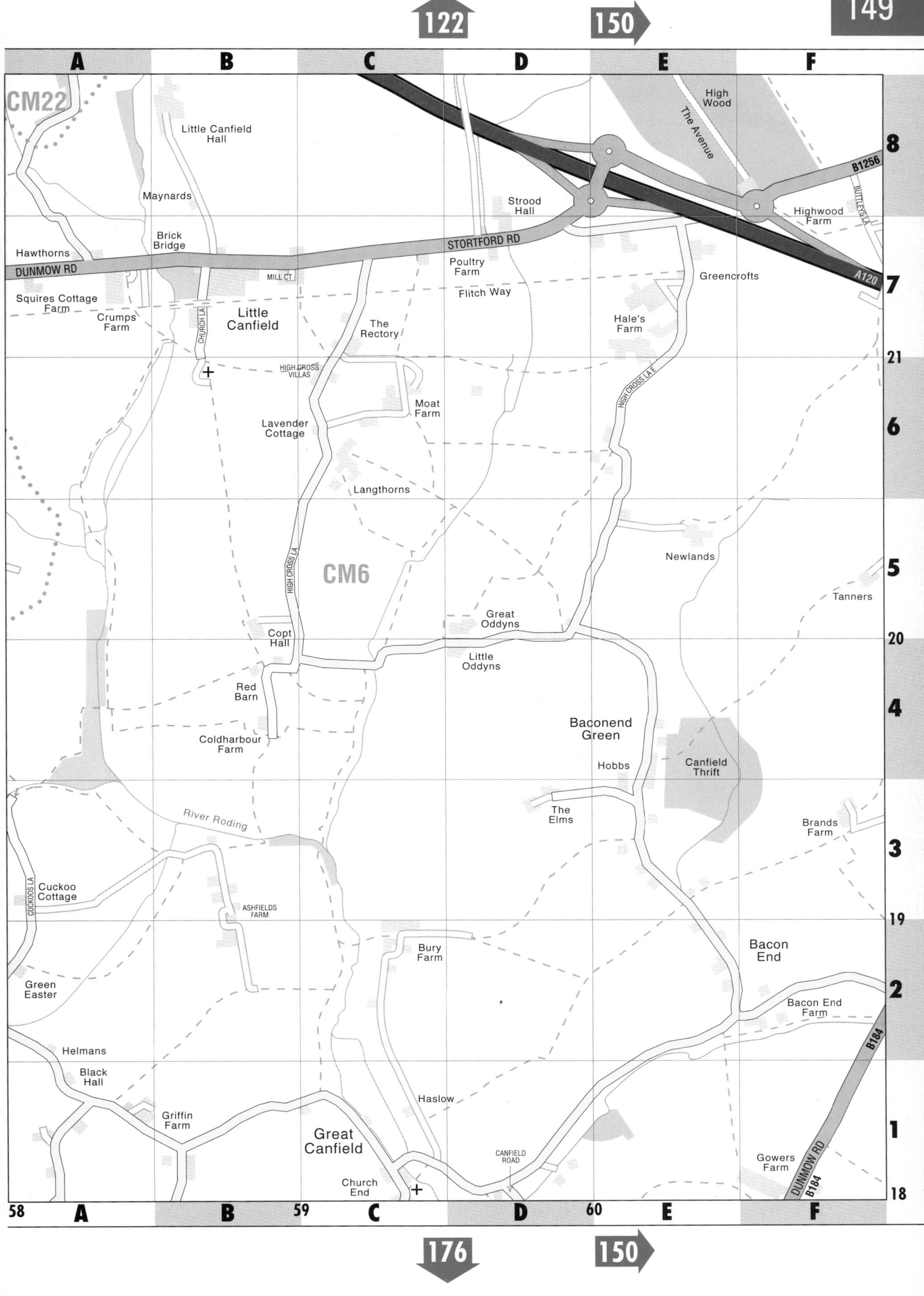

122
150
176
150

CM22

CM6

High Wood

The Avenue

B1256

Little Canfield Hall

Maynards

Strood Hall

Highwood Farm

BUTTLES LA

Brick Bridge

STORTFORD RD

A120

Hawthorns

DUNMOW RD

Poultry Farm

Greencrofts

MILL CT

Flitch Way

Squires Cottage Farm

CHURCH LA

Little Canfield

The Rectory

Hale's Farm

Crumps Farm

HIGH CROSS VILLAS

HIGH CROSS LA E

Lavender Cottage

Moat Farm

Langthorns

HIGH CROSS LA

Newlands

Tanners

Great Oddyns

Copt Hall

Little Oddyns

Red Barn

Baconend Green

Canfield Thrift

Coldharbour Farm

Hobbs

Brands Farm

River Roding

The Elms

CUCKOO LA

Cuckoo Cottage

ASHFIELDS FARM

Bacon End

Green Easter

Bury Farm

Bacon End Farm

B184

Helmans

Black Hall

Griffin Farm

Haslow

Great Canfield

Church End

Canfield Road

Gowers Farm

DUNMOW RD

B184

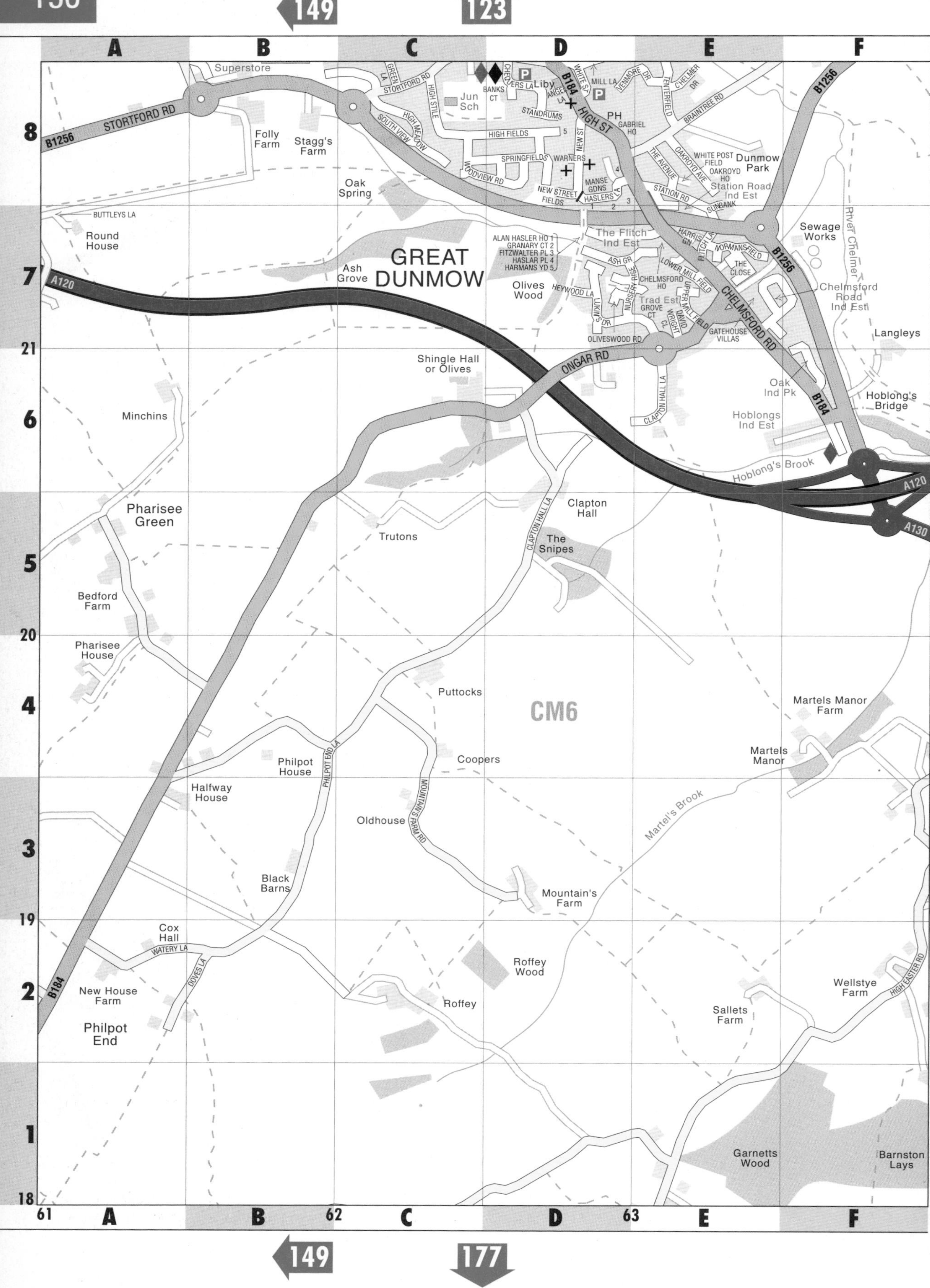

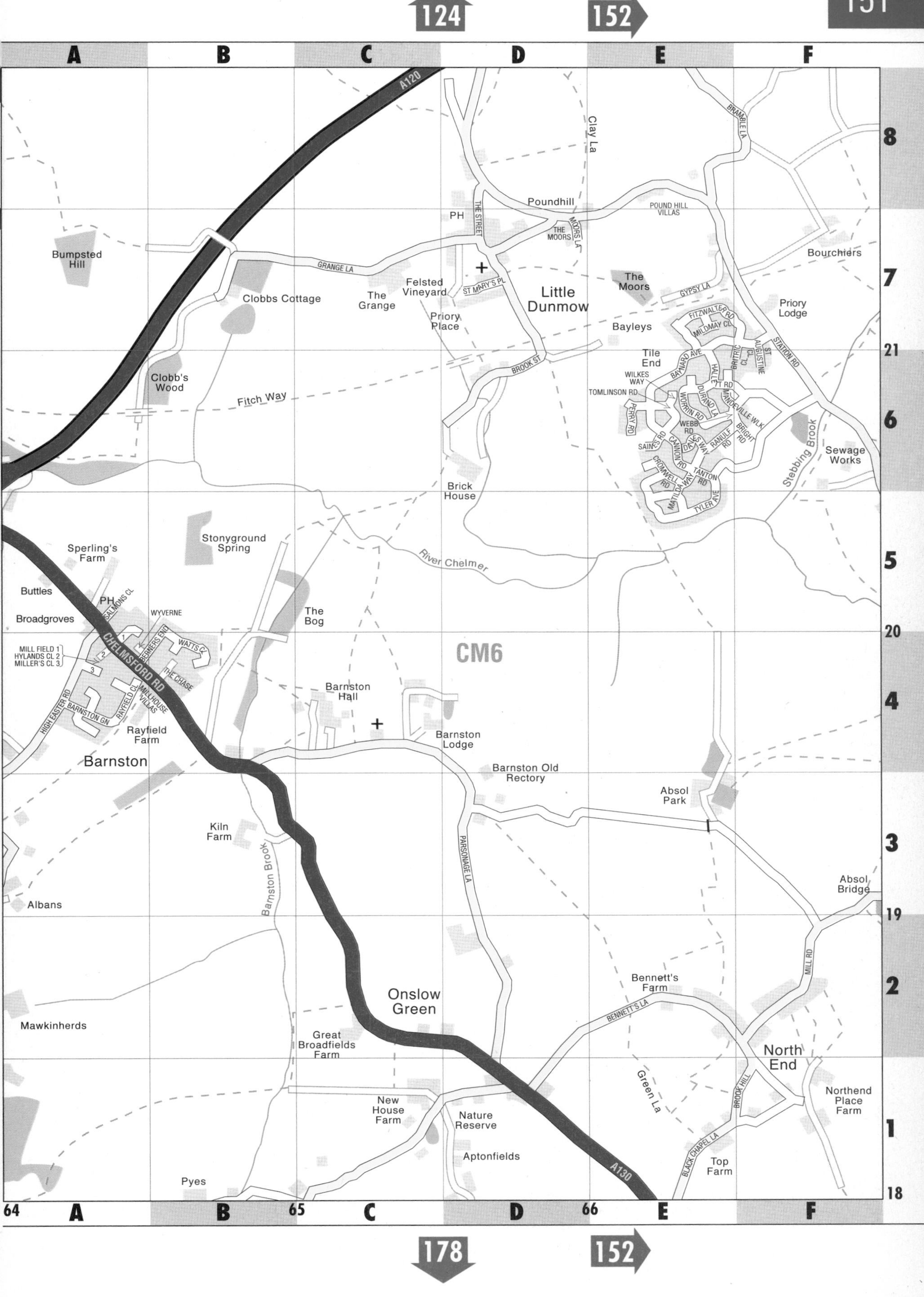
124
152
178
152
A
B
C
D
E
F
8
7
21
6
5
20
4
3
19
2
1
18
64
65
66
A120
A130
Clay La
Poundhill
PH
THE STREET
THE MOORS
MOORS LA
POUND HILL VILLAS
BRAMBLE LA
Bumpsted Hill
GRANGE LA
Clobbs Cottage
The Grange
Felsted Vineyard
ST MARY'S PL
Little Dunmow
The Moors
GYPSY LA
Bourchiers
Priory Lodge
Priory Place
Bayleys
FITZWALTER RD
MILDMAY CL
Tile End
BAYNARD AVE
BRITRIC CL
ST AUGUSTINE
STATION RD
BROOK ST
Clobb's Wood
Fitch Way
WILKES WAY
TOMLINSON RD
PERRY RD
WORRIN RD
DURAND LA
MANDEVILLE WLK
WEBB RD
SAINES RD
CANNON RD
DAVIES WAY
RANULF RD
BRIGHT RD
CROMWELL RD
TANTON RD
MATILDA WAY
TYLER AVE
Stebbing Brook
Sewage Works
Brick House
Stonyground Spring
Sperling's Farm
River Chelmer
Buttles
PH
SALMONS CL
Broadgroves
WYVERNE
The Bog
MILL FIELD 1
HYLANDS CL 2
MILLER'S CL 3
CHELMSFORD RD
BEMERS END
WATTS CL
THE CHASE
CM6
Barnston Hall
HIGH EASTER RD
BARNSTON GN
RAYFIELD CL
MILLHOUSE VILLAS
Rayfield Farm
Barnston Lodge
Barnston
Barnston Old Rectory
Absol Park
Kiln Farm
Barnston Brook
PARSONAGE LA
Absol Bridge
Albans
MILL RD
Bennett's Farm
Onslow Green
BENNETT'S LA
Mawkinherds
Great Broadfields Farm
North End
Green La
BROOK HILL
Northend Place Farm
New House Farm
Nature Reserve
BLACK CHAPEL LA
Aptonfields
Top Farm
Pyes

151 125

A B C D E F

8

Stebbing Brook

Brook Farm
Gifford House

Fitch Way

Great Greenfields

B1417

Weavers Farm

7

Felmoor Farm

Miniature Rifle Range

Stebbing Rd

Sunnybrook Farm

Watch House Green

WATCH HOUSE VILLAS

21

Wr Twr

Felsted Prim Sch

RAVENS CRES

OXNEY VILLAS

BANNISTER GREEN VILLAS

CRESSAGES

CHESTNUT WLK

PLAYERS CT

CHAFFIX CL

GARNETTS LA

CHAFFIX

Chaffix Farm

BANNISTER RD

STEVENS LA

6

Felsted Sch

ALDERTON CL

BRAINTREE RD

Chaffix

Oxney's Farm

THE CO

PH

Bannister Green

Bury Farm

FELSTED ALMSHOUSES

THE ORCHARD

JOLLYBOYS LA

GARNETTS BGLWS

+

+

+

STATION RD

BURY FIELDS

PO

GARNETTS VILLAS

5

RICHE CL

CROMWELL PK

Felsted Pl

Felsted Prep Sch

Hotel

Playing Field

CM6

Cleveland's Farm

20

Mariskalls

THE TERRACE

Felsted

BAKERS LA

Jollyboys

Cock Green

Mill Moorings

CHELMSFORD RD

JOLLYBOYS LA

Potash Farm

Brick House Farm

4

MILL RD

BRICKBURN CL

Mill House

LADYSMITH COTTS

CAUSEWAY END RD

Cobler's Green

Pondpark Farm

3

Causeway End

River Chelmer

Glanfield's Farm

19

Millbank's Farm

LEEZ LA

2

CM3

The Gate House

1

B1417

Prior's Green

CAUSEWAY

18

67 A B 68 C D 69 E F

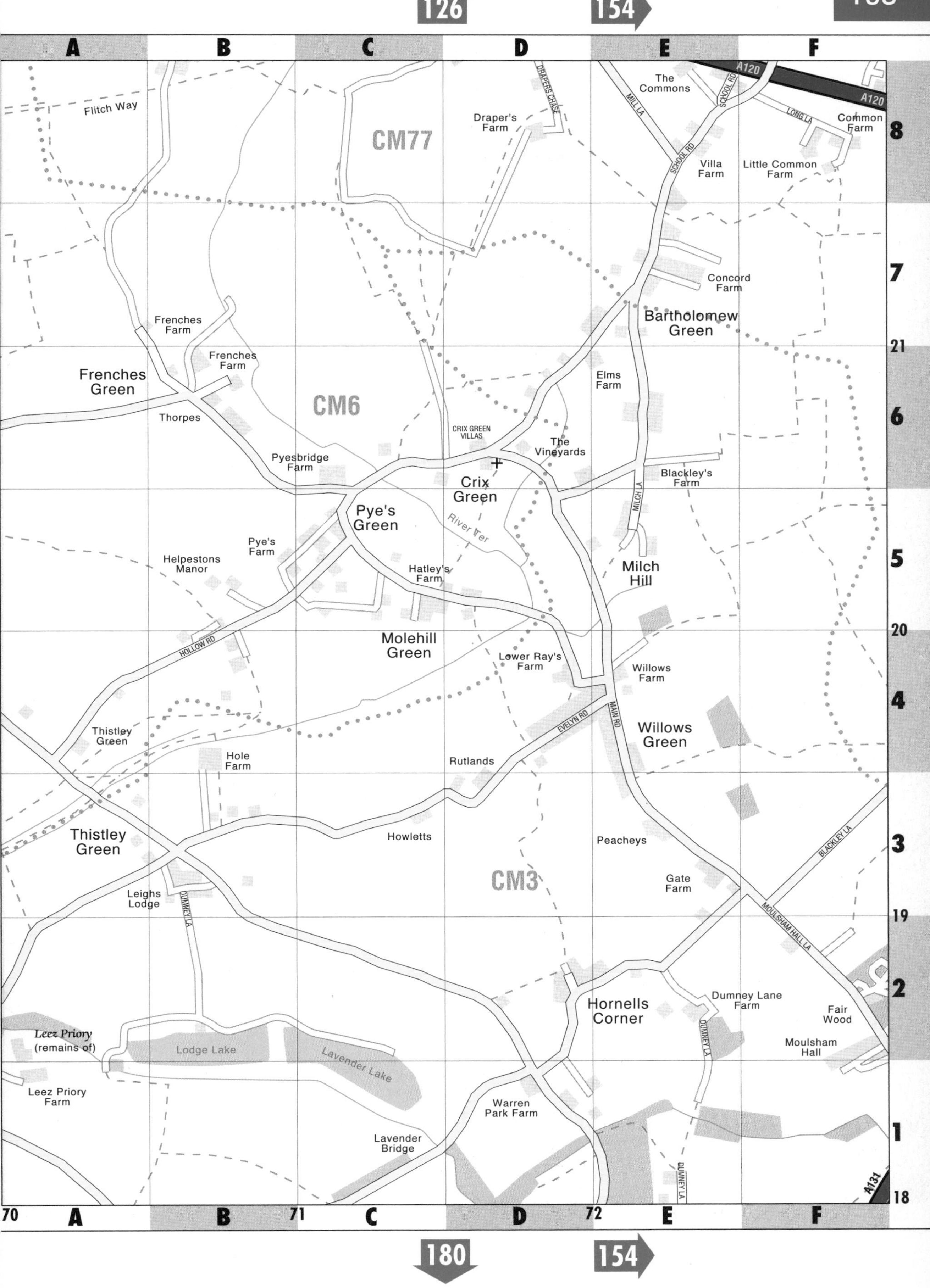

126

154

A120
A120

A B C D E F

The Commons

Draper's
Farm

CM77

SCHOOL RD

MILL LA

LONG LA

Common
Farm

8

Villa
Farm

Little Common
Farm

Concord
Farm

7

Frenches
Farm

Bartholomew
Green

21

Frenches
Farm

Frenches
Green

Elms
Farm

6

CM6

Thorpes

Pyesbridge
Farm

CRIX GREEN
VILLAS

The Vineyards

Blackley's
Farm

MILCH LA

Pye's
Green

Crix
Green

Helpestons
Manor

Pye's
Farm

River Ter

Milch
Hill

5

Hatley's
Farm

HOLLOW RD

Molehill
Green

20

Lower Ray's
Farm

Willows
Farm

4

Thistley
Green

Hole
Farm

EVELYN RD

MAIN RD

Willows
Green

Rutlands

Howletts

Peacheys

BLACKLEY LA

Thistley
Green

CM3

Gate
Farm

3

MOULSHAM HALL LA

Leighs
Lodge

DUMNEY LA

19

Dumney Lane
Farm

2

Leez Priory
(remains of)

Lodge Lake

Lavender Lake

Hornells
Corner

DUMNEY LA

Fair
Wood

Moulsham
Hall

Leez Priory
Farm

Warren
Park Farm

Lavender
Bridge

DUMNEY LA

A131

1

18

180

154

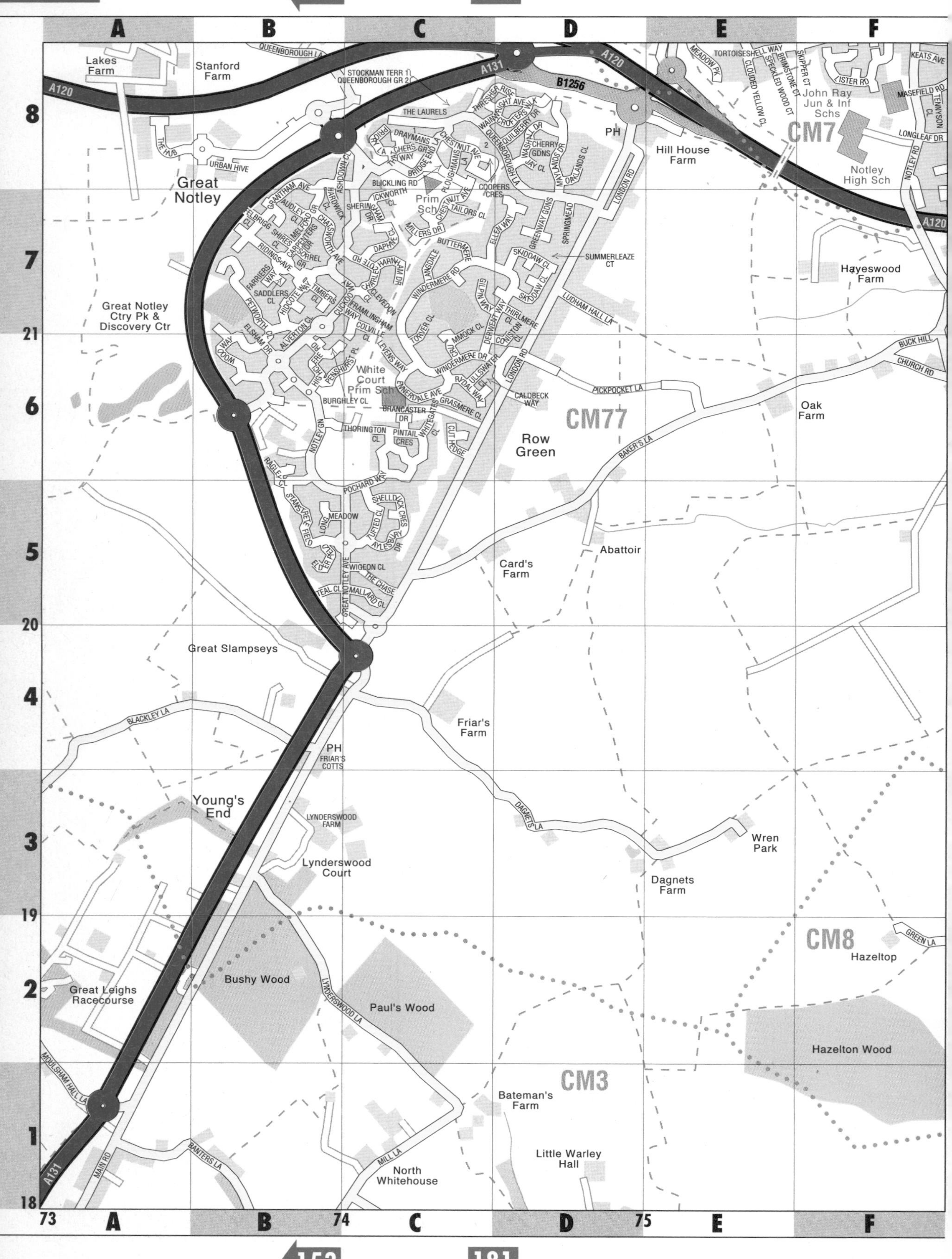

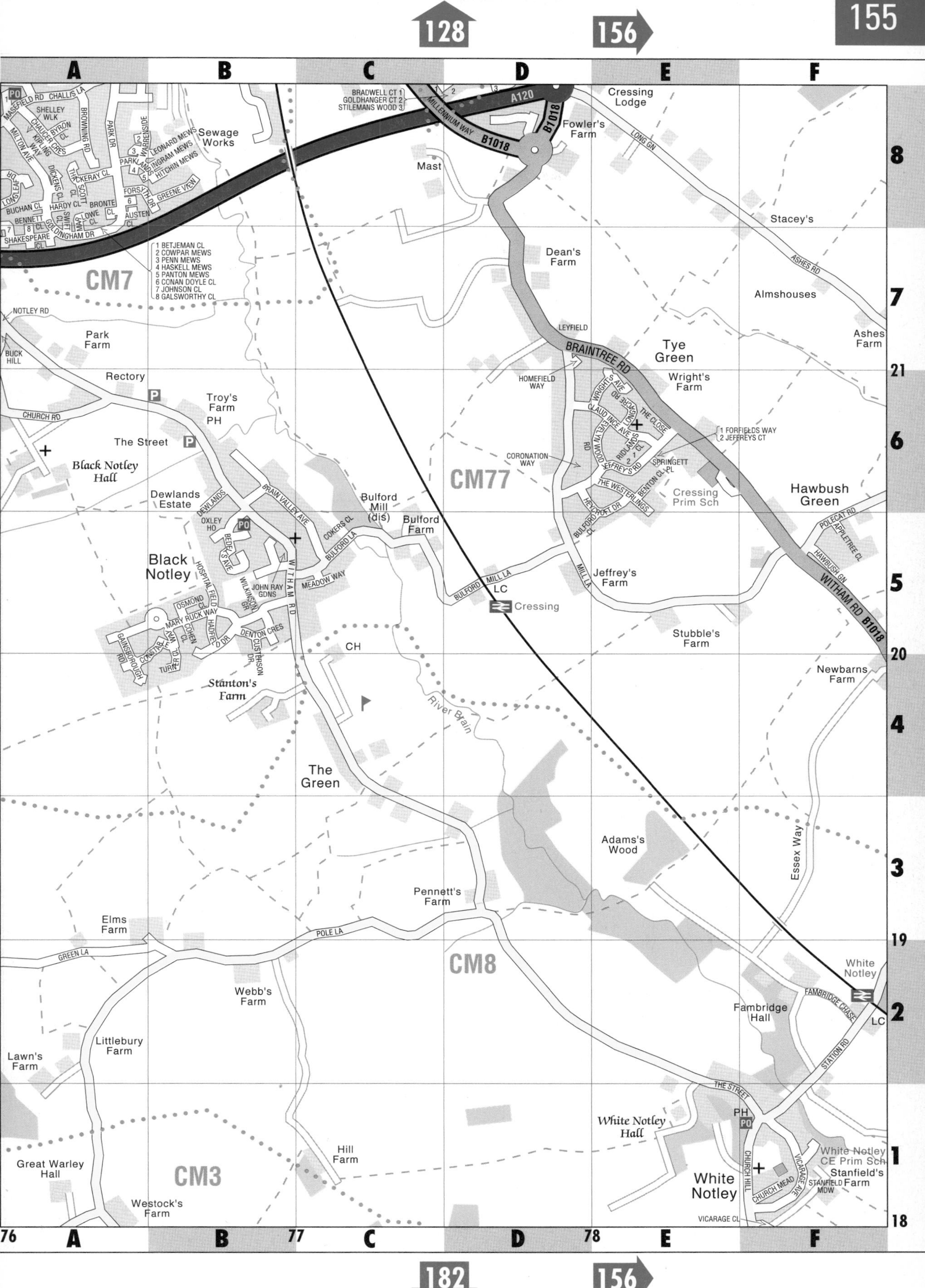

A B C D E F

8
Lanham Manor Farm
Sand & Gravel Pit
LANHAM FARM RD
Wr Twr
Lanham Green
Jubilee Plantation
Clapdog Green
LINKS RD

7
Ashes Farm
PH
ASHES RD
Schills Farm
Link's Farm
Link's Wood
Gosling's Farm

21
LANHAM GREEN RD
Essex Way

6
Cressing
THE STREET
Wright's Farm
Airfield (disused)
Mast
Sheepcotes Farm

POLECAT RD
Egypts Farm
Rolphs Farmhouse
BOARS TYE RD
ROLPHS COTTS

5
Shardloes Bsns Pk
CHURCH RD
CM77
Broomfield
The Goslings
SHEEPCOTES LA

20
COUNCIL HOUSES
PETTITT LA
Weaversfield
Francis Ct
Runnacles St
Walter Way
Broadway Ct
Broadway
Silver St
Rachael Gdns
Silver End

4
B1018
Manors Way
Francis Ct
Liby
PO
The Shops
Hotel
Daniel Way
Rebecca Gdns
Joseph Gdns
Daniel Way
Grooms La
New House
Manors
Works
Valentine Way
Bower Hall
WESTERN RD
Park House

3
STATION RD
Sheepcote Wood
WITHAM RD
TEMPLE LA
Magdalene Cres
Leicester Ct
Stretford Ct
Bristol Ct
School Rd
Silver End Prim Sch
PH
Bowers Cl
Western Cl
Western La
CM8
Rivenhall Place

19

2
Cressing Temple
Cressing Temple Barns
Old Court Room
P
Rivenhall Thicks

Essex Way
Sewage Works

1
B1018
Hungry Hall

18
79 A B 80 C D 81 E F

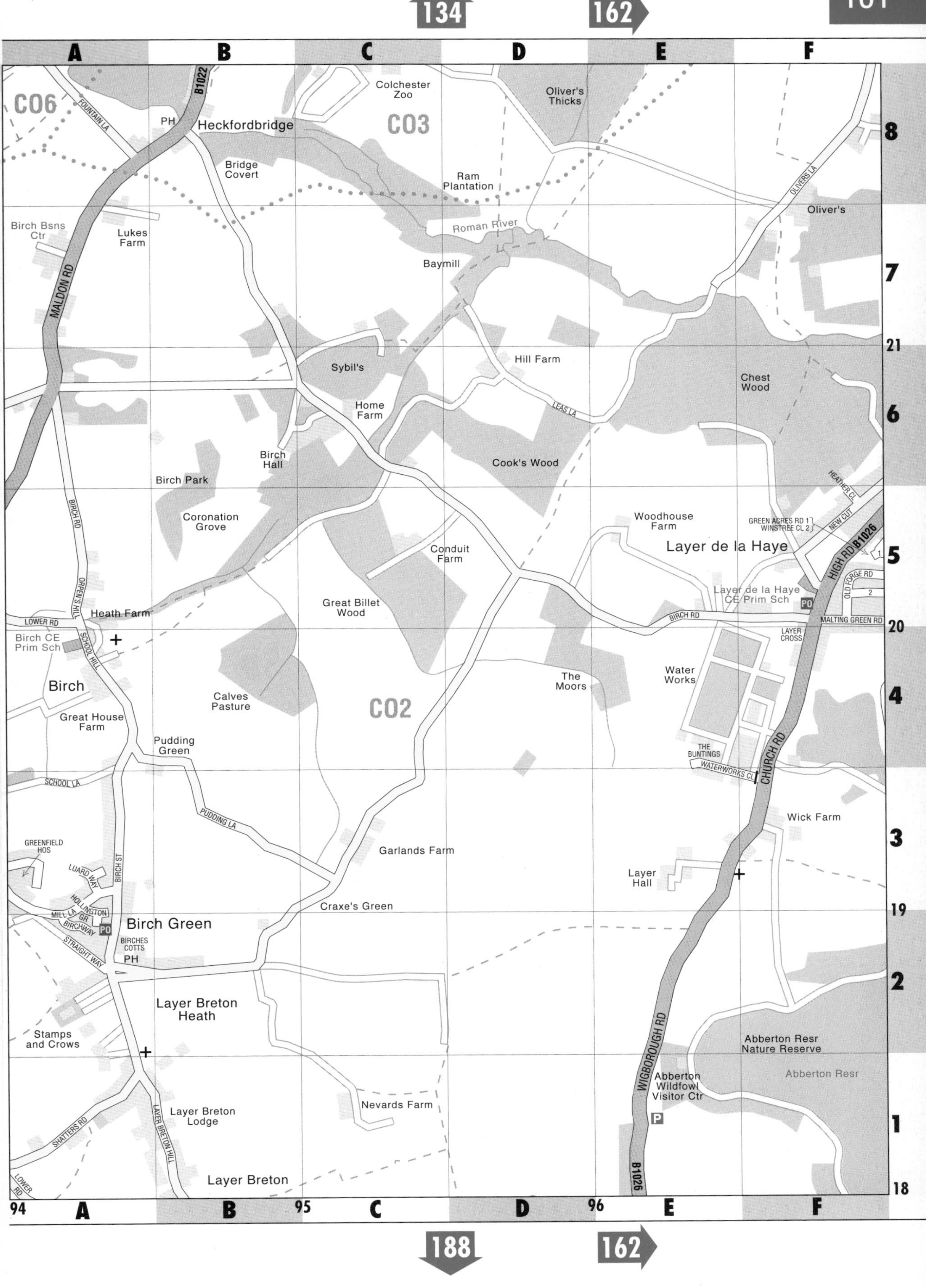
134
162
A
B
C
D
E
F
CO6
FOUNTAIN LA
B1022
PH
Heckfordbridge
Colchester Zoo
CO3
Oliver's Thicks
8
Bridge Covert
Ram Plantation
OLIVERS LA
Oliver's
Birch Bsns Ctr
Lukes Farm
Roman River
Baymill
7
MALDON RD
21
Hill Farm
Sybil's
Chest Wood
Home Farm
LEAS LA
6
Birch Hall
Cook's Wood
Birch Park
HEATHER CL
Coronation Grove
Woodhouse Farm
GREEN ACRES RD 1
WINSTREE CL 2
NEW CUT
B1026
BIRCH RD
Layer de la Haye
Conduit Farm
HIGH RD
5
ORPEN'S HILL
OLD FORGE RD
Layer de la Haye CE Prim Sch
PO
Great Billet Wood
LOWER RD
Heath Farm
BIRCH RD
MALTING GREEN RD
20
Birch CE Prim Sch
SCHOOL HILL
LAYER CROSS
The Moors
Water Works
Birch
Calves Pasture
4
Great House Farm
CO2
Pudding Green
THE BUNTINGS
WATERWORKS CL
CHURCH RD
SCHOOL LA
PUDDING LA
Wick Farm
GREENFIELD HOS
3
LUARD WAY
Garlands Farm
BIRCH ST
Layer Hall
HOLLINGTON
MILL LA
GR
BIRCHWAY
Craxe's Green
19
PO
Birch Green
BIRCHES COTTS
STRAIGHT WAY
PH
2
Layer Breton Heath
Stamps and Crows
WIGBOROUGH RD
Abberton Resr Nature Reserve
Abberton Resr
Abberton Wildfowl Visitor Ctr
SHATTERS RD
LAYER BRETON HILL
Layer Breton Lodge
Nevards Farm
P
1
LOWER RD
Layer Breton
B1026
18
94
95
96
188
162

161
135

A B C D E F

8

Sodoms

CH

THOMAS BENOLD WLK 1 2 3 4

King's Ford Park Hotel

BERECHURCH RD PH

BERECHURCH HALL RD

BERECHURCH HALL RD

JOHN HAMMOND CL 1
WILLIAM HARRIS WAY 2
AGNES SILVERSIDE CL 3
ROSE ALLEN AVE 4

Berechurch Hall Camp

LETHE GR

FRIDAY WOOD GN

B1026

7

Kingsford Farm

Fridaywood Farm

BOUNSTEAD RD

21

King's Ford Bridge

PH

NIGHTINGALE CORNER

P

CO2

6

THE FIRS

THE HEATH

NEW GUT

HIGH RD

Mill House

Bounstead Bridge

Friday Wood

Park Farm

BALL LA

CHERRY TREE LA

B1026

LES BOIS

THE FOLLY

MILL LA

BOUNSTEAD RD

Roman River

OAKS END

WOOD FIELD END

GREETE HOUSE FARM RD

ABBERTON RD

5

MARTIN END

MALLARD CL

UPPER COTTS

Lower End

OLD FORGE

SWALLOW CL

1 2

Malting Green

20

MALTING GREEN RD

YPRES COTTS

Lower Houses

Abberton Manor

1 WINSTREE CL
2 GREEN ACRES RD

Malting Green House

Wellhouse

LAYER RD

4

RYE LA

FIELDS FARM RD

Hill Farm

OXLEY HILL

Rye Farm

Abberton Hall

RECTORY LA

3

Layer Fields House

CO5

19

Blind Knights

2

1

Abberton Reservoir

18

97 A B 98 C D 99 E F

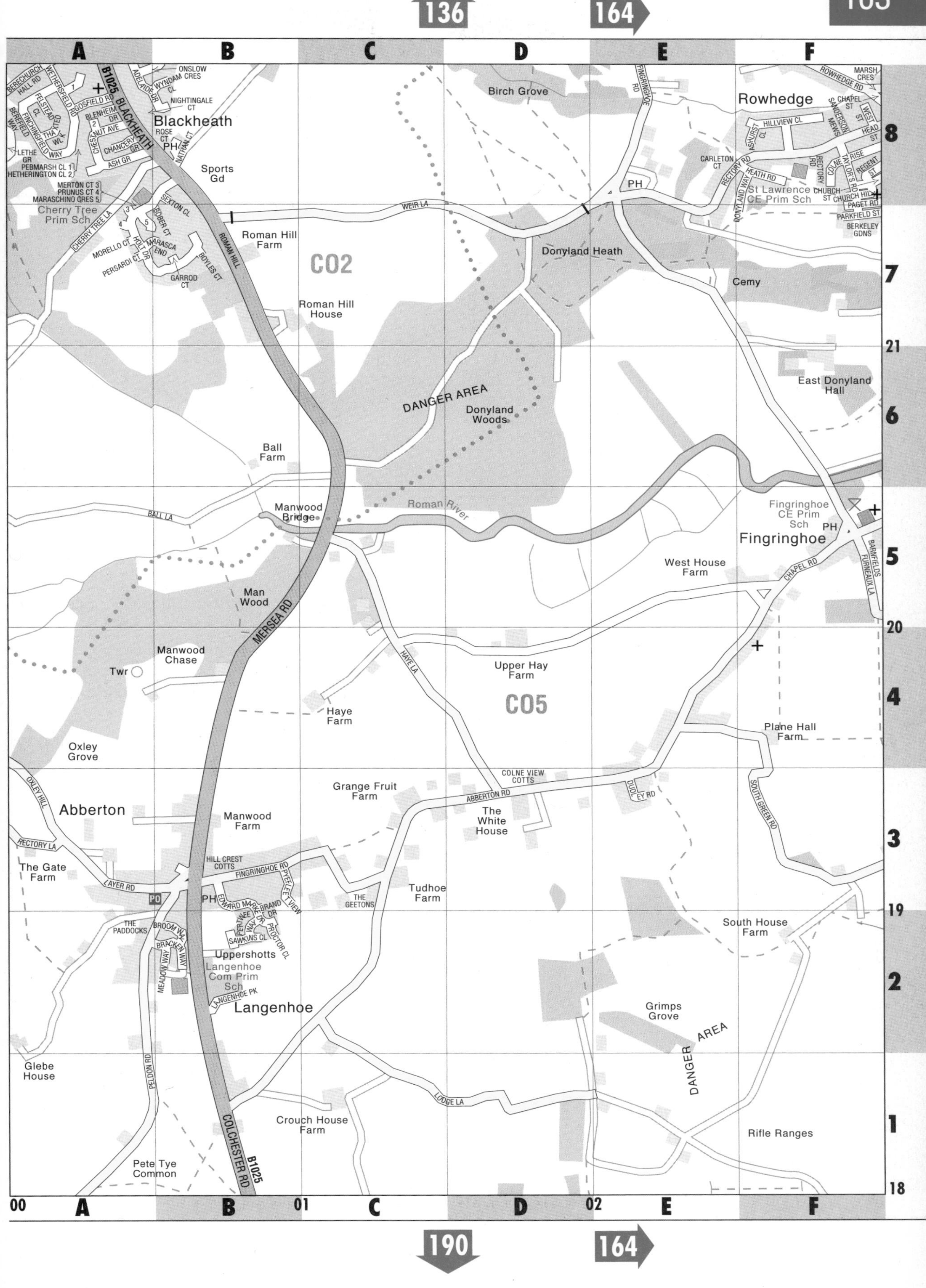

A B C D E F

8

7

21

6

5

20

4

3

19

2

1

18

Blackheath
Berechurch Hall
WETHERSFIELD
CROSSFIELD RD
B1025
ADELAIDE DR
ONSLOW CL
WYNDAM CRES
NIGHTINGALE CT
BLENHEIM DR
CHESTNUT AVE
CHANCERY
ASH GR
NATIONAL CT
ROSE PH
Sports Gd
HALSTEAD RD
BOREHAM WAY
PINCHPOOLS RD
THA WLK
WAY
LETHE GR
PEBMARSH CL 1
HETHERINGTON CL 2
MERTON CT 3
PRUNUS CT 4
MARASCHINO CRES 5
Cherry Tree Prim Sch
CHERRY TREE LA
MORELLO CT
PERSARDI CT
IMRASCA END
SEXTON CL
BOBER CT
BOYLES CT
GARROD CT
Roman Hill Farm
ROMAN HILL
WEIR LA

Birch Grove

Rowhedge
MARSH CRES
ROWHEDGE RD
HILLVIEW CL
ASHURST
SANDERSON MEWS
CHAPEL ST
WEST ST
HEAD ST
REGENT ST
NE RISE
NE TAYLORS
CARLETON CT
HEATH RD
DOWNLAND WAY
RECTORY RD
St Lawrence CE Prim Sch
CHURCH HILL
PAGET RD
PARKFIELD ST
BERKELEY GDNS

CO2

Roman Hill House

Donyland Heath

PH

Cemy

East Donyland Hall

DANGER AREA
Donyland Woods

Ball Farm

BALL LA

Manwood Bridge
Roman River

Fingringhoe CE Prim Sch
PH
Fingringhoe
BARNFIELDS
FURNEAUX LA

Man Wood

MERSEA RD

West House Farm

CHAPEL RD

Manwood Chase
Twr

Upper Hay Farm

Haye Farm
HAYE LA

CO5

Plane Hall Farm

Oxley Grove

Grange Fruit Farm

COLNE VIEW COTTS
ABBERTON RD
DUDLEY RD
SOUTH GREEN RD

Abberton

The White House

RECTORY LA
The Gate Farm
LAYER RD
PO
PH

Manwood Farm

HILL CREST COTTS
FINGRINGHOE RD
PEELEY'S VIEW
The Geetons

Tudhoe Farm

South House Farm

THE PADDOCKS
EDWARD M...
BRAND...
PENTREE WAY
SR DR
PROCTOR CL
SAWKINS CL
BROOM WLK
MEADOW WAY
BRACKEN WAY
Uppershotts
Langenhoe Com Prim Sch
LANGENHOE PK
Langenhoe

Grimps Grove

DANGER AREA

Glebe House

PELDON RD

COLCHESTER RD
B1025

Crouch House Farm

LODGE LA

Rifle Ranges

Pete Tye Common

00 A B 01 C D 02 E F

163
137

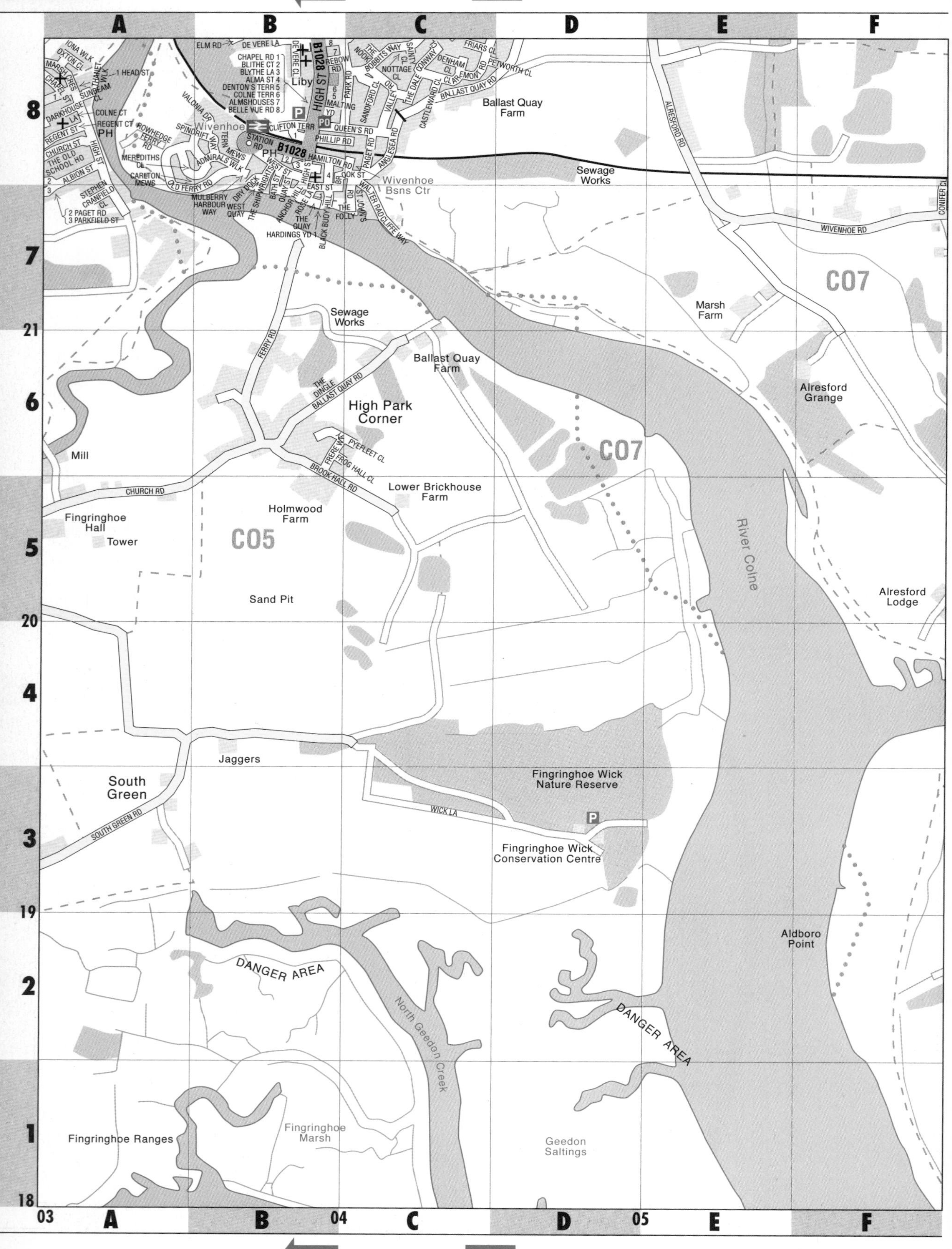

163
191

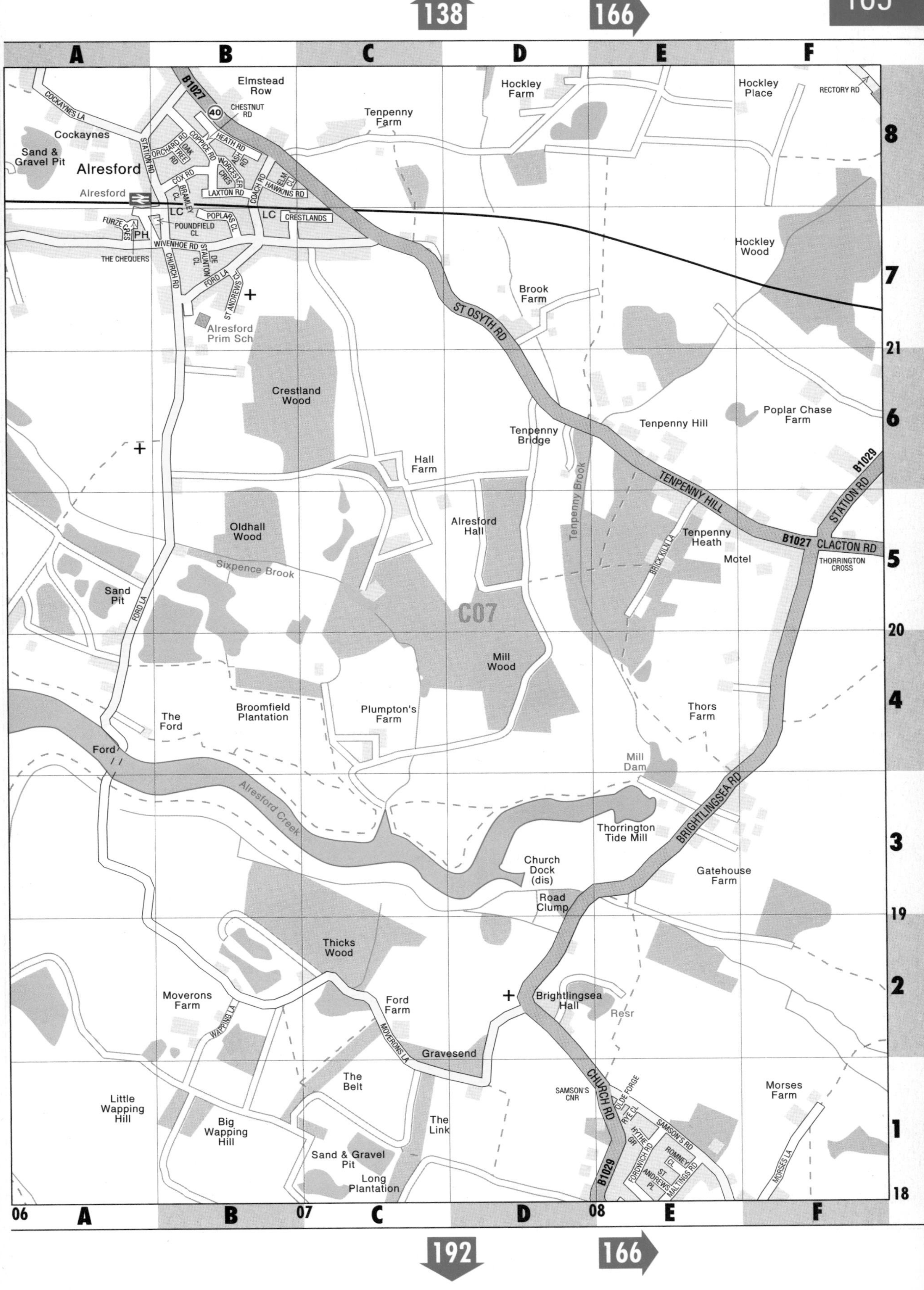
138
166
A
B
C
D
E
F
Elmstead Row
Hockley Farm
Hockley Place
RECTORY RD
B1027
CHESTNUT RD
Tenpenny Farm
COCKAYNES LA
Cockaynes
Sand & Gravel Pit
Alresford
Alresford
STATION RD
ORCHARD RD
OAK TREE RD
COPPICE RD
HEATH RD
WORCESTER CRES
COX RD
BRAMLEY CL
LAXTON RD
COACH RD
ELM CL
HAWKINS RD
LC
POPLARS CL
CRESTLANDS
FURZE CRES
PH
POUNDFIELD CL
WIVENHOE RD
THE CHEQUERS
CHURCH RD
STAUNTON CL
FORD LA
ST ANDREWS CL
Alresford Prim Sch
Hockley Wood
Brook Farm
ST OSYTH RD
Crestland Wood
Tenpenny Bridge
Tenpenny Hill
Poplar Chase Farm
Hall Farm
Oldhall Wood
Alresford Hall
Tenpenny Brook
TENPENNY HILL
Tenpenny Heath
BRICK KILN LA
B1029
STATION RD
B1027
CLACTON RD
THORRINGTON CROSS
Motel
Sixpence Brook
Sand Pit
FORD LA
C07
Mill Wood
The Ford
Broomfield Plantation
Plumpton's Farm
Thors Farm
Ford
Mill Dam
Alresford Creek
Thorrington Tide Mill
BRIGHTLINGSEA RD
Church Dock (dis)
Gatehouse Farm
Road Clump
Thicks Wood
Moverons Farm
WAPPING LA
Ford Farm
MOVERONS LA
Brightlingsea Hall
Resr
Gravesend
CHURCH RD
The Belt
Little Wapping Hill
Big Wapping Hill
The Link
SAMSON'S CNR
OLDE FORGE
RYE CL
HYTHE GR
SAMSON'S RD
ROMNEY CL
FORDWICH RD
ST ANDREWS PL
MALTINGS RD
Morses Farm
MORSES LA
Sand & Gravel Pit
Long Plantation
B1029
8
7
21
6
5
20
4
3
19
2
1
18
06
07
08
192
166

A B C D E F

8

SCHOOL LA
B1029
STATION RD
Burr's Farm
GREAT BENTLEY RD
Hill House Farm
THORRINGTON RD
WREN CL
DE VERE EST
STURRICK LA
CHERRYWOODS
ROBIN CL
LINNET WAY
THE PATH
HECKFORD'S RD
Bentley Green
WEELEY RD
LABURNUM
THE GREEN
PH
MILL ON THE GREEN
SYCAMORE PL
GODWINS MEWS
CEDAR WAY
ELM CL
BIRCH AVE
PINE CL
ROWAN CL
Great Bentley
PO
MORELLA CL
NEW CUT
STATION RD
HALL VIEW RD
KEEBLE CT
Great Bentley Prim Sch
LC
Great Bentley
Ind Est

7

FRATING RD
Lufkins Farm
GREAT BENTLEY RD
FRATING CROSS
LC
PLOUGH RD
St Mary's Farm

21

LC
Mast
B1029 STATION RD
The Talbots
Frating Abbey
Bentley Brook
Lodge Plantation
COUNCIL HOUSES
WEELEY RD
ST MARY'S RD
ST MARY'S RD
AINGERS GREEN RD
PH

6

Whitehouse Farm
CHURCH RD
ACORN WLK 1
THELMA DR 2
HAZEL CL
CLOVER DR
HEATHLANDS
HONEYSUCKLE WAY
CAPEL LA
PO
Thorrington
ROSEMARY LA
PH
VICTORY CL
Aingers Green
THE PADDOCKS
WOOD GREEN EST
Thicket Grove
High Barns
Carpenter's Farm

5
B1027

20

Glebe Farm
Thorrington Hall
CLACTON RD
CO7
The Lodge
Colles Brook
COLLES BROOK RD
STRAIGHT RD
SOUTH HEATH LA

4

Thorringtonhall Wood
Saltwater Brook Cottages
Saltwater Bridge
DIAL RD
DIAL CNR
HOLLYBUSH HILL
Lady Wood
Kellands Farm

3

19

Crocky Grove
MARSH FARM LA
Greatmarsh Farm
Saltwater Brook
Cottage Farm
HILL COTTS
BEDE LA
CO16 →
Hollybush Hill

2

1

FOLKARDS LA
Lowermarsh Farm
Thorrington Creek
Caravan Site
CH
Dines Farm
FLAG HILL
B1027

18
09 A B 10 C D 11 E F

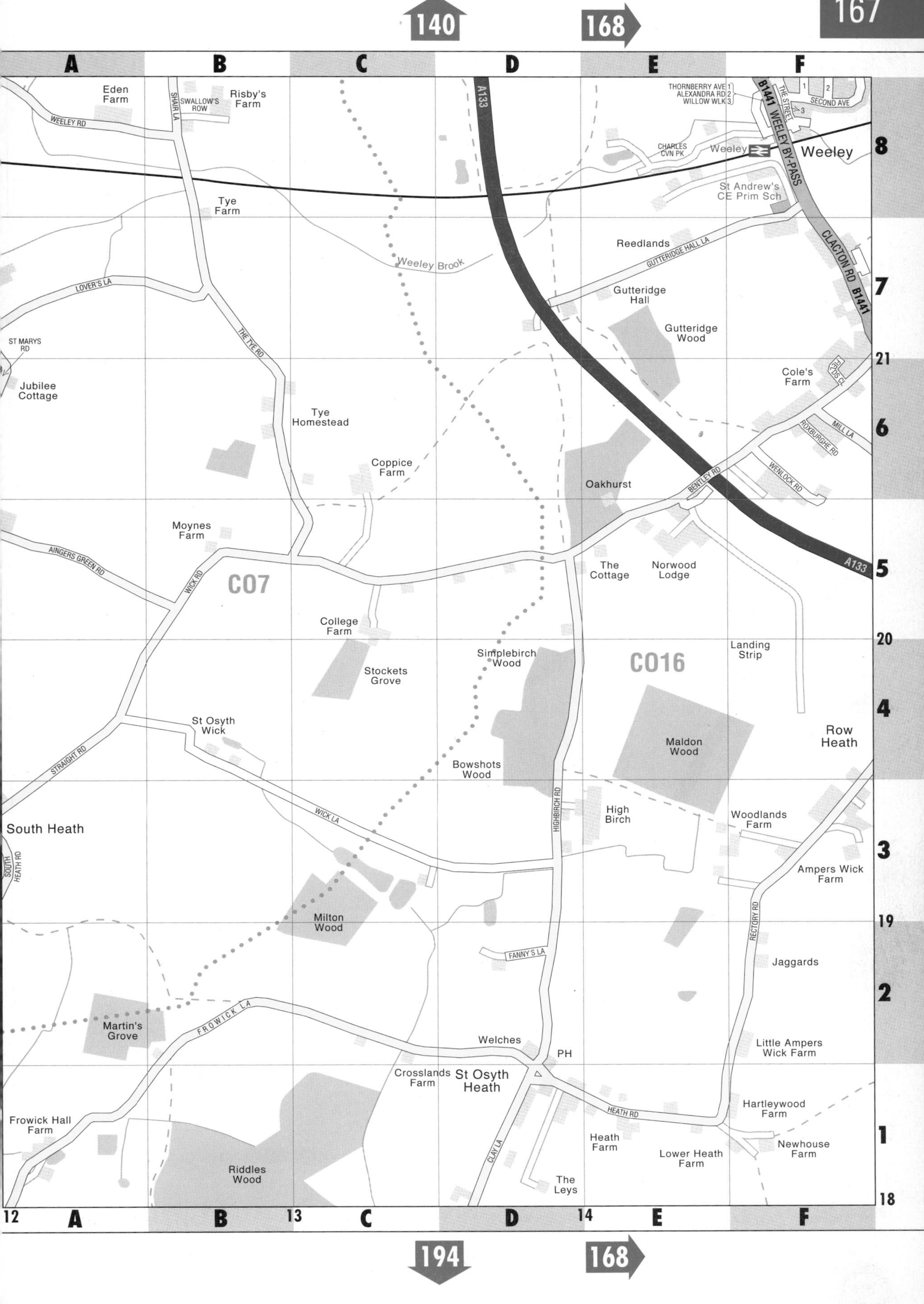

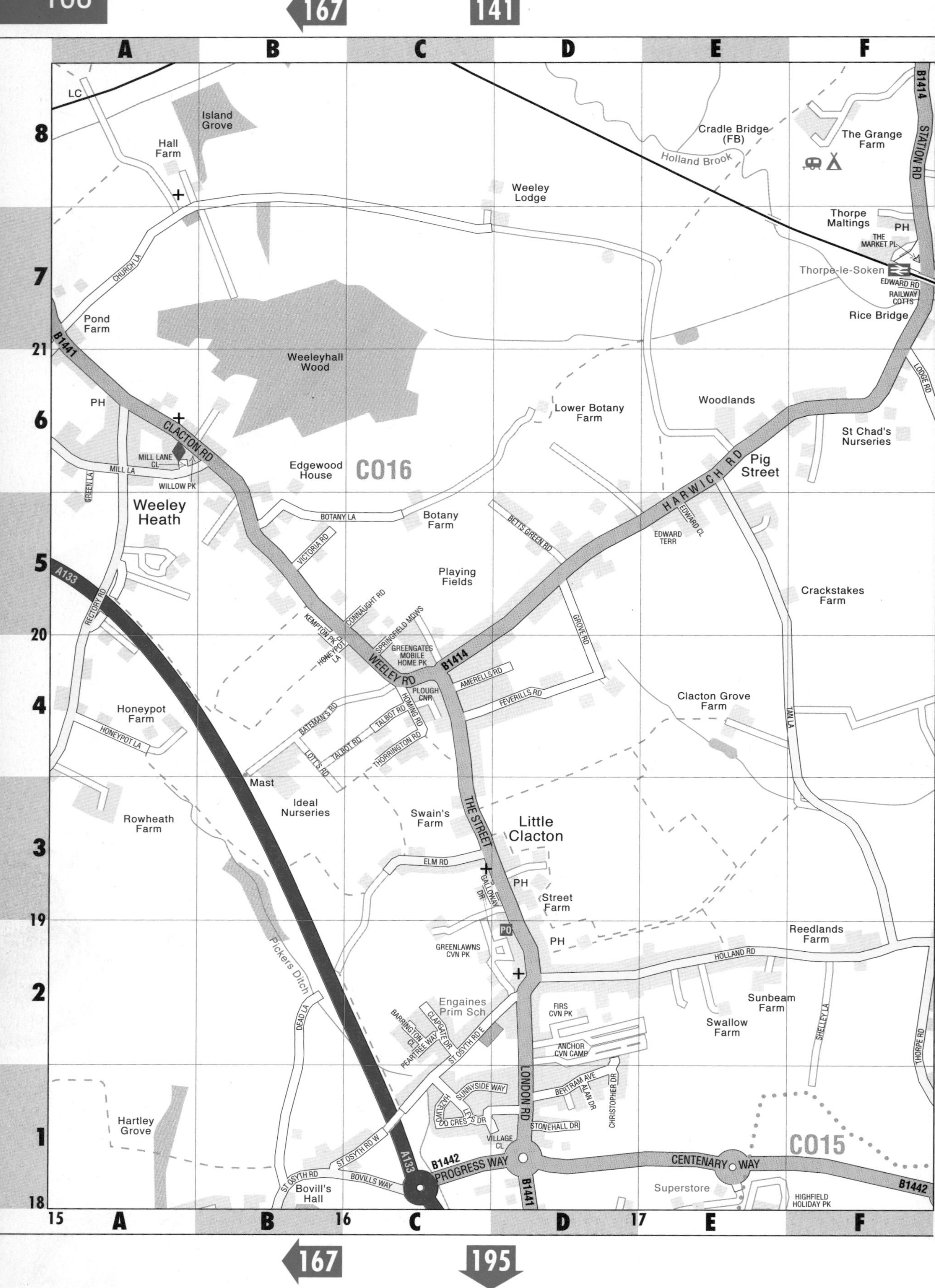

167
141

A B C D E F

8
7
21
6
5
20
4
3
19
2
1
18

15 A B 16 C D 17 E F

167
195

LC

Island Grove

Hall Farm

Weeley Lodge

Cradle Bridge (FB)

Holland Brook

The Grange Farm

Thorpe Maltings

PH

THE MARKET PL.

Thorpe-le-Soken

EDWARD RD

RAILWAY COTTS

Rice Bridge

B1414

STATION RD

CHURCH LA

Pond Farm

B1441

PH

CLACTON RD

MILL LA

MILL LANE CL

WILLOW PK

GREEN LA

Weeley Heath

Weeleyhall Wood

Edgewood House

CO16

Lower Botany Farm

Woodlands

St Chad's Nurseries

HARWICH RD

Pig Street

EDWARD CL

EDWARD TERR

BOTANY LA

Botany Farm

BETTS GREEN RD

VICTORIA RD

Playing Fields

Crackstakes Farm

A133

RECTORY RD

KEMPTON PK CL

CONNAUGHT RD

SPRINGFIELD MDWS

HONEYPOT LA

GREENGATES MOBILE HOME PK

WEELEY RD

B1414

AMERELLS RD

GROVE RD

FEVERILLS RD

Clacton Grove Farm

TAN LA

Honeypot Farm

HONEYPOT LA

BATEMAN'S RD

LOTT'S RD

TALBOT RD

TALBOT RD

BOWLING RD

THORRINGTON RD

PLOUGH CNR

Mast

Ideal Nurseries

Swain's Farm

THE STREET

Little Clacton

Rowheath Farm

Pickers Ditch

ELM RD

BALLOWN DR

PH

Street Farm

Reedlands Farm

HOLLAND RD

PO

PH

Sunbeam Farm

Swallow Farm

SHELLEY LA

THORPE RD

GREENLAWNS CVN PK

FIRS CVN PK

Engaines Prim Sch

BARRINGTON CL

CLAPGATE DR

PEARTREE WAY

ST OSYTH RD E

ANCHOR CVN CAMP

BERTRAM AVE

ALAN DR

CHRISTOPHER DR

SUNNYSIDE WAY

HALSTEAD RD

LEE'S DR

PO CRES

Village CL

STONEHALL DR

CENTENARY WAY

CO15

Hartley Grove

LAID DE LA

ST OSYTH RD W

ST OSYTH RD

BOVILL'S WAY

A133

B1442

PROGRESS WAY

B1441

LONDON RD

Superstore

HIGHFIELD HOLIDAY PK

B1442

Bovill's Hall

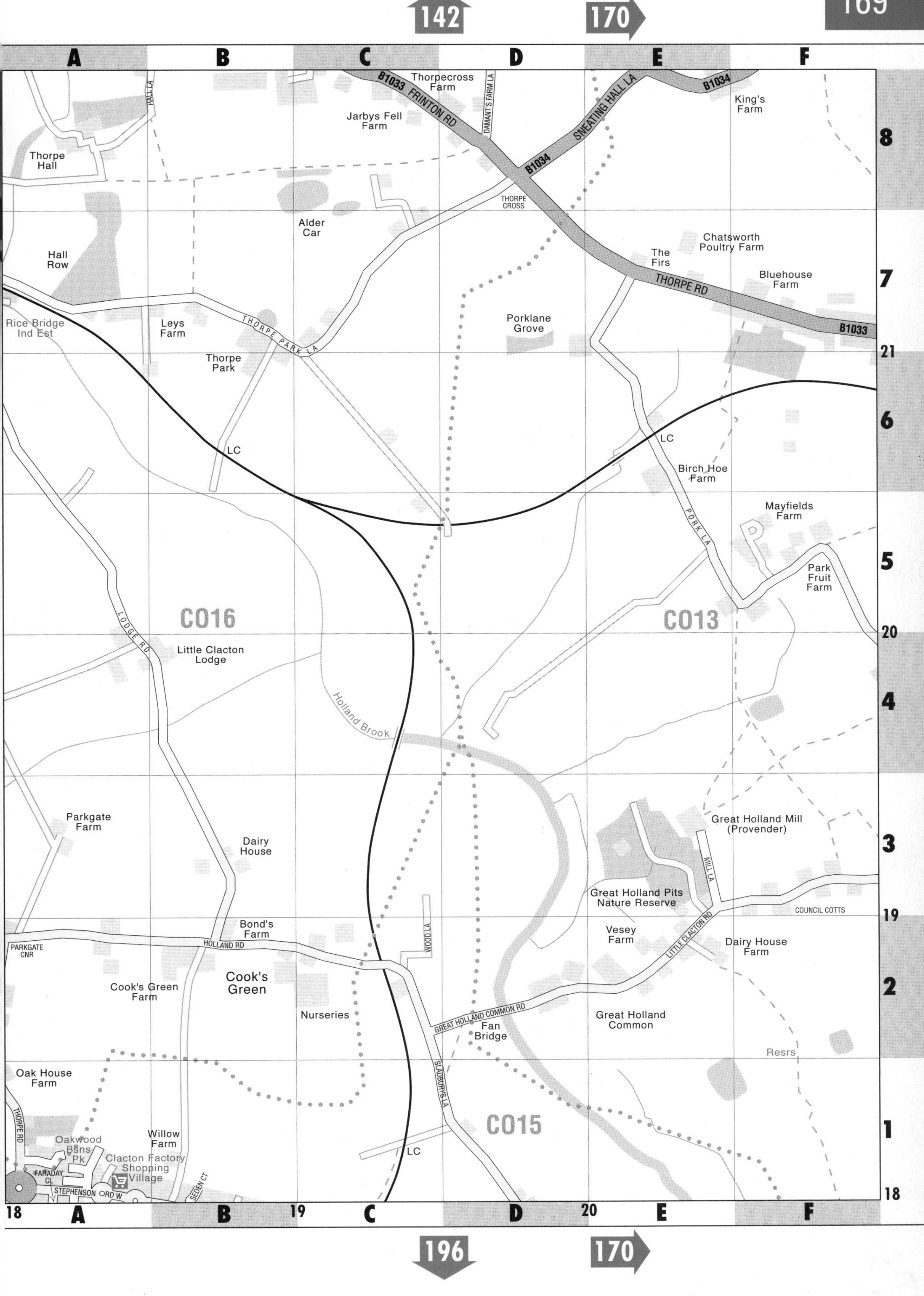

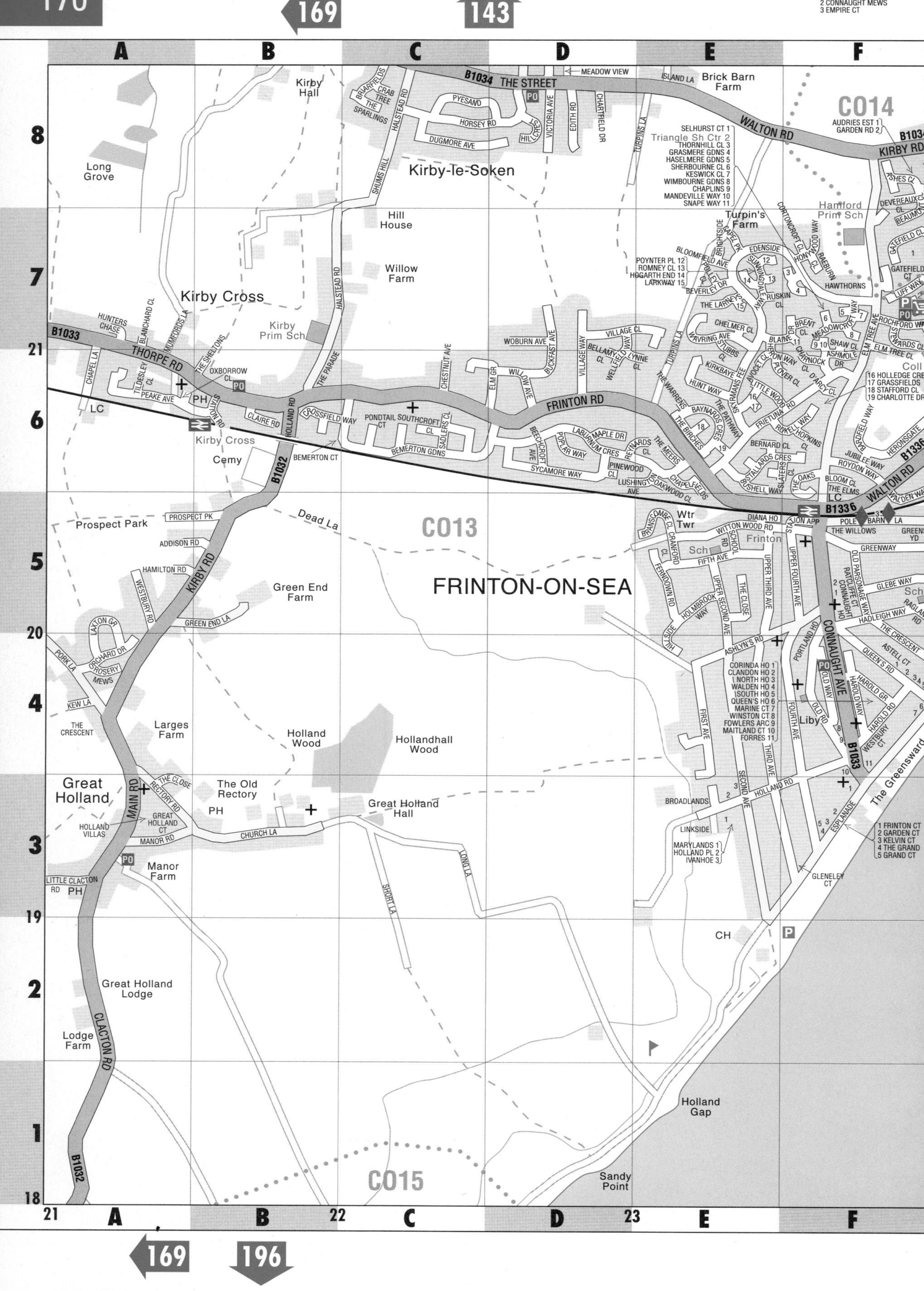

169 143

F5
1 HAMMOND CT
2 CONNAUGHT MEWS
3 EMPIRE CT

CO14

CO13

FRINTON-ON-SEA

CO15

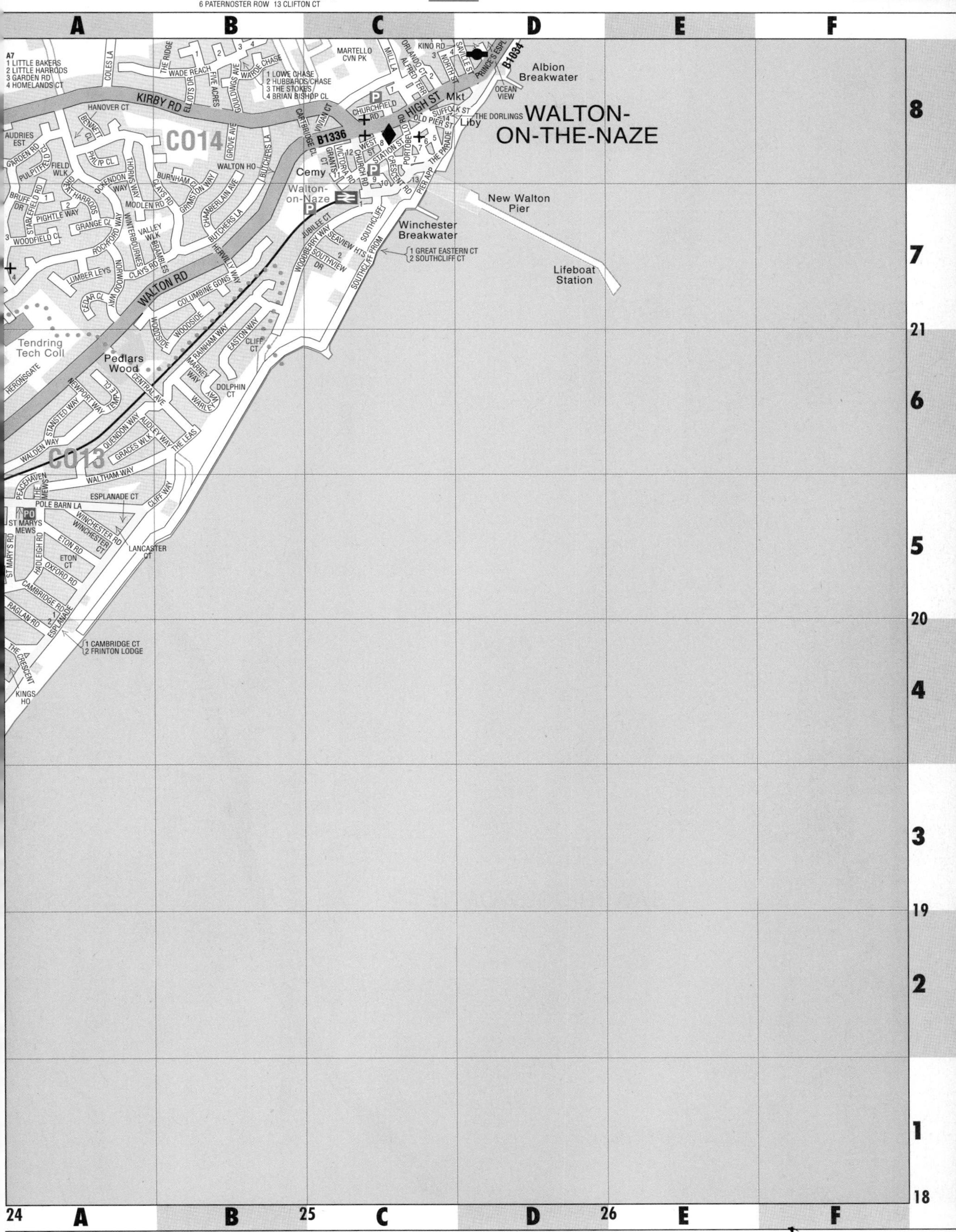

C8
1 MARINA MEWS
2 VICARAGE LA
3 HAVENCROFT CT
4 STRATFORD PL
5 NEWGATE ST
6 PATERNOSTER ROW

7 NEW PIER ST
8 MARTELLO RD
9 AGAR RD
10 AGAR ROAD APP
11 ST BOTOLPH'S TERR
12 CHURCHVIEW CT
13 CLIFTON CT

14 MARINE BLDGS

A7
1 LITTLE BAKERS
2 LITTLE HARRODS
3 GARDEN RD
4 HOMELANDS CT

1 LOWE CHASE
2 HUBBARDS CHASE
3 THE STOKES
4 BRIAN BISHOP CL

WALTON-
ON-THE-NAZE

1 GREAT EASTERN CT
2 SOUTHCLIFF CT

1 CAMBRIDGE CT
2 FRINTON LODGE

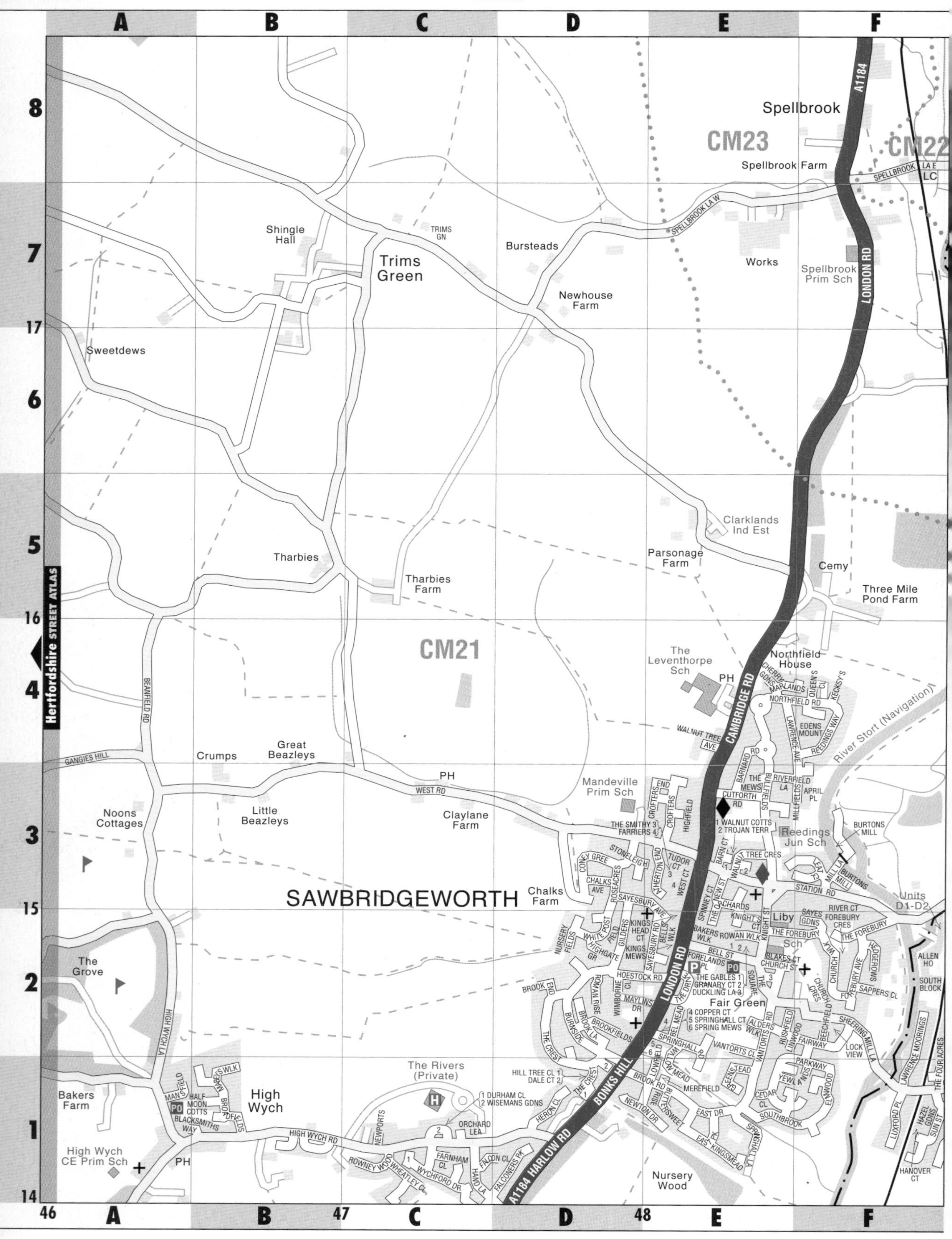

A B C D E F

8 7 17 6 5 16 4 3 15 2 1 14

46 47 48

Hertfordshire STREET ATLAS

Spellbrook
CM23
CM22
Spellbrook Farm
Spellbrook LA E LLC
Works
Spellbrook Prim Sch
LONDON RD
A1184

Shingle Hall
TRIMS GN
Trims Green
Bursteads
Newhouse Farm

Sweetdews

Clarklands Ind Est

Tharbies
Parsonage Farm
Cemy
Three Mile Pond Farm

Tharbies Farm

CM21
The Leventhorpe Sch
Northfield House
PH
CAMBRIDGE RD
River Stort (Navigation)

Crumps
Great Beazleys
PH
WEST RD
Walnut Tree AVE

Noons Cottages
Little Beazleys
Claylane Farm
Mandeville Prim Sch
Reedings Jun Sch
Burtons Mill

The Grove
SAWBRIDGEWORTH
Chalks Farm
Liby Sch
Units D1-D2

Bakers Farm
High Wych
Fair Green

The Rivers (Private)
High Wych CE Prim Sch
PH
A1184 HARLOW RD
BONKS HILL
LONDON RD
Nursery Wood

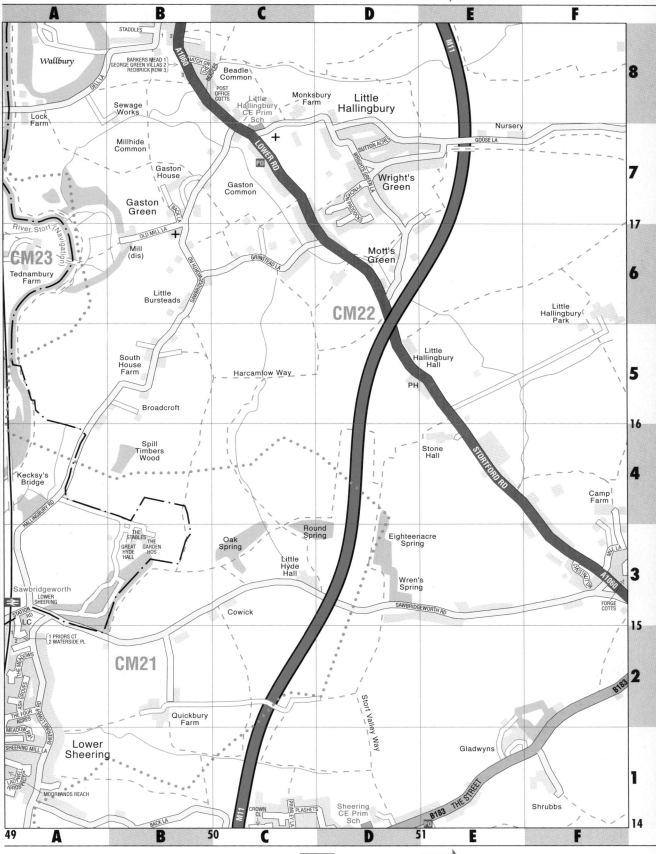

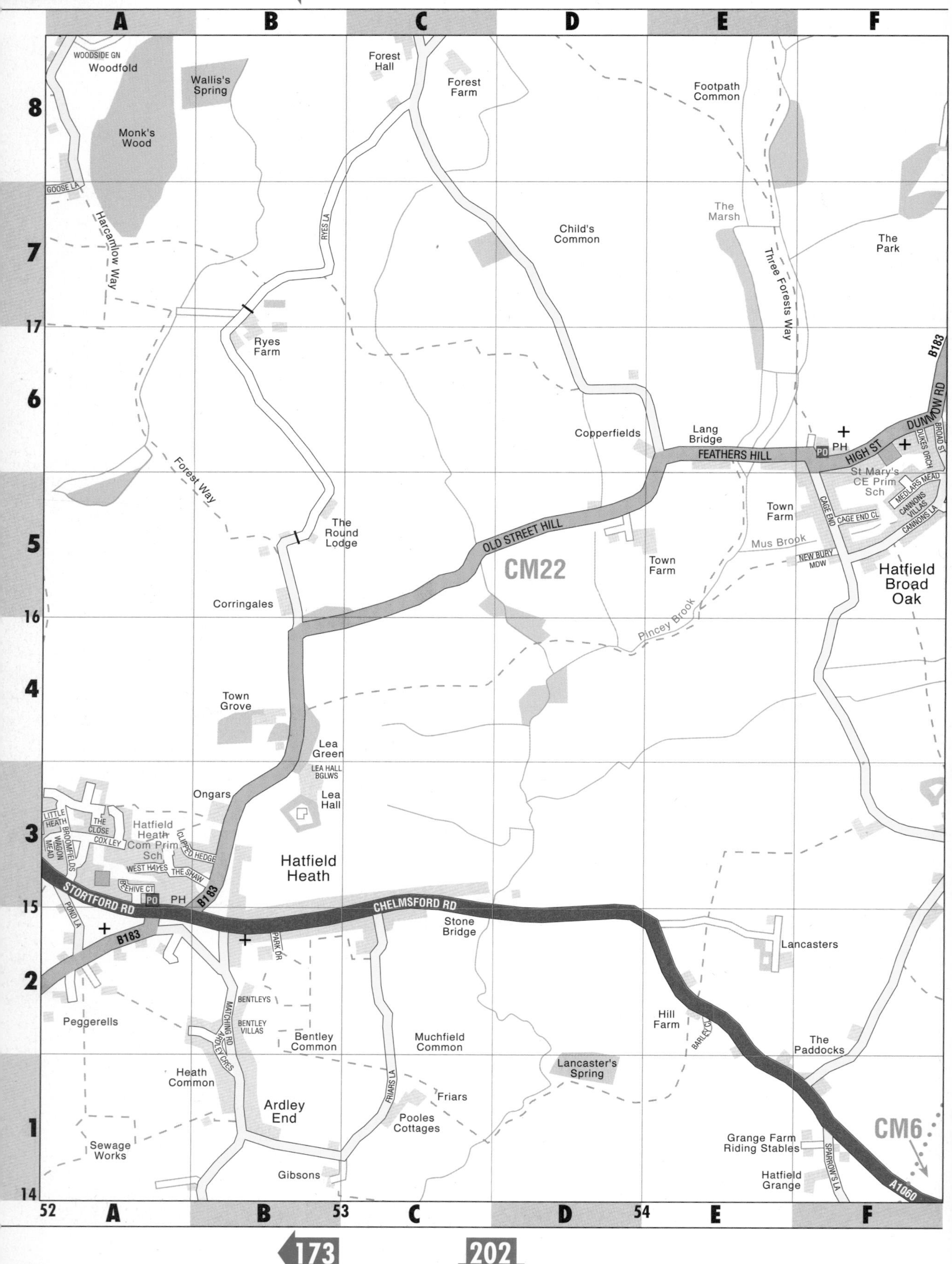

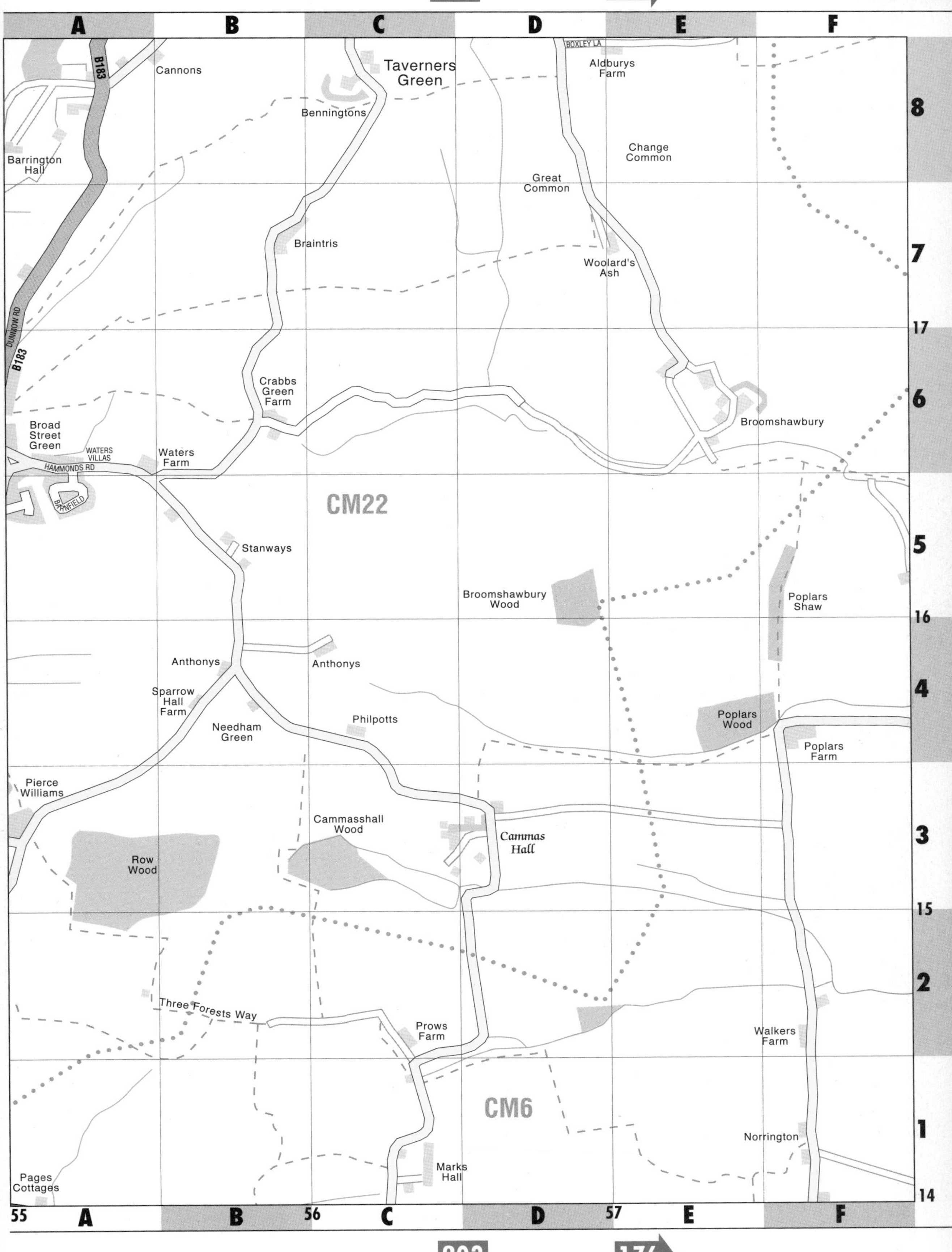
148
176
A
B
C
D
E
F
BOXLEY LA
Cannons
B183
Taverners
Green
Aldburys
Farm
Benningtons
8
Barrington
Hall
Change
Common
Great
Common
Braintris
7
Woolard's
Ash
DUNMOW RD
B183
17
Crabbs
Green
Farm
6
Broad
Street
Green
Broomshawbury
WATERS
VILLAS
Waters
Farm
HAMMONDS RD
BARNFIELD
CM22
5
Stanways
Broomshawbury
Wood
Poplars
Shaw
16
Anthonys
Anthonys
4
Sparrow
Hall
Farm
Needham
Green
Philpotts
Poplars
Wood
Poplars
Farm
Pierce
Williams
Cammasshall
Wood
3
Cammas
Hall
Row
Wood
15
2
Three Forests Way
Prows
Farm
Walkers
Farm
CM6
1
Norrington
Marks
Hall
Pages
Cottages
14
55
A
B
56
C
D
57
E
F
203
176

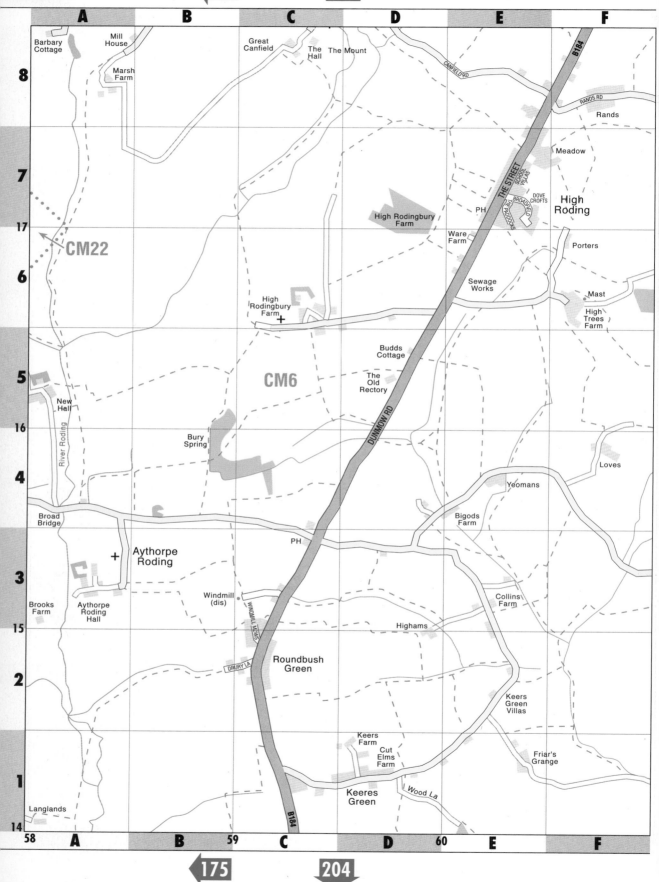

Barbary
Cottage
Mill
House
Marsh
Farm
Great
Canfield
The
Hall
The Mount
CANFIELD RD
B1184
RANDS RD
Rands
Meadow
THE STREET
SCHOOL
VILLAS
DOVE
CROFTS
High
Roding
PH
BROADFIELD
THE PADDOCKS
High Rodingbury
Farm
Ware
Farm
Porters
CM22
Sewage
Works
Mast
High
Trees
Farm
High
Rodingbury
Farm
Budds
Cottage
CM6
The
Old
Rectory
New
Hall
River Roding
Bury
Spring
Loves
Yeomans
Broad
Bridge
Bigods
Farm
Aythorpe
Roding
PH
Collins
Farm
Windmill
(dis)
WINDMILL MDWS
Highams
Brooks
Farm
Aythorpe
Roding
Hall
DRURY LA
Roundbush
Green
Keers
Green
Villas
Keers
Farm
Cut
Elms
Farm
Friar's
Grange
Keeres
Green
Wood La
Langlands
B1184

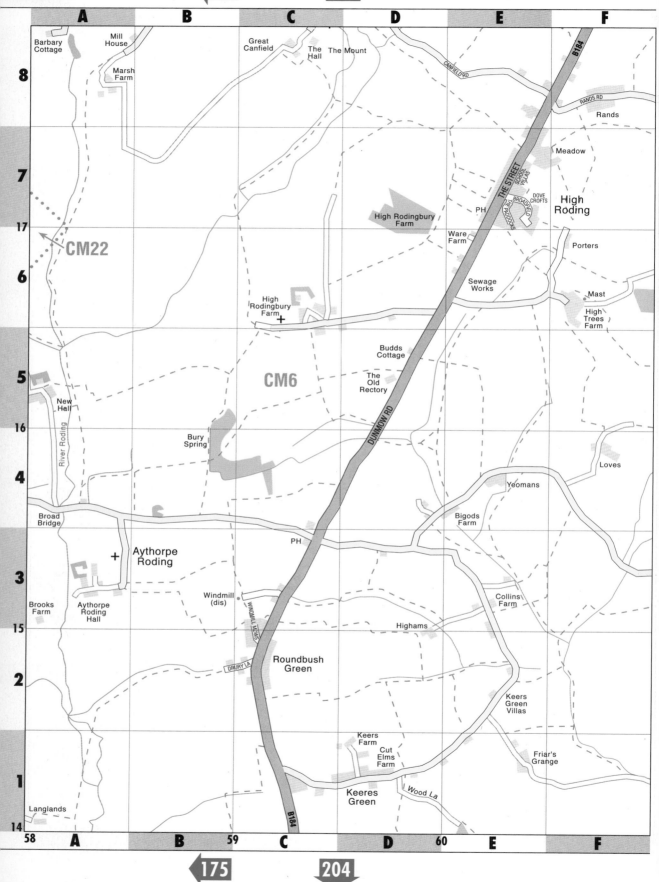

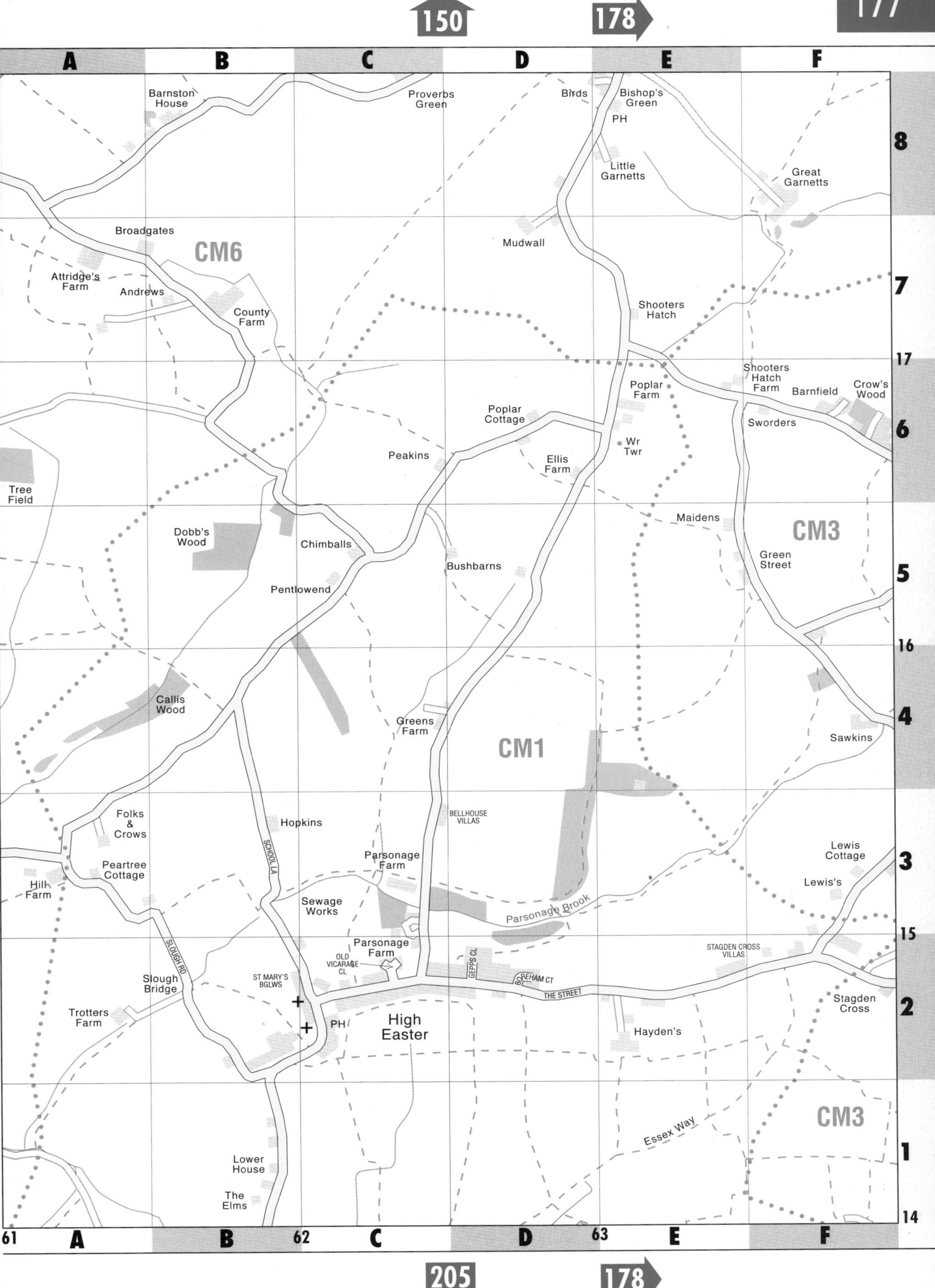

150
178

A B C D E F

8

7

17

6

CM6

Barnston House

Broadgates

Attridge's Farm

Andrews

County Farm

Proverbs Green

Birds

Bishop's Green
PH

Little Garnetts

Mudwall

Shooters Hatch

Great Garnetts

Shooters Hatch Farm

Barnfield

Crow's Wood

Sworders

Poplar Farm

Wr Twr

Poplar Cottage

Peakins

Ellis Farm

Tree Field

Dobb's Wood

Chimballs

Pentlowend

Bushbarns

Maidens

CM3

Green Street

5

16

4

Callis Wood

Greens Farm

CM1

Sawkins

Folks & Crows

Peartree Cottage

Hill Farm

Hopkins

SCHOOL LA

Parsonage Farm

Sewage Works

Parsonage Farm

BELLHOUSE VILLAS

Parsonage Brook

Lewis Cottage

Lewis's

3

15

Stagden Cross Villas

SLOUGH RD

Slough Bridge

Trotters Farm

ST MARY'S BGLWS

OLD VICARAGE CL

PH

High Easter

GEPPS CL

BOREHAM CT

THE STREET

Hayden's

Stagden Cross

2

CM3

Lower House

The Elms

Essex Way

1

14

61 A B 62 C D 63 E F

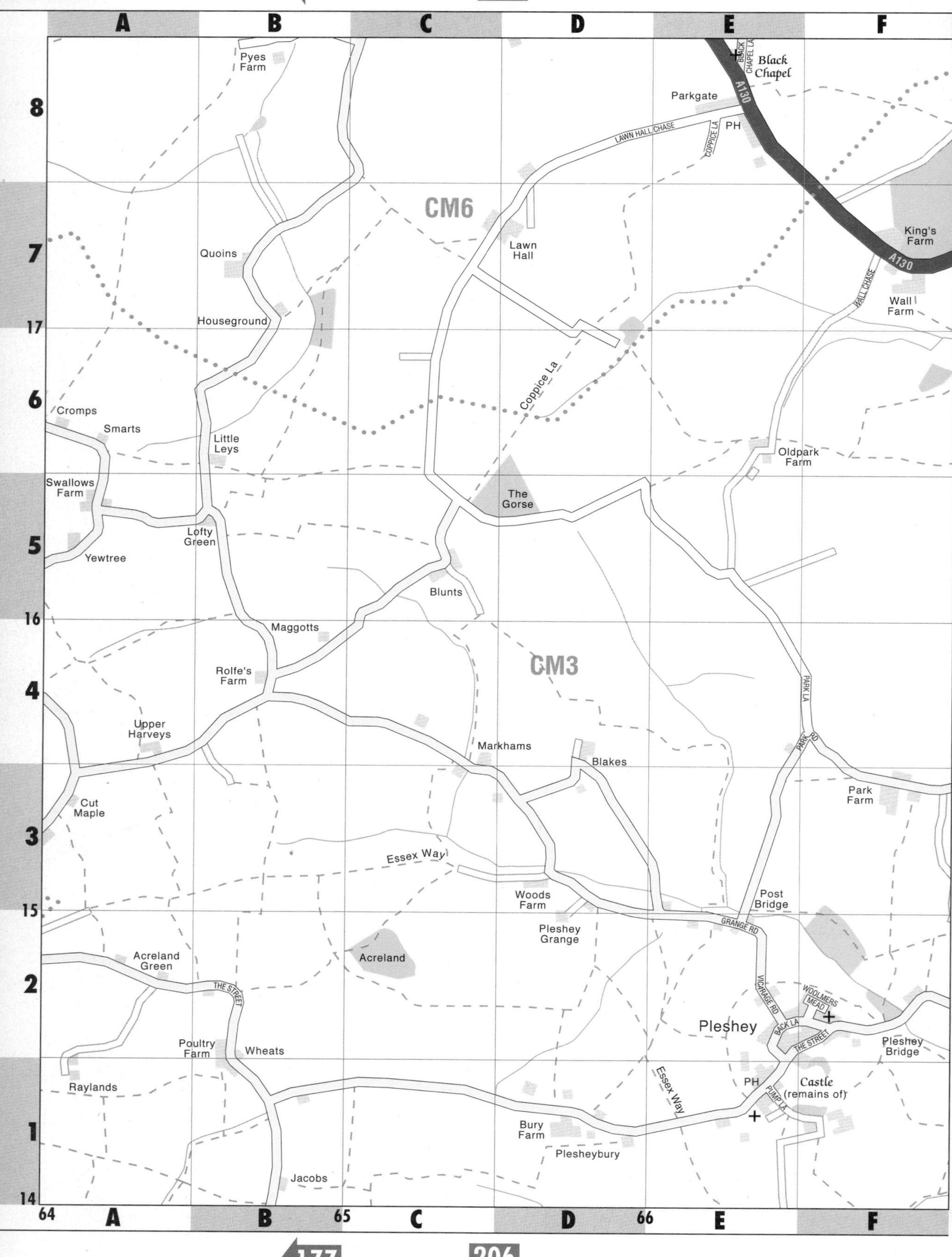

A   B   C   D   E   F

8

7

17

6

CM6

Pyes Farm

Quoins

Houseground

Little Leys

Cromps

Smarts

Swallows Farm

Lofty Green

Yewtree

Lawn Hall

Coppice La

The Gorse

Black Chapel

Parkgate

PH

LAWN HALL CHASE

COPPICE LA

A130

King's Farm

WALL CHASE

Wall Farm

Oldpark Farm

5

16

4

3

15

2

1

14

Blunts

Maggotts

Rolfe's Farm

Upper Harveys

Cut Maple

CM3

Markhams

Blakes

Park Farm

PARK LA

PARK RD

Essex Way

Woods Farm

Pleshey Grange

Acreland Green

Acreland

THE STREET

Poultry Farm

Wheats

Raylands

Jacobs

Bury Farm

Pleshey

Post Bridge

GRANGE RD

VICARAGE RD

BACK LA

WOOLMERS MEAD

THE STREET

Pleshey Bridge

PH

PUMP LA

Castle (remains of)

Essex Way

Plesheybury

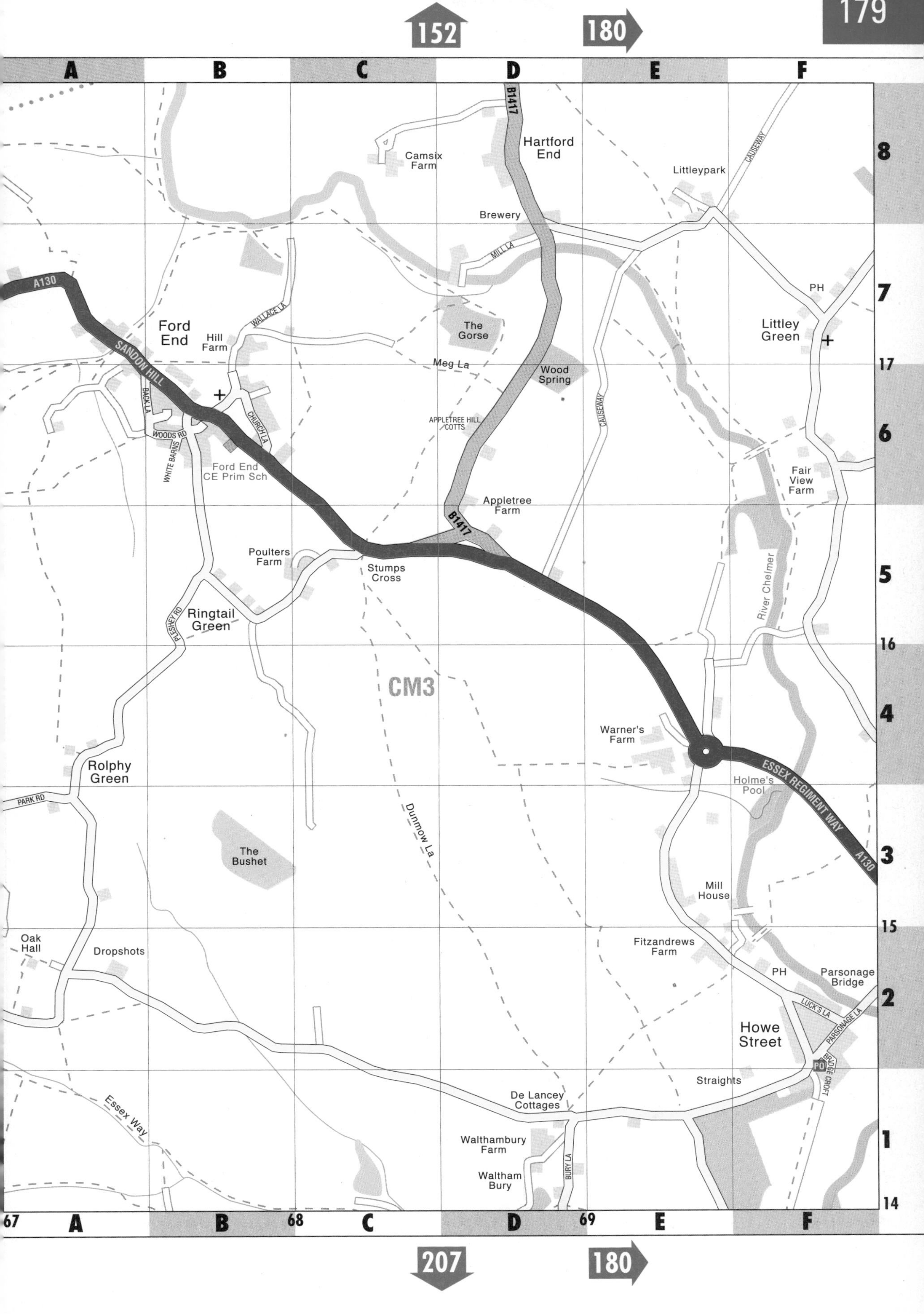
152
180
A
B
C
D
E
F
8
7
17
6
5
16
4
3
15
2
1
14
67
68
69
B1417
Hartford End
Camsix Farm
Littleypark
CAUSEWAY
Brewery
MILL LA
A130
PH
Littley Green
Ford End
Hill Farm
WALLACE LA
The Gorse
Meg La
Wood Spring
SANDON HILL
BACK LA
CHURCH LA
WOODS RD
WHITE BARNS
APPLETREE HILL COTTS
CAUSEWAY
Ford End CE Prim Sch
Fair View Farm
Appletree Farm
B1417
Poulters Farm
Stumps Cross
River Chelmer
Ringtail Green
PLESHEY RD
CM3
Warner's Farm
ESSEX REGIMENT WAY
Rolphy Green
Holme's Pool
PARK RD
Dunmow La
The Bushet
A130
Mill House
Oak Hall
Dropshots
Fitzandrews Farm
PH
Parsonage Bridge
LUCK'S LA
PARSONAGE LA
Howe Street
PO
BRIDGE CROFT
Straights
De Lancey Cottages
Essex Way
Walthambury Farm
Waltham Bury
BURY LA

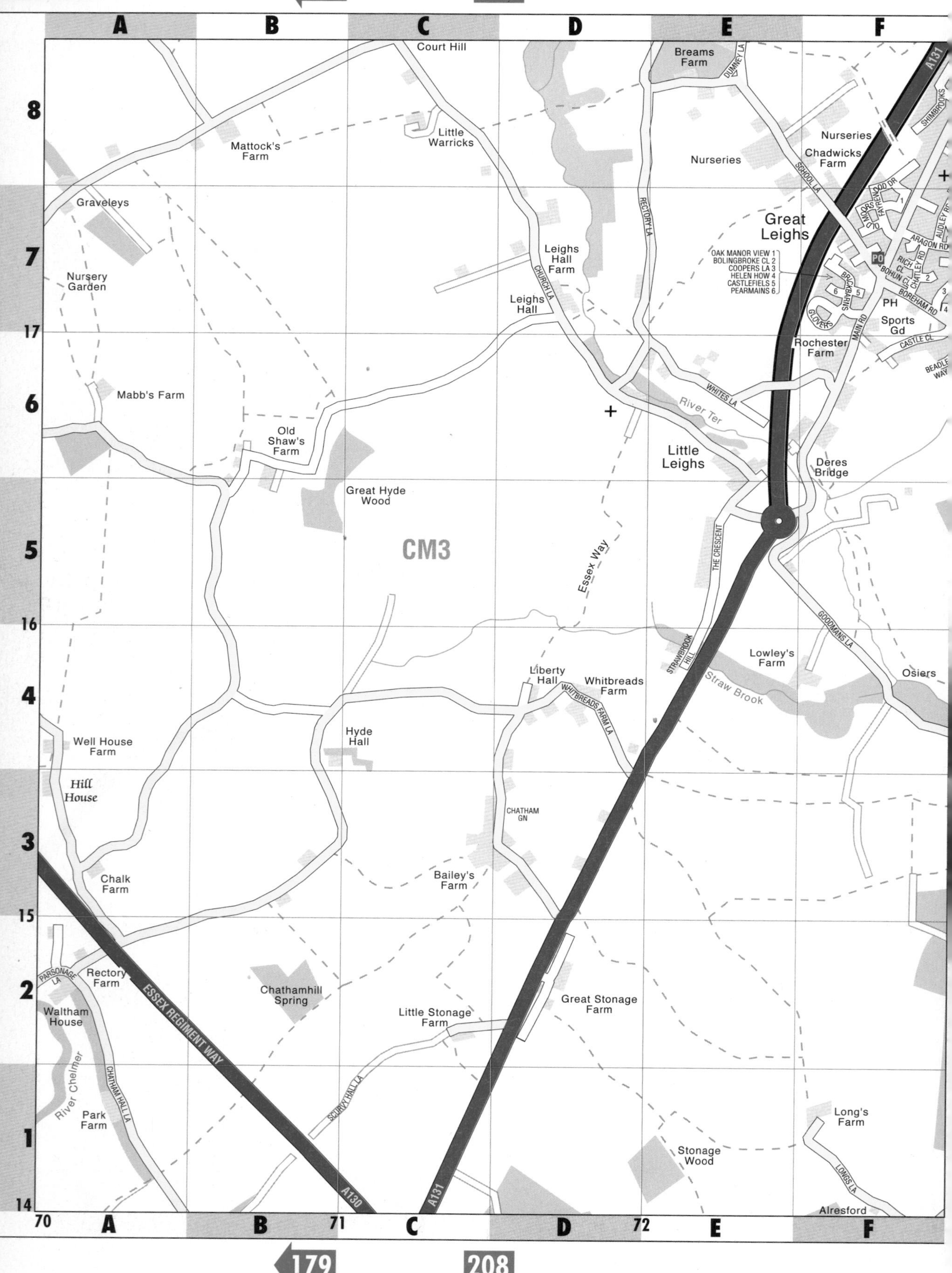

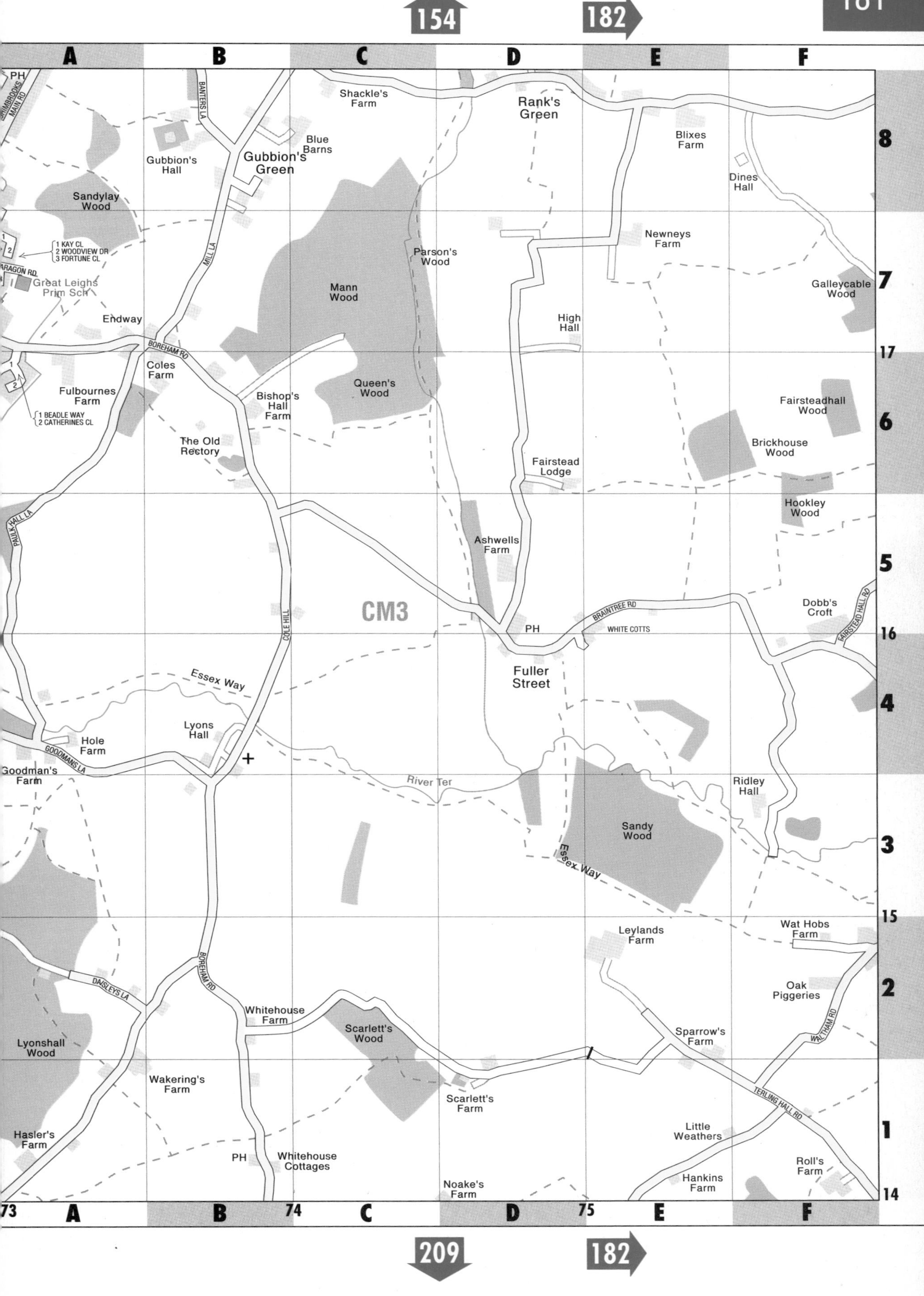

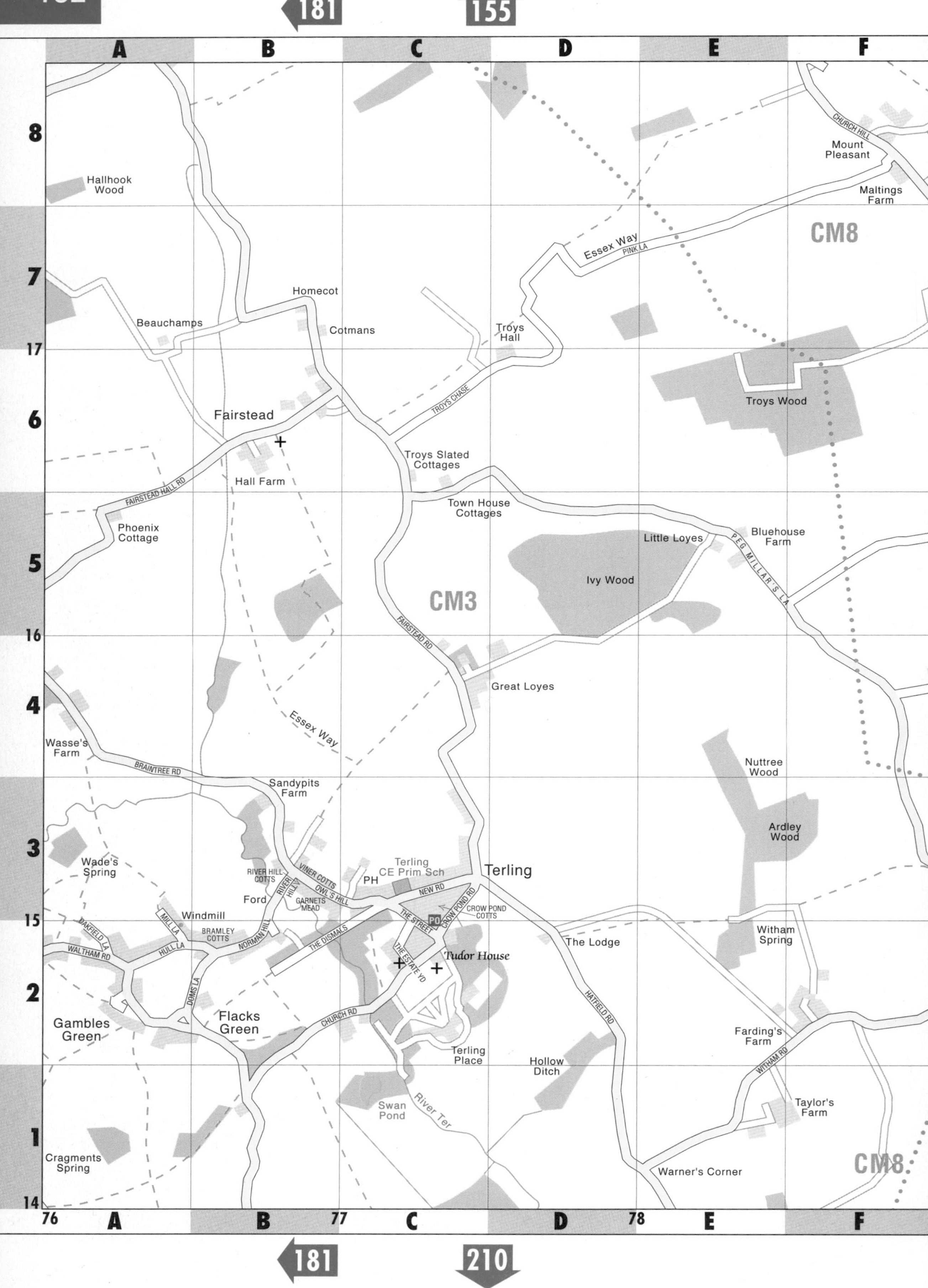

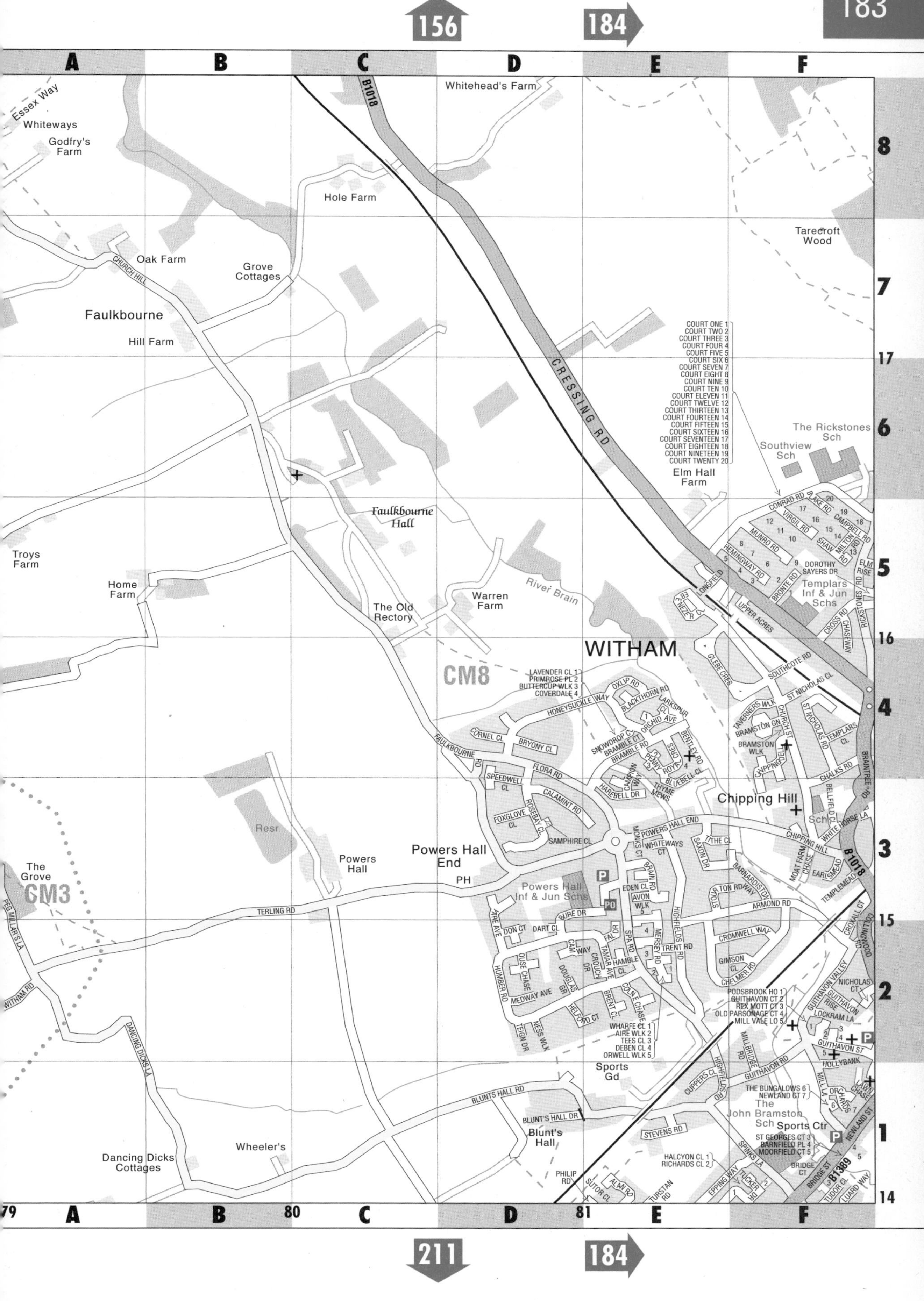

A   B   C   D   E   F

Essex Way

Whiteways

Godfry's Farm

Whitehead's Farm

Hole Farm

Oak Farm

Grove Cottages

Tarecroft Wood

Church Hill

Faulkbourne

Hill Farm

COURT ONE 1
COURT TWO 2
COURT THREE 3
COURT FOUR 4
COURT FIVE 5
COURT SIX 6
COURT SEVEN 7
COURT EIGHT 8
COURT NINE 9
COURT TEN 10
COURT ELEVEN 11
COURT TWELVE 12
COURT THIRTEEN 13
COURT FOURTEEN 14
COURT FIFTEEN 15
COURT SIXTEEN 16
COURT SEVENTEEN 17
COURT EIGHTEEN 18
COURT NINETEEN 19
COURT TWENTY 20

The Rickstones Sch

Southview Sch

Elm Hall Farm

CRESSING RD

B1018

Troys Farm

Home Farm

Faulkbourne Hall

River Brain

CONRAD RD
LAKE RD
CAMPBELL
VIRGIL RD
MUNRO RD
BRONTE RD
SHAW
MILTON
HEMINGWAY RD
DOROTHY SAYERS DR
ELM RISE
CROSS RD
CHASEWAY
Templars Inf & Jun Schs

The Old Rectory

Warren Farm

WITHAM

UPPER ACRES
LONGFIELD

LUPPER ACRES

CM8

LAVENDER CL 1
PRIMROSE PL 2
BUTTERCUP WLK 3
COVERDALE 4

OXLIP RD
BLACKTHORN RD
LARKSPUR
HONEYSUCKLE WAY
CORNEL CL
BRYONY CL
SNOWDROP CL
ORCHID AVE
BRAMBLE RD
BRAMBLE CL
FLORA RD
HAREBELL DR
BLUEBELL CL
THYME
BENTLY RD
ROYDS

SOUTHCOTE RD
GLEBE CRES

ST NICHOLAS CL
ST NICHOLAS RD
TEMPLARS
CHIPPINGS
BRAMSTON GN
BRAMSTON WLK
CHURCH ST
CHALKS RD
BELLFIELD
WHITE HORSE LA
BRAINTREE RD

SPEEDWELL CL
ROSEBAY CL
CALAMINT RD
FOXGLOVE CL
SAMPHIRE CL

MONKS CT
WHITEWAYS
POWERS HALL END
SAXON DR
THE CL
CHIPPING HILL
Sch
MOAT FARM CHASE
EARLS MEAD
TEMPLEMEAD

Chipping Hill

The Grove
CM3

Resr

Powers Hall

Powers Hall End

PH

FAULKBOURNE RD

Powers Hall Inf & Jun Schs

P
PO

BRAIN RD
EDEN CL
AVON WLK
HIGHFIELDS
UPTON RD
BARNARDISTON
CROMWELL WAY
GIMSON CL
ARMOND RD
B1018
TEMPLEMEAD
CROWOOD
CROWHURST

PEG MILLAR LA

TERLING RD

SURE DR
DON CT
DART CL
CARE AVE
CAM WAY
TAMAR GR
HAMBLE
FAL
SPA RD
TRENT RD
MERSEY RD
CHELMER RD

CROBALD CT
GUITHAVON VALLEY
GUITHAVON RISE
NICHOLAS CL
LOCKRAM LA

WITHAM RD

DANCING DICKS LA

HUMBER RD
OUSE CHASE
MEDWAY AVE
DOUGLAS GR
NESS WLK
TEIGN DR
HELIC GR
DOON CHASE
CAN CHASE
BRENT CL

PODSBROOK HO 1
GUITHAVON CT 2
REX MOTT CT 3
OLD PARSONAGE CT 4
MILL VALE LO 5

GUITHAVON ST

HOLLYBANK

WHARFE CL 1
AIRE WLK 2
TEES CL 3
DEBEN CL 4
ORWELL WLK 5

Sports Gd

CUPPERS CL
HIGHFIELDS RD
MILLBRIDGE RD
GUITHAVON RD
SPRING LA

The Bungalows 6
Newland Ct 7

ORCHARD
MILL LA
NEWLAND ST

The John Bramston Sch Sports Ctr

P

BLUNTS HALL RD

BLUNT'S HALL DR

Blunt's Hall

STEVENS RD

ST GEORGES CT 3
BARNFIELD PL 4
MOORFIELD CT 5

P

BRIDGE ST

Dancing Dicks Cottages

Wheeler's

PHILIP RD

SUTOR CL
ALME RD
TURSTAN RD

HALCYON CL 1
RICHARDS CL 2

EPPING WAY
FLICKER
BRIDGE CT
B1389
TUDOR CL
LUARD WAY

79   A   B   80   C   D   81   E   F

8

17

7

6

5

16

4

3

15

2

1

14

A   **B**   **C**   **D**   **E**   **F**

8

Rivenhall CE Prim Sch

Rivenhall

Tarecroft Wood

Hoo Hall

7

Hare Lodge

Hole Farm

17

Stovern's Hall

Rickstone's Farm

CH

Oak Rd

Durwards Hall

6

Rivenhall Bridge

Glebe Farm

The Old Rectory

Henry Dixon Rd

Foxmead

Foxden

Rivenhall End

5

1 WIMSEY CT
2 VANE CT
3 HAWTHORNE RISE

Whitelands

The Matchyn's

Hotel

Sewage Works

Rose Cottage

Appleford Farm

CM8

16

Cemy

PO

HOLLY WLK

YEW CL

ALDER WLK

CHESTNUT WLK

JUNIPER CRES

Waterside Bsns Pk

Braxted Park Rd

Colemans Resr

Appleford Bridge

4

Superstore

CRITTALL CT

HOMEFIELD RD

BIRCH CL

TEAK WLK

WALNUT DR

HORNBEAM WLK

HAZEL CL

CYPRESS RD

LC

MOTTS LA

EASTWAYS

Eastways Ind Est

B1389

22

B1389

Coleman's Bridge

River Blackwater

Commodity Ctr

Workhouse Plantation

Hall Broad House

CHURCH CHASE

3

Witham Junction

Witham

STATION RD

ATLANTIC

CROFT WAY

1 Enterprise Ct
2 Europa Pk
3 Swanbridge Ind Pk

COLCHESTER RD

Coleman's Farm

LITTLE BRAXTED LA

Elm Springs

15

THE AVENUE

THE PADDOCKS

CHEQUERS CT

ARMIGER

BEVINGTON MEWS

Cromwell Ctr

MOSS RD

STEFIELD

FREEBOURNES RD

2

Swan Vale Ind Est

Ct

THE GROVE

CHARLOTTE WAY

1 KYNASTON PL
2 RICHARDSON WLK

Hall

Little Braxted

Lea Lane Wood

Liby

MAYLAND RD

WHEATON RD

Lea Lane Fruit Farm

Broomfield's Farm

1

NEWLAND ST

KING'S CHASE

MALDON RD

B1018

TH

The Grove Ctr

The Retreat

PASTURE RD

GREENFIELD

PERRY WAY

LEA LA

Wheater Ind Est

Briarsford Ind Est

PERRY WAY

14

B1018

BLACKMAN WAY

HANOVER CT

Sewage Works

A12

A2
1 GROVE COTTS
2 FOSTER CT
3 DU CANE PL
4 HORNER PL
5 FREEBOURNES CT
6 HEWITT WLK
7 LOCKRAM LA
8 NEWLANDS PREC
9 PENHALIGON CT

10 COACH HOUSE WAY
11 GUITHAVON ST

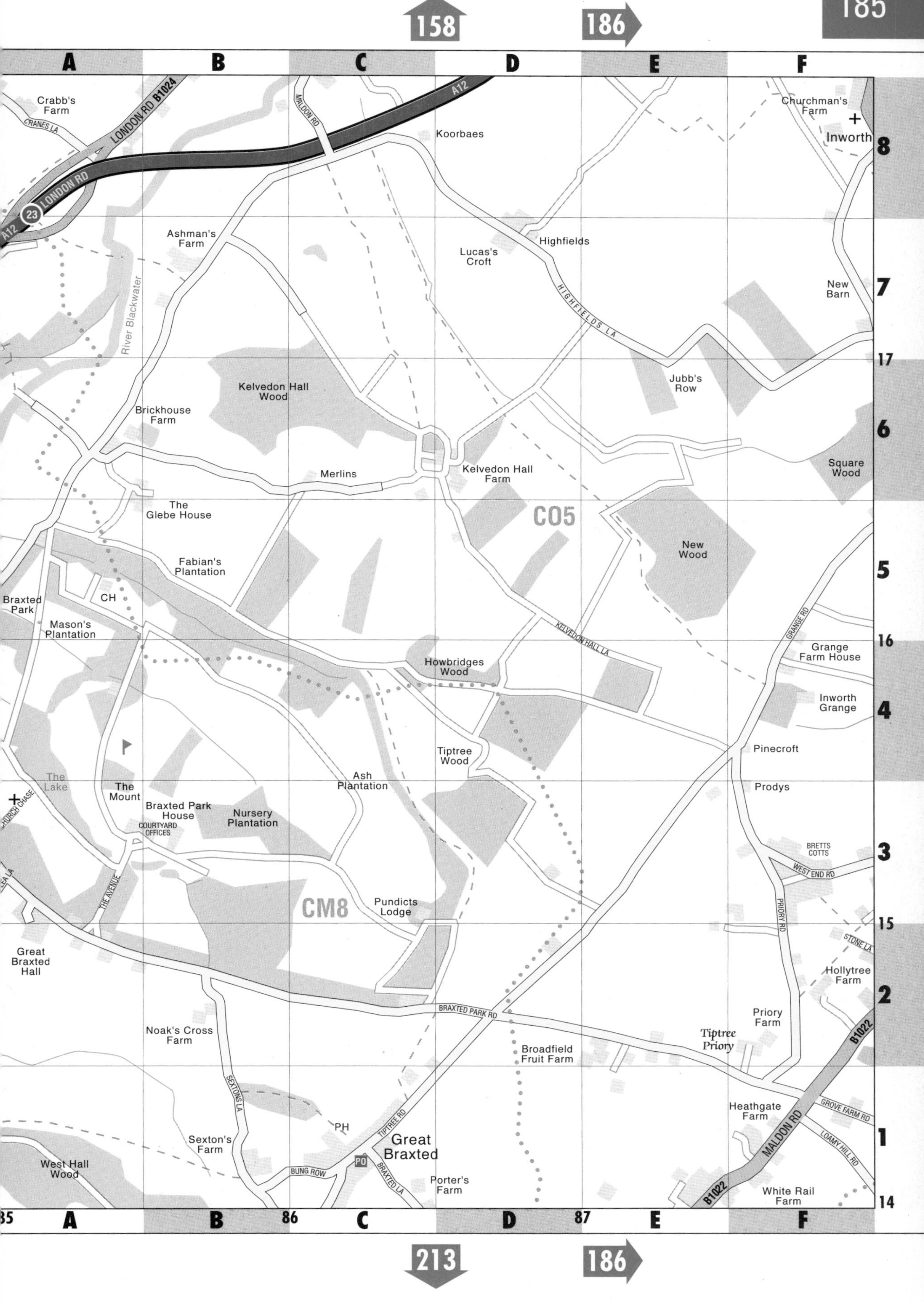
158
186
A
B
C
D
E
F
Crabb's Farm
CRANES LA
LONDON RD B1024
LONDON RD
A12
23
MALDON RD
Koorbaes
Churchman's Farm
Inworth
8
Ashman's Farm
Highfields
Lucas's Croft
River Blackwater
HIGHFIELDS LA
New Barn
7
17
Kelvedon Hall Wood
Brickhouse Farm
Jubb's Row
6
Merlins
Kelvedon Hall Farm
Square Wood
The Glebe House
CO5
New Wood
Fabian's Plantation
5
Braxted Park
CH
Mason's Plantation
KELVEDON HALL LA
GRANGE RD
16
Grange Farm House
Howbridges Wood
Inworth Grange
4
Tiptree Wood
Pinecroft
The Lake
The Mount
Ash Plantation
Prodys
CHURCH CHASE
Braxted Park House
COURTYARD OFFICES
Nursery Plantation
BRETTS COTTS
3
WEST END RD
THE AVENUE
LEA LA
CM8
Pundicts Lodge
PRIORY RD
15
STONE LA
Great Braxted Hall
Hollytree Farm
2
BRAXTED PARK RD
Priory Farm
B1022
Tiptree Priory
Noak's Cross Farm
Broadfield Fruit Farm
SEXTONS LA
Heathgate Farm
GROVE FARM RD
PH
TIPTREE RD
1
Sexton's Farm
Great Braxted
LOAMY HILL RD
MALDON RD
West Hall Wood
BUNG ROW
PO
BRAXTED LA
Porter's Farm
B1022
White Rail Farm
14
85
86
87
213
186

A B C D E F

8

PH
THE STREET
Hill
House
B1023
HAPPY
GDNS

Messing
Park
Farm

B1022

Pods Wood

Haynes
Green

The Elms

The Rampart

Hill
Farm

Bishops
Cottage

COLCHESTER RD

PH

Woodview
Farm

Napiers
Farm

7

Perry's
Wood

KELVEDON RD

Baynard's
Prim Sch

BISHOPS LA
BROKEN HALL
OAK RD
WILLOW WLK
MAPLE LEAF
WALNUT TREE WAY
CEDAR AVE
SIMONS
FLATS
ELM CL
CHESTNUT
ALMOND

MAYPOLE RD

Thurstable
Sch

MAYTREE
CT

Milldene
Prim Sch

Poyston

CO5

Viners
Farm

17

6

Hill Wood

WATERWORKS
COTTS

GRANGE RD

Vine
Farm

LANSDOWNE LA
VINE RD
KINGSWAY
QUEENSWAY
ROWAN
CHASE
STOKES RD
WINDMILL VIEW
PIT LA
MILL WLK
MILLFIELDS
WRIGHT'S
GREEN LA

SPINNEYFIELDS
HEATON WAY
BARBROOK LA
ARNOLD
VILLAS
BLUE CL
MUSCADE
ELEANOR CL
LISSMAN
GLOBE CL
BEDFORD
GROVE RD

WARREN LANE
WILKIN DR
SOUTHGATE CRES
KEYLEY
TIFFIN DR
WALLIS WAY
LUTHER DR
HADBROOKE WLK
NEWBRIDGE RD
KILTIE RD
CHURCHILL
BLENHEIM
WAY

Viners
Farm

1 DOWNTON WLK
2 ST JEAN WLK
3 ELEANOR WLK
4 TALISMAN WLK
5 GLOBE WLK
6 ELTON WLK

1 BROCK CL
2 OLLEY WLK

Ransome's
Grove

Sewage
Works

Windmill HIll

MEADOW
VIEW
HARRINGTON CL
BLUE RD
PERRY RD
PENNSYLVANIA LA
ROSEMARY CRES
THYME CL
HOLLY WAY
THE CUT
RANSOM RD
PIERCE
GLADE

CHURCH RD

CAROLINA WAY
GROSVENOR CT
SELDON RD

Tiptree
Windmill

Tiptree

P

Liby

BROOK MDWS
SAGE WLK
CLARKES HEAD
RECTORY RD
ROSEMARY
CT
ST LUKE'S CHASE
BRYANITA
CT
PO

New RD
ELWIN RD
GAGER DR

Birch Wood

BLENHEIM
WAY

5

16

4

Sand & Gravel Pit

PEAKES CL
FRANCES CL
SPRING RD
SAFFRON WAY
LAVENDER CL
ANCHOR RD
BULL LA
BACK LA
STURRY LA
CHERRY CHASE
GORSE LA
ORCHARD
LODGE
CHERRY CHASE

P
JUBILEE
CT

CEDAR TREE CT
CHAPEL RD
BIRCHWOOD WAY
SILVERTHORN CL

Factory

Tiptree
Mus

FACTORY HILL

Brook Hall

3

15

Villa
Farm

WEST END RD

MALDON RD

PH

Tiptree Heath
Prim Sch

Gate
House

Layer Brook

BRUCE CT

BROOK RD
KNIGHTS
PO

Tolleshunt
Knights

PH

THE FOLLY

2

Manor House
Farm

STONE LA
SIMPSONS LA

P

Tiptree
Heath

TIPTREE HALL LA
HALL RD

Tiptree Hall

STRAWBERRY LA
TUDWICK RD

D'ARCY RD

B1023

Oxley
Farm

1

GROVE FARM RD
LOAM HILL RD

CM9

Hawthorn Farm

Wilkin's
Grove

Venn Farm

Elmwood
Farm

GREEN LA

Wr Twr

CM9

14

88 A 89 B C 89 D 90 E F

160
188

A B C D E F

8

White Lodge

Layer Woodlands
Farm

WOODVIEW
COTTS

Layer Marney

CO2

Layer Marney
Tower

HAYNES GREEN RD

STOCKHOUSE RD

Parkhouse
Farm

Wick Farm

Oak Farm

Parkgate
Farm

7

Hall Farm

17

CO5

NEWBRIDGE RD

Layer Brook

6

Stockridge
Farm

Silverthorn

Rockingham's
Farm

5

Cadgers Wood

16

Long Wood

4

Park Farm

Beatbush
Wood

PARK LA

CM9

3

Paternoster Heath

15

BROOK RD

Gobolt's
Farm

Barn Hall Farm

HAWTHORN RD

STOCKHOUSE CL

HAWTHORN WAY

Tolleshunt
Knights

ELIZABETH
VILLAS

BARNHALL RD

2

Palmers
Farm

TOP RD

P

RECTORY RD

The
Plough Inn
(PH)

D'ARCY RD

BLAND LA

HONEYPOT LA

Wigborough
Springs

1

B1023

Krissimon
Farm

Manifold Wick
Farm

Oxley Green

OXLEY HILL

Lovedowns Farm

14

91 A B 92 C D 93 E F

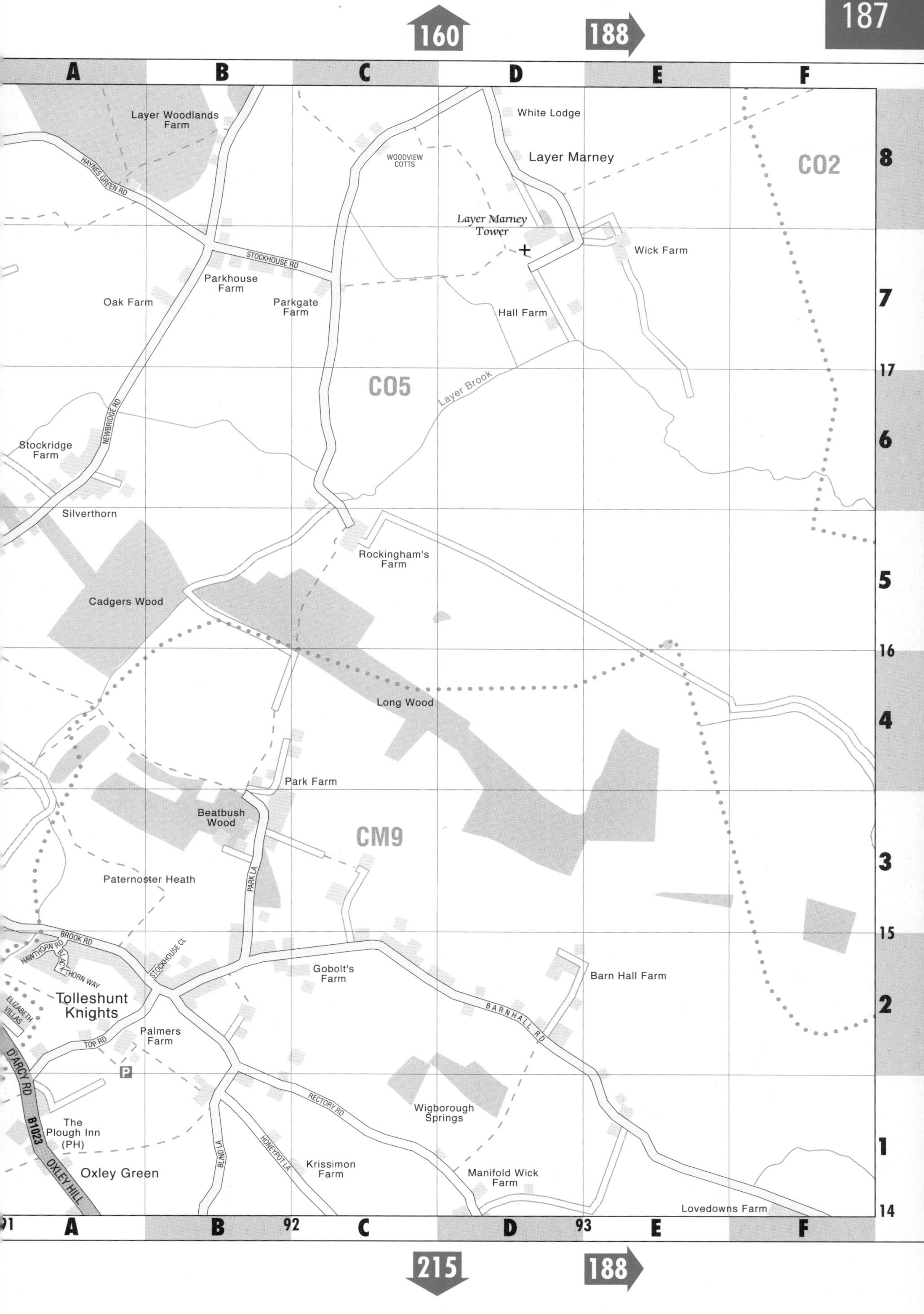

215
188

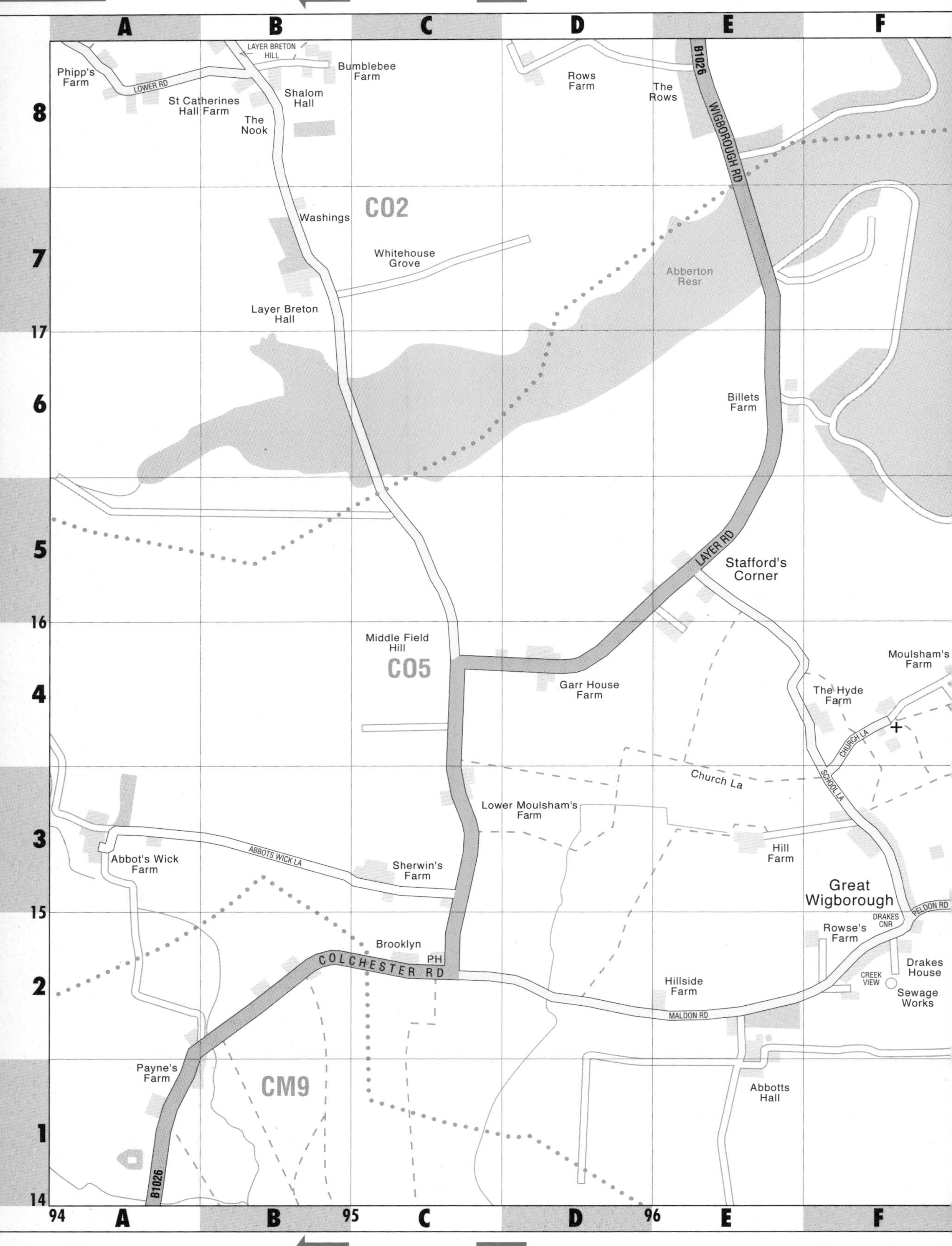

Phipp's Farm
LOWER RD
St Catherines Hall Farm
The Nook
Shalom Hall
LAYER BRETON HILL
Bumblebee Farm

CO2

Washings
Whitehouse Grove
Layer Breton Hall

Rows Farm
The Rows
B1026
WIGBOROUGH RD

Abberton Resr

Billets Farm

Stafford's Corner
LAYER RD

Middle Field Hill
CO5
Garr House Farm

Moulsham's Farm
The Hyde Farm
CHURCH LA
SCHOOL LA
Church La
Hill Farm

Lower Moulsham's Farm

Abbot's Wick Farm
ABBOTS WICK LA
Sherwin's Farm

Great Wigborough
DRAKES CNR
FELDON RD
Rowse's Farm
CREEK VIEW
Drakes House

Brooklyn
PH
COLCHESTER RD

Hillside Farm
MALDON RD
Sewage Works

Payne's Farm
CM9
B1026

Abbotts Hall

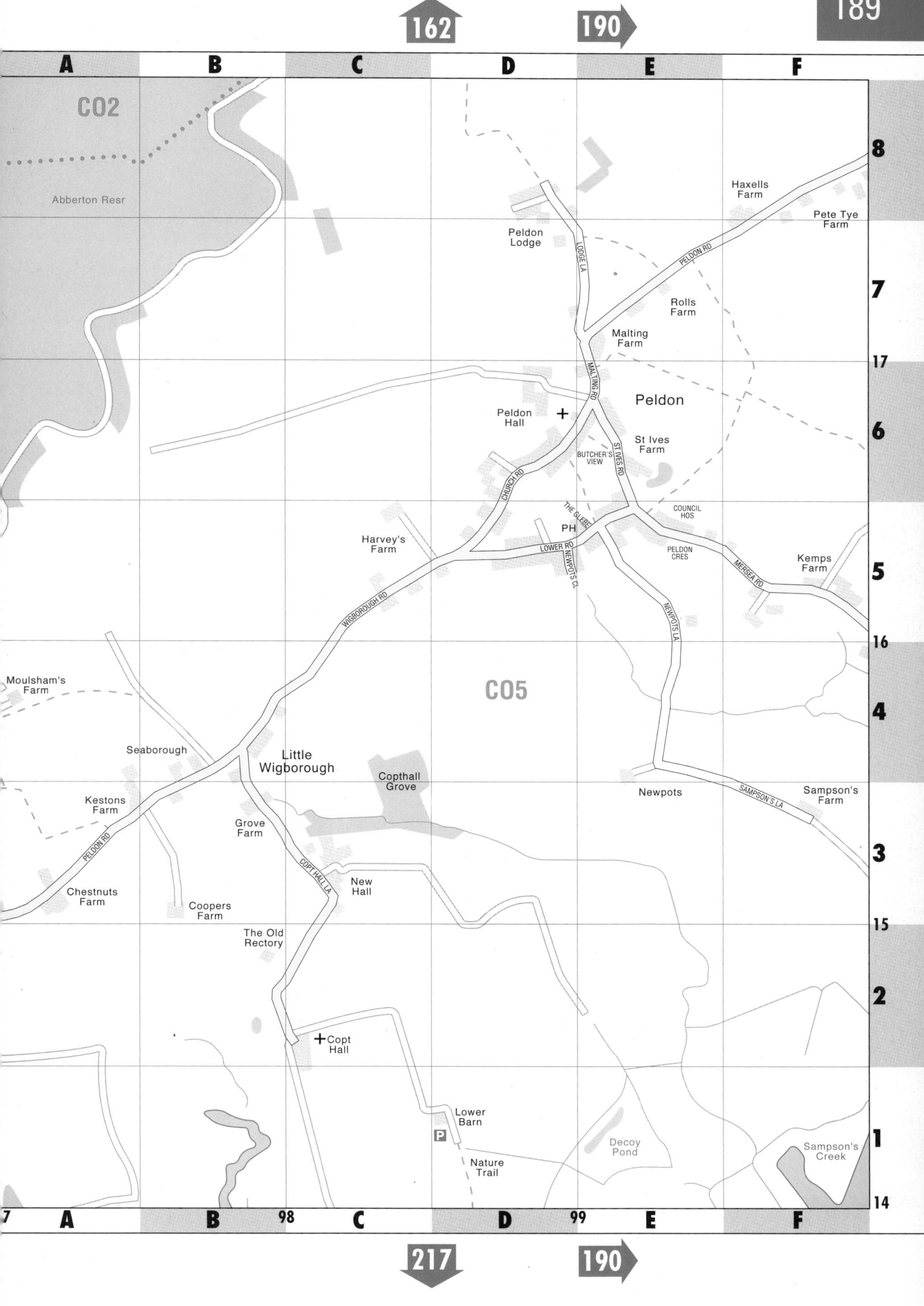

162
190

A **B** **C** **D** **E** **F**

CO2

Abberton Resr

8

Haxells
Farm

Pete Tye
Farm

PELDON RD

Peldon
Lodge

LODGE LA

Rolls
Farm

7

Malting
Farm

MALTING RD

17

Peldon

6

Peldon
Hall

St Ives
Farm

ST IVES RD

BUTCHER'S
VIEW

CHURCH RD

COUNCIL
HOS

Harvey's
Farm

THE GLEBE

PH

PELDON
CRES

Kemps
Farm

LOWER RD

NEWPOTS CL

MERSEA RD

5

WIGBOROUGH RD

NEWPOTS RD

16

Moulsham's
Farm

CO5

NEWPOTS LA

4

Seaborough

Little
Wigborough

Copthall
Grove

Kestons
Farm

Grove
Farm

Newpots

SAMPSON'S LA

Sampson's
Farm

PELDON RD

COPT HALL LA

New
Hall

3

Chestnuts
Farm

Coopers
Farm

The Old
Rectory

15

2

+ Copt
Hall

Lower
Barn

P

Decoy
Pond

Sampson's
Creek

1

Nature
Trail

14

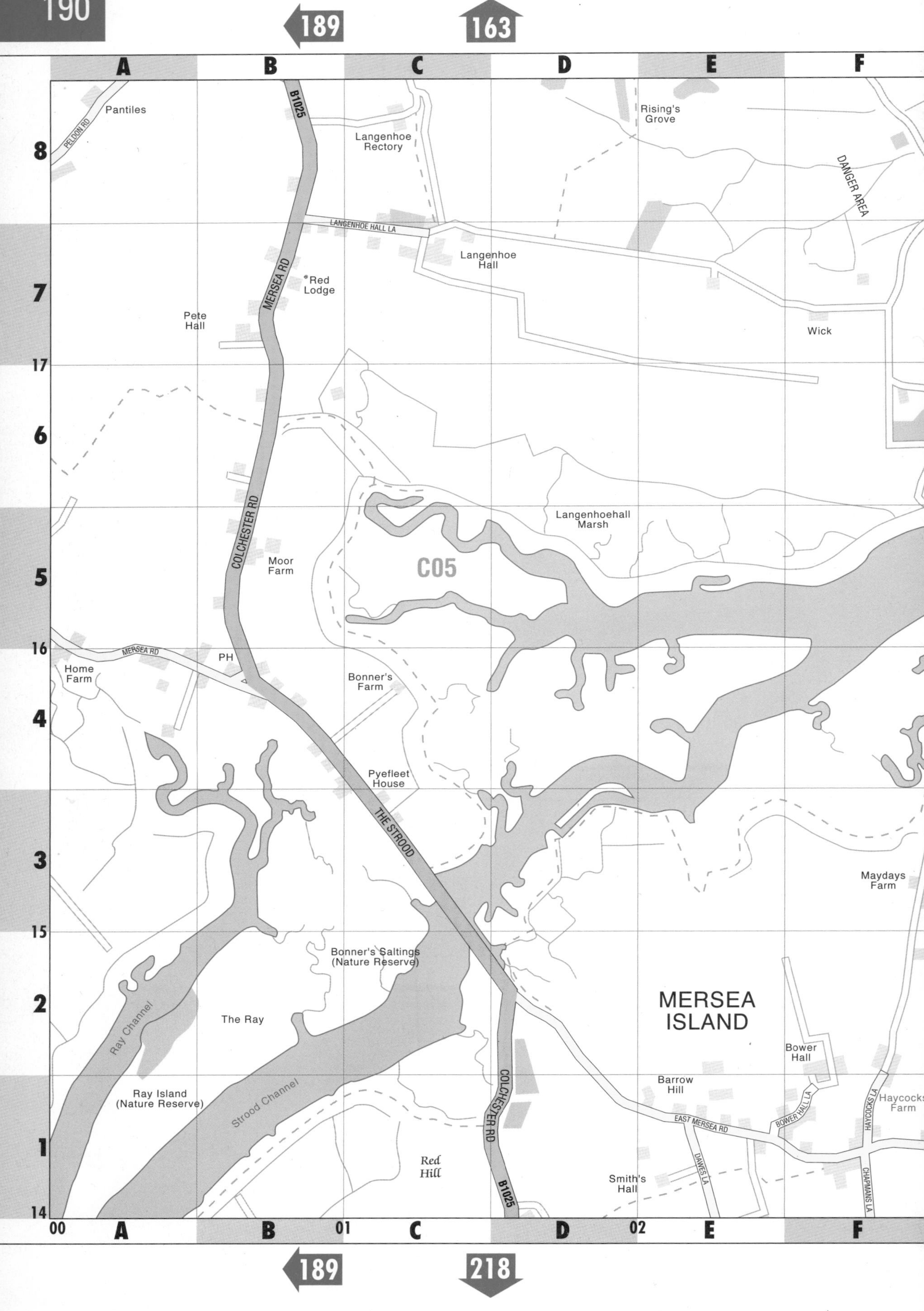

A   B   C   D   E   F

8

7

17

6

5

16

4

3

15

2

1

14

Pantiles

PELDON RD

B1025

Langenhoe Rectory

Rising's Grove

DANGER AREA

LANGENHOE HALL LA

Red Lodge

MERSEA RD

Langenhoe Hall

Pete Hall

Wick

COLCHESTER RD

Langenhoehall Marsh

Moor Farm

C05

Home Farm

MERSEA RD

PH

Bonner's Farm

Pyefleet House

THE STROOD

Maydays Farm

Ray Channel

Bonner's Saltings (Nature Reserve)

MERSEA ISLAND

The Ray

Bower Hall

Barrow Hill

Ray Island (Nature Reserve)

Strood Channel

COLCHESTER RD

EAST MERSEA RD

BOWER HALL LA

HAYCOCKS LA

Haycocks Farm

CHAPMANS LA

Red Hill

B1025

Smith's Hall

DAWES LA

00   A   B   01   C   D   02   E   F

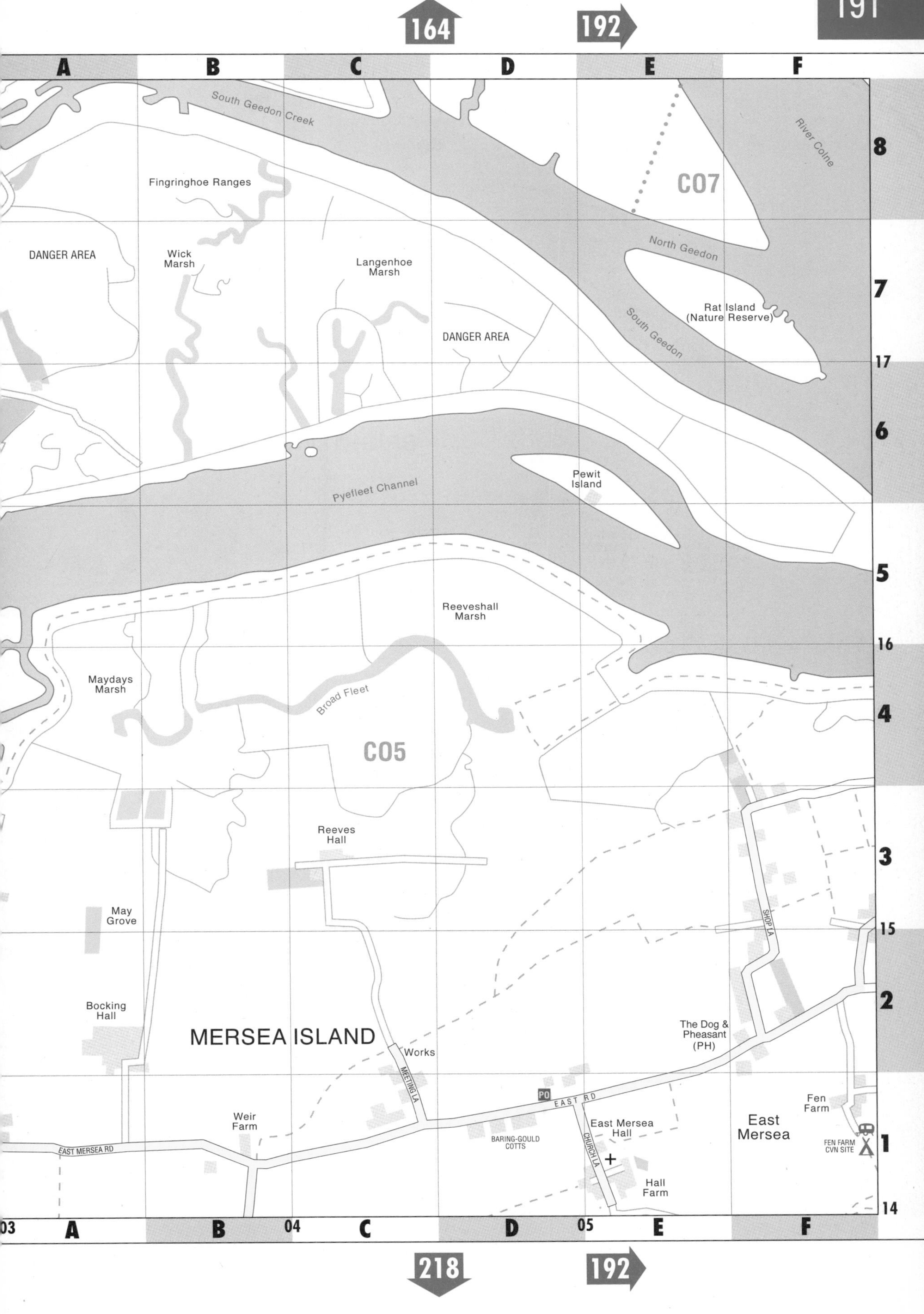

164
192

A   B   C   D   E   F

South Geedon Creek

8

Fingringhoe Ranges

CO7

River Colne

North Geedon

DANGER AREA

Wick Marsh

Langenhoe Marsh

7

Rat Island (Nature Reserve)

South Geedon

17

DANGER AREA

6

Pyefleet Channel

Pewit Island

5

Reeveshall Marsh

16

Maydays Marsh

Broad Fleet

4

CO5

Reeves Hall

3

May Grove

SHOP LA

15

Bocking Hall

2

The Dog & Pheasant (PH)

MERSEA ISLAND

Works

MEETING LA

PO

EAST RD

Fen Farm

East Mersea

Weir Farm

East Mersea Hall

CHURCH LA

FEN FARM CVN SITE

EAST MERSEA RD

BARING-GOULD COTTS

Hall Farm

1

14

218
192

191
165

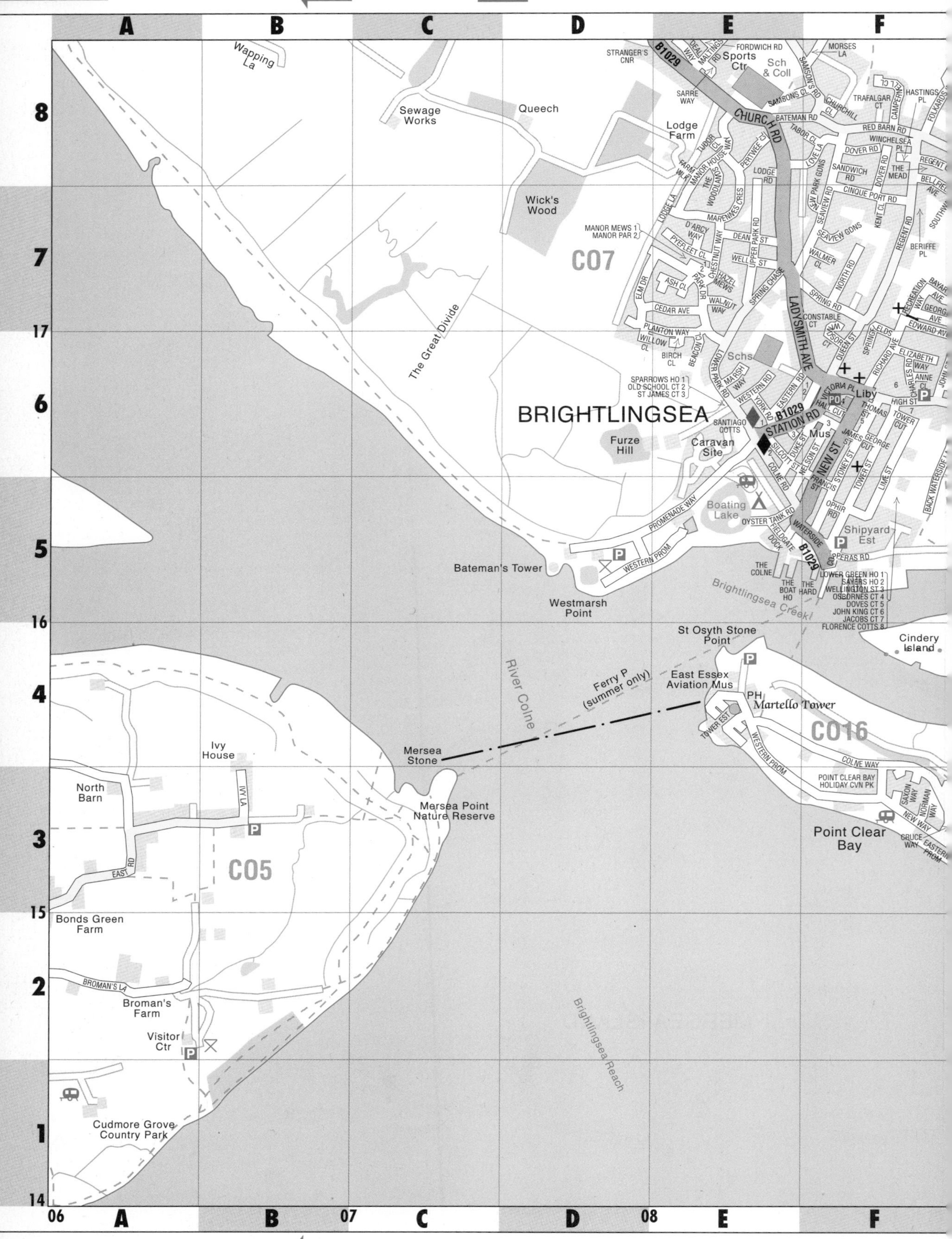
A
B
C
D
E
F
8
7
17
6
5
16
4
3
15
2
1
14
06
07
08
Wapping La
Sewage Works
Queech
Lodge Farm
Wick's Wood
C07
The Great Divide
BRIGHTLINGSEA
Furze Hill
Caravan Site
Boating Lake
Shipyard Est
Bateman's Tower
Westmarsh Point
Brightlingsea Creek
St Osyth Stone Point
Cindery Island
East Essex Aviation Mus
Martello Tower
CO16
River Colne
Ferry P (summer only)
Mersea Stone
Mersea Point Nature Reserve
Ivy House
North Barn
CO5
Point Clear Bay
Bonds Green Farm
Broman's Farm
Visitor Ctr
Brightlingsea Reach
Cudmore Grove Country Park
B1029
CHURCH RD
LADYSMITH AVE
STATION RD
NEW ST
Sports Ctr
Sch & Coll
Schs
Liby
Mus
PO
PROMENADE WAY
WESTERN PROM
WATERSIDE
COLNE WAY
POINT CLEAR BAY HOLIDAY CVN PK
EAST RD
BROMAN'S LA
IVY LA

191

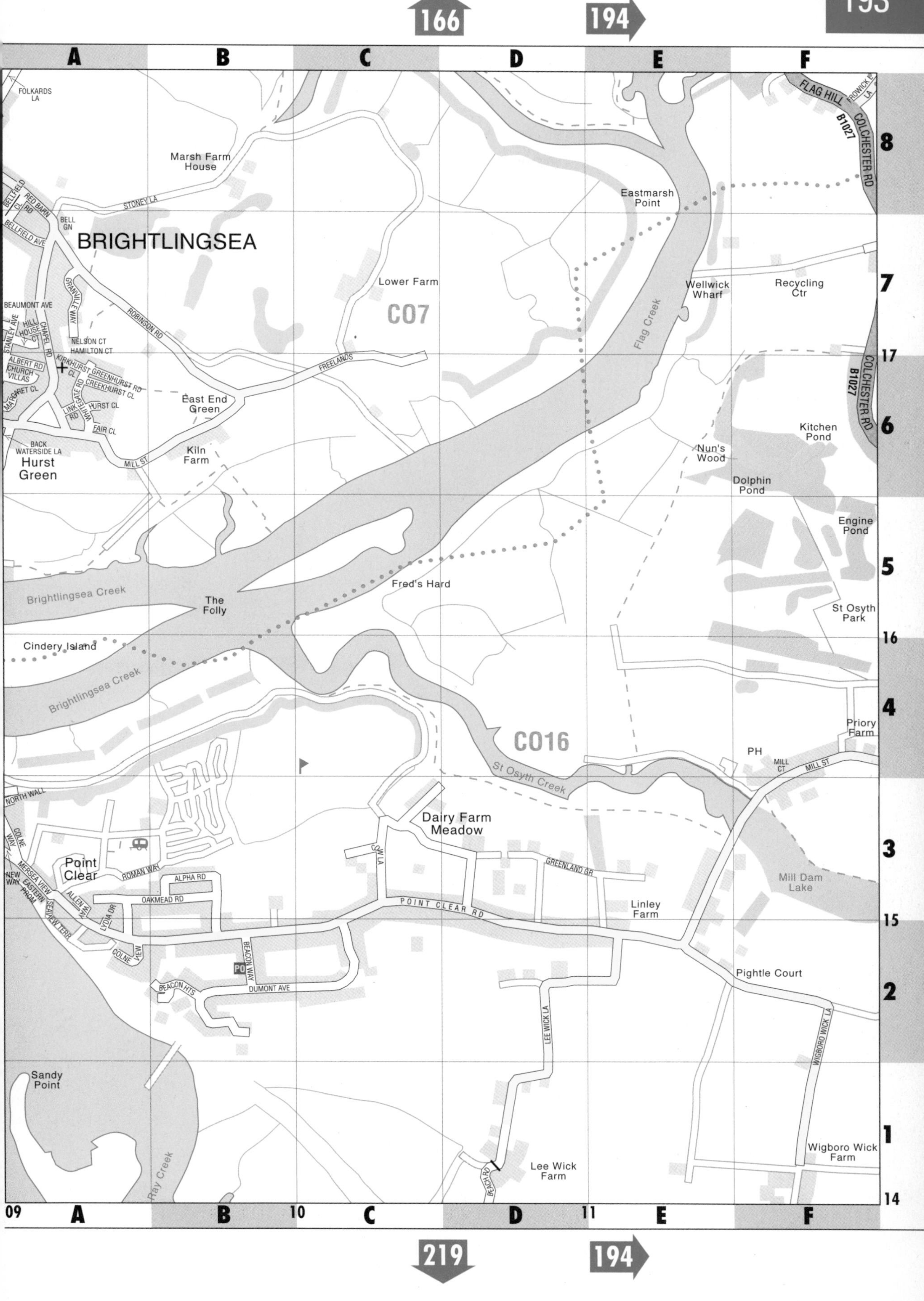

A B C D E F

8

FROWICK LA

CO7

7

B1027 COLCHESTER RD

Caravan Park

17

Riddles Wood

Sandyhayes

Kiln Cottage

High Grove

6

Wellwick Farm

Park Farm Cottages

Park Farm

Earls Hall

CLAY LA

Lamb Farm

COLCHESTER RD

Cemy

GOLDING WAY

PARK CHASE

Lower Barn

EARLS HALL DR

5

Deer Park

PARK COTTS

NEWTON GDNS

NEWTON

TUNSTALL CL

BOTANICAL WAY

WITHRICK WLK

DEEPING WLK

BROADSTROOD

ST CLAIR'S DR

D'ARCY RD

MANI ELD GDNS

NASSAU

VINES GDNS

ABBOTS GDNS

BYPASS RD

Bush Paddock

CO16

Nursery

Duchess Farm

16

St Osyth Priory

PRIORY PK ACRES

THREE ACRES

CASTLE WAY

KINCAID RD

MAYPOLE

LONGFIELDS

STANMORE

ST CLAIR'S RD

CLACTON RD

PUMP HILL

Pump Hill Farm

PUMP HILL CVN PK

ST JOHN'S RD

B1027

4

VYNTONER PH HO

JOHNSON RD

MEADOW VIEW

RIDGEHORD RD

LODGE FARM LA

ROUSES LA

THE BURY

MILL ST

CHURCH SQ

NORMAN CL

CHAPEL LA

St Osyth

St Osyth CE Prim Sch

PARK RD

OLD SCHOOL CL

JAMES RD

SPRING RD

BROOK VALE

DALTES LA

St Osyth Lodge Farm

Rouses Farm

3

Warren Farm

ST CLERES HALL LA

Brazier's Farm

Daltes Farm

15

Warren La

Reed Pond

Botany La

2

St Clere's Hall

BEACH RD

SACKETTS GROVE CVN PK

CO15

LEICESTER CL

SEYMOUR RD

FROBISHER DR

SOMERSET WAY

SPENSER WAY

Sch

1

Top Barns

PH

PARR CL

PARK SQ E

Sewage Works

PARK SQ W

Whyers Hall Farm

COCKETT WICK LA

Cockett Wick Farm

TUDOR GV

14

12 A 13 B C 14 D E F

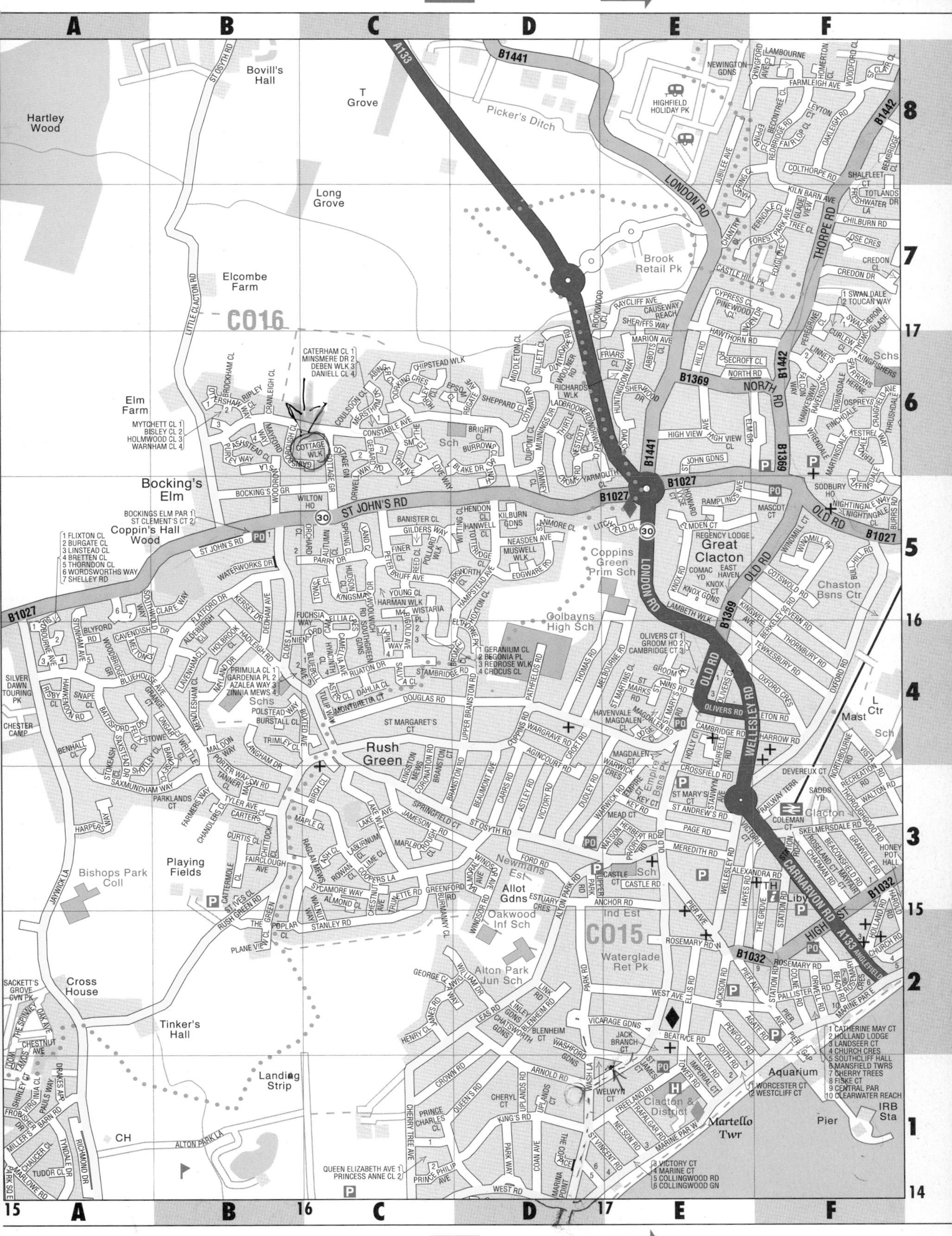

Danbury H3
75 Wash Ln.

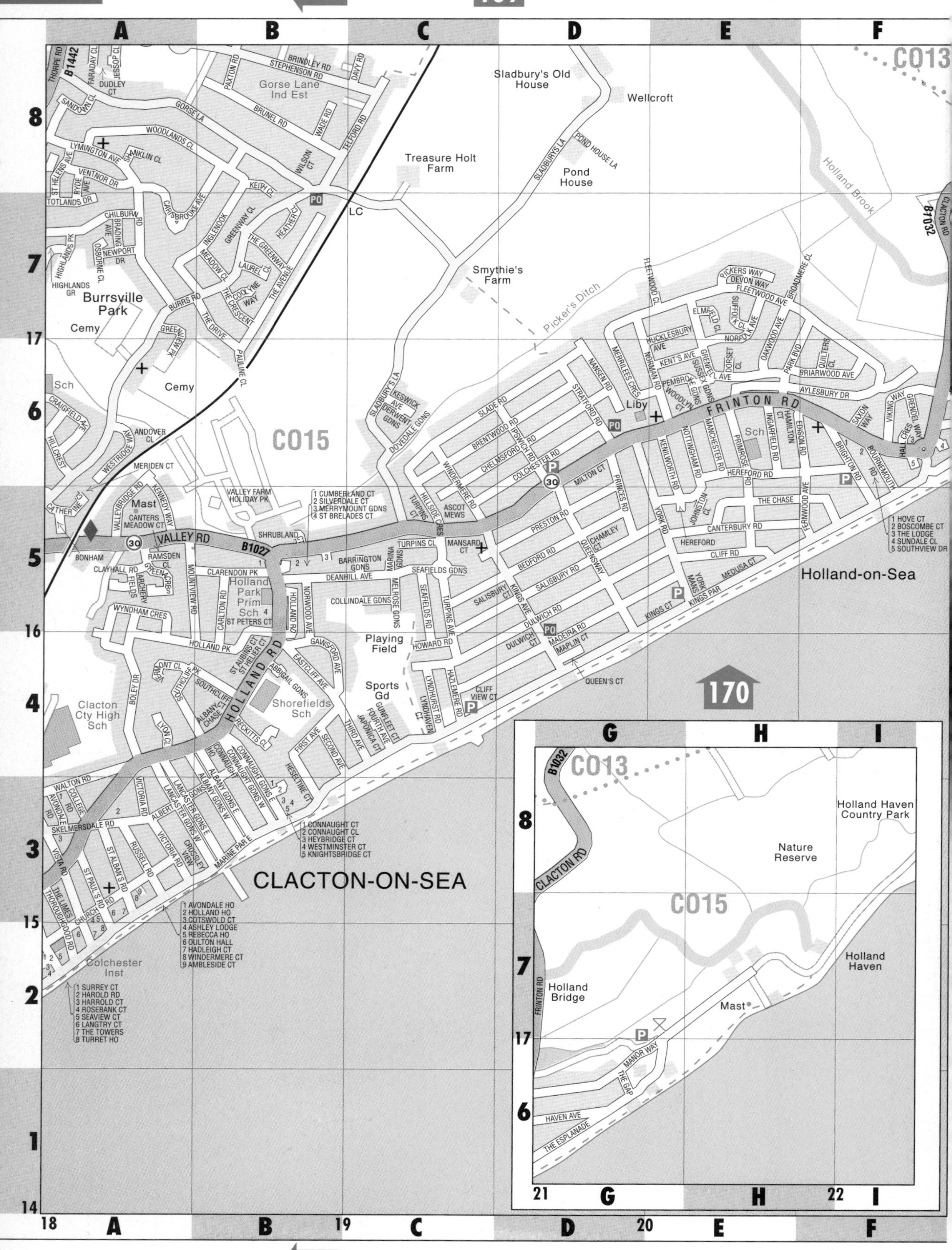

CO13

8

Sladbury's Old House

Wellcroft

Treasure Holt Farm

Pond House

17

Smythie's Farm

Picker's Ditch

7

Burrsville Park

Cemy

CO15

Cemy

FRINTON RD

6

Holland Brook

B1032 CLACTON RD

Pickers Way
Devon Way
Fleetwood Ave

1 CUMBERLAND CT
2 SILVERDALE CT
3 MERRYMOUNT GDNS
4 ST BRELADES CT

VALLEY RD

B1027

1 HOVE CT
2 BOSCOMBE CT
3 THE LODGE
4 SUNDALE CL
5 SOUTHVIEW DR

5

Holland Park Prim Sch

Holland-on-Sea

16

Playing Field

Sports Gd

4

Clacton Cty High Sch

Shorefields Sch

170

Queen's Ct

1 CONNAUGHT CT
2 CONNAUGHT CL
3 HEYBRIDGE CT
4 WESTMINSTER CT
5 KNIGHTSBRIDGE CT

3

15

1 AVONDALE HO
2 HOLLAND HO
3 COTSWOLD CT
4 ASHLEY LODGE
5 REBECCA HO
6 OULTON HALL
7 HADLEIGH CT
8 WINDERMERE CT
9 AMBLESIDE CT

Colchester Inst

2

1 SURREY CT
2 HAROLD RD
3 HARROLD CT
4 ROSEBANK CT
5 SEAVIEW CT
6 LANGTRY CT
7 THE TOWERS
8 TURRET HO

CLACTON-ON-SEA

1

14

18 A **B 19** C **D 20** E **F**

195

Inset (G–I)

B1032 CLACTON RD CO13

8

Holland Haven Country Park

Nature Reserve

CO15

7

FRINTON RD

Holland Bridge

Holland Haven

17

Mast

MANOR WAY
THE GAP

6

HAVEN AVE

THE ESPLANADE

21 G **H 22** I

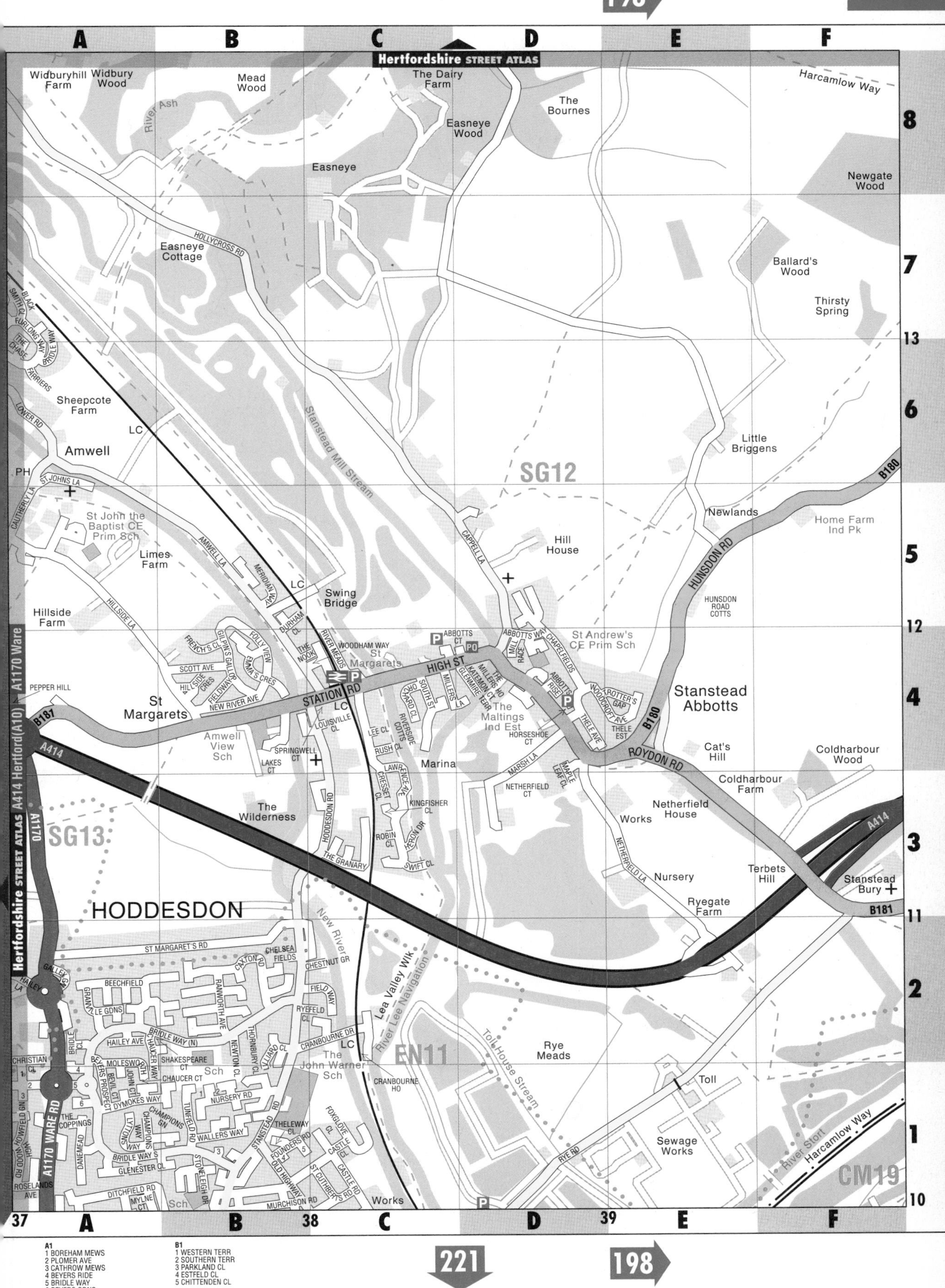

A1
1 BOREHAM MEWS
2 PLOMER AVE
3 CATHROW MEWS
4 BEYERS RIDE
5 BRIDLE WAY
6 BEYERS GDNS

B1
1 WESTERN TERR
2 SOUTHERN TERR
3 PARKLAND CL
4 ESTFELD CL
5 CHITTENDEN CL

197

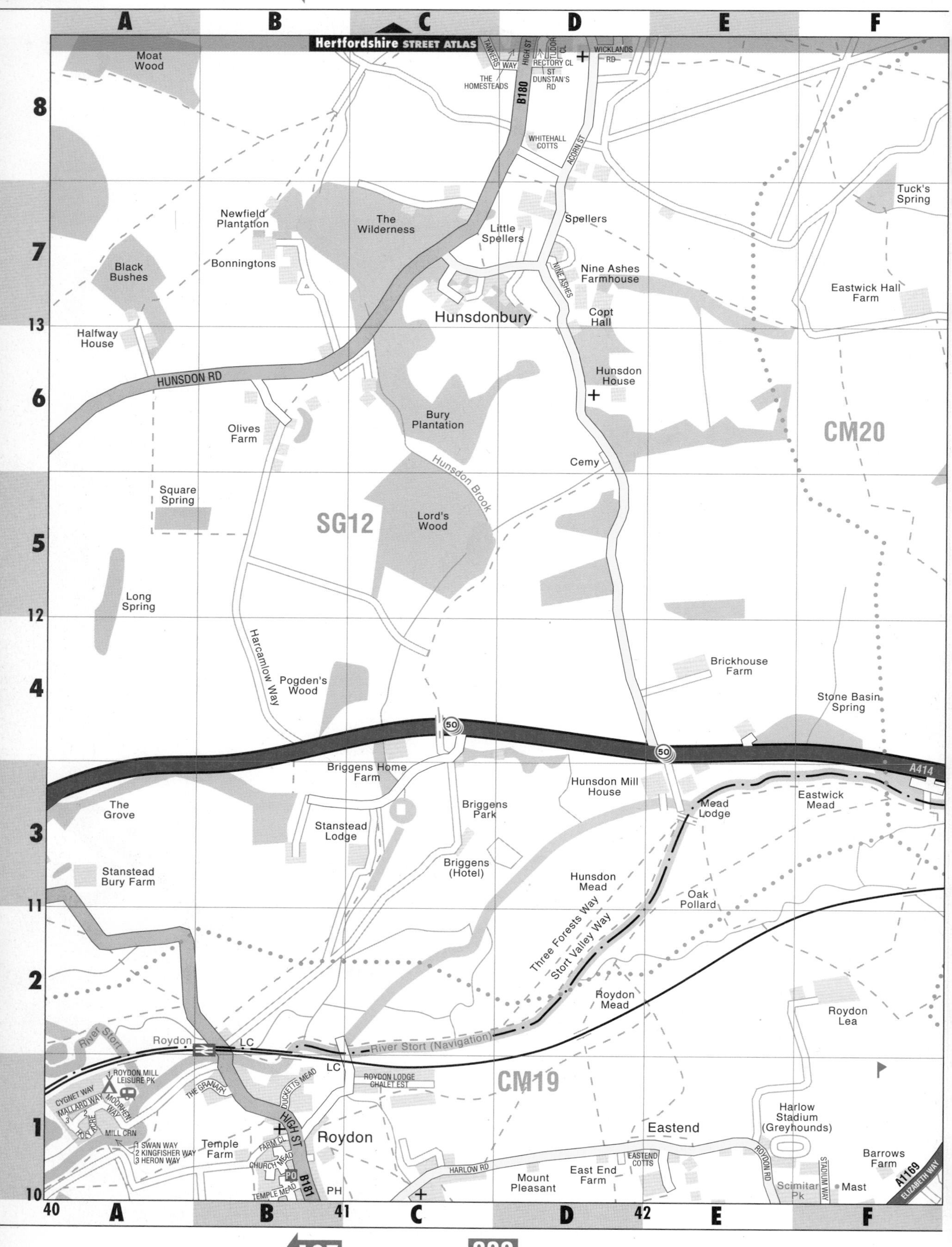
Hertfordshire STREET ATLAS
A
B
C
D
E
F
8
7
13
6
5
12
4
3
11
2
1
10
40
41
42
Moat Wood
TANNERS WAY
HIGH ST
B180
TUDOR CL
RECTORY CL
ST DUNSTAN'S RD
WICKLANDS RD
THE HOMESTEADS
WHITEHALL COTTS
ACORN ST
Tuck's Spring
Newfield Plantation
The Wilderness
Little Spellers
Spellers
Black Bushes
Bonningtons
NINE ASHES
Nine Ashes Farmhouse
Eastwick Hall Farm
Hunsdonbury
Copt Hall
Halfway House
HUNSDON RD
Hunsdon House
Olives Farm
Bury Plantation
CM20
Cemy
Hunsdon Brook
Square Spring
SG12
Lord's Wood
Long Spring
Harcamlow Way
Brickhouse Farm
Pogden's Wood
Stone Basin Spring
50
A414
Briggens Home Farm
Hunsdon Mill House
The Grove
Briggens Park
Mead Lodge
Eastwick Mead
Stanstead Lodge
Briggens (Hotel)
Stanstead Bury Farm
Hunsdon Mead
Oak Pollard
Three Forests Way
Stort Valley Way
Roydon Mead
Roydon Lea
River Stort
Roydon
LC
River Stort (Navigation)
ROYDON LODGE CHALET EST
CM19
1 ROYDON MILL LEISURE PK
CYGNET WAY
MALLARD WAY
MOORHEN WAY
THE GRANARY
DUCKETTS MEAD
HIGH ST
MILL CRN
1 SWAN WAY
2 KINGFISHER WAY
3 HERON WAY
Temple Farm
FARM CL
CHURCH MEAD
TEMPLE MEAD
PO
B181
PH
Roydon
Harlow Stadium (Greyhounds)
Eastend
HARLOW RD
EASTEND COTTS
East End Farm
Mount Pleasant
ROYDON RD
STADIUM WAY
Barrows Farm
Scimitar Pk
Mast
A1169
ELIZABETH WAY

197
222

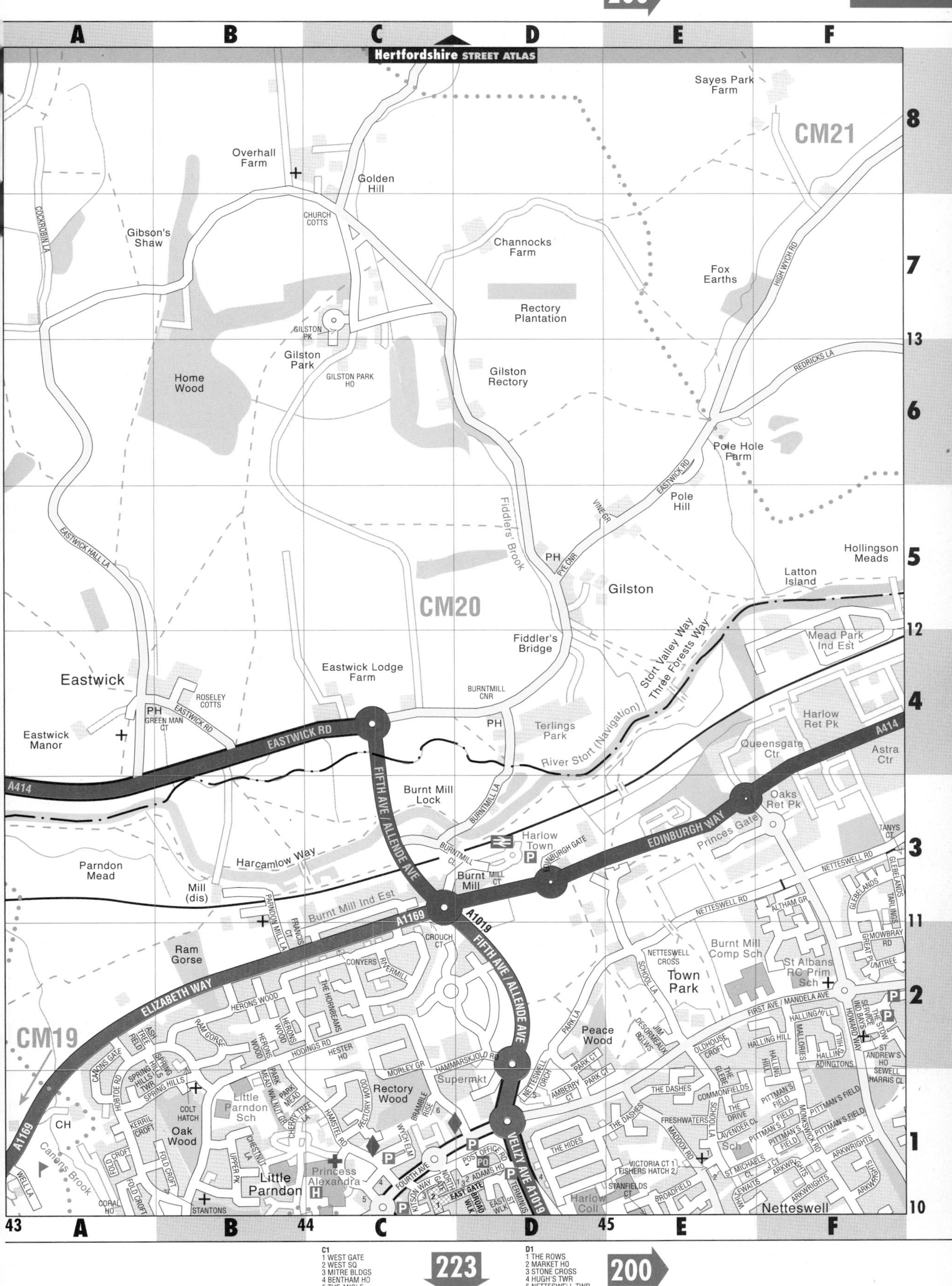

Hertfordshire STREET ATLAS

CM21

CM20

CM19

Sayes Park Farm

Overhall Farm

Golden Hill

Gibson's Shaw

CHURCH COTTS

Channocks Farm

Fox Earths

Rectory Plantation

GILSTON PK

Gilston Park

GILSTON PARK HO

Gilston Rectory

Home Wood

Pole Hole Farm

Pole Hill

Hollingson Meads

Fiddlers Brook

PH

PYE CNR

Gilston

Latton Island

Mead Park Ind Est

Eastwick

Eastwick Lodge Farm

BURNTMILL CNR

Fiddler's Bridge

Stort Valley Way

Three Forests Way

Harlow Ret Pk

PH Green Man Ct

Roseley Cotts

Terlings Park

PH

Queensgate Ctr

Astra Ctr

Eastwick Manor

EASTWICK RD

River Stort (Navigation)

Oaks Ret Pk

A414

Burnt Mill Lock

EDINBURGH WAY

Princes Gate

TANYS CT

Parndon Mead

Harcamlow Way

Harlow Town

Burnt Mill

Burnt Mill Ind Est

MILL CT

BURNTMILL LA

NETTESWELL RD

GLEBELANDS

Mill (dis)

A1169

A1019

FIFTH AVE / ALLENDE AVE

Nettswell Cross

Burnt Mill Comp Sch

St Albans RC Prim Sch

MOWBRAY RD

Ram Gorse

CROUCH CT

CONYERS CT

Town Park

ELIZABETH WAY

FRANCIS

PERMILL

SCHOOL LA

FIRST AVE

MANDELA AVE

HERONS WOOD

THE HORNBEAMS

HODINGS RD

HESTER HO

MORLEY GR

HAMMARSKJOLD RD

Peace Wood

JIM DESMOREAUX BLDGS

OLDHOUSE CROFT

HALLING HILL

ST ANDREW'S HO

CM19

Little Parndon Sch

Rectory Wood

Supermkt

PARK LA

AMBERLY CT

PARK CT

THE DASHES

COMMONFIELDS CT

PITTMAN'S FIELD

Oak Wood

Colt Hatch

CHERRY TREE LA

BRAMBLE

THE HIDES

FRESHWATERS

MAXDOX RD

LAVENDER CT

Little Parndon

Princess Alexandra H

EAST GATE

BROAD WLK

Harlow Coll

Victoria Ct

Stanfields Ct

Netteswell

Nettswell

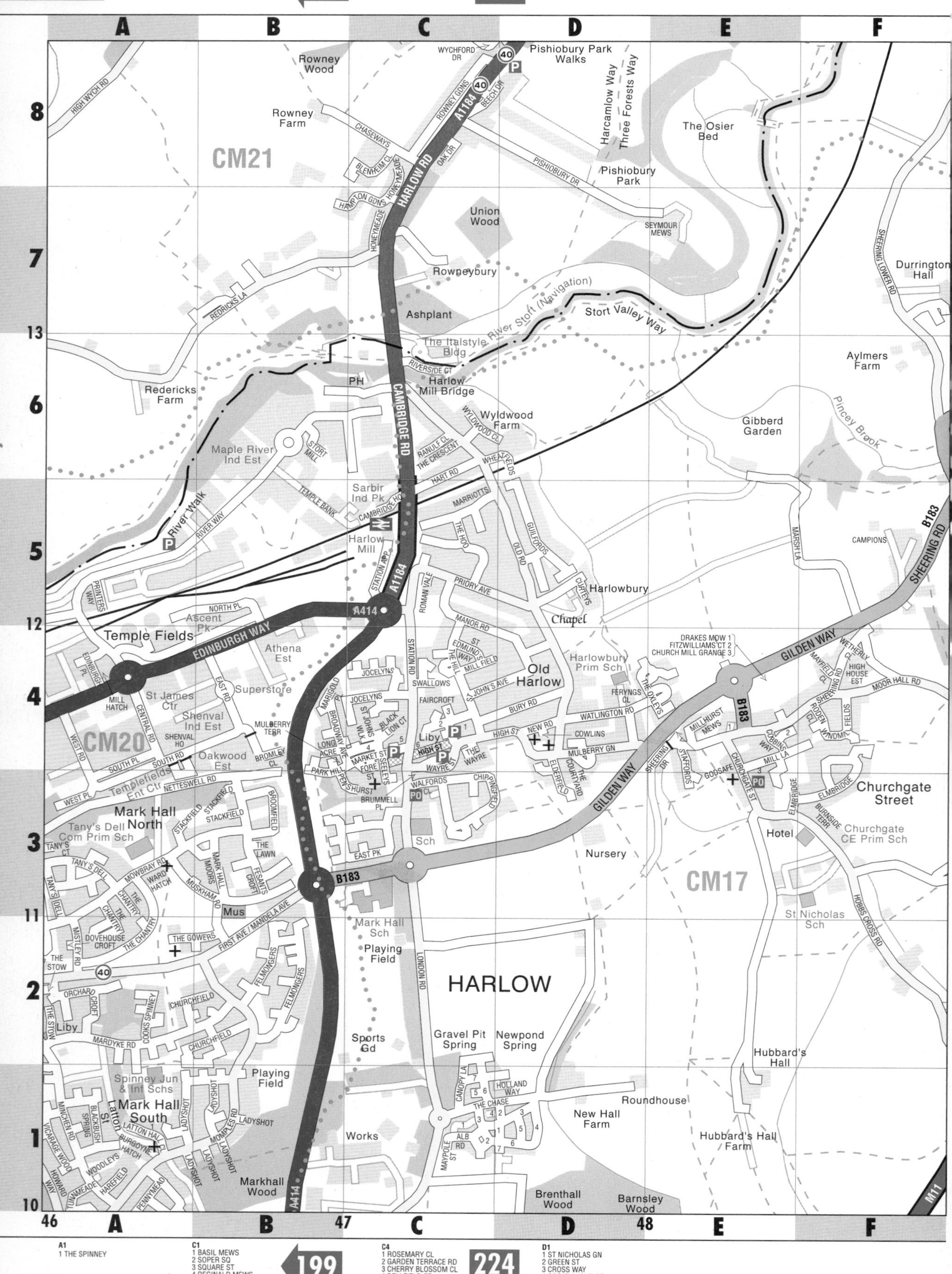

A1
1 THE SPINNEY

C1
1 BASIL MEWS
2 SOPER SQ
3 SQUARE ST
4 REGINALD MEWS
5 ALLIS MEWS
6 TATTON ST
7 HARROWBAND RD

C4
1 ROSEMARY CL
2 GARDEN TERRACE RD
3 CHERRY BLOSSOM CL
4 DELLFIELD CT
5 OAKWOOD MEWS
6 DARLINGTON CT

D1
1 ST NICHOLAS GN
2 GREEN ST
3 CROSS WAY
4 GREAT AUGUR ST
5 RAMBLERS LA
6 SIMPLICITY LA
7 HONOR ST

199

224

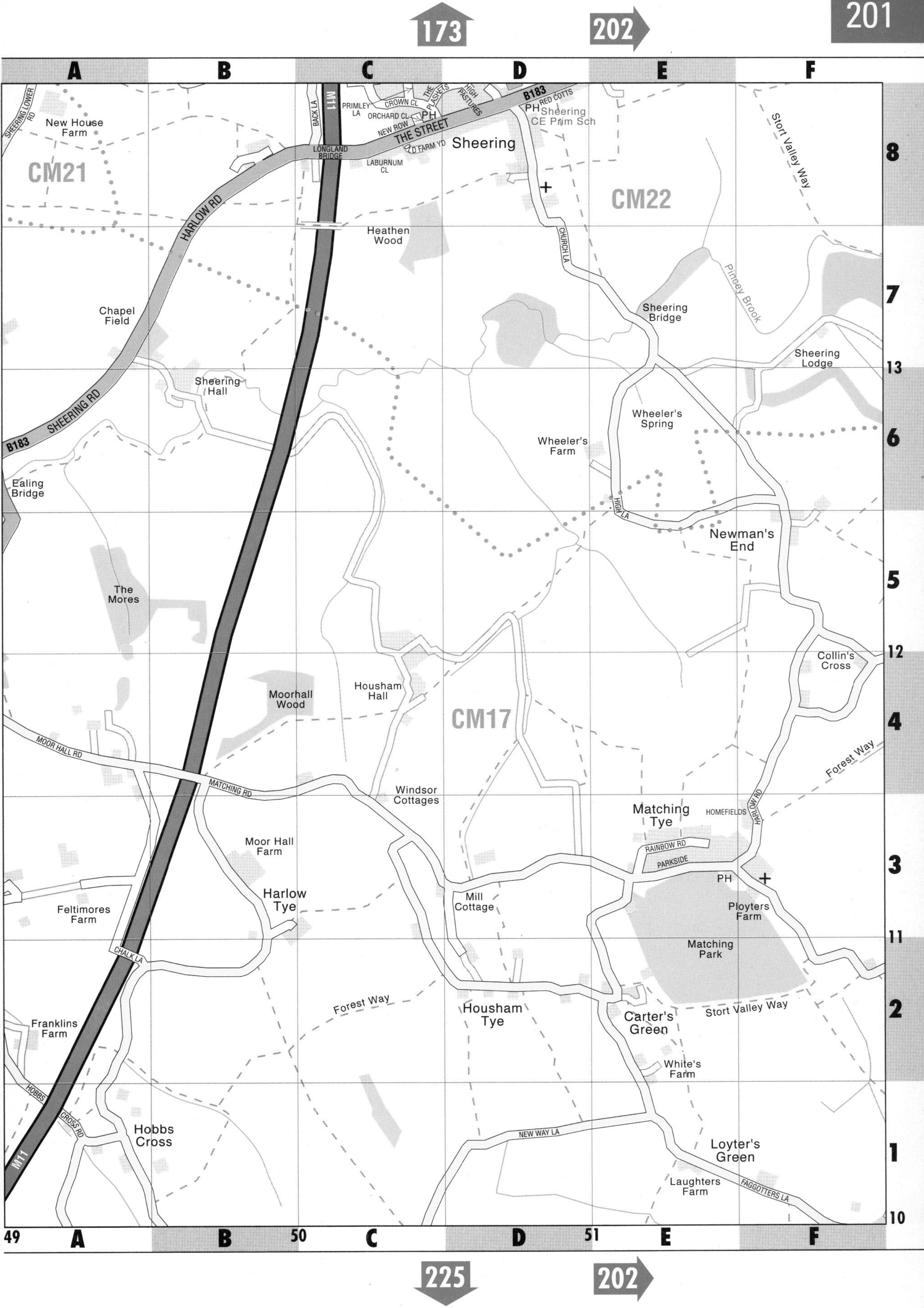

A B C D E F

8
7
13
6
5
12
4
11
3
2
1
10

New House Farm
SHEERING LOWER RD
CM21
HARLOW RD
Chapel Field
SHEERING RD
B183
Ealing Bridge
The Mores
MOOR HALL RD
MATCHING RD
Moorhall Wood
Moor Hall Farm
Harlow Tye
Feltimores Farm
CHALK LA
Franklins Farm
HOBBS CROSS RD
M11
Hobbs Cross

BACK LA
M11
LONGLAND BRIDGE
PRIMLEY LA
CROWN CL
THE PLASHETS
HIGH PASTURES
ORCHARD CL
NEW ROW
PH
THE STREET
OLD FARM YD
LABURNUM CL
Sheering
B183
RED COTTS
PH
Sheering CE Prim Sch
CM22
Heathen Wood
Stort Valley Way
CHURCH LA
Pincey Brook
Sheering Bridge
Sheering Hall
Wheeler's Spring
Wheeler's Farm
Sheering Lodge
HIGH LA
Newman's End
Collin's Cross
CM17
Housham Hall
Forest Way
Windsor Cottages
Matching Tye
HOMEFIELDS
RAINBOW RD
MATCH HALL RD
PARKSIDE
PH
Ployters Farm
Mill Cottage
Matching Park
Forest Way
Housham Tye
Carter's Green
Stort Valley Way
White's Farm
NEW WAY LA
Loyter's Green
Laughters Farm
FAGGOTTERS LA

201
174

A1060

A **B** **C** **D** **E** **F**

8

CM22

CM6

Downhall Wood

Downhall Bridge

Thorn Springs

Parvilles

7

Down Hall (Hotel)

13

Bob's Alley

The Gorse

Forest Way

Merry Meads

Manwood Green

6

The Gorse Wood

Stonehall Bsns Pk

Stone Hall Farm

Kingston Farm Ind Units

KINGSTONS FARM

Peartree Green

Man Wood

5

Stort Valley Way

Matching Pond

DOWNHALL RD

12

Matching

Matching Hall

Brick House

CM17

POTASH RD

CM5

Airfield (disused)

4

Stock Hall

3

Matching Green

11

More Spring

Newhouse Farm

COLLIERS

PER RYFIELD

PH

Matching Green CE Prim Sch

HULL GN

Watersmans End

Hull Green

Park Woods

2

WATERY LA

LITTLE LAVER RD

Little Laver Hall

1

Faggotters Farm

Leather Bottle

Clarksmead Spring

10

52 **A** **B** 53 **C** **D** 54 **E** **F**

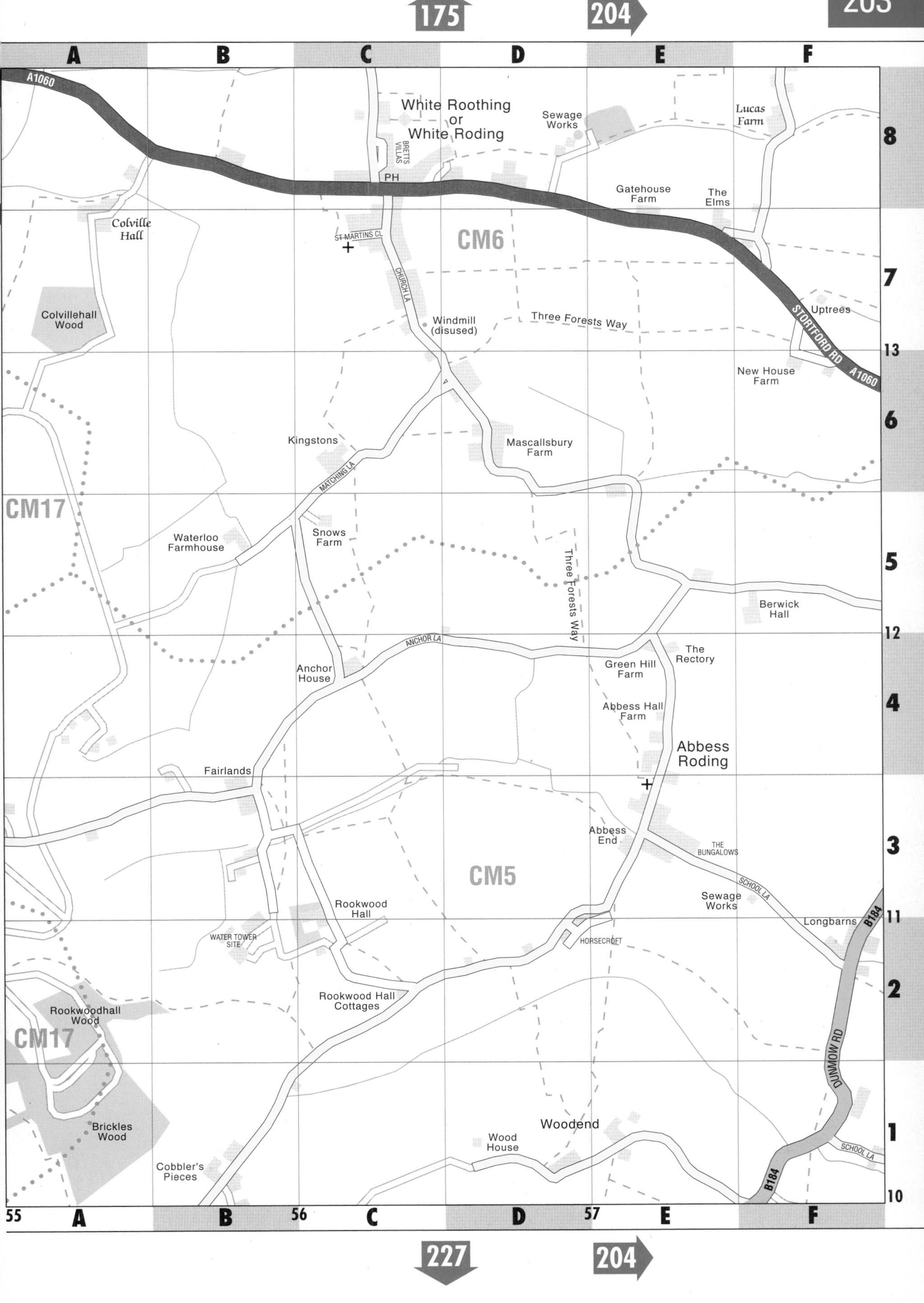
A
B
C
D
E
F
A1060
White Roothing
or
White Roding
BRETTS VILLAS
PH
Sewage
Works
Lucas
Farm
Gatehouse
Farm
The
Elms
8
Colville
Hall
ST MARTINS CL
CM6
CHURCH LA
7
Colvillehall
Wood
Windmill
(disused)
Three Forests Way
STORTFORD RD
Uptrees
A1060
13
New House
Farm
6
Kingstons
Mascallsbury
Farm
MATCHING LA
CM17
Snows
Farm
Waterloo
Farmhouse
Three Forests Way
5
Berwick
Hall
12
ANCHOR LA
The
Rectory
Anchor
House
Green Hill
Farm
4
Abbess Hall
Farm
Abbess
Roding
Fairlands
Abbess
End
3
THE
BUNGALOWS
CM5
SCHOOL LA
Sewage
Works
Rookwood
Hall
Longbarns
B184
11
WATER TOWER
SITE
HORSECROFT
2
Rookwood Hall
Cottages
Rookwoodhall
Wood
CM17
DUNMOW RD
Brickles
Wood
Woodend
1
Wood
House
SCHOOL LA
Cobbler's
Pieces
B184
10
55
A
B
56
C
D
57
E
F

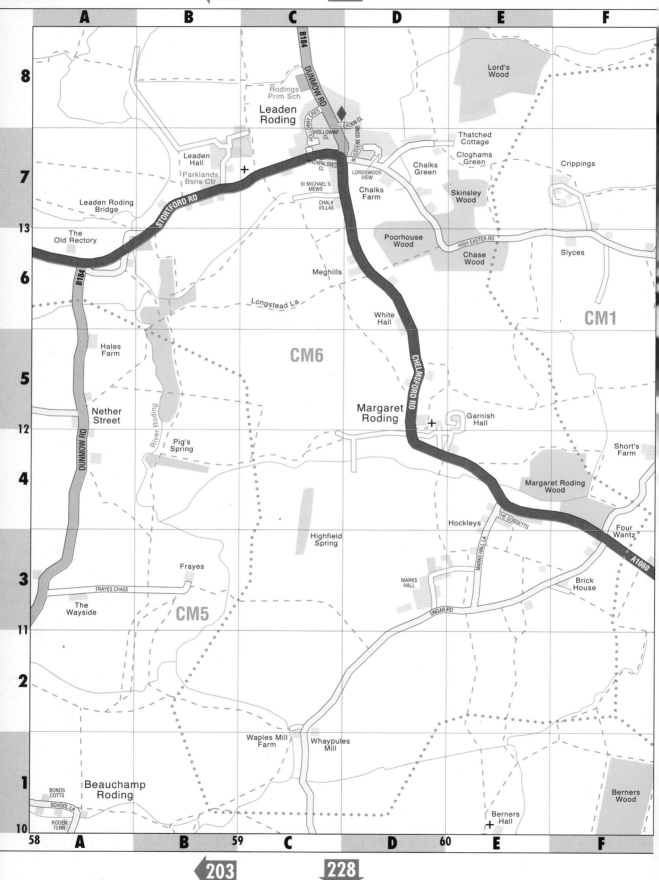

203
176

A   B   C   D   E   F

8

Lord's
Wood

B184

DUNMOW RD

Rodings
Prim Sch

Leaden
Roding

Thatched
Cottage

Cloghams
Green

Crippings

7

HOLLOWAY CL

LEADEN CL

RAGSTONE GDNS

Leaden
Hall

Parklands
Bsns Ctr

CROWNLOWS CL

St MICHAEL'S
MEWS

LORDSWOOD
VIEW

Chalks
Green

Skinsley
Wood

Leaden Roding
Bridge

STORTFORD RD

CHALK
VILLAS

Chalks
Farm

13

The
Old Rectory

Poorhouse
Wood

HIGH EASTER RD

6

B184

Meghills

Chase
Wood

Slyces

Longstead La

White
Hall

CM1

CM6

CHELMSFORD RD

5

Hales
Farm

River Roding

Margaret
Roding

Garnish
Hall

Nether
Street

12

Pig's
Spring

Short's
Farm

4

Margaret Roding
Wood

Highfield
Spring

Hockleys

THE GOSSETTS

MARKS HALL LA

Four
Wantz

A1060

Frayes

FRAYES CHASE

MARKS
HALL

Brick
House

3

The
Wayside

CM5

ONGAR RD

11

2

Waples Mill
Farm

Whaypules
Mill

1

Beauchamp
Roding

Berners
Wood

BONDS
COTTS

SCHOOL LA

Berners
Hall

RODEN
TERR

10

58   A   B   59   C   D   60   E   F

203
228

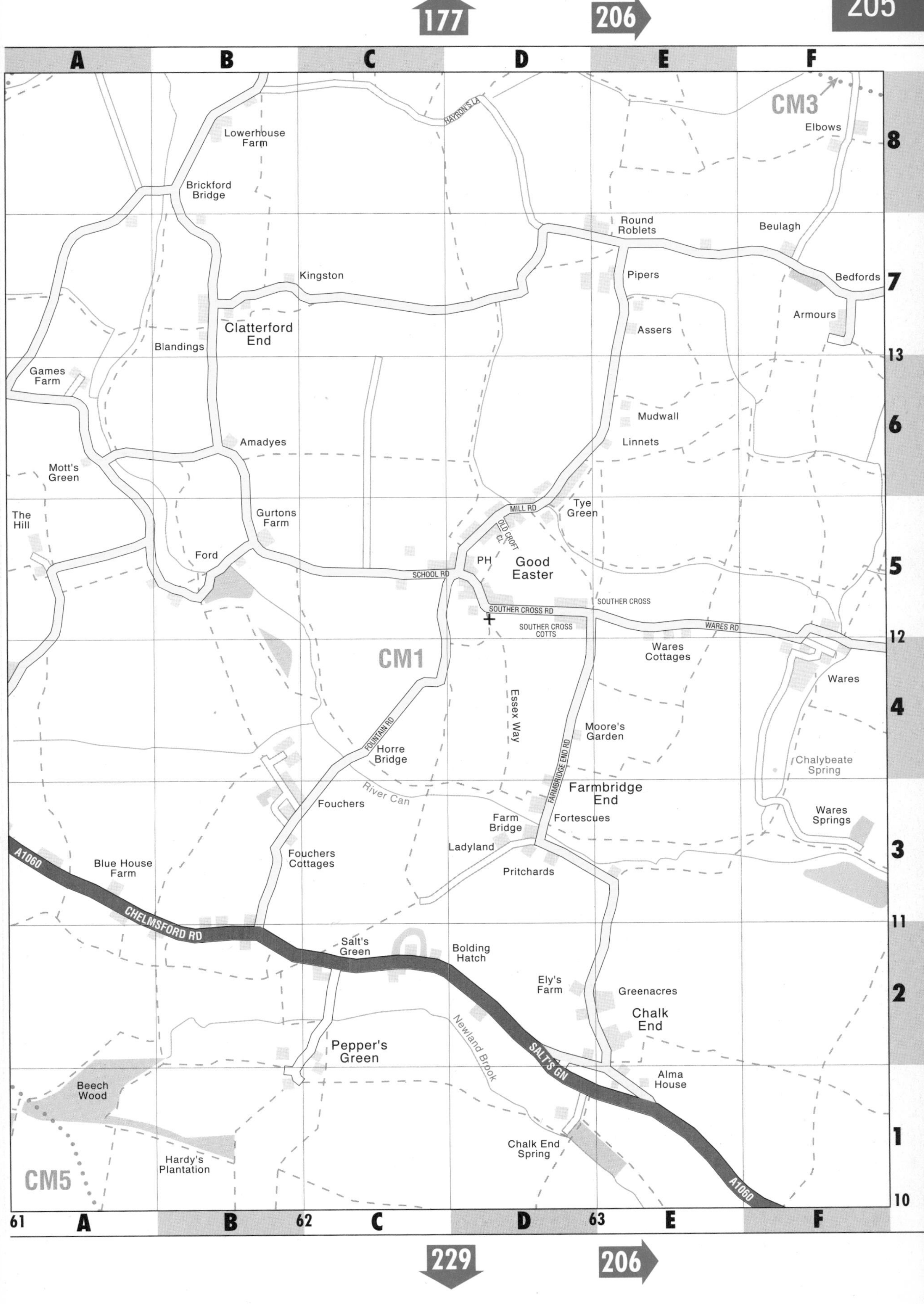
177
206
A
B
C
D
E
F
CM3
Elbows
HAYRON'S LA
Lowerhouse Farm
Brickford Bridge
8
Round Roblets
Beulagh
Kingston
Pipers
Bedfords
7
Armours
Clatterford End
Assers
Blandings
13
Games Farm
Mudwall
6
Amadyes
Linnets
Mott's Green
Tye Green
MILL RD
The Hill
Gurtons Farm
OLD CROFT CL
Ford
PH
Good Easter
5
SCHOOL RD
SOUTHER CROSS
SOUTHER CROSS RD
SOUTHER CROSS COTTS
WARES RD
12
CM1
Wares Cottages
Wares
Essex Way
4
Moore's Garden
FOUNTAIN RD
Horre Bridge
FARMBRIDGE END RD
Chalybeate Spring
Farmbridge End
River Can
Fouchers
Wares Springs
Farm Bridge
Fortescues
Ladyland
3
A1060
Blue House Farm
Fouchers Cottages
Pritchards
CHELMSFORD RD
11
Salt's Green
Bolding Hatch
Ely's Farm
Greenacres
2
Chalk End
Newland Brook
Pepper's Green
SALT'S GN
Alma House
Beech Wood
1
Chalk End Spring
Hardy's Plantation
CM5
A1060
10
61
62
63
229
206

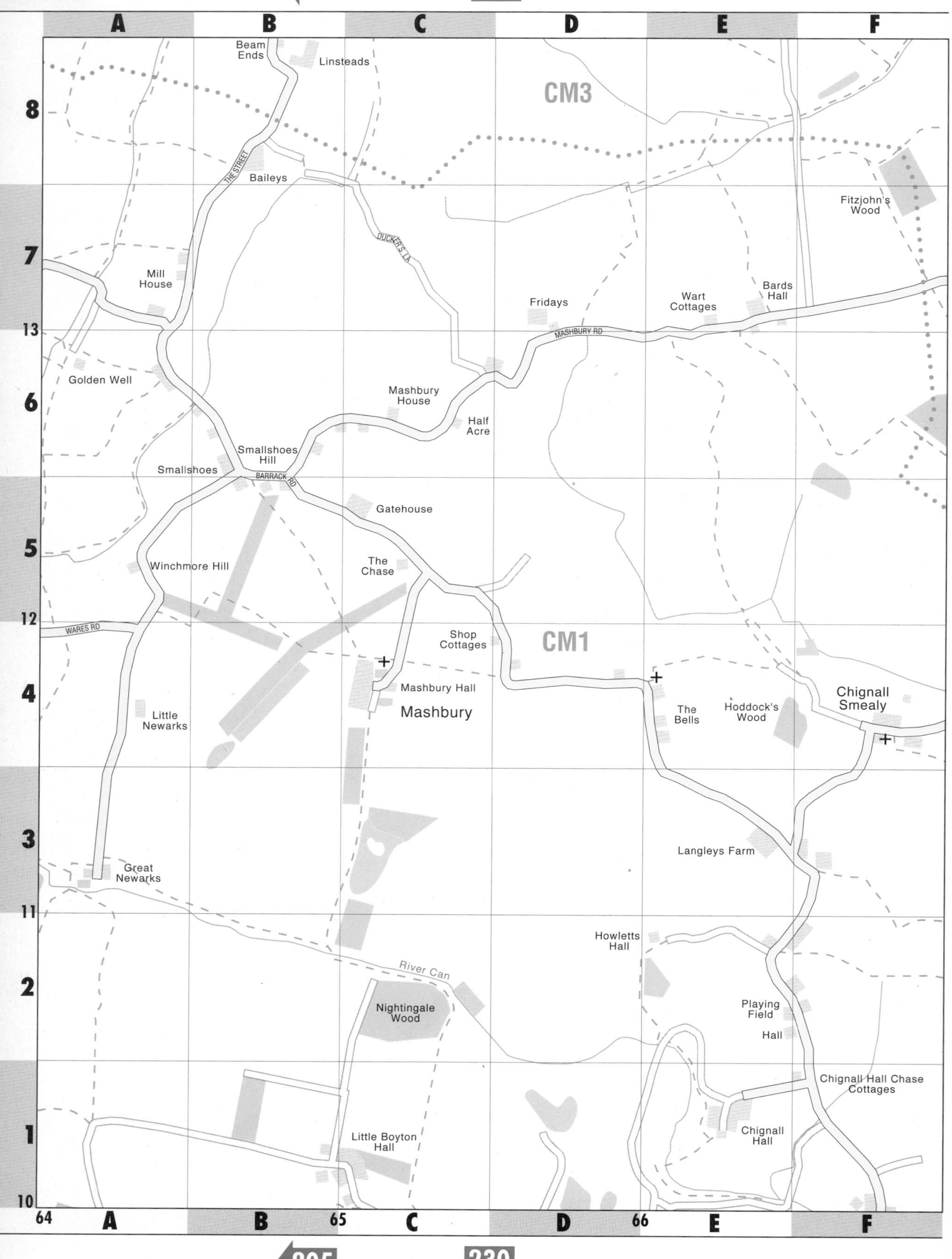

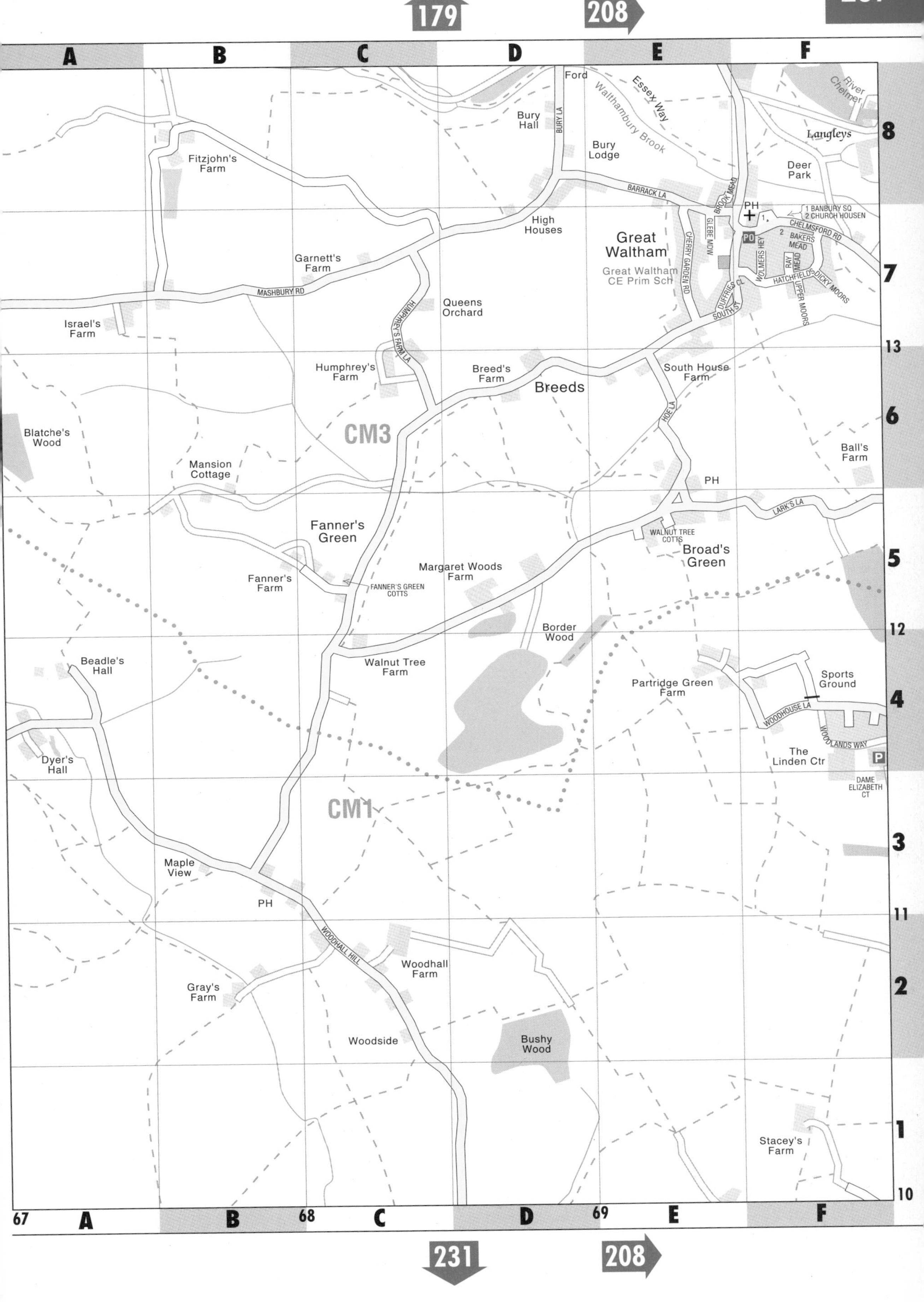

179
208

A　B　C　D　E　F

8

River Chelmer

Langleys

Ford

Essex Way

Bury Hall

Bury Lodge

Walthambury Brook

BURY LA

BARRACK LA

Deer Park

Fitzjohn's Farm

1 BANBURY SQ
2 CHURCH HOUSES

CHELMSFORD RD

PH

High Houses

Great Waltham

PO

2

BAKERS MEAD

BROOK MEAD

GLEBE MDW

WOLMERS HEY

7

Garnett's Farm

MASHBURY RD

Great Waltham CE Prim Sch

RAY

HATCHFIELDS

DUCKY MOORS

UPPER MOORS

DUFFRIES CT

SOUTHS

Queens Orchard

HUMPHREY'S FARM LA

13

Israel's Farm

Humphrey's Farm

Breed's Farm

Breeds

South House Farm

6

CM3

HOE LA

Ball's Farm

Blatche's Wood

Mansion Cottage

PH

LARK'S LA

Fanner's Green

Margaret Woods Farm

WALNUT TREE COTTS

Broad's Green

5

Fanner's Farm

FANNER'S GREEN COTTS

12

Border Wood

Beadle's Hall

Walnut Tree Farm

Partridge Green Farm

Sports Ground

WOODHOUSE LA

WOODLANDS WAY

4

Dyer's Hall

The Linden Ctr

DAME ELIZABETH CT

CM1

3

Maple View

PH

11

Gray's Farm

WOODHALL HILL

Woodhall Farm

2

Woodside

Bushy Wood

Stacey's Farm

1

10

231
208

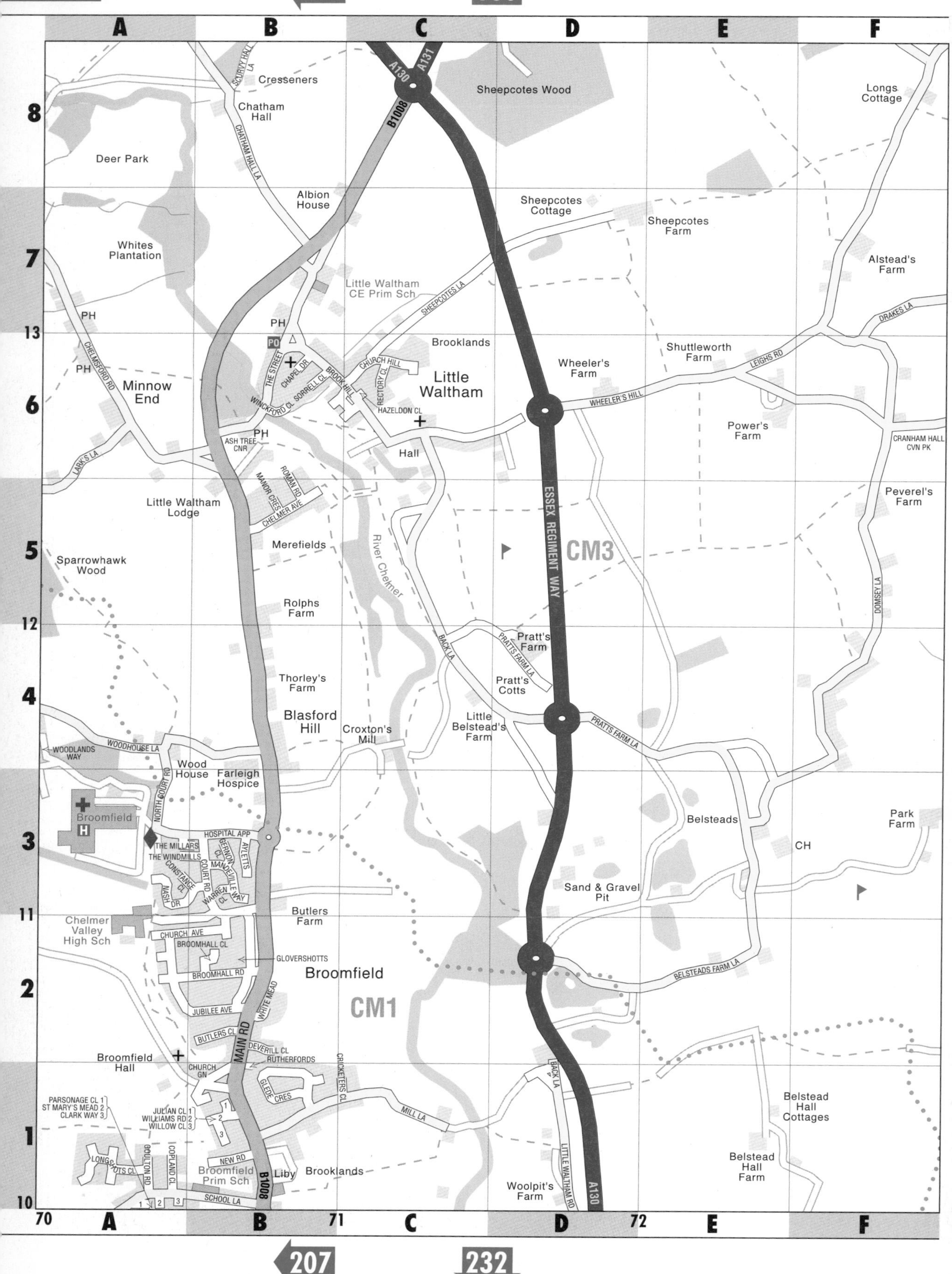

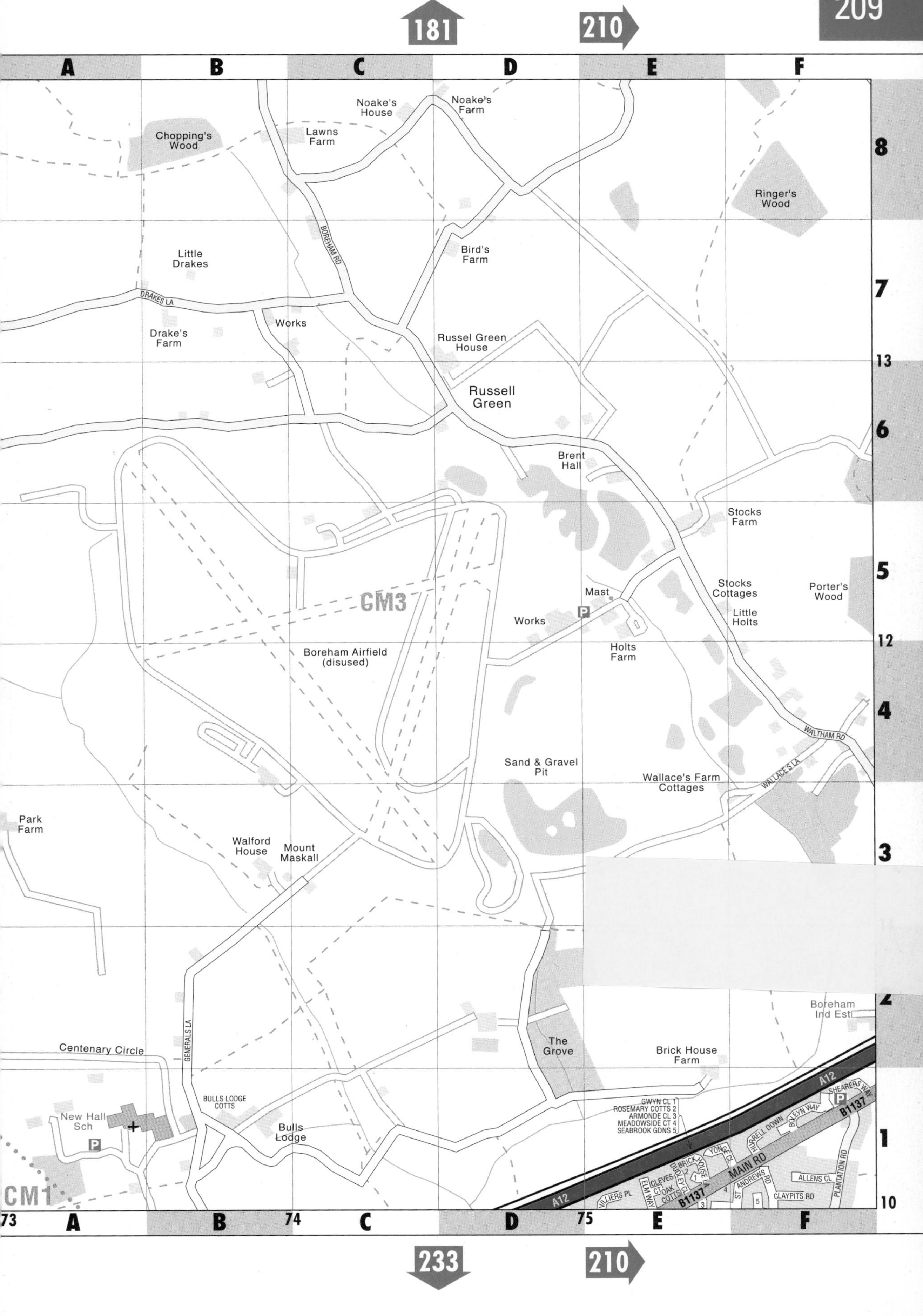

181
210

A B C D E F

8

7

13

6

5

12

4

3

2

1

10

Chopping's Wood

Noake's House

Noake's Farm

Lawns Farm

Ringer's Wood

Little Drakes

Bird's Farm

DRAKES LA

BOREHAM RD

Drake's Farm

Works

Russel Green House

Russell Green

Brent Hall

Stocks Farm

Stocks Cottages

Porter's Wood

CM3

Mast

Little Holts

Works

Holts Farm

WALTHAM RD

Boreham Airfield (disused)

Sand & Gravel Pit

Wallace's Farm Cottages

WALLACE'S LA

Park Farm

Walford House

Mount Maskall

Centenary Circle

GENERALS LA

The Grove

Brick House Farm

Boreham Ind Est

A12

SHEARER

B1137

Bulls Lodge Cotts

New Hall Sch

Bulls Lodge

GWYN CL 1
ROSEMARY COTTS 2
ARMONDE CT 3
MEADOWSIDE CT 4
SEABROOK GDNS 5

VILLIERS PL
ELM WAY
CLOAK COTTS
OAK
DUDLEY
CLEVES
BRICK HOUSE
YONG

MAIN RD

SHERRELL DOWN

ST ANDREWS RD

ALLENS CL

PLANTATION RD

CLAYPITS RD

B1137

A12

CM1

73 A B 74 C D 75 E F

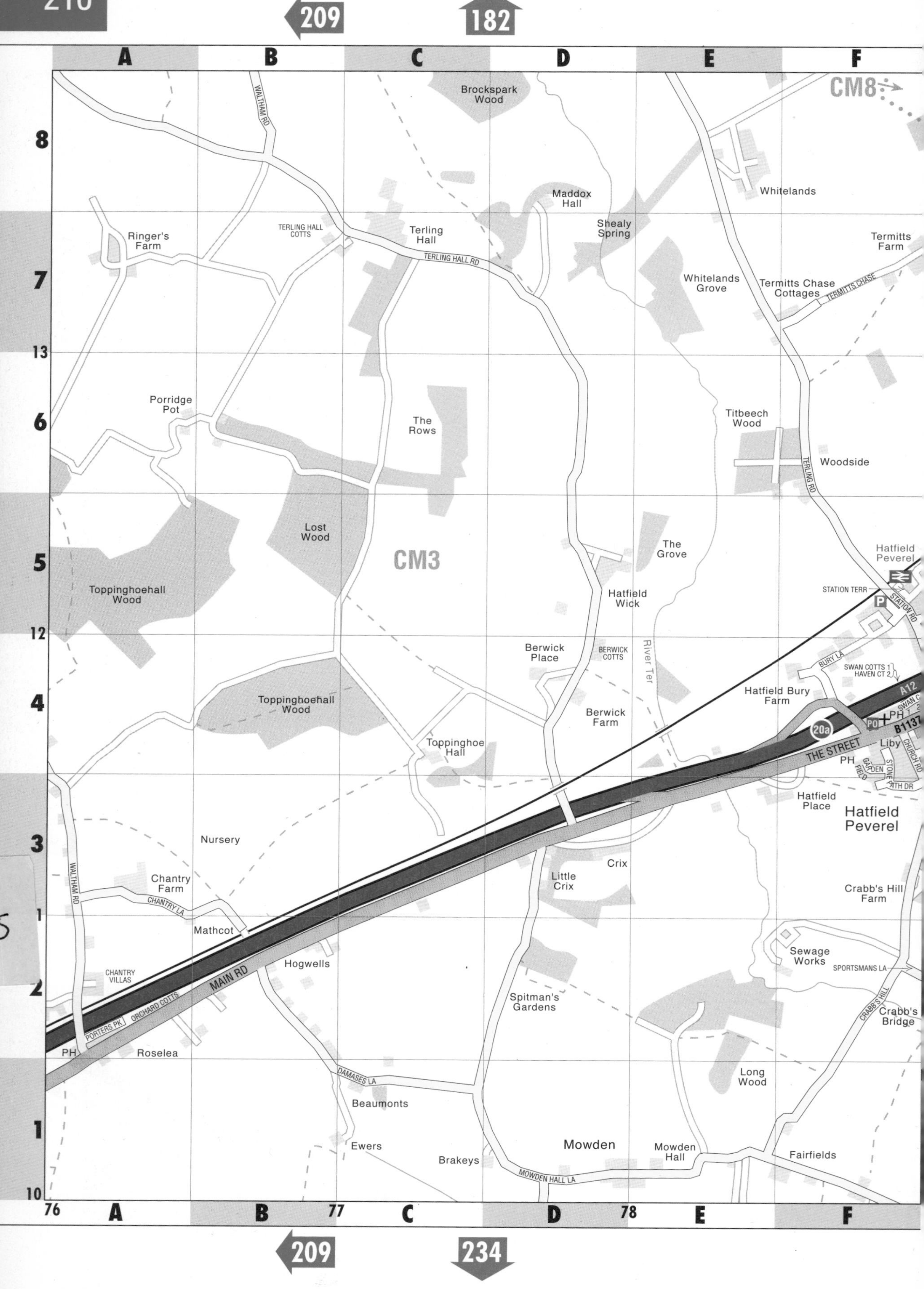

183
212

E8
1 PHILIP RD
2 ALUF CL
3 BARWELL HO
4 FORTIS HO

F7
1 STAINER CL
2 PONDHOLTON DR
3 JUVINA CL
4 KINLOCH CHASE

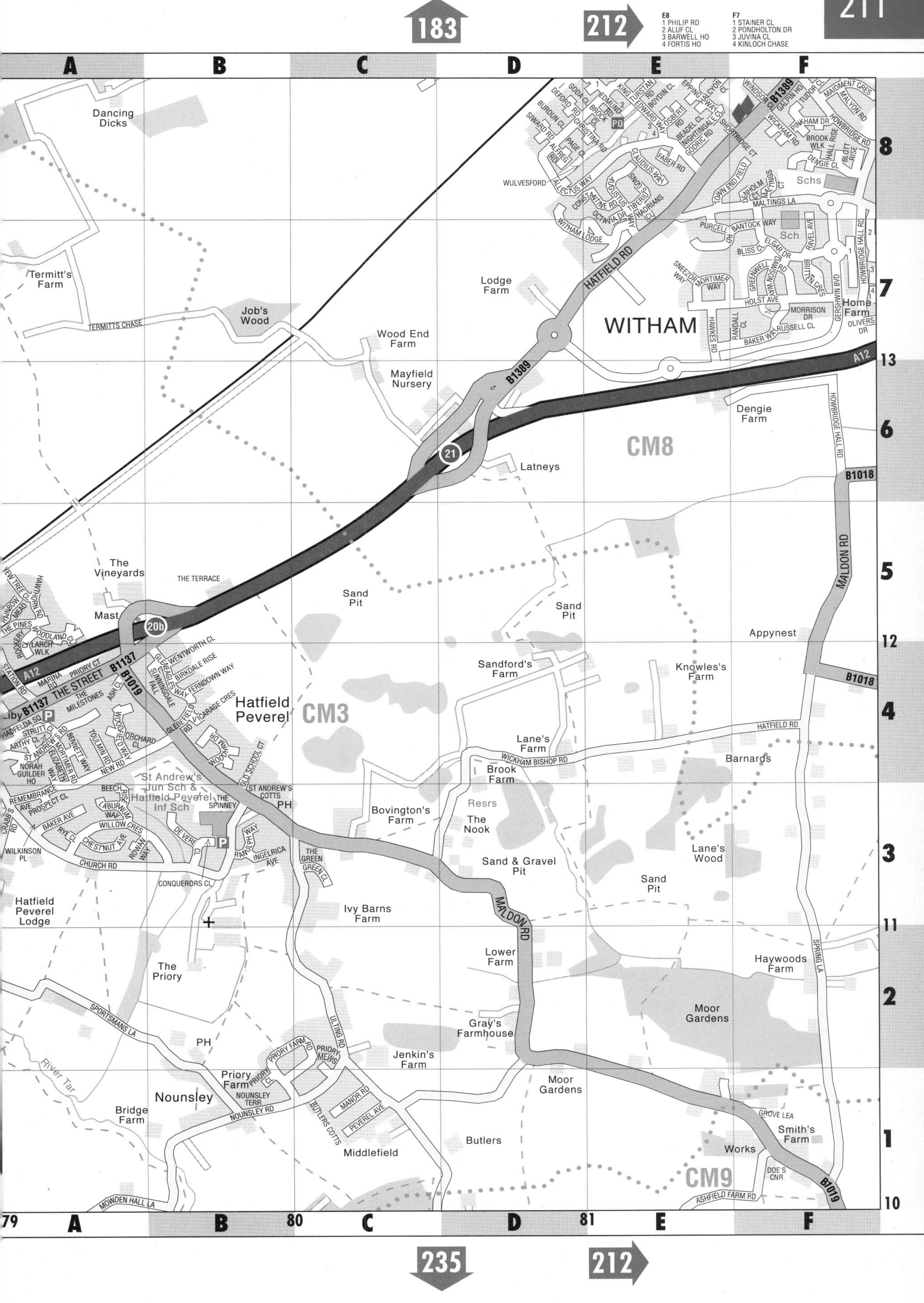

235
212

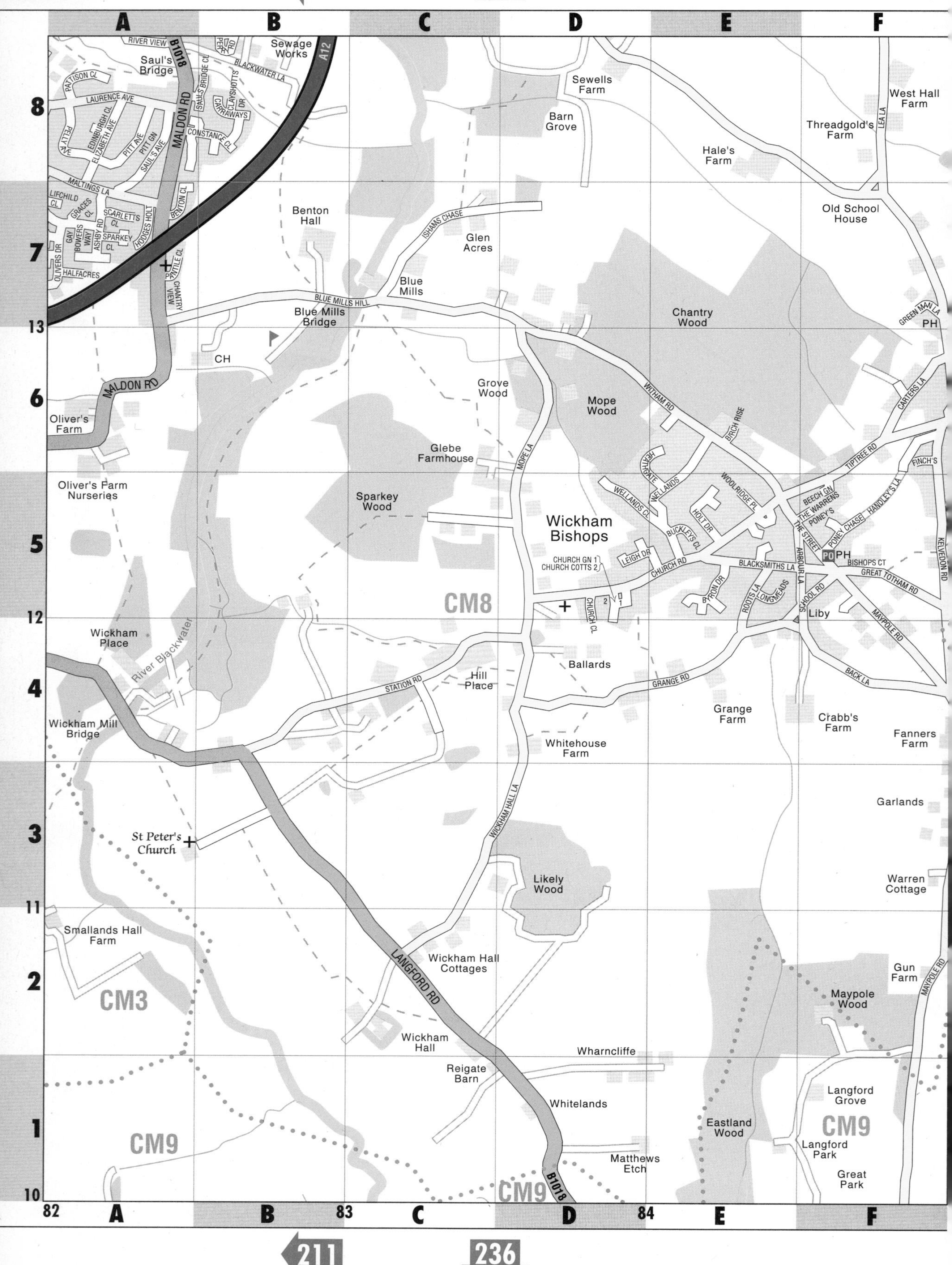

A B C D E F

8

7

13

6

River View
Saul's Bridge
Sewage Works
Blackwater La
PATTISON CL
LAURENCE AVE
EDINBURGH CL
ELIZABETH AVE
PITT AVE
PITT GN
SAUL SLADE
MALDON RD
B1018
A12
BISHOPS BRIDGE CL
HAYSHOTTS DR
CARRAWAYS
CONSTANCE CL
PERRY CL
LIFCHILD CL
GRACES CL
SCARLETTS CL
ASHBY RD
HODGES HOLT
BENTON CL
SPARKEY CL
MALTINGS LA
GAY BOWERS WAY
OLIVERS DR
HALFACRES
PITTLE CL
CHANTRY VIEW

Benton Hall
Sewells Farm
Barn Grove
Hale's Farm
West Hall Farm
Threadgold's Farm
Old School House

ISHAMS CHASE
Glen Acres
Blue Mills
BLUE MILLS HILL
Blue Mills Bridge
CH
Grove Wood
Mope Wood
Chantry Wood
WITHAM RD
BIRCH RISE
GREEN MAN LA
PH
CARTERS LA

MALDON RD

Oliver's Farm

Oliver's Farm Nurseries

Glebe Farmhouse
MOPE LA
Sparkey Wood
Wickham Bishops
CHURCH GN 1
CHURCH COTTS 2
WELLANDS CL
NEWLANDS
SKREENS
HOLT DR
WOOLRIDGE PL
LEIGH DR
CHURCH RD
BLACKSMITHS LA
BUCKLEYS CL
BYRON DR
ROOTS LA
LONGMEADS
THE STREET
ARBOUR LA
SCHOOL RD
PO PH
BISHOPS CT
GREAT TOTHAM RD
TIPTREE RD
HANDLEY'S LA
PONEYS
BEECH GN
THE WARRENS
PONEY CHASE
FINCH'S
KELVEDON RD
Liby
MAYPOLE RD
BACK LA

CM8

5

12

4

Wickham Place
River Blackwater
Wickham Mill Bridge

STATION RD
Hill Place
Ballards
Whitehouse Farm
GRANGE RD
Grange Farm
Crabb's Farm
Fanners Farm

3

11

St Peter's Church
Smallands Hall Farm

WICKHAM HALL LA
Likely Wood
Garlands
Warren Cottage

CM3

2

LANGFORD RD
Wickham Hall Cottages
Wickham Hall
Reigate Barn
Wharncliffe
Whitelands
Eastland Wood
Maypole Wood
Langford Grove
Gun Farm
Langford Park
Great Park
MAYPOLE RD
CM9

CM9

1

10

82
A
B
83
C
D
84
E
F

B1018
CM9

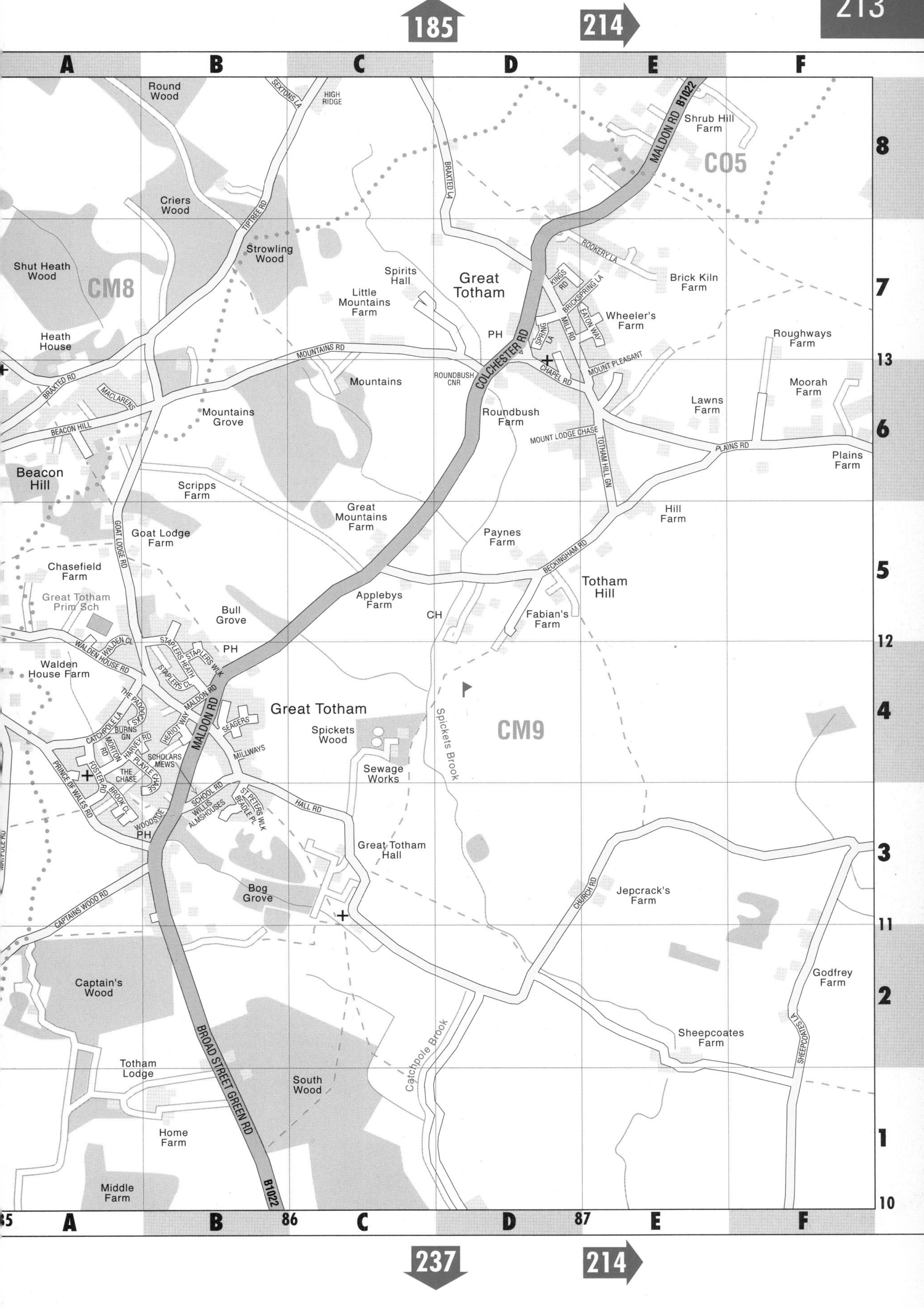

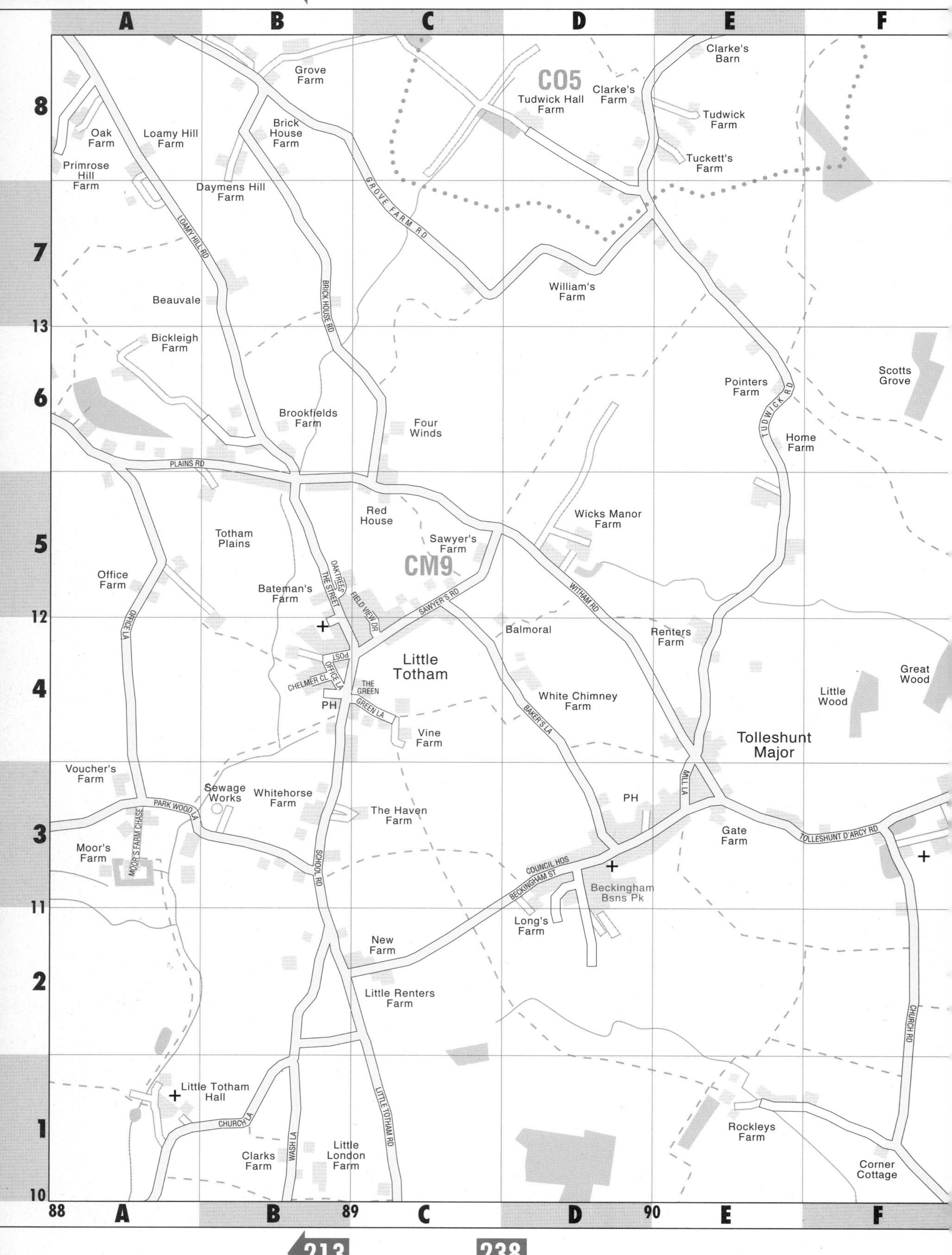

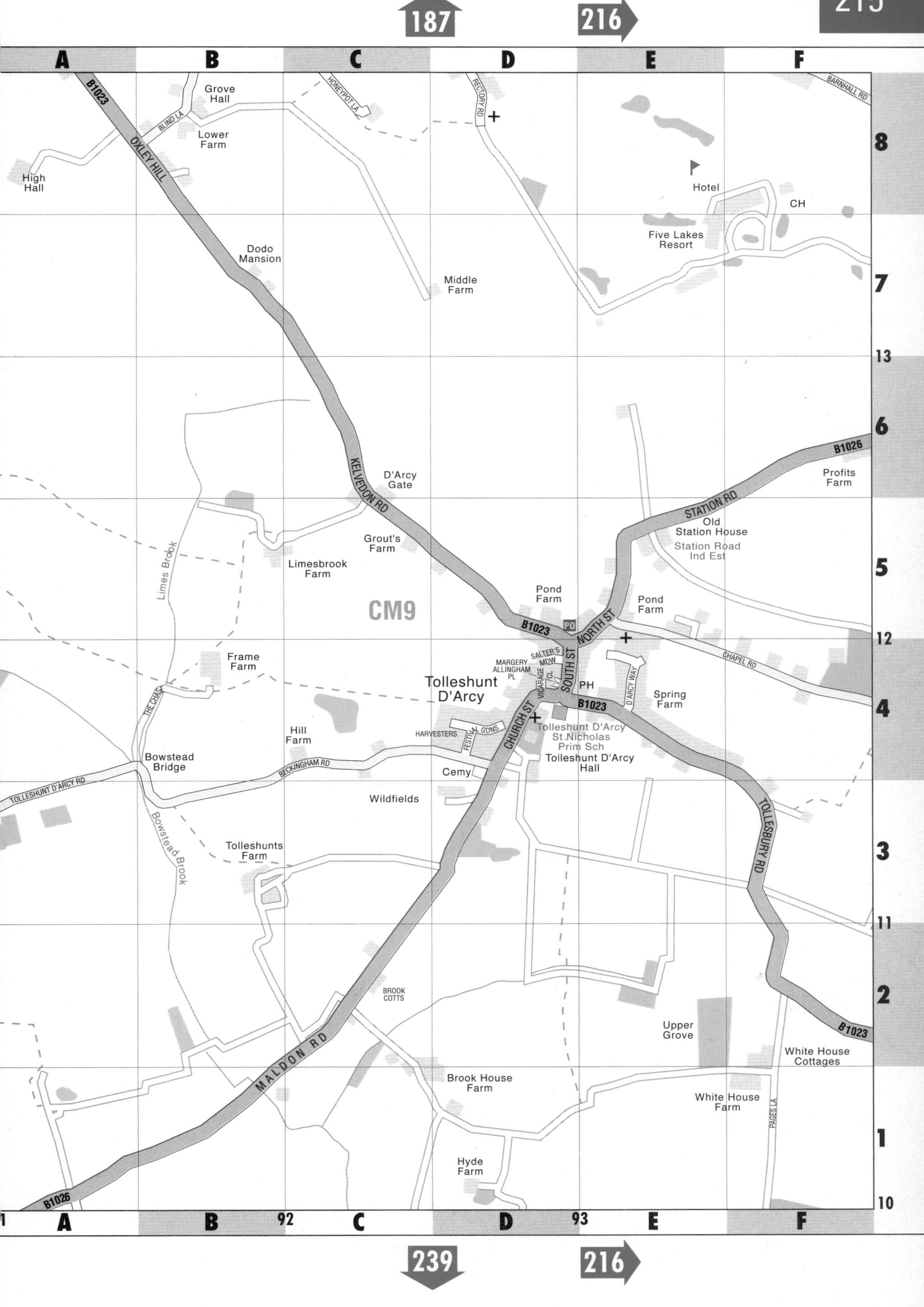
187
216
A
B
C
D
E
F
B1023
Grove Hall
Lower Farm
BLIND LA
OXLEY HILL
High Hall
HONEYPOT LA
RECTORY RD
BARNHALL RD
Hotel
CH
Five Lakes Resort
Dodo Mansion
Middle Farm
8
7
13
6
B1026
Profits Farm
KELVEDON RD
D'Arcy Gate
STATION RD
Old Station House
Station Road Ind Est
Grout's Farm
Limesbrook Farm
Limes Brook
5
CM9
Pond Farm
Pond Farm
B1023
PO
NORTH ST
12
CHAPEL RD
Frame Farm
MARGERY ALLINGHAM PL
SALTER'S MDW
VICARAGE CL
SOUTH ST
PH
D'ARCY WAY
Spring Farm
Tolleshunt D'Arcy
THE CHASE
B1023
4
Hill Farm
HARVESTERS
FESTIVAL GDNS
CHURCH ST
Tolleshunt D'Arcy St Nicholas Prim Sch
Tolleshunt D'Arcy Hall
Bowstead Bridge
BECKINGHAM RD
Cemy
TOLLESHUNT D'ARCY RD
Wildfields
Bowstead Brook
TOLLESBURY RD
Tolleshunts Farm
3
11
2
BROOK COTTS
MALDON RD
Upper Grove
B1023
White House Cottages
Brook House Farm
White House Farm
PAGES LA
1
Hyde Farm
B1026
10
1
A
B
92
C
D
93
E
F
239
216

215
188

A **B** **C** **D** **E** **F**

8

CO5

B1026

BARNHALL RD

COLCHESTER RD

SHARLANDS ROW

THE STREET

The Rectory

MILL LA

Fourways Farm

Horn Farm

ROSE LA

SALCOTT ST

Marsh Farm

Salcott Creek

Salcott-cum-Virley

7

WHITEHOUSE HILL

Green Farm

Sewage Works

13

Spital Farm

Bridge Farm

6

STATION RD

COLCHESTER RD

Old Hall Marsh Farm

Old Hall Farm

5

CM9

OLD HALL LA

12

The Grove

Bourchier's Farm

CHAPEL RD

Bourchier's Hall

Old Hall Creek

4

GUISNES CT

BACK RD

The Rookery

Red Hill

3

Gorwell Hall

11

Carrington Farm

Tollesbury

2

MALLARD CL

GENISTA CL

SHAMROCK CL

ENDEAVOUR CL

VALKYRIE CL

THURSTABLE CL

THURSTABLE WAY

ESTUARY MEWS 1
ST MARYS MEWS 2

WATERWORKS RD

STATION RD

KISSLER RD

SCEPTRE CL

THURSTABLE RD

Oyster Bsns Ctr

Woodrolfe Creek

NORTH RD

NEW RD

THE CHASE

KENTS GRASS

WOODROLFE RD

WOODROLFE PK

Works

Woodrolfe Farm

Garland's Farm

HIGH ST

ORCHARD CL

CRESCENT RD

KINGS WLK

HYACINTH CL

Marina

TOLLESBURY RD

WEST ST

PO

B1023 EAST ST

PH

MELL RD

DARNET RD

Woodrolfe Farm

1

Garlands Farm

Cemy

ST JOHN'S ST

ELYSIAN GDNS

ST JOHN'S CT

CHURCH ST

CHURCHACRE

THE MOUNT

Tollesbury Sch

WOODROLFE FARM LA

PRENTICE HALL LA

Prentice Hall Farm

Bohuns Hall

WYCKE LA

10

94 **A** **B** 95 **C** **D** 96 **E** **F**

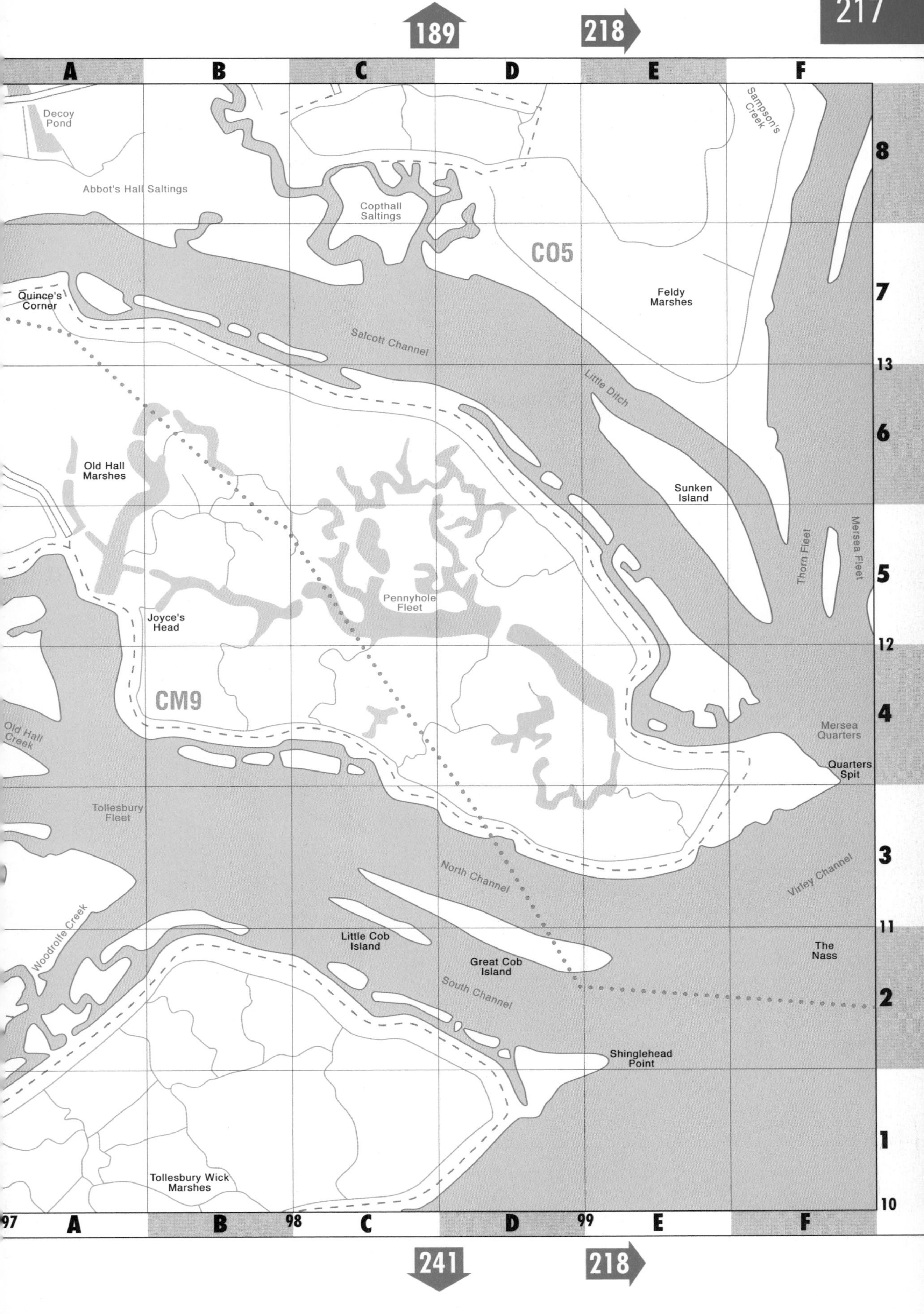

A   B   C   D   E   F

8

Decoy
Pond

Abbot's Hall Saltings

Copthall
Saltings

CO5

Sampson's
Creek

Feldy
Marshes

7

Quince's
Corner

Salcott Channel

Little Ditch

13

6

Old Hall
Marshes

Sunken
Island

Thorn Fleet

Mersea Fleet

5

Joyce's
Head

Pennyhole
Fleet

12

CM9

Mersea
Quarters

4

Quarters
Spit

Old Hall
Creek

Tollesbury
Fleet

North Channel

Virley Channel

3

11

Woodrolfe Creek

Little Cob
Island

Great Cob
Island

The
Nass

2

South Channel

Shinglehead
Point

1

Tollesbury Wick
Marshes

10

97   A   B   98   C   D   99   E   F

217
190

A B C D E F

8

MERSEA
ISLAND

Strood Channel

B1025

Wellhouse
Farm

Weathercock

COLCHESTER RD

PAEONY CHASE

PYEFLEET HO 1
CARRINGTON HO 2
CARRINGTON CT 3
WINDSOR HO 4
RAY HO 5

CO5

BARROW
MEWS

DAVIES LA

CHAPMANS LA

Mortimers
Farm

7

FIRS CHASE
CVN PK

GLEBE VIEW

STABLE MEWS
STABLINGS
CRES

EAST RD

WELLHOUSE RD

BEVERLEY AVE

CROSS WAY

PH

THE
CROSS

BRIERLEY
PADDOCKS

BRICKHOUSE

GUNFLEET CL
BULEY CL

COLCHESTER RD

CHANDLERS

CHASWORTH

TRINITY
MEWS

CLOCK
TOWN

TRINITY CL

LAWNS CL

CONSTABLE CL

GOSSEN AVE

WIVEN RD

NORFOLK AVE

SUFFOLK CL

KEENE CL

WINDSOR RD

FARTHINGS CHASE

WHITTAKER WAY
CYPRESS MEWS

SPRUCE

HIGH ST N

UPLAND
CRES

BRAMBLEDOWN

QUEENS
RD

QUEENS
CL

OAKWOOD RD

BEVERLEY
AVE

CARRIERS CL

THE LANE

STONEHILL
WAY

A STROUD CL

WOODFIELD

PINE GR

TUDOR
CT

CLAIRE RD

RETMEAD CL

UPLAND RD

MILLCROFT
Wr Twr MEWS

ORCHARD CL

KINGSLAND RD

MILL RD

OAKWOOD DR

OAKWOOD
GDNS

EMPRESS AVE

FAIRHAVEN AVE

SEAVIEW AVE

CROSS LA

13

IRB
Sta

CITY RD

FIRS RD

FIRS RD

MERSEA CT

MERSEA AVE

VINCE CL

GRAYS CL

BIRCHWOOD CL 1
THORNWOOD CL 2

ACORN
MEWS

QUEEN
ANNE RD

AINSMERE CL

HOGARTH

ESTUARY PARK RD

WESTWOOD

6

ROSEBANK RD

BLACKWOOD
DR

VICTORY RD

ST PETER'S RD

KENISTON
CT

NEW CAPTAINS
RD

CAPTAINS
RD

BARFIELD RD

AKERSLOOT
PL

RAINBOW

KINGSLAND
HTS

Mersea
Island
Sch

RUSHMERE CL

QUEEN
ANNE DR

LEA
SIDE

THE
PADDOCKS

CARRIERS
CHASE

KING
CHARLES
RD

OSBORNE RD

SEAVIEW
CVN PK

Sewage
Works

PH

FIRS HAMLET

THE
SQUARE

ROSEBANK

THE
SEEDFIELD

HIGH ST

B1025

MELROSE RD

1 AKHURST CT
2 PLEASANT MEWS
3 HARRISON CT

YORICK CT

Mersea
Island
Mews

VICTORIA
MEWS

HILYBROOM

PRINCE ALBERT RD

WILLOUGHBY AVE

BLOSSOM
MEWS

ALEXANDRA RD

ORCHID
FIELD

CHARLESTON

GALIOTS

COAST RD

PHOENIX
CL

CHURCH RD

PH

Liby

HALL
BARN

THE CHASE

YORICK RD

PHAROS LA

GROVE AVE

FIVE
GABLES
CHASE

VICTORIA ESPL

FAIRHAVEN
CT

New
ORLEANS
FLATS

Mus

MEADOW
LA

BEACH RD

LOWER
KINGSLAND
RD

KINGSLAND
BEACH

SHEARS
CT

St Peter's
Well

5

WEST MERSEA

Besom Fleet

Cobmarsh
Island

12

191

G H I J K

4

West
Barn

Rewsalls
Farm

CO5

Works

8

WALDEGRAVES LA

Mersea Island
Vineyard

3

Waldegraves
Farm

Works

Mersea Flats

7

11

Youth
Camp

13

WALDEGRAVES FARM
CVN SITE

2

6

1

03 G 01 H 04 I J 05 K

10

00 A B 01 C D 02 E F

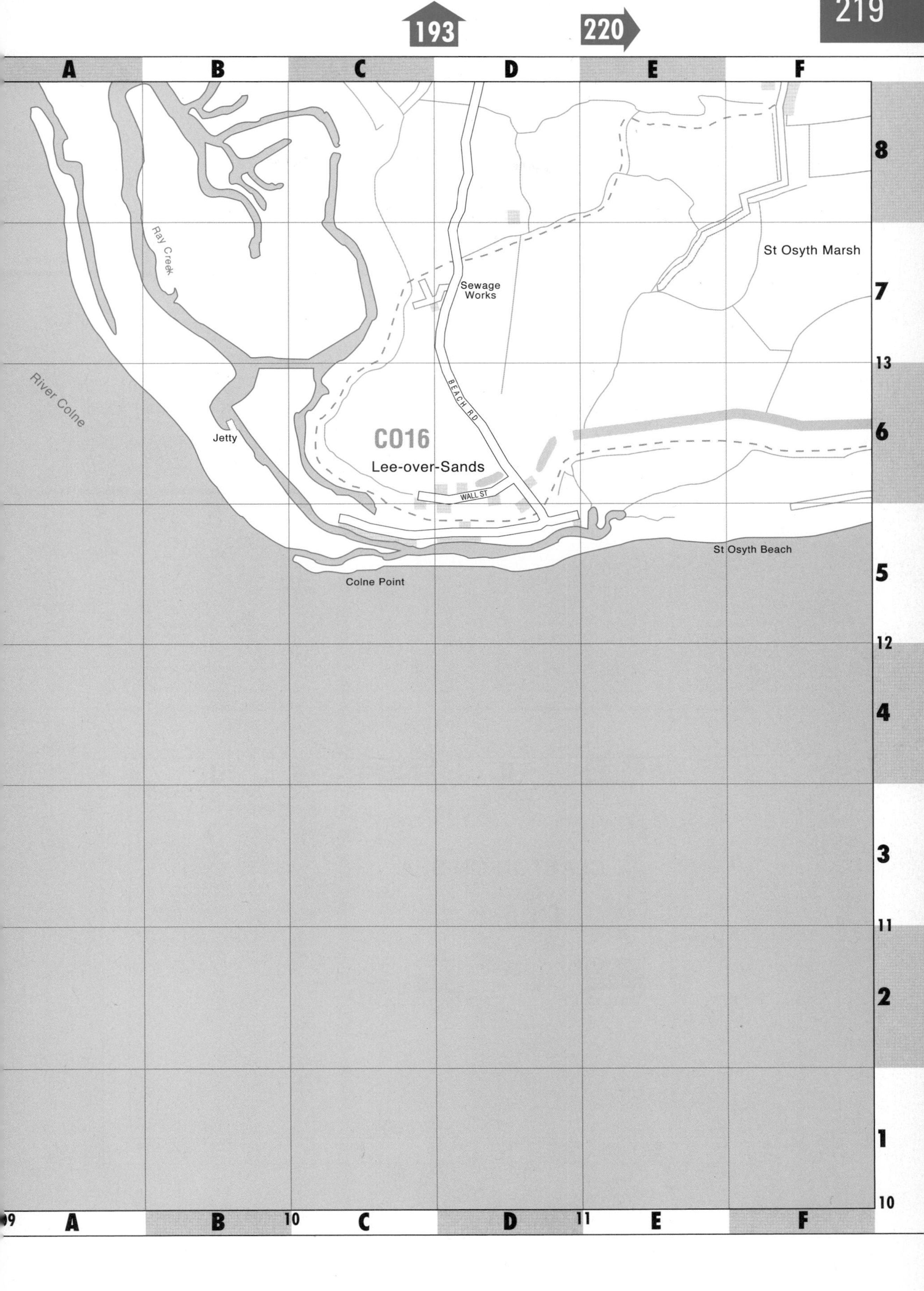

193

220

St Osyth Marsh

Ray Creek

River Colne

Sewage Works

BEACH RD

Jetty

CO16
Lee-over-Sands

WALL ST

Colne Point

St Osyth Beach

219
194
195

A **B** **C** **D** **E** **F**

8

Marsh
Cottage

CO16

CO15

Jaywick

Decoy Pond

7

Seawick
Holiday Park

Seawick

BEACH RD

SEAVIEW RD

PO

13

THE
GREEN

LILAC AVE

WILLOW AVE

LINKS RD

SEAWICK RD

FOURTH AVE

THIRD AVE

SECOND AVE

FIRST AVE

HUNTLEY'S
CVN PK (E)

TOWER
CVN PK

LANCHESTER AVE

DAIMLER AVE

CROSSLEY AVE

SINGER AVE

ROVER AVE

TRIUMPH AVE

LOTUS WAY

GORSE WAY

FERN WAY

YEW WAY

LAKE WAY

MEADOW WAY

BROADWAY

BISHOPS
GDNS

BEL-AIR
EST

ROSE GDNS

BELAIR DR

BISHOPS DR

CLUB PAR

BEACH
APP

HUNTLEY'S
CVN PK (W)

PH

BEL-AIR
BEACH
CVN PK

BUICK AVE

NAPIER AVE

LINCOLN AVE

BELSIZE AVE

STANDARD AVE

WOLSELEY AVE

MORRIS AVE

HILLMAN AVE

SUNBEAM AVE

TALBOT AVE

SWIFT AVE

AUSTIN AVE

HUMBER AVE

RILEY AVE

ESSEX AVE

VAUXHALL AVE

BENTLEY AVE

ALVIS AVE

ANSON AVE

INGRAM

BROOKLANDS

HARVEY CT 1
YEW WAY 2
ELVINA HO 3
BEACH CRES 4.

TAMARISK WAY

BROOME
WAY

SEA WAY

PO

6

Martello
Tower

PROMENADE

P

APRILS VIEW 1
STEDMAN CT 2
LANCIA AVE 3.

5

12

4

G **H** **I** **J**

MARLOWE RD

TUDOR
PAR

The Three Jays
(PH)

WEST RD

P

CH

SPINNAKER
CL

KINGS PROM

ALLEYNE WAY

PARK SQ E

DINNE DR

THE APPROACH

THE CROSSWAYS

UNION RD

JAYWICK LA

LULWORTH
CL

PENZANCE
CL

DAMLIN DR

KENSEY
RD

SANDWICH
RD

PORTSMOUTH
RD

WEYMOUTH
CL

Slipway
Martello Tower

3

8

CLACTON-ON-SEA

CO15

1 DOVER CL
2 PLYMOUTH RD
3 HYTHE CL
4 SHAMROCK HO
5 AQUILINE HO
6 LITTLE STONE CT
7 WORTHING MEWS

11

Jaywick

JASMINE WAY

GOLF GREEN RD

PO

BARCLAY
SQ

BRIXHAM
CL

SHIRBER

HASTINGS AVE

DEAL CL

SELSEY
CL

BELHILL CL

BURNHAM RD

P

P

2

7

MEADOW WAY

CORNFLOWER RD

GLEBE WAY

ROSEMARY WAY

GARDEN RD

BADMINTON RD

THE CLS

1 BRANSTON CT
2 BADMINTON CT

Martello Tower

13

CHRISTOPHER
WAY

LAVENDER WLK

TINKERS WAY

WILLOW WAY

BROADWAY

SEA GLEBE WAY

SEA FLOWERS WAY

SEA PRIMACY WAY

6

FIR WAY

SEA PINK WAY

SEA HOLLY WAY

SEA SHELL WAY

SEA LAVENDER WAY

SEA THISTLE WAY

15 16 17

1

10

12 13 14

A **B** **C** **D** **E** **F**

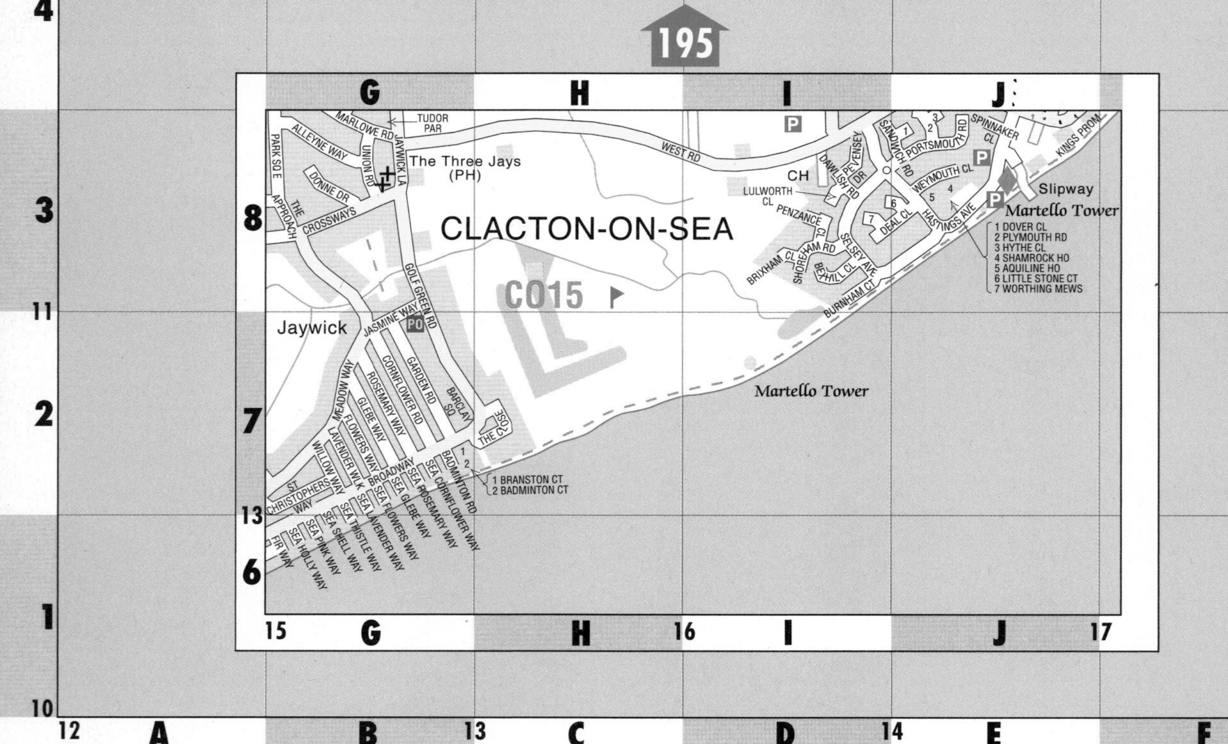

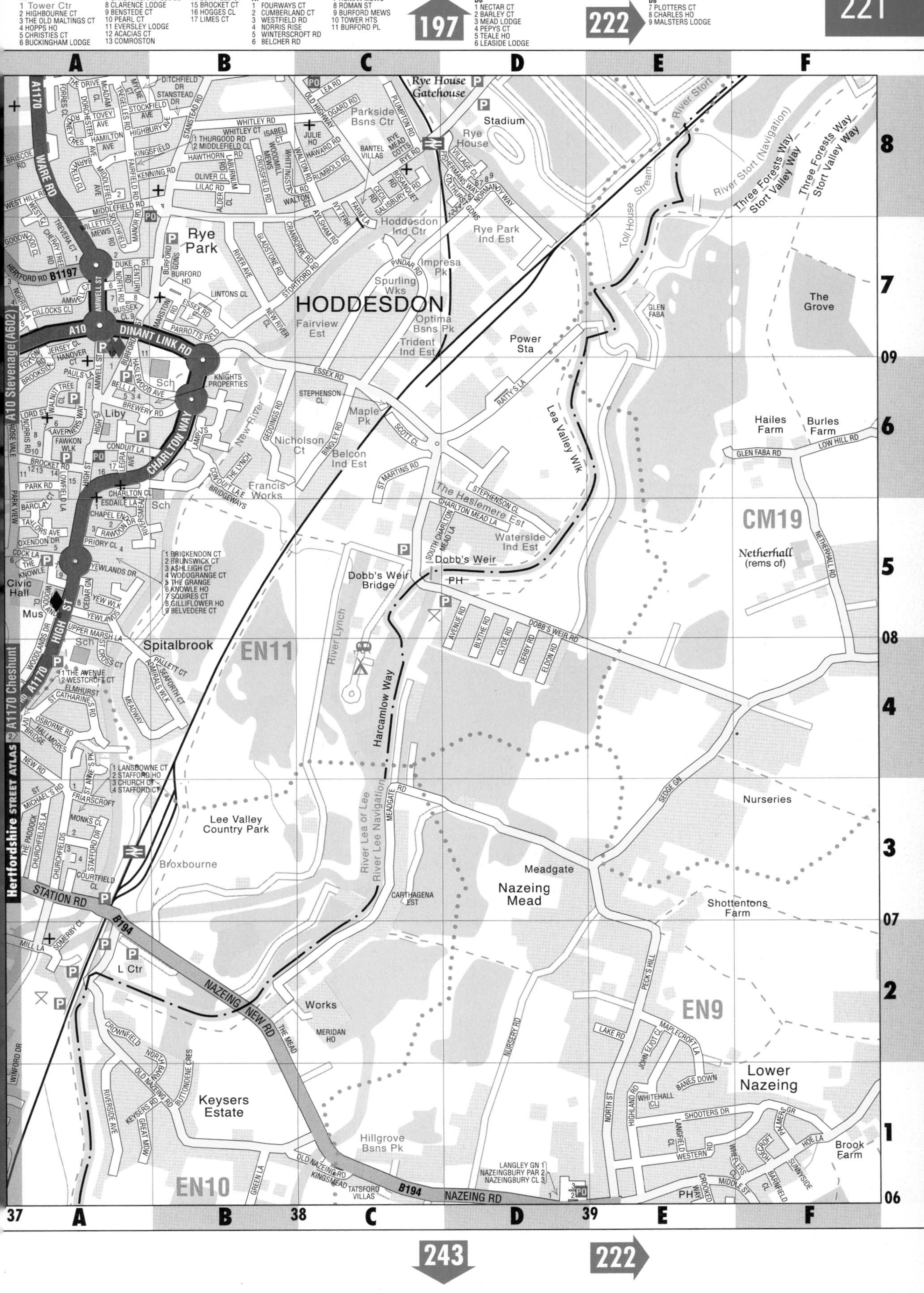
A6
1 Tower Ctr
2 HIGHBOURNE CT
3 THE OLD MALTINGS CT
4 HOPPS HO
5 CHRISTIES CT
6 BUCKINGHAM LODGE
7 SANDRINGHAM LODGE
8 CLARENCE LODGE
9 BENSTEDE CT
10 PEARL CT
11 EVERSLEY LODGE
12 ACACIAS CT
13 COMROSTON
14 LOWFIELD CT
15 BROCKET CT
16 HOGGES CL
17 LIMES CT
A7
1 FOURWAYS CT
2 CUMBERLAND CT
3 WESTFIELD RD
4 NORRIS RISE
5 WINTERSCROFT RD
6 BELCHER RD
7 ROMAN MEWS
8 ROMAN ST
9 BURFORD MEWS
10 TOWER HTS
11 BURFORD PL
197
D8
1 NECTAR CT
2 BARLEY CT
3 MEAD LODGE
4 PEPYS CT
5 TEALE HO
6 LEASIDE LODGE
222
D8
7 PLOTTERS CT
8 CHARLES HO
9 MALSTERS LODGE
A
B
C
D
E
F
Rye House Gatehouse
Stadium
Rye House
Parkside Bsns Ctr
River Stort
River Stort (Navigation)
Three Forests Way
Stort Valley Way
Toll House Stream
Hoddesdon Ind Ctr
Rye Park Ind Est
Rye Park
Impresa Pk
Spurling Wks
HODDESDON
Optima Bsns Pk
Trident Ind Est
Fairview Est
Power Sta
Glen Faba
The Grove
Knights Properties
Liby
Sch
Maple Pk
Nicholson Ct
Belcon Ind Est
Lea Valley Wlk
Hailes Farm
Burles Farm
Francis Works
The Haslemere Est
Waterside Ind Est
CM19
Netherhall (rems of)
Dobb's Weir
Dobb's Weir Bridge
PH
Civic Hall
Mus
Spitalbrook
EN11
River Lynch
Harcamlow Way
Lee Valley Country Park
Broxbourne
Nurseries
Meadgate
Nazeing Mead
Shottentons Farm
River Lea or Lee
River Lee Navigation
Carthagena Est
L Ctr
Works
Meridan Ho
EN9
Keysers Estate
Lower Nazeing
Hillgrove Bsns Pk
Brook Farm
EN10
A1170
WARE RD
A10
DINANT LINK RD
CHARLTON WAY
HIGH ST
AMWELL ST
B1197
HERTFORD RD
STATION RD
B194
NAZEING NEW RD
NAZEING RD
ESSEX RD
DOBB'S WEIR RD
GLEN FABA RD
LOW HILL RD
NETHERHALL RD
SEDGE GN
PECK'S HILL
NORTH ST
NURSERY RD
MEADGATE RD
A10 Stevenage (A602)
A1170 Cheshunt
Hertfordshire STREET ATLAS
1 BRICKENDON CT
2 BRUNSWICK CT
3 ASHLEIGH CT
4 WOODGRANGE CT
5 THE GRANGE
6 KNOWLE HO
7 SQUIRES CT
8 GILLIFLOWER HO
9 BELVEDERE CT
1 LANSDOWNE CT
2 STAFFORD HO
3 CHURCH OF
4 STAFFORD CT
1 THE AVENUE
2 WESTCROFT CT
LANGLEY GN 1
NAZEINGBURY PAR 2
NAZEINGBURY CL 3
8
7
09
6
5
08
4
3
07
2
1
06
37
38
39
243
222

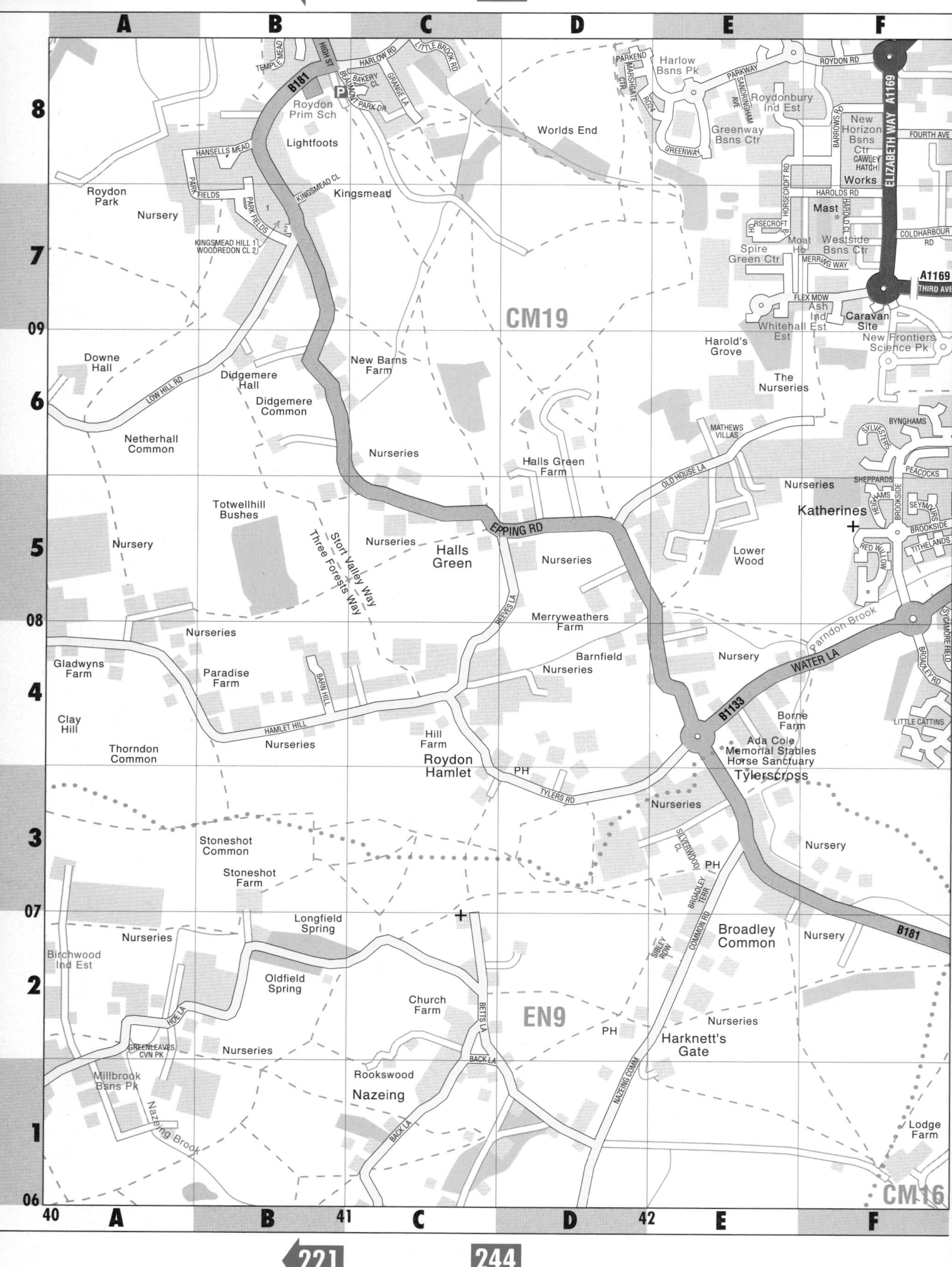

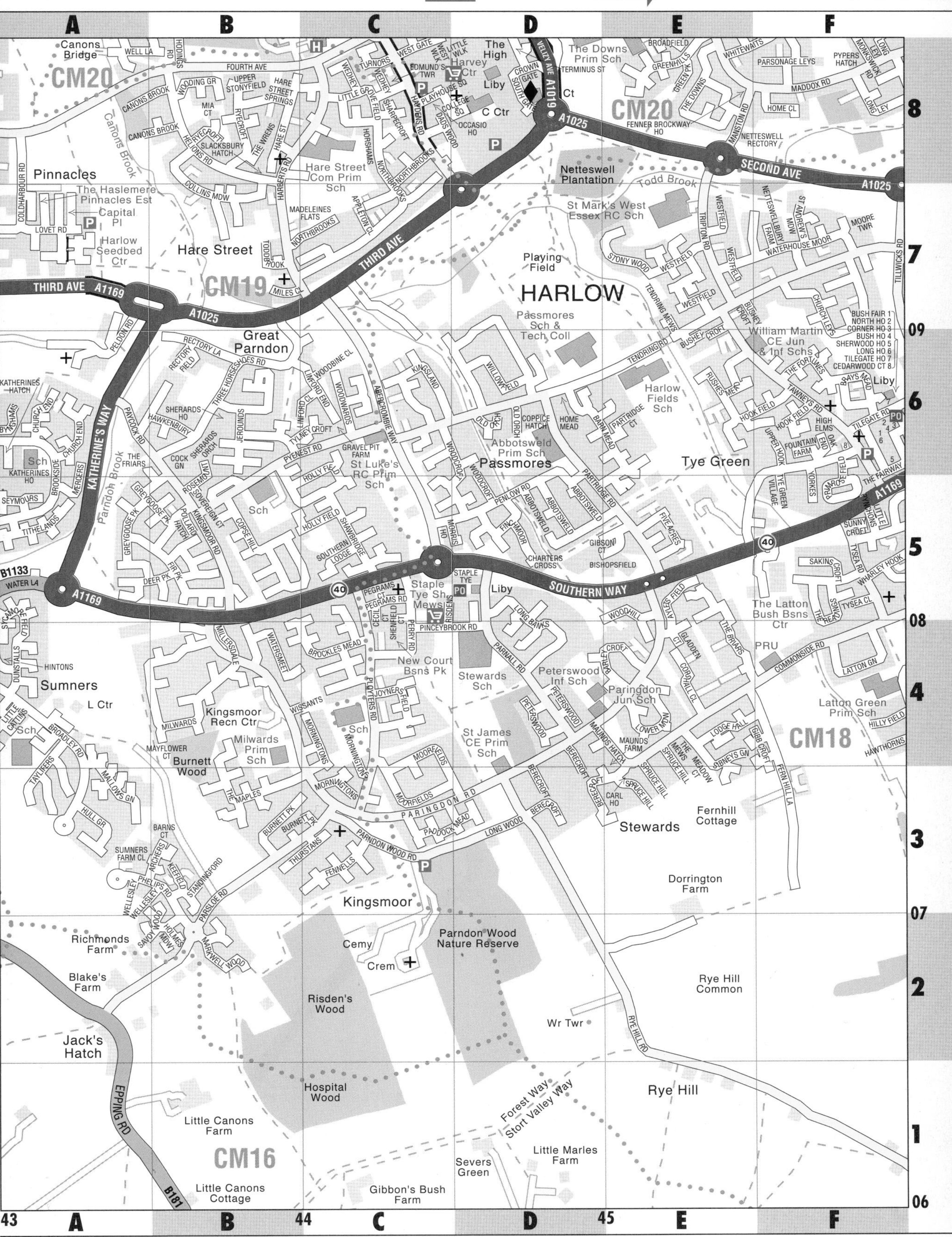

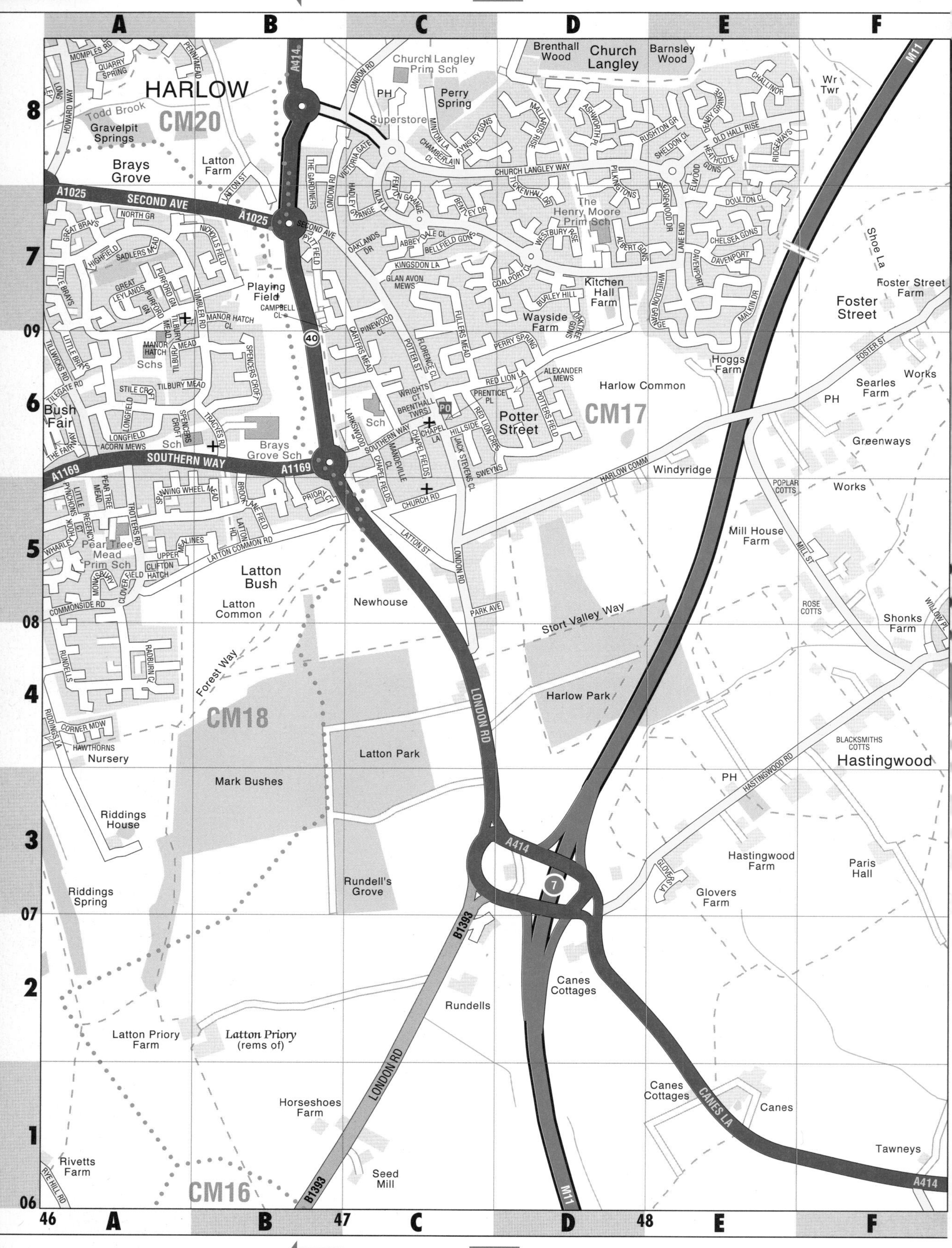

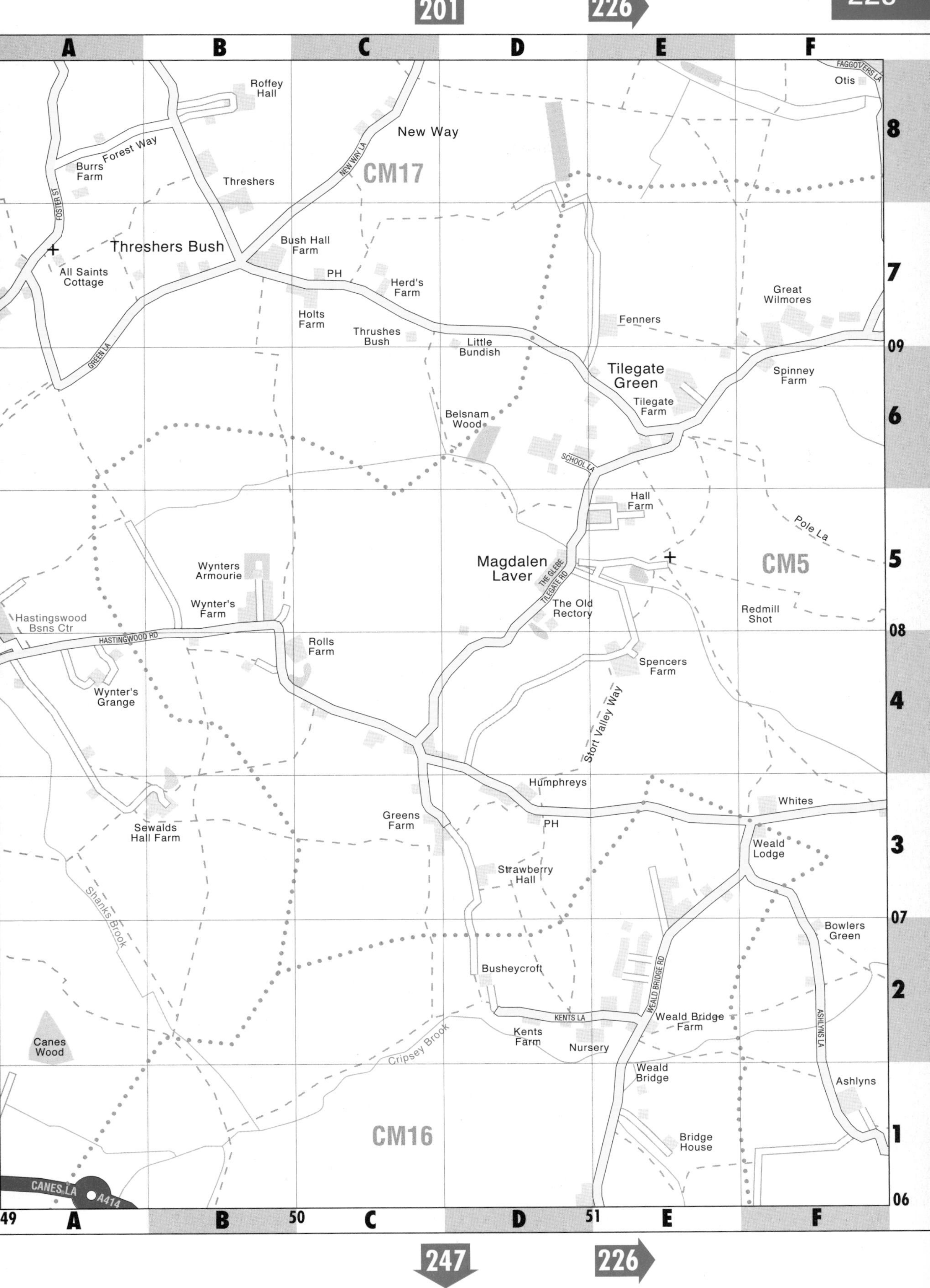

A B C D E F

8
7
6
5
4
3
2
1

09
08
07
06

FAGGOTERS LA
Otis

New Way

CM17

Roffey
Hall

Burrs
Farm

Forest Way

Threshers

FOSTER ST

All Saints
Cottage

Threshers Bush

GREEN LA

Bush Hall
Farm

PH

Herd's
Farm

Holts
Farm

Thrushes
Bush

NEW WAY LA

Little
Bundish

Belsnam
Wood

Fenners

Great
Wilmores

Tilegate
Green

Spinney
Farm

Tilegate
Farm

SCHOOL LA

Hall
Farm

Pole La

CM5

Wynters
Armourie

Wynter's
Farm

Magdalen
Laver

THE GLEBE

TILEGATE RD

The Old
Rectory

Redmill
Shot

Hastingswood
Bsns Ctr

HASTINGWOOD RD

Wynter's
Grange

Rolls
Farm

Spencers
Farm

Stort Valley Way

Humphreys

Whites

Sewalds
Hall Farm

Shanks Brook

Greens
Farm

PH

Strawberry
Hall

Weald
Lodge

Bowlers
Green

Busheycroft

WEALD BRIDGE RD

ASHLYNS LA

Canes
Wood

Cripsey Brook

KENTS LA

Kents
Farm

Nursery

Weald Bridge
Farm

Ashlyns

Weald
Bridge

CM16

CANES LA

A414

Bridge
House

49 A B 50 C D 51 E F

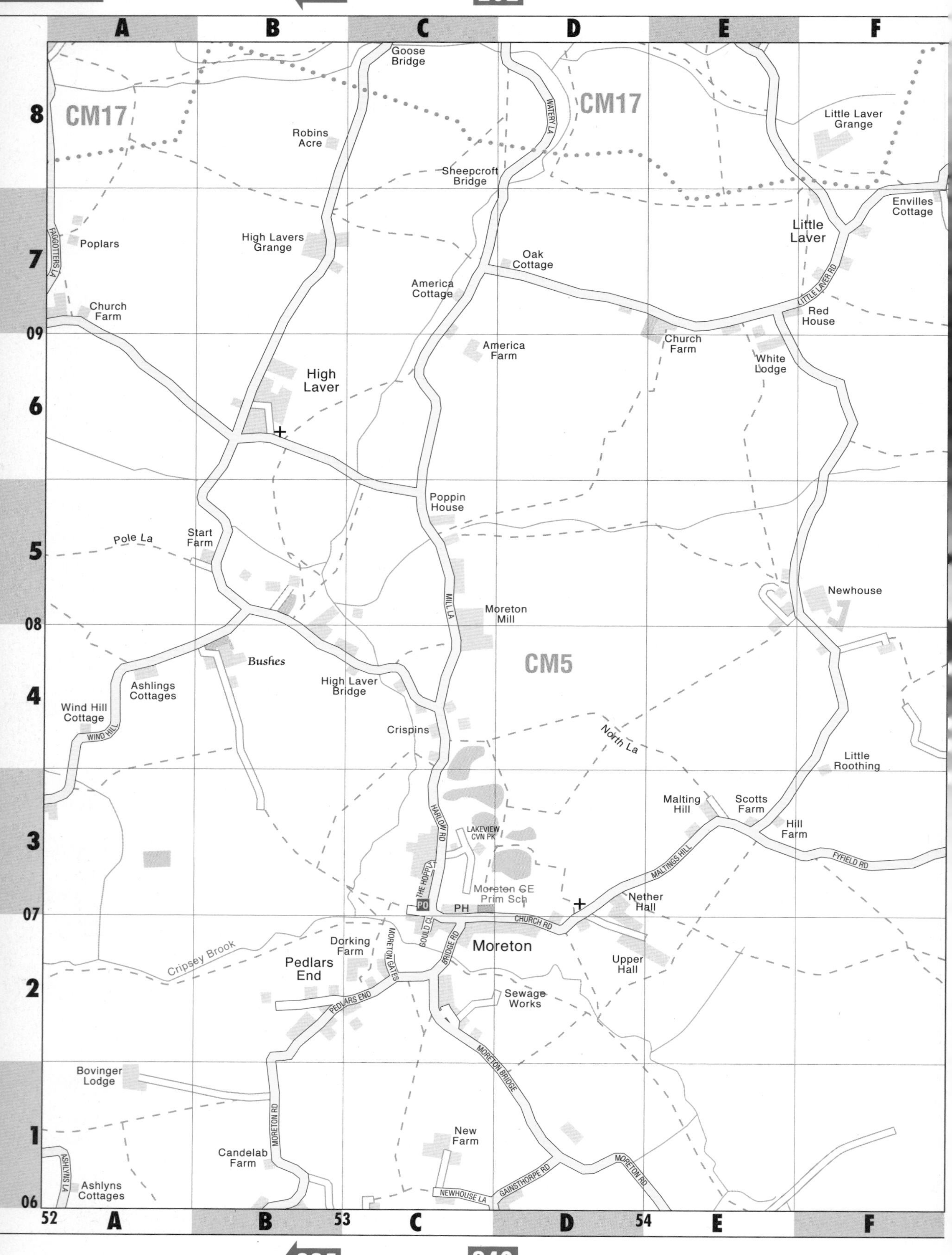

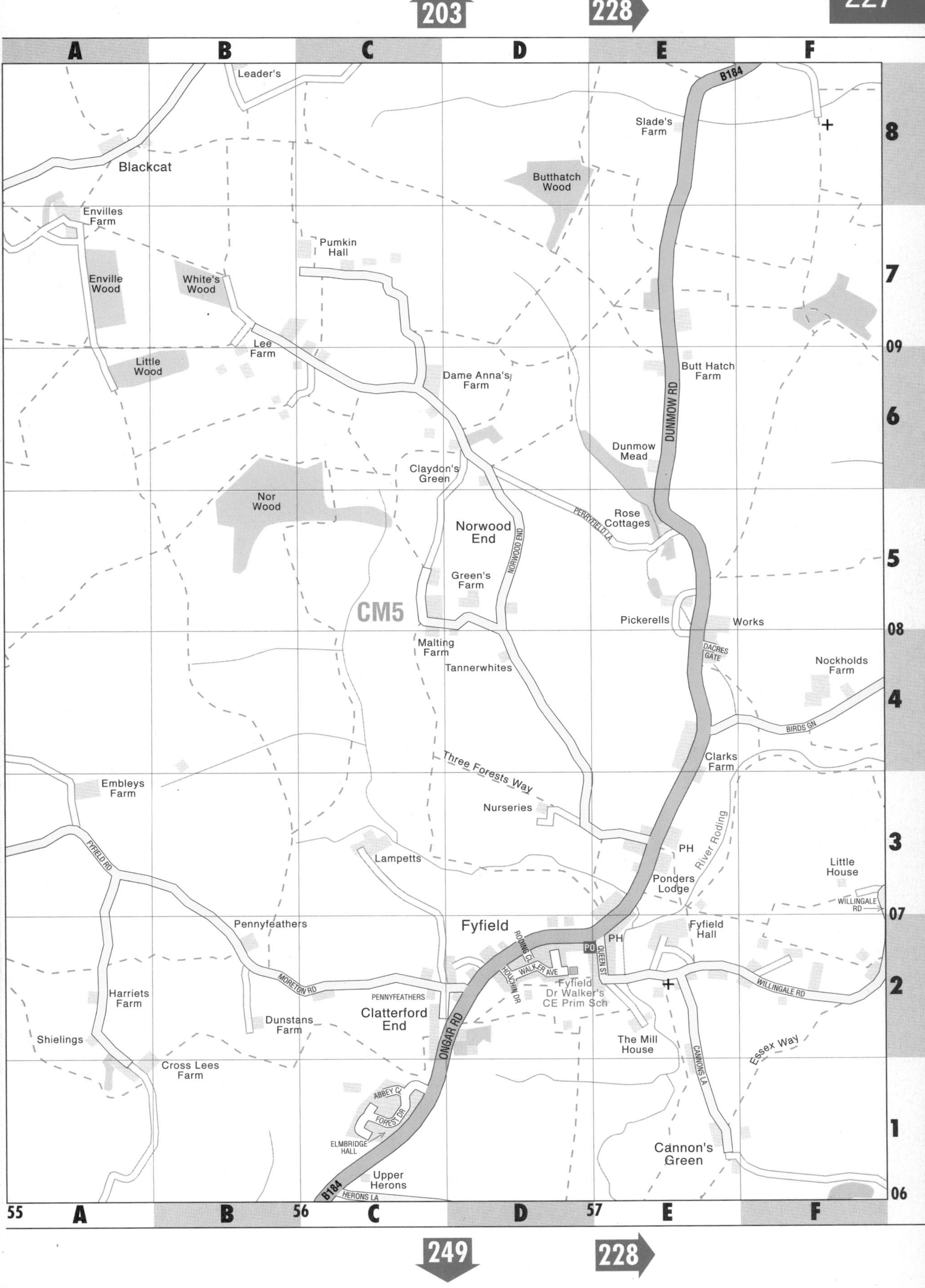

A B C D E F

8

B184

Slade's Farm

Blackcat

Butthatch Wood

Envilles Farm

Pumkin Hall

7

Enville Wood

White's Wood

09

Little Wood

Lee Farm

Dame Anna's Farm

Butt Hatch Farm

DUNMOW RD

6

Nor Wood

Claydon's Green

Dunmow Mead

Norwood End

PERRYFIELD LA

Rose Cottages

5

CM5

Green's Farm

NORWOOD END

Pickerells

Works

08

Malting Farm

DACRES GATE

Nockholds Farm

Tannerwhites

4

BIRDS GN

Three Forests Way

Clarks Farm

Embleys Farm

Nurseries

River Roding

Little House

3

FYFIELD RD

Lampetts

PH

Ponders Lodge

WILLINGALE RD

07

Pennyfeathers

Fyfield

PO

PH

Fyfield Hall

2

MORETON RD

PENNYFEATHERS

RODING LA

WALKER AVE

HOLDEN DR

Fyfield Dr Walker's CE Prim Sch

QUEEN ST

WILLINGALE RD

Essex Way

Harriets Farm

Clatterford End

ONGAR RD

CANNONS LA

Shielings

Dunstans Farm

The Mill House

Cross Lees Farm

ABBEY C

FOREST DR

1

ELMBRIDGE HALL

Cannon's Green

Upper Herons

B184

HERONS LA

06

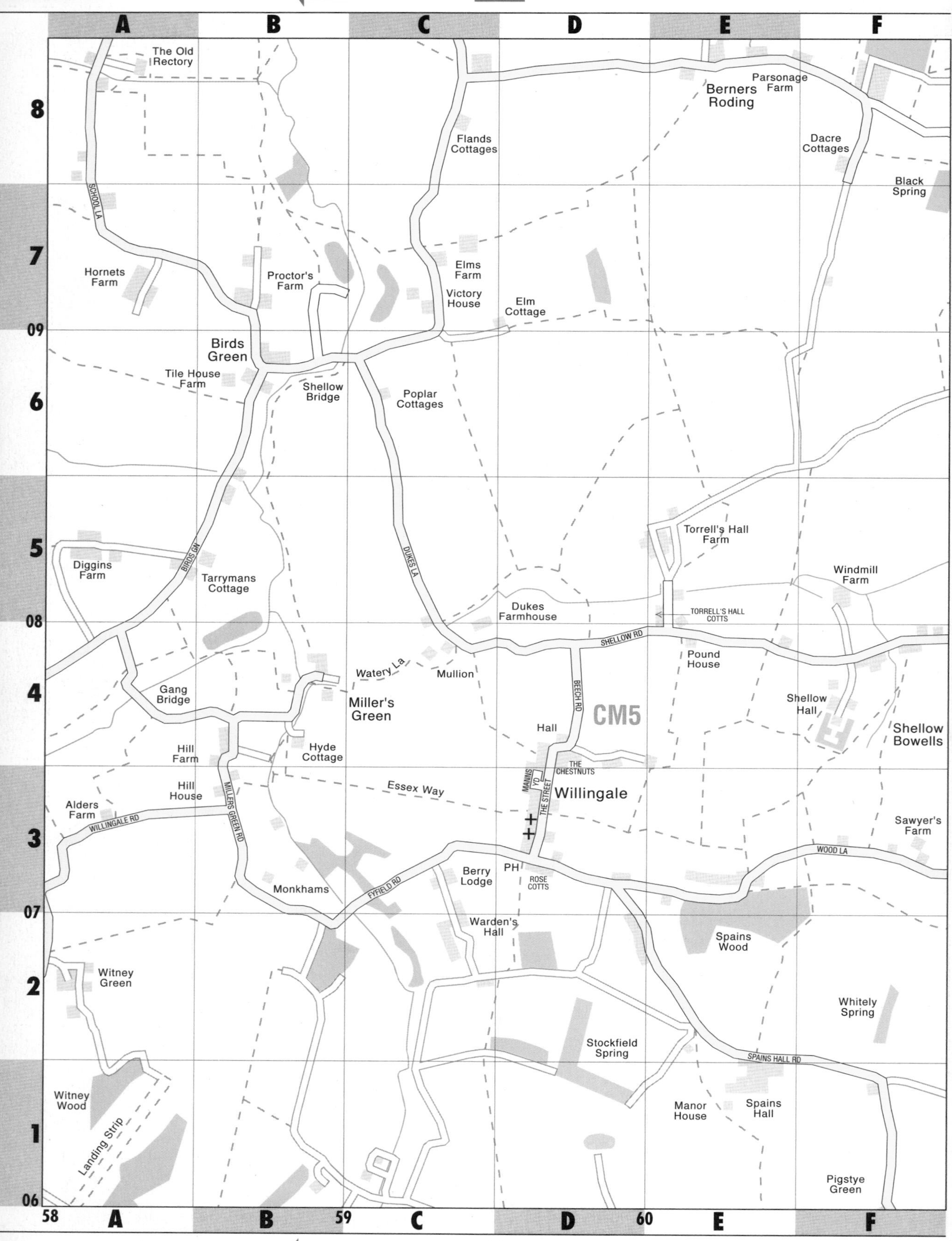

The Old Rectory

Berners Roding

Parsonage Farm

Flands Cottages

Dacre Cottages

Black Spring

Hornets Farm

SCHOOL LA

Proctor's Farm

Elms Farm

Victory House

Elm Cottage

Birds Green

Tile House Farm

Shellow Bridge

Poplar Cottages

Torrell's Hall Farm

Windmill Farm

Diggins Farm

BIRDS GRN

Tarrymans Cottage

DUKES LA

Dukes Farmhouse

SHELLOW RD

TORRELL'S HALL COTTS

Pound House

Shellow Hall

Shellow Bowells

Watery La

Mullion

Gang Bridge

Miller's Green

BEECH RD

CM5

Hill Farm

Hyde Cottage

Hall

THE CHESTNUTS

MILLERS GREEN RD

Essex Way

MANNS YD

THE STREET

Willingale

Alders Farm

Hill House

WILLINGALE RD

Sawyer's Farm

Monkhams

EYFIELD RD

Berry Lodge

PH

ROSE COTTS

WOOD LA

Warden's Hall

Spains Wood

Witney Green

Whitely Spring

Stockfield Spring

SPAINS HALL RD

Witney Wood

Landing Strip

Manor House

Spains Hall

Pigstye Green

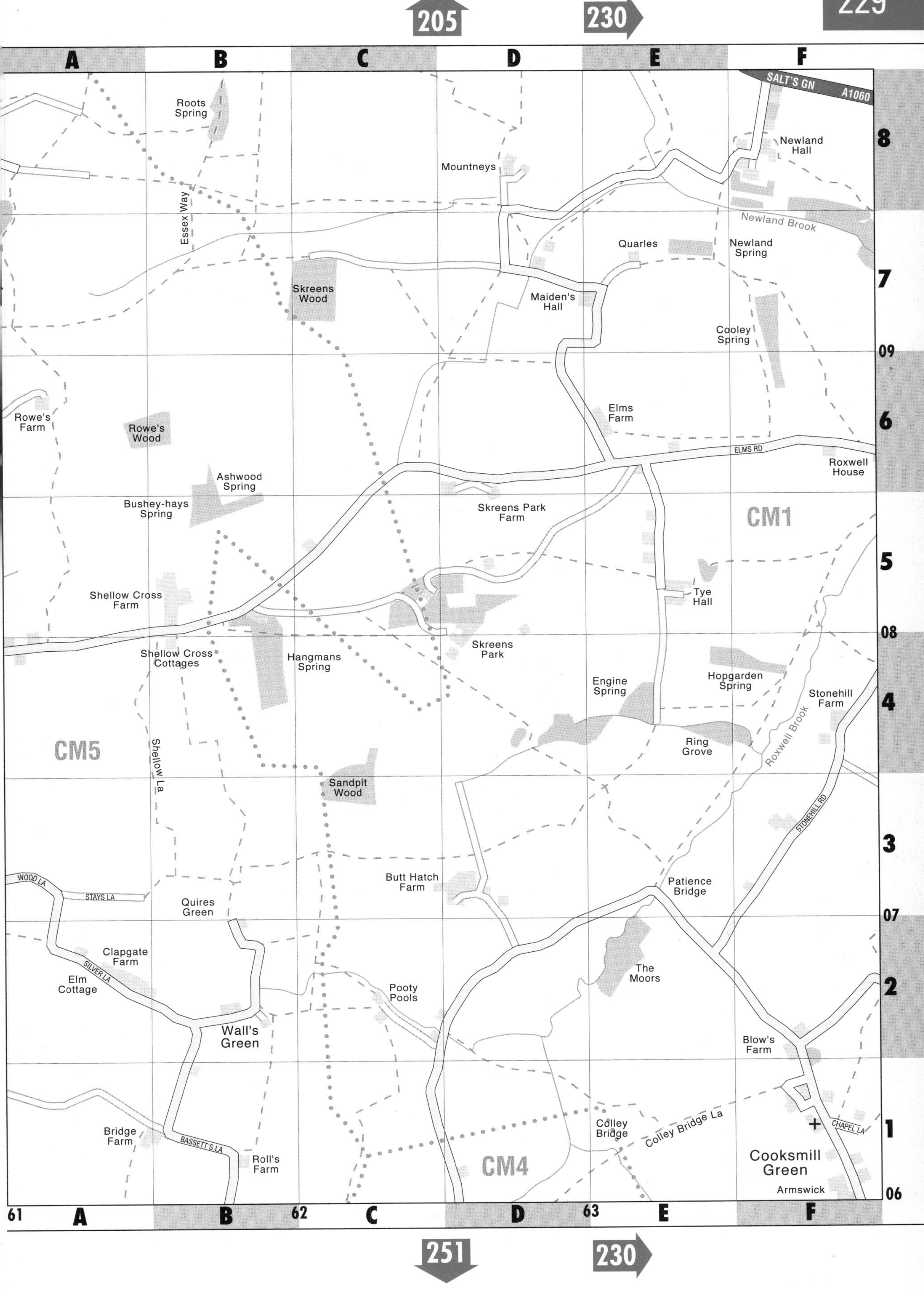

229
206

A   B   C   D   E   F

A1060

Hill Farm

Stevens Farm

8

Greenwich Terrace

Boyton Hall

BOYTON HALL LA

Newland Osiers

Newland Brook

Pengymill

River Can

7

Boyton Cross

PH

Ash Tree Farm

HOOK COTTS

09

Boggis Farm

Lightfoots

ELMS RD

Dukes Farm

Sewage Works

6

Roxwell CE Prim Sch

PO

Roxwell

CM1

THE STREET

PH

Ropers House

Thatcher's Farm

PH

Blackwall Bridge

ROXWELL RD

Reed's Spring

MILL CL

CHURCH GN

ST MICHAEL'S DR

VICARAGE RD

5

STONEHILL RD

MILL VIEW CT

SCHOOL BGLWS

VICARAGE CL

GALLEONS HILL VICARAGE RD

VICARAGE RD

HOE ST

Roxwell Brook

08

4

GREEN LA

Hoestreet

A1060

ROXWELL RD

The Hickerage

Green Lane Farm

Hillcroft

GRAVELLY LA

The Orchards

Reeds Farm

3

Sturgeons Farm

COW WATERING LA

07

PH

Benedict Otes

Newney Green

Newney Hall

Writtle Coll (Cow Watering Campus)

2

Christopher's Farm

VICTORIA RD

PH

FOSTERS CL

BACK RD

DAWS CL

Moor Hall

Hassenbrook

Great Oxney Green

TOWER RD

EAST TREND

ONGAR RD

CHEQUERS RD

MAN'S FIELDS

REDWOOD

DR

1

Green La

GREAT GODFREYS

Bush House Farm

LONG BRANDOCKS

06

64   A   B   65   C   D   66   E   F

A414

229
252

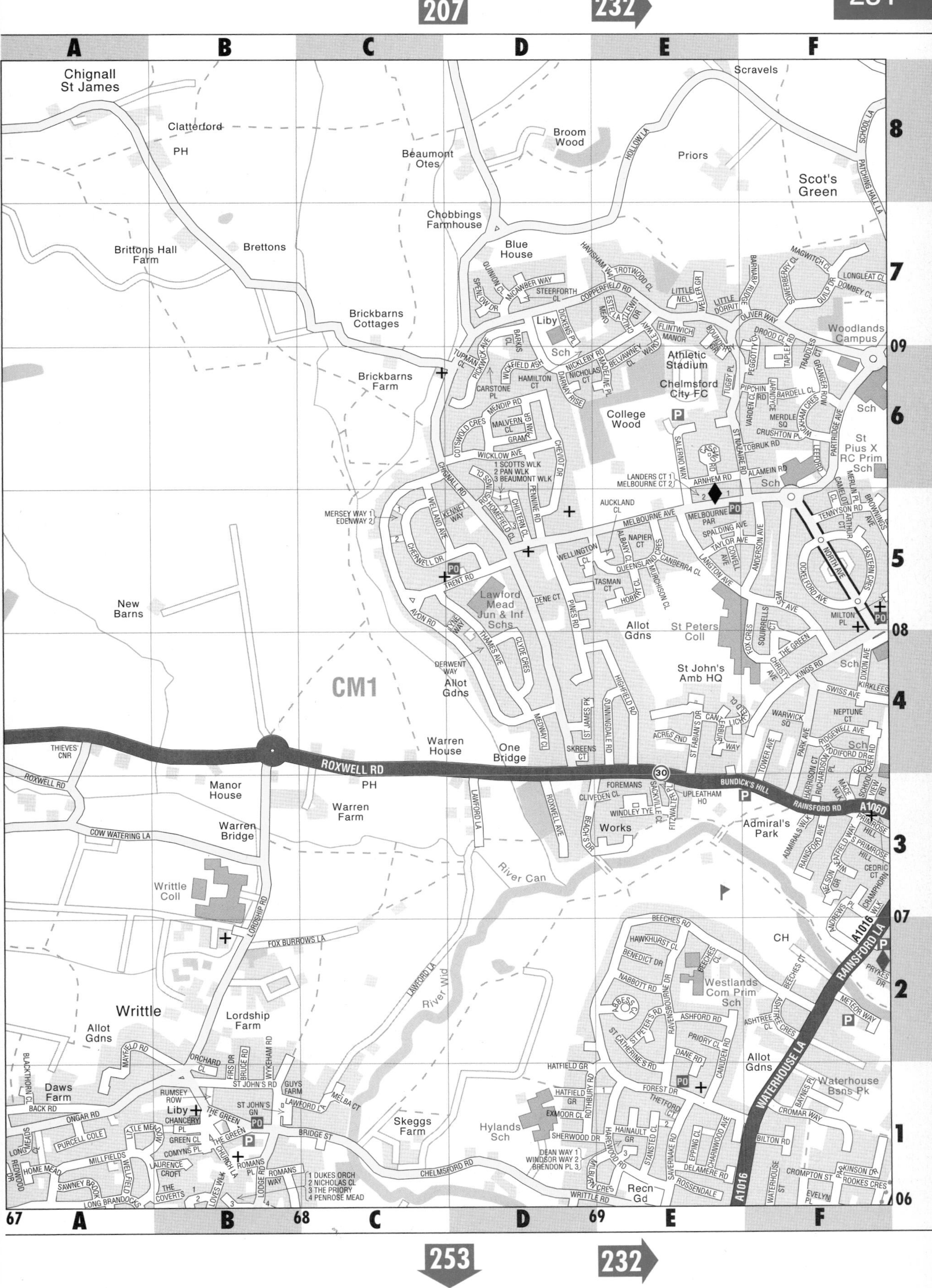

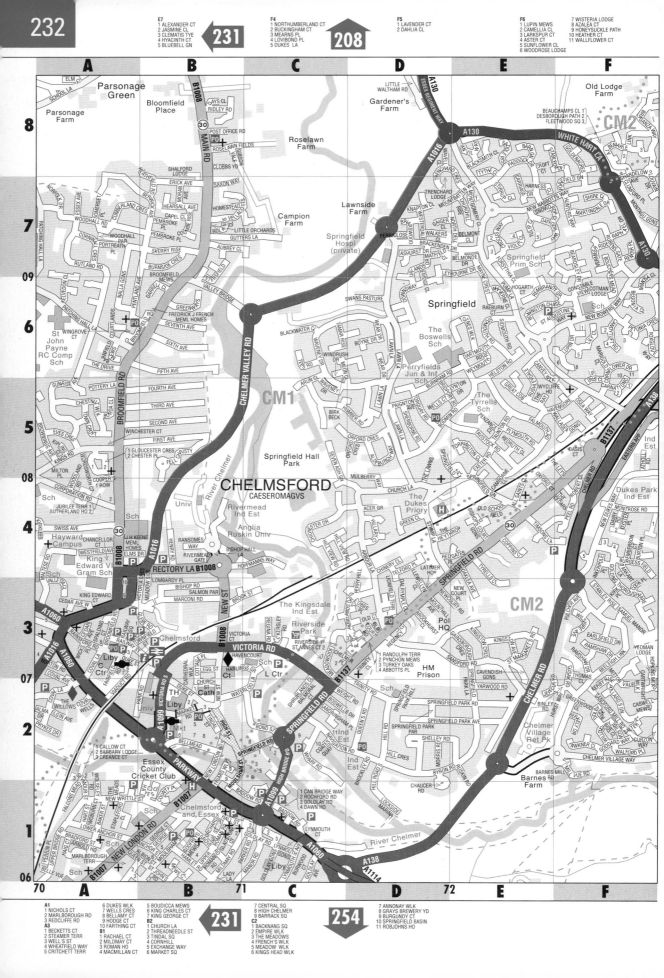

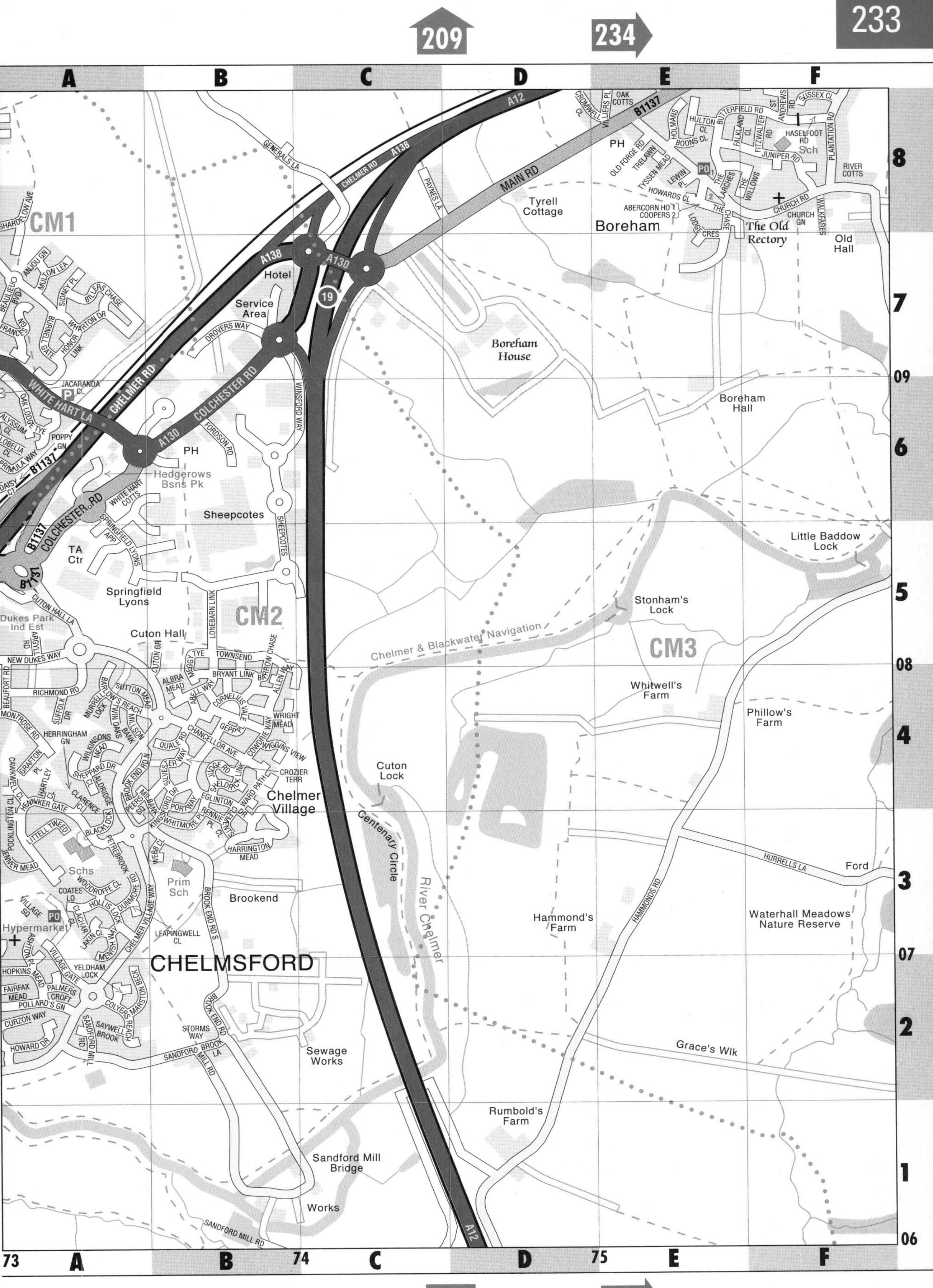

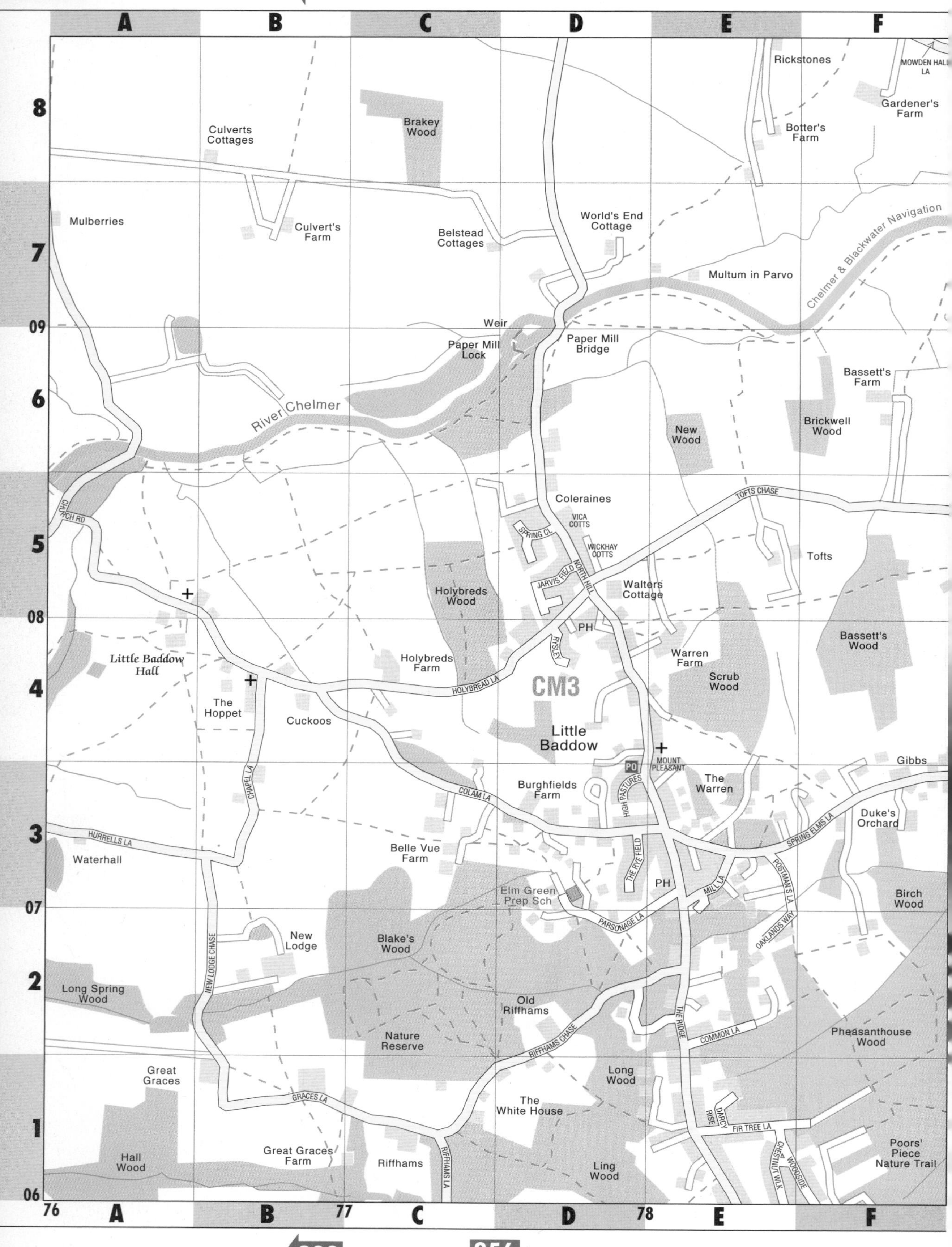

A   B   C   D   E   F

8

Rickstones

MOWDEN HALL LA

Culverts Cottages

Brakey Wood

Botter's Farm

Gardener's Farm

7

Mulberries

Culvert's Farm

Belstead Cottages

World's End Cottage

Multum in Parvo

Chelmer & Blackwater Navigation

09

Weir

Paper Mill Lock

Paper Mill Bridge

Bassett's Farm

6

River Chelmer

New Wood

Brickwell Wood

Coleraines

TOFTS CHASE

5

CHURCH RD

VICA COTTS

WICKHAY COTTS

SPRING CL

JARVIS FIELD

NORTH HILL

Walters Cottage

Tofts

08

Holybreds Wood

PH

Bassett's Wood

4

Little Baddow Hall

The Hoppet

Holybreds Farm

RYSLEY

HOLYBREAD LA

CM3

Warren Farm

Scrub Wood

Cuckoos

Little Baddow

MOUNT PLEASANT

Gibbs

3

HURRELLS LA

CHAPEL LA

COLAM LA

Burghfields Farm

HIGH PASTURES

The Warren

SPRING ELMS LA

Duke's Orchard

Waterhall

Belle Vue Farm

THE RYE FIELD

PH

MILL LA

POSTMAN'S LA

OAKLANDS WAY

Birch Wood

07

NEW LODGE CHASE

Elm Green Prep Sch

PARSONAGE LA

2

New Lodge

Blake's Wood

Long Spring Wood

Old Riffhams

THE RIDGE

COMMON LA

Pheasanthouse Wood

Nature Reserve

RIFFHAMS CHASE

Long Wood

1

Great Graces

GRACES LA

RIFFHAMS LA

The White House

DARCY RISE

FIR TREE LA

Poors' Piece Nature Trail

Hall Wood

Great Graces Farm

Riffhams

Ling Wood

CHESTNUT WALK

WOODSIDE

06

76   A   B   77   C   D   78   E   F

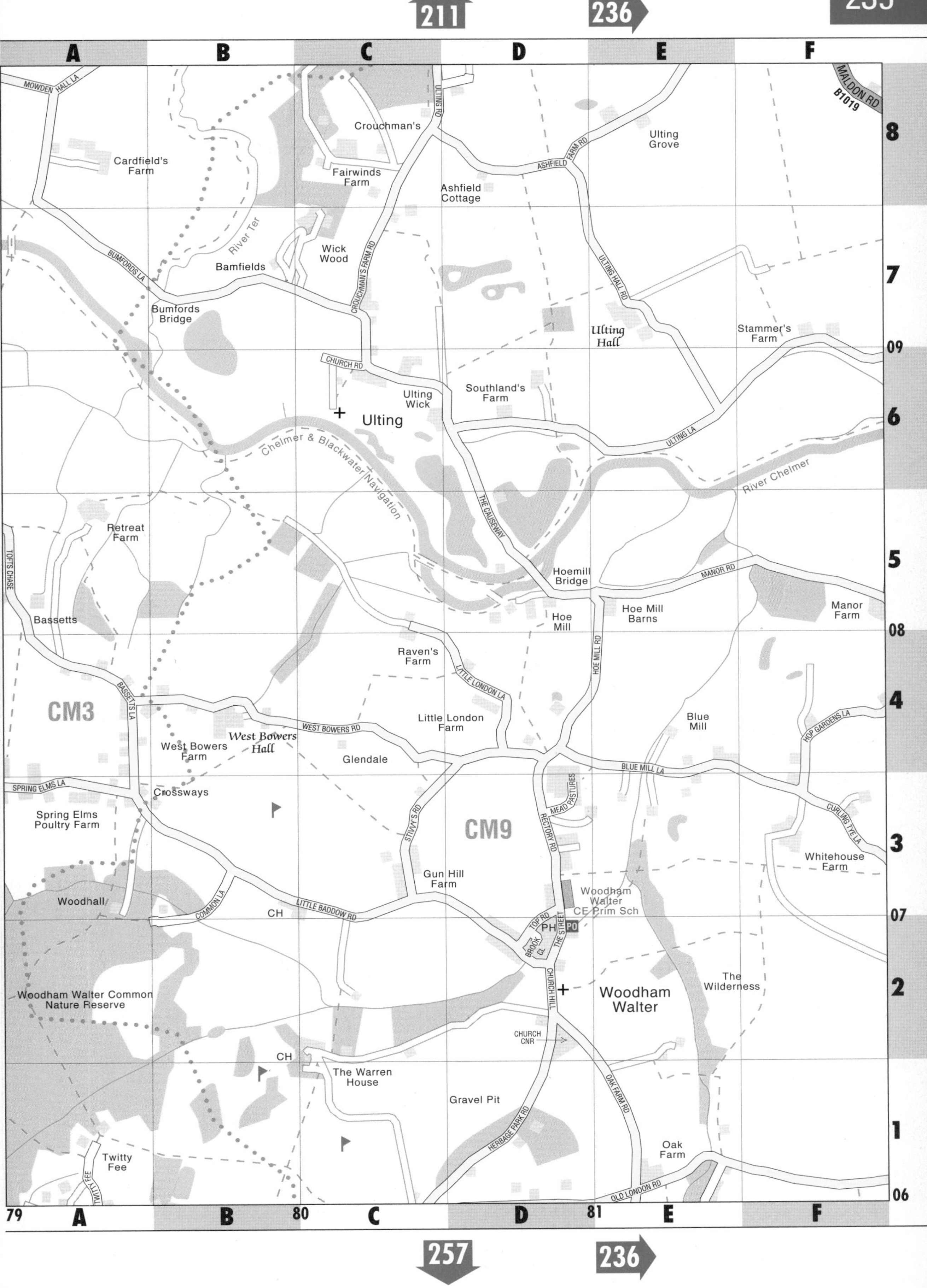

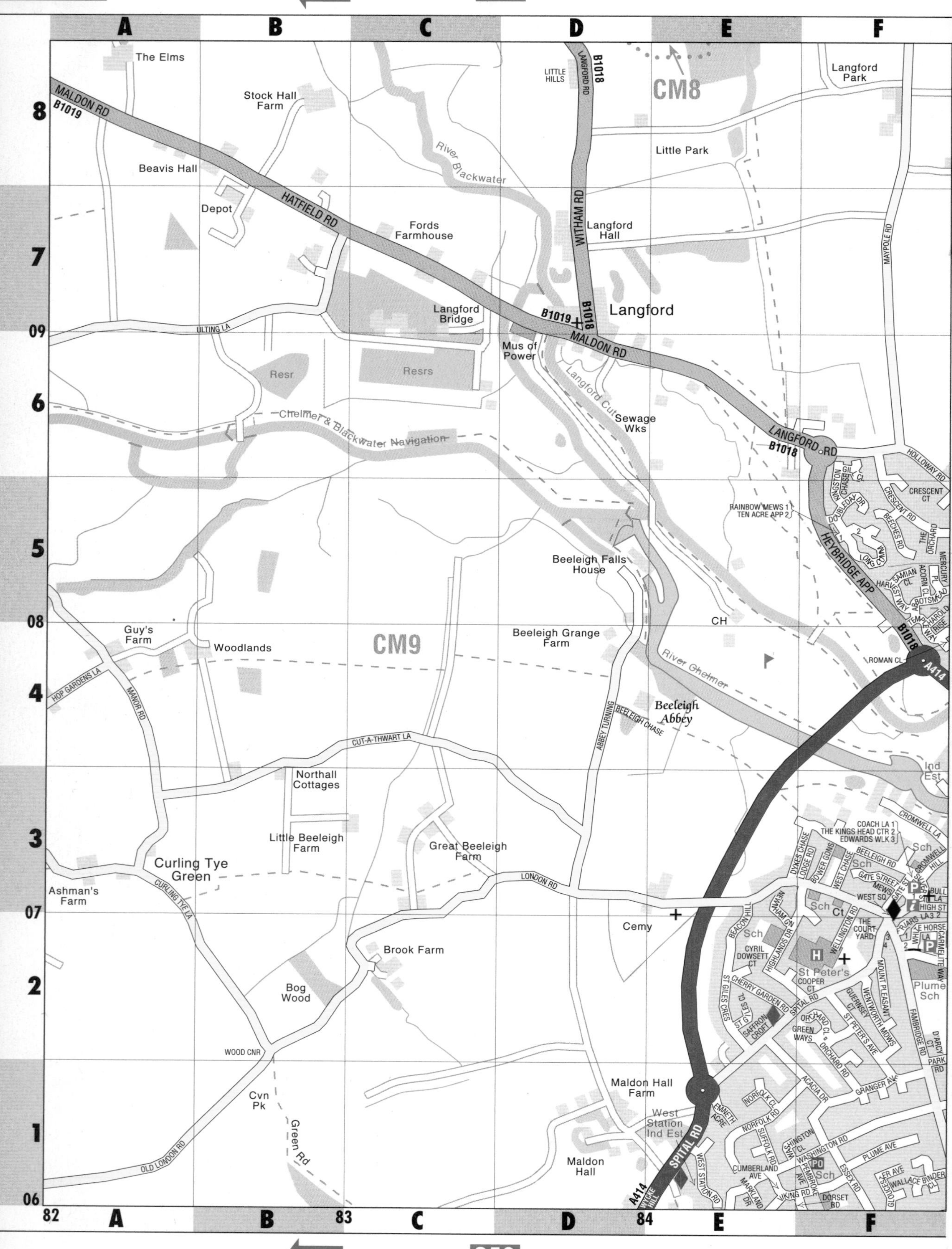

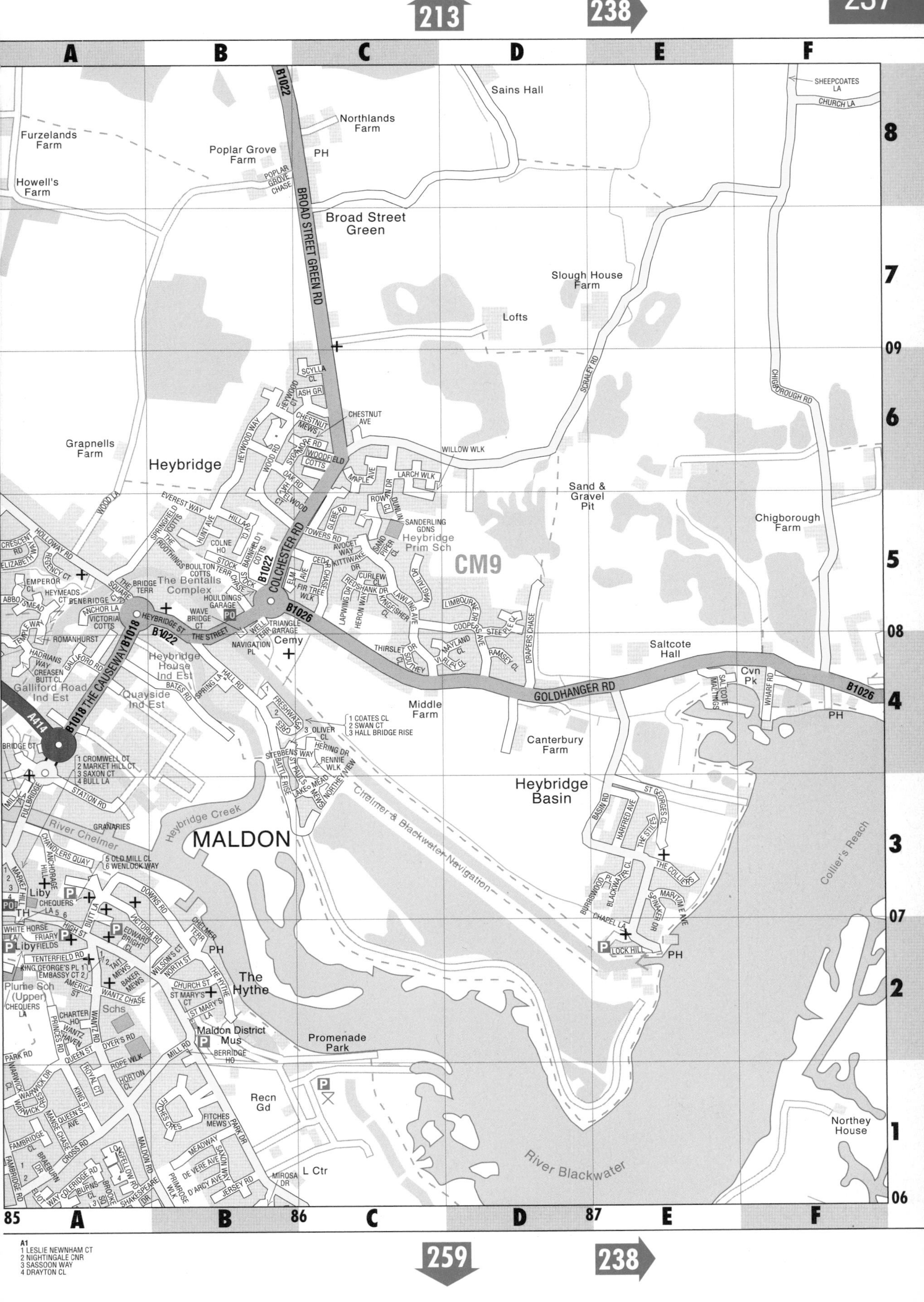

A B C D E F

8

7

09

6

5

08

4

3

07

2

1

06

SHEEPCOATES LA
CHURCH LA

Sains Hall

Northlands Farm

Poplar Grove Farm

PH

Broad Street Green

Slough House Farm

Lofts

Chigborough Farm

Grapnells Farm

Heybridge

Sand & Gravel Pit

Chigborough Farm

CM9

CHIGBOROUGH RD

SCHRAFT RD

WILLOW WLK

LARCH WLK

Heybridge Prim Sch

The Bentalls Complex

Houldings Garage

Triangle Garage

Navigation PL

Cemy

GOLDHANGER RD

Saltcote Hall

Cvn Pk

SALCOTE MALTINGS

WHARF RD

B1026

PH

Middle Farm

1 COATES CL
2 SWAN CT
3 HALL BRIDGE RISE

Canterbury Farm

Heybridge Basin

Chelmer & Blackwater Navigation

BASIN RD

ST GEORGES CL

HARFRED AVE

THE STIFES

THE COLLIERS

Colliers Reach

BURBWOOD

BLACKWATER CL

MARITIME AVE

SPARKER DR

CHAPEL LA

Lock Hill

PH

MALDON

River Chelmer

Heybridge Creek

GRANARIES

5 OLD MILL CL
6 WENLOCK WAY

Liby

CHEQUERS

P

WHITE HORSE

FRIARY

Libyfields

Tenterfield Rd

KING GEORGE'S PL 1
EMBASSY CT 2

Plume Sch (Upper)

CHEQUERS LA

Schs

The Hythe

PH

Maldon District Mus

Promenade Park

Recn Gd

Northey House

River Blackwater

L Ctr

A1
1 LESLIE NEWNHAM CT
2 NIGHTINGALE CNR
3 SASSOON WAY
4 DRAYTON CL

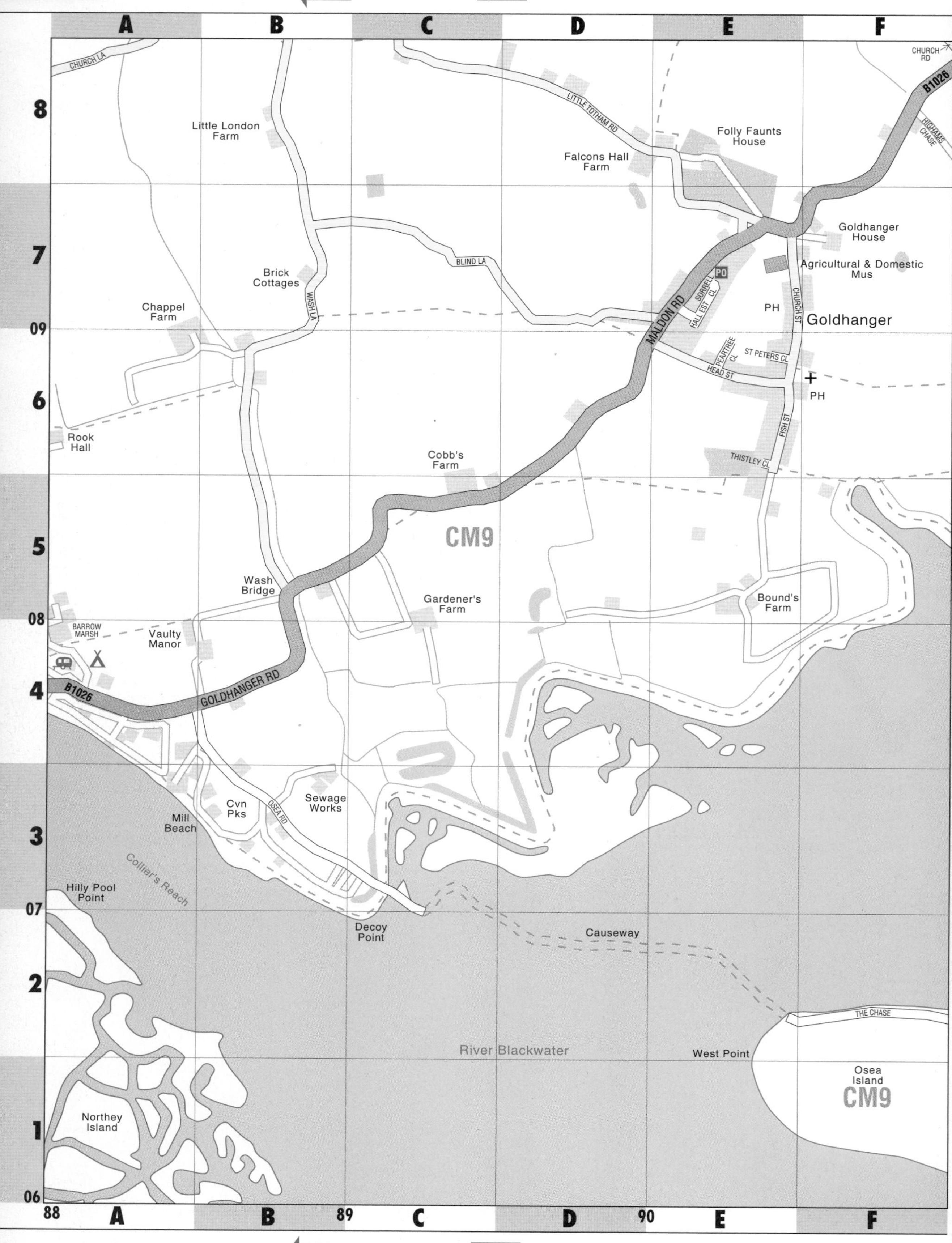

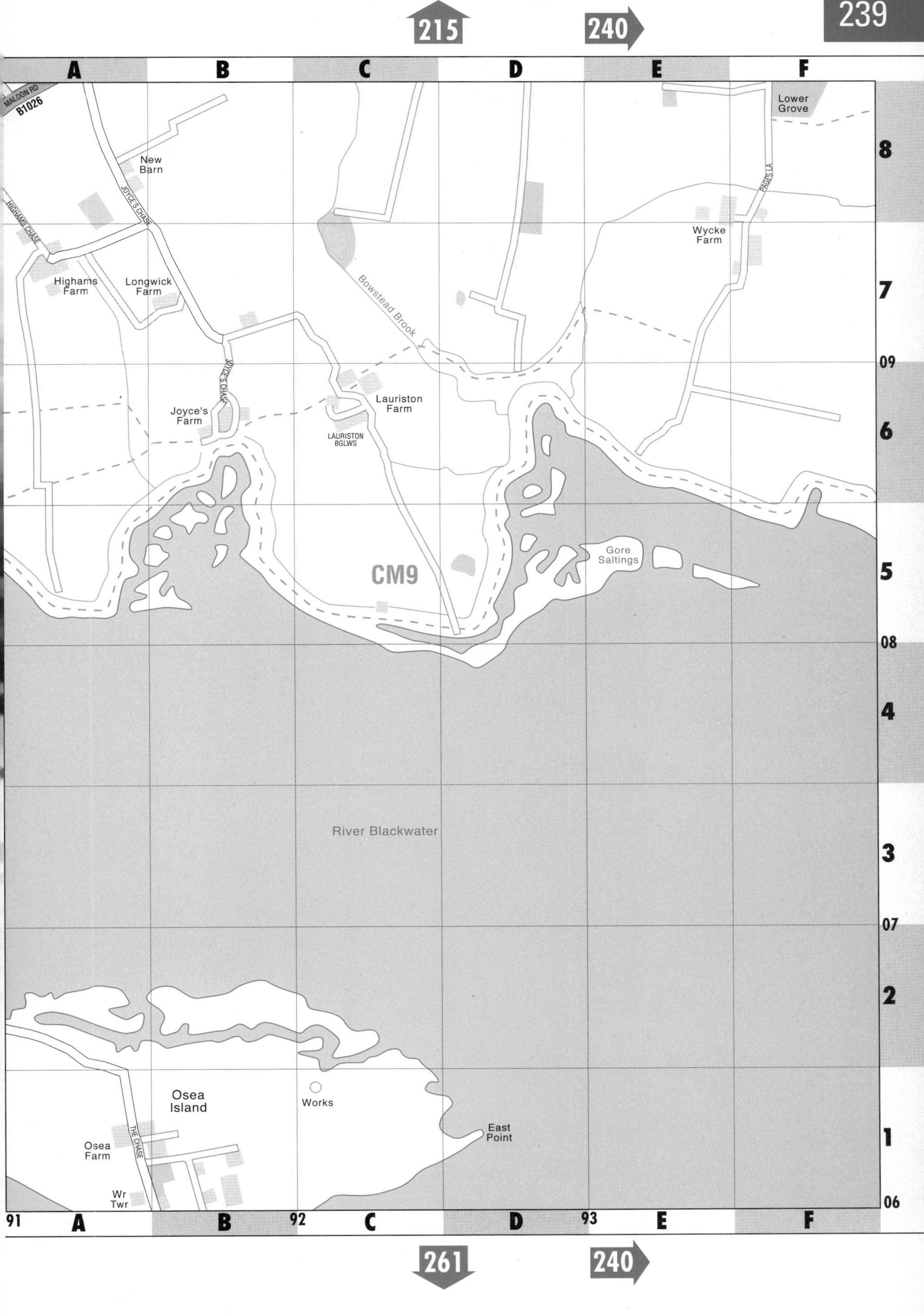

A   B   C   D   E   F

8

7

CM9

09

6

Boreham & Profits Farm

Rolls Farm

Bohuns Hall

Thistly Rd

Tollesbury

Mell Rd   MONKS WLK   WYCKE LA

Mell Farm

Wick Farm

Decoy Farm

Left Decoy Marshes

Mill Farm Marshes

Mill Creek

Mill Point

5

08

4

River Blackwater

3

07

2

1

St Lawrence

CM0   MOUNTVIEW PH   The Stone

SEA VIEW PROM   OYSTER COTTS

RIVERTON DR   MAIN RD

ST LAWRENCE DR   SEA VIEW PAR

TINNOCKS LA

06

94   A   B   95   C   D   96   E   F

PRENTICE HALL LA

A B C D E F

8
7
09
6
5
08
4
3
07
2
1
06

CM9

River Blackwater

Jetty

Pewet
Island

SHOEMENDERS
LA

Cvn
Pk
PARKER
CT

PO

Bradwell
Waterside

B1021

OLD
COASTGUARD
COTTS

PH

Mast

Marina

Bradwell Creek

TRUSSES RD

Westwick
Farm

WATERSIDE RD

WOODYARDS

Down
Westwick

CM0

Orplands

ORPLANDS
COTTS

Kennel
Barn

MALDON RD

MALDON RD

B1021

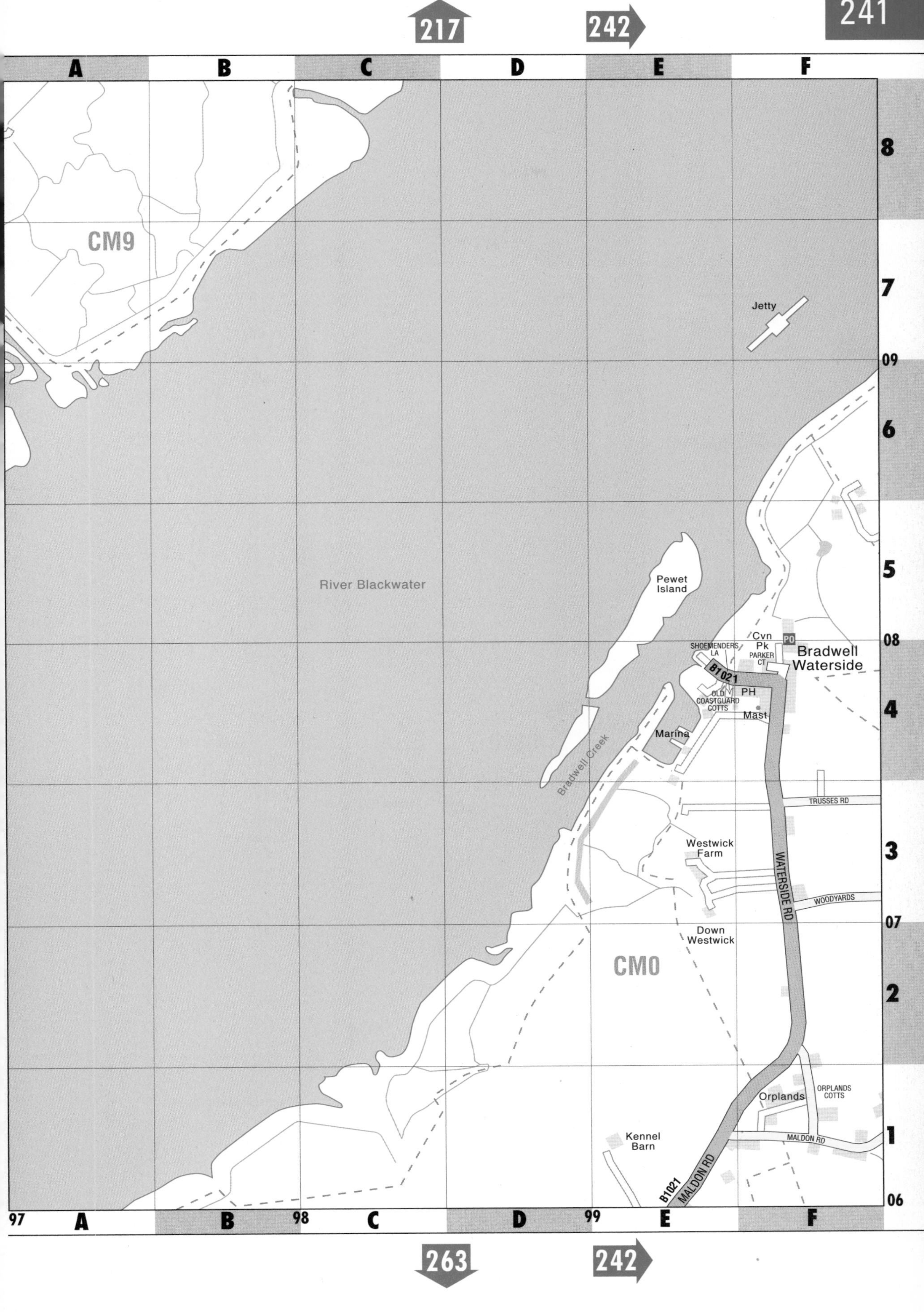

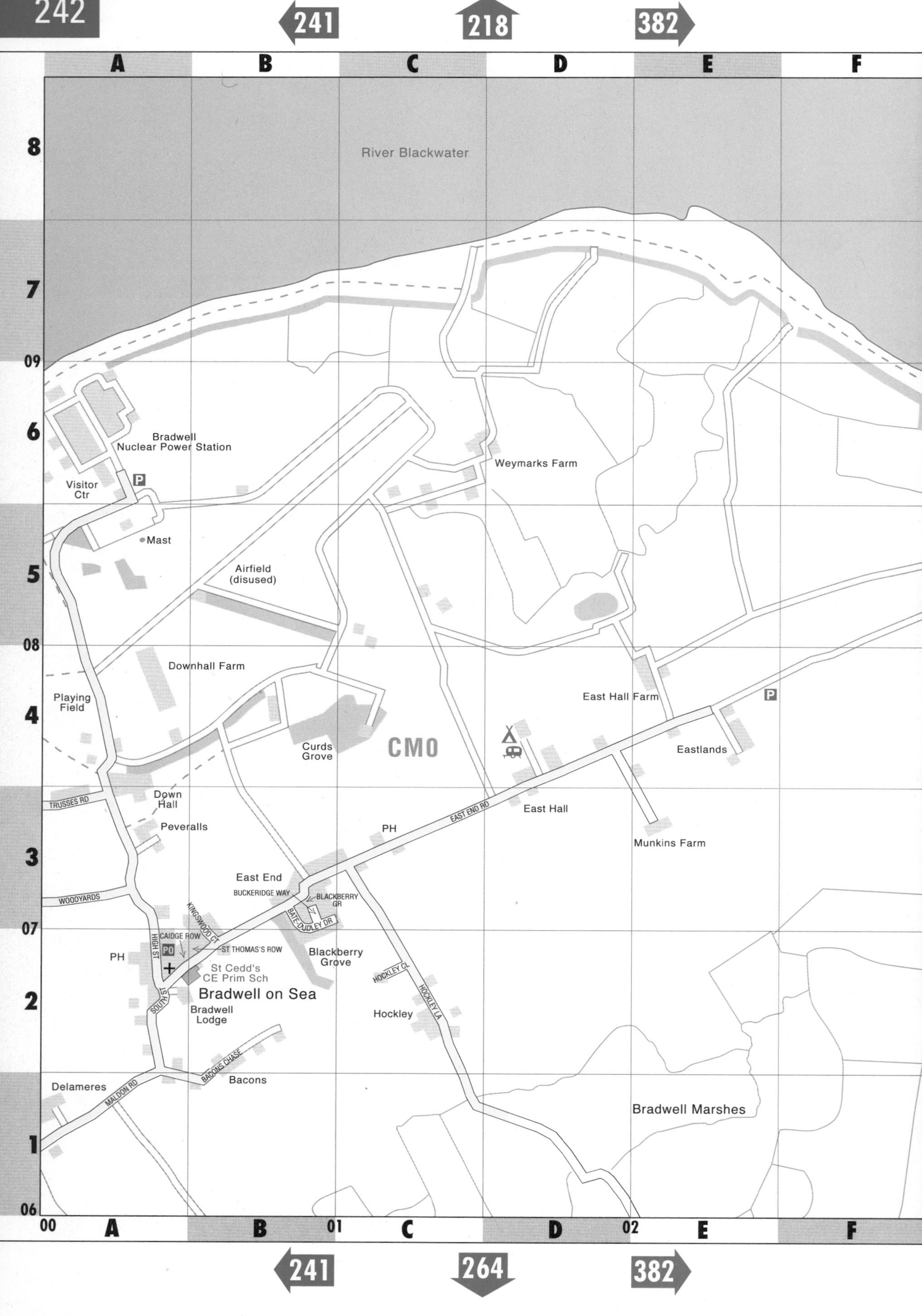

A B C D E F

8

River Blackwater

7

09

6

Bradwell
Nuclear Power Station

Visitor
Ctr

P

Mast

Weymarks Farm

5

Airfield
(disused)

08

Downhall Farm

East Hall Farm

P

Playing
Field

4

CMO

Curds
Grove

Eastlands

TRUSSES RD

Down
Hall

Peveralls

PH

EAST END RD

East Hall

3

East End

BUCKERIDGE WAY

WOODYARDS

BLACKBERRY
GR

Munkins Farm

07

KINGSWOOD CT

KATE DUDLEY DR

CAIDGE ROW

PO

ST THOMAS'S ROW

Blackberry
Grove

PH

HIGH ST

St Cedd's
CE Prim Sch

HOCKLEY CL

HOCKLEY LA

2

Bradwell on Sea

SOUTH ST

Bradwell
Lodge

Hockley

BACONS CHASE

MALDON RD

Bacons

Delameres

Bradwell Marshes

1

06

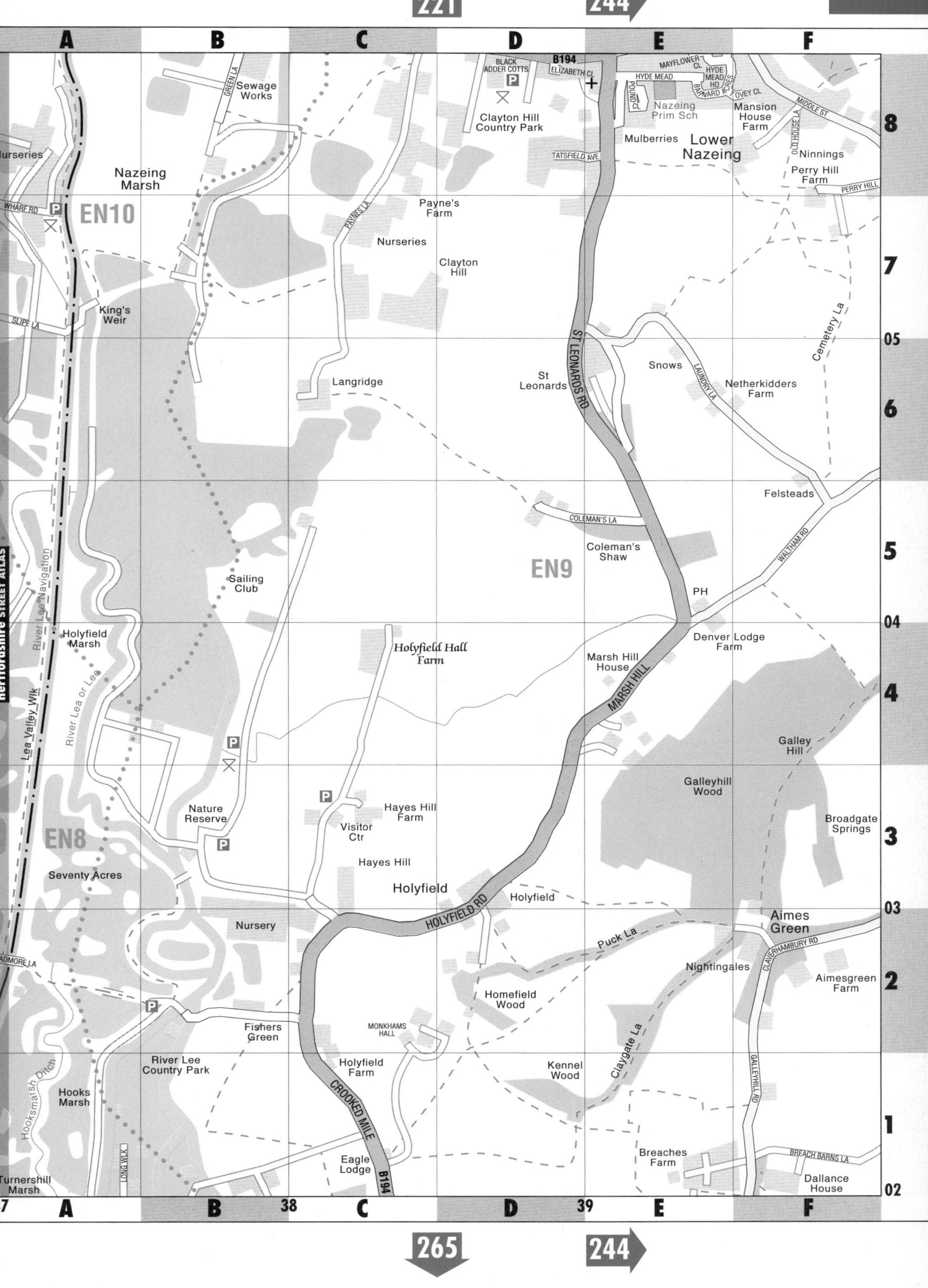

A B C D E F

8

7

05

6

5

04

4

3

03

2

1

02

Nurseries

Nazeing
Marsh

WHARF RD

EN10

SLIPE LA

King's
Weir

GREEN LA

Sewage
Works

PAYNES LA

Langridge

Sailing
Club

Nature
Reserve

EN8

Seventy Acres

Nursery

Fishers
Green

River Lee
Country Park

Hooks
Marsh

Turnershill
Marsh

CADMORE LA

Hooksmash Ditch

LONGS WLK

Lea Valley Wlk

River Lee Navigation

River Lea or Lee

Hertfordshire STREET ATLAS

BLACK
ADDER COTTS

Clayton Hill
Country Park

TATSFIELD AVE

Payne's
Farm

Nurseries

Clayton
Hill

Holyfield Hall
Farm

Holyfield
Marsh

Hayes Hill
Farm

Visitor
Ctr

Hayes Hill

Holyfield

MONKHAMS
HALL

Holyfield
Farm

CROOKED MILE

Eagle
Lodge

B194

HOLYFIELD RD

Homefield
Wood

Kennel
Wood

B194
ELIZABETH CL

Nazeing
Prim Sch

HYDE MEAD

POUND CL

MAYFLOWER
CL

HYDE
MEAD
HO

BYNARD K

OVEY CL

Mulberries

Lower
Nazeing

Mansion
House
Farm

MIDDLE ST

OLD HOUSE LA

Ninnings

Perry Hill
Farm

PERRY HILL

ST LEONARDS RD

St
Leonards

Snows

LAUNDRY LA

Netherkidders
Farm

Cemetery La

EN9

COLEMAN'S LA

Coleman's
Shaw

PH

WALTHAM RD

Felsteads

Denver Lodge
Farm

Marsh Hill
House

MARSH HILL

Galley
Hill

Galleyhill
Wood

Broadgate
Springs

Holyfield

Puck La

Aimes
Green

CLAVERHAMBURY RD

Nightingales

Aimesgreen
Farm

Claygate La

GALLEYHILL RD

Breaches
Farm

BREACH BARNS LA

Dallance
House

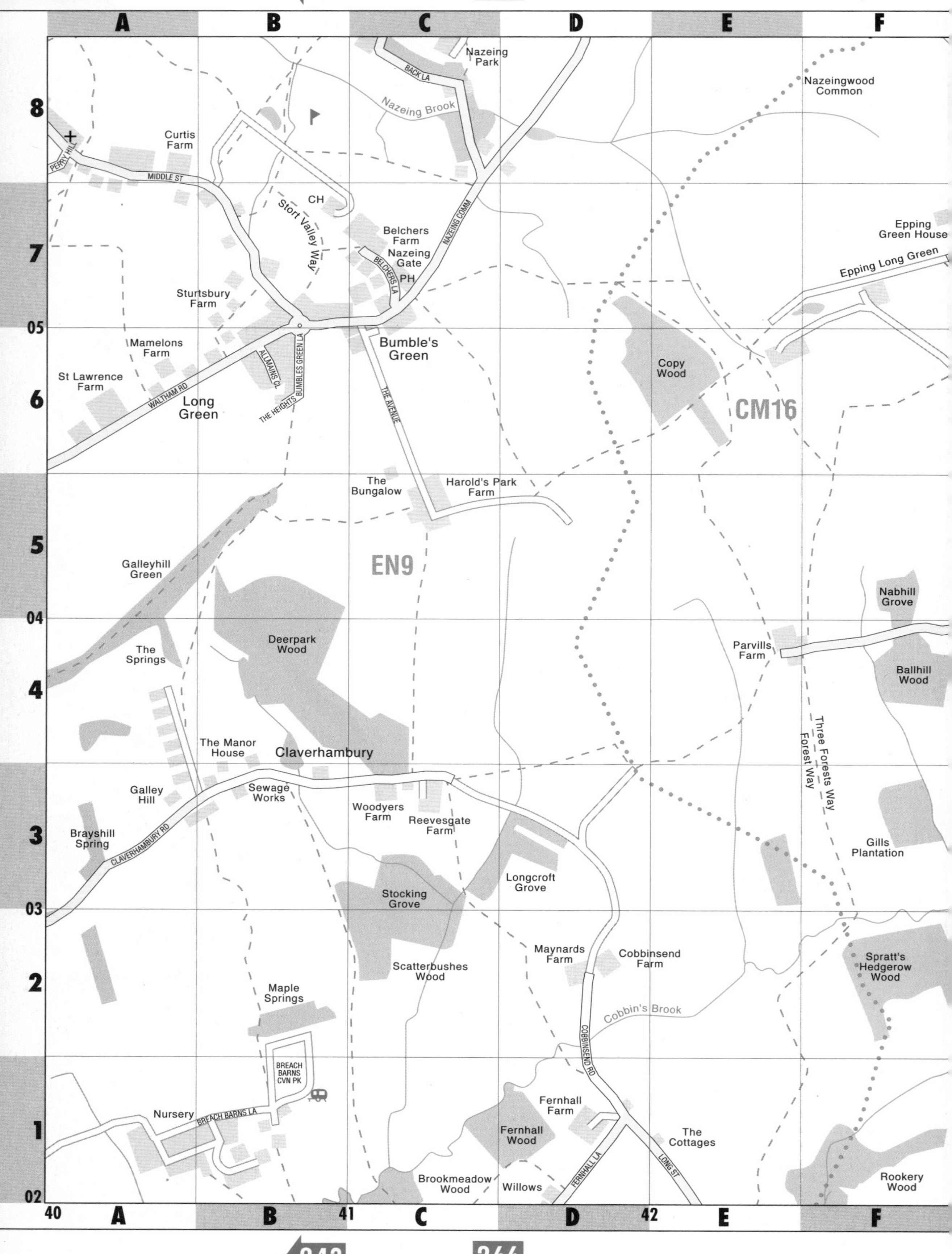

Nazeing Park
Nazeingwood Common
BACK LA
Nazeing Brook
Curtis Farm
CH
Stort Valley Way
Belchers Farm
Nazeing Gate
PH
Epping Green House
Epping Long Green
MIDDLE ST
PERRY HILL
Sturtsbury Farm
BELCHERS LA
NAZEING COMM
Mamelons Farm
ALLMAINS CL
BUMBLES GREEN LA
Bumble's Green
Copy Wood
CM16
St Lawrence Farm
WALTHAM RD
Long Green
THE HEIGHTS
THE AVENUE
The Bungalow
Harold's Park Farm
Galleyhill Green
EN9
Nabhill Grove
The Springs
Deerpark Wood
Parvills Farm
Ballhill Wood
The Manor House
Claverhambury
Three Forests Way
Forest Way
Galley Hill
Sewage Works
Woodyers Farm
Reevesgate Farm
Gills Plantation
Brayshill Spring
CLAVERHAMBURY RD
Longcroft Grove
Stocking Grove
Scatterbushes Wood
Maynards Farm
Cobbinsend Farm
Spratt's Hedgerow Wood
Maple Springs
Cobbin's Brook
COBBINSEND RD
BREACH BARNS CVN PK
Nursery
BREACH BARNS LA
Fernhall Farm
Fernhall Wood
FERNHALL LA
The Cottages
LONG ST
Brookmeadow Wood
Willows
Rookery Wood

40 A B 41 C D 42 E F

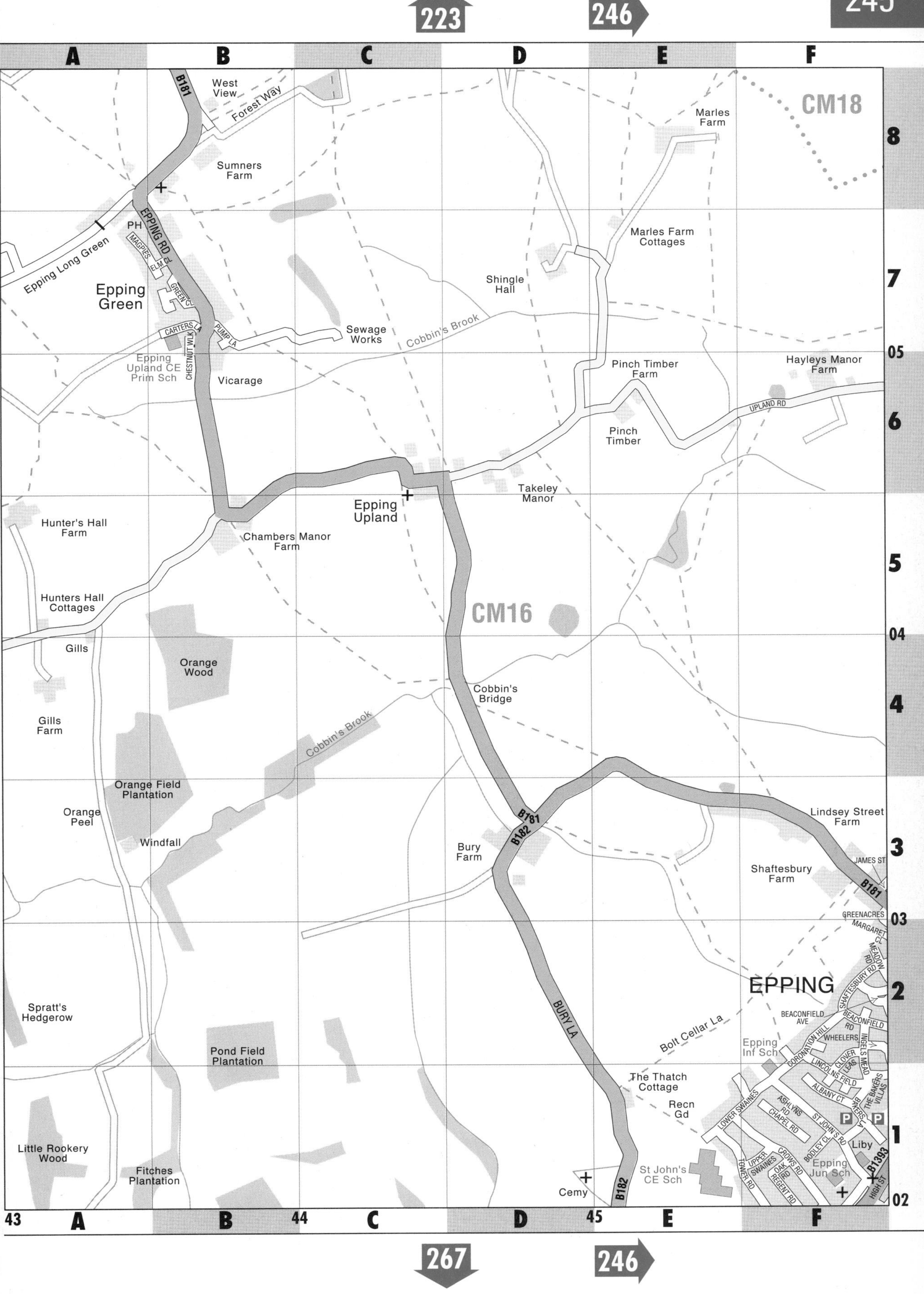

CM18

CM16

CM18 is the postcode area shown

West View
Forest Way
Sumners Farm
Epping Long Green
PH
EPPING RD
MAGPIES
ELM PL
GREEN LA
Epping Green
CARTERS LA
CHESTNUT WLK
PUMP LA
Epping Upland CE Prim Sch
Vicarage
Sewage Works
Cobbin's Brook
Shingle Hall
Marles Farm
Marles Farm Cottages
Pinch Timber Farm
Pinch Timber
Takeley Manor
Hayleys Manor Farm
UPLAND RD
Epping Upland
Hunter's Hall Farm
Chambers Manor Farm
Hunters Hall Cottages
Gills
Orange Wood
Gills Farm
Orange Field Plantation
Orange Peel
Windfall
Cobbin's Brook
Cobbin's Bridge
B181
B182
Bury Farm
Lindsey Street Farm
Shaftesbury Farm
JAMES ST
B181
GREENACRES
MARGARET
MEADOW RD
EPPING
SHAFTESBURY RD
BEACONFIELD AVE
BEACONFIELD RD
WHEELERS
Epping Inf Sch
CORONATION HILL
INGLES MEAD
THE BAKERS
VILLAS
Spratt's Hedgerow
Pond Field Plantation
Bolt Cellar La
LINCOLNS FIELD
CLOVER
ALBANY CT
ST JOHN'S RD
BRAYS LA
The Thatch Cottage
Recn Gd
LOWER SWAINES
ASHLYNS
CHAPEL RD
CROWS RD
BODLEY CL
Epping Jun Sch
Liby
B1393
Little Rookery Wood
Fitches Plantation
UPPER SWAINES
TOWER RD
OAK LA
REGENT RD
St John's CE Sch
B182
Cemy
HIGH ST

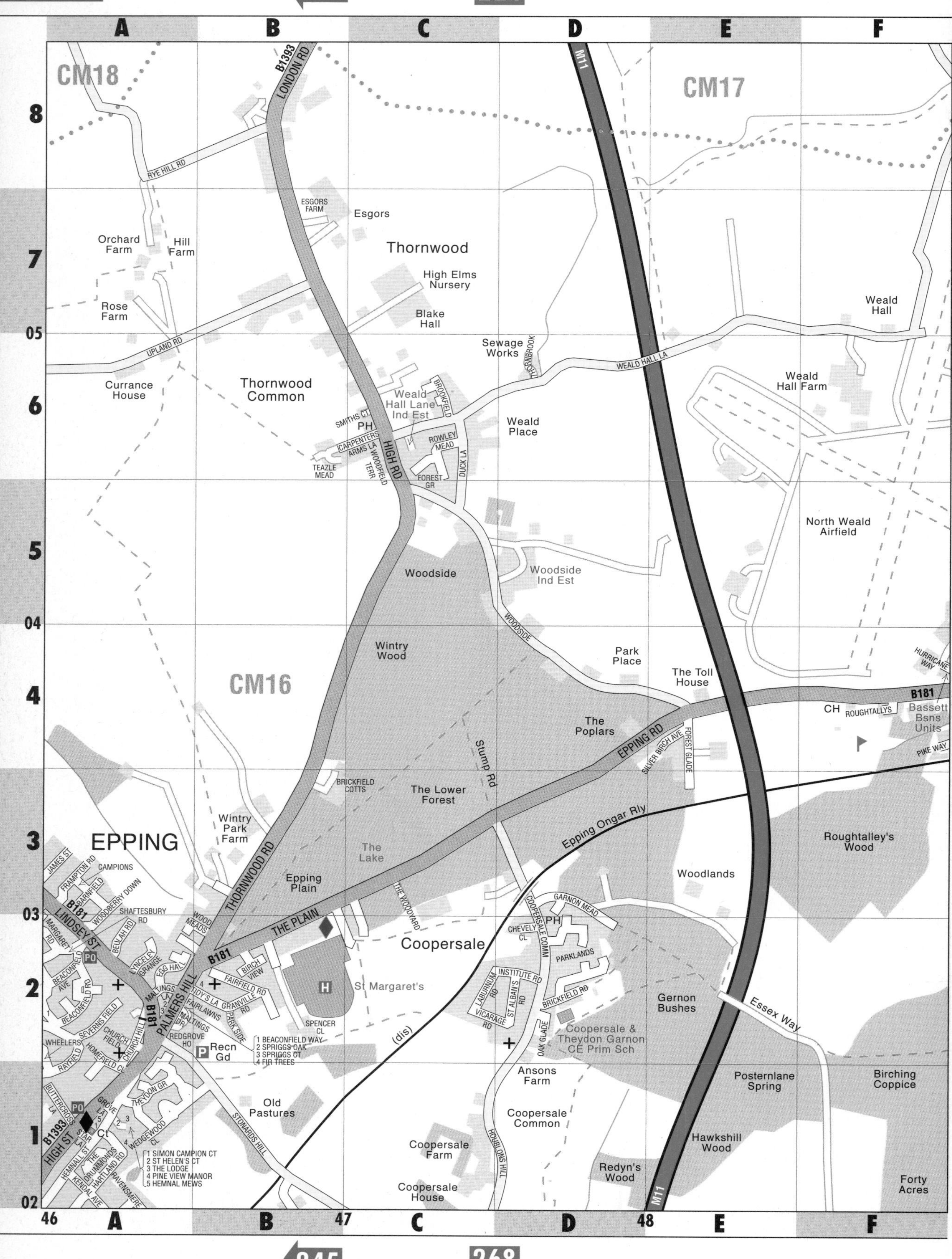

CM18

RYE HILL RD

Orchard
Farm

Hill
Farm

Rose
Farm

UPLAND RD

Currance
House

Thornwood
Common

SMITHS CTS

PH

CARPENTERS
ARMS LA

TEAZLE
MEAD

WOODFIELD
TERR

HIGH RD

LONDON RD

B1393

ESGORS
FARM

Esgors

Thornwood

High Elms
Nursery

Blake
Hall

Sewage
Works

Weald
Hall Lane
Ind Est

BROOMFIELD

ROWLEY
MEAD

FOREST
GR

DUCK LA

HUSSENBROOK

WEALD HALL LA

Weald
Place

Weald
Hall

CM17

Weald
Hall Farm

Weald Place

North Weald
Airfield

Woodside

Woodside
Ind Est

WOODSIDE

CM16

Wintry
Wood

Park
Place

The Toll
House

HURRICANE
WAY

Roughtalley's
Wood

The
Poplars

EPPING RD

SILVER BIRCH AVE

FOREST GLADE

CH ROUGHTALLYS

B181

Bassett
Bsns
Units

PIKE WAY

EPPING

Wintry
Park
Farm

Stump Rd

The Lower
Forest

Epping Ongar Rly

Woodlands

JAMES ST

FRAMPTON RD

CAMPIONS

BARFIELD

WOODBERRY DOWN

SHAFTESBURY
RD

B181

LINDSEY ST

THORNWOOD RD

The
Lake

Epping
Plain

THE PLAIN

THE WOODYARD

Coopersale

GARNON MEAD

COOPERSALE COMMON

PH

Parklands

Gernon
Bushes

Essex Way

Posternlane
Spring

Birching
Coppice

BELLAIR RD

CSG HALL

KINGS
GRANGE

LINDSEY'S LA

BIRCH
SIDE

GRANVILLE
CL

FAIRLAWNS

BIRCH
VIEW

FAIRFIELD RD

WOOD
MEADS

MALTINGS

REDGROVE
HO

PALMERS HILL

CHURCH HILL

BASIN SIDE

SPENCER
CL

H

St Margaret's

1 BEACONFIELD WAY
2 SPRIGGS OAK
3 SPRIGGS CT
4 FIR TREES

Recn
Gd

P

(dis)

LABURNUM
CL

ST ALBAN'S
RD

INSTITUTE RD

VICARAGE

BRICKFIELD RD

CHEVELY
CL

OAK GLADE

Coopersale &
Theydon Garnon
CE Prim Sch

Ansons
Farm

Coopersale
Common

HOBBONS HILL

Coopersale
Farm

Coopersale
House

Redyn's
Wood

Hawkshill
Wood

Forty
Acres

BEACONSFIELD
AVE

SEVERNS FIELD

WHEELERS

CHURCH
FIELD

HOMEFIELD CL

RATFIELD

BUTTERCROFT

B1393

HIGH ST

CT

HEMNAL ST

THE
BRUMMELLS

HARTLAND RD

KENDAL AVE

RAVENSMERE

PO

GROVE
LA

THEYDON GR

WEDGEWOOD
CL

STONARDS HILL

Old
Pastures

1 SIMON CAMPION CT
2 ST HELEN'S CT
3 THE LODGE
4 PINE VIEW MANOR
5 HEMNAL MEWS

MT11

M11

Brickfield
Cotts

BRICKFIELD
COTTS

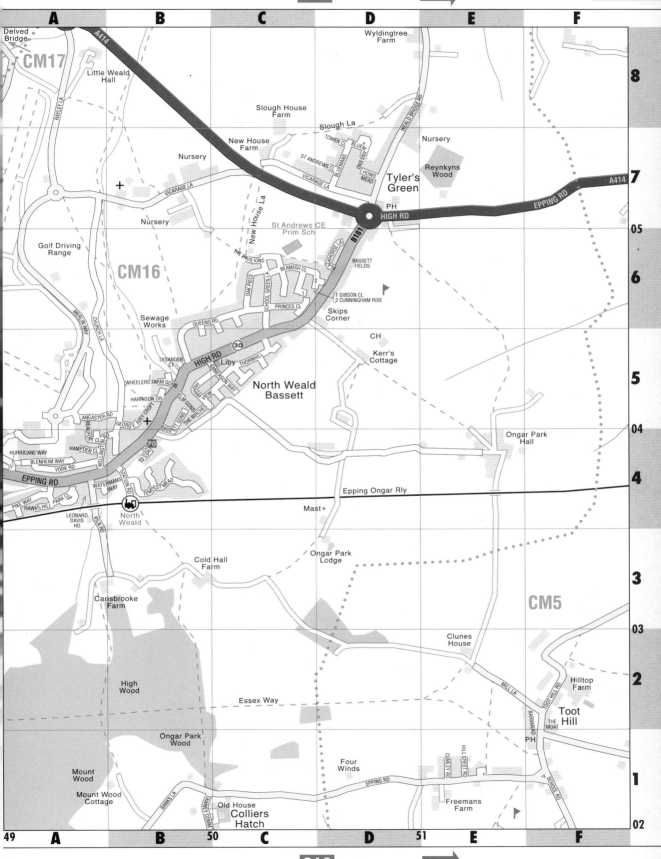

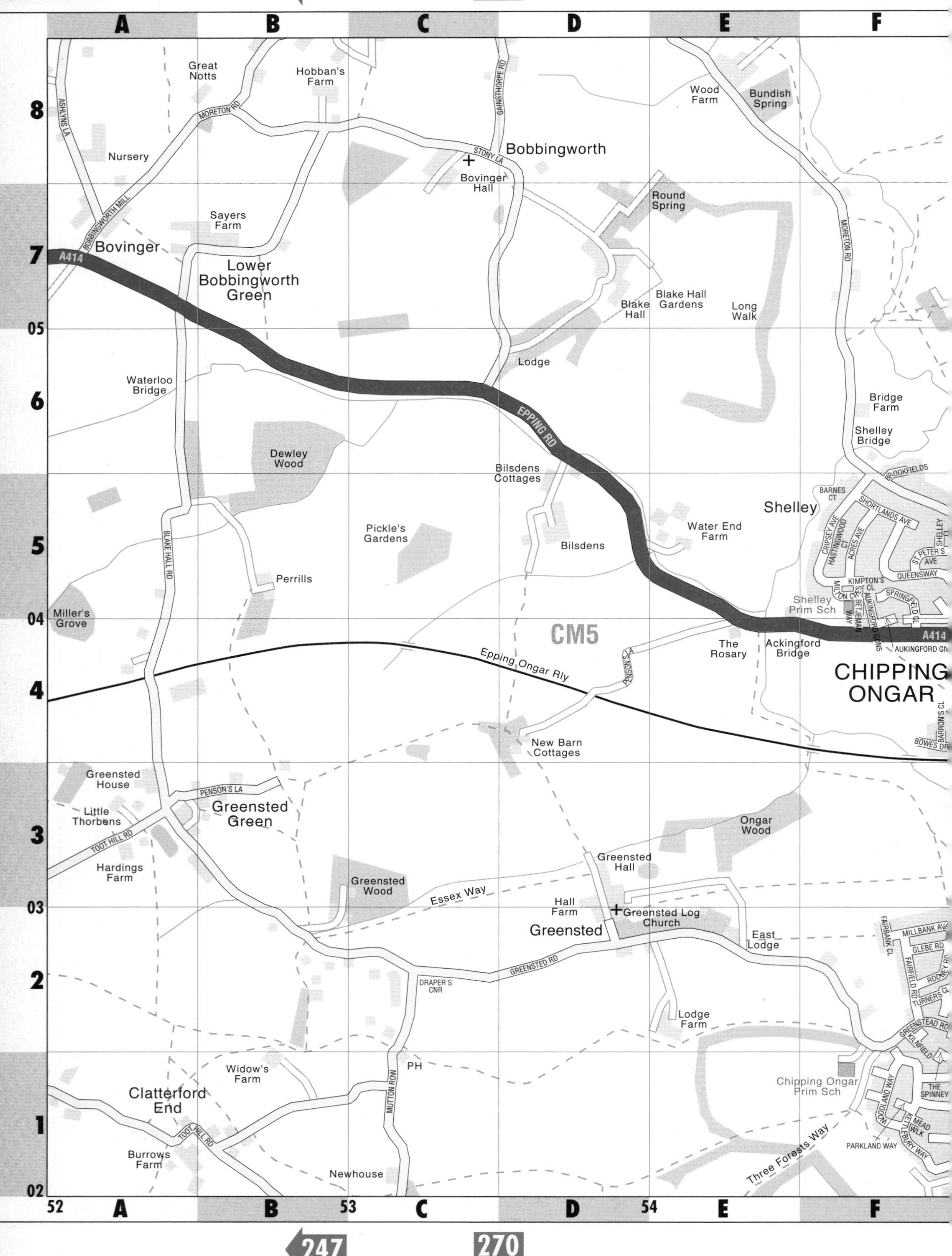
A
B
C
D
E
F
8
7
05
6
5
04
4
3
03
2
1
02
52
53
54
Great Notts
Hobban's Farm
GAINSTHORPE RD
Wood Farm
Bundish Spring
ASHLYNS LA
MORETON RD
Nursery
Bobbingworth
STONY LA
Bovinger Hall
Round Spring
BOBBINGWORTH MILL
Sayers Farm
MORETON RD
Bovinger
A414
Lower Bobbingworth Green
Blake Hall Gardens
Blake Hall
Long Walk
Lodge
Waterloo Bridge
Bridge Farm
EPPING RD
Shelley Bridge
Dewley Wood
Bilsdens Cottages
BROOKFIELDS
BARNES CT
Shelley
SHORTLANDS AVE
Pickle's Gardens
Water End Farm
Bilsdens
BLAKE HALL RD
Perrills
QUEENSWAY
Shelley Prim Sch
Miller's Grove
CM5
A414
The Rosary
Ackingford Bridge
AUKINGFORD GN
Epping Ongar Rly
PENSON'S LA
CHIPPING ONGAR
New Barn Cottages
BOWES DR
BARRON'S CL
Greensted House
PENSON'S LA
Little Thorbens
Greensted Green
TOOT HILL RD
Ongar Wood
Hardings Farm
Greensted Hall
Greensted Wood
Essex Way
Hall Farm
Greensted Log Church
Greensted
East Lodge
FAIRBANK CL
MILLBANK AVE
GLEBE RD
FAIRFIELD RD
GREENSTED RD
DRAPER'S CNR
Lodge Farm
GREENSTEAD RD
KILNFIELD
PH
Widow's Farm
Chipping Ongar Prim Sch
Clatterford End
MUTTON ROW
WOODLAND WAY
THE SPINNEY
Three Forests Way
TOOT HILL RD
PARKLAND WAY
KETTLEBURY WAY
Burrows Farm
Newhouse

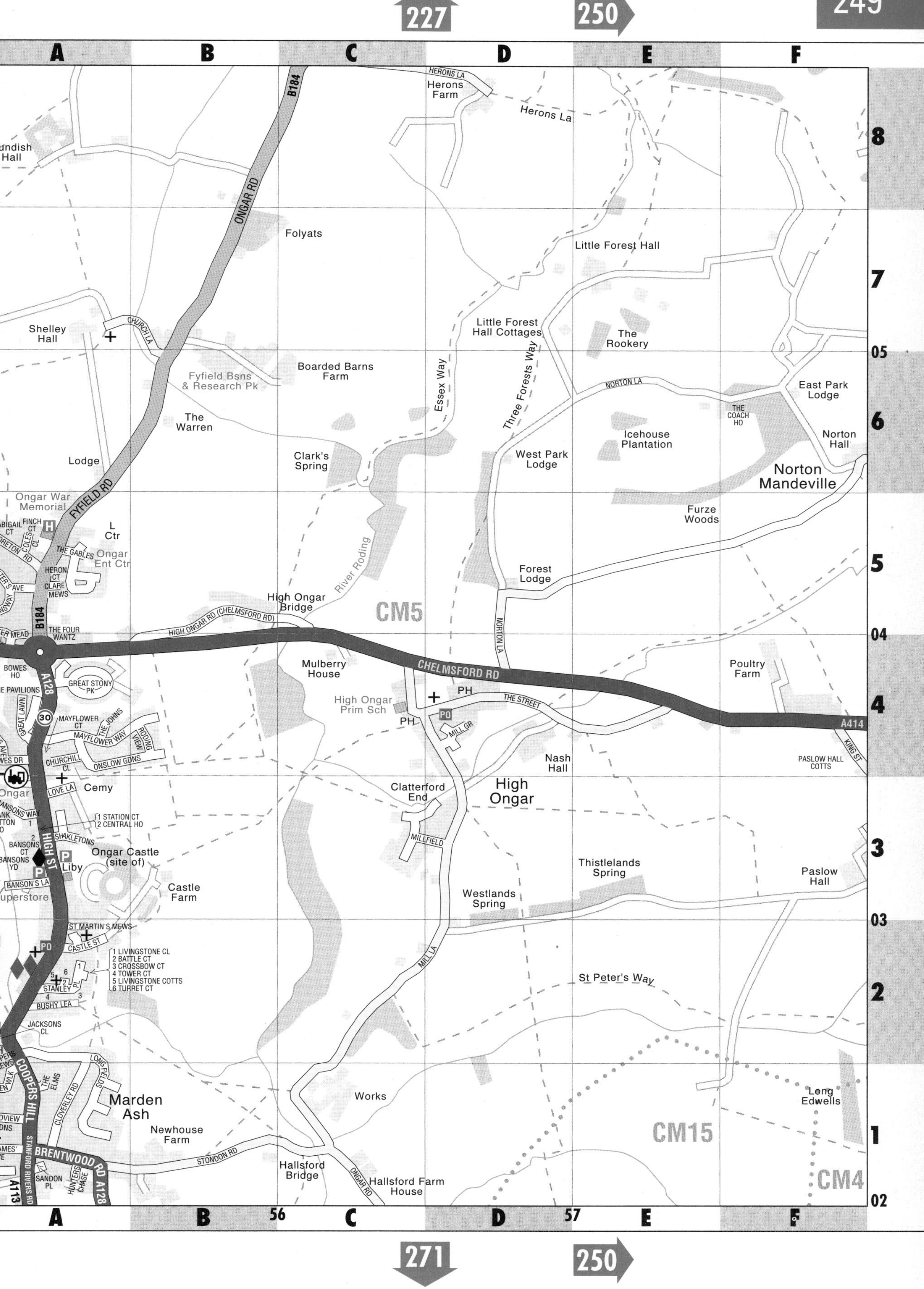

249
228

A B C D E F

8

7

05

6

Hedge Rows

Rockhills

Hodgkins Farm

NORTON HEATH RD

Hulke's Farm

Bonsgrove

Rockhill Cottages

Spriggs

Offin's Cottages

WILLINGALE RD

Long Spring

Norton Glebe House

NORTON LA

Dodd's Farm

Ladylands

+ Norton Mandeville

5

04

CM5

Chevers Hall

Norton Manor

Norton Heath

Tyler's Farm

Readings Farm

PH

A41

CM4

Dovefields Farm

FINGRITH HALL LA

Spurriers

The Orchard

4

Cozen's Farm

A414

CHELMSFORD RD

Blewgates Farm

The Manor House

3

03

Old Wythers Farm

KING ST

Lodge

King Street Farm

ROOKERY RD

Rookery Farm

FINGRITH HALL COTTS

SPRIGGS LA

FINGRITH HALL

Saybridge Lodge

Saybridge Cottage

PH

2

NINE ASHES FARM COTTS

Nine Ashes Farm

Nine Ashes

Orchard Manor

1

St Peter's Way

Sparks Farm

Larkins Farm

NINE ASHES RD

NINE ASHES RD

Wells Farm

Redrose Farm

REDROSE LA

ELM COU PK

02

Blackmore Prim Sch

WOOLARD WAY

WOOLARD WAY

FINGRITH RD

ORCHARD PIECE

CHELMSFORD RD

58 A 59 B C 60 D E F

A B C D E F

8 7 6 5 4 3 2 1

05 04 03 02

Brookend Farm
PIGSTYE GREEN RD
Telfords
CM5
Butlers Farm
Radley Green Farm
Colleybridge Farm
Home Farm
Red House
Radley Green
Lucas's La
Parnells
BASSETT'S LA
PH
Brainwood Farm
RADLEY GREEN RD
Ewson's Farm
Bassett's Farm
RADLEY GREEN RD
A414
PH
ONGAR RD
Hawkin Smith's Farmhouse
WYSE'S RD
Ewson's Bridge
Hand's Farm
CM1
Horsfrith Park Farm
Ewson's Brook
Horsfrithpark Wood
Fithlers Hall Farm
CM4
INGRAM COTTS
Ward's Farm
HIGHWOOD RD
Cat & Kittens Cottages
POOL'S LA
Fingrith Hall Farm
Gorrell's Farm
Awes Farm
Old Barns
HIGHWOOD COTTS
OLD BARNS LA
Budd's Farm
BLACKMORE RD
COCK LA
METSONS LA
INGATESTONE RD
Ellis Wood
High Woods
Barrow Farm
Parsons Spring
SPRIGGS LA
Barrow Wood
Highwood Cottage
New Farm
Sprigg's Farm
Quince Hall
Birch Spring
Monk's & Barrow's Farm
Elm Farm
Howlett's Hall
Deerslade Wood
CHELMSFORD RD

61 A B 62 C D 63 E F

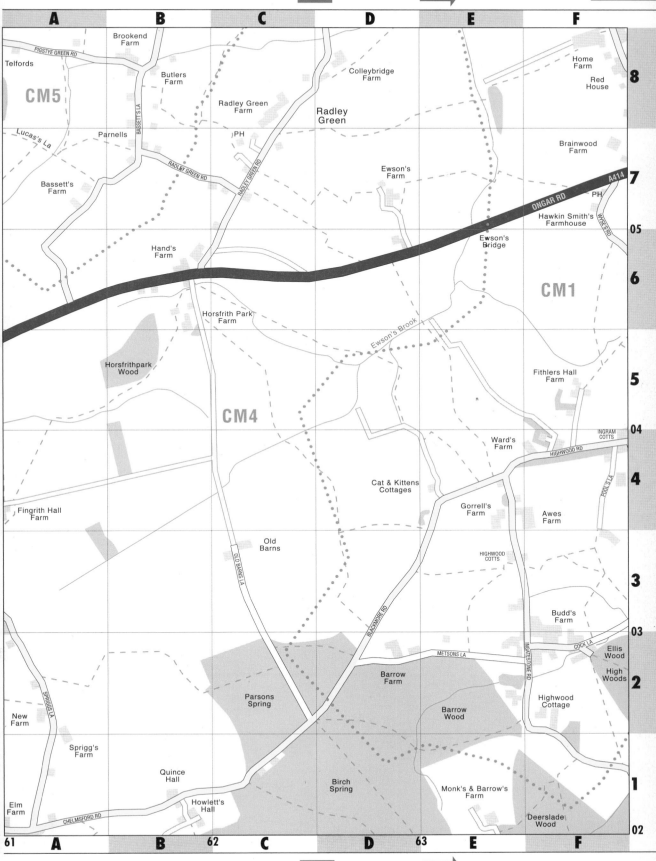

251 230

| | A | B | C | D | E | F |

8

Wellington House
Cooksmill Nursery

Range Cottage
ONGAR RD
A414
A414
ONGAR RD
BULMERS WAY
CHEQUERS RD
OXNEY MEAD
LODGE RD
HIGHWOOD RD
ROLLESTONS
THE SHRUBBERIES

Little Moor Hall

Little Oxney Green

7
Landview House
A414
Four Gables

Lady Grove

Halfway House

HIGHWOOD RD
CAUSEWAY COTTS

Roper's Farm

05
Wyse's Cottage

Lee Cottages
THE CAUSEWAY

Montpelier's Farm

6
WYSE'S RD
Bramwood Farm
Southridge Farm
Lee Wood
Lee Farm

Nursery
HIGHWOOD RD
Edney Common

5
Montague Farm
SPARROWS CL
Loves Green
PH
WOODSIDE COTTS
Sewage Works
Jordan's Farm
CM1
ENDER WOOD
NATHAN'S LA

04
Highwood Prim Sch
BUCKNELLS MEAD
Highwood
Little Edney Wood

4
Writtle Park Cotts
Writtle Park Farm
Writtle Park
Great Edney Wood

3
Chalk Hill
COCK LA
Mast
Baker's Wood
King Wood

03
Writtlepark Wood
Coptfold Hall
Coptfoldhall Farm
WRITTLE RD

2
High Woods
Parkponds Wood
Furness Wood
Hockley Shaw
Furness Farm
CM4
Park Lodge
Coptfold Farm Cottages

1
Whitegates
INGATESTONE RD
Redindyke Farm
Wells & Sheds
IVY BARNS LA
Chatterbox Wood
Bearman's Farm
Furze Hill
Hotel
A12
MAIN RD

02
Dawes Farm
Handley Green Farm

| 64 | A | B | 65 | C | D | 66 | E | F |

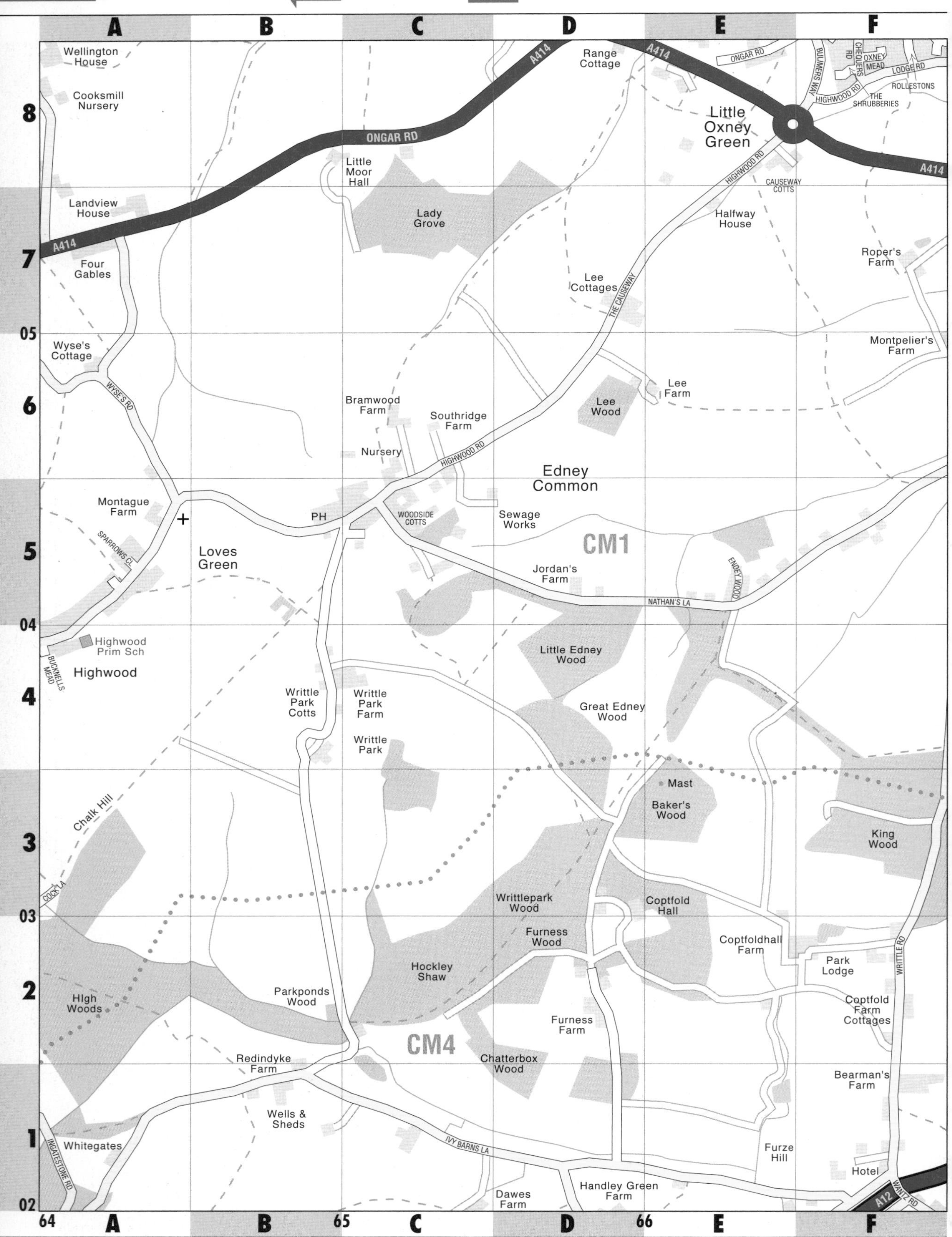

231

254

A B C D E F
8 7 05 6 5 04 4 3 03 2 1 02
68 69
Writtle
CHELMSFORD
Writtle Jun & Inf Schs
New Rollestons Farm
Lower Shakestons
Upper Shakestons
Cemy Crem
Widford Ind Est
WESTWAY
A1016
LONDON RD
A1114
A414
B1007
CM1
CM2
CM4
Britleys
Montpelier's Farm
Swanpond Plantation
Widford
St John's
Writtle Belt
Bumpstead's Farm
Widford Bridge
Moulsham Thrift Wood
Gable Cottages
Hylands Park
Hylands
South Wood
Home Farm
Elm Farm
Southwood Farm
Tower Belt
Lightfoot Spring
Elm Cottages
River Wid
Lower Belt
Chapel Wood
Killegrews Cottages
THREE MILE HILL
Killegrews
The Haven Farm
Lodge Farm
Hill Farm
A12
B1002
White's Place Farm
Bishopscourt
Durrant's Farm
White's Bridge
MALDON RD
WHITESBRIDGE LA
MARGARETTING RD
LONDON HILL
GOAT HALL LA
BEKESWELL LA
MILL HILL
BUTTS WAY
Sandy Brook
ROPER'S CHASE
MARGARETTING RD

275
254

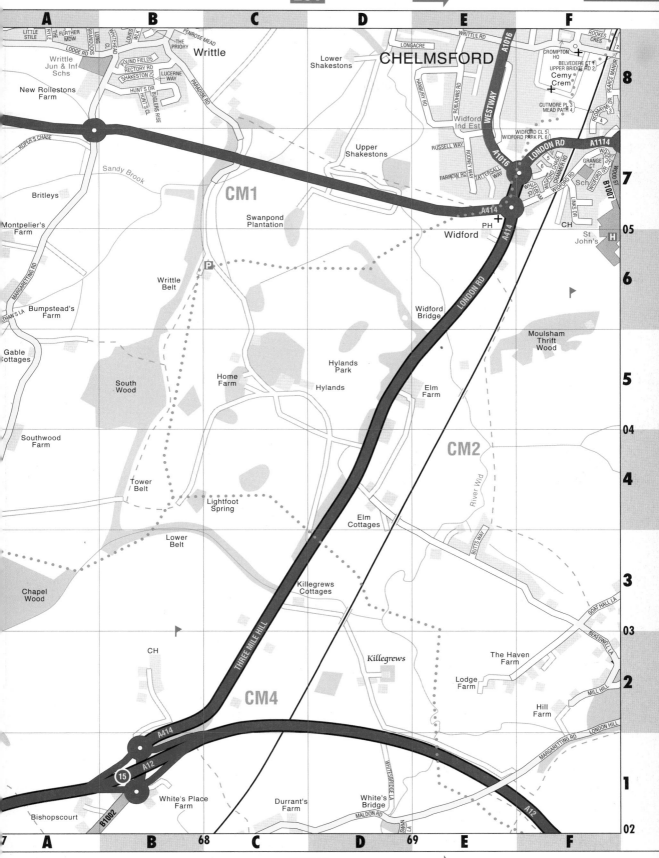

253
232

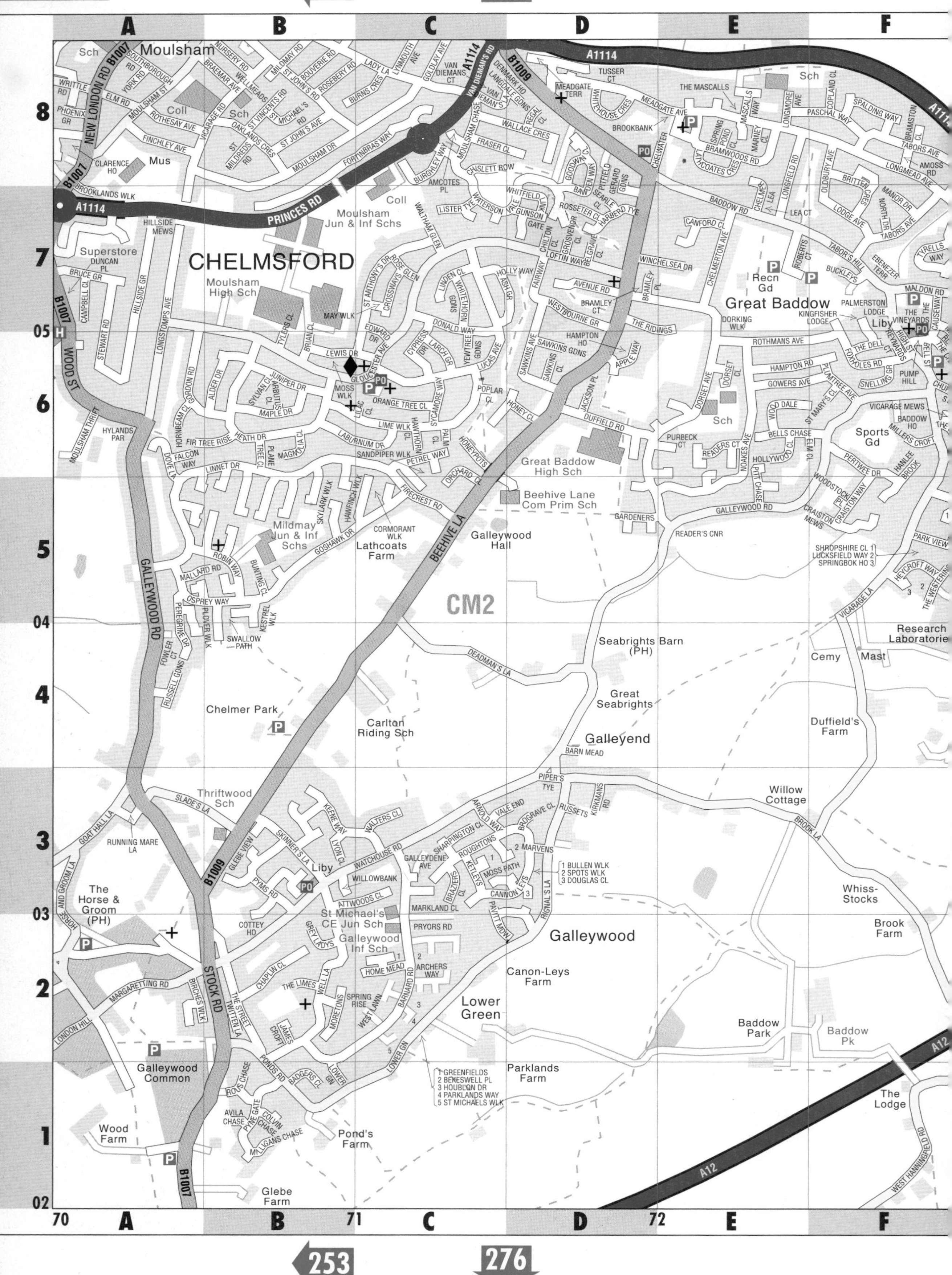
A
B
C
D
E
F
Moulsham
CHELMSFORD
Great Baddow
Galleyend
Galleywood
Lower Green
CM2
A1114
PRINCES RD
B1007
B1009
BEEHIVE LA
GALLEYWOOD RD
STOCK RD
A12
Moulsham Jun & Inf Schs
Moulsham High Sch
Mildmay Jun & Inf Schs
Lathcoats Farm
Galleywood Hall
Great Baddow High Sch
Beehive Lane Com Prim Sch
Seabrights Barn (PH)
Great Seabrights
Chelmer Park
Carlton Riding Sch
Thriftwood Sch
The Horse & Groom (PH)
St Michael's CE Jun Sch
Galleywood Inf Sch
Canon-Leys Farm
Parklands Farm
Galleywood Common
Wood Farm
Pond's Farm
Glebe Farm
Willow Cottage
Whiss-Stocks
Brook Farm
Baddow Park
Baddow Pk
The Lodge
Duffield's Farm
Research Laboratorie
Cemy
Mast
Recn Gd
Sports Gd
Superstore
1 BULLEN WLK
2 SPOTS WLK
3 DOUGLAS CL
1 GREENFIELDS
2 BEKESWELL PL
3 HOUBLON DR
4 PARKLANDS WAY
5 ST MICHAELS WLK
SHROPSHIRE CL 1
LUCKSFIELD WAY 2
SPRINGBOK HO 3
8
7
05
6
5
04
4
3
03
2
1
02
70
71
72

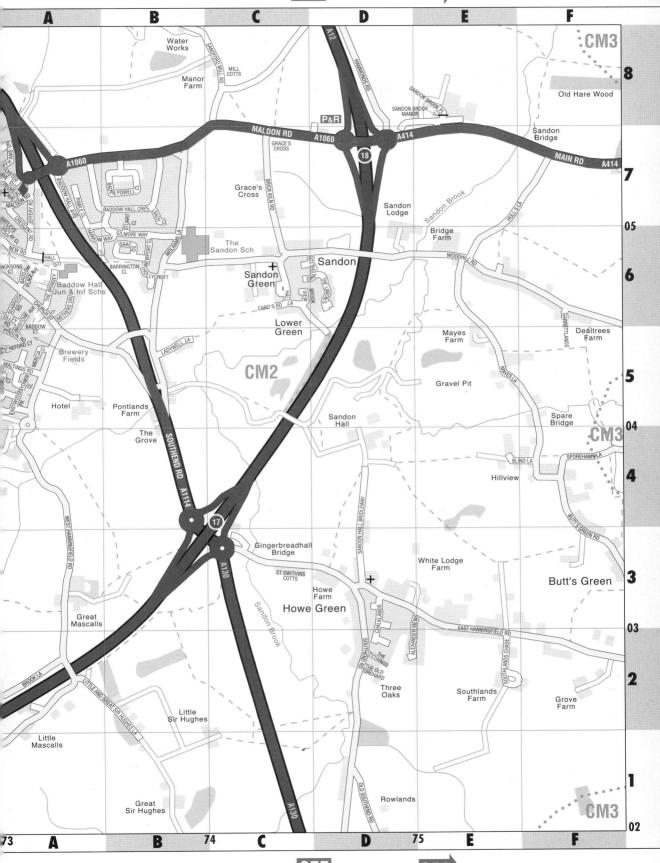

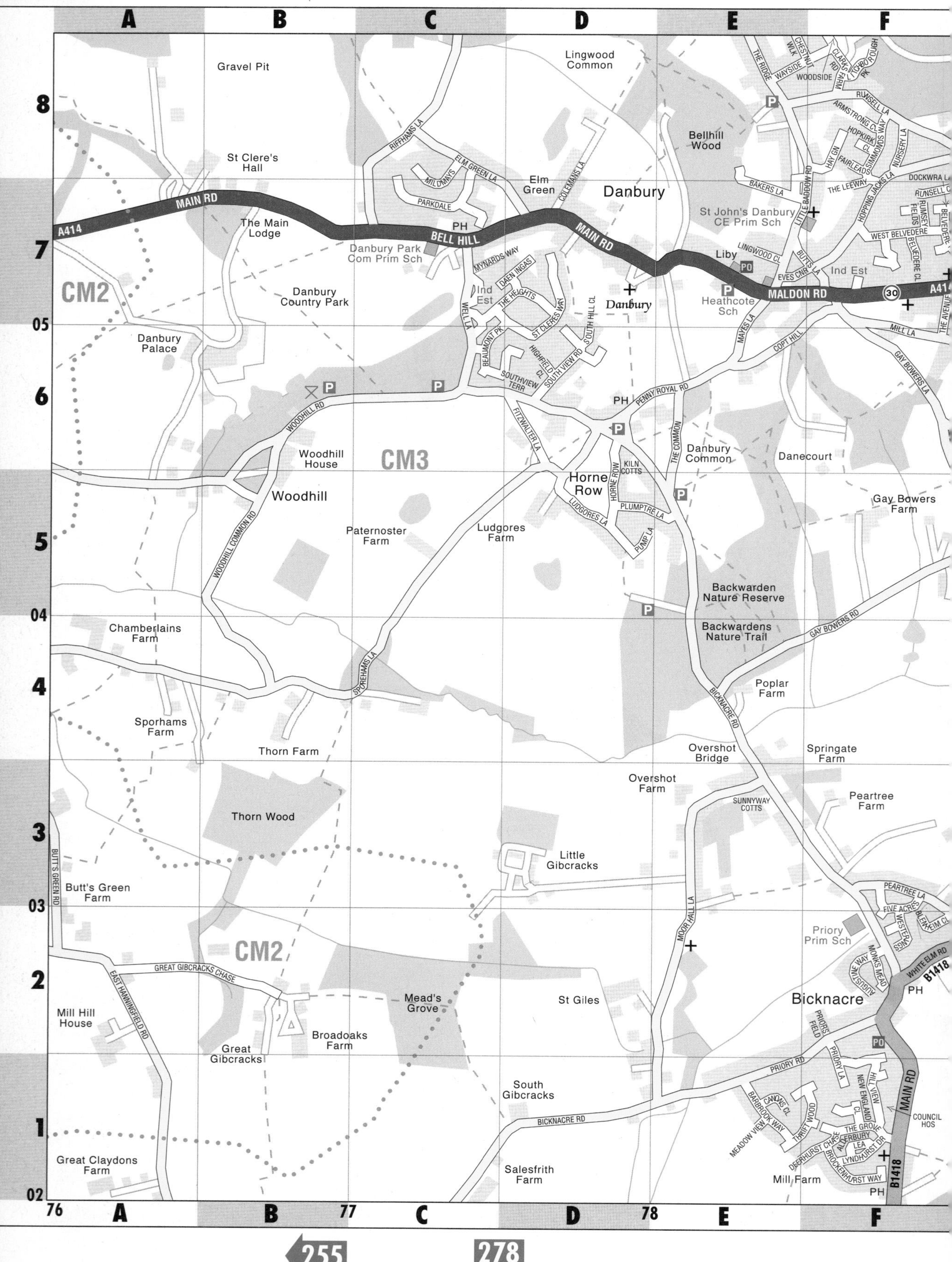

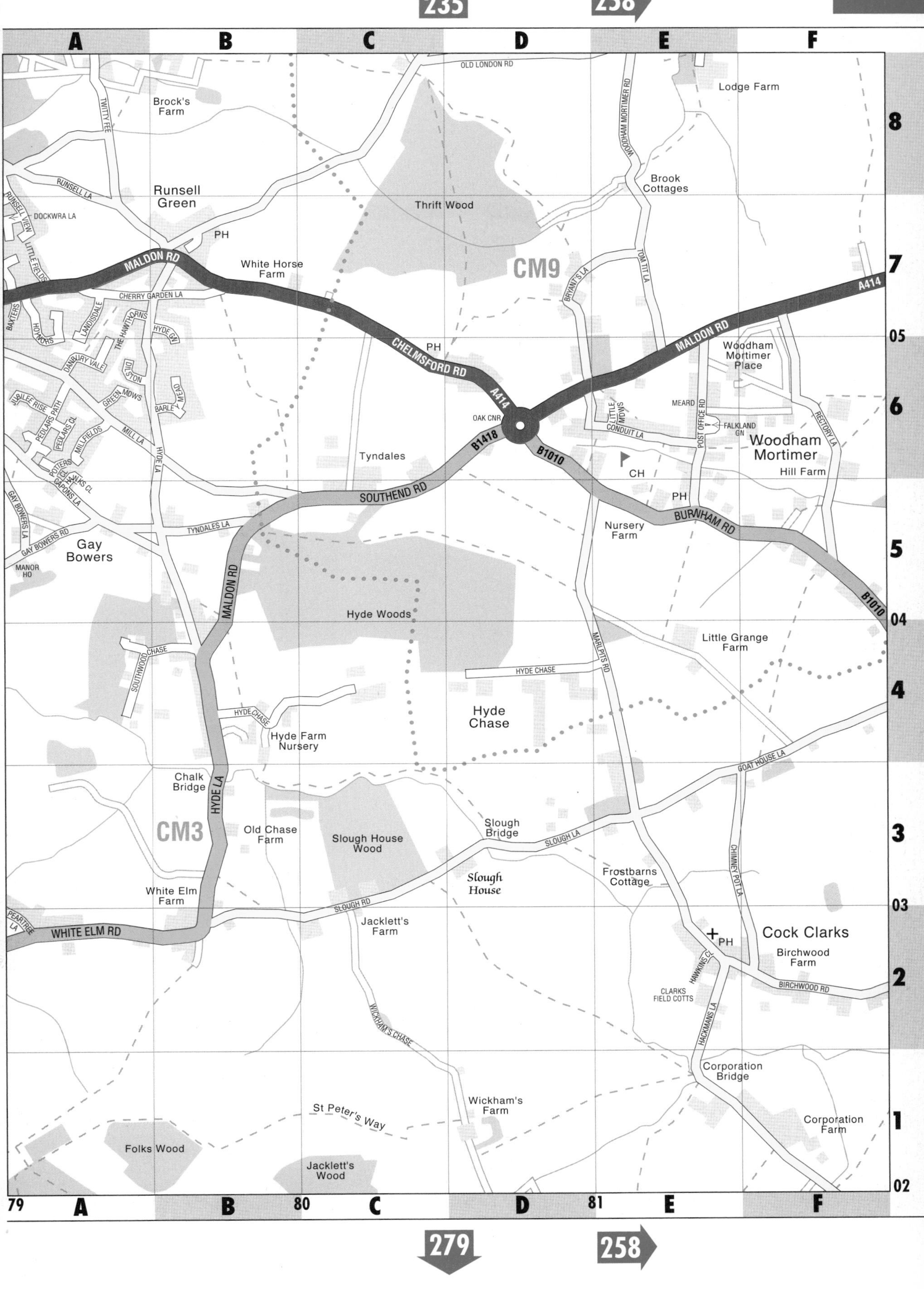

257
236

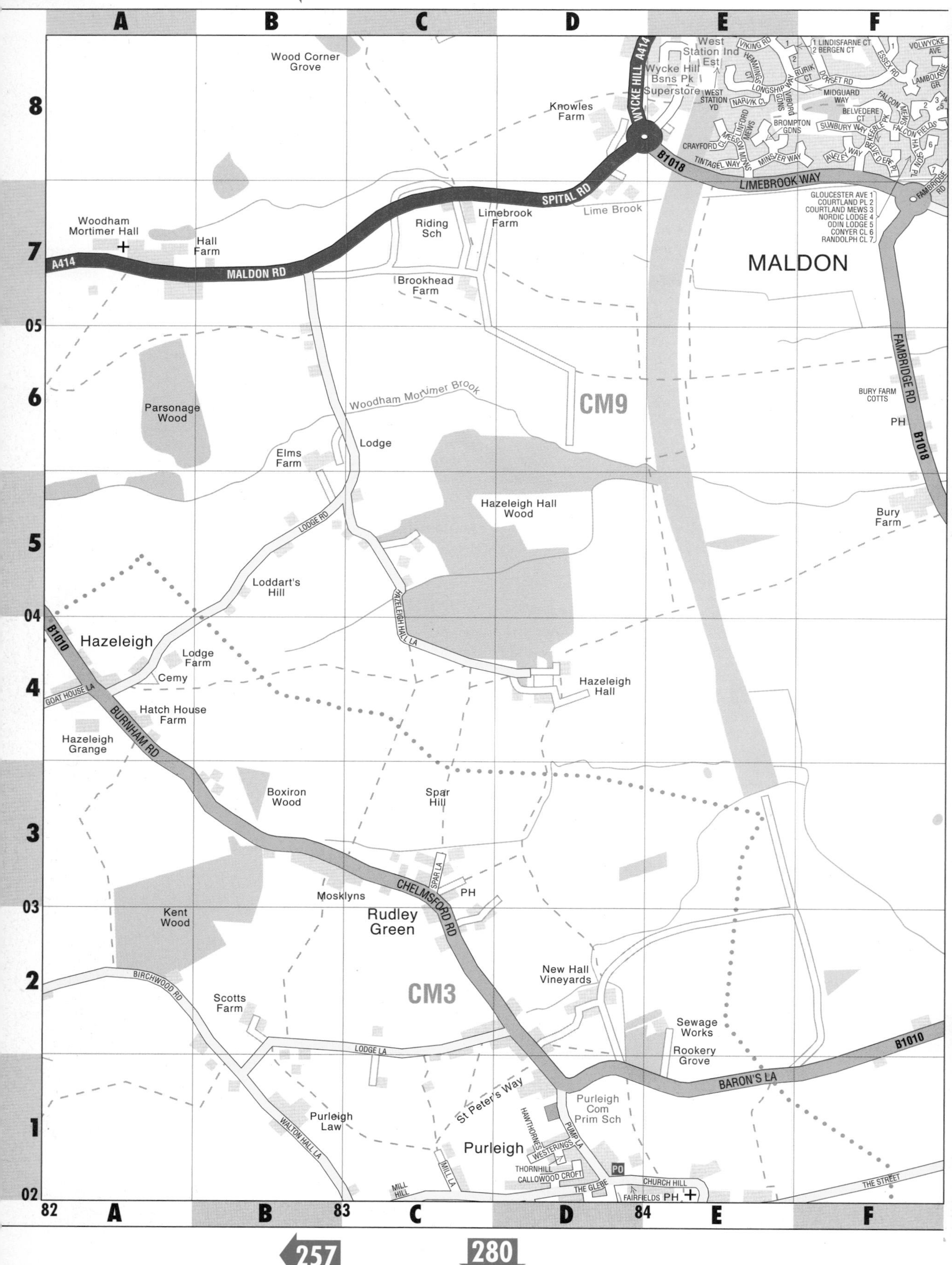

A B C D E F

8

Wood Corner Grove

West Station Ind Est

1 Lindisfarne Ct
2 Bergen Ct

Volwycke Ave
Lambourne Gr

Wycke Hill Bsns Pk Superstore

WYCKE HILL A414

Knowles Farm

West Station YD

MALDON

MIDGUARD WAY
BELVEDERE

7

Woodham Mortimer Hall

Hall Farm

Riding Sch

Limebrook Farm

SPITAL RD

Lime Brook

B1018

LIMEBROOK WAY

GLOUCESTER AVE 1
COURTLAND PL 2
COURTLAND MEWS 3
NORDIC LODGE 4
ODIN LODGE 5
CONYER CL 6
RANDOLPH CL 7

MALDON

A414

MALDON RD

Brookhead Farm

FAMBRIDGE RD

05

6

Parsonage Wood

Woodham Mortimer Brook

CM9

BURY FARM COTTS

PH

B1018

Lodge

Elms Farm

Hazeleigh Hall Wood

Bury Farm

5

Loddart's Hill

HAZELEIGH HALL LA

04

B1010

Hazeleigh

Lodge Farm

Cemy

Hazeleigh Hall

4

GOAT HOUSE LA

Hatch House Farm

BURNHAM RD

Hazeleigh Grange

Boxiron Wood

Spar Hill

3

Kent Wood

Mosklyns

CHELMSFORD RD

SPAR LA

PH

Rudley Green

03

New Hall Vineyards

BIRCHWOOD RD

Scotts Farm

CM3

Sewage Works

B1010

2

LODGE LA

Rookery Grove

BARON'S LA

WALTON HALL LA

Purleigh Law

St Peter's Way

Purleigh Com Prim Sch

1

HAWTHORNES

PUMP LA

WESTERINGS

Purleigh

PO

THORNHILL
CALLOWOOD CROFT

THE GLEBE

Church Hill

THE STREET

02

MILL HILL

MILL LA

FAIRFIELDS

PH

82 A 83 B C 84 D E F

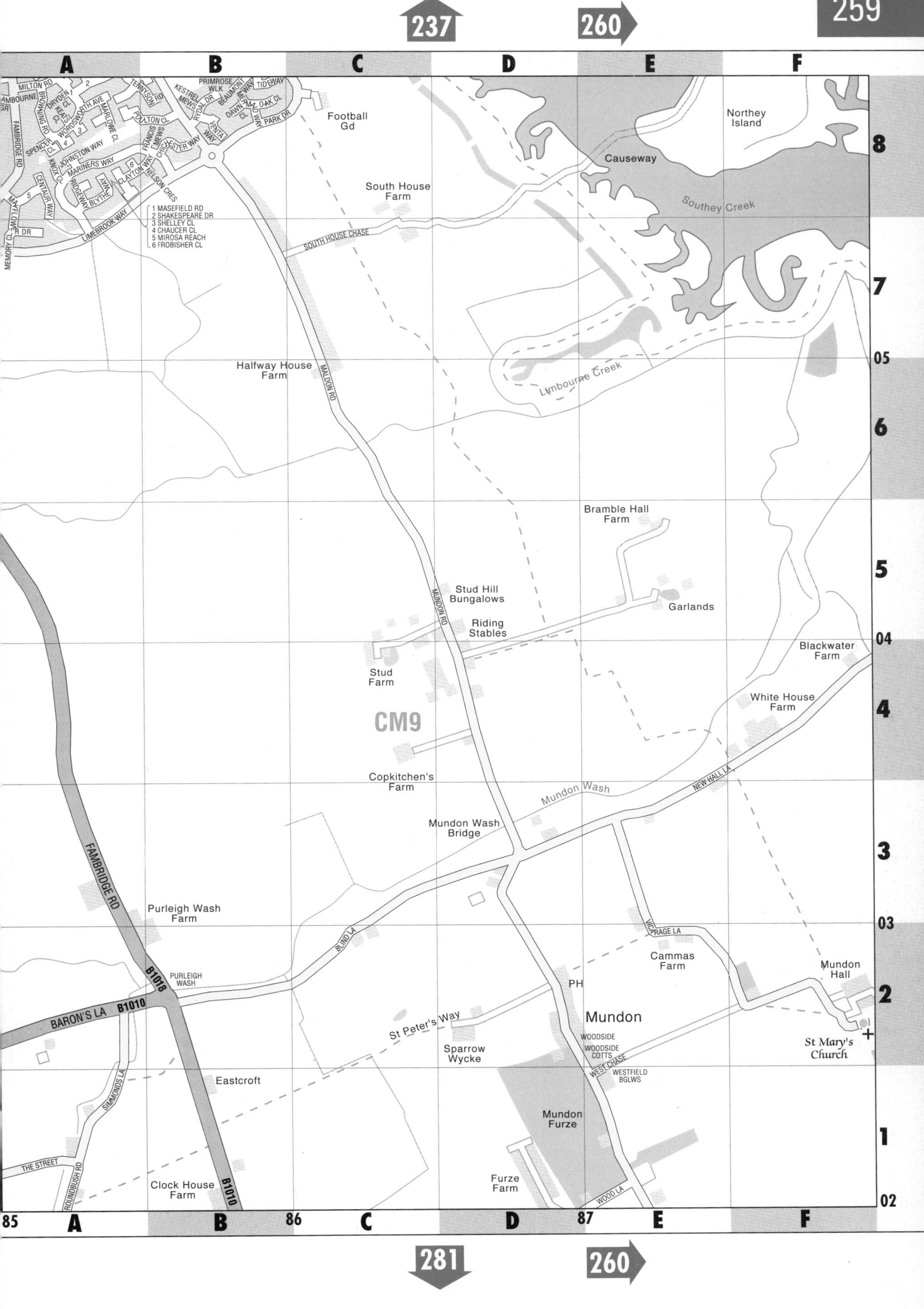

237 260

A B C D E F

8

Northey
Island

Causeway

Southey Creek

7

05

6

Football
Gd

South House
Farm

SOUTH HOUSE CHASE

MALDON RD

Halfway House
Farm

Limbourne Creek

1 MASEFIELD RD
2 SHAKESPEARE DR
3 SHELLEY CL
4 CHAUCER CL
5 MIROSA REACH
6 FROBISHER CL

MILTON RD
LAMBOURNE RD
BROWNING RD
SPENCER
WORDSWORTH AVE
KNOX
DRYDEN
TENNYSON RD
MARLOWE CL
RYTALL DR
CLAYTON
CHUCER WAY
KEATS WAY
DAWN RD
BEAUMONT DR
OAK CL
PARK DR
TIDEWAY
KESTREL DR
MEWS
PRIMROSE WLK
VISTA
FAMBRIDGE RD
HAYFLOWER DR
CENTAUR WAY
MEMORY CL
JOHNSTON WAY
MARINERS WAY
RIDGEWAY
LYNNE
BLYTHE
LIMEBROOK WAY
FRANCIS WAY
NELSON CRES

Bramble Hall
Farm

5

Stud Hill
Bungalows

Garlands

Riding
Stables

04

Blackwater
Farm

Stud
Farm

White House
Farm

4

CM9

Copkitchen's
Farm

Mundon Wash

NEW HALL LA

3

Mundon Wash
Bridge

FAMBRIDGE RD

BLIND LA

Purleigh Wash
Farm

VICARAGE LA

03

Cammas
Farm

Mundon
Hall

B1018

PURLEIGH
WASH

PH

2

BARON'S LA

B1010

St Peter's Way

Mundon

St Mary's
Church

SMALLINS LA

Sparrow
Wycke

WOODSIDE
WOODSIDE
COTTS
WEST CHASE
WESTFIELD
BGLWS

Eastcroft

1

THE STREET

ROUNDBUSH RD

Clock House
Farm

B1010

Mundon
Furze

Furze
Farm

WOOD LA

02

85 A B 86 C D 87 E F

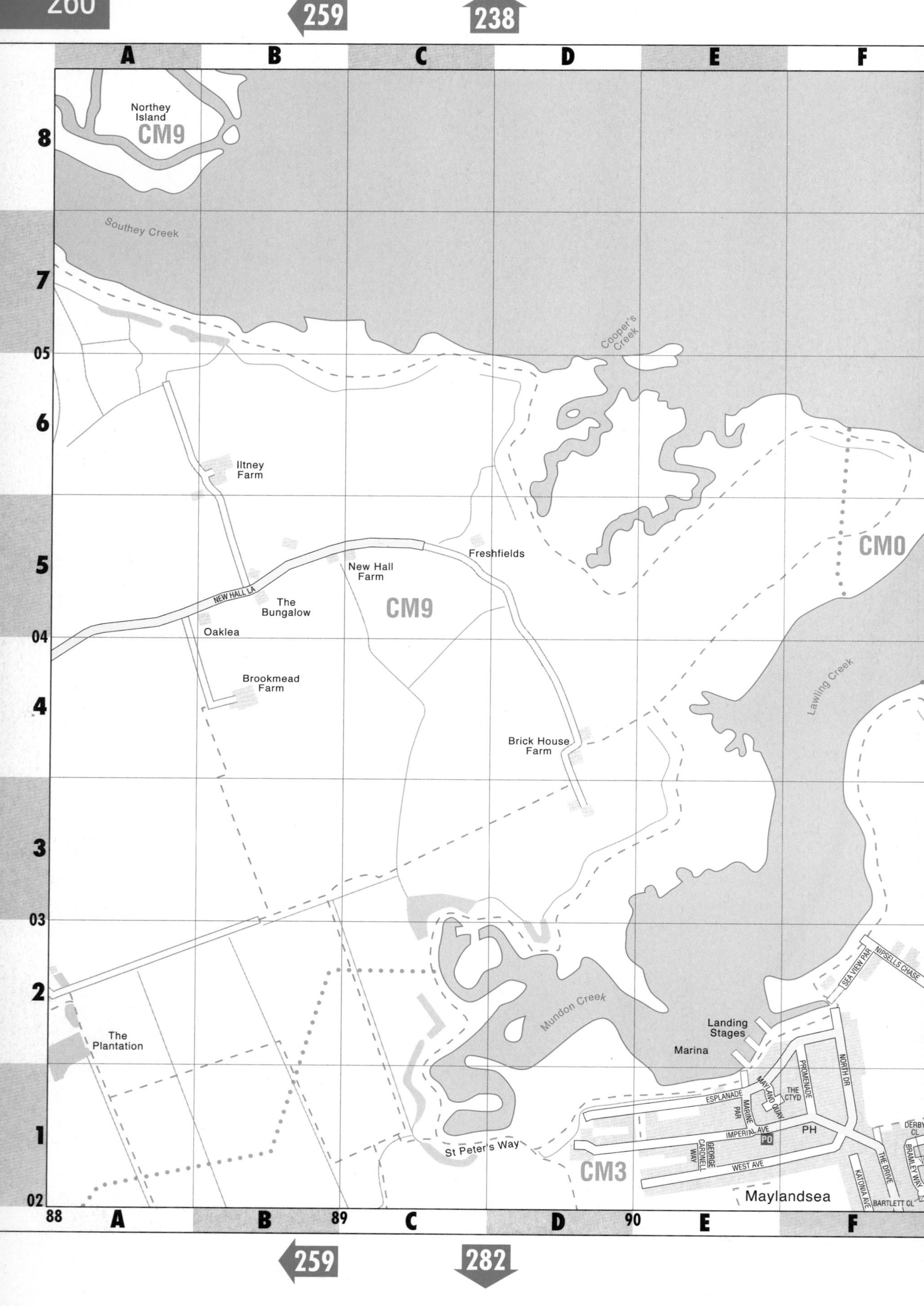

259
238

A **B** **C** **D** **E** **F**

Northey Island
CM9

8

Southey Creek

7

Cooper's Creek

05

6

Iltney Farm

CM0

Freshfields

5
New Hall Farm

NEW HALL LA
The Bungalow
CM9

04
Oaklea

Lawling Creek

Brookmead Farm

4

Brick House Farm

3

03

2

Mundon Creek

The Plantation

Landing Stages

Marina

SEA VIEW PAR
NIPSELLS CHASE

ESPLANADE
MAYLAND QUAY
THE CTYD
PROMENADE
NORTH DR
MARINE PAR

1
IMPERIAL AVE
PO
PH
DERBY CL
BRAMLEY WAY
THE DRIVE

GEORGE CROMELL WAY
WEST AVE
KATONIA AVE
BARTLETT CL

St Peter's Way
CM3
Maylandsea

02

88 **A** **B** 89 **C** **D** 90 **E** **F**

259
282

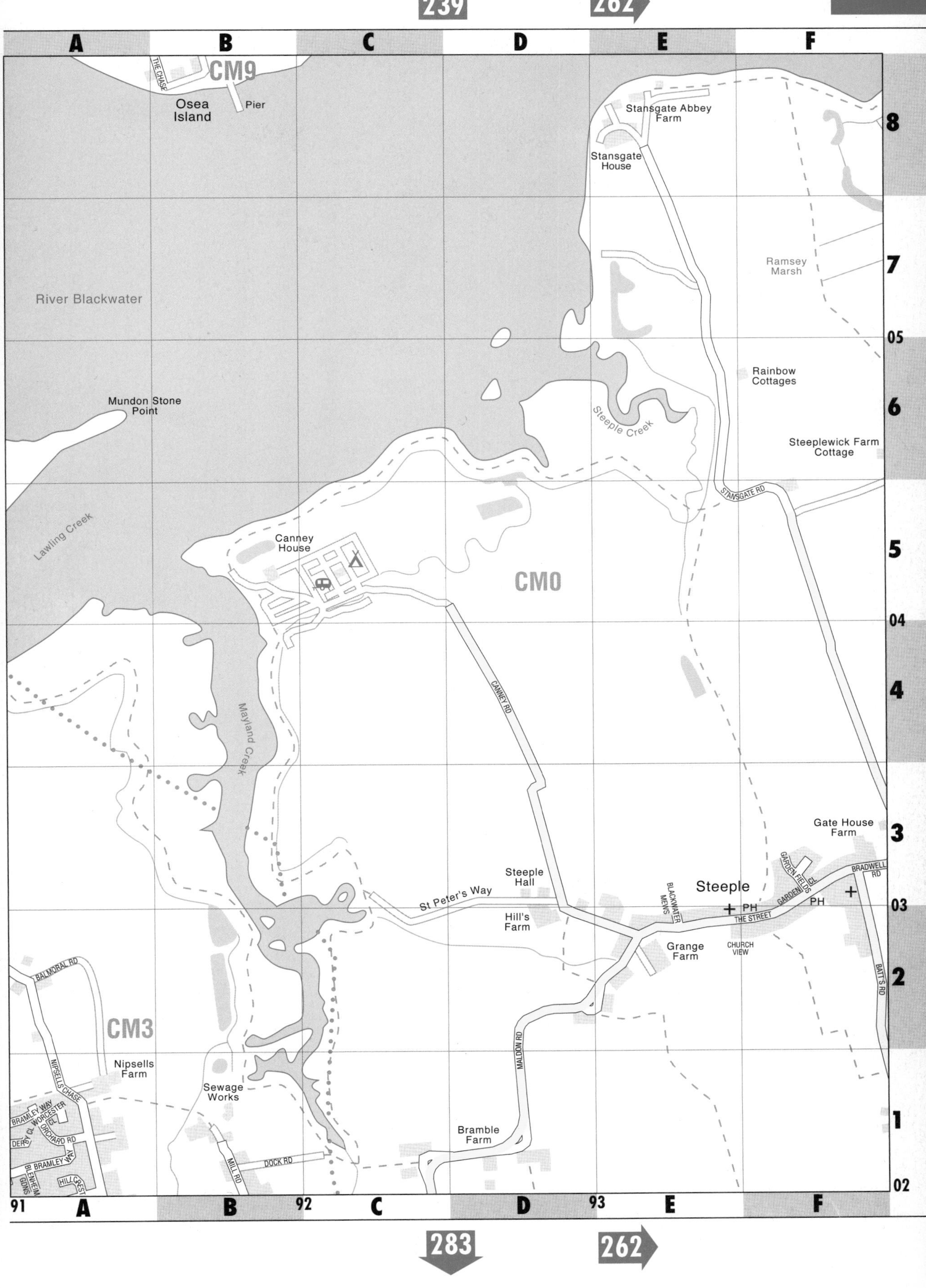

A B C D E F

8

7

05

6

05

5

04

4

04

3

03

2

03

1

02

91 A B 92 C D 93 E F

CM9
Osea
Island
Pier
THE CHASE

River Blackwater

Mundon Stone
Point

Lawling Creek

Canney
House

Mayland Creek

CM0

CANNEY RD

Steeple Creek

STANSGATE RD

Stansgate Abbey
Farm

Stansgate
House

Ramsey
Marsh

Rainbow
Cottages

Steeplewick Farm
Cottage

Gate House
Farm

Steeple
Hall

St Peter's Way

Hill's
Farm

Steeple
PH
BLACKWATER MEWS
THE STREET
Grange
Farm
CHURCH
VIEW
GARDEN FIELDS CL
PH
BRADWELL RD

BATT'S RD

CM3

Nipsells
Farm

Sewage
Works

MALDON RD

Bramble
Farm

BALMORAL RD
NIPSELLS CHASE
BRAMLEY WAY
WORCESTER CL
DERBY CL
ORCHARD RD
BRAMLEY WAY
HILL CREST
BLENHEIM GDNS

MILL RD
DOCK RD

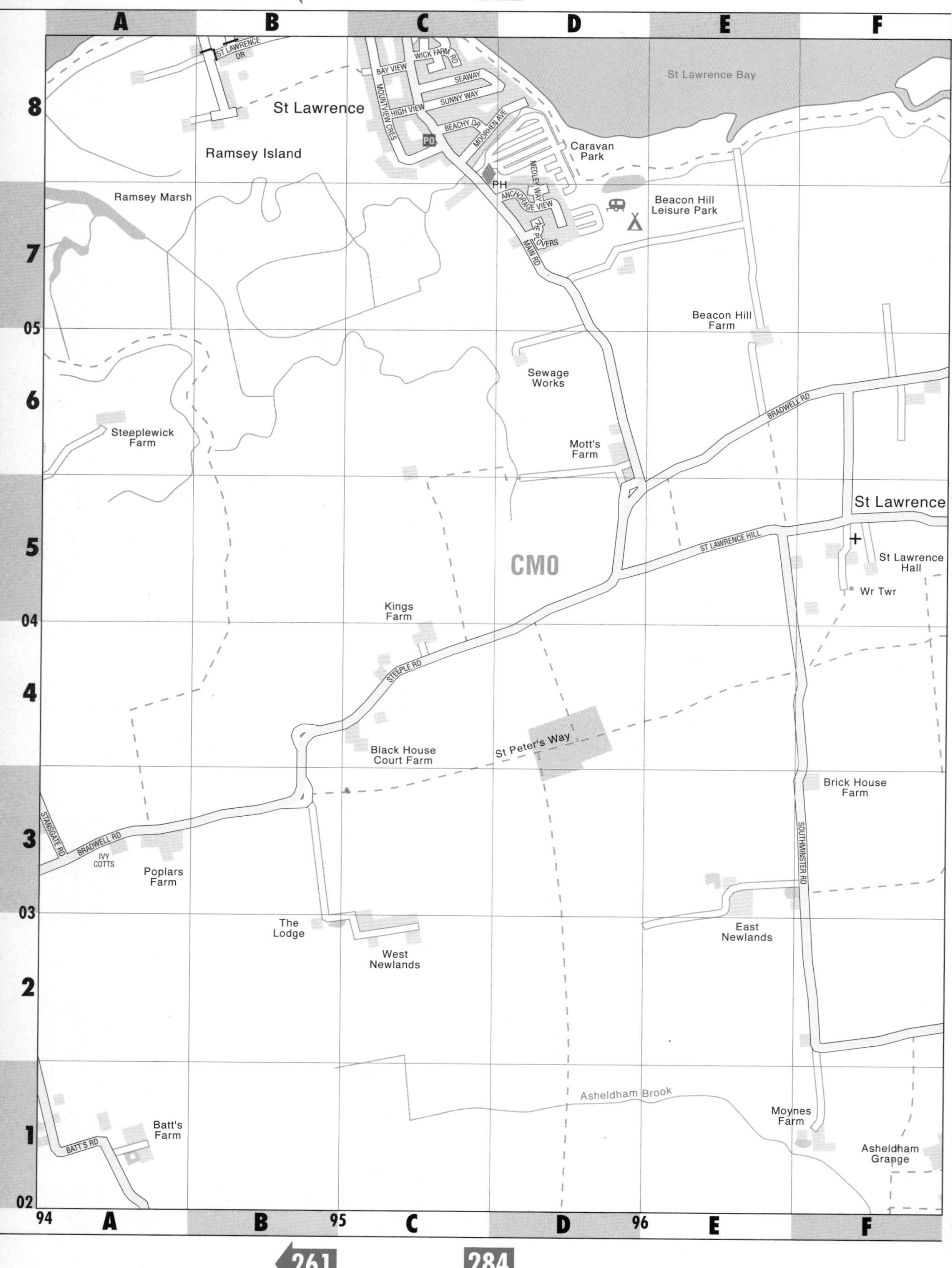

A B C D E F

8

St Lawrence

St Lawrence Bay

St Lawrence Dr

BAY VIEW

WICK FARM RD

SEAWAY

SUNNY WAY

HIGH VIEW

MOUNTVIEW CRES

BEACHY DR

MOURNE'S AVE

PO

Ramsey Island

Caravan Park

PH

MEDLEY WAY

ANCHORAGE VIEW

THE PLOVERS

MAIN RD

Beacon Hill Leisure Park

Ramsey Marsh

7

05

Beacon Hill Farm

Sewage Works

6

Steeplewick Farm

BRADWELL RD

Mott's Farm

St Lawrence

5

CMO

St Lawrence Hill

St Lawrence Hall

Wr Twr

04

Kings Farm

STEEPLE RD

4

Black House Court Farm

St Peter's Way

Brick House Farm

3

STANSGATE RD

BRADWELL RD

IVY COTTS

Poplars Farm

SOUTHMINSTER RD

03

The Lodge

West Newlands

East Newlands

2

Asheldham Brook

Moynes Farm

1

Batt's Farm

BATT'S RD

Asheldham Grange

02

94 A B 95 C D 96 E F

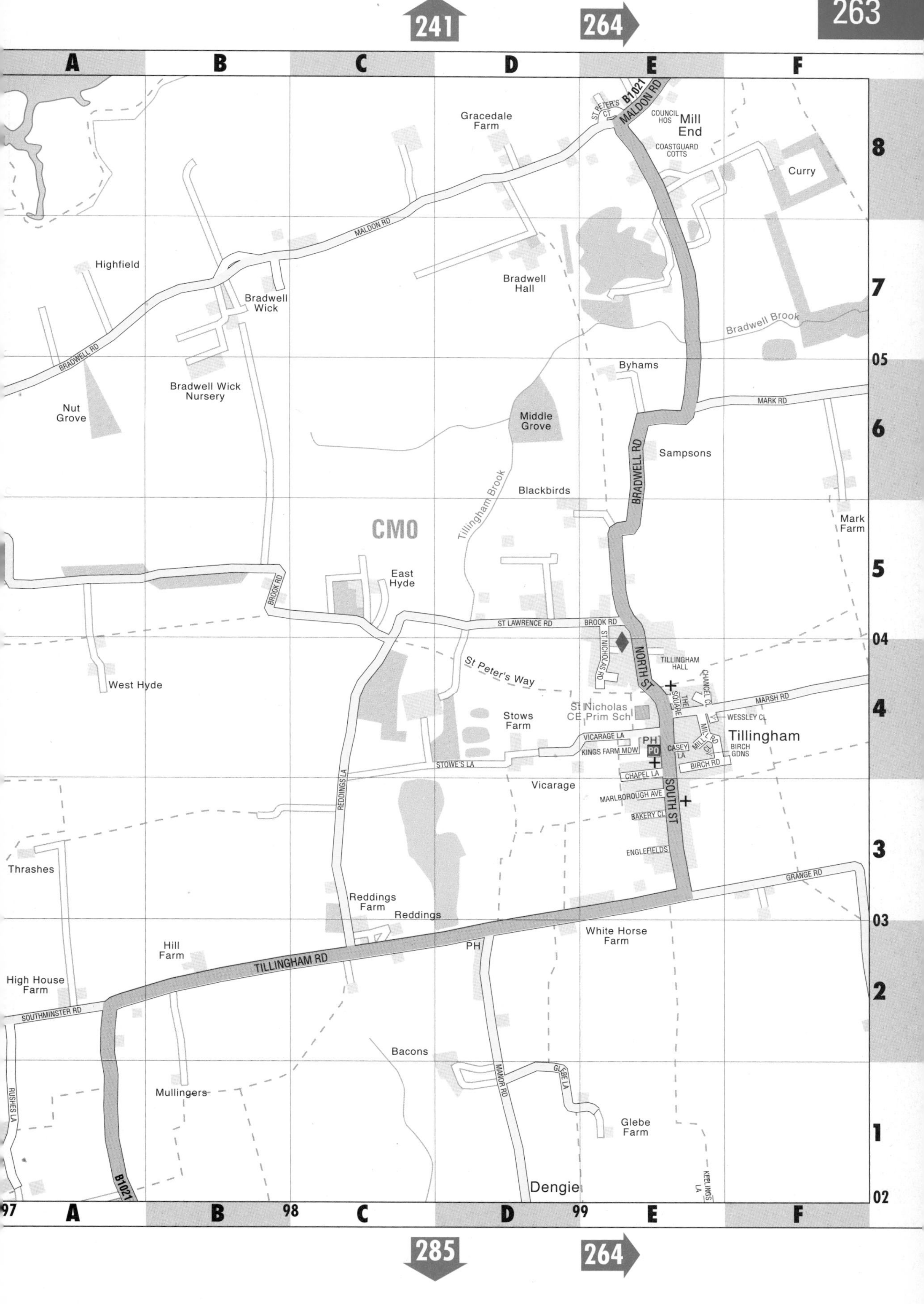

A B C D E F

8
05
7
6
5
04
4
3
03
2
02
1

97 A B 98 C D 99 E F

Nut Grove

Highfield

Bradwell Wick

Bradwell Wick Nursery

MALDON RD

BRADWELL RD

Gracedale Farm

Bradwell Hall

ST PETER'S CT

B1021 MALDON RD

COUNCIL HOS

Mill End

COASTGUARD COTTS

Curry

Byhams

Bradwell Brook

MARK RD

Middle Grove

Sampsons

Mark Farm

Blackbirds

BRADWELL RD

CMO

Tillingham Brook

East Hyde

West Hyde

BROOK RD

St Peter's Way

ST LAWRENCE RD

BROOK RD

ST NICHOLAS RD

NORTH ST

Tillingham Hall

CHANCEL CO

MARSH RD

Tillingham

WESSLEY CL

BIRCH GDNS

St Nicholas CE Prim Sch

THE SQUARE

MILL RD

CASEY LA

BIRCH RD

Stows Farm

VICARAGE LA

KINGS FARM MDW

PH PO

CHAPEL LA

Vicarage

MARLBOROUGH AVE

BAKERY CL

SOUTH ST

REDDINGS LA

STOWE'S LA

ENGLEFIELDS

GRANGE RD

Thrashes

Reddings Farm

Reddings

White Horse Farm

Hill Farm

PH

TILLINGHAM RD

High House Farm

SOUTHMINSTER RD

RUSHES LA

B1021

Bacons

MANOR RD

GLEBE LA

Mullingers

Glebe Farm

KEPLINGS LA

Dengie

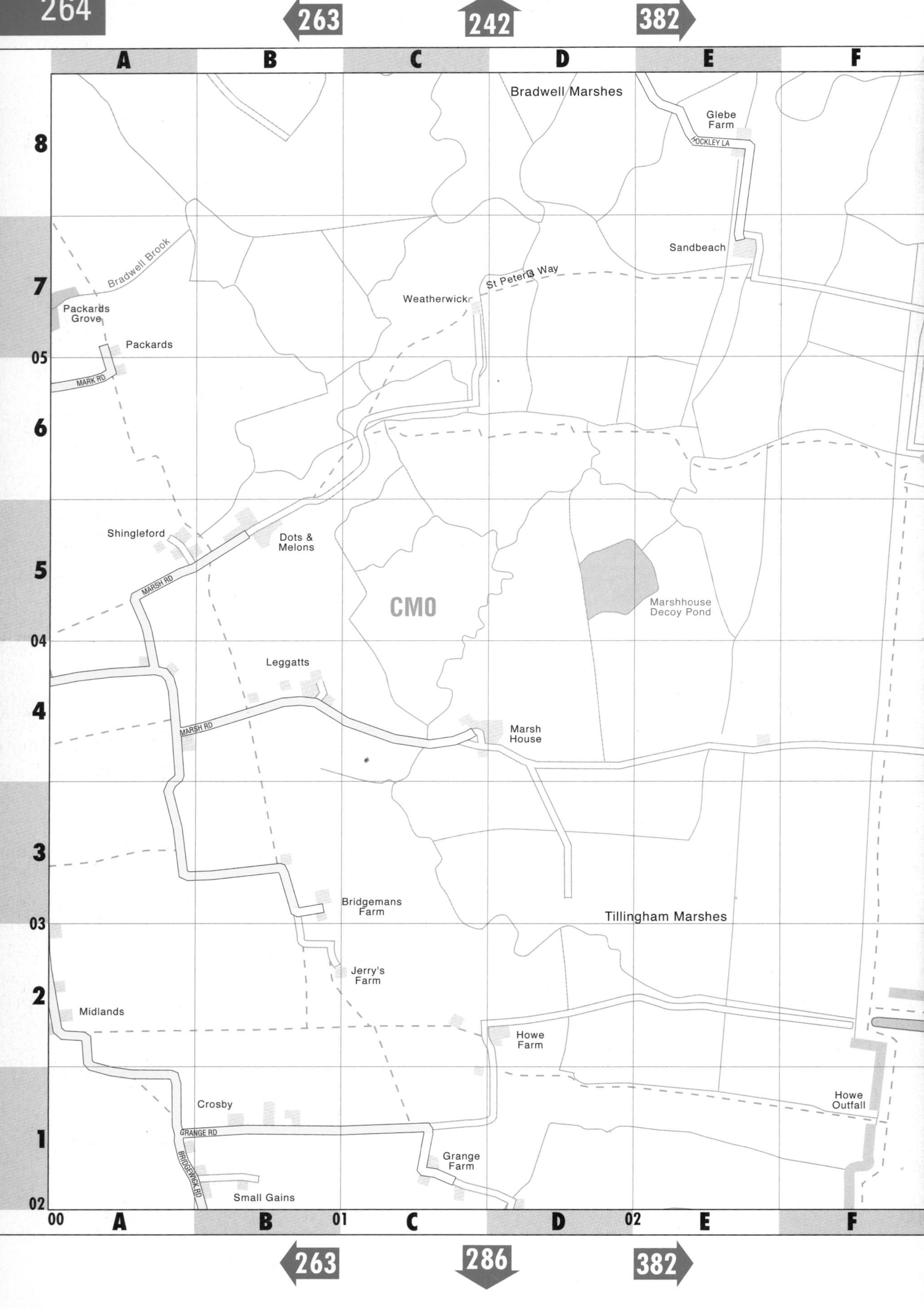

A B C D E F

8

7

05

6

04

5

04

4

03

3

03

2

1

02

Bradwell Marshes

Glebe Farm

HOCKLEY LA

Sandbeach

Bradwell Brook

Packards Grove

Packards

MARK RD

St Peter's Way

Weatherwick

Shingleford

Dots & Melons

CMO

Marshhouse Decoy Pond

MARSH RD

Leggatts

MARSH RD

Marsh House

Bridgemans Farm

Tillingham Marshes

Jerry's Farm

Midlands

Howe Farm

Howe Outfall

Crosby

GRANGE RD

BRIDGEWICK RD

Grange Farm

Small Gains

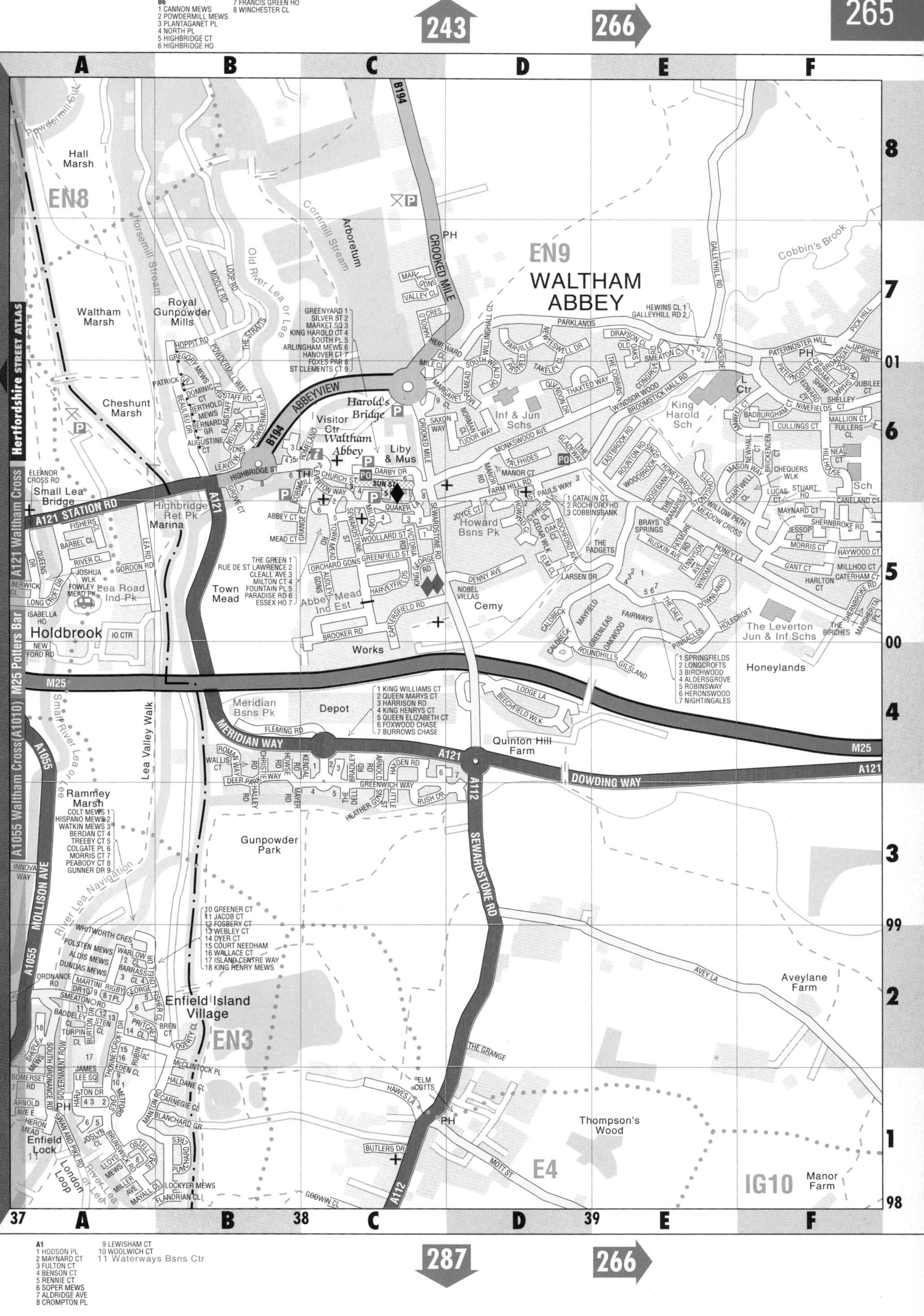

B6
1 CANNON MEWS
2 POWDERMILL MEWS
3 PLANTAGANET PL
4 NORTH PL
5 HIGHBRIDGE CT
6 HIGHBRIDGE HO

7 FRANCIS GREEN HO
8 WINCHESTER CL

EN8

Hertfordshire Street Atlas

Hall Marsh

Waltham Marsh

Royal Gunpowder Mills

Cheshunt Marsh

Small Lea Bridge

A1055 Waltham Cross

A121 Waltham Cross

M25 Potters Bar

Eleanor Cross Rd

Fowley Mead Pk

Holdbrook

Lea Road Ind Pk

Highbrige Ret Pk

Marina

A1 STATION RD

A121

Town Mead

THE GREEN 1
RUE DE ST LAWRENCE 2
CLEALL AVE 3
MILTON CT 4
FOUNTAIN PL 5
PARADISE RD 6
ESSEX HO 7

Abbey Mead Ind Est

Works

Meridian Bsns Pk

MERIDIAN WAY

Depot

Lea Valley Walk

Rammey Marsh

COLT MEWS 1
HISPANO MEWS 2
WATKIN MEWS 3
BERDAN CT 4
TREEBY CT 5
COLGATE PL 6
MORRIS CT 7
PEABODY CT 8
GUNNER DR 9

Gunpowder Park

10 GREENER CT
11 JACOB CT
12 FOSBERY CT
13 WEBLEY CT
14 DYER CT
15 COURT NEEDHAM
16 WALLACE CT
17 ISLAND CENTRE WAY
18 KING HENRY MEWS

WHITWORTH CRES
POLSTEN MEWS
ALDIS MEWS
DUNDAS MEWS

Enfield Island Village

EN3

MOLLISON AVE

A1055

INNOVA WAY

Enfield Lock

London Loop

River Lea Navigation

WALTHAM ABBEY
EN9

CROOKED MILE
B194

Arboretum

Cornmill Stream

Old River Lea or Lea

GREENYARD 1
SILVER ST 2
MARKET SQ 3
KING HAROLD CT 4
SOUTH PL 5
ARLINGHAM MEWS 6
HANOVER CT 7
FOXES PAR 8
ST CLEMENTS CT 9

ABBEYVIEW

Harold's Bridge

Visitor Ctr
Waltham Abbey

Liby & Mus

SUN ST

QUAKER LA

Howard Bsns Pk

1 CATALIN CT
2 ROCHFORD HO
3 COBBINSBANK

Cemy

NOBEL VILLAS

King Harold Sch

Inf & Jun Schs

The Padgets

BRAYS SPRINGS

1 SPRINGFIELDS
2 LONGCROFTS
3 BIRCHWOOD
4 ALDERSGROVE
5 ROBINSWAY
6 HERONSWOOD
7 NIGHTINGALES

Honeylands

The Leverton Jun & Inf Schs

The Birches

M25

Quinton Hill Farm

DOWDING WAY
A121

1 KING WILLIAMS CT
2 QUEEN MARYS CT
3 HARRISON RD
4 KING HENRYS CT
5 QUEEN ELIZABETH CT
6 FOXWOOD CHASE
7 BURROWS CHASE

SEWARDSTONE RD

THE GRANGE

Aveylane Farm

AVEY LA

Thompson's Wood

E4

IG10

Manor Farm

A1
1 HODSON PL
2 MAYNARD CT
3 FULTON CT
4 BENSON CT
5 RENNIE CT
6 SOPER MEWS
7 ALDRIDGE AVE
8 CROMPTON PL

9 LEWISHAM CT
10 WOOLWICH CT
11 Waterways Bsns Ctr

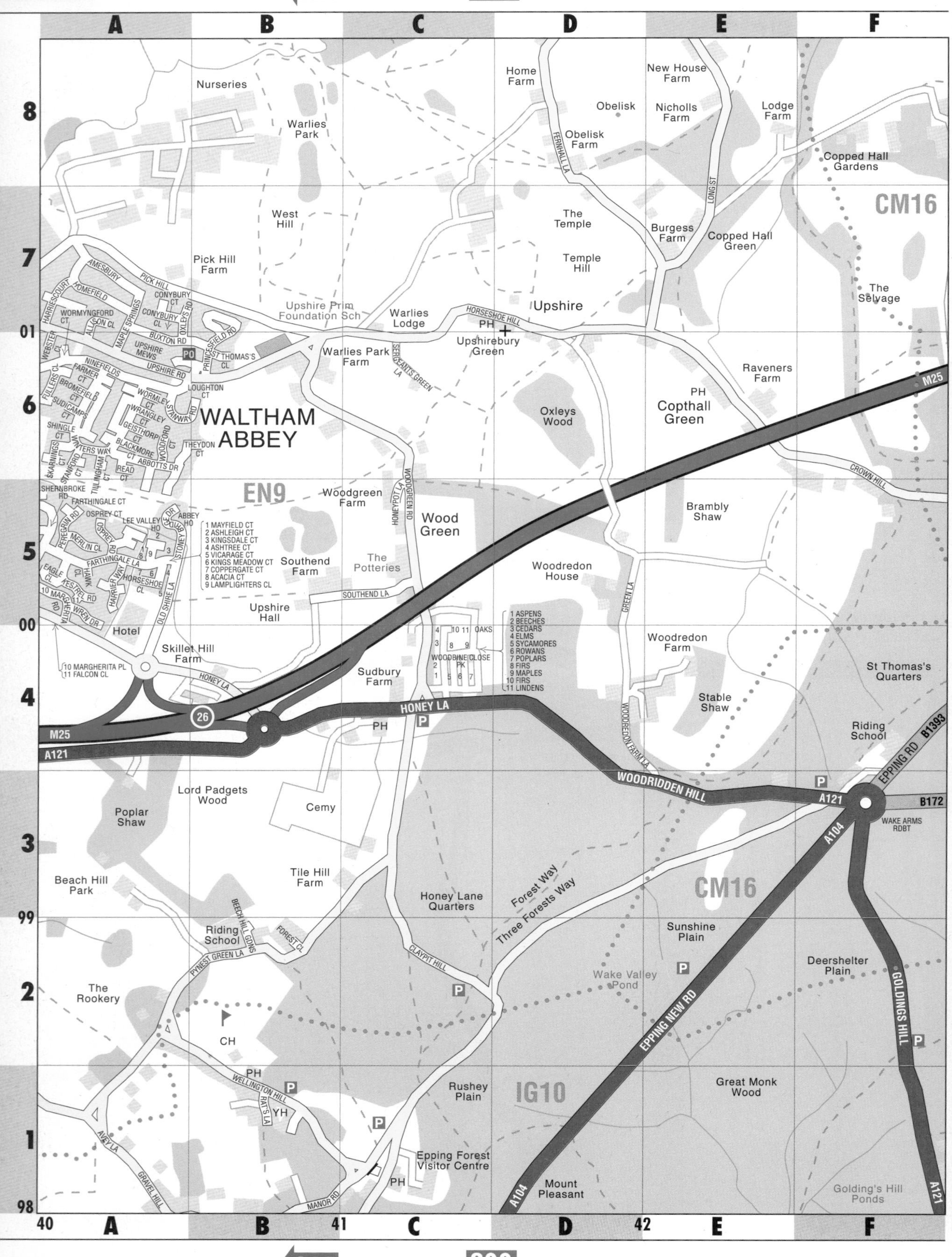

265
244

A   B   C   D   E   F

8

CM16

7

Nurseries

Warlies Park

Home Farm

Obelisk

New House Farm

Nicholls Farm

Lodge Farm

Copped Hall Gardens

West Hill

Obelisk Farm

The Temple

Burgess Farm

Copped Hall Green

The Selvage

Pick Hill Farm

Temple Hill

Upshire

01

AMESBURY
HARRISCOURT
POMEFIELD
CONYBURY CT
CONYBURY CT
Pick Hill
Upshire Prim Foundation Sch
Warlies Lodge
HORSESHOE HILL
PH
Upshirebury Green

Ravenens Farm

WORMYNGFORD CT
WEBSTER
ALLISON CT
SUDICAMPS
BROMEFIELD
FARMER
NINEFIELDS
UPSHIRE MEWS
UPSHIRE RD
PRINCESFIELD RD
ST THOMAS'S CL
BUXTON RD
OXLEYS RD
LOUGHTON CT
PO

Warlies Park Farm

SERJEANTS GREEN

PH Copthall Green

6

FULLERS CT
SHINGLE CT
STANFORD
WATERS WAY
WORMLEY CT
WRANGLEY CT
GEISTHORPE CT
BLACKMORE CT
ABBOTTS DR
THEYDON CT
READ CT

WALTHAM ABBEY

Oxleys Wood

CROWN HILL

SKARNINGS
SHERNBROKE RD
FARTHINGALE LA
OSPREY CT
PETERGATE RD
LEE VALLEY
MERLIN CL

EN9

Woodgreen Farm

HONEYLANE
WOODGREEN RD

Wood Green

Brambly Shaw

5

EAGLE CT
HAWK CT
KESTREL RD
FARTHINGALE LA
HORSESHOE CL
MARSH
WREN DR
ABBEY HO
OLD SHIRE LA
STONEY

1 MAYFIELD CT
2 ASHLEIGH CT
3 KINGSDALE CT
4 ASHTREE CT
5 VICARAGE CT
6 KINGS MEADOW CT
7 COPPERGATE CT
8 ACACIA CT
9 LAMPLIGHTERS CL

Southend Farm

The Potteries

Woodredon House

GREEN LA

00

10 MARGHERITA PL
11 FALCON CL
Hotel

Skillet Hill Farm

SOUTHEND LA

Upshire Hall

Sudbury Farm

4 10 11 OAKS
3   9
PK
WOODBINE CLOSE
1   5 6 7

1 ASPENS
2 BEECHES
3 CEDARS
4 ELMS
5 SYCAMORES
6 ROWANS
7 POPLARS
8 FIRS
9 MAPLES
10 FIRS
11 LINDENS

Woodredon Farm

Woodredon House

St Thomas's Quarters

4

M25
A121

26

HONEY LA

PH

P

HONEY LA

Stable Shaw

Riding School

WOODREDON FARM LA

WOODRIDDEN HILL

A121

P

EPPING RD
B1393
B172

Lord Padgets Wood

Cemy

WOODRIDDEN HILL

A104

WAKE ARMS RDBT

3

Poplar Shaw

Tile Hill Farm

Honey Lane Quarters

Forest Way

Three Forests Way

CM16

Deershelter Plain

Beach Hill Park

99

BEECH HILL GDNS
FOREST CL
Riding School
PYNEST GREEN LA

CLAYPIT HILL

Sunshine Plain

P

Wake Valley Pond

GOLDINGS HILL

2

The Rookery

CH

P

EPPING NEW RD

Great Monk Wood

P

1

AVEY LA
WELLINGTON HILL
PH
P
RAYS LA
YH

Rushey Plain

IG10

98

GRAVEL HILL
MANOR RD
PH

Epping Forest Visitor Centre

A104

Mount Pleasant

42

Golding's Hill Ponds

A121

40   A   B   41   C   D   42   E   F

265
288

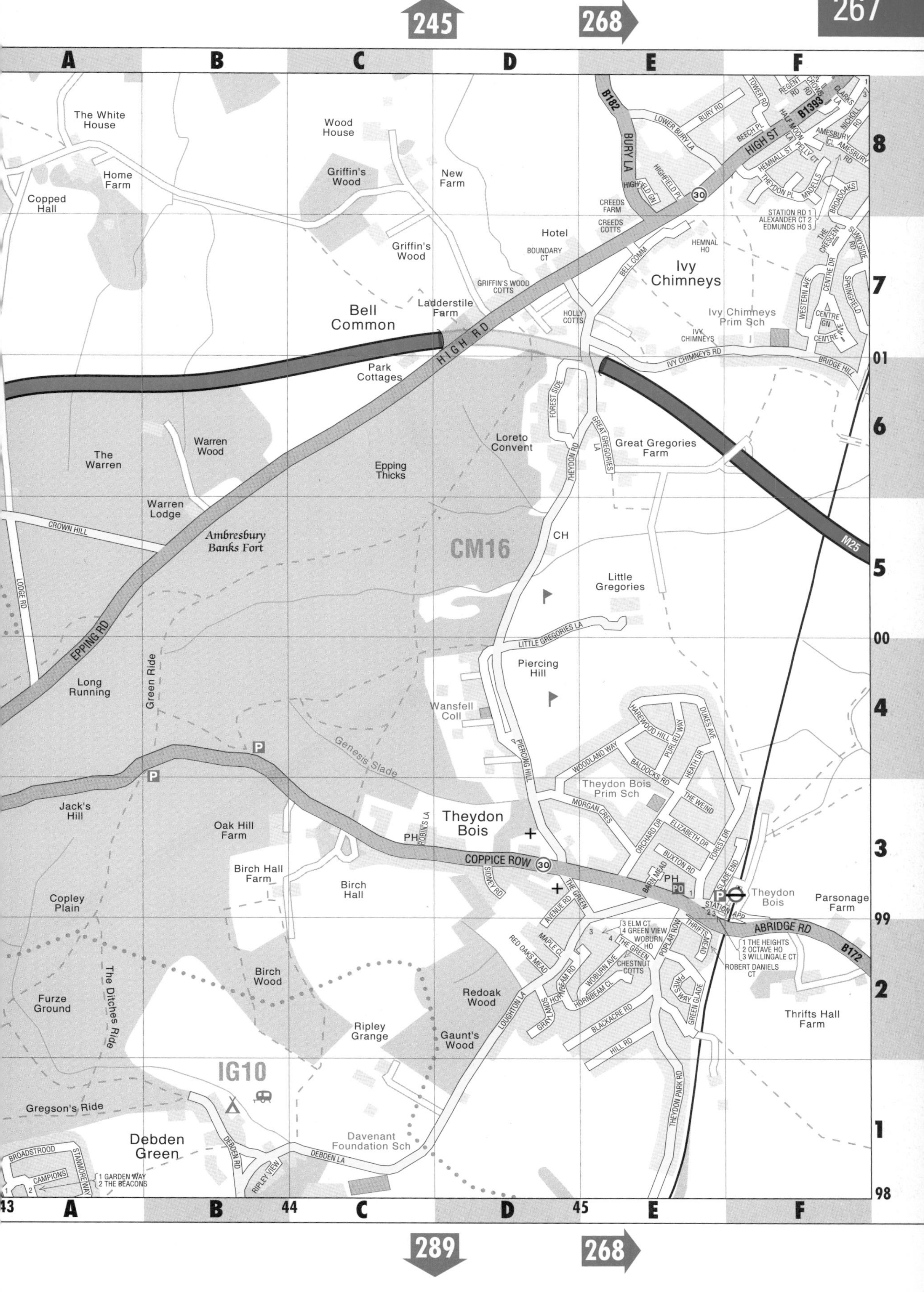
245
268
A
B
C
D
E
F
The White House
Home Farm
Copped Hall
Wood House
Griffin's Wood
New Farm
Griffin's Wood
Hotel
Bell Common
Ladderstile Farm
Park Cottages
HIGH RD
Ivy Chimneys
Ivy Chimneys Prim Sch
IVY CHIMNEYS RD
BRIDGE HILL
BURY LA
LOWER BURY LA
BURY RD
HIGH ST
B1393
B182
HIGHFIELD PL
HEMNALL ST
THEYDON PL
BELL COMM
The Warren
Warren Wood
Warren Lodge
Epping Thicks
Loreto Convent
Great Gregories Farm
FOREST SIDE
THEYDON RD
GREAT GREGORIES LA
CROWN HILL
Ambresbury Banks Fort
CM16
CH
M25
Little Gregories
LITTLE GREGORIES LA
Piercing Hill
LODGE RD
EPPING RD
Long Running
Green Ride
Wansfell Coll
Genesis Slade
Jack's Hill
Oak Hill Farm
Theydon Bois
Theydon Bois Prim Sch
COPPICE ROW
PH
Birch Hall Farm
Birch Hall
Copley Plain
Theydon Bois
Parsonage Farm
ABRIDGE RD
B172
Furze Ground
The Ditches Ride
Birch Wood
Redoak Wood
Ripley Grange
Gaunt's Wood
Thrifts Hall Farm
IG10
Gregson's Ride
Debden Green
DEBDEN RD
DEBDEN LA
Davenant Foundation Sch
THEYDON PARK RD
BROADSTROOD
CAMPIONS
STANMORE WAY
1 GARDEN WAY
2 THE BEACONS
8
7
01
6
5
00
4
3
99
2
1
98
43
44
45
289
268

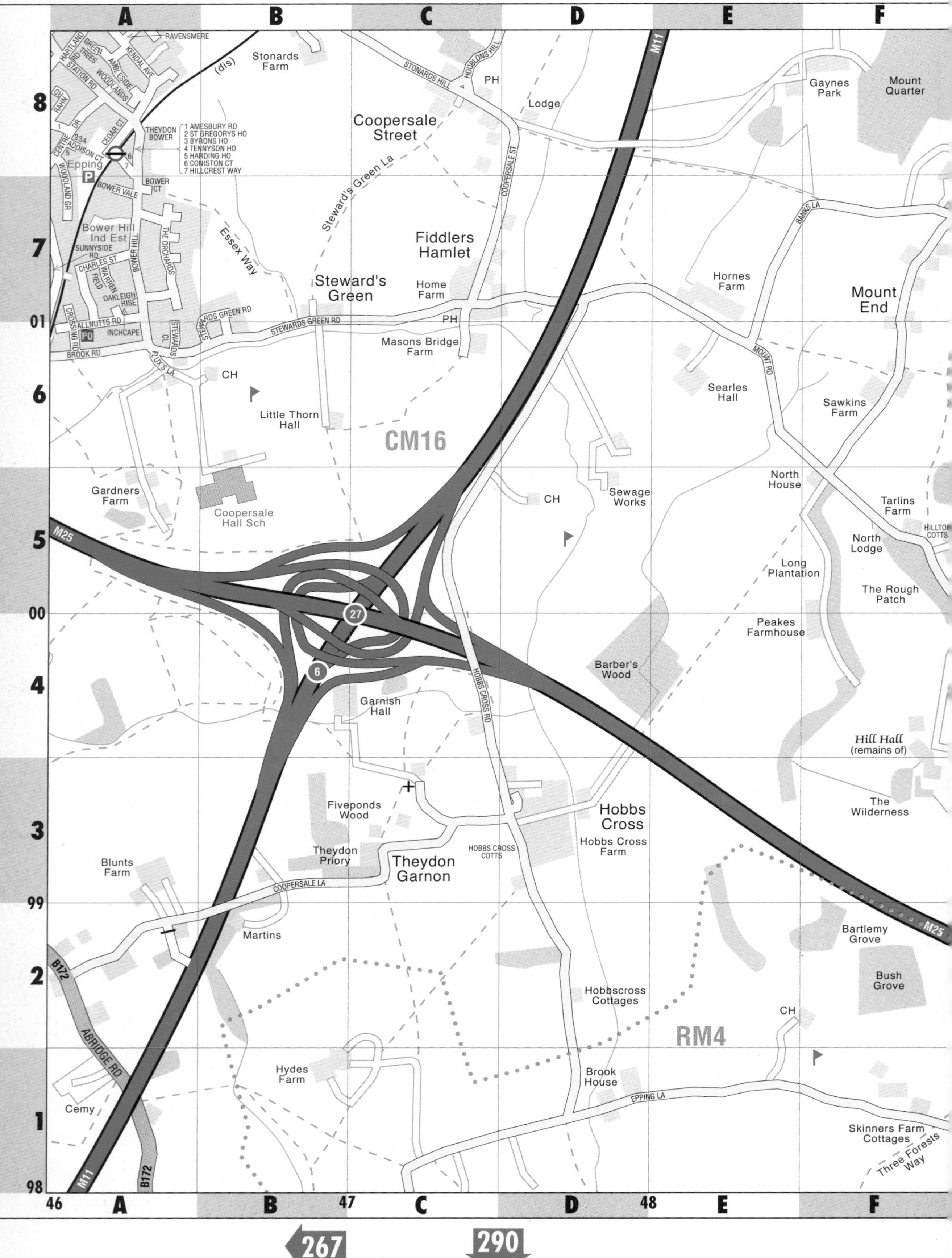

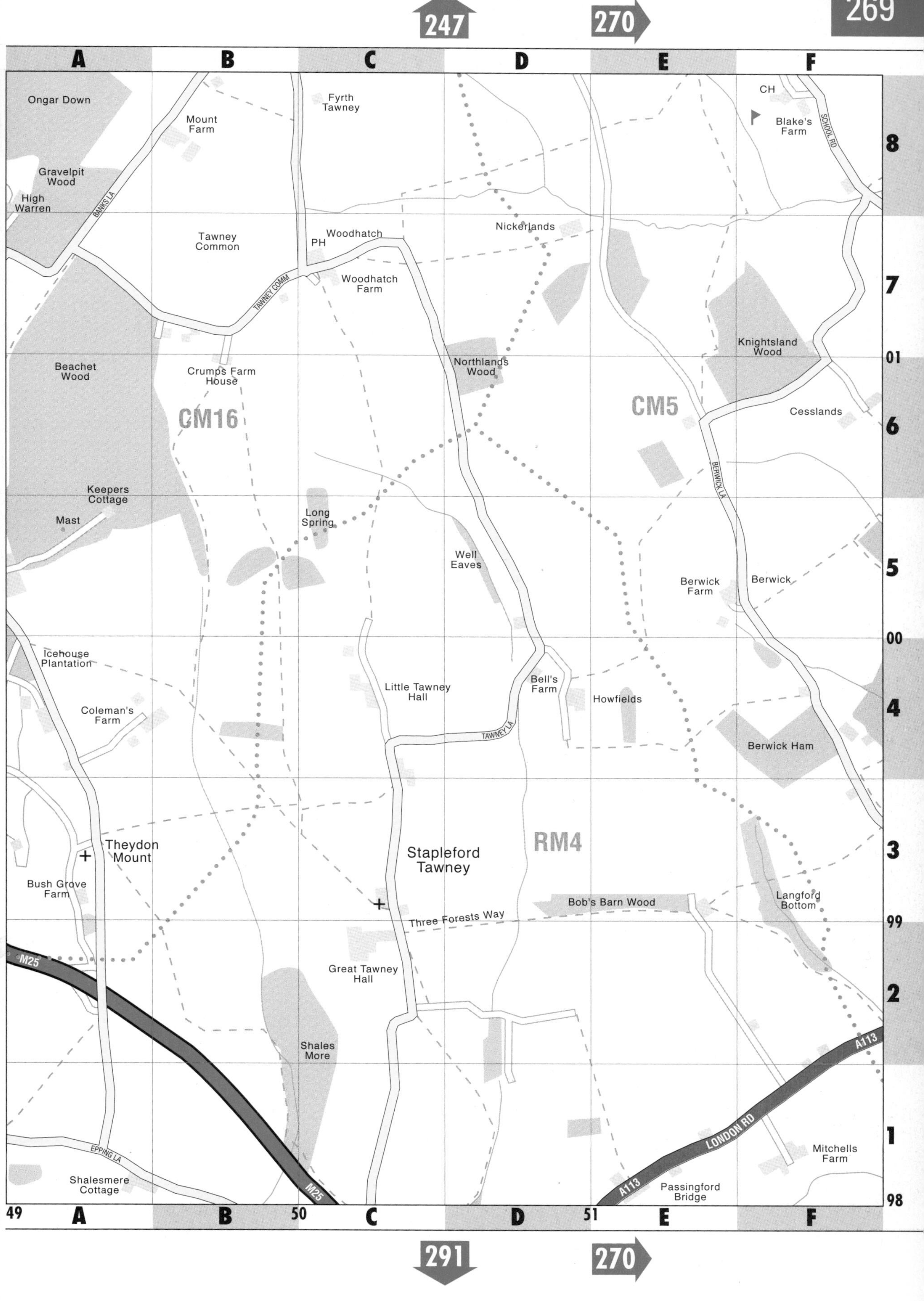

269
248

A **B** **C** **D** **E** **F**

8

Coleman's Farm

Clark's Farm

Kettlebury Spring

A113

Great Colemans

Stewart's Farm

MUTTON ROW

7

HOP GDNS

SCHOOL RD

Three Forests Way

Summerhill

ROMFORD RD

Little Colemans

01

Three Forests Way

CHURCH COTTS

THE HALL BARNS

Hall Cottages

Bridge Farm

6

Stanford Rivers

CM5

CHURCH RD

Wash Bridge

Park Wood

The Old Rectory

OLD RECTORY RD

Little End

5

Icehouse Wood

SANDERS FIELDS

HARE ST

Works

Sewage Works

00

White Bear (PH)

4

Twentyacre Wood

Murrells Farm

LONDON RD

River Roding

Ireland Grove

Traceys Farm

Aspen Wood

Hollingford Spring

3

Tenacre Wood

BERWICK LA

Stoneyrocks Plantation

Little Aspen Wood

Red Wood

CM14

Wayletts

99

Broom Wood

Lady's Pond

2

A113

Lawns

Church Wood

1

RM4

Navestock Hall Farm

LADY'S HILL

DUDBROOK ROAD

Fortification Wood

Shank's Mill Bridge

MILL LA

SHONKS MILL RD

Rose Hall Farm

Hook Wood

CHURCH RD

PRINCE'S RD

98

52 **A** **B** 53 **C** **D** 54 **E** **F**

A B C D E F

8 7 01 6 5 00 4 3 99 2 1 98

STANFORD RIVERS RD
A113
A128
BRENTWOOD RD
Gray's Farm
Hallsford Bridge Ind Est
Stondon Hall
Stondon Hall Farm
CM4
Chestnut Walk
Little Myles
ONGAR RD
Church Wood
Langford Bridge
River Roding
Round Spring
CM5
The Lodge
Churchfields Farm
Littlebury
Great Myles
Stondon Massey House
Mill
Stondon Manor
Langford Bridge Farm
Courtfield Wood
Menageria Wood
Stondon Place
Park Wood
Clapgate Estate
Kelvedon Hall Lodge
Round Wood
CM15
Pump House Farm
Kelvedon Grange
Kelvedon Hall
Priors Wood
CHIVERS RD
The Bungalow
Pole's Wood
ONGAR RD
KELVEDON HALL LA
Germains Farm
Cartshead Wood
Mellow Purgess Farm
Kelvedon Hatch Nuclear Bunker
Mast
Chivers
Cook's Wood
CM14
The Coppice
Merlincock Wood
Kelvedon Hatch Com Prim Sch
THE COPPICE
SCHOOL RD
Mast
Beaconhill Farm
1 LITTLEBURY CT
2 BARLEY FIELD
3 MATCHING FIELD
CHURCH CL
PO
Kelvedon Hatch
BEACON HILL
CHURCH RD
Beacon Hill
LUTHERS CL
MILL LA
CHANDLERS WLK
ROMAN DR
HORSEMAN CT
WINDMILL WAY
The Eagle (PH)
EAGLE LA
KELVEDON GN
GLOVERS FIELD
BRIARWOOD
LYNDALE
ELMTREE AVE
MOWBRAY CROFT
BEACON HILL RD
HOWARD LODGE RD
THE FINCHINGFIELDS
SWAN LA
CYGNET CT
BLACKMORE RD
STOCKSFIELD
Peniel Acad
SWAN WLK
FOX HATCH
BURROWS HO
BROAD MDW
STOCKS LA
SHORTCROFT
GREAT FOX MDW
Dudbrook
DUDBROOK RD
Fox Hatch
Brizes Wood
Twostile Wood
Bois Hall
A128

55 A B 56 C D 57 E F

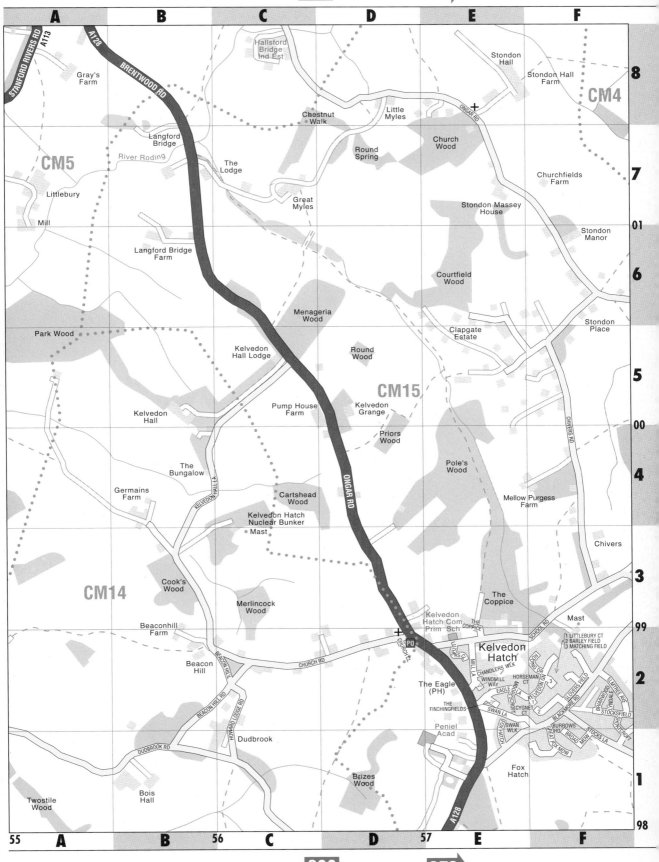

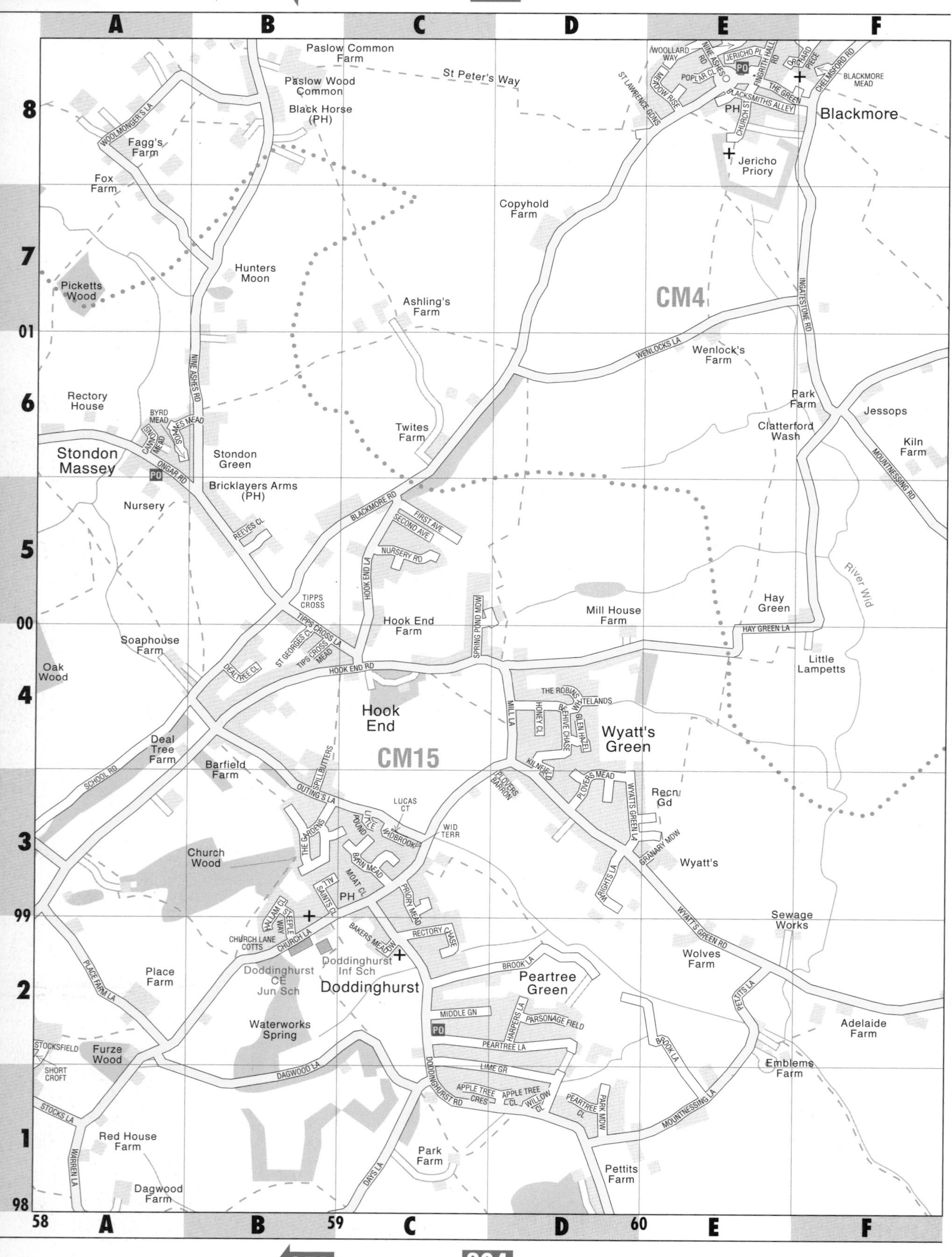

251
274

| A | B | C | D | E | F |

8

Ganders Hall

College Wood

Stoneymore Wood

Marple Tree Farm

St Peter's Way

WOODSIDE COTTS

MAPLETREE LA

MILL GREEN RD

7

Fryerning Wood

Bell Grove

Brick House Farm

Beggar Hill

Mill Green

P

PH

Mapletree La

Mill Green Park

HARDING'S LA

Woodcock Lodge

Whitehouse Farm

+

01

INGATESTONE RD

Portsmoorhall Wood

Furze Hall

Barns Pond

Lyndsey's Farm

Blanket Hall

Nursery

Wr Twr

Wood Barns Farm

BECKCHILL

Redcote

Windmill

6

St Leonards Farm

St Leonards

BLACKMORE RD

Delamas

CM4

Spring Farm

5

Stubbers Farm

Woodbarns Spring

Fryerning Hall

PH

The Hyde

Little Woodbarns

Cemy

+

00

Wasketts

4

Green St

Green Street

MOUNTNESSING RD

Green Street Farm

BAG LA

Dodd's Farm

3

Orchard Farm

Dunstead's Farm

Trueloves

Ray Place Farm

Mandawel

99

TRUELOVES LA

Swallows Cross Farm

CM15

Thoby Priory

Kettles Place

B1002

13

2

WYATT'S GREEN RD

Chiver's Farm

HARE BRIDGE CRES

A12

Swallows Cross

Woodland Cottages

Woodlands Farmhouse

Thoby Priory Farm

INGATESTONE BY-PASS

MARKS CL

COURT VIEW

HEYBRIDGE RD

1

THOBY LA

Master John's Farm

ST ANNE'S RD

RYDAN RD

THE HILL WAY

B1002

A12

BURNTHOUSE LA

98

| A | | B | | C | | D | | E | | F |

61

62

63

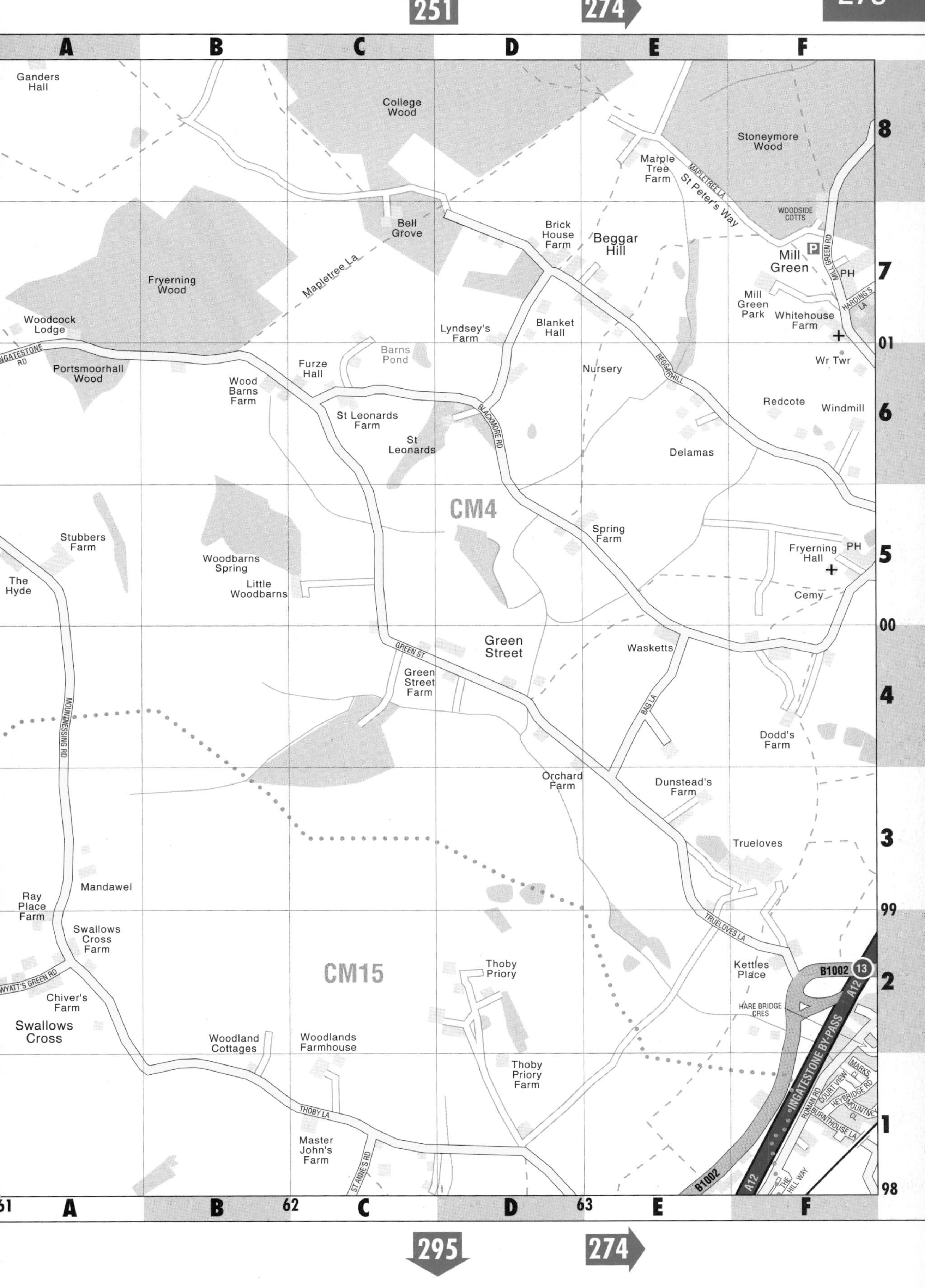

295
274

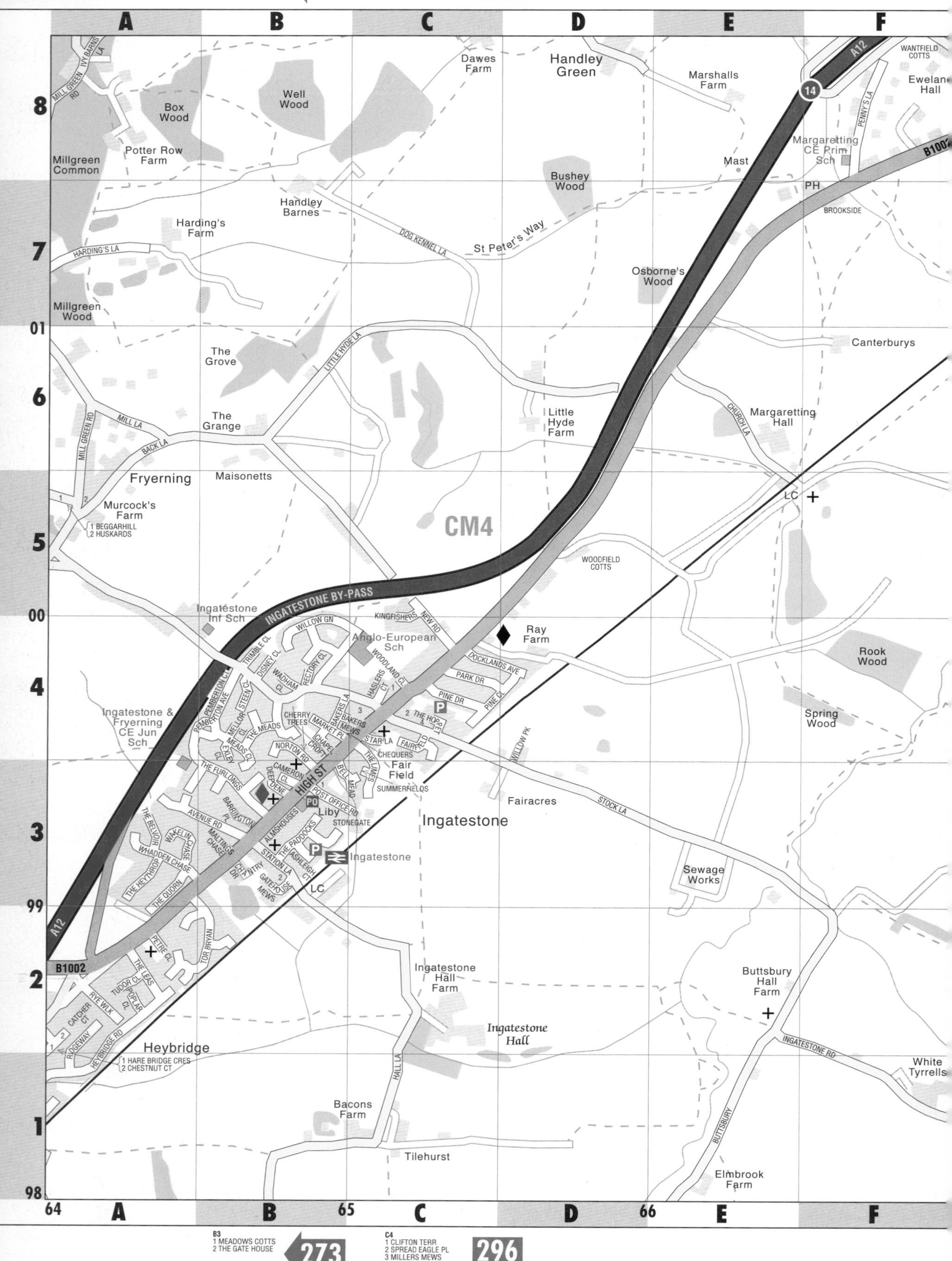

273

252

A B C D E F

8

Mill Green Rd
IVY BARTS LA

Box
Wood

Well
Wood

Dawes
Farm

Handley
Green

Marshalls
Farm

WANTFIELD
COTTS

Ewelan
Hall

A12

14

Millgreen
Common

Potter Row
Farm

Handley
Barnes

Bushey
Wood

Mast

Margaretting
CE Prim
Sch

B1002

7

HARDING'S LA

Harding's
Farm

DOG KENNEL LA

St Peter's Way

Osborne's
Wood

PH

BROOKSIDE

01

Millgreen
Wood

The
Grove

LITTLE HYDE LA

Little
Hyde
Farm

Canterburys

6

MILL LA

The
Grange

BACK LA

Margaretting
Hall

CHURCH LA

LC

MILL GREEN RD

Fryerning

Maisonetts

CM4

Woodfield
Cotts

5

1 2

Murcock's
Farm

1 BEGGARHILL
2 HUSKARDS

Rook
Wood

INGATESTONE BY-PASS

Ingatestone
Inf Sch

KINGFISHERS

NEW RD

WILLOW GN

Anglo-European
Sch

Ray
Farm

00

THIMBLE CL

DISNEY CL

WALSHAM
CL

RECTORY CL

WOODLAND CL

DOCKLANDS AVE

PARK DR

PINE CL

4

Ingatestone &
Fryerning
CE Jun Sch

PEMBERTON AVE

MELLOR CL

STEEN CL

THE MEADS

HASLERS LA

MARKET PL

BAKERS MEWS

P

PINE DR

THE HOP

WILLOW PK

Spring
Wood

CHERRY
TREES

CHAPEL

STAR LA

FAIRY

CHEQUERS

MEADS CL

NORTON RD

CROFT

Fair
Field

HIGH ST

SUMMERFIELDS

3

THE FURLONGS

CAMERON CL

DEEP DENE

BELL MEAD

POST OFFICE RD

PO
Liby
STONEGATE

Fairacres

STOCK LA

Sewage
Works

Buttsbury
Hall
Farm

AVENUE RD

BARRINGTON

MALTINGS CHASE

ALMSHOUSES

THE PADDOCKS

THE ASHLEIGHS

Ingatestone

WAKELIN CHASE

THE BEAULIEUS

WHADDEN CHASE

STATION LA

P

Ingatestone

99

PETRE CL

THE QUORN

GATE RD

LC

THE HEYTHROPS

COX BRYAN

A12

2

B1002

TUDOR CL

RYE WALK

THE LEAS

POPLAR

Ingatestone
Hall
Farm

HALL LA

INGATESTONE RD

White
Tyrrells

CATCHER
CT

RIDGEWAY

HEYBRIDGE RD

Heybridge

1 HARE BRIDGE CRES
2 CHESTNUT CT

Ingatestone
Hall

BUTTSBURY

Elmbrook
Farm

1

Bacons
Farm

Tilehurst

98

64 A 65 B C 66 D E F

B3
1 MEADOWS COTTS
2 THE GATE HOUSE

273

C4
1 CLIFTON TERR
2 SPREAD EAGLE PL
3 MILLERS MEWS
4 INGLETON HO

296

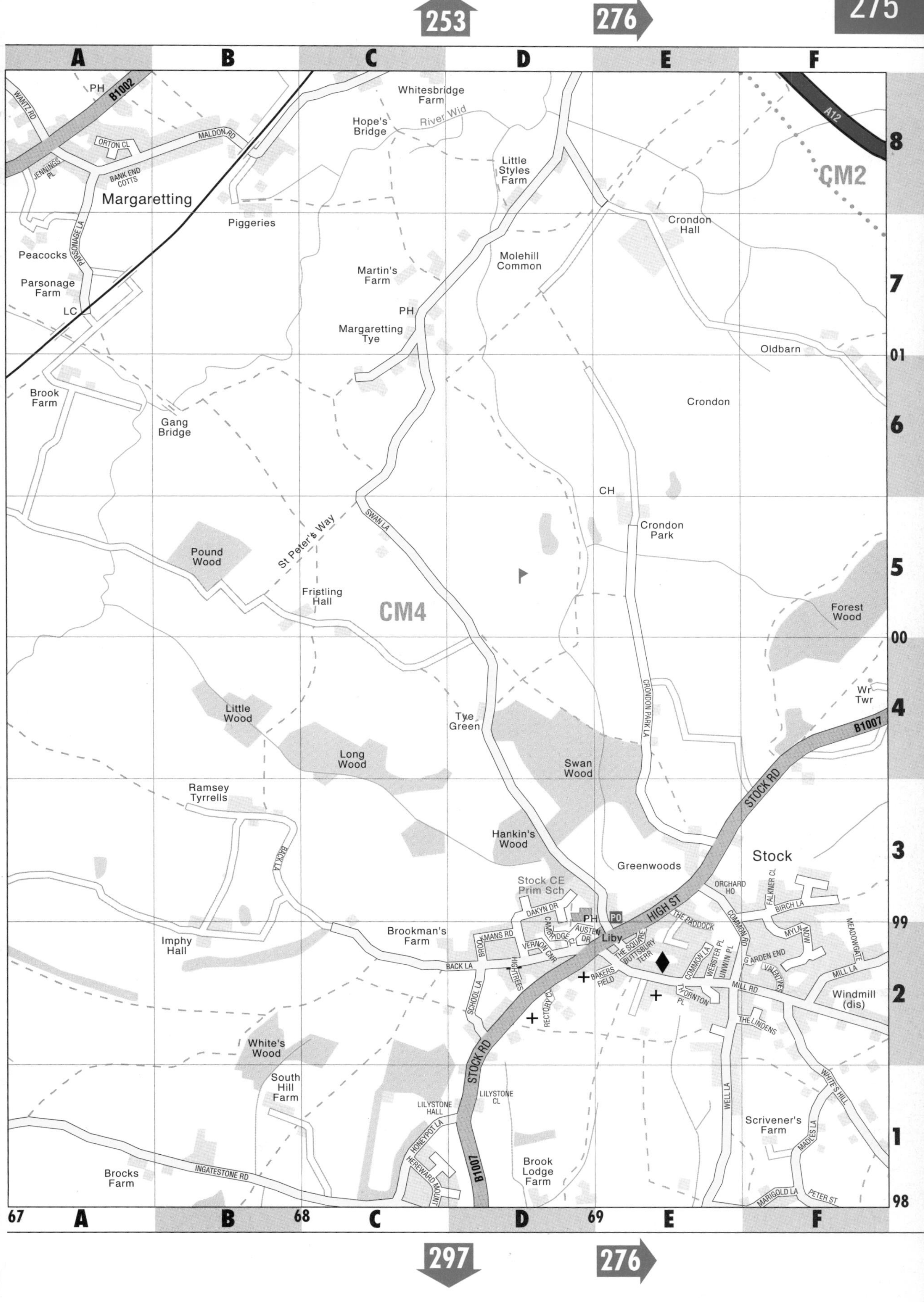

253
276

A B C D E F

8

7

01

6

5

00

4

3

99

2

1

98

CM2

CM4

A12

B1002

Margaretting

WANTZ RD

PH

ORTON CL

MALDON RD

JENNINGS PL

BANK END COTTS

PARSONAGE LA

Peacocks

Parsonage Farm

LC

Brook Farm

Gang Bridge

Pound Wood

St Peter's Way

SWAN LA

Fristling Hall

Piggeries

Hope's Bridge

Whitesbridge Farm

River Wid

Little Styles Farm

Martin's Farm

PH

Margaretting Tye

Molehill Common

Crondon Hall

Oldbarn

Crondon

CH

Crondon Park

Forest Wood

Wr Twr

B1007

STOCK RD

Little Wood

Long Wood

Tye Green

Swan Wood

CRONDON PARK LA

Ramsey Tyrrells

BACK LA

Hankin's Wood

Greenwoods

Stock

Stock CE Prim Sch

ORCHARD HO

FALKNER CL

BIRCH LA

COMMON RD

MEADOWGATE

Imphy Hall

Brookman's Farm

BROOKMANS RD

DAKYN DR

VERNON CNR

CAMBRIDGE

AUSTEN DR

PH

PO

Liby

THE SQUARE

BUTTSBURY TERR

HIGH ST

THE PADDOCK

COMMON LA

WEBSTER PL

UNWIN PL

G ARDEN END

VANEMKES

MYLN

MILL LA

BACK LA

HIGHTREES

SCHOOL LA

RECTORY RD

BAKERS FIELD

THORNTON PL

UNWIN PL

MILL RD

Windmill (dis)

THE LINDENS

White's Wood

South Hill Farm

STOCK RD

LILYSTONE HALL

LILYSTONE CL

HONEYPOT LA

MEREWARD MOUNT

B1007

Brook Lodge Farm

WELL LA

Scrivener's Farm

WHITE'S HILL

MADLES LA

MARIGOLD LA

PETER ST

Brocks Farm

INGATESTONE RD

67 68 69

297
276

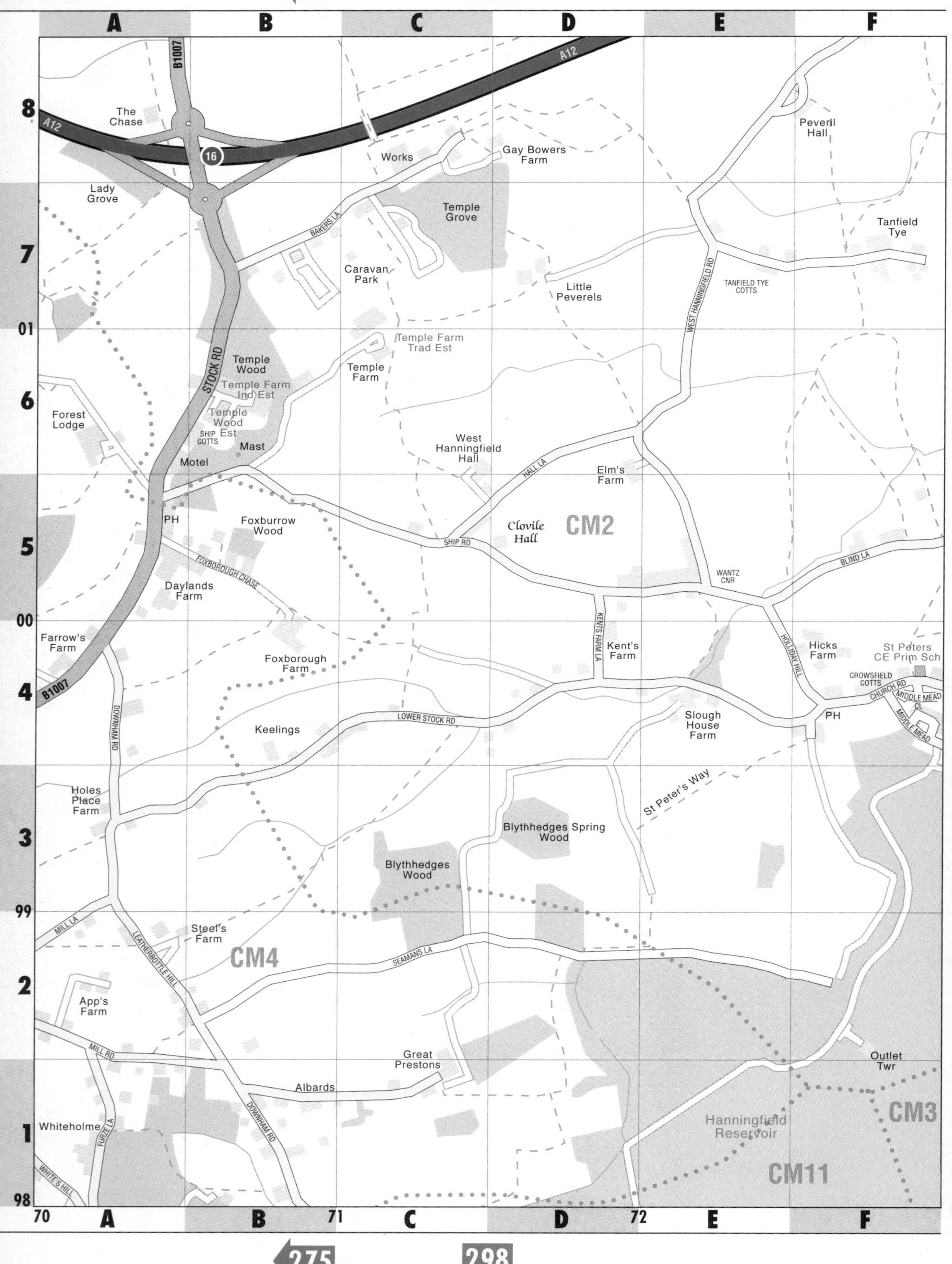

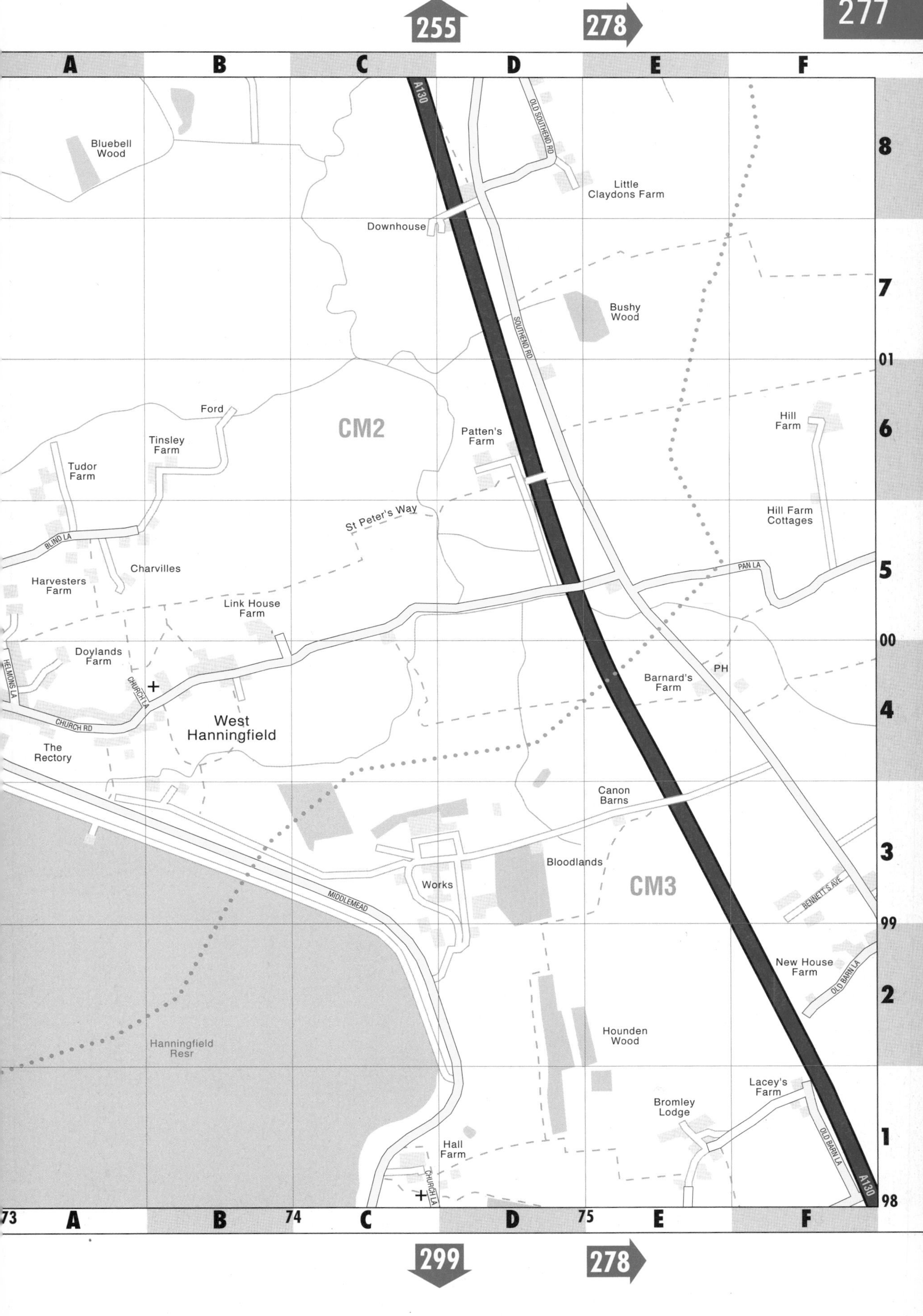

255
278

A B C D E F

8
7
01
6
5
00
4
3
99
2
1
98

A130

Bluebell
Wood

OLD SOUTHEND RD

Downhouse

Little
Claydons Farm

SOUTHEND RD

Bushy
Wood

Hill
Farm

CM2

Ford

Patten's
Farm

Tinsley
Farm

Hill Farm
Cottages

Tudor
Farm

St Peter's Way

PAN LA

BLIND LA

Charvilles

Harvesters
Farm

Link House
Farm

Barnard's
Farm

PH

Doylands
Farm

CHURCH LA

West
Hanningfield

CHURCH RD

Canon
Barns

The
Rectory

Bloodlands

CM3

BENNETT'S AVE

MIDDLEMEAD

Works

New House
Farm

OLD BARN LA

Hanningfield
Resr

Hounden
Wood

Lacey's
Farm

Bromley
Lodge

Hall
Farm

CHURCH LA

A130

HELMONS LA

73 A B 74 C D 75 E F

299
278

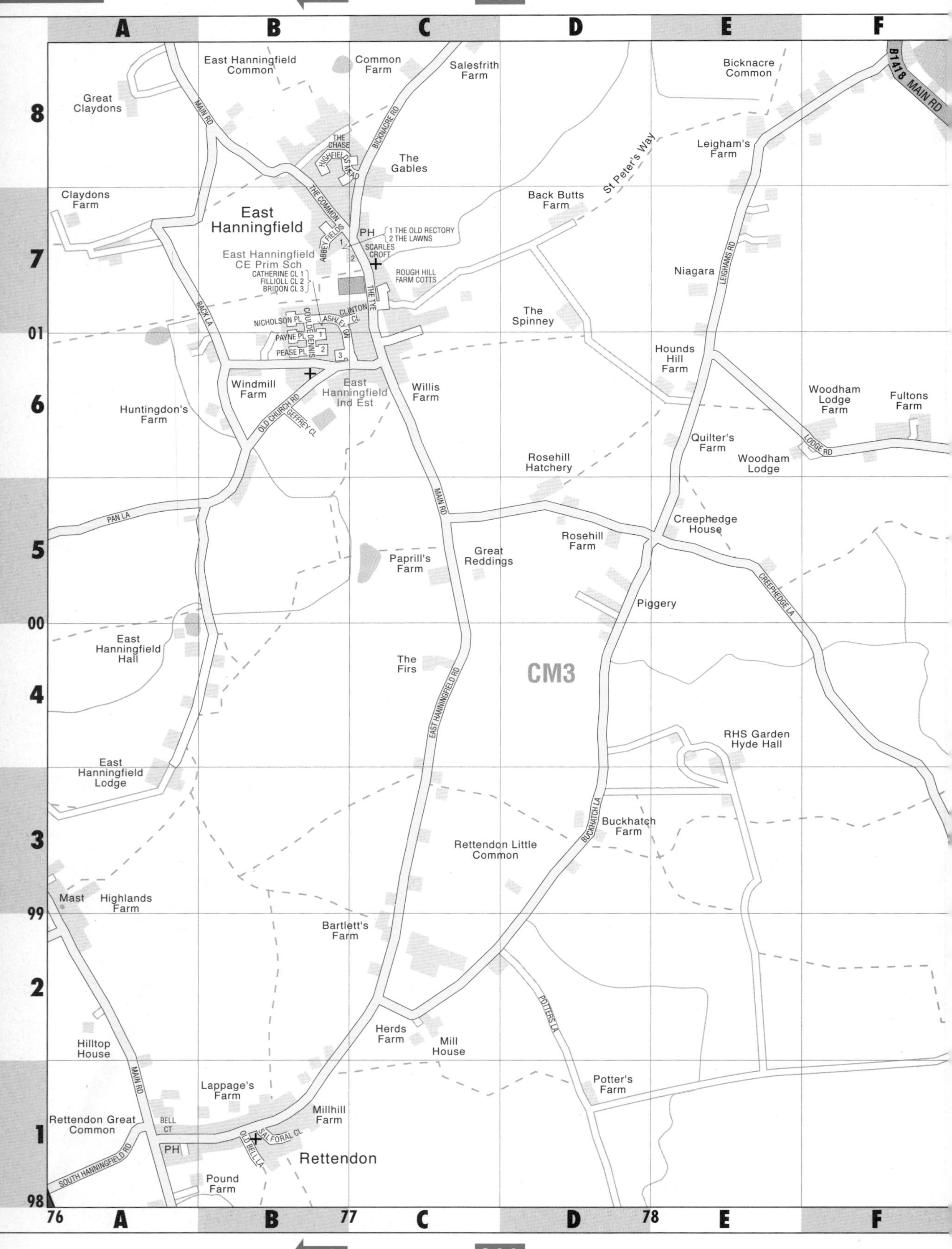

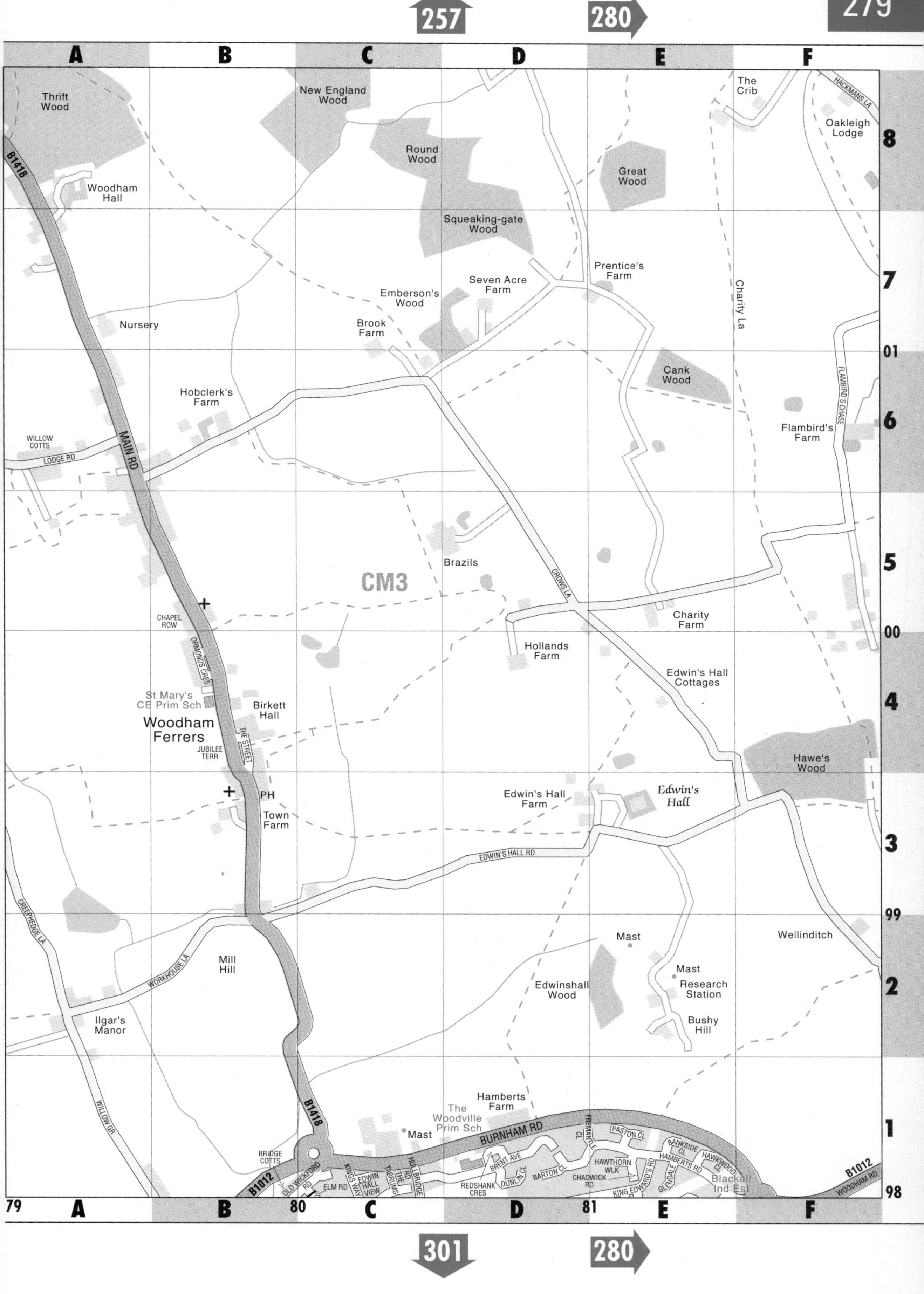
257
280
A
B
C
D
E
F
Thrift Wood
New England Wood
The Crib
HACKMANS LA
Oakleigh Lodge
8
Round Wood
Great Wood
B1418
Woodham Hall
Squeaking-gate Wood
Prentice's Farm
Seven Acre Farm
7
Emberson's Wood
Charity La
Nursery
Brook Farm
01
Cank Wood
FLAMBIRD'S CHASE
Hobclerk's Farm
6
Flambird's Farm
WILLOW COTTS
LODGE RD
MAIN RD
Brazils
5
CM3
CROWS LA
CHAPEL ROW
Charity Farm
Hollands Farm
00
ORMONDS CRES
Edwin's Hall Cottages
St Mary's CE Prim Sch
Birkett Hall
4
Woodham Ferrers
THE STREET
JUBILEE TERR
Hawe's Wood
PH
Edwin's Hall Farm
Edwin's Hall
Town Farm
3
EDWIN'S HALL RD
CREEPHEDGE LA
99
Mast
Wellinditch
Mill Hill
WORKHOUSE LA
Mast
Research Station
Edwinshall Wood
2
Ilgar's Manor
Bushy Hill
WILLOW GR
B1418
Hamberts Farm
The Woodville Prim Sch
1
Mast
BURNHAM RD
FREMANTLE CL
PASTON CL
BANKSIDE CL
HAWKWOOD CL
HAMBERTS RD
BRIDGE COTTS
OLD WICKFORD RD
KINGS WAY
EDWIN HALL VIEW
THE TABRUMS
HULLBRIDGE RD
BRENT AVE
DUNLIN CL
BARTON CL
HAWTHORN WLK
KING EDWARD'S RD
GLENDALE
Blackall Ind Est
B1012
ELM RD
REDSHANK CRES
CHADWICK RD
B1012
WOODHAM RD
98
79
80
81
301
280

CM9

CM3

8
7
01
6
00
5
4
99
2
1
98

A B C D E F

82 83 84

MILL HILL
Walton Hall
Hill Farm
THE GLEBE
THE STREET
Purleigh Hall
CHAPEL LA
Landing Strip (Private)
Howegreen
St Peter's Way
FLAMBIRD'S CHASE
HOWE GREEN RD
Farther Howegreen
Howegreen Farm
Howe Wood
Cold Norton
CHERRY BLOSSOM LA
CROWN RD
BRENNAN CL
VICTORIA RD
KEMEY CL
GREEN TREES AVE
HACKMANS LA
Great Whitmans
Little Whitmans
Wr Twr
LATCHINGDON RD
CLARKE RISE
Blue House Farm
Great Canney
CHARTERHOUSE COTTS 1
EAST CANNEY COTTS 2
PH
FERRIS AVE
Cold Norton Prim Sch
STATION CRES
CH
Beacon Hill
STOW RD
HAGG HILL
ST STEPHENS RD
THE FAIRWAYS
Canney Wood
New Farm
PH
Wright's Ley Wood
PH
THE STREET
1 SMYTHE ROW
2 STOW VILLAS
1
2
Stow Maries
Stow Hall Farm
Honeywood Farm
PH
RIDLEY COTTS
WOODHAM RD
Poorhouse Wood
HONEY POT LA
Pantile Wood
Brookmead Grove
99
CHURCH LA
B1012
LOWER BURNHAM RD
High Hall Cottages
Great Hayes
Rookery Farm
ROOKERY LA
Yondah
FRENCH RD
Morris Farm
HOGWELL CHASE
Slate Hall Cottages
LITTLE HAYES CHASE
Skinner's Wick
B1012

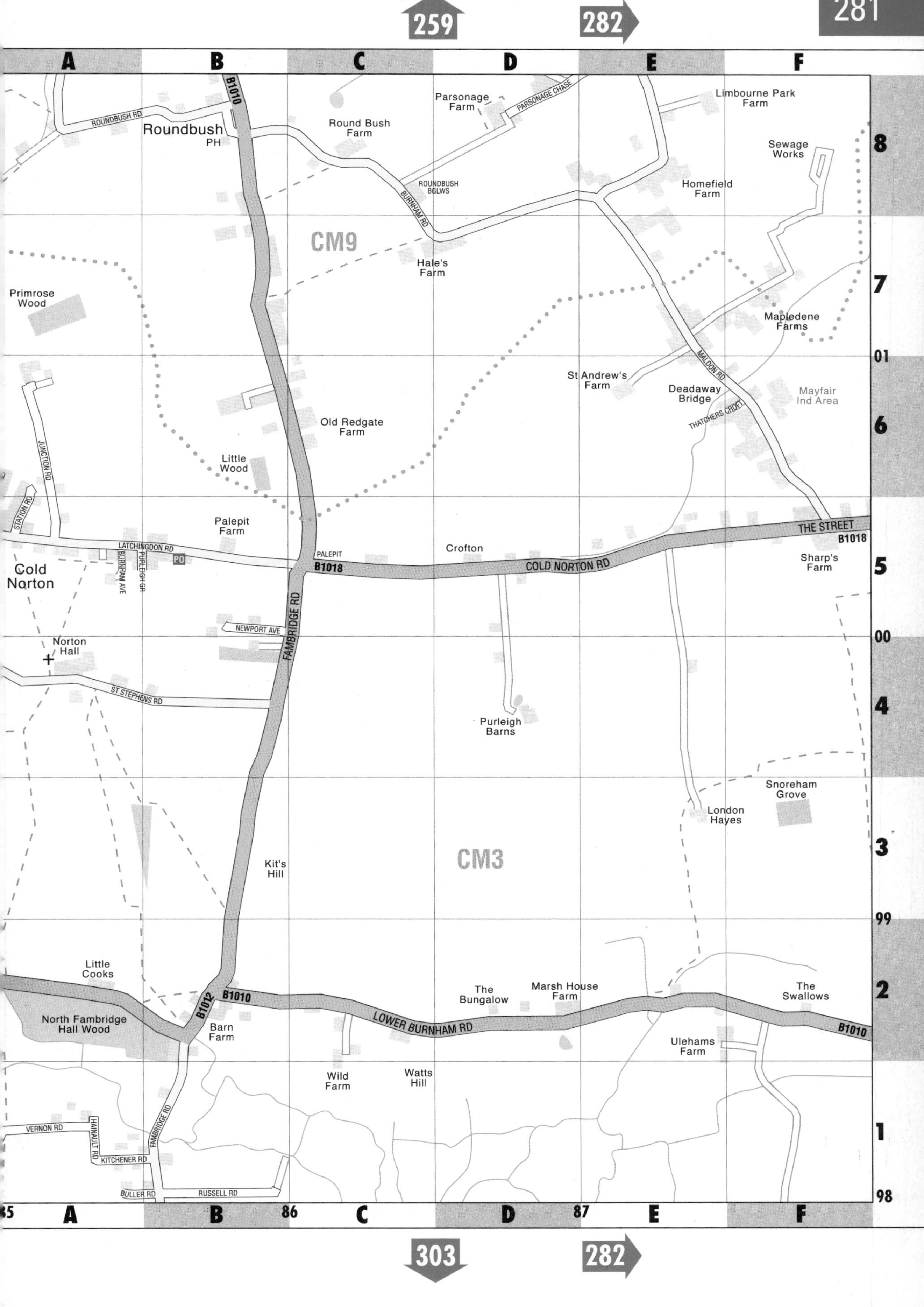

A B C D E F

ROUNDBUSH RD
Roundbush
PH
B1010
Round Bush
Farm
Parsonage
Farm
PARSONAGE CHASE
Limbourne Park
Farm

8

Sewage
Works

CM9
ROUNDBUSH
BGLWS
BURNHAM RD
Hale's
Farm
Homefield
Farm

Primrose
Wood

7

MALDON RD
Mapledene
Farms

01

JUNCTION RD
Old Redgate
Farm
St Andrew's
Farm
Deadaway
Bridge
THATCHERS CROFT
Mayfair
Ind Area

6

Little
Wood

STATION RD
Palepit
Farm
THE STREET
B1018

Cold
Norton
LATCHINGDON RD
PURLEIGH GR
BURNHAM AVE
PO
PALEPIT
B1018
Crofton
COLD NORTON RD
Sharp's
Farm

5

FAMBRIDGE RD
NEWPORT AVE

Norton
Hall
+

00

ST STEPHENS RD

4

Purleigh
Barns

Snoreham
Grove

CM3
Kit's
Hill
London
Hayes

3

99

Little
Cooks
B1012
B1010
The
Bungalow
Marsh House
Farm
LOWER BURNHAM RD
The
Swallows
B1010

2

North Fambridge
Hall Wood
Barn
Farm
Ulehams
Farm

FAMBRIDGE RD
VERNON RD
HAINAULT RD
KITCHENER RD
Wild
Farm
Watts
Hill

1

BULLER RD
RUSSELL RD

98

85 A B 86 C D 87 E F

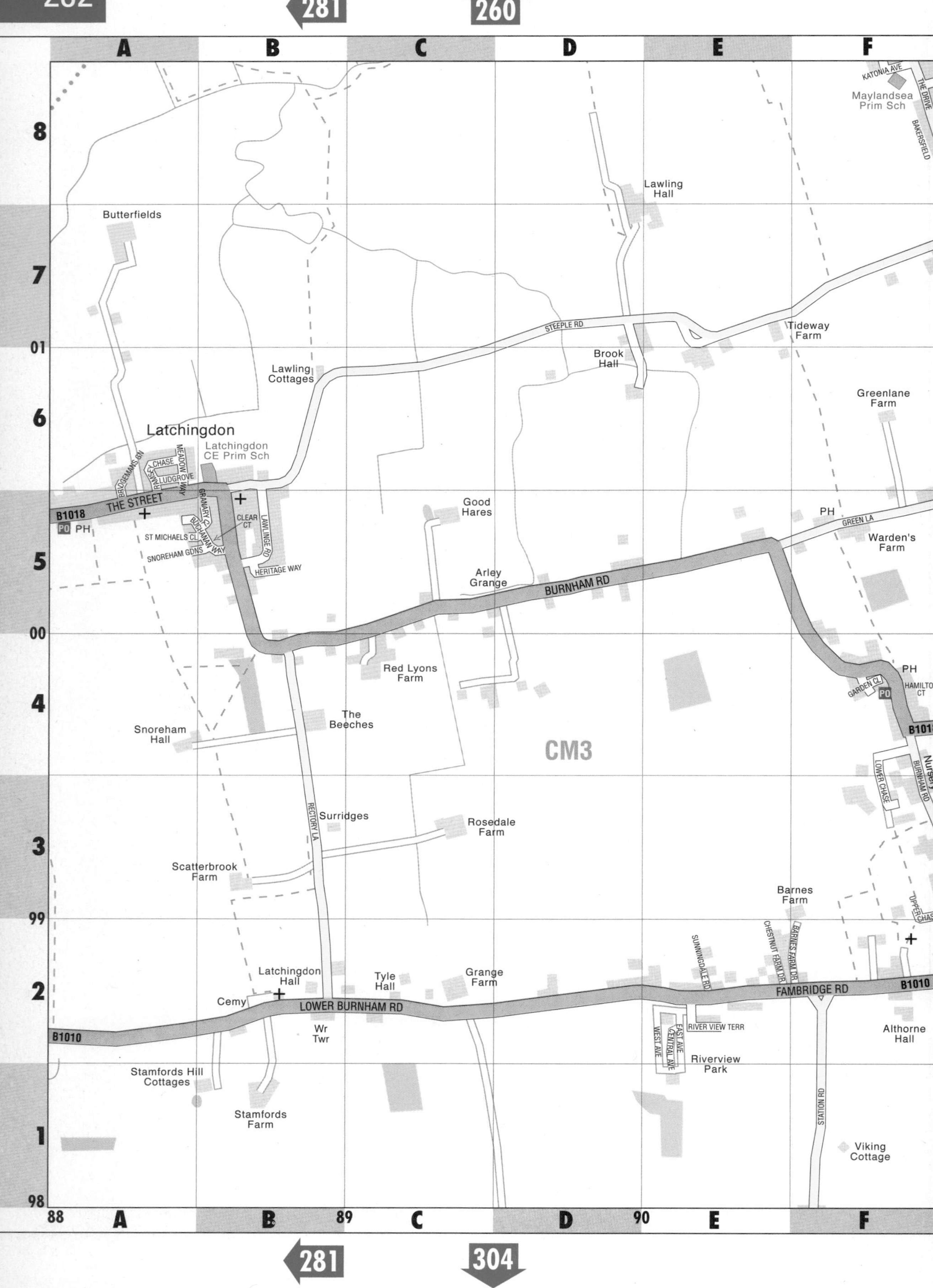

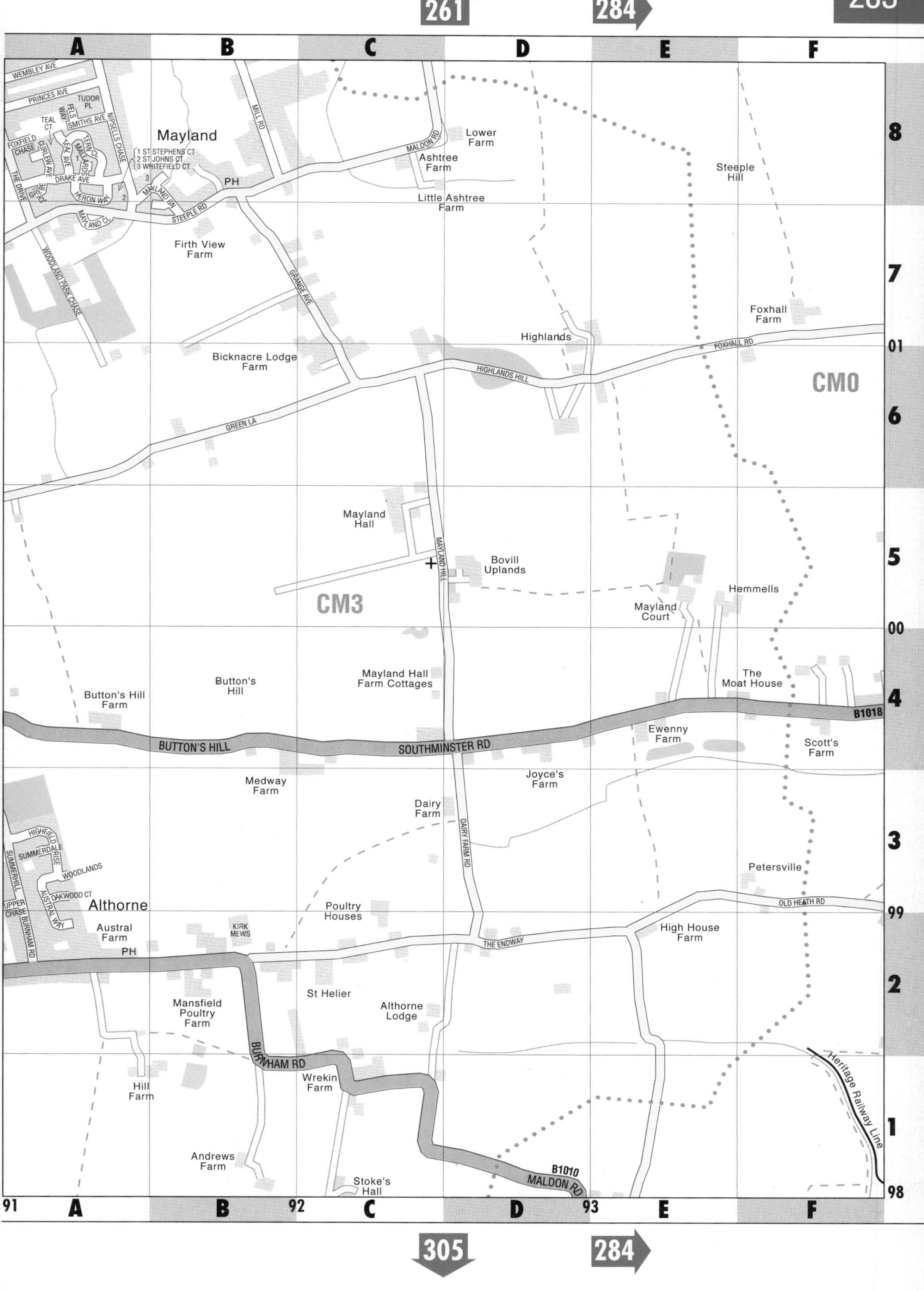
261
284
A
B
C
D
E
F
8
7
01
6
5
00
4
3
99
2
1
98
91
92
93
Mayland
WEMBLEY AVE
PRINCES AVE
TUDOR PL
FELS WAY
SMITHS AVE
TEAL CT
FOXFIELD CHASE
CURLEW AVE
TEAL AVE
MALLARDS
TERN CL
NIPSELLS CHASE
1 ST STEPHENS CT
2 ST JOHNS CT
3 WHITEFIELD CT
THE DRIVE
DRAKE AVE
HERON WAY
MAYLAND GN
MAYLAND CL
STEEPLE RD
MILL RD
MALDON RD
PH
Lower Farm
Ashtree Farm
Little Ashtree Farm
Steeple Hill
Firth View Farm
WOODLAND PARK CHASE
GRANGE AVE
Foxhall Farm
Highlands
FOXHALL RD
HIGHLANDS HILL
Bicknacre Lodge Farm
GREEN LA
CM0
Mayland Hall
MAYLAND HILL
Bovill Uplands
CM3
Hemmells
Mayland Court
Button's Hill Farm
Button's Hill
Mayland Hall Farm Cottages
The Moat House
B1018
BUTTON'S HILL
SOUTHMINSTER RD
Ewenny Farm
Scott's Farm
Medway Farm
Joyce's Farm
Dairy Farm
DAIRY FARM RD
HIGHFIELD RISE
SUMMERDALE
WOODLANDS
SUMMERHILL
OAKWOOD CT
AUSTRAL WAY
UPPER CHASE
BURNHAM RD
Althorne
Petersville
Poultry Houses
OLD HEATH RD
Austral Farm
KIRK MEWS
PH
THE ENDWAY
High House Farm
St Helier
Mansfield Poultry Farm
Althorne Lodge
BURNHAM RD
Wrekin Farm
Heritage Railway Line
Hill Farm
Andrews Farm
Stoke's Hall
B1010
MALDON RD
305
284

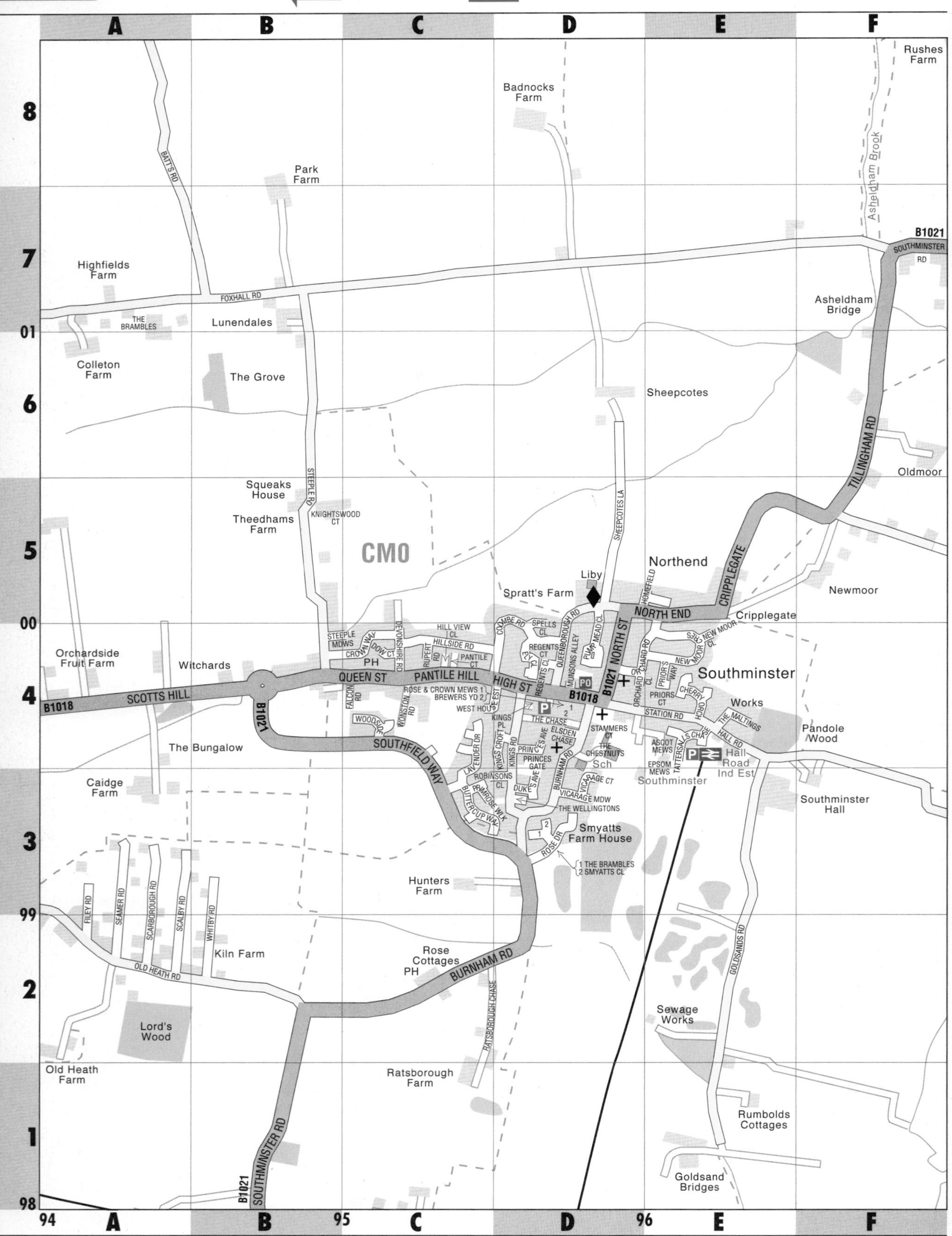

283 262

283 306

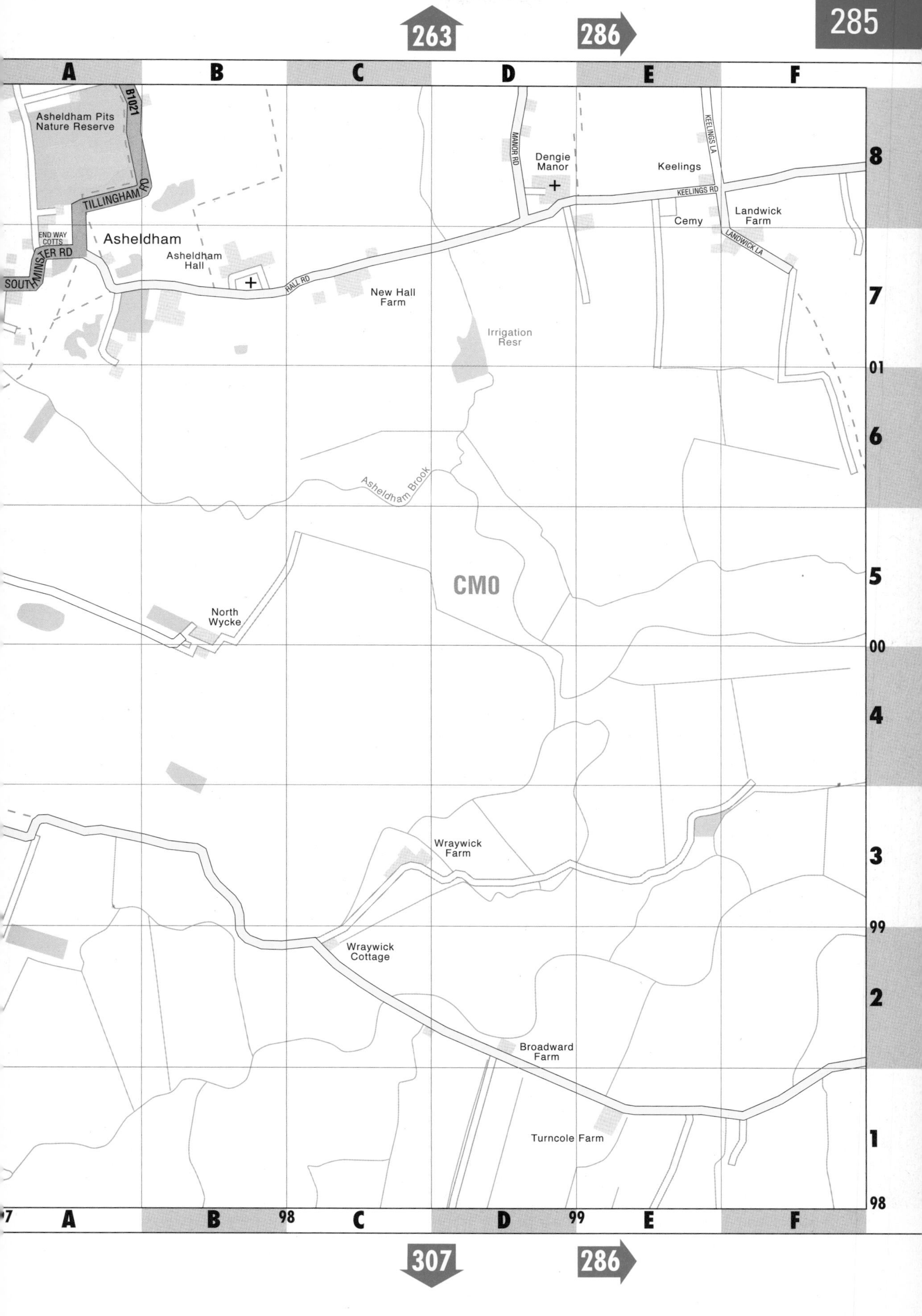

263
286

A B C D E F

8

7

01

6

5

00

4

3

99

2

1

98

Asheldham Pits Nature Reserve

B1021

Asheldham

TILLINGHAM RD

END WAY COTTS

SOUTHMINSTER RD

Asheldham Hall

HALL RD

New Hall Farm

MANOR RD

Dengie Manor

Keelings

KEELINGS LA

KEELINGS RD

Cemy

Landwick Farm

LANDWICK LA

Irrigation Resr

Asheldham Brook

CMO

North Wycke

Wraywick Farm

Wraywick Cottage

Broadward Farm

Turncole Farm

A B C D E F

7 98 99

285
264
383

A   B   C   D   E   F

8   Bushey Piece
East Ware Farm
KEELINGS RD

Grange Outfall

7   Round Barn
Asheldham Brook

01

BRIDGEWICK RD

6

5   Brook Farm

CMO

00   Dengie Marshes

4   Bridgewick Arts Ctr

3

Court Farm

99

Middle Wick

2   Middle Wick Cottage

1   Montsale Bungalow

98
00   A   B   01   C   D   02   E   F

285
308
383

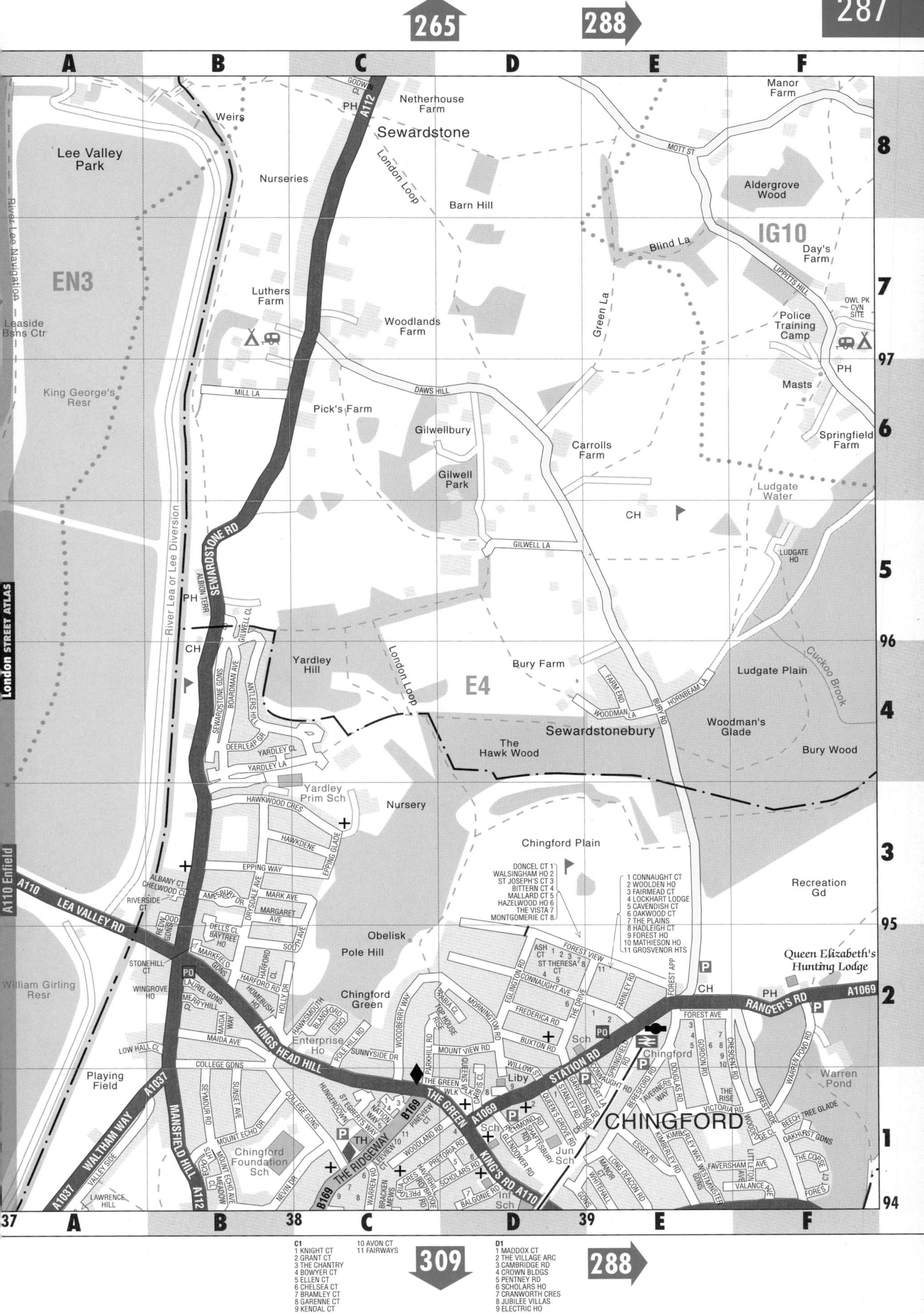

C1
1 KNIGHT CT
2 GRANT CT
3 THE CHANTRY
4 BOWYER CT
5 ELLEN CT
6 CHELSEA CT
7 BRAMLEY CT
8 GARENNE CT
9 KENDAL CT
10 AVON CT
11 FAIRWAYS

D1
1 MADDOX CT
2 THE VILLAGE ARC
3 CAMBRIDGE RD
4 CROWN BLDGS
5 PENTNEY RD
6 SCHOLARS HO
7 CRANWORTH CRES
8 JUBILEE VILLAS
9 ELECTRIC HO

287
266

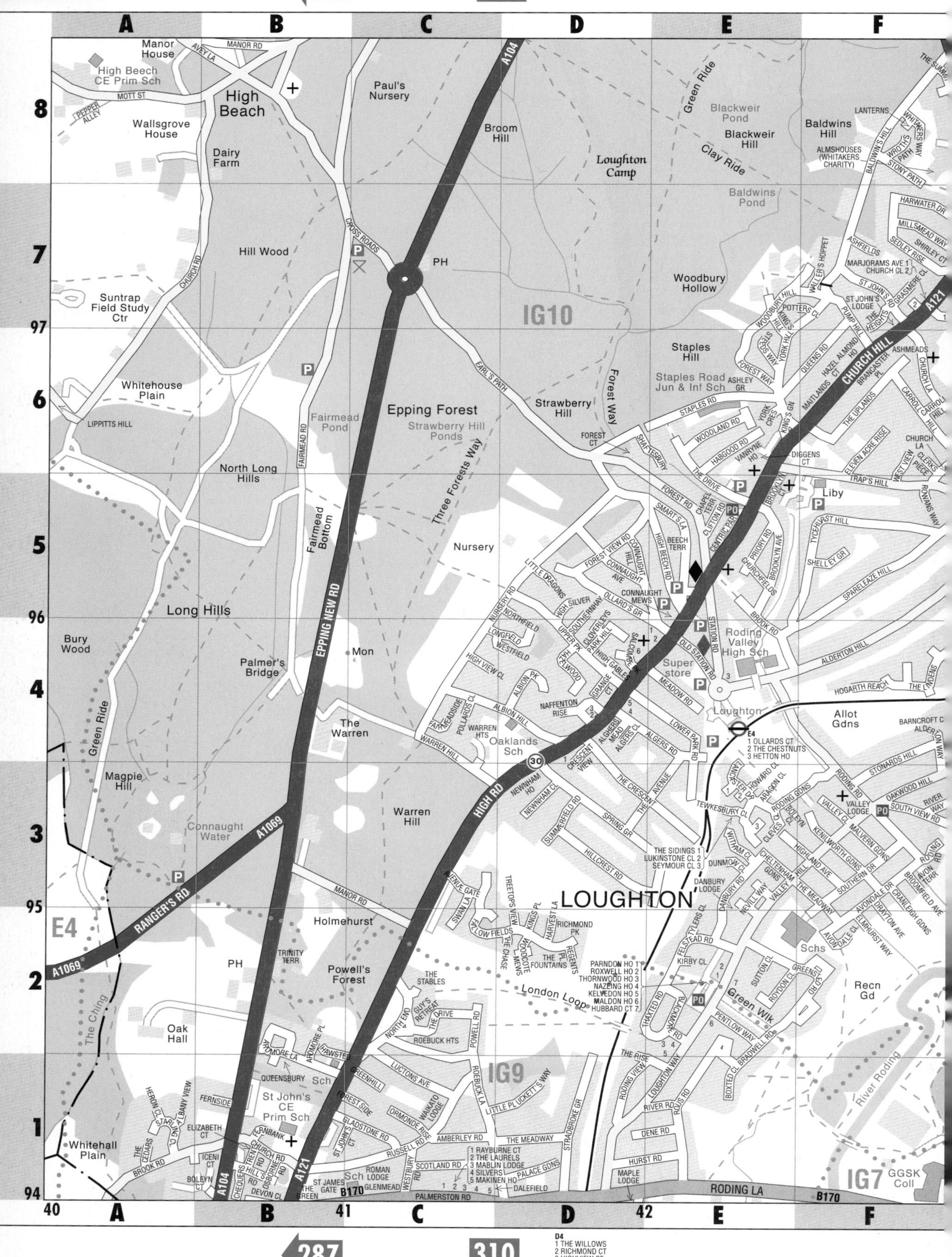

287
310

D4
1 THE WILLOWS
2 RICHMOND CT
3 HIGHVIEW CT
4 CARLTON HO
5 COLLINS CT
6 HOMECHERRY HO

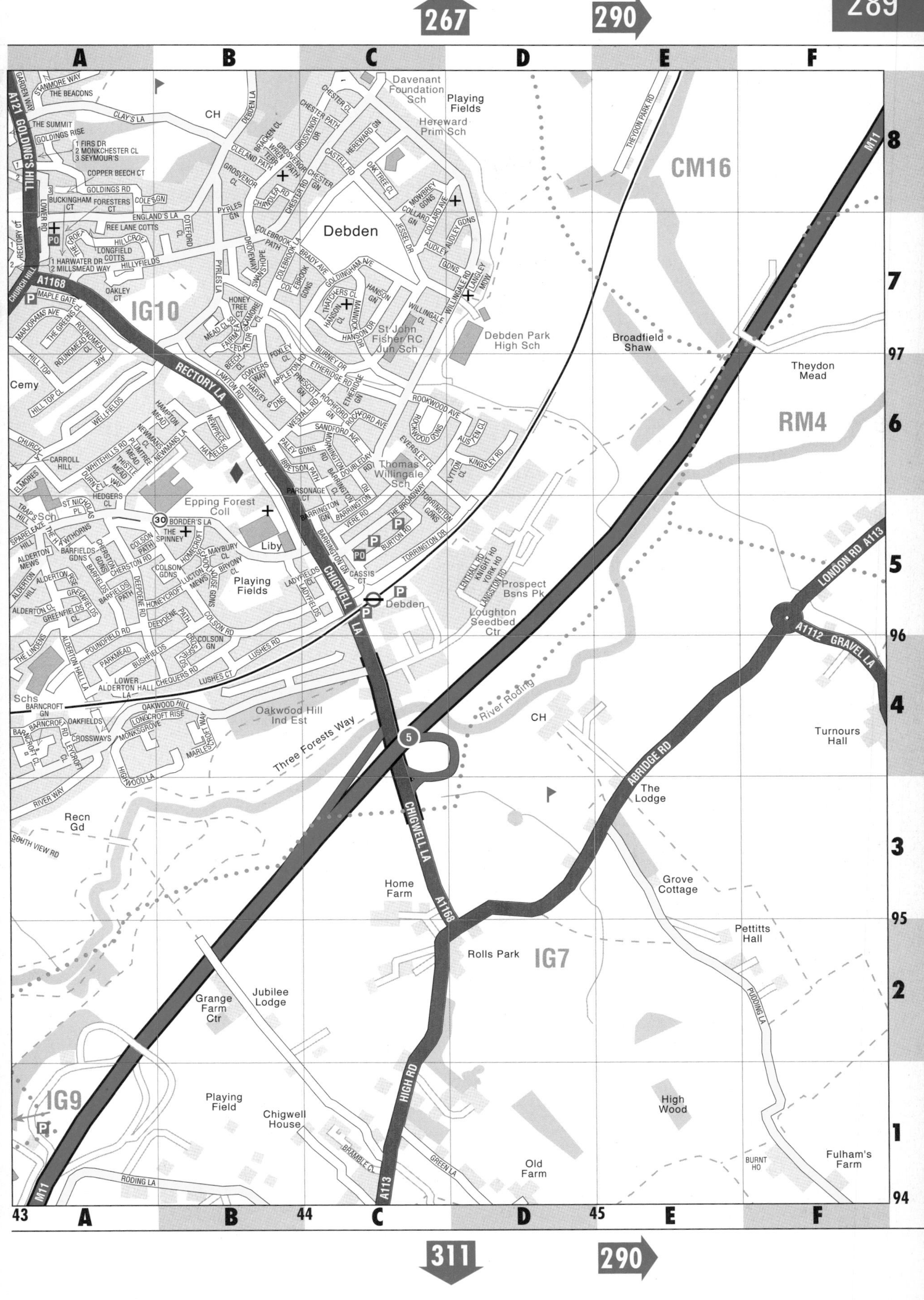

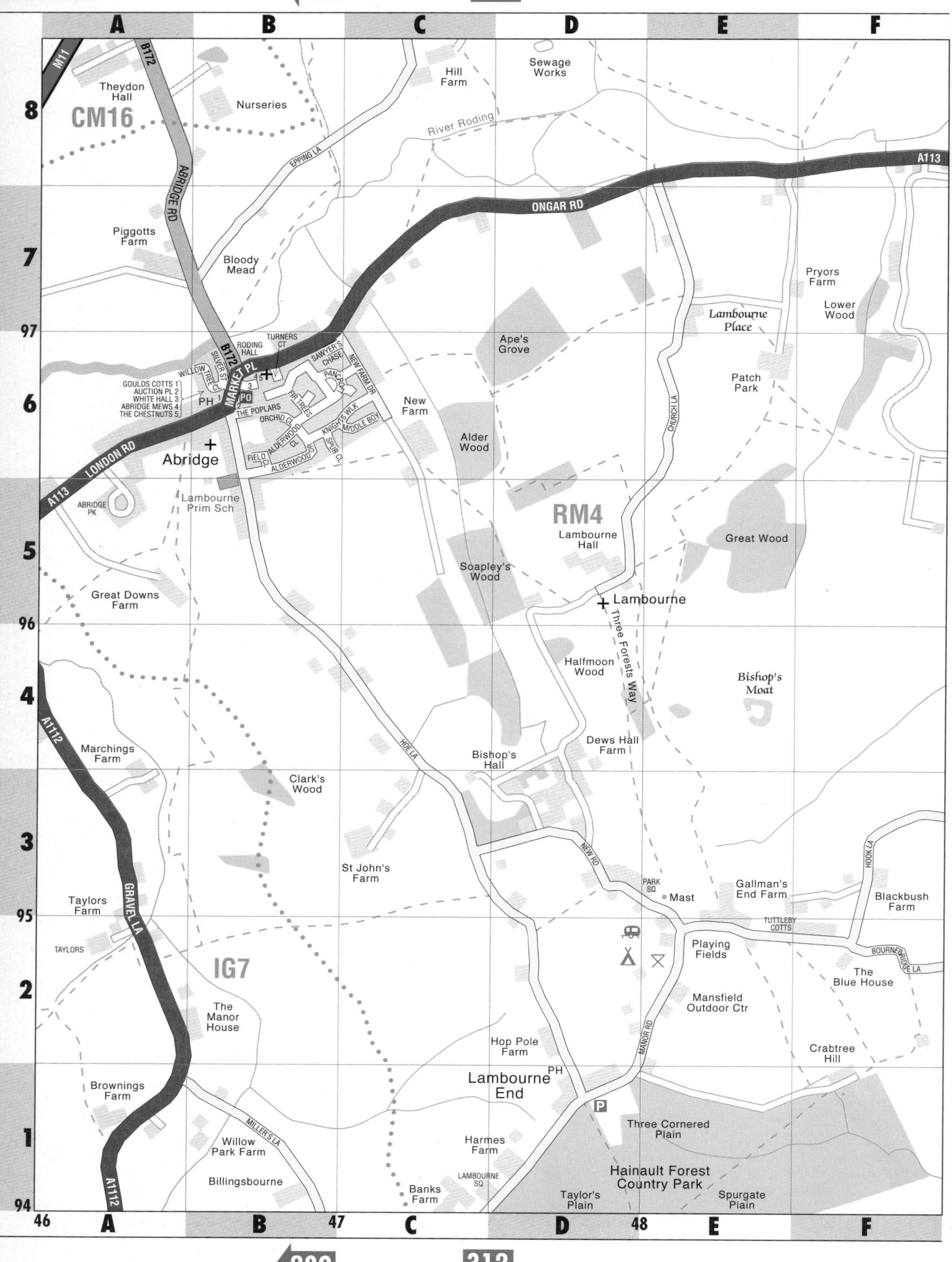

A B C D E F

8

CM16

Theydon Hall

Nurseries

Hill Farm

Sewage Works

River Roding

A113

ONGAR RD

7

Piggotts Farm

Bloody Mead

Pryors Farm

Lower Wood

97

Lambourne Place

Patch Park

Roding Hall

TURNERS CT

SAWYER'S CHASE

Ape's Grove

6

GOULDS COTTS 1
AUCTION PL 2
WHITE HALL 3
ABRIDGE MEWS 4
THE CHESTNUTS 5

MARKET PL

SILVER ST

WILLOW TREE CL

B172

PH

PO

THE POPLARS

ORCHID CL

FIR TREES

NEW FARM DR

PANS CT

KNIGHTS WLK

MIDDLE BDY

New Farm

Alder Wood

CHURCH LA

Abridge

London Rd

A113

LONDON RD

FIELD

ALDERWOOD CL

ALDERWOOD

ALDERWOOD

SPUR CL

RM4

Lambourne Hall

Great Wood

ABRIDGE PK

Lambourne Prim Sch

Soapley's Wood

Lambourne

5

Great Downs Farm

Three Forests Way

96

Halfmoon Wood

Bishop's Moat

4

A1112

HOPE LA

Bishop's Hall

Dews Hall Farm

Marchings Farm

Clark's Wood

NEW RD

HOOK LA

3

GRAVEL LA

St John's Farm

Gallman's End Farm

Blackbush Farm

95

Taylors Farm

PARK SQ

Mast

TUTTLEBY COTTS

BOURNEBRIDGE LA

TAYLORS

Playing Fields

The Blue House

2

IG7

The Manor House

Mansfield Outdoor Ctr

Crabtree Hill

MANOR RD

Hop Pole Farm

PH

Brownings Farm

Lambourne End

Three Cornered Plain

1

MILLER'S LA

Willow Park Farm

P

Harmes Farm

Hainault Forest Country Park

Spurgate Plain

A1112

Billingsbourne

Banks Farm

LAMBOURNE SQ

Taylor's Plain

94

46 A B 47 C D 48 E F

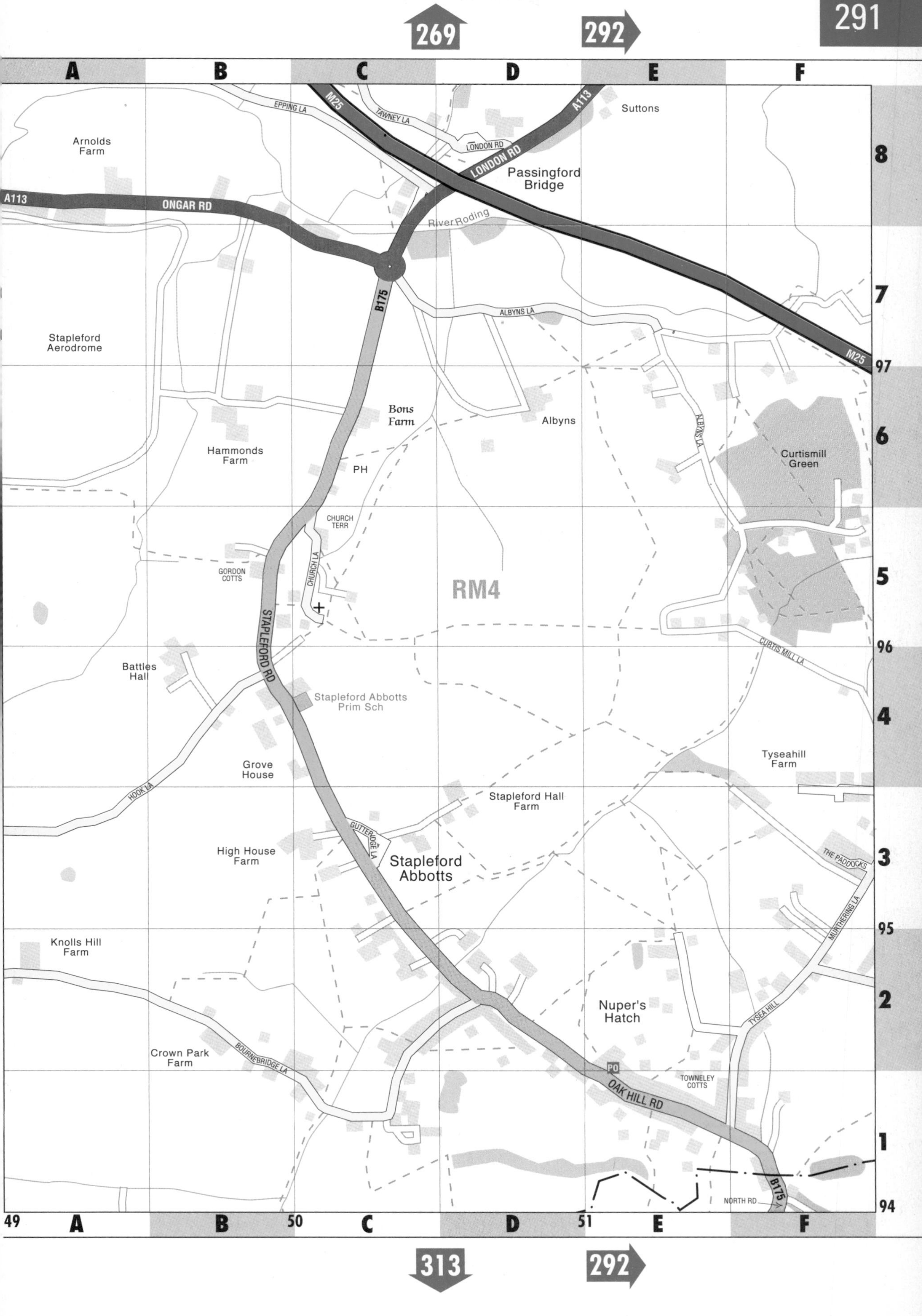

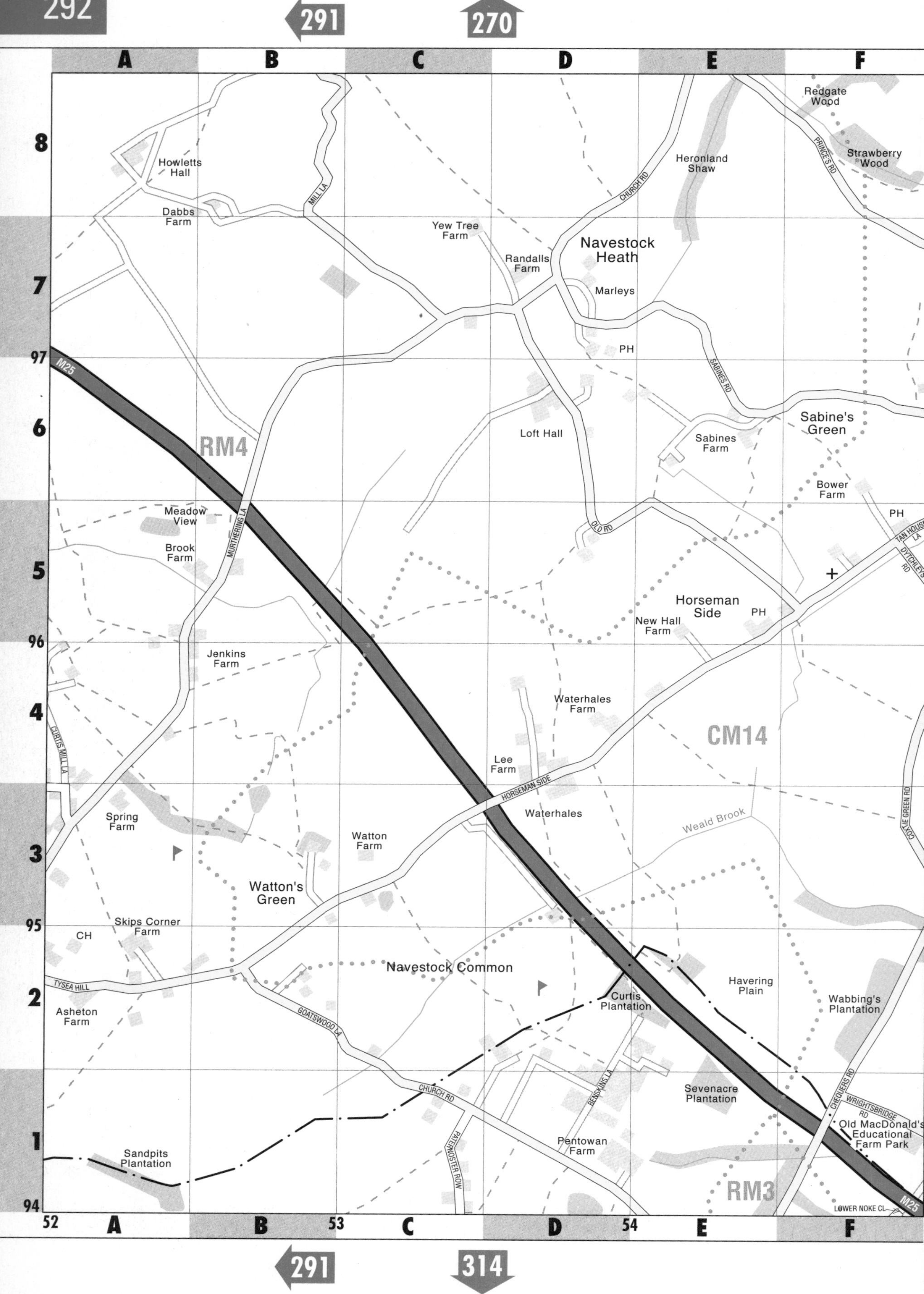

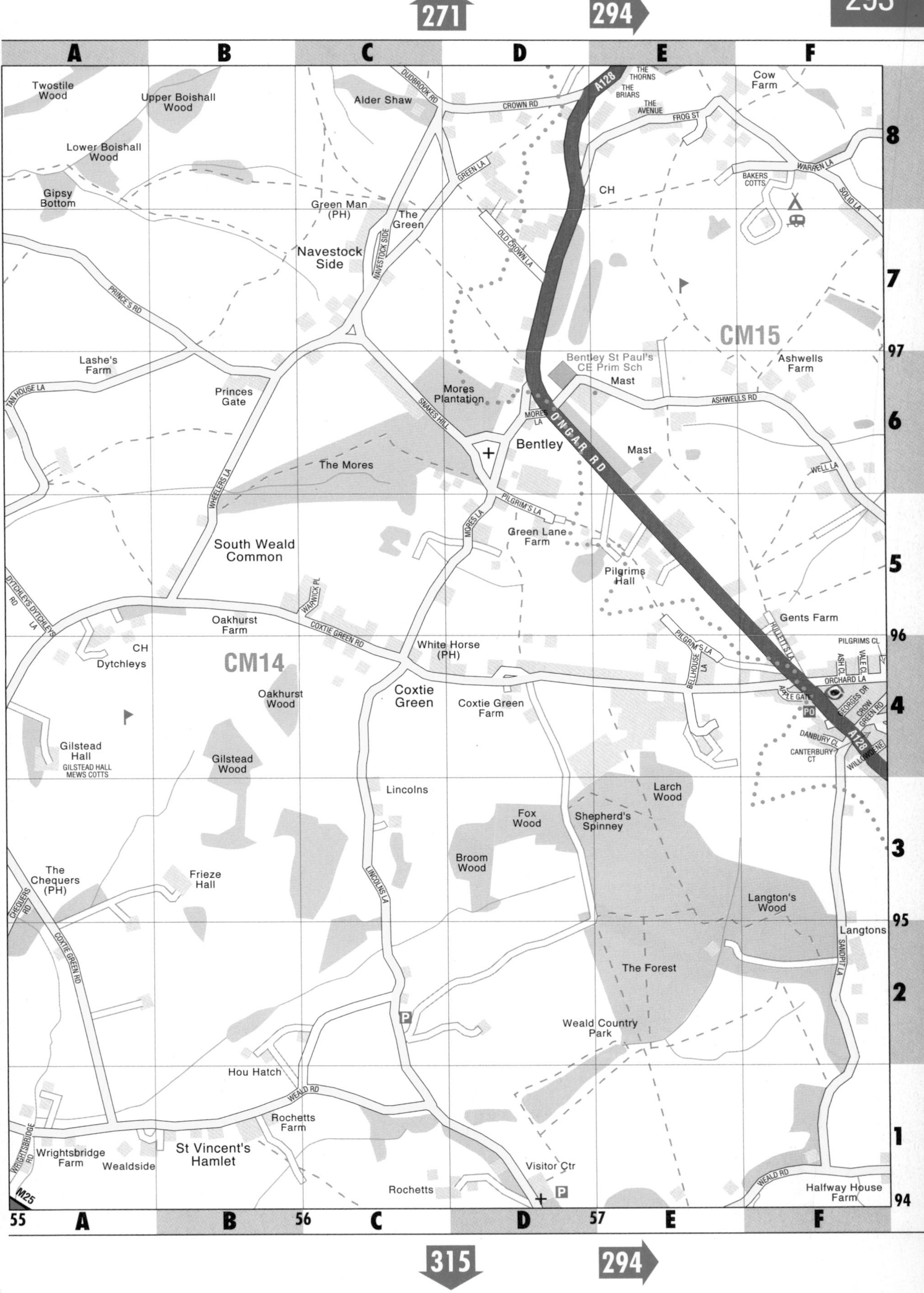

271
294

A   B   C   D   E   F

Twostile
Wood

Upper Boishall
Wood

Lower Boishall
Wood

Gipsy
Bottom

Green Man
(PH)

The
Green

Alder Shaw

DUDBROOK RD

CROWN RD

A128

THE
THORNS

THE
BRIARS

THE
AVENUE

FROG ST

Cow
Farm

WARREN LA

SOLID LA

8

NAVESTOCK SIDE

Navestock
Side

PRINCE'S RD

Lashe's
Farm

Princes
Gate

TAN HOUSE LA

GREEN LA

OLD CROWN LA

CH

BAKERS
COTTS

7

CM15

97

Mores
Plantation

Bentley St Paul's
CE Prim Sch

Mast

ASHWELLS RD

Ashwells
Farm

6

SNAKES HILL

The Mores

MORES
LA

Bentley

Mast

WELL LA

WHEELERS LA

South Weald
Common

PILGRIM'S LA

Green Lane
Farm

Pilgrims
Hall

ONGAR RD

MORES LA

5

WARWICK PL

Oakhurst
Farm

COXTIE GREEN RD

White Horse
(PH)

Gents Farm

PILGRIM'S LA

PILGRIMS CL

ASH CL

VALE CL

96

DITCHLEYS
RD

DITCHLEYS
LA

CH
Dytchleys

CM14

Oakhurst
Wood

Coxtie
Green

Coxtie Green
Farm

BELLHOUSE LA

RILLETT'S LA

APPLE GATE

ORCHARD LA

ST GEORGE'S DR

CROWN
GREEN RD

PO

A128

4

Gilstead
Hall

GILSTEAD HALL
MEWS COTTS

Gilstead
Wood

Lincolns

Fox
Wood

Shepherd's
Spinney

Larch
Wood

DANBURY CL

CANTERBURY
CT

WILLOW LA

3

The
Chequers
(PH)

CHEQUERS
RD

COXTIE GREEN RD

Frieze
Hall

LINCOLNS LA

Broom
Wood

The Forest

Langton's
Wood

Langtons

SANDPIT LA

95

2

Hou Hatch

WEALD RD

Rochetts
Farm

Weald Country
Park

WRIGHTSBRIDGE
RD

Wrightsbridge
Farm

Wealdside

St Vincent's
Hamlet

Rochetts

Visitor Ctr

P

WEALD RD

Halfway House
Farm

1

M25

94

55   A   56   B   C   57   D   E   F

315
294

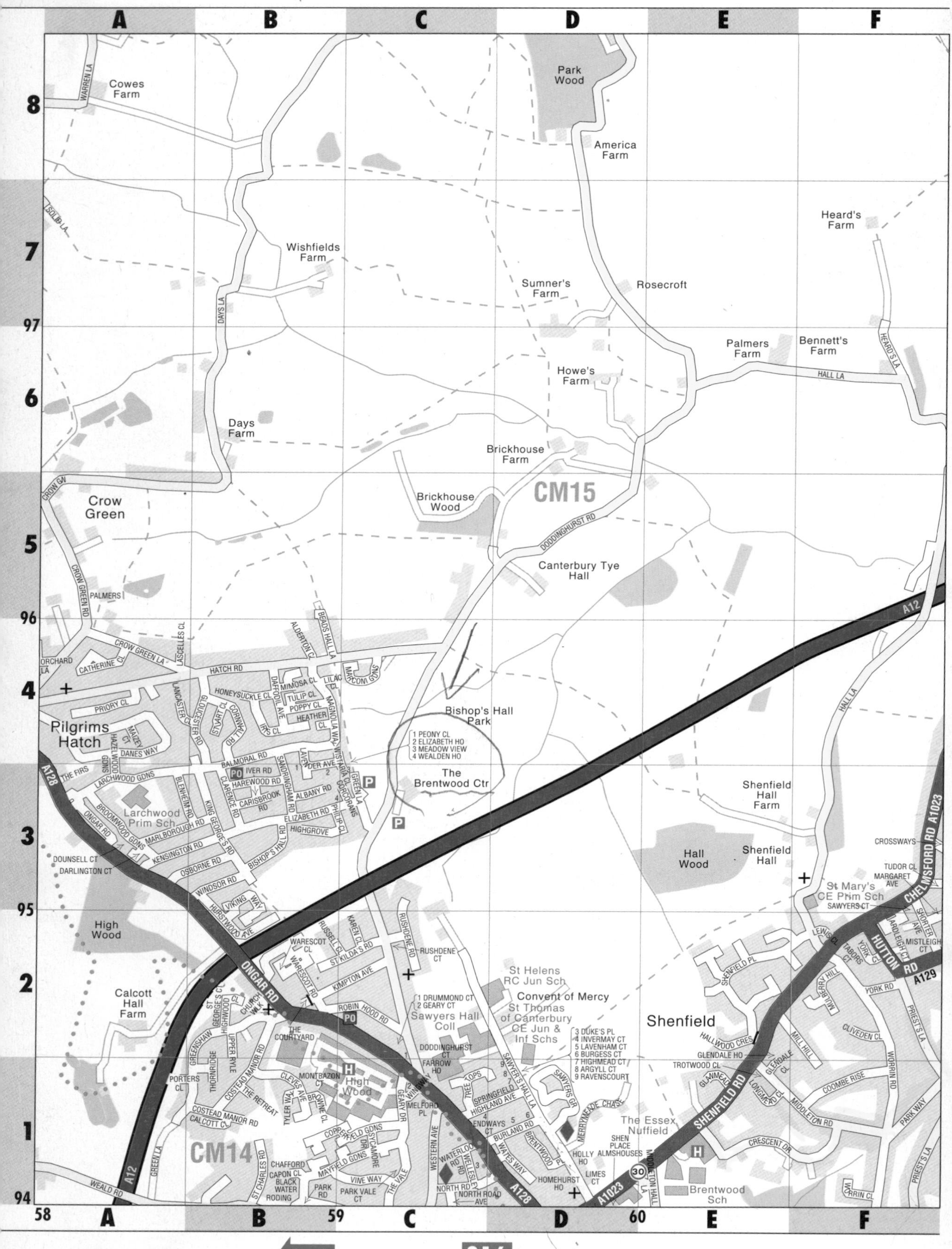

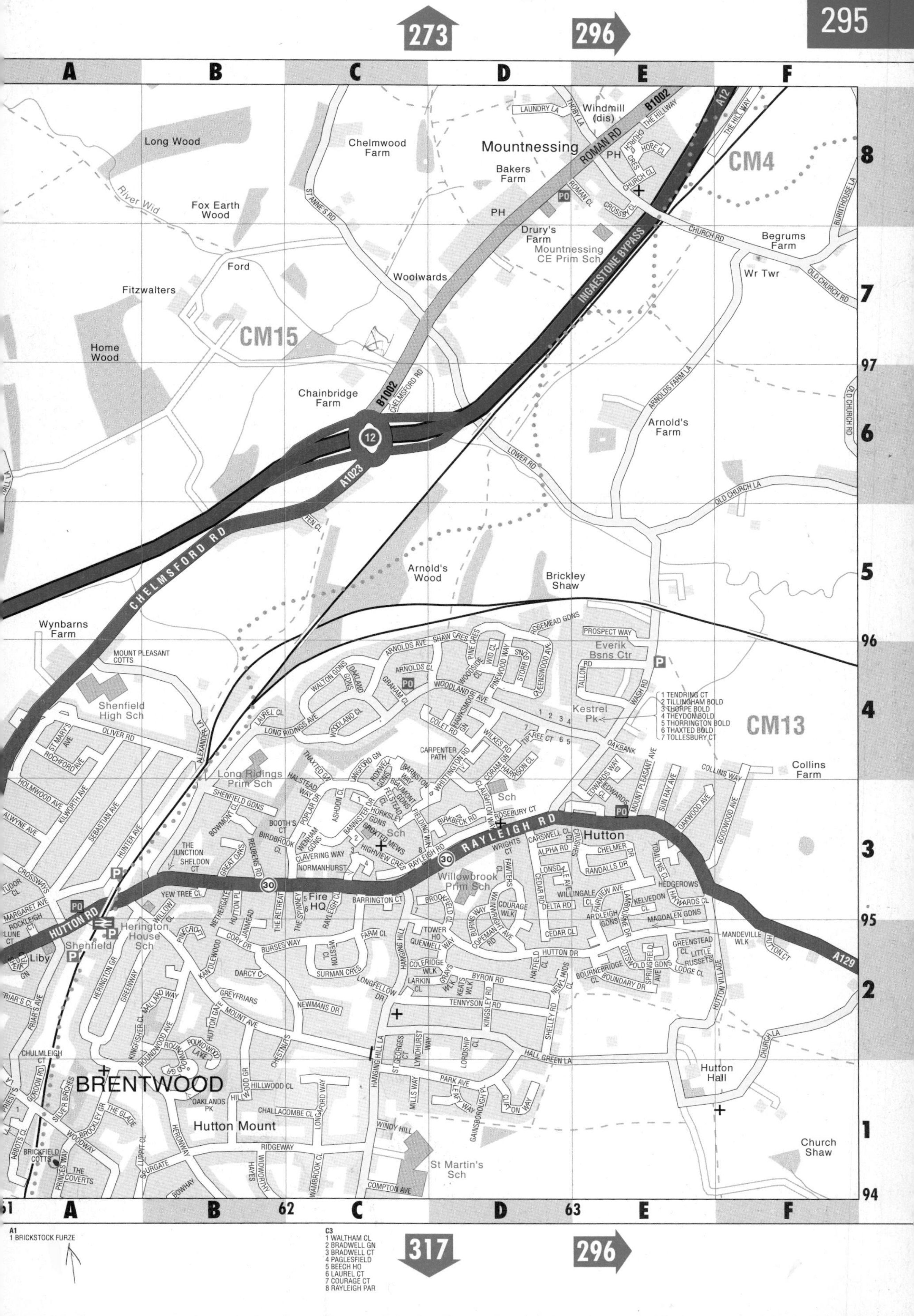
273
296
A
B
C
D
E
F
8
7
97
6
5
96
4
3
95
2
1
94
61
62
63
Long Wood
River Wid
Fox Earth Wood
Chelmwood Farm
Mountnessing
Bakers Farm
Windmill (dis)
LAUNDRY LA
THOBY LA
ROMAN RD
B1002
THE HILLWAY
A12
THE HILL WAY
CM4
PH
PO
ROMAN CL
CHURCH CL
HOPE CL
CROSSBY CL
CHURCH RD
Begrums Farm
BURNTHOUSE LA
Drury's Farm
Mountnessing CE Prim Sch
INGATESTONE BYPASS
Wr Twr
OLD CHURCH RD
Woolwards
Ford
Fitzwalters
CM15
Home Wood
ST ANNE'S RD
Chainbridge Farm
CHELMSFORD RD
12
A1023
LOWER RD
ARNOLDS FARM LA
Arnold's Farm
OLD CHURCH LA
FEN CL
CHELMSFORD RD
Arnold's Wood
Brickley Shaw
Wynbarns Farm
MOUNT PLEASANT COTTS
Shenfield High Sch
ROSEMEAD GDNS
PROSPECT WAY
Everik Bsns Ctr
ARNOLDS AVE
SHAW CRES
PINE CRES
WID CL
PINEWOOD WAY
QUEENSWOOD AVE
ARNOLDS CL
WOODLAND AVE
OAKLAND GDNS
WALTON GDNS
GRAHAM CL
WOODLAND CL
LONG RIDINGS AVE
LAUREL CL
TALLON RD
WASH RD
Kestrel Pk
1 TENDRING CT
2 TILLINGHAM BOLD
3 THORPE BOLD
4 THEYDON BOLD
5 THORRINGTON BOLD
6 THAXTED BOLD
7 TOLLESBURY CT
CM13
OAKBANK
COLLINS WAY
Collins Farm
OLIVER RD
ST MARY'S AVE
ROCHFORD AVE
ALEXANDER LA
Long Ridings Prim Sch
HOLMWOOD AVE
KILWORTH AVE
SEBASTIAN AVE
HUNTER AVE
ALWYNE AVE
SHENFIELD GDNS
BOWMONT CL
BOOTH'S CT
BIRDBROOK CL
CARPENTER PATH
WHITTINGTON RD
COLET RD
WILKES RD
TREE CT
EDWARDS WAY
MOUNT PLEASANT AVE
SUN RAY AVE
OAKWOOD AVE
GOODWOOD AVE
Sch
ROSEBURY CT
RAYLEIGH RD
30
Hutton
CARSWELL CL
CRUSHES
CHELMER DR
ALPHA RD
RANDALLS DR
TOMLYNS CL
HEDGEROWS
HAYWARDS CL
THE JUNCTION
SHELDON CT
GREAT OAKS
REUBENS RD
CLAVERING WAY
NORMANHURST
HIGHVIEW CRES
Willowbrook Prim Sch
WRIGHTS CT
FAWTERS
CEDAR RD
WILLINGALE CL
FAIRVIEW AVE
KELVEDON CL
MAGDALEN GDNS
LAMBOURNE DR
ARDLEIGH GDNS
DELTA RD
CEDAR CL
GREENSTEAD CL
LITTLE RUSSETS
LODGE CL
MANDEVILLE WLK
HUTTON CT
A129
CROSSWAYS
TUDOR CL
MARGARET AVE
ROCKLEIGH CT
HUTTON RD
PO
P
YEW TREE CL
WILLOW CL
NETHERGATE
HUTTON PL
JAMMEAD
THE RETREAT
THE SPINNEY
Fire HQ
RAYLEIGH CL
BARRINGTON CT
Herington House Sch
Shenfield
Liby
PINECROFT
CORY DR
BURSES WAY
WESTON CL
FARM CL
HANGING HILL
TOWER HO
QUENNELL WAY
COURAGE WLK
HUTTON DR
HATFIELD CL
BOURNEBRIDGE CL
BOUNDARY DR
SPRINGFIELD AVE
COTSWOLD GDNS
HUTTON VILLAGE
HERINGTON GR
GREENWAY
KANDLEWOOD
DARCY CL
SURMAN CRES
LONGFELLOW DR
COLERIDGE WLK
LARKIN CL
BYRON RD
KEATS WLK
GRAYS WLK
TENNYSON RD
KINGSLEY RD
SHELLEY RD
NEWLANDS CL
RIAR'S CL
FRIAR'S AVE
MALLARD WAY
GREYFRIARS
MOUNT AVE
NEWMANS DR
KINGFISHER CL
ROUNDWOOD AVE
ROUNDWOOD LAKE
HUTTON GATE
CHESTNUTS
HANGING HILL LA
ST GEORGES CT
LYNDHURST WAY
LORDSHIP CL
HALL GREEN LA
CHURCH LA
CHULMLEIGH CT
BRENTWOOD
GORDON RD
SILVER BIRCHES
THE GLADE
HILLWOOD GR
HILLWOOD CL
OAKLANDS PK
HERONWAY
LONGFORD WAY
CHALLACOMBE CL
PARK AVE
LEAFY WAY
GAINSBOROUGH PL
CLIFTON WAY
MILLS WAY
WINDY HILL
Hutton Hall
Hutton Mount
WOODWAY
BROCKLEY GR
ABBOTS CL
BRICKFIELD COTTS
PRINCES WAY
THE COVERTS
LUPPITT CL
SPURGATE
BOWHAY
HAYES
WIDWORTHY
RIDGEWAY
WAMBROOK CL
St Martin's Sch
COMPTON AVE
Church Shaw
A1
1 BRICKSTOCK FURZE
C3
1 WALTHAM CL
2 BRADWELL GN
3 BRADWELL CT
4 PAGLESFIELD
5 BEECH HO
6 LAUREL CT
7 COURAGE CT
8 RAYLEIGH PAR
317
296

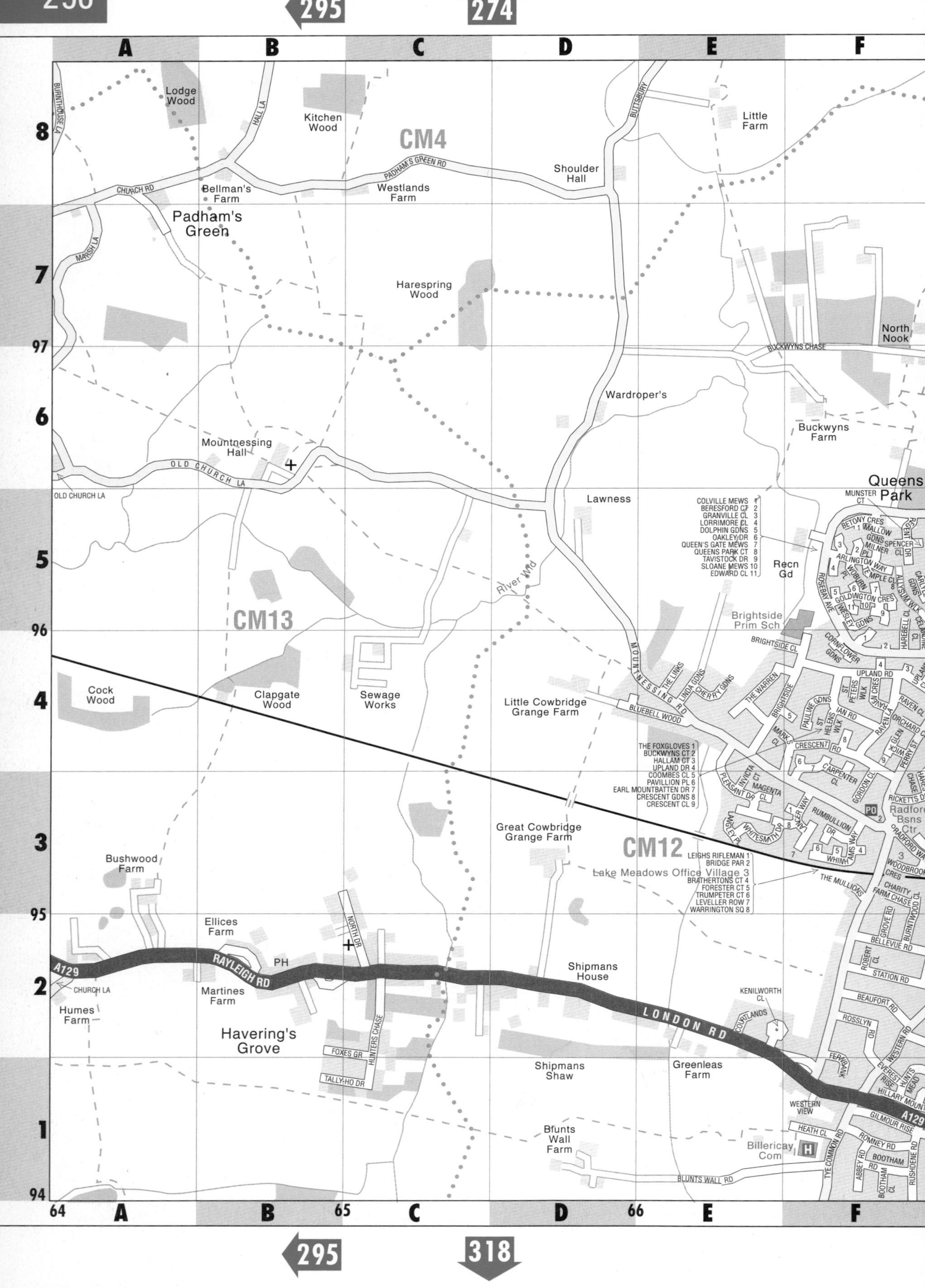

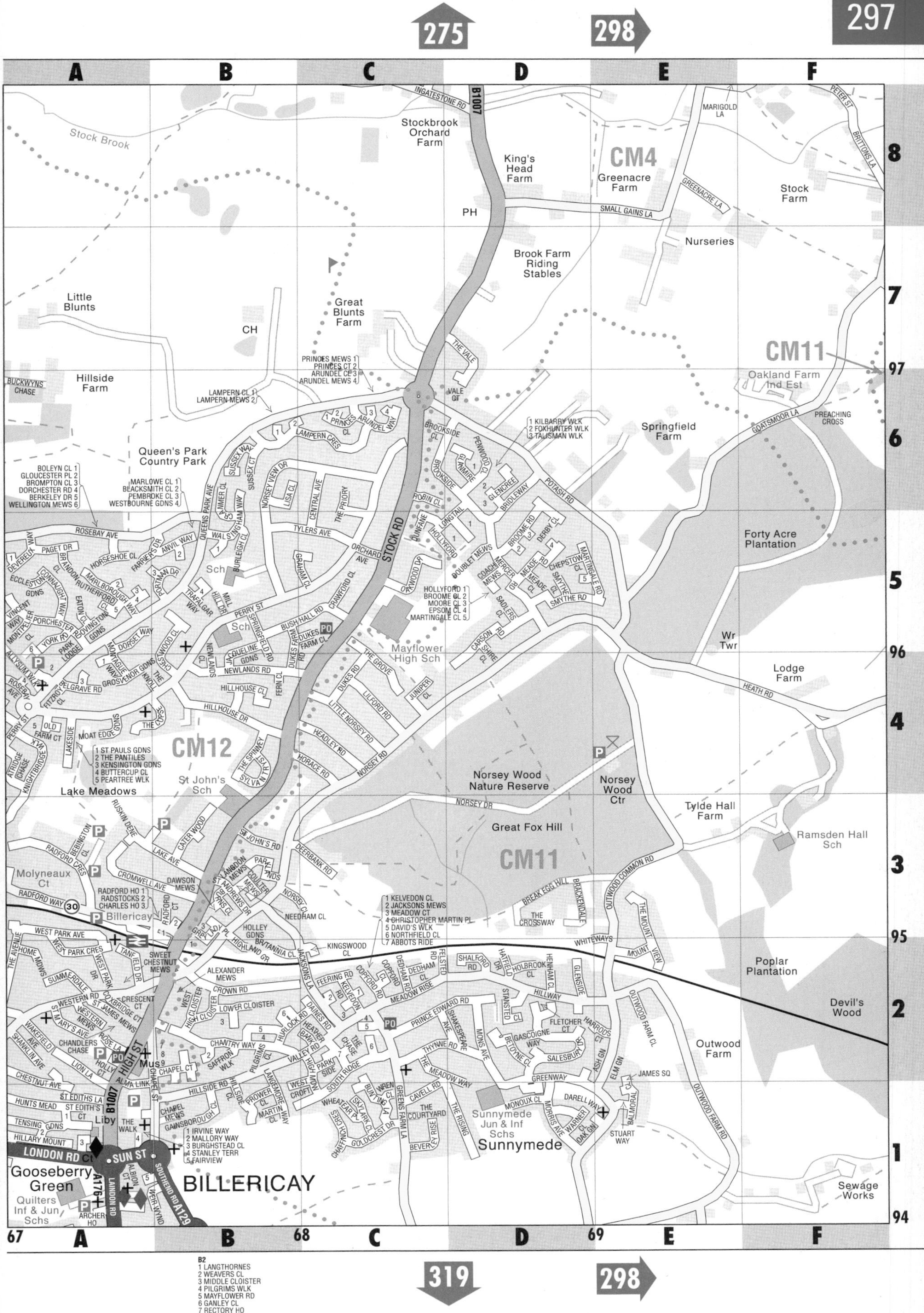

B2
1 LANGTHORNES
2 WEAVERS CL
3 MIDDLE CLOISTER
4 PILGRIMS WLK
5 MAYFLOWER RD
6 GANLEY CL
7 RECTORY HO
8 VICARAGE CT
9 HAWKLEY CT

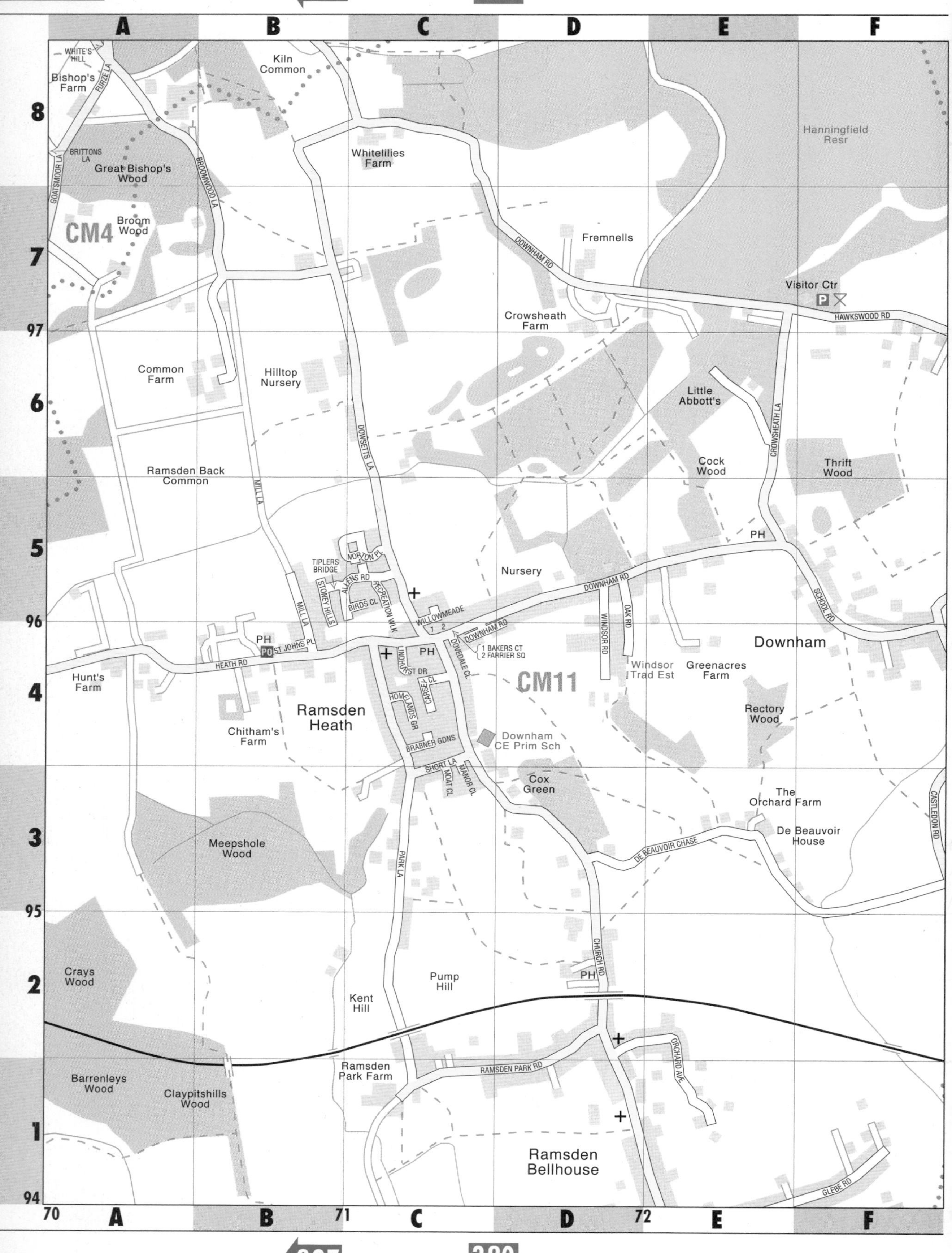

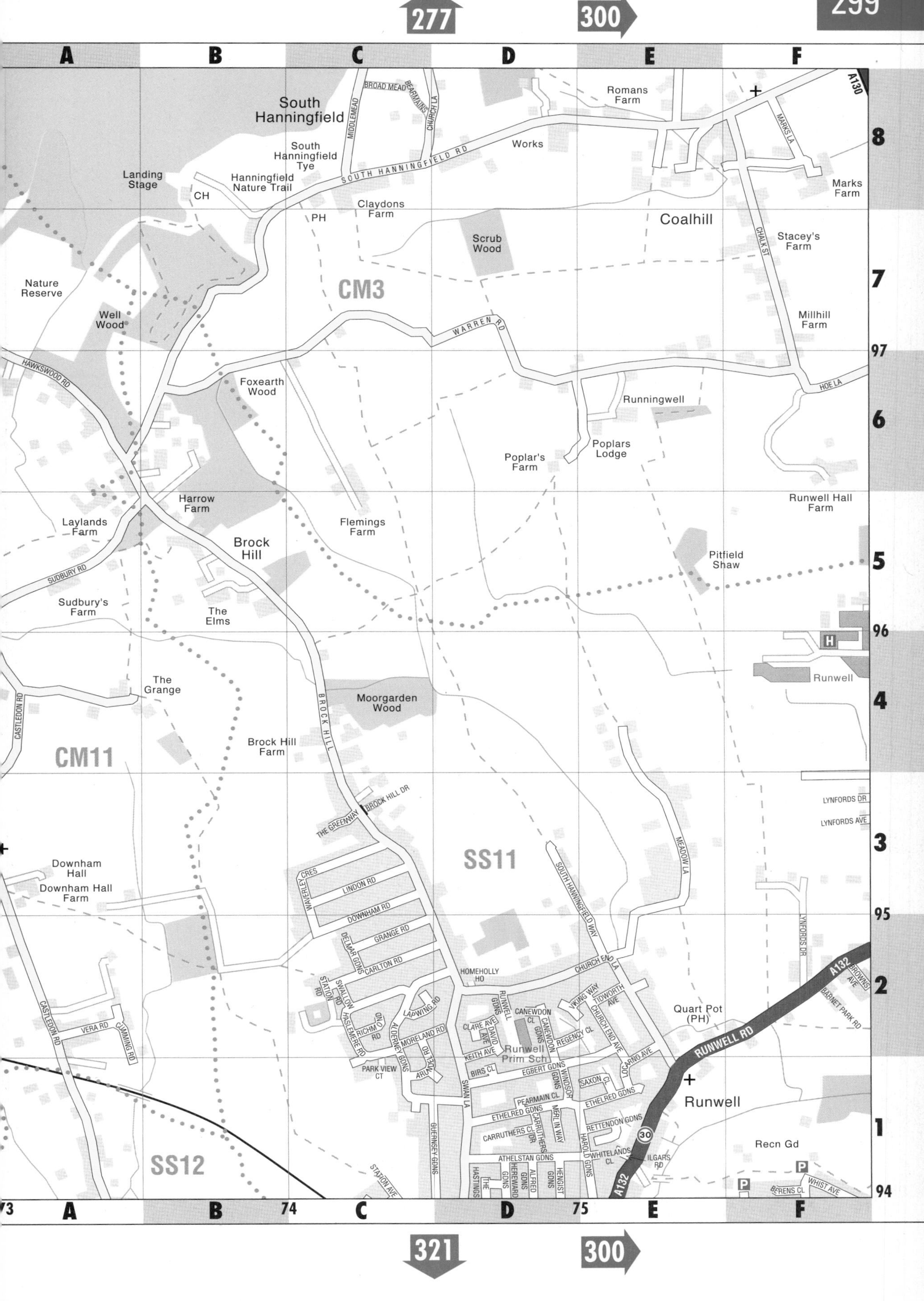

277
300

A B C D E F

A130

8

South
Hanningfield

Romans
Farm

Broad Mead

MIDDLEMEAD

BEARMANS

V'LD CHURCH

South Hanningfield
Tye

South
Hanningfield
Nature Trail

Landing
Stage

CH

PH

Claydons
Farm

SOUTH HANNINGFIELD RD

Works

Coalhill

Marks
Farm

MARKS LA

Scrub
Wood

Stacey's
Farm

CM3

7

CHALK ST

Nature
Reserve

Well
Wood

Foxearth
Wood

WARREN RD

Millhill
Farm

HAWKSWOOD RD

97

HOE LA

6

Runningwell

Poplars
Lodge

Poplar's
Farm

Harrow
Farm

Flemings
Farm

Runwell Hall
Farm

Laylands
Farm

Brock
Hill

Pitfield
Shaw

5

SUDBURY RD

Sudbury's
Farm

The
Elms

96

H

The
Grange

Runwell

4

CASTLEDON RD

CM11

Brock Hill
Farm

Moorgarden
Wood

BROCK HILL

LYNFORDS DR

LYNFORDS AVE

3

Downham
Hall

Downham Hall
Farm

BROCK HILL DR

THE GREENWAY

SS11

MEADOW LA

95

LYNFORDS DR

A132

2

CASTLEDON RD

VERA RD

CUMMING RD

WAYLETTS

CRES

LINDON RD

DOWNHAM RD

GRANGE RD

CARLTON RD

DELMAR GDNS

SWALLOW STATION RD

SOUTH HANNINGFIELD WAY

CHURCH END LA

Quart Pot
(PH)

BROWNS AVE

BARNET PARK RD

HOMEHOLLY
HO

RUNWELL RD

Runwell

LAPWING RD

MORELAND RD

OLD RICHM'D RD

HASLMERE RD

CANEWDON
GDNS

VIKING WAY

CHURCH END AVE

1

ALDERNEY GDNS

PARK VIEW
CT

SWAN LA

ARUN

RUNWELL
GDNS

CLARE AVE

DAVID CL

CANEWDON
GDNS

REGENCY CL

TIDWORTH AVE

WINDSOR

SAXON

CARINO AVE

Runwell
Prim Sch

30

A132

KEITH AVE

BIRS CL

EGBERT GDNS

ETHELRED GDNS

Recn Gd

GUERNSEY GDNS

PEARMAIN CL

CARRUTHERS CL DR

ETHELRED GDNS

MGR IN WAY

RETTENDON GDNS

WHITELANDS
CL

ILGARS
RD

P

WHIST AVE

SS12

THE HASTINGS

ATHELSTAN GDNS

HEREWARD GDNS

ALFRED GDNS

HENGIST GDNS

HAROLD GDNS

BERENS AVE

P

94

73 A B 74 C D 75 E F

321
300

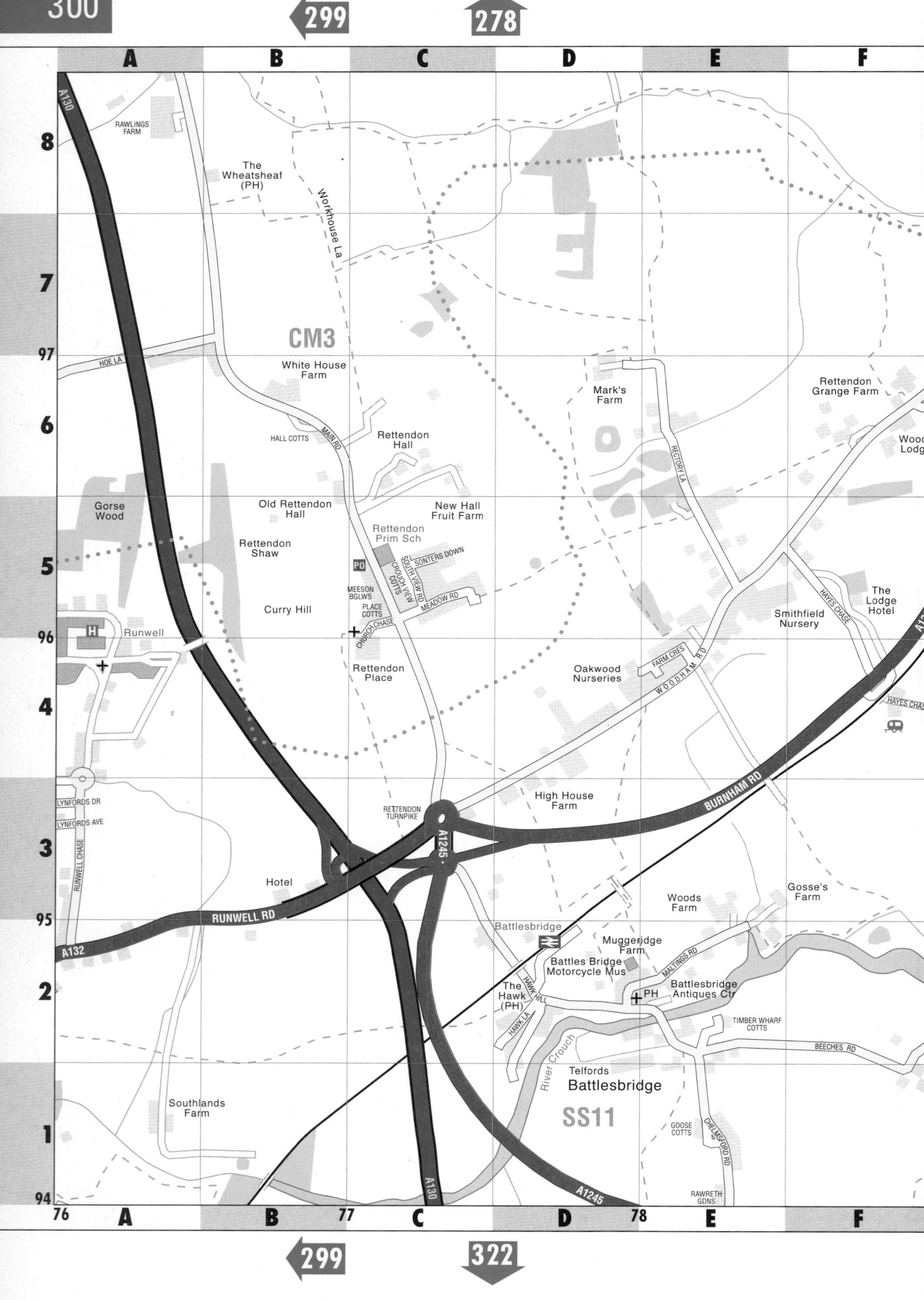

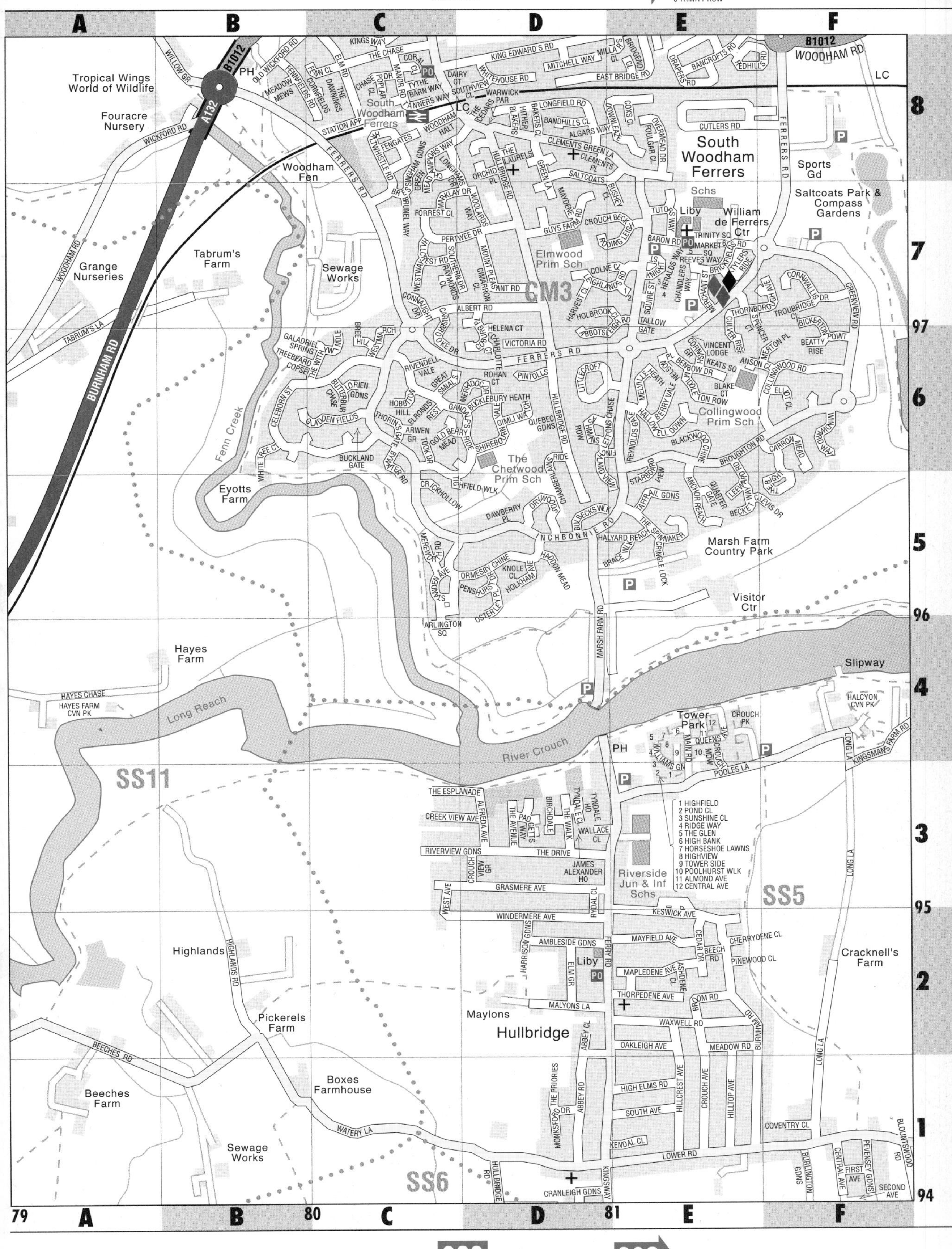

279

302
E7
1 AKENFIELD CL
2 WOODHAM CT
3 GUILD WAY
4 QUEEN ELIZABETH II SQ
5 CHIPPING ROW
6 TRINITY ROW

301

A B C D E F

Tropical Wings
World of Wildlife

Fouracre
Nursery

Grange
Nurseries

Tabrum's
Farm

Woodham Fen

Sewage
Works

South
Woodham
Ferrers

Woodham Rd
B1012

South
Woodham
Ferrers

Sports
Gd

Saltcoats Park &
Compass
Gardens

GM3

Elmwood
Prim Sch

Liby

William
de Ferrers
Ctr

Collingwood
Prim Sch

The Chetwood
Prim Sch

8

7

97

6

5

96

4

Marsh Farm
Country Park

Visitor
Ctr

Slipway

Halcyon
CVN PK

Eyotts
Farm

Hayes
Farm

Long Reach

River Crouch

SS11

Tower
Park

PH

1 HIGHFIELD
2 POND CL
3 SUNSHINE CL
4 RIDGE WAY
5 THE GLEN
6 HIGH BANK
7 HORSESHOE LAWNS
8 HIGHVIEW
9 TOWER SIDE
10 POOLHURST WLK
11 ALMOND AVE
12 CENTRAL AVE

Crouch
Pk

Riverside
Jun & Inf
Schs

James
Alexander
Ho

SS5

Cracknell's
Farm

3

95

2

Highlands

Liby
PO

Maylons

Hullbridge

Pickerels
Farm

Boxes
Farmhouse

Beeches
Farm

Sewage
Works

SS6

1

94

79 A B 80 C D 81 E F

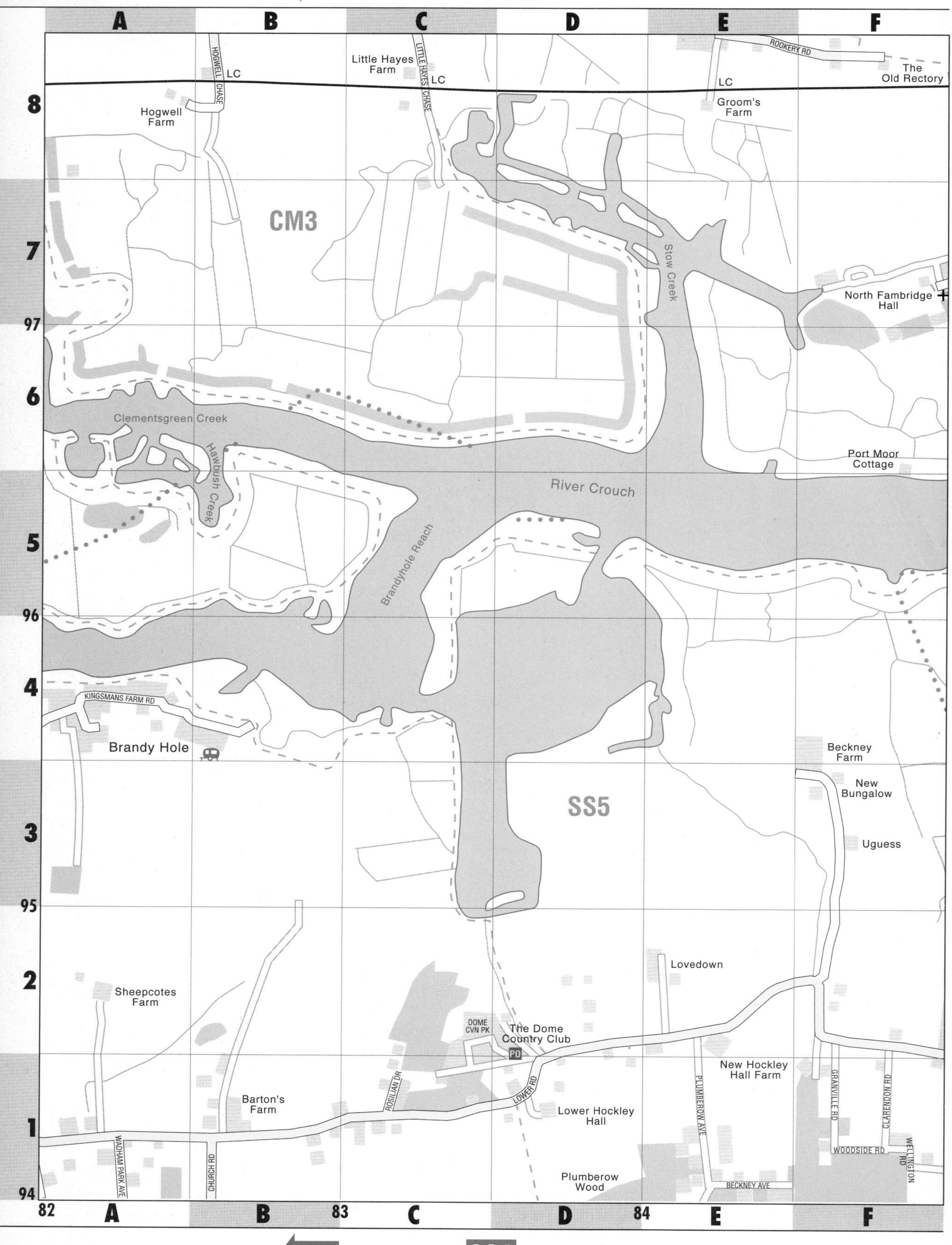

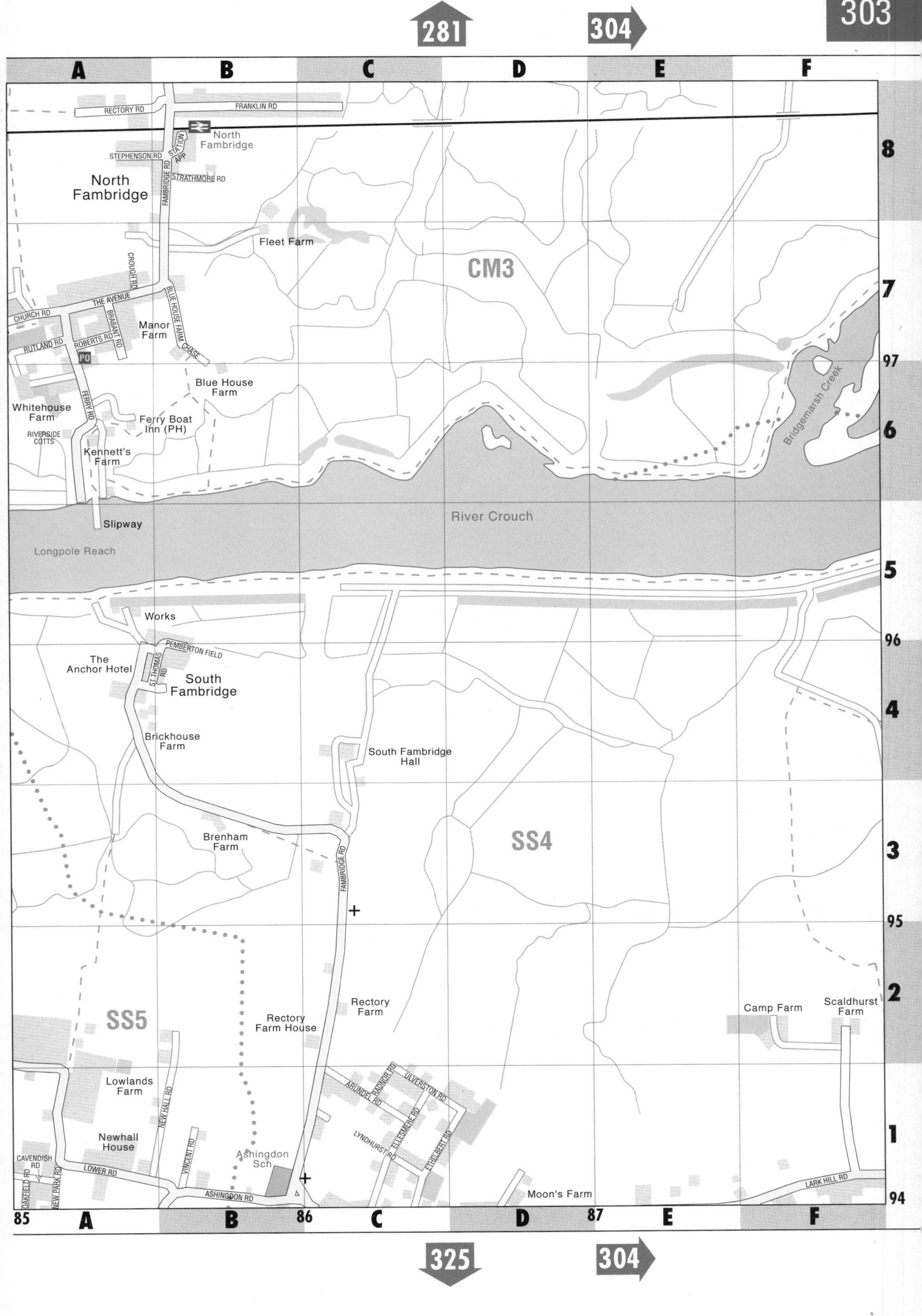

A B C D E F

8

CM3

→ STATION RD
Althorne   LC

Bridgemarsh LA

Marina

Althorne Creek

7

Bridgemarsh Creek

97

Bridgemarsh
Island

6

Shortpole   Reach

Raypits Reach

Landsend
Point

5

River Crouch

Easter Reach

96

Upper Raypits
Farm

4

Old Fleet

3

SS4

Pudsey Hall

Market
Hill

95

Butts Hill

New Hall
Farm

2

Bolt Hall

Beacon Hill

GAYS LA

Canewdon Hall
Farm

BUTTS PADDOCK

Crouch View
Villas

ALTHORNE WAY

Canewdon Hall

DUCKETTS MEAD

HIGH ST

DANTE CL

LAMBOURNE HALL RD

PUDSEY HALL LA

CHESTNUT PATH

VILLAGE
GN

CHURCH
GN

BIRCH CL

PO

REST COTTS

Canewdon
CE Prim Sch

ORCHARD
BGLWS

LARKHILL AVE

ROWAN WAY

ANCHOR
PAR

SYCAMORE WAY

ASH GN

WILLOW WLK

CEDAR WLK

ANCHOR LA

GARDENERS LA

1

LARK HILL RD

SCOTTS HALL RD

ANCHOR LANE
COTTS

Gardeners

White House
Farm

Canewdon

94

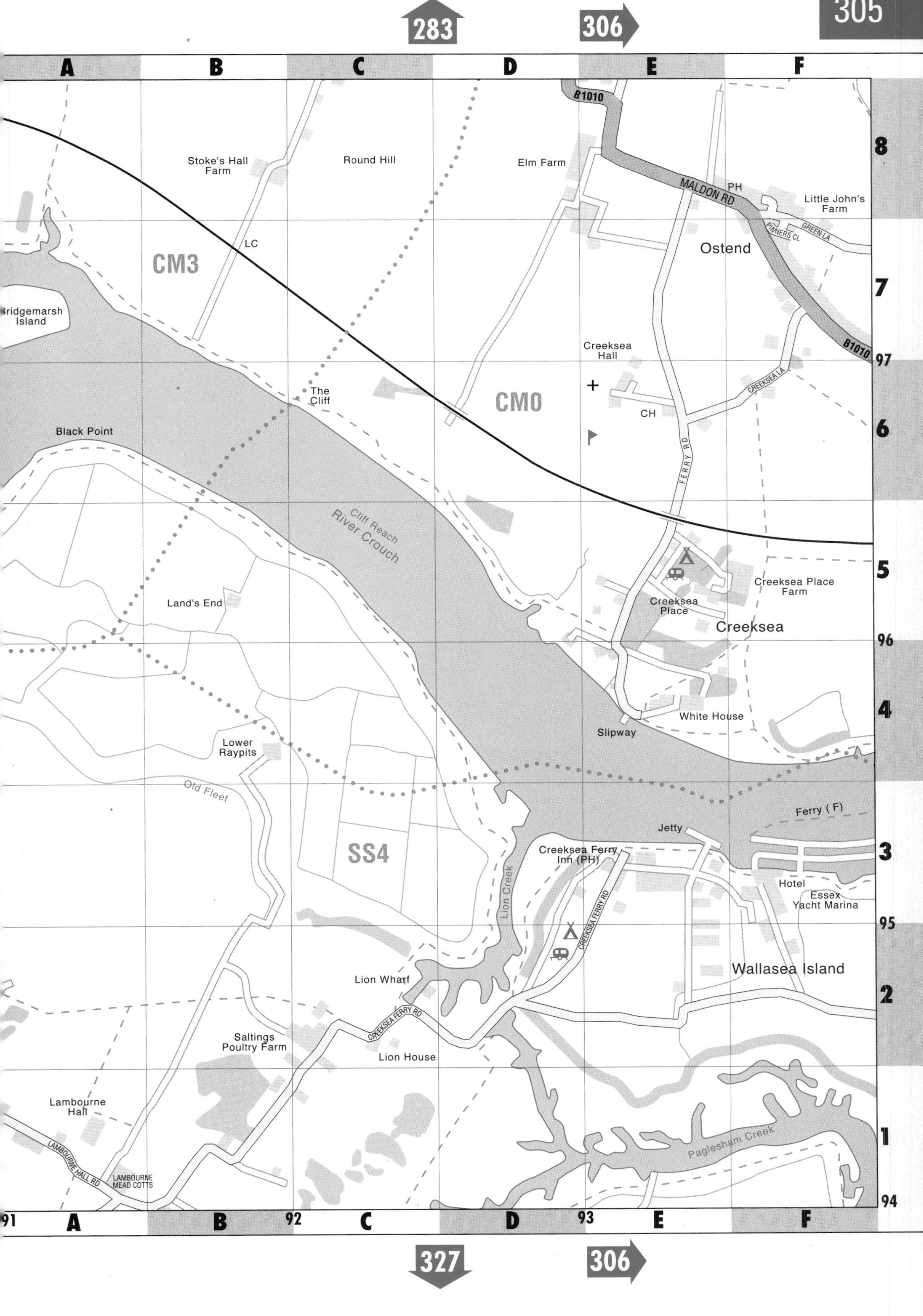

305
284

A B C D E F

8

Mangapps Rly Mus

B1021

Cemy

COBBINS CHASE

Stoneyhills

BEAUCHAMPS

MANGAPP CHASE

SOUTHMINSTER RD

THE COBBINS

COBBINS GR

BADGERS KEEP

BOUVEL DR

WOODCUTTERS

Mill Farm

Stoney Hills

MILL GRANGE

CROXON WAY

ROMAN WAY

MILL RD

BARNFIELD WAY

GREEN LA

Newman's Farm

7

EVES CNR

ASHWOOD CL

ROMANS FARM CHASE

Romans Farm

Pannel's Bridge

MEADOW WAY

THE HAWTHORNS

ST PETER'S RD

St Peter's High Sch

Hall Farm

St Mary's CE Prim Sch

ROMANS FARM CHASE

Brook Farm Abattoir

Pannel's Brook

97

CINDLERS

B1010

COMPASS GDNS

MALDON RD

WELLAND RD

1 DEBDEN WAY
2 CHELMER WAY
3 EMBER WAY

B1010

B1021 CHURCH RD

GLENDALE CL

GLEBE WAY

THE LEAS

LEAS CT

MARSH RD

DAMMERWICK COTTS

DAMMER WICK

Muscle Bridge

6

Burnham Bsns Pk

Springfield Ind Est

THAMES RD

SPRINGFIELD RD

MEDWAY

ORWELL RD

TRENT WAY

KING EDWARD AVE

HAMBLE WAY

PLANE TREE

LIME WAY

MAPLE WAY

WILLOW

Burnham-on-Crouch

CEDAR GR

BEECH

ST MARY'S RD

D'ARCY CL

PRINCES RD

WORCESTER RD

PIPPINS

PIPPINS

RUSSET WAY

CMO

BURNHAM-ON-CROUCH

Springfield Nursery Est

Sand Island Ctr

Mayfield Ctr

Springfield Ind Est

Station Ind Est

POPLAR

CHESTNUT CL

HOLLY CL

STATION APP

FOUNDRY LA

ASH GR

ALEXANDRA RD

BLACKWATER CL

DEVONSHIRE RD

EASTERN RD

CHESTER RD

Allot Gdns

5

SHEERWATER CL
GALAHAD CL 2
HERMES DR 3
MILDMAY HO 4
Mildmay Ind Est 5

DRAGON CL

HORNET WAY

WAYFARER GDNS

FERNLEA RD

HILLSIDE RD

PARK SIDE

WINSTREE RD

FELKLANDS RD

WILLIAM RD

NEW RD

ESSEX RD

DORSET RD

ARCADIA RD

BOOTH PL

NORMANDY AVE

WESLEY

Burnham-on-Crouch Prim Sch

Super store

P

PO

Station App

CROUCH RD

ALPHA RD

96

IRB Sta

P

Country Park

Caravan Site

Dengie Hundred Sports Ctr

Sports Gd

Liby

WARWICK CT

MILLFIELD

MILL GN

BRICKWALL

DILLIWAY CT

WESTERN RD

QUEEN'S RD

ALBERT RD

ALAMEIN RD

ARNHEIM RD

DUNKIRK RD

Burnham Wick

WICK RD

4

P

Marina

Burnham-on-Crouch & District Mus

REMEMBRANCE AVE

QUEENS CT

CORONATION RD

YORK RD

CHAPEL RD

WITNEY RD

PROVIDENCE

ORCHARD RD

SHIP RD

RIVERSIDE RD

P

SILVER RD

10

ARGYLE RD

RAMBLERS WAY

HIGH RD ST

B1021

KINGS RD

REGENTS RD

i

PROMENADE QUAY

THE BELVEDERE

PH

Sewage Works

SEA-END CVN SITE

Gardenness Point

Ferry (F)

C4
1 CURLEW HO
2 NELSON CT
3 HAMILTON CT
4 GRANVILLE TERR
5 STEBBINGS CT
6 ST MARY'S HO
7 AUGERS
8 HARDINGS-REACH
9 CALMPATCH
10 SUNNYMEAD FLATS
11 BUCKINGHAM SQ

Slipways

12 BELVEDERE CT
13 THE CROWSNEST
14 THE ANCHORAGE
15 PETTICROW QUAYS

3

River Crouch

Ringwood Bar

95

Overland Point

Grassland Point

Fleet Point

2

Grapnells

Wallasea Wetlands Scheme

GRAPNELLS FARM COTTS

1

SS4

WALLASEA ISLAND

CMO

94

94 A B 95 C D 96 E F

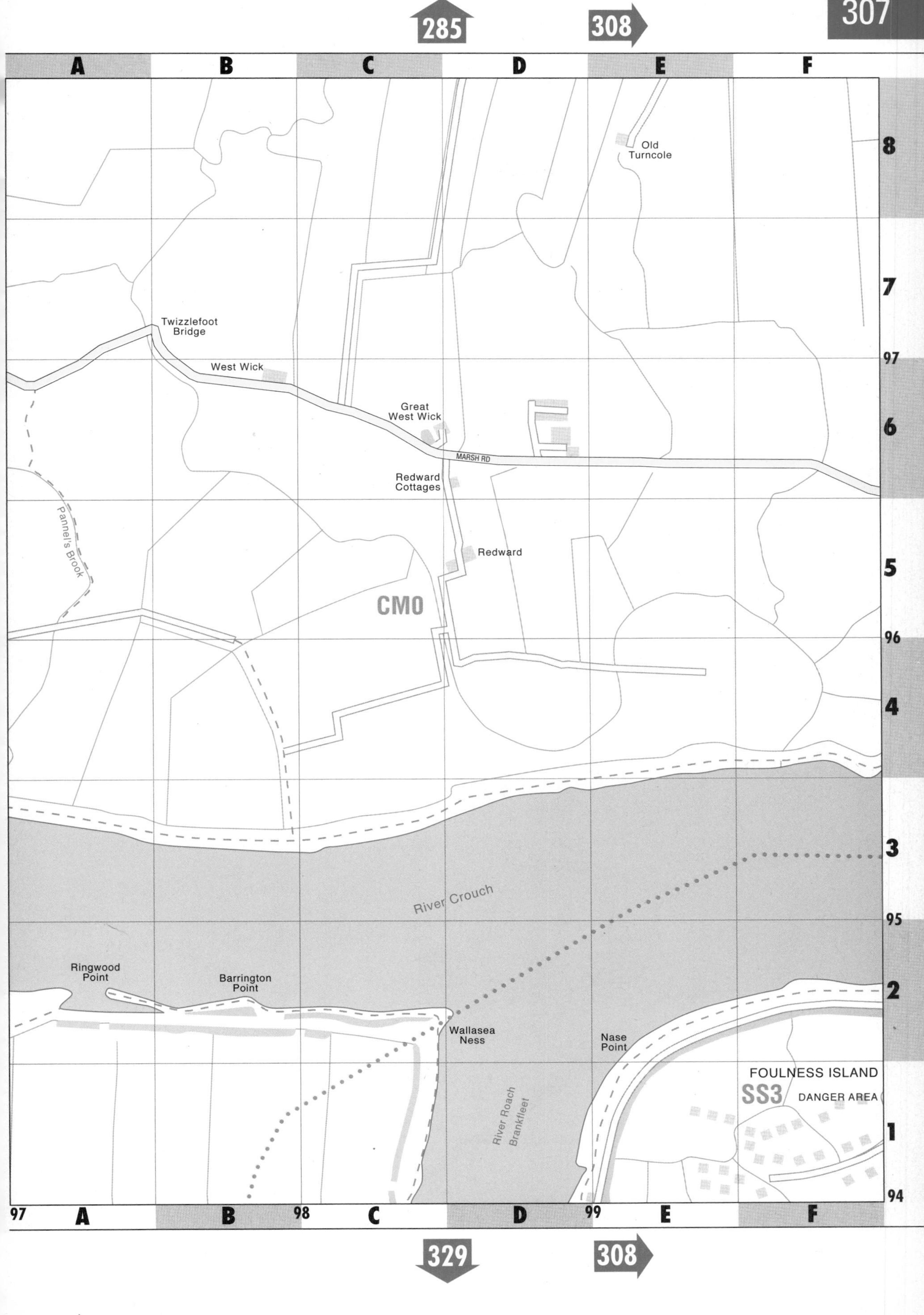

285

308

A B C D E F

8

7

97

6

Old Turncole

Twizzlefoot
Bridge

West Wick

Great
West Wick

MARSH RD

Redward
Cottages

Redward

CMO

96

5

4

Pannel's Brook

River Crouch

3

95

Ringwood
Point

Barrington
Point

2

Wallasea
Ness

Nase
Point

FOULNESS ISLAND

SS3 DANGER AREA

River Roach
Branktleet

1

94

97 A B 98 C D 99 E F

329

308

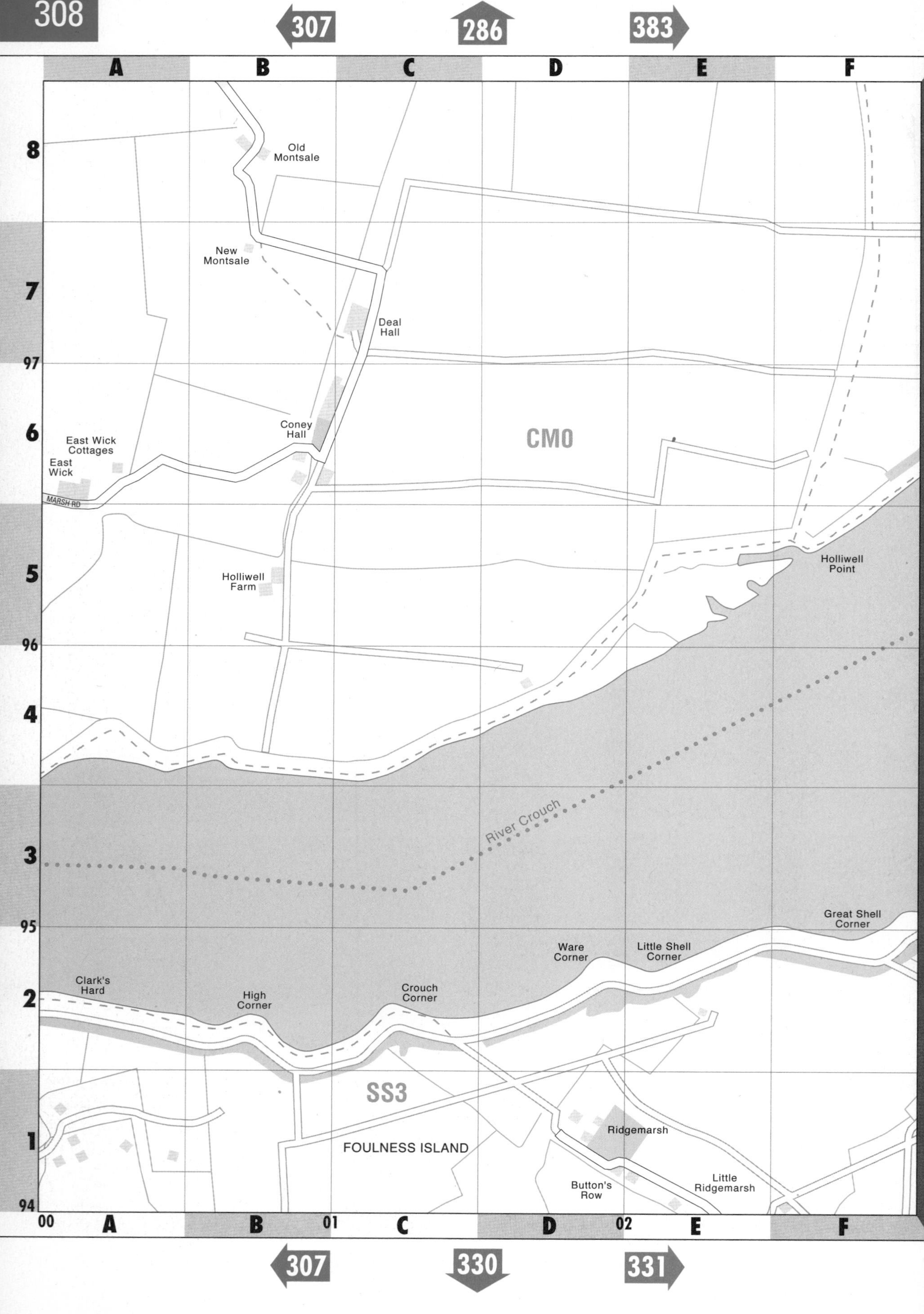

307 286 383

8

Old Montsale

New Montsale

7

Deal Hall

97

Coney Hall

6

CM0

East Wick Cottages

East Wick

MARSH RD

5

Holliwell Point

Holliwell Farm

96

4

River Crouch

3

95

Great Shell Corner

Ware Corner

Little Shell Corner

Clark's Hard

2

High Corner

Crouch Corner

SS3

1

Ridgemarsh

FOULNESS ISLAND

Button's Row

Little Ridgemarsh

94

307 330 331

C8
1 LEA CT
2 PARK CT
3 CONFERENCE CL
4 BERRYBANK CL
5 RUSSELL LODGE
6 BRUNSWICK LODGE
7 KENILWORTH CT
8 TRINITY CT
9 KINGSMEAD LODGE
10 FAIRLAWNS

287

D5
1 HEDGEMOOR CT
2 HEWITT HO
3 CASTLE HO
4 BAILEY CT
5 WENTWORTH CT
6 HARCOURT HO
7 GERBOA CT
8 HAVELOCK HO

310

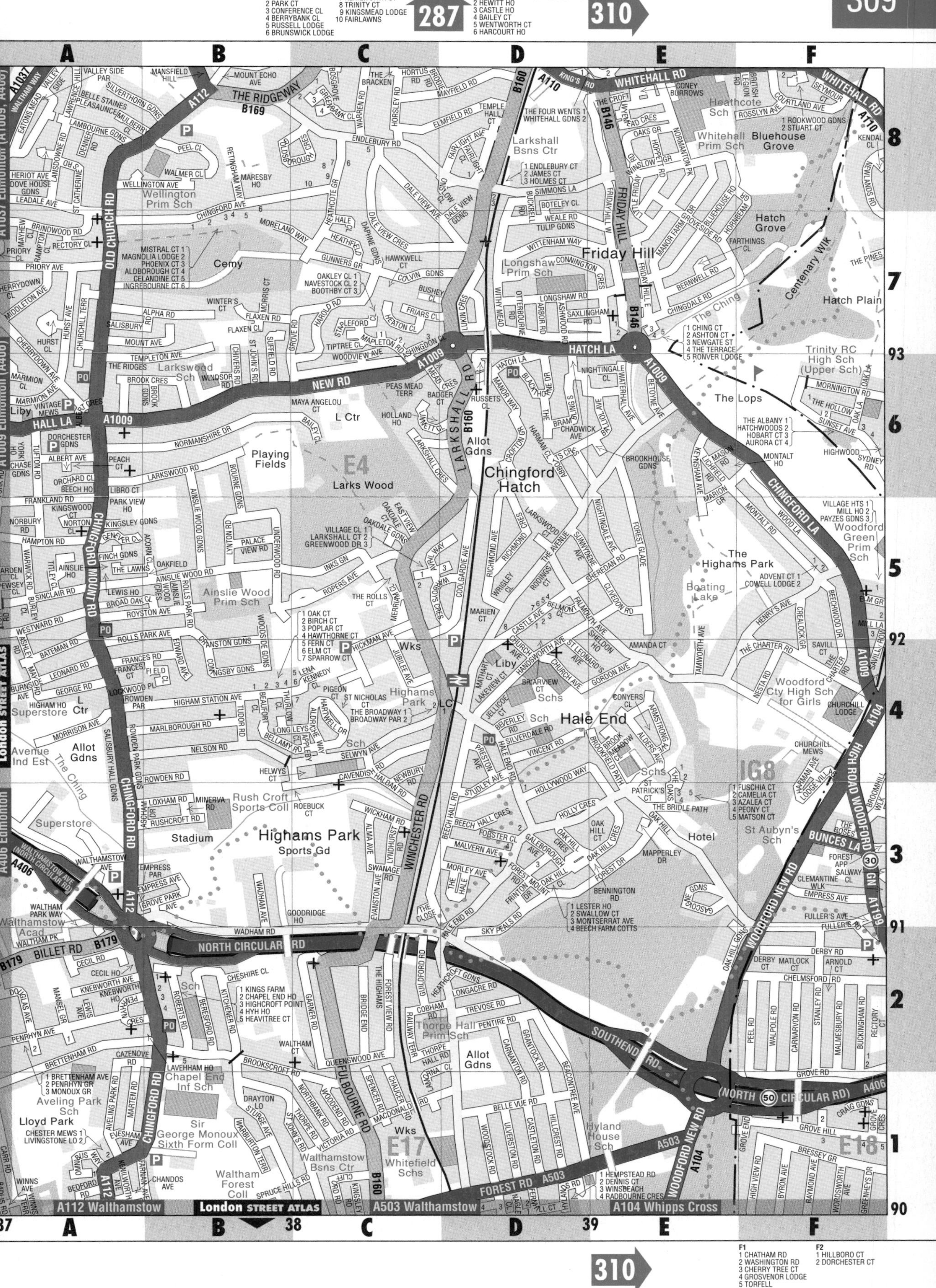

310

F1
1 CHATHAM RD
2 WASHINGTON RD
3 CHERRY TREE CT
4 GROSVENOR LODGE
5 TORFELL

F2
1 HILLBORO CT
2 DORCHESTER CT

309

C8
1 WESTBURY CT
2 WESTBURY RD
3 PALMERSTON CT
4 IBROX CT
5 RICHARD BURTON CT
6 QUEENS MEWS

288

C8
7 MIRRAVALE CT
8 GUNNELS CT & HASTINGWOOD CT
9 SOMERSET CT
10 MARLBOROUGH CT
11 THE AVENUE
12 TORA CT

D8
1 REGENCY LODGE
2 BUCKHURST CT
3 KINGS CT
4 SALISBURY GDNS
5 PEGASUS CT
6 BEECH CT
7 SYCAMORE HO
8 GEORGE CT
9 ATRIUM

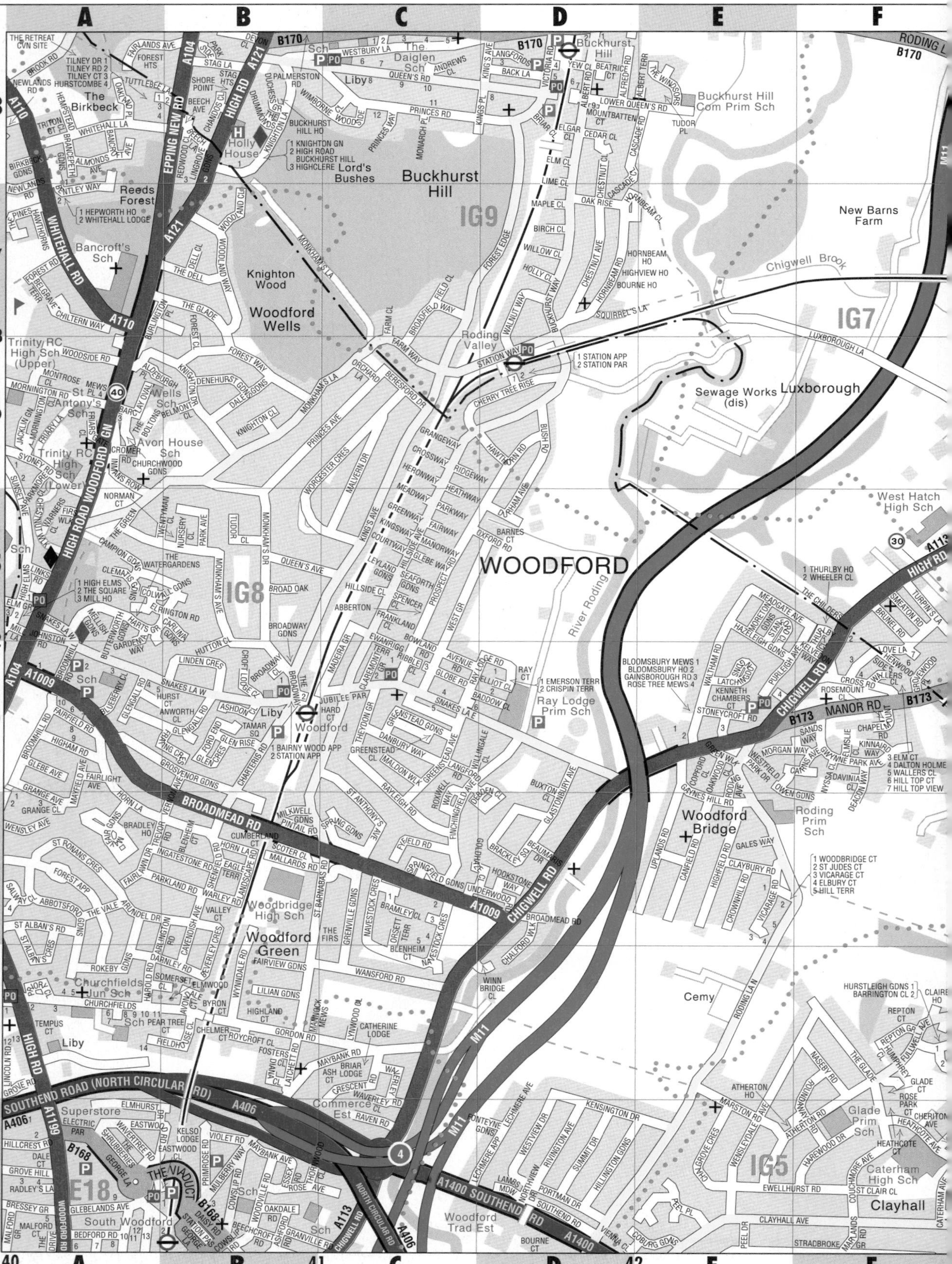

309

332

A1
1 ESTON CT
2 REGENCY CT
3 COWLEY CT
4 THE CHILTONS
5 HIGH OAKS LODGE
6 MILLBROOK
7 LANSDOWNE RD
8 WOBURN CT
9 ULLSWATER CT
10 CLEVELAND RD
11 LEIGH CT
12 ALVESTON SQ
13 MARLBOROUGH RD

A2
1 LINDAL CT
2 HOCKLEY CT
3 WOODLEIGH
4 MILNE CT
5 CEDAR CT
6 ELIZABETH CT
7 SILVERMEAD
8 LAUREL MEAD CT
9 MITRE CT
10 PEVENSEY CT
11 LYNDHURST CT
12 RECTORY CT
13 MANOR COURT LODGE
14 QUEEN MARY VILLAS

A3
1 NEW JUBILEE CT
2 CHARTWELL CT
3 GREENWOOD
4 CLEMENTINE WLK

A4
1 THE TERRACE
2 BROOMHILL CT
3 CLIFTON CT
4 FAIRSTEAD LODGE

A4
5 HADLEIGH LODGE
6 BROADMEAD CT
7 WILTON CT
8 FAIRFIELD CT
9 HIGHAM CT
10 ASTON CT

A6
1 TREE TOPS
2 CRANFIELD CT
3 PERCIVAL HO
4 RAINE GDNS

B1
1 Station Est
2 STATION APP
3 JAMES CT

C3
1 LISTON WAY
2 ELIZABETH CT
3 COOPERSALE CL
4 SUNSET CT
5 LAMBOURNE CT

C4
1 COWAN LODGE
2 HOPE CL
3 REX PAR
4 SHALFORD
5 THE RODINGS
6 LAWRENCE CT

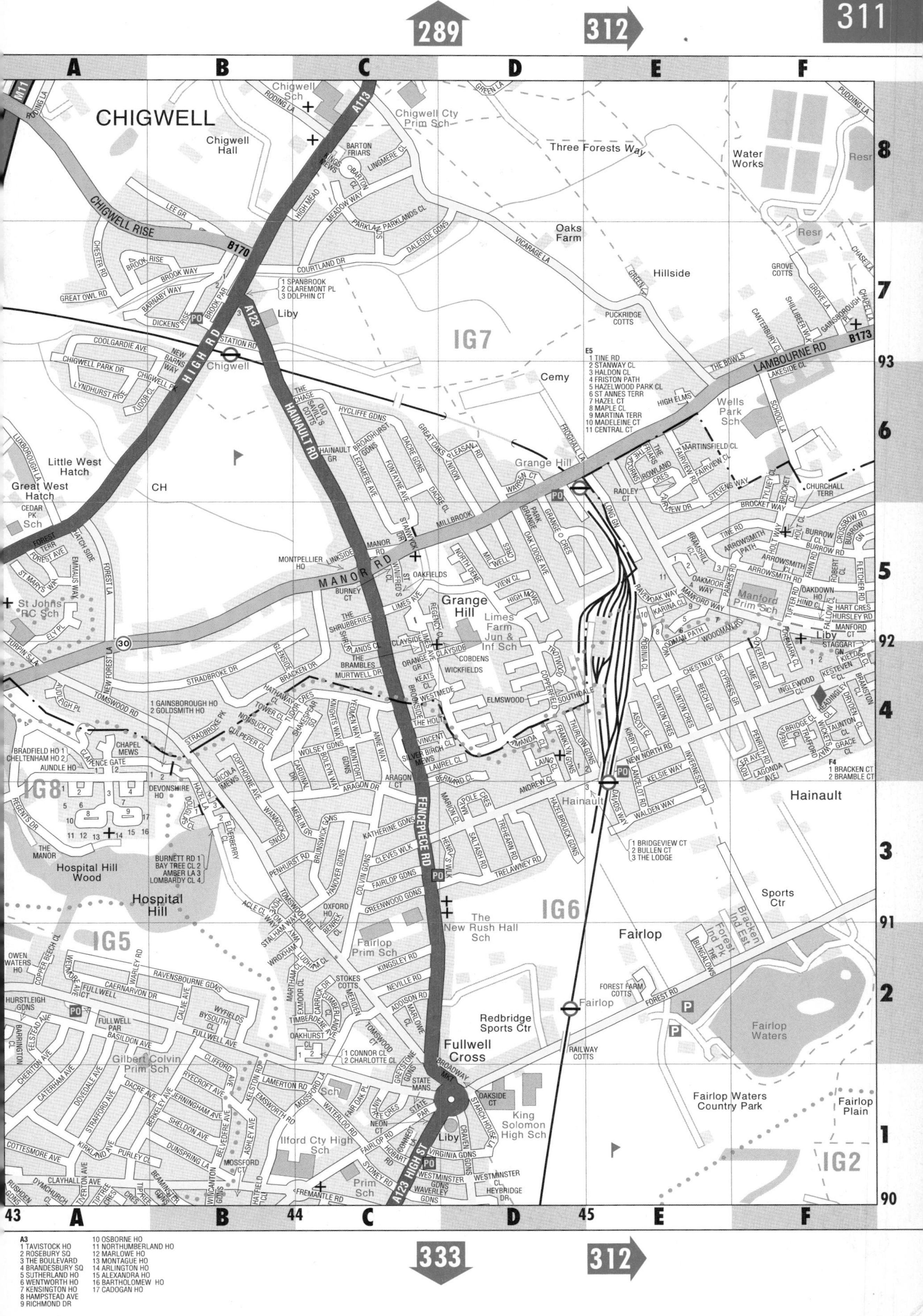
289
312
A
B
C
D
E
F
CHIGWELL
Chigwell Hall
Chigwell Sch
Chigwell Cty Prim Sch
Three Forests Way
Water Works
Resr
Oaks Farm
Hillside
IG7
Chigwell
Cemy
Wells Park Sch
Grange Hill
Little West Hatch
Great West Hatch
CH
Cedar Pk Sch
St Johns RC Sch
Grange Hill
Limes Farm Jun & Inf Sch
Manford Prim Sch
Liby
IG8
Hospital Hill Wood
Hospital Hill
IG5
IG6
Hainault
Sports Ctr
Fairlop
The New Rush Hall Sch
Fairlop Prim Sch
Redbridge Sports Ctr
Fullwell Cross
Fairlop Waters
Gilbert Colvin Prim Sch
Ilford Cty High Sch
King Solomon High Sch
Fairlop Waters Country Park
Fairlop Plain
IG2
Prim Sch
MANOR RD
HAINAULT RD
FENCEPIECE RD
HIGH RD
LAMBOURNE RD
CHIGWELL RISE
A123 HIGH ST
43
44
45
90
91
92
93
1
2
3
4
5
6
7
8
A3
1 TAVISTOCK HO
2 ROSEBURY SQ
3 THE BOULEVARD
4 BRANDESBURY SQ
5 SUTHERLAND HO
6 WENTWORTH HO
7 KENSINGTON HO
8 HAMPSTEAD AVE
9 RICHMOND DR
10 OSBORNE HO
11 NORTHUMBERLAND HO
12 MARLOWE HO
13 MONTAGUE HO
14 ARLINGTON HO
15 ALEXANDRA HO
16 BARTHOLOMEW HO
17 CADOGAN HO
333
312

B6
1 THE RIDINGS
2 LARCHWOOD HO
3 HAWKESBURY CL
4 BUCKTHORNE HO

311

290

A   B   C   D   E   F

8

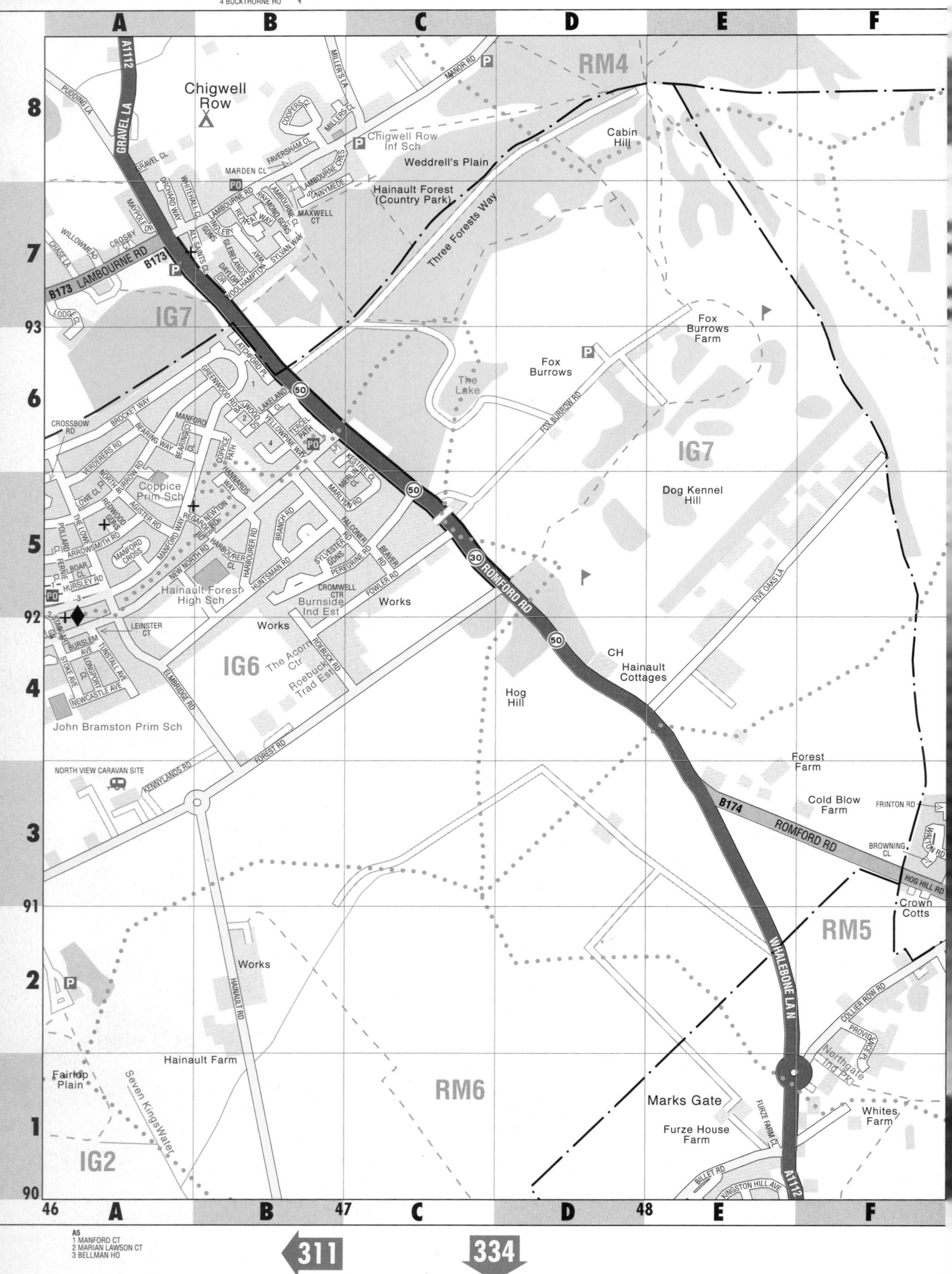

Chigwell Row

RM4

Cabin Hill

Chigwell Row Inf Sch

Weddrell's Plain

Hainault Forest (Country Park)

Three Forests Way

7

93

IG7

Fox Burrows Farm

The Lake

Fox Burrows

Fox Burrow Rd

6

IG7

Dog Kennel Hill

Coppice Prim Sch

5

Hainault Forest High Sch

Burnside Ind Est

Works

Works

Cromwell Ctr

ROMFORD RD

CH Hainault Cottages

92

The Acorn Ctr

Roebuck Trad Est

IG6

Hog Hill

John Bramston Prim Sch

4

Forest Farm

Cold Blow Farm

Frinton Rd

NORTH VIEW CARAVAN SITE

Kennylands Rd

B174 ROMFORD RD

Browning Cl

Walton Rd

Hog Hill Rd

3

91

Crown Cotts

RM5

Works

Hainault Rd

WHALEBONE LA N

2

Hainault Farm

Northgate Ind Pk

Fairlop Plain

Seven Kingswater

Marks Gate

Whites Farm

1

Furze House Farm

Firze Farm Ct

Provident

Collier Row Rd

IG2

RM6

Billet Rd

Kingston Hill Ave

A1112

90

46   A   B   47   C   D   48   E   F

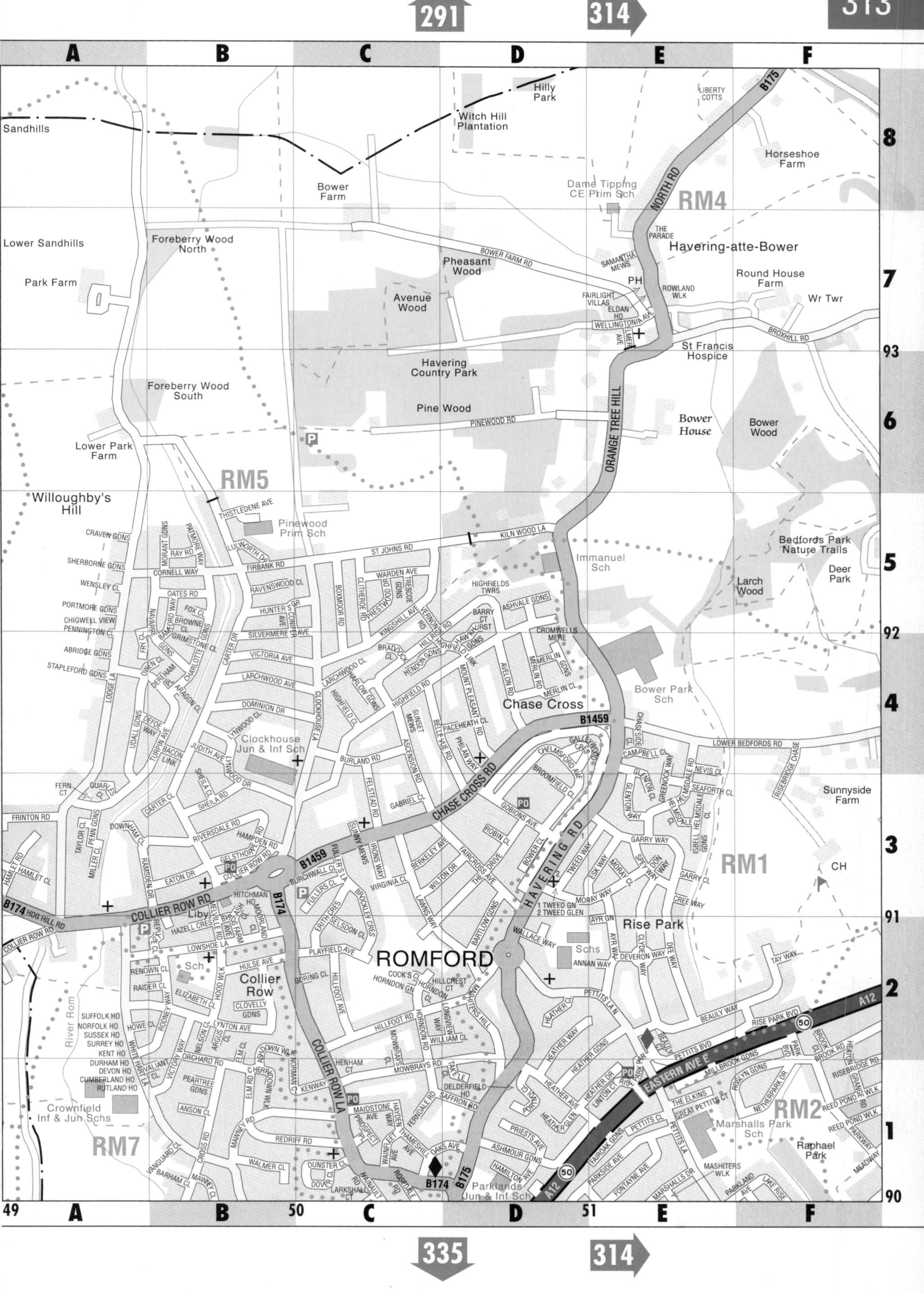

313
292

D5
1 ANGMERING HO
2 AMPTHILL HO
3 THORNBURY HO
4 CARDIGAN HO
5 UPTON HO
6 DEVIZES HO

D5
7 BARNSTAPLE PATH
8 OUNDLE HO
9 KIRKHAM HO
10 ACCRINGTON HO
11 RADSTOCK HO
12 STROUD HO
13 SOUTHSEA HO
14 ALCESTER HO
15 NORTHALLERTON WAY
16 DARLINGTON PATH
17 ABERCROMBIE HO
18 THE ARCADE

E5
1 WOLVERTON HO
2 NEWMARKET HO
3 NELSON HO
4 NANTWICH HO
5 MORECAMBE HO
6 MINEHEAD HO
7 MACCLESFIELD HO
8 LYNMOUTH HO
9 LUTON HO
10 THRAPSTON HO
11 HASLINGDEN HO
12 HALIFAX HO
13 GLOSSOP HO
14 GILLINGHAM HO
15 EPSOM HO

E6
1 CAMELFORD HO
2 PORTMADOC HO
3 WILMSLOW HO
4 NORTHAMPTON HO

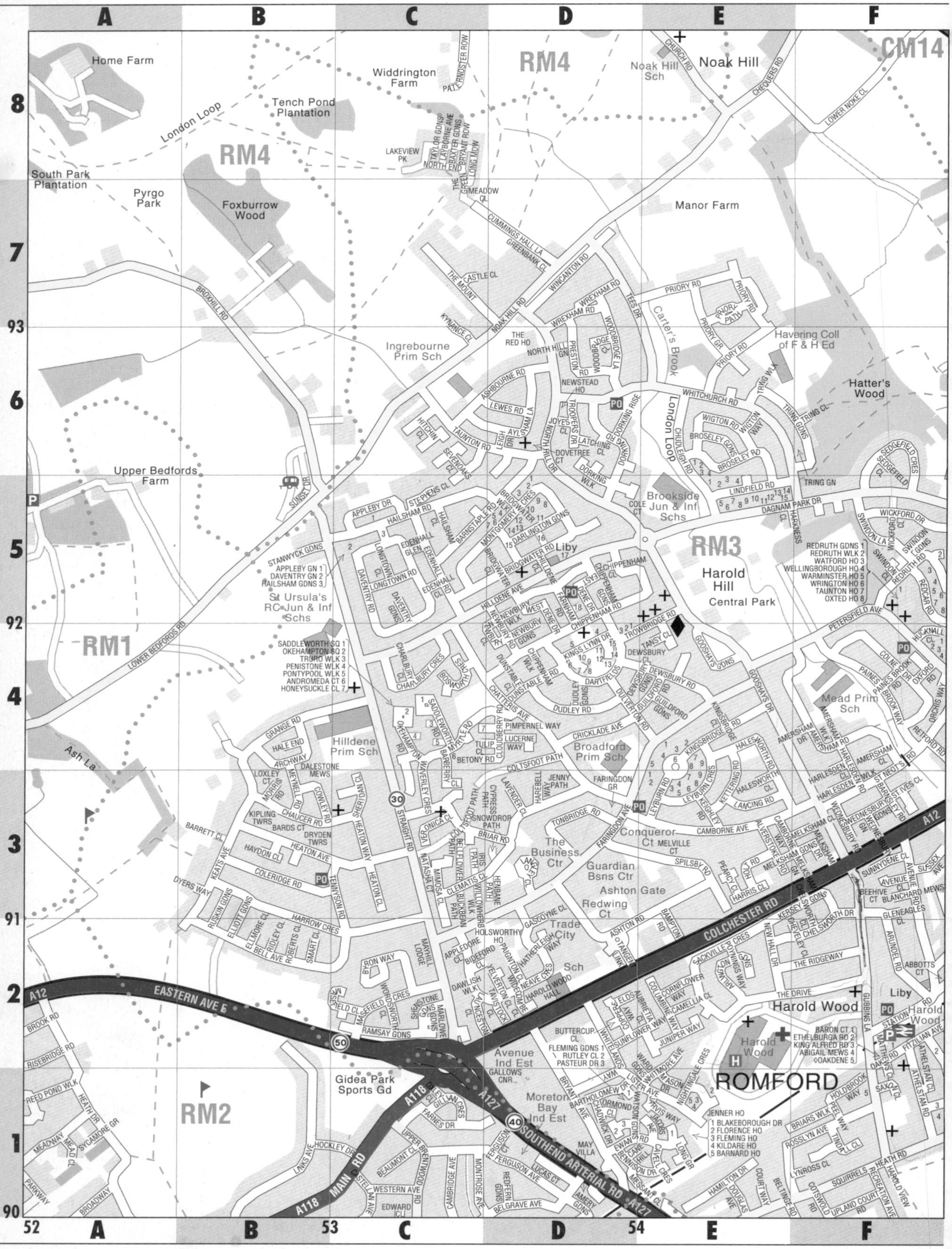

313
336

D4
1 MILLOM HO
2 ECCLES HO
3 TREGARON HO
4 CREDITON HO
5 ROTHBURY HO
6 STRATFORD HO
7 RIPON HO
8 MORPETH HO
9 RINGWOOD HO
10 WANTAGE HO
11 INGLETON HO
12 LINCOLN HO
13 MATLOCK HO
14 KESWICK HO
15 HALSTEAD HO

E3
1 PULBOROUGH HO
2 ORTON HO
3 LANGPORT HO
4 LAMPETER HO
5 HELMSLEY HO
6 ENFIELD HO
7 MIDDLESBOROUGH HO
8 ATHERTON HO
9 HAVANT HO

E4
1 ULVERSTON HO
2 WALLINGFORD HO
3 TALGARTH HO
4 SOUTHALL HO
5 RUNCORN HO
6 KINGSBRIDGE CIR
7 COLEFORD HO
8 DENBIGH HO
9 CHESHAM HO

F4
1 MARSDEN HO
2 CARNFORTH HO
3 BRACKNELL HO
4 BRACKLEY HO

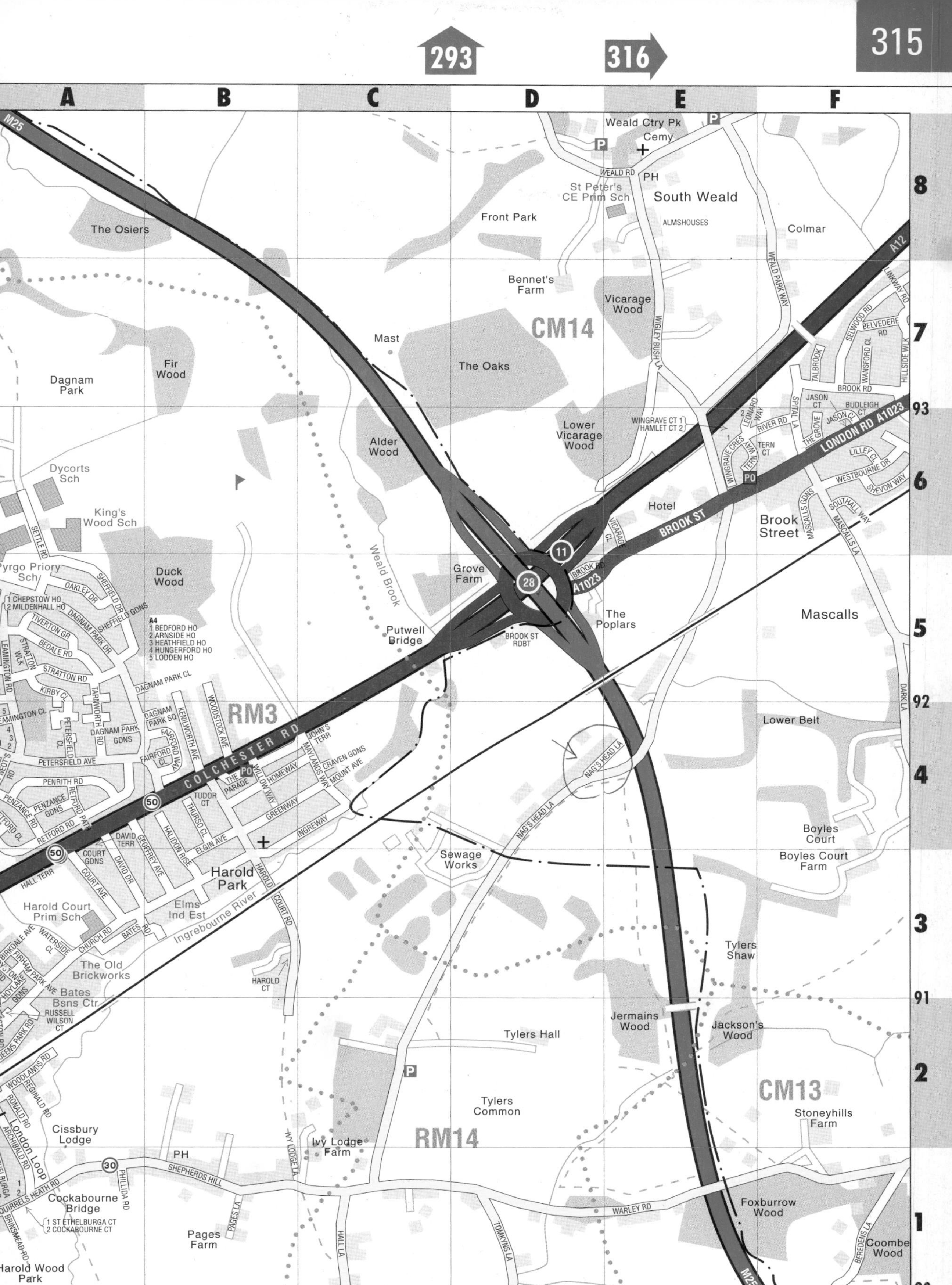

8

7

93

6

5

92

4

3

91

2

1

90

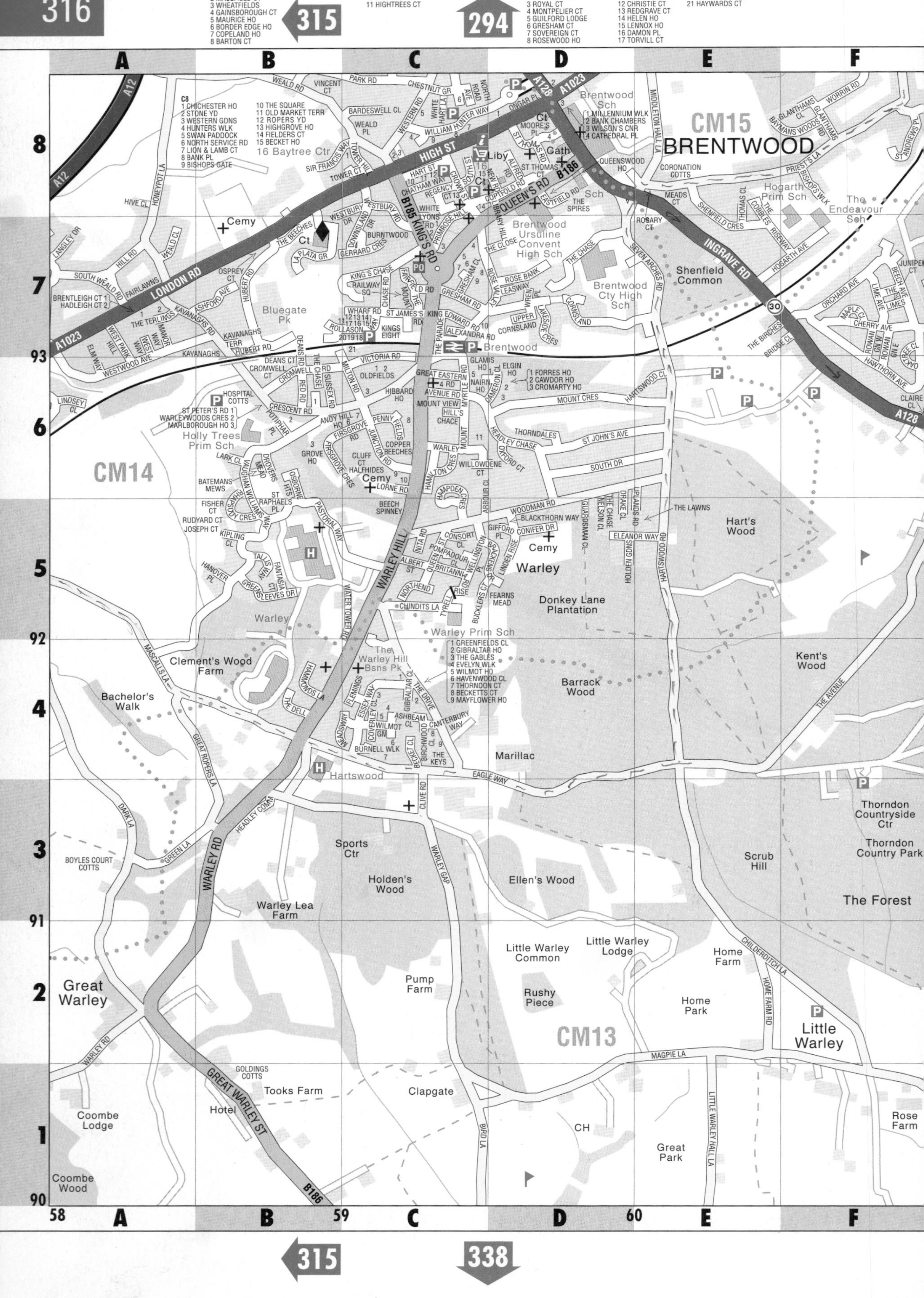

C6
1 VICTORIA CT
2 MASEFIELD CT
3 WHEATFIELDS
4 GAINSBOROUGH CT
5 MAURICE HO
6 BORDER EDGE HO
7 COPELAND HO
8 BARTON CT
315
C6
9 TYLERS CT
10 HOWERD HO
11 HIGHTREES CT
294
C7
1 DOUGLAS MATTHEW HO
2 PRIMROSE CT
3 ROYAL CT
4 MONTPELIER CT
5 GUILFORD LODGE
6 GRESHAM CT
7 SOVEREIGN CT
8 ROSEWOOD HO
9 SWALLOW CT
10 CORNSLAND CT
11 WHITBREAD CT
12 CHRISTIE CT
13 REDGRAVE CT
14 HELEN HO
15 LENNOX HO
16 DAMON PL
17 TORVILL CT
18 WATSON CT
19 TOMLINSON HO
20 MACARTHUR PL
21 HAYWARDS CT
A
B
C
D
E
F
C8
1 CHICHESTER HO
2 STONE YD
3 WESTERN GDNS
4 HUNTERS WLK
5 SWAN PADDOCK
6 NORTH SERVICE RD
7 LION & LAMB CT
8 BANK PL
9 BISHOPS GATE
10 THE SQUARE
11 OLD MARKET TERR
12 ROPERS YD
13 HIGHGROVE HO
14 FIELDERS CT
15 BECKET HO
16 Baytree Ctr
1 MILLENNIUM WLK
2 BANK CHAMBERS
3 WILSON'S CNR
4 CATHEDRAL PL
8
CM15
BRENTWOOD
Brentwood Sch
HIGH ST
LONDON RD
A12
A1023
A128
B186
B185 KING'S RD
QUEEN'S RD
INGRAVE RD
Liby
Cath
Cemy
Ct
PO
Brentwood Ursuline Convent High Sch
Brentwood Cty High Sch
Shenfield Common
Hogarth Prim Sch
The Endeavour Sch
7
Bluegate Pk
93
Brentwood
6
CM14
Holly Trees Prim Sch
HOSPITAL COTTS
ST PETER'S RD 1
WARLEYWOODS CRES 2
MARLBOROUGH HO 3
1 FORRES HO
2 CAWDOR HO
3 CROMARTY HO
5
Hart's Wood
Warley
Donkey Lane Plantation
WARLEY HILL
92
Warley Prim Sch
Clement's Wood Farm
The Warley Hill Bsns Pk
1 GREENFIELDS CL
2 GIBRALTAR HO
3 THE GABLES
4 EVELYN WLK
5 WILMOT HO
6 HAVENWOOD CL
7 THORNDON CT
8 BECKETTS CT
9 MAYFLOWER HO
Barrack Wood
Kent's Wood
Bachelor's Walk
4
Marillac
Hartswood
EAGLE WAY
3
Thorndon Countryside Ctr
Thorndon Country Park
BOYLES COURT COTTS
Sports Ctr
Holden's Wood
Ellen's Wood
Scrub Hill
WARLEY RD
Warley Lea Farm
The Forest
91
Little Warley Common
Little Warley Lodge
Home Farm
2
Great Warley
Pump Farm
Rushy Piece
Home Park
CM13
Little Warley
MAGPIE LA
GOLDINGS COTTS
Tooks Farm
Clapgate
GREAT WARLEY ST
Hotel
Coombe Lodge
1
CH
Great Park
Rose Farm
Coombe Wood
90
58
59
60
315
338

295
318

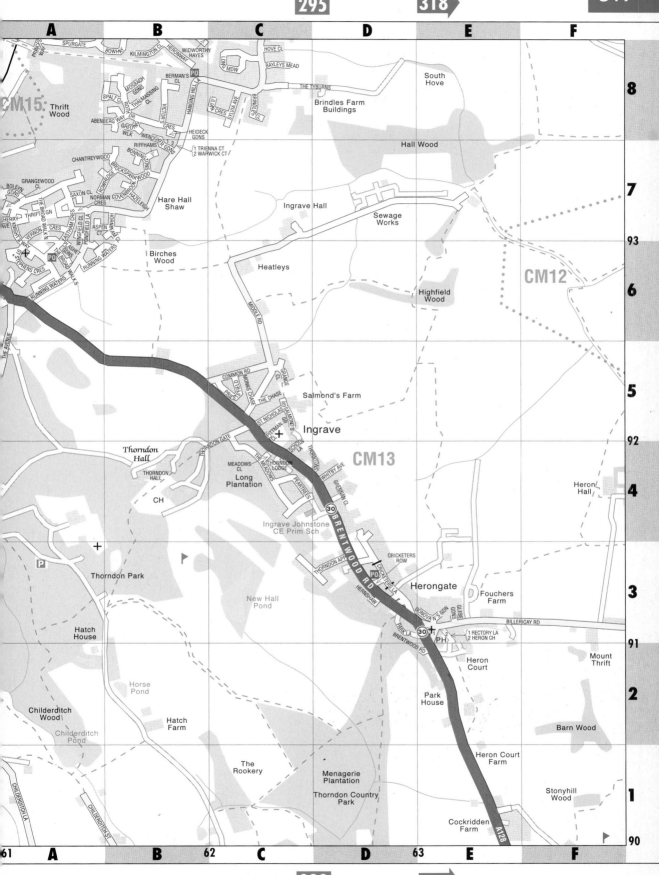
A
B
C
D
E
F
8
7
93
6
5
92
4
3
91
2
1
90
61
62
63
CM15
CM12
CM13
Thrift Wood
South Hove
Brindles Farm Buildings
Hall Wood
Hare Hall Shaw
Ingrave Hall
Sewage Works
Birches Wood
Heatleys
Highfield Wood
Salmond's Farm
Ingrave
Thorndon Hall
Long Plantation
CH
Ingrave Johnstone CE Prim Sch
Heron Hall
Thorndon Park
New Hall Pond
Herongate
Fouchers Farm
Hatch House
Heron Court
Mount Thrift
Horse Pond
Park House
Childerditch Wood
Childerditch Pond
Hatch Farm
Barn Wood
The Rookery
Menagerie Plantation
Thorndon Country Park
Heron Court Farm
Stonyhill Wood
Cockridden Farm
BRENTWOOD RD
BILLERICAY RD
MIDDLE RD
A128
CHILDERDITCH LA
CHILDERDITCH ST
THE AVENUE
RUNNING WATERS
HANGING HILL LA
THE TYBURNS
SPURGATE
KILMINGTON CL
HERONWAY
WIDWORTHY HAYES
HOVE CL
BAYLEYS MEAD
LONG MDW
BERMAN'S CL
LILIAN CRES
SYLVIA AVE
BRINDLES CL
HEIDECK GDNS
1 TRIENNA CT
2 WARWICK CT
CHANTREYWOOD
GRANGEWOOD CL
SAXON CL
COMMON RD
GRANGE CL
THE CHASE
ST NICHOLAS GR
THORNDON GATE
MEADOWS CL
THE MEADOWS
THORNDON LODGE
WHITBY AVE
GRENMAN CL
CRICKETERS ROW
CRICKETERS LA
HERNSHAW
THORNDON APP
PARK LA
BRENTWOOD RD
1 RECTORY LA
2 HERON CH
PH

317 296

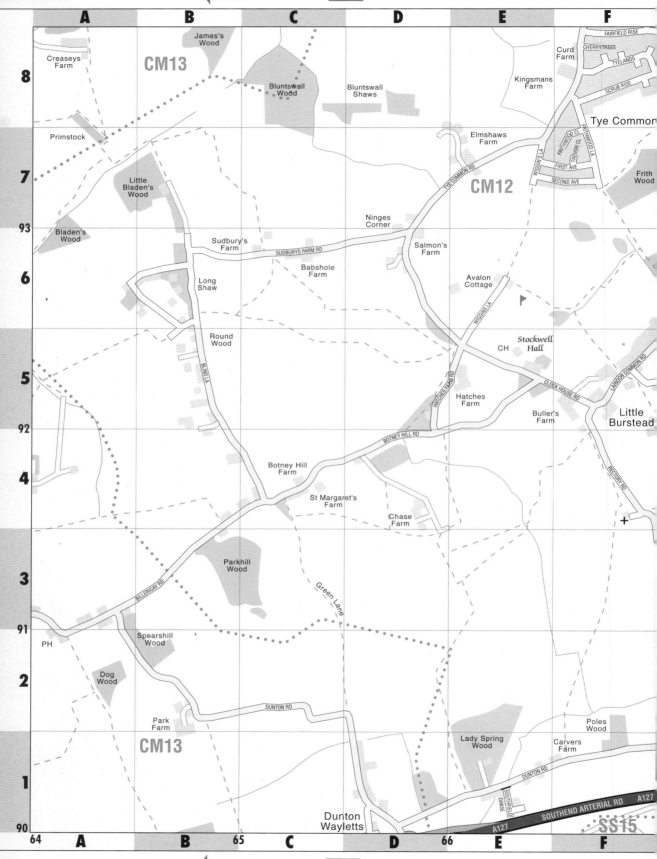

Creaseys Farm

CM13

James's Wood

Bluntswall Wood

Bluntswall Shaws

Curd Farm

FAIRFIELD RISE

CHERRYTREES

TYELANDS

Kingsmans Farm

SCRUB RISE

Tye Common

Primstock

Little Bladen's Wood

Elmshaws Farm

TYE COMMON RD

WIGGINS LA

FRITHWOOD CL

TREVOR CL

FRITHWOOD LA

FIRST AVE

SECOND AVE

CM12

Frith Wood

Bladen's Wood

Sudbury's Farm

SUDBURYS FARM RD

Ninges Corner

Salmon's Farm

Long Shaw

Babshole Farm

Avalon Cottage

WIGGINS LA

Round Wood

Stockwell Hall

BLIND LA

CH

HATCHES FARM RD

Hatches Farm

CLOCK HOUSE RD

LANGDON COMMON RD

Little Burstead

Buller's Farm

BOTNEY HILL RD

Botney Hill Farm

St Margaret's Farm

RECTORY RD

Chase Farm

Parkhill Wood

BILLERICAY RD

Green Lane

PH

Spearshill Wood

Dog Wood

DUNTON RD

Park Farm

CM13

Lady Spring Wood

Poles Wood

Carvers Farm

DUNTON RD

Dunton Wayletts

SOUTHFIELD CHASE

SOUTHEND ARTERIAL RD

A127

A127

SS15

317 340

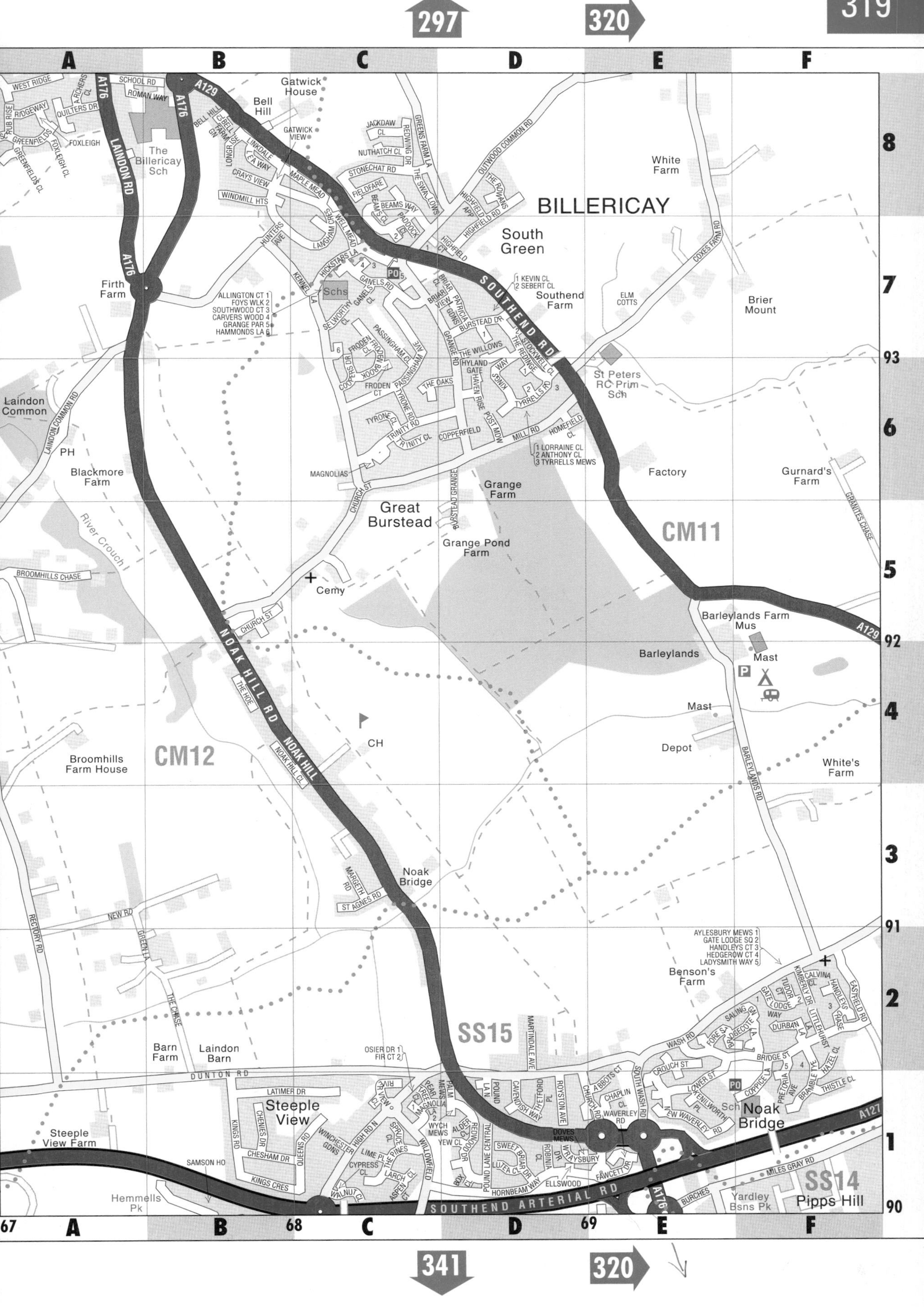

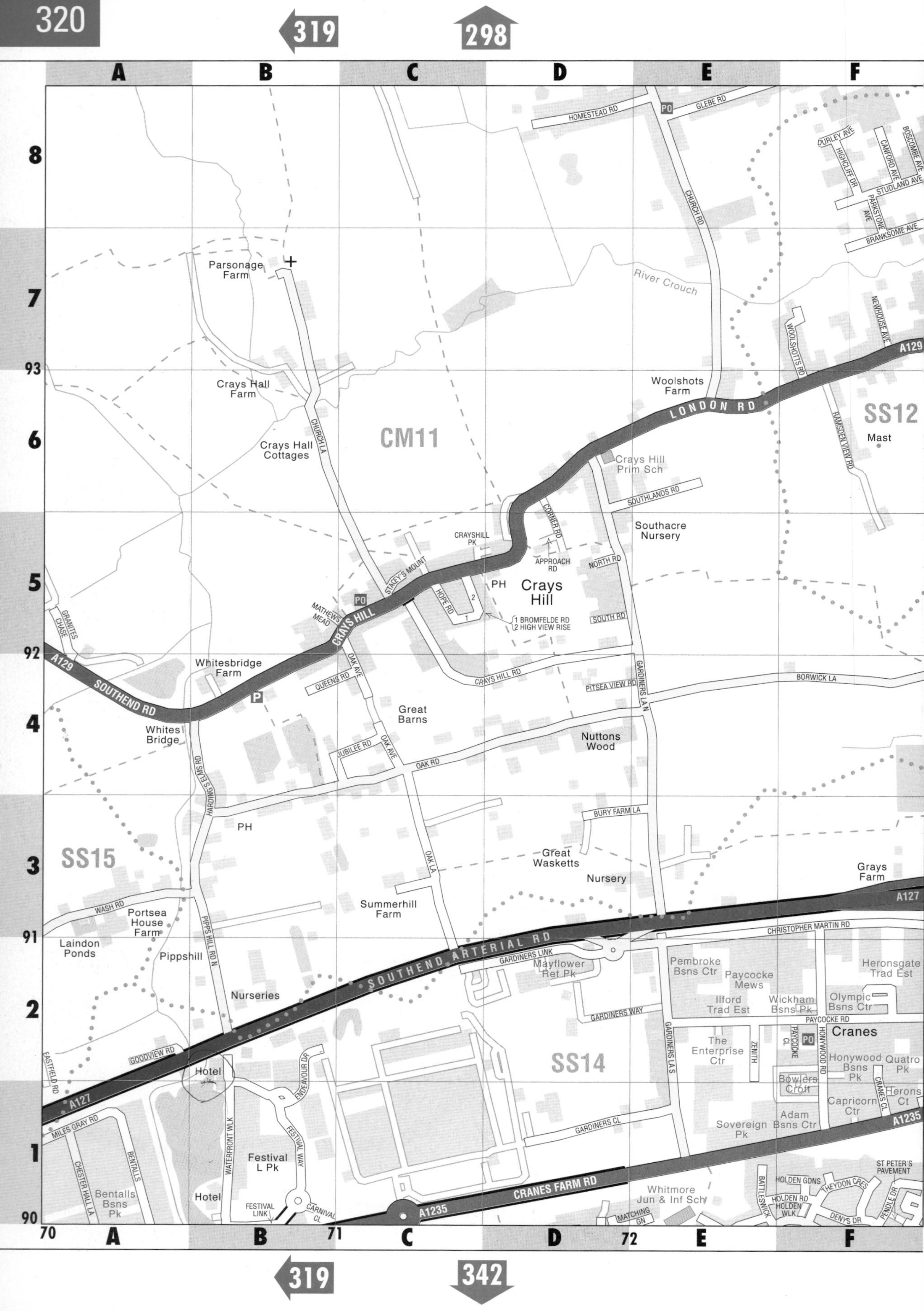

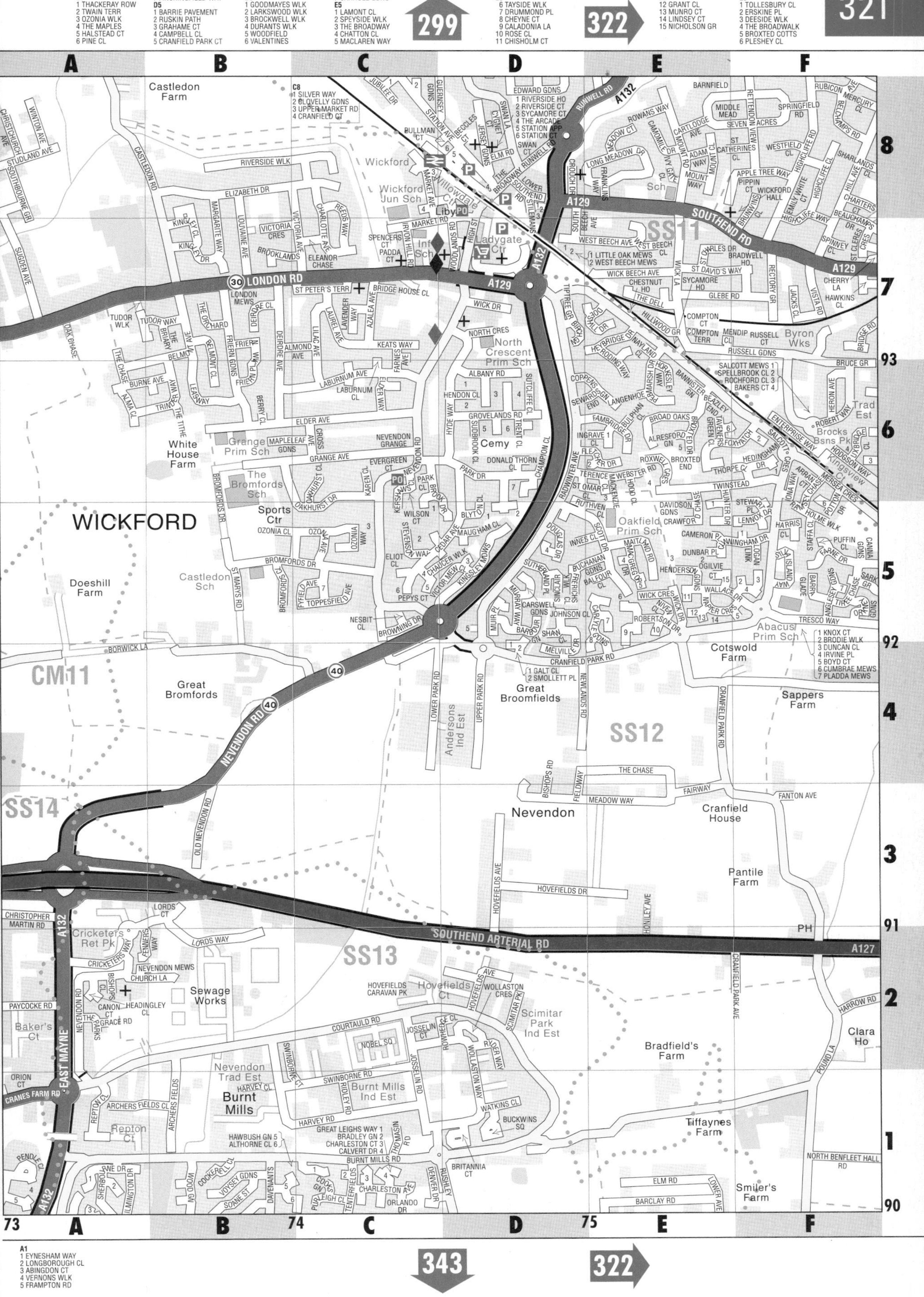

299
322

343
322

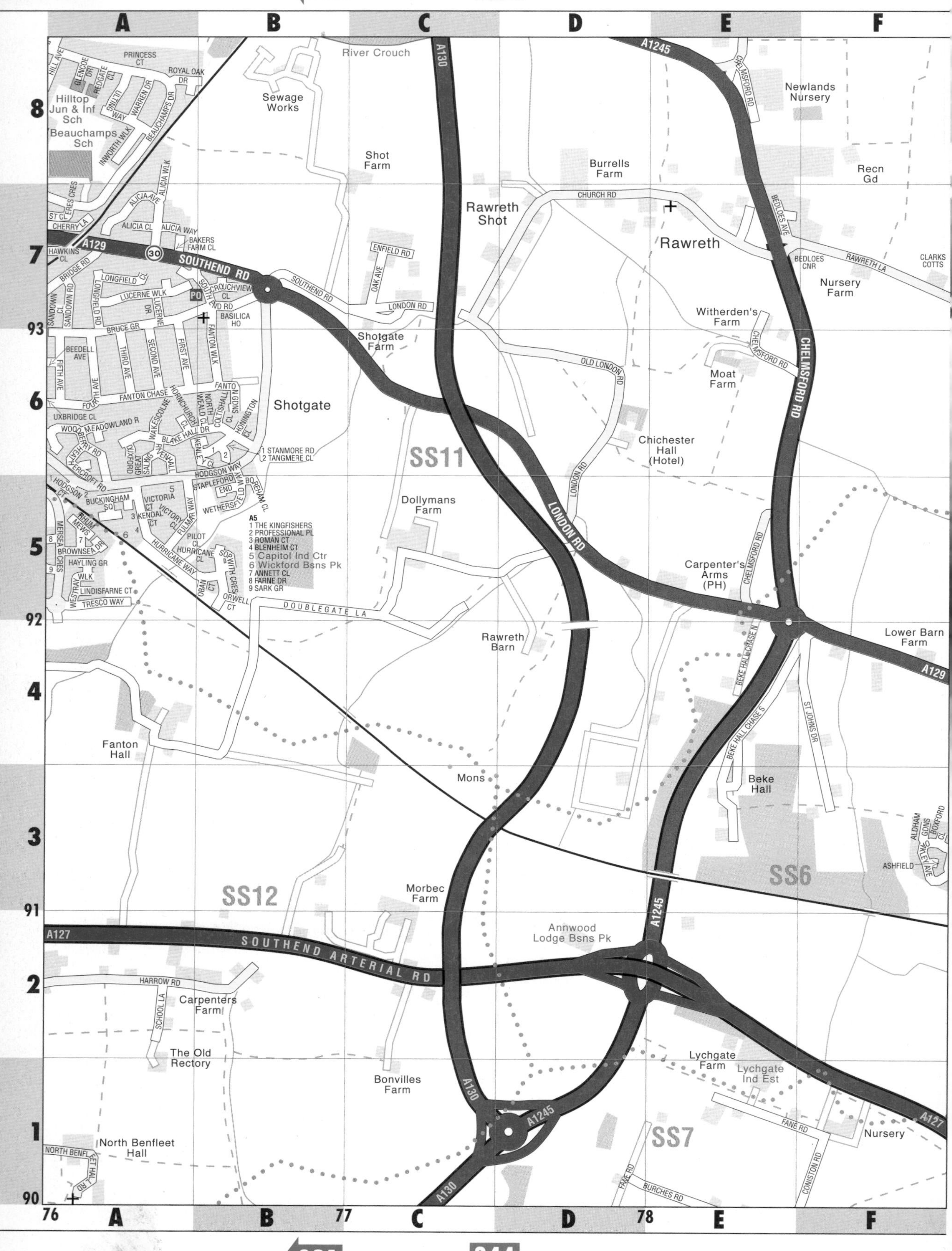

321
300

River Crouch

A130

A1245

Newlands
Nursery

Sewage
Works

Shot
Farm

Burrells
Farm

Recn
Gd

CHURCH RD

Rawreth
Shot

Rawreth

CLARKS
COTTS

ENFIELD RD

Nursery
Farm

RAWRETH LA

BEDLOES
CNR

Witherden's
Farm

Shotgate
Farm

OLD LONDON RD

Moat
Farm

Shotgate

SS11

Chichester
Hall
(Hotel)

1 STANMORE RD
2 TANGMERE CL

Dollymans
Farm

LONDON RD

Carpenter's
Arms
(PH)

A5
1 THE KINGFISHERS
2 PROFESSIONAL PL
3 ROMAN CT
4 BLENHEIM CT
5 Capitol Ind Ctr
6 Wickford Bsns Pk
7 ANNETT CL
8 FARNE DR
9 SARK GR

Lower Barn
Farm

A129

DOUBLEGATE LA

Rawreth
Barn

Fanton
Hall

Beke
Hall

SS6

ASHFIELD

Mons

SS12

Morbec
Farm

A1245

SS7

Annwood
Lodge Bsns Pk

Carpenters
Farm

SOUTHEND ARTERIAL RD

A127

HARROW RD

Lychgate
Farm

Lychgate
Ind Est

SCHOOL LA

The Old
Rectory

Bonvilles
Farm

A130

A1245

A127

Nursery

North Benfleet
Hall

NORTH BENFL

BURCHES RD

301
324

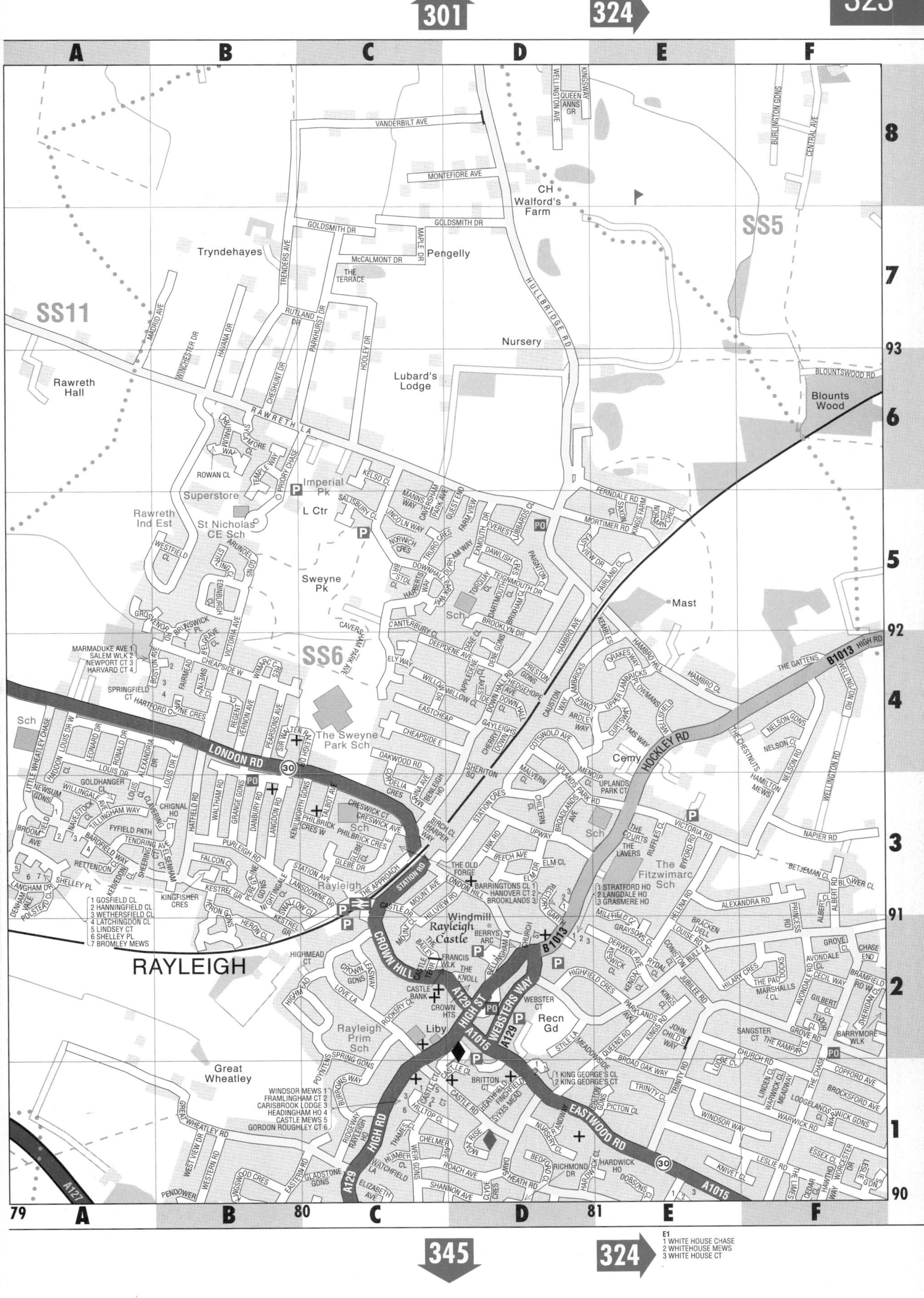

345
324

E1
1 WHITE HOUSE CHASE
2 WHITEHOUSE MEWS
3 WHITE HOUSE CT

A B C D E F

8

7

93

6

5

92

4

3

91

2

1

90

82 A 83 B C 84 D E F

Plumberow Wood

Beckney Wood

Plumberow Mount

WOOD AVE WOOD AVE

ETHELDORE AVE

Crabtree Wood

Vicarage Farm

Wadham Park Farm

MERTON RD

WADHAM PARK AVE

BLOUNTSWOOD RD

CHURCH RD

Mill Hill

Hockleyhall Wood

APPLEYARD

BLENHEIM CL

BRANKSOME CL

ASH WAY
PEACH AVE
ORCHARD AVE

RUSSET WAY
BLACKTHORN

MALVERN RD

TONBRIDGE RD

HARROGATE DR

PULPITS CL

Hockley Hall

MURRELS LA

ST PETERS RD

Nurseries

Marylands Wood

BRACKENDALE CL

MERRYFIELDS AVE

OAK WLK

Plumberow Prim Sch

The Greensward Coll

CHELTENHAM

GREENSWARD LA

MAPLELEAF CL

93

Blounts Farm

Nurseries

Hockley Prim Sch

HANOVER MEWS 1
SANDRINGHAM AVE 2
LAMBETH MEWS 3
KENSINGTON WAY 4
CEDAR MEWS 5
THE MEWS 6
ST JAMES'S WLK 7
CHEVENING GDNS 8

MOUNT AVE

MOUNT CRES

WESTMINSTER DR
CAERNARVON CL

WOODSTOCK CRS

ROMSEY CL

ALTHORPE CL

POPLAR CT

LIME CL

Hockley

Foundry Bsns Pk

RSSLYN CL

SELBOURNE RD

SEDDONS WLK

BROADLANDS

BEACHES

WILLOW

WILLOW

ELM

BROAD WLK

CHESTNUT CL

Home Farm

FRINTON LA

SILVERTREE

GAY BOWERS

FOLLY CHASE

FOLLY LA

HAWTHORNE GDNS

SUNNYFIELD GDNS

LABURNUM CL

LABURNUM

BALMORAL GDNS

HAMPTON CT

BUCKINGHAM RD

MARLBOROUGH GDNS

OSBOURNE AVE

BREAK AVE

BULL LA

BELVEDERE

BETTS LA

GATSCOMBE CT

HEVER

REY CL

BARNWELL DR

PICKWORTH DR

SUDLEY GDNS

BULLWOOD RD

MAIN RD

Hockley

Eldon Way Ind Est

FOUNDRY

ELDON WAY

CLAYSWELL

ELDON WAY CT

MEADOW

SPA RD

SPA CT

STATION RD

REGENCY CL

RETREAT

ODDLEY RD

HAWKWELL RD

HIGHAMS RD

WHITE HART LA

GLENCROFT

ALDERMANS HILL

30

HIGH RD

HILLSIDE RD

BULLWOOD APP

CROWN RD

WOODSIDE RD

Hockley Woods Forest Walks

PH

BADGERS MOUNT

WOODLANDS PAR

WOODLANDS CL

THE SPINNEYS

THE HYLANDS

BULLWOOD RD

PO

Liby

HOLLY CT

WOODPOND

HILLCREST RD

HARRIS CL

SHEPHERDS CT

HOCKLEY RISE

BELCHAMPS WAY

SOUTHEND RD

EVELYN RD

GLADSTONE RD

EASTERN RD

KEN GREEN AVE

HAWK LA

IRVING CL

VICTOR GDNS

GLENWOOD AVE

HEYCROFT RD

HAWTHORN CL

92

B1013

BULLWOOD HALL LA

Northlands Farm

Great Bull Wood

KILNWOOD AVE

WOOD END

BRICK WAY

TYRELL'S

THE WESTERINGS

HIGH ELMS RD

SUNNY RD

JUBILEE CL

30

HELENA CL

HILL CL

HILLSIDE AVE

WELBECK CL

BISFORTH CL

PO

HAWKWELL PARK DR

HAZELWOOD

Turret Farm

Beeches Wood

Hockley Woods

SS5

The Westerings Prim Sch

HAWKWELL CHASE

ELIZABETH CL

GREGORY CL

SUDBURY CL

TUDOR WAY

ELMWOOD CHASE

WOODSIDE CHASE

BROOKSIDE

MARTIN WLK

MAIN RD

HM Young Offender Inst & Prison (Bulwood Hall)

Belchamps Scout Ctr

POPLARS AVE

THORPE RD

THORPE CL

THORPE GDNS

HOLYOAK LA

Mount Bovers

MOUNT BOVERS LA

B1073

3

Stevens Farm

GUSTEDHALL LA

Honeypots Farm

Potash Wood

91

BULL LA

SS6

Fisher's Farm

1 POPES WLK
2 BARRYMORE WLK
3 WALPOLE WLK
4 HOLTON RD

Rawreth-hall Wood

Gustedhall Wood

Gusted Hall

2

MILTON CL

BLACKMORE WLK

KEATS WLK

BRAMFIELD RD

DOROTHY FARM RD

THORNINGTON RD

THE SPINNEYS

SHAKESPEARE AVE

BROOKSIDE AVE

ALBANY RD

GROVE RD

CONNAUGHT RD

CATHERINE CL

Sewage Works

The Scrubs

Primrose Wood

SS4

1

WARWICK GDN

CLARENCE RD

GROVE RD

P

GORDON CT

THE DRIVE

KATHERINE CL

RATELEIGH AVE

EASTWOOD RISE

New England Wood

Cottons

Grove Wood Prim Sch

LILLYVILLE WLK

MINSTER RD

WARWICK RD

DISRAELI RD

SS9

90

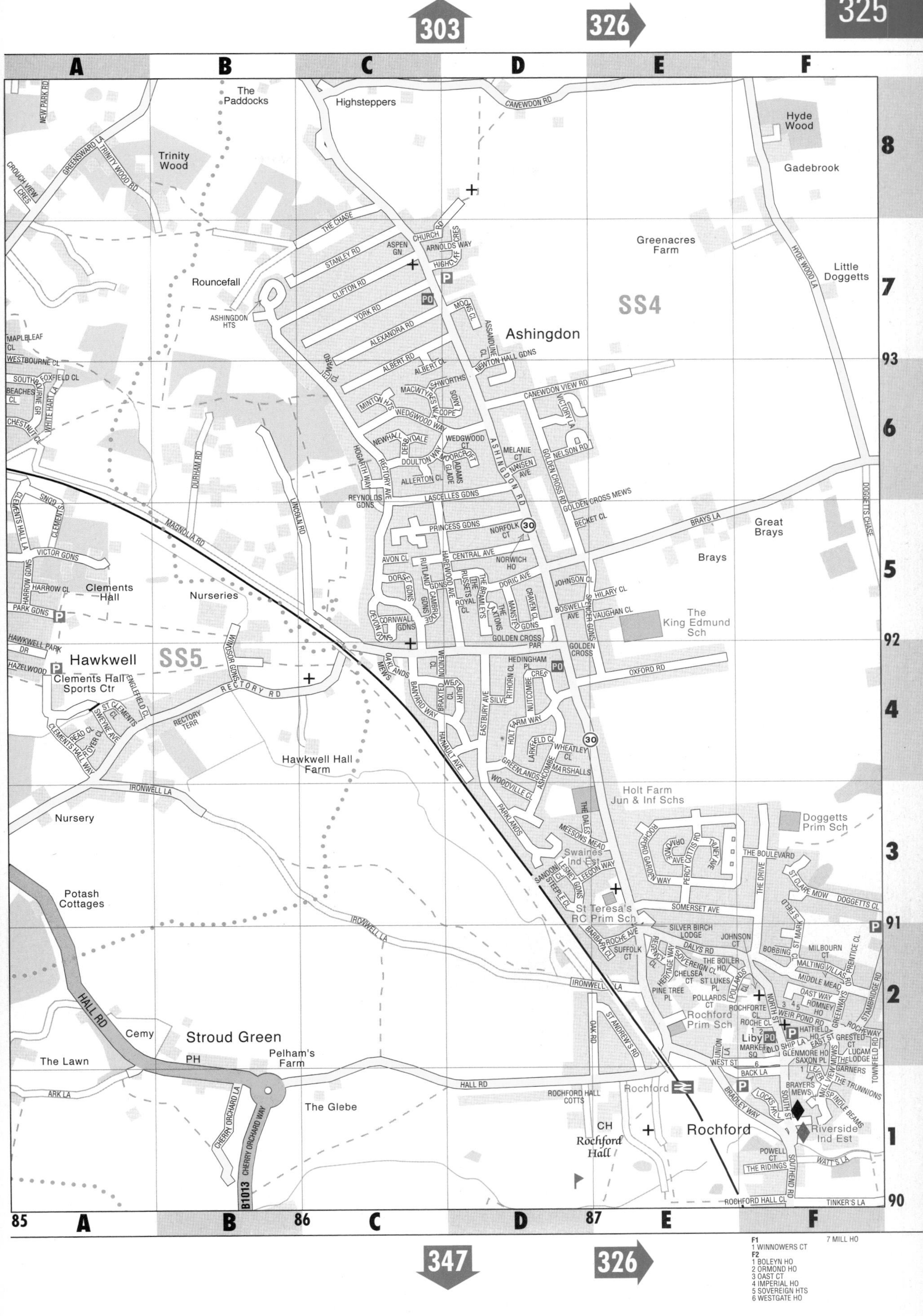
303
326
A
B
C
D
E
F
The Paddocks
Highsteppers
CANEWDON RD
Hyde Wood
Gadebrook
Trinity Wood
GREENSWARD LA
TRINITY WOOD RD
NEW PARK RD
CROUCH VIEW CRES
THE CHASE
CHURCH RD
ARNOLDS WAY
HIGHCLIFF CRES
ASPEN GN
STANLEY RD
CLIFTON RD
YORK RD
ALEXANDRA RD
ALBERT RD
ALBERT CL
Greenacres Farm
Little Doggetts
HYDE WOOD LA
Rouncefall
ASHINGDON HTS
SS4
Ashingdon
MAPLELEAF CL
WESTBOURNE CL
FOXFIELD CL
SOUTHBOURNE GR
BEACHES CL
WHITE HART LA
CHESTNUT CL
NEWTON HALL GDNS
ASSANDUNE CL
CANEWDON VIEW RD
VICTORY LA
ASHWORTHS
MACWILLIAMS WAY
MINTON HTS
WEDGWOOD WAY
COPE
NEWHALL
DERBYDALE
WEDGWOOD CT
DOULTON WAY
MOORCROFT
ADAMS GLADE
ALLERTON CL
HOGARTH WAY
RECTORY AVE
MELANIE CT
NANSEN AVE
NELSON RD
ASHINGDON RD
GOLDEN CROSS RD
GOLDEN CROSS MEWS
BECKET CL
BRAYS LA
Great Brays
Brays
DOGGETTS CHASE
REYNOLDS GDNS
LASCELLES GDNS
PRINCESS GDNS
NORFOLK CT
NORWICH HO
CENTRAL AVE
AVON CL
DORSET GDNS
RUTLAND GDNS
CAMBRIDGE GDNS
HAREWOOD AVE
RUSSETS
THE BRAMBLEYS
ROYAL CL
THE PAXTONS
MANSTEAD GDNS
CRAVEN CL
DORIC AVE
JOHNSON CL
HILARY CL
BOSWELL AVE
SPENCER GDNS
VAUGHAN CL
The King Edmund Sch
DEVON GDNS
CORNWALL GDNS
GOLDEN CROSS PAR
GOLDEN CROSS
OXFORD RD
HEDINGHAM PL
CLEMENTS HALL LA
CLEMENTS GDNS
MAGNOLIA RD
DURHAM RD
LINCOLN RD
VICTOR GDNS
HARROW GDNS
HARROW CL
Clements Hall
Nurseries
PARK GDNS
HAWKWELL PARK DR
HAZELWOOD
Hawkwell
SS5
Clements Hall Sports Ctr
WINDSOR GDNS
RECTORY RD
RECTORY TERR
ENGLEFIELD CL
ST CLEMENTS CL
SWEYNE AVE
READ CL
ROYER CL
CLEMENTS HALL WAY
OAKLANDS MEWS
BANYARD WAY
WENDON CL
BRAXTED CL
WEDBURY
EASTBURY AVE
SILVER
RITHORN CL
NUTCOMBE CRES
HAINAULT AVE
HOLT FARM WAY
LARKFIELD CL
WHEATLEY CL
GREENLANDS
ASHCOMBE
MARSHALLS
WOODVILLE CL
PARKLANDS
Hawkwell Hall Farm
IRONWELL LA
Nursery
Holt Farm Jun & Inf Schs
THE DALES
MEESONS MEAD
Swaines Ind Est
LEEDON WAY
LESNEY GDNS
SANDON CL
STEEPLE CL
ROCHFORD GARDEN WAY
ORMONDE AVE
PERCY COTTIS RD
TINNEY AVE
THE BOULEVARD
THE DRIVE
Doggetts Prim Sch
ST CLARE MDW
DOGGETTS CL
Potash Cottages
St Teresa's RC Prim Sch
SOMERSET AVE
BARBARA CL
ROCHE AVE
SUFFOLK CT
SILVER BIRCH LODGE
JOHNSON CT
DALYS RD
REGENCY CL
HERITAGE WAY
SOVEREIGN CL
THE BOILER HO
CHELSEA CT
ST LUKES PL
PINE TREE PL
POLLARDS CT
POLLARDS CL
BOBBING CL
ST MARKS FIELD
MILBOURN CT
PRENTICE CL
MALTINGS VILLAS
MIDDLE MEAD
OAST WAY
ROMNEY HO
STAMBRIDGE RD
ROCHEWAY
NORTH ST
ROCHFORTE CL
ROCHE CL
WEIR POND RD
HATFIELD HO
GRESTED CT
Rochford Prim Sch
HALL RD
Cemy
Stroud Green
PH
Pelham's Farm
The Lawn
ARK LA
STANDREWS RD
OAK RD
Liby
MARKET SQ
OLD SHIP LA
EAST ST
GLENMORE HO
SAXON PL
LUCAM LODGE
UNION LA
WEST ST
BACK LA
GARNERS
THE TRUNNIONS
TOWNFIELD RD
BRAYERS MEWS
MILL VIEW MDWS
SPINDLE BEAMS
LOCKS HILL
BRADLEY WAY
SOUTH ST
Riverside Ind Est
Rochford
CHERRY ORCHARD LA
CHERRY ORCHARD WAY
B1013
The Glebe
ROCHFORD HALL COTTS
CH
Rochford Hall
POWELL CT
THE RIDINGS
WATTS LA
SOUTHEND RD
ROCHFORD HALL CL
TINKER'S LA
8
7
93
6
5
92
4
3
91
2
1
90
85
86
87
347
326
F1
1 WINNOWERS CT
F2
1 BOLEYN HO
2 ORMOND HO
3 OAST CT
4 IMPERIAL HO
5 SOVEREIGN HTS
6 WESTGATE HO
7 MILL HO

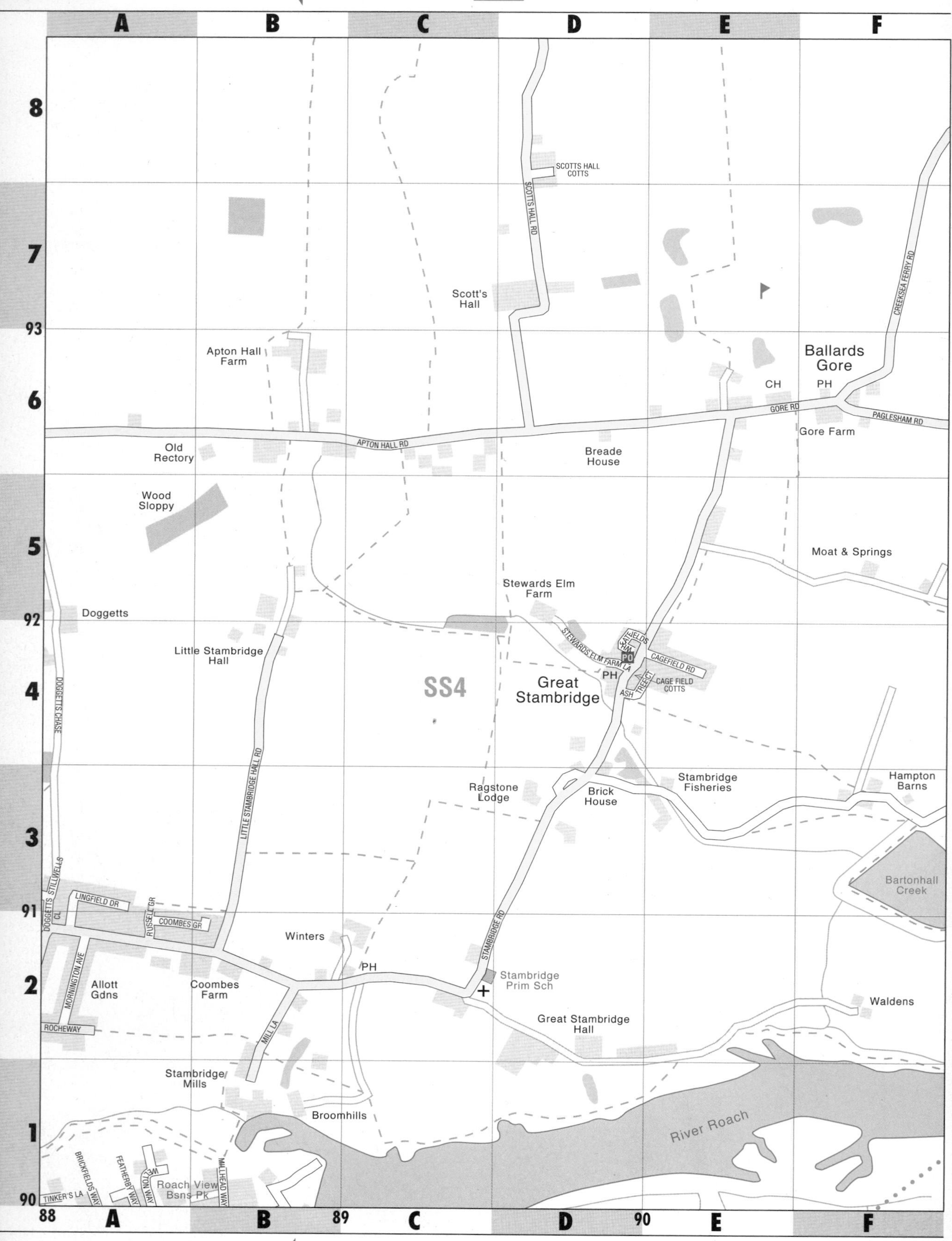

325
304

SCOTTS HALL COTTS

SCOTTS HALL RD

Scott's Hall

CREEKSEA FERRY RD

Ballards Gore

CH   PH

Apton Hall Farm

GORE RD   PAGLESHAM RD

Gore Farm

Old Rectory

APTON HALL RD

Breade House

Wood Sloppy

Moat & Springs

Stewards Elm Farm

Doggetts

DOGGETTS CHASE

Little Stambridge Hall

LITTLE STAMBRIDGE HALL RD

SS4

STEWARDS ELM FARM LA

FIELDS
PO

CAGEFIELD RD

PH

ASH TREE CT

CAGE FIELD COTTS

Great Stambridge

Ragstone Lodge

Brick House

Stambridge Fisheries

Hampton Barns

STAMBRIDGE RD

Bartonhall Creek

DOGGETTS

STILLWELLS

LINGFIELD DR

CL

RUSSEL GR

COOMBES GR

Winters

PH

MORNINGTON AVE

Allott Gdns

Coombes Farm

Stambridge Prim Sch

Waldens

ROCHEWAY

MILL LA

Great Stambridge Hall

Stambridge Mills

Broomhills

River Roach

BRICKFIELDS WAY

FEATHERBY WAY

MALLHEAD WAY

Roach View Bsns Pk

TINKER'S LA

325
348

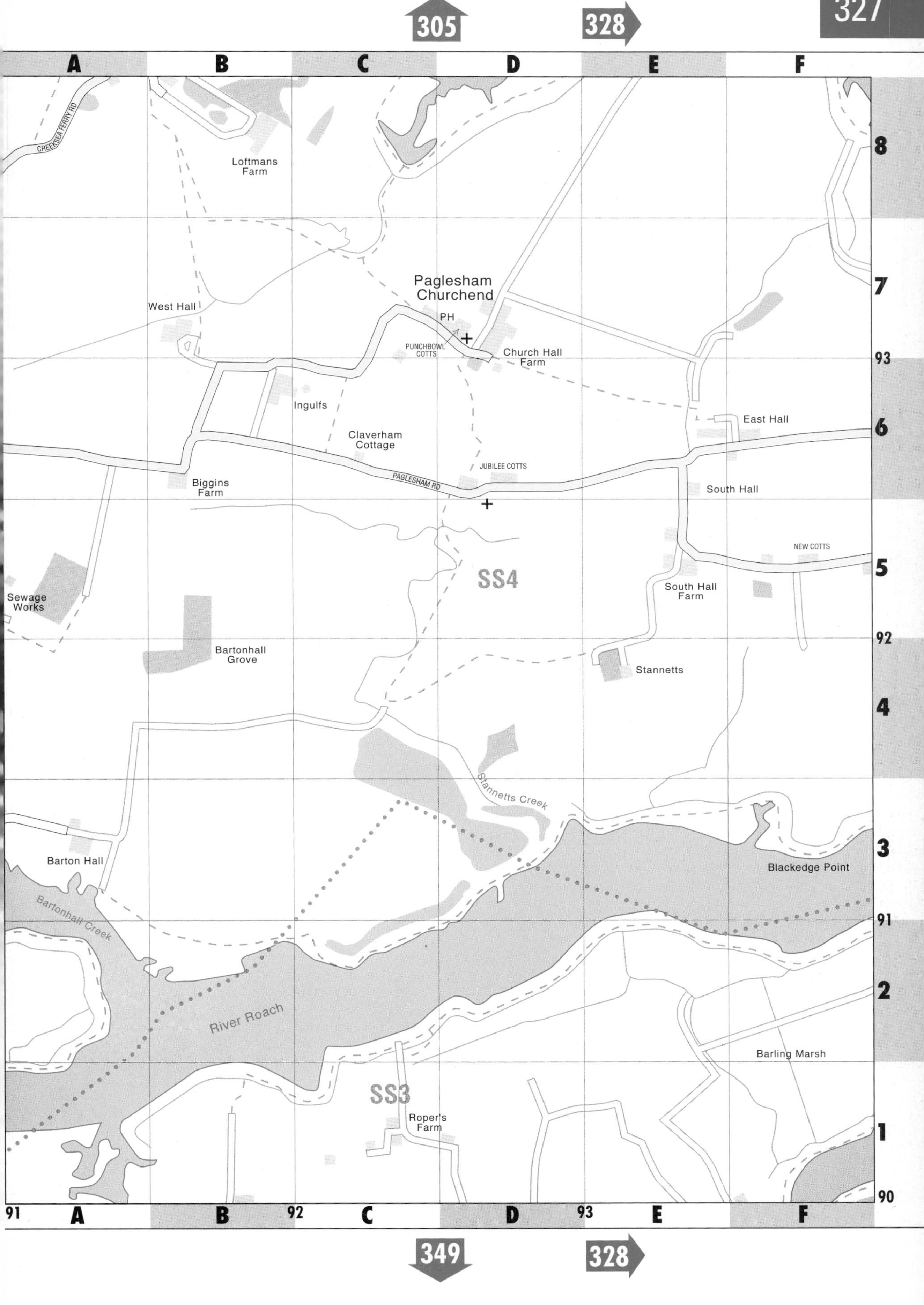

A B C D E F

8

Loftmans
Farm

7

Paglesham
Churchend

West Hall

PH

93

PUNCHBOWL
COTTS

Church Hall
Farm

Ingulfs

East Hall

6

Claverham
Cottage

Biggins
Farm

PAGLESHAM RD

JUBILEE COTTS

South Hall

+

Sewage
Works

SS4

NEW COTTS

5

South Hall
Farm

92

Bartonhall
Grove

Stannetts

4

Stannetts Creek

Barton Hall

3

Blackedge Point

Bartonhall Creek

91

River Roach

2

Barling Marsh

SS3

Roper's
Farm

1

90

91 A B 92 C D 93 E F

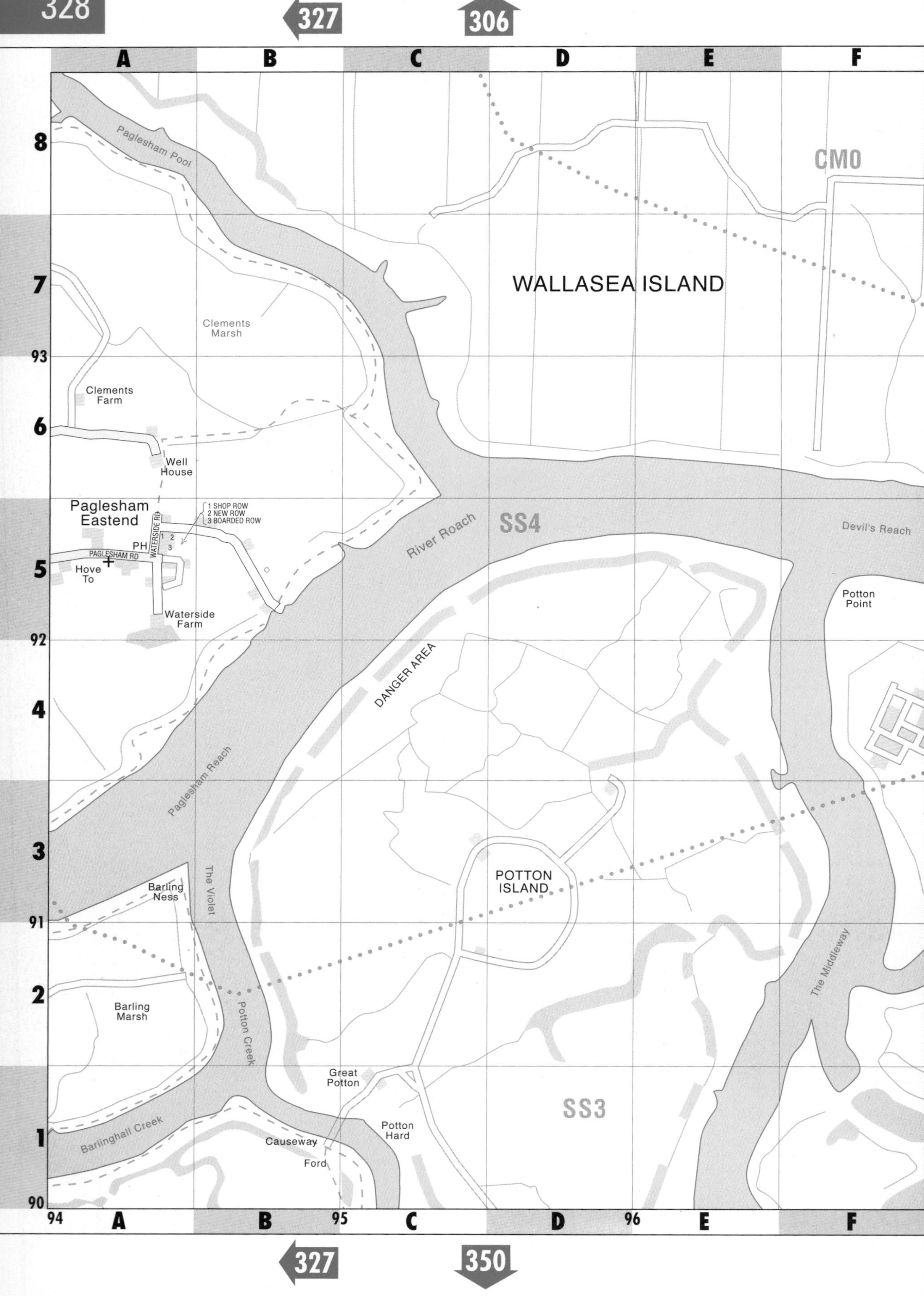

A   B   C   D   E   F

8

Paglesham Pool

7

Clements Marsh

93

Clements Farm

6

Well House

Paglesham Eastend

1 SHOP ROW
2 NEW ROW
3 BOARDED ROW

PH

PAGLESHAM RD

WATERSIDE RD

Hove To

5

Waterside Farm

92

WALLASEA ISLAND

CM0

River Roach

SS4

Devil's Reach

Potton Point

4

DANGER AREA

Paglesham Reach

The Violet

3

Barling Ness

POTTON ISLAND

The Middleway

91

Barling Marsh

2

Potton Creek

Great Potton

Potton Hard

SS3

1

Barlinghall Creek

Causeway

Ford

90

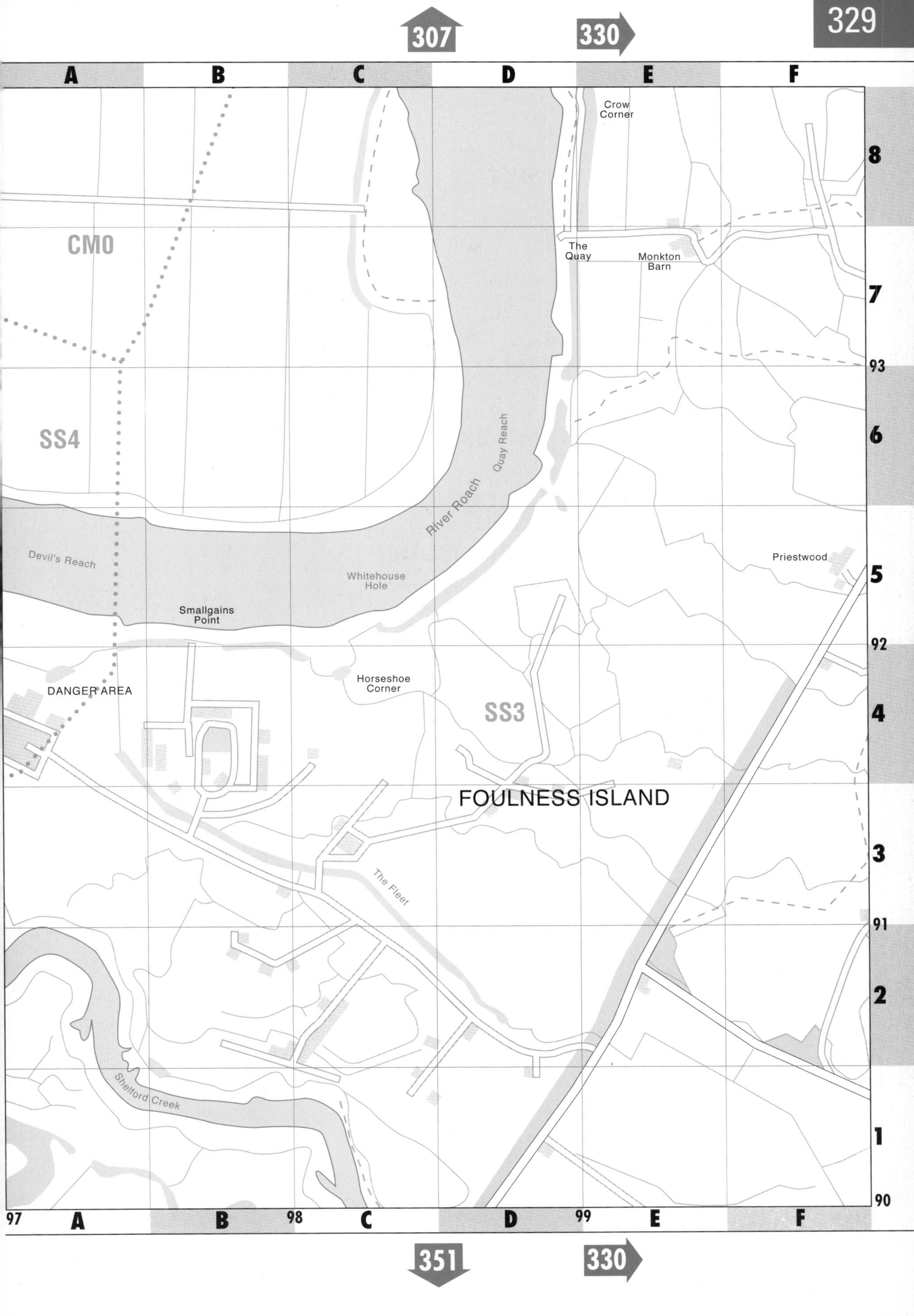

307
330

A B C D E F

8

CMO

7

93

SS4

6

River Roach

Quay Reach

Crow
Corner

The
Quay

Monkton
Barn

Devil's Reach

Whitehouse
Hole

Priestwood

5

92

Smallgains
Point

Horseshoe
Corner

DANGER AREA

SS3

4

FOULNESS ISLAND

3

The Fleet

91

2

Shelford Creek

1

90

351
330

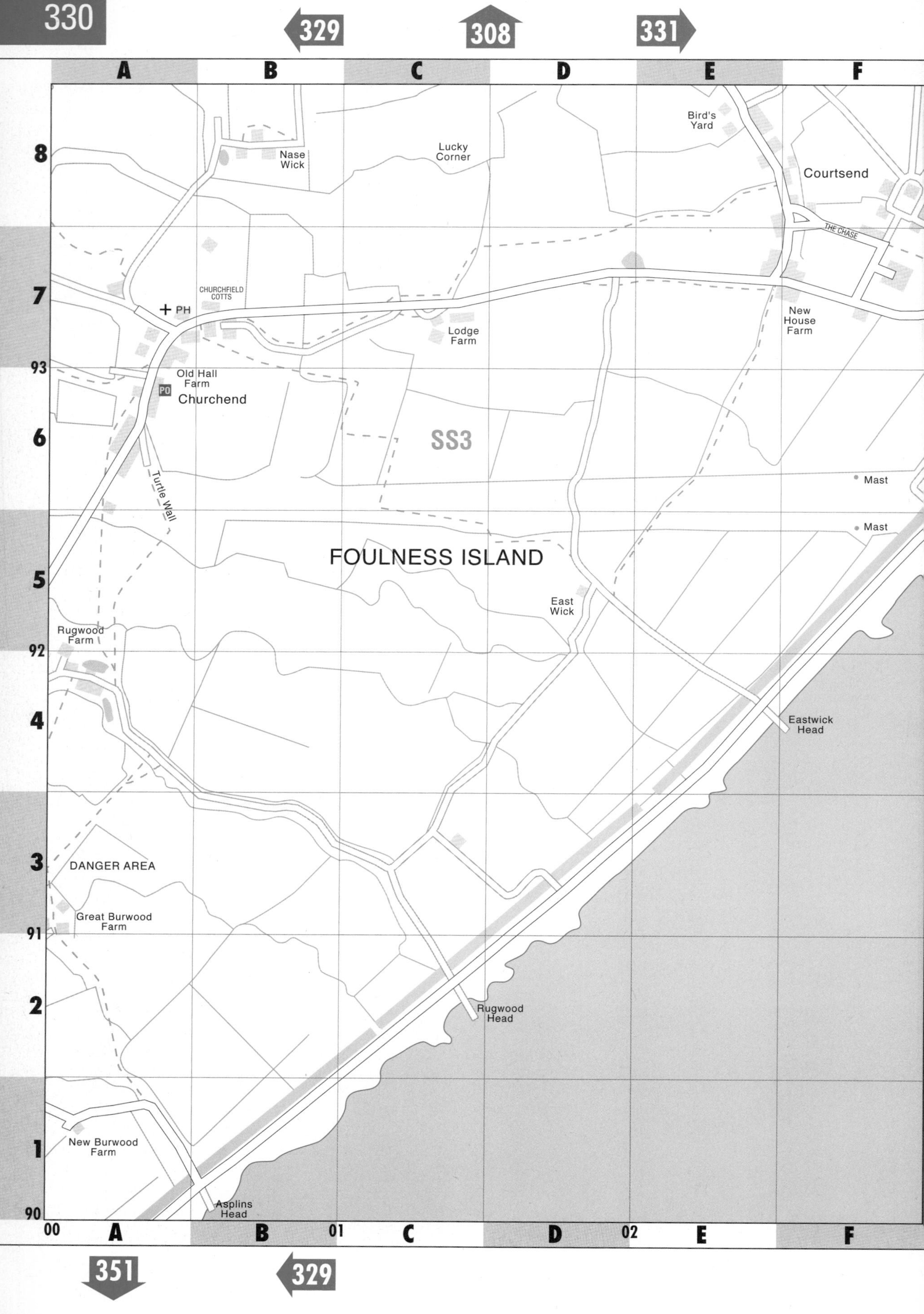

A   B   C   D   E   F

8

Nase Wick

Lucky Corner

Bird's Yard

Courtsend

THE CHASE

7

CHURCHFIELD COTTS

+ PH

Lodge Farm

New House Farm

93

Old Hall Farm

PO

Churchend

SS3

6

Turtle Wall

Mast

Mast

FOULNESS ISLAND

5

East Wick

Rugwood Farm

92

Eastwick Head

4

3

DANGER AREA

Great Burwood Farm

91

2

Rugwood Head

1

New Burwood Farm

90

Asplins Head

00   A   B   01   C   D   02   E   F

308

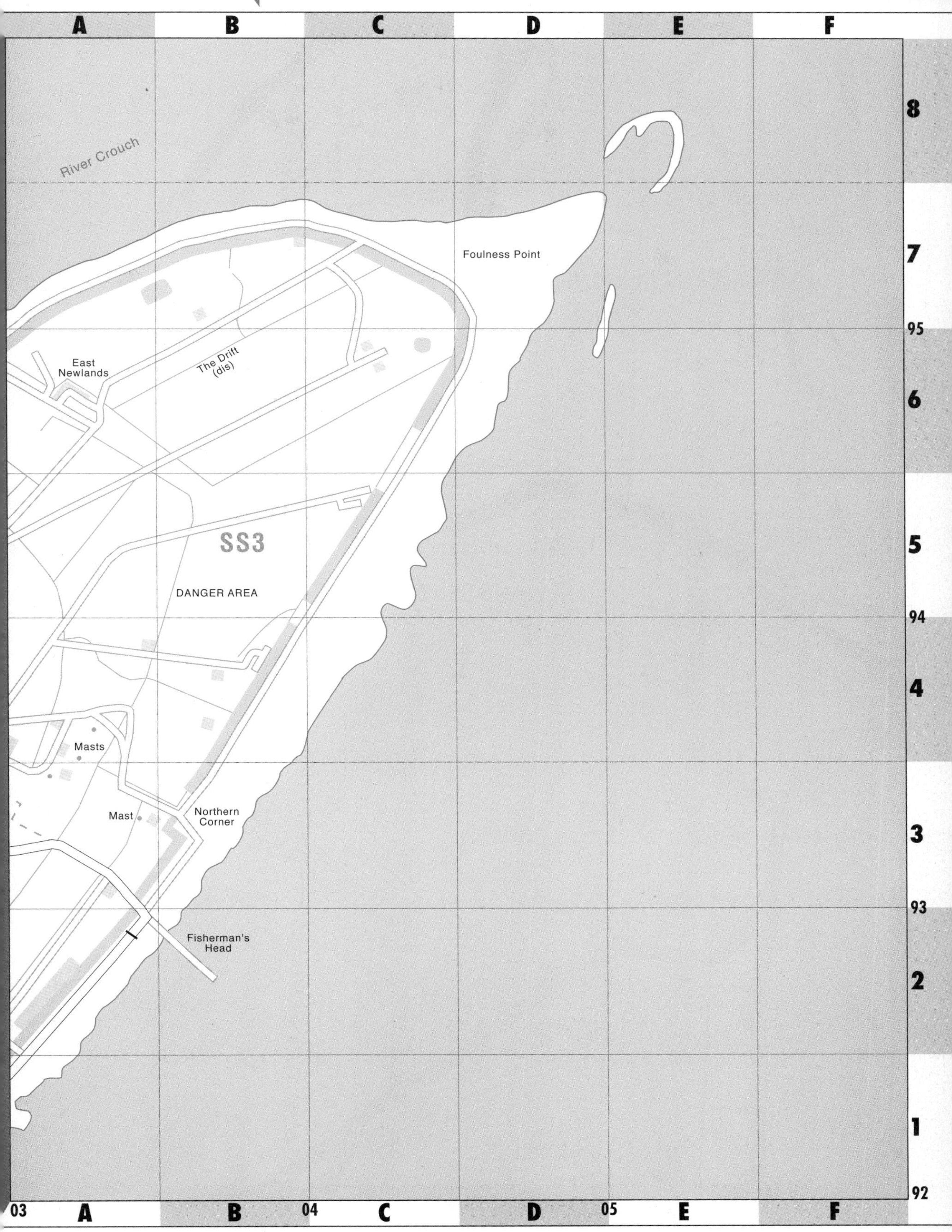

River Crouch

Foulness Point

East
Newlands

The Drift
(dis)

SS3

DANGER AREA

Masts

Mast

Northern
Corner

Fisherman's
Head

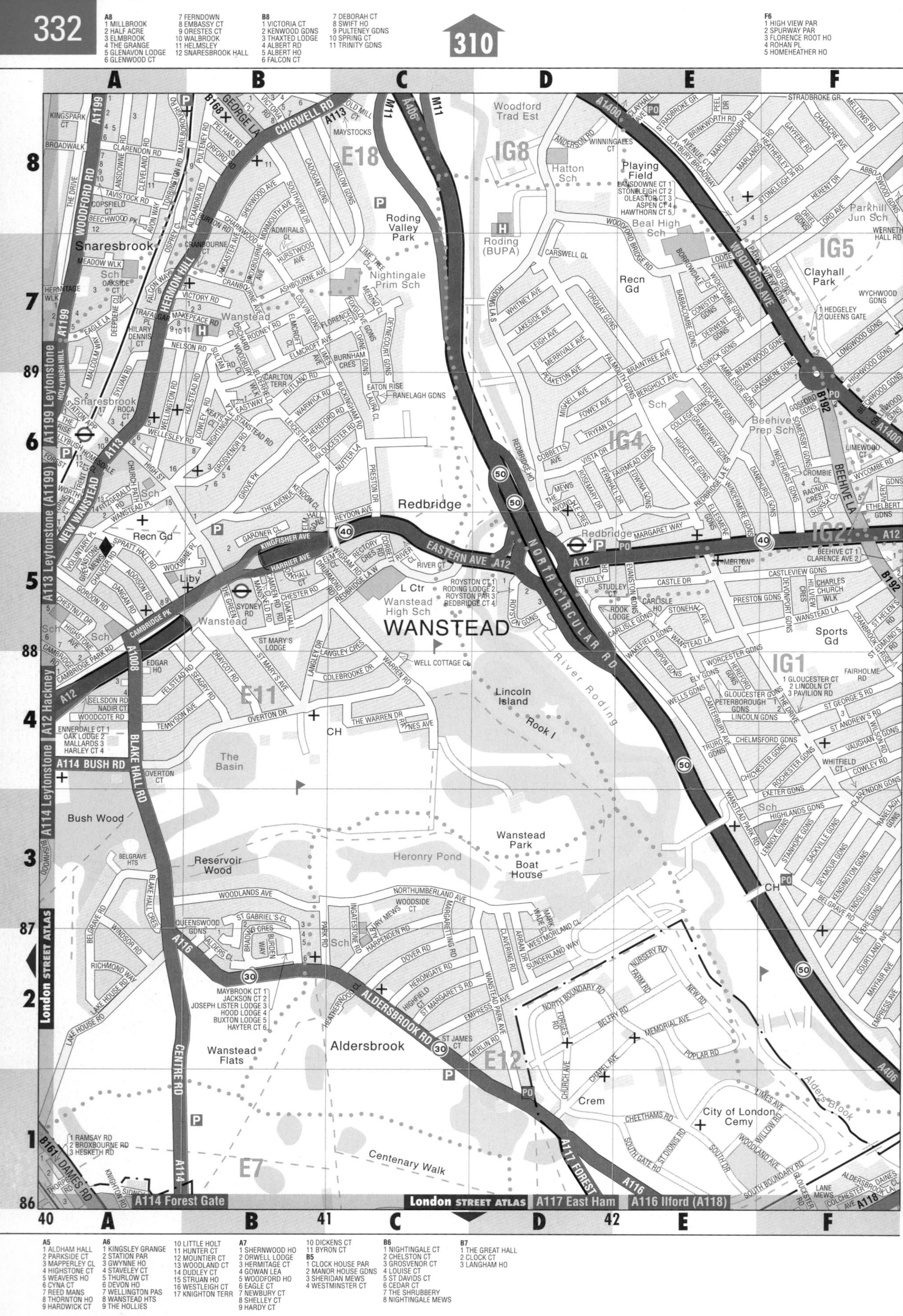

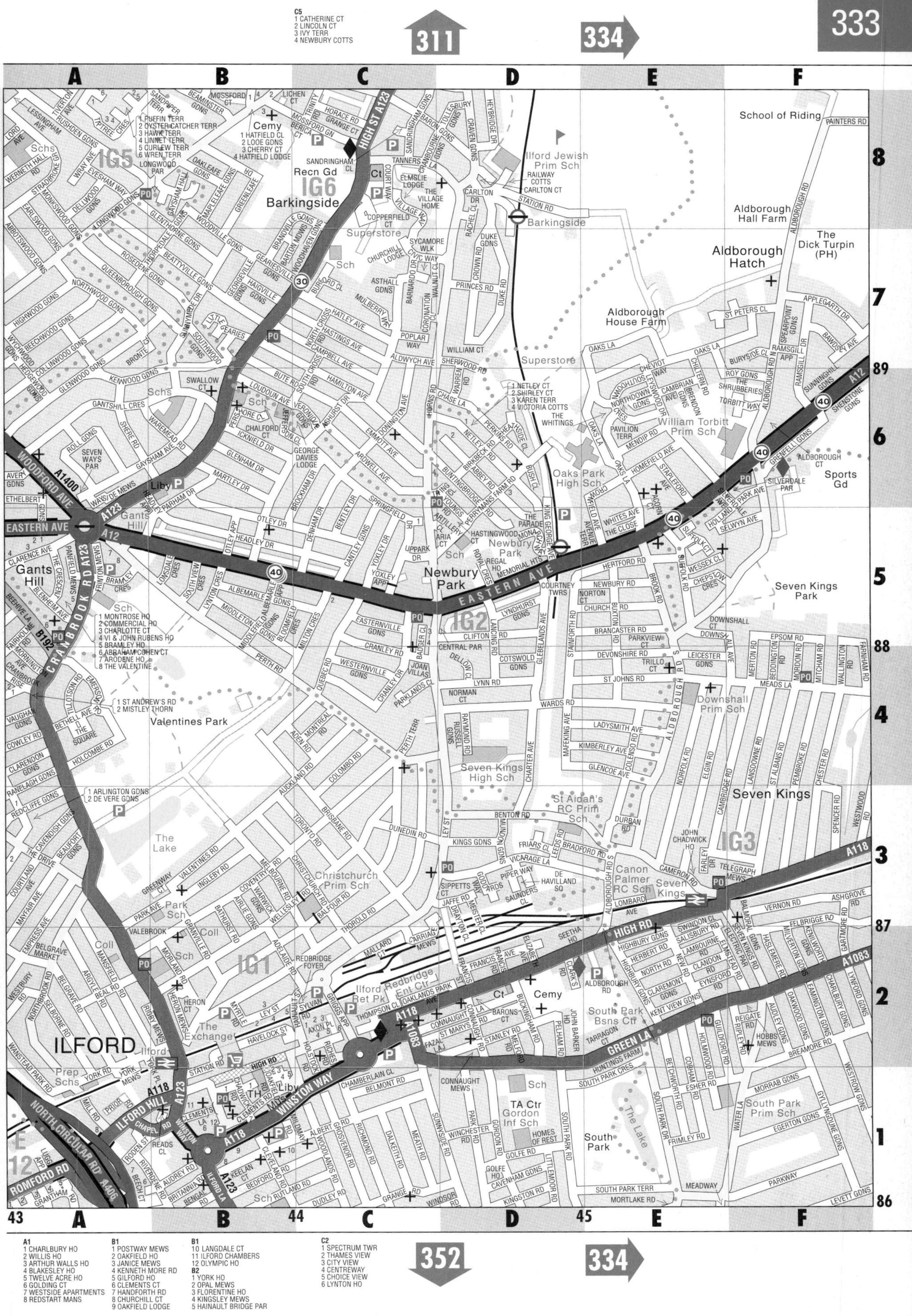
C5
1 CATHERINE CT
2 LINCOLN CT
3 IVY TERR
4 NEWBURY COTTS
311
334
A
B
C
D
E
F
8
7
89
6
5
88
4
3
87
2
1
86
43
44
45
School of Riding
PAINTERS RD
Cemy
1 HATFIELD CL
2 LOOE GDNS
3 CHERRY CT
4 HATFIELD LODGE
1 PUFFIN TERR
2 OYSTER CATCHER TERR
3 HAWK TERR
4 LINNET TERR
5 CURLEW TERR
6 WREN TERR
LONGWOOD PAR
IG5
IG6
Schs
Recn Gd
Barkingside
HIGH ST A123
SANDRINGHAM CL
TANNERS LA
ELMSLIE LODGE
THE VILLAGE HOME
Ilford Jewish Prim Sch
RAILWAY COTTS
CARLTON CT
STATION RD
Barkingside
Superstore
Sch
COPPERFIELD CT
SYCAMORE WLK
CHURCHILL LODGE
CIVIC WAY
ASTHALL GDNS
PRINCES RD
Aldborough Hall Farm
The Dick Turpin (PH)
Aldborough Hatch
Aldborough House Farm
ST PETERS CL
APPLEGARTH DR
OAKS LA
Superstore
WILLIAM CT
POPLAR WAY
ALDWYCH AVE
1 NETLEY CT
2 SHIRLEY CT
3 KAREN TERR
4 VICTORIA COTTS
THE WHITINGS
William Torbitt Prim Sch
ALDBOROUGH CT
SILVERDALE PAR
Sports Gd
Oaks Park High Sch
Seven Ways Par
Liby
Gants Hill
EASTERN AVE
WOODFORD AVE
A1400
A12
A123
Gants Hill
1 MONTROSE HO
2 COLERIDGE HO
3 CHARLOTTE CT
4 VI & JOHN RUBENS HO
5 BRAMLEY HO
6 ABRAHAM COHEN CT
7 ARODENE HO
8 THE VALENTINE
CRANBROOK RD A123
B192
1 ST ANDREW'S RD
2 MISTLEY THORN
Valentines Park
Newbury Park
HASTINGWOOD CT
Sch
REGAL HO
MEMORIAL HTS
COURTNEY TWRS
IG2
EASTERN AVE
CENTRAL PAR
Seven Kings Park
DOWNSHALL AVE
Downshall Prim Sch
Seven Kings High Sch
St Aidan's RC Prim Sch
Seven Kings
IG3
JOHN CHADWICK HO
TELEGRAPH MEWS
A118
Canon Palmer RC Sch
Seven Kings
1 ARLINGTON GDNS
2 DE VERE GDNS
The Lake
Christchurch Prim Sch
Park Sch
Coll
Coll
Sch
IG1
REDBRIDGE FOYER
Ilford Ret Pk
Redbridge Ent Ctr
HIGH RD
A1083
Cemy
Ct
South Park Bsns Ctr
GREEN LA
ILFORD
The Exchange
Ilford
Prep Schs
TH
Mus
Liby
WINSTON WAY
ILFORD HILL
A118
A123
NORTH CIRCULAR RD
A406
ROMFORD RD
Sch
TA Ctr
Gordon Inf Sch
HOMES OF REST
South Park
The Lake
South Park Prim Sch
HOBBS MEWS
SOUTH PARK TERR
MORTLAKE RD
MEADWAY
PARKWAY
LEVETT GDNS
E12
A1
1 CHARLBURY HO
2 WILLIS HO
3 ARTHUR WALLS HO
4 BLAKESLEY HO
5 TWELVE ACRE HO
6 GOLDING CT
7 WESTSIDE APARTMENTS
8 REDSTART MANS
B1
1 POSTWAY MEWS
2 OAKFIELD HO
3 JANICE MEWS
4 KENNETH MORE RD
5 GILFORD HO
6 CLEMENTS CT
7 HANDFORTH RD
8 CHURCHILL CT
9 OAKFIELD LODGE
B1
10 LANGDALE CT
11 ILFORD CHAMBERS
12 OLYMPIC HO
B2
1 YORK HO
2 OPAL MEWS
3 FLORENTINE HO
4 KINGSLEY MEWS
5 HAINAULT BRIDGE PAR
C2
1 SPECTRUM TWR
2 THAMES VIEW
3 CITY VIEW
4 CENTREWAY
5 CHOICE VIEW
6 LYNTON HO
352
334

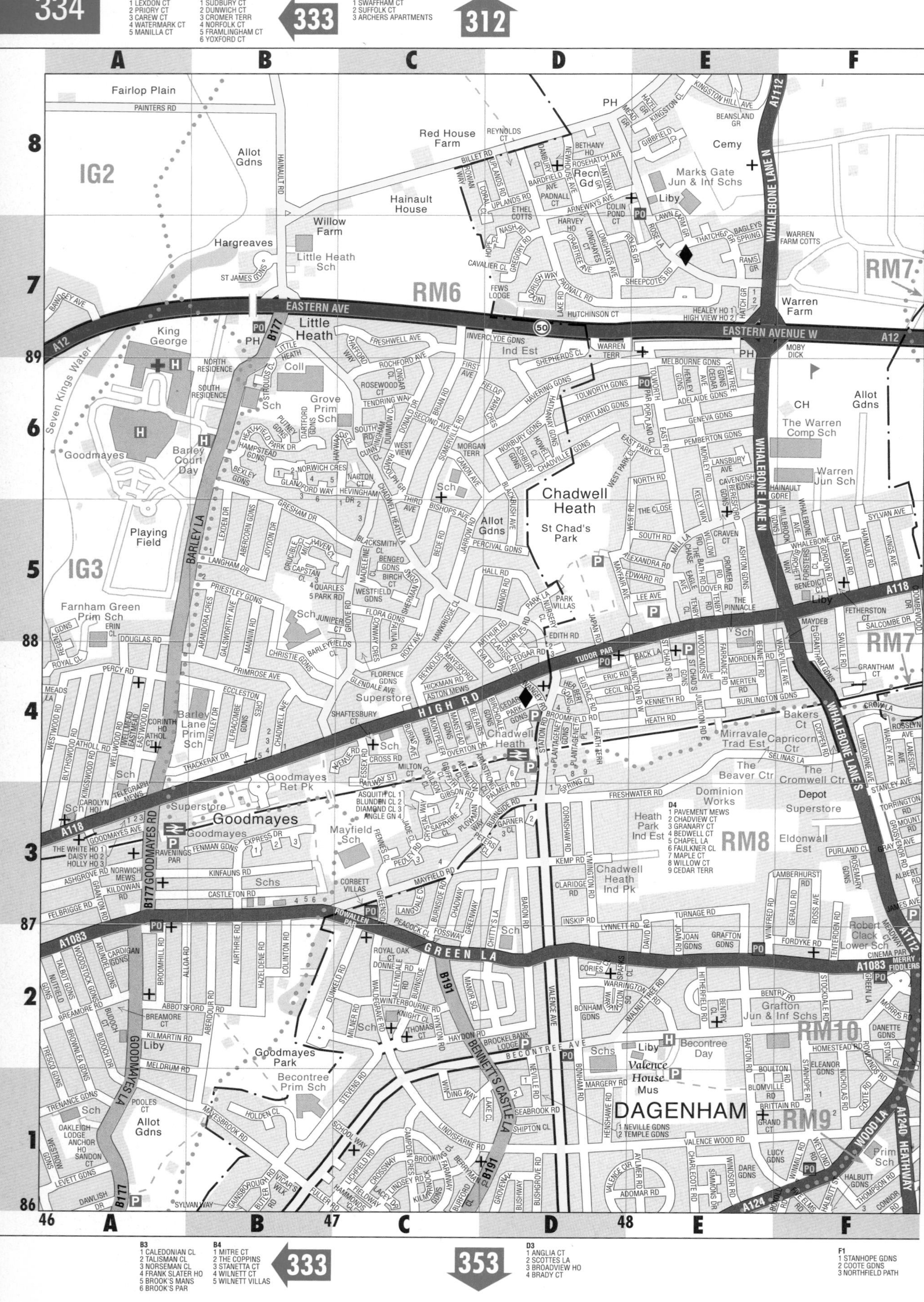

333 312

333 353

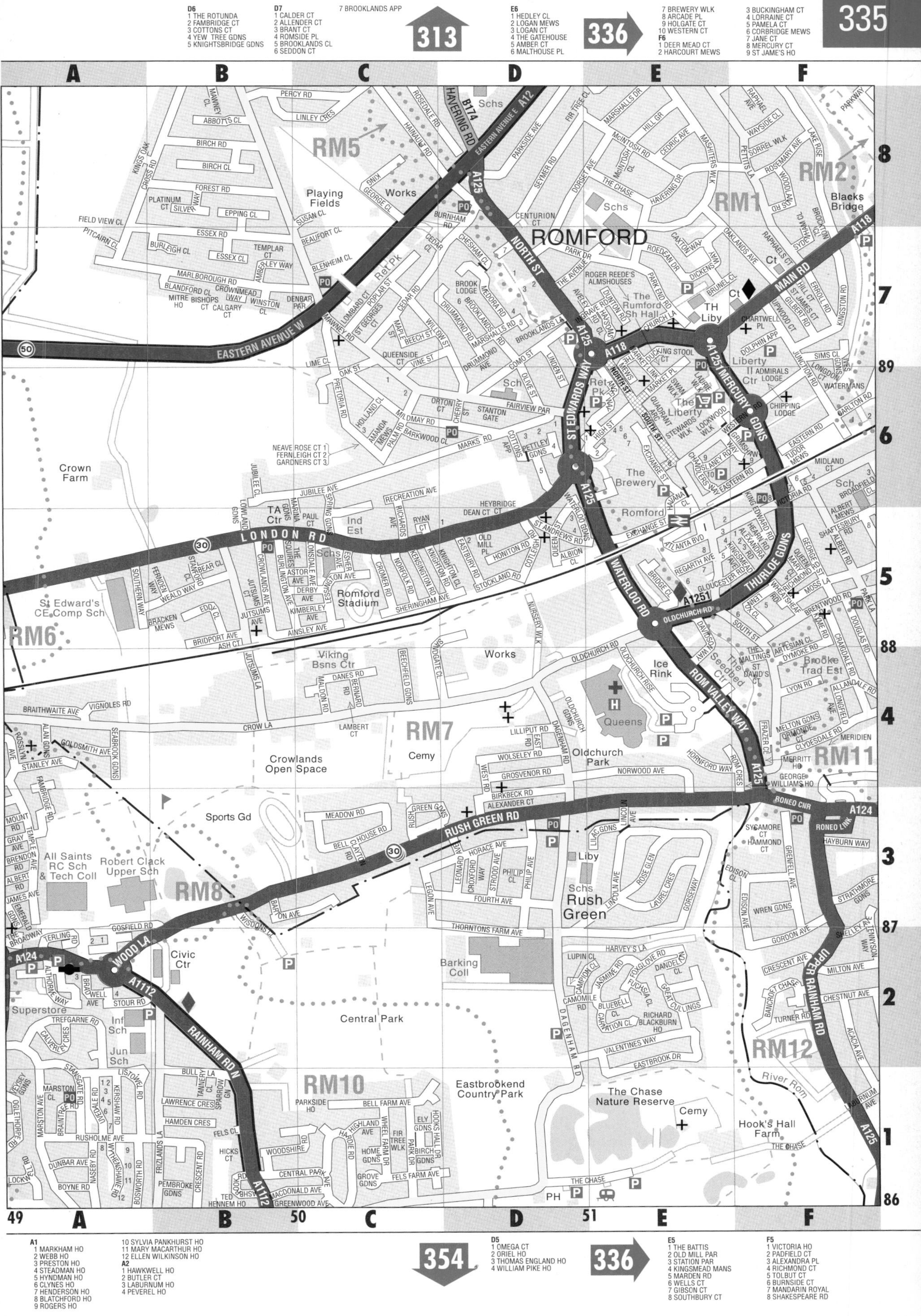

335
D6
1 THE ROTUNDA
2 FAMBRIDGE CT
3 COTTONS CT
4 YEW TREE GDNS
5 KNIGHTSBRIDGE GDNS
D7
1 CALDER CT
2 ALLENDER CT
3 BRANT CT
4 ROMSIDE PL
5 BROOKLANDS CL
6 SEDDON CT
7 BROOKLANDS APP
313
E6
1 HEDLEY CL
2 LOGAN MEWS
3 LOGAN CT
4 THE GATEHOUSE
5 AMBER CT
6 MALTHOUSE PL
336
7 BREWERY WLK
8 ARCADE PL
9 HOLGATE CT
10 WESTERN CT
F6
1 DEER MEAD CT
2 HARCOURT MEWS
3 BUCKINGHAM CT
4 LORRAINE CT
5 PAMELA CT
6 CORBRIDGE MEWS
7 JANE CT
8 MERCURY CT
9 ST JAME'S HO
A B C D E F
8 7 89 6 5 88 4 3 87 2 1 86
49 50 51
ROMFORD
RM1
RM2
RM5
RM6
RM7
RM8
RM10
RM11
RM12
EASTERN AVENUE W
EASTERN AVENUE E
LONDON RD
RUSH GREEN RD
RAINHAM RD N
UPPER RAINHAM RD
WATERLOO RD
ROM VALLEY WAY
NORTH ST
ST EDWARDS WAY
MERCURY GDNS
THURLOE GDNS
MAIN RD
A12
A118
A124
A125
A1112
A1251
B174
Crown Farm
St Edward's CE Comp Sch
Romford Stadium
Crowlands Open Space
Sports Gd
All Saints RC Sch & Tech Coll
Robert Clack Upper Sch
Civic Ctr
Superstore
Central Park
Barking Coll
Eastbrookend Country Park
The Chase Nature Reserve
Hook's Hall Farm
River Rom
Rush Green
Oldchurch Park
Queens
Ice Rink
The Brewery
The Liberty
Roger Reede's Almshouses
The Rumford Sh Hall
Playing Fields
Blacks Bridge
Brooke Trad Est
Viking Bsns Ctr
A1
1 MARKHAM HO
2 WEBB HO
3 PRESTON HO
4 STEADMAN HO
5 HYNDMAN HO
6 CLYNES HO
7 HENDERSON HO
8 BLATCHFORD HO
9 ROGERS HO
10 SYLVIA PANKHURST HO
11 MARY MACARTHUR HO
12 ELLEN WILKINSON HO
A2
1 HAWKWELL HO
2 BUTLER CT
3 LABURNUM HO
4 PEVEREL HO
354
D5
1 OMEGA CT
2 ORIEL HO
3 THOMAS ENGLAND HO
4 WILLIAM PIKE HO
336
E5
1 THE BATTIS
2 OLD MILL PAR
3 STATION PAR
4 KINGSMEAD MANS
5 MARDEN RD
6 WELLS CT
7 GIBSON CT
8 SOUTHBURY CT
F5
1 VICTORIA HO
2 PADFIELD CT
3 ALEXANDRA PL
4 RICHMOND CT
5 TOLBUT CT
6 BURNSIDE CT
7 MANDARIN ROYAL
8 SHAKESPEARE RD

336

B6
1 ACADEMY SQ
2 SCHOLARS CT
3 MASTERS CT
4 SCHOLARS WAY
5 COLLEGE CT
6 HAVERSTOCK PL

◁ **335**

C7
1 EDINBURGH HO
2 VICTORIA HO
3 ELIZABETH HO
4 MOUNTBATTEN HO
5 SNOWDON CT

△ **314**

B3
1 PRIORY MEWS
2 THE LODGE
3 HARROW CL
4 CHELSEA MEWS
5 THE CHAPEL

◁ **335**

▽ **355**

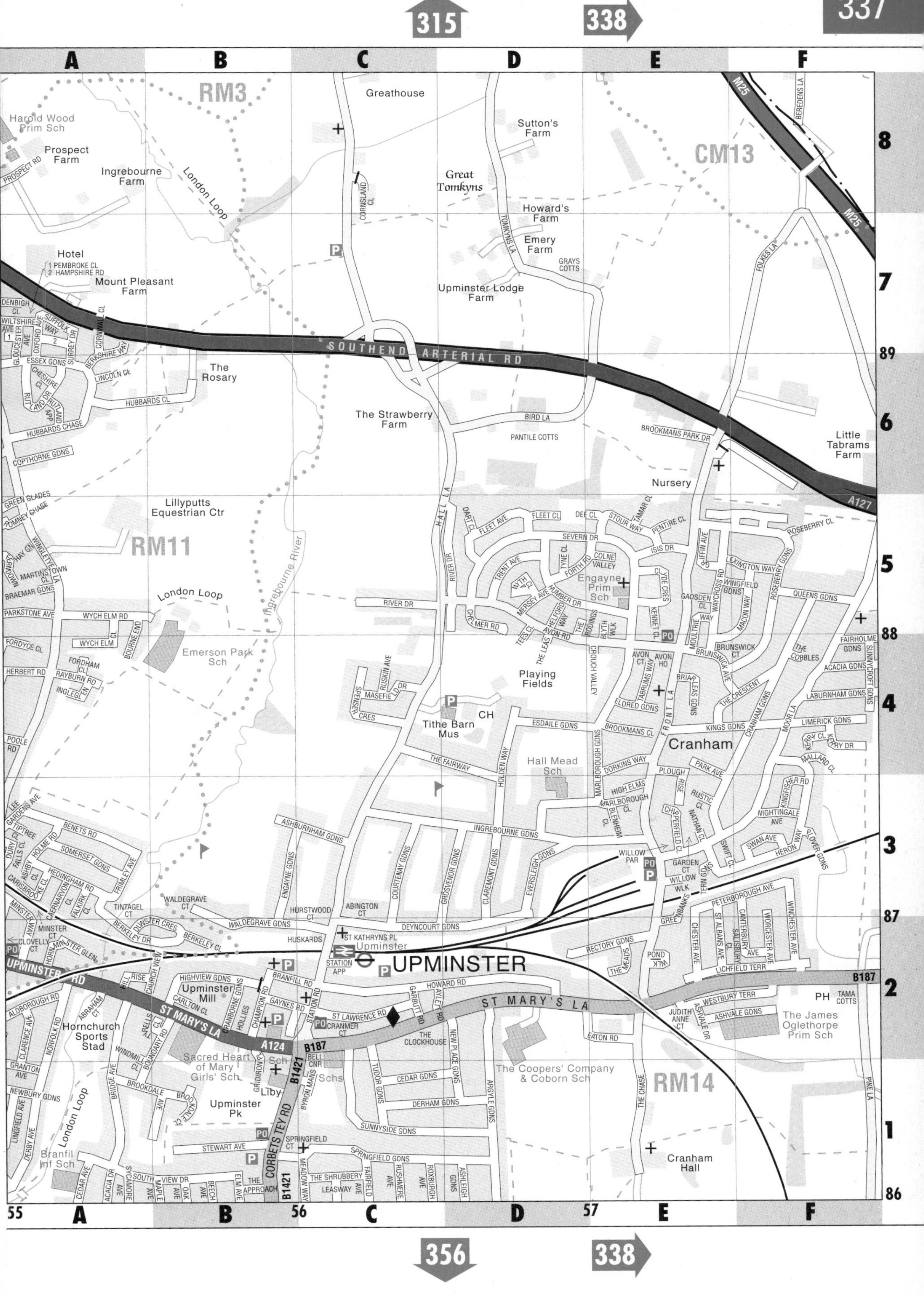

337
316

A B C D E F

8 7 89 6 5 88 4 3 87 2 1 86

Sewage Works
Hole Farm
Normans
B186 GREAT WARLEY ST
BIRD LA
Parker's Shaw
Childerditch Ind Pk
RECTORY CHASE
St Peter's Rectory
M25
CODHAM HALL LA
CM13
Woodlands Sch
LITTLE WARLEY HALL LA
Hotel
Codham Hall Wood
Codham Hall
A127
SOUTHEND ARTERIAL RD
FOLKES LA
Folkes Farm
Great Warley Hall
Little Warley Hall
Hall Lane Farm
A127
29
CHURCH LA
WARLEY ST
Prettigate Farm
Hobbs Hole
Abattoir
FAIRHOLME GDNS
ACACIA GDNS
SAXON HO
LABURNHAM GDNS
LABURNHAM CL
Upminster Trad Pk
WARLEY HALL LA
Franks Wood
Playing Field
Franks Farm
Monks Farm
Old England
RM14
Puddle Dock
Westbury Farm
FRANKS COTTS
B187
ST MARY'S LA
Nursery
Clay Tye Wood
B187
BURY FARM COTTS
Sewage Works
Bury Farm
CLAY TYE RD
Clay Tye Farm
Thames Chase Forest Centre
M25
B186
Fairplay Farm

58 A B 59 C D 60 E F

337
357

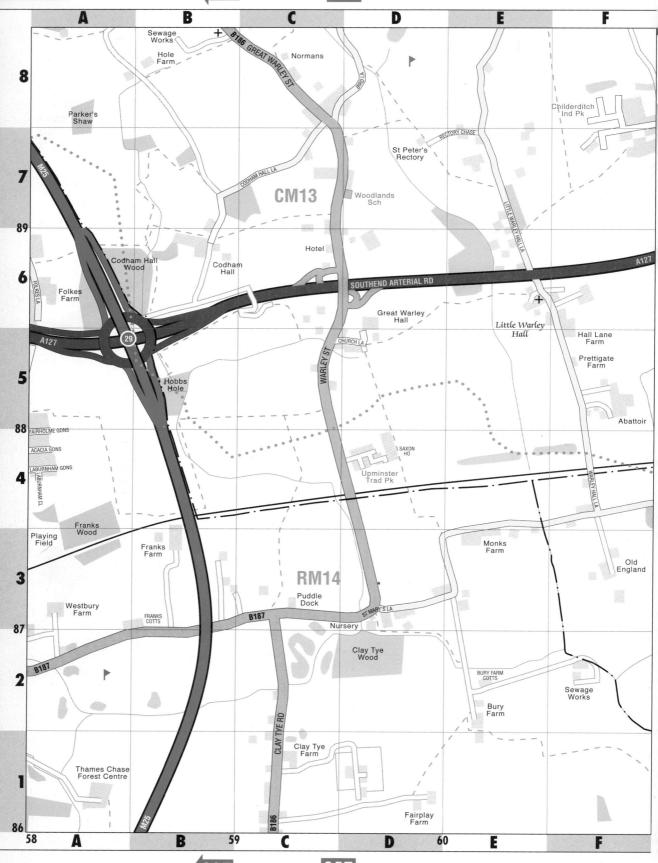

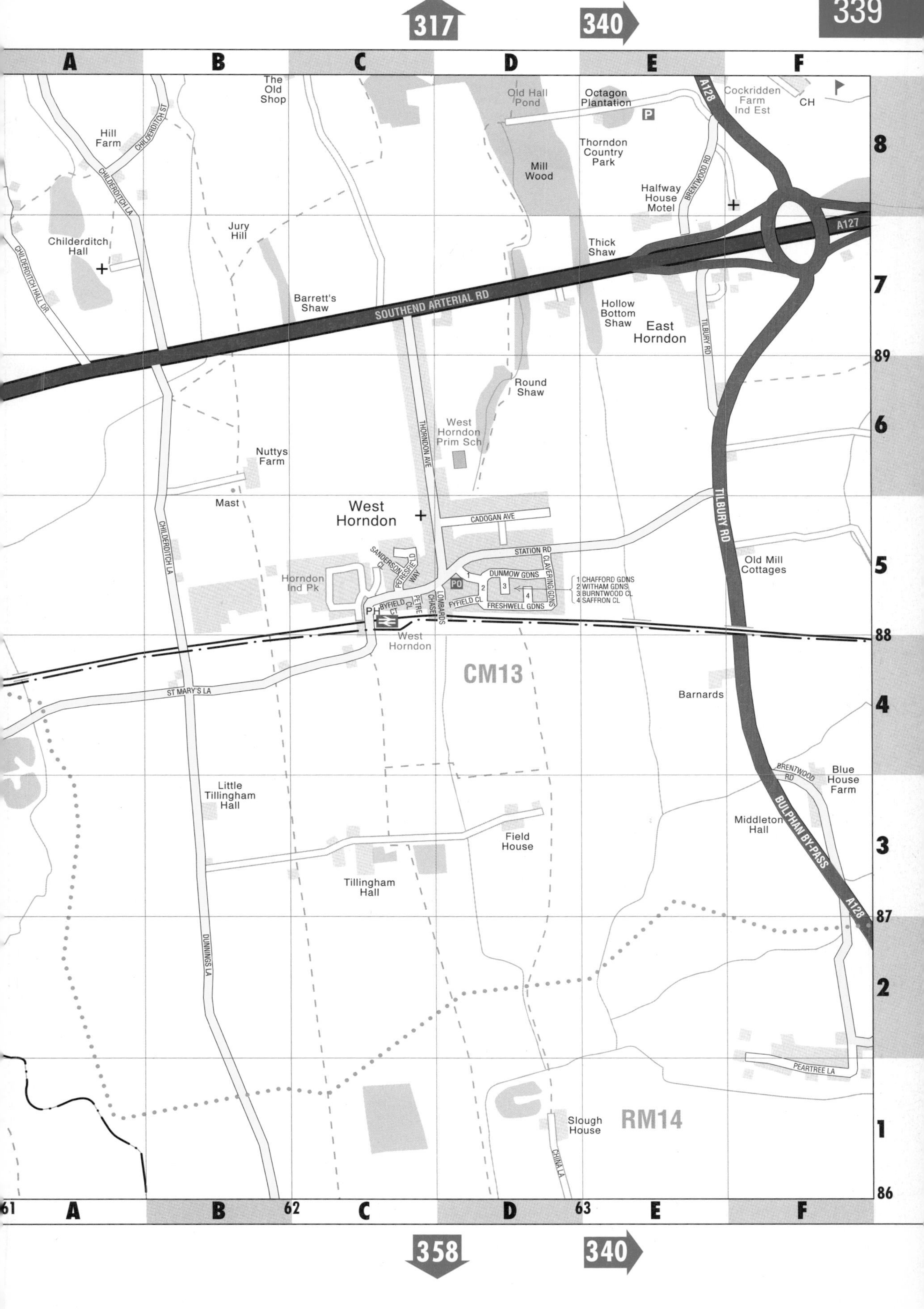

A B C D E F

The Old Shop

Old Hall Pond

Octagon Plantation

P

A128

Cockridden Farm Ind Est

CH

8

Hill Farm

CHILDERDITCH ST

CHILDERDITCH LA

Mill Wood

Thorndon Country Park

Thorndon Country Park

BRENTWOOD RD

Halfway House Motel

+

A127

Jury Hill

CHILDERDITCH HALL DR

Childerditch Hall

+

Thick Shaw

7

Barrett's Shaw

SOUTHEND ARTERIAL RD

Hollow Bottom Shaw

East Horndon

TILBURY RD

89

Nuttys Farm

THORNDON AVE

West Horndon Prim Sch

Round Shaw

6

Mast

CHILDERDITCH LA

West Horndon

+

CADOGAN AVE

TILBURY RD

Old Mill Cottages

5

SANDERSON CL

PETRIE WAY

OLD CL

Station Rd

CLAVERING GDNS

Horndon Ind Pk

PH

BYFIELD CL

PETRIE CL

PYFIELD CL

LOMBARDS CHASE

PO

DUNMOW GDNS

1 2 3 4

FRESHWELL GDNS

1 CHAFFORD GDNS
2 WITHAM GDNS
3 BURNTWOOD CL
4 SAFFRON CL

West Horndon

88

ST MARY'S LA

CM13

Barnards

4

Little Tillingham Hall

BRENTWOOD RD

Blue House Farm

DUNNINGS LA

Field House

Middleton Hall

BULPHAN BY-PASS

A128

3

Tillingham Hall

87

2

PEARTREE LA

Slough House

CHINA LA

RM14

1

86

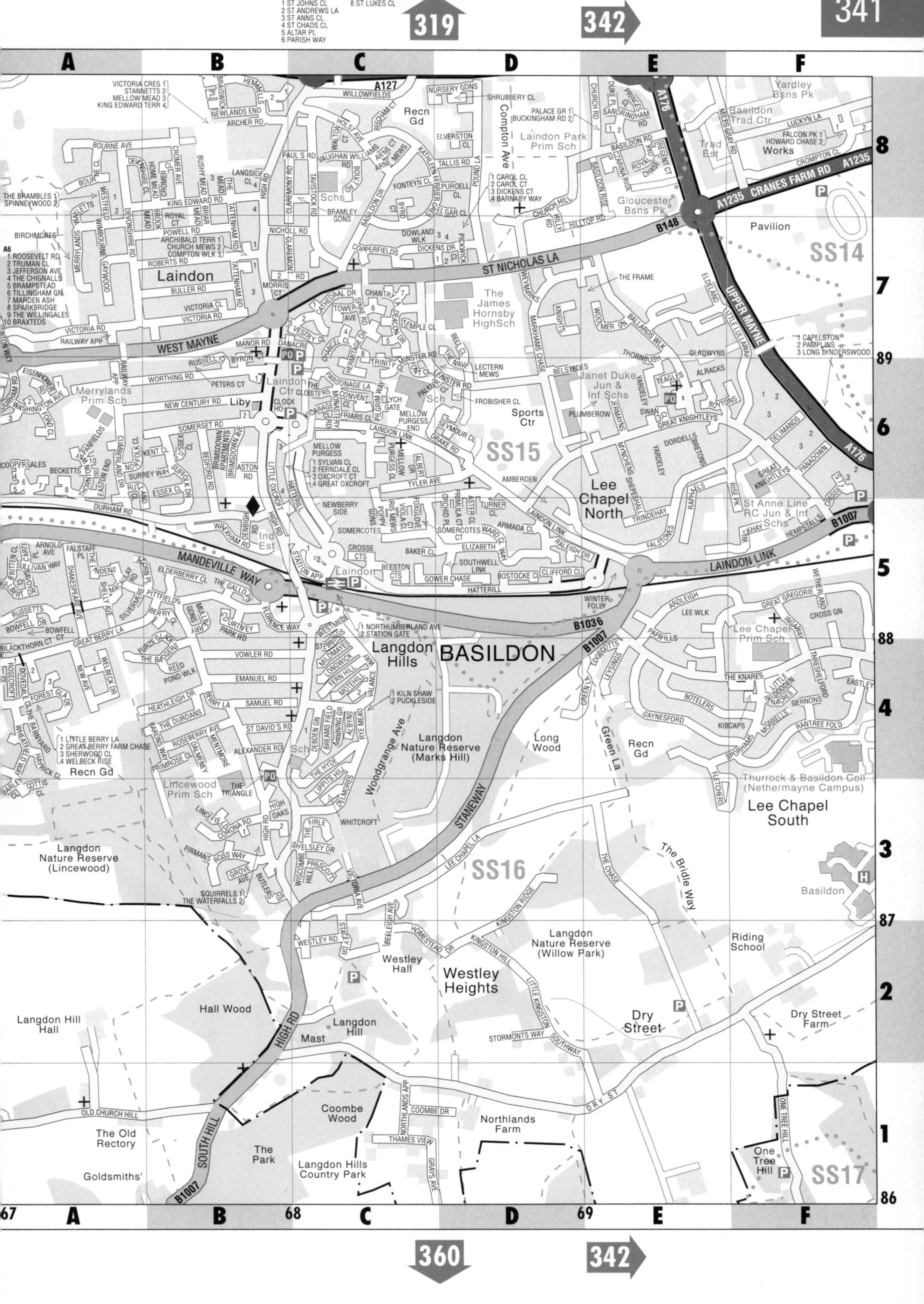
C7
1 ST JOHNS CL
2 ST ANDREWS LA
3 ST ANNS CL
4 ST CHADS CL
5 ALTAR PL
6 PARISH WAY
7 WALSINGHAM CL
8 ST LUKES CL
319
342
A
B
C
D
E
F
8
7
89
6
5
88
4
3
87
2
1
86
67
68
69
360
342
VICTORIA CRES 1
STANNETTS 2
MELLOW MEAD 3
KING EDWARD TERR 4
THE BRAMBLES 1
SPINNEYWOOD 2
A6
1 ROOSEVELT RD
2 TRUMAN CL
3 JEFFERSON AVE
4 THE CHIGNALLS
5 BRAMPSTEAD
6 TILLINGHAM GN
7 MARDEN ASH
8 SPARKBRIDGE
9 THE WILLINGALES
10 BRAXTEDS
1 CAROL CL
2 CAROL CT
3 DICKENS CT
4 BARNABY WAY
PALACE GR 1
BUCKINGHAM RD 2
FALCON PK 1
HOWARD CHASE 2
1 CAPELSTON
2 PAMPLINS
3 LONG LYNDERSWOOD
1 SYLVAN CL
2 FERNDALE CL
3 OXCROFT CT
4 GREAT OXCROFT
1 NORTHUMBERLAND AVE
2 STATION GATE
1 KILN SHAW
2 PUCKLESIDE
1 LITTLE BERRY LA
2 GREAT BERRY FARM CHASE
3 SHERWOOD CL
4 WELBECK RISE
SQUIRRELS 1
THE WATERFALLS 2
A127
WILLOWFIELDS
NURSERY GDNS
SHRUBBERY CL
Recn Gd
Compton Ave
Laindon Park Prim Sch
Yardley Bsns Pk
Basildon Trad Ctr
Trad Est
Works
LUCKYN LA
CROMPTON CL
A1235 CRANES FARM RD
A1235
A176
Gloucester Bsns Pk
Pavilion
SS14
B148
ST NICHOLAS LA
Laindon
BOURNE AVE
KING EDWARD RD
ROBERTS RD
BULLER RD
VICTORIA CL
VICTORIA RD
RAILWAY APP
WEST MAYNE
MANOR RD
DANACRE
PO
Laindon Ctr
Schs
The James Hornsby HighSch
THE FRAME
UPPER MAYNE
Janet Duke Jun & Inf Schs
Sports Ctr
SS15
Lee Chapel North
Merrylands Prim Sch
Liby
WORTHING RD
NEW CENTURY RD
SOMERSET RD
DURHAM RD
Ind Est
MANDEVILLE WAY
LAINDON LINK
Laindon
HATTERILL
WINTER FOLLY
B1036
B1007
St Anne Line RC Jun & Inf Schs
Lee Chapel Prim Sch
Langdon Hills
BASILDON
VOWLER RD
EMANUEL RD
SAMUEL RD
ST DAVID'S RD
ALEXANDER RD
Recn Gd
Lincewood Prim Sch
Langdon Nature Reserve (Marks Hill)
Woodgrange Ave
Long Wood
Green La
Recn Gd
Thurrock & Basildon Coll (Nethermayne Campus)
Lee Chapel South
STANEWAY
LEE CHAPEL LA
SS16
The Bridle Way
Langdon Nature Reserve (Lincewood)
Basildon
WHITCROFT
Langdon Nature Reserve (Willow Park)
Riding School
Westley Hall
Westley Heights
Hall Wood
Langdon Hill Hall
HIGH RD
Langdon Hill
Mast
Dry Street
Dry Street Farm
STORMONTS WAY
SOUTHWAY
OLD CHURCH HILL
Coombe Wood
COOMBE DR
Northlands Farm
DRY ST
The Old Rectory
The Park
Langdon Hills Country Park
Goldsmiths'
SOUTH HILL
B1007
THAMES VIEW
One Tree Hill
ONE TREE HILL
SS17

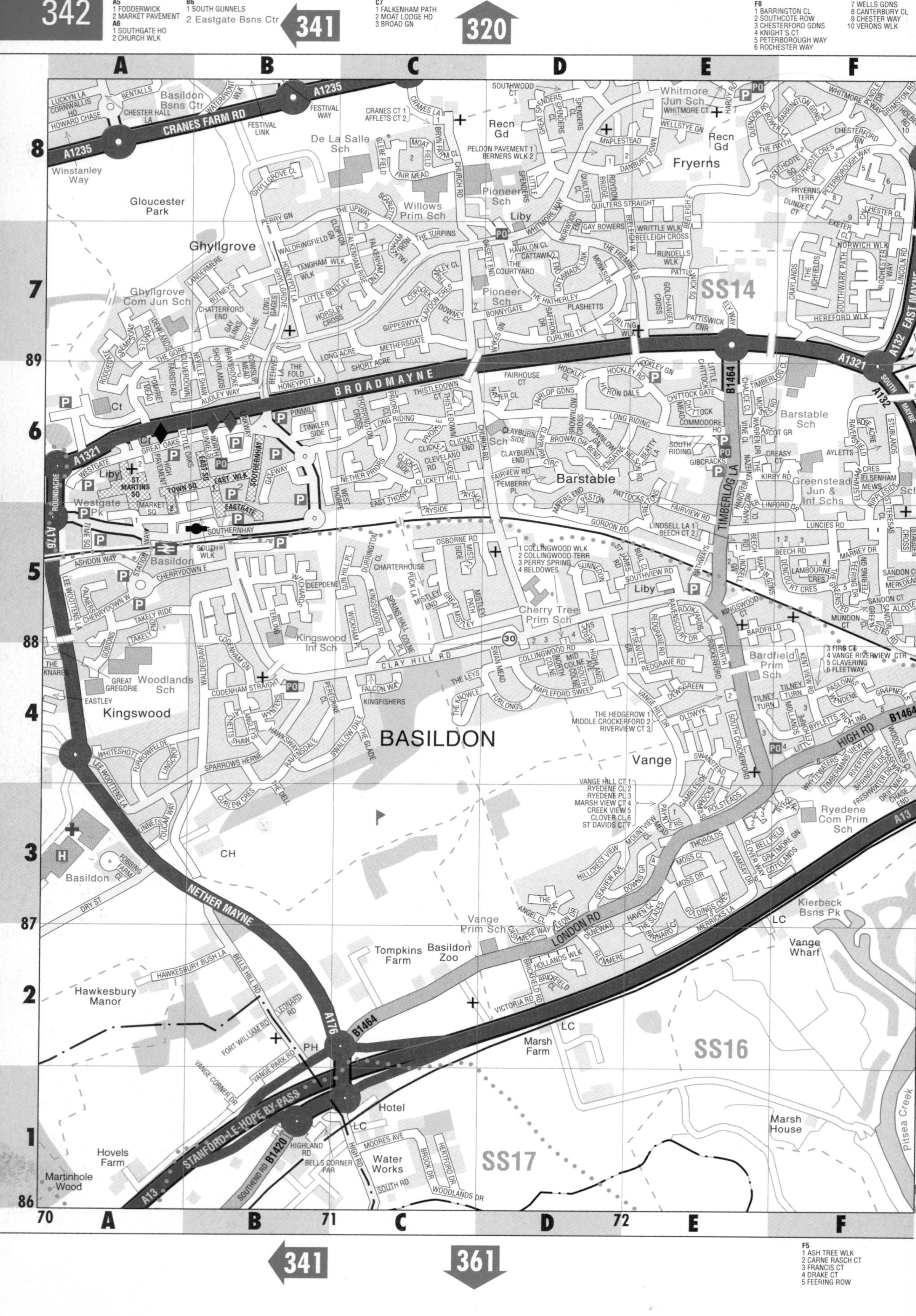
A5
1 FODDERWICK
2 MARKET PAVEMENT
A6
1 SOUTHGATE HO
2 CHURCH WLK
B6
1 SOUTH GUNNELS
2 Eastgate Bsns Ctr
341
C7
1 FALKENHAM PATH
2 MOAT LODGE HO
3 BROAD GN
320
F8
1 BARRINGTON CL
2 SOUTHCOTE ROW
3 CHESTERFORD GDNS
4 KNIGHT'S CT
5 PETERBOROUGH WAY
6 ROCHESTER WAY
7 WELLS GDNS
8 CANTERBURY CL
9 CHESTER WAY
10 VERONS WLK
A
B
C
D
E
F
8
7
89
6
5
88
4
3
87
2
1
86
70
71
72
A1235
CRANES FARM RD
Basildon Bsns Ctr
Winstanley Way
Gloucester Park
De La Salle Sch
Willows Prim Sch
Pioneer Sch
Recn Gd
Whitmore Jun Sch
Fryerns
Ghyllgrove
Ghyllgrove Com Jun Sch
SS14
A1321
BROADMAYNE
B1464
TIMBERLOG LA
A132
EAST MAYNE
Barstable Sch
Barstable
Greenstead Jun & Inf Schs
Westgate Pk
Basildon
Cherry Tree Prim Sch
Kingswood Inf Sch
Woodlands Sch
Kingswood
BASILDON
Bardfield Prim Sch
Vange
Ryedene Com Prim Sch
A13
A176
NETHER MAYNE
Basildon
LONDON RD
Vange Prim Sch
Basildon Zoo
Tompkins Farm
Kierbeck Bsns Pk
Vange Wharf
Hawkesbury Manor
Marsh Farm
SS16
STANFORD-LE-HOPE BY-PASS
B1420
Hotel
Water Works
SS17
Marsh House
Pitsea Creek
Hovels Farm
Martinhole Wood

F5
1 ASH TREE WLK
2 CARNE RASCH CT
3 FRANCIS CT
4 DRAKE CT
5 FEERING ROW

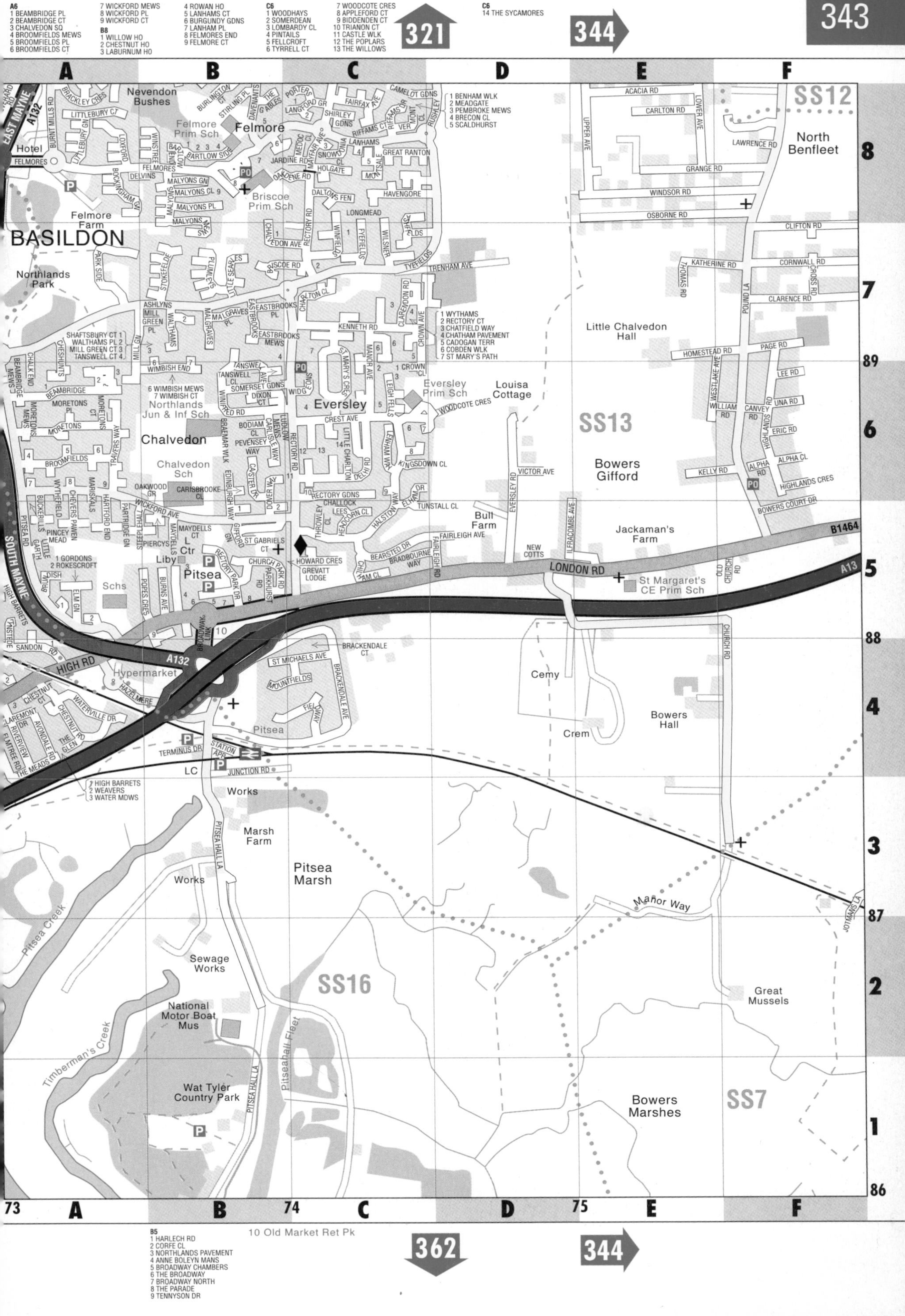
A6
1 BEAMBRIDGE PL
2 BEAMBRIDGE CT
3 CHALVEDON SQ
4 BROOMFIELDS MEWS
5 BROOMFIELDS PL
6 BROOMFIELDS CT
7 WICKFORD MEWS
8 WICKFORD PL
9 WICKFORD CT
B8
1 WILLOW HO
2 CHESTNUT HO
3 LABURNUM HO
4 ROWAN HO
5 LANHAMS CT
6 BURGUNDY GDNS
7 LANHAM PL
8 FELMORES END
9 FELMORE CT
C6
1 WOODHAYS
2 SOMERDEAN
3 LOMBARDY CL
4 PINTAILS
5 FELLCROFT
6 TYRRELL CT
7 WOODCOTE CRES
8 APPLEFORD CT
9 BIDDENDEN CT
10 TRIANON CT
11 CASTLE WLK
12 THE POPLARS
13 THE WILLOWS
321
C6
14 THE SYCAMORES
344
A
B
C
D
E
F
SS12
North Benfleet
Nevendon Bushes
Felmore
Felmore Prim Sch
Hotel
FELMORES
Briscoe Prim Sch
Felmore Farm
BASILDON
Northlands Park
1 BENHAM WLK
2 MEADGATE
3 PEMBROKE MEWS
4 BRECON CL
5 SCALDHURST
ACACIA RD
CARLTON RD
LAWRENCE RD
GRANGE RD
WINDSOR RD
OSBORNE RD
CLIFTON RD
KATHERINE RD
CORNWALL RD
CLARENCE RD
TRENHAM AVE
1 WYTHAMS
2 RECTORY CT
3 CHATFIELD WAY
4 CHATHAM PAVEMENT
5 CADOGAN TERR
6 COBDEN WLK
7 ST MARY'S PATH
Little Chalvedon Hall
HOMESTEAD RD
PAGE RD
1 SHAFTSBURY CT
2 WALTHAMS PL
3 MILL GREEN CT
4 TANSWELL CT
6 WIMBISH MEWS
7 WIMBISH CT
Northlands Jun & Inf Sch
Eversley
Eversley Prim Sch
Louisa Cottage
SS13
Chalvedon
Chalvedon Sch
Bowers Gifford
Bull Farm
Jackaman's Farm
B1464
1 GORDONS
2 ROKESCROFT
Pitsea
Schs
LONDON RD
St Margaret's CE Prim Sch
A13
A132
Hypermarket
Cemy
Crem
Bowers Hall
Pitsea
1 HIGH BARRETS
2 WEAVERS
3 WATER MDWS
Works
Marsh Farm
Pitsea Marsh
Manor Way
Pitsea Creek
Sewage Works
SS16
National Motor Boat Mus
Great Mussels
Timberman's Creek
Wat Tyler Country Park
Bowers Marshes
SS7
8
89
7
6
88
5
4
3
87
2
1
86
73
74
75
B5
1 HARLECH RD
2 CORFE CL
3 NORTHLANDS PAVEMENT
4 ANNE BOLEYN MANS
5 BROADWAY CHAMBERS
6 THE BROADWAY
7 BROADWAY NORTH
8 THE PARADE
9 TENNYSON DR
10 Old Market Ret Pk
362
344

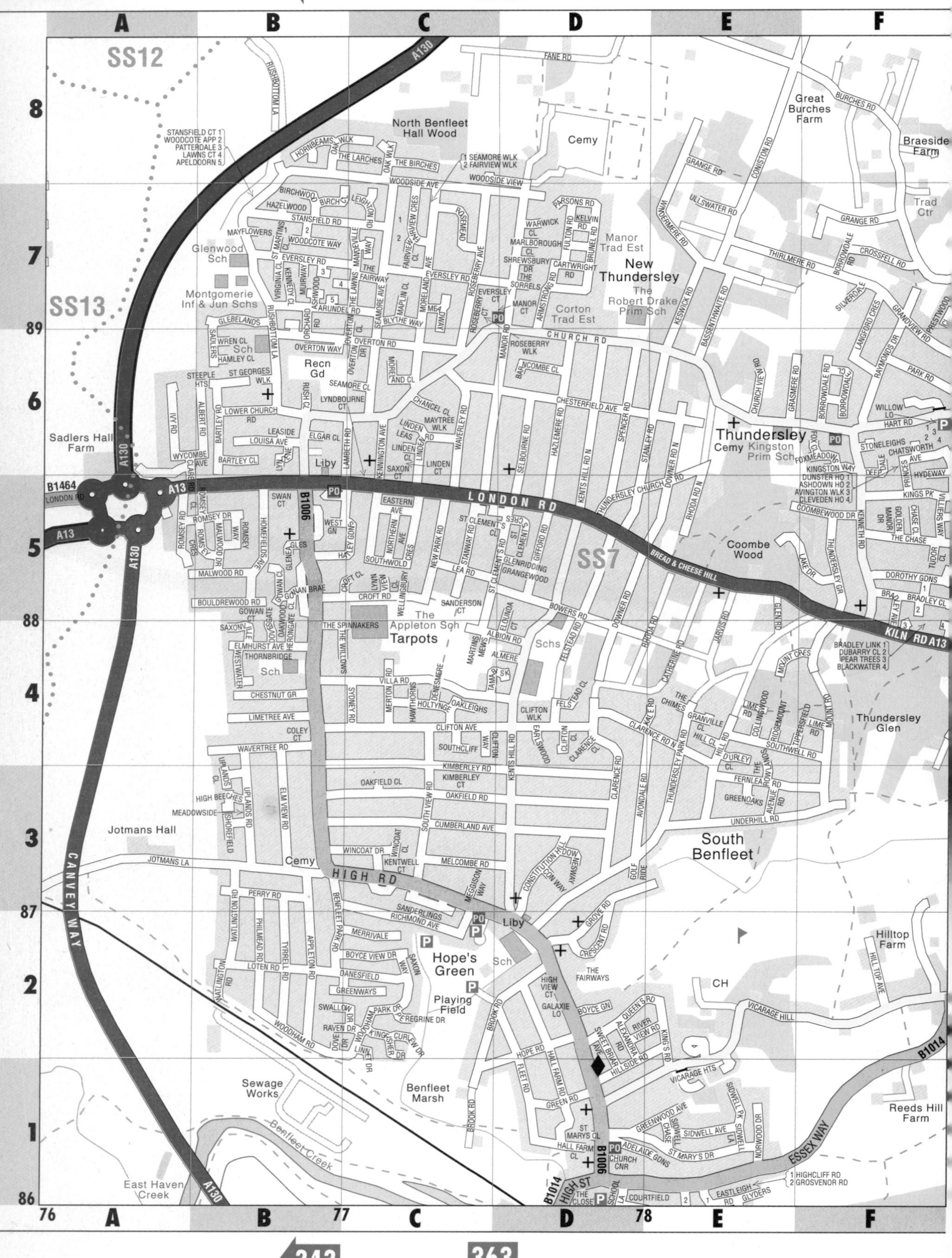

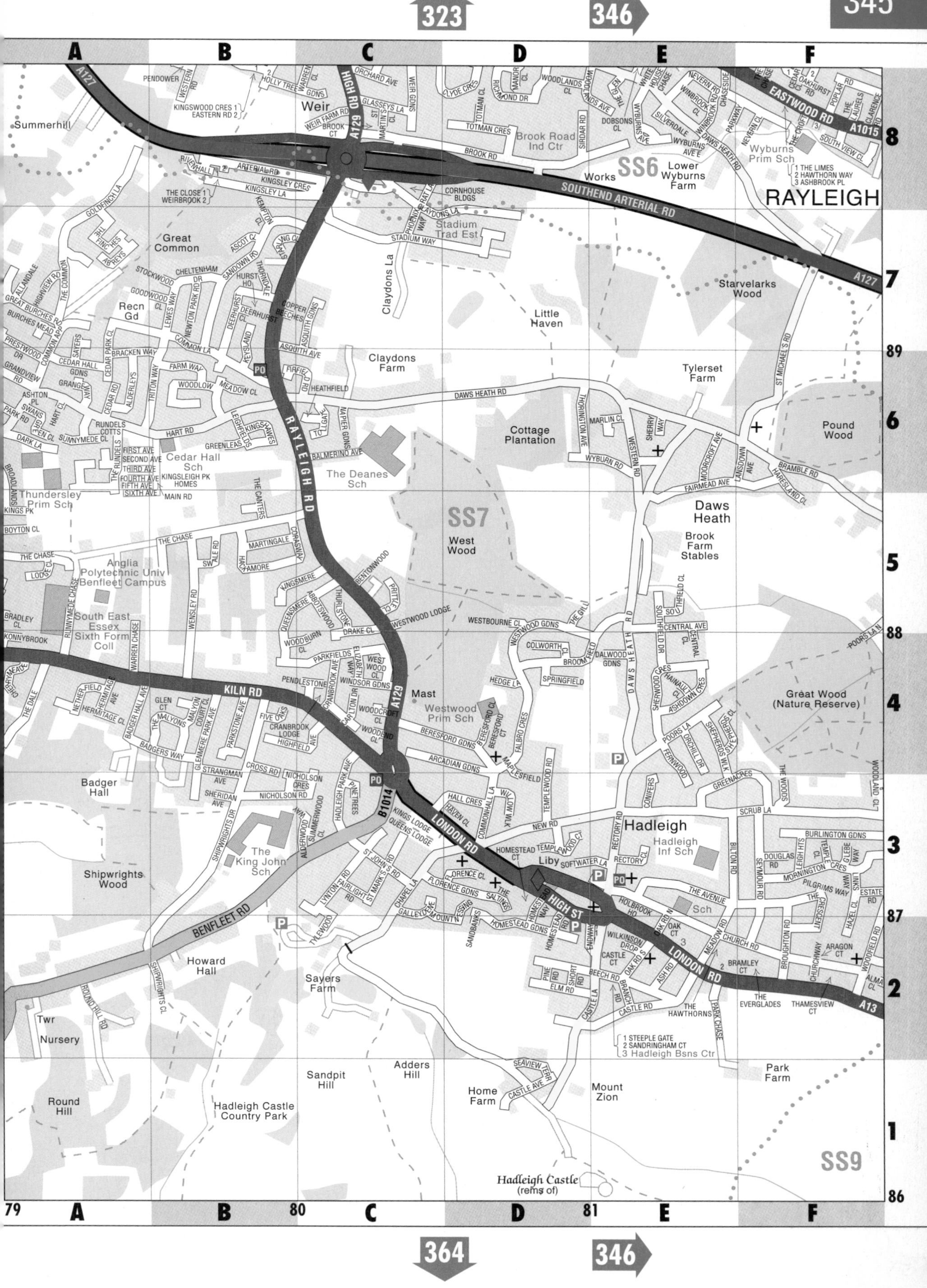

345
324

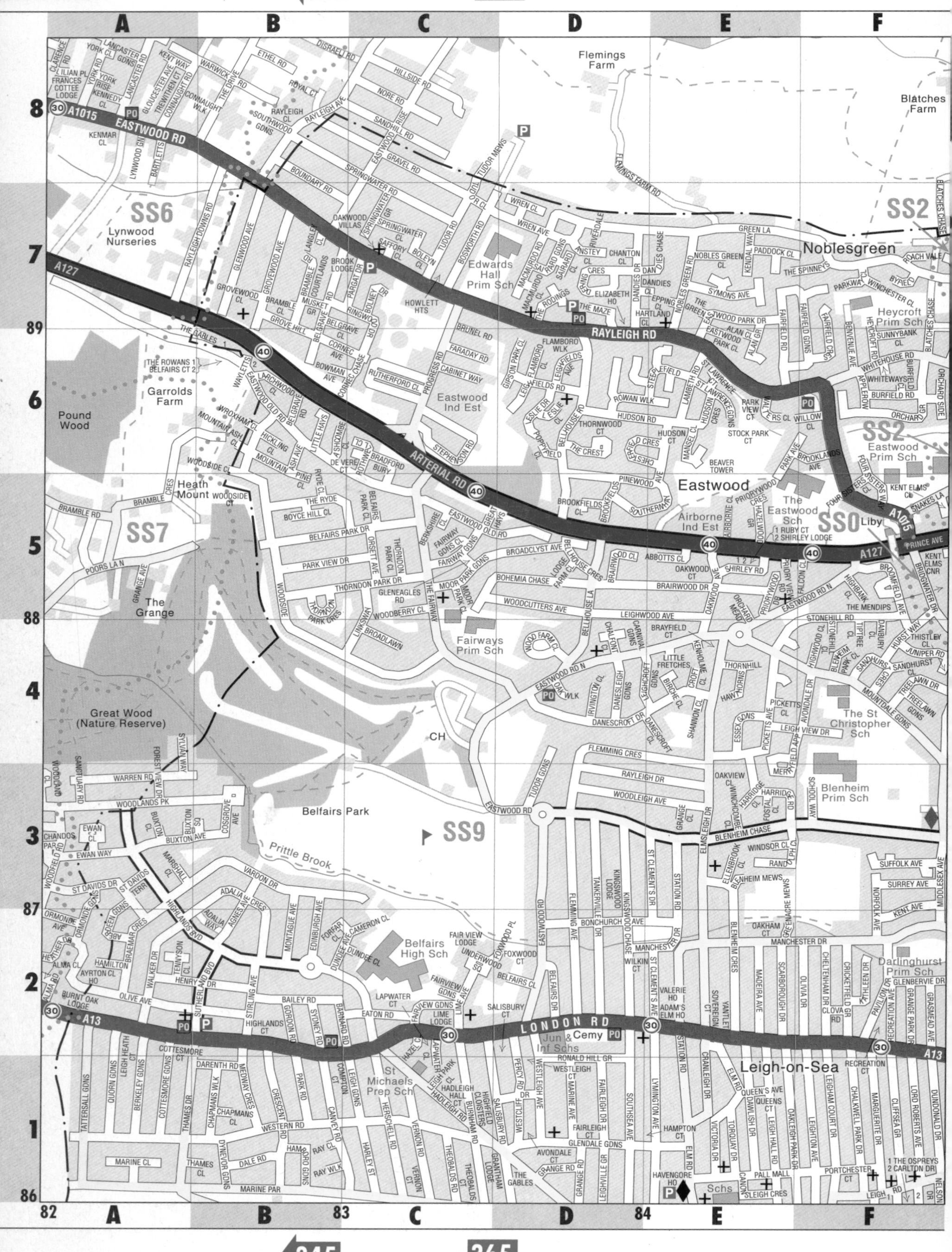
A
B
C
D
E
F
8
7
89
6
5
88
4
3
87
2
1
86
82
83
84
Flemings Farm
Blatches Farm
SS6
Lynwood Nurseries
SS2
Noblesgreen
A1015
EASTWOOD RD
A127
RAYLEIGH RD
ARTERIAL RD
Edwards Hall Prim Sch
Heycroft Prim Sch
Eastwood Ind Est
Garrolds Farm
Pound Wood
Eastwood Prim Sch
Heath Mount
Eastwood
The Eastwood Sch
SS0
Liby
Airborne Ind Est
SS7
The Grange
Fairways Prim Sch
Great Wood (Nature Reserve)
CH
The St Christopher Sch
Blenheim Prim Sch
Belfairs Park
SS9
Prittle Brook
Belfairs High Sch
Darlinghurst Prim Sch
A13
LONDON RD
Jun & Inf Schs
Cemy
St Michaels Prep Sch
Leigh-on-Sea
Schs
EASTWOOD RD N
BLENHEIM CHASE
EASTWOOD OLD RD
BELFAIRS PARK DR
THORNDON PARK DR
LEIGHWOOD AVE
WOODCUTTERS AVE
BRAIRWOOD DR
RAYLEIGH DR
WOODLEIGH AVE
FLEMMING CRES
HIGHLANDS BLVD
MARINE PAR
WESTERN RD
MANCHESTER DR
GLENDALE GDNS
PALL MALL

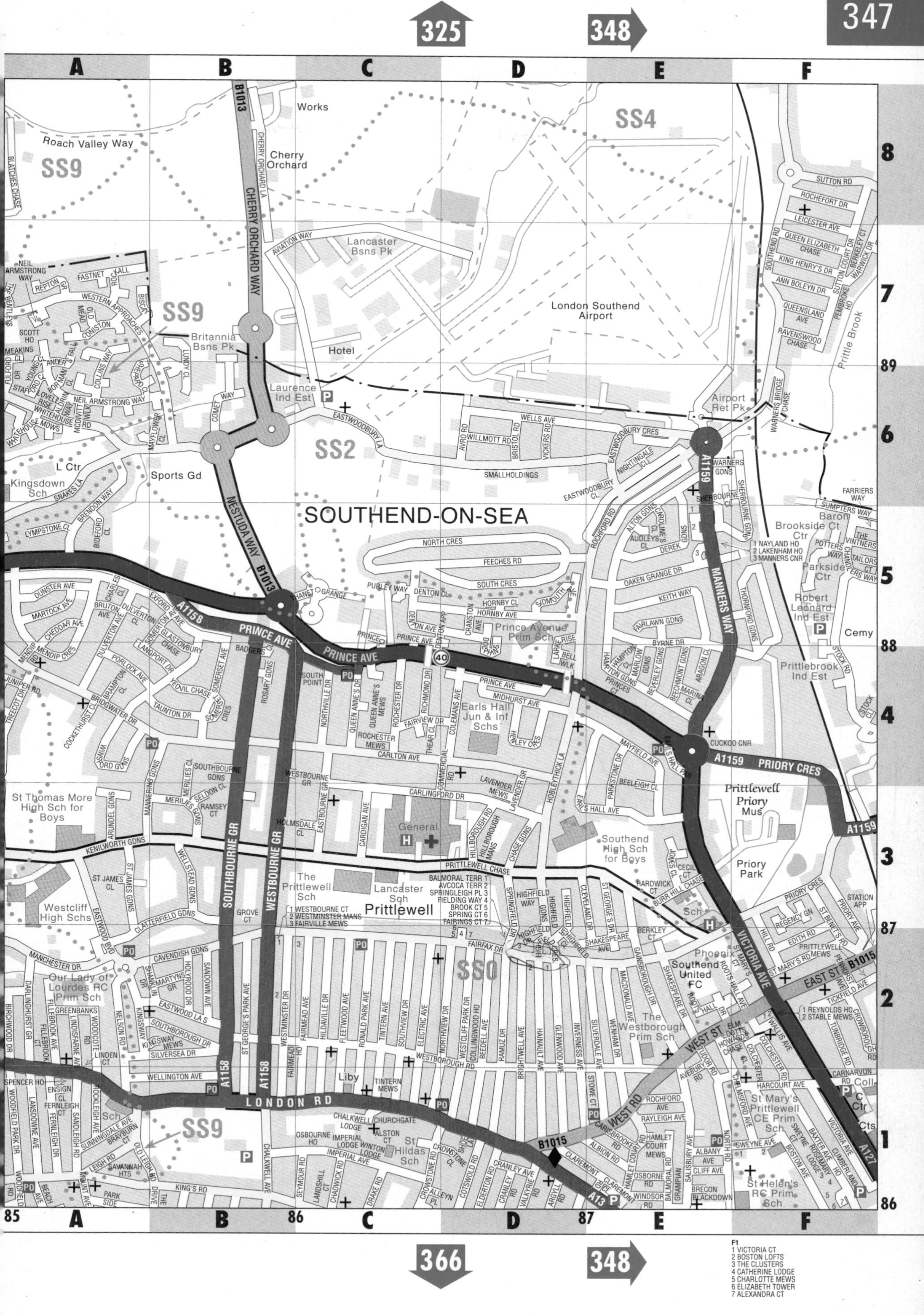

347
326

A
B
C
D
E
F
8
7
89
6
5
88
4
3
87
2
1
86
88
89
90
River Roach
ROCHEHALL WAY
PURDEYS WAY
BRICKFIELDS WAY
MILLHEAD WAY
ROSE WAY
FLEETHALL RD
MAGNOLIA WAY
Sutton Ford Bridge
Sutton Bridge Farm
Crowstone (Sutton) Prep Sch
Fleet Hall
WARWICK DR
BROOK CL
SUTTON FORD COTTS
FLEET HALL COTTS
Prittle Brook
SS4
SHOPLAND RD
Butler's Farm
Sutton Hall
Slated Row
New Hall
SUTTON RD
Rectory Lodge
SS3
Beauchamps Cottages
SHOPLAND HALL RD
Temple Farm
THE CANDLEMAKERS
JOURNEYMANS WAY
THE CORDWAINERS
THE WHEELWRIGHTS
FLETCHERS SQ
CRAFTSMANS SQ
COOPERS WAY
CHANDLERS WAY
TEMPLE GATE COTTS
SMITHER'S CHASE
Smither's Farm
THE FORUM
Shopland Hall
Beauchamps
Cemy
Crem
Stock Ind Pk
STOCK RD
SOUTHEND-ON-SEA
Rosshill Ind Pk
Priory Park Ind Est
BENTALLS CL
Works
EASTERN CL
CH
Sports Ctr
REBELS LA
FOSSETTS WAY
BUPA Wellesley
Cecil Jones Coll (Upper Sch)
Garon Park
A1159
EASTERN AVE
THE MULBERRYS
CROMWELL RD
WEYBOURNE GDNS
WALTHAM CRES
EASTERN AVE
WEYBOURNE CL
Temple Sutton Prim Sch
PRIORY MEWS
Coll
ENNISMORE GDNS
RAILWAY TERR
STATION AVE
WENTWORTH RD
LEWES RD
LEWES CT
LORNES CL
EASTERN AVE
LLOYD WISE CL
ARCHER AVE
APPLETREE CL
TA Ctr
ROYSTON AVE
GRAHAME HO
TEMPLE CT
COKEFIELD AVE
LONSDALE CT
EASTCOTE GR
LINCOLN CHASE
ARCHER CL
ROYAL ARTILLERY WAY
Prittlewell
EAST ST
B1015
STUART RD
STUART CL
CLUNY SQ
SELBOURNE RD
PANTILE AVE
ST EDMUND'S CL
SUTTON CT
PEARTREE CL
CANTERBURY AVE
SHERWOOD WAY
LONGBOW
VALLANCE CL
WELCH CL
ELDBERT CL
DICKENS CL
RUSKIN AVE
LYNDALE AVE
WALSINGHAM RD
ST LUKE'S RD
NORWICH AVE
NORWICH CL
CUMBERLAND AVE
STOWE PL
NEWINGTON AVE
CHANGATE AVE
WICKHAM RD
RYLANDS RD
BETJEMAN MEWS
ELIOT MEWS
KIPLING MEWS
BRONTE MEWS
GLENHURST RD
WORDSWORTH CL
CHESTNUT GR
CEDAR CL
LAWN AVE
TENNYSON AVE
BOURNEMOUTH PARK RD
SS2
WESTBOURNE HO
SEAFORTH AVE
SEAFORTH GR
LONSDALE RD
CROSSFIELD RD
NEWINGTON GDNS
KENWAY
BROWNING AVE
SHELLEY SQ
SYCAMORE GR
PHILPOTT AVE
BEWLEY CT
STOKES CT
WHITTINGHAM AVE
LOCKSLEY CL
CLATERS CL
BOYDEN CL
TOWNFIELDS
VALE AVE
Victoria Bsns Pk
BIRCHAM RD
GAYTON RD
THE JORDANS
MAPLE SQ
BYRON AVE
DURHAM RD
WESTBURY RD
GROVELANDS RD
HAMSTEL RD
Hamstel Jun & Inf Schs
St Nicholas Sch
A1159
ASHURST AVE
PETWORTH GDNS
SUTTON RD
Sch
CHURCH VIEW CL
ELY RD
THE GROVE
FERNDALE RD
SELWYN RD
NORTH AVE
YEOVIL CT
POYNINGS AVE
ROEDEAN GDNS
ROEDEAN CL
REDSTOCK RD
DRYDEN AVE
CROMBOROUGH RD
Coll
GRAINGER CL
STANFIELD RD
STADIUM RD
MARTIN'S CT
CENTRAL AVE
THURSTON AVE
ARLINGTON RD
STEYNING AVE
WICK CHASE
GLYNDE WAY
Grainger Road Ind Est
GREYHOUND WAY
Greyhound Pk
1 MILTON CL
2 CARLTON VILLAS
3 GUILDFORD CT
4 CENTRE REACH
5 ROYAL CT
SOUTH AVE
SOUTH MEWS
LYMINGTON RD
TRINITY RD
TRINITY LODGE
HAMSTEL MEWS
VAUGHAN AVE
CASTLETON RD
SACKVILLE RD
SS1
A13
FORTESCUE CHASE
GREAT EASTERN AVE
CARLTON CT
GRAINGER RD
Cts
MALDON RD
KINGSCROFT
BRANKSOME RD
STORNOWAY RD
LOVELACE VILLAS
PAVILION CL
PELHAM RD
SOUTHCHURCH BVD
BOVINGER WAY
SHORT ST
GREYHOUND WAY
ST ANN'S RD
SWANAGE RD
CHRISTCHURCH RD
OBAN RD
STROMNESS RD
ST FRANCIS CT
BELLEVUE RD
BELLEVUE MEWS
ILFRACOMBE RD
LOVELACE GDNS
SURBITON RD
RICHMOND ST
MOSELEY ST
BEAUFORT ST
DROITWICH AVE
SOUTHCHURCH RECTORY CHASE
COPTFOLD CL
WANSFIELD GDNS
Liby
Mus
MILTON ST
GUILDFORD RD
WIMBORNE RD
GLENMORE ST
A127
Victoria
COLEMAN ST
PRITTLEWELL ST
MALVERN
B1015
Porters Town
BOSCOMBE RD
A13
Liby
OLD RECTORY CT
PILGRIMS CL
Southend High Sch for Girls
NAVESTOCK GDNS

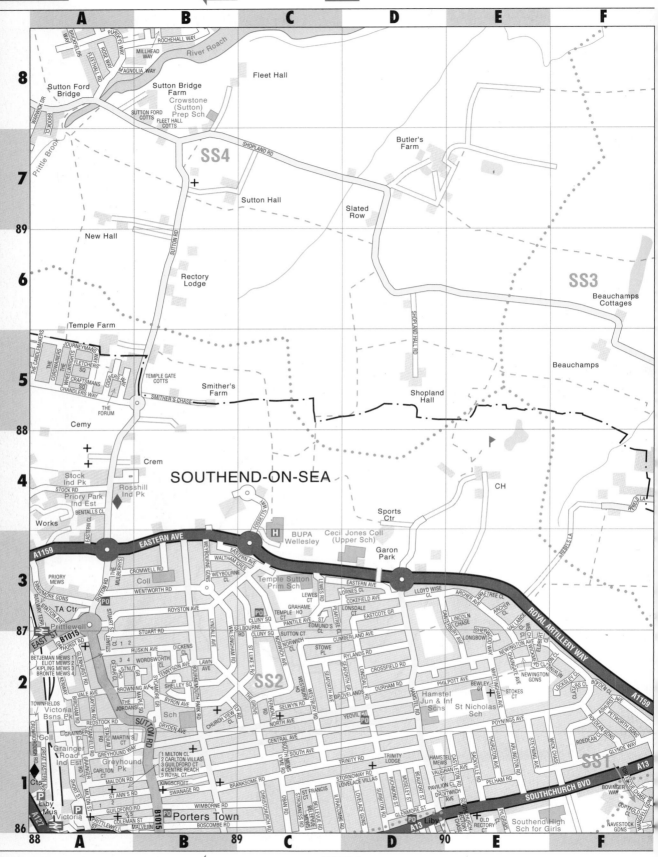

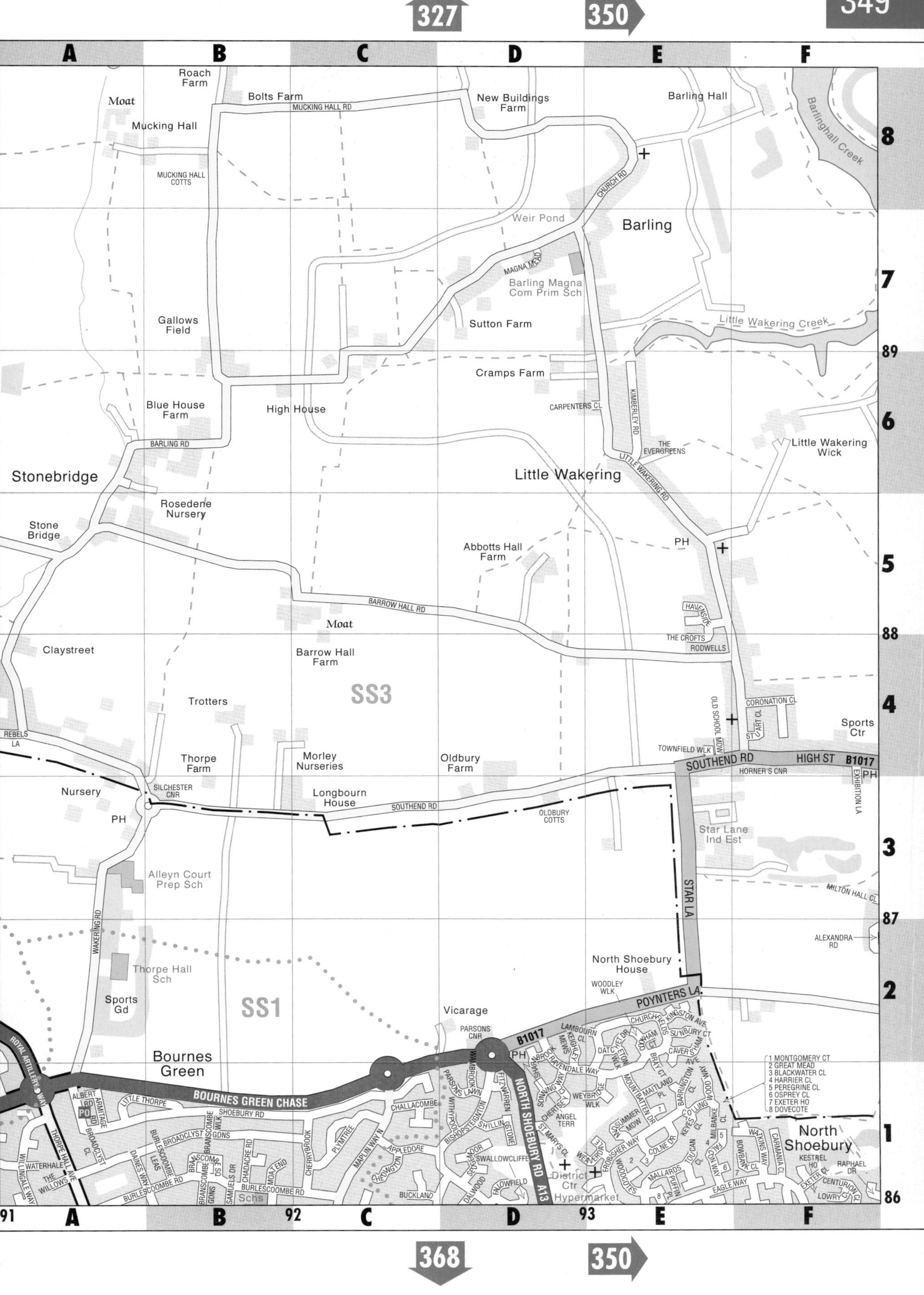
A B C D E F
8 7 89 6 5 88 4 3 87 2 1 86
91 92 93
Roach Farm
Moat
Bolts Farm
MUCKING HALL RD
New Buildings Farm
Barling Hall
Barlinghall Creek
Mucking Hall
MUCKING HALL COTTS
CHURCH RD
Weir Pond
Barling
MAGNA MEAD
Barling Magna Com Prim Sch
Sutton Farm
Gallows Field
Little Wakering Creek
Cramps Farm
Blue House Farm
High House
CARPENTERS CL
KIMBERLEY RD
BARLING RD
THE EVERGREENS
Little Wakering Wick
Stonebridge
Little Wakering
LITTLE WAKERING RD
Rosedene Nursery
Stone Bridge
Abbotts Hall Farm
PH
BARROW HALL RD
HAVENSIDE
Moat
THE CROFTS
RODWELLS
Claystreet
Barrow Hall Farm
SS3
Trotters
OLD SCHOOL MDW
CORONATION CL
STUART CL
Sports Ctr
REBELS LA
TOWNFIELD WLK
SOUTHEND RD
HIGH ST
B1017
HORNER'S CNR
PH
EXHIBITION LA
Thorpe Farm
Morley Nurseries
Oldbury Farm
Nursery
SILCHESTER CNR
Longbourn House
SOUTHEND RD
OLDBURY COTTS
PH
Star Lane Ind Est
Alleyn Court Prep Sch
STAR LA
MILTON HALL CL
WAKERING RD
ALEXANDRA RD
Thorpe Hall Sch
North Shoebury House
WOODLEY WLK
POYNTERS LA
Sports Gd
SS1
Vicarage
PARSONS CNR
B1017
Bournes Green
BOURNES GREEN CHASE
ROYAL ARTILLERY WAY
1 MONTGOMERY CT
2 GREAT MEAD
3 BLACKWATER CL
4 HARRIER CL
5 PEREGRINE CL
6 OSPREY CL
7 EXETER HO
8 DOVECOTE
North Shoebury
NORTH SHOEBURY RD A13
ALBERT RD
ARMITAGE RD
LITTLE THORPE
SHOEBURY RD
BROADCLYST CL
BROADCLYST GDNS
CHALLACOMBE
PLYMTREE
CHERRYBROOK
APPLEDORE
SWALLOWCLIFFE
FALLOWFIELD
BUCKLAND
WATERHALE
THE WILLOWS
THORPE HALL AVE
WILLINGALE WAY
DAINES WAY
BURLESCOMBE RD
SAMUELS DR
CHADACRE RD
MOAT END
ANGEL TERR
WEYBRIDGE WLK
FROBISHER WAY
WOODCOTES
COLNE DR
MALLARDS
PUFFIN PL
TOUCAN
MILBANKE CL
BOWBANK CL
WATKINS WAY
CARMANIA CL
KESTREL HO
RAPHAEL DR
CENTURION CL
LOWRY CL
EXETER CL
EAGLE WAY
KINGSTON AVE
SUNBURY CT
CAVERSHAM AVE
LAMBOURN CL
District Ctr
Hypermarket
Schs
PO

A B C D E F

8

7

89

6

5

88

4

3

87

2

1

86

94 A B 95 C D 96 E F

DANGER AREA

Farm Cottages

Swing Bridge

Fleet Head

POTTON ISLAND

The Middleway

Narrow Guts

Brimstone Hill

Fleethead Creek

Wakering Creek

Rushley Island

Halfway House Farm

Mill Head

Rushley Farm

Ford

Havengore Creek

Little Wakering Hall

Millhead Cottages

Oxenham Farm

Sewage Works

Millhead Villas

SS3

Great Wakering

LITTLE WAKERING HALL LA

HOME FARM CL

WEDDS WAY

Great Wakering Common

LANDWICK COTTS

BRIDGE RD

STAIRS RD

THE MALLARDS

B1017 HIGH ST B1017

Liby

NEW RD

SAMUEL'S CNR

Great Wakering Prim Sch

PO

CONNAY AVE

1 LION FIELDS
2 SOUTHGATE MEWS
3 ST JOHN'S CL
4 THE ANCHORAGE
5 RODING CL
6 THE CEDARS

GLEBE CL

MORRIN'S CL

STAIRS RD

ALEXANDRA RD

MILTON HALL CL

OLD HALL CT 7
CROUCHMANS AVE 8

LC

Shoeburyness New Ranges

MORRIN'S CHASE

Crouchmans Farm

SHOEBURY RD

MARINERS CT

BEACH CT

BRACKMANS

HAVENGORE CT

SEAVIEW DR

ESTUARY GDNS

DANGER AREA

Crouchmans Cottage

The Lansdowne

BROADSIDE AVE

GOLDSWORTHY DR

VICTORIA DR

NEW ENGLAND CRES

Morrin's Point

CUPIDS CHASE

POYNTERS LA

CUPID'S CNR

SUTTONS RD

CHERRYTREE CHASE

Poynter's Point

PICASSO WAY

RAPHAEL DR

BRODIE RD

BUTTS RD

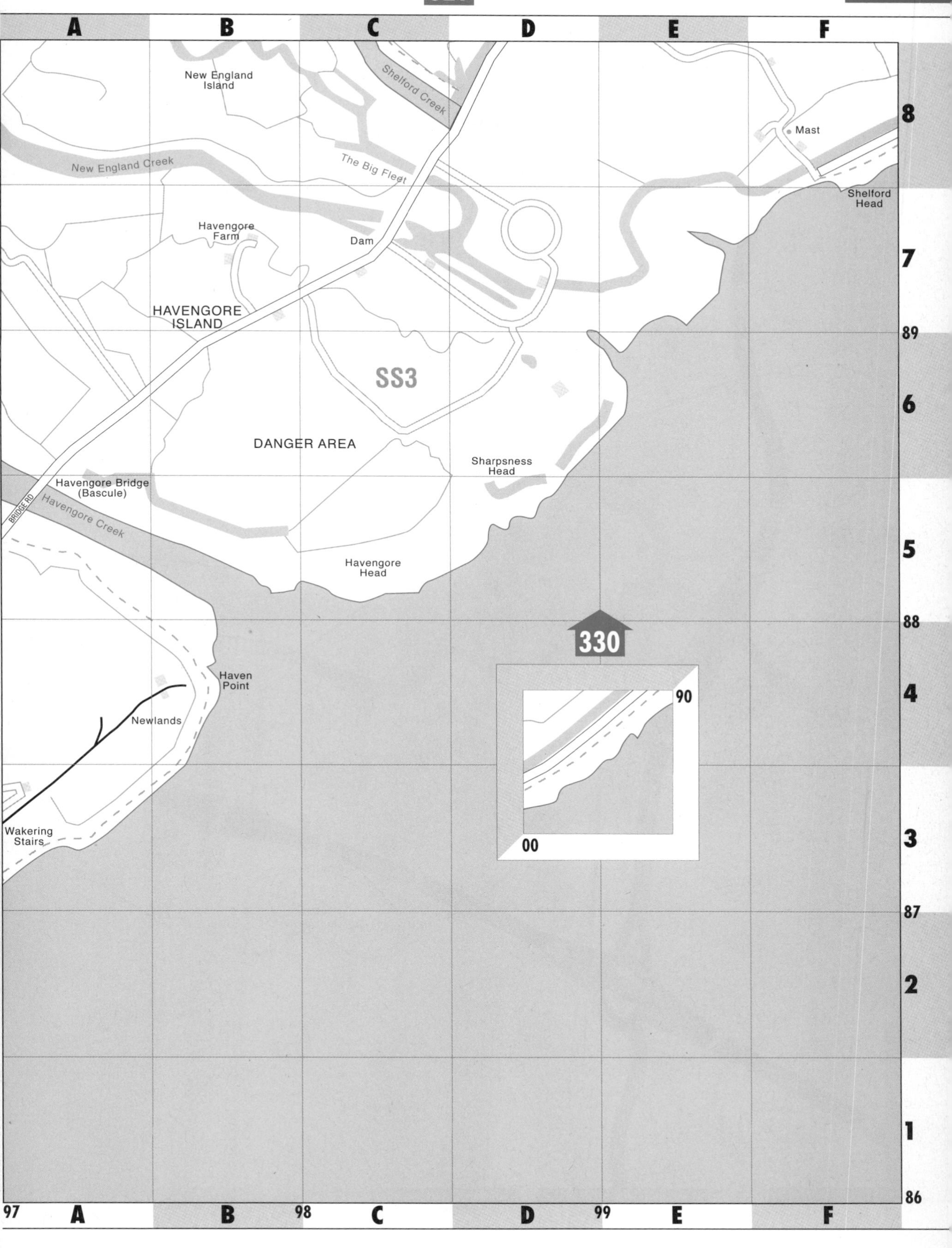

A B C D E F

New England
Island

Shelford Creek

8

Mast

New England Creek

The Big Fleet

Shelford
Head

Havengore
Farm

Dam

7

HAVENGORE
ISLAND

89

SS3

6

DANGER AREA

Sharpsness
Head

Havengore Bridge
(Bascule)

BRIDGE RD

Havengore Creek

5

Havengore
Head

88

330

Haven
Point

4

90

Newlands

00

Wakering
Stairs

3

87

2

1

86

97 A B 98 C D 99 E F

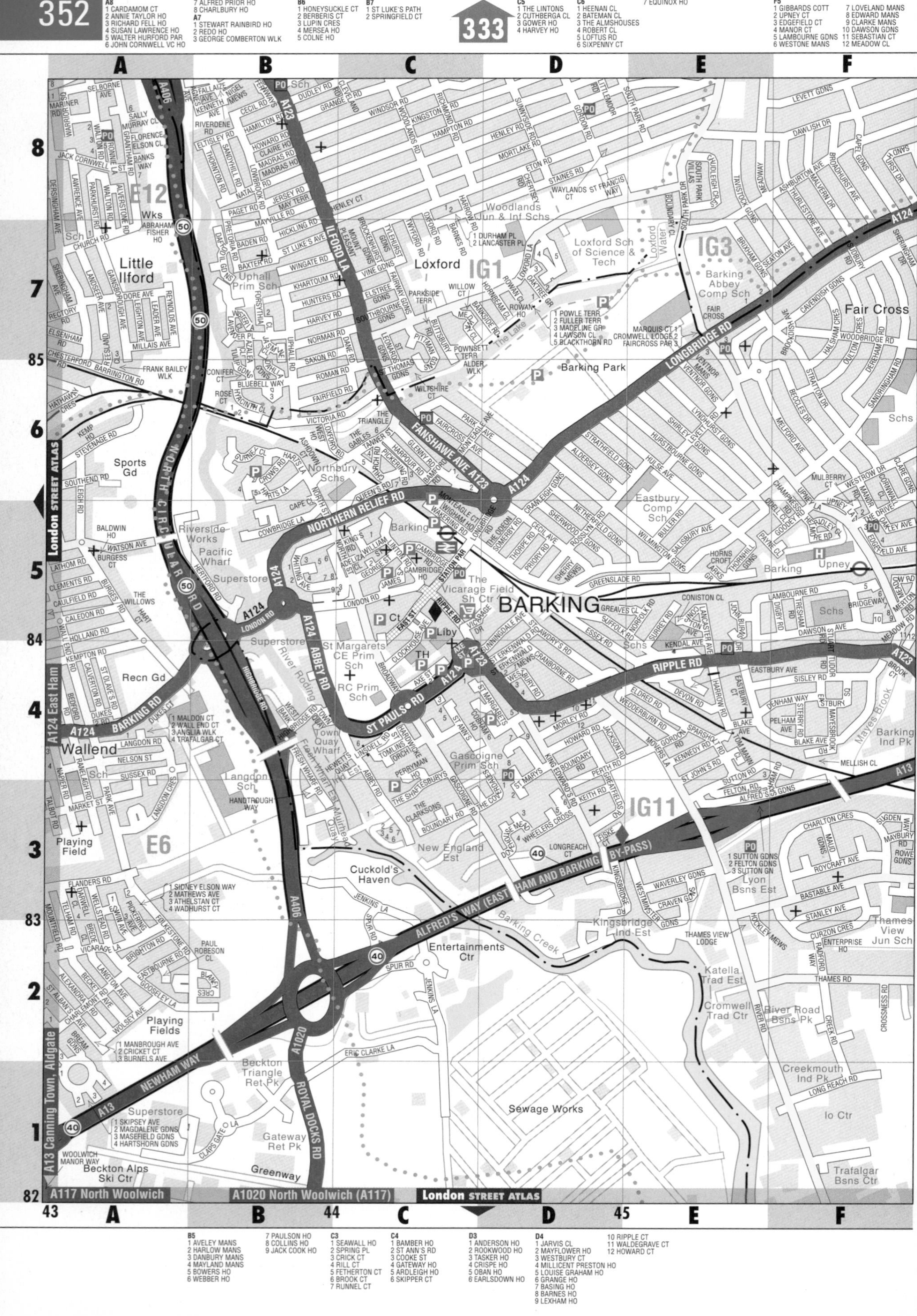

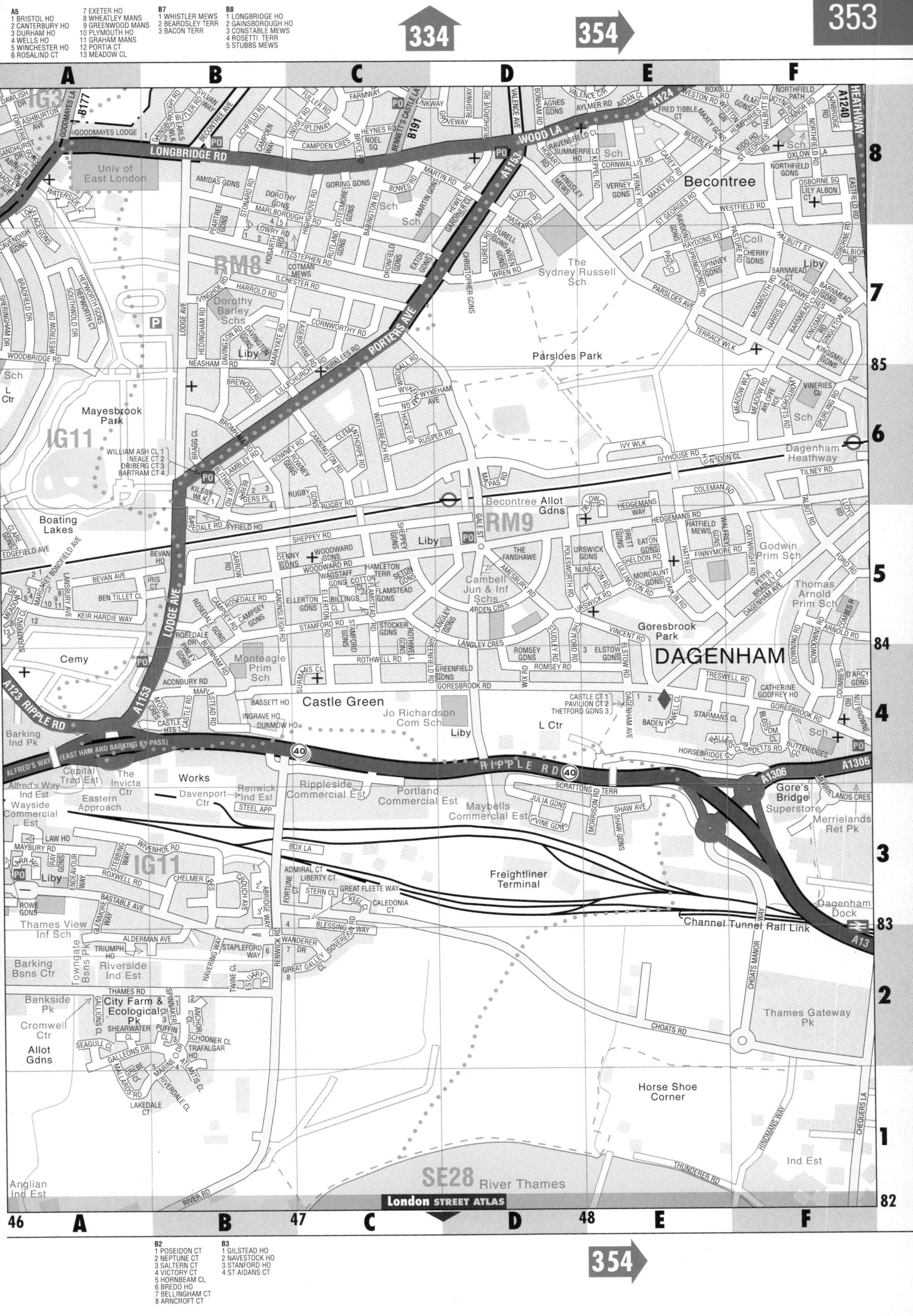

A5
1 BRISTOL HO
2 CANTERBURY HO
3 DURHAM HO
4 WELLS HO
5 WINCHESTER HO
6 ROSALIND CT
7 EXETER HO
8 WHEATLEY MANS
9 GREENWOOD MANS
10 PLYMOUTH HO
11 GRAHAM MANS
12 PORTIA CT
13 MEADOW CL
B7
1 WHISTLER MEWS
2 BEARDSLEY TERR
3 BACON TERR
B8
1 LONGBRIDGE HO
2 GAINSBOROUGH HO
3 CONSTABLE MEWS
4 ROSETTI TERR
5 STUBBS MEWS
334
354
353
A
B
C
D
E
F
8
7
85
6
5
84
4
3
83
2
1
82
46
47
48
LONGBRIDGE RD
WOOD LA
A124
A1240
HEATHWAY
B177
B191
A1153
Univ of East London
Becontree
The Sydney Russell Sch
RM8
Dorothy Barley Schs
PORTERS AVE
Parsloes Park
Mayesbrook Park
IG11
Boating Lakes
Dagenham Heathway
Becontree
Allot Gdns
RM9
Liby
Cambell Jun & Inf Schs
Godwin Prim Sch
Thomas Arnold Prim Sch
Goresbrook Park
DAGENHAM
Cemy
Monteagle Prim Sch
LODGE AVE
Castle Green
Jo Richardson Com Sch
L Ctr
A123 RIPPLE RD
ALFRED'S WAY
(EAST HAM AND BARKING BY-PASS)
RIPPLE RD
A1306
Barking Ind Pk
Capital Trad Est
The Invicta Ctr
Works
Alfred's Way Ind Est
Eastern Approach
Wayside Commercial Est
Davenport Ctr
Renwick Ind Est
Rippleside Commercial Est
Portland Commercial Est
Maybells Commercial Est
Gore's Bridge Superstore
Merrielands Ret Pk
Freightliner Terminal
Channel Tunnel Rail Link
Dagenham Dock
A13
Thames View Inf Sch
Barking Bsns Ctr
Towngate Bsns Pk
Riverside Ind Est
Bankside Pk
City Farm & Ecological Pk
Cromwell Ctr
Allot Gdns
CHOATS RD
CHOATS MANOR WAY
Thames Gateway Pk
Horse Shoe Corner
THUNDERER RD
Ind Est
SE28
River Thames
Anglian Ind Est
RIVER RD
London STREET ATLAS
B2
1 POSEIDON CT
2 NEPTUNE CT
3 SALTERN CT
4 VICTORY CT
5 HORNBEAM CL
6 BREDO HO
7 BELLINGHAM CT
8 ARNCROFT CT
B3
1 GILSTEAD HO
2 NAVESTOCK HO
3 STANFORD HO
4 ST AIDANS CT
354

A6
1 JACKSON CT
2 MONTGOMERY CT
3 LUDLOW CT
4 STANTON CT
5 HESTER CT

B6
1 FORSYTH CT
2 ELDRIDGE CT
3 MADISON CT
4 BOWERY CT
5 RIVINGTON CT
6 PICADOR HO

353

B6
7 CENTURION LODGE
8 LOUIS CT
9 WATSONS LODGE
10 CARPENTERS CT
11 BELL HO
12 ROUNDERS CT

335

B6
13 OLDMEAD HO
14 JERVIS CT
15 BARTLETTS HO
16 ROYAL PAR
17 RICHARDSON GDNS

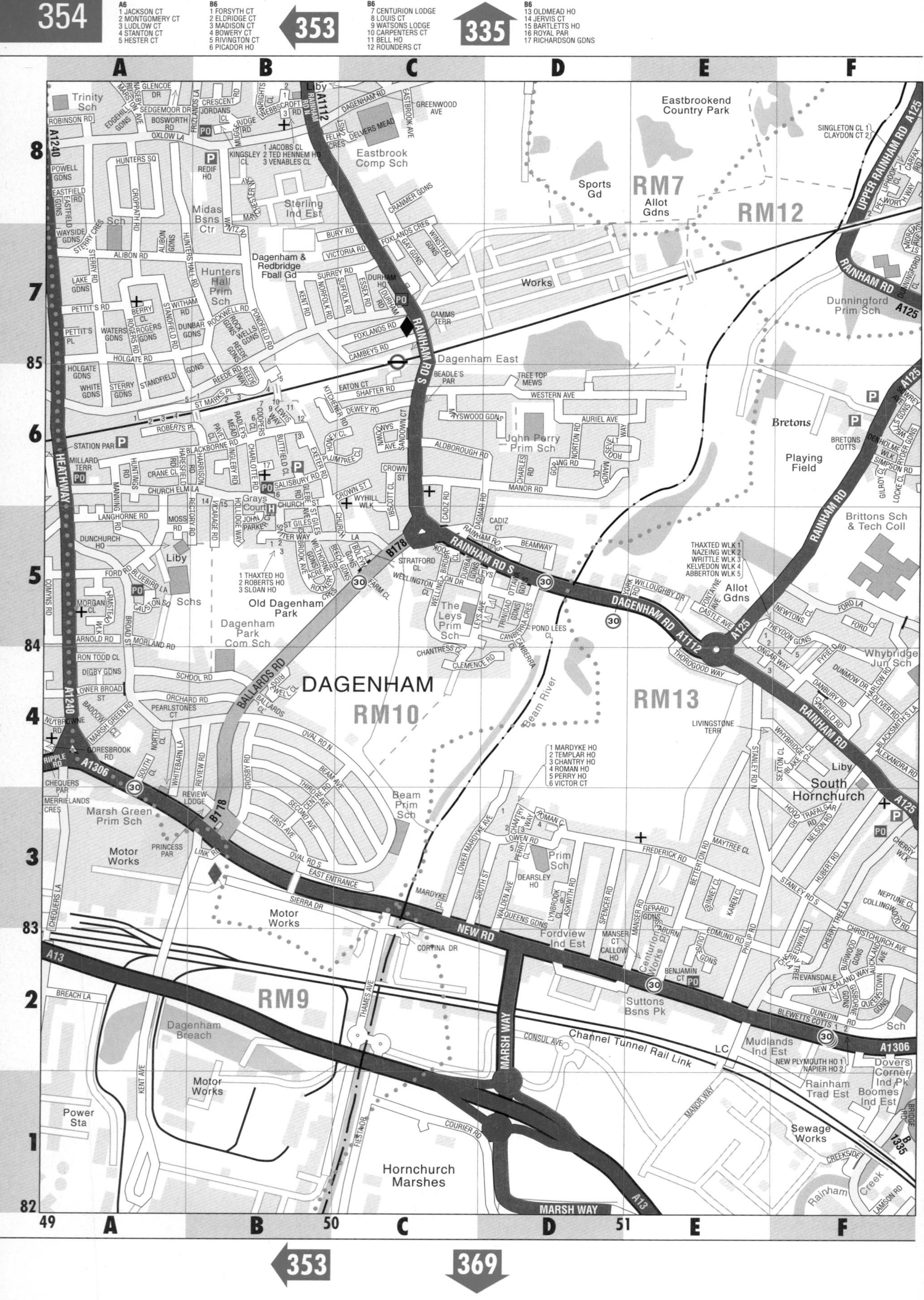

353
369

A6
1 CLOISTERS
2 BOUCHIER WLK
3 BROADHURST WLK
4 FLAMINGO WLK
5 HUGO GDNS
6 PARK MEWS

B6
1 CONCORDE HO
2 ASTRA CT W
3 ASTRA CT E
4 DEBDEN WLK
5 SWALLOW WLK
6 PEREGRINE WLK

7 DOVE WLK
8 CORMORANT WLK

C7
1 DIGBY WLK
2 MAYBANK LODGE
3 GENOTIN MEWS

336   356

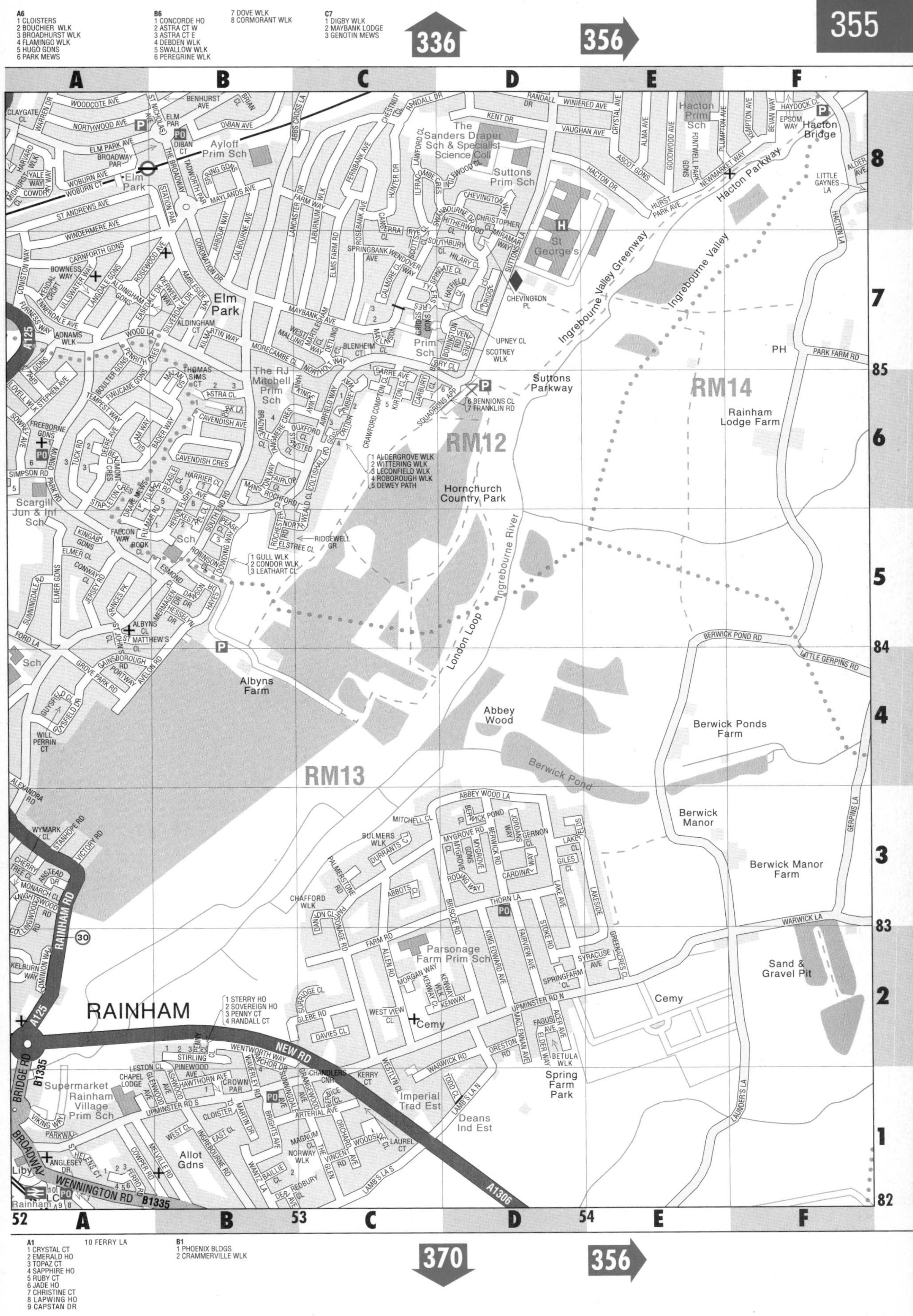

A1
1 CRYSTAL CT
2 EMERALD HO
3 TOPAZ CT
4 SAPPHIRE HO
5 RUBY CT
6 JADE HO
7 CHRISTINE CT
8 LAPWING HO
9 CAPSTAN DR

10 FERRY LA

B1
1 PHOENIX BLDGS
2 CRAMMERVILLE WLK

370   356

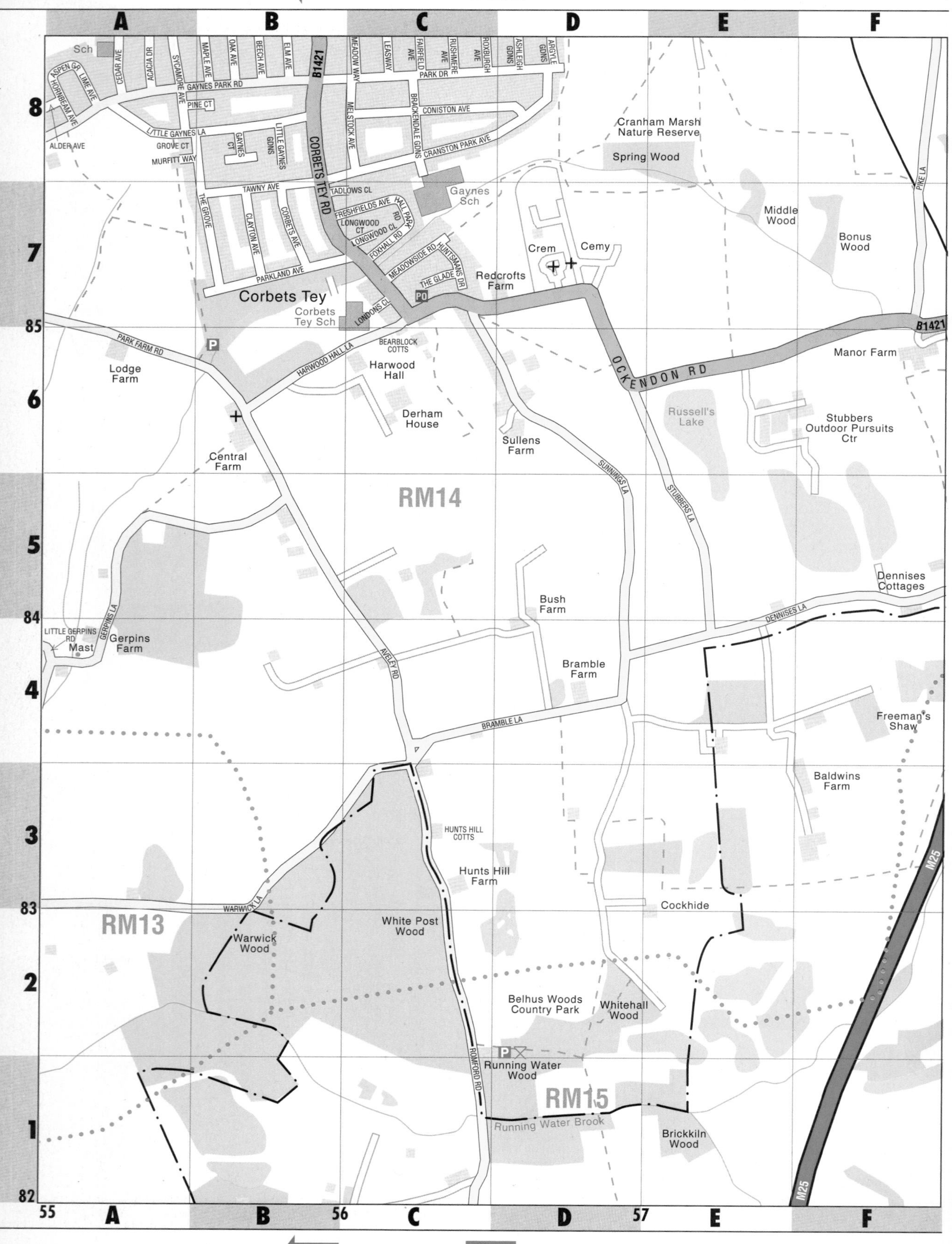

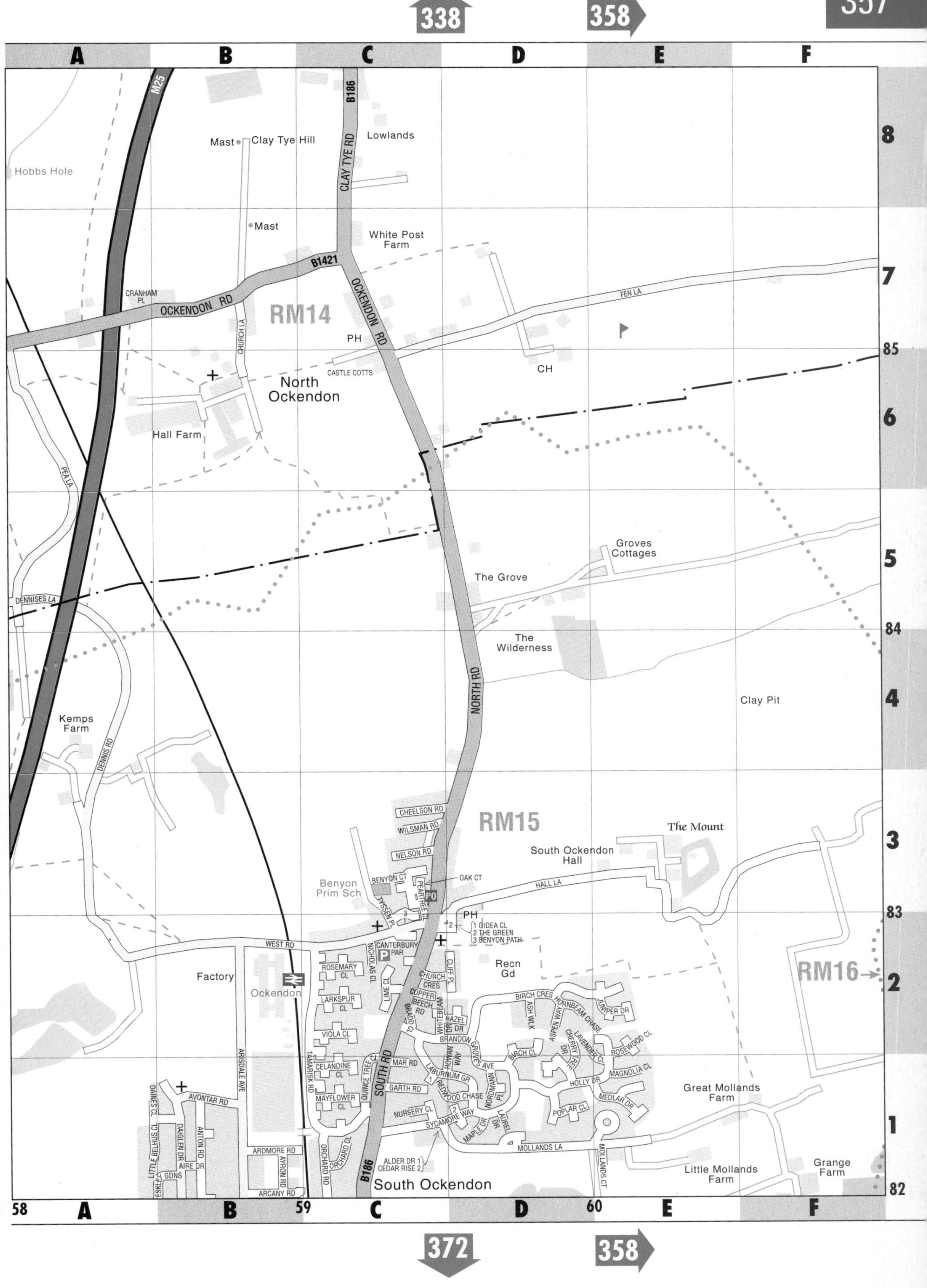
338
358
A B C D E F
8 7 6 5 4 3 2 1
85 84 83 82
58 59 60
M25
B186
CLAY TYE RD
Mast
Clay Tye Hill
Lowlands
Hobbs Hole
Mast
White Post Farm
B1421
OCKENDON RD
CRANHAM PL
RM14
CHURCH LA
PH
FEN LA
CASTLE COTTS
CH
North Ockendon
Hall Farm
PEA LA
Groves Cottages
The Grove
DENNISES LA
The Wilderness
NORTH RD
Clay Pit
Kemps Farm
DENNIS RD
CHEELSON RD
WILSMAN RD
RM15
The Mount
NELSON RD
South Ockendon Hall
OAK CT
BENYON CT
Benyon Prim Sch
PO
HALL LA
PEARTREE CL
TYSSEN PL
PH
1 GIDEA CL
2 THE GREEN
3 BENYON PATH
WEST RD
CANTERBURY PAR
Recn Gd
RM16
NICHOLAS CL
ROSEMARY CL
CLIFF PL
Factory
Ockendon
CHURCH CRES
LIME CL
COPPER BEECH RD
BIRCH CRES
HORNBEAM CHASE
JUNIPER DR
LARKSPUR CL
ASH WLK
ASPEN WAY
HAZEL DR
WHITEBEAM DR
BRADD CL
VIOLA CL
CHERRY TREE DR
LAVENDER CL
ROSEWOOD CL
BRANDON GROVES AVE
ROWAN WAY
BIRCH CL
MAGNOLIA CL
CELANDINE CL
TAMARISK RD
MAR RD
LABURNUM GR
QUINCE TREE CL
SOUTH RD
HOLLY DR
Great Mollands Farm
ARISDALE AVE
MAYFLOWER CL
GARTH RD
REDWOOD CHASE
NORDMANN PL
MEDLAR DR
AVONTAR RD
DAINES CL
NURSERY CL
SYCAMORE WAY
POPLAR CL
MAPLE DR
LAUREL DR
LITTLE BELHUS CL
DAIGLEN DR
ANTON RD
ORCHARD CL
ORCHARD RD
MOLLANDS LA
ARDMORE RD
AYRON RD
AIRE DR
ALDER DR 1
CEDAR RISE 2
MOLLANDS CT
Little Mollands Farm
Grange Farm
ESKLEY GDNS
ARCANY RD
B186
South Ockendon
372
358

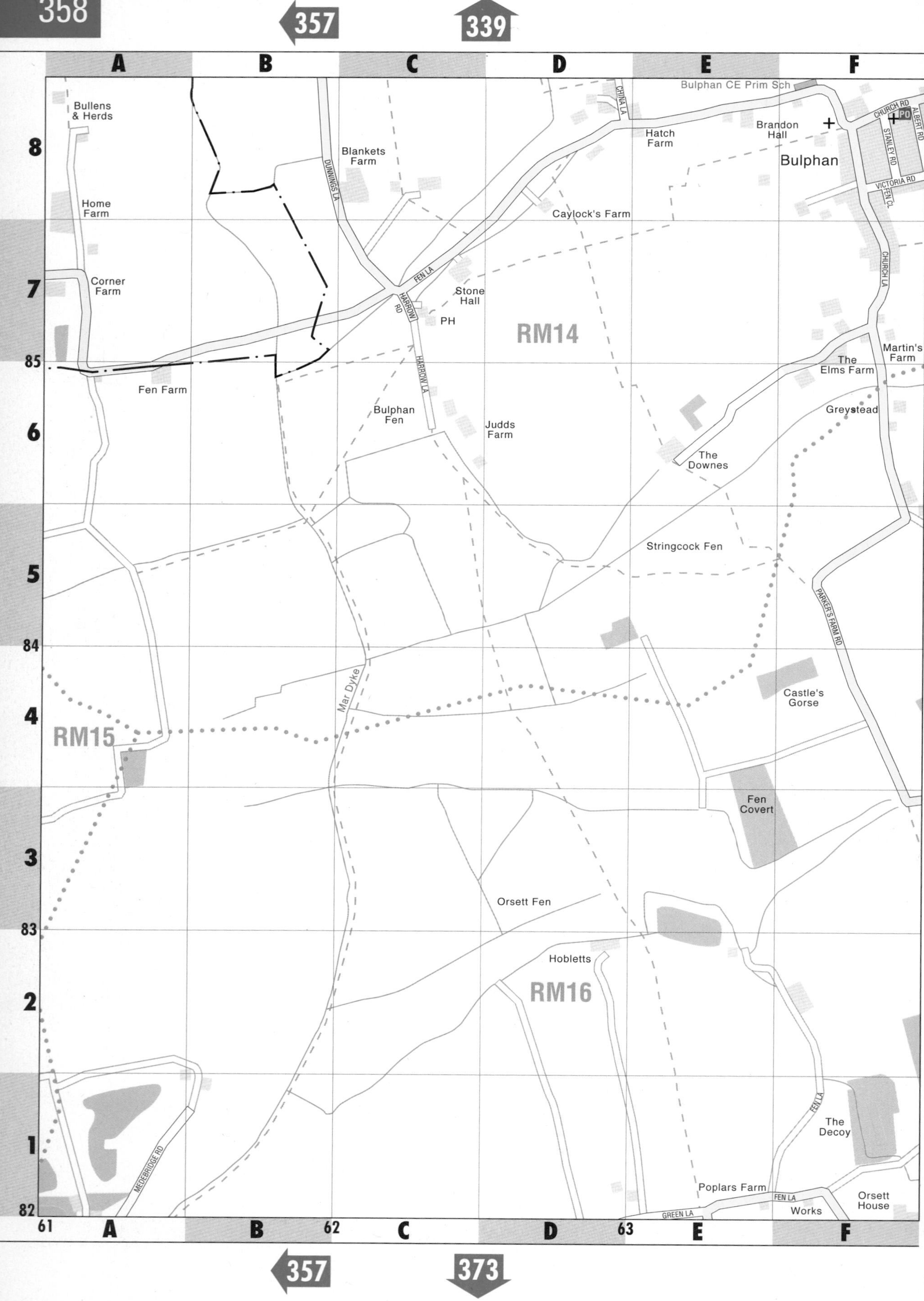

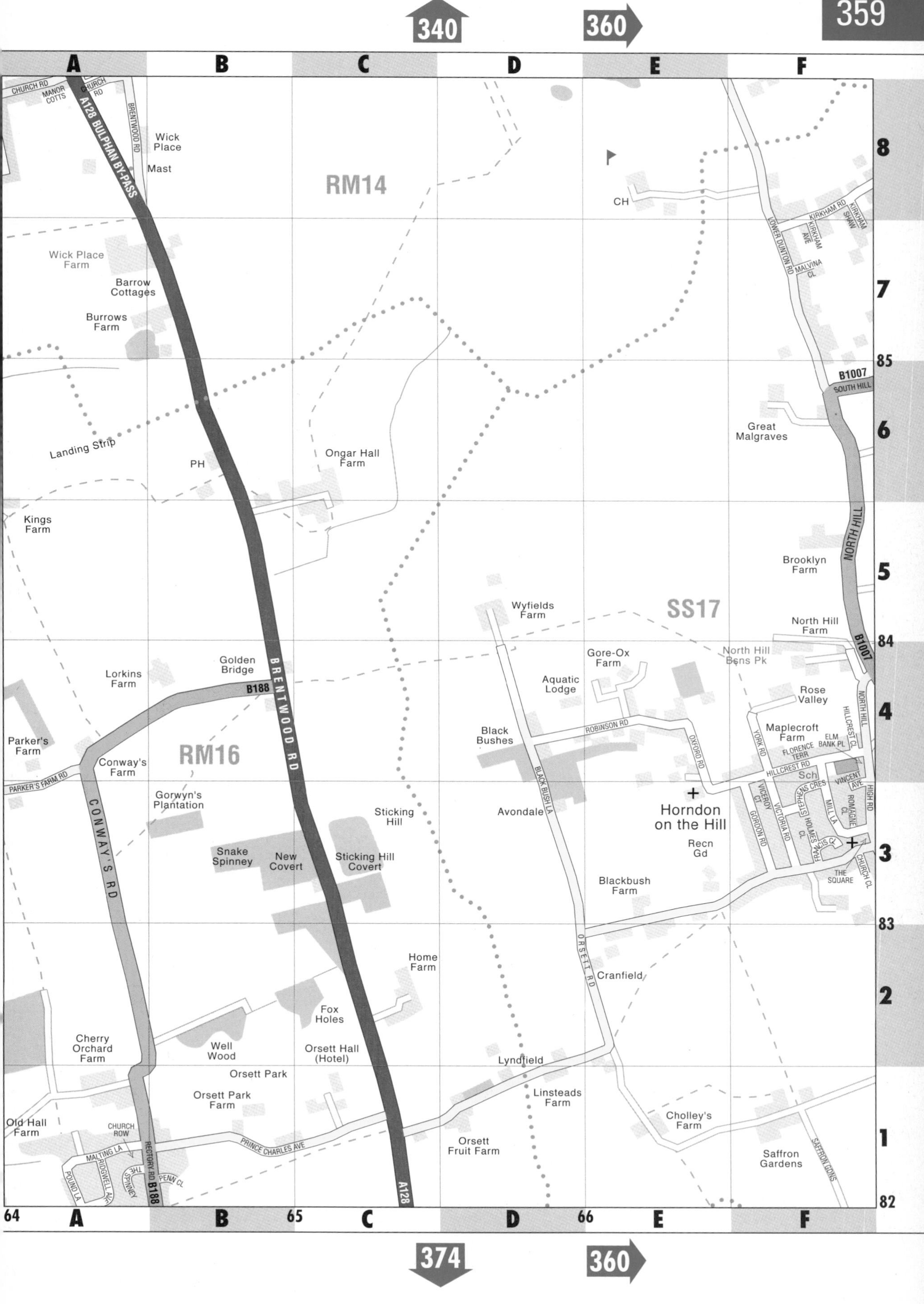

8
7
85
6
5
84
4
83
3
2
1
82

A B C D E F

CHURCH RD
MANOR COTTS
CHURCH RD
BRENTWOOD RD
A128 BULPHAN BY-PASS

Wick Place
Mast

RM14

CH

Wick Place Farm

Barrow Cottages

Burrows Farm

KIRKHAM RD
KIRKHAM SPINNEY
LOWER DUNTON RD
KIRKHAM AVE
MALVINA CL

B1007
SOUTH HILL

Landing Strip

PH

Ongar Hall Farm

Great Malgraves

NORTH HILL

Kings Farm

Brooklyn Farm

SS17

Wyfields Farm

North Hill Farm

B1007

Lorkins Farm

Golden Bridge
B188
BRENTWOOD RD

Gore-Ox Farm

Aquatic Lodge

North Hill Bens Pk

Rose Valley

North Hill

Parker's Farm

Black Bushes

Maplecroft Farm
FLORENCE TERR
ELM BANK PL
HILLCREST RD

Conway's Farm

RM16

ROBINSON RD

OXFORD RD

YORK RD
HILLCREST RD
Sch
VINCENT AVE
HIGH RD

Gorwyn's Plantation

Sticking Hill

Avondale

BLACK BUSH LA

Horndon on the Hill

VICEROY CT
VICTORIA RD
GORDON RD
THOMAS CRES
HOLMES
ROMAGNE CL
MILL LA

PARKER'S FARM RD

CONWAY'S RD

Snake Spinney

New Covert

Sticking Hill Covert

Recn Gd

THE SQUARE
CHURCH CL

Blackbush Farm

83

Home Farm

ORSETT RD

Cranfield

Cherry Orchard Farm

Well Wood

Fox Holes

Orsett Hall (Hotel)

Lyndfield

Linsteads Farm

Cholley's Farm

SAFFRON GDNS

Old Hall Farm

CHURCH ROW

Orsett Park

Orsett Park Farm

PRINCE CHARLES AVE

Orsett Fruit Farm

Saffron Gardens

POUND LA
MALTING LA
RIDGWELL AVE
THE SPINNEY
RECTORY RD
PENN CL
B188

A128

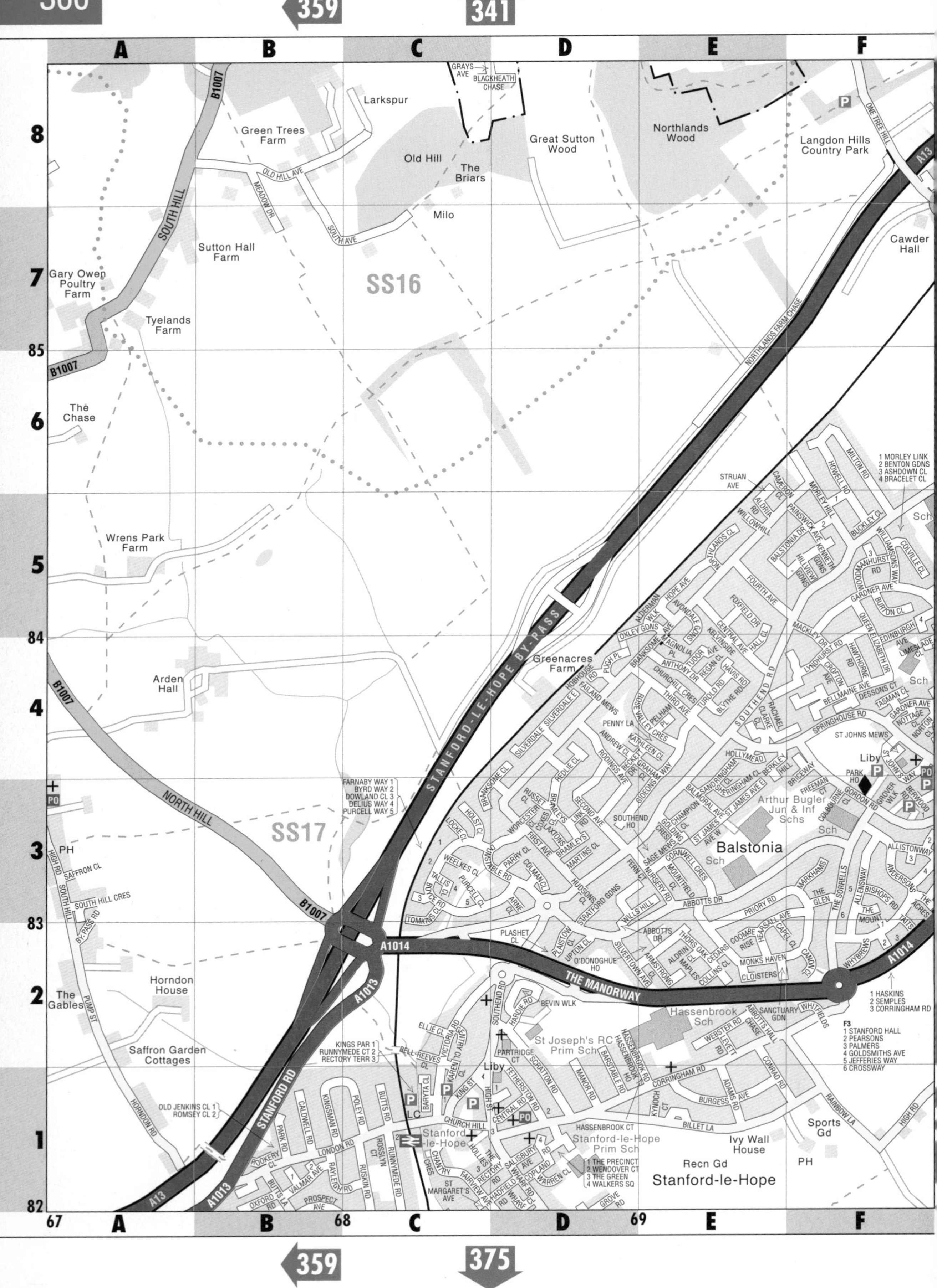

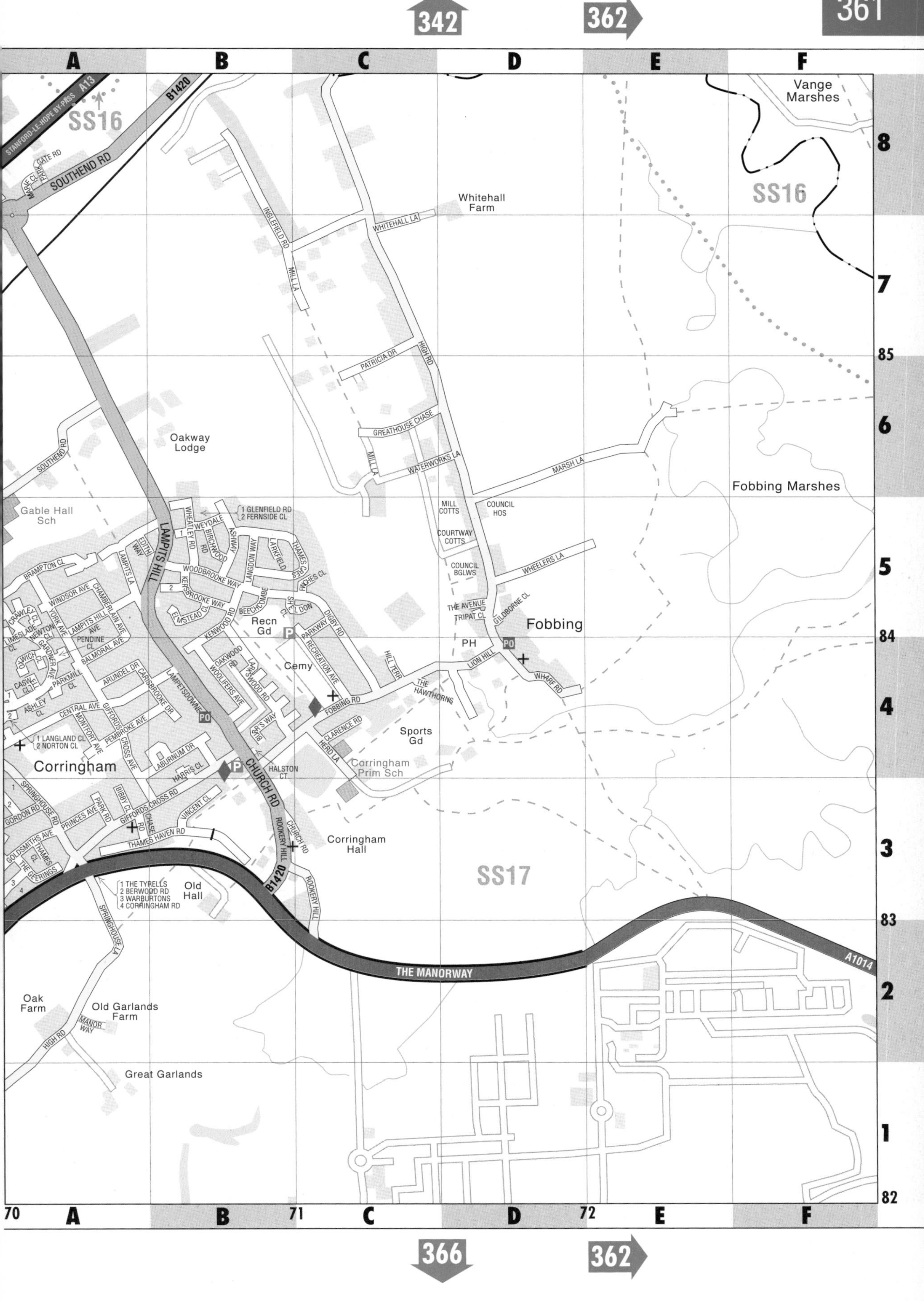

361 343

	A	B	C	D	E	F

8 Pitsea Wharf — Wat Tyler Country Park — Wharf — SS7

SS16

WATTYLER WAY

Vange Creek

Wharf

7 Parting Gut

85 Fobbing Creek

6 Fobbing Horse — East Haven Creek

5 Movable Flood Barrier — Movable Flood Barrier — SS8 — Northwick

84 NORTHWICK RD

4 SS17

3 Oozedam — Flare — Flare — Upper Horse

83 Flare — Jetty — Holehaven Creek

2 A1014 — Manorway Fleet — THE MANORWAY — LC — Coryton — Oil Refineries — A1014

Chy

1 THE MANORWAY — SS8

82 LC

361 367

344
364

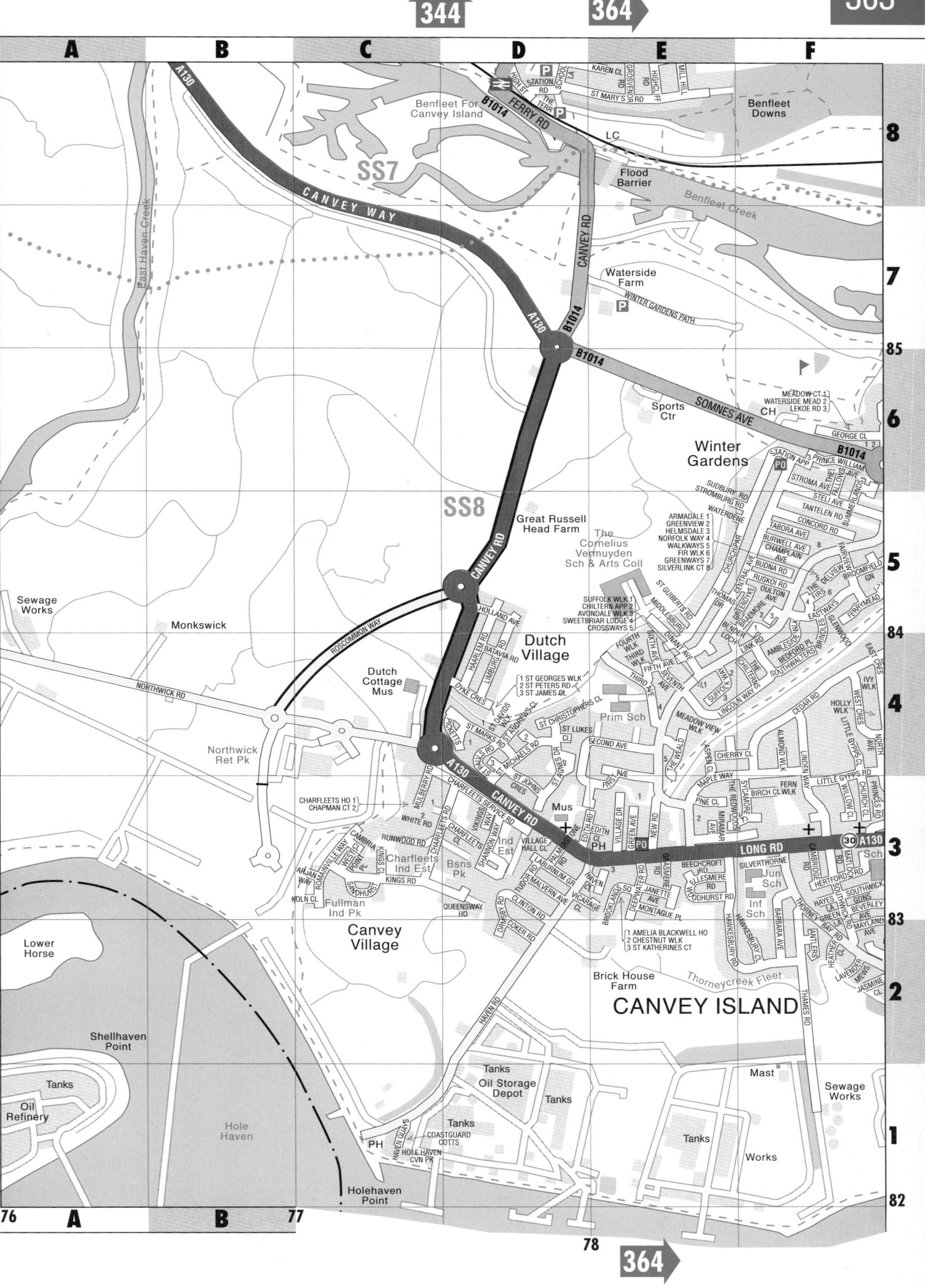
A
B
C
D
E
F
8
7
85
6
5
84
4
3
83
2
1
82
76
77
78
SS7
SS8
A130
CANVEY WAY
B1014
FERRY RD
CANVEY RD
Benfleet For Canvey Island
STATION RD
HIGH ST
SCHOOL LA
KAREN CL
GROSVENOR RD
HIGHCLIFF RD
MILL HILL
ST MARY'S RD
THE TERR
LC
Benfleet Downs
Flood Barrier
Benfleet Creek
East Haven Creek
Waterside Farm
WINTER GARDENS PATH
SOMNES AVE
Sports Ctr
CH
MEADOW CT 1
WATERSIDE MEAD 2
LEKOE RD 3
GEORGE CL
Winter Gardens
STATION APP
PRINCE WILLIAM AVE
STROMA AVE
STELI AVE
TANTELEN RD
CONCORD RD
TABORA AVE
BURWELL AVE
CHAMPLAIN AVE
BUDNA RD
RUSKOI RD
OULTON AVE
SUDBURY RD
STROMBURG RD
WATERDENE
ARMADALE 1
GREENVIEW 2
HELMSDALE 3
NORFOLK WAY 4
WALKWAYS 5
FIR WLK 6
GREENWAYS 7
SILVERLINK CT 8
Great Russell Head Farm
The Cornelius Vermuyden Sch & Arts Coll
SUFFOLK WLK 1
CHILTERN APP 2
AVONDALE WLK 3
SWEETBRIAR LODGE 4
CROSSWAYS 5
Sewage Works
Monkswick
ROSCOMMON WAY
NORTHWICK RD
Northwick Ret Pk
HOLLAND AVE
HARLEM RD
LIMBURG RD
BATAVIA RD
Dutch Village
Dutch Cottage Mus
DYKE CRES
1 ST GEORGES WLK
2 ST PETERS RD
3 ST JAMES CL
ST CHRISTOPHERS CL
Prim Sch
ST LUKES CL
SECOND AVE
MEADOW VIEW WLK
THE WEALD
ASPEN CL
CHERRY CL
MAPLE WAY
PINE CL
BIRCH CL
FERN WLK
LINDEN WAY
ALMOND WLK
CEDAR RD
HOLLY WLK
IVY WLK
WEST CRES
LITTLE GYPPS CL
LITTLE GYPPS RD
NORTH AVE
EAST CRES
CHURCH CL
WILLOW CL
PRINCES RD
PICKETTS
ST MARKS RD
ST MICHAELS RD
ST JOHNS CRES
ST AGNES DR
FIRS AVE
MULBERRY RD
CHARFLEETS SERVICE RD
CHARFLEETS HO 1
CHAPMAN CT 2
WHITE RD
RUNWOOD RD
Charfleets Ind Est
Bsns Pk
Ind Est
VILLAGE HALL CL
Mus
PH
PO
LONG RD
EDITH RD
VILLAGE DR
GREEN AVE
NEW RD
GRASMERE RD
BEECHCROFT RD
ELLESMERE RD
SILVERTHORNE
Jun Sch
Inf Sch
CAMBRIDGE RD
HERTFORD RD
MATLOCK RD
SOUTHWICK GDNS
BEVERLEY AVE
MAYLAND AVE
30
A130
Sch
ARJAN WAY
KOLN CL
Fullman Ind Pk
KINGS RD
SANDHURST
QUEENSWAY HO
Canvey Village
TUDOR RD
MALVERN AVE
CLINTON RD
COKER RD
ORMSBY RD
VICARAGE CL
BROOKLANDS
DEEPWATER RD
JANETTE AVE
MONTAGUE PL
1 AMELIA BLACKWELL HO
2 CHESTNUT WLK
3 ST KATHERINES CT
HAWKESBURY RD
BARBARA AVE
ANTLERS
HEATHER CL
LAVENDER MEWS
JASMINE CL
Brick House Farm
Thorneycreek Fleet
CANVEY ISLAND
THAMES RD
Lower Horse
Shellhaven Point
Tanks
Oil Refinery
Hole Haven
HAVEN RD
Oil Storage Depot
Mast
Sewage Works
Works
HAVEN QUAYS
COASTGUARD COTTS
HOLE HAVEN CVN PK
Holehaven Point

364

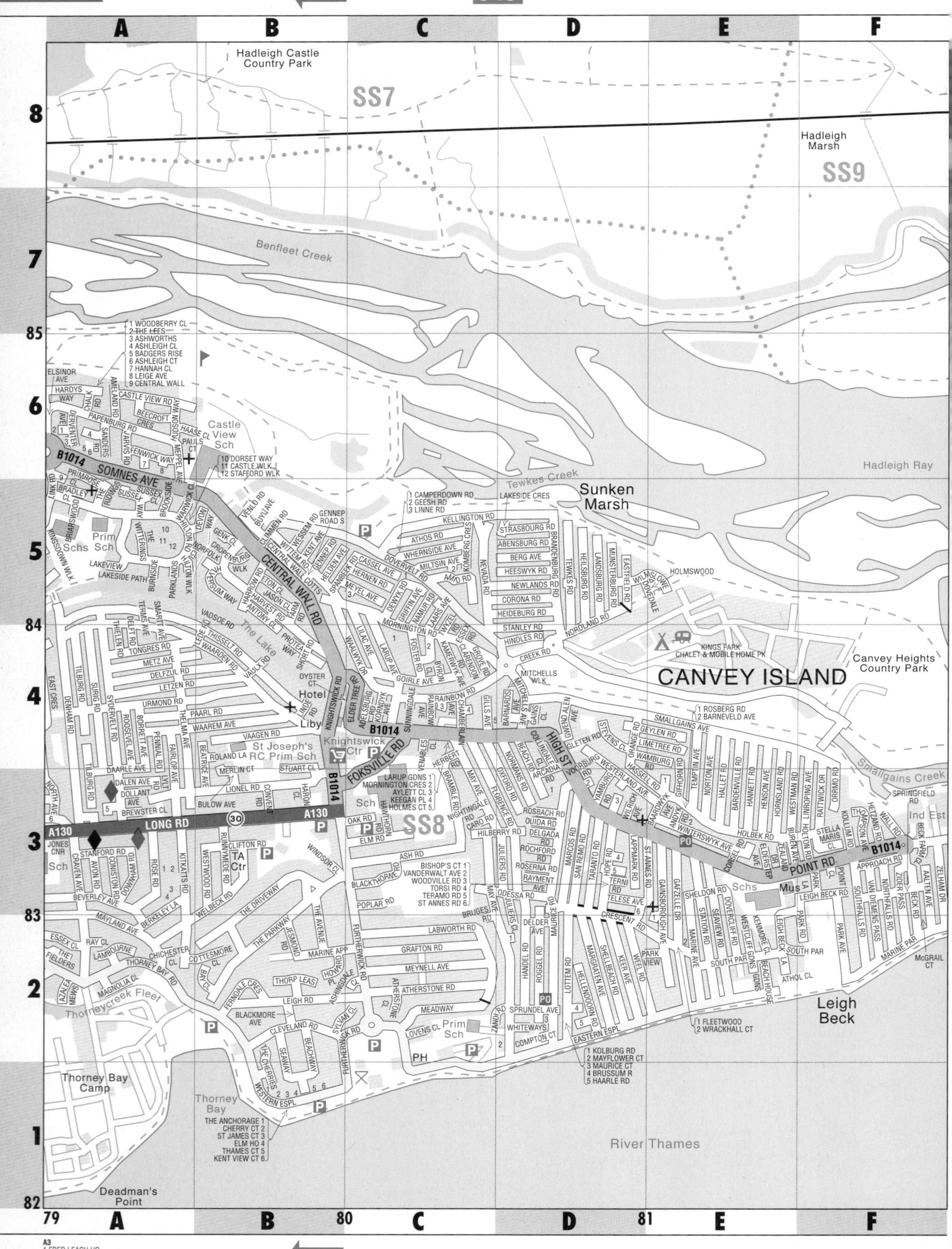

A3
1 FRED LEACH HO
2 FLORENCE NEALE HO
3 SUSAN FIELDER COTTS
4 CLAIRE JAMES COTTS
5 REMBRANDT CL
6 THAMESIDE CRES

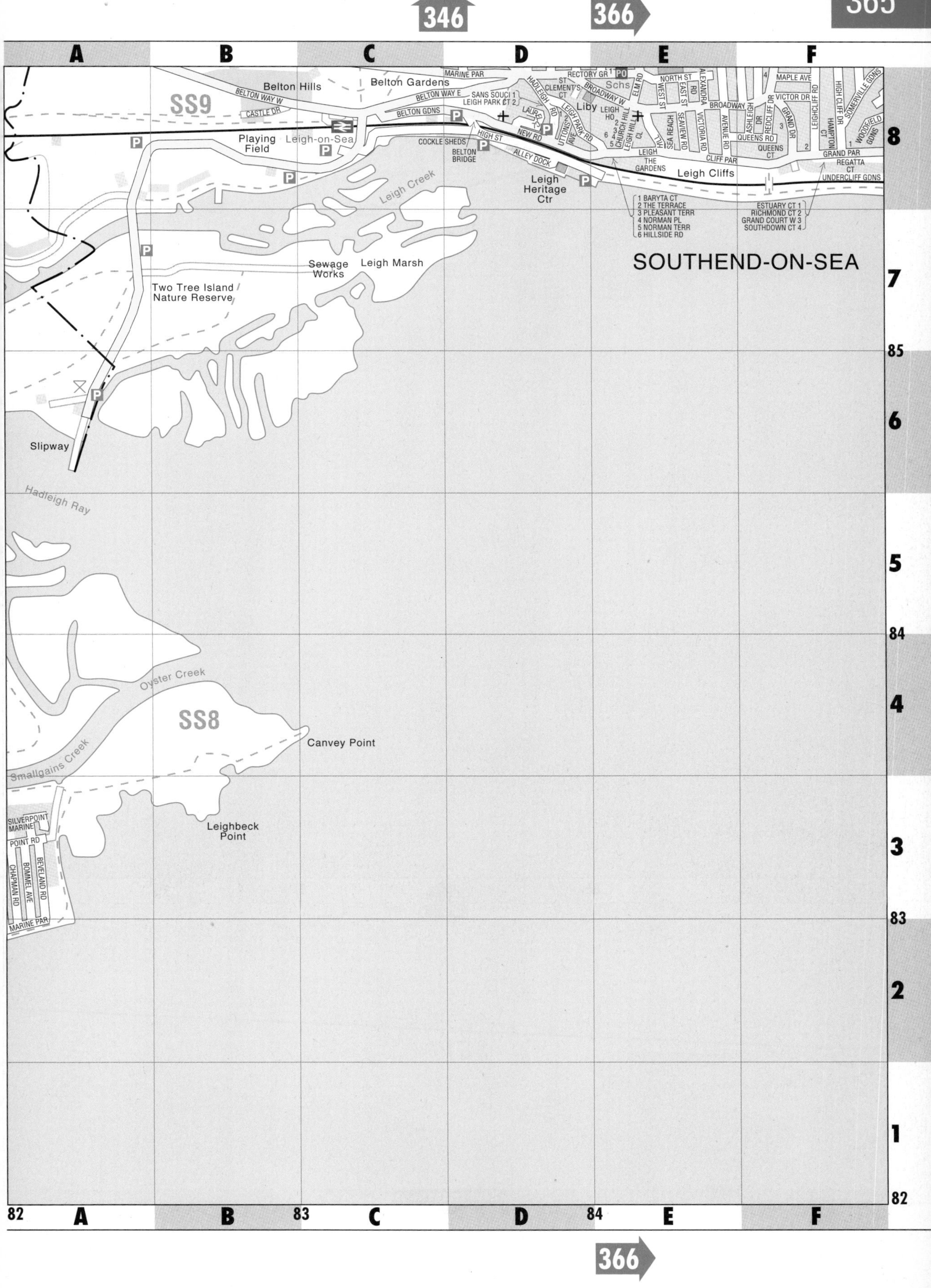
A
B
C
D
E
F
SS9
Belton Hills
Belton Gardens
BELTON WAY W
CASTLE DR
BELTON WAY E
BELTON GDNS
MARINE PAR
SANS SOUCI 1
LEIGH PARK CT 2
Playing Field
Leigh-on-Sea
COCKLE SHEDS
BELTON BRIDGE
HIGH ST
ALLEY DOCK
NEW RD
Leigh Heritage Ctr
RECTORY GR
PO
ST CLEMENT'S CT
Schs
BROADWAY W
Liby
LEIGH HO
LEIGH PARK RD
HADLEIGH RD
LAUREL
UTTONS AVE
CHURCH HILL
LEIGH HILL
ELM RD
WEST ST
NORTH ST
EAST ST
SEA REACH
SEAVIEW RD
VICTORIA RD
ALEXANDRA RD
AVENUE RD
BROADWAY
ASHLEIGH DR
REDCLIFF DR
GRAND DR
QUEENS RD
QUEENS CT
LEIGHCLIFF RD
HIGH CLIFF DR
HAMPTON CT
SOMERVILLE GDNS
WOODFIELD GDNS
MAPLE AVE
VICTOR DR
LEIGH
THE GARDENS
CLIFF PAR
GRAND PAR
REGATTA CT
UNDERCLIFF GDNS
Leigh Cliffs
1 BARYTA CT
2 THE TERRACE
3 PLEASANT TERR
4 NORMAN PL
5 NORMAN TERR
6 HILLSIDE RD
ESTUARY CT 1
RICHMOND CT 2
GRAND COURT W 3
SOUTHDOWN CT 4
Leigh Creek
Sewage Works
Leigh Marsh
Two Tree Island Nature Reserve
SOUTHEND-ON-SEA
Slipway
Hadleigh Ray
Oyster Creek
SS8
Canvey Point
Smallgains Creek
Leighbeck Point
SILVERPOINT MARINE
POINT RD
CHAPMAN RD
BOMMEL AVE
BEVELAND RD
MARINE PAR
8
7
85
6
5
84
4
3
83
2
1
82
82
83
84

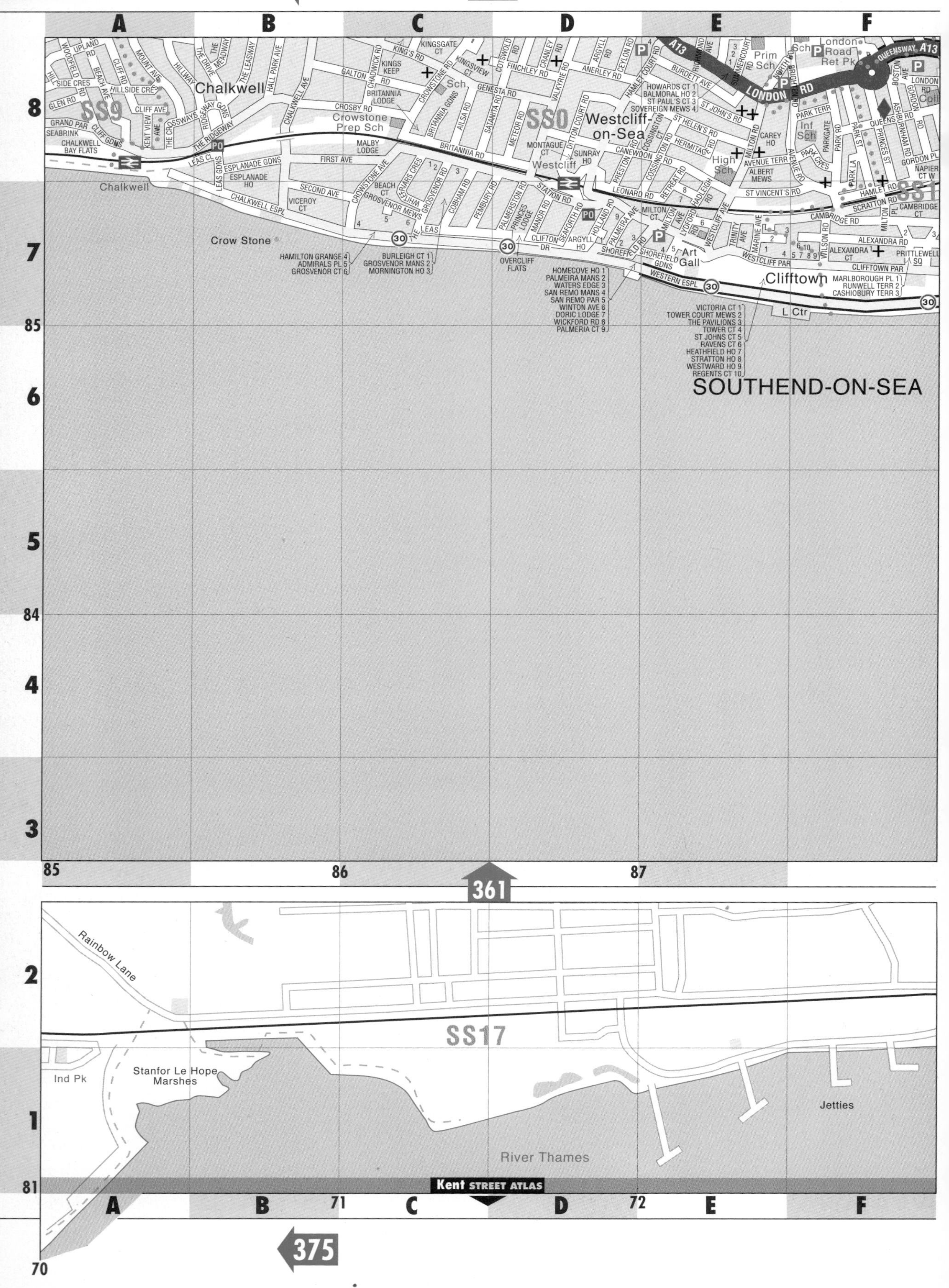

Chalkwell

SS9

Chalkwell

Crow Stone

HAMILTON GRANGE 4
ADMIRALS PL 5
GROSVENOR CT 6

BURLEIGH CT 1
GROSVENOR MANS 2
MORNINGTON HO 3

OVERCLIFF
FLATS

HOMECOVE HO 1
PALMEIRA MANS 2
WATERS EDGE 3
SAN REMO MANS 4
SAN REMO PAR 5
WINTON AVE 6
DORIC LODGE 7
WICKFORD RD 8
PALMERIA CT 9

VICTORIA CT 1
TOWER COURT MEWS 2
THE PAVILIONS 3
TOWER CT 4
ST JOHNS CT 5
RAVENS CT 6
HEATHFIELD HO 7
STRATTON HO 8
WESTWARD HO 9
REGENTS CT 10

MARLBOROUGH PL 1
RUNWELL TERR 2
CASHIOBURY TERR 3

Westcliff-
on-Sea

SS0

Westcliff

Clifftown

SOUTHEND-ON-SEA

HOWARDS CT 1
BALMORAL HO 2
ST PAUL'S CT 3
SOVEREIGN MEWS 4

SS1

Rainbow Lane

SS17

Ind Pk

Stanfor Le Hope
Marshes

Jetties

River Thames

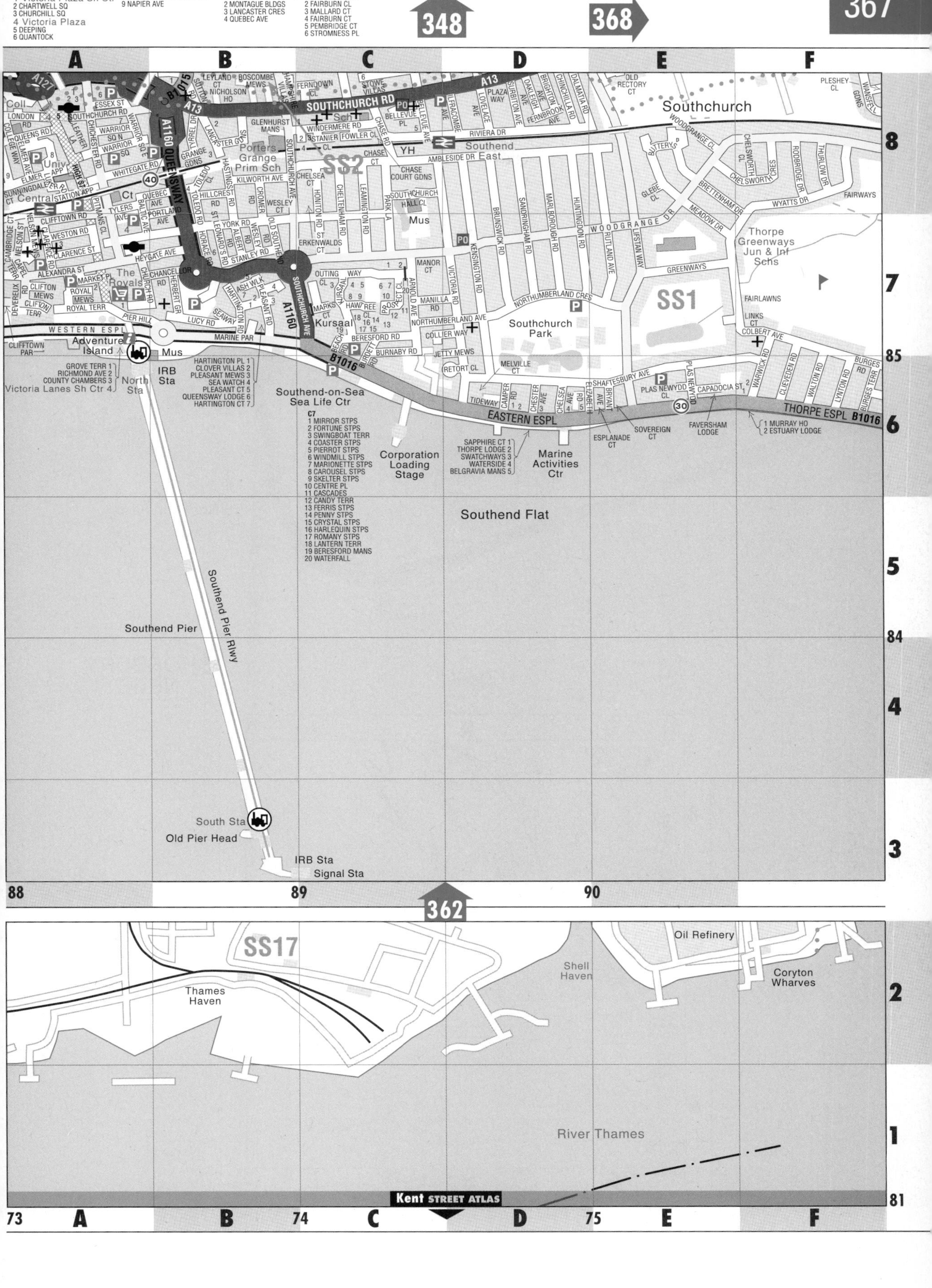
A8
1 Victoria Plaza Sh Ctr
2 CHARTWELL SQ
3 CHURCHILL SQ
4 Victoria Plaza
5 DEEPING
6 QUANTOCK
7 WARRIOR HO
8 FARRINGDON SERVICE RD
9 NAPIER AVE
B8
1 CHILTERN
2 MONTAGUE BLDGS
3 LANCASTER CRES
4 QUEBEC AVE
C8
1 LAURISTON PL
2 FAIRBURN CL
3 MALLARD CT
4 FAIRBURN CT
5 PEMBRIDGE CT
6 STROMNESS PL
348
368
A
B
C
D
E
F
8
7
85
6
5
84
4
3
88
89
90
A127
A13
SOUTHCHURCH RD
B1015
A1160
QUEENSWAY
Southchurch
Southend East
SS2
Porters Grange Prim Sch
Univ
Central
YH
Mus
SOUTHCHURCH HALL CL
WOODGRANGE DR
Thorpe Greenways Jun & Inf Schs
GREENWAYS
SS1
Southchurch Park
FAIRLAWNS
LINKS CT
COLBERT AVE
NORTHUMBERLAND CRES
NORTHUMBERLAND AVE
Kursaal
The Royals
WESTERN ESPL
MARINE PAR
CLIFFTOWN PAR
Adventure Island
Mus
North Sta
IRB Sta
B1016
EASTERN ESPL
THORPE ESPL
SHAFTESBURY AVE
PLAS NEWYDD CL
CAPADOCIA ST
GROVE TERR 1
RICHMOND AVE 2
COUNTY CHAMBERS 3
Victoria Lanes Sh Ctr 4
HARTINGTON PL 1
CLOVER VILLAS 2
PLEASANT MEWS 3
SEA WATCH 4
PLEASANT CT 5
QUEENSWAY LODGE 6
HARTINGTON CT 7
Southend-on-Sea Sea Life Ctr
C7
1 MIRROR STPS
2 FORTUNE STPS
3 SWINGBOAT TERR
4 COASTER STPS
5 PIERROT STPS
6 WINDMILL STPS
7 MARIONETTE STPS
8 CAROUSEL STPS
9 SKELTER STPS
10 CENTRE PL
11 CASCADES
12 CANDY TERR
13 FERRIS STPS
14 PENNY STPS
15 CRYSTAL STPS
16 HARLEQUIN STPS
17 ROMANY STPS
18 LANTERN TERR
19 BERESFORD MANS
20 WATERFALL
Corporation Loading Stage
SAPPHIRE CT 1
THORPE LODGE 2
SWATCHWAYS 3
WATERSIDE 4
BELGRAVIA MANS 5
Marine Activities Ctr
ESPLANADE CT
SOVEREIGN CT
FAVERSHAM LODGE
1 MURRAY HO
2 ESTUARY LODGE
Southend Flat
Southend Pier
Southend Pier Rlwy
South Sta
Old Pier Head
IRB Sta
Signal Sta
362
SS17
Thames Haven
Shell Haven
Oil Refinery
Coryton Wharves
River Thames
2
1
81
73
74
75
Kent STREET ATLAS

367
349

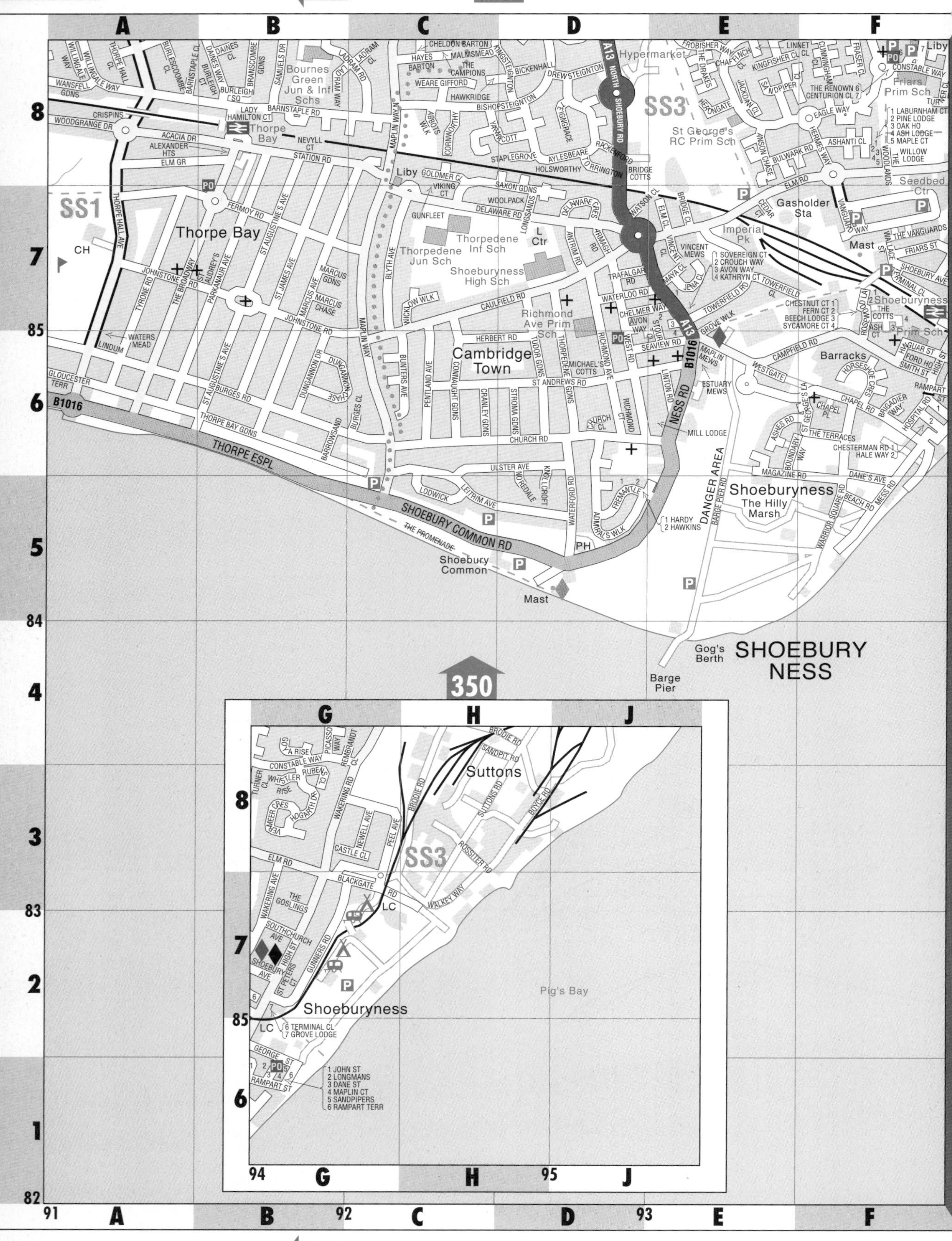
A
B
C
D
E
F
8
7
6
5
4
3
2
1
85
84
83
82
91
92
93
SS1
SS3
Thorpe Bay
Bournes Green Jun & Inf Schs
Hypermarket
St George's RC Prim Sch
Friars Prim Sch
Seedbed Ctr
Gasholder Sta
Imperial Pk
Mast
Shoeburyness
Prim Sch
Barracks
Thorpedene Inf Sch
Thorpedene Jun Sch
Shoeburyness High Sch
L Ctr
Richmond Ave Prim Sch
Cambridge Town
Liby
CH
Shoeburyness The Hilly Marsh
DANGER AREA
Shoebury Common
Gog's Berth
Barge Pier
SHOEBURY NESS
A13
NORTH SHOEBURY RD
B1016
NESS RD
THORPE ESPL
SHOEBURY COMMON RD
THE PROMENADE
THORPE HALL AVE
WOODGRANGE DR
CRISPINS
ACACIA DR
ELM GR
STATION RD
NEVYLL CT
BARNSTAPLE RD
FERMOY RD
JOHNSTONE RD
THE BROADWAY
PARKANAUR AVE
ST AUGUSTINE'S AVE
ST JAMES AVE
MARCUS AVE
MARCUS CHASE
BURGES RD
THORPE BAY GDNS
DUNGANNON DR
DUNGANNON CHASE
BURGES CL
BARROWSAND
MAPLIN WAY
MAPLIN WAY N
BLYTH AVE
BUNTERS AVE
PENTLAND AVE
CONNAUGHT GDNS
CRANLEY GDNS
STROMA GDNS
HERBERT RD
ST ANDREWS RD
CHURCH RD
ULSTER AVE
LODWICK
LEITRIM AVE
WATERFORD RD
CAULFIELD RD
WICKLOW WLK
GUNFLEET
DELAWARE RD
WOOLPACK
SAXON GDNS
VIKING CT
GOLDMER CL
HOLSWORTHY
STAPLEGROVE
AYLESBEARE
BISHOPSTEIGNTON
DREWSTEIGNTON
BICKENHALL
HAWKRIDGE
WEARE GIFFORD
TRAFALGAR RD
WATERLOO RD
CHELMER WAY
SEAVIEW RD
RICHMOND AVE
WEST RD
LINTON RD
ANTRIM RD
ARMAGH RD
TOWERFIELD RD
GROVE WLK
CAMPFIELD RD
WESTGATE
CHAPEL RD
THE TERRACES
MAGAZINE RD
DANE'S AVE
BEACH RD
MESS RD
WARRIOR SQUARE RD
BARGE PIER RD
MILL LODGE
ESTUARY MEWS
MAPLIN MEWS
1 HARDY
2 HAWKINS
1 SOVEREIGN CT
2 CROUCH WAY
3 AVON WAY
4 KATHRYN CT
CHESTNUT CT 1
FERN CT 2
BEECH LODGE 3
SYCAMORE CT 4
1 LABURNHAM CT
2 PINE LODGE
3 OAK HO
4 ASH LODGE
5 MAPLE CT
CHESTERMAN RD 1
HALE WAY 2
THE RENOWN 6
CENTURION CL 7
EAGLE WAY
BULWARK RD
ELM RD
350
G
H
J
Suttons
SS3
BRODIE RD
SANDPIT RD
SUTTONS RD
BOYCE RD
ROSSITER RD
WALKEY WAY
CONSTABLE WAY
WAKERING RD
PEEL AVE
NEWELL AVE
CASTLE CL
ELM RD
BLACKGATE RD
WAKERING AVE
THE GOSLINGS
SOUTHCHURCH AVE
GUNNERS RD
HIGH ST
ST PETERS CT
SHOEBURY AVE
LC
Shoeburyness
Pig's Bay
6 TERMINAL CL
7 GROVE LODGE
GEORGE ST
RAMPART ST
1 JOHN ST
2 LONGMANS
3 DANE ST
4 MAPLIN CT
5 SANDPIPERS
6 RAMPART TERR
94
95

367

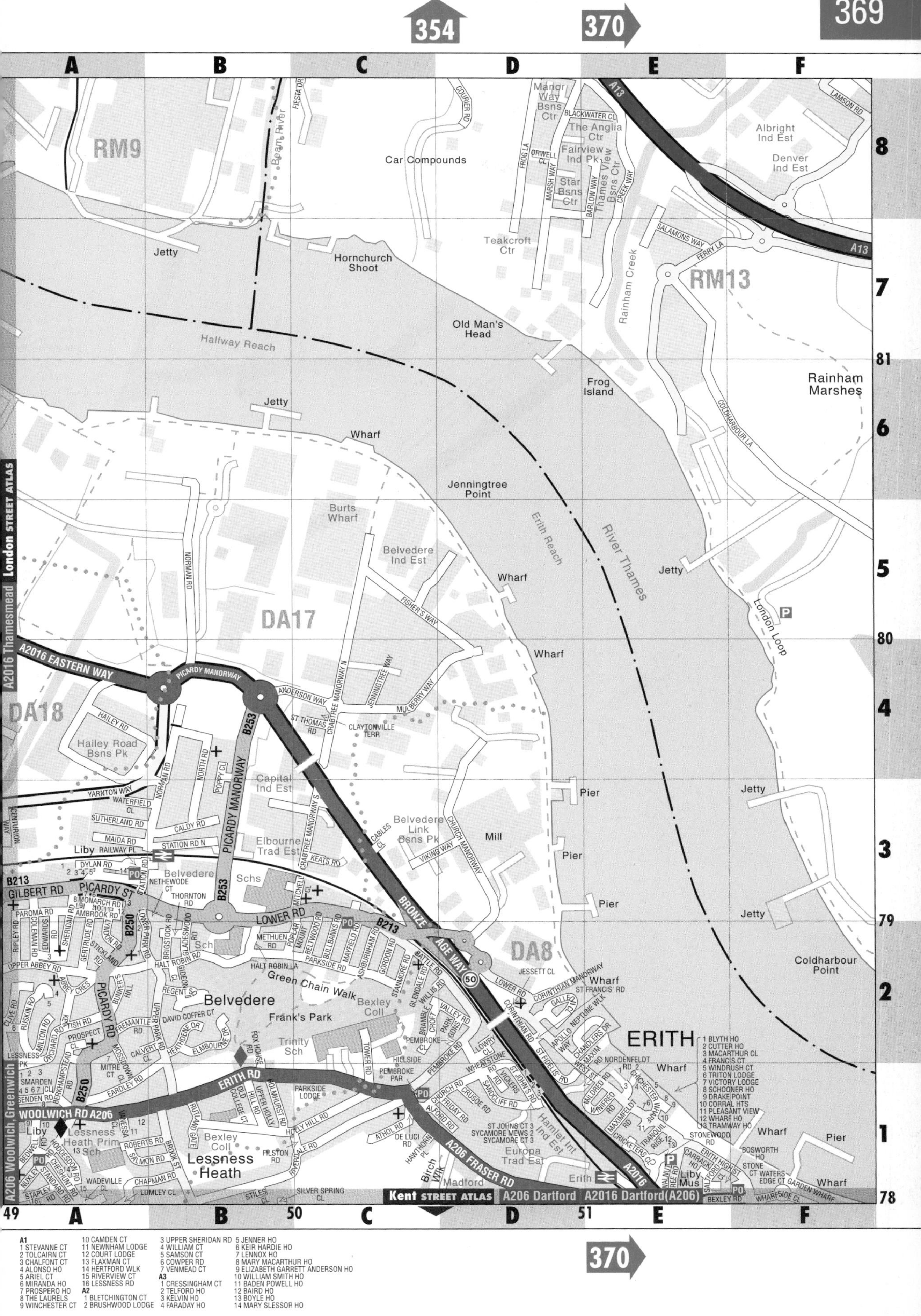

RM9

Jetty

Car Compounds

Hornchurch Shoot

Manor Way Bsns Ctr
The Anglia Ctr
BLACKWATER CL
Fairview Ind Pk
ORWELL CL
FROG LA
Marsh Bsns Ctr
Star Bsns Ctr
Thames View Bsns Ctr
BARLOW WAY
CREEK WAY
SALAMONS WAY
FERRY LA
Albright Ind Est
Denver Ind Est
LAMSON RD
A13

Teakcroft Ctr

RM13

8

7

Halfway Reach

Old Man's Head

Frog Island

Rainham Creek

Rainham Marshes

COLDHARBOUR LA

81

Jetty

Wharf

Jenningtree Point

Burts Wharf

Belvedere Ind Est

FISHER'S WAY

Wharf

Wharf

Erith Reach

River Thames

Jetty

London Loop

P

6

5

80

London STREET ATLAS

A2016 Thamesmead

DA17

DA18

A2016 EASTERN WAY

PICARDY MANORWAY

Hailey Road Bsns Pk
HAILEY RD
NORMAN RD
NORTH RD
POPPY CL
ANDERSON WAY
CRABTREE MANORWAY N
JENNINGTREE WAY
St THOMAS RD
CLAYTONVILLE TERR
MULBERRY WAY
Capital Ind Est
Belvedere Link Bsns Pk
CHURCH MANORWAY
VIKING WAY
Mill

Pier

Pier

Pier

Jetty

Jetty

Coldharbour Point

4

3

79

B253

B253

PICARDY MANORWAY

YARNTON WAY
WATERFIELD CL
SUTHERLAND RD
MAIDA RD
CALDY RD
STATION RD N
DYLAN RD
Liby RAILWAY PL
Belvedere
NETHEWODE CT
THORNTON RD
Schs
Elbourne Trad Est
CRABTREE MANORWAY S
KEATS RD
CABLES
MITCHELL

B213
GILBERT RD
PICARDY ST
PAROMA RD
AMBROOK RD
RIPLEY RD
GRAHAM RD
EDWARDS
B250
SHERIDAN RD
GERTRUDE RD
STICKLAND RD
HALT ROBIN RD
BRIGSTOCK RD
GLADESWOOD RD
LOWER RD
METHUEN RD
BERWOOD RD
MOUNT RD
BILL BANKS RD
MAYFIELD RD
AGGBOROUGH RD
ASHBURNHAM RD
GORDON RD
Sch

BRONZE AGE WAY

DA8

LOWER RD
CORINTHIAN MANORWAY
JESSETT CL
St FRANCIS' RD
CALLOW
APOLLO
NEPTUNE WLK
Wharf

ERITH

1 BLYTH HO
2 CUTTER HO
3 MACARTHUR CL
4 FRANCIS CT
5 WINDRUSH CT
6 TRITON LODGE
7 VICTORY LODGE
8 SCHOONER HO
9 DRAKE POINT
10 CORRAL HTS
11 PLEASANT VIEW
12 WHARE HO
13 TRAMWAY HO

Wharf

2

UPPER ABBEY RD
ABBEY CRES
RUSKIN RD
CLIVE RD
MILTON RD
LESSNESS PK
SMARDEN
BENDEN CL
PICARDY RD
B250
FREMANTLE RD
DAVID COFFER CT
HEATHDENE DR
CALVERT RD
EARDLEY RD
MITRE CT
REGENT SQ
Belvedere
Frank's Park
Green Chain Walk
HALT ROBIN LA
Bexley Coll
Trinity Sch
HILLSIDE
PEMBROKE PAR
GLENDALE RD
WILLIS RD
STANMORE RD
BATTLE RD
BRAMBLE CROFT
PEMBROKE RD
VALLEY RD
LOWRY
WHEATSTONE
St JOHN'S RD
St JOHN'S CT 1
MAXIM RD
NORDENFELDT
MILFORD RD
CHICHESTER RD
WINIFRED RD
TRANQUIL
MAXIMFIELD RD
CRICKETERS RD
STONEWOOD RD
Liby Mus
CARRBROOK
STONE CT

WOOLWICH RD A206
Liby
Lessness Heath Prim Sch
ROBERTS RD
BROOK ST
SALMON RD
WADEVILLE CL
CHAPMAN RD
LUMLEY CL
Lessness Heath
Bexley Coll
FILSTON RD
ATHOL RD
DE LUCI RD
RAVENSBOURNE RD
HAWTHORN
SILVER SPRING CL
STILES
Birch WLK
Madford
A206 FRASER RD
Europa Trad Est
Erith
A2016

ERITH RD
A206
RUTLAND RD
WOOLHURST AVE
BIRCH WLK
HOLLY HILL RD
AVEDON RD
CHURCH RD
FRIDAY RD
CRUSOE RD
Hamlet Int Ind Est
BOSWORTH RD
EDGE CT
GARDEN WHARF
WATERS CT
SALTFORD
WHARFSIDE CL
BEXLEY RD
Pier

Wharf

79

78

A206 Woolwich, Greenwich

A1
1 STEVANNE CT
2 TOLCAIRN CT
3 CHALFONT CT
4 ALONSO HO
5 ARIEL CT
6 MIRANDA HO
7 PROSPERO HO
8 THE LAURELS
9 WINCHESTER CT
10 CAMDEN CT
11 NEWNHAM LODGE
12 COURT LODGE
13 FLAXMAN CT
14 HERTFORD WLK
15 RIVERVIEW CT
16 LESSNESS RD
A2
1 BLETCHINGTON CT
2 BRUSHWOOD LODGE
3 UPPER SHERIDAN RD
4 WILLIAM CT
5 SAMSON CT
6 COWPER RD
7 VENMEAD CT
A3
1 CRESSINGHAM CT
2 TELFORD HO
3 KELVIN HO
4 FARADAY HO
5 JENNER HO
6 KEIR HARDIE HO
7 LENNOX HO
8 MARY MACARTHUR HO
9 ELIZABETH GARRETT ANDERSON HO
10 WILLIAM SMITH HO
11 BADEN POWELL HO
12 BAIRD HO
13 BOYLE HO
14 MARY SLESSOR HO

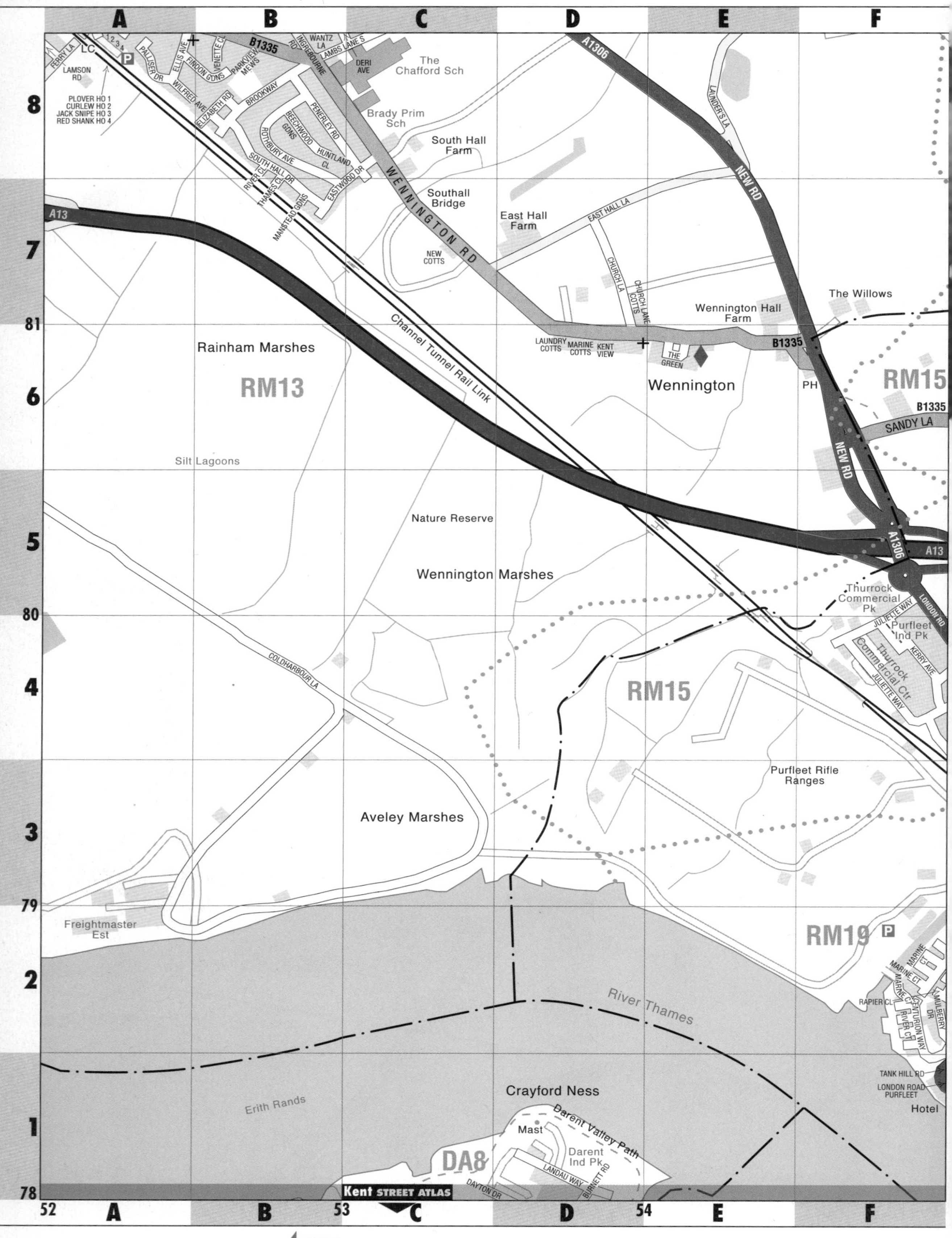

A B C D E F

8

PLOVER HO 1
CURLEW HO 2
JACK SNIPE HO 3
RED SHANK HO 4

LAMSON RD

FERRY LA

B1335

WANTZ LA

LAMBS LANE S

DERI AVE

The Chafford Sch

A1306

WENNINGTON RD

Brady Prim Sch

South Hall Farm

Southall Bridge

East Hall Farm

East Hall La

NEW RD

SAUNDERS LA

7

A13

NEW COTTS

7

81

Rainham Marshes

RM13

Channel Tunnel Rail Link

CHURCH LANE COTTS

The Willows

Wennington Hall Farm

LAUNDRY COTTS

MARINE COTTS

KENT VIEW

THE GREEN

PH

B1335

SANDY LA

B1335

RM15

6

Wennington

NEW RD

6

Silt Lagoons

Nature Reserve

A1306

A13

5

Wennington Marshes

Thurrock Commercial Pk

Purfleet Ind Pk

Thurrock Commercial Ctr

LONDON RD

KERRY AVE

JULIETTE WAY

JULIETTE WAY

5

80

COLDHARBOUR LA

RM15

4

Purfleet Rifle Ranges

4

Aveley Marshes

3

3

79

Freightmaster Est

RM19

MARINE DR

MARINE CT

RAPIER CL

CENTURION WAY

RIVER CT

AMBERLEY

2

River Thames

TANK HILL RD

LONDON ROAD PURFLEET

Hotel

2

1

Erith Rands

Crayford Ness

Darent Valley Path

Mast

Darent Ind Pk

DARENT RD

LANDAU WAY

DAYTON DR

BIRRELL RD

DA8

1

78

Kent STREET ATLAS

52 A 53 B C 54 D E F

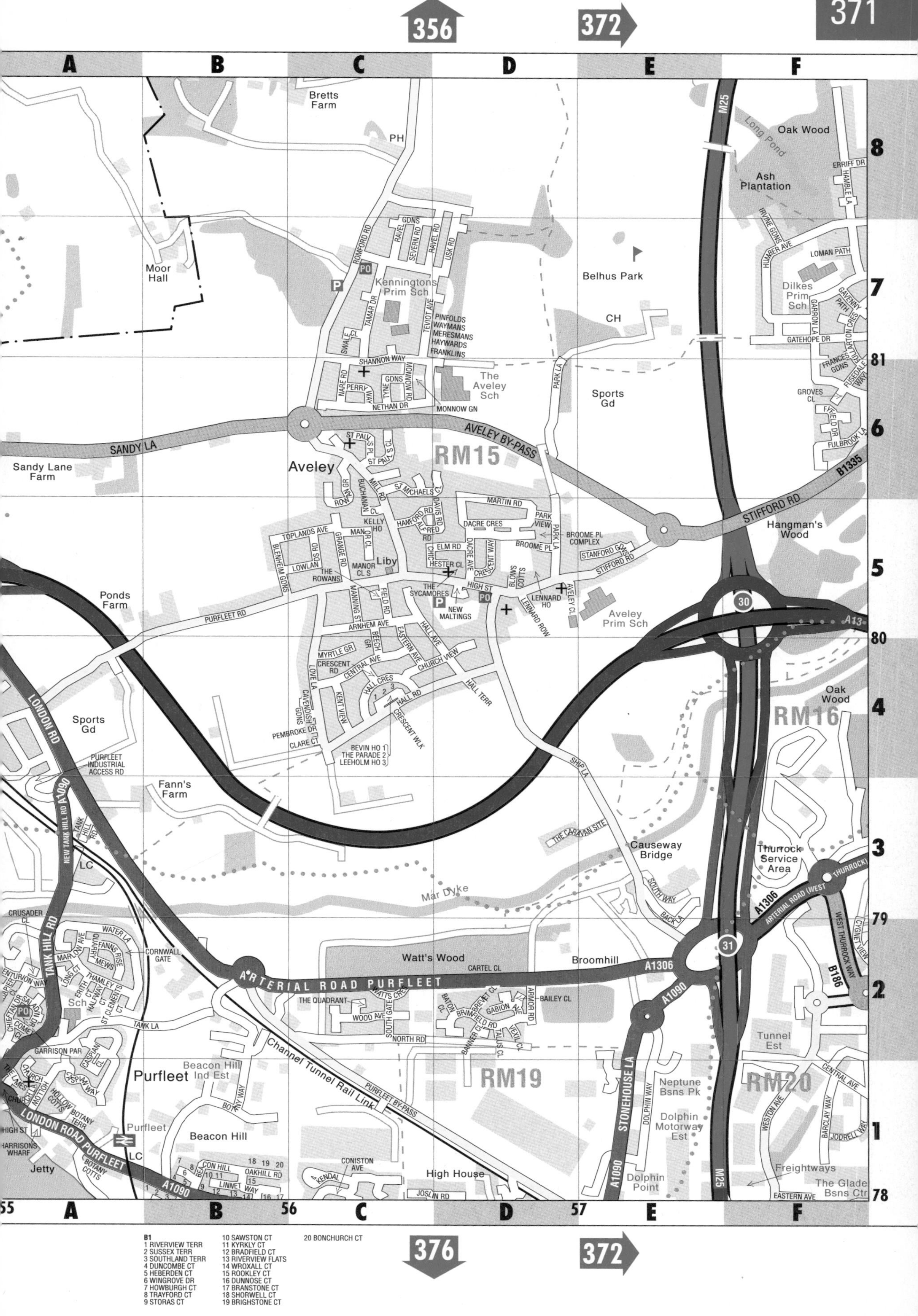

B1
1 RIVERVIEW TERR
2 SUSSEX TERR
3 SOUTHLAND TERR
4 DUNCOMBE CT
5 HEBERDEN CT
6 WINGROVE DR
7 HOWBURGH CT
8 TRAYFORD CT
9 STORAS CT
10 SAWSTON CT
11 KYRKLY CT
12 BRADFIELD CT
13 RIVERVIEW FLATS
14 WROXALL CT
15 ROOKLEY CT
16 DUNNOSE CT
17 BRANSTONE CT
18 SHORWELL CT
19 BRIGHSTONE CT
20 BONCHURCH CT

371
357

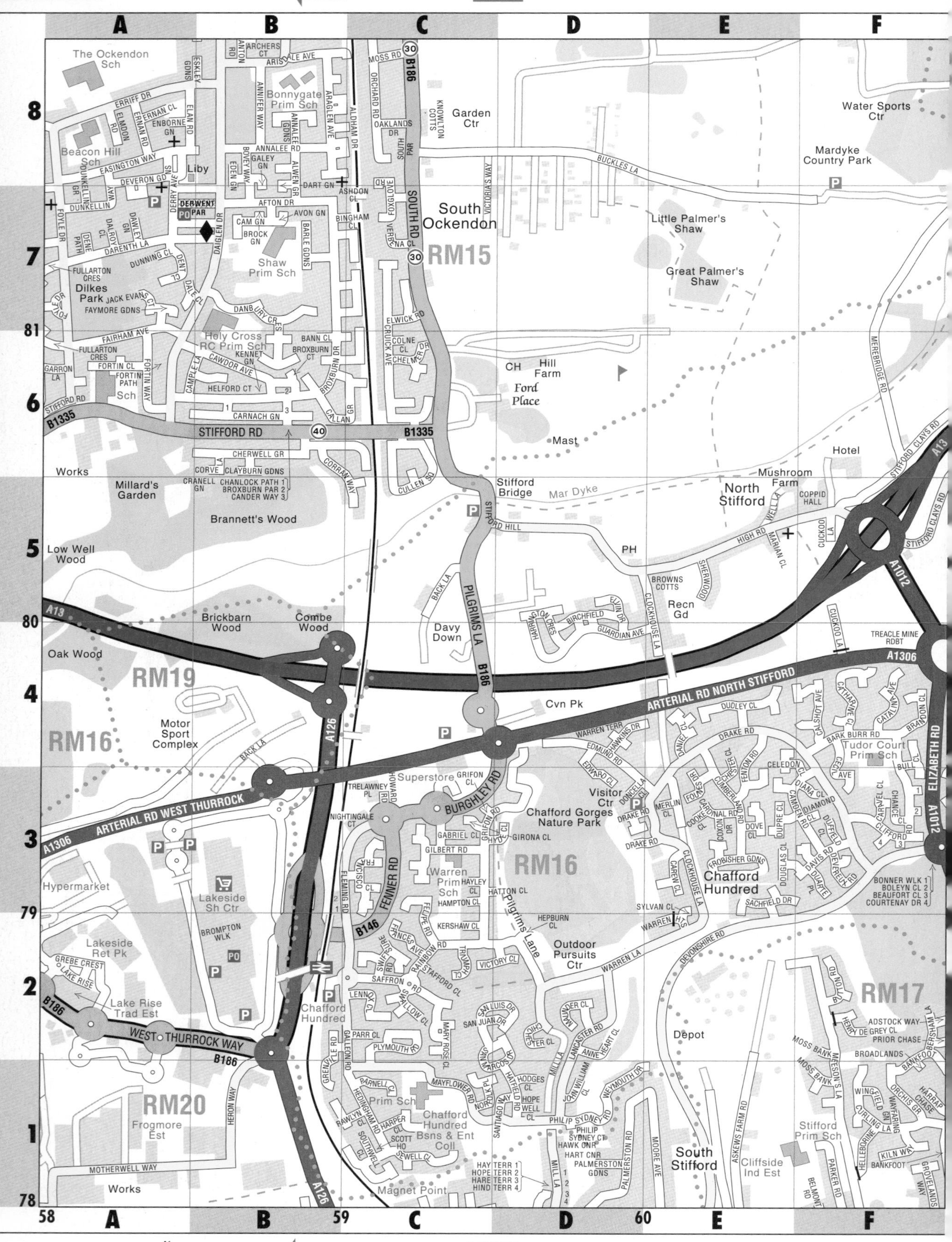

A1
1 GOWER PL
2 Ascension Bsns Pk

371
377

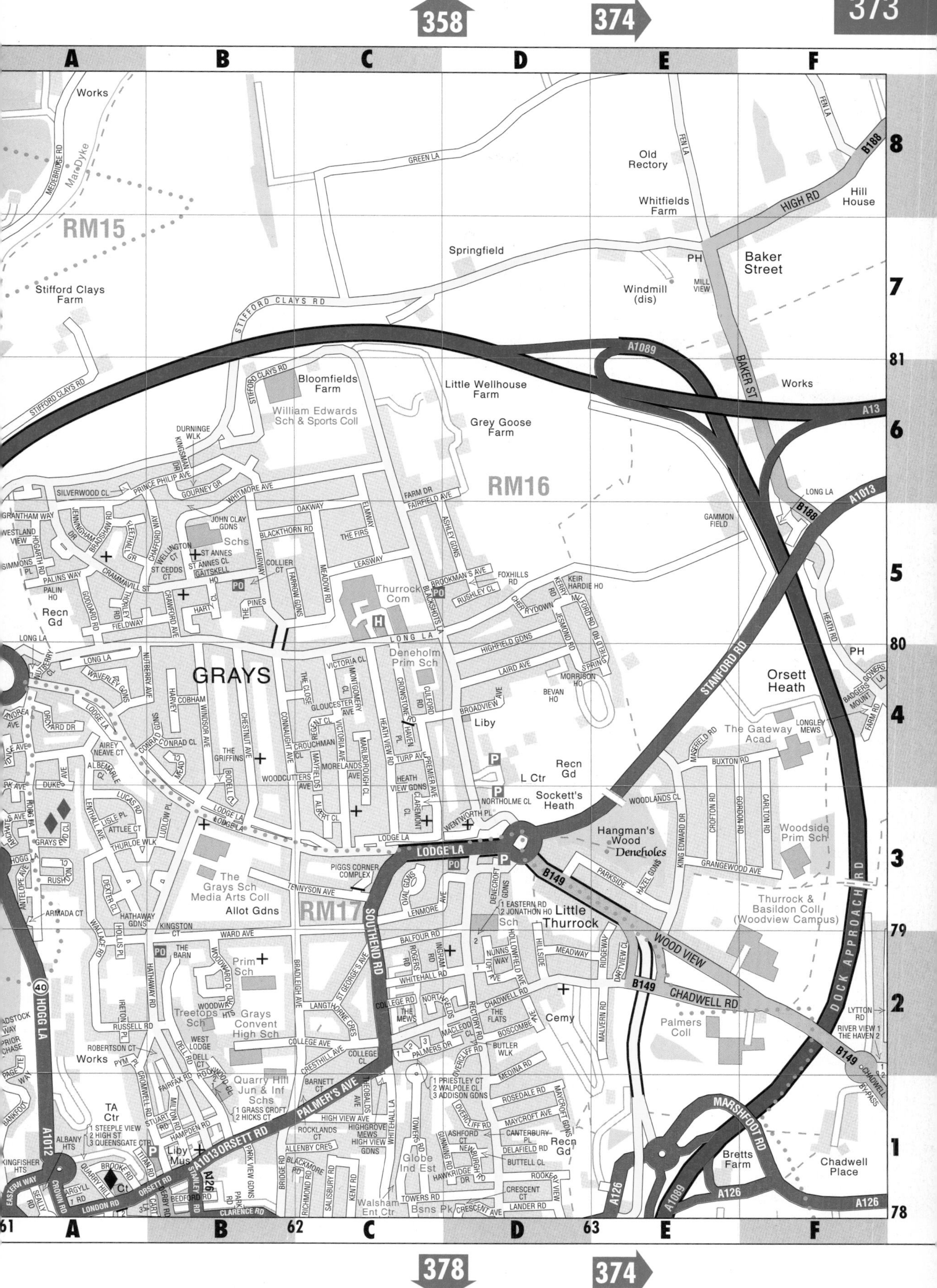
358
374
A
B
C
D
E
F
8
7
81
6
5
80
4
3
79
2
1
78
61
62
63
RM15
RM16
RM17
GRAYS
Works
Stifford Clays Farm
STIFFORD CLAYS RD
GREEN LA
Springfield
Old Rectory
Whitfields Farm
Windmill (dis)
PH
Baker Street
Hill House
HIGH RD
B188
FEN LA
BAKER ST
A1089
A13
Bloomfields Farm
William Edwards Sch & Sports Coll
Little Wellhouse Farm
Grey Goose Farm
LONG LA
A1013
GAMMON FIELD
Thurrock Com
Deneholm Prim Sch
Recn Gd
Liby
L Ctr
Sockett's Heath
STANFORD RD
Orsett Heath
The Gateway Acad
Woodside Prim Sch
Hangman's Wood Deneholes
LODGE LA
The Grays Sch Media Arts Coll
Allot Gdns
SOUTHEND RD
Little Thurrock
Thurrock & Basildon Coll (Woodview Campus)
WOOD VIEW
B149
CHADWELL RD
DOCK APPROACH RD
Palmers Coll
Cemy
Prim Sch
Treetops Sch
Grays Convent High Sch
Quarry Hill Jun & Inf Schs
TA Ctr
Liby Mus
HOGG LA
A1012
A1013 ORSETT RD
PALMER'S AVE
Globe Ind Est
Walsham Ent Ctr
Bsns Pk
MARSHFOOT RD
Bretts Farm
Chadwell Place
A126
378
374

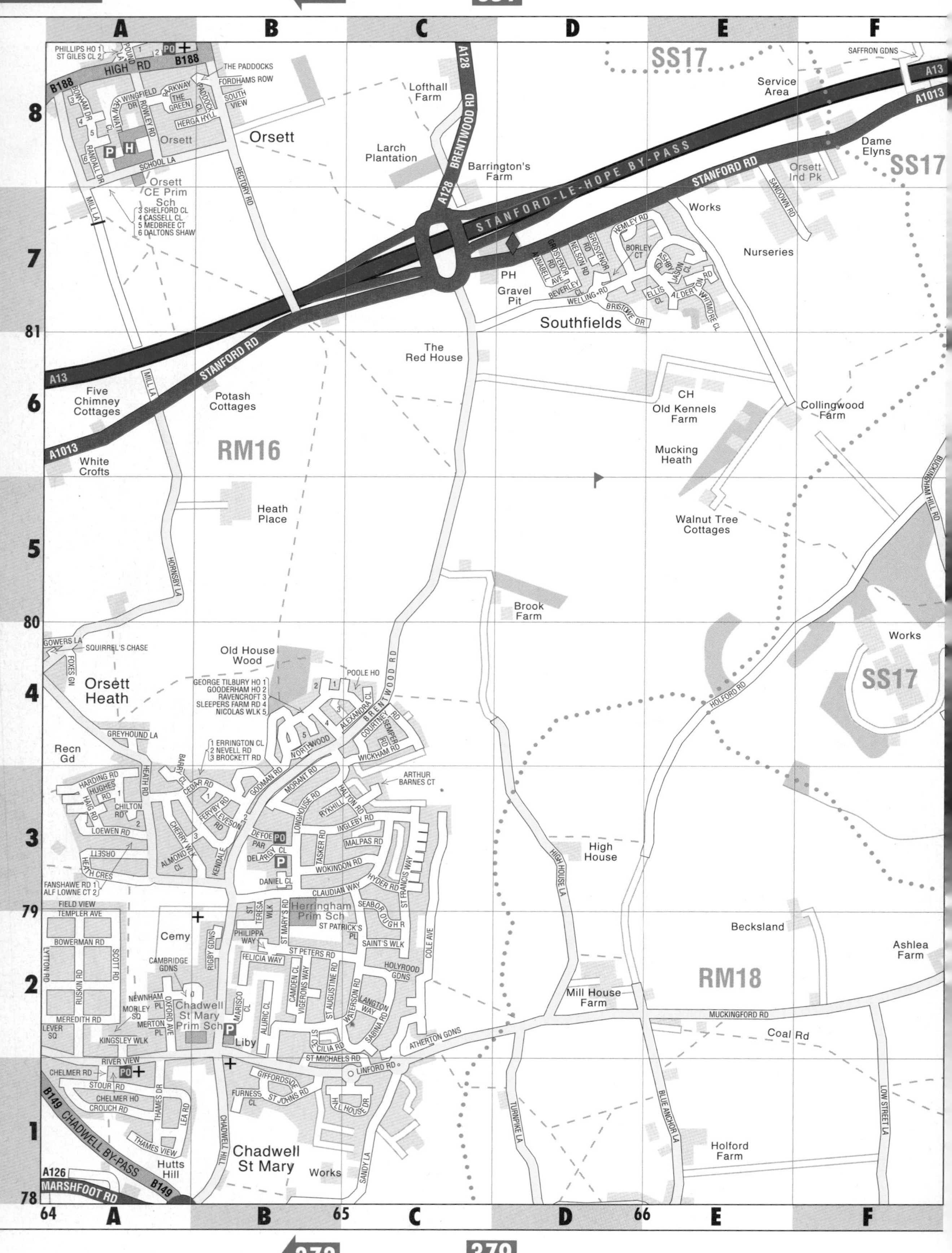

373
359

A **B** **C** **D** **E** **F**

8

SS17

SAFFRON GDNS

Phillips Ho 1
St Giles Cl 2
HIGH RD
B188
PO
B188
THE PADDOCKS
FORDHAMS ROW
SOUTH VIEW
HERGA HYL
A13
A1013
Service Area
Dame Elyns
SS17

Orsett

Lofthall Farm

Larch Plantation

A128
BRENTWOOD RD

Barrington's Farm

STANFORD-LE-HOPE BY-PASS
STANFORD RD

Works

Orsett Ind Pk

Nurseries

Orsett CE Prim Sch
3 SHELFORD CL
4 CASSELL CL
5 MEDBREE CT
6 DALTONS SHAW
SCHOOL LA
RECTORY RD
MILL LA

7

A128

PH
Gravel Pit

HEMLEY RD
BORLEY CT
GROSVENOR RD
NELSON RD
CROSTON
ANNABEL
BEVERLEY GL
WELLING RD
BRISTOW DR
ASHLEY
ALDER
ELLIS
WILBUR CL

Southfields

81

The Red House

CH
Old Kennels Farm

Collingwood Farm

6

A13
STANFORD RD
MILL LA

Five Chimney Cottages

Potash Cottages

RM16

Mucking Heath

A1013

White Crofts

Heath Place

Walnut Tree Cottages

5

Works

80

GOWERS LA
SQUIRREL'S CHASE
FOXES GN
HORNSBY LA

Old House Wood

Brook Farm

SS17

4

Orsett Heath

GEORGE TILBURY HO 1
GOODERHAM HO 2
RAVENSCROFT 3
SLEEPERS FARM RD 4
NICOLAS WLK 5

POOLE HO
ALEXANDRA CL
BRENTWOOD RD
COURTNEY RD
NORTHWOOD
KEMPER

HOLFORD RD

GREYHOUND LA

1 ERRINGTON CL
2 NEVELL RD
3 BROCKETT RD

WICKHAM RD

ARTHUR BARNES CT

High House

HIGH HOUSE LA

Recn Gd

HARDING RD
HUGHES RD
HAIG RD
CHILTON RD
LOEWEN RD
HEATH RD
ORSETT
HEATH CRES
BARRY CL
CEDAR RD
CHERRY WLK
ALMOND CL
FERRYBY RD
KEMDALE
LEVESON RD
DEFOE PAR
DELARGY CL
PO
GODMAN RD
LONGHOUSE RD
MORANT RD
RYKHILL RD
TASKER RD
MALPAS RD
WOKINDON RD
HYDER CL
CLAUDIAN WAY
ST FRANCIS WAY
INGLEBY RD
SEABOR CL
DANIEL CL

3

FANSHAWE RD 1
ALF LOWNE CT 2
FIELD VIEW

Becksland

Ashlea Farm

79

TEMPLER AVE
BOWERMAN RD
LYTTON RD
RUSKIN RD
SCOTT RD
MEREDITH RD
LEVER SQ
NEWNHAM
MORLEY
SQ
PL
KINGSLEY WLK

Cemy

CAMBRIDGE GDNS
MERTON AVE

Chadwell St Mary Prim Sch

RIGBY GDNS
PHILIPPA WAY
FELICIA WAY
MARISCO
VIGERONS WAY
CAMDEN CL
ALLURIC CL
ST TERESA RD
ST MARY'S RD
ST PATRICK'S PL
ST PETERS RD
SAINT'S WLK
WATHERSON WAY
ST AUGUSTINE RD
LANGTON WAY
SABINA RD
HOLYROOD GDNS

Herringham Prim Sch

COLE AVE

Mill House Farm

RM18

MUCKINGFORD RD

Coal Rd

2

RIVER VIEW
CHELMER RD
PO
STOUR RD
CHELMER HO
CROUCH RD
THAMES DR
LEA RD
CHADWELL HILL
Liby
GIFFORDS CL
ST JOHNS RD
FURNESS CL
CILIA ST
ST MICHAELS RD
ATHERTON GDNS
LINFORD RD
HILL HOUSE DR

TURNPIKE LA
BLUE ANCHOR LA

Holford Farm

1

B149 CHADWELL BY-PASS
B149
THAMES VIEW

Hutts Hill

Chadwell St Mary

SANDY LA

Works

LOW STREET LA

A126
MARSHFOOT RD

78

64
A **B** 65 **C** **D** 66 **E** **F**

360
366

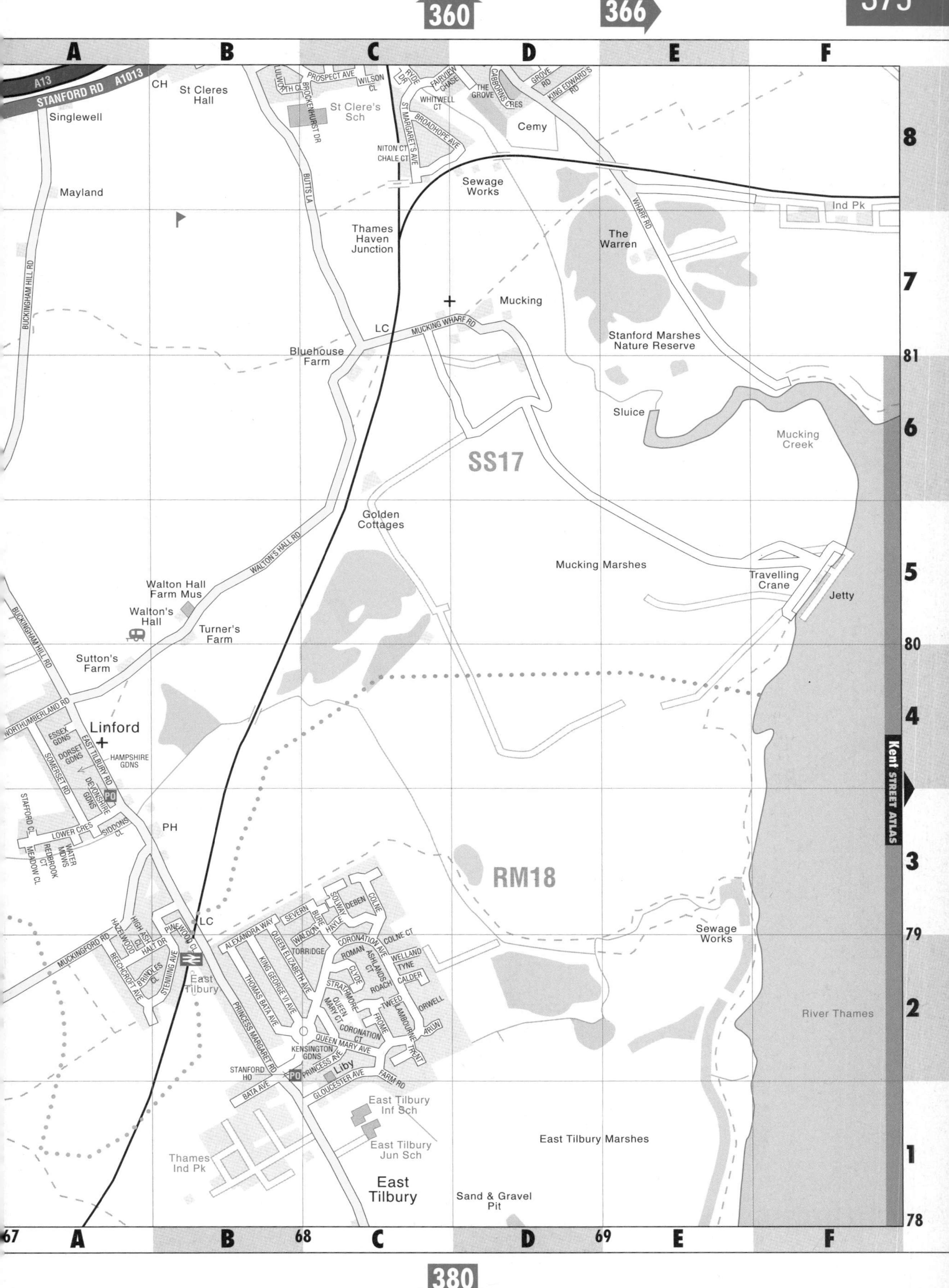
A13
A1013
STANFORD RD
CH
St Cleres Hall
Singlewell
Mayland
St Clere's Sch
Cemy
Sewage Works
Thames Haven Junction
The Warren
Ind Pk
Mucking
LC
Bluehouse Farm
Stanford Marshes Nature Reserve
Sluice
Mucking Creek
SS17
Golden Cottages
Mucking Marshes
Travelling Crane
Jetty
Walton Hall Farm Mus
Walton's Hall
Turner's Farm
Sutton's Farm
Linford
PH
RM18
Sewage Works
East Tilbury
River Thames
Liby
East Tilbury Inf Sch
East Tilbury Jun Sch
Thames Ind Pk
East Tilbury Marshes
East Tilbury
Sand & Gravel Pit
Kent STREET ATLAS

380

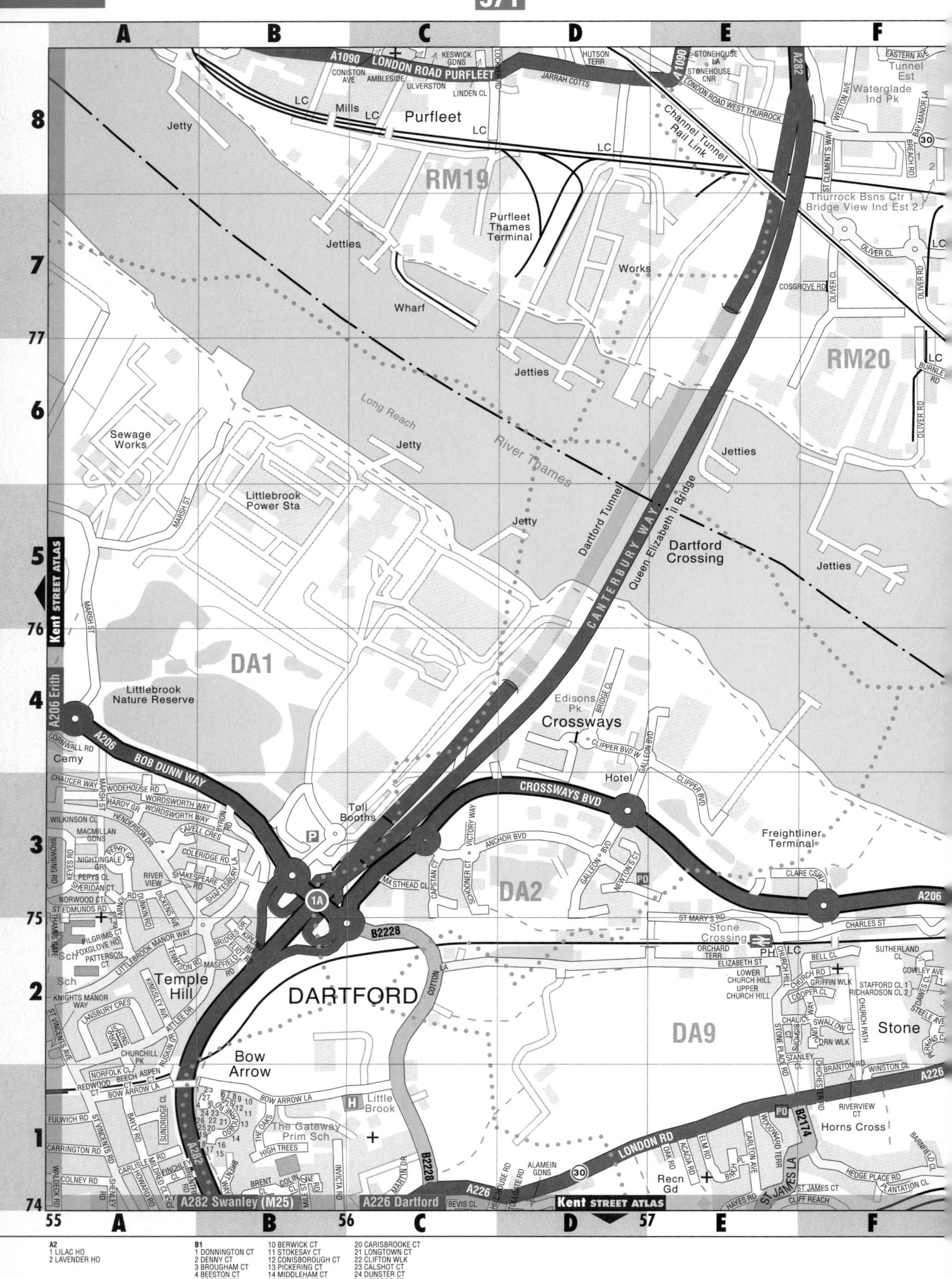

371

A2
1 LILAC HO
2 LAVENDER HO

B1
1 DONNINGTON CT
2 DENNY CT
3 BROUGHAM CT
4 BEESTON CT
5 ORFORD CT
6 ALNWICK CT
7 BRAMBER CT
8 KENILWORTH CT
9 WARDOUR CT
10 BERWICK CT
11 STOKESAY CT
12 CONISBOROUGH CT
13 PICKERING CT
14 MIDDLEHAM CT
15 PRUDHOE CT
16 NORHAM CT
17 BOWES CT
18 BARNARD CT
19 TATTERSHALL CT
20 CARISBROOKE CT
21 LONGTOWN CT
22 CLIFTON WLK
23 CALSHOT CT
24 DUNSTER CT
25 LYDFORD CT
26 PEVERIL CT
27 HARDWICK CRES
28 GRANGE CRES

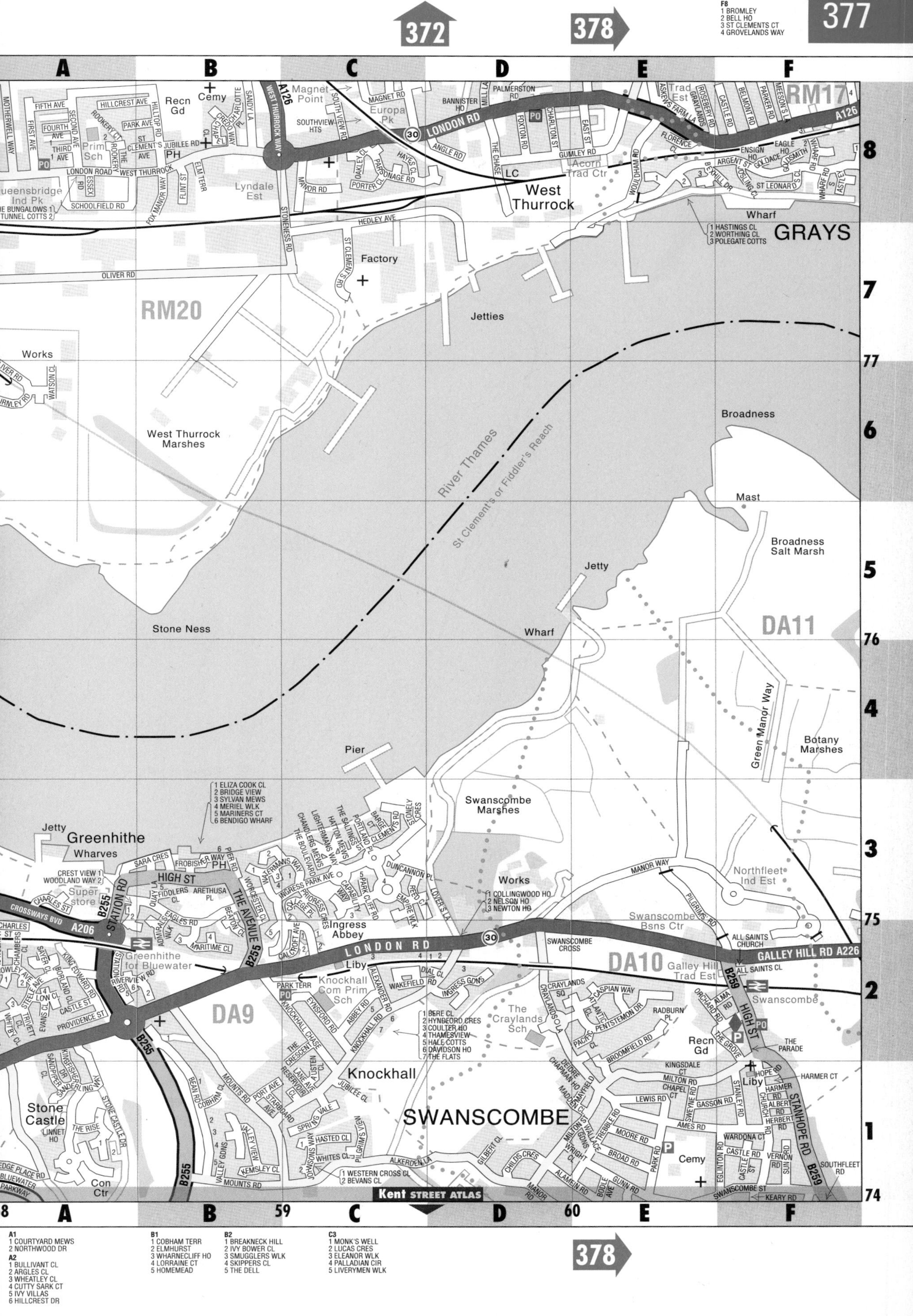

377
372
378
F8
1 BROMLEY
2 BELL HO
3 ST CLEMENTS CT
4 GROVELANDS WAY
A
B
C
D
E
F
8
7
77
6
5
76
4
3
75
2
1
74
58
59
60
RM17
RM20
DA11
DA10
DA9
GRAYS
West Thurrock
Lyndale Est
Recn Gd
Cemy
Prim Sch
PH
Magnet Point
Europa Pk
Trad Est
Acorn Trad Ctr
LC
Wharf
1 HASTINGS CL
2 WORTHING CL
3 POLEGATE COTTS
Factory
Jetties
Works
West Thurrock Marshes
River Thames
St Clement's or Fiddler's Reach
Broadness
Mast
Broadness Salt Marsh
Jetty
Wharf
Stone Ness
Green Manor Way
Botany Marshes
Pier
Swanscombe Marshes
Northfleet Ind Est
Swanscombe Bsns Ctr
Greenhithe
Wharves
Jetty
1 ELIZA COOK CL
2 BRIDGE VIEW
3 SYLVAN MEWS
4 MERIEL WLK
5 MARINERS CT
6 BENDIGO WHARF
1 COLLINGWOOD HO
2 NELSON HO
3 NEWTON HO
Ingress Abbey
Super store
Greenhithe for Bluewater
LONDON RD
HIGH ST
THE AVENUE
STATION RD
CROSSWAYS BVD
A206
B255
A126
GALLEY HILL RD A226
Galley Hill Trad Est
Swanscombe
Liby
Knockhall Com Prim Sch
1 BERE CL
2 HYNDFORD CRES
3 COULTER HO
4 THAMESVIEW
5 HALE COTTS
6 DAVIDSON HO
7 THE FLATS
The Craylands Sch
Knockhall
SWANSCOMBE
Recn Gd
Cemy
Stone Castle
Con Ctr
1 WESTERN CROSS CL
2 BEVANS CL
Kent STREET ATLAS
A1
1 COURTYARD MEWS
2 NORTHWOOD DR
A2
1 BULLIVANT CL
2 ARGLES CL
3 WHEATLEY CL
4 CUTTY SARK CT
5 IVY VILLAS
6 HILLCREST DR
B1
1 COBHAM TERR
2 ELMHURST
3 WHARNECLIFF HO
4 LORRAINE CT
5 HOMEMEAD
B2
1 BREAKNECK HILL
2 IVY BOWER CL
3 SMUGGLERS WLK
4 SKIPPERS CL
5 THE DELL
C3
1 MONK'S WELL
2 LUCAS CRES
3 ELEANOR WLK
4 PALLADIAN CIR
5 LIVERYMEN WLK
378

377

373

C8
1 ALFRED ST
2 PERCY ST
3 HENRY ST
4 ST THOMAS'S PL
5 RICHMOND RD
6 SALISBURY RD

C8
7 HARWOOD CT
8 KENSINGTON CT
9 TRASA CT
10 CEMENT BLOCK COTTS
11 SPURGEON CL
12 ARTHUR CT

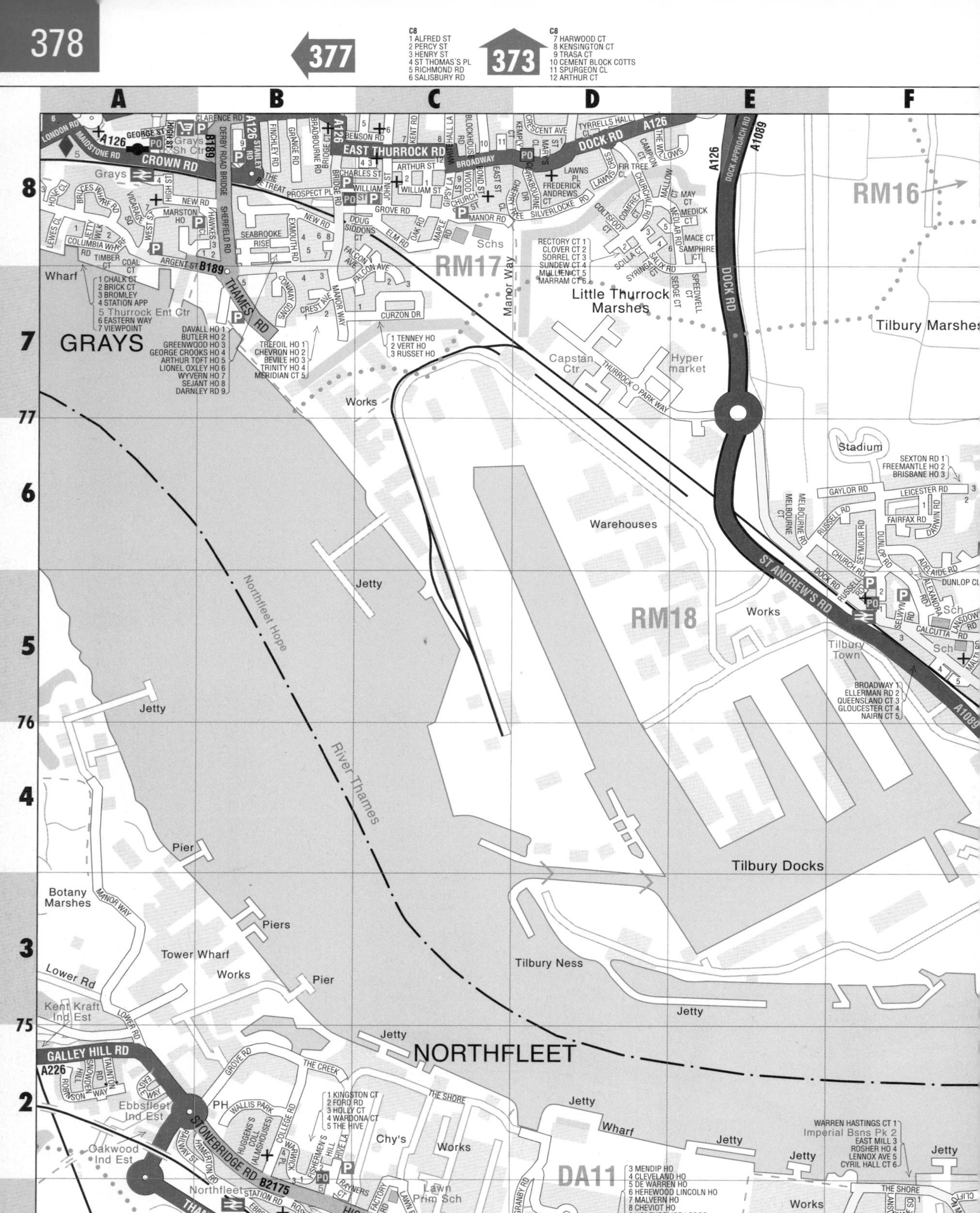

377

374
380

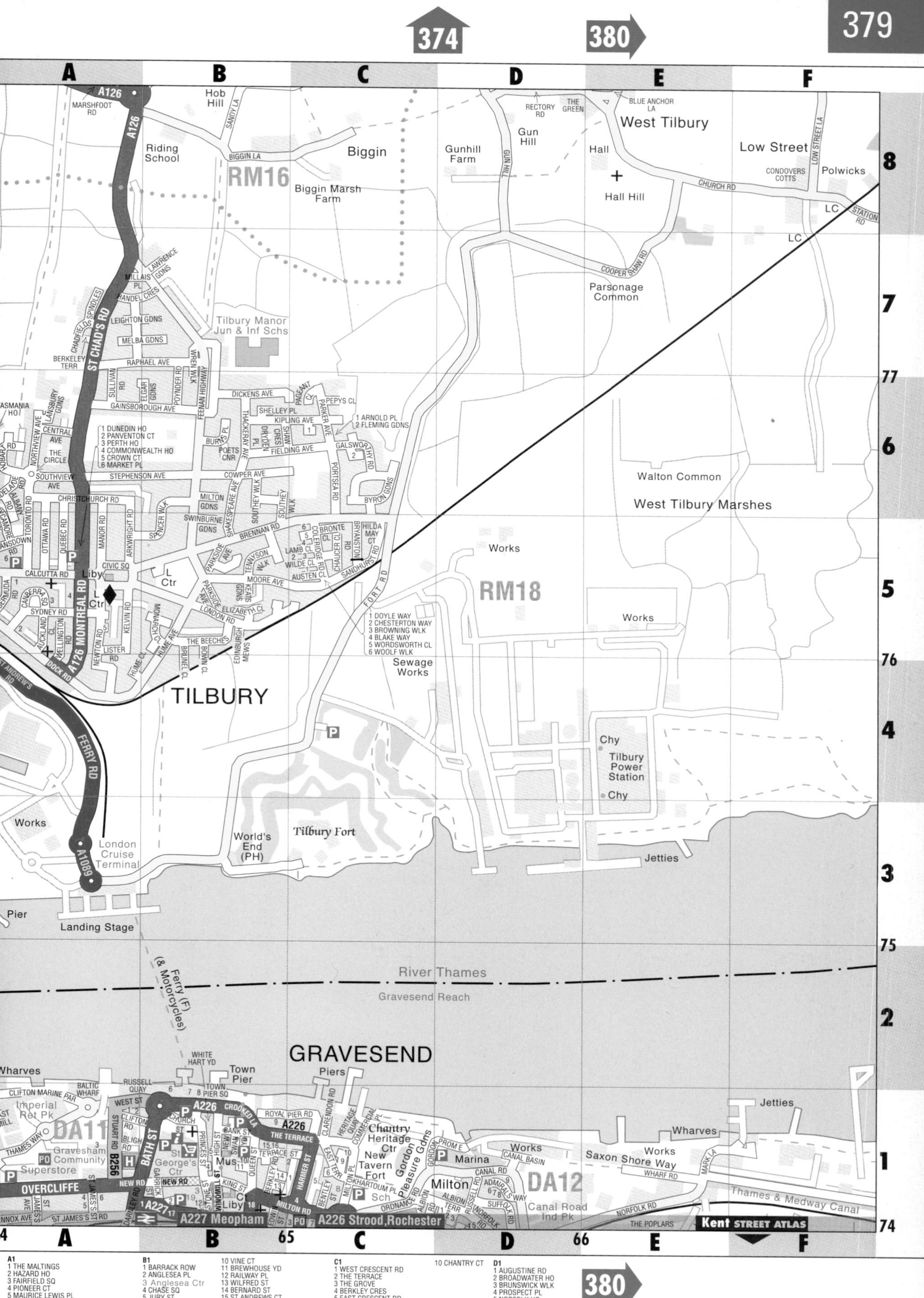

A1
1 THE MALTINGS
2 HAZARD HO
3 FAIRFIELD SQ
4 PIONEER CT
5 MAURICE LEWIS PL
6 ELIZABETH CT

B1
1 BARRACK ROW
2 ANGLESEA PL
3 Anglesea Ctr
4 CHASE SQ
5 JURY ST
6 CRAWLEY CT
7 REGENTS CT
8 MELBOURNE QUAY
9 ROYAL PIER MEWS
10 VINE CT
11 BREWHOUSE YD
12 RAILWAY PL
13 WILFRED ST
14 BERNARD ST
15 ST ANDREWS CT
16 CROSS ST
17 CLIVE RD
18 PARROCK ST
19 Thamesgate Sh Ctr

C1
1 WEST CRESCENT RD
2 THE TERRACE
3 THE GROVE
4 BERKLEY CRES
5 EAST CRESCENT RD
6 PILOTS PL
7 PEACOCK ST
8 Bentley Street Ind Est
9 GORDON PL
10 CHANTRY CT

D1
1 AUGUSTINE RD
2 BROADWATER HO
3 BRUNSWICK WLK
4 PROSPECT PL
5 NORFOLK HO
6 RAVENS CT
7 MEDUZA CT
8 AMAZON CT
9 FISGARD CT

380

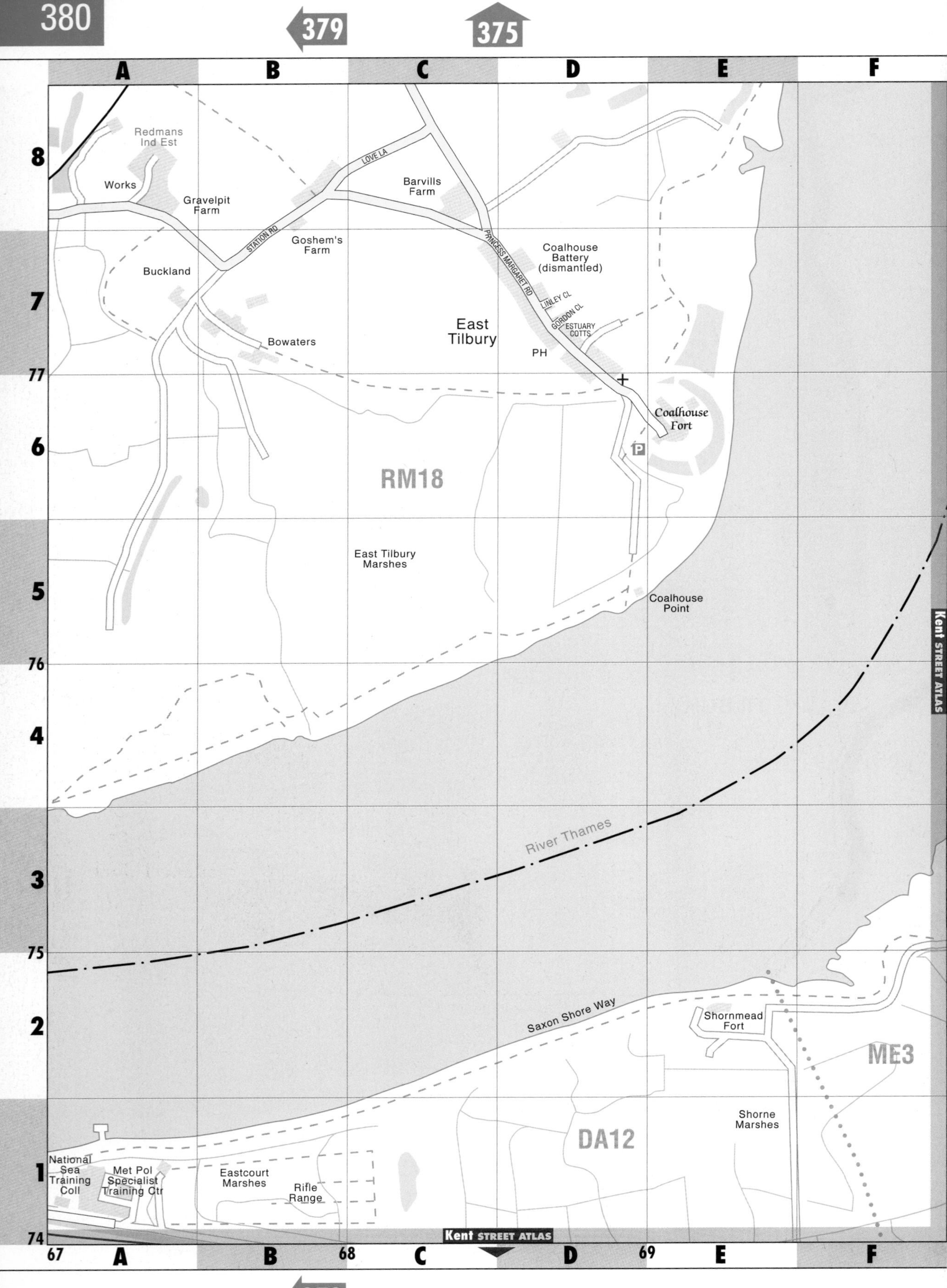

A B C D E F

8

Redmans
Ind Est

Works

LOVE LA

Gravelpit
Farm

Barvills
Farm

STATION RD

Goshem's
Farm

PRINCESS MARGARET RD

Coalhouse
Battery
(dismantled)

7

Buckland

Bowaters

East
Tilbury

LINLEY CL

GORDON CL

ESTUARY
COTTS

PH

77

Coalhouse
Fort

6

P

RM18

5

East Tilbury
Marshes

Coalhouse
Point

76

4

River Thames

3

75

2

Saxon Shore Way

Shornmead
Fort

ME3

1

National
Sea
Training
Coll

Met Pol
Specialist
Training Ctr

Eastcourt
Marshes

Rifle
Range

DA12

Shorne
Marshes

74

Kent STREET ATLAS

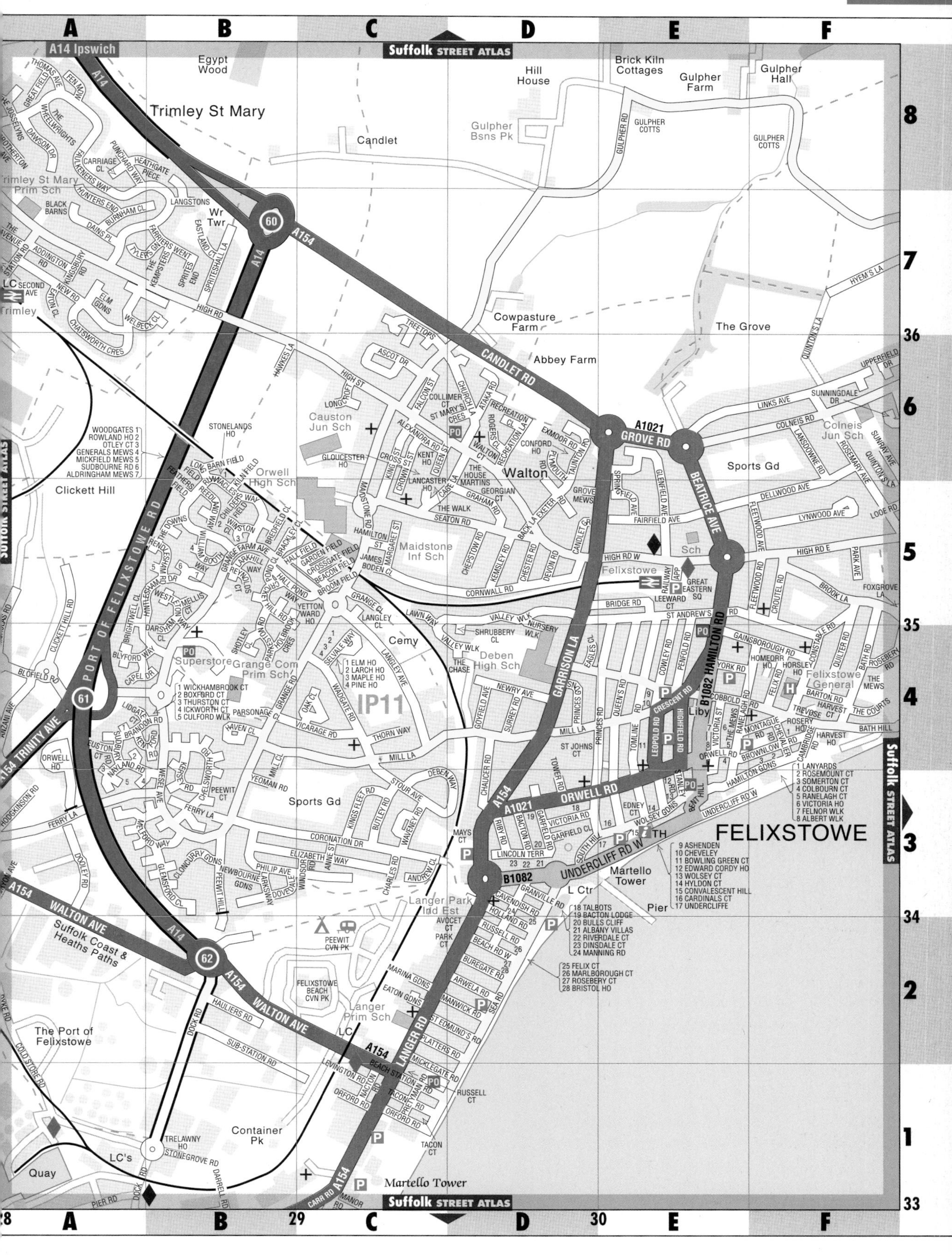

FELIXSTOWE

IP11

1 LANYARDS
2 ROSEMOUNT CT
3 SOMERTON CT
4 COLBOURN CT
5 RANELAGH CT
6 VICTORIA HO
7 FELNOR WLK
8 ALBERT WLK
9 ASHENDEN
10 CHEVELEY
11 BOWLING GREEN CT
12 EDWARD CORDY HO
13 WOLSEY CT
14 HYLDON CT
15 CONVALESCENT HILL
16 CARDINALS CT
17 UNDERCLIFFE
18 TALBOTS
19 BACTON LODGE
20 BULLS CLIFF
21 ALBANY VILLAS
22 RIVERDALE CT
23 DINSDALE CT
24 MANNING RD
25 FELIX CT
26 MARLBOROUGH CT
27 ROSEBERY CT
28 BRISTOL HO

1 WICKHAMBROOK CT
2 BOXFORD CT
3 THURSTON CT
4 ICKWORTH CT
5 CULFORD WLK

WOODGATES 1
ROWLAND HO 2
OTLEY CT 3
GENERALS MEWS 4
MICKFIELD MEWS 5
SUDBOURNE RD 6
ALDRINGHAM MEWS 7

1 ELM HO
2 LARCH HO
3 MAPLE HO
4 PINE HO

242

264

Sales
Point

Tip
Head

Community
Settlement

St Peter's
Chapel

St Peter's Flat
Nature Reserve

Gunner's Creek

CMO

St Peter's Way

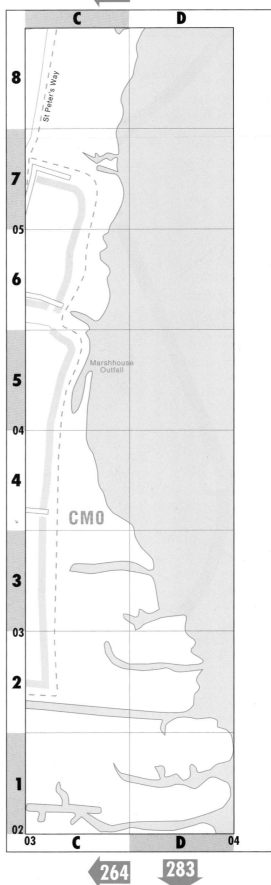

St Peter's Way

Marshhouse
Outfall

CMO

242

264   283

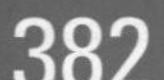

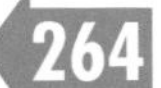

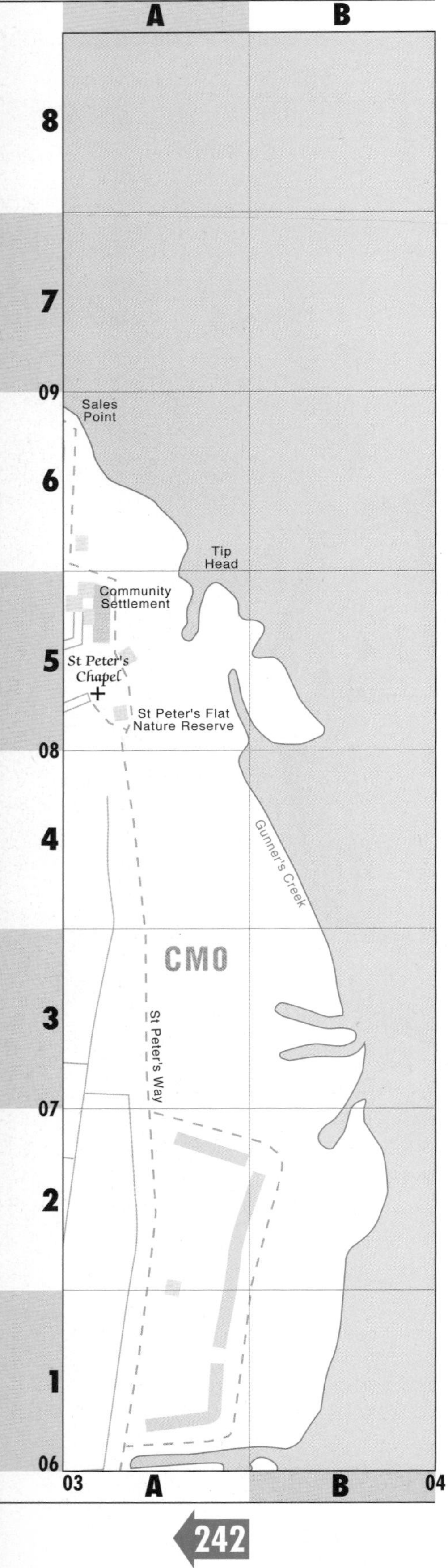

A **B**

C **D**

8

01

7

97

6

CMO

CMO

5

River Crouch

00

Ray Sand

96

4

3

95

East
Newlands

The Drift
(dis)

99

SS3

2

1

DANGER AREA

98

94

Index

Place name May be abbreviated on the map

Location number Present when a number indicates the place's position in a crowded area of mapping

Locality, town or village Shown when more than one place has the same name

Postcode district District for the indexed place

Page and grid square Page number and grid reference for the standard mapping

Church Rd 6 Beckenham BR2.........**53** C6

Cities, towns and villages are listed in CAPITAL LETTERS

Public and commercial buildings are highlighted in magenta   **Places of interest** are highlighted in blue with a star★

Abbreviations used in the index

Acad	Academy	Comm	Common	Gd	Ground	L	Leisure	Prom	Promenade
App	Approach	Cott	Cottage	Gdn	Garden	La	Lane	Rd	Road
Arc	Arcade	Cres	Crescent	Gn	Green	Liby	Library	Recn	Recreation
Ave	Avenue	Cswy	Causeway	Gr	Grove	Mdw	Meadow	Ret	Retail
Bglw	Bungalow	Ct	Court	H	Hall	Meml	Memorial	Sh	Shopping
Bldg	Building	Ctr	Centre	Ho	House	Mkt	Market	Sq	Square
Bsns, Bus	Business	Ctry	Country	Hospl	Hospital	Mus	Museum	St	Street
Bvd	Boulevard	Cty	County	HQ	Headquarters	Orch	Orchard	Sta	Station
Cath	Cathedral	Dr	Drive	Hts	Heights	Pal	Palace	Terr	Terrace
Cir	Circus	Dro	Drove	Ind	Industrial	Par	Parade	TH	Town Hall
Cl	Close	Ed	Education	Inst	Institute	Pas	Passage	Univ	University
Cnr	Corner	Emb	Embankment	Int	International	Pk	Park	Wk, Wlk	Walk
Coll	College	Est	Estate	Intc	Interchange	Pl	Place	Wr	Water
Com	Community	Ex	Exhibition	Junc	Junction	Prec	Precinct	Yd	Yard

Index of towns, villages, streets, hospitals, industrial estates, railway stations, schools, shopping centres, universities and places of interest

Albert Cres E4 .... 309 A6
Albert Ct CM7 .... 128 A3
Albert Dr SS15 .... 341 C6
Albert Gdns
Clacton-on-S CO15 .... 196 B3
Coggeshall CO6 .... 131 A2
Harlow CM17 .... 224 D7
Albert Ho Ipswich IP2 .... 17 B4
5 Wanstead E18 .... 332 B8
Albertine Cl CO3 .... 134 C6
Albert Mews Romford RM1 335 F5
Southend-on-S SS0 .... 366 E8
Albert Pl CO6 .... 131 A2
Albert Rd Braintree CM7 .. 128 A3
Brightlingsea CO7 .... 193 A6
Buckhurst Hill IG9 .... 310 D8
Bulphan RM14 .... 358 F8
Burnham-on-C CM0 .... 306 C4
Dagenham RM8 .... 335 A3
Ilford IG1 .... 333 C1
Rayleigh SS6 .... 323 F3
Rochford SS4 .... 325 C7
Romford RM1 .... 335 F5
South Benfleet SS7 .... 344 B6
Southend-on-S, Bournes Green
SS1 .... 349 A1
Southend-on-S SS1 .... 367 B7
South Woodham Ferrers
CM3 .... 301 D7
Swanscombe DA10 .... 377 F1
4 Wanstead E18 .... 332 B8
Witham CM8 .... 184 A3
Albert St Brentwood CM14 .. 316 C5
Colchester CO1 .... 135 E8
Harwich CO12 .... 91 D5
Albert Terr IG9 .... 310 E8
Albert Wlk IP11 .... 381 E4
Albion Cl RM7 .... 335 D5
Albion Ct Billericay CM12 .. 297 A1
Chelmsford CM2 .... 232 B1
Albion Gr CO2 .... 136 A5
Albion Hill Ipswich IP4 .... 17 F7
Loughton IG10 .... 288 D4
Albion Pk IG10 .... 288 D4
Albion Rd Dagenham RM10 . 353 F7
Gravesend DA12 .... 379 D1
South Benfleet SS7 .... 344 D4
Southend-on-S SS0 .... 347 E1
Albion St CO5 .... 164 A8
Albion Terr
Gravesend DA12 .... 379 D1
Sewardstone E4 .... 287 B5
Albra Mead CM2 .... 233 B4
Albright Ind Est RM13 .... 369 F8
Albrighton Croft CO4 .... 110 C4
Albury Mews E12 .... 332 C2
Albyns SS16 .... 341 C4
Albyns Cl RM13 .... 355 A5
Albyns La RM4 .... 291 D7
Alcester Ho 14 RM3 .... 314 D5
Alconbury CM23 .... 119 B1
Alcorns The CM24 .... 119 E7
Alcotes SS14 .... 342 F5
Aldborough Ct
Chingford E4 .... 309 B7
Ilford IG2 .... 333 F6
ALDBOROUGH HATCH 333 F7
Aldborough Rd
Dagenham RM10 .... 354 C6
Ilford, Aldborough Hatch
IG2 .... 333 F8
Ilford IG1 .... 333 E2
Upminster RM14 .... 337 A2
Aldborough Rd N IG2 .... 333 F6
Aldborough Rd S IG3 .... 333 E4
Aldeburgh Cl
Clacton-on-S CO16 .... 195 B4
Haverhill CB9 .... 8 E7
Aldeburgh Gdns
Colchester CO4 .... 110 B4
Ipswich IP4 .... 18 A6
Aldeburgh Pl IG8 .... 310 A6
Aldeburgh Way CM1 .... 232 D5
Alder Ave RM14 .... 355 F8
Alderbury Lea CM3 .... 256 F1
Alderbury Rd CM24 .... 119 E8
Aldercar Rd CO6 .... 133 F1
Alder Cl Basildon SS15 .... 319 D1
Bishop's Stortford CM23 .. 145 D4
Hoddesdon EN11 .... 221 B8
Alde Rd CB9 .... 9 A8
Alder Dr Chelmsford CM2 .. 254 B6
South Ockendon RM15 .... 357 C1
Alderford Maltings CO9 .... 75 E8
Alderford St CO9 .... 75 E8
Aldergrove Wlk RM12 .... 355 C6
Alderlee IP2 .... 36 F8
Alderleys SS7 .... 345 A6
Alderman Ave IG11 .... 353 A2
Alderman Blaxhill Sch
CO2 .... 135 B3
Alderman Howe Lodge
CO4 .... 110 B4
Alderman Rd IP1 .... 17 B5
Aldermans Hill SS5 .... 324 C5
Alderman Wlk SS17 .... 360 E5
Alderney Gdns SS11 .... 299 C2
Alders Ave IG8 .... 309 E4
ALDERSBROOK 332 C2
Aldersbrook La E12 .... 332 F1
Aldersbrook Prim Sch
E12 .... 332 C2
Aldersbrook Rd E12 .... 332 C2
Alders Cl E11 .... 332 B2
Aldersey Gdns IG11 .... 352 D6
Aldersgrove EN9 .... 265 E5
Alders Wlk CM21 .... 172 E2
Alderton Cl Felsted CM6 .. 152 C6
Loughton IG10 .... 289 A5
Pilgrims Hatch CM15 .... 294 B4
Alderton Hall La IG10 .... 289 A5
Alderton Hill IG10 .... 288 F4
Alderton Jun & Inf Schs The
IG10 .... 289 A4
Alderton Mews IG10 .... 289 A5
Alderton Rd
Colchester CO4 .... 136 C8
Orsett RM16 .... 374 E7
Alderton Rise IG10 .... 289 A5
Alderton Way IG10 .... 288 F4
Alder Way CO10 .... 33 F8
Alder Wlk Ilford IG1 .... 352 D7
Witham CM8 .... 184 B4
Alderwood Cl RM4 .... 290 B6
Alderwood Dr RM4 .... 290 B6
Alderwood Way SS7 .... 345 A6
ALDHAM 133 B8
Aldham Ct 18 CB9 .... 8 E7
Aldham Dr RM15 .... 372 C8
Aldham Gdns SS6 .... 322 F3
Aldham Hall 1 E11 .... 332 A5
Aldingham Ct RM12 .... 355 B7
Aldingham Gdns RM12 .... 355 A7
Aldington Cl RM8 .... 334 C3
Aldis Mews EN3 .... 265 A2
Aldon Cl CO12 .... 90 C1
Aldous Cl CO7 .... 59 C3
Aldria Rd SS17 .... 360 E5
Aldriche Way E4 .... 309 C4
Aldridge Ave 7 EN3 .... 265 A1
Aldridge Cl CM2 .... 233 A4
Aldrin Cl SS17 .... 360 E2
Aldringham Mews IP11 .... 381 B5
Aldrin Way SS9 .... 347 A6
Aldwych Ave IG6 .... 333 C7
Aldwych Cl RM12 .... 336 B2
Alec Kay Ct CO2 .... 135 C2
Aletha Farm Pl CO9 .... 29 D6
Alexander Ct
1 Chelmsford CM1 .... 232 E7
Epping CM16 .... 267 F8
Romford RM7 .... 335 D3
Alexander Hts SS1 .... 368 B8
Alexander La CM15 .... 295 B4
Alexander Mews
Billericay CM12 .... 297 B2
Harlow CM17 .... 224 D6
Howe Green CM2 .... 255 D2
Alexander Rd
Basildon SS16 .... 341 B4
Braintree CM7 .... 127 E4
Greenhithe DA9 .... 377 C2
Alexandra Ave CO5 .... 218 E6
Alexandra Cl RM16 .... 374 C4
Alexandra Ct
Southend-on-S, Clifftown
SS1 .... 366 F7
7 Southend-on-S SS2 .... 347 F1
Alexandra Dr CO7 .... 137 C3
Alexandra Ho 15 IG8 .... 311 A3
Alexandra Mews 7 CM7 .. 128 A2
Alexandra Pl 3 RM1 .... 335 F5
Alexandra Rd
Brentwood CM14 .... 316 C7
Burnham-on-C CM0 .... 306 C5
Clacton-on-S CO15 .... 195 F3
Colchester CO3 .... 135 E6
Dagenham RM6 .... 334 E5
Felixstowe IP11 .... 381 C6
Great Wakering SS3 .... 350 A3
Harwich CO12 .... 91 D5
Ipswich IP4 .... 17 E6
Rainham RM13 .... 354 F4
Rayleigh SS6 .... 323 F3
Rochford SS4 .... 325 C7
Romford RM1 .... 335 F5
Sible Hedingham CO9 .... 51 D1
South Benfleet SS7 .... 344 D2
Southend-on-S, Clifftown
SS1 .... 366 F7
Southend-on-S, Leigh Cliffs
SS9 .... 365 E8
Sudbury CO10 .... 34 A7
Tilbury RM18 .... 378 F5
Wallend E6 .... 352 A2
Wanstead E18 .... 332 B8
Weeley CO16 .... 140 F1
Alexandra St Harwich CO12 . 91 D5
Southend-on-S SS1 .... 367 A7
Alexandra Terr 9 CO3 .... 135 E6
Alexandra Way RM18 .... 375 B3
Alexandria Dr SS6 .... 323 A4
Alexia Ho CM6 .... 123 D1
Alfefounder Cl CO4 .... 136 E6
Alfells Rd CO7 .... 137 F6
Alf Lowne Ct RM16 .... 374 A3
Alford Rd DA8 .... 369 C1
Alfreda Ave SS5 .... 301 D3
Alfred Gdns SS11 .... 299 D2
Alfred Prior Ho 7 E12 .... 352 A8
Alfred Rd Aveley RM15 .... 371 C5
Brentwood CM14 .... 316 D8
Buckhurst Hill IG9 .... 310 D8
Alfred's Gdns IG11 .... 352 E3
Alfred St 1 RM17 .... 378 C8
Alfred's Way (East Ham & Barking By-Pass) IG11 .352 D3
Alfred's Way Ind Est IG11 353 A4
Alfred Terr CO14 .... 171 C8
Alfreg Rd CM8 .... 211 D8
Algars Way CM3 .... 301 D8
Algers Cl IG10 .... 288 D4
Algers Rd IG10 .... 288 E4
Alghers Mead IG10 .... 288 D4
Alibon Gdns RM10 .... 354 A7
Alibon Rd RM10 .... 354 A7
Alicia Ave SS11 .... 322 A7
Alicia Cl SS11 .... 322 A7
Alicia Way SS11 .... 322 A7
Alicia Wlk SS11 .... 322 A7
Alienor Ave CM7 .... 72 B1
Alkerden La DA9, DA10 .... 377 C1
Allandale SS7 .... 345 A7
Allandale Rd RM11 .... 335 F4
Allectus Way CM8 .... 211 D8
Allenby Cres RM17 .... 373 C1
Allenby Dr RM11 .... 336 F3
Allenby Rd IP2 .... 16 F6
Allen Cotts CO6 .... 106 E5
Allendale Dr CO6 .... 133 D4
Allender Ct 2 RM1 .... 335 D7
Allen Ho Braintree CM7 .... 128 A5
Sawbridgeworth CM21 .... 172 F2
Allen Rd RM13 .... 355 C2
Allens Cl CM3 .... 209 F1
Allens Rd CM11 .... 298 C5
Allensway SS17 .... 360 F3
Allen Way Chelmsford CM2 . 233 B4
Point Clear B CO16 .... 193 A3
Allerton Cl SS4 .... 325 C6
Alley Dock SS9 .... 365 D8
Alleyn Court Prep Sch
SS3 .... 349 A3
Alleyn Court Sch SS0 .... 347 C1
Alleyndale Rd RM8 .... 334 C2
Alleyne Way CO15 .... 220 G8
Alleyn Pl SS0 .... 347 C1
Allfields CO12 .... 91 A2
All Hallows Ct IP3 .... 18 A1
Allington Cl IP4 .... 17 F7
Allington Ct CM11 .... 319 C7
Allington Wlk CB9 .... 8 E8
Allis Mews 5 CM17 .... 200 C1
Allison Cl EN9 .... 266 A7
Allistonway SS17 .... 360 F3
Allmains Cl EN9 .... 244 B6
Allnutts Rd CM16 .... 268 A6
Alloa Rd IG3 .... 334 A2
All Saints Ave CO3 .... 135 A4
All Saints CE Prim Sch
Bishop's Stortford CM23 .... 146 B8
Great Oakley CO12 .... 116 C3
Harwich CO12 .... 90 F3
All Saints Church DA10 .... 377 F2
All Saints Cl Ashdon CB10 .... 23 F7
Bishop's Stortford CM23 .... 146 A8
Chelmsford CM1 .... 232 E4
Chigwell IG7 .... 312 A7
Doddinghurst CM15 .... 272 B3
Swanscombe DA10 .... 377 F2
All Saints Maldon CE Prim
Sch CM9 .... 236 E2
All Saints RC Sch & Tech Coll
RM8 .... 335 A3
All Saints' Rd IP1 .... 17 A8
Allshots Enterprises CO5 . 157 B5
Allysum Wlk CM12 .... 296 F5
Alma Ave Chingford E4 .... 309 C3
Hornchurch RM12 .... 336 E1
Alma Cl South Benfleet SS7 . 346 A2
Wickford SS12 .... 321 A6
Alma Dr CM1 .... 232 A2
Alma Link CM12 .... 297 A1
Alma Rd South Benfleet SS7 346 A2
Swanscombe DA10 .... 377 F2
Alma Sq 4 CO11 .... 86 D4
Alma St CO7 .... 164 B8
Almere SS7 .... 344 D4
Almond Ave Hullbridge SS5 301 E4
Wickford SS12 .... 321 C7
Almond Cl
Clacton-on-S CO15 .... 195 C3
Grays RM16 .... 374 A3
Tiptree CO5 .... 186 C6
Wivenhoe CO7 .... 137 C2
Almondhayes IP2 .... 17 B3
Almond Ho IG10 .... 288 F6
Almonds Ave IG9 .... 310 A8
Almond Way CO4 .... 136 E8
Almond Wlk SS8 .... 363 F4
ALMSHOUSE GREEN 74 E7
Almshouses
Brentwood CM14 .... 315 E8
Wivenhoe CO7 .... 164 B8
Almshouses The 3 IG11 .. 352 C6
Almshouses (Whitakers Charity) IG10 .... 288 F8
Alnesbourn Cres IP3 .... 38 D7
Al-Noor Muslim Prim Sch
IG3 .... 334 B3
Alnwick Cl SS16 .... 340 F5
Alnwick Ct 6 DA2 .... 376 B1
Alonso Ho 4 DA17 .... 369 A1
Alp Ct SS3 .... 350 A3
Alpe St IP1 .... 17 B7
Alpha Cl Basildon SS13 .... 343 F6
Braintree CM7 .... 128 A2
ALPHAMSTONE 54 F3
Alphamstone Rd CO8 .... 55 B4
Alpha Pl
4 Bishop's Stortford
CM23 .... 145 F8
2 Saffron Walden CB11 .... 22 E1
Alpha Rd Basildon SS13 .... 343 F6
Brentwood CM13 .... 295 D3
Burnham-on-C CM0 .... 306 C5
Chingford E4 .... 309 B7
Point Clear B CO16 .... 193 B3
Alpha Terr IP3 .... 18 E1
Alport Ave CO2 .... 135 C4
Alracks SS15 .... 341 A6
ALRESFORD 165 A8
Alresford Gn SS12 .... 321 E6
Alresford Prim Sch CO7 .. 165 B7
Alresford Rd CO7 .... 164 E8
Alresford Sta CO7 .... 165 A8
Alsa Bsns Pk CM24 .... 93 F1
Alsa Gdns CM22 .... 94 C2
Alsa Leys CM22 .... 94 C2
Alsa St CM24 .... 93 F1
Alston Cres CO10 .... 2 E6
Alston Ct SS0 .... 347 C1
Alston Rd IP3 .... 17 F4
Alstons Ct IP3 .... 18 D1
Altar Pl 5 SS15 .... 341 C7
Altbarn Cl CO4 .... 110 C5
Altbarn Rd CO2 .... 136 D5
Altham Gr CM20 .... 199 F3
ALTHORNE 283 A3
Althorne Cl SS13 .... 321 B1
Althorne Sta CM3 .... 304 F8
Althorne Way
Canewdon SS4 .... 304 E2
Dagenham RM10 .... 335 A2
Althorpe Cl SS5 .... 324 D6
Altitude Bsns Pk IP3 .... 18 C1
Alton Dr CO3 .... 135 B6
Alton Gdns SS2 .... 347 E5
Alton Gn IP9 .... 63 A2
Alton Hall La IP9 .... 61 F3
Alton Park Jun Sch CO15 .. 195 D2
Alton Park La CO15 .... 195 B1
Alton Park Rd CO15 .... 195 D3
Alton Rd CO15 .... 195 C2
Alton Water (Resr)* IP9 .. 62 A4
Alton Water Visitor Ctr*
IP9 .... 62 B3
Aluf Cl 2 CM8 .... 211 E8
Aluric Cl RM16 .... 374 B2
Alverstoke Rd RM3 .... 314 E3
Alverstone Rd E12 .... 352 A8
Alverton Cl CM77 .... 154 B6
Alverton Way CO4 .... 110 B3
Alveston Sq 12 E18 .... 310 A1
Alvis Ave CO15 .... 220 E6
Alwen Gr RM15 .... 372 B8
Alwyne Ave CM15 .... 295 A3
Alyssum Cl CM1 .... 233 A6
Alyssum Wlk CO4 .... 136 D8
Amanda Cl IG7 .... 311 D4
Amanda Ct E4 .... 309 E4
Amanda Mews RM7 .... 335 C6
Amazon Ct 8 DA12 .... 379 D1
Amber Ct 5 RM1 .... 335 E6
Amberden SS15 .... 341 D5
Amber La IG6 .... 311 B3
Amberley Cl CO7 .... 137 D1
Amberley Rd IG9 .... 288 C1
Amberley Way RM7 .... 335 B7
Amberry Ct CM20 .... 199 D1
Ambleside Epping CM16 .... 268 A8
Purfleet RM19 .... 376 C8
Ambleside Ave RM12 .... 355 B7
Ambleside Ct CO15 .... 196 A3
Ambleside Dr SS1 .... 367 D8
Ambleside Gdns
Hullbridge SS5 .... 301 D2
Redbridge IG4 .... 332 E6
Ambleside Wlk SS8 .... 363 F5
Ambridge Rd CO6 .... 130 E3
Ambrook Rd DA17 .... 369 A3
Ambrose Ave CO3 .... 134 F4
Ambrose Ct CO6 .... 133 D4
Ambrose Ho CO2 .... 135 D2
Amcotes Pl CM2 .... 254 C8
Ameland Rd SS8 .... 364 A6
Amelia Blackwell Ho SS8 . 363 E3
Amerells Rd CO16 .... 168 C4
America Rd CO6 .... 105 C2
America St CM9 .... 237 A2
Amersham Ave SS16 .... 340 F5
Amersham Cl RM3 .... 314 F4
Amersham Dr RM3 .... 314 F5
Amersham Rd RM3 .... 314 F4
Amersham Wlk RM3 .... 314 F4
Amery Gdns RM2 .... 336 D8
Amesbury EN9 .... 266 A7
Amesbury Cl CM16 .... 267 F8
Amesbury Dr E4 .... 287 B3
Amesbury Rd
Dagenham RM9 .... 353 D5
Epping CM16 .... 267 F8
Ames Rd DA10 .... 377 E1
Amherst Lo 6 CM20 .... 199 C1
Amidas Gdns RM8 .... 353 B8
Amid Rd SS8 .... 364 C5
Amos Hill CO10 .... 54 B8
Amoss Rd CM2 .... 254 F8
Ampers End SS14 .... 342 D6
Ampthill Ho 2 RM3 .... 314 D5
AMWELL 197 A6
Amwell Ct Hoddesdon EN11 221 A7
Waltham Abbey EN9 .... 265 E6
Amwell La SG12 .... 197 B5
Amwell St EN11 .... 221 A7
Amwell View Sch SG12 .... 197 B4
Ancaster Rd IP2 .... 17 B4
Anchorage Hill CM9 .... 237 A3
Anchorage The
Burnham-on-C CM0 .... 306 C3
Canvey Island SS8 .... 364 B1
Great Wakering SS3 .... 350 B4
Harwich CO12 .... 90 F5
Anchorage View CM0 .... 262 D7
Anchor Bvd DA2 .... 376 D3
Anchor Cl IG11 .... 353 B2
Anchor Cvn Camp CO16 .... 168 D2
Anchor Dr RM13 .... 355 B2
Anchor End CO11 .... 87 A4
Anchor Hill CO7 .... 164 B7
Anchor Ho Colchester CO2 . 135 E2
Ilford IG3 .... 334 A1
Anchor La
Abbess Roding CM5 .... 203 C4
Canewdon SS4 .... 304 E1
Dedham CO7 .... 85 A4
Heybridge CM9 .... 237 A5
New Mistley CO11 .... 87 A4
Anchor Lane Cotts SS4 .... 304 E1
Anchor Par SS4 .... 304 E1
Anchor Rd
Clacton-on-S CO15 .... 195 E3
Tiptree CO5 .... 186 C4
Anchor Reach CM3 .... 301 E5
Anchor St
Bishop's Stortford CM23 .... 146 A6
Chelmsford CM2 .... 232 B1
Ipswich IP3 .... 17 E4
Anders Fall SS9 .... 347 A6
Anderson Ave CM1 .... 231 F5
Anderson Cl CM23 .... 92 F2
Anderson Ho 1 IG11 .... 352 D3
Anderson Rd IG8 .... 332 D8
Andersons SS17 .... 360 F3
Andersons Ind Est SS12 .... 321 D4
Anderson Way DA17 .... 369 C4
Andover Cl CO15 .... 196 A6
Andrea Ave RM16 .... 373 A4
Andrew Cl Braintree CM7 .. 127 F5
Felixstowe IP11 .... 381 C3
Redbridge IG6 .... 311 D3
Stanford-le-H SS17 .... 360 D4
Andrews Cl IG9 .... 310 C8
Andrews Farm La CM6 .... 123 C8
Andrews Pl CM1 .... 231 F3
Andromeda Ct RM3 .... 314 C4
Andros Cl IP3 .... 38 A8
Andy Hill Ho CM14 .... 316 B6
Andyk Rd SS8 .... 364 E3
Anemone Ct CO4 .... 109 C2
Anerley Rd SS0 .... 366 D8
Angel Cl SS16 .... 342 D3
Angelgate CO12 .... 91 E6
Angelgate Cotts CO12 .... 91 E6
Angel La Glemsford CO10 .... 2 B4
Great Dunmow CM6 .... 150 D8
17 Ipswich IP4 .... 17 D5
Angel Mdw CO10 .... 2 B4
Angel Terr SS3 .... 349 D1
Angel Way RM1 .... 335 E6
Anglefield CO15 .... 195 F2
Angle Gn RM8 .... 334 C3
Angle Rd RM20 .... 377 D8
Anglesea Ctr 3 DA11 .... 379 B1
Anglesea Pl 2 DA11 .... 379 B1
Anglesea Rd Ipswich IP1 .... 17 B7
Wivenhoe CO7 .... 164 C8
Anglesey Cl CM23 .... 145 C7
Anglesey Dr RM13 .... 355 A1
Anglesey Gdns SS12 .... 321 F5
Angle Side CM7 .... 128 B2
Angle The 5 CM20 .... 199 C1
Anglia Cl CO2 .... 135 B3
Anglia Ct 1 RM8 .... 334 D3
Anglia Ctr The RM13 .... 369 E8
Anglian Ind Est IG11 .... 353 A1
Anglia Polytechnic Univ
Benfleet Campus SS7 .. 345 A5
Anglia Poly Univ
Chelmsford CM1 .... 232 B2
Chelmsford CM1 .... 232 B4
Anglia Way CM7 .... 128 B2
Anglia Wlk E6 .... 352 A4
Anglo-European Sch
CM4 .... 274 C4
Angmering Ho 1 RM3 .... 314 D5
Anita Cl E IP2 .... 16 E5
Anita Cl W IP2 .... 16 E5
Anjou Gn CM1 .... 233 A7
Annabel Ct RM12 .... 336 C3
Annabell Ave RM16 .... 374 D7
Annalee Gdns RM15 .... 372 B8
Annalee Rd RM15 .... 372 B8
Annan Way RM1 .... 313 E2
Ann Boleyn Dr SS4 .... 347 F7
Annbrook Rd IP2 .... 16 E1
Ann Coles Cl CB9 .... 27 C6
Anne Boleyn Mans 4
SS13 .... 343 B5
Anne Cl CO7 .... 192 F6
Anne Heart Cl RM16 .... 372 D2
Anne Nastri Ct RM2 .... 336 B6
Anne St IP11 .... 381 C3
Annett Cl 7 SS12 .... 322 A5
Anne Way IG6 .... 311 C4
Annie Taylor Ho 2 E12 .... 352 A8
Annifer Way RM15 .... 372 B8
Annonay Wlk 7 CM2 .... 232 C2
Ann St IP1 .... 17 B7
Annwood Lodge Bsns Pk
SS6 .... 322 D2
Ansgar Rd CB11 .... 43 E7
Anson Chase SS3 .... 368 E8
Anson Cl Harwich CO12 .... 91 A2
Romford RM7 .... 313 B1
South Woodham Ferrers
CM3 .... 301 F6
Anson Way CM7 .... 128 C4
Anstead Dr RM13 .... 355 A3
Anstey Cl SS9 .... 346 D7
Antelope Ave RM16 .... 373 A3
Anthony Cl Billericay CM11 . 319 D6
Colchester CO4 .... 110 D2
Anthony Dr SS17 .... 360 E4
Antlers SS8 .... 363 F2
Antlers Hill E4 .... 287 B4
Antonia Cl CB9 .... 9 E7
Antonio Wlk CO4 .... 136 F7
Antonius Way CO4 .... 110 B6
Anton Rd RM15 .... 357 B1
Antony Cl SS8 .... 364 B5
Antrim Rd SS3 .... 368 D7
Anvil Way Billericay CM12 .. 297 B5
Chelmsford CM1 .... 232 E8
Anworth Cl IG8 .... 310 B4
Anzani Ave IP11 .... 381 A4
Anzio Cres CO2 .... 135 C3
Apeldoorn SS7 .... 344 B7
Apex Ct SS5 .... 324 E7
Apollo Cl RM12 .... 336 B2
Apollo Ho IP2 .... 16 D1
Apollo Mews CO2 .... 135 C1
Apollo Way DA8 .... 369 D2
Appleby Cl Chingford E4 .... 309 C4
Ipswich IP2 .... 16 D1
Appleby Dr Basildon SS16 .. 340 F5
Romford RM3 .... 314 C5
Appleby Gn RM3 .... 314 C5
Appledene Cl SS6 .... 323 D4
Appledore SS3 .... 349 C1
Appledore Cl RM3 .... 314 C2
Appleford Ct 8 SS13 .... 343 C6
Applegarth Dr IG2 .... 333 F7
Apple Gate CM14 .... 293 F4
Applegates Mdw CO9 .... 29 F2
Applerow SS9 .... 346 F6
Appleton Cl CM19 .... 223 C7
Appleton Ct RM12 .... 336 D3
Appleton Fields CM23 .... 145 E4
Appleton Rd
Loughton IG10 .... 289 B6
South Benfleet SS7 .... 344 B2
Appleton Sch The SS7 .... 344 C5
Appleton Way RM11 .... 336 D3
Appletree Cl
Cressing CM77 .... 155 F5
Southend-on-S SS2 .... 348 E3
Apple Tree Cl
Doddinghurst CM15 .... 272 D1
Halstead CO9 .... 77 A2
Apple Tree Cres CM15 .... 272 C1
Appletree Hill Cotts CM3 .. 179 D6
Apple Tree Way SS11 .... 321 F8
Appletree Wlk CM7 .... 128 A1
Apple Way CM2 .... 254 D6
Appleyard Ave SS5 .... 324 E8
Approach Rd
Canvey Island SS8 .... 364 F3
Crays Hill CM11 .... 320 D5
Approach The
Clacton-on-S CO15 .... 220 G8
Rayleigh SS6 .... 323 C3
Upminster RM14 .... 337 B1
April Pl CM21 .... 172 F3
Aprils View CO15 .... 220 D6
Apsley Cl CM23 .... 145 F4
Apsley Ct 3 IP1 .... 17 A7
Apton Ct CM23 .... 145 F7
Apton Fields 7 CM23 .... 145 F6
Apton Hall Rd SS4 .... 326 C6
Apton Rd CM23 .... 145 F7
Aquiline Ho CO15 .... 220 J8
Arabia Cl E4 .... 287 D2
Araglen Ave RM15 .... 372 B8
Aragon Cl
Clacton-on-S CO15 .... 220 F8
Loughton IG10 .... 288 E3
Romford RM5 .... 313 B4
Southend-on-S SS2 .... 347 E4
Aragon Ct Hadleigh SS7 .... 345 F2
Redbridge IG6 .... 311 C4
Aragon Dr IG6 .... 311 C3
Aragon Rd
Great Leighs CM3 .... 180 F7
Haverhill CB9 .... 8 D6
Arakan Cl CO2 .... 135 B1
Arandora Cres RM6 .... 334 B5
Arbor Rd E4 .... 309 D7
Arbour Cl CM14 .... 316 C5
Arbour La Chelmsford CM1 . 232 D4
Wickham Bishops CM8 .... 212 F5
Arbour Way
Colchester CO4 .... 110 C4
Hornchurch RM12 .... 355 B7
Arbutus Cl CM2 .... 254 B6
Arcade Pl 8 RM1 .... 335 E6
Arcade St 15 IP1 .... 17 C6
Arcade The
Clacton-on-S CO15 .... 195 F2
18 Romford RM3 .... 314 D5
Wickford SS11 .... 321 D8
Arcadian Gdns SS7 .... 345 D4
Arcadia Rd
Burnham-on-C CM0 .... 306 C5
Canvey Island SS8 .... 364 D3
Arcany Rd RM15 .... 357 B1
Archangel Gdns IP2 .... 16 E4
Archates Ave RM16 .... 373 A3
Archer Ave SS2 .... 348 E3
Archer Cl SS2 .... 348 E3
Archer Cres CO5 .... 186 E5
Archer Ho CM12 .... 297 A1
Archer Rd SS15 .... 341 B8
Archers CM19 .... 223 B3
Archers Apartments 3
RM6 .... 334 C5
Archers Cl CM12 .... 319 A8
Archers Ct RM15 .... 372 B8
Archers Fields SS13 .... 321 B1
Archers Fields Cl SS13 .... 321 A1
Archers Way CM2 .... 254 C2
Archery Fields CO15 .... 196 A5
Archibald Rd RM3 .... 315 A1
Archibald Terr SS15 .... 341 B7
Archway RM3 .... 314 B4
Arden Cl CO4 .... 110 C3
Arden Cres RM9 .... 353 D5
Arderne Cl CO12 .... 90 F2
ARDLEIGH 111 E7
Ardleigh SS16 .... 341 E5
Ardleigh Cl RM11 .... 336 D8
Ardleigh Ct Ardleigh CO7 .. 111 E8
Shenfield CM15 .... 294 F2
Ardleigh Gdns CM13 .... 295 E3
ARDLEIGH GREEN 336 D7
Ardleigh Green Inf Sch
RM11 .... 336 D8
Ardleigh Green Jun Sch
RM11 .... 336 D8
Ardleigh Green Rd RM11 .. 336 D7
ARDLEIGH HEATH 84 D1
Ardleigh Ho 5 IG11 .... 352 C4
Ardleigh Rd Dedham CO7 .... 84 D3
Great Bromley CO7 .... 112 B4
Little Bromley CO11 .... 112 E5
Ardley Cres CM22 .... 174 B2
ARDLEY END 174 B1
Ardley Way SS6 .... 323 D4
Ardmore La IG9 .... 288 B2
Ardmore Pl IG9 .... 288 B2
Ardmore Rd RM15 .... 357 B1
Ardwell Ave IG6 .... 333 C6
Arethusa Pl DA9 .... 377 B3
Argent Ct SS15 .... 340 F7
Argents La CO3 .... 108 C2
Argent St RM17 .... 378 A8
Argles Cl DA9 .... 377 A2
Argus Cl RM7 .... 313 B2
Argyle Ct CO5 .... 158 C2
Argyle Gdns RM14 .... 337 D1
Argyle Rd
Burnham-on-C CM0 .... 306 D4
Ilford IG1 .... 333 A2
Thorpe-le-S CO16 .... 141 F2
Argyle St IP4 .... 17 D6
Argyll Ct Brentwood CM15 .. 294 D1
10 Haverhill CB9 .... 8 F7
Argyll Ho SS0 .... 366 D7
Argyll Rd Chelmsford CM2 .. 233 A5
Grays RM17 .... 373 A1
Southend-on-S SS0 .... 347 D1
Aria Ct IG2 .... 333 D5
Ariel Cl CO4 .... 136 F7
Ariel Ct 5 DA17 .... 369 A1
Arisdale Ave RM15 .... 357 B1
Arjan Way SS8 .... 363 C3
Ark Ave RM16 .... 373 A4
ARKESDEN 41 E2
Arkesden Rd CB11 .... 65 E6
Ark La SS4 .... 325 A1
Arkwright Rd Ipswich IP2 .... 16 E7
Tilbury RM18 .... 379 B5
Arkwrights CM20 .... 199 F1
Arlesford Ct CO4 .... 136 F4
Arlingham Mews EN9 .... 265 C6
Arlington Gdns Ilford IG1 .. 333 A3
Romford RM3 .... 314 E2
Arlington Ho 14 IG8 .... 311 A3
Arlington Rd
Southend-on-S SS2 .... 348 E1
Woodford IG8 .... 310 B3
Arlington Sq CM3 .... 301 C4
Arlington Way CM12 .... 296 F5
Armada Cl SS15 .... 341 D5
Armada Ct RM16 .... 373 A3
Armadale SS8 .... 363 F5
Armagh Rd SS3 .... 368 D7

Armath Pl SS16 340 F4
Armidale Wlk CO2 136 A2
ARMIGERS 96 D6
Armiger Way CM8 184 B2
Armitage Rd SS1 349 A1
Armonde Cl CM3 209 E1
Armond Rd CM8 183 F3
Armor Rd RM19 371 D2
Armourers Cl CM23 145 B4
Armoury Rd CO6 108 F4
Armstead Wlk RM10 354 A5
Armstrong Ave IG8 309 E4
Armstrong Cl
Dagenham RM8 334 D4
Danbury CM3 256 F8
Stanford-le-H SS17 360 E2
Armstrong Rd SS7 344 D7
Armstrong Way CO9 30 A2
Arncroft Ct 8 IG11 353 B2
Arne Cl SS17 360 D3
Arne Ct SS15 341 C8
Arne Mews SS15 341 C8
Arneways Ave RM6 334 D8
Arnheim Rd CM0 306 C4
Arnhem Ave RM15 371 C5
Arnhem Gr CM7 127 E5
Arnhem Rd CM1 231 E6
Arnold Ave Basildon SS16 341 A5
Southend-on-S SS1 367 C7
Arnold Ave E EN3 265 A1
Arnold Ct E18 309 F2
Arnold Dr CO4 136 E6
Arnold Ho CM2 232 A1
Arnold Pl RM18 379 C6
Arnold Rd
Clacton-on-S CO15 195 D1
Dagenham RM9 353 F5
Dagenham RM10 354 A5
Waltham Abbey EN9 265 C4
Arnolds Ave CM13 295 C4
Arnolds Cl CM13 295 C4
Arnolds Farm La CM13 295 E6
Arnolds Way SS4 325 D7
Arnold Villas CO5 186 C6
Arnold Way CM2 254 C3
Arnside Ho 2 RM3 315 A4
Arnstones Cl CO4 136 C8
Arodene Ho IG2 333 A5
ARP Shelter Mus* IP4 17 F5
Arran Ct SS12 321 F6
Arran Dr E12 332 D2
Arras Sq 12 IP1 17 C6
Arrow Rd CO4 136 F7
Arrowsmith Cl IG7 311 F5
Arrowsmith Path IG7 311 F5
Arrowsmith Rd IG7 311 F5
Arrowsmith Wlk CO4 110 A6
Arterial Ave RM13 355 C1
Arterial Rd
Southend-on-S SS6, SS9 346 C6
Thundersley SS6 345 B8
Arterial Rd North Stifford
RM16 372 E4
Arterial Rd West Thurrock
RM20 372 A3
Arterial Road Purfleet
RM19 371 C2
Artesian Cl RM11 335 F4
Arthur Barnes Ct RM16 374 C3
Arthur Bugler Inf Sch
SS17 360 E3
Arthur Bugler Jun Sch
SS17 360 E3
Arthur Ct Chelmsford CM1 231 F5
12 Grays RM17 378 C8
Arthur Rd RM6 334 D5
Arthur St
5 Colchester CO2 135 F6
Grays RM17 378 C8
Arthur's Terr IP4 17 E6
Arthur Toft Ho RM17 378 B8
Arthur Walls Ho 3 E12 333 A1
Arthy Cl CM3 211 A4
Artillery Cl IG2 333 D5
Artillery Dr CO12 90 D1
Artillery St CO1 136 B6
Arun RM18 375 C2
Arun Cl CM1 232 C5
Arundel Cl CM12 297 C6
Arundel Dr
Corringham SS17 361 A3
Woodford IG8 310 A3
Arundel Gdns Ilford IG3 334 A2
Rayleigh SS6 323 B5
Southend-on-S SS0 347 A3
Arundel Mews CM12 297 C6
Arundel Rd Rochford SS4 303 C1
Romford RM3 314 F2
South Benfleet SS7 344 B7
Wickford SS11 299 C1
Arundel Way
Billericay CM12 297 C6
Ipswich IP3 18 E3
Arundel Wlk 1 CB9 8 E8
Arwela Rd IP11 381 D2
Arwen Gr CM3 301 C6
Asbury Cl CO4 136 D8
Ascension Bsns Pk 2
RM16 372 B3
Ascension Rd RM5 313 C4
Ascent Pk CM20 200 B5
Ascham Dr E4 309 A3
Ascot Cl
Bishop's Stortford CM23 146 C8
Redbridge IG6 311 E4
Thundersley SS7 345 B7
Ascot Dr Felixstowe IP11 381 C6
Ipswich IP3 18 B3
Ascot Gdns Colchester CO3 134 E7
Hornchurch RM12 355 E8
Ascot Gr SS14 342 E6
Ascot Mews
Clacton-on-S CO15 196 C5
Southminster CM0 284 E4
Ashanti Cl SS3 368 F8
Ashbeam Cl CM13 316 C4
Ash Bglws CM7 127 E3
Ashbourne Ave E18 332 B7
Ashbourne Rd RM3 314 D6
Ashbrook Pl SS6 345 F8
Ashbrook Rd RM10 335 B1
Ashburnham Gdns RM14 337 C3
Ashburnham Rd
Belvedere DA17 369 C2
Southend-on-S SS1 366 F8
Ashburton Ave IG3 352 F8
Ashbury Dr CO6 132 F3
Ashbury Gdns RM6 334 D6
Ashby Cl Hornchurch RM11 337 A3
Orsett RM16 374 E7
Ashby Rd CM8 212 A7
Ashby Rise CM23 119 B1
Ash Cl Brightlingsea CO7 192 E7
Clacton-on-S CO15 195 C3
Hatfield Peverel CM3 211 A4
Ipswich IP3 18 F1
Pilgrims Hatch CM15 293 F4
Romford RM5 313 B3
Ashcombe SS4 325 D4
Ashcombe Cl SS9 346 B6
Ash Ct Chingford E4 287 D2
Harwich CO12 90 E2
Romford RM7 335 B5
Southend-on-S SS3 368 F7
Woodford E18 310 C2
Ashdale CM23 145 D4
Ashdene Cl SS5 301 E2
ASHDON 6 B1
Ashdon Cl
Brentwood CM13 295 C3
South Ockendon RM15 372 C7
Woodford IG8 310 B4
Ashdon Mus The* CB10 24 B8
Ashdon Prim Sch CB10 6 B1
Ashdon Rd Ashdon CB10 24 E3
Saffron Walden CB10 23 C3
Ashdon Road Commercial Ctr
CB10 23 A3
Ashdon Way SS16 342 A5
Ashdown Cl
Great Notley CM77 154 B8
Stanford-le-H SS17 360 F5
Ashdown Cres SS7 345 E4
Ashdown Ct IG11 352 B6
Ashdown Ho SS7 344 F6
Ashdown Way
Colchester CO4 136 D7
Ipswich IP3 18 D3
Ashdown Wlk RM7 313 B2
ASHELDHAM 285 A7
Asheldham Pits Nature
Reserve* CM0 285 A8
ASHEN 11 D1
Ashen Cl CO10 11 D1
Ashenden IP11 381 E4
Ashen Hill CO10 11 C2
Ashen La CO10 11 C3
Ashen Rd Ashen CO10 12 A1
Clare CO10 12 B5
Ridgewell CO9 29 B8
Ashes Cl CO14 170 F8
Ashes Rd Cressing CM77 155 F7
Southend-on-S SS3 368 E6
Ash Fall CM8 184 A5
Ashfield SS6 322 F3
Ashfield Cl CM6 123 C1
Ashfield Ct IP4 18 A6
Ashfield Farm Rd CM9 235 D8
Ashfields Basildon SS13 343 C8
Loughton IG10 288 F7
Ashfields Farm CM6 149 B3
Ashford Ave CM14 316 B7
Ashford Ct RM17 373 D1
Ashford Rd
Chelmsford CM1 231 E2
Wallend E6 352 A5
Woodford E18 310 B1
Ash Gn Billericay CM11 297 E2
Canewdon SS4 304 D1
Great Chesterford CB10 3 D1
Ash Gr Blackheath CO2 163 A8
Burnham-on-C CM0 306 B6
Capel St M IP9 35 A2
Chelmsford CM2 254 D7
Great Cornard CO10 34 C5
Great Dunmow CM6 150 D7
Heybridge CM9 237 C6
Wivenhoe CO7 137 C3
Ash Ground Cl CO11 86 D8
Ashgrove Rd IG3 334 A3
Ash Groves CM21 173 A2
Ash Ho IP2 16 D2
Ash Ind Est CM19 222 F7
Ashingdale Cl SS8 364 C2
ASHINGDON 325 D7
Ashingdon Cl E4 309 C7
Ashingdon Hts SS4 325 B7
Ashingdon Rd SS4 325 D6
Ashingdon Sch SS4 303 B1
Ashlands Ct RM18 375 C2
Ashlea Cl CB9 9 B6
Ashlea Rd CB9 9 B6
Ashleigh Cl SS8 364 A6
Ashleigh Ct
Canvey Island SS8 364 A6
Hoddesdon EN11 221 A5
Ingatestone CM4 274 B3
Waltham Abbey EN9 266 A5
Ashleigh Dr SS9 365 F8
Ashleigh Gdns RM14 337 D1
Ashley Ave IG6 311 B1
Ashley Cl SS17 361 A3
Ashley Ct CO12 91 B3
Ashley Gdns
Colchester CO3 135 C6
Grays RM16 373 D5
Ashley Gn CM3 278 B7
Ashley Gr IG10 288 E6
Ashley Lodge CO15 196 A8
Ashley Rd Chingford E4 309 A4
Harwich CO12 91 B3
Ashley St IP2 17 C4
Ash Lodge SS3 368 F8
Ashlong Gr CO9 76 E3
Ashlyn Gr RM11 336 D8
Ashlyns SS13 343 B7
Ashlyns La CM5 225 F2
Ashlyns Rd CM16 245 F1
Ashlyn's Rd CO13 170 E4
Ashmans Row CM3 301 D6
Ashmeads IG10 288 F6
Ashmere Gr IP4 17 F6
Ashmere Rise CO10 34 A8
Ashmole Dr CO13 170 F6
Ashmour Gdns RM1 313 D1
Ashpole Rd CM7 102 B1
Ash Rd Alresford CO7 165 B8
Canvey Island SS8 364 C3
Hadleigh SS7 345 E2
Ash Rise CO9 103 F8
Ashstead Cl CO16 195 B6
Ashton Cl IP2 16 C2
Ashton Ct E4 309 E7
Ashton Gate RM3 314 D3
Ashton Gdns RM6 334 E5
Ashton Pl Chelmsford CM2 233 A3
Thundersley SS7 345 A6
Ashton Rd RM3 314 D2
Ash Tree Cl CM1 231 F2
Ash Tree Cnr CM3 208 B6
Ash Tree Cres CM1 231 F2
Ashtree Ct EN9 266 A5
Ash Tree Ct Rochford SS4 326 D4
Romford RM1 336 A6
Ash Tree Field CM20 199 A2
Ash Tree Wlk 1 SS14 342 F5
Ashurst Ave SS2 348 F2
Ashurst Cl CO5 163 F8
Ashurst Dr
Chelmsford CM1 232 D7
Ilford IG6 333 C6
Ashvale Dr RM14 337 E2
Ashvale Gdns
Romford RM5 313 D5
Upminster RM14 337 F2
Ashway SS17 361 B4
Ash Way Colchester CO3 134 F3
Hockley SS5 324 F8
Ashwells Mdw CO6 105 B6
Ashwells Rd CM15 293 E6
Ashwin Ave CO6 133 D4
Ash Wlk Southend-on-S SS1 367 B7
South Ockendon RM15 357 D2
Ashwood SS7 345 B1
Ashwood Ave RM13 355 B1
Ashwood Cl CM0 306 B7
Ashwood Rd E4 309 D7
Ashworth Pl CM17 224 D8
Ashworths
Canvey Island SS8 364 A6
Rochford SS4 325 C6
Askews Farm Rd RM17 372 E1
Askins Rd CO7 59 C3
Askwith Rd RM13 354 D3
Aspen Cl SS8 363 E4
Aspen Ct Basildon SS15 319 C1
Brentwood CM13 317 A7
Dartford DA1 376 A1
Redbridge IG5 332 E8
Aspen Gn SS4 325 C7
Aspen Gr RM14 356 A8
Aspens EN9 266 C4
Aspens The CM23 119 B3
Aspen Way
3 Colchester CO4 136 D8
Little Oakley CO12 117 B7
South Ockendon RM15 357 D2
Aspin Mews CB10 22 E3
Asquith Ave SS7 345 B7
Asquith Cl RM8 334 C3
Asquith Dr CO4 110 C5
Asquith Gdns SS7 345 C7
Assandune Cl SS4 325 D7
Astell Ct CO13 170 F4
Aster Cl Basildon SS15 341 D5
Bishop's Stortford CM23 145 D6
4 Chelmsford CM1 232 F6
Clacton-on-S CO16 195 C4
Aster Rd IP2 16 E4
Asthall Gdns IG6 333 C7
Astley RM17 377 F8
Astley Rd CO15 195 D3
Aston Ct 10 IG8 310 A4
Aston Mews RM6 334 C4
Aston Rd SS15 341 B6
Astor Ave RM7 335 C5
Astra Cl RM12 355 B6
Astra Ct E 3 RM12 355 B6
Astra Ctr CM20 199 F4
Astra Ct W 2 RM12 355 B6
Ataka Rd IP11 381 D6
Athelstan Cl RM3 314 F1
Athelstan Ct E6 352 A3
Athelstan Gdns SS11 299 D1
Athelstan Rd
Colchester CO3 135 C5
Romford RM3 314 F1
Athena Est CM20 200 B4
Atherstone Cl SS8 364 C2
Atherstone Rd SS8 364 C2
Atherton End CM21 172 E3
Atherton Gdns RM16 374 C2
Atherton Ho
8 Romford RM3 314 E3
Woodford IG5 310 E1
Atherton Rd Ipswich IP2 16 D2
Woodford IG5 310 F1
Athol Cl SS8 364 E2
Athol Ct IG3 334 A4
Atholl Rd Chelmsford CM2 232 F5
Ilford IG3 334 A4
Athol Rd DA17 369 C1
Athos Rd SS8 364 C5
Atlanta Bvd RM1 335 E5
Atlantic Cl DA10 377 E2
Atlantic Sq CM8 184 A3
Atlantis Cl IG11 353 B2
Atlas Bglws CO6 105 A6
Atlas Ct CO6 105 A7
Atlas Ho 3 IP4 17 E6
Atlas Rd CO6 104 F7
Atlas Works CO6 105 B6
Atridge Chase CM12 297 A4
Atrium 9 IG9 310 D8
Attlee Ct RM17 373 A3
Attlee Dr DA1 376 A2
Attlee Gdns 7 CO1 136 A6
Attwood Cl CO4 110 B5
Attwoods Cl CM2 254 C3
Aubrey Buxton Nature
Reserve* CM24 94 A1
Aubrey Cl CM1 232 B7
Aubrietia Cl RM3 314 E2
Auckland Ave RM13 354 F2
Auckland Cl
Chelmsford CM1 231 E5
Tilbury RM18 379 A5
Auckland Rd IG1 333 C4
Auction Pl RM4 290 B6
Audleigh Pl IG7 311 A4
Audley Cl CM77 154 B7
Audley Ct CB11 22 D1
AUDLEY END
Castle Hedingham 52 E8
Saffron Walden 43 B8
Audley End House &
Gardens* CB11 22 B1
Audley End Miniature Rly*
CB11 43 A8
Audley End Rd CB11 43 C8
Audley End Sta CB11 42 F5
Audley Gdns Ilford IG3 333 F2
Loughton IG10 289 D7
Waltham Abbey EN9 265 C5
Audley Gr IP4 18 B5
Audley Rd Colchester CO3 135 C5
Great Leighs CM3 180 F7
Saffron Walden CB11 22 E1
Audleys Cl SS2 347 E5
Audley Way Basildon SS14 342 B6
Frinton-on-S CO13 171 B6
Audrey Gdns CM23 145 F4
Audrey Rd IG1 333 B1
Audries Est CO14 171 A8
Augers 7 CM0 306 C4
Augusta Cl IP3 38 E7
Augusta Ct EN9 265 B6
Augustine Rd 1 DA12 379 D1
Augustine Way CM3 256 F2
Augustus Cl
Colchester CO4 110 B6
Haverhill CB9 9 D7
Augustus Mews CM7 127 E2
Augustus Way CM8 211 E8
Aukingford Gdns CM5 248 F5
Aukingford Gn CM5 248 F4
Aundle Ho IG8 311 A4
Auriel Ave RM10 354 D6
Aurora Ct IG8 309 F6
Austen Cl Braintree CM7 155 A8
Greenhithe DA9 377 C1
Loughton IG10 289 D6
Tilbury RM18 379 C5
Austen Dr CM4 275 D2
Austin Ave CO15 220 E6
Austin St IP2 17 C4
Austral Dr RM11 336 D4
Austral Way CM3 283 A3
Auton Croft CB11 43 D7
Autoway CO4 110 C5
Autumn Cl CO16 195 C5
Avcoca Terr SS0 347 D2
Avebury Rd SS0 347 E2
AVELEY 371 C6
Aveley By-Pass RM15 371 D6
Aveley Cl RM15 371 D5
Aveley Mans 1 IG11 352 B5
Aveley Prim Sch RM15 371 E5
Aveley Rd Romford RM1 335 E7
Upminster RM14 356 C4
Aveley Sch The RM15 371 D6
Aveley Way CM9 258 F8
Aveline Rd CO7 111 E7
Aveling Park Rd E17 309 A1
Aveling Park Sch E17 309 A1
Avelon Rd Rainham RM13 355 A4
Romford RM5 313 D4
Avenue Cl RM3 314 F3
Avenue Ct IG5 332 E8
Avenue Gate IG10 288 C3
Avenue Ind Est
Chingford E4 309 A4
Romford RM3 314 D2
Avenue Pl CM23 146 A6
Avenue Rd
Bishop's Stortford CM23 146 B6
Brentwood CM14 316 C6
Chelmsford CM2 254 D7
Hoddesdon EN11 221 D5
Ilford RM6 334 C4
Ingatestone CM4 274 B3
Romford RM3 314 F3
South Benfleet SS7 344 E3
Southend-on-S, Clifftown
SS0 366 F8
Southend-on-S, Leigh Cliffs
SS9 365 E8
Theydon Bois CM16 267 D3
Witham CM8 184 A3
Woodford IG8 310 C4
Avenue Terr Ilford IG2 333 E5
Southend-on-S SS0 366 E8
Avenue The
Billericay CM12 297 A2
Braintree CM7 127 F3
Brentwood CM13 316 F4
11 Buckhurst Hill IG9 310 C8
Canvey Island SS8 364 B2
Chingford E4 309 D5
Clacton-on-S CO15 196 B7
Colchester CO3 135 C6
Danbury CM3 256 F7
Fobbing SS17 361 D4
Great Braxted CM8 185 A3
Great Dunmow CM6 150 E8
Great Oakley CO12 116 B3
Greenhithe DA9 377 B2
Hadleigh SS7 345 E3
Hoddesdon EN11 221 A4
Hornchurch RM12 336 D2
Hullbridge SS5 301 D3
Ipswich IP1 17 C8
Kelvedon Hatch CM15 293 E8
Loughton IG10 288 E3
Lower Nazeing EN9 244 C6
North Fambridge CM3 303 A7
Romford RM1 335 D7
Avenue The *continued*
Trimley St M IP11 381 A7
Wanstead E11 332 B6
Washbrook IP8 35 F7
West Bergholt CO6 108 D3
Witham CM8 184 A2
Wivenhoe CO7 137 B1
Avery Gdns Ilford IG2 333 A6
Redbridge IG2 332 F6
Avey La High Beach IG10 288 A8
Waltham Abbey EN9 265 E2
Aviation Way SS2 347 B7
Avignon Cl CO2 136 B4
Avila Chase CM2 254 B1
Avington Wlk SS7 344 F6
Avitus Way CO4 110 B5
Avocet Cl
Frinton-on-S CO13 170 E6
Kelvedon CO5 158 D2
West Mersea CO5 218 D7
Avocet Ct IP11 381 D2
Avocet Way CM9 237 C5
Avon Cl SS4 325 C5
Avon Ct 10 Chingford E4 287 C1
Upminster RM14 337 E4
Avondale Cl Loughton IG10 288 F2
Rayleigh SS6 323 F2
Avondale Cres IG4 332 D6
Avondale Ct
Southend-on-S SS9 346 D1
Woodford E18 310 B2
Avondale Dr Loughton IG10 288 F3
Southend-on-S SS9 346 F4
Avondale Gdns SS17 360 E5
Avondale Ho CO15 196 A3
Avondale Rd Basildon SS16 343 A4
Clacton-on-S CO15 196 A3
Ipswich IP3 18 A2
Rayleigh SS6 323 F2
South Benfleet SS7 344 D3
Avondale Wlk SS8 363 E4
Avon Gn RM15 372 B7
Avon Ho RM14 337 E4
Avon House Sch IG8 310 A6
Avon Rd Canvey Island SS8 364 A3
Chelmsford CM1 231 C5
Upminster RM14 337 D5
Avontar Rd RM15 357 B1
Avon Terr IG10 288 F3
Avon Way Colchester CO4 136 F6
Southend-on-S SS3 368 E7
Wanstead E18 332 A8
Avon Way Ho CO4 136 F6
Avon Wlk CM8 183 E3
Avril Way E4 309 C5
Avro Rd SS2 347 D6
Axe St IG11 352 C4
Axial Way CO4 110 B6
Axon Pl IG1 333 C2
Aylesbeare SS3 368 D8
Aylesbury Dr Basildon SS16 340 F4
Great Notley CM77 154 C5
Holland-on-S CO15 196 F6
Aylesbury Mews SS15 319 F2
Aylets Field CM18 223 E5
Aylett Cl SS8 364 C4
Aylett Rd RM14 337 C2
Ayletts Basildon SS14 342 F6
Broomfield CM1 208 B3
Aylmer Rd RM8 334 E1
Ayloffe Rd Colchester CO4 110 C1
Dagenham RM9 353 F6
Ayloff Prim Sch RM12 355 B8
Ayloffs Cl RM11 336 E6
Ayloff's Wlk RM11 336 E6
Aylsham La RM3 314 D6
Aylsham Rd EN11 221 C8
Aynsley Gdns CM17 224 C8
Aynsworth Ave CM23 119 B2
Ayr Gn RM1 313 E2
Ayron Rd RM15 357 B1
Ayrton Ho SS9 346 A2
Ayr Way RM1 313 E2
AYTHORPE RODING 176 B3
Azalea Ave SS12 321 C7
Azalea Cl IG1 352 B7
Azalea Ct
8 Chelmsford CM1 232 F6
Chingford IG8 309 E3
Colchester CO4 136 D8
Azalea Mews SS8 364 A2
Azalea Way CO16 195 C4

B

Baardwyk Ave SS8 364 E3
Babbacombe Gdns IG4 332 E7
Babington Rd
Dagenham RM8 353 C8
Hornchurch RM12 336 B3
Baburgh Ho CO10 33 F7
Back Hamlet IP3 17 E5
Back Hill Hadstock CB1 5 B6
Holbrook IP9 62 E4
Back La Broomfield CM1 208 D1
Buckhurst Hill IG9 310 D8
Colchester CO3 134 E7
Dagenham RM6 334 E4
East Hanningfield CM3 278 B7
Felixstowe IP11 381 D5
Ford End CM3 179 B6
Grays RM20 372 B4
Great Oakley CO12 116 C3
Ickleton CB10 3 A3
Ingatestone CM4 274 A6
Little Hallingbury CM22 173 B7
Little Waltham CM3 208 C4
Lower Nazeing EN9 222 C1
Pleshey CM3 178 E2
Purfleet RM19 371 E3
Ramsey CO12 90 A1
Rochford SS4 325 F1
Sheering CM22 173 B1
South Ockendon RM16 372 C5
Stisted CM77 129 C7
Stock CM4 275 D2
Tattingstone IP9 61 C6
Washbrook IP8 35 E8
Wickham Bishops CM8 212 F4
Back La E CO7 139 A6
Back La W CO7 138 F7
Backnang Sq 1 CM2 232 C2
Back Rd Ardleigh CO7 112 B5
Tollesbury CM9 216 C4
Writtle CM1 231 A1
Backwarden Nature Reserve*
CM3 256 E5
Backwardens Nature Trail*
CM3 256 E4
Back Waterside La CO7 192 F5
BACON END 149 F2
BACONEND GREEN 149 E4
Bacon Link RM5 313 B4
Bacons Chase CM0 242 B2
Bacons Green Cotts CO7 58 E7
Bacon's La CO6 106 C3
Bacon Terr 3 RM8 353 B7
Bacton Lodge IP11 381 D3
Bacton Rd IP11 381 D3
Badburgham Ct EN9 265 F6
Baddeley Cl EN3 265 A2
Baddow Cl
Dagenham RM10 354 A4
Woodford IG8 310 D4
Baddow Ct CM2 255 A6
Baddow Hall Ave CM2 255 A7
Baddow Hall Cres CM2 255 B7
Baddow Hall Jun & Inf Sch
CM2 255 A6
Baddow Place Ave CM2 255 A6
Baddow Rd
Chelmsford CM2 232 C1
Great Baddow CM2 254 E7
Baden Powell Cl RM9 353 E4
Baden Powell Dr CO3 135 A4
Baden Powell Ho 11
DA17 369 A3
Baden Rd IG1 352 B7
Bader Cl IP3 18 C2
Bader Way RM13 355 B6
Badger Cl IG2 333 C4
Badger Ct E4 309 D6
Badger Gr CM7 128 B3
Badger Hall Ave SS7 345 A4
Badgers CM23 145 E5
Badgers Bank IP2 16 E1
Badgers Cl
Galleywood CM2 254 B1
Southend-on-S SS0 347 B4
Badgers Gn CO6 132 E3
Badgers Holt CO3 134 D6
Badgers Keep CM0 306 B8
Badgers Mount
Chadwell St M RM16 373 F4
Hockley SS5 324 D5
Badgers Rise SS8 364 A6
Badgers The SS16 341 B4
Badgers Way SS7 345 B4
Badley Hall Rd CO7 112 F2
Badlis Rd E17 309 A1
Badminton Ct CO15 220 G7
Badminton Rd CO15 220 G7
Badshah Ave IP3 18 B3
Bag La CM4 273 E4
Bagleys Spring RM6 334 E7
Bagshaw Rd CO12 91 D4
Bailey Bridge Rd CM7 127 E5
Bailey Cl Chingford E4 309 C6
Haverhill CB9 9 D7
Ipswich IP2 16 E6
Purfleet RM19 371 D2
Bailey Ct 4 E4 309 D5
Bailey Dale CO3 134 C4
BAILEY HILL 28 B5
Bailey La CO10 12 C7
Bailey Rd SS9 346 B2
Bailey The SS6 323 C2
Baillie Cl RM13 355 B1
Bainbridge Dr CO5 186 D4
Bainbridge Rd RM9 353 F8
Baines Cl CO3 135 A5
Baird Cl IP2 16 F7
Baird Ho 12 DA17 369 A3
Bairny Wood App IG8 310 B4
Baker Ave CM3 211 A3
Baker Cl SS15 341 C5
Baker Mews CM9 237 A2
Baker Rd IP9 91 A8
Bakers Almshouses IP9 61 F3
Bakers Cl CM3 301 D8
Bakers Cotts CM15 293 F8
Bakers Ct
5 Bishop's Stortford
CM23 146 A7
Colchester CO1 109 E1
Bakers Ct RM8 334 F4
Bakers Ct
Ramsden Heath CM11 298 C4
Wickford SS11 321 F6
Baker's Ct SS14 321 A2
Bakers Farm Cl SS11 322 A7
Bakersfield CM3 282 F8
Bakers Field CM4 275 E2
Bakers La Danbury CM3 256 E7
Epping CM16 245 F1
Felsted CM6 152 C4
Ingatestone CM4 274 B4
West Hanningfield CM2 276 B7
Baker's La Colchester CO4 109 A2
Great Notley CM77 154 D6
Tolleshunt Major CM9 214 D4
Bakers Mdw CM15 272 C2
Bakers Mead CM3 207 F7
Bakers Mews CM4 274 B4
Baker's Rd CO10 12 F2
Baker St Chelmsford CM2 232 A1
Orsett RM16 373 F6
BAKER STREET 373 F7
Bakers Villas The CM16 245 F1
Bakers Wlk CM21 172 E2
Baker Way CM8 211 F7
Bakery Cl Roydon CM19 222 C8
Tillingham CM0 263 E3
Bakery Ct CM24 119 D6
Baldocks Rd CM16 267 E4
Baldry Cl IP8 16 C1
Baldwin Ho E6 352 A5
Baldwin's Hill IG10 288 F8
Baldwin's La CO6 131 E8

Bale Cl CO3 134 E4
Balfe Ct CO4 136 E6
Balfour Cl SS12 321 E5
Balfour Rd Grays RM17 373 C2
Ilford IG1 333 C3
Balfour Terr IP3 38 C8
Balgonie Rd E4 287 D1
Balgores Cres RM2 336 B8
Balgores La RM2 336 B7
Balgores Sq RM2 336 B7
Balkerne Gdns CO1 135 E7
Balkerne Hill CO3 135 E7
Balkerne Pas CO1 135 E7
Ball Alley 3 CO1 135 F7
Ballantyne Dr CO2 136 D5
Ballards Cl RM10 354 B3
BALLARDS GORE 326 F6
Ballards Rd RM10 354 B3
Ballards Wlk SS15 341 E7
Ballast Quay Rd
Fingringhoe CO5 164 B6
Wivenhoe CO7 137 D1
BALLINGDON 33 D6
Ballingdon Gr CO10 33 D5
Ballingdon Hill CO10 33 C5
Ballingdon Hill Ind Est CO10 33 C6
Ballingdon St CO10 33 D6
Ballingdon Trad Est CO10 33 C6
Balliol Ave E4 309 E6
Ball La Abberton CO2 162 F5
Blackheath CO2 163 B5
Ball's Chace CO8 79 F2
Ball's Chase CO9 76 F1
Ball's Farm CO7 137 E7
Balmerino Ave SS7 345 C6
Balmoral Ave
Clacton-on-S CO15 195 D3
Corringham SS17 361 A3
Stanford-le-H SS17 360 E3
Balmoral Cl
Billericay CM11 297 E1
Ipswich IP2 16 F1
Balmoral Ct Braintree CM7 128 C4
Chelmsford CM2 232 C2
Balmoral Dr CB9 8 E8
Balmoral Gdns
Hockley SS5 324 C6
Ilford IG3 333 F3
Balmoral Ho SS0 366 E8
Balmoral Rd
Hornchurch RM12 336 D1
Mayland CM3 261 A2
Pilgrims Hatch CM15 294 B4
Romford RM2 336 B6
Southend-on-S SS0 347 E1
Balmoral Terr SS0 347 D2
Balstonia Dr SS17 360 F5
Baltic Ave SS1 367 A8
Baltic Wharf DA11 379 A1
Balton Way CO12 90 F2
Bamber Ho 1 IG11 352 C4
BAMBER'S GREEN 121 F3
Bamford Rd IG11 352 C6
Bamford Way RM5 313 B5
Bampton Rd RM3 314 E2
Bancroft Ave IG9 310 A8
Bancroft Chase RM12 335 F2
Bancrofts Rd CM3 301 E8
Bancroft's Sch IG8 310 A7
Bandhills Cl CM3 301 D8
Banes Down EN9 221 E1
Bangs Cl CB21 7 A7
Banham Dr CO10 33 F8
Banister Cl CO16 195 C5
Bankart La CM2 232 F4
Bank Bldgs 13 CO10 33 E7
Bank Chambers CM15 316 D8
Bank End Cotts CM4 275 A8
Bankfoot RM17 373 A1
Bank Pas CO1 135 E7
Bank Pl 8 CM14 316 C8
Bank Rd IP4 17 E6
Banks Ct CM6 150 D8
Bankside DA11 378 C1
Bankside Cl CM3 279 E1
Bankside Pk IG11 353 A2
Bankside Rd IG1 352 D7
Banks La Epping CM16 268 F7
Stapleford Tawney CM16 269 A8
Bank St Braintree CM7 127 F3
Gravesend DA11, DA12 379 B1
Banks Way E12 352 A8
Bann Cl RM15 372 B6
Banner Cl RM19 371 D2
Bannister Dr CM13 295 C3
Bannister Gn SS12 321 E6
BANNISTER GREEN 152 F6
Bannister Green Villas CM6 152 E6
Bannister Ho RM20 377 D8
Bansons Ct CM5 249 A3
Banson's La CM5 249 A3
Bansons Way CM5 249 A3
Bansons Yd CM5 249 A3
Bantel Villas EN11 221 C8
Banters La CM3 154 B1
Bantock Way CM8 211 F7
Bantoft Terr IP3 18 C2
Banyards RM11 336 E7
Banyard Way SS4 325 C4
Barbara Ave SS8 363 F2
Barbara Cl SS4 325 E2
Barbary Lodge CM2 232 A2
Barbel Cl EN8 265 A5
Barbel Rd CO4 110 F1
Barberry Cl RM3 314 C3
Barbour Gdns CO2 134 F2
Barbour Gn SS12 321 D5
Barbrook La CO5 186 D6
Barbrook Way CM3 256 E1
Barclay Cl CM2 255 A6
Barclay Ct EN11 221 A5
Barclay Oval IG8 310 A6
Barclay Rd SS13 321 E1
Barclay Sq CO15 220 G7
Barclay Way RM20 371 F1
Bardell Cl CM1 231 F6
Bardenville Rd SS8 364 E3
Bardeswell Cl CM14 316 C8
Bardfield SS16 342 E5
Bardfield Ave RM6 334 D8
Bardfield Ctr CM7 72 B1
BARDFIELD END GREEN 70 C2
Bardfield End Villas CM6 70 C2
Bardfield Prim Sch SS16 342 E4
Bardfield Rd
Bardfield Saling CM7 99 F1
Colchester CO2 136 A1
Finchingfield CM7 72 C5
Thaxted CM6 70 D2
BARDFIELD SALING 99 C2
Bardfield Way
Frinton-on-S CO13 170 F6
Rayleigh SS6 323 A3
Bards Ct RM3 314 B3
Bardsley Cl 2 CO4 109 E2
Bardsley Rd 2 CO4 109 E2
Barfield Rd CO5 218 C6
Barfields IG10 289 A5
Barfields Gdns IG10 289 A5
Barfields Path IG10 289 A5
Barfields Row CO5 159 D2
Bargate La CO7 85 C3
Barge Ct DA9 377 C3
Barge Pier Rd SS3 368 E5
Barham Cl RM7 313 B1
Baring-Gould Cotts CO5 191 D1
Bark Burr Rd RM16 372 F4
Barker Cl Ipswich IP2 16 D5
Lawford CO11 86 B4
Steeple Bumpstead CB9 27 B6
Barker Rd CO10 15 E2
Barkers Mead CM22 173 B8
Barkers Terr CO7 85 A5
BARKING 352 D5
Barking Abbey Comp Sch (Lower Sch) IG11 352 E7
Barking Abbey Sch IG11 352 F6
Barking Bsns Ctr IG11 353 A2
Barking Coll RM7 335 D2
Barking Hospl IG11 352 F5
Barking Ind Pk IG11 353 A4
Barking Rd E6 352 A4
BARKINGSIDE 333 C8
Barkingside Sta IG6 333 D8
Barking Sta IG11 352 C5
Barkis Cl CM1 231 D7
Barkstead Rd CO4 110 C1
Barkwood Cl RM7 335 C6
Barlee Cl CB11 65 C3
Barle Gdns RM15 372 B7
Barley Cl Basildon SS16 341 A3
Hatfield Heath CM22 174 E2
New Mistley CO11 87 A4
Barleycorn Way RM11 336 F5
Barley Court Day Hospl IG3 334 B6
Barley Croft CM18 223 E4
Barley Ct
2 Hoddesdon EN11 221 D8
Saffron Walden CB11 22 D1
Wivenhoe CO7 137 C3
Barley Field CM15 271 F2
Barleyfields CM8 184 A1
Barleyfields Cl RM6 334 C4
Barleyhayes CL IP2 17 B2
Barley Hills CM23 145 E4
Barley Ho CO10 15 B5
Barley La IG3, RM6 334 B5
Barleylands Farm Mus★ CM11 319 F5
Barleylands Rd CM11, SS15 319 F4
Barley Lane Prim Sch RM6 334 B4
Barley Mead CM3 257 B6
Barley Way CO3 134 E5
BARLING 349 E7
Barling Magna Com Prim Sch SS3 349 D7
Barling Rd SS3 349 B6
Barlon Rd CO11 112 F4
Barlow Road Cotts CB10 6 B2
Barlow's Reach CM2 233 A4
Barlow Way RM13 369 E8
Barnaby Rudge CM1 231 F7
Barnaby Way
Basildon SS15 341 D7
Chigwell IG7 311 B7
Barnard Acres EN9 243 E8
Barnard Cl Basildon SS16 342 E2
Newport CB11 66 F8
Barnard Ct 18 DA2 376 B1
Barnard Ho RM3 314 E1
Barnardiston Rd CO4 110 C1
Barnardiston Way CM8 183 F3
Barnardo Dr IG6 333 C7
Barnard Rd
Galleywood CM2 254 C2
Sawbridgeworth CM21 172 E4
Southend-on-S SS9 346 C2
Barnards Ave SS8 364 D4
Barnards Ct CB10 22 D2
Barnards Field CM6 70 B2
Barnards Orch CM77 126 F2
Barnards Yd CB10 22 D1
Barnby Cl CB9 8 C8
Barncombe Cl SS7 344 D6
Barncroft Cl
Colchester CO4 110 B3
Loughton IG10 289 A4
Barncroft Gn IG10 289 A4
Barncroft Rd IG10 289 A4
Barn Ct CM21 172 E3
Barnes Ct
Chipping Ongar CM5 248 F5
Woodford IG8 310 D5
Barnes Farm Dr CM3 282 F2
Barnes Farm Jun & Inf Schs CM2 233 A3
Barnes Ho 8 IG11 352 D4
Barnes Mill Rd CM2 232 F2
Barnes Rd IG1 352 C7
Barnet Park Rd SS11 299 F2
Barnett Ct RM17 373 C1
Barnett Reach CO14 144 E2
Barneveld Ave SS8 364 E3
Barnfield Capel St M IP9 35 B1
Epping CM16 246 A3
Barnfield *continued*
Feering CO5 158 D3
Hatfield Broad Oak CM22 175 A5
Manningtree CO11 86 D4
Wickford SS11 321 E8
Barn Field IP11 381 B6
Barnfield Cl
Greenhithe DA9 376 F1
Hoddesdon EN11 221 A8
Lower Nazeing EN9 221 F1
Barnfield Cotts CM9 237 B5
Barnfield Mews CM1 232 A6
Barnfield Pl CM8 183 F1
Barnfield Rd CO6 109 C6
Barnfields CO5 163 F5
Barn Fields CO3 134 C6
Barn Gn CM1 232 E8
Barn Hall Ave CO2 136 C4
Barnhall Rd CM9 187 D2
Barnham Pl IP5 18 F6
Barn Hill CM19 222 B4
Barn La CO11 112 F7
Barnmead CM5 247 F2
Barn Mead Braintree CM7 128 D2
Doddinghurst CM15 272 C3
Harlow CM18 223 E6
Theydon Bois CM16 267 E3
Barnmead Ct RM9 353 F7
Barnmead Gdns RM9 353 F7
Barnmead Rd RM9 353 F7
Barnmead Way CM0 306 B8
Barns Ct CM19 223 B3
Barnsley Rd RM3 314 F3
Barnstaple Cl SS1 368 A8
Barnstaple Path 7 RM3 314 D5
Barnstaple Rd
Romford RM3 314 C5
Southend-on-S SS1 368 B8
BARNSTON 151 A4
Barnston Gn CM6 151 A4
Barnston Way CM13 295 C4
Barn The RM17 373 B2
Barn View Rd CO6 131 A1
Barnwell Dr SS5 324 D6
Barnyard The SS16 341 A4
Baron Ct RM3 314 F2
Baron Ct SS2 347 F5
Baron Gdns IG6 333 C8
Baronia Croft CO4 110 C3
Baron Rd Dagenham RM8 334 D3
South Woodham Ferrers CM3 301 E7
Barons Court Inf Sch SS0 366 F8
Barons Ct IG1 333 D2
Baron's Ct 5 CB9 8 E7
Baron's La CM3, CM9 258 E1
Barons The CM23 145 D5
Barons Way SS16 341 B4
Baronswood Way CO2 135 D2
Barrack Cnr 5 IP1 17 B6
Barrack La
Great Waltham CM3 207 E8
Harwich CO12 91 E4
Ipswich IP1 17 B6
Barrack Rd CM1 206 B5
Barrack Row 1 DA11 379 B1
Barrack Sq 10 CM2 232 B2
Barrack St Bradfield CO11 114 D8
Colchester CO1 136 B6
Barracks The CM7 73 C3
Barra Glade SS12 321 F5
Barrass Cl EN3 265 A2
Barr Cl CO7 137 C1
Barrel Cl CO7 139 A3
Barrells Down Rd CM23 118 E1
Barrett Cl RM3 314 B3
Barrett La 5 CM23 145 F7
Barrie Pavement 1 SS12 321 D5
Barrington Cl
1 Basildon SS14 342 F8
Great Baddow CM2 255 A6
Little Clacton CO16 168 C2
Loughton IG10 289 C5
Southend-on-S SS3 349 E1
Woodford IG5 310 F2
Barrington Ct CM13 295 C3
Barrington Gdns
Basildon SS14 342 F8
Clacton-on-S CO15 196 C5
Barrington Gn IG10 289 C5
Barrington Ho CO2 136 A5
Barrington Pl CM4 274 B3
Barrington Rd
Colchester CO2 136 A5
Little Ilford E12 352 A6
Loughton IG10 289 C5
Barringtons Cl SS6 323 D3
Barron's Cl CM5 248 F4
Barrow Chase CM2 233 B4
Barrow Hall Rd SS3 349 C5
Barrow Marsh CM9 238 A4
Barrow Mews CO5 218 E8
Barrowsand SS1 368 B6
Barrows Rd CM19 222 F8
Barry Cl RM16 374 A3
Barry Ct RM5 313 D5
Barryfields CM7 100 E7
Barrymore Wlk SS6 324 A2
BARSTABLE 342 D6
Barstable Rd SS17 360 D1
Barstable Sch SS14 342 F6
Bartholomew Cl CB10 3 E2
Bartholomew Ct CO4 109 E3
Bartholomew Dr RM3 314 D1
BARTHOLOMEW GREEN 153 E7
Bartholomew Ho 16 IG8 311 A3
Bartholomew Rd 8 CM23 145 F6
Bartholomew St IP4 17 F6
Bartlett Cl CM3 260 F1
Bartletts Rayleigh SS6 346 A8
Saffron Walden CB10 22 D1
Bartletts Ho 15 RM10 354 B6
Bartley Cl SS7 344 B6
Bartley Rd SS7 344 B6
BARTLOW 6 B7
Bartlow End SS13 343 B8
Bartlow Gdns RM5 313 D2
Bartlow Rd
Castle Camps CB21 7 D4
Hadstock CB1 5 D7
Bartlow Side SS13 343 B8
Barton Ave RM7 335 B3
Barton Cl Chigwell IG7 311 C8
Ipswich IP2 16 E2
South Woodham Ferrers CM3 279 D1
Barton Ct 8 CM14 316 C6
Barton Friars IG7 311 C8
Barton Mdws IG6 333 B7
Barton Rd Felixstowe IP11 381 F4
Hornchurch RM12 336 A3
Bartram Ave N CM7 128 C3
Bartram Ave S CM7 128 C3
Bartram Ct RM8 353 B6
Barwell Ho 3 CM8 211 E8
Barwell Way CM8 184 B2
Baryta Cl SS17 360 C1
Baryta Ct SS9 365 E8
Basbow La 2 CM23 145 F7
Basedale Rd RM9 353 B5
BASILDON 342 C4
Basildon Ave IG5 311 A1
Basildon Bsns Ctr SS14 342 A8
Basildon Dr SS15 341 C8
Basildon Hospl SS16 342 A3
Basildon Rd SS15 341 E8
Basildon Rise SS15 341 E8
Basildon Sta SS14 342 A5
Basildon Trad Ctr SS14 341 F8
Basildon Zoo★ SS16 342 C2
Basilica Ho SS11 322 B7
Basil Mews 1 CM17 200 C1
Basing Ho 7 IG11 352 D4
Basin Rd CM9 237 E3
Bassenthwaite Rd SS7 344 E7
Bassett Bsns Units CM16 246 F4
Bassett Fields CM16 247 D6
Bassett Gdns CM16 247 B5
Bassett Ho RM9 353 B4
Bassetts La CM3, CM9 235 A4
Bassett's La CM5 251 B8
Bassingbourn Rd CM24 121 A3
Bassingham Cres CO5 186 E5
Bastable Ave IG11 353 A3
Bata Ave RM18 375 B1
Batavia Rd SS8 363 D4
Bate-Dudley Dr CM0 242 B3
Bateman Cl 2 IG11 352 C6
Bateman Rd
Brightlingsea CO7 192 E8
Chingford E4 309 A4
Batemans Mews CM14 316 B6
Bateman's Rd CO16 168 B4
Bates Bsns Ctr RM3 315 A3
Bates Rd Maldon CM9 237 B4
Romford RM3 315 A3
Bath Ct CB9 8 F6
Bath Hill IP11 381 F4
Bath Rd Dagenham RM6 334 E5
Felixstowe IP11 381 F4
BATH SIDE 91 D5
Bath St Gravesend DA11 379 B1
Ipswich IP2 17 D3
Wivenhoe CO7 164 B8
Bathurst Cl 11 CO2 136 A1
Bathurst Rd IG1 333 B3
Baton Cl RM19 371 D2
Battery La IP9 91 B8
Batt Hall CO10 33 B6
Battisford Dr CO16 195 A4
Battis The 1 RM1 335 E5
Battle Ct CM5 249 A2
Battle Rd DA17 369 C2
BATTLESBRIDGE 300 D1
Battlesbridge Antiques Ctr★ SS11 300 E2
Battles Bridge Motorcycle Mus★ SS11 300 D2
Battlesbridge Sta SS11 300 D2
Battlesbrook Rd CO2 136 D2
Battleswick SS14 320 E1
Batt's Rd CM0 284 A8
Bawden Way CM2 254 D8
Bawdsey Ave IG2 333 F7
Bawdsey Cl CO16 195 B3
Bawn Cl CM7 128 A4
Bawtree Way CO3 135 A5
Baxter Ave SS2 347 F1
Baxter Gdns RM3 314 C8
Baxter Rd IG1 352 B7
Baxters CM3 257 A7
Bayard Ave CO7 192 F7
Bay Cl SS8 364 B2
Bay Ct CO12 91 D5
Bayleys Mead CM13 317 C8
Bayley St CO9 51 F4
Baylis Rd DA1 376 A1
Bay Manor La RM20 376 F8
Baymans Woods CM15 316 F8
Baynard Ave CM6 151 E6
Baynard Gn CO2 135 F4
Baynards Cres CO13 170 E6
Baynard's Prim Sch CO5 186 B7
Bayning Ho CO7 139 F8
Bay Rd CO12 91 D4
Bays Dr CO9 76 E2
Baytree Cl Rayne CM77 126 F2
Wix CO11 115 C5
Bay Tree Cl IG6 311 B3
Baytree Ctr 16 CM14 316 C8
Baytree Ho E4 287 B2
Bay View CM0 262 C8
Bay View Cres
Harwich CO12 90 C1
Little Oakley CO12 117 C8
Baywood Sq IG7 312 B6
Beach App CO16 220 B6
Beach Ave SS9 366 A8
Beach Cres CO15 220 F6
Beach Ct
Great Wakering SS3 350 C3
Southend-on-S SS0 366 C7
Beaches Cl SS5 325 A6
Beach House Gdns SS8 364 E2
Beach Rd
Canvey Island SS8 364 D4
Clacton-on-S CO15 195 F2
Harwich CO12 91 C2
Lee-o-S CO16 219 D6
Seawick CO16 220 C7
Beach Rd *continued*
Southend-on-S, Shoeburyness SS1 368 F5
Southend-on-S SS1 367 C7
St Osyth CO16 194 B2
West Mersea CO5 218 C5
Beach Rd W IP11 381 D2
Beach's Dr CM1 231 D3
Beach Station Rd IP11 381 C1
Beachway SS8 364 B2
Beach Way CO15 220 F6
Beachy Dr CM0 262 C8
Beacon Cl CO7 192 E6
BEACON END 134 D6
Beacon End Ctyd CO3 134 C6
Beacon Field IP11 381 C5
Beaconfield Ave CM16 246 A2
Beaconfield Rd CM16 246 A2
Beaconfield Way CM16 246 A2
BEACON HILL 213 A6
Beacon Hill
Kelvedon Hatch CM14 271 C2
Maldon CM9 236 E2
Purfleet RM19 371 B1
Wickham Bishops CM8 213 A6
Beacon Hill Ave CO12 91 E4
Beacon Hill Ind Est RM19 371 B1
Beacon Hill Rd CM14 271 B2
Beacon Hill Sch Ipswich IP2 16 F3
South Ockendon RM15 372 A8
Beacon Hts CO16 193 B2
Beaconsfield Ave CO3 135 E6
Beaconsfield Cl CO10 33 E8
Beaconsfield Ct 7 CB9 8 F7
Beaconsfield Rd
Clacton-on-S CO15 195 F3
Ipswich IP1 16 F7
Sudbury CO10 33 E8
Beacons The IG10 267 A1
Beacontree Ave E17 309 D1
Beacon Way
Colchester CO3 134 C6
Point Clear B CO16 193 B2
Beadel Cl CM8 211 E8
Beadle Pl CM9 213 B3
Beadle's Par RM10 354 C6
Beadles The CM22 173 B8
Beadle Way CM3 181 A6
Beadon Dr CM7 128 A1
Beads Hall La CM15 294 B4
Beal High Sch IG4 332 E7
Beal Rd IG1 333 A2
Beam Ave RM10 354 B4
Beambridge SS13 343 A6
Beambridge Ct 2 SS13 343 A6
Beambridge Mews SS13 343 A6
Beambridge Pl 1 SS13 343 A6
Beaminster Gdns
Ilford IG6 333 B8
Redbridge IG6 311 B1
Beamish Cl CM16 247 C6
Beam Prim Sch RM10 354 C3
Beams Cl CM11 319 C8
Beams Way CM11 319 C8
Beamway RM10 354 D5
Beanfield Rd CM21 172 A4
Bean Rd DA9 377 B1
Beansland Gr RM6 334 E8
Bearblock Cotts RM14 356 C6
Bear Cl RM7 335 B5
Beard's La CB11 41 A4
Beardsley Dr CM1 232 F7
Beardsley Terr 2 RM8 353 B7
Beard's Terr CO6 131 A3
Bearing Cl IG7 312 A6
Bearing Way IG7 312 A6
Bearmains CM3 299 C8
Bear St CO6 56 A1
Bearsted Dr SS13 343 C5
Bearwalden Bsns Pk CB11 42 F5
Beaton Cl DA9 377 B2
Beatrice Ave
Canvey Island SS8 364 B4
Felixstowe IP11 381 E5
Beatrice Cl Hockley SS5 324 D6
Ipswich IP3 18 A3
Beatrice Ct IG9 310 D8
Beatrice Rd
Clacton-on-S CO15 195 E2
Walton-on-t-N CO14 144 D2
Beatty Gdns CM7 128 C4
Beatty La SS14 342 E6
Beatty Rd IP3 18 B2
Beatty Rise CM3 301 F6
Beattyville Gdns IG6 333 B7
BEAUCHAMP RODING 204 A1
Beauchamps CM0 306 B8
Beauchamps Cl CM1 232 F8
Beauchamps Dr SS11 322 A8
Beauchamps Sch SS11 322 A8
Beaufort Cl Chingford E4 309 B4
Grays RM16 372 F3
North Weald Bassett CM16 247 A4
Romford RM7 335 C7
Beaufort Ct 5 CB9 8 F7
Beaufort Gdns
Braintree CM7 128 A4
Ilford IG1 333 A3
Beaufort Rd
Billericay CM12 296 F2
Chelmsford CM2 233 A4
Beaufort St Ipswich IP1 17 A7
Southend-on-S SS2 348 D1
Beaulieu Bvd CM1 233 A7
Beaulieu Dr EN9 265 B6
Beauly Ct RM1 313 E2
Beauly Way RM1 313 E2
Beaumaris Dr IG8 310 D3
BEAUMONT 141 F7
Beaumont Ave
Brightlingsea CO7 193 A7
Clacton-on-S CO15 195 D3
Beaumont Cl
Colchester CO4 109 F4
Romford RM2 314 C1
Walton-on-t-N CO14 170 F7
Beaumont Cres RM13 355 A6
Beaumont Ct CB9 9 B6
Beaumont Gdns CM13 295 C3
Beaumont Hill CM6 123 D2
Beaumont Ho CO6 131 A3
Beaumont Park Dr CM19 222 B8
Beaumont Pk CM3 256 C6
Beaumont Pl CM7 128 B3
Beaumont Rd CO12 116 C3
Beaumont Vale CB9 9 B6
Beaumont Way CM9 259 B8
Beaumont Wlk CM1 231 D5
Beaver Cl CO3 134 E7
Beaver Ct IP4 18 B7
Beaver Ctr The RM8 334 E4
Beaver Rd IG6 312 C5
Beaver Twr SS9 346 E6
BEAZLEY END 101 C6
Beazley End SS12 321 E6
Bebington Cl CM12 297 A3
Beccles Ct SS11 321 D8
Beccles Dr IG11 352 F6
Beche Ho CO2 135 E4
Beche Rd CO2 136 B5
Becker Rd CO3 134 E4
Beckers Green Prim Sch CM7 128 D2
Beckers Green Rd CM7 128 D2
Becket Ave E6 352 A2
Becket Cl Brentwood CM13 316 C4
Rochford SS4 325 D5
Becket Ho 15 CM14 316 C8
Beckett Dr SS17 360 D4
Becketts SS15 341 A6
Becketts Ct
Brentwood CM13 316 C4
Chelmsford CM1 232 A3
Becketts La IP7 57 D8
Becket Way CM3 301 E5
Beck Farm Cl SS8 364 F3
Beckford Rd CO11 87 A4
Beckingham Bsns Pk CM9 214 D3
Beckingham Rd
Great Totham CM9 213 D5
Tolleshunt D'arcy CM9 215 C4
Beckingham St CM9 214 D3
Beckney Ave SS5 302 E1
Beck Rd Canvey Island SS8 364 F3
Saffron Walden CB11 22 D1
Beckton Alps Ski Ctr★ E6 352 A1
Beckton Triangle Ret Pk E6 352 B1
BECONTREE 353 E8
Becontree Ave RM8 334 D2
Becontree Cl CO15 195 F8
Becontree Day Hospl RM8 334 E2
Becontree Prim Sch RM8 334 B1
Becontree Sta RM9 353 D6
Bedale Rd RM3 315 A5
Beddington Rd IG3 333 F4
Bedells Ave CM77 155 B5
Bede Rd RM6 334 C5
Bedford Cl Braintree CM7 128 B4
Rayleigh SS6 323 D1
Tiptree CO5 186 D5
Bedford Ct 9 CB9 8 F7
Bedford Gdns RM12 336 C2
Bedford Ho 1 RM3 315 A4
Bedford Pl SS8 363 F4
Bedford Rd Basildon SS15 341 B6
Chingford E17 309 A1
Colchester CO4 109 F5
Grays RM17 373 B1
Holland-on-S CO15 196 D5
Ilford IG1 333 B1
Wallend E6 352 A4
Woodford IG8 310 A1
Bedfords Pk Nature Trails★ RM4 313 F5
Bedford St IP1 17 B6
Bedloes Ave SS11 322 E7
Bedloes Cnr SS11 322 F7
Bedwell Ct 4 RM6 334 D4
Bedwell Rd
Belvedere DA17 369 A1
Ugley CM22 94 B3
Beecham Ct SS15 341 C8
Beech Ave Braintree CM7 127 F5
Brentwood CM13 316 F7
Halstead CO9 77 A2
Rayleigh SS6 323 D3
Upminster RM14 356 B8
Wivenhoe CO7 137 B1
Woodford IG9 310 B8
Beech Cl
Burnham-on-C CM0 306 B6
Hornchurch RM12 336 B1
Loughton IG10 289 B6
Sproughton IP8 16 A6
Takeley CM22 148 C8
Beechcombe SS17 361 B4
Beechcroft Ave
Kirby Cross CO13 170 D6
Linford SS17 375 A2
Beechcroft Rd
Canvey Island SS8 363 E3
Woodford E18 310 B1
Beech Ct Basildon SS14 342 E5
6 Buckhurst Hill IG9 310 D8
Dartford DA1 376 A1
Ilford E12 333 A1
Beech Dr CM21 200 C8
Beeches EN9 266 C4
Beeches Cl
Chelmsford CM1 231 E2
Saffron Walden CB11 43 C7
Beeches Rd
Chelmsford CM1 231 E2
Heybridge CM9 236 F5
Rawreth SS11 301 A2
Beeches The
Brentwood CM14 316 B7
Ipswich IP3 17 F4
Lawford CO11 86 C3
Tilbury RM18 379 B5
Wendens Ambo CB11 42 E6
Beech Farm Cotts IG8 309 D3
Beechfield
Hoddesdon EN11 197 A2

Bla–Bra 389

Blackbush Ave RM6 334 D6
Blackbushe CM23 119 C1
Black Bush La SS17 359 D3
Blackbush Spring CM20 200 A1
BLACKCAT 227 A8
Black Chapel La
North End CM6 151 E1
Pleshey CM6 178 E8
Blackdown SS0 347 B8
Blackdown Ave IP5 18 F6
Blackfriars CO10 33 D6
Blackfriars Ct 8 IP4 17 D5
Blackgate Rd SS3 368 G7
BLACKHALL 64 B4
BLACKHEATH 163 B8
Blackheath CO2 163 A8
Blackheath Chase SS16 360 D8
Blackhorse La CM16 247 D6
Black Horse La IP1 17 C6
Blackhouse La CO10 34 C3
Black La CM7 71 F2
Blacklands Cl CB11 43 C7
Blackley La Braintree CM3 153 F3
Great Notley CM77 154 A4
Black Lion Ct CM17 200 C4
Blacklock CM2 233 A3
Blackman Way CM8 184 A1
BLACKMORE 272 F8
Blackmore Ave SS8 364 B2
Blackmore Ct EN9 266 A6
BLACKMORE END 74 B2
Blackmore Mead CM4 272 F8
Blackmore Prim Sch CM4 250 E1
Blackmore Rd
Blackmore CM1 251 D3
Buckhurst Hill IG9 288 E2
Grays RM17 373 C1
Hook End CM15 272 C5
Ingatestone CM4 273 D6
Kelvedon Hatch CM15 271 F2
Blackmores SS15 340 F6
Blackmore Wlk SS6 324 A2
BLACK NOTLEY 155 B5
Blackshots La RM16 373 C5
Blacksmith Cl
Billericay CM12 297 B5
Chelmsford CM1 232 E8
Dagenham RM6 334 C5
Blacksmiths Alley CM4 272 E8
Blacksmiths Cl CM23 145 B5
Black Smiths Cl SG12 197 A7
Blacksmith's Cnr CO6 109 B8
Blacksmith's Cnr CO4 83 D4
BLACKSMITH'S CORNER 36 C6
Blacksmiths Cotts CM17 224 F4
Blacksmiths Hill CO10 11 B4
Blacksmiths La
Bulmer Tye CO10 32 F2
Shudy Camps CB21 7 C6
Wickham Bishops CM8 212 E5
Blacksmith's La
Harwich CO12 90 F2
Rainham RM13 354 F4
Blacksmiths Way CM21 172 B1
Blackthorn Ave CO4 136 E7
Blackthorn Cl Ipswich IP3 18 E1
Writtle CM1 231 A1
Blackthorn Ct SS16 341 A4
Blackthorne Dr E4 309 D6
Blackthorne Rd SS8 364 C3
Blackthorn Rd Barking IG1 352 D7
Grays RM16 373 B5
Harwich CO12 90 F2
Hockley SS5 324 F8
Witham CM8 183 E4
Blackthorn Way
Brentwood CM14 316 D5
Tolleshunt Knights CM9 187 A2
Blackwater SS7 344 F4
Black Water CM14 294 B1
Blackwater Ave CO4 110 E1
Blackwater Cl
Burnham-on-C CM0 306 C5
Chelmsford CM1 232 C6
Heybridge Basin CM9 237 E3
Rainham RM13 369 E8
Southend-on-S SS3 349 E1
Blackwater Cotts CM77 129 D3
Blackwater Dr CO5 218 A6
Blackwater La CM8 212 B8
Blackwater Mews CM0 261 E2
Blackwater Way CM7 128 A4
Blackwell Dr CM7 127 C4
Blackwood Chine CM3 301 E6
Bladen Dr IP4 18 F5
Bladon Cl Braintree CM7 127 E7
Tiptree CO5 186 E5
Blaine Dr CO13 170 F7
Blair Cl
Bishop's Stortford CM23 145 C7
Rushmere St A IP4 18 E5
Blair Par CB9 8 E8
Blake Ave IG11 352 F4
Blakeborough Dr RM3 314 E1
Blake Cl Lawford CO11 86 B4
Rainham RM13 354 F4
Blake Ct CM3 301 E6
Blake Dr Braintree CM7 128 C4
Clacton-on-S CO16 195 D6
BLAKE END 126 A2
Blake Hall Cres E11 332 A3
Blake Hall Dr SS11 322 A6
Blake Hall Gdns★ CM5 248 E7
Blake Hall Rd
Chipping Ongar CM5 248 A5
Wanstead E11 332 A4
Blake Rd CM8 183 F5
Blakes Ct CM21 172 E2
Blakesley Ho 4 E12 333 A1
Blake Way RM18 379 C5
Blamsters Cres CO9 103 D8
Blamsters Rise CM6 97 A2
Blanchard Cl CO13 170 A7
Blanchard Gr EN3 265 B1
Blanchard Mews RM3 314 F3
Blanche St IP4 17 D6
Blandford Cl RM7 335 B7
Blandford Cres E4 287 C2
Blandford Rd IP3 18 D3
Blaney Cres E6 352 B2
Blatches Chase
Rayleigh SS2 346 F7
Southend-on-S SS2 347 A8
Blatchford Ho 8 RM10 335 A1
Blaxhall Ct 17 CB9 8 E7
Blenheim Ave IG2 333 A5
Blenheim Chase SS9 346 E3
Blenheim Cl Bicknacre CM3 256 F2
Braintree CM7 127 E7
Brantham CO11 60 D1
Hockley SS5 324 E8
Romford RM7 335 C7
Sawbridgeworth CM21 200 C8
Upminster RM14 337 E3
Blenheim Cres SS9 346 E2
Blenheim Ct
Bishop's Stortford CM23 145 C7
Clacton-on-S CO15 195 D2
Hornchurch RM12 355 C7
3 Ipswich IP1 17 A7
4 Wickford SS11 322 A5
Woodford IG8 310 B3
Woodford IG8 310 C2
Blenheim Dr CO2 163 A8
Blenheim Gdns
Aveley RM15 371 B5
Mayland CM3 261 A1
Blenheim Mews SS9 346 E3
Blenheim Park Cl SS9 346 F4
Blenheim Prim Sch SS9 346 F3
Blenheim Rd
Clacton-on-S CO15 195 D2
Ipswich IP1 17 A7
Pilgrims Hatch CM15 294 A3
Blenheim Way
North Weald Bassett
CM16 247 A4
Tiptree CO5 186 F5
Blessing Way IG11 353 C3
Bletchington Ct 1 DA17 369 A2
Blewetts Cotts RM13 354 F2
Blickling Cl IP2 17 B2
Blickling Rd CM77 154 C8
Bligh Rd DA11 379 A1
Blind La Easthorpe CO2 160 B4
Eight Ash G CO6 134 A8
Goldhanger CM9 238 C7
Howe Green CM2 255 F4
Little Burstead CM12 318 B5
Mundon CM9 259 C2
Tolleshunt Knights CM9 187 B1
West Hanningfield CM2 276 F5
Bliss Cl CM8 211 F7
Blithbury Rd RM9 353 B6
Blithe Ct CO7 164 B8
Blockhouse Rd RM17 378 C8
Blofield Rd IP11 381 A4
Blois Meadows Bsns Ctr
CB9 27 C8
Blois Rd
Steeple Bumpstead CB9 27 D8
Sturmer CB9 9 F1
Blomville Rd RM8 334 E1
Bloom Cl CO13 170 F6
Bloomfield Ave CO13 170 F7
Bloomfield Cres IG2 333 B5
Bloomfield Ct CO10 12 B7
Bloomfield St IP4 18 B6
Bloomsbury Ho IG8 310 E4
Bloomsbury Mews IG8 310 E4
Blooms Hall La CO10 2 F8
Blossom Cl RM9 353 F4
Blossom Mews CO5 218 D6
Blott Rise CM8 211 F8
Blountswood Rd
Hockley SS5 324 A8
Hullbridge SS5 323 F6
Blower Cl SS6 323 F3
Blows Cotts RM15 371 D5
Bloyers Mews CO1 109 F1
Blue Anchor La RM18 374 E1
Bluebell Ave CO16 195 C4
Bluebell Cl Ipswich IP2 16 E4
Romford RM7 335 E2
Witham CM8 183 E3
Bluebell Gn 5 CM1 232 E7
Bluebell Way
Colchester CO4 109 C2
Ilford IG1 352 B6
Bluebell Wood CM12 296 E4
Blueberry Cl IG8 310 A4
Bluebird La RM10 354 A5
Bluebridge Cotts CO9 77 A1
Bluebridge Ind Est CO9 77 B1
Bluegate La IP9 60 B7
Bluegate Pk CM14 316 B7
Bluehouse Ave CO16 195 A4
Blue House Farm Chase
CM3 303 B7
Bluehouse Rd E4 309 E7
Bluemans CM16 247 D7
Bluemans End CM16 247 D7
Blue Mill La CM9 235 E4
Blue Mills Hill CM8 212 B7
Blue Rd CO5 186 C5
Bluestem Rd IP3 38 E8
Blunden Cl RM8 334 C3
Blundens The CO6 56 C6
Blunt's Hall Dr CM8 183 D1
Blunts Hall Rd CM8 183 D1
Blunts Wall Rd CM12 296 E1
Blyford Rd CO16 195 A4
Blyford Way IP11 381 A4
Blyth Ave SS3 368 C7
Blyth Cl IP2 17 A1
Blyth Ct CB11 43 E8
Blythe La CO7 164 B8
Blythe Rd Hoddesdon EN11 221 D5
Stanford-le-H SS17 360 E4
Blythe Way Maldon CM9 259 A8
South Benfleet SS7 344 C7
Blyth Ho DA8 369 E1
Blyth's Mdw CM7 127 F3
Blyth's Way CM77 126 F2
Blythswood Rd IG3 334 A4
Blyth Wlk RM14 337 E5
Blythwood Gdns CM24 119 D6
Blyton Cl SS12 321 D5
Boadicea Cotts CO8 79 F6
Boadicea Way CO2 135 C4
Boar Cl IG7 312 A5
Boarded Row SS4 328 A5
Boardman Ave E4 287 B4
Boars Tye Rd CM8 156 D6
Boat Ho The CO7 192 E5
Boat House Mews The
CO10 12 B7
Boatman Cl IP8 36 E8
Bobbing Cl SS4 325 F2
BOBBINGWORTH 248 D8
Bobbingworth Mill CM5 248 A7
Bobbits La IP9 36 F8
Bobbits Way CO7 164 C8
Bob Dunn Way DA1 376 A4
Bober Ct CO2 163 B7
Bob Russell Ho CO2 136 A5
BOCKING 127 F4
BOCKING
CHURCHSTREET 127 F8
Bocking Church Street Prim
Sch CM7 127 F8
Bocking End CM7 127 F3
Bockingham Gn SS13 343 A8
Bocking Pl CM7 127 F3
BOCKING'S ELM 195 B5
Bockings Elm Par CO16 195 B5
Bocking's Gr CO16 195 B5
Bocking Windmill★ CM7 128 A8
Bodell Cl RM16 373 B3
Bodiam Cl Basildon SS13 343 B6
Ipswich IP3 18 D4
Bodiam Rd IP3 18 D4
Bodiam Wlk 3 CB9 8 E8
Bodle Ave DA10 377 E1
Bodley Cl CM16 245 F1
Bodmin Rd CM1 232 D5
Bogmoor Rd SG8 39 A8
Bohemia Chase SS9 346 D5
Bohun Cl CM3 180 F7
Boiler Ho The SS4 325 E2
Bois Field Terr CO9 76 E2
Bois Hall Gdns CO9 76 F3
Boley Dr CO15 196 A4
Boleyn Cl Billericay CM12 297 A5
Grays RM16 372 F3
Loughton IG10 288 E3
Southend-on-S SS9 346 C7
Boleyn Ct IG9 288 B1
Boleyn Gdns
Brentwood CM13 317 A7
Dagenham RM10 354 C5
Boleyn Ho 1 SS4 325 F2
Boleyns Ave CM7 127 F6
Boleyn Way Boreham CM3 209 F1
Clacton-on-S CO15 220 F8
Haverhill CB9 8 D7
Redbridge IG6 311 C4
Boley Rd CO6 106 A8
Bolford St CM6 69 F2
Bolingbroke Cl CM3 180 F7
Bolney Dr SS9 346 C7
Bolsin Dr CO4 109 E4
Bolton La IP4 17 D6
Boltons The IG8 310 A6
Bommel Ave SS8 365 A3
Bonchurch Ave SS9 346 D2
Bonchurch Ct 20 RM19 371 B1
Bonds Cotts CM5 204 A1
Bond St Chelmsford CM2 232 C2
Grays RM17 378 C8
Ipswich IP4 17 D5
Bonham Cl CO15 196 A5
Bonham Dr RM16 374 A8
Bonham Gdns RM8 334 D2
Bonham Rd RM8 334 D1
Bonington Chase CM1 232 E6
Bonington Rd RM12 355 D7
Bonks Hill CM21 172 D1
Bonner Wlk RM16 372 F3
Bonneting La CM23 92 B8
Bonnett Mews RM11 336 E3
Bonnington Rd IP3 17 F1
Bonningtons CM13 317 B7
Bonny Cres IP3 38 C8
Bonnygate SS14 342 D7
Bonnygate Prim Sch
RM15 372 B8
Boomes Ind Est RM13 354 F1
Boone Pl CM8 184 A2
Boons Cl CM3 233 E8
BOOSE'S GREEN 77 F2
Bootham Cl CM12 296 F1
Bootham Rd CM12 296 F1
Booth Ave CO4 136 C8
Booth Ct E4 309 C7
Booth Pl CM0 306 C5
Booth's Ct CM13 295 B3
Borda Cl CM1 232 A5
Border Edge Ho 6 CM14 316 C6
Border's La IG10 289 B5
BOREHAM 233 E8
Boreham Cl SS11 322 B5
Boreham Ct CM1 177 D2
Borehamgate CO10 33 F7
Boreham Ind Est CM3 209 F2
Boreham Mews 1 EN11 197 A1
Boreham Pl CO9 10 B2
Boreham Prim Sch CM3 233 F8
Boreham Rd
Great Leighs CM3 181 B7
Little Waltham CM3 181 B2
Borland Cl DA9 377 A2
BORLEY 14 F3
Borley Ct RM16 374 D7
BORLEY GREEN 14 D2
Borley Rd CO10 15 B4
Borman Cl SS9 347 A6
Borough La CB11 43 D8
Borradale Ct CB9 27 B6
Borrett Ave SS8 364 A4
Borrowdale Ave IP4 17 E8
Borrowdale Cl
Redbridge IG4 332 E7
Thundersley SS7 344 F6
Borrowdale Rd
Thundersley SS7 344 F6
Thundersley SS7 344 F7
Borwick La Crays Hill CM11 320 F4
Wickford CM11, SS12 321 A4
Bosanquet Rd EN11 221 C8
Boscawen Gdns CM7 128 C4
Boscombe Ave
Grays RM17 373 D2
Hornchurch RM11 336 D4
Wickford SS12 320 F8
Boscombe Ct CO15 196 F6
Boscombe Mews SS2 367 B8
Boscombe Rd SS2 348 B1
Bosgrove E4 309 C8
Boss Hall Bsns Pk IP1 16 E7
Boss Hall Rd IP1 16 E7
Bostocke Cl SS15 341 D5
Bostock Rd IP2 17 C1
Boston Ave Rayleigh SS6 323 B4
Southend-on-S SS2 347 F1
Boston Lofts 2 SS2 347 F1
Boston Rd IP4 17 F7
Boswell Ave SS4 325 D5
Boswells Dr CM2 232 C2
Boswells Sch The CM1 232 D6
Bosworth Cl SS5 324 F4
Bosworth Cres RM3 314 C4
Bosworth Ho DA8 369 E1
Bosworth Rd
Dagenham RM10 335 A1
Southend-on-S SS9 346 C7
Botanical Way CO16 194 A5
Botany Cotts RM19 371 A1
Botany Dr CM7 128 D3
Botany La CO16 168 B5
Botany Terr RM19 371 A1
Botany Way RM19 371 B1
Botelers SS16 341 E4
Boteley Cl E4 309 D8
Botney Hill Rd CM12 318 D4
Bouchers Mead CM1 232 F7
Bouchiers Barn Visitors Ctr★
CO6 130 D7
Bouchiers Pl CO5 159 D2
Bouchier Wlk 2 RM13 355 A6
Boudicca Mews 5 CM2 232 B1
Boudicca Wlk CO7 137 C3
Bouldrewood Rd SS7 344 B5
Boulevard The
Greenhithe DA9 377 C3
3 Redbridge IG8 311 A3
Rochford SS4 325 F3
Boulter Gdns RM13 355 A7
Boulton Cotts CM9 237 B5
Boulton Rd RM8 334 F2
Boult Rd SS15 341 C8
Boundary Cl
Bishop's Stortford CM23 146 A5
Ilford IG3 352 E8
Boundary Ct CM16 267 D7
Boundary Dr CM13 295 E2
Boundary Rd Barking IG11 352 C3
Barking IG11 352 D4
Bishop's Stortford CM23 146 A5
Colchester CO4 136 F4
Romford RM1 336 A5
Southend-on-S SS9 346 B8
Sturmer CB9 9 D5
Upminster RM14 337 B2
Wivenhoe CO7 137 A4
Boundary Way SS3 368 E6
Bounderby Gr CM1 231 E7
Bounstead Hill CO2 162 C5
Bounstead Rd CO2 162 D7
Bourchier Ave CM7 128 D5
Bourchier Way CO9 103 D8
Bourne Ave SS15 341 A8
Bournebridge Cl CM13 295 E2
Bournebridge Hill CO9 103 B6
Bournebridge La RM4 291 B2
Bourne Cl Basildon SS15 341 A8
Halstead CO9 103 D8
Bourne Ct Braintree CM7 128 D1
Colchester CO2 136 A4
Wanstead E11 332 A6
Woodford IG8 310 D1
Bourne End RM11 337 A4
Bourne Gdns E4 309 B6
Bourne Hill IP2 37 B7
Bourne Ho IG9 310 D7
Bourne Mill★ CO2 136 B4
Bournemouth Park Prim Sch
SS2 348 B2
Bournemouth Park Rd
SS2 348 B2
Bournemouth Rd CO15 196 F6
Bourne Park Residential Pk
IP2 17 B1
Bourne Rd Colchester CO2 136 B4
Haverhill CB9 9 B8
West Bergholt CO6 108 E2
BOURNES GREEN 349 B1
Bournes Green Chase
SS3 349 B1
Bournes Green Inf Sch
SS1 368 B8
Bournes Green Jun Sch
SS1 368 B8
Bourne Terr IP2 37 B8
Bourne The CM23 146 A8
Bouvel Dr CM0 306 B8
Bouverie Rd CM2 254 B8
Bovey Way RM15 372 B8
Bovills Way CO16 168 C1
Bovingdon Rd CM7 101 D2
BOVINGER 248 A7
Bovinger Way SS1 348 F1
BOW ARROW 376 B1
Bow Arrow La
Dartford DA1 376 A1
Dartford DA2 376 B1
Bowbank Cl SS3 349 F1
Bowden Dr RM11 336 E3
Bowdens La CO6 80 F7
Bower Cl RM5 313 D3
Bower Ct CM16 268 A7
Bower Farm Rd RM4 313 D7
Bower Gdns CM9 236 F3
Bower Hall Dr CB9 27 B6
Bower Hall La CO5 190 F1
Bower Hill CM16 268 A7
Bower Hill Ind Est CM16 268 A7
Bower La SS14 342 E8
Bowerman Rd RM16 374 A2
Bower Park Sch RM1 313 E4
Bowers Cl CM8 156 E3
Bowers Court Dr SS13 343 F5
BOWERS GIFFORD 343 E6
Bowers Ho 5 IG11 352 B5
Bowers Rd SS7 344 D5
Bower Vale CM16 268 A7
Bowery Ct 4 RM10 354 B6
Bowes Ct 17 DA2 376 B1
Bowes Dr CM5 249 A4
Bowes Ho CM5 249 A4
Bowes Rd Dagenham RM8 353 C8
Wivenhoe CO7 137 D1
Bowfell Ct SS16 341 A5
Bowfell Dr SS16 341 A5
Bowhay CM13 317 B8
Bowland Dr IP8 16 C1
Bowland Rd IG8 310 C4
Bowlers Croft SS14 320 F2
Bowling Cl 14 CM23 145 F6
Bowling Green Ct IP11 381 E4
Bowls The IG7 311 F7
Bowman Ave SS9 346 B6
Bowmans Pk CO9 51 E4
Bowmont Cl CM13 295 B3
Bown Cl RM18 379 B5
Bowness Way RM12 355 A7
Bowsers La CB10 5 C3
Bowthorpe Cl IP1 17 B7
Bowyer Ct 4 E4 287 C1
Box Cl SS15 319 D1
Boxford Cl SS6 322 F3
Boxford Ct Felixstowe IP11 381 A4
Haverhill CB9 8 E7
Boxhouse La CO7 84 C5
Box La IG11 353 C3
Boxley La CM22 175 D8
Box Mill La CO9 76 E3
Boxmoor Rd RM5 313 C5
Boxoll Rd RM9 334 F1
BOXTED 82 F7
Boxted Ave CO16 195 C4
Boxted Church Rd CO6 82 C5
Boxted Cl IG9 288 E1
BOXTED CROSS 83 B5
Boxted Rd Colchester CO4 109 E6
Great Horkesley CO6 82 C3
Boxted St Peter's CE Prim Sch
CO4 82 F7
Boxted Straight Rd CO4 83 A5
Boyce Gn SS7 344 D2
Boyce Hill Cl SS9 346 B5
Boyce Rd
Southend-on-S SS3 368 H8
Stanford-le-H SS17 360 C3
Boyce View Dr SS7 344 C2
Boyd Cl 1 CM23 146 B8
Boyd Ct SS12 321 F5
Boydell's Dairy Farm★
CM7 100 E8
Boyden Cl SS2 348 F2
Boydin Cl CM8 211 E8
Boydlands IP9 35 A1
Boyes Croft CM6 123 D1
Boyle Ho 13 DA17 369 A3
Boyles Court Cotts CM14 316 A3
Boyles Ct CO2 163 B7
Boyne Dr CM1 232 D6
Boyne Rd RM10 335 A1
Boysenberry Wlk IP3 38 C7
Boyton Cl SS7 345 A5
BOYTON CROSS 230 B7
BOYTON END 70 C5
Boyton Hall La CM1 230 C8
Boyton Rd IP3 18 B1
Boytons SS15 341 E6
Boytons Acre CB11 43 D8
Boyton's La CB10 26 A1
Boyton Vineyard★ CO10 10 D5
Brabant Rd CM3 303 A7
Brabner Gdns CM11 298 C4
Bracelet Cl SS17 360 F5
Brace Wlk CM3 301 E5
Brackenbury Cl IP1 17 B8
Bracken Cl IG10 289 B8
Bracken Ct 1 IG6 311 F4
Brackendale CM11 297 D3
Brackendale Ave SS13 343 C4
Brackendale Cl SS5 324 E7
Brackendale Ct SS13 343 C4
Brackendale Gdns RM14 356 C8
Bracken Dell SS6 323 E2
Brackenden Dr CM1 232 D7
Bracken Dr IG7 311 C4
Brackenhayes Cl IP2 17 B3
Bracken Ind Est IG6 311 F2
Bracken Mews
Chingford E4 287 C1
Romford RM7 335 B5
Brackens Dr CM14 316 D5
Brackens The CO4 110 B3
Bracken The E4 309 C8
Bracken Way
Abberton CO5 163 B2
Thundersley SS7 345 A6
Brackley Cl IP11 381 C5
Brackley Cres SS13 343 A8
Brackley Ho 4 RM3 314 F4
Brackley Sq IG8 310 D3
Bracknell Ho 3 RM3 314 F4
Bracks La CO6 131 F3
Bradbourne Rd RM17 378 B8
Bradbourne Way SS13 343 C5
Bradbrook Cotts CO6 108 F4
Bradbury Dr CM7 127 D3
Bradd Cl RM15 357 C2
Braddock Cl RM5 313 C4
Braddy Ct CO5 158 C2
BRADFIELD 87 F2
Bradfield Ct 12 RM19 371 B1
Bradfield Dr IG11 353 A7
BRADFIELD HEATH 114 D8
Bradfield Ho IG8 311 A4
Bradfield Prim Sch CO11 87 E1
Bradfield Rd CO11 115 B7
Bradford Bury SS9 346 C6
Bradford Dr CO4 109 E2
Bradford Rd IG1 333 D3
Bradfords Ct CM7 128 A4
Bradford St Braintree CM7 128 A4
Chelmsford CM2 232 A1
Brading Ave CO15 196 A7
Brading Cres E11 332 B2
Bradleigh Ave RM17 373 C2
Bradley Ave SS7 344 F5
Bradley Cl
Canvey Island SS8 364 A5
Great Dunmow CM6 123 C2
Thundersley SS7 344 F5
Bradley Comm CM23 119 C3
Bradley Gn SS13 321 C1
Bradley Ho IG8 310 A3
Bradley Link SS7 344 F5
Bradley Mews 1 CB10 22 F2
Bradley Rd EN9 265 C4
Bradley St 6 IP2 17 C4
Bradley Way SS4 325 F1
Bradshaw Rd RM16 373 A5
BRADWELL 129 D2
Bradwell Ave RM10 335 A2
Bradwell Cl RM12 355 B6
Bradwell Ct
Braintree CM77 155 C8
3 Brentwood CM13 295 C3
Bradwell Gn 2 CM13 295 C3
Bradwell Ho SS11 321 F7
BRADWELL-ON-SEA 242 B2
Bradwell Power Sta Visitor
Ctr★ CM0 242 A6
Bradwell Rd
Buckhurst Hill IG9 288 E2
Steeple CM0 262 A3
St Lawrence CM0 262 E6
Tillingham CM0 263 E6
BRADWELL WATERSIDE 241 F4
Brady Ave IG10 289 C7
Brady Ct 4 RM8 334 D3
Brady Prim Sch RM13 370 C8
Braemar Ave CM2 254 B8
Braemar Cres SS9 346 A2
Braemar Gdns RM11 337 A5
Braemar Wlk SS13 343 B6
Braemore SS8 363 F5
Braemore Cl CO4 110 D3
Braeside Sch
Buckhurst Hill IG9 288 B1
Buckhurst Hill IG9 310 C8
Bragg Cl RM8 353 B6
Braggon's Hill IP29 2 B8
Braiding Cres CM7 128 C3
Brain Rd CM8 183 E3
BRAINTREE 128 B5
Braintree Ave IG4 332 E7
Braintree Cnr CO9 75 F6
Braintree Coll CM7 128 A5
Braintree Ent Ctr CM7 127 D5
Braintree Foyer The 7
CM7 127 F2
Braintree Mus & Heritage
Ctr★ CM7 127 F3
Braintree Rd
Cressing CM77 155 E7
Dagenham RM10 335 A1
Felsted CM6 152 C6
Gosfield CO9 102 E5
Great Bardfield CM7 72 B1
Great Dunmow CM6 124 A1
Shalford CM7 100 E6
Terling CM3 181 E5
Wethersfield CM7 73 D2
Witham CM8 183 F4
Braintree Sta CM7 128 A2
Braintree Town FC CM7 128 C2
Brain Valley Ave CM77 155 B6
Brairwood Cl SS9 346 D5
BRAISWICK 109 B2
Braiswick CO4 109 C2
Braiswick La CO4 109 D4
Braiswick Pl Basildon SS15 341 B8
Colchester CO4 109 C3
Braithwaite Ave RM7 335 A4
Braithwaite Dr CO4 109 F2
Bramber Ct 7 DA2 376 B1
Bramble Cl Chigwell IG7 289 C1
Southend-on-S SS9 346 B7
Bramble Cres SS7 346 A5
Bramble Croft DA8 369 C2
Bramble Ct
2 Redbridge IG6 311 F4
Witham CM8 183 E4
Brambledown CO5 218 C7
Bramble Dr IP3 18 E1
Bramble La
Little Dunmow CM6 151 F8
Upminster RM14 356 D4
Bramble Rd
Canvey Island SS8 364 C3
Hadleigh SS7 345 F6
Southend-on-S SS9 346 B7
Witham CM8 183 E4
Bramble Rise CM20 199 C1
Brambles CO14 171 B7
Brambles The
Basildon SS15 341 A8
Bishop's Stortford CM23 145 C6
Braintree CM7 127 E3
Chigwell IG7 311 C4
Colchester CO3 134 F3
Southminster CM0 284 D3
Steeple CM0 284 A7
Bramble Tye Basildon SS15 319 F1
Harwich CO12 90 D1
Bramblewood 1 IP8 16 C2
Bramblings The E4 309 D6
Bramerton Rd SS5 324 D6
Bramfield Rd E SS6 324 A2
Bramfield Rd W SS6 323 F2
Bramford La IP1 16 F8
Bramford Rd IP1 16 E8
Bramhall Cl IP2 16 D1
Bramley Chase IP4 18 B7
Bramley Cl Alresford CO7 165 B8
Braintree CM7 128 A1
Colchester CO3 135 B7
Woodford IG8 310 C3
Bramley Cotts CM3 182 B2
Bramley Cres IG2 333 A5

Brook Par IG7 311 B7
Brook Pl CO9 76 E1
Brook Rd Aldham CO6 133 B7
Brentwood, Brook Street CM14 315 F7
Brentwood CM14 315 D5
Buckhurst Hill IG9 288 A1
Epping CM16 268 A6
Great Tey CO6 132 C7
Ilford IG2 333 E5
Loughton IG10 288 E4
Rayleigh SS6 345 D8
Romford RM2 313 F2
Sawbridgeworth CM21 172 E1
South Benfleet SS7 344 C2
Stansted Mountfitchet CM24 119 E6
St Lawrence CM0 263 B5
Tillingham CM0 263 E5
Tiptree CO5 186 F3
Tolleshunt Knights CM9, CO5 187 A2
Brook Retail Pk CO16 195 E7
Brook Rise IG7 311 A7
Brook Road Ind Ctr SS6 345 D8
Brook St Rdbt CM14 315 D5
Brookscroft Rd E17 309 B2
Brook Service Rd CB9 9 A7
Brooks Hall Rd IP1 17 A7
Brookside Billericay CM11 297 C6
Canvey Island SS8 364 A5
Harlow CM19 223 A5
Hockley SS5 324 F4
Hoddesdon EN11 221 A6
Hornchurch RM11 336 E6
Margaretting CM4 274 F7
Redbridge IG6 311 C4
Waltham Abbey EN9 265 E7
Brookside Ave SS3 350 C2
Brookside Cl
Billericay CM11 297 C6
Colchester CO2 136 B4
Brookside Ctr SS2 347 F5
Brookside Jun & Inf Schs RM3 314 E5
Brooksies CB11 40 F6
Brooks Malting 3 CO11 86 D4
Brook's Mans 5 IG3 334 B3
Brook's Par 6 IG3 334 B3
Brook St Belvedere DA17 369 B1
Brentwood CM14 315 E6
Chelmsford CM1 232 B3
Colchester CO1 136 B7
Colne Engaine CO6 77 F1
Dedham CO7 84 F7
Glemsford CO10 2 B6
Great Bardfield CM7 72 B2
Great Bromley CO7 112 E1
Little Dunmow CM6 151 D6
Manningtree CO11 86 D4
Wivenhoe CO7 164 C8
BROOK STREET 2 B6
315 F6
Brook Street Bsns Ctr CO1 136 B6
Brook Terr CO9 51 E1
Brook Vale CO16 194 B3
Brookview IP2 36 E8
Brook View
Chelmsford CM2 255 C6
Stansted Mountfitchet CM24 119 E5
Thaxted CM6 70 A3
Brookway RM13 370 B8
Brook Way IG7 311 B7
Brook Wlk CM8 211 F8
Broomclose Villas CM7 100 E5
Broom Cres IP3 17 F1
Broome Cl CM11 297 D5
Broome Gr CO7 137 B2
Broome Pl RM15 371 D5
Broome Pl Complex RM15 371 D5
Broome Rd CM11 297 D5
Broome Way CO15 220 F6
Broom Farm Rd CM22 94 C2
BROOMFIELD 208 B2
Broomfield Hadleigh SS7 345 D4
Harlow CM20 200 B3
Silver End CM8 156 C5
Broom Field IP11 381 C5
Broomfield Ave
Loughton IG10 288 F3
Rayleigh SS6 323 A3
Southend-on-S SS9 346 F5
Broomfield Cl RM5 313 D3
Broomfield Comm IP8 16 B6
Broomfield Cres CO7 137 B2
Broomfield Ctyd CB9 8 F8
Broomfield Gn SS8 363 F5
Broomfield Hospl CM1 208 A3
Broomfield Prim Sch CM1 208 B1
Broomfield Rd
Chelmsford CM1 232 A5
Dagenham RM6 334 D4
Swanscombe DA10 377 E2
Broomfields Basildon SS13 343 A6
Hatfield Heath CM22 174 A3
Broomfields Ct 6 SS13 343 A6
Broomfields Mews 4 SS13 343 A6
Broomfields Pl 5 SS13 343 A6
Broomgrove Inf & Jun Schs CO7 137 B2
Broomhall Cl CM1 208 B2
Broomhall Rd CM1 208 B2
Broomhayes IP2 17 A2
Broomhill IP9 62 D6
Broomhill Ct 2 IG8 310 A4
Broomhill Rd Ilford IG3 334 A2
Woodford IG8 310 A4
Broom Hill Rd IP1 17 A8
Broomhills Chase CM12 319 A5
Broomhills Ind Est CM7 127 D2
Broomhills Rd CO5 218 D5
Broomhill Wlk IG8 309 F3
Broom Knoll CO7 60 C2
Broom Rd SS5 301 E2
Broom St CO10 34 B5
Broomstick Hall Rd EN9 265 E6
Broom Way Abberton CO5 163 B2
Capel St M IP9 35 B2
Broomways SS3 350 C3
Broomwood Gdns CM15 294 A3
Broomwood La CM11 298 B8
Broseley Gdns RM3 314 E6
Broseley Rd RM3 314 E6
Brotherton Ave IP11 381 A8
Broton Dr CO9 76 E2
Brougham Cl SS3 350 A4
Brougham Ct 3 DA2 376 B1
Brougham Glades CO3 134 D5
Broughton Cl CO2 135 C4
Broughton Rd
Hadleigh SS7 345 F2
Ipswich IP1 17 B7
South Woodham Ferrers CM3 301 E6
Browne Cl
Brentwood CM14 294 B1
Romford RM5 313 B5
Browning Ave SS2 348 B2
Browning Cl
Colchester CO3 134 F6
Romford RM5 312 F3
Browning Dr SS12 321 C5
Browning Rd
Braintree CM7 155 A8
Brantham CO11 86 C7
Dartford DA1 376 A3
Maldon CM9 259 A8
Brownings Ave CM1 232 A5
Browning Wlk RM18 379 C5
Brownlea Gdns IG3 334 A2
Brownlow Bend SS14 342 D6
Brownlow Cross SS14 342 D6
Brownlow Gn SS14 342 D6
Brownlow Rd IP11 381 F4
Brownlows Cl CM6 204 C7
Browns Ave SS11 299 F2
Browns Cotts RM16 372 E5
Brownsea Dr SS12 322 A5
Brownsea Way CO3 135 A4
Brown's End Rd CM6 121 F7
Broxbourne Ave E18 332 B7
Broxbourne Rd E7 332 A1
Broxbourne Sta EN10 221 A3
Broxburn Ct RM15 372 B6
Broxburn Dr RM15 372 B6
Broxburn Par RM15 372 B6
Broxhill Rd
Havering-atte-B RM4 314 B7
Romford RM4 313 F7
BROXTED 95 F2
Broxted Cotts 5 SS12 321 E6
Broxted Dr SS12 321 E6
Broxted End SS12 321 E6
Broxted Mews CM13 295 C3
Bruce Ave RM12 336 D2
Bruce Gr Chelmsford CM2 254 F7
Wickford SS11 322 A7
Bruce Rd CM1 231 B1
Bruces Wharf Rd RM17 378 A8
Bruff Cl CO4 109 E2
Bruff Dr CO14 171 A7
Bruff Rd IP2 17 C3
Bruges Cl CO12 91 A1
Bruges Rd SS8 364 C3
Brummell Pl CM17 200 C3
Brundells Rd CO7 139 A5
Brundish SS13 343 A5
BRUNDON 15 C1
Brundon La CO10 33 C7
Brunel Cl Romford RM1 335 E7
Tilbury RM18 379 B5
Brunel Ct CO4 110 C6
Brunel Rd Braintree CM7 128 A1
Chigwell IG8 310 F5
Clacton-on-S CO15 196 B8
Ipswich IP2 16 F6
South Benfleet SS7 344 D7
Southend-on-S SS9 346 C7
Brunel Way Colchester CO4 110 C6
South Woodham Ferrers CM3 301 C7
Brunswick Ave RM14 337 E4
Brunswick Ct
Hoddesdon EN11 221 A5
Upminster RM14 337 E4
Brunswick Gdns IG6 311 C3
Brunswick House Cut CO11 87 A3
Brunswick Lodge 6 E4 309 C8
Brunswick Pl SS6 323 B5
Brunswick Rd
Holdbrook EN3 265 A1
Ipswich IP4 17 F8
Southend-on-S SS1 367 D7
Brunswick Wlk 3 DA12 379 D1
Brunwin Rd CM77 126 F2
Brunwins Cl SS11 321 F8
Brushwood Lodge 2 DA17 369 A2
Brussels Cl CO12 91 B1
Brussum Rd SS8 364 D2
Bruton Ave SS0 347 A5
Bryanita Ct CO5 186 D5
Bryan Rd CM23 145 F8
Bryanstone Mews CO3 134 E5
Bryanston Rd RM18 379 C5
Bryant Ave Romford RM3 314 D1
Southend-on-S SS1 367 E6
Bryant Link CM2 233 B4
Bryant Row RM3 314 C8
Bryant's La CM9 257 D7
Bryce Rd RM8 353 C8
Bryn Farm Cl SS14 342 C8
Bryon Ave IP11 381 A3
Bryony Cl Loughton IG10 289 B5
Witham CM8 183 D4
Buchanan Cl RM15 371 C5
Buchanan Gdns SS12 321 E5
Buchanan Way CM3 282 B5
Buchan Cl CM7 155 A8
Buckbean Path RM3 314 C3
Buckenhoe Rd CB10 22 E3
Buckeridge Way CM0 242 B3
Buckerills SS13 343 A6
Buckfast Ave CO13 170 D6
Buckfast Cl 5 IP2 17 A2
Buckhatch La CM3 278 D3
Buck Hill CM77 154 F6
Buckhurst Ct 2 IG9 310 D8
BUCKHURST HILL 310 C8
Buckhurst Hill Com Prim Sch IG9 310 E8
Buckhurst Hill Ho IG9 310 B8
Buckhurst Hill Sta IG9 310 D8
Buckhurst Way IG9 310 D7
Buckingham Cl RM11 336 D6
Buckingham Ct
2 Chelmsford CM2 232 F4
Loughton IG10 289 A7
3 Romford RM1 335 F6
Buckingham Dr CO4 136 E7
Buckingham Hill Rd
Linford SS17, RM16 374 F5
Stanford-le-H SS17 375 A7
Buckingham Lodge 6 EN11 221 A6
Buckingham Rd
Basildon SS15 341 E8
Haverhill CB9 8 E6
Hockley SS5 324 D6
Ilford IG1 333 D2
Wanstead E11 332 C6
Woodford E18 309 F2
Buckinghamshire Sq SS11 322 A5
Buckingham Sq 11 CM0 306 C4
Buckland SS3 349 C1
Buckland Gate CM3 301 C6
Bucklebury Heath CM3 301 D6
Bucklers Ct CM14 316 C5
Bucklesham Rd IP3 18 E2
Buckles La RM15 372 D8
Buckley Cl SS17 360 F5
Buckleys CM2 254 F7
Buckleys Cl CM8 212 E5
Buckley's La CO6 131 E6
Bucknells Mead CM1 252 A4
Buckrell Rd E4 309 D8
Buck's Horns La IP8 36 B6
Bucks La CO10 12 B7
Buckthorne Ho 4 IG7 312 B6
Buckwins Sq SS13 321 D1
Buckwoods Rd CM7 128 A1
Buckwyns Chase CM12 296 F6
Buckwyns Ct CM12 296 F4
Buddleia Cl IP2 16 E4
Buddleia Ct CO7 137 A2
Budleigh Ct CM14 315 F6
Budna Rd SS8 363 F5
Budoch Ct IG3 334 A2
Budoch Dr IG3 334 A2
Buffett Way CO4 136 E6
Buglers Rise CM1 253 B8
Buick Ave CO15 220 D6
BUILDING END 40 B8
Building End Rd
Chrishall SG8 19 C1
Duddenhoe End SG8 40 B8
Bulbecks Wlk CM3 301 D5
Bulford Cl CM77 155 D5
Bulford La CM77 155 C5
Bulford Mill La CM77 155 D5
Bullace Cl CO4 110 D3
Bullbanks Rd DA17 369 C2
Bull Cl Basildon SS16 342 E5
Grays RM16 372 F4
Bullen Ct IG6 311 E4
Bullen Wlk CM2 254 C3
Buller Rd Barking IG11 352 E5
Basildon SS15 341 B7
North Fambridge CM3 281 A1
Bullfields Newport CB11 67 A8
Sawbridgeworth CM21 172 E3
Bullfinch Cl Colchester CO4 136 F8
Harwich CO12 90 E1
Bullfinch Dr CO9 77 A1
Bull Hill Rd CO15 195 F5
Bullivant Cl DA9 377 A2
Bull La Dagenham RM10 335 B1
Hockley SS5 324 C6
Langley CB11 40 C2
Long Melford CO10 15 E8
Maldon CM9 237 A3
Rayleigh SS6 323 E2
Tiptree CO5 186 C3
Bullocks La CO10 33 E6
Bullocks Terr CO10 33 E6
Bullock Wood Cl CO4 110 D4
Bull Rd IP3 18 B4
Bulls Cliff IP11 381 D3
Bulls Lodge Cotts CM3 209 B1
Bullwood App SS5 324 B5
Bullwood Hall La SS5 324 A4
Bullwood Rd SS5 324 D5
BULMER 32 F5
Bulmer Rd CO10 33 C6
Bulmer Road Ind Est CO10 33 C6
Bulmer St CO10 32 D4
Bulmers Wlk RM13 355 C3
BULMER TYE 32 F2
Bulow Ave SS8 364 B3
BULPHAN 358 F8
Bulphan By-Pass RM14 340 A1
Bulphan CE Prim Sch RM14 358 F8
Bulphan Cl SS12 321 E6
Bulphan View CM13 340 E5
Bulrush Cl CM7 128 B1
Bulstrode Rd IP2 17 D4
Bulwark Rd SS3 368 E8
Bulwer Rd IP1 17 A6
BUMBLE'S GREEN 244 C6
Bumbles Green La EN9 244 B6
Bumfords La CM3, CM9 235 A7
Bumpstead Rd CB9 9 B4
Bunces La IG8 309 F3
Bundick's Hill CM1 231 F3
Bungalows The
Abbess Roding CM5 203 E3
Grays RM20 377 A8
Redbridge IG6 311 D1
Witham CM8 183 F1
Bung Row CM8 185 C1
Bunker's Hill DA17 369 A2
Bunters Ave SS3 368 C6
Buntingbridge Rd IG2 333 D6
Bunting Cl CM2 254 B5
Buntingford Ct 2 CO2 136 A1
Bunting La CM11 297 C1
Bunting Rd IP2 16 D3
BUNTING'S GREEN 77 D1
Buntings The CO2 161 E4
Bunyan Rd CM7 127 E3
Burches SS14 319 E1
Burches Mead SS7 345 A7
Burches Rd SS7 344 F8
Burchett Way RM6 334 F5
Burch Rd DA11 378 F1
Burchwall Cl RM5 313 C3
Burden Way E11 332 B2
Burdett Ave SS0 366 E8
Burdett Rd SS1 367 C7
Burdetts Rd RM9 353 F4
Burdun Cl CM8 211 D8
Bure RM18 375 C3
Bure Dr CM8 183 D3
Buregate Rd IP11 381 D2
Buren Ave SS8 364 E3
BURES 79 E8
Bures CE Prim Sch CO8 79 F8
Bures Ct 16 CB9 8 E7
Bures Ho CO8 79 F8
Bures Rd
Great Cornard CO10 34 B3
Nayland CO6 81 B8
Wakes Colne CO6 106 D7
West Bergholt CO6 108 D7
White Colne CO6 105 E8
Bures Sta CO8 79 E8
Burfield Cl SS9 346 F6
Burfield Rd SS9 346 F6
Burford Cl Dagenham RM8 334 C1
Ilford IG6 333 C7
Burford Gdns EN11 221 B7
Burford Ho EN11 221 B7
Burford Mews 9 EN11 221 A7
Burford Pl 11 EN11 221 A7
Burford St EN11 221 A7
Burgate Cl CO16 195 A4
Burgate Lane Cotts CO7 85 B3
Burges Cl Hornchurch RM11 336 F5
Southend-on-S SS1 368 C6
Burges Rd
Southend-on-S SS1 368 B6
Wallend E6 352 A5
Burgess Ave SS17 360 E1
Burgess Ct
Brentwood CM15 294 D1
Wallend E12 352 A5
Burgess Field CM2 232 F4
Burges Terr SS1 367 F6
Burghley Ave CM23 145 C7
Burghley Cl
Great Notley CM77 154 B6
4 Ipswich IP2 17 A2
Burghley Rd RM16 372 C3
Burghley Way CM2 254 C8
Burghstead Cl CM12 297 A1
Burgoyne Hatch CM20 200 A1
Burgundy Ct CM2 232 C2
Burgundy Gdns 6 SS13 343 B8
Burkitts Ct 8 CO10 33 E7
Burkitts La CO10 33 E7
Burland Rd
Brentwood CM15 294 D1
Romford RM5 313 C4
Burleigh Cl Billericay CM12 297 B5
Romford RM7 335 B7
Burleigh Ct
Southend-on-S SS0 366 C8
Southend-on-S, Thorpe Bay SS1 368 B8
Burleigh Sq SS1 368 B8
Burlescoombe Cl SS1 368 A8
Burlescoombe Leas SS1 349 B1
Burlescoombe Rd SS1 349 A1
Burley Cl E4 309 A5
Burley Hill CM17 224 D7
Burley Rd CM23 146 A4
Burlingham Ho IP2 17 B4
Burlington Ave RM7 335 B5
Burlington Ct SS13 343 B8
Burlington Gdns
Dagenham RM6 334 E4
Hadleigh SS7 345 F3
Hullbridge SS5 301 F1
Burlington Pl IG8 310 A7
Burlington Rd
Colchester CO3 135 E6
Ipswich IP1 17 B6
Burmanny Cl CO15 195 C3
Burnaby Rd
Gravesend DA11 378 E1
Southend-on-S SS1 367 C7
Burne Ave SS12 321 A6
Burnell Gate CM1 233 A7
Burnells Way CM24 119 E7
Burnell Wlk CM13 316 C4
Burnels Ave E6 352 A2
Burnet Cl IP8 36 D8
Burnett Pk CM19 223 B3
Burnett Rd Erith DA8 370 D1
Redbridge IG6 311 B3
Burney Ct IG7 311 C5
Burney Dr IG10 289 C6
Burnham Ave CM3 281 A5
Burnham Bsns Pk CM0 306 A6
Burnham Cl Ipswich IP4 17 F7
Trimley St M IP11 381 A7
Walton-on-t-N CO14 171 B8
Burnham Cres E11 332 C7
Burnham Ct CO15 220 I8
Burnham Lodge IP4 18 A6
BURNHAM-ON-CROUCH 306 D6
Burnham-on-Crouch & District Mus★ CM0 306 B4
Burnham-on-Crouch Prim Sch CM0 306 D5
Burnham-on-Crouch Sta CM0 306 B6
Burnham Rd Althorne CM3 283 B1
Battlesbridge SS11 300 E3
Chelmsford CM1 232 D5
Dagenham RM9 353 B4
Hullbridge SS5 301 E2
Burnham Rd continued
Latchingdon CM3 282 D5
Mundon CM9 281 C8
Romford RM7 335 D8
Southend-on-S SS9 346 C1
Southminster CM0 284 C2
Southminster CM0 284 D3
South Woodham Ferrers CM3 279 D1
Woodham Mortimer CM9, CM3 257 E5
Burnley Rd RM20 377 A6
Burnsall Cl CB11 43 F8
Burns Ave Basildon SS13 343 B5
Colchester CO3 134 F6
Dagenham RM6 334 C4
Burns Cl Billericay CM11 297 B3
Maldon CM9 237 A1
Burns Cres CM2 254 C8
Burns Gn CM9 213 A4
Burnside Canvey Island SS8 364 A5
Dagenham RM8 334 C2
Sawbridgeworth CM21 172 D2
Burnside Ave E4 309 A4
Burnside Cres CM1 232 B7
Burnside Ct 6 RM1 335 F5
Burnside Ind Est IG6 312 B5
Burnside Rd RM8 334 C3
Burnside Terr CM17 200 F3
Burns Pl RM18 379 B6
Burnstie Rd CM6 152 F6
Burns Way CM13 295 D3
Burnt Dick Hill CO4 82 D7
BURNT HEATH 112 B4
Burnt Ho IG7 289 F1
Burnthouse La
Ingatestone CM4 273 F1
Mountnessing CM4, CM13 296 A8
Burnthouse Rd CO6 105 E2
Burntmill Cl CM20 199 C3
Burntmill Cnr CM20 199 D4
Burnt Mill Comp Sch CM20 199 E2
Burnt Mill Ind Est CM20 199 C3
Burntmill La CM20 199 D3
BURNT MILLS 321 B1
Burnt Mills Ind Est SS13 321 C1
Burnt Mills Rd SS13 321 C1
Burnt Oak Cnr CO7 59 D1
Burnt Oak Lodge SS9 346 A2
Burntwood CM14 316 C7
Burntwood Ave RM11 336 E5
Burntwood Cl
Billericay CM12 296 F2
West Horndon CM13 339 D5
Burnway RM11 336 E4
Burr Cl Basildon SS16 340 E5
Harwich CO12 90 C1
Burrell Rd IP2 17 C4
Burr Hill Chase SS2 347 E3
Burroughs Piece Rd CO10 33 F7
Burrow Cl IG7 311 F5
Burrow Gn IG7 311 F5
Burrow Rd IG7 312 A5
Burrows Chase EN9 265 D4
Burrows Cl
Clacton-on-S CO16 195 D6
Lawford CO11 86 B4
Burrows Ho CM15 271 F1
Burrow's Rd CO6 105 B7
Burrows Way SS6 323 C1
Burrs Rd CO15 196 A7
Burrsville Com Inf Sch CO15 195 F6
BURRSVILLE PARK 196 A7
Burr's Way SS17 361 B3
Burrswood Pl CM9 237 E3
Burses Way CM13 295 C2
Burslem Ave IG6 312 A4
Burstall Cl CO16 195 B4
Burstall La IP8 16 A6
Burstead Dr CM11 319 D7
Burstead Grange CM11 319 D6
Burton Cl Corringham SS17 360 F5
Haverhill CB9 8 E7
Burton Dr EN3 265 A2
BURTON END 120 C4
Burton End CB9 8 E7
Burton End Prim Sch CB9 8 D7
Burton Pl CM2 232 F4
Burton Rd Loughton IG10 289 C5
Wanstead E18 332 B8
BURTON'S GREEN 104 B2
Burton's Green Rd CO9 104 B4
Burtons Mill CM21 172 F3
Burts Wharf DA17 369 C5
Burwell Ave SS8 363 F5
Burwood Ct CM2 232 C1
Burwood Gdns RM13 354 F2
Bury Cl Colchester CO1 136 A8
Marks Tey CO6 132 F4
Bury Farm Cotts RM14 338 E2
Bury Farm La CM11 320 D3
Bury Fields CM6 152 A5
Bury Gdns CB11 20 A4
Bury La Chrishall SG8 19 D1
Epping CM16 245 D2
Great Waltham CM3 207 D8
Hatfield Peverel CM3 210 F4
Bury Lodge La
Great Hallingbury CM22 147 C7
Stansted Mountfitchet CM24 120 A2
Bury Rd Chingford E4 287 E4
Dagenham RM10 354 C7
Epping CM16 267 E8
Harlow CM17 200 D4
Buryside Cl IG3 333 F7
Bury The CO16 194 A4
Bury Villas CM22 121 E3
Burywater Cotts CB11 42 F1
Bury Water La CB11 42 E1
Burywoods CO4 109 B3
Bush Cl IG2 333 D6
Bushell Way CO13 170 E6
Bush Elms Rd RM11 336 A4
BUSH END 148 A4
Bushey Cl Capel St M IP9 35 A1
Chingford E4 309 C7
Bushey Cl continued
South Woodham Ferrers CM3 301 E7
Bushey Croft CM18 223 E7
Bushey Ley CM7 128 D3
BUSH FAIR 224 A6
Bush Fair CM18 223 F6
Bushfields IG10 289 A4
Bush Gr CO10 33 C6
Bushgrove Rd RM8 334 D1
Bush Hall Rd CM12 297 C5
Bush Ho CM18 223 F6
Bush Rd
Great Sampford CB10 46 E2
Wanstead E11 332 A4
Woodford IG9 310 D6
Bushway RM8 334 D1
Bushwood E11 332 A3
Bushy Lea CM5 249 A2
Bushy Mead SS15 341 B8
Business Ctr The RM3 314 D3
BUSTARD GREEN 98 B6
Butcher Row CB10 22 D1
Butcher's Hill CB10 3 A4
Butchers La Capel St M IP9 35 B1
Walton-on-t-N CO14 171 B7
Butchers Pasture CM6 122 F5
Butcher's View CO5 189 E6
Bute Ct CB9 8 F6
Bute Rd IG6 333 B6
Butler Cl CB11 22 E1
Butler Ct 2 RM8 335 A2
Butler Ho RM17 378 B8
Butler Rd Dagenham RM8 353 B8
Halstead CO9 76 D2
Butlers Cl CM1 208 B2
Butlers Cotts CM3 211 C1
Butlers Dr E4 265 C1
Butlers Gr SS16 341 B3
Butler's Hall La CM23 145 B3
Butlers La CB10 23 C5
Butler's La CO11 88 E1
Butlers Way CO9 30 A1
Butler Wlk RM17 373 D2
Butley Cl IP2 36 F8
Butley Ct 1 CB9 8 E6
Butley Rd IP11 381 C3
Butneys SS14 342 B7
Buttell Cl RM17 373 D1
Butterbur Chase CM3 301 C6
Buttercross La CM16 246 A1
Buttercup Cl
Billericay CM12 297 A4
Ipswich IP8 16 C2
Romford RM3 314 D2
Buttercup Way CM0 284 C3
Buttercup Wlk CM8 183 E4
Butterfield Rd CM3 233 E8
Butterfly Gdns IP4 18 E5
Butteridges Cl RM9 353 F4
Butter Market IP1 17 C6
Buttermarket Sh Ctr 3 IP1 17 C5
Buttermere CM77 154 C7
Buttersweet Rise CM21 172 E1
Butterworth Gdns IG8 310 A5
Butterys SS1 367 E8
Buttfield Cl RM10 354 B6
Butt La Maldon CM9 237 A3
Manuden CM23 92 E2
Buttleys La CM6 149 F8
Buttondene Cres EN10 221 B1
Button Rd RM17 372 F2
Button's Hill CM3 283 B4
Butt Rd Colchester CO3 135 E5
Great Cornard CO10 34 B6
Stoke-by-N CO6 56 C5
Buttsbury CM4 274 E1
Buttsbury Inf Sch CM12 297 B5
Buttsbury Jun Sch The CM12 297 B5
Buttsbury Rd IG1 352 C7
Buttsbury Terr CM4 275 E2
BUTTS GREEN 64 E8
Butts Green Rd RM11 336 D5
Butt's Green Rd CM2 255 F3
Butts La Danbury CM3 256 F7
Stanford-le-H SS17 375 C8
Butts Paddock SS4 304 D2
Butts Rd SS17 360 C1
Butts Way CM2 253 E3
Buxey Cl CO5 218 B7
Buxton Ave SS9 346 A3
Buxton Cl
Southend-on-S SS9 346 A3
Woodford IG8 310 D4
Buxton Cotts CO6 132 A3
Buxton Link SS15 340 E6
Buxton Lodge E11 332 B2
Buxton Rd Chingford E4 287 D2
Coggeshall CO6 130 F3
Colchester CO2 136 A3
Grays RM16 373 E4
Ilford IG2 333 E5
Theydon Bois CM16 267 E3
Waltham Abbey EN9 266 A6
Buxton Sq SS9 346 A3
Buyl Ave SS8 364 B5
Byfield SS9 346 F7
Byfield Ct CM13 339 C5
Byfletts SS16 342 F4
Byford Rd SS6 323 E3
Bylam La IP9 63 C6
Byland Cl IP2 17 A2
Bylands Cl CM23 145 D6
Byng Cl CO16 142 B1
Byng Cres CO16 142 B1
Byng Ct CO2 136 A1
Byng Gdns CM7 128 C4
Bynghams CM19 222 F6
Byng Ho CO16 142 B1
Bypass Rd CO16 194 B5
By-Pass Rd SS17 360 A2
Byrd Ct SS15 341 C8
Byrd Mead CM15 272 A6
Byrd's Farm La CB10 22 E3
Byrd Way SS17 360 C3

Cavendish Ho CB9 8 F7
Cavendish La CO10 1 F3
Cavendish Rd Chingford E4 309 C4
Clare CO10 12 D7
Felixstowe IP11 381 D3
Hockley SS5 303 A1
Rochford SS5 303 A1
Cavendish St IP3 17 F5
Cavendish Way
Basildon SS15 319 D1
Sudbury CO10 33 F7
Cavenham Gdns
Hornchurch RM11 336 C6
Ilford IG1 333 D1
Caversham Ave SS3 349 E2
Caversham Park Ave SS6 323 C4
Cawdor Ave RM15 372 B6
Cawdor Ho CM14 316 D6
Cawkell Cl CM24 119 D7
Cawkwell Cl CM2 233 A4
Cawley Hatch CM19 222 F8
Caxton Cl CO5 186 D4
Caxton Ct CO4 110 C6
Caxton Pl CO9 76 E2
Caxton Rd EN11 197 B2
Caxton Way RM1 335 E7
Cazenove Rd E17 309 A2
Cecil Ave Barking IG11 352 D5
Grays RM16 372 F4
Hornchurch RM11 336 E8
Cecil Cl CM23 146 D7
Cecil Ct Harlow CM18 223 C5
Southend-on-S SS2 347 E3
Cecil Ho E17 309 A2
Cecilia St IP1 17 C5
Cecil Jones Coll (Lower Sch)
SS2 348 B3
Cecil Jones Coll (Upper Sch)
SS2 348 D3
Cecil Rd Chingford E17 309 A2
Dagenham RM6 334 D4
Hoddesdon EN11 221 C8
Ilford IG1 352 B8
Ipswich IP1 17 B7
Cecil Way SS6 323 F2
Cedar Ave
Brightlingsea CO7 192 E7
Chelmsford CM1 232 A3
Dagenham RM6 334 E6
Tiptree CO5 186 C7
Upminster RM14 356 A8
Wickford SS12 321 D5
Cedar Ave W CM1 232 A3
Cedar Chase CM9 237 C5
Cedar Cl Brantham CO11 60 D1
Brentwood CM13 295 D2
Buckhurst Hill IG9 310 D8
Great Dunmow CM6 123 A1
Rayleigh SS6 323 F1
Romford RM7 335 C7
Sawbridgeworth CM21 172 E1
Southend-on-S SS2 348 A2
Walton-on-t-N CO14 171 A7
Cedar Cres CO11 86 C3
Cedar Ct
Bishop's Stortford CM23 118 F1
Epping CM16 268 A8
Southend-on-S SS3 368 E7
6 Wanstead E11 332 B6
West Bergholt CO6 108 D5
5 Woodford E18 310 A2
Cedar Dr Hullbridge SS5 301 E2
Loughton IG10 289 B7
Witham CM8 184 A5
Cedar Gdns RM14 337 C1
Cedar Gn EN11 221 A5
Cedar Gr CM0 306 B6
Cedar Hall Gdns SS7 345 A6
Cedar Hall Sch SS7 345 B6
Cedar Ho IP2 17 A3
Cedar Mews SS5 324 C6
Cedar Park Cl SS7 345 A6
Cedar Park Gdns RM6 334 D4
Cedar Pk
Bishop's Stortford CM23 145 D4
Chigwell IG7 311 A5
Cedar Rd Brentwood CM13 295 D3
Canvey Island SS8 363 F4
Grays RM16 374 B3
Hornchurch RM12 336 C1
Romford RM7 335 C7
Thundersley SS7 345 A6
Cedar Rise RM15 357 D1
Cedars Stanford-le-H SS17 360 E2
Waltham Abbey EN9 266 C4
Cedars Rd 13 CO2 135 F6
Cedars The
Buckhurst Hill IG9 288 A1
Gosfield CO9 102 E7
Great Wakering SS3 350 B4
South Woodham Ferrers
CM3 301 D8
Stansted Mountfitchet
CM24 119 D6
Cedar Terr 9 RM8 334 D4
Cedar Way CO7 166 E8
Cedar Wlk Canewdon SS4 304 D1
Waltham Abbey EN9 265 D5
Cedarwood Ct CM18 223 F6
Cedric Ave RM1 335 E8
Celandine Cl
Billericay CM12 296 F4
South Ockendon RM15 357 C1
Celandine Ct Chingford E4 309 B7
Colchester CO4 109 C2
Celeborn St CM3 301 B6
Celedon Cl RM16 372 E4
Celestion Dr IP3 18 B4
Cement Block Cotts 10
RM17 378 C8
Cemetery La
East Bergholt CO7 59 B2
Ipswich IP4 17 E8
Cemetery Rd
Bishop's Stortford CM23 145 F6
Ipswich IP4 17 E6
Centaur Way CM9 259 A8
Centaury Cl CO3 134 C7
Centenary Way CO15,
CO16 168 E1
Central Arc CB10 22 D1
Central Ave Althorne CM3 282 E2
Aveley RM15 371 C4
Basildon SS16 340 E4
Billericay CM12 297 C6
Canvey Island SS8 363 F5
Corringham SS17 361 A3
Frinton-on-S CO13 171 A6
Grays RM20 371 F1
Hadleigh SS7 345 E5
Hullbridge SS5 301 F1
Hullbridge, Tower Park SS5 301 E4
Ipswich IP3 38 E8
Rochford SS4 325 D5
Southend-on-S SS2 348 C1
Stanford-le-H SS17 360 E4
Tilbury RM18 379 A6
Central Cl SS7 345 E4
Central Ct 11 IG7 311 E5
Central Dr RM12 336 E1
Central Ho
Chipping Ongar CM5 249 A3
Harwich CO12 91 D4
Central Maltings The 5
CO11 86 D4
Central Par
Clacton-on-S CO15 195 F2
Ilford IG2 333 D5
Central Park Ave RM10 335 C1
Central Rd Harlow CM20 200 A4
Stanford-le-H SS17 360 D1
Central Sq 7 CM1 232 B2
Central Wall SS8 364 A6
Central Wall Cotts SS8 364 B5
Central Wall Rd SS8 364 B5
Centre Ave CM16 267 F7
Centre Dr CM16 267 F7
Centre Gn CM16 267 F7
Centre Pl 10 SS1 367 C7
Centre Rd Dagenham RM10 354 B3
Wanstead E11 332 A2
Centre Reach SS2 348 A1
Centre The
2 Colchester CO4 136 E7
Halstead CO9 76 E2
Centre The IP2 17 A1
Centre The CO5 186 D5
Centreway 4 IG1 333 C2
Centric Par IG10 288 E5
Centrum Ct IP2 17 B4
Centurian Ho 2 CO2 135 F6
Centurion Cl SS3 368 F8
Centurion Ct RM1 335 D8
Centurion Lodge 7 RM10 354 B6
Centurion Way
Belvedere DA18 369 A3
Colchester CO2 135 A3
Purfleet RM19 370 F2
Centurion Works RM13 354 E2
Century Dr CM7 128 B2
Century Rd EN11 221 A7
Ceylon Rd SS0 366 D8
Chadacre Ave
Redbridge IG5 332 F8
Woodford IG5 310 F1
Chadacre Rd SS1 349 B1
Chadburn Rd CO10 15 D8
Chadfields RM18 379 A7
Chadview Ct 2 RM6 334 D4
Chadville Gdns RM6 334 D6
Chadway RM8 334 C3
Chadwell Ave RM6 334 B4
Chadwell By-Pass RM16 374 A1
CHADWELL HEATH 334 D5
Chadwell Heath Foundation
Sch The RM6 334 B5
Chadwell Heath Ind Pk
RM8 334 D3
Chadwell Heath La RM6 334 C5
Chadwell Heath Sta RM6 334 D4
Chadwell Hill RM16 374 B1
Chadwell Prim Sch RM6 334 C4
Chadwell Rd RM16, RM17 373 D2
CHADWELL ST MARY 374 B1
Chadwell St Mary Prim Sch
RM16 374 B2
Chadwick Ave E4 309 D6
Chadwick Dr
Braintree CM7 127 E3
Romford RM3 314 D1
Chadwick Rd Ilford IG1 333 B1
Southend-on-S SS0 366 C8
South Woodham Ferrers
CM3 279 E1
Chaffinch Cl SS3 368 E8
Chaffinch Cres CM11 297 C1
Chaffinch Dr CO12 90 E1
Chaffinch Gdns CO4 136 F8
Chaffinch Way CO9 77 A1
Chaffix CM6 152 C6
Chaffix Cl CM6 152 C6
Chafford CM14 294 B1
Chafford Gdns CM13 339 D5
Chafford Gorges Nature
Park★ RM15 372 D3
CHAFFORD HUNDRED 372 E3
Chafford Hundred Bsns & Ent
Coll RM16 372 C1
Chafford Hundred Prim Sch
RM16 372 C1
Chafford Hundred Sta
RM16 372 B2
Chafford Sch The RM13 370 C8
Chafford Way Grays RM16 373 B5
Ilford RM6 334 C7
Chafford Wlk RM13 355 C3
Chainey Pieces 12 CB9 8 F7
Chaingate Ave SS2 348 E2
Chale Ct SS17 375 C8
Chalfont Cl SS9 346 D4
Chalfont Ct 3 DA17 369 A1
Chalfont Rd CO4 110 C3
Chalfont Sq 15 IP4 17 D6
Chalford Ct IG2 333 B6
Chalforde Gdns RM2 336 B7
Chalford Wlk IG8 310 D3
Chalgrove Cres IG5 310 E1
Chalice Cl SS14 342 E6
Chalice Way DA9 376 F2
Chalk Ct RM17 378 A8
CHALK END 205 E2
Chalk End SS13 343 A7
Chalk La CM17 201 A2
Chalklands
Howe Green CM2 255 D3
Saffron Walden CB10 22 E3
Chalkners Cl 2 IP9 35 A1
Chalk Rd SS8 364 A6
Chalks Ave CM21 172 D3
Chalks Rd CM8 183 F4
Chalk St CM3 299 F7
Chalkstone Mid Sch CB9 9 A8
Chalkstone Way CB9 9 D7
Chalk Villas CM6 204 C7
CHALKWELL 366 B8
Chalkwell Ave SS0 366 B8
Chalkwell Bay Flats SS9 366 A8
Chalkwell Espl SS0 366 B7
Chalkwell Hall Jun & Inf Schs
SS0 347 A1
Chalkwell Lodge SS0 347 C1
Chalkwell Park Dr SS9 346 F1
Chalkwell Sta SS9 366 A8
Chalky La SG8 19 D2
Challacombe SS1 349 C1
Challacombe Cl CM13 295 C1
Challenge Way CO1 136 B6
Challinor CM17 224 E8
Challis La CM7 155 A8
Challock Lees SS13 343 C5
Chalon St IP1 17 B5
CHALVEDON 343 B6
Chalvedon Ave SS13 343 B7
Chalvedon Sch SS13 343 B6
Chalvedon Sq 3 SS13 343 A6
Chamberlain Ave
Canvey Island SS8 364 C4
Corringham SS17 361 A4
Walton-on-t-N CO14 171 B7
Chamberlain Cl
Harlow CM17 224 C8
Ilford IG1 333 C1
Chamberlains Ride CM3 301 D6
Chamberlain Way IP8 16 C2
Chambers Cl DA9 377 A2
Chamley Ct CO15 196 D5
Champion Cl
Stanford-le-H SS17 360 E3
Wickford SS12 321 D6
Champion Rd RM14 337 B2
Champions Gn EN11 197 A1
Champions Way
Hoddesdon EN11 197 A1
South Woodham Ferrers
CM3 301 C8
Champlain Ave SS8 363 F5
Champness Rd IG11 352 F5
Chance Cl RM16 372 F3
Chancel Cl Basildon SS15 341 C7
South Benfleet SS7 344 C6
Tillingham CM0 263 E4
Chancellor Ave CM2 233 B4
Chancellor Rd SS1 367 B7
Chancery Gr CO2 163 A8
Chancery Pl CM1 231 B1
Chancery Rd IP1 17 B5
Chandler Rd IG10 289 B8
Chandlers CM0 306 A6
Chandlers Chase CM12 297 A2
Chandlers Cl
Bishop's Stortford CM23 145 C4
Clacton-on-S CO16 195 B3
West Mersea CO5 218 C7
Chandlers Cnr RM13 355 C1
Chandlers Dr DA8 369 E2
Chandlers Mews DA9 377 C3
Chandlers Quay CM9 237 A3
Chandlers Row CO1 136 C5
Chandlers Way
Romford RM1 335 E6
Southend-on-S SS2 348 A5
South Woodham Ferrers
CM3 301 E7
Chandlers Wlk CM15 271 E2
Chandos Ave E17 309 A1
Chandos Cl IG9 310 B8
Chandos Par SS7 346 A3
Chaney Rd CO7 137 A2
Chanlock Path RM15 372 B6
Channing Cl RM11 336 F4
Chant Ct CO4 110 D3
Chanterelle CO4 110 B3
Chanton Cl SS9 346 D7
Chantress Cl RM10 354 C4
Chantreywood CM13 317 B7
CHANTRY 16 E3
Chantry Cl
Bishop's Stortford CM23 145 E8
Clacton-on-S CO16 195 E7
Chantry Cres SS17 360 C1
Chantry Ct 10 DA12 379 C1
Chantry Dr
Ingatestone CM4 274 B3
Wormingford CO6 80 E4
Chantry Gn IP2 16 D3
Chantry Heritage Ctr★
DA12 379 C1
Chantry High Sch & Sixth
Form Ctr IP2 16 F3
Chantry Ho RM13 354 D3
Chantry Home Farm Pk
IP2 16 E5
Chantry La Basildon SS15 341 C7
Boreham CM3 210 A3
Chantry Mount CM23 145 E8
Chantry Prim Sch DA12 379 C1
Chantry Rd CM23 145 E8
Chantry The
6 Bishop's Stortford
CM23 145 F8
3 Chingford E4 287 C1
Colchester CO3 135 C7
Harlow CM20 200 A2
Chantry View CM8 212 A7
Chantry Villas CM3 210 A2
Chantry Way
Billericay CM11 297 B2
Rainham RM13 354 D3
Chanute Ave CM7 73 D7
Chapel Ave E12 332 D1
Chapel Cl Capel St M IP9 35 A1
Grays RM20 377 B8
Chapel Corner CO6 80 F4
Chapel Croft Ardleigh CO7 111 E7
Ingatestone CM4 274 B4
Chapel Ct Billericay CM12 297 B2
Swanscombe DA10 377 E1
Chapel Cut CO11 87 A4
Chapel Dr CM3 208 B6
CHAPELEND 23 A8
CHAPEL END 121 C7
Chapel End EN11 221 A5
Chapel End Ho E17 309 B2
Chapel End Inf Sch E17 309 B1
Chapel End Jun Sch E17 309 B2
CHAPELEND WAY 28 B2
Chapel End Way CO9 28 B2
Chapelfields
Kirby Cross CO13 170 E6
Stanstead Abbotts SG12 197 D4
Chapel Fields
Harlow CM17 224 C6
Takeley CM22 148 B7
Chapel High CM14 316 C8
Chapel Hill
Belchamp Walter CO10 31 D4
Braintree CM7 128 B2
Halstead CO9 76 D2
Stansted Mountfitchet
CM24 119 E6
Chapel Hill Bsns & Ret Pk
CM77 128 C1
Chapel La Belstead IP8 36 C7
Boxted CO4 83 A3
Chigwell IG7 311 F7
Colchester CO7 111 B1
5 Dagenham RM6 334 D4
Elmstead Market CO7 138 A6
Great Bromley CO7 139 A5
Great Cornard CO10 34 C2
Great Wakering SS3 350 B4
Hadleigh SS7 345 C3
Harlow CM17 224 C6
Heybridge Basin CM9 237 E2
Kirby Cross CO13 170 A6
Little Baddow CM3 234 B3
Newport CB11 67 A8
Purleigh CM3 280 D8
Roxwell CM1 229 B5
St Osyth CO16 194 A4
Tendring CO16 140 E8
Thorington Street CO6 57 D6
Thorrington CO7 166 B5
Tillingham CM0 263 E4
Tiptree CO5 186 E5
Washbrook IP8 16 A1
West Bergholt CO6 108 E3
Chapel Lodge RM13 355 A1
Chapel Mews
Billericay CM12 297 B1
Chigwell IG8 311 A4
18 Ipswich IP4 17 D6
Chapel Pl SS3 368 F6
Chapel Rd Beaumont CO16 141 E7
Boxted CO4 83 A3
Brightlingsea CO7 193 A7
Burnham-on-C CM0 306 C4
Colchester CO3 134 C6
Epping CM16 245 F1
Great Totham CM9 213 D6
Ilford IG1 333 B1
Langham CO4 83 D4
Ridgewell CO9 29 B7
Southend-on-S SS3 368 F6
Tiptree CO5 186 E4
Tolleshunt D'arcy CM9 215 F4
West Bergholt CO6 108 E4
Wivenhoe CO7 164 B8
Chapel Rise CM77 129 D2
Chapel Row
3 Bishop's Stortford
CM23 145 F6
Woodham Ferrers CM3 279 B5
Chapel St N 2 CO2 135 E6
Chapel St S 3 CO2 135 E6
Chapel St Billericay CM12 297 A2
Halstead CO9 76 E2
Rowhedge CO5 164 A8
Steeple Bumpstead CB9 27 C7
Stoke by C CO10 11 A3
Chapel Terr IG10 288 E5
Chapel The 5 RM11 336 B3
Chaplaincy Gdns RM11 336 E3
Chaplemount Rd IG8 310 F4
Chaplin Cl Basildon SS15 319 E1
Galleywood CM2 254 B2
Chaplin Dr CO4 110 D1
Chaplin Rd Dagenham RM9 353 E5
East Bergholt CO7 59 D3
Chaplins CO13 170 F7
Chaplin Wlk CO10 34 D5
Chapman Ct SS8 363 C3
Chapman La IP1 17 B6
Chapman Pl CO4 110 B6
Chapman Rd
Belvedere DA17 369 B1
Canvey Island SS8 365 A3
Clacton-on-S CO15 195 F3
Chapmans Cl SS9 346 B1
Chapmans La CO5 218 F8
Chapmans Wlk SS9 346 B1
CHAPPEL 106 C5
Chappel CE Prim Sch
CO6 106 D5
Chappel Cnr CO6 106 D6
Chappel Hill CO6 106 C5
Chappel Rd Bures CO6, CO8 79 E3
Fordham CO6 107 D7
Great Tey CO6 106 C1
Chappel & Wakes Colne Sta
CO6 106 D6
Charfleets Cl SS8 363 D3
Charfleets Farm Ind Est
SS8 363 D3
Charfleets Ho SS8 363 C3
Charfleets Ind Est SS8 363 C3
Charfleets Rd SS8 363 C3
Charfleets Service Rd
SS8 363 D3
Chariot Dr CO2 135 F3
Charity Farm Chase CM12 296 F3
Charlbury Cl RM3 314 C4
Charlbury Cres RM3 314 C4
Charlbury Gdns IG3 333 F2
Charlbury Ho 1 Ilford E12 333 A1
8 Little Ilford E12 352 A8
Charlecote Rd
Dagenham RM8 334 E1
Great Notley CM77 154 C7
Charlemont Rd E6 352 A2
Charles Church Wlk IG1 332 F5
Charles Cl SS0 347 A5
Charles Ct Colchester CO3 134 D6
Wivenhoe CO7 137 C3
Charles Cvn Pk CO16 167 E8
Charles Hall CO4 109 F4
Charles Ho Billericay CM11 297 B3
Colchester CO1 135 F8
8 Hoddesdon EN11 221 D8
Charles Pell Rd CO4 136 E7
Charles Rd
Brightlingsea CO7 192 F6
Dagenham RM10 354 D6
Felixstowe IP11 381 C3
Ilford RM6 334 D5
Charles Smith Ho CO2 136 A3
Charles St Colchester CO1 136 A6
Epping CM16 268 A7
Grays RM17 378 C8
Greenhithe DA9 377 A3
Greenhithe, Stone DA9 376 F2
Ipswich IP1 17 C6
Charleston Ave SS13 321 C1
Charleston Ct
Basildon SS13 321 C1
West Mersea CO5 218 E6
Charlotte Ave SS12 321 C7
Charlotte Cl IG6 311 C2
Charlotte Ct
Hornchurch RM11 336 D4
Ilford IG2 333 A5
South Woodham Ferrers
CM3 301 D6
Charlotte Dr CO13 170 E6
Charlotte Gdns RM5 313 B4
Charlotte Mews 5 SS2 347 F1
Charlotte Pl RM20 377 B8
Charlotte Rd RM10 354 B6
Charlotte Way CM8 184 B2
Charlton Cl Basildon SS13 343 C7
Hoddesdon EN11 221 A6
Charlton Cres IG11 352 F3
Charlton Mead La EN11 221 D5
Charlton St RM20 377 D8
Charlton Way EN11 221 B6
Charnock Cl CO13 170 F6
Charnwood Ave CM1 231 E1
Charnwood Ct IP2 17 B4
Charnwood Dr E18 332 B7
Charrington Cl CB9 9 C6
Charter Ave IG2 333 D4
Charter Ct CO4 110 C6
Charter Ho CM9 237 A2
Charterhouse SS16 342 C5
Charterhouse Cotts CM3 280 F5
Charteris Rd IG8 310 B4
Charter Rd The IG8 309 F4
Charters Cross CM18 223 D5
Charters Ct SS11 321 F8
Charters The CM6 123 D2
Charter Way
Braintree CM77 128 C1
Colchester CO4 109 F4
Chartfield Dr CO13 170 D8
Chartwell Cl Braintree CM7 127 E7
Ipswich IP4 18 A5
Waltham Abbey EN9 265 E6
Chartwell Ct 2 IG8 310 A3
Chartwell Pl
Bishop's Stortford CM23 119 B1
Romford RM1 335 F7
Chartwell Sq 2 SS1 367 A8
Chase Cl SS7 344 F5
Chase Court Gdns SS1 367 C8
CHASE CROSS 313 D3
Chase Cross Rd RM5 313 D3
Chase Ct Colchester CO4 136 D7
Harwich CO12 90 E2
Southend-on-S SS1 367 C8
Chase Dr CM3 301 C8
Chase End Basildon SS16 342 F3
Rayleigh SS6 323 F2
Chase Gdns Chingford E4 309 A6
Southend-on-S SS0 347 D3
Chase High Sch SS0 347 C3
Chase House Gdns RM11 336 F6
Chase La Chigwell IG7 312 A7
Harwich CO12 90 E2
Ilford IG6 333 D6
Chase Lane Prim Sch CO12 90 E2
Chase Nature Reserve The★
RM7 335 E1
Chaser Cl IP3 38 C8
Chase Rd Brentwood CM14 316 C7
Corringham SS17 361 A2
Southend-on-S SS1 367 C8
Chase Rd E CO7 139 C8
Chase Rd W CO7 139 A6
Chaseside SS6 345 E8
Chaseside Cl RM1 313 E4
Chase Sq 4 DA11 379 B1
Chase The Aldham CO6 133 B8
Barnston CM6 151 B4
Basildon, Langdon Hills
SS16 341 E3
Basildon, Steeple View SS15,
CM12 319 B2
Billericay CM11 297 C2
Bishop's Stortford CM23 145 F6
Boreham CM3 233 E8
Braintree CM7 128 A7
Brantham CO11 60 F1
Brentwood CM14 316 D7
Brentwood, Warley CM14 316 B6
Brentwood, Warley CM14 316 D5
Chigwell IG7 311 C6
Colchester CO1 136 B7
6 Colchester, Greenstead
CO1 136 D7
Dagenham RM6 334 E5
Chase The *continued*
Dagenham RM7 335 D1
East Hanningfield CM3 278 B8
Elmstead Market CO7 138 B6
Felixstowe IP11 381 D4
Foulness Island SS3 330 F7
Foxearth CO10 14 C6
Grays RM20 377 D8
Great Amwell SG12 197 A6
Great Baddow CM2 254 F6
Great Notley CM77 154 C5
Great Tey CO6 132 C8
Great Totham CM9 213 A4
Hadleigh SS7 345 B5
Harlow CM17 200 C1
Henham CM22 94 F6
Holland-on-S CO15 196 E5
Hornchurch RM7, RM12 335 F1
Ingrave CM13 317 C5
Kelvedon CO5 158 C2
Loughton IG10 288 D2
Manningtree CO11 86 D3
Osea Island CM9 239 A1
Rayleigh SS6 323 F1
Rochford SS4 325 C8
Romford RM1 335 E8
Southminster CM0 284 D4
South Woodham Ferrers
CM3 301 C8
Steeple Bumpstead CB9 27 B7
Thaxted CM6 70 A2
Tollesbury CM9 216 D2
Tolleshunt D'Arcy CM9 215 B4
Upminster RM14 337 E1
West Mersea CO5 218 C6
Wickford, Nevendon SS12 321 E4
Wickford, Runwell SS12 321 A6
Chaseway Basildon SS16 342 F4
Witham CM8 183 F5
Chaseways CM21 200 C8
Chaseway The CM7 128 C2
Chase Way The
Colchester CO3 109 C1
Colchester, Lexden CO3 109 B1
Chaston Bsns Ctr CO15 195 F5
Chaters Hill CB10 22 E2
Chatfield Way SS13 343 C7
Chatham Gn CM3 180 D3
Chatham Hall La CM3 208 B8
Chatham Pavement SS13 343 C7
Chatham Rd 1 E18 309 F1
Chatham Way CM14 316 C8
Chatley Rd CM3 180 F7
Chatsworth SS7 344 F6
Chatsworth Ave CM77 154 B7
Chatsworth Cl CM23 145 C7
Chatsworth Cres
Ipswich IP2 17 B2
Trimley St M IP11 381 A6
Chatsworth Dr IP4 18 E5
Chatsworth Gdns
Clacton-on-S CO15 195 D2
Hockley SS5 324 D6
Chatsworth Rd CO5 218 C7
CHATTER END 118 C7
Chatterford End SS14 342 B7
Chatteris Ave RM3 314 D4
Chattisham Rd IP8 35 C8
Chatton Cl 4 SS12 321 E5
Chaucer Cl Jaywick CO15 195 A1
Maldon CM9 259 A8
Tilbury RM18 379 C5
Chaucer Cres CM7 155 A8
Chaucer Ct EN11 197 A1
Chaucer Rd
Chelmsford CM2 232 D1
Chingford E17 309 C1
Felixstowe IP11 381 D3
Romford RM3 314 B3
Sudbury CO10 15 D2
Wanstead E11 332 A5
Chaucer Way
Colchester CO3 134 F6
Dartford DA1 376 A3
Hoddesdon EN11 197 A2
Chaucer Wlk SS12 321 D5
Chauntry Rd CB9 8 F7
Chauntry The 2 CB9 9 A7
Cheapside E SS6 323 C4
Cheapside W SS6 323 B4
Chedburgh Pl 3 CB9 9 A8
Cheddar Ave SS0 347 A5
Chedington SS3 349 C1
Chedworth Pl IP9 61 D7
Cheelson Rd RM15 357 C3
Cheethams Rd E12 332 E1
Cheldon Barton SS1 368 C8
Chelmer Ave
Little Waltham CM3 208 B5
Rayleigh SS6 323 C1
Chelmer Cl
Kirby Cross CO13 170 E7
Little Totham CM9 214 B4
Chelmer Cres IG11 353 B3
Chelmer Ct E18 310 B2
Chelmer Dr
Brentwood CM13 295 E3
Great Dunmow CM6 150 E8
South Ockendon RM15 372 C6
Chelmer Ho RM16 374 A1
Chelmer Lea CM2 254 E7
Chelmer Pl CM2 232 D3
Chelmer Rd Braintree CM7 128 D1
Chelmsford CM2 232 E2
Grays RM16 374 A1
Haverhill CB9 9 B8
Upminster RM14 337 D5
Witham CM8 183 F2
Chelmer Terr CM9 237 B2
Chelmerton Ave CM2 254 E7
Chelmer Valley High Sch
CM1 208 A2
Chelmer Valley Rd CM1 232 B5
CHELMER VILLAGE 233 B4
Chelmer Village Ret Pk
CM2 232 E2

Cotton Cl RM9 353 C5
Cotton La DA2, DA9 376 C2
Cottons App RM7 335 D6
Cottons Ct 3 RM7 335 D6
Cottonwood Cl CO2 135 D2
Couchmore Ave IG5 310 F1
Coulde Dennis CM3 278 B7
Coulsdon Cl CO16 195 C6
Coulson Cl RM8 334 C3
Coulter Ho DA9 377 C2
Coulter Mews CM11 297 B3
Council Ave DA11 378 C1
Council Bglws
Braintree CM7 127 F7
Fobbing SS17 361 D4
Council Cotts
Great Holland CO13 169 F3
Helions Bumpstead CB9 8 E1
Council Hos Bicknacre CM3 256 F1
Bradwell on S CM0 263 E8
Corringham SS17 361 D4
Finchingfield CM7 72 C6
Great Bromley CO7 139 A6
Hadstock CB1 5 B6
Holbrook IP9 62 D6
Peldon CO5 189 E5
Shudy Camps CB21 7 B6
Thorington Street CO6 57 B3
Thorpe-le-S CO16 141 E2
Tolleshunt Major CM9 214 D3
Wakes Colne CO6 79 C1
Wix CO11 115 B5
Wrabness CO11 88 F2
Council Houses
Cressing CM77 156 A4
Great Bentley CO7 166 F5
COUNTESS CROSS 78 D3
Counting House La CM6 123 D1
County Chambers SS1 367 A7
County Pl CM2 232 B1
Coupals Cl CB9 9 C6
Coupals Com Prim Sch CB9 9 D7
Coupals Ct CB9 9 C6
Coupals Rd CB9 9 E6
Courage Cl RM11 336 C5
Courage Ct 7 CM13 295 C3
Courage Wlk CM13 295 D3
Courtauld Cl CO9 76 F1
Courtauld Homes of Rest
CO9 76 E3
Courtauld Mews 1 CM7 127 F2
Courtauld Rd
Basildon SS13 321 C2
Braintree CM7 128 A4
Court Ave RM3 315 A3
Court Cl CM23 145 E5
Court Eight CM8 183 F5
Court Eighteen CM8 183 F5
Court Eleven CM8 183 F5
Courtenay Cl CO10 15 D2
Courtenay Dr RM16 372 F3
Courtenay Gdns RM14 337 C3
Court Farm CO11 61 A1
Courtfield SS7 344 D1
Courtfield Cl EN10 221 A3
Court Fifteen CM8 183 F5
Court Five CM8 183 E5
Court Four CM8 183 F5
Court Fourteen CM8 183 F5
Court Gdns RM3 315 A3
Court Ind Est CM2 232 C2
Courtland Ave
Chingford E4 309 F8
Ilford IG1 333 A3
Redbridge IG1 332 F2
Courtland Dr IG7 311 C7
Courtland Mews CM9 258 F8
Courtland Pl CM9 258 F8
Courtlands Billericay CM12 296 E2
Chelmsford CM1 232 A6
Halstead CO9 103 D8
Southend-on-S SS9 346 B7
Court Lodge 12 DA17 369 A1
Court Mews DA11 378 B1
Court Needham EN3 265 A2
Courtney Park Rd SS16 341 B5
Courtney Rd RM16 374 C4
Courtney Twrs IG2 333 D5
Court Nine CM8 183 F5
Court Nineteen CM8 183 F5
Court One CM8 183 F5
Court Rd CM1 208 B3
COURTSEND 330 F8
Court Seven CM8 183 F5
Court Seventeen CM8 183 F5
Court Six CM8 183 F5
Court Sixteen CM8 183 F5
Court St CO6 56 A1
Courts The Felixstowe IP11 381 F4
Rayleigh SS6 323 E3
Court Ten CM8 183 F5
Court The CO7 59 B2
Court Thirteen CM8 183 F5
Court Three CM8 183 F5
Court Twelve CM8 183 F5
Court Twenty CM8 183 F5
Court Two CM8 183 F5
Court View CM4 273 F1
Courtway IG8 310 C5
Court Way Ilford IG6 333 C8
Romford RM3 314 E1
Courtway Cotts SS17 361 D4
Courtyard Mews 1 DA9 377 A1
Courtyard Offices CM8 185 B3
Courtyard The
Basildon SS14 342 D7
Billericay CM11 297 C1
Braintree CM7 128 A4
Brentwood CM15 294 B2
Harlow CM17 200 D4
Ipswich IP1 17 B7
Maldon CM9 236 F2
Mayland CM3 260 F1
Coval Ave CM1 232 A2
Coval La CM1 232 A2
Coval Wells CM1 232 A2
Covehite Ct 3 CB9 8 E6
Covenbrook CM13 317 B7
Coventry Cl Colchester CO1 136 A8
Hullbridge SS5 301 F1
Coventry Rd IG1 333 B3
Coverdale CM8 183 E4
Coverdales The IG11 352 D3
Coverley Cl CM13 316 C4
Covert Rd IG6 311 F4
Coverts The
Brentwood CM13 295 A1
West Mersea CO5 218 D6
Writtle CM1 231 B1
Cowan Lodge 1 IG8 310 C4
Cowbridge La IG11 352 B5
Cowdray Ave CO1 109 F1
Cowdray Cres CO1 135 F7
Cowdray Ctr The CO1 110 A1
Cowdray Way RM12 355 A8
Cowdrie Way CM2 233 B4
Cowell Ave CM1 231 E5
Cowell Lodge IG8 309 F5
Cowell St IP2 17 C3
Cowels Farm La CM6 97 E5
COW GREEN 294 A5
Cow La
Great Chesterford CB10 4 A5
Point Clear B CO16 193 C3
Cowley Ave DA9 377 A2
Cowley Ct 3 E18 310 A1
Cowley Rd Felixstowe IP11 381 E4
Ilford IG1 333 A4
Redbridge IG1 332 F4
Romford RM3 314 B3
Wanstead E11 332 B6
Cowlins CM17 200 D4
Cowpar Mews CM7 155 A8
Cowper Ave RM18 379 B6
Cowper Rd
6 Belvedere DA17 369 A2
Rainham RM13 355 A1
Cowper St IP4 18 B6
Cowslip Cl IP2 16 E4
Cowslip Ct CO3 134 C7
Cowslip Mead SS14 342 B6
Cowslip Rd E18 310 B1
Cow Watering La CM1 230 E2
Coxbridge Ct CM12 297 A2
Coxes Cl SS17 360 D3
Coxes Farm Rd CM11 319 E7
Coxhall Rd IP9 36 E1
Cox La IP4 17 D5
Cox Ley CM22 174 A3
Coxon Dr RM16 372 E3
Cox Rd CO7 165 B8
Coxs Cl Haverhill CB9 8 D7
South Woodham Ferrers
CM3 301 E8
Cox's Ct CO12 91 E5
Cox's Gdns CM23 145 E5
Cox's Hill CO11 86 B4
COXTIE GREEN 293 C4
Coxtie Green Rd
Pilgrims Hatch CM14 293 C5
South Weald CM14 293 A2
Coytes Gdns 2 IP1 17 C5
Crabbe St IP4 18 A6
Crabbs Gn CM22 148 C1
Crabb's Hill CM3 210 F2
Crabs Croft CM7 128 D3
Crabtree CO13 170 C8
Crabtree Ave RM6 334 D7
Crabtree Hill CB11 67 C3
Crabtree La CO6 81 C1
Crabtree Manorway N
DA17 369 C5
Crabtree Manorway S
DA17 369 C3
Crabtrees CB11 43 E8
Cracknell Cl CO7 137 B2
Crafton Gn CM24 119 E7
Craftsmans Sq SS2 348 A5
Craig Ct CO2 135 B3
Craigdale Rd RM11 335 F4
Craigfield Ave CO15 196 A6
Craig Gdns E18 309 F1
Craig Ho CM7 128 A3
CRAIG'S END 49 D8
Craig's Hill CO8 79 E6
Craigs La CO8 79 E6
Craiston Way CM2 254 F5
Crammavill St RM16 373 A5
Crammerville Wlk 2
RM13 355 B1
Cramphorn Wlk CM1 231 F3
Cramswell Cl CB9 8 E6
Cranberry Sq IP3 38 C7
Cranborne Cl CO4 109 F2
Cranborne Gdns RM14 337 B2
Cranborne Rd
Barking IG11 352 D4
Hoddesdon EN11 221 C7
Cranbourne Ave E11 332 B7
Cranbourne Ct E18 332 B7
Cranbourne Dr EN11 197 C2
Cranbourne Gdns IG6 333 C8
Cranbourne Ho EN11 197 C2
Cranbourne Prim Sch The
EN11 197 B2
Cranbrook Ave SS7 345 C4
Cranbrook Coll (Boys)
IG1 333 A2
Cranbrook Dr RM2 336 C7
Cranbrook La CO10 2 F1
Cranbrook Lodge SS7 345 C4
Cranbrook Rd IG1, IG2 333 A5
Cranbrook Rise Ilford IG1 333 A4
Redbridge IG1 332 F5
Crane Ave CO3 134 B4
Crane Cl RM10 354 A6
Crane Hill IP2 16 E4
Cranell Gn RM15 372 B5
CRANES 320 F2
Cranes Cl SS13 320 F1
Cranes Ct SS14 342 C8
Cranes Farm Rd SS14 320 D1
Cranes La SS14 342 C8
Crane's La CO5 157 F1
Cranfield Ct
4 Wickford SS12 321 C8
2 Woodford IG8 310 A6
Cranfield Park Ave SS12 321 F2
Cranfield Park Ct 5 SS12 321 D5
Cranfield Park Rd SS12 321 D4
Cranford Cl CO13 170 E5
CRANHAM 337 E4
Cranham Gdns RM14 337 F4
Cranham Hall Cvn Pk
CM3 208 F6
Cranham Pl RM14 357 A7
Cranham Rd Broxted CM6 95 F3
Hornchurch RM11 336 B5
Cranleigh Cl CO16 195 B6
Cranleigh Dr SS9 346 E1
Cranleigh Gdns
Barking IG11 352 D6
Hullbridge SS5 301 D1
Loughton IG10 288 F3
Cranley Ave SS0 347 D1
Cranley Dr IG2 333 C4
Cranley Gdns SS3 368 C6
Cranley Rd Ilford IG2 333 C4
Southend-on-S SS0 347 D1
Cranmer Cl CM12 297 B6
Cranmer Cl RM14 337 C2
Cranmere Ct CO1 136 A7
Cranmer Gdns RM10 354 C8
Cranmer Ho CM2 253 F7
Cranmer's La CO6 131 E6
Cranmore Cl CM22 94 C2
Cranmoregreen La CO10 2 F3
Cranston Ave SS0 347 D5
Cranston Gdns E4 309 B4
Cranston Park Ave RM14 356 C8
Cranwell Cres IP3 18 C1
Cranwell Gdns CM23 119 C1
Cranworth Cres 7 E4 287 D1
Craven Ave SS8 364 A3
Craven Cl SS4 325 D5
Craven Ct RM6 334 E5
Craven Dr CO4 110 C3
Craven Gdns Barking IG11 352 E3
Ilford IG6 333 D8
Redbridge IG6 311 D1
Romford, Harold Park RM3 315 C4
Romford, Willoughby's Hill
RM5 313 A5
Crawford Ave RM16 373 B5
Crawford Chase SS12 321 E5
Crawford Cl CM12 297 C5
Crawford Compton Cl
RM12 355 C6
Crawley Cl SS17 361 A4
Crawley Ct 6 DA11 379 B1
CRAWLEY END 19 D4
Crawley End SG8 19 D4
Crayfields CM6 123 E1
Crayford Cl CM9 258 E8
Crayford Rd CO10 15 D2
Craylands SS14 342 F7
Craylands La DA10 377 D2
Craylands Sch The DA10 377 D2
Craylands Sq DA10 377 D2
CRAYS HILL 320 D5
Crays Hill CM11 320 C5
Crayshill Pk CM11 320 C5
Crays Hill Prim Sch CM11 320 D6
Crays Hill Rd CM11 320 D4
Crays View CM12 319 B8
Crealock Gr IG8 309 F5
Creance Ct CM2 232 A2
Creasen Butt Cl CM9 237 A4
Creasey Cl RM11 336 B2
Creasy Ct SS14 342 E6
Crediton Ho 4 RM3 314 D4
Credon Cl CO15 195 F7
Credon Dr CO15 195 F7
Credo Way RM20 377 B8
Creeds Cotts CM16 267 E7
Creeds Farm CM16 267 E7
Creek Cotts CO14 144 E4
Creekhurst Cl CO7 193 A6
Creekmouth Ind Pk IG11 352 F1
Creek Rd Barking IG11 352 F2
Canvey Island SS8 364 D4
CREEKSEA 305 F5
Creeksea Ferry Rd SS4 305 C2
Creeksea La CM0 305 F6
Creekside RM13 354 F1
Creek The DA11 378 B2
Creek View Basildon SS16 342 E3
Great Wigborough CO5 188 F2
Creek View Ave SS5 301 D3
Creekview Rd CM3 301 F7
Creek Way RM13 369 E8
Creephedge La CM3 278 E5
Cree Way RM1 313 E3
Creffield Rd CO3 135 D6
Crepping Hall Dr IP9 61 F1
Crescent Ave Grays RM17 378 D8
Hornchurch RM12 335 F2
Crescent Cl CM12 296 F4
Crescent Ct
Billericay CM12 297 A2
Grays RM17 373 D1
Heybridge CM9 236 F5
Crescent Dr CM15 294 E1
Crescent Gdns CM12 296 F4
Crescent Rd Aveley RM15 371 C4
Billericay CM12 296 F4
Bishop's Stortford CM23 146 A6
Brentwood CM14 316 B6
Canvey Island SS8 364 D2
Chingford E4 287 E2
Dagenham RM10 335 B1
Felixstowe IP11 381 E4
Great Baddow CM2 255 A7
Heybridge CM9 236 F5
Ipswich IP1 17 B6
South Benfleet SS7 344 D2
Southend-on-S SS9 346 B1
Tollesbury CM9 216 E1
Walton-on-t-N CO14 171 C8
Woodford E18 310 C2
Crescent The
Clacton-on-S CO15 196 B7
Colchester CO4 110 C7
Epping CM16 267 F7
Frinton-on-S CO13 170 F4
Gestingthorpe CO9 31 F2
Great Holland CO13 170 A4
Great Horkesley CO6 82 B1
Great Leighs CM3 180 E5
Greenhithe DA9 377 C2
Crescent The *continued*
Hadleigh SS7 345 F3
Harlow CM17 200 C6
Ilford IG2 333 A5
Loughton IG10 288 D3
Marks Tey CO6 133 A3
Steeple Bumpstead CB9 27 B7
Thorpe-le-S CO16 141 F2
Upminster RM14 337 F4
West Bergholt CO6 108 D5
Crescent View IG10 288 D4
Crescent Way RM15 371 D5
Crescent Wlk RM15 371 C4
Cressages Cl CM6 152 F6
Cress Croft CM7 128 D1
Cressells SS15 341 F6
Cresset Cl SG12 197 C3
CRESSING 156 A6
Cressingham Ct 1 DA17 369 A3
Cressing Prim Sch CM77 155 E6
Cressing Rd Braintree CM7 128 D6
Witham CM8 183 D6
Cressing Sta CM77 155 D5
Cressing Temple Barns*
CM77 156 B2
Crest Ave Basildon SS13 343 C6
Grays RM17 378 B7
Cresthill Ave RM17 373 C2
Crestlands CO7 165 B7
Crest The
Sawbridgeworth CM21 172 D2
Southend-on-S SS9 346 D6
Crest View DA9 377 A3
Creswick Ave SS6 323 C3
Creswick Ct SS6 323 C3
Crete Hall Rd DA11 378 E1
Crick Ct 3 IG11 352 C3
Cricket Ct E6 352 A2
Cricketers Cl
Broomfield CM1 208 C1
Erith DA8 369 E1
Sudbury CO10 33 E6
Cricketers La CM13 317 D3
Cricketers Ret Pk SS13 321 A2
Cricketers Row CM13 317 D3
Cricketers Way SS13 321 A2
Cricketfield Gr SS9 346 F2
Cricketfield La CM23 145 E8
Cricket Hill Rd IP11 381 B5
Crickhollow CM3 301 C5
Cricklade Ave RM3 314 D4
Cringle Lock CM3 301 E5
CRIPPLE CORNER 54 B2
Cripplegate CM0 284 E5
Cripsey Ave CM5 248 F5
Crispe Ho 4 IG11 352 D3
Crispin Cl CB9 8 D7
Crispins SS1 368 A8
Crispin Terr IG8 310 D4
Critchett Terr 1 CM1 232 A3
Crittal Ct CM7 127 D4
Crittall Cl CM8 156 E4
Crittall Ct CM8 184 A3
Crittall Dr CM7 127 D4
Crittall Rd CM8 184 B3
CRIX GREEN 153 D6
Crix Green Villas CM6 153 D6
Croasdaile Rd CM24 119 E8
Croasdale Cl CM24 119 E8
Crocklands CO9 104 A5
CROCKLEFORD HEATH 111 C2
Crocus Cl
Clacton-on-S CO16 195 C4
Ipswich IP2 16 F4
Crocus Fields CB10 22 E3
Crocus Way CM1 232 E7
Croft Cl Braintree CM7 128 A3
South Benfleet SS7 344 C5
Southend-on-S SS9 346 E2
Croft Ct Chelmsford CM1 232 E8
20 Sudbury CO10 33 E7
Crofters CM21 172 E3
Crofters End CM21 172 E3
Crofters Wlk CM77 154 D8
Croft Ho 4 CO9 76 F2
Croft La CB9 9 B6
Croft Lodge Cl IG8 310 B4
Crofton Ave SS17 360 F4
Crofton Cl IP4 18 B7
Crofton Gr E4 309 D6
Crofton Ho 6 CO10 33 E8
Crofton Rd Grays RM16 373 E3
Ipswich IP4 18 B7
Croft Rd Clacton-on-S CO15 195 D4
Kelvedon CO5 158 B2
South Benfleet SS7 344 C5
Sudbury CO10 33 E8
Croftside CO8 55 F1
Croft St IP2 17 C3
Crofts The SS3 349 E4
Croft The Bures CO8 55 F1
Chingford E4 309 E8
Earls Colne CO6 105 A6
Elsenham CM22 94 C1
Glemsford CO10 2 C4
Great Yeldham CO9 30 A2
Loughton IG10 289 A7
Rayleigh SS6 345 F8
Croft Villas CO10 2 C3
Croft Way CM8 184 A3
Cromarty Ho CM14 316 D6
Cromarty Rd IP4 18 B8
Cromar Way CM1 231 F1
Crombie Cl IG4 332 F6
Crome Cl CO3 135 A5
Cromer Ave SS15 341 B8
Cromer Cl SS15 341 B8
Crome Rd CO16 195 D5
Cromer Mews CO4 109 E3
Cromer Rd Dagenham RM6 334 E5
Hornchurch RM11 336 D4
Ipswich IP1 16 F8
Romford RM7 335 C5
Southend-on-S SS1 367 B8
Woodford IG8 310 A6
Cromer Terr 3 RM6 334 B6
Crompton Cl SS14 341 F8
Crompton Pl 8 EN3 265 A1
Crompton Rd IP2 16 F7
Crompton St CM1 231 F1
Cromwell Ave CM12 297 A3
Cromwell Cl
Bishop's Stortford CM23 145 B7
Boreham CM3 233 D8
Cromwell Ct
Brentwood CM14 316 B6
11 Ipswich IP1 17 C5
Maldon CM9 237 A3
Cromwell Ctr Barking IG11 353 A2
Redbridge IG6 312 B5
Witham CM8 184 B2
Cromwell Ctr The RM8 334 F4
Cromwell Hill CM9 236 F3
Cromwell Ho CO4 109 F4
Cromwell La CM9 236 F3
Cromwell Lodge IG11 352 E7
Cromwell Pk CM6 152 B5
Cromwell Rd
Brentwood CM14 316 B6
16 Colchester CO2 135 F6
Grays RM17 373 A1
Hockley SS5 324 E6
Little Dunmow CM6 151 E6
Saffron Walden CB11 43 E7
Southend-on-S SS2 348 B3
Cromwells Mere RM5 313 D4
Cromwell Sq 8 IP1 17 C5
Cromwell Trad Ctr IG11 352 E2
Cromwell Way CM8 183 F2
Crondon Park La CM4 275 E4
Crooked La DA11, DA12 379 B1
Crooked Mile
Waltham Abbey EN9 265 C6
Waltham Abbey EN9 265 C7
Crooked Way EN9 221 E1
Cropenburg Wlk SS8 364 B5
Croppath Rd RM10 354 A8
Croquet Gdns CO7 137 C1
Crosby Ct IG7 312 A7
Crosby Rd Dagenham RM10 354 B4
Southend-on-S SS0 366 C8
Cross Ave SS12 321 C6
Crossbow Ct CM5 249 A2
Crossbow Rd IG7 311 F5
Crossby Cl CM15 295 E8
Cross Cotts CO4 83 B6
Crosse Cts SS15 341 C5
CROSS END 78 C8
Crossfell Rd SS7 344 F7
Crossfield Rd
Clacton-on-S CO15 195 E3
Hoddesdon EN11 221 B8
Southend-on-S SS2 348 D2
Crossfields Halstead CO9 103 F8
Loughton IG10 289 B4
Stoke-by-N CO6 56 C5
Crossfield Way CO13 170 B6
Cross Field Way CO4 83 B5
Crossgate Field IP11 381 C5
Cross Gn SS16 341 F5
Cross Hill CO12 116 D1
Crossing Rd CM16 268 A6
Cross La CO5 218 F7
Crossley Ave CO15 220 E7
Crossley View CO15 196 B3
Crossness Rd IG11 352 F2
Cross Rd Basildon SS13 343 F7
Chingford E4 287 E1
Dagenham RM6 334 C4
Gravesend DA11 378 F1
Hadleigh SS7 345 B4
Maldon CM9 237 A1
Romford RM7 335 B8
Witham CM8 183 F5
Woodford IG8 310 F4
Crossroads CO9 31 E2
Cross Roads IG10 288 C7
Cross St Felixstowe IP11 381 C6
16 Gravesend DA11 379 B1
Saffron Walden CB10 22 D1
Sudbury CO10 33 D7
Cross The
West Mersea CO5 218 E7
Wivenhoe CO7 137 B2
Crosstree Wlk CO2 136 A3
Crossway Dagenham RM8 334 C1
6 Stanford-le-H SS17 360 F3
Woodford IG8 310 C6
Cross Way
3 Harlow CM17 200 D1
West Mersea CO5 218 E7
CROSSWAYS 376 D4
Crossways
Canvey Island SS8 363 E4
Chelmsford CM2 254 C7
Clacton-on-S CO15 220 G8
Colne Engaine CO6 77 F1
Loughton IG10 289 A4
Romford RM2 336 B8
Shenfield CM15 295 A3
Crossways Bvd DA2 376 C3
Crossways The SS0 366 A8
Crossway The CM11 297 D3
Crotchets Cl IP9 35 A1
Crouch Ave Barking IG11 353 B3
Hullbridge SS5 301 E1
Crouch Beck CM3 301 E7
Crouch Ct Braintree CM7 128 D1
Harlow CM20 199 C3
Crouch Dr Wickford SS11 321 D8
Witham CM8 183 E2
CROUCH GREEN 51 C4
Crouchman Cl RM16 373 C4
Crouchmans Ave SS3 350 A4
Crouchman's Farm Rd
CM9 235 C7
Crouch Mdw SS5 301 E4
Crouch Pk SS5 301 E4
Crouch Rd
Burnham-on-C CM0 306 C5
Grays RM16 374 A1
Crouch St Basildon SS15 319 E2
Colchester CO3 135 E6
Crouch Valley RM14 337 E4
Crouchview Cl SS11 322 B7
Crouch View Cotts CM3 300 C5
Crouch View Cres SS5 325 A8
Crouch View Gr SS5 301 D3
Crouch View Villas SS4 304 E2
Crouch Way SS3 368 E7
Crough Rd CM3 303 A7
Croutel Rd IP11 381 F5
Crowborough Rd SS2 348 A2
Crowe Hall La IP9 62 A1
Crow Gn CM15 294 A5
Crow Green La CM15 294 A4
Crow Green Rd CM15 294 A5
Crowhall La CO11 87 E1
Crowhurst Ct CO3 135 E7
Crowhurst Rd CO3 135 E7
Crow La Romford RM7 335 B4
Tendring CO16 141 A3
Crowland Cl 7 IP2 17 A2
Crowland Rd CB9 8 F8
Crowlands Ave RM7 335 B5
Crowlands Jun & Inf Schs
RM7 335 C5
Crown Ave SS13 343 C7
Crown Bays Rd CO4 136 C8
Crown Bldgs 4 E4 287 D1
Crown Cl Basildon SS13 343 C6
Sheering CM22 201 C8
Crown Ct RM18 379 A5
Crownfield EN10 221 A2
Crownfield Ave IG2 333 E6
Crownfield Jun & Inf Schs
RM7 313 A1
Crownfield Rd CO10 2 B6
Crownfields CO7 84 F6
Crown Gate
Colchester CO4 110 D6
Harlow CM20 223 D8
Crown Gdns SS6 323 C2
Crown Hill Ashdon CB10 6 B1
Loughton CM16 267 A5
Rayleigh SS6 323 C2
Waltham Abbey EN9, CM20 266 F6
Crownhill Rd IG8 310 E3
Crown Hts SS6 323 D2
Crown La Harwich CO12 91 D4
Tendring CO16 140 D3
Crown La N CO7 110 F7
Crown La S CO7 111 A4
Crown Mdw CM7 128 D4
Crownmead Way RM7 335 B7
Crown Par RM13 355 B1
Crown Rd Billericay CM11 297 B2
Clacton-on-S CO15 195 C1
Cold Norton CM3 280 F6
Grays RM17 378 A8
Hockley SS5 324 B5
Ilford IG6 333 D7
Kelvedon Hatch CM14 293 D8
Crown St Brentwood CM14 316 C8
Castle Hedingham CO9 51 E4
Dagenham RM10 354 C6
Dedham CO7 84 F6
Felixstowe IP11 381 C6
Great Bardfield CM7 72 B2
Ipswich IP1 17 C6
Crown Terr CM23 146 A7
Crown Way CM0 284 C4
Crow Pond Cotts CM3 182 C3
Crow Pond Rd CM3 182 C3
Crowsfield Cotts CM2 276 F4
CROW'S GREEN 125 E8
Crowsheath La CM11 298 E6
Crows La CM3 279 D5
Crowsnest The CM0 306 C3
Crows Rd Barking IG11 352 B6
Epping CM16 245 F1
Crow St CM22 94 F5
Crowstone Ave SS0 366 C8
Crowstone Cl SS0 347 D1
Crowstone Prep Sch SS0 366 C8
Crowstone Rd Grays RM16 373 C4
Southend-on-S SS0 366 C8
Crowstone (Sutton) Prep Sch
SS4 348 B8
Croxall Ct CM8 183 F2
Croxford Way RM7 335 D3
Croxon Way CM0 306 B7
Crozier Ave CM23 145 C8
Crozier Mews IP4 18 B6
Crozier Terr CM2 233 B4
Cruce Way CO16 192 F3
Crucible Cl RM6 334 B5
Cruick Ave RM15 372 C6
Crummock Cl CM77 154 C6
Crunch Croft CB9 9 E5
Crusader Cl RM19 371 A2
Crusader Way CM7 128 D2
Crushes Cl CM13 295 E3
Crushton Pl CM1 231 F6
Crusoe Rd DA8 369 D1
Crystal Ave RM12 336 E1
Crystal Ct 1 RM13 355 A1
Crystal Stps 15 SS1 367 C7
Crystal Way RM8 334 C3
Cuckfield Ave IP3 18 E3
Cuckoo Cnr SS2 347 E4
Cuckoo Farm Bsns Pk
CO4 110 A7
Cuckoo Hill Bures CO8 55 F1
Sible Hedingham CO9 75 B8
Cuckoo La RM16 372 F5
Cuckoos La
Great Canfield CM6 149 A3
Takeley CM6 148 F2
Cuckoo Way CM77 154 C7
Cudmore Grove Ctry Pk*
CO5 192 A1
Culford Pl IP3 17 F4
Culford Rd RM16 373 C4
Culford Wlk IP11 381 A3
Cullen Sq RM15 372 C5
Cullingham Rd IP1 17 A5
Cullings Ct EN9 265 F6
Culpeper Cl IG6 311 B4
Culverdown SS14 342 A6
Culver Rise CM3 301 E6
Culver St E CO1 135 F7
Culver St W CO1 135 F7
Culvert Cl CO6 130 F1
Culver Wlk 21 CO1 135 F7
Cumberland Ave
Hornchurch RM12 336 E1

Francisco Cl RM16 372 C3
Francis Ct
3 Basildon SS14 342 F5
Copford CO6 133 C4
Erith DA8 369 E1
Francis Ct CM20 199 B2
Francis Ct CM8 156 C5
Francis Green Ho 7 EN9 265 B6
Francis Kellerman Wlk CO3 135 E7
Francis Mews CM9 259 B8
Francis Rd Braintree CM7 127 D2
Ilford IG1 333 D2
14 Sudbury CO10 33 E7
Francis St
Brightlingsea CO7 192 F5
Ilford IG1 333 D2
Francis Way
Colchester CO4 110 D1
Silver End CM8 156 C4
Francis Wks EN11 221 B6
Francis Wlk SS6 323 D2
Francombe Gdns RM1 336 A5
Frank Bailey Wlk E12 352 A6
Frank Bretton Ho CM5 249 A3
Frank Clater Cl CO4 136 C8
Frankland Cl IG8 310 C5
Frankland Rd E4 309 A5
Franklin Rd
Hornchurch RM12 355 C6
Ipswich IP3 18 B2
North Fambridge CM3 303 B8
Franklins RM15 371 D7
Franklins Way SS11 321 E8
Franklyn Gdns IG6 311 D4
Frank Naylor Ct 11 CO1 135 F7
Franks Cotts RM14 338 B3
Frank Slater Ho 4 IG3 334 B3
Franmil Rd RM12 336 A3
Fraser Cl Basildon SS15 340 F6
Chelmsford CM2 254 C8
Southend-on-S SS3 368 F8
Fraser Rd Erith DA8 369 D1
Ipswich IP1 16 F7
Frating Abbey Farm Rd CO7 166 C6
Frating Cres IG8 310 B4
Frating Cross CO7 166 B7
Frating Ct CM7 128 D1
FRATING GREEN 139 A3
Frating Hill CO7 138 D3
Frating Rd Ardleigh CO7 111 F6
Great Bromley CO7 138 F6
Thorrington CO7 166 A7
Frayes Chase CM5 204 A3
Frazer Cl RM1 335 F4
Frederica Rd E4 287 D2
Frederick Andrews Ct RM17 378 D8
Frederick Rd RM13 354 E3
Fred Leach Ho 1 SS8 364 A3
Fredrick J French Meml Homes CM1 232 B6
Fredricks Cl CO11 115 B5
Fred Tibble Ct RM9 353 E8
Freeborne Gdns RM13 355 A6
Freebournes Ct 5 CM8 184 A2
Freebournes Rd CM8 184 B2
Freehold Rd IP4 18 B6
Freeland Rd CO15 195 E1
Freelands
Brightlingsea CO7 193 C6
Ipswich IP4 18 B6
Freeman Cl CO4 110 A6
Freeman Ct SS17 360 F3
Freemantle Ho RM18 378 F6
Freeman Way RM11 336 F5
Freeport Designer Outlet CM77 128 C1
Freeport Office Village CM7 128 B1
Freeport Sta CM77 128 B1
Free Rodwell Ho CO11 86 F4
Freewood La CB11 20 B3
Freezes Barns CB9 27 B7
Freightmaster Est RM13 370 A2
Freightways RM20 371 F1
Fremantle SS3 368 D5
Fremantle Cl CM3 279 D1
Fremantle Rd
Belvedere DA17 369 A2
Colchester CO2 136 B1
Ilford IG6 311 C1
Redbridge IG6 311 C1
Fremnells The SS14 342 D7
FRENCHES GREEN 153 A6
French Rd CM3 280 F1
French's Cl SG12 197 B4
French's Wlk 4 CM2 232 C2
Frensham Cl CO3 134 D7
Frere Ct CM23 118 F1
Frere Way CO5 164 B6
Frerichs Cl SS12 321 D5
Freshfields CO12 90 F1
Freshfields Ave RM14 356 C7
Freshfields Rd CO12 91 A4
Freshwater Cres CM9 237 B4
Freshwater Dr SS16 342 F4
Freshwater La CO15 195 F7
Freshwater Rd RM8 334 E3
Freshwaters CM20 199 E1
Freshwell Ave RM6 334 C7
Freshwell Gdns
Saffron Walden CB10 22 C2
West Horndon CM13 339 D5
Freshwell St CB10 22 D2
Fresh Wharf Est IG11 352 B4
Fresh Wharf Rd IG11 352 B3
FRESTON 37 E3
Freston Hill IP9 37 E4
Freston Rd IP3 38 C8
Freston St IP9 37 E3
Frettons SS14 342 E6
Friars IP9 60 B8
Friar's Ave CM15 295 A2
Friars Bridge Rd IP1 17 B5
Friars Cl Basildon SS15 341 C6
Chingford E4 309 C7
Clacton-on-S CO15 195 E6
Colchester CO4 110 C2
Friars Cl continued
Ilford IG1 333 D3
Sible Hedingham CO9 51 D2
Wivenhoe CO7 164 C8
Friar's Cl CM15 295 A2
Friar's Cotts CM77 154 B4
Friarscroft EN10 221 A3
Friars Ct Colchester CO2 136 C3
15 Sudbury CO10 33 E7
Friars Ctyd 1 IP1 17 C5
Friars Gate Cl IG8 310 A6
Friars Grove Jun & Inf Schs CO4 110 C2
Friars La Braintree CM7 127 F4
Hatfield Heath CM22 174 C1
Maldon CM9 236 F2
Friars Mead CB9 9 F4
Friars Prim Sch SS3 368 F8
Friars St Ipswich IP1 17 C5
Southend-on-S SS3 368 F7
Sudbury CO10 33 E7
Friars The Chigwell IG7 311 E6
Harlow CM19 223 A6
Friars Wlk CM2 232 B1
Friars Wood CM23 146 C8
Friary Fields CM9 237 A2
Friary La IG8 310 A6
FRIDAY HILL 309 E7
Friday Hill E4 309 E7
Friday Hill E E4 309 E7
Friday Hill W E4 309 E8
Friday Rd DA8 369 D1
Friday Wood Gn CO2 162 F8
Friedberg Ave CM23 145 D4
Friends Field CO8 55 F1
Friends Sch CB11 43 D8
Friends Wlk CB11 43 D7
Friern Gdns SS12 321 B7
Friern Pl SS12 321 B6
Friern Wlk SS12 321 B7
Friesian Cl CM7 127 D2
Frietuna Rd CO13 170 E6
Frimley Ave RM11 337 A3
Frimley Rd IG3 333 E1
Frinton Ct CO13 170 F3
Frinton Dr IG8 309 D3
Frinton Lodge CO13 171 A4
Frinton Mews IG2 333 A5
FRINTON-ON-SEA 170 D5
Frinton-on-Sea Prim Sch CO13 170 E5
Frinton Rd
Holland-on-S CO15 196 E6
Kirby Cross CO13 170 D6
Romford RM5 313 A3
Thorpe-le-S CO16 142 B1
Frinton Sta CO13 170 F5
Friston Path 4 IG6 311 E5
Frithwood Cl CM12 318 F7
Frithwood La CM12 318 F7
Fritillary Cl IP8 36 E8
Fritton Cl IP2 17 A1
Fritton Ct 19 CB9 8 E7
Frizlands La RM10 335 B1
Frobisher Cl Basildon SS15 341 D6
Maldon CM9 259 A8
Frobisher Dr CO15 194 F1
Frobisher Gdns RM16 372 E3
Frobisher Prim Sch CO15 194 F1
Frobisher Rd Harwich CO12 90 F1
Ipswich IP3 17 E1
Frobisher Way
Braintree CM7 128 C4
Greenhithe DA9 377 B3
Southend-on-S SS3 349 E1
Froden Brook CM11 319 C7
Froden Cl CM11 319 C7
Froden Ct CM11 319 C6
Frogge St CB10 3 B3
Frog Hall Cl CO5 164 B6
Froghall La IG7 311 D6
Frog La RM13 369 D8
Frog Mdw CO7 84 F7
Frogmore Est RM20 372 A1
Frog St CM15 293 E8
Frome RM18 375 C2
Fronk's Ave CO12 91 C2
Fronk's Rd CO12 91 B2
Front La RM14 337 E4
Front Rd IP3 38 D8
Frowick La CO16 167 B2
Fryatt Ave CO12 91 A4
Fryatt Hospl CO12 91 A3
Fry Cl RM5 313 A4
FRYERNING 274 A5
Fryerning La CM4 274 B4
FRYERNS 342 E8
Fryerns Terr SS14 342 F8
Fryth The SS14 342 E8
Fuchsia Cl RM7 335 E2
Fuchsia Ct 6 CO4 136 D8
Fuchsia La IP4 18 A5
Fuchsia Way CO16 195 C5
Fulbourne Rd E17 309 C1
Fulbrook La RM15 371 F6
Fulcher Ave CM2 232 F3
Fulfen Way CB11 43 D7
Fulford Dr SS9 347 A6
Fullarton Cres RM15 371 F7
Fullbridge CM9 237 A3
Fuller Ct 3 CM23 146 A7
Fuller Rd RM8 353 C8
Fuller's Almshouses CM24 119 F6
Fuller's Ave IG8 309 F3
Fullers Cl Romford RM5 313 C3
Waltham Abbey EN9 266 A6
Fuller's Cl CO5 158 B2
Fullers Ct CM7 128 A3
FULLER'S END 120 D8
Fullers Gate CO5 158 B2
Fuller's La RM5 313 C3
Fullers Mead CM17 224 C7
Fullers Rd CO2 136 D2
Fuller's Rd E18 309 F3
FULLER STREET 181 D4
Fuller Terr IG1 352 D7
Fullman Ind Pk SS8 363 C3
Fullwell Ave IG5 311 B2
FULLWELL CROSS 311 D2
Fullwell Ct IG5 311 A2
Fullwell Par IG5 311 A2
Fullwood Prim Sch IG6 333 C7
Fulmar Cl CO4 137 A8
Fulmar Rd RM12 355 B6
Fulmar Way SS11 322 A5
Fulton Cres CM23 146 C8
Fulton Ct 3 EN3 265 A1
Fulton Rd SS7 344 D7
Fulwich Rd DA1 376 A1
Furlongs SS16 342 D4
Furlongs The CM4 274 B3
Furlong Way SG12 197 A7
Furneaux La CO5 163 F5
Furness Cl Grays RM16 374 B1
Ipswich IP2 36 F8
Furness Way RM12 355 A7
Furriers Cl CM23 145 C5
Furrow Cl CO3 134 E5
Furrowfelde SS16 342 A4
FURTHER FORD END 64 D6
Further Mdw CM1 253 A8
Furtherwick Park Sch SS8 364 C3
Furtherwick Rd SS8 364 C2
Furze Cres CO7 165 A7
Furze Farm Cl RM6 312 E1
Furze Glade SS16 341 B4
Furze Inf Sch RM6 334 E5
Furze La
Great Bromley CO7 139 A5
Stock CM4 276 A1
Fuschia Ct IG8 309 E4
Fusedale Way RM15 371 F6
Fyefields SS13 343 C7
FYFIELD 227 D2
Fyfield Ave SS12 321 C5
Fyfield Bsns & Research Pk CM5 249 B6
Fyfield Cl CM13 339 D5
Fyfield Dr RM15 371 F6
Fyfield Dr Walker's CE Prim Sch CM5 227 D2
Fyfield Ho RM9 353 B5
Fyfield Path SS6 323 A3
Fyfield Rd
Chipping Ongar CM5 249 A5
Moreton CM5 226 F3
Rainham RM13 354 F4
Willingale CM5 228 C3
Woodford IG8 310 C3

G

Gabion Ave RM19 371 D2
Gablefields CM2 255 D6
Gable Hall Sch SS17 361 A4
Gable Ho IP4 17 F6
Gables The Barking IG11 352 C6
Basildon SS13 343 B8
Brentwood CM13 316 C4
Chipping Ongar CM5 249 A5
Haverhill CB9 9 F4
Sawbridgeworth CM21 172 E2
Southend-on-S, Eastwood SS9 346 B6
Southend-on-S SS9 346 D1
Gabriel Cl Grays RM16 372 C3
Romford RM5 313 C3
Gabriel Ho CM6 150 D8
Gaces Acre CB11 43 A1
Gadsden Cl RM14 337 E5
Gadwall Reach CO5 158 D2
Gafzelle Dr SS8 364 E3
Gager Dr CO5 186 E5
Gage's Rd
Belchamp St P CO10 13 A1
Little Yeldham C10 30 F8
Gaiger Cl CM1 232 D7
GAINSBOROUGH 38 B8
Gainsborough Ave
Canvey Island SS8 364 E3
Little Ilford E12 352 A7
Tilbury RM18 379 B6
Gainsborough Cl
Billericay CM11 297 B1
Clacton-on-S CO16 195 B6
West Mersea CO5 218 D6
Gainsborough Cres CM2 232 E3
Gainsborough Ct
4 Brentwood CM14 316 C6
17 Sudbury CO10 33 E7
Gainsborough Dr
Lawford CO11 86 C4
Southend-on-S SS0 347 E2
Gainsborough Ho
2 Barking RM8 353 B8
Redbridge IG8 311 B4
Gainsborough La IP3 37 F7
Gainsborough Pl
Brentwood CM13 295 D1
Chigwell IG7 311 F7
Gainsborough Rd
Black Notley CM77 155 A4
Colchester CO3 135 B5
Dagenham RM8 334 B1
Felixstowe IP11 381 F4
Ipswich IP4 17 D8
Rainham RM13 355 A4
Sudbury CO10 33 E8
Woodford IG8 310 E4
Gainsborough's House Mus* CO10 33 E7
Gainsborough St CO10 33 E7
Gains Cl SS8 364 D4
GAINSFORD END 49 F4
Gainsford End Rd CO9 50 B6
Gainsthorpe Rd CM5 248 D8
Gaitskell Ho RM16 373 B5
Galadriel Spring CM3 301 C6
Galahad Cl CM0 306 B5
Galaxie Lo SS7 344 D2
Galeborough Ave IG8 309 D3
Gale St RM9 353 D5
Gales Way IG8 310 E3
Galey Gn RM15 372 B8
Galiots CO5 218 A6
Gall End La CM24 119 F7
Galleon Bvd DA2 376 D3
Galleon Cl DA8 369 D2
Galleon Rd RM16 372 C2
Galleons Dr IG11 353 A2
Galleydene SS7 345 C3
Galleydene Ave CM2 254 C3
GALLEYEND 254 D4
Galley Gn SG13 197 A2
Galleyhill Rd EN9 265 E7
Galley Hill Rd
Northfleet DA11 378 A2
Swanscombe DA10 377 F2
Galley Hill Trad Est DA10 377 E2
GALLEYWOOD 254 D2
Galleywood Cres RM5 313 D4
Galleywood Inf Sch CM2 254 C2
Galleywood Rd
Chelmsford CM2 254 A5
Great Baddow CM2 254 E5
Galliford Rd CM9 237 A4
Galliford Road Ind Est CM9 237 A4
Gallions Cl IG11 353 A2
Gallops The SS16 341 B5
Galloway Cl 1 CM23 145 F8
Galloway Dr CO16 168 D3
Galloway Rd CM23 118 F1
Gallows Cnr RM3 314 C2
GALLOWS GREEN
Fordham Heath 107 C1
Great Easton 97 D2
Gallows Green Rd CM6 97 F2
Gallows Hill CB11 43 C7
Galpin Ho CM8 211 F8
Galsworthy Ave RM6 334 B5
Galsworthy Cl CM7 155 A7
Galsworthy Rd RM18 379 C6
Galt Cl SS12 321 D4
Galton Rd SS0 366 C8
GAMBLES GREEN 182 A2
Gambleside SS16 342 E3
Gamma Terr IP3 18 E1
Gammon Field RM16 373 E5
Gandalf's Ride CM3 301 D6
Gandish Cl CO7 59 D1
Gandish Rd CO7 59 E2
Ganels Cl CM11 319 C7
Ganels Rd CM11 319 C7
Ganges Rd IP9 91 B8
Gangies Hill CM21 172 A4
Ganley Cl 6 CM11 297 B2
Gannet Cl CB9 9 C8
Gannet Rd IP2 16 E3
Gant Ct EN9 265 F5
GANTS HILL 333 A5
Gantshill Cres IG2 333 A6
Gants Hill Sta IG2 333 A5
Ganymede Cl IP1 16 D7
Gaol La CO10 33 E7
Gap The Arkesden CB11 41 F1
Holland-on-S CO15 196 G6
Garbutt Rd RM14 337 C2
Garden Cl Althorne CM3 282 F4
Chingford E4 309 A5
Steeple CM0 261 F3
Garden Cotts CO6 131 A2
Garden Ct
Frinton-on-S CO13 170 F3
Upminster RM14 337 E3
Garden Dr CO3 134 E6
Garden End CM4 275 F2
Gardeners CM2 254 D5
Gardeners La SS4 304 F1
Gardeners Rd CO9 76 F1
Gardeners Row CO6 131 A2
Garden Farm CO5 218 D7
Garden Field
Felixstowe IP11 381 C5
Hatfield Peverel CM3 210 F4
Garden Field Cotts CO6 81 E5
Garden Fields
Great Tey CO6 132 C8
Stebbing CM6 124 D6
Steeple CM0 261 F3
Garden Hos The CM21 173 B3
Gardenia Pl CO16 195 B4
Gardenia Way IG8 310 A5
Gardenia Wlk CO4 136 E7
Garden Pl CO10 33 D7
Garden Rd
Clacton-on-S CO15 220 G7
Walton-on-t-N CO14 171 A7
Gardens Fields CM5 270 E5
Gardens The
Doddinghurst CM15 272 B3
Southend-on-S SS9 365 E8
Garden Terr CO9 76 F2
Garden Terrace Rd 2 CM17 200 C4
Garden Way IG10 267 A1
Garden Wharf DA8 369 F1
Gardiner Cl RM8 353 D8
Gardiners Cl SS14 320 D1
Gardiners La N CM11 320 E4
Gardiners La S SS14 320 E2
Gardiners Link SS14 320 D2
Gardiners The CM17 224 B8
Gardiners Way SS14 320 D2
Gardner Ave SS17 361 A3
Gardner Cl E11 332 B5
Gardners Ct RM7 335 C6
Garenne Ct 8 E4 287 C1
Garfield Cl IP11 381 D3
Garfield Rd Chingford E4 287 D1
Felixstowe IP11 381 D3
Garland Rd CO12 90 F5
Garland Way RM11 336 E7
Garling Wlk CO6 108 E3
Garner Cl RM8 334 D3
Garner Rd E17 309 C2
Garners The SS4 325 F2
Garnets Mead CM3 182 B3
Garnetts CM22 94 B2
Garnetts Bglws CM6 152 C5
Garnetts La CM6 152 C6
Garnetts Villas CM6 152 C5
Garnon Mead CM16 246 D3
Garnons Chase CO6 81 A5
Garret Pl CO6 108 F4
Garrettlands CM2 255 F6
Garrick Ho RM12 336 A2
Garrick St DA11 379 B1
Garrison La IP11 381 D4
Garrison Par RM19 371 A2
Garrod Ct CO2 163 B7
Garrods IP9 35 B1
Garron La
South Ockendon RM15 371 F7
South Ockendon RM15 372 A6
Garry Cl RM1 313 E3
Garry Way RM1 313 E3
Garth Rd RM15 357 C1
Garthwood Cl CO6 108 E4
Gartmore Rd IG3 333 F2
Gascoigne Gdns IG8 309 E3
Gascoigne Prim Sch IG11 352 C4
Gascoigne Rd
Barking IG11 352 C3
Colchester CO4 136 C8
Gascoigne Way CM11 297 D2
Gascoyne Cl RM3 314 D2
Gasfield 14 CO11 86 D4
Gasgoine Ho CO4 109 F4
Gasson Rd DA10 377 E1
Gaston End CO7 59 C3
GASTON GREEN 173 B7
Gaston St CO7 59 C3
Gatacre Ct CO2 135 B3
Gatacre Rd IP1 17 A7
Gatefield Cl CO14 170 F7
Gatefield Ct CO14 170 F7
Gatehope Dr RM15 371 F7
Gatehouse Mews CM4 274 B3
Gatehouse The 4 RM1 335 E6
Gate House The 2 CM4 274 B3
Gatehouse Villas CM6 150 E7
Gatekeeper Cl
8 Braintree CM7 127 F1
Ipswich IP8 36 E8
Gate Lodge Sq SS15 319 F2
Gate Lodge Way SS15 319 F2
Gate St CM9 236 F3
Gate Street Mews CM9 236 F3
Gateway SS14 342 B6
Gateway Acad The RM16 373 F4
Gateway Ho 4 IG11 352 C4
Gateway Prim Sch The DA1 376 B1
Gateway Ret Pk E6 352 B1
Gatscombe Cl SS5 324 D6
Gattens The SS6 323 F4
Gatwick Cl CM23 119 B1
Gatwick View CM12 319 B8
Gatwick Way RM12 336 F1
Gauden Rd CM7 127 F7
GAUNT'S END 120 F7
Gavenny Path RM15 371 F7
Gavin Way CO4 110 B6
Gawlers CM23 92 B8
GAY BOWERS 257 A5
Gay Bowers Basildon SS14 342 D7
Hockley SS5 324 B6
Gay Bowers La CM3 256 F6
Gay Bowers Rd CM3 256 F4
Gay Bowers Way CM8 212 A7
Gaye St 1 IP1 17 B6
Gayfere Rd IG5 332 F8
Gay Gdns RM10 354 C7
Gayleighs SS6 323 D4
Gay Links SS14 342 B7
Gaylor Rd RM18 378 F6
Gaynes Ct RM14 356 B8
Gaynesford SS16 341 E4
Gaynes Hill Rd IG8 310 E3
Gaynes Park Rd RM14 356 B8
Gaynes Rd RM14 337 B2
Gaynes Sch RM14 356 C7
Gaysham Ave IG2 333 B6
Gaysham Hall IG5 333 B8
Gays La SS4 304 E2
Gayton Rd SS2 348 A2
Gaywood SS15 341 A7
Gazelle Ct CO4 110 C4
Gearies Inf Sch IG2 333 B6
Gearies Jun Sch IG2 333 B6
Geariesville Gdns IG6 333 B7
Geary Ct CM14 294 C1
Geary Dr CM14 294 C1
Geddings Rd EN11 221 B6
Geddy Ct RM2 336 B7
Geerings The SS17 361 A2
Geesh Rd SS8 364 C5
Geetons The CO5 163 C3
Geffrey Cl CM3 278 B6
Geisthorp Ct EN9 266 A6
Gelsthorpe Rd RM5 313 B3
General Hospl SS0 347 C3
Generals La CM3 209 B2
Generals Mews IP11 381 B5
Genesta Cl CM9 216 D2
Genesta Rd SS0 366 D8
Geneva Gdns RM6 334 E6
Geneva Rd IP1 17 B7
Genever Cl E4 309 A5
Genevyll Cl CO10 1 D2
Genk Cl SS8 364 B5
Gennep Rd SS8 364 B5
Gennep Rd S SS8 364 B5
Genotin Mews 3 RM12 355 C7
Gentian Ct CO4 109 C2
Gentry Cl SS17 360 C2
Geoffrey Ave RM3 315 B3
Geoff Seaden Cl 2 CO1 136 C6
George Ave CO7 192 F7
George Avey Croft CM16 247 B5
George Cardnell Way CM3 260 E1
George Cl
Canvey Island SS8 363 F6
Clacton-on-S CO15 195 C2
George Comberton Wlk 3 E12 352 A7
George Crooks Ho RM17 378 B8
George Ct
8 Buckhurst Hill IG9 310 D8
Chelmsford CM2 232 B1
George Cut CO7 192 F6
George Davies Lodge IG6 333 C6
George Frost Cl IP4 17 D7
George Gent Cl CB9 27 B6
George Green Bglws CM22 146 B1
George Green Villas CM22 173 B8
George La Glemsford CO10 2 B3
Wanstead E18 332 B8
Woodford E18 310 A1
George Lovell Dr EN3 265 A2
George Rd Braintree CM7 127 D2
Chingford E4 309 A4
Georges Dr CM15 293 F4
George St Barking IG11 352 C5
Chelmsford CM2 232 B1
12 Colchester CO1 135 F7
Grays RM17 378 A8
Harwich CO12 91 D6
Romford RM1 335 F5
Saffron Walden CB10 22 D1
Southend-on-S SS3 368 G6
George Tilbury Ho RM16 374 B4
Georgeville Gdns IG6 333 B7
George Williams Ho RM7 335 F4
George Williams Way CO1 136 A6
George Yard Sh Ctr 8 CM7 127 F3
Georgian Ct IP11 381 D5
Georgian Ho CM7 128 A4
Gepp Pl CM2 233 B4
Gepps Cl CM1 177 D2
Gerald Rd RM8 334 F3
Geralds Ave IP4 18 A5
Geranium Cl CO16 195 C4
Geranium Wlk CO4 136 D7
Gerard Ave CM23 145 E4
Gerard Gdns RM13 354 E3
Gerard Rd CO16 195 C6
Gerboa Ct 7 E4 309 D5
Gernon Cl Broomfield CM1 208 B3
Rainham RM13 355 D3
Gernon Rd CO7 111 E7
Gernons SS16 341 F4
Gerpins La RM14 356 A4
Gerrard Cres CM14 316 C7
Gershwin Bvd CM8 211 F7
Gertrude Rd DA17 369 A2
GESTINGTHORPE 31 E1
Gestingthorpe Rd CO10 31 F4
Geylen Rd SS8 364 E4
GHYLLGROVE 342 B7
Ghyllgrove SS14 342 B7
Ghyllgrove Cl SS14 342 B8
Ghyllgrove Com Jun Sch SS14 342 A7
Gibbards Cott 1 IG11 352 F5
Gibb Croft CM18 223 F4
Gibbfield Cl RM6 334 E8
Gibbons Ct CM6 123 D1
Gibbons St 3 IP1 17 A6
Gibbs Field CM23 145 D5
Gibcracks SS14 342 E6
Gibraltar Cl CM13 316 C4
Gibraltar Ho CM13 316 C4
Gibson Cl Ipswich IP3 18 C2
North Weald Bassett CM16 247 C6
Saffron Walden CB10 22 D1
Gibson Ct Harlow CM18 223 E5
7 Romford RM1 335 E5
Gibson Gdns CB10 22 D2
Gibson Rd Dagenham RM8 334 C3
Sible Hedingham CO9 51 D1
Gibson Vale CM1 232 B8
Gibson Way CB10 22 D1
Gidea Ave RM2 336 A8
Gidea Cl Romford RM2 336 A8
South Ockendon RM15 357 C2
Gidea Lodge RM2 336 B8
Gidea Park Coll RM2 336 A8
Gidea Park Prim Sch RM2 336 A8
Gidea Park Sta RM2 336 B7
Gideon Ct DA17 369 B2
Gideons Way SS17 360 E3
Giffards Prim Sch SS17 360 F4
Giffins Cl CM7 127 F1
Gifford Cl IP9 62 D5
Gifford Gn SS13 343 B5
Gifford Pl CM14 316 D5
Gifford Rd SS7 344 D5
Giffords Cross Ave SS17 361 A3
Giffords Cross Rd SS17 361 B2
Giffordside RM16 374 B1
Giffords Pl IP4 18 F6
Gifhorn Rd SS8 364 E3
Gilberd Ct CO4 110 C6
Gilberd Ho CO3 135 A7
Gilberd Rd CO2 136 B4
Gilberd Sch The CO4 110 B5
Gilbert Calvin Prim Sch IG5 311 A1
Gilbert Cl Rayleigh SS6 323 F2
Swanscombe DA10 377 D1
Gilbert Dr SS16 341 A5
Gilbert Rd Belvedere DA17 369 A3
Clare CO10 12 B8
Grays RM16 372 C3
Romford RM1 335 F7
Gilbert Way CM7 128 C5
Gilbey Ave CM23 146 B6
Gilbey Cotts CM22 94 C1
Gilbey Cres CM24 119 E8
Gilbey Gn CB11 42 F1
Gilchrist Way CM7 127 E4
Gilda Terr CM77 127 B2
Gildborne Cl SS17 361 D4
Gilden Cl CM17 200 E4
Gilden Way CM17 200 D3
Gilderdale Cl CO4 110 D3
Gilders CM21 172 D2
Gilders Way CO16 195 C5
Giles Cl RM13 355 D3
Gilford Ho 5 IG1 333 B1
Gillam Way RM13 355 A6
Gill Cl CM9 236 F6
Gillian Cres RM2 314 C1
Gilliflower Ho EN11 221 A5
Gillingham Ho 14 RM3 314 E5

Gills Ave SS8 364 C4
Gill The SS7 345 D5
Gilmore Way CM2 255 B6
Gilmour Rise CM12 296 F1
Gilpin's Gallop SG12 197 B4
Gilpin Way CM77 154 C7
Gilroy Cl RM13 354 F6
Gilsland EN9 265 E4
Gilson Cl CM2 232 F2
Gilstead Hall Mews Cotts CM14 293 A4
Gilstead Ho 1 IG11 353 B3
GILSTON 199 E5
Gilston Park Ho CM20 199 C6
Gilston Pk CM20 199 C7
Gilwell Cl E4 287 B5
Gilwell La E4 287 D5
Gilwell Park Cl CO3 135 A4
Gimli Watch CM3 301 D6
Gimson Cl CM8 183 F2
Gippeswyk SS14 342 C7
Gippeswyk Ave IP2 17 A4
Gippeswyk Rd IP2 17 B4
Gipping Cl CB9 8 E6
Gipping Way IP8 16 B6
Gipson Park Cl SS9 346 D6
Gipsy La
 Bishop's Stortford CM23, CM24 119 C4
 Grays RM17 378 C8
Girling St CO10 33 E8
Girona Cl RM16 372 C3
Girton Rd CB9 9 B7
Girton Way IP2 16 F1
Gisborne Gdns RM13 354 F2
Gladden Ct CM18 223 E4
Gladden Fields CM3 301 C6
Glade Bsns Ctr The RM20 371 F1
Glade Ct IG5 310 F2
Glade Prim Sch IG5 310 F1
Gladeswood Rd DA17 369 B2
Glade The Basildon SS16 342 C4
 Brentwood CM13 295 A1
 Colchester CO4 110 F2
 Upminster RM14 356 C7
 Woodford, Clayhall IG5 310 F2
 Woodford, Woodford Wells IG8 310 B7
Gladeview CO15 195 F7
Gladeway The EN9 265 D6
Gladiator Way CO2 135 A2
Gladstone Ct CM2 232 B1
Gladstone Gdns SS6 323 C1
Gladstone Rd
 Buckhurst Hill IG9 288 C1
 Colchester CO1 136 B5
 Hockley SS5 324 E6
 Hoddesdon EN11 221 B7
 Ipswich IP3 17 F5
 Tiptree CO5 186 D4
Gladwin Rd CO2 135 D4
Gladwyns SS15 341 E7
Glamis Cl CB9 8 D8
Glamis Dr RM11 336 E3
Glamis Ho CM14 316 C6
Glamorgan Rd IP2 17 B1
Glan Avon Mews CM17 224 C7
Glandford Way RM6 334 B6
Glanmead CM15 294 E1
Glanmire CM11 297 D6
Glanthams Cl CM15 316 F8
Glanthams Rd CM15 316 F8
Glanville Dr RM11 336 F3
Glasseys La SS6 345 C8
Glastonbury Ave IG8 310 D4
Glastonbury Chase SS0 347 B5
Glastonbury Cl IP2 16 F1
Glebe Ave Braintree CM7 127 F6
 Woodford IG8 310 A4
Glebe Cl
 Elmstead Market CO7 138 A6
 Great Wakering SS3 350 D3
 Rayleigh SS6 323 C3
 Southend-on-S SS1 367 E8
 Sproughton IP8 16 B6
 Tattingstone IP9 61 C7
 Wix CO11 115 D6
Glebe Cres Broomfield CM1 208 B1
 Witham CM8 183 E4
Glebe Ct CM23 146 B8
Glebe Dr SS6 323 C3
Glebe End Capel St M IP9 35 B2
 Elsenham CM22 94 D1
Glebe Field SS14 342 C8
Glebefield Rd CM3 211 B4
Glebe Gdns Feering CO5 158 E5
 Ingrave CM13 317 E3
Glebe Jun & Inf Sch SS6 323 C3
Glebe La Chelmondiston IP9 63 A8
 Dengie CM0 263 D1
 Little Easton CM6 122 F5
 Woolverstone IP9 38 B1
Glebelands Chigwell IG7 312 B7
 Great Horkesley CO6 82 B1
 Harlow CM20 199 F3
 South Benfleet SS7 344 B7
Glebelands Ave Ilford IG2 333 D5
 Woodford E18 310 A1
Glebe Mdw CM3 207 E7
Glebe Rd Chelmsford CM1 232 B3
 Chipping Ongar CM5 248 F2
 Colchester CO2 135 C2
 Dagenham RM10 354 B6
 Heybridge CM9 237 C5
 Kelvedon CO5 158 B2
 Rainham RM13 355 C2
 Ramsden Bellhouse CM11 298 F1
 Tiptree CO5 186 C5
 Wickford SS11 321 E7
Glebe The Elmdon CB11 20 A4
 Elsenham CM22 94 C1
 Harlow CM20 199 E1
 Magdalen Laver CM5 225 D5
 Peldon CO5 189 E5
 Purleigh CM3 258 D1
 Saffron Walden CB11 43 E7
Glebe View
 Galleywood CM2 254 B3
 West Mersea CO5 218 E8
Glebe Way
 Burnham-on-C CM0 306 C6
 Clacton-on-S CO15 220 G7
 Frinton-on-S CO13 170 F5
 Hadleigh SS7 345 F3
 Hornchurch RM11 336 E3
 Woodford IG8 310 C5
Glemham Dr IP4 18 F4
GLEMSFORD 2 C4
Glemsford Cl IP11 381 B3
Glemsford Com Prim Sch CO10 2 B5
Glemsford Pl 3 CB9 9 B8
Glenarm Coll IG1 333 B2
Glen Ave CO3 135 B7
Glenavon Lodge 5 E18 332 A8
Glenavon Rd IP4 18 D7
Glenbervie Dr SS9 346 F2
Glencoe Ave IG2 333 E4
Glencoe Dr
 Dagenham RM10 354 A8
 Wickford SS11 322 A8
Glencoe Rd IP4 18 C8
Glencree CM11 297 D6
Glen Cres IG8 310 B4
Glencrofts SS5 324 F6
Glen Ct SS7 345 B4
Glendale CM3 279 E1
Glendale Ave RM6 334 C4
Glendale Cl
 Burnham-on-C CM0 306 C6
 Shenfield CM15 294 E1
Glendale Gdns SS9 346 D1
Glendale Gr CO4 110 C3
Glendale Ho CM15 294 E2
Glendale Rd
 Burnham-on-C CM0 306 C6
 Erith DA8 369 C2
Glendower Rd E4 287 D1
Gleneagles SS7 344 B5
Gleneagles Cl RM3 314 F3
Gleneagles Dr IP4 18 D5
Gleneagles Rd SS9 346 C5
Gleneagles Way CM3 211 B4
Gleneley Ct CO13 170 F3
Glenester Cl EN11 197 A1
Glen Faba CM19 221 E7
Glen Faba Rd CM19 221 F6
Glenfield Ave IP11 381 E5
Glenfield Rd SS17 361 B4
Glengall Rd IG8 310 B4
Glenham Dr IG2 333 B6
Glen Hazel CM15 272 D4
Glenhurst Ave IP4 18 B8
Glenhurst Mans SS1 367 B8
Glenhurst Rd SS2 348 A2
Glenmead IG9 288 C1
Glenmere SS16 342 D2
Glenmere Park Ave SS7 345 B4
Glenmire Terr SG12 197 D4
Glenmore Ho SS4 325 F2
Glenmore St SS2 348 D1
Glenmore Way IG11 353 A3
Glenny Rd IG11 352 C6
Glen Rd South Benfleet SS7 344 E5
 Southend-on-S SS9 366 A8
Glenridding SS7 344 D5
Glen Rise IG8 310 B4
Glenside Billericay CM11 297 D2
 Chigwell IG7 311 B4
 Great Cornard CO10 34 A6
Glen The Basildon SS16 343 A4
 Hullbridge SS5 301 E4
 Rainham RM13 355 C1
 Rayleigh SS6 345 E8
 Stanford-le-H SS17 360 F3
Glenthorne Gdns IG6 333 B7
Glenton Cl RM1 313 E3
Glenton Way RM1 313 E3
Glentress Cl CO4 110 D3
Glenway Cl CO6 82 B1
Glenway Ct CO6 82 B1
Glenwood SS8 363 F5
Glenwood Ave Hockley SS5 324 F5
 Rainham RM13 355 B1
 Southend-on-S, Eastwood SS9 346 B7
 Southend-on-S, Prittlewell SS0 347 D2
Glenwood Ct 6 E18 332 A8
Glenwood Dr RM2 336 A7
Glenwood Gdns
 Basildon SS16 340 E4
 Ilford IG2 333 A6
Glenwood Sch SS7 344 B7
Gleten Rd SS8 364 D4
Glisson Sq CO2 135 B4
Globe Cl CO5 186 D6
Globe Cres CM23 118 D6
Globe Ind Est RM17 373 C1
Globe Rd Hornchurch RM11 336 A5
 Woodford IG8 310 C4
Globe Wlk CO5 186 D6
Globe Yd 4 CO10 33 E8
Glossop Ho 13 RM3 314 E5
Gloucester Ave
 Chelmsford CM2 254 C6
 Colchester CO2 135 C3
 East Tilbury RM18 375 C1
 Grays RM16 373 C4
 Hornchurch RM11 337 A7
 Maldon CM9 236 F1
 Rayleigh SS6 346 A8
Gloucester Bsns Pk SS15 341 E8
Gloucester Cres CM1 232 A5
Gloucester Ct
 Redbridge IG1 332 F4
 Tilbury RM18 378 F5
Gloucester Gdns
 Braintree CM7 128 B4
 Redbridge IG1 332 E4
Gloucester Ho IP11 381 C6
Gloucester Pl CM12 297 A5
Gloucester Rd Haverhill CB9 8 F6
 Ipswich IP3 18 B2
 Little Ilford E12 332 F1
 Pilgrims Hatch CM15 294 B4
Gloucester Rd *continued*
 Romford RM1 335 F5
 Wanstead E11 332 C6
Gloucester Terr SS1 368 A6
Gloucester Way CO10 15 D2
Glovers CM3 180 F7
Glovers Field CM15 271 F2
Glovershotts CM1 208 B2
Glovers La CM17 224 E3
Glyders SS7 344 E1
Glynde Way SS2 348 F1
Glynn Rd CM0 306 B5
Goat Hall La
 Chelmsford CM2 253 F3
 Galleywood CM2 254 A3
Goat House La CM3 257 F4
Goat Lodge Rd CM8, CM9 213 A5
Goatsmoor La
 Billericay CM4, CM11 297 F6
 Stock CM4 298 A8
Goatswood La RM4 292 B2
Gobions SS16 342 A4
Gobions Ave RM5 313 D3
Goda Cl CM8 211 D8
Goddard Rd RM16 373 A5
Goddards Way IG1 333 D3
Goddard Way
 Chelmsford CM2 232 F2
 Saffron Walden CB10 22 E3
Godfreys Mews CM2 232 B1
Godfrey Way CM6 123 C1
Godlings Way CM7 127 F2
Godman Rd RM16 374 B3
Godmans La CO6 132 E3
Godric Pl CM7 127 E3
Godric Rd CM8 211 E8
Godsafe CM17 200 E4
Godwin Cl Halstead CO9 76 D1
 Sewardstone E4 265 C1
Godwin Prim Sch RM9 353 E5
Godwit Ct CO5 158 D2
Goff's La CO16 141 F8
Goings La CO5 218 D6
Goirle Ave SS8 364 C4
Goldace RM17 377 F8
Gold Berry Mead CM3 301 C6
Gold Cl CM22 94 B3
Goldcrest Cl CO4 137 A8
Goldcrest Ct IP2 16 D3
Goldcrest Dr CM11 297 C1
Goldcrest Rd IP2 16 C3
Goldenacres CM1 232 F8
Golden Cross SS4 325 D4
Golden Cross Mews SS4 325 D5
Golden Cross Par SS4 325 D5
Golden Cross Rd SS4 325 D6
Golden Dawn Way CO4 109 E2
Golden Jubilee Ct RM12 336 A3
Golden La Radwinter CB10 25 A2
 Thorpe-le-S CO16 141 F3
Golden Lion La CO12 91 E6
Goldenlonds CO6 56 C5
Golden Manor Dr SS7 344 F5
Golden Noble Hill CO1 136 A6
Goldfinch Cl CO4 136 F7
Goldfinch La SS7 345 A8
GOLDHANGER 238 F7
Goldhanger Cl SS6 323 A3
Goldhanger Cross SS14 342 E7
Goldhanger Ct CM7 128 D1
Goldhanger Rd CM9 237 D4
Goldhaze Cl IG8 310 D3
Golding Cres SS17 360 E3
Golding Ct 6 IG1 333 A1
Goldingham Ave IG10 289 C7
Goldingham Dr CM7 155 A7
Goldings CM23 146 B8
Goldings Cotts CM13 316 B1
Goldings Cres SS16 342 E3
Goldings Hill IG10, CM16 266 F2
Goldings Rd IG10 289 A8
Goldings Rise IG10 289 A8
Golding Thoroughfare CM2 232 F3
Goldington Cres CM12 296 F5
Golding Way Glemsford CO10 2 B4
 St Osyth CO16 194 A5
Goldlay Ave CM2 254 C8
Goldlay Gdns CM2 232 C1
Goldlay Rd CM2 232 C1
Goldmer Cl SS3 368 C8
Goldsands Rd CM0 284 E2
Goldsborough Cres E4 309 C8
Goldsmere Ct RM11 336 E3
Goldsmith RM17 377 F8
Goldsmith Ave RM7 335 A4
Goldsmith Dr SS6 323 D7
Goldsmith Ho IG8 311 B4
Goldsmiths Ave
 Corringham SS17 361 A2
 4 Stanford-le-H SS17 360 F3
Golds Nursery Bsns Pk CM22 94 C3
Gold St CB10 22 D1
Goldsworthy Dr SS3 350 C2
Golfe Ho IG1 333 D1
Golfe Rd IG1 333 D1
Golf Green Rd CO15 220 G8
Golf Ride SS7 344 D3
Goodchild Way CO9 30 A2
GOOD EASTER 205 D5
Gooderham Ho RM16 374 B4
Goodey Cl CO1 136 A6
Goodey Rd IG11 352 F5
Goodier Rd CM1 231 F4
Goodlake Cl CO12 90 F2
Goodliffe Pk CM23 119 B2
Goodmans SS3 350 B3
Goodmans La CM3 180 F4
GOODMAYES 334 B3
Goodmayes Ave IG3 334 A3
Goodmayes Hospl IG3 334 A6
Goodmayes La IG3 334 A1
Goodmayes Lodge RM8 353 A8
Goodmayes Prim Sch IG3 334 B3
Goodmayes Rd IG3 334 A3
Goodmayes Ret Pk IG3 334 B3
Goodmayes Sta IG3 334 A3
Goodmayes Wlk 1 SS12 321 D6
Goodridge Ho E17 309 C3
Goodrington Sch RM11 336 D5
Goodview Rd SS14 320 A2
Goodwin Cl CM2 254 D8
Goodwins Cl CB11 21 E3
Goodwin Stile CM23 145 D5
Goodwood Ave
 Brentwood CM13 295 F3
 Hornchurch RM12 355 E8
Goodwood Cl
 Hoddesdon EN11 221 A7
 Thundersley SS7 345 B7
Goodwyns Mews CO7 166 E8
Goojerat Rd CO2 135 D5
GOOSEBERRY GREEN 297 A1
Goose Cotts SS11 300 E1
GOOSE GREEN
 Tendring Green 140 E7
 Wix 114 E3
Goose La CM22 173 E7
Gooseley La E6 352 A2
Gooshays Dr RM3 314 E4
Gooshays Gdns RM3 314 E4
Gordian Wlk CO4 110 B5
Gordon Ave Chingford E4 309 E4
 Hornchurch RM12 335 F2
Gordon Cl Billericay CM12 296 F3
 East Tilbury RM18 380 D7
Gordon Cotts RM4 291 B5
Gordon Dr CO4 110 C5
Gordon Inf Sch IG1 333 D1
Gordon Pl
 9 Gravesend DA12 379 C1
 Southend-on-S SS1 366 F8
Gordon Prom E DA12 379 C1
Gordon Rd Barking IG11 352 E4
 Basildon SS14 342 D5
 Belvedere DA17 369 C2
 Brentwood CM15 295 A1
 Chelmsford CM2 254 A6
 Chingford E4 287 E2
 Corringham SS17 360 F3
 Dagenham RM6 334 F5
 Gravesend DA11 378 E1
 Grays RM16 373 F3
 Harwich CO12 91 B2
 Holdbrook EN9 265 A5
 Horndon on t H SS17 359 F3
 Ilford IG1 333 D1
 Ipswich IP4 18 A7
 Southend-on-S SS9 346 B2
 Southend-on-S, Westcliff-on-S SS1 366 F8
 Wanstead E11 332 A5
 Woodford E18 310 B2
Gordon Roughley Ct SS6 323 C1
Gordons SS13 343 A5
Gordon Way CO12 91 B2
Gorefield CM22 148 C7
Gorefield Rd CM22, CM24 121 B5
Gorefield Rdbt CM24 121 B4
Gore La CM77 127 A2
GORE PIT 158 E4
Gore Rd Rayne CM77 127 A2
 Rochford SS4 326 E6
Goresbrook Rd RM9 353 D4
Gore Terr CM77 127 A2
Gore The SS14 342 A7
Goring Cl RM5 313 C2
Goring Gdns RM8 353 C8
Goring Ho CO4 109 E4
Goring Rd Colchester CO4 110 C1
 Dagenham RM10 354 D6
 Ipswich IP4 18 C6
Gorsehayes IP2 17 B3
Gorse La Clacton-on-S CO15 196 A8
 Tiptree CO5 186 D4
Gorse Lane Ind Est CO15 196 B8
Gorse Rd IP3 18 B2
Gorseway RM7 335 E3
Gorse Way
 Clacton-on-S CO15 220 F7
 Colchester CO3 134 D4
Gorse Wlk CO4 136 D7
Gosbecks Bsns Pk CO2 135 B2
Gosbecks Prim Sch CO2 135 A3
Gosbecks Rd CO2 135 A2
Gosbecks View CO2 135 A2
GOSFIELD 102 E7
Gosfield Cl SS6 323 A3
Gosfield Com Prim Sch CO9 102 E8
Gosfield Hall* CO9 102 C8
Gosfield Rd
 Blackheath CO2 163 A8
 Braintree CM7 102 D3
 Dagenham RM8 335 A3
Gosfield Sch CO9 75 F2
Gosford Cl CO10 12 B8
Gosford Gdns IG4 332 F6
Goshawk Dr CM2 254 B5
Goslings The
 Silver End CM8 156 C5
 Southend-on-S SS3 368 G7
Gosport Dr RM12 355 C6
Gossetts The CM6 204 E4
Gould Cl CM5 226 C2
Gouldings Ave CO14 171 B8
Goulds Cotts RM4 290 B6
Goulds Rd CO8 54 F2
Goul La CB10 22 D1
Goulton Rd CM1 208 A1
Gourney Gr RM16 373 B6
Government Ct CO12 91 E5
Government Row EN3 265 A2
Gowan Brae SS7 344 B5
Gowan Cl SS7 344 B5
Gowan Ct SS7 344 B5
Gowan Lea 4 E18 332 A7
Gower Chase SS15 341 D5
Gower Ho 3 IG11 352 C5
Gower Pl 1 RM16 372 B3
Gowers Ave CM2 254 E6
Gowers End CO10 2 C5
Gowers La RM16 374 A4
Gower St IP2 17 C4
Gowers The CM20 200 B2
Goya Rise SS3 368 G8
Goyfield Ave IP11 381 D4
Grace Cl IG6 311 F4
Grace Gdns CM23 145 F4
Grace Rd SS13 321 A2
Graces Cl CM8 212 A7
Grace's Cross CM2 255 C7
Graces La CM3 234 B1
Graces Wlk CO13 171 A6
Grafton Gdns RM8 334 E2
Grafton Inf Sch RM8 334 F2
Grafton Jun Sch RM8 334 F2
Grafton Pl CM2 233 A4
Grafton Rd
 Canvey Island SS8 364 C2
 Dagenham RM8 334 E2
 Harwich CO12 91 D4
Grafton Way IP1 17 C5
Graham Ave IP1 17 B8
Graham Cl Billericay CM12 297 C5
 Brentwood CM13 295 C4
 Hockley SS5 324 E7
 Stanford-le-H SS17 360 E4
Grahame Ct 3 SS12 321 D5
Grahame Ho SS2 348 C3
Graham James Prim Sch SS17 360 F3
Graham Mans 11 IG11 353 A5
Graham Rd
 Felixstowe IP11 381 D5
 Ipswich IP1 17 B7
Grailands CM23 145 D8
Grainger Cl SS2 348 A1
Grainger Rd SS2 348 A1
Grainger Road Ind Est SS2 348 A1
Grammar School Pl 11 CO10 33 E7
Grampian SS0 347 E1
Grampian Gr CM1 231 D6
Granaries The EN9 265 E5
Granary Cl CM3 282 B5
Granary Ct
 12 Colchester CO1 136 C6
 3 Dagenham RM6 334 D4
 Great Dunmow CM6 150 D7
 Sawbridgeworth CM21 172 E2
Granary Mdw CM15 272 E3
Granary The Bures CO8 55 F1
 Clare CO10 12 B6
 Roydon CM19 198 B1
 Stanstead Abbotts SG12 197 C3
Granby Rd DA11 378 D1
Granchester Ct CO4 110 C4
Grand Court W SS9 365 F8
Grand Ct Dagenham RM8 334 E1
 Frinton-on-S CO13 170 F3
Grand Dr SS9 365 F8
Grand Par SS9 365 F8
Grand The CO13 170 F3
Grandview Rd SS7 344 F7
Grange Ave Mayland CM3 283 C7
 South Benfleet SS7 346 A5
 Wickford SS12 321 C6
 Woodford IG8 310 A3
Grange Cl Felixstowe IP11 381 C5
 Halstead CO9 103 E7
 Ingrave CM13 317 C5
 Southend-on-S SS9 346 E3
 Walton-on-t-N CO14 171 A7
 Woodford IG8 310 A3
Grange Com Prim Sch IP11 381 B4
Grange Cres Chigwell IG7 311 D5
 28 Dartford DA2 376 B1
Grange Ct Chelmsford CM2 253 F7
 Clacton-on-S CO16 195 A4
 Ilford IG6 333 C8
 Loughton IG10 288 D4
 Waltham Abbey EN9 265 C5
Grange Farm CO2 136 D4
Grange Farm Ave IP11 381 B5
Grange Farm Rd CO2 136 D4
Grange Gdns Rayleigh SS6 323 B3
 Southend-on-S SS1 367 B8
GRANGE HILL 311 D5
Grange Hill CO6 130 F1
Grange Hill Sta IG7 311 D6
Grange Ho 6 IG11 352 D4
Grange La
 Little Dunmow CM6 151 C7
 Roydon CM19 222 C8
Grange Mill CO6 130 F1
Grange Par CM11 319 C7
Grange Park Dr SS9 346 F2
Grange Pk CM23 118 F1
Grange Prim Sch SS12 321 B6
Granger Ave CM9 236 F1
Grange Rd Aveley RM15 371 C5
 Basildon SS13 343 E8
 Billericay CM11 319 D7
 Bishop's Stortford CM23 146 A7
 Felixstowe IP11 381 B4
 Grays RM17 378 B8
 Great Horkesley CO6 109 B7
 Harwich CO12 91 A3
 Ickleton CB10 20 A8
 Ilford IG1 352 C8
 Ipswich IP4 17 E6
 Lawford CO11 85 F1
 Little Bromley CO11 112 E7
 Pleshey CM3 178 E2
 Romford RM3 314 B4
 Southend-on-S SS9 346 D1
 Thundersley SS7 344 F7
 Tillingham CM0 264 A1
 Tiptree CO5 186 A6
 Wickford SS11 299 C2
 Wickham Bishops CM8 212 E4
Granger Row CM1 231 F6
Granger Way RM1 336 A5
Grangeside CM23 119 A2
Grange The
 Bishop's Stortford CM23 118 F1
 Hoddesdon EN11 221 A5
 Waltham Abbey EN9 265 D2
 4 Wanstead E18 332 A8
Grangeway
 Thundersley SS7 345 A6
 Woodford IG8 310 C6
Grange Way CO2 136 D3
Grange Way Bsns Pk CO2 136 D3
Grangeway Gdns IG4 332 E6
Grange Wlk CM23 146 A7
Grangewood SS7 344 D5
Grangewood Ave
 Grays RM16 373 E3
 Rainham RM13 355 C1
Grangewood Cl CM13 317 A7
Granites Chase CM11 319 F5
GRANSMORE GREEN 125 F1
Granta Cl CB10 3 D1
Granta Cotts CB10 3 C2
Grant Cl 12 SS12 321 E5
Grant Ct 2 E4 287 C1
Grantham Ave CM77 154 B7
Grantham Cres IP2 17 A4
Grantham Ct
 Colchester CO1 136 A7
 Dagenham RM6 334 F4
Grantham Gdns RM6 334 F4
Grantham Lodge SS9 346 D1
Grantham Rd
 Great Horkesley CO6 109 B7
 Ilford E12 333 A1
 Little Ilford E12 352 A8
Grantham Way RM16 373 A5
Grantley Cl CO6 133 D5
Grantock Rd E17 309 D2
Granton Ave RM14 336 F2
Granton Rd IG3 334 A3
Grants Ct CO14 171 C8
Granville Cl Billericay CM12 296 F5
 South Benfleet SS7 344 E4
 West Bergholt CO6 108 E3
Granville Gdns EN11 197 A2
Granville Rd
 Clacton-on-S CO15 195 F3
 Colchester CO1 136 B5
 Epping CM16 246 B2
 Felixstowe IP11 381 D3
 Hockley SS5 302 F1
 Ilford IG1 333 B2
 Woodford E18 310 B1
Granville St 2 IP1 17 B6
Granville Terr 4 CM0 306 C4
Granville Way CO7 193 A7
Grapnells SS16 342 F4
Grapnells Farm Cotts SS4 306 A2
Grasby Cl CO7 137 B2
Grasmead Ave SS9 346 F2
Grasmere Ave SS5 301 D3
Grasmere Cl
 Great Notley CM77 154 C6
 Ipswich IP3 18 B1
 Loughton IG10 288 F7
Grasmere Gdns
 Kirby Cross CO13 170 F7
 Redbridge IG4 332 F6
Grasmere Ho SS6 323 D2
Grasmere Rd
 Canvey Island SS8 363 E3
 Thundersley SS7 344 E6
Grass Croft RM17 373 B1
Grassfields CO13 170 E6
GRASS GREEN 29 B1
Grassmere CO4 110 B5
Grassmere Rd RM11 336 F7
Gratian Cl CO4 110 B5
Gratmore Gn SS16 342 F3
Gravel Cl IG7 312 A8
Gravel Ct CO6 130 F2
Gravel Hill Loughton IG10 266 A1
 Nayland CO6 56 A2
Gravel Hill Way CO12 90 F1
Gravel La IG7 290 A3
Gravelly La CM1 230 C3
Gravel Pit Farm CM19 223 C6
Gravel Pit La CO11 60 E2
Gravel Rd SS9 346 C8
Gravel The CO6 130 F2
GRAVESEND 379 C2
Gravesend Sta DA11 379 B1
Gravesham Com Hospl DA11 379 A1
Gravesham Mus* DA11 379 B1
Gray Ave RM8 334 F3
Gray Gdns RM13 355 A6
Graylands Grays RM17 377 E8
 Theydon Bois CM16 267 D2
Grayling Cl CM7 127 E1
Grayling Dr CO4 110 F1
Grayling Rd IP8 36 E8
Gray Rd CO3 135 D6
GRAYS 378 A7
Grays Ave SS16 341 C1
Grays Cl CO5 218 C6
Grays Convent High Sch RM17 373 B2
Grays Cotts RM14 337 D7
Gray's Cotts CO1 136 B7
Grays Court Hospl RM10 354 B5
Grays Ct CM23 145 E8
Grays End Cl RM17 373 A3
Gray's La CM7 73 E4
Grays Mead CO9 51 D2
Graysons Cl SS6 323 E2
Grays Sch Media Arts Coll The RM17 373 B3
Grays Sh Ctr RM17 378 A8
Grays Sta RM17 378 A8
Grays Wlk CM13 295 D2
Great Augur St 4 CM17 200 D1
GREAT BADDOW 254 E7
Great Baddow High Sch CM2 254 D6
GREAT BARDFIELD 72 C1
Great Bardfield Cage* CM7 72 B2
Great Bardfield Cottage Mus* CM7 72 A1
Great Bardfield Prim Sch CM7 72 B2
GREAT BENTLEY 166 D8
Great Bentley Prim Sch CO7 166 E7
Great Bentley Rd CO7 166 A8
Great Bentley Sta CO7 166 E7
GREAT BERRY 340 F4
Great Berry Farm Chase SS16 341 A4
Great Berry La SS16 341 A5
Great Berry Prim Sch SS16 340 F4

Great Bradfords Jun & Inf Schs CM7 128 B4
GREAT BRAXTED 185 C1
Great Brays CM18 224 A7
GREAT BROMLEY 112 F1
Great Burches Rd SS7 345 A7
GREAT BURSTEAD 319 C5
GREAT CANFIELD 149 C1
GREAT CHESTERFORD 3 D2
Great Chesterford CE Prim Sch CB10 3 D2
Great Chesterford Ct CB10 3 C2
Great Chesterford Sta CB10 3 C1
GREAT CLACTON 195 E5
Great Clacton CE Jun Sch CO15 195 F6
Great Cob CM1 232 E5
Great Colman St [14] IP4 17 D6
GREAT CORNARD 34 B5
Great Cornard Ctry Pk* CO10 34 C3
Great Cornard Mid Sch CO10 34 C4
Great Cornard Upper Sch & Tech Coll CO10 34 B4
Great Cullings RM7 335 E2
GREAT DAWKINS 25 F4
GREAT DUNMOW 150 C7
Great Dunmow Mus* CM6 123 D1
Great Dunmow Prim Sch CM6 123 B1
Great Eastern Ave SS2 348 A1
Great Eastern Cl CM23 146 A6
Great Eastern Ct CO14 171 C7
Great Eastern Rd
Brentwood CM14 316 C6
Hockley SS5 324 E6
Sudbury CO10 33 F7
Great Eastern Sq IP11 381 E5
GREAT EASTON 122 F7
Great Easton CE Prim Sch CM6 123 A8
Greate House Farm Rd CO2 162 A5
Great Field IP11 381 A8
Greatfields Rd IG11 352 D3
Great Fleete Way IG11 353 C3
Great Fox Mdw CM15 271 F1
Great Galley Cl IG11 353 C2
Great Gardens Rd RM11 336 C5
Great Gibcracks Chase CM2 256 A2
Great Gipping St IP1 17 B5
Great Godfreys CM1 230 F1
Great Gregorie SS16 341 F5
Great Gregories La CM16 267 E6
Great Hadham Rd CM23 145 C5
GREAT HALLINGBURY 146 E4
Great Hall The [1] E11 332 B7
Great Harrods CO14 171 A7
Great Havers Ct CM23 145 E5
Great Hays SS9 346 C5
GREAT HENNY 54 C8
GREAT HOLLAND 170 A3
Great Holland Common Rd CO13 169 D2
Great Holland Ct CO13 170 A3
GREAT HORKESLEY 82 A1
Greathouse Chase SS17 361 C5
Great Hyde Hall CM21 173 B3
Great Knightleys SS15 341 E6
Great Lawn CM5 249 A4
GREAT LEIGHS 180 E7
Great Leighs Prim Sch CM3 181 A7
Great Leighs Way SS13 321 C1
Great Leylands CM18 224 A7
GREAT MAPLESTEAD 52 D2
Great Mdw EN10 221 A1
Great Mead SS3 349 E1
Great Mistley SS16 342 C5
Great Nelmes Chase RM11 336 F6
GREAT NOTLEY 154 B8
Great Notley Ave CM77 154 C5
Great Notley Country Park & Discovery Ctr* CM77 154 A7
Great Oak Ct CO9 30 A1
GREAT OAKLEY 116 C4
Great Oaks Basildon SS14 342 A6
Brentwood CM13 295 B3
Chigwell IG7 311 C6
Great Owl Rd IG7 311 A7
Great Oxcroft SS15 341 B6
GREAT OXNEY GREEN 230 E1
GREAT PARNDON 223 B6
Great Pettits Ct RM1 313 E1
Great Pitchers CO6 105 A7
Great Plumtree CM20 199 F2
Great Priory Cotts CM7 127 C8
Great Ranton SS13 343 C8
Great Ropers La CM13 316 B4
GREAT SALING 126 A8
Great Saling SS11 322 A6
GREAT SAMPFORD 47 B4
Great Sampford Prim Sch CB10 47 A3
Great Smials CM3 301 C6
Great Spenders SS14 342 D8
Great Sq [10] CM7 127 F3
GREAT STAMBRIDGE 326 D4
Great Stony Pk CM5 249 A4
GREAT TEY 132 C8
Great Tey CE Prim Sch CO6 106 C1
Great Tey Rd CO6 132 C4
GREAT TOTHAM 213 C4
Great Totham Prim Sch CM9 213 A5
Great Totham Rd CM8 212 F5
Great Tufts IP9 35 B1
GREAT WAKERING 350 A4
Great Wakering Prim Sch SS3 350 A3
GREAT WALTHAM 207 E7
Great Waltham CE Prim Sch CM3 207 E7
GREAT WARLEY 316 A2
Great Warley St CM13 316 B1
Great Wheatley Rd SS6 323 B1
Great Whip St IP2 17 C4
GREAT WIGBOROUGH 188 F3
GREAT YELDHAM 30 A1
Great Yeldham Rd CO9 50 D7
Greaves Cl IG11 352 E5
Grebe Cl Barking IG11 353 A1
Ipswich IP2 16 E2
Mayland CM3 283 A8
Grebe Crest RM20 372 A2
Greding Wlk CM13 317 B8
Greenacre La CM4 297 E8
Greenacre Mews SS9 346 E2
Greenacres
Clacton-on-S CO15 196 A5
Coggeshall CO6 130 F1
Colchester CO4 109 E3
Epping CM16 245 F3
Hadleigh SS7 345 E3
Greenacres Cl RM13 355 E2
Greenacres Cvn Pk CO12 91 A1
Green Acres Rd CO2 162 A5
Green Ave SS8 363 E3
Greenbank Cl Chingford E4 309 C8
Romford RM3 314 D7
Greenbanks
Southend-on-S SS9 347 A2
Upminster RM14 337 E2
Green Cl Chelmsford CM1 232 D4
Epping Green CM16 245 B7
Hatfield Peverel CM3 211 C3
Writtle CM1 231 B1
Green Cnr CO7 139 E1
Green Ct CO6 109 A7
Greendyke SS8 363 F5
Green End La CO13 170 B5
Greener Ct EN3 265 A2
Greene View CM7 155 B8
Green Farm Rd CO6 78 B2
Greenfield CM8 184 A1
Greenfield Cotts CO4 82 E6
Greenfield Dr CO6 106 B1
Greenfield Gdns RM9 353 C4
Greenfield Hos Birch CO2 161 A3
Birch Green CO2 160 F3
Greenfield Rd RM9 353 C4
Greenfields
Billericay CM12 319 A8
Galleywood CM2 254 C2
Gosfield CO9 102 F7
Loughton IG10 289 A5
Stansted Mountfitchet CM24 119 E7
Greenfields Cl
Billericay CM12 319 A8
Brentwood CM13 316 C4
Loughton IG10 289 A5
Greenfield St EN9 265 C5
Greenfields Way CB9 8 E6
Greenfinch Ave IP2 16 D3
Greenfinch End CO4 136 F8
Greenford Rd CO15 195 C3
Greengates Mobile Home Pk CO16 168 C4
Green Glade CM16 267 E2
Green Glades RM11 337 A5
Greenheys Dr E18 309 F1
Greenhill IG9 288 C1
Greenhill Pk CM23 145 D5
Greenhills CM20 223 E8
GREENHITHE 377 A3
Greenhithe for Bluewater Sta DA9 377 A2
Greenhurst Rd CO7 193 A6
Greenhythe Ct CO4 136 D6
Green La Aldham CO6 107 C1
Ardleigh CO7 111 D6
Basildon, Lee Chapel South SS16 341 E4
Basildon, Steeple View CM12 319 A2
Black Notley CM8 155 A2
Boxted CO4 82 D5
Brentwood CM14 294 A1
Burnham-on-C CM0 306 A7
Canvey Island SS8 363 F3
Chigwell, Grange Hill IG7 311 E7
Chigwell IG7 289 C1
Colchester CO4 110 E2
Colchester, Crockleford Heath CO7 111 C1
Dagenham IG3, RM8 334 C2
Great Dunmow CM6 150 C8
Great Horkesley CO6 109 C6
Great Notley CM8 154 F2
Great Warley CM13, CM14 316 A3
Hoddesdon EN10 243 B8
Ilford IG1, IG3 333 E2
Kelvedon Hatch CM14 293 D8
Little Totham CM9 214 C4
Mayland CM3 283 B6
Orsett RM16 373 C8
Pilgrims Hatch CM15 294 C3
Roxwell CM1 230 A4
Southend-on-S SS9 346 E7
South Woodham Ferrers CM3 301 D8
Stratford St M CO7 58 C4
Tattingstone IP9 61 D7
Threshers Bush CM17 225 A6
Tiptree CO5 186 D6
Tolleshunt Knights CO5 186 E1
Waltham Abbey EN9 266 D4
Walton-on-t-N CO14 144 D2
Weeley Heath CO16 168 A6
Greenland Gr CO16 193 D3
Greenlands SS4 325 D4
Greenlawns Cvn Pk CO16 168 C2
Greenleafe Dr IG6 333 B8
Greenleas Thundersley SS7 345 B6
Waltham Abbey EN9 265 E5
Greenleaves Cvn Pk EN9 222 A2
Green Man Ct CM20 199 A4
Green Man La CM8 212 F7
Green Mdws CM3 257 A6
Green Mead CM3 301 C8
Green Oak Glade IP8 36 D8
Greenoaks SS7 344 E3
Greenock Way RM1 313 E3
Green Pk CM20 223 E8
Green Rd SS7 344 D1
Greens Cl The IG10 289 A7
Greens Farm La CM11 297 C1
Greenshaw CM15 294 B2
Greenside RM8 334 C3
Greenslade Rd IG11 352 D5
Greensleeves Dr CM14 316 B5
Greensmill CO11 86 C5
Greenspire Gr IP8 16 B2
Green St [2] Harlow CM17 200 D1
Ingatestone CM4 273 C4
Takeley CM6 148 F2
GREENSTEAD 136 E7
Greenstead CM21 172 E1
Greenstead Ave IG8 310 C4
Greenstead Cl
Brentwood CM13 295 E2
Woodford IG8 310 C4
Greenstead Ct CO1 136 D6
Greenstead Gdns IG8 310 C4
GREENSTEAD GREEN 104 A5
Greenstead Jun & Inf Schs SS14 342 F6
Greenstead Rd
Chipping Ongar CM5 248 F2
Colchester CO1 136 D7
Greenstead Rdbt CO4 136 D6
GREENSTED 248 D2
Greensted Cl SS14 342 F5
GREENSTED GREEN 248 B3
Greensted Log Church* CM5 248 D2
Greensted Rd
Chipping Ongar CM5 248 D2
Loughton IG10 288 F2
Greensted The SS14 342 F5
Greens The IP4 18 F4
Greenstone Mews E11 332 A5
GREEN STREET 273 D4
Greensward Coll The SS5 324 F7
Greensward La SS5 324 F7
Greens Yd CO13 170 F5
Green's Yd CO1 135 E7
GREEN THE 155 C4
Green The
Bishop's Stortford CM23 145 F4
Blackmore CM4 272 E8
Buckhurst Hill IG9 288 B1
Chelmsford CM1 231 F4
Chingford E4 287 D1
Chrishall SG8 19 D3
Clacton-on-S CO16 195 B2
Colne Engaine CO6 78 A2
Feering CO5 158 E5
Great Bentley CO7 166 D8
Hatfield Peverel CM3 211 C3
Little Totham CM9 214 C4
Mistley CO11 86 F4
Orsett RM16 374 A8
Romford RM3 314 C7
Saffron Walden CB10 22 E2
Seawick CO16 220 B6
Southend-on-S SS9 346 E7
South Ockendon RM15 357 D2
Stanford-le-H SS17 360 D1
Stanstead CO10 2 E7
Theydon Bois CM16 267 D3
Theydon Bois CM16 267 E2
Waltham Abbey EN9 265 C5
Wanstead E11 332 B5
Wennington RM13 370 E6
West Tilbury RM18 379 D8
Wickham St P CO9 53 C5
Woodford IG8 310 A5
Writtle CM1 231 B1
Green Trees CM16 268 A8
Green Trees Ave CM3 280 F5
Greenview SS8 363 F5
Green View CM16 267 E2
Greenview Pk CO15 196 A7
Greenway Billericay CM11 297 D2
Bishop's Stortford CM23 146 C6
Brentwood CM13 295 A2
Dagenham RM8 334 C3
Frinton-on-S CO13 170 F5
Harlow CM19 222 E8
Romford RM3 315 B4
Woodford IG8 310 C5
Green Way CO6 78 A2
Greenway Bsns Ctr CM19 222 E8
Greenway Cl CO15 196 B7
Greenway Ct IG1 333 B3
Greenway Gdns CM77 154 D7
Greenways
Canvey Island SS8 363 F5
Chelmsford CM1 232 B6
Feering CO5 158 D3
Gosfield CO9 102 F7
Maldon CM9 236 F2
Rochford SS4 325 F2
Saffron Walden CB11 43 E7
South Benfleet SS7 344 C2
Southend-on-S SS1 367 E7
Greenways Cl IP1 17 B8
Greenways Ct RM11 336 D5
Greenways The CO6 131 A3
Greenway The
Clacton-on-S CO15 196 B7
Wickford SS11 299 C3
Greenwell Rd CM8 211 F7
GREENWICH 17 E1
Greenwich Bsns Pk IP3 17 E2
Greenwich Cl IP3 17 E2
Greenwich Rd IP3 17 E2
Greenwich Way EN9 265 C3
Green Wlk
Chipping Ongar CM5 249 A1
Woodford IG8 310 E4
Green Wlk The E4 287 D1
Greenwood [3] IG8 310 A3
Greenwood Ave
Dagenham RM10 354 B8
South Benfleet SS7 344 E1
Greenwood Cl CB9 8 E7
Greenwood Dr E4 309 D5
Greenwood Gdns IG6 311 C3
Greenwood Gr CO4 110 C3
Greenwood Ho RM17 378 B8
Greenwood Mans [9] IG11 353 A5
Greenwood Rd IG7 312 B6
Greenyard EN9 265 C6
Gregory Cl SS5 324 F4
Gregory Mews EN9 265 B7
Gregory Rd RM6 334 D7
Gregory St CO10 33 E7
Grenadier Rd CB9 8 C8
Grendel Way CO15 196 F6
Grenfell Ave
Holland-on-S CO15 196 E6
Hornchurch RM12 335 F3
Grenfell Cl CO4 110 C1
Grenfell Gdns IG2 333 F6
Grennan Cl CM13 317 D4
Grenville Gdns IG8 310 C3
Grenville Rd Braintree CM7 127 E2
Grays RM16 372 B1
Sudbury CO10 15 F2
Gresham Cl CM14 316 C7
Gresham Ct
[6] Brentwood CM14 316 C7
Ipswich IP1 17 B8
Gresham Dr RM6 334 B5
Gresham Pl CM7 127 F4
Gresham Rd CM14 316 C7
Gresley Cl CO4 109 F2
Gresley Dr [2] CM7 128 A2
Gresley Gdns IP2 17 C3
Grested Ct SS4 325 F2
Gretna Gdns IP4 18 B8
Grevatt Lodge SS13 343 C5
Greville Cl CO14 144 E2
Greyfriars CM13 295 B2
Grey Friars Rd [10] IP1 17 C5
Greygoose Pk CM19 223 A5
Greyhound Hill CO4 83 E5
Greyhound La RM16 374 A4
Greyhound Pk SS2 348 A1
Greyhound Rd CO10 2 B3
Greyhound Way SS2 348 A1
Grey Lady Pl CM11 297 B3
Grey Ladys CM2 254 B2
Greys Cl CO10 1 C1
Greys Hollow CB11 93 D8
Greystone Gdns IG6 311 C1
Greystones Cl CO3 135 A3
Grey Towers Ave RM11 336 D3
Grey Towers Gdns RM11 336 C3
Gridiron Pl RM14 337 B2
Grieves Ct CO3 134 C4
Griffin Ave
Canvey Island SS8 364 C5
Upminster RM14 337 E5
Griffin Ct IP2 17 D3
Griffins The RM16 373 B4
Griffin's Wood Cotts CM16 267 D7
Griffin Wlk DA9 376 F2
Griffith Cl RM8 334 C3
Grifon Cl RM16 372 C3
Grifon Rd RM16 372 C3
Griggs App IG1 333 C2
Griggs Bsns Ctr CO6 130 E1
Griggs Gdns RM12 355 C7
Grimshaw Way RM1 335 F6
Grimstone Cl RM5 313 B4
Grimston Rd Basildon SS14 342 F8
Colchester CO2 136 A4
Grimston Way CO14 171 B7
Grimwade Cl CO11 86 D7
Grimwade St IP4 17 D5
Grimwood Cnr [18] CO10 33 E7
Grindle The IP8 16 A7
Grinstead La CM22 173 C6
Groome Ct [2] CO4 136 D7
Groom Ho CO15 195 E4
Groom Pk CO15 195 E4
Groomside [5] CM7 128 A2
Grooms La CM8 156 E4
Grosvenor Cl
Bishop's Stortford CM23 145 D4
Chelmsford CM2 254 D7
Ipswich IP4 17 E8
Loughton IG10 289 B8
Tiptree CO5 186 D5
Grosvenor Ct Ipswich IP3 18 B1
Southend-on-S SS0 366 C7
[3] Wanstead E11 332 B6
Grosvenor Dr
Hornchurch RM11 336 C4
Loughton IG10 289 B8
Grosvenor Gdns
Billericay CM12 297 A4
Upminster RM14 337 D3
Woodford IG8 310 B4
Grosvenor Ho [4] CM23 146 B8
Grosvenor Hts E4 287 E2
Grosvenor Lodge [4] E18 309 F1
Grosvenor Mans SS0 366 C8
Grosvenor Mews SS0 366 C7
Grosvenor Path IG10 289 B8
Grosvenor Pl CO1 136 B7
Grosvenor Rd
Dagenham RM8 334 F3
Ilford IG1 333 C1
Orsett RM16 374 D7
Rayleigh SS6 323 B5
Romford RM7 335 D4
South Benfleet SS7 363 E8
Southend-on-S SS0 366 C7
Sudbury CO10 15 D2
Wanstead E11 332 B6
Grove Ave Basildon SS16 341 B3
Walton-on-t-N CO14 171 B8
West Mersea CO5 218 C5
Grove Cl SS6 323 F2
Grove Cotts Chigwell IG7 311 F7
[1] Witham CM8 184 A2
Grove Cres E18 309 F1
Grove Ct
Great Dunmow CM6 150 E7
Hornchurch RM11 336 A3
Rayleigh SS6 324 B1
Southend-on-S SS0 347 B3
Upminster RM14 356 A8
Waltham Abbey EN9 265 B6
Grove Ctr The CM8 184 A1
Grove End E18 309 F1
Grove Farm Rd
Little Totham CM9 214 C7
Tiptree CO5, CM9 186 A1
Grove Field CM7 102 C1
Grove Gdns RM10 335 C1
Grove Hill Belstead IP8 36 C7
Dedham CO7 84 D4
Langham CO4 83 F5
Southend-on-S SS9 346 B7
Stansted Mountfitchet CM24 119 F7
Woodford E18 309 F1
Grove Ho CM14 316 B6
Grove La Chelmondiston IP9 63 E5
Chigwell IG7 311 F7
Epping CM16 246 A1
Ipswich IP4 17 E5
Grovelands SS2 348 D2
Grovelands Rd SS12 321 D6
Grovelands Way RM17 372 F1
Grove Lea CM9 211 F1
Grove Lodge SS3 368 G7
Grove Mews IP11 381 D5
Grove Orch CM7 102 C1
Grove Park Ave E4 309 B3
Grove Park Rd RM13 355 A4
Grove Pk
Bishop's Stortford CM23 145 C8
Wanstead E11 332 B6
Grove Pl [19] CM23 145 F7
Grove Prim Sch RM6 334 C6
Grove Rd Bentley IP9 60 E6
Billericay CM12 296 F2
Brantham CO11 86 D8
Canvey Island SS8 364 C4
Chelmsford CM2 232 B1
Chingford E4 309 C7
Felixstowe IP11 381 E6
Grays RM17 378 C8
Ilford RM6 334 C5
Little Clacton CO16 168 D5
Northfleet RM17 378 B2
Rayleigh SS6 323 F2
South Benfleet SS7 344 D2
Stanford-le-H SS17 375 D8
Tiptree CO5 186 E6
Woodford E18 309 F1
Grover Wlk SS17 360 F3
Groves Cl Colchester CO4 109 E2
South Ockendon RM15 371 F6
Groveside Rd E4 309 E7
Grove Terr SS1 367 A7
Grove The Bicknacre CM3 256 F1
Billericay CM11 297 C4
Brentwood CM14 315 F6
Clacton-on-S CO15 195 F2
Earls Colne CO6 105 B6
[3] Gravesend DA12 379 C1
Great Hallingbury CM22 146 F4
Southend-on-S SS2 348 C2
Stanford-le-H SS17 375 D8
Swanscombe DA10 377 F2
Upminster RM14 356 B7
Witham CM8 184 A2
Grove Villas CM7 126 A8
Groveway RM8 353 D8
Grove Wlk Ipswich IP8 36 D8
Southend-on-S SS3 368 E7
Grovewood Ave SS9 346 B7
Grovewood Cl SS9 346 B7
Grovewood Pl IG8 310 F4
Grove Wood Prim Sch SS6 324 A1
Gryme's Dyke Ct CO3 134 D6
Gryme's Dyke Way CO3 134 E3
Gryphon Way CO2 135 E3
Gryps Cl CO2 135 E1
Guardian Ave RM16 372 D4
Guardian Bsns Ctr RM3 314 D3
Guardian Cl RM11 336 B2
Guardsman Cl CM14 316 D5
Gubbins La RM3 314 F2
GUBBION'S GREEN 181 B8
Guelph's La CM6 70 A3
Guernsey Ct CM9 236 F2
Guernsey Gdns SS11 299 D1
Guernsey Way CM7 127 D2
Guildford Ct SS2 348 A1
Guildford Gdns RM3 314 E4
Guildford Rd Chingford E17 309 C2
Colchester CO1 136 A8
Ilford IG3 333 E2
Romford RM3 314 E4
Southend-on-S SS2 348 A1
Guildhall Way CB10 24 A7
Guild Way [3] CM3 301 E7
Guilford Lodge [5] CM14 316 C7
Guilfords CM17 200 D5
Guinea Cl CM7 128 D4
Guisnes Ct CM9 216 A4
Guithavon Ct CM8 183 F2
Guithavon Rd CM8 183 F1
Guithavon Rise CM8 183 F2
Guithavon St CM8 183 F2
Guithavon Valley CM8 183 F2
Gull Cotts CO16 142 D4
Gull Ct CO15 141 F1
Gulls Croft CM7 128 D3
Gull's La CO7 85 A3
Gull Wlk RM12 355 B5
Gulpher Bsns Pk IP11 381 D8
Gulpher Cotts IP11 381 E8
Gulpher Rd IP11 381 E8
Gumley Rd RM20 377 E8
Gunfleet SS3 368 C7
Gunfleet Cl CO5 218 B7
Gunfleet Ct CO15 196 C4
Gun Hill Dedham CO7 84 C7
West Tilbury RM18 379 D8
Gun Hill Pl SS16 342 C5
Gunnels Ct & Hastingwood Ct [8] IG9 310 C8
Gunner Dr EN3 265 A2
Gunners Gr E4 309 C7
Gunners Rd SS3 368 G7
Gunning Rd RM17 373 D1
Gunn Rd DA10 377 E1
Gunpowder Park* EN9 265 B3
Gunson Gate CM2 254 D7
Gurdon Rd CO2 135 F3
Gurney Benham Cl CO2 135 B4
Gurney Cl IG11 352 B6
Gurton Rd CO6 131 A3
Guru Gobind Singh Khalsa Coll IG7 288 F1
Gusford Com Prim Sch IP2 16 D1
Gustedhall La SS5 324 E3
Gutteridge Hall La CO16 167 E7
Gutteridge La RM4 291 C3
Gutters La CM1 232 C7
Guy Cook Cl CO10 34 C4
Guys Farm CM1 231 B1
Guys Farm Rd CM3 301 D7
Guysfield Cl RM13 355 A4
Guysfield Dr RM13 355 A4
Guy's Retreat IG9 288 C2
Gwend Alen Ave SS8 364 D4
Gwendoline Cl IP4 18 F4
Gwent Ho IP2 17 B3
Gwyn Cl CM3 209 E1
Gwynne Ho [3] E11 332 A6
Gwynne Park Ave IG8 310 F4
Gwynne Rd CO12 91 D4
Gyllyngdune Gdns IG3 333 F1
Gymnasium St IP1 17 B7
Gypsy La Feering CO5 159 C6
Little Dunmow CM6 151 E7
Sudbury CO10 33 C6

H

Haarlem Rd SS8 363 D4
Haarle Rd SS8 364 D2
Haase Cl SS8 364 A6
Habgood Rd IG10 288 E6
Hackamore SS7 345 B5
Hackmans La
Cock Clarks CM3 257 E2
Cold Norton CM3 280 B6
Hacton Dr RM12 355 E8
Hacton La RM14 355 F8
Hacton Par RM12 336 F1
Hacton Prim Sch RM12 355 E8
Haddon Cl SS6 323 A4
Haddon Mead CM3 301 D5
Haddon Pk CO1 136 C6
Hadfelda Sq CM3 211 A4
Hadfield Dr CM77 155 B5
Hadfield Rd SS17 360 D1
Hadham Ct CM23 145 E8
Hadham Gr CM23 145 C8
Hadham Rd CM23 145 D8
HADLEIGH 345 E3
Hadleigh Bsns Ctr SS7 345 E2
Hadleigh Castle* SS7 345 D1
Hadleigh Castle Ctry Pk* SS7 345 B1
Hadleigh Ct
Brentwood CM14 316 A7
Chingford E4 287 E2
Clacton-on-S CO15 196 A3
[4] Saffron Walden CB10 22 F2
Hadleigh Hall Ct SS9 346 C1
Hadleigh Inf Sch SS7 345 E3
Hadleigh Jun Sch SS7 345 E3
Hadleigh Lodge [5] IG8 310 A4
Hadleigh Park Ave SS7 345 C3
Hadleigh Rd
Clacton-on-S CO16 195 B4
East Bergholt CO7 59 B3
Frinton-on-S CO13 171 A5
Ipswich IP2 16 D5
Southend-on-S SS9 346 C1
Southend-on-S, Westcliff-on-S SS0 366 E7
Stratford St M CO7 58 A6
Hadleigh Road Ind Est IP2 16 F7
Hadleigh Way CO13 170 F5
Hadley Cl CM7 102 B1
Hadley Grange CM17 224 C7
Hadrian Cl Colchester CO4 110 B6
Haverhill CB9 9 D7
Hadrians Cl CM8 211 E8
Hadrians Way CM9 237 A4
HADSTOCK 5 C6
Hadstock Rd CB1 5 B8
Haggars La CO7 138 F3
Haggers Cl CB10 3 D2
Hagg Hill CM3 280 D5
Haig Ct CM2 232 A1
Haig Rd RM16 374 A3
Haigville Gdns IG6 333 B7
Hailes Wood CM22 94 D1
Hailes Wood Cl CM22 94 D1
Hailey Ave EN11 197 A2
Hailey La SG13 197 A2
Hailey Rd DA18 369 A4
Hailey Road Bsns Pk DA18 369 A4
Hailsham Cl RM3 314 C5
Hailsham Gdns RM3 314 C5
Hailsham Rd RM3 314 C5
HAINAULT 311 F3
Hainault Ave Rochford SS4 325 D4
Southend-on-S SS0 347 D2
Hainault Bridge Par [5] IG1 333 B2
Hainault Cl SS7 345 E4
Hainault Forest Ctry Pk* IG7 312 C7
Hainault Forest High Sch IG6 312 B5
Hainault Gore RM6 334 E6
Hainault Gr
Chelmsford CM1 231 E1
Chigwell IG7 311 C6
Hainault Rd Chigwell IG7 311 C6
Dagenham RM6 334 F5
Ilford RM6 334 B8
North Fambridge CM3 281 A1
Redbridge RM6 312 B2
Romford RM5 335 C8
Hainault St IG1 333 B2
Hainault Sta IG6 311 E3
Hakewill Way CO4 109 E3
Halbutt Gdns RM9 334 F1
Halbutt St RM9 353 F7
Halcyon Cl CM8 183 F1

408 Hig–Hol

High Beech Rd IG10 ... **288** E5
Highbirch Rd CO16 ... **167** D3
Highbourne Ct 2 EN11 ... **221** A6
Highbridge Ct 5 EN9 ... **265** B6
Highbridge Ho 6 EN9 ... **265** B6
Highbridge Rd IG11 ... **352** B4
High Bridge Rd CM2 ... **232** C1
Highbridge Ret Pk EN9 ... **265** B5
Highbridge St EN9 ... **265** B6
Highbury Ave EN11 ... **221** A8
Highbury Gdns IG3 ... **333** E2
Highbury Terr 1 CO9 ... **76** F2
Highbury Way CO10 ... **34** B5
High Chelmer 8 CM1 ... **232** B2
High Cl SG8 ... **19** A5
Highclere IG9 ... **310** B8
Highclere Rd
Colchester CO4 ... **110** B4
Great Notley CM77 ... **154** B6
Highcliff Cres SS4 ... **325** D7
Highcliff Dr SS12 ... **320** F8
High Cliff Dr SS9 ... **365** F8
Highcliffe Cl SS11 ... **321** F8
Highcliffe Gdns IG4 ... **332** E6
Highcliffe Rd SS11 ... **321** F8
Highcliffe Way SS11 ... **321** F8
Highcliff Rd SS7 ... **363** E8
High Cloister CM11 ... **297** B2
High Croft CO6 ... **78** A2
Highcroft Point E17 ... **309** B2
High Cross La CM6 ... **149** B5
High Cross La E CM6 ... **149** E6
High Cross Villas CM6 ... **149** C6
HIGH EASTER ... **177** C2
High Easter Rd
Barnston CM6 ... **150** F2
Leaden Roding CM6 ... **204** E6
High Elms Chigwell IG7 ... **311** E6
Harlow CM18 ... **223** F6
Upminster RM14 ... **337** E3
Woodford IG8 ... **310** A5
High Elms Rd SS5 ... **301** E1
Highfield Clare CO10 ... **12** D7
Harlow CM18 ... **224** A7
Hullbridge SS5 ... **301** E3
Sawbridgeworth CM21 ... **172** E3
Highfield App CM11 ... **319** D8
Highfield Ave
Bishop's Stortford CM23 ... **146** C6
Hadleigh SS7 ... **345** C4
Harwich CO12 ... **91** B3
Highfield Cl Braintree CM7 **128** A6
Danbury CM3 ... **256** D6
Romford RM5 ... **313** C4
Southend-on-S SS0 ... **347** D2
Highfield Cloisters SS99 ... **346** C1
Highfield Cres
Hornchurch RM12 ... **336** F2
Rayleigh SS6 ... **323** D2
Southend-on-S SS0 ... **347** D2
Highfield Ct
Billericay CM11 ... **319** D7
Harwich CO12 ... **91** B3
Wanstead E12 ... **332** C2
Highfield Dr
Colchester CO3 ... **135** C7
Southend-on-S SS0 ... **347** D2
Highfield Gdns
Grays RM16 ... **373** D5
Southend-on-S SS0 ... **347** D3
Highfield Gn CM16 ... **267** E8
Highfield Gr SS0 ... **347** D3
Highfield Holiday Pk
Clacton-on-S CO16 ... **195** E8
Little Clacton CO15 ... **168** F1
Highfield Link RM5 ... **313** D4
Highfield Pl CM16 ... **267** E8
Highfield Rd
Billericay CM11 ... **319** D7
Chelmsford CM1 ... **231** E4
Felixstowe IP11 ... **381** E4
Hornchurch RM12 ... **336** F2
Romford RM5 ... **313** C4
Sudbury CO10 ... **34** A8
Woodford IG8 ... **310** E3
Highfield Rise CM3 ... **283** A3
Highfields Bentley IP9 ... **60** E6
Debden CB11 ... **68** B7
Great Yeldham CO9 ... **30** A2
Halstead CO9 ... **103** F8
Henham CM22 ... **94** F6
Langley CB11 ... **40** D2
Saffron Walden CB10 ... **22** E2
High Fields CM6 ... **150** D8
Highfields La CO5 ... **185** E7
Highfields Mead CM3 ... **278** B8
Highfields Prim Sch CO11 ... **86** C4
Highfields Rd CM8 ... **183** E1
Highfield Stile Rd CM7 ... **128** A6
Highfields Twrs RM5 ... **313** D5
Highfield Way
Hornchurch RM12 ... **336** F2
Southend-on-S SS0 ... **347** D3
High Gables IG10 ... **288** D4
HIGH GARRETT ... **102** D2
High Garrett CM7 ... **102** C2
Highgate Gr CM21 ... **172** D2
Highgates CO9 ... **102** E8
Highgrove CM15 ... **294** B3
Highgrove Ho 13 CM14 ... **316** C8
Highgrove Mews RM17 ... **373** C1
Highgrove Rd RM8 ... **353** C8
High House Est CM17 ... **200** F4
High House La RM18 ... **374** D3
High La
Bishop's Stortford CM24 ... **119** F8
Sheering CM17 ... **201** E6
Highland Ave
Brentwood CM15 ... **294** D1
Dagenham RM10 ... **335** C1
Loughton IG10 ... **288** F3
Highland Ct E18 ... **310** B2
Highland Gr CM11 ... **297** B2
Highland Rd Basildon SS17 **342** B1
Bishop's Stortford CM23 ... **145** F3
Lower Nazeing EN9 ... **221** E1
Highlands CO9 ... **75** E1
Highlands Ave SS16 ... **342** D4
Highlands Bvd SS9 ... **346** A2
Highlands Cres SS13 ... **343** F6
Highlands Ct SS9 ... **346** B2
Highlands Dr CM9 ... **236** E2
Highlands Gdns IG1 ... **332** F3
Highlands Gr CO15 ... **196** A7
Highlands Hill CM3 ... **283** D6
Highlands Pk CO15 ... **196** A7
Highlands Prim Sch IG1 ... **332** F3
Highlands Rd
Basildon SS13 ... **343** F6
Rawreth SS11 ... **301** B2
HIGH LAVER ... **226** B6
High Lift Villas CO4 ... **83** D8
High Mdw Billericay CM11 ... **297** C2
Great Dunmow CM6 ... **150** C8
High Mdws IG7 ... **311** D5
Highmead Rayleigh SS6 ... **323** B2
Stansted Mountfitchet CM24 ... **119** E8
High Mead Chigwell IG7 ... **311** C8
Hockley SS5 ... **324** E5
Highmead Ct
Brentwood CM15 ... **294** D1
Rayleigh SS6 ... **323** C2
High Oaks Basildon SS16 ... **341** B3
Harwich CO12 ... **90** B2
High Oaks Lodge 5 E18 ... **310** A1
HIGH ONGAR ... **249** D3
High Ongar Prim Sch CM5 ... **249** C4
High Ongar Rd (Chelmsford Rd) CM5 ... **249** B5
HIGH PARK CORNER ... **164** C6
High Pastures
Little Baddow CM3 ... **234** D3
Sheering CM22 ... **201** D8
High Pavement SS14 ... **342** A6
High Rd
Basildon, Laindon SS16, SS15 ... **341** B6
Basildon, Pitsea SS16 ... **343** A4
Basildon, Westley Heights SS16 ... **341** B2
Chigwell IG7 ... **311** B7
Corringham SS17 ... **361** C5
Dagenham RM6, IG3 ... **334** C4
Epping CM16 ... **267** D7
Hockley SS5 ... **324** A5
Hoddesdon EN10 ... **221** A4
Horndon on t H SS17 ... **359** F3
Ilford IG1 ... **333** B2
Ilford, Seven Kings IG1, IG3 ... **333** E2
Layer de la H CO2 ... **161** F5
Loughton IG9, IG10 ... **288** C3
North Weald Bassett CM16 **247** B5
Orsett RM16 ... **374** A8
Rayleigh SS6 ... **323** C1
South Benfleet SS7 ... **344** C3
South Ockendon RM16 ... **372** E5
Stanford-le-H SS17 ... **360** F1
Thornwood CM16 ... **246** C6
Trimley St M IP11 ... **381** B7
Woodford E18 ... **310** A2
High Rd E IP11 ... **381** F5
High Rd N SS15 ... **319** C1
High Rd W IP11 ... **381** D5
High Ridge CM8 ... **213** C8
High Road Buckhurst Hill 2 IG9 ... **310** B8
High Road Woodford Gn IG8 ... **310** A6
HIGH RODING ... **176** F7
High St N CO5 ... **218** C7
High Silver IG10 ... **288** D5
High St Aveley RM15 ... **371** D5
Billericay CM12 ... **297** A2
Bishop's Stortford CM23 ... **145** F7
Bradwell on S CM0 ... **242** A2
Braintree CM7 ... **127** F3
Brentwood CM14 ... **316** C8
Brightlingsea CO7 ... **192** F6
Bures CO8 ... **55** F1
Burnham-on-C CM0 ... **306** C4
Canewdon SS4 ... **304** D2
Canvey Island SS8 ... **364** D4
Castle Camps CB21 ... **7** E3
Cavendish CO10 ... **1** D2
Chelmsford CM1 ... **232** B2
Chipping Ongar CM5 ... **249** A3
Chrishall SG8 ... **19** D3
Clacton-on-S CO15 ... **195** F2
Clare CO10 ... **12** B7
Clavering CB11 ... **65** D4
Colchester CO1 ... **135** F7
Debden CB11 ... **68** B7
Dedham CO7 ... **84** F7
Earls Colne CO6 ... **105** B6
Elsenham CM22 ... **94** D1
Epping CM16 ... **267** F8
Felixstowe IP11 ... **381** C6
Gravesend DA11 ... **379** B1
Grays RM17 ... **378** A8
Great Baddow CM2 ... **254** F6
Great Bardfield CM7 ... **72** A1
Great Chesterford CB10 ... **3** E2
Great Dunmow CM6 ... **150** D8
Great Oakley CO12 ... **116** C4
Great Wakering SS3 ... **350** A4
Great Yeldham CO9 ... **30** A1
Greenhithe DA9 ... **377** B3
Hadleigh SS7 ... **345** D3
Halstead CO9 ... **76** E2
Harlow CM17 ... **200** C4
Harwich CO12 ... **91** D4
Hatfield Broad Oak CM22 ... **174** F6
Haverhill CB9 ... **9** A7
Hempstead CB10 ... **25** F1
Henham CM22 ... **94** F5
Hinxton CB10 ... **3** B7
Hoddesdon EN11 ... **221** A5
Hornchurch RM11, RM12 ... **336** D3
Ilford IG6 ... **333** C8
Ingatestone CM4 ... **274** B3
Ipswich IP1 ... **17** C6
Kelvedon CO5 ... **158** C2
Langham CO4 ... **83** D4
Littlebury CB11 ... **21** F4
High St *continued*
Little Chesterford CB10 ... **21** F8
Little Wakering SS3 ... **349** F4
Maldon CM9 ... **237** A2
Manningtree CO11 ... **86** D4
Mistley CO11 ... **86** F4
Nayland CO6 ... **56** B1
Newport CB11 ... **67** A8
Northfleet RM17 ... **378** C1
Purfleet RM19 ... **371** A1
Rayleigh SS6 ... **323** D2
Redbridge IG6 ... **311** C1
Romford RM1 ... **335** E6
Rowhedge CO5 ... **164** A8
Roydon CM19 ... **198** B1
Saffron Walden CB10 ... **22** D1
South Benfleet SS7 ... **344** D1
Southend-on-S, Leigh-on-S SS9 ... **365** D8
Southend-on-S, Shoeburyness SS3 ... **368** F6
Southend-on-S, Shoeburyness SS3 ... **368** G7
Southend-on-S SS1 ... **367** A8
Southminster CM0 ... **284** D4
Sproughton IP8 ... **16** A6
Stanford-le-H SS17 ... **360** C1
Stanstead Abbotts SG12 ... **197** C4
Stebbing CM6 ... **124** E5
Stock CM4 ... **275** E3
Swanscombe DA10 ... **377** F2
Thorpe-le-S CO16 ... **141** F1
Tollesbury CM9 ... **216** D1
Walton-on-t-N CO14 ... **171** C8
Wanstead E11 ... **332** A6
West Mersea CO5 ... **218** B6
Wethersfield CM7 ... **73** C3
Wickford SS12 ... **321** D7
Widdington CB11 ... **67** D4
Wivenhoe CO7 ... **164** B8
High Stile CM6 ... **150** C8
Highstone Ave E11 ... **332** A5
Highstone Ct 4 E11 ... **332** A5
HIGHSTREET GREEN ... **51** A2
High Tree La CO14 ... **144** D2
Hightrees CM4 ... **275** D2
High Trees DA2 ... **376** B1
Hightrees Ct 11 CM14 ... **316** C6
Highview SS5 ... **301** E4
High View
Birchanger CM23 ... **119** D3
St Lawrence CM0 ... **262** C8
Highview Ave SS16 ... **340** F5
High View Ave
Clacton-on-S CO15 ... **195** E6
Grays RM17 ... **373** C1
Highview Cl CO10 ... **15** E2
High View Cl
Clacton-on-S CO15 ... **195** E6
Loughton IG10 ... **288** C4
Highview Cres CM13 ... **295** C3
Highview Ct 3 IG10 ... **288** D4
High View Ct SS7 ... **344** D2
Highview Gdns RM14 ... **337** B2
High View Gdns RM17 ... **373** C1
Highview Ho IG9 ... **310** D7
High View Ho RM6 ... **334** E7
High View Par 1 IG4 ... **332** F6
Highview Rd SS7 ... **345** A7
High View Rd Ipswich IP1 ... **16** D8
Woodford E18 ... **309** F1
High View Rise CM11 ... **320** C5
HIGHWOOD ... **252** A4
Highwood IG8 ... **309** F6
Highwood Cl
Brentwood CM14 ... **294** B2
Southend-on-S SS9 ... **346** F4
Highwood Cotts CM1 ... **251** E3
Highwood Gdns Ilford IG5 **333** A7
Redbridge IG5 ... **332** F7
High Wood Hospl CM14 ... **294** C1
Highwood La IG10 ... **289** A3
Highwood Prim Sch CM1 ... **252** A4
Highwood Rd
Edney Common CM1 ... **252** C6
Roxwell CM1 ... **251** F4
High Wood Rd EN11 ... **197** A1
Highwoods App CO4 ... **110** C4
Highwoods Com Prim Sch CO4 ... **110** B4
High Woods Country Park Visitor Ctr* CO4 ... **109** F3
High Woods Ctry Pk* CO4 ... **110** A3
Highwoods Sq CO4 ... **110** B4
HIGH WYCH ... **172** B1
High Wych CE Prim Sch CM21 ... **172** A1
High Wych La CM21 ... **172** A2
High Wych Rd
Gilston CM21 ... **199** F7
High Wych CM21 ... **172** B1
Hilary Cl Hornchurch RM12 ... **355** D7
Rochford SS4 ... **325** E5
Hilary Cres SS6 ... **323** E2
Hilary Dennis Ct E18 ... **332** A7
Hilberry Rd SS8 ... **364** D3
Hildabrook Cl 2 IP2 ... **16** E1
Hilda May Ct RM18 ... **379** C5
Hildaville Dr SS0 ... **347** C2
Hillary Cl Bradwell CM77 ... **129** D2
Chelmsford CM1 ... **232** D4
Heybridge CM9 ... **237** B5
Ipswich IP4 ... **18** A5
Hillary Mount CM12 ... **297** A1
Hill Ave SS11 ... **321** F8
Hillboro Ct 1 E18 ... **309** F2
Hillborough Mans SS0 ... **347** D3
Hillborough Rd SS0 ... **347** D3
Hill Cl Long Melford CO10 ... **15** D8
South Benfleet SS7 ... **344** E4
Hill Cotts CO7 ... **166** E1
Hillcourt RM11 ... **336** F2
Hill Cres Chelmsford CM2 ... **232** D2
Hornchurch RM11 ... **336** C5
Hillcrest Clacton-on-S CO15 **196** A6
Kirby-le-S CO13 ... **170** D8
Mayland CM3 ... **261** A1
Hillcrest Ave Basildon SS16 **340** E3
Grays RM20 ... **377** A8
Hillcrest Ave *continued*
Hullbridge SS5 ... **301** E1
Hillcrest Cl SS17 ... **359** F4
Hillcrest Ct CO4 ... **83** E6
Hill Crest Cotts CO5 ... **163** B3
Hillcrest Ct Harwich CO12 ... **91** C3
Romford RM5 ... **313** C2
Hillcrest Dr DA9 ... **377** A2
Hillcrest Rd Chingford E17 ... **309** D1
Hockley SS5 ... **324** E5
Hornchurch RM11 ... **336** A4
Horndon on t H SS17 ... **359** F4
Loughton IG10 ... **288** D3
Southend-on-S SS1 ... **367** B8
South Woodham Ferrers CM3 ... **301** C7
Sudbury CO10 ... **15** E2
Woodford E18 ... **310** A1
Hill Crest Rd CM5 ... **247** E1
Hillcrest View SS16 ... **342** D3
Hillcrest Way CM16 ... **268** A8
Hillcroft IG10 ... **289** A7
Hill Ct RM1 ... **335** F7
Hilldene Ave RM3 ... **314** D5
Hilldene Cl RM3 ... **314** D5
Hilldene Prim Sch RM3 ... **314** C4
Hill Farm La IP9 ... **63** F7
Hillfield CO5 ... **158** D4
Hillfoot Ave RM5 ... **313** C2
Hillfoot Rd RM5 ... **313** C2
Hill Gr RM1 ... **335** E8
HILL GREEN ... **65** E6
Hillgrove Bsns Pk EN10 ... **221** C1
Hill Hall* CM16 ... **268** F4
Hillhouse EN9 ... **265** F6
Hillhouse CE Prim Sch EN9 ... **265** F6
Hillhouse Cl CM12 ... **297** B4
Hill House Ct CO7 ... **193** A7
Hillhouse Dr CM12 ... **297** B4
Hill House Dr RM16 ... **374** C1
Hillhouse La CO16 ... **141** B3
Hill House Rd
Dartford DA2 ... **376** C1
Ipswich IP3 ... **17** E5
Hilliards Rd CO7 ... **113** C2
Hillie Bunnies CO6 ... **105** B7
Hillington Gdns IG8 ... **310** D1
Hill La Hockley SS5 ... **324** F5
Sturmer CB9 ... **9** F4
Hillman Ave CO15 ... **220** E6
Hillman Cl RM11 ... **336** D8
Hillmead Prim Sch CM23 ... **145** C7
Hill Rd Brentwood CM14 ... **316** A7
Chelmsford CM2 ... **232** D2
Clacton-on-S CO15 ... **195** E6
Coggeshall CO6 ... **131** B2
Harwich CO12 ... **91** C4
Hempstead CB10 ... **46** D8
Ramsey CO12 ... **116** E8
South Benfleet SS7 ... **344** E4
Southend-on-S SS2 ... **347** F2
Theydon Bois CM16 ... **267** E2
Hill Rd S CM2 ... **232** D2
Hillridge CO4 ... **110** B3
Hill Rise RM14 ... **337** A2
Hillrise Rd RM5 ... **313** C4
Hill's Chace CM14 ... **316** C6
Hills Cl CM7 ... **127** F4
Hills Cres CO3 ... **135** A5
Hillside Belvedere DA8 ... **369** C2
Frinton-on-S CO13 ... **170** E4
Grays RM17 ... **373** D2
Harlow CM17 ... **224** C6
Hillside Ave
Bishop's Stortford CM23 ... **146** A7
Hockley SS5 ... **324** F5
Woodford IG8 ... **310** C5
Hillside Cl Billericay CM11 ... **297** B1
Woodford IG8 ... **310** C5
Hillside Com Prim Sch IP2 **17** C3
Hillside Cotts
Birchanger CM23 ... **119** C3
Ipswich IP9 ... **37** E4
Sudbury CO10 ... **34** A7
Hillside Cres
Holland-on-S CO15 ... **196** C5
Ipswich IP3 ... **18** C3
Southend-on-S SS9 ... **366** A8
Stanstead Abbotts SG12 ... **197** B4
Hillside End CM23 ... **119** C3
Hillside Gdns CM7 ... **127** F1
Hillside Gr CM2 ... **254** A7
Hillside Ho 2 CM7 ... **127** F1
Hillside La SG12 ... **197** A5
Hillside Mews CM2 ... **254** A7
Hillside Rd Billericay CM11 ... **297** B1
Burnham-on-C CM0 ... **306** B5
Hockley SS5 ... **324** B5
Rayleigh SS9 ... **346** C8
South Benfleet SS7 ... **344** D1
Southend-on-S SS9 ... **365** E8
Southminster CM0 ... **284** C4
Sudbury CO10 ... **34** A7
Hillside Specl Sch CO10 ... **15** F1
Hillside Terr 1 CM7 ... **127** F1
Hillside Wlk CM14 ... **315** F7
Hillsleigh Mews CO1 ... **136** A7
Hills Rd CO9 ... **75** D8
Hill's Rd IG9 ... **288** B1
Hill St CB10 ... **22** D1
Hillston Cl CO2 ... **136** B2
Hill Terr Clare CO10 ... **12** C8
Corringham SS17 ... **361** C3
Woodford IG8 ... **310** E3
Hill The Harlow CM17 ... **200** C4
Northfleet DA11 ... **378** C1
Hill Top IG10 ... **289** A6
Hilltop Ave SS5 ... **301** E1
Hill Top Ave SS7 ... **344** F2
Hilltop Cl Colchester CO2 ... **136** D4
Rayleigh SS6 ... **323** C1
Hill Top Cl IG10 ... **289** A6
Hilltop Cotts H 6 CM16 ... **268** F5
Hilltop Cres CO16 ... **140** F1
Hill Top Ct IG8 ... **310** F4
Hilltop Jun & Inf Sch SS11 ... **322** A8
Hill Top La CB11 ... **43** E7
Hilltop Rd Basildon SS15 ... **341** E7
Hilltop Rd *continued*
Grays RM20 ... **377** B8
Hilltop Rise CO16 ... **140** E1
Hill Top Rise SS16 ... **340** F4
Hill Top View IG8 ... **310** F4
Hill Tree Cl CM21 ... **172** D1
Hill View CM3 ... **256** F1
Hillview Ave RM11 ... **336** D5
Hillview Cl CO5 ... **163** F8
Hill View Cl CM0 ... **284** C4
Hillview Cres IG1 ... **332** F5
Hillview Gdns SS17 ... **360** F5
Hillview Rd SS6 ... **323** C3
Hill View Rd CM1 ... **232** C4
Hillway Billericay CM11 ... **297** D2
Southend-on-S SS0 ... **366** A8
Hillway The CM15 ... **295** E8
Hill Way The CM4 ... **273** F1
Hillwood Cl CM13 ... **295** B1
Hillwood Gr
Brentwood CM13 ... **295** B1
Wickford SS11 ... **321** E7
Hillybroom Gdns CO5 ... **218** D6
Hilly Field CM18 ... **223** F4
Hillyfields IG10 ... **289** A7
Hilly Rd SS15 ... **341** D7
Hilton Cl CO11 ... **86** D4
Hilton Rd
Canvey Island SS8 ... **364** A5
Ipswich IP3 ... **18** C1
Hilton Way CO9 ... **75** E8
Hilton Wlk
Canvey Island SS8 ... **364** A5
Sible Hedingham CO9 ... **75** E8
Hilversum Way SS8 ... **364** B5
Hind Cl IG7 ... **311** F5
Hindles Rd SS8 ... **364** D4
Hindmans Way RM9 ... **353** F1
Hind Terr RM20 ... **372** D1
Hines Cl CO6 ... **133** B8
Hines Rd IP3 ... **18** A4
Hinguar Com Prim Sch SS3 ... **368** F6
Hinguar St SS3 ... **368** F6
Hintlesham Cl IP4 ... **18** F5
Hintlesham Dr IP11 ... **381** B5
Hintons CM19 ... **223** A4
HINXTON ... **3** B7
Hinxton Mill* CB10 ... **3** A7
Hinxton Rd CB10 ... **3** A7
Hipkins CM23 ... **145** E4
Hispano Mews EN3 ... **265** A2
Histon Cl IP5 ... **18** F7
Hitcham Rd CO6 ... **130** F3
Hitchcock Pl CO10 ... **15** E1
Hitch Common Rd CB11 ... **66** F8
Hitchin Cl RM3 ... **314** C6
Hitchin Mews CM7 ... **155** B8
Hitchman Ho RM5 ... **313** B3
Hither Blakers CM3 ... **301** D8
Hitherfield Rd RM8 ... **334** E2
Hitherwood Cl RM12 ... **355** D8
Hive Cl CM14 ... **316** A8
Hive La DA11 ... **378** B2
Hive The DA11 ... **378** B1
HMS Ganges Assoc Mus* CO12 ... **91** C8
Hobart Cl CM1 ... **231** E5
Hobart Ct IG8 ... **309** F6
Hobart Rd Dagenham RM9 ... **353** D8
Redbridge IG6 ... **311** C1
Tilbury RM18 ... **379** A6
Hobbiton Hill CM3 ... **301** C6
HOBBS CROSS Epping ... **268** D3
Harlow ... **201** A1
Hobbs Cross Cotts CM16 ... **268** D3
Hobbs Cross Rd
Epping CM16 ... **268** C4
Harlow CM17 ... **200** F3
Hobbs Dr CO4 ... **83** A5
Hobbs La CO10 ... **2** D2
Hobbs Mews IG3 ... **333** F2
Hobhouse Rd SS17 ... **360** D4
Hobleythick La SS0 ... **347** D4
Hoblongs Ind Est CM6 ... **150** E6
Hobtoe Rd CM20 ... **199** A1
HOCKERILL ... **146** A6
Hockerill Anglo-European Coll CM23 ... **146** B7
Hockerill Ct 6 CM23 ... **146** A7
Hockerill St CM23 ... **146** A7
HOCKLEY ... **324** D6
Hockley Cl Basildon SS14 ... **342** D6
Bradwell on S CM0 ... **242** C2
Shudy Camps CB21 ... **7** B5
Hockley Ct 2 E18 ... **310** A2
Hockley Dr RM2 ... **314** C1
Hockley Gn SS14 ... **342** E6
Hockley La CM0 ... **242** C2
Hockley Mews IG11 ... **352** E2
Hockley Prim Sch SS5 ... **324** C6
Hockley Rd Basildon SS14 ... **342** D6
Rayleigh SS6 ... **323** E4
Hockley Rise SS5 ... **324** E5
Hockley Sta SS5 ... **324** E6
Hockley Woods* SS5 ... **324** C4
Hockney Gdns IP3 ... **38** A8
HODDESDON ... **221** C7
Hoddesdon Ind Ctr EN11 ... **221** C7
Hoddesdon Rd
Belvedere DA17 ... **369** A1
Stanstead Abbotts SG12 ... **197** C3
Hodges Cl RM16 ... **372** D1
Hodges Holt CM8 ... **212** A7
Hodgkinson Rd IP11 ... **381** A3
Hodgson Ct SS11 ... **322** A5
Hodgson Way SS11 ... **322** B6
Hodings Rd CM20 ... **199** C2
Hodson Pl 1 EN3 ... **265** A1
Hoecroft EN9 ... **221** F1
Hoe Dr CO3 ... **135** A5
Hoe La Abridge RM4 ... **290** C4
Great Waltham CM3 ... **207** E6
Lower Nazeing EN9 ... **222** A2
Pentlow CO10 ... **13** F8
Rettendon CM3 ... **300** A6
Hoe Mill Rd CM9 ... **235** E4
Hoe St CM1 ... **230** D4
Hoestock Rd CM21 ... **172** D2
Hoe The CM12 ... **319** B4
Hoffmanns Way CM1 ... **232** B4
Hogarth Ave CM15 ... **316** F7
Hogarth Cl CO5 ... **218** D6
Hogarth Ct CM1 ... **232** E6
Hogarth Dr SS3 ... **368** G8
Hogarth End CO13 ... **170** E7
Hogarth Prim Sch CM15 ... **316** F7
Hogarth Rd
Dagenham RM8 ... **353** B7
Grays RM16 ... **373** A5
Ipswich IP3 ... **18** A1
Hogarth Reach IG10 ... **288** F4
Hogarth Sq IP3 ... **18** A1
Hogarth Way SS4 ... **325** C6
Hogges Cl 16 EN11 ... **221** A6
Hogg La RM16, RM17 ... **373** A2
Hog Hill Rd RM5 ... **313** A3
Hog's La SG8 ... **19** D3
Hogwell Chase
Hullbridge CM3 ... **302** B8
South Woodham Ferrers CM3 ... **280** B1
Holbech Rd SS14 ... **342** F8
Holbek Rd SS8 ... **364** E3
Holborough Cl CO4 ... **136** F7
HOLBROOK ... **62** D5
Holbrook Cl
Billericay CM11 ... **297** D2
Clacton-on-S CO16 ... **195** B4
South Woodham Ferrers CM3 ... **301** E7
Holbrook Cres IP11 ... **381** B4
Holbrooke Wlk CO5 ... **186** E5
Holbrook High Sch IP9 ... **62** D6
Holbrook Ho SS7 ... **345** E3
Holbrook Prim Sch IP9 ... **62** D6
Holbrook Rd Harkstead IP9 ... **63** A2
Haverhill CB9 ... **8** E6
Ipswich IP3 ... **17** F1
Stutton IP9 ... **62** A2
Holcombe Cres IP2 ... **16** D2
Holcombe Rd IG1 ... **333** A4
HOLDBROOK ... **265** A5
Holdbrook Way RM3 ... **314** F1
Holden Cl Braintree CM7 ... **128** A2
Dagenham RM8 ... **334** B1
Ipswich IP2 ... **17** D3
HOLDEN END ... **6** B2
Holden Gdns Basildon SS14 **320** F1
Brentwood CM14 ... **316** D5
Holden Rd Basildon SS14 ... **320** F1
Colchester CO4 ... **109** F2
Holden Way RM14 ... **337** D4
Holden Wlk SS14 ... **320** F1
HOLDER'S GREEN ... **97** E6
Holdsworth Cl CO10 ... **2** B3
Holecroft EN9 ... **265** E5
Hole Haven Cvn Pk SS8 ... **363** C1
Holford Rd SS17, RM18 ... **374** E4
Holgate SS13 ... **343** C8
Holgate Ct 9 RM1 ... **335** E6
Holgate Gdns RM10 ... **354** A6
Holgate Rd RM10 ... **354** A7
Holkham Ave CM3 ... **301** D5
Holkham Cl IP4 ... **18** F5
Holland Ave SS8 ... **363** D5
Holland Cl RM7 ... **335** C6
Holland Haven Ctry Pk* CO15 ... **196** I8
Holland Haven Prim Sch CO15 ... **196** E6
Holland Ho Chingford E4 ... **309** C6
Clacton-on-S CO15 ... **196** A3
Holland Lodge CO15 ... **195** F3
HOLLAND-ON-SAND ... **196** F5
Holland Park Ave IG3 ... **333** F6
Holland Park Prim Sch CO15 ... **196** B5
Holland Pk CO15 ... **196** B4
Holland Pl CO13 ... **170** E3
Holland Rd
Clacton-on-S, Rush Green CO15 ... **195** F2
Felixstowe IP11 ... **381** D3
Frinton-on-S CO13 ... **170** E3
Holland-on-S CO15 ... **196** B4
Ipswich IP4 ... **17** F6
Kirby Cross CO13 ... **170** B6
Little Clacton CO16 ... **168** E2
Southend-on-S SS0 ... **366** D7
Wallend E6 ... **352** A5
Hollands Rd CB9 ... **9** A6
Hollands Wlk SS16 ... **342** D2
Holland Villas CO13 ... **170** A3
Holland Way CM17 ... **200** D1
Holledge Cres CO13 ... **170** E6
Hollesley Ave CB9 ... **8** C8
Holley Gdns CM11 ... **297** B3
Holliday Hill CM2 ... **276** F4
Hollidge Way RM10 ... **354** B5
Hollies RM14 ... **337** B2
Hollies Rd CM77 ... **129** C3
Hollies The
Stanford-le-H SS17 ... **360** D1
9 Wanstead E11 ... **332** A6
Holliland Croft CO6 ... **132** C8
Hollington Gr CO2 ... **161** A3
Hollis Lock CM2 ... **233** A3
Hollis Pl RM17 ... **373** A2
Holliwell Cl CO3 ... **134** D6
Holloway Cl CM6 ... **204** C7
Holloway Cres CM6 ... **204** C8
Holloway Rd CM9 ... **237** A5
Hollow Cotts RM19 ... **371** A1
Hollowfield Ave RM17 ... **373** D2
Hollow La Broomfield CM1 ... **231** E8
Bures CO8 ... **55** F3
Chelmondiston IP9 ... **63** F7
Hollow Rd Ashen CO10 ... **11** E3
Braintree CM6 ... **153** B4
Chrishall SG8 ... **19** D2
Elmdon CB11 ... **20** C4
Kelvedon CO5 ... **157** F2
Washbrook IP8 ... **35** D8
Widdington CB11 ... **67** C3
Hollow The IG8 ... **309** F6
Hollybank Basildon SS16 ... **340** F4
Witham CM8 ... **183** F1
Holly Blue Cl IP8 ... **36** E8
Holly Brook CM7 ... **128** A4

Mallard Way *continued*
Roydon CM19 . . . . .198 A1
Mallinson Cl RM12 . . . . .355 C7
Mallion Ct EN9 . . . . .265 F6
Mallories CM20 . . . . .199 F2
Mallory Way CM12 . . . . .297 A1
Mallow Ct RM17 . . . . .378 E8
Mallow Gdns CM12 . . . . . . .296 F5
Mallowhayes Cl IP2 . . . . 17 B3
Mallows Field CO9 . . . . 76 F2
Mallows Gn CM19 . . . . .223 A3
MALLOWS GREEN 92 D2
Mallows Green Rd CM23 . . .92 D1
Mallows La CO9 . . . . 49 F3
Mallow Wlk CB9 . . . . 8 D8
Mall The RM11 . . . . .336 B3
Malmesbury Cl IP2 . . . . 17 A1
Malmesbury Rd E18 . . . . . . .309 F2
Malmsmead SS3 . . . . .368 C8
Malpas Rd Dagenham RM9 .353 D6
Grays RM16 . . . . .374 C3
Malsters Lodge 9 EN11 . . .221 D8
Malta Rd RM18 . . . . .378 F5
Maltese Rd CM1 . . . . .232 A4
Malthouse Pl 6 RM1 . . . . . .335 E6
Malthouse Rd CO11 . . . . 86 D4
Malthouse The CO10 . . . . 15 B5
Malting Cotts CB9 . . . . 9 F4
Malting Farm La CO7 . . . . 84 D2
MALTING GREEN 162 B5
Malting Green Rd CO2 . . . .162 A5
Malting La Clare CO10 . . . . . . 12 B7
Kirby-le-S CO13 . . . . .143 C1
Orsett RM16 . . . . .359 A1
Malting Rd Colchester CO2 .135 C1
Peldon CO5 . . . . .189 E6
Maltings Chase CM4 . . . . . . .274 B3
Maltings Cl CO8 . . . . 55 E1
Maltings Ct CM8 . . . . .211 F8
Maltings Dr CM16 . . . . .246 A2
Maltings Hill CM5 . . . . .226 E3
Maltings Ind Est The
SG12 . . . . .197 D4
Maltings La Epping CM16 . .246 A2
Witham CM8 . . . . .211 F8
Maltings Rd
Battlesbridge SS11 . . . . . . .300 E2
Brightlingsea CO7 . . . . .165 E1
Great Baddow CM2 . . . . . . .255 A5
Maltings The The Cavendish CO10 1 D2
1 Gravesend DA11 . . . . . . .379 A1
Great Dunmow CM6 . . . . . . .123 D1
Great Easton CM6 . . . . 96 A2
Ramsey CO12 . . . . .116 E8
Rayne CM77 . . . . .127 A2
Romford RM1 . . . . .335 F4
Saffron Walden CB10 . . . . 22 D1
Southminster CM0 . . . . .284 E4
Thaxted CM6 . . . . 70 A2
Maltings View CM7 . . . . . . .128 A3
Maltings Wharf CO11 . . . . . . 86 D4
Malting Terr IP2 . . . . 17 D4
Malting Villas Rd SS4 . . . . .325 F2
Malting Yd CO7 . . . . .164 B8
Maltings Park Rd CO6 . . . . .108 F4
Malvern SS2 . . . . .348 B1
Malvern Ave
Canvey Island SS8 . . . . .363 D3
Chingford E4 . . . . .309 D3
Malvern Cl
Chelmsford CM1 . . . . .231 D6
Ipswich IP3 . . . . 18 B4
Rayleigh SS6 . . . . .323 D4
Rushmere St A IP5 . . . . 18 F7
Malvern Dr Ilford IG3 . . . . . .352 F8
Woodford IG8 . . . . .310 C6
Malvern Gdns IG10 . . . . . . .288 F3
Malvern Ho DA11 . . . . .378 D1
Malvern Rd Grays RM17 . . .373 E2
Hockley SS5 . . . . .324 F8
Hornchurch RM11 . . . . .336 A5
Malvern Way CO6 . . . . .109 B7
Malvina Cl SS16 . . . . .359 F7
Malwood Dr SS7 . . . . .344 B5
Malwood Rd SS7 . . . . .344 B5
Malyon Cl CM7 . . . . .127 E3
Malyon Court Cl SS7 . . . . . . .345 B4
Malyon Rd CM8 . . . . .211 F8
Malyons SS13 . . . . .343 B8
Malyons Cl SS13 . . . . .343 B8
Malyons Gn SS13 . . . . .343 B8
Malyons La SS5 . . . . .301 D2
Malyons Mews SS13 . . . . . . .343 B8
Malyons Pl SS13 . . . . .343 B8
Malyons The SS7 . . . . .345 B4
Manbrough Ave E6 . . . . .352 A2
Manchester Dr SS9 . . . . .346 F2
Manchester Rd
Holland-on-S CO15 . . . . .196 E6
Ipswich IP2 . . . . 16 D2
Manchester Way RM10 . . . .354 B8
Mandarin Royal 7 RM1 . . .335 F5
Mandeville Cl CM17 . . . . . . .224 C6
Mandeville Prim Sch
CM21 . . . . .172 D3
Mandeville Rd
Marks Tey CO6 . . . . .132 E3
Saffron Walden CB11 . . . . 43 D8
Mandeville Way
Basildon SS15, SS16 . . . . . .341 B5
Broomfield CM1 . . . . .208 B3
Kirby Cross CO13 . . . . .170 F6
South Benfleet SS7 . . . . . . .344 C7
Mandeville Wlk
Brentwood CM13 . . . . .295 E2
Little Dunmow CM6 . . . . . . .151 E6
Mandy Cl IP4 . . . . 18 A6
Manfield 2 CO9 . . . . 76 F2
Manfield Gdns CO16 . . . . . .194 B5
Manford Cl IG7 . . . . .312 B6
Manford Cross IG7 . . . . .312 A5
Manford Ct Chigwell IG7 . . .311 F5
1 Redbridge IG7 . . . . .312 A5
Manford Prim Sch IG7 . . . . .311 E5
Manford Way Chigwell IG7 311 E5
Redbridge IG7 . . . . .312 A5
Mangapp Chase CM0 . . . . . .306 A8
Mangapps Rly Mus★ CM0 306 A8
Manilla Ct 5 RM6 . . . . .334 B5
Manilla Rd SS1 . . . . .367 C7
Mannering Gdns SS0 . . . . . .347 A3
Manners Cnr SS2 . . . . .347 E5
Manners Way SS2 . . . . .347 E5
Manning Gr SS16 . . . . .341 C4
Manning Rd
Dagenham RM10 . . . . .354 A5
Felixstowe IP11 . . . . .381 D3
Mannings Cl CB11 . . . . 43 E7
Mannings La IP9 . . . . 38 A2
Manning St RM15 . . . . .371 C5
Mannington Cl IP4 . . . . 18 F5
MANNINGTREE 86 E4
Manningtree Ct CO7 . . . . . .136 F4
Manningtree High Sch
CO11 . . . . 86 B3
Manningtree Mus★ CO11 . . 86 D4
Manningtree Rd
Brantham CO11 . . . . 86 A8
Dedham CO7 . . . . 85 B6
East Bergholt CO7 . . . . 59 F1
Little Bentley CO7 . . . . .139 F8
Stutton IP9 . . . . 61 F2
Manningtree Sta CO11 . . . . . 86 A5
Mannin Rd RM6 . . . . .334 B5
Mannock Dr IG10 . . . . .289 C7
Mannock Mews E18 . . . . . . .310 B2
Manns Way SS6 . . . . .323 C5
Manor Ave Basildon SS13 . .343 C7
Hornchurch RM11 . . . . .336 C6
Manor Cl Aveley RM15 . . . . .371 C5
Cavendish CO10 . . . . 1 C2
Dagenham RM10 . . . . .354 D6
Great Horkesley CO6 . . . . . .109 C7
Ramsden Heath CM11 . . . . .298 C3
Rayleigh SS6 . . . . .345 D8
Romford RM1 . . . . .336 A6
Manor Cl S RM15 . . . . .371 C5
Manor Cotts RM14 . . . . .359 A8
Manor Court Lodge 13
E18 . . . . .310 A2
Manor Cres
Hornchurch RM11 . . . . .336 C6
Little Waltham CM3 . . . . . . .208 B5
Manor Ct 4 Barking IG11 . .352 F5
Chingford E4 . . . . .287 E1
South Benfleet SS7 . . . . . . .344 D7
Southend-on-S SS1 . . . . .367 C7
Waltham Abbey EN9 . . . . . . .265 D6
Manor Dr CM2 . . . . .254 F7
Manor Farm Cl CB9 . . . . 9 B7
Manor Farm Dr E4 . . . . .309 E7
Manor Fields Prim Sch
CM23 . . . . .145 D5
Manor Hatch CM18 . . . . .224 A7
Manor Hatch Cl CM18 . . . . . .224 B7
Manor Ho CM3 . . . . .257 A5
Manor House Gdns 2
E11 . . . . .332 B6
Manor House Way CO7 . . . .192 E8
Manor Inf Sch IG11 . . . . . . .352 F6
Manor Jun Sch IG11 . . . . . .352 F6
Manor La
Great Chesterford CB10 . . . . . 3 D2
Harwich CO12 . . . . 91 B2
Stutton IP9 . . . . 61 E2
Manor Links CM23 . . . . .146 C7
Manor Mews CO7 . . . . .192 E7
Manor Par CO7 . . . . .192 E7
Manor Pl CM7 . . . . .128 A3
Manor Prim Sch The RM1 335 F6
Manor Rd Abridge RM4 . . . .290 E2
Barking IG11 . . . . .352 F6
Basildon SS15 . . . . .341 B7
Bishop's Stortford CM23 . . .146 A7
Chelmsford CM2 . . . . .232 C1
Chigwell IG7 . . . . .311 C5
Colchester CO3 . . . . .135 E7
Dagenham RM10 . . . . .354 D6
Dengie CM0 . . . . .263 D1
Felixstowe IP11 . . . . .381 C1
Grays, Little Thurrock Marshes
RM17 . . . . .378 C8
Grays, West Thurrock
RM20 . . . . .377 C8
Great Holland CO13 . . . . . . .170 A3
Harlow CM17 . . . . .200 C5
Harwich CO12 . . . . 91 B3
Hatfield Peverel CM3 . . . . . .211 C1
Haverhill CB9 . . . . 9 B7
High Beach IG10 . . . . .288 B8
Hockley SS5 . . . . .324 C6
Hoddesdon EN11 . . . . .221 A7
Ilford RM6 . . . . .334 D5
Ipswich IP4 . . . . 17 D8
Little Easton CM6 . . . . .122 F5
Loughton IG10 . . . . .288 C3
Maldon CM9 . . . . .236 A4
Romford RM1 . . . . .336 A6
South Benfleet SS7 . . . . . . .344 D6
Southend-on-S SS0 . . . . .366 D7
South Woodham Ferrers
CM3 .301 C8
Stanford-le-H SS17 . . . . . . .360 D1
Stansted Mountfitchet
CM24 . . . . .119 E5
Sudbury CO10 . . . . 15 E1
Swanscombe DA10 . . . . . . .377 D1
Tilbury RM18 . . . . .379 A5
Waltham Abbey EN9 . . . . . . .265 D6
West Bergholt CO6 . . . . .108 E5
Witham CM8 . . . . .184 A4
Wivenhoe CO7 . . . . .137 C1
Woodham Walter CM9 . . . . .235 E5
Manors CM8 . . . . .156 D4
Manor Sq RM8 . . . . .334 C2
Manor St CM7 . . . . .128 A3
Manors Way CM8 . . . . .156 C4
Manor The IG8 . . . . .311 A3
Manor Trad Est SS7 . . . . . . .344 D7
Manorway IG8 . . . . .310 C5
Manor Way
Brentwood CM14 . . . . .316 A7
Chingford E4 . . . . .309 D6
Corringham SS17 . . . . .361 A1
Holland-on-S CO15 . . . . .196 G6
Northfleet RM17 . . . . .378 A3
Rainham RM13 . . . . .354 E1
Swanscombe DA10 . . . . . . .377 E3
Manor Way Bsns Ctr
RM13 . . . . .369 D8
Manorway The
Corringham SS17 . . . . .361 D1
Stanford-le-H SS17 . . . . . . .360 D2
Mansard Cl RM12 . . . . .336 A2
Mansard Ct CO15 . . . . .196 C5
Mansbrook Bvd IP3 . . . . 38 D7
Man's Cross CO9 . . . . 29 E2
Manse Chase CM9 . . . . .237 A1
Manse Gdns CM6 . . . . .150 D8
Mansel Cl SS9 . . . . .346 E6
Mansel Gr E17 . . . . .309 A2
Manser Ct RM13 . . . . .354 E2
Manser Rd RM13 . . . . .354 E3
Mansfield CM21 . . . . .172 A1
Mansfield Gdns RM12 . . . . .336 D2
Mansfield Hill E4 . . . . .287 B1
Mansfield Rd Ilford IG1 . . . .333 A2
Wanstead E11 . . . . .332 B5
Mansfields CM1 . . . . .230 F1
Mansfield Twrs CO15 . . . . . .195 F2
Manstead Gdns
Dagenham RM6 . . . . .334 C4
Rainham RM13 . . . . .370 B7
Mansted Cl CM13 . . . . .340 E5
Mansted Gdns SS4 . . . . .325 D5
Manston Dr CM23 . . . . .119 B1
Manston Rd CM20 . . . . .223 E8
Manston Way RM12 . . . . . . .355 B6
Manton Rd EN3 . . . . .265 A1
MANUDEN 92 F2
Manuden Prim Sch CM23 . . 93 A2
Manwick Rd IP11 . . . . .381 D2
MANWOOD GREEN 202 F5
Maple Ave
Bishop's Stortford CM23 . . .145 D8
Braintree CM7 . . . . .127 D2
Heybridge CM9 . . . . .237 C6
Southend-on-S SS9 . . . . .365 F8
Upminster RM14 . . . . .356 B8
Maple Cl
Bishop's Stortford CM23 . . .145 D8
Brentwood CM13 . . . . .316 F7
Buckhurst Hill IG9 . . . . .310 D7
Clacton-on-S CO15 . . . . .195 C3
Halstead CO9 . . . . 77 A2
Harwich CO12 . . . . 91 B3
Hornchurch RM12 . . . . .336 B1
Ipswich IP2 . . . . 17 A3
8 Redbridge IG6 . . . . .311 E5
Theydon Bois CM16 . . . . . . .267 D2
Maplecroft La EN9 . . . . .221 E2
Maple Ct
7 Dagenham RM8 . . . . .334 D4
Southend-on-S SS3 . . . . .368 F8
Stanstead Abbotts SG12 . . .197 D3
Mapledene Ave SS5 . . . . . . .301 E2
Maple Dr Chelmsford CM2 . .254 B6
Kirby Cross CO13 . . . . .170 D6
Rayleigh SS6 . . . . .323 C7
South Ockendon RM15 . . . . .357 D1
Witham CM8 . . . . .184 A5
MAPLE END 45 D7
Mapleford Sweep SS16 . . . .342 D4
Maple Gate IG10 . . . . .289 A7
Maple Gr CM23 . . . . .145 D8
Maple Ho IP11 . . . . .381 C4
Maple La CB10 . . . . 45 C5
Maple Leaf CO5 . . . . .186 C7
Mapleleaf Cl SS5 . . . . .324 F7
Maple Leaf Cl SG12 . . . . . . .197 D4
Mapleleafe Gdns IG6 . . . . . .333 B8
Mapleleaf Gdns SS12 . . . . . .321 B6
Maple Lodge IG9 . . . . .288 D1
Maple Mead CM12 . . . . .319 C8
Maple Pk EN11 . . . . .221 C6
Maple Rd Grays RM17 . . . . .378 C8
Great Cornard CO10 . . . . 34 B5
Maple River Ind Est CM20 200 B6
Maples Stanford-le-H SS17 . .360 E2
Waltham Abbey EN9 . . . . . . .266 C4
Maplesfield SS7 . . . . .345 D4
Maple Spring CM23 . . . . .145 D8
Maple Springs EN9 . . . . .266 A7
Maple Sq SS2 . . . . .348 B2
Maple St RM7 . . . . .335 C7
Maplestead SS14 . . . . .342 D8
Maplestead Ct CO9 . . . . 53 D2
Maplestead Rd RM9 . . . . . . .353 B4
Maples The The Harlow CM19 . .223 B3
Rushmere St A IP4 . . . . 18 E8
4 Wickford SS12 . . . . .321 C5
Mapleton Rd E4 . . . . .309 C7
Mapletree La CM4 . . . . .273 E8
Maple Tree La SS16 . . . . .340 F5
Maple Way
Burnham-on-C CM0 . . . . . . .306 A6
Canvey Island SS8 . . . . .363 E3
Colchester CO2 . . . . .136 A4
Great Dunmow CM6 . . . . . . .123 B1
Maplin Cl SS7 . . . . .344 C7
Maplin Ct
Clacton-on-S CO15 . . . . .196 D4
Southend-on-S SS3 . . . . .368 G6
Maplin Gdns SS14 . . . . .342 E5
Maplin Mews SS3 . . . . .368 E6
Maplin Way SS1 . . . . .368 C6
Maplin Way N SS1 . . . . .349 C1
Mapperley Cl 3 E11 . . . . . . .332 A5
Mapperley Dr IG8 . . . . .309 E3
Marasca End CO2 . . . . .163 A7
Maraschino Cres CO2 . . . . . .163 A7
Marbled White Dr IP8 . . . . . . 36 E8
Marchmant Cl RM12 . . . . . . .336 C1
Marconi Gdns CM15 . . . . . . .294 C4
Marconi Rd CM1 . . . . .232 B3
Marcos Rd SS8 . . . . .364 D3
Marcus Ave SS1 . . . . .368 B7
Marcus Chase SS1 . . . . .368 B7
Marcus Cl Colchester CO4 . . .110 B6
Haverhill CB9 . . . . 9 D7
Marcus Gdns SS1 . . . . .368 B7
MARDEN ASH 249 A1
Marden Ash 7 SS15 . . . . . . .341 A6
Marden Cl IG7 . . . . .312 B8
Marden Rd 5 RM1 . . . . .335 E5
Marden Rd RM13 . . . . .354 C3
Mardyke Country Pk★
RM15 . . . . .372 F8
Mardyke Ho RM13 . . . . .354 D3
Mardyke Rd CM20 . . . . .200 A2
Marennes Cres CO7 . . . . . . .192 E7
Maresby Ho E4 . . . . .309 B8
Mareth Rd CO2 . . . . .135 C2
Margaret Ave
Brentwood CM15 . . . . .295 A3
Chingford E4 . . . . .287 B3
Margaret Bondfield Ave
IG11 .353 A5
Margaret Cl
Brightlingsea CO7 . . . . .193 A6
Epping CM16 . . . . .245 F2
Romford RM2 . . . . .336 B6
Waltham Abbey EN9 . . . . . . .265 D6
Margaret Dr RM11 . . . . .336 F4
Margaret Rd
Colchester CO1 . . . . .135 F8
Epping CM16 . . . . .246 A2
Romford RM2 . . . . .336 B6
MARGARET RODING 204 D5
Margaret St
Felixstowe IP11 . . . . .381 C5
Thaxted CM6 . . . . 70 A3
MARGARETTING 275 A8
Margaretting CE Prim Sch
CM4 .274 F8
Margaretting Rd
Chelmsford CM2 . . . . .253 F1
Galleywood CM2 . . . . .254 A2
Wanstead E12 . . . . .332 C3
Writtle CM1 . . . . .253 A6
Margaret Way
Redbridge IG4 . . . . .332 E5
Saffron Walden CB10 . . . . 22 D1
Margarite Way SS12 . . . . . . .321 B7
Margate Rd IP3 . . . . 18 C3
Margery Allingham Pl
CM9 .215 D4
Margery Rd RM8 . . . . .334 D1
Margeth Rd CM12 . . . . .319 C3
Margherita Pl EN9 . . . . .266 A5
Margherita Rd EN9 . . . . .266 A5
Margraten Ave SS8 . . . . .364 D2
Margrave Gdns 4 CM23 . . .145 E5
Marguerite Dr SS9 . . . . .346 F1
Marguerite Way CM23 . . . . .145 C6
Maria Ct CO2 . . . . .136 C5
Mariam Gdns RM12 . . . . . . .336 F2
Marian Cl RM16 . . . . .372 E5
Marian Lawson Ct 2 IG7 . .312 A5
Maria St CO12 . . . . 91 D5
Marie Cl SS17 . . . . .361 A7
Marien Ct E4 . . . . .309 D5
Marigold Ave
Clacton-on-S CO16 . . . . .195 C4
Ipswich IP2 . . . . 16 E3
Marigold Cl
Chelmsford CM1 . . . . .232 F6
Colchester CO4 . . . . .136 E8
Marigold La CM4 . . . . .275 F1
Marigold Pl CM17 . . . . .200 B4
Marina Ave SS6 . . . . .323 C3
Marina Cl SS2 . . . . .347 E4
Marina Dr DA11 . . . . .378 F1
Marina Gdns
Clacton-on-S CO15 . . . . .196 C5
Felixstowe IP11 . . . . .381 C2
Romford RM7 . . . . .335 C6
Marina Mews 1 CO14 . . . . .171 C8
Marina Point CO15 . . . . .195 D1
Marina Rd CM3 . . . . .211 A4
Marine App SS8 . . . . .364 B2
Marine Ave
Canvey Island SS8 . . . . .364 E2
Southend-on-S, Clifftown
SS0 .366 E7
Southend-on-S SS9 . . . . .346 D1
Marine Bldgs 14 CO14 . . . .171 C8
Marine Cl SS9 . . . . .346 A1
Marine Cotts RM13 . . . . .370 D6
Marine Ct
Clacton-on-S CO15 . . . . .195 E1
Frinton-on-S CO13 . . . . .170 F4
Purfleet RM19 . . . . .370 F2
Marine Dr IG11 . . . . .353 B2
Marine Par
Canvey Island SS8 . . . . .364 F2
Harwich CO12 . . . . 91 D3
Mayland CM3 . . . . .260 E1
Southend-on-S, Leigh-on-S
SS9 .346 B1
Southend-on-S SS1 . . . . .367 B7
Marine Par E CO15 . . . . .196 B3
Marine Par W CO15 . . . . .195 E1
Mariner Rd E12 . . . . .352 A8
Mariners Ct
Great Wakering SS3 . . . . . . .350 C3
Greenhithe DA9 . . . . .377 B3
Mariners The CO12 . . . . 91 C3
Mariners Way CM9 . . . . .259 A8
Marion Ave CO15 . . . . .195 E6
Marion Cl IG6 . . . . .311 D3
Marionette Stps 7 SS1 . . . .367 C7
Marion Gr IG8 . . . . .309 E6
Mario Way CO2 . . . . .135 F3
Marisco Cl RM16 . . . . .374 B2
Mariskals SS13 . . . . .343 A6
Maritime Ave CM9 . . . . .237 E3
Maritime Cl DA9 . . . . .377 B2
Maritime Ct 12 IP4 . . . . 17 D5
Maritime Gate DA11 . . . . . . .378 E1
Marjorams Ave IG10 . . . . . . .289 A7
Mark Ave E4 . . . . .287 B3
Market Ave SS12 . . . . .321 C8
Market Cl CO1 . . . . .135 E8
Market End CO6 . . . . .130 F2
Market Field Sch CO7 . . . . .138 A5
Market Gr CO9 . . . . 30 A1
Market Hill Clare CO10 . . . . . 12 B7
Coggeshall CO6 . . . . .131 A2
Halstead CO9 . . . . 76 E2
Haverhill CB9 . . . . 9 A8
Maldon CM9 . . . . .237 A3
Saffron Walden CB10 . . . . 22 D2
Sudbury CO10 . . . . 33 E7
Market Hill Ct CM9 . . . . . . .237 A3
Market Ho 2 CM20 . . . . . . .199 D1
Market Link RM1 . . . . .335 E7
Market Pavement 2
SS14 .342 A5
Market Pl Abridge RM4 . . . .290 B6
Market Pl *continued*
12 Braintree CM7 . . . . .127 F3
Great Dunmow CM6 . . . . . . .123 D1
Ingatestone CM4 . . . . .274 B4
Maldon CM9 . . . . .236 F2
Romford RM1 . . . . .335 E6
Saffron Walden CB10 . . . . 22 D2
Southend-on-S SS1 . . . . .367 A7
Tilbury RM18 . . . . .379 A5
Market Pl The CO16 . . . . . . .168 F7
Market Rd Chelmsford CM1 232 B2
Wickford SS12 . . . . .321 C7
Market Row CB10 . . . . 22 D1
Market Sq Basildon SS14 . . .342 A5
6 Bishop's Stortford CM23 145 F7
6 Chelmsford CM1 . . . . .232 B2
Rochford SS4 . . . . .325 F2
South Woodham Ferrers
CM3 .301 E7
Waltham Abbey EN9 . . . . . . .265 C6
Market St
7 Bishop's Stortford
CM23 . . . . .145 F7
11 Braintree CM7 . . . . .127 F3
Harlow CM17 . . . . .200 C4
Harwich CO12 . . . . 91 E6
Saffron Walden CB10 . . . . 22 D2
Wallend E6 . . . . .352 A3
Market Wlk CB10 . . . . 22 D1
Markfield Gdns E4 . . . . .287 B2
Mark Hall Cycle Mus & Gdns★
CM20 . . . . .200 B3
Mark Hall Moors CM20 . . . . .200 B3
MARK HALL NORTH 200 A3
Mark Hall Sch CM17 . . . . . . .200 C3
MARK HALL SOUTH 200 A1
Markham Ho 1 RM10 . . . . .335 A1
Markhams SS17 . . . . .360 F3
Markhams Chase SS15 . . . . .341 D7
Marking's Field CB10 . . . . . . 22 E2
Mark La DA12 . . . . .379 E1
Markland Cl CM2 . . . . .254 C3
Markland Dr CM9 . . . . .236 E1
Marklay Dr CM3 . . . . .301 C7
Mark Rd CM0 . . . . .263 F6
Mark's Ave CM5 . . . . .249 A4
Marks Cl Billericay CM12 . . .296 F4
Ingatestone CM4 . . . . .273 F1
Marks Ct SS1 . . . . .367 C7
MARKS GATE 312 E1
Marks Gate Inf Sch RM6 . . .334 E8
Marks Gate Jun Sch RM6 . .334 E8
Marks Gdns CM7 . . . . .128 C3
Marks Hall CM6 . . . . .204 D3
Marks Hall Ctry Est★ CO6 130 E7
Marks Hall La CM6 . . . . .204 E3
Marks Hall Rd CO6 . . . . .130 E6
Marks La CM3 . . . . .299 F8
Marks Rd RM7 . . . . .335 D6
MARKS TEY 132 E4
Marks Tey Rdbt CO6 . . . . . . .133 A4
Marks Tey Sta CO6 . . . . .133 B4
Mark Wade Cl E12 . . . . .332 D2
Markwells CM22 . . . . 94 D2
Markwell Wood CM19 . . . . .223 B2
Markyate Rd RM8 . . . . .353 B7
Marlands CM21 . . . . .172 E4
Marlands Rd
Redbridge IG5 . . . . .332 E8
Woodford IG5 . . . . .310 F1
Marlborough Ave CM0 . . . . .263 E3
Marlborough Cl
Bishop's Stortford CM23 . . .145 F5
Clacton-on-S CO15 . . . . .195 C3
Grays RM16 . . . . .373 C4
South Benfleet SS7 . . . . .344 D7
Upminster RM14 . . . . .337 E3
Marlborough Ct
10 Buckhurst Hill IG9 . . . . .310 C8
Felixstowe IP11 . . . . .381 D2
Haverhill CB9 . . . . 8 E7
Marlborough Dr
Redbridge IG5 . . . . .332 E8
Sudbury CO10 . . . . 33 F8
Marlborough Gdns RM14 . .337 E4
Marlborough Ho CM14 . . . . .316 B6
Marlborough Pl SS1 . . . . . . .366 F7
Marlborough Rd
Braintree CM7 . . . . .128 A4
2 Chelmsford CM2 . . . . .232 A1
Chingford E4 . . . . .309 B4
Dagenham RM8 . . . . .353 C8
Ipswich IP4 . . . . 18 A6
Pilgrims Hatch CM15 . . . . . .294 A3
Romford RM7 . . . . .335 B7
Southend-on-S SS1 . . . . .367 D8
Wanstead E18 . . . . .332 A8
13 Woodford E18 . . . . .310 A1
Marlborough Terr CM2 . . . .232 A1
Marlborough Way CM12 . . .297 A5
Marlborough Wlk SS5 . . . . .324 C6
Marle Gdns EN9 . . . . .265 C7
Marlescroft Way IG10 . . . . .289 B4
Marlin Cl SS7 . . . . .345 E6
Marlow Ave RM19 . . . . .371 A2
Marlowe Cl Billericay CM12 297 B5
Braintree CM7 . . . . .155 A8
Maldon CM9 . . . . .259 A8
Redbridge IG6 . . . . .311 C2
Marlowe Gdns RM3 . . . . . . .314 C2
Marlowe Ho 12 IG8 . . . . . . .311 A3
Marlowe Rd
Clacton-on-S CO15 . . . . .220 G8
Jaywick CO15 . . . . .195 A1
Marlowe Way CO3 . . . . .134 F6
Marlow Gdns SS2 . . . . .347 E4
Marlpits Rd CM3, CM9 . . . . .257 E4
Marlyon Rd IG6 . . . . .312 B5
Marmaduke Ave SS6 . . . . . . .323 B4
Marmion App E4 . . . . .309 A6
Marmion Ave E4 . . . . .309 A6
Marmion Cl E4 . . . . .309 A6
Marney Cl CM2 . . . . .254 E8
Marney Dr SS14 . . . . .342 F5
Marney Way CO13 . . . . .171 B6
Marquis Cl CM23 . . . . .145 B7
Marquis Ct IG11 . . . . .352 E7
Marram Cl CO3 . . . . .134 B6
Marram Ct RM17 . . . . .378 E8
Mar Rd RM15 . . . . .357 C1
Marriages Yard CO1 . . . . . . .136 B7
Marriotts CM17 . . . . .200 C5
Marsden Ct CO3 . . . . .134 E4
Marsden Ho 1 RM3 . . . . . . .314 F4
Marshall Cl Feering CO5 . . .158 D4
Southend-on-S SS9 . . . . .346 A3
Marshalls SS4 . . . . .325 D4
Marshalls Cl SS6 . . . . .323 F2
Marshalls Dr RM1 . . . . .335 E8
Marshalls Park Sch RM1 . . .313 E1
Marshalls Piece CM6 . . . . . .124 D6
Marshalls Rd
Braintree CM7 . . . . .127 E1
Romford RM7 . . . . .335 D7
Marshbarns CM23 . . . . .145 C8
Marsh Cres CO5 . . . . .164 A8
Marsh Farm Ctry Pk★
CM3 .301 E5
Marsh Farm La CO7 . . . . . . .166 D3
Marsh Farm Rd CM3 . . . . . . .301 D4
Marshfoot Rd RM16, RM17 373 F1
Marshgate Ctr CM19 . . . . . .222 D8
Marsh Green Prim Sch
RM10 . . . . .354 A3
Marsh Green Rd RM10 . . . . .354 A4
Marsh Hill EN9 . . . . .243 E4
Marsh La Fobbing SS17 . . . . .361 D5
Harlow CM17 . . . . .200 E5
Mountnessing CM13 . . . . . . .296 A7
Stanstead Abbotts SG12 . . .197 D4
Marsh Rd
Burnham-on-C CM0 . . . . . . .307 B7
Thorington Street CO6, CO7 . 57 E6
Tillingham CM0 . . . . .264 B4
Marsh St Dartford DA1 . . . . .376 A3
Dartford DA1 . . . . .376 A5
Marsh View Ct SS16 . . . . . . .342 E3
Marsh Way
Brightlingsea CO7 . . . . .192 E6
Rainham RM13 . . . . .369 D8
Marston Ave RM10 . . . . .335 A1
Marston Beck CM2 . . . . .233 A2
Marston Cl RM10 . . . . .335 A1
Marston Ho RM17 . . . . .378 A8
Marston Rd
Hoddesdon EN11 . . . . .221 B7
Woodford IG5 . . . . .310 E1
Martello Cvn Pk CO14 . . . . .171 C8
Martello Rd 8 CO14 . . . . . .171 C8
Marten Rd E17 . . . . .309 A1
Marten's La CO6 . . . . 56 F8
Martens Mdw CM7 . . . . .128 D3
Martham Cl IG6 . . . . .311 B2
Martina Terr 9 IG6 . . . . . . .311 E5
Martin Cl CM11 . . . . .297 B1
Martindale Ave SS15 . . . . . .319 D2
Martin Dr Dartford DA2 . . . .376 C1
Rainham RM13 . . . . .355 B1
Martin End CO2 . . . . .162 A5
Martinet Gn IP3 . . . . 18 C1
Martingale SS7 . . . . .345 B5
Martingale Cl CM11 . . . . . . .297 D5
Martingale Dr CM1 . . . . .232 F7
Martingale Rd CM11 . . . . . . .297 D5
Martin Gdns RM8 . . . . .353 D8
Martini Dr EN3 . . . . .265 A2
Martin Rd Aveley RM15 . . . .371 D5
Dagenham RM8 . . . . .353 D8
Ipswich IP2 . . . . 17 C4
Martins Cl SS17 . . . . .360 D3
Martin's Ct SS2 . . . . .348 A1
Martinsdale CO15 . . . . .195 F6
Martinsfield Cl IG7 . . . . .311 E6
Martins Mews Haverhill CB9 . . 8 C8
South Benfleet SS7 . . . . .344 C4
Martin's Rd CO9 . . . . 76 E1
Martinstown Cl RM11 . . . . . .337 A5
Martin Wlk SS5 . . . . .324 F4
Martlesham Cl RM12 . . . . . . .355 C7
Martley Dr IG2 . . . . .333 B6
Martock Ave SS0 . . . . .347 A5
Martyns Gr SS0 . . . . .347 B2
Martyns Rise CO10 . . . . 15 C5
Marvens CM2 . . . . .254 D3
Marvens The IP8 . . . . 16 A1
Marwell Cl RM1 . . . . .336 A6
Maryborough Gr CO2 . . . . . .136 B2
Mary Frank Ho CO4 . . . . . . .136 C8
Mary La N CO7 . . . . .139 A8
Maryland Ct 1 CO2 . . . . . . .136 A1
Marylands CO13 . . . . .170 E3
Marylands Ave SS5 . . . . .324 D7
Mary La S CO7 . . . . .139 B6
Mary Macarthur Ho
8 Belvedere DA17 . . . . .369 A3
11 Dagenham RM10 . . . . . . .335 A1
Mary McArthur Pl CM24 . . .119 E8
Maryon Rd IP3 . . . . 18 B1
Mary Park Gdns CM23 . . . .145 F4
Mary Rose Cl RM16 . . . . . . .372 C2
Mary Ruck Way CM77 . . . . .155 B5
Marys Ho CO5 . . . . .158 C2
Mary Slessor Ho 14 DA17 .369 A3
Mary Warner Rd CO7 . . . . . .111 E7
MASCALLS 315 F5
Mascalls Gdns CM14 . . . . . .315 F6
Mascalls La
Brentwood CM14 . . . . .315 F6
Great Warley CM14 . . . . .316 A4
Mascalls The CM2 . . . . .254 E8
Mascalls Way CM2 . . . . .254 E8
Mascot Ct CO15 . . . . .195 F5
Mascot Sq CO4 . . . . .136 D5
Masefield Cl RM3 . . . . .314 C2
Masefield Cres RM3 . . . . . . .314 C2
Masefield Ct 2 CM14 . . . . .316 C6
Masefield Dr
Colchester CO3 . . . . .134 F6
Upminster RM14 . . . . .337 C4
Masefield Gdns E6 . . . . .352 A1
Masefield Rd
Braintree CM7 . . . . .155 A8
Dartford DA1 . . . . .376 B2
Grays RM16 . . . . .373 E4
Maldon CM9 . . . . .259 A8
Mashay Rd CO9 . . . . 30 D5
MASHBURY 206 C4

Mashbury Rd
Great Waltham CM3 207 B7
Mashbury CM1 206 D6
Mashiters Hill RM1 313 D2
Mashiters Wlk RM1 335 E8
Mason Cl CO2 135 B3
Mason Dr RM3 314 E1
Mason Rd
Clacton-on-S CO16 195 B3
Colchester CO1 109 F1
Woodford IG8 309 E6
Masons Cl IP4 17 F6
Masons Ct
Bishop's Stortford CM23 145 E7
Stansted Mountfitchet CM24 119 D6
Mason Way EN9 265 F6
Massingham Dr CO6 105 A6
Masterlord Bsns Pk IP3 18 E1
Masterman Wharf 12 CM23 145 F7
Masters Ct 3 RM2 336 B6
Masthead Cl DA2 376 C3
Matchett Dr CO4 110 B6
MATCHING 202 B4
Matching Field CM15 271 F2
Matching Gn SS14 320 D1
MATCHING GREEN 202 D3
Matching Green CE Prim Sch CM17 202 D2
Matching La
Bishop's Stortford CM23 145 D8
White Roding or White Roding CM5, CM6 203 C6
Matching Rd
Harlow, Harlow Tye CM17 201 B4
Harlow, Matching CM22 202 B8
Hatfield Heath CM22 174 B2
MATCHING TYE 201 E3
Matfield Cl CM1 232 D7
Mathams Dr CM23 145 D5
Mathart Ct E4 309 D4
Mather Way IP2 17 D4
Mathews Ave E6 352 A3
Mathews Cl CO9 77 A3
Mathews Mead CM11 320 B5
Mathews Villas CM19 222 E6
Mathieson Ho E4 287 E2
Matilda Way CM6 151 E6
Matlock Cl 8 IP2 16 C2
Matlock Ct E18 309 F2
Matlock Gdns RM12 336 E1
Matlock Ho 13 RM3 314 D4
Matlock Rd SS8 363 F3
Matson Ct IG8 309 E3
Matson Rd IP1 16 F8
Matthews Cl Romford RM3 314 F2
Stratford St M CO7 58 C1
Maude St IP3 17 E4
Maud Gdns IG11 352 F3
Maudlyn Rd CO1, CO4 136 C6
Maugham Cl SS12 321 D5
Maunder Cl RM16 372 D2
Maunds Farm CM18 223 E4
Maunds Hatch CM18 223 E4
Maurice Cl CB10 45 B1
Maurice Ct SS8 364 D2
Maurice Ho 5 CM14 316 C6
Maurice Lewis Pl 5 DA11 379 A1
Maurice Rd SS8 364 D3
Mavis Gr RM12 336 E2
Mawney Cl RM7 313 B1
Mawney Rd RM7 335 C7
Mawney Sch The RM7 335 D6
Maxey Gdns RM9 353 E8
Maxey Rd RM9 353 E8
Maximfeldt Rd DA8 369 E1
Maxim Rd DA8 369 D2
Maximus Dr CO4 110 B6
Maxwell Ct IG7 312 B7
Maya Angelou Ct E4 309 C6
Maya Cl SS3 368 E7
Mayall Cl EN3 265 A1
May Ave SS8 364 C3
Maybank Ave
Hornchurch RM12 355 C7
Woodford E18 310 B1
Maybank Lodge 2 RM12 355 C7
Maybank Rd E18 310 C2
Maybells Commercial Est IG11 353 D3
Mayberry Wlk CO2 136 A3
Maybrick Rd RM11 336 C5
Maybrook Ct E11 332 B2
Maybury Cl Loughton IG10 289 B5
Marks Tey CO6 132 F3
Maybury Rd Barking IG11 353 A3
Ipswich IP3 18 B1
Maybush Rd RM11 336 E4
Maycroft Ave RM17 373 D1
Maycroft Gdns RM17 373 D1
May Ct RM17 378 E8
Mayda Cl CO9 76 D1
Maydeb Ct RM6 334 F5
Maydells SS13 343 B5
Maydells Ct SS13 343 B5
Maydene CM3 301 D7
Mayer Rd EN9 265 B3
Mayesbrook Rd
Barking IG11 352 F4
Dagenham IG3, RM8 334 B1
Mayes Cl CM23 146 D8
Mayesford Rd RM6 334 C4
Mayes La Chelmsford CM2 255 E5
Danbury CM3 256 E6
Harwich CO12 90 C1
Mayespark Prim Sch IG3 334 A1
Mayes Pl CM6 97 A6
Mayfair Ave Basildon SS13 343 C8
Dagenham RM6 334 D5
Ilford IG1 333 A3
Mayfair Ct CO15 195 F3
Mayfair Gdns IG8 310 A3
Mayfair Ind Area CM3 281 F6
Mayfield Swanscombe DA10 377 E1
Mayfield *continued*
Waltham Abbey EN9 265 D5
Mayfield Ave
Hullbridge SS5 301 E2
Southend-on-S SS2 347 E4
Woodford IG8 310 A4
Mayfield Cl Colchester CO4 110 C2
Harlow CM17 200 F4
Mayfield Ct EN9 266 A5
Mayfield Ctr CM0 306 A5
Mayfield Gdns CM14 294 C1
Mayfield Pk CM23 145 D3
Mayfield Rd
Belvedere DA17 369 C2
Chingford E4 309 D8
Dagenham RM8 334 C3
Ipswich IP4 18 C7
Writtle CM1 231 A2
Mayfields RM16 373 C4
Mayfield Sch RM8 334 C3
Mayflower Ave CO12 91 E5
Mayflower Cl
Colchester CO3 134 D6
Lower Nazeing EN9 243 E8
Southend-on-S SS2 347 B6
South Ockendon RM15 357 C1
Mayflower Ct
Canvey Island SS8 364 D2
Chipping Ongar CM5 249 A4
Harlow CM19 223 B4
Mayflower Dr CM9 259 A7
Mayflower Gdns CM23 145 B6
Mayflower High Sch CM12 297 C5
Mayflower Ho
2 Barking IG11 352 D4
Brentwood CM13 316 C4
Harwich CO12 91 D6
Mayflower Prim Sch The CO12 91 B4
Mayflower Rd
5 Billericay CM11 297 B2
Grays RM16 372 C1
Mayflower Ret Pk SS14 320 D2
Mayflowers SS7 344 B7
Mayflower Way
Chipping Ongar CM5 249 A4
Sudbury CO10 15 F2
Mayfly Cl IP8 36 E8
Mayford Way CO16 195 B6
Maygreen Cres RM11 336 A4
Mayhew Cl E4 309 A7
Mayhill Lodge RM3 314 C2
MAYLAND 283 B8
Mayland Ave SS8 364 A2
Mayland Cl Heybridge CM9 237 D4
Mayland CM3 283 A7
Mayland Gn CM3 283 B8
Mayland Hill CM3 283 C5
Mayland Mans 4 IG11 352 B5
Mayland Quay CM3 260 E1
Mayland Rd CM8 184 A2
Maylands Ave RM12 355 B8
Maylands Dr CM77 154 D8
MAYLANDSEA 260 F1
Maylandsea Prim Sch CM3 282 F8
Maylands Way RM3 315 C4
Maylins Dr CM21 172 D2
Maynard Cl CM6 123 D1
Maynard Ct
2 Holdbrook EN3 265 A1
Waltham Abbey EN9 265 F5
Maynards RM11 336 E4
Maynards Villas CM6 122 F5
Mayne Crest CM1 232 E6
Maypole Cl CB11 43 C7
Maypole Cres IG6 311 D3
Maypole Dr Chigwell IG7 312 A7
St Osyth CO16 194 B4
MAYPOLE GREEN 135 D1
Maypole Green Rd CO2 135 C1
Maypole Rd Tiptree CO5 186 C6
Wickham Bishops CM8, CM9 212 F2
Maypole St CM17 200 C1
Maypole Terr CB9 9 A7
Maypole The CM6 69 F3
May Rd Chingford E4 309 A4
Ipswich IP3 18 C2
Mays Ct IP11 381 D3
Maysent Ave CM7 127 F5
May's La CO7 84 E4
Maystocks E18 332 C8
Mayswood Gdns RM10 354 C6
May Terr IG1 352 B8
Maytime Prep Sch E12 333 A1
Maytree Cl RM13 354 E3
Maytree Ct CO5 186 C6
Maytree Gdns CM22 94 B3
Maytree Wlk SS7 344 C6
May Villa RM2 314 D1
Mayville Rd IG1 352 B7
Maywin Dr RM11 336 F3
May Wlk Chelmsford CM2 254 C7
Elsenham CM24 94 A1
Maze Green Hts CM23 145 C7
Maze Green Rd CM23 145 D7
Mazers Ct 14 CM7 127 F2
Maze The SS9 346 D7
Mazoe Cl CM23 145 F5
Mazoe Rd CM23 145 F5
Meachen Rd CO2 136 C5
Mead Cl Grays RM16 373 B4
Loughton IG10 289 B7
Romford RM2 314 A1
Mead Cres E4 309 C6
Mead Ct Clacton-on-S CO15 195 E3
Stansted Mountfitchet CM24 119 D7
Waltham Abbey EN9 265 B5
Meade Cl CM11 297 D5
Meade Rd CM11 297 D5
Meadgate SS13 343 C8
Meadgate Ave
Great Baddow CM2 254 D8
Woodford IG8 310 E5
Meadgate Prim Sch CM2 254 E8
Meadgate Rd EN9 221 C3
Meadgate Terr CM2 254 D8
Mead Gr RM6 334 D8
Mead Lodge 3 EN11 221 D8
Meadowbrook Ct CO1 136 B7
Meadow Brown Ct CM7 127 E1
Meadow Cl
12 Barking IG11 352 F5
Chelmondiston IP9 63 F7
Chingford E4 287 B1
Clacton-on-S CO15 196 B7
Elmstead Market CO7 137 F6
Great Bromley CO7 139 A6
Halstead CO9 103 F8
Linford SS17 375 A3
Panfield CM7 127 A7
Romford RM3 314 C7
Thundersley SS7 345 B6
Meadow Cres IP3 18 F1
Meadowcroft CM24 119 E7
Meadowcroft Way CO13 170 F7
Meadow Cross EN9 265 E5
Meadow Ct Billericay CM11 297 C2
Canvey Island SS8 363 F6
Harlow CM18 223 E4
Wickford SS11 321 E8
Meadow Dr Basildon SS16 360 B8
Southend-on-S SS1 367 E7
MEADOWEND 29 C5
Meadowford CB11 42 F1
Meadowgate CM4 275 F2
Meadow Grass Cl CO3 134 B6
Meadow La Sudbury CO10 33 E7
West Mersea CO5 218 C5
Wickford SS11 299 E3
Meadowland Rd SS11 322 A6
Meadowlands
Bishop's Stortford CM23 119 A2
Hornchurch RM11 336 E4
Meadow Mews CM3 301 B8
Meadow Pk CM7 154 E8
Meadow Pl CO10 33 E6
Meadow Rd Barking IG11 353 A5
Colchester CO2 135 D1
Dagenham RM9 353 F6
Epping CM16 245 F2
Grays RM16 373 C5
Great Chesterford CB10 3 D3
Hadleigh SS7 345 E2
Hullbridge SS5 301 E2
Loughton IG10 288 E4
Rettendon CM3 300 C5
Romford RM7 335 C3
Meadow Rise
Billericay CM11 297 C2
Blackmore CM4 272 E8
Meadows Cl CM13 317 C4
Meadows Cotts 1 CM4 274 B3
Meadowside
Braintree CM7 127 E5
Chelmsford CM2 232 C3
Rayleigh SS6 323 D2
South Benfleet SS7 344 B3
Meadow Side CM1 232 B3
Meadowside Ct CM3 209 E1
Meadowside Gdns IP4 18 E8
Meadowside Rd RM14 356 C7
Meadows The
Bishop's Stortford CM23 145 E5
3 Chelmsford CM2 232 C2
Ingrave CM13 317 C4
Sawbridgeworth CM21 173 A2
Meadowsweet Cl CM23 145 C6
Meadowvale Cl IP4 17 F7
Meadow View
Basildon SS16 340 E4
Bicknacre CM3 256 E1
Great Bardfield CM7 72 B2
Kirby-le-S CO13 143 D1
Pilgrims Hatch CM15 294 C3
St Osyth CO16 194 B4
Tiptree CO5 186 B5
Meadow View Cl CO3 134 E5
Meadow View Rd CO10 33 D5
Meadow View Wlk SS8 363 E4
Meadow Way
Abberton CO5 163 B2
Black Notley CM77 155 C5
Burnham-on-C CM0 306 A7
Chigwell IG7 311 C8
Clacton-on-S CO15 220 G7
Hockley SS5 324 E6
Latchingdon CM3 282 A6
Sawbridgeworth CM21 173 A1
Upminster RM14 337 C1
Wickford SS12 321 E3
Meadow Way The CM11 297 C2
Meadow Wlk
5 Chelmsford CM2 232 C2
Dagenham RM9 353 F6
Wanstead E18 332 A7
Mead Park Ind Est CM20 199 F4
Mead Pastures CM9 235 D3
Mead Path CM2 253 F8
Mead Prim Sch RM3 314 F4
Meads Cl CM4 274 B4
Meads Ct CM15 316 E8
Meadside CM7 73 B3
Meads La IG3 333 F4
Meads The Basildon SS16 343 A4
Chelmsford CM2 232 A1
Ingatestone CM4 274 B4
Stansted Mountfitchet CM24 119 F6
Upminster RM14 337 E2
Wicken Bonhunt CB11 66 A7
Meadsway CM13 316 C4
Mead The Basildon SS15 341 B8
Brightlingsea CO7 192 F8
Great Cornard CO10 34 B4
Great Dunmow CM6 123 C2
Hoddesdon EN10 221 B2
Thaxted CM6 70 A3
Meadway
Canvey Island SS8 364 C2
Gosfield CO9 102 E8
Grays RM17 373 D2
Hoddesdon EN11 221 A4
Ilford IG3 352 E8
Lawford CO11 86 B3
Maldon CM9 237 B1
Rayleigh SS6 323 E1
Meadway *continued*
Romford RM2 314 A1
South Benfleet SS7 344 C7
Woodford IG8 310 C5
Meadway Ct RM8 334 F2
Meadway The
Buckhurst Hill IG9 288 D1
Loughton IG10 288 F3
Southend-on-S SS0 366 B8
Mead Wlk CM5 248 F1
Meakins Cl SS9 347 A7
Mealings Mead CM16 246 A6
Meals Pl 3 CM2 232 F4
Meath Rd IG1 333 C1
Medbree Ct RM16 374 A8
Medebridge Rd
Grays RM15, RM16 373 A8
South Ockendon RM16 358 A1
Mede Way CO7 137 C3
Medick Ct RM17 378 E8
Medina Bsns Ctr CB11 22 F1
Medina Rd RM17 373 D2
Medlar Cl CM8 184 A4
Medlar Dr RM15 357 E1
Medlar Rd RM17 378 E8
Medlars Mead CM22 174 F5
Medley Rd CM77 126 F2
Medley Way CM0 262 D7
Medoc Cl SS13 343 C8
Medora Rd RM7 335 D7
Medusa Ct Harwich CO12 91 B2
Holland-on-S CO15 196 E5
Meduza Ct 7 DA12 379 D1
Medway CM0 306 A6
Medway Ave CM8 183 D2
Medway Cl
Chelmsford CM1 231 D4
Ilford IG1 352 C7
Medway Cres SS9 346 B1
Medway Rd IP3 17 F2
Meekings Rd CO10 34 B8
Meers The CO13 170 E6
MEESDEN 64 A6
Meeson Bglws CM3 300 C5
Meeson Mdws CM9 258 E8
Meeson's La RM17 372 F1
Meesons Mead SS4 325 E3
Meeting Field CO10 15 C7
Meeting La
East Mersea CO5 191 C1
Ridgewell CO9 29 B7
Meeting Wlk CB9 9 B7
Meggison Way SS7 344 C3
Meggy Tye CM2 233 B5
Megs Way CM7 128 B2
Meister Cl IG1 333 D3
Melanie Ct SS4 325 D6
Melba Ct CM1 231 C1
Melba Gdns RM18 379 B7
Melbourne Ave CM1 231 E5
Melbourne Chase CO2 136 B1
Melbourne Ct
Chelmsford CM1 231 E5
Tilbury RM18 378 E6
Melbourne Gdns RM6 334 E6
Melbourne Par CM1 231 E5
Melbourne Park Prim Sch CM1 231 F6
Melbourne Quay 8 DA11 379 B1
Melbourne Rd
Clacton-on-S CO15 195 E4
Ilford IG1 333 B3
Ipswich IP4 18 D7
Tilbury RM18 378 E6
Melcombe Rd SS7 344 C3
Meldrum Rd IG3 334 A2
Melford Ave IG11 352 F6
Melford Cl IP4 18 F5
Melford Gr CM77 154 B7
Melford Pl CM14 294 C1
Melford Rd Cavendish CO10 1 E2
Ilford IG1 333 D2
Sudbury CO10 15 D2
Melford Way IP11 381 A3
Melksham Cl RM3 314 F3
Melksham Dr RM3 314 F3
Melksham Gdns RM3 314 F3
Melksham Gn RM3 314 F3
Mellings CO6 130 F3
Mellis Ct IP11 381 B5
Mellish Cl IG11 352 F4
Mellish Gdns IG8 310 A5
Mellish Way RM11 336 C6
Mellor Chase CO3 134 E7
Mellor Cl CM4 274 B4
Mellow Mead SS15 341 B8
Mellow Purgess SS15 341 C6
Mellow Purgess Cl SS15 341 C6
Mellow Purgess End SS15 341 C6
Mellows Rd IG5 332 F8
Mell Rd CM9 216 E1
Melplash Cl IP3 18 E4
Melplash Rd IP3 18 E4
Melrose Gdns
Clacton-on-S CO15 196 C5
Ipswich IP4 18 B8
Melrose Rd CO5 218 C6
Melso Cl CO10 34 A5
Melstock Ave RM14 356 C8
Melton Cl CO16 195 A4
Melton Gdns RM1 335 F4
Melville Ct Romford RM3 314 E3
Southend-on-S SS1 367 D6
Melville Dr SS12 321 D4
Melville Heath CM3 301 E6
Melville Rd Ipswich IP4 17 F5
Rainham RM13 355 B1
Romford RM5 313 B2
Memnon Ct CO2 135 F3
Memorial Ave E12 332 E2
Memorial Hts IG2 333 D5
Memory Cl CM9 259 A7
Menai Ct IP1 17 B7
Mendip Cl Rayleigh SS6 323 D4
Wickford SS11 321 E7
Mendip Cres SS0 347 A4
Mendip Dr IP5 18 F6
Mendip Ho DA11 378 D1
Mendip Rd
Chelmsford CM1 231 D6
Mendip Rd *continued*
Hornchurch RM11 336 A4
Ilford IG2 333 E6
Southend-on-S SS0 347 A4
Mendips The SS9 346 F5
Mendlesham Cl CO16 195 B4
Mendoza Cl RM11 336 E6
Menin Rd CO2 135 D4
Menish Way CM2 233 A3
Menthone Pl RM11 336 D4
Mentmore SS16 341 B4
Menzies Ave SS15 340 F6
Meon Cl CM1 232 C6
Meopham Ct CO2 136 B4
Meppel Ave SS8 364 A6
Mercantile Ho 1 CO1 135 F6
Mercer Ave SS3 350 A4
Mercer Rd CM11 297 D5
Mercers CM19 223 A5
Mercers Ave CM23 145 C4
Mercers Row CB10 22 D1
Mercers Way 2 CO1 135 E8
Merchant St CM3 301 E7
Mercia Cl CM2 255 A5
Mercury Cl Colchester CO2 135 A3
Wickford SS11 321 F8
Mercury Ct 8 RM1 335 F6
Mercury Gdns RM1 335 F6
Mercury Pl CM9 236 F5
Merdle Sq CM1 231 F6
Merebridge Rd RM16 372 F6
Meredene SS14 342 F5
Meredith Rd
Clacton-on-S CO15 195 E3
Grays RM16 374 A2
Merediths Cl CO7 164 B8
Merefield CM21 172 E1
Mere Gdns IP4 18 F4
Meresmans RM15 371 D7
Mereworth Rd CM3 301 C5
Meriadoc Dr CM3 301 D6
Meridan Ho EN10 221 C2
Meriden Cl IG6 311 C2
Meriden Ct CO15 196 A5
Meridian Bsns Pk EN9 265 B4
Meridian Ct RM17 378 B7
Meridian Way
Stanstead Abbotts SG12 197 B5
Waltham Abbey EN9 265 B4
Meridien RM1 335 F4
Meriel Wlk DA9 377 B3
Merilies Cl SS0 347 B4
Merilies Gdns SS0 347 B3
Merino Cl E11 332 C7
Merivale Cl CO11 86 C3
Merivale Rd CO11 86 B3
Merlin Cl Grays RM16 372 E3
Redbridge IG6 312 C6
Romford RM5 313 D4
Waltham Abbey EN9 266 A5
Merlin Ct
Canvey Island SS8 364 B3
Ipswich IP2 17 B4
Merlin End CO4 110 F1
Merlin Gdns RM5 313 D4
Merlin Gr IG6 311 C3
Merlin Pl CM1 231 F5
Merlin Rd Ipswich IP2 16 C3
Romford RM5 313 D4
Wanstead E12 332 D2
Merlin Way
North Weald Bassett CM16 247 A6
Wickford SS11 299 D1
Mermagen Dr RM13 355 B5
Mermaid Way CM9 259 B8
Merriam Cl Brantham CO11 86 D8
Chingford E4 309 C5
Merricks La SS16 342 E3
Merrielands Cres RM9 353 F3
Merrielands Ret Pk RM9 353 F3
Merrilees Cres CO15 196 D6
Merrill Hts IP2 17 C3
Merrill Pl 2 CM23 145 E5
Merring Way CM19 222 F7
Merrion Cl 7 IP2 16 C2
Merritt Ho RM1 335 F4
Merrivale SS7 344 C2
Merrivale Ave IG4 332 D7
Merry Fiddlers RM8 334 F2
Merryfield App SS9 346 E4
Merryfields Ave SS5 324 D7
Merryhill Cl E4 287 B2
Merrylands SS15 341 A7
Merrylands Chase CM13 340 D7
Merrylands Prim Sch SS15 341 A6
Merrymeade Chase CM15 294 D1
Merrymount Gdns CO15 196 B5
Mersea Ave CO5 218 B6
Mersea Cres SS12 321 F6
Mersea Ct CO5 218 B7
Mersea Fleet Way CM7 128 C1
Mersea Ho 4 IG11 352 B6
Mersea Island Mus* CO5 218 B6
Mersea Island Sch CO5 218 C6
Mersea Island Vineyard* CO5 218 H8
Mersea Point Nature Reserve* CO5 192 C3
Mersea Rd
Abberton CO2, CO5 163 B5
Colchester CO2 136 A3
Peldon CO5 189 F5
Mersea View CO16 193 A3
Mersey Ave RM14 337 D5
Mersey Rd Ipswich IP3 17 F2
Witham CM8 183 E2
Mersey Way CM1 231 C5
Merstham Dr CO16 195 C6
Merten Rd RM6 334 E4
Merton Ct Blackheath CO2 163 A7
Redbridge IG4 332 E5
Merton Pl Grays RM16 374 A2
Littlebury CB11 21 E4
South Woodham Ferrers CM3 301 F6
Merton Rd Barking IG11 352 F5
Hockley SS5 324 A8
Ilford IG3 333 F4
Merton Rd *continued*
South Benfleet SS7 344 C4
Messant Cl RM3 314 D1
Messines Rd CO2 135 D5
MESSING 159 D3
Messing-cum-Inworth Prim Sch CO5 159 C2
Messing Gn CO5 159 D2
Mess Rd SS3 368 F5
Meteor Rd SS0 366 D8
Meteor Way CM1 231 F2
Metford Cres EN3 265 A1
Methersgate SS14 342 C7
Methuen Rd DA17 369 B2
Metsons La CM1 251 E2
Metz Ave SS8 364 A4
Mews Ct CM2 232 B1
Mews Pl IG8 310 A6
Mews The
Bishop's Stortford CM22 146 A3
Felixstowe IP11 381 E4
Felixstowe IP11 381 F4
Frinton-on-S CO13 171 A5
Grays RM17 373 C2
Harlow CM18 223 E4
Harwich CO12 91 C3
Hockley SS5 324 C6
Panfield CM7 126 A7
Redbridge IG4 332 D6
Romford RM1 335 E7
Sawbridgeworth CM21 172 E3
Stansted Mountfitchet CM24 119 F7
Meyel Ave SS8 364 C5
Meynell Ave SS8 364 C2
Meynell Rd RM3 314 B3
Meyrick Cres CO2 135 F5
Mey Wlk SS5 324 C6
Mia Ct CM19 223 B8
Micawber Way CM1 231 D7
Michael Gdns RM11 336 D7
Michael's Cotts SS3 368 D6
Michaels Rd CM23 119 B2
Michaelstowe Cl CO12 90 C2
Michaelstowe Dr CO12 90 C2
Mickfield Mews IP11 381 B5
Micklegate Rd IP11 381 C1
Midas Bsns Ctr RM10 354 B8
Mid Colne SS16 342 D4
Middleborough CO1 135 E8
Middlebury RM4 290 C6
Middle Cloister 3 CM11 297 B2
Middle Crockerford SS16 342 E4
Middlefield CO9 76 F1
Middlefield Ave EN11 221 A8
Middlefield Cl EN11 221 A8
Middlefield Gdns IG2 333 B5
Middlefield Rd
Hoddesdon EN11 221 A8
New Mistley CO11 87 A3
Middle Gn
Doddinghurst CM15 272 C2
Wakes Colne CO6 79 C1
Middleham Ct 14 DA2 376 B1
Middle King CM7 128 D1
Middlemead
South Hanningfield CM3 299 C8
West Hanningfield CM2 277 C3
Middle Mead Rochford SS4 325 F2
Wickford SS11 321 E8
Middle Mead Cl CM2 276 F4
Middle Mill Rd CO1 135 F8
Middle Rd Ingrave CM13 317 C6
Waltham Abbey EN9 265 B7
Middle Row 5 CM23 145 F6
Middlesborough Ho 7 RM3 314 E3
Middlesburg SS8 363 E5
Middlesex Ave SS9 346 F3
Middleside Cvn Pk CM24 120 A4
Middle St Clavering CB11 65 C4
Lower Nazeing EN9 244 A8
MIDDLETON 33 E4
Middleton Ave E4 309 A7
Middleton Cl
Clacton-on-S CO16 195 D6
Ipswich IP2 16 D2
Middleton Gdns IG2 333 B5
Middleton Hall La CM15 316 E8
Middleton Rd
Shenfield CM15 294 F1
Sudbury CO10 33 D5
Middleton Row CM3 301 E6
Middle Way CO10 15 D8
MIDDLEWICK 136 B2
Middlewick Cl 4 CO2 136 A1
Midguard Way CM9 258 F8
Midhurst Ave SS0 347 D4
Midhurst Cl RM12 355 A8
Midland Cl CO2 135 F4
Midland Ct RM1 335 F6
Midland Ho CO12 91 C4
Midsummer Mdw SS3 349 E1
Midway CO15 220 E6
Midway Rd CO2 135 C2
Mighell Ave IG4 332 D6
Milbank CM2 233 B4
Milbanke Cl SS3 349 E1
Milbourn Ct SS4 325 F2
Milburn Cres CM1 231 D1
MILCH HILL 153 E5
Milch La CM3 153 E6
Mildenhall Ho RM3 315 A5
Mildenhall Pl 16 CB9 9 B8
Milden Rd IP2 16 E5
Mildmay Cl CM6 151 E7
Mildmay Ct 2 CM2 232 B1
Mildmayes SS16 341 C4
Mildmay Ho CM0 306 B5
Mildmay Ind Est CM0 306 B5
Mildmay Jun & Inf Schs CM2 254 B5
Mildmay Rd
Burnham-on-C CM0 306 C5
Chelmsford CM2 232 B1
Ilford IG1 333 B1
Ipswich IP3 18 B1
Romford RM7 335 C6
Mildmays CM3 256 C7
Mildred Cl DA1 376 A1

Niton Ct SS17 . . . 375 C8
Niven Cl SS12 . . . 321 E5
Noah's Ark La CO10 . . . 33 D7
NOAK BRIDGE . . . 319 F1
Noak Bridge Prim Sch SS15 . . . 319 F1
Noakes Ave CM2 . . . 254 E6
NOAK HILL . . . 314 E8
Noak Hill CM12 . . . 319 C4
Noak Hill Cl CM12 . . . 319 B4
Noak Hill Rd
Basildon CM12 . . . 319 B4
Romford RM3 . . . 314 D7
Noak Hill Sch RM4 . . . 314 E8
Noaks Rd IP7 . . . 58 D8
Nobel Sq SS13 . . . 321 C2
Nobel Villas EN9 . . . 265 D5
NOBLESGREEN . . . 346 F7
Nobles Green Cl SS9 . . . 346 E7
Nobles Green Rd SS9 . . . 346 E7
Nobles The CM23 . . . 145 D6
Noel Sq RM8 . . . 353 C8
Nonancourt Way CO6 . . . 105 A6
Nonesuch Mdw CO10 . . . 33 E6
Nonsuch Cl IG6 . . . 311 B4
Nonsuch Mdw CO10 . . . 33 E7
Nook The
Stanstead Abbotts SG12 . . . 197 B4
Wivenhoe CO7 . . . 164 C8
Norah Guilder Ho CM3 . . . 211 A4
Norbury Cl CO6 . . . 132 F3
Norbury Gdns RM6 . . . 334 D6
Norbury Rd Chingford E4 . . . 309 A5
Ipswich IP4 . . . 18 B8
Nordenfeldt Rd DA8 . . . 369 D1
Nordic Lodge CM9 . . . 258 F8
Nordland Rd SS8 . . . 364 D5
Nordmann Pl RM15 . . . 357 D1
Noredale SS3 . . . 368 D5
Nore Rd SS9 . . . 346 C8
Nore View SS16 . . . 340 F4
Norfolk Ave
Clacton-on-S CO15 . . . 196 E7
Southend-on-S SS9 . . . 346 F3
West Mersea CO5 . . . 218 D7
Norfolk Cl Basildon SS15 . . . 341 A6
Canvey Island SS8 . . . 364 A5
Dartford DA1 . . . 376 A1
Maldon CM9 . . . 236 E1
Norfolk Cres CO4 . . . 110 B1
Norfolk Ct 4 Ilford RM6 . . . 334 B6
Rochford SS4 . . . 325 D5
Norfolk Dr CM1 . . . 232 A7
Norfolk Gdns CM7 . . . 128 B4
Norfolk Ho
5 Gravesend DA12 . . . 379 D1
Romford RM7 . . . 313 A2
Norfolk Pl RM16 . . . 372 C1
Norfolk Rd Barking IG11 . . . 352 E5
Dagenham RM10 . . . 354 B7
Gravesend DA12 . . . 379 E1
Ilford IG3 . . . 333 E4
Ipswich IP4 . . . 17 D6
Maldon CM9 . . . 236 E1
Romford RM7 . . . 335 C5
Upminster RM14 . . . 337 A2
Wallend E6 . . . 352 A4
Norfolk Way
Bishop's Stortford CM23 . . . 145 F5
Canvey Island SS8 . . . 363 F5
Norham Ct 16 DA2 . . . 376 B1
Norman Ave CM23 . . . 145 D6
Norman Cl Marks Tey CO6 . . . 132 E3
Romford RM5 . . . 313 B1
St Osyth CO16 . . . 194 A4
Waltham Abbey EN9 . . . 265 D6
Norman Cres
Brentwood CM13 . . . 317 A7
Ipswich IP3 . . . 18 A2
Rayleigh SS6 . . . 323 E5
Norman Ct Ilford IG1 . . . 333 D4
Stansted Mountfitchet CM24 . . . 119 E7
Woodford IG8 . . . 310 B5
Normandie Way CO8 . . . 79 E8
Normandy Ave
Burnham-on-C CM0 . . . 306 C5
Colchester CO2 . . . 136 A3
Normandy Way EN11 . . . 221 D8
Norman Hill CM3 . . . 182 B2
Normanhurst CM13 . . . 295 C3
Normanhurst Sch E4 . . . 287 D2
Norman Pl SS9 . . . 365 E8
Norman Rd
Belvedere DA17 . . . 369 B3
Clacton-on-S CO15 . . . 196 E6
Hornchurch RM11 . . . 336 B4
Ilford IG1 . . . 352 B7
Manningtree CO11 . . . 86 D4
Normansfield CM6 . . . 150 E7
Normanshire Dr E4 . . . 309 B6
Normans Rd SS8 . . . 364 D4
Norman's Way CM24 . . . 119 E7
Norman Terr SS9 . . . 365 E8
Normanton Pk E4 . . . 309 E8
Norman Way
Colchester, Lexden CO3 . . . 135 B6
Colchester, Shrub End CO3 . . . 135 B4
Point Clear B CO16 . . . 192 F3
Norris Cl
Bishop's Stortford CM23 . . . 146 C7
Braintree CM7 . . . 128 C5
Norris La EN11 . . . 221 A7
Norris Rd EN11 . . . 221 A6
Norris Rise 4 EN11 . . . 221 A7
Norseman Cl 3 IG3 . . . 334 B3
Norsey Cl CM11 . . . 297 B3
Norsey Dr CM11 . . . 297 D3
Norsey Rd CM11 . . . 297 C4
Norsey View Dr CM12 . . . 297 B6
Norsey Wood Nature Reserve* CM11 . . . 297 D4
Northallerton Way 15 RM3 . . . 314 D5
Northampton Cl CM7 . . . 128 D5
Northampton Gr SS16 . . . 340 F4
Northampton Ho 4 RM3 . . . 314 E6
Northampton Mdw CM7 . . . 72 B2
North Ave
Canvey Island SS8 . . . 364 A3
North Ave continued
Chelmsford CM1 . . . 231 F5
Haverhill CB9 . . . 8 E8
Southend-on-S SS2 . . . 348 C2
Northbank Rd E17 . . . 309 C1
North Barn EN10 . . . 221 B1
NORTH BENFLEET . . . 343 F8
North Benfleet Hall Rd
Basildon SS12 . . . 322 A1
North Benfleet SS12 . . . 321 F1
North Boundary Rd E12 . . . 332 D2
Northbourne Rd CO15 . . . 195 F4
Northbrook Rd IG1 . . . 333 A2
Northbrooks CM19 . . . 223 C7
Northbury Jun & Inf Schs IG11 . . . 352 C6
North Circular Rd
Chingford E17 . . . 309 B2
Ilford IG1, E12 . . . 333 A1
Wallend E6, E12 . . . 352 A5
Wanstead IG1 . . . 332 D5
Woodford E18 . . . 310 C1
North Cl Dagenham RM10 . . . 354 A4
Ipswich IP4 . . . 17 E8
Redbridge IG7 . . . 312 A5
North Colne SS16 . . . 342 D4
North Court Rd CM1 . . . 208 A3
North Cres
Southend-on-S SS2 . . . 347 D5
Steeple Bumpstead CB9 . . . 27 B7
Wickford SS12 . . . 321 D7
North Crescent Prim Sch SS12 . . . 321 D7
North Crockerford SS16 . . . 342 E4
Northcroft CO10 . . . 33 E7
North Cross Rd IG6 . . . 333 C7
North Dell CM1 . . . 232 E7
North Dene IG7 . . . 311 D5
Northdown Gdns IG2 . . . 333 E6
Northdown Rd RM11 . . . 336 B4
North Dr Brentwood CM13 . . . 296 C2
Great Baddow CM2 . . . 254 F7
Mayland CM3 . . . 260 F1
Romford RM2 . . . 336 C8
NORTHEND
Saffron Walden CB11 . . . 22 A3
Southminster CM0 . . . 284 E5
NORTH END Felsted . . . 151 F2
Great Yeldham . . . 30 F3
Northend CM14 . . . 316 C5
North End
Buckhurst Hill IG9 . . . 288 C2
Romford RM3 . . . 314 C8
Southminster CM0 . . . 284 E5
North End Rd
Gestingthorpe CO9, CO10 . . . 31 C2
Hinxton CB10 . . . 3 B8
Little Yeldham CO9 . . . 30 E2
Northern App CO4 . . . 109 E3
Northern Ave SS7 . . . 344 C5
Northern Rd CO10 . . . 34 B8
Northern Relief Rd IG11 . . . 352 C5
Northfalls Rd SS8 . . . 364 F3
NORTH FAMBRIDGE . . . 303 A8
North Fambridge Sta CM3 . . . 303 B8
Northfield
Great Bardfield CM7 . . . 72 B3
Loughton IG10 . . . 288 D5
Northfield Cl CM11 . . . 297 C2
Northfield Cres SS3 . . . 350 B4
Northfield Gdns
Colchester CO4 . . . 110 A4
Dagenham RM9 . . . 353 F8
Northfield Path RM9 . . . 353 F8
Northfield Rd
Dagenham RM9 . . . 353 F8
Saffron Walden CB11 . . . 43 E8
Sawbridgeworth CM21 . . . 172 E4
Northfields Grays RM17 . . . 373 D2
Stansted Mountfitchet CM24 . . . 119 E7
NORTHFLEET . . . 378 C2
Northfleet Ind Est DA10 . . . 377 F3
Northfleet Sta DA11 . . . 378 B1
North Gate CM20 . . . 199 C1
Northgate End CM23 . . . 145 F8
Northgate Ind Pk RM5 . . . 312 F1
Northgate Prim Sch CM23 . . . 145 E8
Northgate St
Colchester CO1 . . . 135 F8
Ipswich IP1 . . . 17 C6
North Gr CM18 . . . 224 A7
North Hall Rd Henham CM22 . . . 94 B7
Rickling Green CB11 . . . 67 A2
North Hill Colchester CO1 . . . 135 E7
Horndon on t H SS17 . . . 360 A3
Little Baddow CM3 . . . 234 D5
North Hill Bsns Pk SS17 . . . 359 F4
North Hill Dr RM3 . . . 314 D6
North Hill Gdns 1 IP4 . . . 17 E6
North Hill Gn RM3 . . . 314 D6
North Hill Rd IP4 . . . 17 E6
North Ho Frinton-on-S CO13 . . . 170 F4
Harlow CM18 . . . 223 F6
North Kent Ave DA11 . . . 378 C1
North La CO6 . . . 133 B5
Northlands App SS16 . . . 341 C1
Northlands Cl SS17 . . . 360 E5
Northlands Farm Chase SS17 . . . 360 E7
Northlands Jun & Inf Sch SS13 . . . 343 B6
Northlands Pavement 3 SS13 . . . 343 B5
North Lawn IP4 . . . 18 C8
North Mill Pl CO9 . . . 76 E3
NORTH OCKENDON . . . 357 B6
Northolme Cl RM16 . . . 373 C3
Northolt Ave CM23 . . . 119 B1
Northolt Way RM12 . . . 355 C7
North Pl Harlow CM20 . . . 200 B5
4 Waltham Abbey EN9 . . . 265 B6
North Prim Sch CO1 . . . 135 E8
North Rd
Belchamp Walter CO10 . . . 31 F6
Belvedere DA17 . . . 369 B4
Brightlingsea CO7 . . . 192 F7
Clacton-on-S CO15 . . . 195 F6
Crays Hill CM11 . . . 320 D5
North Rd continued
Dagenham RM6 . . . 334 E6
Great Yeldham CO9 . . . 30 A2
Havering-atte-B RM4 . . . 291 F1
Hoddesdon EN11 . . . 221 A7
Ilford IG3 . . . 333 E2
Purfleet RM19 . . . 371 C2
Romford RM4 . . . 313 E7
Southend-on-S SS0 . . . 347 E1
South Ockendon RM15 . . . 357 D4
Takeley CM22 . . . 148 C8
Tollesbury CM9 . . . 216 C2
North Residence IG3 . . . 334 B6
North Rise CO10 . . . 34 A6
North Road Ave CM14 . . . 316 C8
North Sea View CO12 . . . 90 F2
North Service Rd 6 CM14 . . . 316 C8
NORTH SHOEBURY . . . 349 F1
North Shoebury Rd SS3 . . . 349 D1
North St Barking IG11 . . . 352 C5
4 Bishop's Stortford CM23 . . . 145 F7
Great Dunmow CM6 . . . 123 D1
Great Wakering SS3 . . . 350 B4
Hornchurch RM11 . . . 336 D4
Lower Nazeing EN9 . . . 221 E1
Maldon CM9 . . . 237 B2
Manningtree CO11 . . . 86 D4
Rochford SS4 . . . 325 F2
Romford RM1 . . . 335 D7
Southend-on-S SS9 . . . 365 E8
Southminster CM0 . . . 284 D4
Steeple Bumpstead CB9 . . . 27 B7
Sudbury CO10 . . . 33 E8
Tillingham CM0 . . . 263 E4
Tolleshunt D'arcy CM9 . . . 215 E5
Walton-on-t-N CO14 . . . 171 C8
North Sta* SS1 . . . 367 A6
North Station Rd CO1 . . . 135 E8
NORTH STIFFORD . . . 372 E5
North Street Par 1 CO10 . . . 33 E7
North Terr 5 CM23 . . . 145 F8
Northumberland Ave
Basildon SS15 . . . 341 C5
Hornchurch RM11 . . . 336 C6
Southend-on-S SS1 . . . 367 D7
Wanstead E12 . . . 332 C3
Northumberland Cl CM7 . . . 128 B4
Northumberland Cres SS1 . . . 367 D7
Northumberland Ct 1 CM2 . . . 232 F4
Northumberland Ho 11 IG8 . . . 311 A3
Northumberland Rd SS17 . . . 375 A4
Northview Ave RM18 . . . 379 A6
North View Cotts CO6 . . . 109 B7
North View Cvn Site IG6 . . . 312 A3
Northview Dr
Southend-on-S SS0 . . . 347 D2
Woodford IG8 . . . 310 D1
Northville Dr SS0 . . . 347 C4
North Wall CO16 . . . 193 A3
NORTH WEALD BASSETT . . . 247 C5
North Weald Cl
Hornchurch RM12 . . . 355 C5
Wickford SS11 . . . 322 B6
North Weald Sta* CM16 . . . 247 B4
Northwick Park Prim Sch SS8 . . . 363 E4
Northwick Rd SS8 . . . 363 B4
Northwick Ret Pk SS8 . . . 363 B4
Northwood RM16 . . . 374 B4
Northwood Ave RM12 . . . 355 A8
Northwood Dr 2 DA9 . . . 377 A1
Northwood Gdns IG5 . . . 333 A7
Norton Ave SS8 . . . 364 E3
Norton Cl Chingford E4 . . . 309 A5
Corringham SS17 . . . 361 A3
Norton Ct IG2 . . . 333 E5
NORTON END . . . 42 E4
NORTON HEATH . . . 250 D5
Norton Heath Rd CM5 . . . 250 E8
Norton La High Ongar CM5 . . . 249 D5
High Ongar, Norton Mandeville CM4, CM5 . . . 250 C6
NORTON MANDEVILLE . . . 249 F6
Norton Pl CM11 . . . 320 B5
Norton Rd Chelmsford CM1 . . . 232 A3
Dagenham RM10 . . . 354 D6
Haverhill CB9 . . . 8 E6
Ingatestone CM4 . . . 274 B4
Norway Cres CO12 . . . 90 F3
Norway Wlk RM13 . . . 355 C1
Norwich Ave SS2 . . . 348 C2
Norwich Cl
Clacton-on-S CO16 . . . 195 E6
Colchester CO1 . . . 136 A8
Southend-on-S SS2 . . . 348 C2
Norwich Cres Ilford RM6 . . . 334 B6
Rayleigh SS6 . . . 323 C5
Norwich Ct 2 IP1 . . . 17 A7
Norwich Ho SS4 . . . 325 D5
Norwich Mews IG3 . . . 334 A3
Norwich Rd IP1 . . . 17 A7
Norwich Wlk SS14 . . . 342 F7
Norwood Ave
Clacton-on-S CO15 . . . 196 B5
Romford RM7 . . . 335 E4
Norwood Ct DA1 . . . 376 A3
Norwood Dr SS7 . . . 344 E1
NORWOOD END . . . 227 D5
Norwood End
Basildon SS14 . . . 342 D7
Fyfield CM5 . . . 227 D5
Norwood Way CO14 . . . 171 A7
NOSTERFIELD END . . . 7 F5
Notcutts CO7 . . . 59 E1
Notley Gn CM77 . . . 154 B6
Notley Green Prim Sch CM77 . . . 154 C8
Notley High Sch CM7 . . . 154 F8
Notley Rd CM7 . . . 154 F8
Nottage Cl
Corringham SS17 . . . 360 F4
Wivenhoe CO7 . . . 164 C8
Nottage Cres CM7 . . . 127 E3
Nottidge Rd IP4 . . . 17 E6
Nottingham Rd CO15 . . . 196 E6
Nottingham Way SS16 . . . 340 F5
NOUNSLEY . . . 211 B1
Nounsley Rd CM3 . . . 211 B1
Nounsley Terr CM3 . . . 211 B1
Nuneaton Rd RM9 . . . 353 E5
Nunnery St CO9 . . . 51 D4
Nunns Cl CO6 . . . 131 A2
Nunn's Rd CO1 . . . 135 E7
Nunns Way RM17 . . . 373 D2
Nun's Mdw CO9 . . . 102 E7
Nuns Wlk CO9 . . . 29 F1
Nunty's La
Greenstead Green CO9 . . . 104 A1
Pattiswick CM77 . . . 129 F8
NUPER'S HATCH . . . 291 E2
Nursery Cl
Bishop's Stortford CM23 . . . 145 F6
Colchester CO3 . . . 134 C5
Ilford RM6 . . . 334 D5
Rayleigh SS6 . . . 323 D1
South Ockendon RM15 . . . 357 C1
Woodford IG8 . . . 310 B5
Nursery Dr CM7 . . . 128 A5
Nursery Fields CM21 . . . 172 D2
Nursery Gdns SS15 . . . 341 D8
Nursery La CM3 . . . 256 F8
Nursery Rd
Bishop's Stortford CM23 . . . 145 F6
Chelmsford CM2 . . . 254 B8
Great Cornard CO10 . . . 34 B5
Hoddesdon EN11 . . . 197 B1
Hook End CM15 . . . 272 C5
Loughton IG10 . . . 288 D5
Lower Nazeing EN9 . . . 221 D2
Stanford-le-H SS17 . . . 360 E3
Wanstead E12 . . . 332 E2
Nursery Rise CM6 . . . 150 D7
Nursery Wlk
Felixstowe IP11 . . . 381 D5
Romford RM7 . . . 335 D5
Nutberry Ave RM16 . . . 373 B4
Nutberry Cl RM16 . . . 373 A4
Nutbrowne Rd RM9 . . . 354 A4
Nutcombe Cres SS4 . . . 325 D4
Nutfield Gdns IG3 . . . 334 A2
NUTHAMPSTEAD . . . 39 A2
Nuthatch Cl CM11 . . . 319 C8
Nutter La E11 . . . 332 C6
Nuxley Rd DA17 . . . 369 A1
Nyall Ct RM2 . . . 336 D8
Nyssa Cl IG8 . . . 310 F4
Nyth Cl RM14 . . . 337 D5

O

Oakapple Cl CO2 . . . 135 D1
Oak Ave Crays Hill CM11 . . . 320 C4
Jaywick CO16 . . . 195 A2
Upminster RM14 . . . 356 B8
Wickford SS11 . . . 322 C7
Oakbank CM13 . . . 295 E4
Oak Bglws CM7 . . . 127 E3
Oak Bsns Pk CO16 . . . 141 F8
Oak Chase SS12 . . . 321 A7
Oak Cl Clacton-on-S CO15 . . . 195 E6
Felixstowe IP11 . . . 381 C4
Maldon CM9 . . . 259 B8
Rushmere St A IP4 . . . 18 E7
Thorpe-le-S CO16 . . . 142 A1
Waltham Abbey EN9 . . . 265 D5
West Bergholt CO6 . . . 108 E4
Oak Cnr Beaumont CO16 . . . 141 F6
Woodham Mortimer CM9 . . . 257 D6
Oak Cotts CM3 . . . 233 E8
Oak Ct Chingford E4 . . . 309 B4
Hadleigh SS7 . . . 345 E2
South Ockendon RM15 . . . 357 C3
Oakdale Ct E4 . . . 309 C5
Oakdale Gdns E4 . . . 309 C5
Oakdale Inf Sch E18 . . . 310 B1
Oakdale Jun Sch E18 . . . 310 B1
Oakdale Rd E18 . . . 310 B1
Oakdene RM3 . . . 314 F1
Oak Dene Cl RM11 . . . 336 B5
Oakdene Rd SS13 . . . 343 C8
Oakdown Ho IG7 . . . 311 F5
Oak Dr CM21 . . . 200 C8
Oak Eggar Chase IP8 . . . 36 D8
Oak End CM18 . . . 223 F6
Oaken Grange Dr SS2 . . . 347 E5
Oak Fall CM8 . . . 184 A5
Oak Farm Rd CM9 . . . 235 E1
Oakfield Chingford E4 . . . 309 B5
Stebbing CM6 . . . 125 A4
Oakfield Cl SS7 . . . 344 C3
Oakfield Dr CO4 . . . 83 A5
Oakfield Ho 2 IG1 . . . 333 B1
Oakfield La CM3 . . . 182 A2
Oakfield Lodge 9 IG1 . . . 333 B1
Oakfield Prim Sch SS12 . . . 321 E5
Oakfield Rd Belstead IP8 . . . 36 A7
Ilford IG1 . . . 333 B1
Rochford SS4 . . . 303 A1
South Benfleet SS7 . . . 344 C3
Washbrook IP8 . . . 35 F6
Oakfields Chigwell IG7 . . . 311 C5
Loughton IG10 . . . 289 A4
Oakfield Wood Nature Reserve* CO11 . . . 88 D4
Oak Glade CM16 . . . 246 D2
Oak Glen RM11 . . . 336 E8
Oak Gn CM11 . . . 297 D1
Oak Gr IP8 . . . 16 A6
Oak Hall CM23 . . . 145 E8
Oakhall Ct E11 . . . 332 B5
Oak Hall Rd E11 . . . 332 B5
Oakham Cl SS16 . . . 340 F5
Oakham Ct SS9 . . . 346 E2
Oakhaven CO12 . . . 90 F1
Oak Hill Beazley End CM7 . . . 101 A8
Chingford IG8 . . . 309 E3
Wethersfield CM7 . . . 73 F1
Oak Hill Cl IG8 . . . 309 D3
Oak Hill Cres IG8 . . . 309 E3
Oak Hill Ct IG8 . . . 309 E3
Oak Hill Gdns IG8 . . . 309 F2
Oak Hill La IP2 . . . 17 B3
Oakhill Prim Sch IG8 . . . 309 E4
Oakhill Rd RM19 . . . 371 B1
Oak Hill Rd RM4 . . . 291 E1
Oak Ho Ipswich IP2 . . . 16 D2
Southend-on-S SS3 . . . 368 F8
Stutton IP9 . . . 61 F2
Oakhurst Cl Redbridge IG6 . . . 311 C2
Wickford SS12 . . . 321 C6
Oakhurst Dr SS12 . . . 321 C5
Oakhurst Gdns E4 . . . 287 F1
Oakhurst Rd Rayleigh SS6 . . . 345 F8
Southend-on-S SS2 . . . 348 A2
Oak Ind Pk CM6 . . . 150 F6
Oak La Crays Hill CM11 . . . 320 C3
Woodford IG8 . . . 309 F6
Oakland Farm Ind Est CM4 . . . 297 F6
Oakland Gdns CM13 . . . 295 C4
Oakland Pl IG9 . . . 310 A8
Oakland Rd CO12 . . . 91 C3
Oaklands Ave
Colchester CO3 . . . 134 E5
Romford RM1 . . . 335 F7
Oaklands Cl
Bishop's Stortford CM23 . . . 119 B2
Great Notley CM77 . . . 154 D8
Oaklands Cres CM2 . . . 254 B8
Oaklands Dr
Bishop's Stortford CM23 . . . 119 B2
Harlow CM17 . . . 224 C7
South Ockendon RM15 . . . 372 C8
Oaklands Inf Sch CM2 . . . 254 B8
Oaklands Mews SS4 . . . 325 C4
Oaklands Park Ave IG1 . . . 333 C2
Oaklands Pk
Bishop's Stortford CM23 . . . 119 B2
Brentwood CM15 . . . 295 B1
Oaklands Sch IG10 . . . 288 D4
Oaklands Way CM3 . . . 234 E2
Oaklea Ave CM2 . . . 232 E3
Oakleafe Gdns IG6 . . . 333 B8
Oaklee IP2 . . . 17 A1
Oakleigh Ave
Hullbridge SS5 . . . 301 E2
Southend-on-S SS1 . . . 367 D8
Oakleigh Ct CM23 . . . 145 D8
Oakleigh Lodge IG3 . . . 334 A1
Oakleigh Park Dr SS9 . . . 346 E1
Oakleigh Rd CO15 . . . 195 F8
Oakleigh Rise CM16 . . . 268 A7
Oakleighs SS7 . . . 344 C4
Oakley Ave Barking IG11 . . . 352 F5
Rayleigh SS6 . . . 322 F3
Oakley Cl Chingford E4 . . . 309 C7
Grays RM20 . . . 377 C8
Oakley Cross CO12 . . . 117 B7
Oakley Ct IG10 . . . 289 A7
Oakley Dr Billericay CM12 . . . 296 F5
Romford RM3 . . . 315 A5
Oakley Rd Braintree CM7 . . . 127 F7
Harwich CO12 . . . 90 D1
Wix CO11 . . . 115 E5
Oak Lodge E11 . . . 332 A4
Oak Lodge Ave IG7 . . . 311 D5
Oak Lodge Tye CM1 . . . 233 A6
Oak Manor View CM3 . . . 180 F7
Oakmead Rd CO16 . . . 193 B3
Oakmoor Way IG7 . . . 311 E5
Oak Piece CM16 . . . 247 C6
Oak Rd Canvey Island SS8 . . . 364 C3
Chappel CO6 . . . 106 B3
Crays Hill CM11 . . . 320 C4
Epping CM16 . . . 245 F1
Grays RM17 . . . 378 C8
Great Cornard CO10 . . . 34 B6
Greenhithe DA9 . . . 376 E1
Halstead CO9 . . . 103 D7
Heybridge CM9 . . . 237 B6
Little Maplestead CO9 . . . 77 A8
Pebmarsh CO9 . . . 77 F8
Ramsden Heath CM11 . . . 298 D5
Rivenhall CM8 . . . 184 C6
Rochford SS4 . . . 325 E2
Romford RM3 . . . 314 F2
Tiptree CO5 . . . 186 C7
Oak Rd N SS7 . . . 345 E2
Oak Rd S SS7 . . . 345 E2
Oak Ridge CO12 . . . 117 B7
Oak Rise IG9 . . . 310 D7
Oakroyd Ave CM6 . . . 150 E8
Oakroyd Ho CM6 . . . 150 E8
Oaks EN9 . . . 266 C4
Oaks Ave RM5 . . . 313 C1
Oaks Com Prim Sch The IP2 . . . 16 E3
Oaks Dr CO3 . . . 135 D7
Oaks End CO2 . . . 162 A5
Oaks Gr E4 . . . 309 E8
Oaks Hospl The CO4 . . . 109 E3
Oakside Ct Redbridge IG6 . . . 311 D1
Wanstead E11 . . . 332 A7
Oaks La IG2 . . . 333 E7
Oaksmere Gdns IP2 . . . 17 A2
Oaks Park High Sch IG2 . . . 333 E6
Oaks Pl CO4 . . . 109 E2
Oaks Ret Pk CM20 . . . 199 F3
Oak St
Bishop's Stortford CM23 . . . 145 F6
Romford RM7 . . . 335 C6
Oakstead Cl IP4 . . . 18 A6
Oaks The Billericay CM11 . . . 319 C6
Chingford IG8 . . . 309 E3
Dartford DA2 . . . 376 B1
Frinton-on-S CO13 . . . 170 F6
Oaktree Cl
14 Bishop's Stortford CM23 . . . 145 F7
Brentwood CM13 . . . 316 F7
Oak Tree Cl IG10 . . . 289 C8
Oak Tree Cotts CO6 . . . 133 B8
Oaktree Gdns CM17 . . . 224 D7
Oaktree Gr IG1 . . . 352 D7
Oak Tree Rd CO7 . . . 165 B8
Oaktrees CM9 . . . 214 B5
Oakview CO12 . . . 90 F1
Oakview Cl SS9 . . . 346 E3
Oak View Cvn Pk CM24 . . . 120 A4
Oak View Sch IG10 . . . 289 A6
Oakway RM16 . . . 373 C5
Oak Wlk Hockley SS5 . . . 324 E7
Sible Hedingham CO9 . . . 51 D2
South Benfleet SS7 . . . 344 B8
Oak Wlk continued
Southend-on-S SS9 . . . 346 D4
Oakwood EN9 . . . 265 E5
Oakwood Ave
Brentwood CM13 . . . 295 E3
Clacton-on-S CO15 . . . 196 E7
Southend-on-S SS9 . . . 346 E5
West Mersea CO5 . . . 218 D7
Oakwood Bsns Pk CO15 . . . 169 A1
Oakwood Chase RM11 . . . 336 F4
Oakwood Cl
Kirby Cross CO13 . . . 170 E6
South Benfleet SS7 . . . 344 B5
Woodford IG8 . . . 310 E4
Oakwood Ct Althorne CM3 . . . 283 A3
Chingford E4 . . . 287 E2
Romford RM2 . . . 336 C8
Southend-on-S SS9 . . . 346 E5
Oakwood Dr
Billericay CM12 . . . 297 C5
West Mersea CO5 . . . 218 D7
Oakwood Est CM20 . . . 200 B4
Oakwood Gdns Ilford IG3 . . . 333 F2
West Mersea CO5 . . . 218 D7
Oakwood Gr SS13 . . . 343 B6
Oakwood Hill IG10 . . . 289 B4
Oakwood Hill Ind Est IG10 . . . 289 B4
Oakwood Ind Est DA11 . . . 378 A2
Oakwood Inf Sch CO15 . . . 195 D2
OakWood Mews 5 CM17 . . . 200 C4
Oakwood Rd
Corringham SS17 . . . 361 B3
Rayleigh SS6 . . . 323 C4
Oakwood Villas SS9 . . . 346 C7
Oak Yd CO9 . . . 76 E2
Oasis Ct CM1 . . . 232 F5
Oast Ct 3 SS4 . . . 325 F2
Oasthouse Ct CB10 . . . 22 D1
Oast House Spinney CM7 . . . 127 F6
Oast Way SS4 . . . 325 F2
Oates Rd RM5 . . . 313 B5
Oatfield Cl CO3 . . . 134 D6
Oatlands CO7 . . . 137 F6
Oban Ct SS11 . . . 322 B5
Oban Ho 5 IG11 . . . 352 D3
Oban Rd SS2 . . . 348 C1
Oban St IP1 . . . 17 B7
Oberon Cl CO4 . . . 136 F7
Obrey Way CM23 . . . 145 E3
Observation Ct IP1 . . . 17 B5
Observer Way CO5 . . . 158 C4
Occasio Ho CM20 . . . 223 C8
Ocean View CO14 . . . 171 D8
Ockelford Ave CM1 . . . 231 F5
Ockendon Rd RM14 . . . 357 B7
Ockendon Sch The RM15 . . . 372 A8
Ockendon Sta RM15 . . . 357 B2
Ockendon Way CO14 . . . 171 A8
Octave Ho CM16 . . . 267 E3
Octavia Dr CM8 . . . 211 E7
Oddcroft CO6 . . . 77 F1
Odell Cl IG11 . . . 352 F5
Odeon The IG11 . . . 352 D5
Odessa Rd SS8 . . . 364 D3
Odin Lodge CM9 . . . 258 F8
O'Donoghue Ho SS17 . . . 360 E2
Office La CM9 . . . 214 A4
Ogard Rd EN11 . . . 221 C8
Ogilvie Ct SS12 . . . 321 E5
Oglethorpe Rd RM10 . . . 335 A1
Okehampton Rd RM3 . . . 314 C4
Okehampton Sq RM3 . . . 314 C4
Old Barn La CM3 . . . 277 F2
Old Barn Rd CO8 . . . 80 A6
Old Barns La CM4 . . . 251 C3
Old Bell Cl CM24 . . . 119 D6
Old Bell La CM3 . . . 278 B1
Old Brickworks The RM3 . . . 315 A3
Oldbury Ave CM2 . . . 254 F8
Oldbury Cotts SS3 . . . 349 D3
Old Burylodge La CM24 . . . 120 A4
Old Camps Castle CB21 . . . 7 E3
Old Cattle Market 5 IP4 . . . 17 C5
Oldchurch Gdns RM7 . . . 335 D4
Old Church Hill SS16 . . . 341 A1
Old Church La Bulmer CO10 . . . 32 F3
Bulmer Tye CO10 . . . 32 F2
Mountnessing CM13 . . . 296 B6
West Bergholt CO6 . . . 108 D5
Oldchurch Rd RM7 . . . 335 E4
Old Church Rd
Basildon SS13 . . . 343 F5
Chingford E4 . . . 309 A7
East Hanningfield CM3 . . . 278 B6
Oldchurch Rise RM7 . . . 335 E4
Old Clements La CB9 . . . 8 F7
Old Coach Rd CO1 . . . 136 B7
Old Coastguard Cotts CM0 . . . 241 E4
Old College Ct DA17 . . . 369 B1
Old Convent The CO5 . . . 158 B1
Old Court Ho 2 CM24 . . . 119 E6
Old Court Rd CM2 . . . 232 D3
Old Croft Cl CM1 . . . 205 D5
Old Crown La CM14 . . . 293 D7
Old Ct Chelmsford CM2 . . . 232 D3
Long Melford CO10 . . . 15 D8
Olde Forge CO7 . . . 165 E1
Old Farm Ct CM12 . . . 297 A4
Old Farm Yd CM22 . . . 201 C8
Old Ferry Rd CO7 . . . 164 B8
Oldfield Rd IP8 . . . 16 B1
Oldfields CM14 . . . 316 C6
Old Forge CO7 . . . 137 C2
Old Forge Rd
Boreham CM3 . . . 233 E8
Layer de la H CO2 . . . 161 F5
Old Forge The SS6 . . . 323 C3
Old Foundry Rd IP4 . . . 17 D6
Old Hall Cl CB9 . . . 27 C7
Old Hall Ct SS3 . . . 350 A4
Old Hall La Capel St M IP9 . . . 35 F3
Tollesbury CM9 . . . 216 C5
Walton-on-t-N CO14 . . . 144 E3
Old Hall Rise CM17 . . . 224 E8
OLD HARLOW . . . 200 D4

Princes Gate CM0 284 D4
Princes Gdns IP11 381 D4
Princes Lodge SS0 366 D7
Princes Mews CM12 297 C6
Princes Pk RM13 355 A5
Princes Rd
Buckhurst Hill IG9 310 C8
Burnham-on-C CM0 306 C6
Canvey Island SS8 363 F3
Chelmsford CM2 254 B7
Clacton-on-S CO15 196 D5
Felixstowe IP11 381 E4
Harwich CO12 91 B3
Ilford IG6 333 D7
Maldon CM9 237 A2
Romford RM1 336 A6
Prince's Rd
Navestock Heath CM14, RM4 292 F8
Navestock Side CM14 293 A7
Princess Alexandra Hospl CM20 199 C1
Princess Anne Cl CO15 195 C1
Princess Ave RM18 375 C2
Princess Ct SS11 322 A8
Princess Dr CO4 110 C5
Princess Gdns SS4 325 D5
Princess Margaret Rd RM18 380 D7
Princess Par RM10 354 A3
Princess Rd SS6 323 F3
Princess St CO12 90 F5
Princes St Gravesend DA11 379 B1
Ipswich IP1 17 B5
Southend-on-S SS1 366 F8
Princess Way CB9 8 E8
Prince St CO10 33 E8
Princes Way
Brentwood CM13 295 A1
Buckhurst Hill IG9 310 C8
Princes Well CB10 45 F7
Princethorpe Rd IP3 18 C4
Princeton Mews CO4 110 B4
Prince William Ave SS8 363 F6
Printers Way CM20 200 A5
Prior Chase RM17 372 F2
Prior Cl CO9 103 D8
Prioress Cres DA9 377 C3
Priories The SS5 301 D1
Prior Rd IG1 333 A1
Priors 8 CM23 146 A7
Priors Cl SS14 342 C6
Priors Ct
Sawbridgeworth CM22 173 A2
Southminster CM0 284 E4
Priors E SS14 342 C6
Prior's Hall Barn★ CB11 67 D4
Priors Pk RM12 336 C1
Priors Way CO6 131 A3
Prior's Way CM0 284 E4
Prior's Wood Rd CM22 148 C7
Prior Way CO4 109 E2
Priory Ave Chingford E4 309 A7
Harlow CM17 200 C5
Haverhill CB9 8 F7
Southend-on-S SS2 347 F3
Priory Chase SS6 323 B6
Priory Cl Chelmsford CM1 231 E2
Chingford E4 309 A7
Hatfield Peverel CM3 211 B1
Hoddesdon EN11 221 A5
Ickleton CB10 3 A3
Pilgrims Hatch CM15 294 A4
Seawick CO16 220 A6
Woodford E18 310 A2
Priory Cotts CO2 160 E6
Priory Cres SS2 347 F4
Priory Ct
Bishop's Stortford CM23 145 F7
Colchester CO1 135 E7
Harlow CM18 224 B5
Hatfield Peverel CM3 211 A4
2 Ilford RM6 334 B5
Ipswich IP10 38 C6
Priory Dr CM24 119 E5
Priory Farm Rd CM3 211 B2
Priory Gdns CO10 33 E6
Priory Gr RM3 314 E6
PRIORY HEATH 18 D1
Priory La Bicknacre CM3 256 F1
Great Notley CM77 154 C8
Priory Mead CM15 272 C3
Priory Mews
Hatfield Peverel CM3 211 C2
1 Hornchurch RM11 336 B3
Southend-on-S SS2 348 A3
Priory Park Ind Est SS2 348 A4
Priory Path RM3 314 E7
Priory Pk Ipswich IP10 38 B6
St Osyth CO16 194 A4
Priory Prim Sch CM3 256 F2
Priory Rd Barking IG11 352 D5
Bicknacre CM3 256 E1
Chappel CO6 106 B3
Clacton-on-S CO15 195 E3
Loughton IG10 288 E5
Romford RM3 314 E7
Stanford-le-H SS17 360 E3
Sudbury CO10 15 D1
Tiptree CO5 185 F3
Priory Sch SS2 347 E3
Priory St Colchester CO1 136 A7
Earls Colne CO6 105 B7
Priory The Billericay CM12 297 C6
Writtle CM1 253 B8
Priory View Rd SS9 346 E5
Priory Wlk
23 Colchester CO1 135 F7
Sudbury CO10 33 E7
Priory Wood CO9 51 E4
Priorywood Cres SS9 346 E5
Priorywood Dr SS9 346 E5
Priory Wood Rdbt CM22 147 A8
Pritchett Cl EN3 265 A2
Prittlebrook Ind Est SS2 347 F4
Prittle Cl SS7 345 C5
PRITTLEWELL 347 C3
Prittlewell CE Jun & Inf Sch SS2 347 F2
Prittlewell Chase SS0 347 D3
Prittlewell Cl IP2 16 F1
Prittlewell Mews SS2 347 F2
Prittlewell Priory Mus★ SS2 347 F3
Prittlewell Sq SS1 366 F7
Prittlewell St SS2 348 A1
Prittlewell Sta SS2 348 A3
Proctor Cl CO5 163 B2
Proctors Way CM23 146 A4
Proctor Way CO6 132 E3
Professional Pl 2 SS11 322 A5
Progress Ct CM7 127 E3
Progress Rd SS9 346 C6
Progress Way CO16 168 C1
Promenade
Clacton-on-S CO15 220 D6
Harwich CO12 91 E4
Harwich, Dovercourt CO12 91 C2
Mayland CM3 260 F1
Promenade The
Burnham-on-C CM0 306 C4
Southend-on-S SS3 368 C5
Promenade Way CO7 192 E5
Propelair Way CO4 109 D2
Prospect Ave SS17 360 B1
Prospect Bsns Pk IG10 289 D5
Prospect Cl
Belvedere DA17 369 A2
Hatfield Peverel CM3 211 A3
Southend-on-S SS1 367 C7
Prospect Hill CO10 34 D3
Prospect Pk CO13 170 A5
Prospect Pl
4 Gravesend DA12 379 D1
Grays RM17 378 B8
Romford RM5 313 C1
Saffron Walden CB11 22 F1
Prospect Rd
Hornchurch RM11 336 F8
Ipswich IP1 17 A7
Woodford IG8 310 C5
Prospect St 1 IP1 17 A6
Prospect Way CM13 295 E5
Prospero Cl CO4 136 F8
Prospero Ho 7 DA17 369 A1
Protea Way SS8 364 B4
Prout Ind Est SS8 364 F3
Provan Ct IP3 18 B4
Provence Cl CO3 134 C7
Providence CM0 306 C4
Providence La IP1 17 A7
Providence Pl
Colchester CO1 136 B6
Dagenham RM5 312 F2
Providence St
Greenhithe DA9 377 A2
6 Ipswich IP1 17 C6
Prower Cl CM11 297 B1
Prudhoe Ct 15 DA2 376 B1
Prunus Ct CO2 163 A7
Prykes Dr CM1 232 A2
Pryor Cl CM8 184 A1
Pryors Cl CM23 146 A6
Pryors Rd CM2 254 C2
Puck La SS16 342 C5
Puckleside SS16 341 C4
Puckridge Cotts IG7 311 E7
Pudding La Birch CO2 161 A5
Chigwell IG7 289 F2
Pudsey Hall La SS4 304 A2
Puffin Cl Barking IG11 353 B2
Wickford SS12 321 F5
Puffin Pl SS3 349 E1
Puffinsdale CO15 195 F5
Puffin Terr IG5 333 A8
Pugh Pl SS17 360 E3
Pulborough Ho 1 RM3 314 E3
Pulford Pl CM6 124 D7
Pullman Ct SS11 321 D8
Pulpitfield Cl CO14 171 A8
Pulpits Cl SS5 324 F7
Pulteney Gdns 9 E18 332 B8
Pulteney Rd E18 332 B8
Pumphill SG9 64 A2
Pump Hill
Great Baddow CM2 254 F6
Loughton IG10 288 F7
St Osyth CO16 194 D4
Pump Hill Cvn Pk CO16 194 C4
Pump Ho The 13 CM23 146 A7
Pump La Chelmsford CM1 232 E6
Danbury CM3 256 D5
Epping Green CM16 245 B7
Pleshey CM3 178 E1
Purleigh CM3 258 D1
Pump Mead Cl CM0 284 D4
Pump St SS17 360 A2
Pumpyard Cotts CO9 31 E1
Punchard Cres EN3 265 B1
Punchard Way IP11 381 A8
Punchbowl Cotts SS4 327 D7
Punders Field CM7 128 D1
Purbeck Ct
4 Colchester CO1 136 D7
Great Baddow CM2 254 E6
Purbeck Rd RM11 336 A4
Purcell Cl Basildon SS15 341 D8
Colchester CO4 136 E6
Stanford-le-H SS17 360 C3
Writtle CM1 231 A1
Purcell Rd CM8 211 E7
Purcell Way SS17 360 C3
Purdeys Way SS4 348 A8
Purdis Ave IP3 18 F2
Purdis Farm La IP3 18 F2
PURFLEET 371 B1
Purfleet By-Pass RM19 371 C1
Purfleet Ind Pk RM15 370 F4
Purfleet Industrial Access Rd RM15 371 A3
Purfleet Prim Sch RM19 371 A2
Purfleet Rd RM15 371 B5
Purford Gn CM18 224 A7
Purford Green Jun & Inf Schs CM18 224 A6
Purland Cl RM8 334 F3
PURLEIGH 258 D1
Purleigh Ave IG8 310 E4
Purleigh Cl SS13 321 C1
Purleigh Gr CM3 281 A5
Purleigh Prim Sch CM3 258 D1
Purleigh Rd SS6 323 B3
Purleigh Wash CM9 259 B2
Purley Cl IG5 311 A1
Purley Way
Clacton-on-S CO16 195 B6
Southend-on-S SS0 347 C5
Purlieu Way CM16 267 E4
Purplett Ho IP2 17 D4
Purplett St IP2 17 D4
Purvis Way CO4 110 B5
Putney Gdns RM6 334 B6
Putticks La CO7 59 E3
PUTTOCK END 31 C6
PUTTOCK'S END 148 E4
Pyecat's Cnr CO7 137 C7
Pye Cnr
Castle Hedingham CO9 51 E4
Gilston CM20 199 D5
Pyefleet Cl
Brightlingsea CO7 192 E7
Fingringhoe CO5 164 C6
Pyefleet Ho CO5 218 D7
Pyefleet View CO5 163 B3
Pye Gdns CM23 145 E8
Pyenest Rd CM19 223 C6
Pyesand CO13 170 C8
PYE'S GREEN 153 C5
Pygot Pl CM7 127 E4
Pym Pl RM17 373 A2
Pyms Rd CM2 254 B3
Pynchbek CM23 145 E3
Pynchon Mews CM1 232 D3
Pynchon Paddocks CM22 173 D7
Pyne Gate CM2 254 B1
Pynest Green La EN9 266 B2
Pypers Hatch CM20 223 F8
Pyrgo Priory Sch RM3 315 A6
Pyrles Gn IG10 289 B8
Pyrles La IG10 289 B7
Pytt Field CM17 224 B7

Q

QM Ind Pk IP3 18 C1
Quadling St IP1 17 C5
Quadrangle Ctr The IP3 18 C1
Quadrant Arc RM1 335 E6
Quadrant The RM19 371 C2
Quaker La EN9 265 C5
Quaker's La CB9 9 A7
Quale Rd CM2 233 B4
Quantock 6 SS1 367 A8
Quantock Cl IP5 18 F7
Quarles Cl RM5 313 A3
Quarles Park Rd RM6 334 B5
Quarry Hill RM17 373 A1
Quarry Hill Inf Sch RM17 373 B1
Quarry Hill Jun Sch RM17 373 B1
Quarry Mews RM19 371 A2
Quarry Spring CM20 224 A8
Quarter Gate CM3 301 E5
Quatro Pk SS14 320 F2
Quay Ctyd 2 CO11 86 D4
Quay La Beaumont CO16 142 B5
Greenhithe DA9 377 B3
Kirby-le-S CO13 143 D1
Sudbury CO10 33 E6
Quayside Dr CO2 136 D5
Quayside Ind Est CM9 237 A4
Quay St
1 Manningtree CO11 86 D4
Wivenhoe CO7 164 B8
Quay The
Burnham-on-C CM0 306 C4
Harwich CO12 91 D6
Wivenhoe CO7 164 B7
Quay Theatre★ CO10 33 E6
Quebec Ave 4 SS1 367 B8
Quebec Gdns CM3 301 D6
Quebec Rd Ilford IG1 333 C4
Tilbury RM18 379 A5
Queech La IP9 87 C8
Queech The IP9 35 B2
Queen Anne Dr CO5 218 D6
Queen Anne Gdns CO5 218 D6
Queen Anne Rd CO5 218 D7
Queen Anne's Dr SS0 347 C4
Queen Anne's Mews SS0 347 C4
Queen Anns Gr SS5 301 E3
Queenborough Gdns IG2 333 A7
Queenborough Gr CM77 154 C8
Queenborough La
Great Notley CM77 154 D8
Rayne CM77 154 B8
Queenborough Rd CM0 284 D4
Queenbury Cl CO5 218 E6
Queen Edith Dr CB9 27 B6
Queen Elizabeth Ave
Clacton-on-S CO15 195 C1
East Tilbury RM18 375 B2
Queen Elizabeth Chase SS4 347 F7
Queen Elizabeth Ct EN9 265 C3
Queen Elizabeth Dr SS17 360 F4
Queen Elizabeth II Sq 4 CM3 301 E7
Queen Elizabeth's Hunting Lodge★ E4 287 F2
Queen Elizabeth Way CO2 136 A2
Queen Mary Ave
Colchester CO2 135 F4
East Tilbury RM18 375 C2
Queen Mary Cl RM1 335 F5
Queen Mary Ct RM18 375 C2
Queen Marys Ct EN9 265 C4
Queen Mary Villas 14 E18 310 A2
Queens Ave SS5 301 E4
Queen's Ave Maldon CM9 237 A1
Southend-on-S SS9 346 E1
Woodford IG8 310 B5
Queensberry Rd IP3 18 A1
Queensbridge Ind Pk RM20 377 A8
Queensbury IG9 288 B1
Queensbury Ave CO6 133 D5
Queens Cl
Stansted Mountfitchet CM24 119 E8
Sudbury CO10 33 E8
Queen's Cl CM21 172 F4
Queenscliffe Rd IP2 17 A3
Queens Cnr CO5 218 D7
Queen's Cotts CO6 105 B7
Queens Cres CM23 145 E5
Queens Ct
Burnham-on-C CM0 306 B4
Southend-on-S, Chalkwell SS9 365 F8
Southend-on-S SS9 346 E1
5 Sudbury CO10 33 F8
West Mersea CO5 218 D7
Queen's Ct
Clacton-on-S CO15 196 D4
6 Haverhill CB9 8 E8
Queen's Dr EN8 265 A5
Queens Gate IG4 332 F7
Queensgate Ctr RM17 373 A1
Queensgate Ctr CM20 199 F4
Queensgate Dr IP4 17 F8
Queen's Gate Mews CM12 296 F5
Queens Gdns
Rainham RM13 354 D3
Upminster RM14 337 F5
Queen's Gdns CM7 127 B7
Queen's Grove Rd E4 287 D1
Queen's Head Rd CO4 82 E3
Queen's Ho CO13 170 F4
Queens Hospl RM7 335 E4
Queenside Ct RM7 335 C7
Queenside Mews RM12 336 E2
Queensland Ave SS4 347 F7
Queensland Cres CM1 231 E5
Queensland Ct RM18 378 F5
Queensland Dr CO2 136 A1
Queens Lodge SS7 345 C3
Queensmere SS7 345 B5
Queens Mews
6 Buckhurst Hill IG9 310 C8
West Mersea CO5 218 B6
QUEENS PARK 296 F5
Queens Park Ave CM12 297 B5
Queens Park Ct CM12 296 F5
Queen's Park Ctry Pk★ CM12 297 B6
Queens Park Rd RM3 315 A2
Queens Rd
Basildon, Steeple View SS15 319 C1
Braintree CM7 127 F5
Crays Hill CM11 320 B4
Loughton IG10 288 F6
North Weald Bassett CM16 247 B6
Rayleigh SS6 323 E2
Southend-on-S, Chalkwell SS9 365 F8
Southend-on-S, Clifftown SS1 366 F8
Sudbury CO10 33 E8
Queen's Rd Barking IG11 352 C6
Brentwood CM14 316 D8
Buckhurst Hill IG9 310 C8
Burnham-on-C CM0 306 C5
Chelmsford CM2 232 D2
Clacton-on-S CO15 195 D1
Colchester CO3 135 C6
Earls Colne CO6 105 B7
Felixstowe IP11 381 E4
Frinton-on-S CO13 170 F4
Harwich CO12 91 A2
South Benfleet SS7 344 D2
West Bergholt CO6 108 D3
Wivenhoe CO7 164 C8
Queens Sq 5 CB9 9 A8
Queen's Sq IP3 18 B4
Queen St Brentwood CM14 316 C5
Brightlingsea CO7 192 F6
Castle Hedingham CO9 51 E3
Chelmsford CM2 232 A1
Coggeshall CO6 131 A2
Colchester CO1 135 F7
Felixstowe IP11 381 C6
Fyfield CM5 227 E2
Gravesend DA12 379 B1
Great Oakley CO12 116 C4
Haverhill CB9 9 A8
Ipswich IP1 17 C5
Maldon CM9 237 A2
Romford RM7 335 D5
Sible Hedingham CO9 75 F6
Southminster CM0 284 C4
Queens Terr CO10 34 A7
Queenstown Gdns RM13 354 F2
Queensway
Chipping Ongar CM5 248 F5
Clacton-on-S CO15 196 D5
Great Cornard CO10 34 B5
Haverhill CB9 8 E8
Lawford CO11 86 C4
Southend-on-S SS1 367 B8
Tiptree CO5 186 C6
Queen's Way IP3 18 B2
Queensway Ho SS8 363 D3
Queensway Lodge SS1 367 B7
Queens Wlk E4 287 D1
Queenswood Ave
Brentwood CM13 295 D4
Chingford E17 309 C2
Queenswood Gdns E11 332 B2
Queenswood Ho CM14 316 D8
Queen Victoria Dr IP9 91 B8
QUENDON 66 F2
Quendon Dr EN9 265 D6
Quendon Pl 17 CB9 9 B8
Quendon Rd SS14 342 E8
Quendon Way CO13 171 A6
Quennell Way CM13 295 D2
Quentin Cl IP1 16 E8
Quest End SS6 323 D5
Quickset Rd CB11 20 C5
Quicksie Hill CB11 41 E2
Quilberry Dr CM77 154 D8
Quilp Dr CM1 231 F7
Quilter Dr IP8 16 C1
Quilter Rd IP11 381 F4
Quilters Cl Basildon SS14 342 D8
Quilters Cl continued
Holland-on-S CO15 196 F6
Quilters Dr CM12 319 A8
Quilter's Gn CO6 107 D6
Quilters Inf Sch CM12 297 A1
Quilters Jun Sch CM12 297 A1
Quilters Straight SS14 342 E8
Quince Cl CO11 60 D1
Quince Ct CO5 186 D4
Quince Tree Cl RM15 357 C1
Quinion Cl CM1 231 D7
Quintons Cnr CO7 59 D4
Quinton's La IP11 381 F7
Quintons Rd CO7 59 D4
Quorn Gdns SS9 346 A1
Quorn The CM4 274 A3

R

R A Butler Jun & Inf Schs CB11 22 E1
RACECOURSE 18 B2
Rachael Clarke Cl SS17 360 E4
Rachael Ct 1 CM2 232 B1
Rachael Gdns CM8 156 E4
Rachel Cl IG6 333 D8
Rachel Ct 6 IP4 17 D6
Rackenford SS3 368 D8
Radbourne Cres E17 309 D1
Radburn Cl CM18 224 A4
Radburn Pl DA10 377 E2
Radcliffe Dr IP2 16 D2
Radford Bsns Ctr CM12 296 F3
Radford Cres CM12 297 A3
Radford Ct CM12 297 B3
Radford Ho CM12 297 B3
Radford Way Barking IG11 352 F2
Billericay CM12 297 A3
Radiator Rd CO10 34 A5
Radley Ave IG3 353 A8
Radley Ct IG7 311 E6
RADLEY GREEN 251 D8
Radley Green Rd CM4, CM5 251 C7
RADLEY'S END 97 A2
Radley's La E18 310 A1
Radleys Mead RM10 354 B6
Radnor Cres IG4 332 F6
Radnor Rd SS4 303 C1
Radstock Ho 11 RM3 314 D5
Radstocks CM12 297 B3
Radveld Chase CO3 134 E4
RADWINTER 45 F8
Radwinter Ave SS12 321 D6
Radwinter CE Prim Sch CB10 45 F7
RADWINTER END 25 B4
Radwinter Rd Ashdon CB10 24 B7
Saffron Walden CB10 23 B1
Sewards End CB10 23 F1
Raeburn Cl CO13 170 F7
Raeburn Rd IP3 18 A1
Raeburn Rd S IP3 17 F1
Raglan Mews CO15 195 C3
Raglan Rd CO13 171 A5
Ragley Cl CM77 154 B6
Rahn Rd CM16 268 A8
Raider Cl RM7 313 B2
Raile Wlk CO10 15 D8
Railey Rd CB11 43 E8
Railstore The RM2 336 C8
Railway App Basildon SS15 341 B4
Felixstowe IP11 381 E5
Railway Cotts Ilford IG6 333 D8
Redbridge IG6 311 D2
Thorpe-le-S CO16 168 F7
Wendens Ambo CB11 42 F5
Railway Pl Belvedere DA17 369 A3
12 Gravesend DA11 379 B1
Railway Sq
Brentwood CM14 316 C7
Chelmsford CM1 232 A3
Railway St Braintree CM7 128 A3
Chelmsford CM1 232 A3
Dagenham RM6 334 C4
Manningtree CO11 86 D4
Northfleet DA11 378 C1
Railway Terr Chingford E17 309 C2
Clacton-on-S CO15 195 F3
11 Manningtree CO11 86 D4
Southend-on-S SS2 348 A3
Rainbow Ave SS8 364 C4
Rainbow Ct CO12 91 D4
Rainbow La SS17 360 F1
Rainbow Mead CM3 211 A5
Rainbow Mews CM9 236 F5
Rainbow Rd
Canvey Island SS8 364 C4
Grays RM16 372 C2
Sheering CM17 201 E3
West Mersea CO5 218 D6
Rainbow Way CO6 77 F1
Raine Ave CB9 8 D8
Raine Gdns 4 IG8 310 A6
RAINHAM 355 A2
Rainham Rd RM13 354 F4
Rainham Rd N RM10 335 B2
Rainham Rd S RM10 354 C7
Rainham Sta RM13 355 A1
Rainham Trad Est RM13 354 F1
Rainham Village Prim Sch RM13 355 A1
Rainham Way CO13 171 B6
Rainsborowe Rd CO2 135 C4
Rainsford Ave CM1 231 F3
Rainsford La CM1 231 F2
Rainsford Rd
Chelmsford CM1 231 F3
Stansted Mountfitchet CM24 119 E8
Rainsford Way RM12 336 A3
Raleigh Dr SS15 341 D5
Rambler Cl CO3 134 D7
Ramblers La 5 CM17 200 D1
Ramblers Way CM0 306 D4
Ram Gorse CM20 199 B2
Rampart Cotts CO6 109 B7
Ramparts Cl CO6 109 B7
Rampart St SS3 368 G6
Ramparts The SS6 323 F2
Rampart Terr SS3 368 G6
Ramplings Ave CO15 195 E5
Rampton Cl E4 309 A7
Ramsay Dr SS16 342 E3
Ramsay Gdns RM3 314 C2
Ramsay Rd E7 332 A1
RAMSDEN BELLHOUSE 298 D1
Ramsden Cl CO15 196 A5
Ramsden Dr RM5 313 A3
Ramsden Hall Sch CM11 297 F3
RAMSDEN HEATH 298 B4
Ramsden Park Rd CM11 298 D1
Ramsden View Rd SS12 320 F6
RAMSEY 90 A2
Ramsey Chase
Latchingdon CM3 282 A6
Wickford SS12 321 F6
Ramsey Cl Heybridge CM9 237 D4
Ipswich IP2 17 A1
Ramsey Ct SS0 347 B3
RAMSEY ISLAND 262 B8
Ramsey Mews CO2 136 A4
Ramsey Rd Halstead CO9 103 D8
Harwich CO12 90 C2
Ramsey Sch (Priory Hall) The CO9 77 A2
Ramsey Sch The CO9 77 A2
Ramsgate Dr IP3 18 B3
Ramsgill App IG2 333 F7
Ramsgill Dr IG2 333 F7
Rams Gr RM6 334 E7
Ramshaw Dr CM2 232 F3
Ramuz Dr SS0 347 D2
Rana Ct CM7 127 F4
Rana Dr CM7 127 F4
Randall Cl
Great Dunmow CM6 123 D1
Witham CM8 211 F7
Randall Ct RM13 355 B2
Randall Dr
Hornchurch RM12 355 D8
Orsett RM16 374 A8
Randalls Dr CM13 295 E3
Randolph Ave CM7 73 C6
Randolph Cl Ipswich IP4 18 B5
Maldon CM9 258 F8
Southend-on-S SS9 346 E3
Randolph Gr RM6 334 C6
Rands Rd CM6 176 F8
Rands Way IP3 18 B2
Randulph Terr CM1 232 D3
Randway SS6 323 D1
Randwell Cl IP4 18 B5
Ranelagh Ct IP11 381 E4
Ranelagh Gdns Ilford IG1 333 A3
Redbridge IG1 332 F3
Wanstead E11 332 C6
Ranelagh Prim Sch IP2 16 F5
Ranelagh Rd
Felixstowe IP11 381 E4
Ipswich IP2 17 A5
Wallend E6 352 A3
Ranger Hts 4 CM7 127 F3
Ranger's Rd
Buckhurst Hill E4, IG9, IG10 288 A2
Chingford E4 287 F2
Ranger Wlk CO2 136 B3
Rangoon Cl CO2 135 B1
RANK'S GREEN 181 D8
Ransome Cl IP8 16 A6
Ransome Cres IP3 18 B2
Ransome Rd IP3 18 B3
Ransomes Europark IP3 38 E8
Ransomes Way
Chelmsford CM1 232 B4
Ipswich IP3 38 D8
Ransom Rd CO5 186 C5
Rantree Fold SS16 341 F4
Ranulf Cl CM17 200 C6
Ranulf Rd CM6 151 E6
Ranulph Way CM3 211 B3
Ranworth Ave EN11 197 B2
Raphael Ave Romford RM1 335 F8
Tilbury RM18 379 B7
Raphael Dr
Chelmsford CM1 232 F7
Southend-on-S SS3 350 A1
Raphael Ind Sch RM11 336 A5
Raphaels SS15 341 E6
Raphaels Ct RM1 335 F7
Rapier Cl RM19 371 A2
Rapier St IP2 17 C3
Ratcliff Ct CO5 158 E2
Ratcliffe Ct Colchester CO1 136 B8
Frinton-on-S CO13 170 F5
Ratcliffe Rd CO3 134 E6
Rat Hill IP9 63 F2
Rat La SS6 345 C8
Ratsborough Chase CM0 284 C2
Rat's La IG10 266 B1
Rattwick Dr SS8 364 F3
Ratty's La EN11 221 D6
Ravel Ave CM8 211 F7
Ravel Gdns RM15 371 C7
Ravel Rd RM15 371 D7
Raven Cl CM12 296 F4
Raven Cres CM12 296 F4
Ravencroft RM16 374 B4
Ravendale Way SS3 349 D1
Raven Dr SS7 344 C2
Ravenings Par IG3 334 A3
Raven La CM12 296 F4
Ravenoak Way IG7 311 E5
Raven Rd E18 310 C1
Ravens Ave CO9 76 F1
Ravensbourne Cres RM3 336 F8
Ravensbourne Dr CM1 231 E2
Ravensbourne Gdns IG5 311 B2
Ravensbourne Sch RM3 314 D2
Ravenscourt CM15 294 D1
Ravenscourt Cl RM12 336 E1
Ravenscourt Dr
Basildon SS16 342 E5
Hornchurch RM12 336 E1
Ravenscourt Gr RM12 336 E2

Riverside Wlk
16 Bishop's Stortford CM23 ... 145 F7
Colchester CO1 ... 135 E8
Wickford SS12 ... 321 B8
Riverside Works IG11 ... 352 B5
Riversmead EN11 ... 221 A5
Rivers St IP4 ... 17 F7
Riverton Dr CM0 ... 240 B1
Rivertons SS16 ... 342 F4
Riverview Basildon SS16 ... 343 A4
Dartford DA1 ... 376 A3
River View Braintree CM7 ... 127 F1
Grays RM16 ... 374 A1
Holbrook IP9 ... 62 D5
Manningtree CO11 ... 86 C4
Witham CM8 ... 212 A8
River View Cl SS15 ... 319 C1
Riverview Ct Basildon SS16 342 E4
15 Belvedere DA17 ... 369 A1
Greenhithe DA9 ... 376 F1
Riverview Flats 13 RM19 ... 371 B1
Riverview Gdns SS5 ... 301 C3
Riverview Rd DA9 ... 377 A2
River View Rd
Harkstead IP9 ... 63 B2
South Benfleet SS7 ... 344 E2
Riverview Terr 1 RM19 ... 371 B1
River View Terr CM3 ... 282 E2
River Way Harlow CM20 ... 200 B5
Loughton IG10 ... 289 A3
Riviera Dr SS1 ... 367 D8
Rivington Ave IG8 ... 310 D1
Rivington Ct 5 RM10 ... 354 B6
Rivish La CO10 ... 15 C7
RJ Mitchell Prim Sch The RM12 ... 355 B6
RO24 CM19 ... 222 D8
Roach RM18 ... 375 C2
Roach Ave SS6 ... 323 D1
Roach Vale Colchester CO4 110 E1
Southend-on-S SS9 ... 346 F7
Roach Vale Prim Sch CO4 110 E1
Roach View Bsns Pk SS4 .. 326 B1
Roast Gn CB11 ... 64 F6
Robeck Rd IP3 ... 17 F1
Robert Cl 4 Barking IG11 .. 352 C6
Billericay CM12 ... 296 F2
Chelmsford CM2 ... 232 F4
Chigwell IG7 ... 311 F5
Robert Clack Lower Sch RM8 ... 334 F2
Robert Clack Upper Sch RM8 ... 335 A3
Robert Daniels Ct CM16 .. 267 E2
Robert Drake Prim Sch The SS7 ... 344 D7
Robert Leonard Ind Est SS2 ... 347 F5
Roberts Cl RM3 ... 314 B2
Roberts Ct CM2 ... 254 E7
Robert's Hill CO8 ... 79 F3
Roberts Ho RM10 ... 354 B5
Robertson Ct RM17 ... 373 B2
Robertson Dr SS12 ... 321 E5
Roberts Pl RM10 ... 354 A6
Roberts Rd Basildon SS15 .. 341 B7
Belvedere DA17 ... 369 A1
Chingford E17 ... 309 B2
Colchester CO1, CO2 ... 136 A5
North Fambridge CM3 ... 303 A7
Robert Suckling Ct CB9 ... 27 B6
Robert Wallace Cl CM23 .. 118 F1
Robert Way Wickford SS11 . 321 F6
Wivenhoe CO7 ... 137 C3
Robin Cl Billericay CM12 ... 297 C6
Great Bentley CO7 ... 166 D8
Haverhill CB9 ... 9 C7
Romford RM5 ... 313 D3
Stanstead Abbotts SG12 .. 197 C3
Robin Cres CO3 ... 134 B4
Robin Dr IP2 ... 16 D3
ROBINHOOD END ... 49 B6
Robin Hood Rd
Brentwood CM15 ... 294 C2
Elsenham CM22 ... 94 C1
Robinia Cl Basildon SS15 .. 319 D1
Redbridge IG6 ... 311 E4
Robinia Ct 1 CO4 ... 136 E7
Robin Jeffrey Ct 10 CM23 . 145 F6
Robinsbridge Rd CO6 ... 130 F2
Robinsdale CO15 ... 195 F6
Robin's La CM16 ... 267 C3
Robinson Cl
Bishop's Stortford CM23 .. 145 F5
Hornchurch RM12 ... 355 B5
Robinson Rd
Brightlingsea CO7 ... 193 A7
Dagenham RM10 ... 354 A8
Horndon on t H SS17 ... 359 E4
Robinsons Cl CM0 ... 284 D3
Robinson Way DA11 ... 378 A2
Robins The CM15 ... 272 D4
Robinsway EN9 ... 265 E5
Robin Way Chelmsford CM2 254 B5
Sudbury CO10 ... 33 C5
Robjohns Rd CM1 ... 253 E8
Robletts Way CO6 ... 80 E4
Roborough Wlk RM12 ... 355 C6
Roca Ct E11 ... 332 A6
Rochdale Way CO4 ... 136 E6
Roche Ave SS4 ... 325 E2
Roche Cl SS4 ... 325 F2
Rochefort Dr SS4 ... 347 F8
Rochehall Way SS4 ... 348 B8
Rochelle Cl CM6 ... 70 A3
Rochester Cl CM7 ... 128 D4
Rochester Ct CB10 ... 22 F2
Rochester Dr SS0 ... 347 C4
Rochester Gdns IG1 ... 332 F4
Rochester Mews SS0 ... 347 C4
Rochester Rd RM12 ... 355 B5
Rochester Way
Basildon SS14 ... 342 F7
6 Basildon SS14 ... 342 F8
Sudbury CO10 ... 15 D2
Rocheway SS4 ... 326 A2
ROCHFORD ... 325 E1
Rochford Ave
Brentwood CM15 ... 295 A4
Rochford Ave *continued*
Ilford RM6 ... 334 C6
Loughton IG10 ... 289 C6
Southend-on-S SS0 ... 347 E1
Waltham Abbey EN9 ... 265 D5
Rochford Cl
Hornchurch RM12 ... 355 B6
Stansted Mountfitchet CM24 ... 119 E5
Wickford SS11 ... 321 F6
Rochford Garden Way SS4 ... 325 E3
Rochford Gn IG10 ... 289 C6
Rochford Hall Cl SS4 ... 325 F1
Rochford Hall Cotts SS4 .. 325 D1
Rochford Ho
Waltham Abbey EN9 ... 265 D6
Walton-on-t-N CO14 ... 144 E2
Rochford Prim Sch SS4 ... 325 E2
Rochford Rd
Bishop's Stortford CM23 .. 119 C1
Canvey Island SS8 ... 364 D3
Chelmsford CM2 ... 232 C1
Southend-on-S SS2 ... 347 E5
St Osyth CO16 ... 194 B4
Rochford Sta SS4 ... 325 E1
Rochford Way
Frinton-on-S CO13 ... 170 F7
Walton-on-t-N CO14 ... 171 A7
Rochforte Cl SS4 ... 325 F2
Rockall SS2 ... 347 A7
Rockall Cl CB9 ... 9 D7
Rockchase Gdns RM11 ... 336 E5
Rockells Farm* CB11 ... 41 B5
Rock Gdns RM10 ... 354 B7
Rockhampton Wlk 10 CO2 ... 136 A1
Rockingham Ave RM11 ... 336 B4
Rockingham Cl CO4 ... 110 D3
Rocklands Ct RM17 ... 373 C1
Rockleigh Ave SS9 ... 347 A1
Rockleigh Ct CM15 ... 295 A2
Rockwell Rd RM10 ... 354 B7
Rockwood Gdns IG10 ... 289 C6
RODBRIDGE CORNER ... 15 C4
Rodbridge Dr SS1 ... 367 F8
Rodbridge Hill CO10 ... 15 B5
Rodbridge Nature Reserve* CO10 ... 15 B4
Roddam Cl CO3 ... 135 C6
Roden Cl CM17 ... 200 F4
Roden St IG1 ... 333 A1
Roden Terr CM5 ... 204 A1
Roding CM14 ... 294 B1
Roding Ave IG8 ... 310 E4
Roding Cl Fyfield CM5 ... 227 D2
Great Wakering SS3 ... 350 B4
Roding Ct CM7 ... 128 D1
Roding Dr CM15 ... 271 F2
Roding Gdns IG10 ... 288 E3
Roding Hall RM4 ... 290 B6
Roding Hospl (BUPA) IG4 ... 332 D8
Roding La
Buckhurst Hill IG9, IG7 .. 288 E1
Chigwell IG7 ... 289 A1
Roding La N IG8 ... 310 E2
Roding La S IG4 ... 332 D7
Roding Leigh CM3 ... 301 E7
Roding Lodge IG1 ... 332 D5
Roding Prim Sch
Barking RM8 ... 353 C7
Woodford IG8 ... 310 E3
Roding Rd IG10 ... 288 F3
Rodings Ave SS17 ... 360 D4
Rodings Ct E4 ... 309 D5
Rodings Prim Sch CM6 .. 204 C8
Rodings The
Southend-on-S SS9 ... 346 D7
Upminster RM14 ... 337 D5
5 Woodford IG8 ... 310 C4
Roding Valley High Sch IG10 ... 288 E4
Roding Valley Sta IG9 ... 310 D6
Roding View
Buckhurst Hill IG9 ... 288 D1
Chipping Ongar CM5 ... 249 B4
Roding Way
Rainham RM13 ... 355 D3
Wickford SS12 ... 321 E7
Rodney Cres EN11 ... 221 A8
Rodney Gdns CM7 ... 128 C4
Rodney Rd
Chipping Ongar CM5 ... 248 F2
Wanstead E11 ... 332 B7
Rodney Way
Chelmsford CM1 ... 253 E7
Romford RM7 ... 313 B2
Rodwells SS3 ... 349 E4
Roebuck Ct E4 ... 309 C3
Roebuck Hts IG9 ... 288 C2
Roebuck La IG9 ... 288 C1
Roebuck Rd IG6 ... 312 B4
Roebuck Trad Est IG6 ... 312 B4
Roedean Cl SS2 ... 348 F1
Roedean Dr RM1 ... 335 E7
Roedean Gdns SS2 ... 348 F2
Rogation Cl CO3 ... 134 D6
Roger Browning Ho 25 CO1 ... 135 F7
Roger Reede's Almshouses RM1 ... 335 E7
Rogers Cl IP11 ... 381 D6
ROGERS END ... 6 B1
Rogers Gdns RM10 ... 354 A7
Rogers Ho 9 RM10 ... 335 A1
Rogers Rd
Dagenham RM10 ... 354 A7
Grays RM17 ... 373 C2
Roggel Rd SS8 ... 364 D2
Rohan Ct SS6 ... 301 D6
Rohan Pl 4 IG4 ... 332 F6
Rokeby Gdns IG8 ... 310 A2
Rokells SS14 ... 342 A7
Rokell Way CO13 ... 170 F6
Rokescroft SS13 ... 343 A5
Roland La SS8 ... 364 B4
Rolands Cl CM1 ... 232 B7
Roles Gr RM6 ... 334 E7
Rollason Way CM14 ... 316 C7
Rollerworld* CO1 ... 136 B7
Rollestons CM1 ... 252 F8
Rolley La CO5 ... 158 C2
Roll Gdns IG2 ... 333 A6
Rolls Ct The E4 ... 309 C5
Rolls Park Ave E4 ... 309 B5
Rolls Park Rd E4 ... 309 B5
Rolph CE Prim Sch CO16 . 141 F1
Rolph Cl CO16 ... 142 A2
Rolphs Cotts CM8 ... 156 D5
ROLPHY GREEN ... 179 A4
Romagne Cl SS17 ... 359 F3
Romainville Way SS8 ... 363 C3
Roman RM18 ... 375 C2
Roman Cl Maldon CM9 ... 236 F4
Mountnessing CM15 ... 295 E8
Rainham RM13 ... 354 D3
Roman Ct Braintree CM7 ... 128 C1
Saffron Walden CB11 ... 43 E7
3 Wickford SS11 ... 322 A5
Roman Hill CO2 ... 163 B7
Roman Ho
3 Chelmsford CM2 ... 232 B1
Rainham RM13 ... 354 D3
Roman La CM24 ... 120 B2
Roman Lodge IG9 ... 288 C1
Roman Mews 7 EN11 ... 221 A7
Roman Rd Colchester CO1 .. 136 A7
Ilford IG1 ... 352 B6
Ingatestone CM4 ... 273 F1
Little Waltham CM3 ... 208 B5
Mountnessing CM15 ... 295 E8
Roman Rise CM21 ... 172 D2
Romans Farm Chase CM0 306 C7
Romanshurst CM9 ... 237 A4
Romans Pl CM1 ... 231 B1
Roman St 8 EN11 ... 221 A7
Romans Way CM1 ... 231 B1
Roman Vale CM17 ... 200 C5
Roman Way
Billericay CM12 ... 319 A8
Burnham-on-C CM0 ... 306 B8
Colchester CO2 ... 135 E3
Haverhill CB9 ... 9 D7
Littlebury CB11 ... 21 F4
Long Melford CO10 ... 15 C6
Point Clear B CO16 ... 193 A3
Waltham Abbey EN9 ... 265 B4
Romany Stps 17 SS1 ... 367 C7
Rom Cres RM7 ... 335 F4
Romeland EN9 ... 265 C6
ROMFORD ... 335 D7
Romford Cl CO4 ... 136 E8
Romford Rd Aveley RM15 .. 371 C7
Chipping Ongar CM5 ... 270 F7
Ilford E12 ... 333 A1
Redbridge IG6 ... 312 C5
Upminster RM15 ... 356 C1
Romford Sta RM1 ... 335 E5
Romney Chase RM11 ... 337 A5
Romney Cl Braintree CM7 .. 127 E6
Brightlingsea CO7 ... 165 E1
Clacton-on-S CO16 ... 195 D5
Kirby Cross CO13 ... 170 E7
Romney Ho SS4 ... 325 F2
Romney Rd Billericay CM12 296 F1
Ipswich IP3 ... 38 A8
Romsey Cl Hockley SS5 ... 324 D6
South Benfleet SS7 ... 344 B5
Stanford-le-H SS17 ... 360 B1
Romsey Cres SS7 ... 344 B5
Romsey Dr SS7 ... 344 B5
Romsey Gdns RM9 ... 353 D4
Romsey Rd Dagenham RM9 353 D4
South Benfleet SS7 ... 344 A5
Romsey Way SS7 ... 344 B4
Romside Pl 4 RM7 ... 335 D7
Romulus Cl CO4 ... 109 F5
Rom Valley Way RM7 ... 335 D5
Ronald Dr SS6 ... 323 A4
Ronald Hill Gr SS9 ... 346 D1
Ronald Park Ave SS0 ... 347 C2
Ronald Rd Halstead CO9 ... 103 E8
Romford RM3 ... 315 A2
Roneo Cnr RM12 ... 335 F3
Roneo Link RM12 ... 335 F3
Ronnie La E12 ... 352 A8
Ron Todd Cl RM10 ... 354 A4
Ronver Lodge E4 ... 309 E7
Roodegate SS14 ... 342 A6
Rook Cl RM13 ... 355 A5
ROOK END ... 68 A5
Rook End La CB11 ... 68 B5
Rookeries The CO6 ... 133 B4
Rookery Chase CO7 ... 84 E2
Rookery Cl
Great Chesterford CB10 ... 3 D3
Hatfield Peverel CM3 ... 211 A5
Rayleigh SS6 ... 323 C2
Stanford-le-H SS17 ... 360 B1
Rookery Cres RM10 ... 354 B5
Rookery Ct RM20 ... 377 A8
Rookery Hill SS17 ... 361 C2
Rookery La
Great Totham CM9 ... 213 E7
North Fambridge CM3 ... 280 E1
Tiptree CO5 ... 186 C7
Wendens Ambo CB11 ... 42 E4
Rookery Rd CM4 ... 250 D3
Rookery The Grays RM20 .. 377 A8
Lawford CO11 ... 86 C4
Stansted Mountfitchet CM24 ... 119 E8
Rookery View RM17 ... 373 D1
Rookes CB10 ... 22 D3
Rookes Cres CM1 ... 253 F8
Rookley Ct 15 RM19 ... 371 B1
Rook Lodge IG1 ... 332 D5
Rookwood Ave IG10 ... 289 C6
Rookwood Cl
Clacton-on-S CO15 ... 195 D7
Grays RM17 ... 373 B2
Rookwood Gdns E4 ... 309 F8
Rookwood Ho 2 IG11 ... 352 D3
Rookwood Way CB9 ... 9 A6
Rookyards SS16 ... 342 E5
Roosevel Ave SS8 ... 364 A4
Roosevelt Rd 1 SS15 ... 341 A6
Roosevelt Way
Colchester CO2 ... 136 B4
Roosevelt Way *continued*
Dagenham RM10 ... 354 D6
Roos Hill Debden Rd CB11 . 43 E5
Roothings The CM9 ... 237 B5
Roots Hall Ave SS2 ... 347 F2
Roots Hall Dr SS2 ... 347 E2
Roots Hall (Southend United F.C.) SS2 ... 347 E2
Roots La CM8 ... 212 E5
Roper Cl CO4 ... 110 B6
Roper Ct IP4 ... 18 C5
Ropers Ave E4 ... 309 C5
Roper's Chase CM1 ... 253 A7
Ropers La CO10 ... 15 B5
Ropers Yd 12 CM14 ... 316 C8
Rope Wlk Ipswich IP4 ... 17 E5
Maldon CM9 ... 237 A1
Rosabelle Ave CO7 ... 137 B1
Rosalind Cl CO4 ... 136 F7
Rosalind Ct 6 IG11 ... 353 A5
Rosary Ct CM15 ... 316 E8
Rosary Gdns SS0 ... 347 B4
Rosbach Rd SS8 ... 364 D3
Rosberg Rd SS8 ... 364 E3
Roscommon Way SS8 ... 363 C4
Rose Acre Basildon SS14 .. 342 F6
Stratford St M CO7 ... 58 F6
Roseacre Cl RM11 ... 336 F4
Roseacres
Sawbridgeworth CM21 ... 172 D3
Takeley CM22 ... 148 C7
Rose Allen Ave CO2 ... 162 F8
Rose Ave Colchester CO3 .. 134 C4
Woodford E18 ... 310 B1
Rosebank Harwich CO12 ... 91 A3
Waltham Abbey EN9 ... 265 E6
West Mersea CO5 ... 218 B6
Rose Bank CM14 ... 316 D7
Rosebank Ave RM12 ... 355 C7
Rosebank Ct CO15 ... 196 A2
Rosebank Rd CO5 ... 218 B6
Rosebay Ave CM12 ... 296 F5
Rosebay Cl CM8 ... 183 D3
Roseberry Ave
Basildon SS16 ... 341 B4
South Benfleet SS7 ... 344 C7
Roseberry Cl RM14 ... 337 F5
Roseberry Ct SS7 ... 344 C7
Roseberry Gdns RM14 ... 337 F5
Roseberry Wlk SS7 ... 344 C7
Rosebery CM23 ... 146 C6
Rosebery Ave CO1 ... 136 A7
Rosebery Ct IP11 ... 381 D2
Rosebery Rd
Chelmsford CM2 ... 254 B8
Felixstowe IP11 ... 381 F4
Grays RM17 ... 377 E8
Ipswich IP4 ... 17 F5
Rosebury Ct CM13 ... 295 D3
Rosebury Sq 2 IG8 ... 311 A3
Rose Cl 10 SS12 ... 321 E5
Rose Cotts
Brent Pelham SG9 ... 64 A5
Great Sampford CM7 ... 47 E5
Harlow CM17 ... 224 F5
Willingale CM5 ... 228 D3
Rose Cres CO4 ... 109 D2
Rosecroft Cl Basildon SS16 341 A4
Clacton-on-S CO15 ... 195 E6
Rose & Crown Mews CM0 284 D4
Rose & Crown Wlk CB10 ... 22 D2
Rose Ct Blackheath CO2 ... 163 B8
Ilford IG1 ... 352 B6
Rosedale Cotts CO3 ... 133 F5
Rosedale Dr RM9 ... 353 B5
Rosedale Gdns RM9 ... 353 B5
Rosedale Rd
Dagenham RM9 ... 353 B5
Grays RM17 ... 373 D1
Romford RM1 ... 335 C8
Rosedene Gdns IG2 ... 333 A7
Rose Dr CM0 ... 284 D3
Rosefinch Cl CB9 ... 9 C7
Rose Gdns Braintree CM7 .. 128 A2
Seawick CO16 ... 220 B6
Rose Glen Chelmsford CM2 . 254 C7
Romford RM7 ... 335 D5
ROSE GREEN ... 106 E5
Rose Green Cotts CO6 ... 106 E5
Rosehatch Ave RM6 ... 334 D8
ROSE HILL ... 18 A4
Rose Hill CM7 ... 128 A2
Rosehill Cres IP3 ... 17 F4
Rose Hill Prim Sch IP3 ... 18 A4
Rosehill Rd IP3 ... 17 F4
Rose Ho 12 CO1 ... 136 A6
Rose La Billericay CM12 ... 297 A2
Dagenham RM6 ... 334 E7
Great Chesterford CB10 ... 3 E2
Ipswich IP1, IP4 ... 17 C5
Salcott-c-V CM9 ... 216 B8
Wivenhoe CO7 ... 164 B7
Roselaine SS14 ... 342 B7
Roseland Ct CO15 ... 195 F3
Roselands Ave EN11 ... 197 A1
Roselawn Fields CM1 ... 232 B8
Roseley Cotts CM20 ... 199 B4
Rosemary Ave
Braintree CM7 ... 127 F4
Felixstowe IP11 ... 381 F6
Romford RM1 ... 335 F8
Rosemary Cl
Great Dunmow CM6 ... 123 C1
1 Harlow CM17 ... 200 C4
South Ockendon RM15 ... 357 C2
Tiptree CO5 ... 186 C5
Rosemary Cotts CM3 ... 209 E1
Rosemary Cres
Clacton-on-S CO15 ... 195 F2
Great Dunmow CM6 ... 123 C1
Tiptree CO5 ... 186 C5
Rosemary Ct
2 Colchester CO4 ... 136 D8
Tiptree CO5 ... 186 C5
Rosemary Dr IG4 ... 332 D6
Rosemary Gdns
Dagenham RM8 ... 334 F3
Sudbury CO10 ... 15 F2
Rosemary La
Castle Hedingham CO9 ... 52 A5
Rosemary La *continued*
Great Dunmow CM6 ... 123 C1
Halstead CO9 ... 76 E2
Stebbing CM6 ... 124 C7
Thorrington CO7 ... 166 B5
Rosemary Lodge SS2 ... 347 F1
Rosemary Rd CO15 ... 195 F2
Rosemary Rd W CO15 ... 195 E2
Rosemary Way CO15 ... 220 G7
Rosemead SS7 ... 344 C7
Rosemead Gdns CM13 ... 295 D5
Rosemount CM19 ... 223 A5
Rosemount Cl IG8 ... 310 F4
Rosemount Ct IP11 ... 381 F4
Rose Park Ct IG5 ... 310 F1
Rose Rd SS8 ... 364 A3
Roserna Rd SS8 ... 364 D3
Rosery Ho IP11 ... 381 F4
Rosery Mews CO13 ... 170 A4
Rose St DA11 ... 378 B1
Roses The IG8 ... 309 F3
Rose Tree Mews IG8 ... 310 E4
Rosetta Cl CO7 ... 137 B2
Rosetti Terr 4 RM8 ... 353 B8
Rose Vale EN11 ... 221 A6
Rose Valley CM14 ... 316 D7
Rose Valley Cres SS17 ... 360 E4
Rose Way SS4 ... 348 A8
Rose Wlk CO9 ... 29 B6
Rosewood Ave RM12 ... 355 A7
Rosewood Cl
Colchester CO4 ... 110 A4
South Ockendon RM15 ... 357 E2
Rosewood Ct RM6 ... 334 C6
Rosewood Ho 8 CM14 ... 316 C7
Rosewood La SS3 ... 368 F7
Rosher Ho DA11 ... 378 F1
ROSHERVILLE ... 378 E1
Rosherville CE Prim Sch DA11 ... 378 E1
Rosherville Way DA11 ... 378 E1
Rosilian Dr SS5 ... 302 C1
Roslings Cl CM1 ... 231 D5
Roslyn Gdns RM2 ... 313 F1
Rossall Cl RM11 ... 336 A5
Ross Ave RM8 ... 334 F3
Ross Cl Haverhill CB9 ... 9 D7
Saffron Walden CB11 ... 43 E6
Rossdene Gdns CM6 ... 204 D7
Rossendale CM1 ... 231 E1
Rossendale Cl CO4 ... 110 D3
Rosshill Ind Pk SS2 ... 348 A4
Rossiter Rd SS3 ... 368 H8
Rosslyn Ave Chingford E4 .. 309 F8
Dagenham RM8 ... 335 A4
Romford RM3 ... 314 F1
Rosslyn Cl SS5 ... 324 E7
Rosslyn Ct SS17 ... 360 C1
Rosslyn Rd Barking IG11 ... 352 D5
Billericay CM12 ... 296 F2
Hockley SS5 ... 324 E7
Rosslyn Terr CO5 ... 158 C3
Ross Way SS16 ... 341 B3
Rotary Way CO3 ... 135 E8
Rothbury Ave RM13 ... 370 B8
Rothbury Ho 5 RM3 ... 314 D4
Rothbury Rd CM1 ... 231 D1
Roth Dr CM13 ... 317 B8
Rothesay Ave CM2 ... 254 A8
Rothmans Ave CM2 ... 254 E6
Rothwell Cl SS9 ... 346 C6
Rothwell Gdns RM9 ... 353 C4
Rothwell Rd RM9 ... 353 C4
ROTTEN END ... 101 A7
Rotunda The 1 RM7 ... 335 D6
Rough Hill Farm Cotts CM3 ... 278 C7
Roughtallys CM16 ... 246 F4
Roughtons CM2 ... 254 C3
Roundacre Basildon SS14 .. 342 A6
Halstead CO9 ... 103 E8
Roundaway Rd IG5 ... 310 F1
ROUNDBUSH ... 281 B8
Roundbush Bglws CM9 ... 281 C8
Roundbush Cnr
Birch Green CO5 ... 160 D3
Great Totham CM9 ... 213 D6
ROUNDBUSH GREEN ... 176 C2
Roundbush Rd
Birch Green CO5 ... 160 D2
Mundon CM9 ... 281 A8
Round Cl CO3 ... 135 B7
Round Coppice Rd
Great Hallingbury CM24 ... 147 A8
Stansted Mountfitchet CM24 ... 120 B1
Rounders Ct 12 RM10 ... 354 B6
Round Hill Rd SS7 ... 345 A2
Roundhills EN9 ... 265 E4
Roundmead Ave IG10 ... 289 A6
Roundmead Cl IG10 ... 289 A7
Roundridge Rd IP9 ... 35 B2
Roundwood Ave CM13 ... 295 B2
Roundwood Gr CM13 ... 295 B2
Roundwood Lake CM13 ... 295 B2
Roundwood Rd IP4 ... 18 A7
Rounton Rd EN9 ... 265 E6
Rous Chase CM2 ... 254 B1
Rouse Way CO1 ... 136 B7
Rous Rd IG9 ... 288 E1
Routh Ave IP3 ... 18 F1
Rover Ave
Clacton-on-S CO15 ... 220 E6
Redbridge IG6 ... 311 F4
Rowallan Cl CO3 ... 135 A3
Rowallen Par RM8 ... 334 C3
Rowan Chase CO5 ... 186 C6
Rowan Cl
Clacton-on-S CO15 ... 195 C3
Colchester CO3 ... 134 D4
Great Bentley CO7 ... 166 F8
Harwich CO12 ... 91 B3
Ilford IG1 ... 352 D7
Ipswich IP3 ... 18 D2
Rayleigh SS6 ... 323 B6
Rowan Dr CM9 ... 237 C5
Rowan Gr RM15 ... 371 C6
Rowan Green E CM13 ... 316 F7
Rowan Green W CM13 ... 316 F7
Rowanhayes Cl IP2 ... 17 B3
Rowan Ho
4 Basildon SS13 ... 343 B8
Ilford IG1 ... 352 D7
Rowan Pl CO1 ... 109 E1
Rowans EN9 ... 266 C4
Rowans The Aveley RM15 .. 371 C5
Billericay CM11 ... 319 D8
Rayleigh SS9 ... 346 B6
Rowans Way
Loughton IG10 ... 288 F5
Wickford SS11 ... 321 E8
Rowan Way Canewdon SS4 304 E1
Great Dunmow CM6 ... 123 C1
Hatfield Peverel CM3 ... 211 A3
Ilford RM6 ... 334 C8
South Ockendon RM15 ... 357 C1
Witham CM8 ... 184 A5
Rowan Wlk
Hornchurch RM11 ... 336 D7
Sawbridgeworth CM21 ... 172 E2
Southend-on-S SS9 ... 346 D6
Rowden Par E4 ... 309 A4
Rowden Park Gdns E4 ... 309 A4
Rowden Rd E4 ... 309 B4
Rowdowns Rd RM9 ... 353 F5
Rowe Gdns IG11 ... 353 A3
Rowenhall SS15 ... 340 F6
ROW GREEN ... 154 D6
ROW HEATH ... 167 F4
ROWHEDGE ... 163 F8
Rowhedge CM13 ... 317 B7
Rowhedge Cl SS13 ... 321 D2
Rowhedge Ct CO7 ... 136 F4
Rowhedge Ferry Rd CO7 .. 164 A8
Rowhedge Rd CO2, CO5 ... 136 E1
Rowherns La CO7 ... 139 F4
Rowland Cres IG7 ... 311 E6
Rowland Ho IP11 ... 381 B5
Rowlands Rd RM8 ... 334 F2
Rowlands The SS7 ... 344 E3
Rowland's Yd CO12 ... 90 E2
Rowland Wlk RM4 ... 313 E7
Rowley Cl CO11 ... 86 D8
Rowley Cotts The CO6 ... 56 D5
Rowley Ct CB9 ... 9 E5
Rowley Hill CB9 ... 9 E5
Rowley Mead CM16 ... 246 C6
Rowley Rd RM16 ... 374 A8
Rowney Ave CB10 ... 44 E2
Rowney Gdns
Dagenham RM9 ... 353 C6
Sawbridgeworth CM21 ... 200 C8
Rowney Rd RM9 ... 353 B6
Rowney Wood CM21 ... 172 C1
Rowntree Way CB11 ... 43 D7
Rows The 1 CM20 ... 199 D1
Row The Hadstock CB1 ... 5 B7
Stratford St M CO7 ... 58 C2
Roxborough Cl CO6 ... 132 E3
Roxburgh Ave RM14 ... 337 C1
Roxburghe Rd CO16 ... 167 F6
ROXWELL ... 230 B6
Roxwell Ave CM1 ... 231 D3
Roxwell CE Prim Sch CM1 ... 230 A6
Roxwell Cres SS12 ... 321 E6
Roxwell Gdns CM13 ... 295 C4
Roxwell Ho IG10 ... 288 E2
Roxwell Rd Barking IG11 ... 353 A3
Chelmsford CM1 ... 231 C4
Roxwell CM1 ... 230 E5
Writtle CM1 ... 231 A4
Roxwell Way IG8 ... 310 C3
Roxy Ave RM6 ... 334 C4
Royal Artillery Way SS2 ... 348 F2
Royal Cl Ilford IG3 ... 334 A4
Rochford SS4 ... 325 D5
Royal Cres IG2 ... 333 D5
Royal Ct Basildon SS15 ... 341 B7
3 Brentwood CM14 ... 316 C7
Colchester CO4 ... 110 E1
Maldon CM9 ... 237 A1
Rayleigh SS9 ... 346 B8
Southend-on-S SS2 ... 348 A1
Royal Docks Rd E6 ... 352 B1
Royal Gunpowder Mills* EN9 ... 265 B7
Royal Hospital Sch IP9 ... 62 D3
Royal Jubilee Ct RM2 ... 336 A8
Royal Liberty Sch The RM2 ... 336 C8
Royal Mews SS1 ... 367 A7
Royal Oak Chase SS15 ... 341 E8
Royal Oak Ct RM8 ... 334 C2
Royal Oak Dr SS11 ... 322 A8
Royal Oak Gdns 6 CM23 .. 145 F6
Royal Par 10 RM10 ... 354 B6
Royal Pier Mews 9 DA11 . 379 B1
Royal Pier Rd DA12 ... 379 C1
Royal Sq CO7 ... 84 F7
Royals The SS1 ... 367 A7
Royal Terr SS1 ... 367 A7
Roy Ave IP3 ... 18 B5
Roycraft Ave IG11 ... 352 F3
Roycroft Cl E18 ... 310 B2
ROYDON ... 198 B1
Roydon Bridge SS14 ... 342 D8
Roydonbury Ind Est CM19 222 B8
Roydon Cl IG10 ... 288 E2
ROYDON HAMLET ... 222 C4
Roydon Lodge Chalet Est CM19 ... 198 C1
Roydon Mill Leisure Pk CM19 ... 198 A1
Roydon Prim Sch CM19 ... 222 B8
Roydon Rd Harlow CM19 ... 198 E1
Stanstead Abbotts SG12 ... 197 E4
Roydon Sta CM19 ... 198 B2
Roydon Way CO13 ... 170 F6
Royer Cl SS5 ... 325 A4
Roy Gdns IG2 ... 333 F6
Royle Cl RM2 ... 336 B6
Royston Ave Basildon SS15 319 D1
Chingford E4 ... 309 B5
Southend-on-S SS2 ... 348 B3
Royston Ct IG1 ... 332 D5
Royston Dr IP2 ... 16 D2

426 Roy–St J

Royston Gdns IG1 332 D5
Royston La CB11 20 C6
Royston Par IG1 332 D5
Royston Rd Romford RM3 315 A3
Wendens Ambo CB11 42 C5
Ruaton Dr CO16 195 C4
Rubens Cl SS3 368 G8
Rubens Gate CM1 232 F7
Rubens Rd IP3 18 A1
Rubicon Ave SS11 321 F8
Rubin Pl EN3 265 A2
Ruby Ct 5 Rainham RM13 355 A1
Southend-on-S SS9 346 E5
Rudd Ct CO4 110 F1
Rudkin Rd CO4 109 F5
Rudlands IP8 16 C1
RUDLEY GREEN 258 C2
Rudsdale Way CO3 134 F5
Rudyard Ct CM14 316 B5
Rue De Jeunes 6 CM7 127 F2
Rue De St Lawrence EN9 265 C5
Ruffels Field CM6 124 E4
Ruffles Cl SS6 323 E3
Ruffles Rd CB9 9 C7
Rugby Gdns RM9 353 C6
Rugby Rd Dagenham RM9 353 C6
Great Cornard CO10 34 B4
Rugosa Cl CO3 134 C7
Rumballs Ct CM23 145 A4
Rumbold Rd EN11 221 C8
Rumbullion Dr CM12 296 F3
Rumford Sh Hall The RM1 335 E7
Rumsey Fields CM3 256 F7
Rumsey Row CM1 231 B1
Runcorn Ho 5 RM3 314 E4
Rundells CM18 224 A4
Rundells Wlk SS14 342 E7
Rundels Cotts SS7 345 A6
Rundels The SS7 345 A6
Runnacles St CM8 156 C5
Runnacles Way IP11 381 B5
Runnel Ct 7 IG11 352 C3
Running Mare La CM2 254 A3
Running Waters CM13 317 A6
Runnymede Chase SS7 345 A5
Runnymede Ct SS17 360 C1
Runnymede Rd
Canvey Island SS8 364 B3
Stanford-le-H SS17 360 C1
Runsell Cl CM3 256 F7
RUNSELL GREEN 257 B7
Runsell La CM3 256 F8
Runsell View CM3 257 A7
RUNWELL 299 E1
Runwell Chase SS11 300 A3
Runwell Gdns SS11 299 D2
Runwell Hospl SS11 300 A5
Runwell Prim Sch SS11 299 D2
Runwell Rd SS11 300 B3
Runwell Terr SS1 366 F7
Runwood Rd SS8 363 C3
Rupert Rd CM0 284 C4
Rural Cl RM11 336 B3
Rural Vale DA11 378 E1
Rurik Ct CM9 258 F8
Rushbottom La SS7 344 B7
Rushbury Cl IP4 18 B8
Rush Cl Rushmere St A IP4 18 F4
South Benfleet SS7 344 B6
Stanstead Abbotts SG12 197 C4
Rushcroft Rd E4 309 B3
Rush Croft Sports Coll E4 309 B3
Rushdene Ct CM15 294 C2
Rushdene Rd
Billericay CM12 296 F1
Brentwood CM15 294 C2
Rushden Gdns Ilford IG5 333 A8
Redbridge IG5 311 A1
Rushdon Cl Grays RM17 373 A3
Romford RM1 336 A6
Rushdon Ct RM1 336 A6
Rush Dr EN9 265 D5
Rushes Ct CM23 146 A5
Rushes La CM0 263 A1
Rushes Mead CM18 223 E6
Rushfield CM21 172 E2
RUSH GREEN 195 C4
Rush Green Gdns RM7 335 C3
Rush Green Inf Sch RM7 335 D3
Rush Green Jun Sch RM7 335 D3
Rush Green Rd
Clacton-on-S CO16 195 B2
Romford RM7 335 D3
Rush La CM22 94 C1
Rushleigh Gn CM23 145 D4
Rushley SS13 321 D1
Rushley Cl Grays RM16 373 D5
Great Wakering SS3 350 A4
Rushleydale CM1 232 E5
RUSHLEY GREEN 51 F6
Rushmere Ave RM14 337 C1
Rushmere Cl CO5 218 D6
Rushmere Pl 11 CB9 9 B8
Rushmere Rd IP4 18 B7
RUSHMERE ST ANDREW 18 E7
Rushmere St
Ipswich IP4, IP5 18 D8
Rushmere St A IP5 18 E8
Rushmoor Dr CM7 128 B1
Rusholme Ave RM10 335 A1
Rushton Gr CM17 224 E8
Ruskin Ave
Southend-on-S SS2 348 B2
Upminster RM14 337 C4
Waltham Abbey EN9 265 E5
Ruskin Cl CO13 170 E7
Ruskin Dene CM12 297 A3
Ruskin Gdns RM3 314 B3
Ruskin Gr DA1 376 A2
Ruskin Path 2 SS12 321 D5
Ruskin Rd Belvedere DA17 369 A2
Chelmsford CM2 232 E2
Grays RM16 374 A2
Ipswich IP4 17 F5
Stanford-le-H SS17 360 C1
Ruskins The CM77 126 F1
Ruskoi Rd SS8 363 F5
Rusper Rd RM9 353 C6
Russell Cl Basildon SS15 341 B6
Brentwood CM15 294 B2
Witham CM8 211 F7
Russell Ct Colchester CO2 136 B4
Felixstowe IP11 381 C1
Wickford SS11 321 F7
Russell Gdns
Chelmsford CM2 254 A4
Ilford IG1 333 D4
Wickford SS11 321 F7
Russell Gr SS4 326 A2
RUSSELL GREEN 209 D6
Russell Lodge 5 E4 309 C8
Russell Quay DA11 379 A1
Russell Rd
Buckhurst Hill IG9 288 C1
Clacton-on-S CO15 196 A3
Felixstowe IP11 381 D2
Gravesend DA12 379 D1
Grays RM17 373 A2
Ipswich IP1 17 B5
North Fambridge CM3 281 B1
Tilbury RM18 378 F5
Tilbury RM18 378 F6
Russell's Rd Gosfield CO9 76 A1
Halstead CO9 103 B8
Russell Way CM1 253 E7
Russell Wilson Ct RM3 315 A2
Russet Cl Braintree CM7 128 A1
Stanford-le-H SS17 360 D3
Russet Ho RM17 378 C7
Russets CM2 254 D3
Russets Cl E4 309 D6
Russets The SS4 325 D5
Russett Cl CB9 8 C8
Russetts Basildon SS16 341 A5
Hornchurch RM11 336 E7
Russet Way
Burnham-on-C CM0 306 C6
Hockley SS5 324 F8
Rustic Cl Braintree CM7 128 C3
Upminster RM14 337 E3
Rutherford Cl
Billericay CM12 297 A5
Southend-on-S SS9 346 C6
Rutherfords CM1 208 B1
Ruthven Cl SS12 321 D6
Rutland App RM11 337 A6
Rutland Ave
Colchester CO2 135 B3
Southend-on-S SS1 367 E7
Rutland Cl SS15 341 A6
Rutland Ct 11 CB9 8 E7
Rutland Dr
Hornchurch RM11 337 A6
Rayleigh SS6 323 C7
Rutland Gate DA17 369 B1
Rutland Gdns
Braintree CM7 128 A4
Dagenham RM8 353 C7
Rochford SS4 325 C5
Rutland Ho RM7 313 A1
Rutland Pl CM7 72 B2
Rutland Rd
Chelmsford CM1 232 A7
Ilford IG1 333 B1
North Fambridge CM3 303 A7
Wanstead E11 332 B6
Rutley Cl RM3 314 D1
Ryan Ct RM7 335 C5
Rydal Cl Hullbridge SS5 301 D3
Rayleigh SS6 323 E2
Rydal Dr CM9 259 B8
Rydal Way CM77 154 C6
Rydal Wlk IP3 18 C2
Ryde Ave CO15 196 A8
Ryde Cl SS9 346 B5
Ryde Dr SS17 375 C8
Ryder Gdns RM13 354 F6
Ryder Way SS13 321 D2
Ryde The SS9 346 B5
Rye Cl Brightlingsea CO7 165 E1
Colchester CO3 134 E5
Hatfield Peverel CM3 211 A3
Hornchurch RM12 355 C7
Ipswich IP3 18 D4
Ryecroft CM19 223 B8
Ryecroft Ave IG5 311 B1
Rye Ct 3 CB9 8 F7
Ryedene SS16 342 F3
Ryedene Cl SS16 342 E3
Ryedene Com Prim Sch SS16 342 F3
Ryedene Pl SS16 342 F3
Ryefeld Cl EN11 197 B2
Rye Field The CM3 234 D3
Ryegate Rd CO1 135 F7
Rye Grass Way CM7 128 B1
RYE HILL 223 E1
Rye Hill Rd CM18 223 E2
Rye Hills CO9 103 F8
Rye House Gatehouse* EN11 221 D8
Rye House Sta EN11 221 C8
Rye La CO2 162 A4
Rye Mead SS16 341 C4
Rye Mead Cotts EN11 221 C8
Rye Mill La CO5 158 D4
RYE PARK 221 B7
Rye Park Ind Est EN11 221 D7
Rye Rd EN11 221 C8
Ryes La Bulmer CO10 33 A2
Hatfield Heath CM22 174 B7
Rye St CM23 118 F1
Rye Wlk CM4 274 A2
Rykhill RM16 374 B3
Rylands IP9 35 A2
Rylands Rd SS2 348 D2
Ryle The CM1 253 A8
Rylstone Way CB11 43 F8
Rysley CM3 234 D4

S

Sabina Rd RM16 374 C2
SABINE'S GREEN 292 F6
Sabines Rd RM4 292 E6
Sable Way SS15 340 F7
Sachfield Dr RM16 372 E3
Sacketts Grove Cvn Pk CO15 194 F2
Sackett's Grove Cvn Pk CO16 195 A2
Sackville Cl CM1 231 E3
Sackville Cres RM3 314 E2
Sackville Gdns IG1 332 F3
Sackville Rd SS2 348 E1
Sackville Way CO6 108 D4
Sacred Heart of Mary Girls' Sch RM14 337 B2
Sacred Heart RC Prim Sch SS1 367 C8
Saddle Mews CO3 134 E6
Saddle Rise CM1 232 E8
Saddlers Cl
Bishop's Stortford CM23 145 C4
Great Notley CM77 154 B7
Saddleworth Rd RM3 314 C4
Saddleworth Sq RM3 314 C4
Sadds Yd CO15 195 F3
Sadler Cl CO2 136 B4
Sadlers SS7 344 B6
Sadlers Cl Billericay CM11 297 D5
Kirby Cross CO13 170 C6
Sadlers Mead CM18 224 A7
Saffory Cl SS9 346 C7
Saffron Bsns Ctr CB10 22 F2
Saffron Cl
Horndon on t H SS17 360 A3
West Horndon CM13 339 D5
Wethersfield CM7 73 C3
Saffron Croft CM9 236 E2
Saffron Ct Basildon SS15 340 F6
Saffron Walden CB11 22 D1
Saffron Dr SS14 342 D7
Saffron Gdns
Stanford-le-H SS17 359 F1
Wethersfield CM7 73 C3
Saffron Rd Grays RM16 372 C2
Romford RM5 313 D1
SAFFRON WALDEN 22 E3
Saffron Walden Cty High Sch CB11 43 C8
Saffron Walden Mus* CB10 22 D2
Saffron Waldon Hospl CB11 23 A2
Saffron Way CO5 186 C4
Saffron Wlk
Billericay CM11 297 B2
Wethersfield CM7 73 B3
Sagehayes Cl IP2 17 B3
Sage Mews SS17 360 E3
Sage Rd CO2 136 A2
Sages CM22 94 F5
Sages End Rd CB9 26 B8
Sage Wlk CO5 186 C4
Saines Rd CM6 151 E6
St Agnes Dr SS8 363 D4
St Agnes Rd CM12 319 C3
St Agnes Way IP5 18 F6
St Aidans Ct 4 IG11 353 B3
St Aidan's RC Prim Sch IG1 333 D3
St Albans Ave RM14 337 E2
St Alban's Ave E6 352 A2
St Alban's Cres IG8 310 A2
St Alban's RC High Sch IP4 18 C7
St Albans RC Prim Sch CM20 199 F2
St Alban's RC Prim Sch RM12 355 B5
St Albans Rd IG3 333 F4
St Alban's Rd
Clacton-on-S CO15 196 A3
Colchester CO3 135 D7
Coopersale CM16 246 D2
Woodford IG8 310 A3
St Andrews Ave
Hornchurch RM12 355 A8
Rainham RM12 354 F7
St Andrew's Ave
Colchester CO4 136 D6
Wivenhoe CO4 137 A5
St Andrews CE Prim Sch CM16 247 C6
St Andrew's CE Prim Sch
Bulmer CO10 32 F3
Great Yeldham CO9 29 F2
Halstead CO9 77 A3
Marks Tey CO6 132 E3
Stanstead Abbotts SG12 197 D4
Weeley CO16 167 F8
Wormingford CO6 80 E5
St Andrews Cl
Alresford CO7 165 B7
Canvey Island SS8 363 D4
Ipswich IP4 18 D5
North Weald Bassett CM16 247 D7
St Andrew's Cotts CM3 211 B3
St Andrews Ct
3 Colchester CO4 136 C8
15 Gravesend DA11 379 B1
St Andrews Dr CM11 297 B3
St Andrew's Dr IP9 63 E7
St Andrews Gdns CO4 136 C8
St Andrew's Ho CM20 199 F2
St Andrew's Jun & Inf Schs CO4 136 D7
St Andrews La 2 SS15 341 C7
St Andrew's Mdw CM18 223 F7
St Andrews Pl
Brentwood CM15 316 F8
Brightlingsea CO7 165 E1
St Andrews Rd
Boreham CM3 209 F1
Great Cornard CO10 34 A6
Halstead CO9 76 F1
Romford RM7 335 D5
Southend-on-S SS3 368 D6
St Andrew's Rd
Clacton-on-S CO15 195 E3
Felixstowe IP11 381 E5
Hatfield Peverel CM3 211 A4
Redbridge IG1 332 F4
Rochford SS4 325 E2
Tilbury RM18 378 E5
Weeley CO16 140 F1
St Andrew's Rise CO10 32 E5
St Andrew Wlk IP4 18 F6
St Anne Line RC Jun & Inf Schs SS15 341 F6
St Annes RM16 373 B5
St Annes Cl Coggeshall CO6 131 B2
Grays RM16 373 B5
St Annes Ct CM1 232 C3
St Anne's Pk EN10 221 A4
St Annes Rd SS8 364 E3
St Anne's Rd
Colchester CO4 136 C8
Mountnessing CM15 295 C8
St Anne's Sch CM2 232 A1
St Annes Terr 6 IG6 311 E5
St Ann's IG11 352 C4
St Anns Cl 3 SS15 341 C7
St Anns Rd CO15 195 E4
St Ann's Rd
2 Barking IG11 352 C4
Southend-on-S SS2 348 A1
St Anselm's RC Prim Sch DA1 376 A2
St Anthony's Ave IG8 310 C3
St Anthonys Cres IP4 17 F6
St Anthony's Dr CM2 254 C7
St Antony's RC Prim Sch IG8 310 A6
St Aubins Ct CO15 196 B4
St Aubyns Rd IP4 18 A5
St Aubyn's Sch IG8 309 F3
St Audrey's SS1 368 B7
St Augustine Cl CM6 151 F6
St Augustine Mews CO1 136 A7
St Augustine Rd
Grays RM16 374 B2
Ipswich IP3 18 D4
St Augustine's Ave SS1 368 B7
St Augustine's Gdns IP3 18 C3
St Augustine's RC Prim Sch
Hoddesdon EN11 221 B6
Ilford IG2 333 B6
St Austell Rd CO4 110 D2
St Austin's La CO12 91 E6
St Awdry's Rd IG11 352 D5
St Barnabas Rd IG8 310 C3
St Bartholomew Cl CO4 110 C3
St Bartholomews La CO10 15 D2
St Bede's RC Prim Sch RM6 334 C6
St Benedict's RC Coll CO3 135 B6
St Benet's Rd SS2 347 F3
St Bernard Rd CO4 110 D2
St Bernard's High Sch & Art Coll SS0 366 E8
St Botolph's Church Wlk 7 CO2 135 F6
St Botolph's Cir 8 CO2 135 F6
St Botolph's Pl 1 CB9 8 F7
St Botolph's St 6 CO2 135 F6
St Botolph's Terr 11 CO13 171 C8
St Botolph's Way CB9 8 F8
St Brelades Ct CO15 196 B5
St Bride Ct CO4 110 D2
St Catharine's Rd EN10 221 A4
St Catherines Cl
Colchester CO2 135 D1
Wickford SS11 321 F8
St Catherines Ct CM23 145 E7
St Catherine's Ct IP2 16 E1
St Catherine's Hoddesdon CE Prim Sch EN11 221 B6
St Catherine's Rd
Chelmsford CM1 231 E2
Chingford E4 309 A8
Long Melford CO10 15 C7
St Cecilia Rd RM16 374 B2
St Cedd's CE Prim Sch CM0 242 B2
St Cedds Ct RM16 373 B5
St Cedd's Sch CM1 232 A4
St Chads Cl 4 SS15 341 C7
St Chad's Gdns RM6 334 E4
St Chad's Rd
Dagenham RM6 334 E4
Tilbury RM16, RM18 379 A7
St Charles Dr SS11 321 E7
St Charles Rd CM14 294 B1
St Christopher Ct CO4 110 D2
St Christopher Rd CO4 110 D2
St Christopher Sch The SS9 346 F4
St Christophers Cl SS8 363 D4
St Christophers Way CO15 220 G7
St Clair Cl
Clacton-on-S CO15 195 F8
Woodford IG5 310 F1
St Clair's Dr CO16 194 B5
St Clair's Rd CO16 194 B5
St Clare Dr CO3 135 A7
St Clare Mdw SS4 325 F3
St Clare Rd CO3 135 A6
St Clare's RC Prim Sch CO16 195 B4
St Clement Rd CO4 110 D2
St Clements CM6 70 A2
St Clement's Ave
Grays RM20 377 B8
Southend-on-S SS9 346 E2
St Clement's Church La 13 IP4 17 D5
St Clements Cl SS5 325 A4
St Clement's Cl SS7 344 D5
St Clement's Cres SS7 344 D5
St Clements Ct
3 Grays RM17 377 F8
Purfleet RM19 371 A2
Waltham Abbey EN9 265 C6
St Clement's Ct
Clacton-on-S CO16 195 B5
Southend-on-S SS9 365 D8
St Clement's Dr SS9 346 E3
St Clement's Hospl IP3 18 B4
St Clements Rd DA9 377 C3
St Clement's Rd
Grays RM20 377 C7
South Benfleet SS7 344 D5
St Clement's Way RM20 376 F8
St Cleres Cres SS11 321 F7
St Cleres Hall La CO16 194 B3
St Clere's Sch SS17 375 C8
St Cleres Way CM3 256 D7
St Columb Ct CO4 110 C2
St Cross Ct EN11 221 A4
St Cross RC Prim Sch EN11 221 A4
St Cuthberts Rd EN11 197 C1
St Cyrus Rd CO4 110 D3
St Davids Cl CO4 136 C7
St Davids Ct Basildon SS16 342 E3
5 Wanstead E11 332 B6
St David's Ct RM1 335 F4
St Davids Dr SS9 346 A3
St David's Rd
Basildon SS16 341 B4
Ipswich IP3 18 B3
St Davids Terr SS9 346 A3
St David's Way SS11 321 E7
St Davids Wlk SS8 363 D4
St Denis Ct CO12 91 A1
St Dionis Rd E12 332 E1
St Dominic Rd CO4 110 D2
St Dunstan's Rd SG12 198 D8
St Edith's Ct CM12 297 A1
St Ediths La CM12 297 A1
St Edmundsbury Ho IP4 17 F6
St Edmunds Cl CO12 91 A1
St Edmund's Cl SS2 348 C3
St Edmunds Croft CM6 123 E1
St Edmund's Ct CO4 136 C8
St Edmunds Fields CM6 123 E2
St Edmund's Hill CO8, CO10 55 D6
St Edmunds Ho CO4 136 E8
St Edmunds La Bures CO8 55 F1
Great Dunmow CM6 123 E1
St Edmund's Pl IP1 17 C8
St Edmunds Rd DA1 376 A3
St Edmund's Rd
Felixstowe IP11 381 D2
Ipswich IP1 17 B8
Redbridge IG1 332 F5
St Edward's Way CM17 200 C4
St Edward's CE Comp Sch RM7 335 A5
St Edward's CE Prim Sch RM1 335 E8
St Edwards Way RM1, RM7 335 D6
St Egberts Way E4 287 C1
SS Peter & Paul's Prim Sch IG1 333 D1
St Erkenwald Mews IG11 352 D4
St Erkenwald Rd IG11 352 D4
St Erkenwalds Ct SS1 367 C8
St Ethelburga Ct RM3 315 A1
St Fabian's Dr CM1 231 E4
St Faith Rd CO4 110 D2
St Felix RC Prim Sch CB9 8 D7
St Fidelis' Rd DA8 369 D1
St Fillan Rd CO4 110 D2
St Francis Ct SS2 348 C1
St Francis RC Prim Sch
Braintree CM7 127 E4
Maldon CM9 236 F3
St Francis' Rd DA8 369 D2
St Francis Way
Grays RM16 374 C3
Ilford IG1 352 D8
St Gabriel's Cl E11 332 B3
St Gabriels Ct SS13 343 B5
St George's Ave
Grays RM17 373 C2
Harwich CO12 91 C2
Hornchurch RM11 336 F4
St George's CE Prim Sch CO7 112 E1
St Georges Cl
Heybridge Basin CM9 237 E3
Hook End CM15 272 B4
St George's Cl CO7 112 E1
St Georges Ct
Brentwood CM13 295 C2
Romford RM7 335 C7
Witham CM8 183 F1
St George's Ct
Brentwood CM14 294 B2
17 Ipswich IP1 17 C6
St George's Ctr DA11 379 B1
St George's Dr SS0 347 E3
St George's Hospl RM12 355 D7
St George's Inf Sch CO2 136 A4
St George's La SS3 368 F6
St George's New Town Jun Sch CO2 136 A5
St George's Park Ave SS0 347 B2
St George's RC Prim Sch SS3 368 E8
St Georges Rd RM9 353 E8
St George's Rd IG1 332 F4
St George's St IP1 17 C6
St Georges Wlk
Canvey Island SS8 363 D4
South Benfleet SS7 344 B6
St Giles Ave RM10 354 B5
St Giles CE Prim Sch CO9 52 D2
St Giles Cl Dagenham RM10 354 B5
Great Maplestead CO9 52 D2
Maldon CM9 236 E2
Orsett RM16 374 A8
St Giles Cres CM9 236 E2
St Gregory CE Prim Sch CO10 33 D7
St Gregory's Ct CO10 33 D8
St Gregorys Ho CM16 268 A8
St Guiberts Rd SS8 363 E5
St Helena Mews CO3 135 D5
St Helena Rd CO3 135 D5
St Helena Sch CO3 135 B8
St Helens Ave CO15 196 A8
St Helens Ct RM13 355 A1
St Helen's Ct CM16 246 A1
St Helen's Gn CO12 91 E5
St Helen's La 7 CO1 135 F7
St Helen's Prim Sch IP4 17 E6
St Helen's RC Inf Sch CM14 316 D8
St Helen's RC Prim Sch SS0 366 F8
St Helen's Rd
Redbridge IG1 332 F5
Southend-on-S SS0 366 E8
St Helen's St IP4 17 D6
St Helens Wlk CM12 296 F4
St Helier Ct CO15 196 B4
St Hildas Sch SS0 347 C1
St Ives Cl
Clacton-on-S CO16 195 B3
Romford RM3 314 F3
St Ives Rd CO5 189 E6
St Ivians Dr RM2 336 A8
St James Ave SS1 368 B7
St James' Ave CM5 249 A1
St James Ave E SS17 360 E3
St James Ave W SS17 360 E3
St James CE Prim Sch CM18 223 D4
St James' CE Prim Sch CO1 136 A7
St James Cl
Canvey Island SS8 363 D4
Southend-on-S SS0 347 A3
St James Ct
Brightlingsea CO7 192 E6
Canvey Island SS8 364 B1
Clacton-on-S CO15 195 E1
Greenhithe DA9 376 F1
Haverhill CB9 8 E8
Romford RM1 335 F7
5 Saffron Walden CB10 22 F2
Wanstead E12 332 C2
St James' Ct 5 CO1 136 A7
St James Ctr CM20 200 A4
St James Gate IG9 288 B1
St James Gdns Ilford RM6 334 B7
Southend-on-S SS0 347 A3
St Jame's Ho 9 RM1 335 F6
St James La DA9 376 E1
St James Mews CM12 297 A2
St James Pk CM1 231 D4
St James Rd Basildon SS16 342 D5
Braintree CM7 127 F5
St James' Rise CO1 136 A7
St James's Ave DA11 379 A1
St James's Rd
Brentwood CM14 316 C7
Gravesend DA11 379 A1
St James's St
Castle Hedingham CO9 51 F4
Gravesend DA11 379 A1
St James's Wlk SS5 324 C6
St James Way CM23 145 C3
St Jean Wlk CO5 186 D6
St John Fisher RC Jun Sch IG10 289 C7
St John Gdns CO15 195 E6
St John Payne RC Comp Sch CM1 231 F6
St Johns Ave CM7 127 F2
St John's Ave
Brentwood CM14 316 D6
Chelmsford CM2 254 B8
12 Colchester CO2 135 F6
Harlow CM17 200 C4
St John's CE Prim Sch
Buckhurst Hill IG9 288 B1
Colchester CO4 110 D4
Ipswich IP4 18 A7
St John's CE Sch CM16 245 E1
St Johns Cl
1 Basildon SS15 341 C7
Great Chesterford CB10 3 D2
Great Wakering SS3 350 B3
Saffron Walden CB11 43 D7
St John's Cl
Colchester CO4 110 D4
Rainham RM13 355 A5
St Johns Cres SS8 363 D3
St John's Cres CM24 119 E7
St Johns Ct Erith DA8 369 D1
Felixstowe IP11 381 D4
Mayland CM3 283 A8
Southend-on-S SS1 366 F7
St John's Ct
Buckhurst Hill IG9 288 B1
Ipswich IP4 18 B6
Tollesbury CM9 216 C1
St John's Danbury CE Prim Sch CM3 256 E7
St Johns Dr SS6 322 F4
St John's Gn
Colchester CO2 135 F6
Writtle CM1 231 B1
St John's Green Prim Sch CO2 135 F6
St John's Hospl CM2 253 F6
St Johns La SG12 197 A6
St John's La CM24 119 E7
St John's Lodge IG10 288 F7
St Johns Mews SS17 360 F4
St John's Pl CM11 298 B4
St John's Pl 14 CO2 135 F6
St Johns RC Sch IG8 311 A5
St Johns Rd Grays RM16 374 B1
Ilford IG2 333 E4
Romford RM5 313 C5
St John's Rd Barking IG11 352 E4
Billericay CM11 297 B3
Chelmsford CM2 254 B8
Chingford E4 309 B6
Chingford, Highams Park E17 309 C1
Clacton-on-S CO16 195 C5
Colchester CO4 110 D3
Epping CM16 245 F1
Erith DA8 369 D1
Great Wakering SS3 350 B3
Hadleigh SS7 345 C3
Ipswich IP4 18 A6
Loughton IG10 288 F7
Southend-on-S SS0 366 E8

St John's Rd *continued*
Stansted Mountfitchet CM24 ... 119 E7
Wivenhoe CO7 ... 164 C7
Writtle CM1 ... 231 B1
St John's Sch CM12 ... 294 B3
St John's St Colchester CO2 135 F6
Tollesbury CM9 ... 216 C1
St John's Terr CM7 ... 72 B2
St John's Way SS17 ... 360 F4
St Johns Wlk CM17 ... 200 C4
St John The Baptist CE Prim Sch
Great Amwell SG12 ... 197 A5
Pebmarsh CO9 ... 78 B8
St Joseph Rd CO4 ... 110 C3
St Joseph's Coll IP2 ... 17 A3
St Joseph's Convent Sch E11 ... 332 A5
St Joseph's Ct E4 ... 287 D2
St Joseph's Prim Sch CO10 33 E8
St Josephs RC Prim Sch IG11 ... 352 C4
St Joseph's RC Prim Sch
Bishop's Stortford CM23 ... 145 E6
Canvey Island SS8 ... 364 B4
Dagenham RM9 ... 353 F8
Harwich CO12 ... 91 B2
South Woodham Ferrers CM3 ... 301 E7
Stanford-le-H SS17 ... 360 D2
Upminster RM14 ... 337 B2
St Joseph The Worker RC Prim Sch CM13 ... 295 C3
St Jude Gdns CO4 ... 110 E2
St Judes Cl CO4 ... 110 D2
St Judes Ct IG8 ... 310 E3
St Julian Gr CO1 ... 136 A6
St Katherine's CE Prim Sch SS8 ... 364 A5
St Katherines Ct SS8 ... 363 E3
St Kathryns Pl RM14 ... 337 C2
St Kilda's Rd CM15 ... 294 C2
ST LAWRENCE ... 262 B8
St Lawrence CE Prim Sch CO2 ... 163 F8
St Lawrence Ct
3 Braintree CM7 ... 127 F3
Southend-on-S SS9 ... 346 E6
St Lawrence Dr
Steeple CM0 ... 262 B8
St Lawrence CM0 ... 240 B1
St Lawrence Gdns
Blackmore CM4 ... 272 E8
Southend-on-S SS9 ... 346 E6
St Lawrence Hill CM0 ... 262 E5
St Lawrence Rd
Colchester CO4 ... 110 D2
Tillingham CM0 ... 263 D5
Upminster RM14 ... 337 C2
St Lawrence St 11 IP1 ... 17 C6
St Leonard's Ave E4 ... 309 D4
St Leonards Cl
Grays RM17 ... 377 F8
Newport CB11 ... 43 A2
St Leonards Gdns IG1 ... 352 C7
St Leonard's Hospl CO10 ... 33 F7
St Leonards Rd Ipswich IP3 . 18 B3
Lower Nazeing EN9 ... 243 D6
St Leonard's Rd
Colchester CO1 ... 136 C6
Southend-on-S SS1 ... 367 B7
St Leonards School Ho 8 CO1 ... 136 C6
St Leonards Terr 7 CO1 ... 136 C6
St Leonards Way RM11 ... 336 B2
St Luke's Ave IG1 ... 352 B7
St Luke's CE Prim Sch CO5 ... 186 D5
St Luke's Chase CO5 ... 186 D5
St Lukes Cl
8 Basildon SS15 ... 341 C7
Canvey Island SS8 ... 363 D4
St Luke's Cl CO4 ... 110 D2
St Luke's Path 1 IG1 ... 352 B7
St Lukes Pl SS4 ... 325 E2
St Luke's RC Prim Sch CM19 ... 223 C6
St Luke's Rd SS2 ... 348 C2
ST MARGARETS ... 197 A4
St Margarets IG11 ... 352 D4
St Margaret's Ave SS17 ... 375 C8
St Margarets CE Prim Sch IG11 ... 352 C5
St Margaret's CE Prim Sch
Basildon SS13 ... 343 E5
Ipswich IP4 ... 17 D6
Toppesfield CO9 ... 50 C7
St Margaret's Cross CO4 ... 83 F4
St Margaret's Ct CO16 ... 195 C4
St Margaret's Gn 2 IP4 ... 17 D6
St Margaret's Hospl CM16 246 B2
St Margaret's Plain 1 IP4 17 D6
St Margaret's Rd
Chelmsford CM2 ... 232 E3
Hoddesdon SG12 ... 197 B2
Wanstead E12 ... 332 C2
St Margaret's Sch CO9 ... 102 D8
St Margaret's St IP4 ... 17 D6
St Margarets Sta SG12 ... 197 C4
St Mark Dr CO4 ... 110 D2
St Mark's Ave DA11 ... 378 F1
St Mark's Field SS4 ... 325 F2
St Marks Pl RM10 ... 354 B6
St Marks RC Prim Sch IP2 . 16 F3
St Marks Rd
Canvey Island SS8 ... 363 D4
Clacton-on-S CO15 ... 195 E4
St Mark's Rd SS7 ... 345 C3
St Mark's West Essex RC Sch CM18 ... 223 E7
St Martins Cl
Clacton-on-S CO15 ... 195 E4
South Benfleet SS7 ... 344 B7
White Roothing or White Roding CM6 ... 203 C7
St Martin's Cl SS6 ... 345 C8
St Martin's Mews CM5 ... 249 A2
St Martins Rd EN11 ... 221 C6
St Martin's Sch CM13 ... 295 C1
St Martins Sq SS14 ... 342 A6
St Mary Magdalen Ho CO1 ... 136 B6
St Marys IG11 ... 352 D4
St Mary's Art Ctr* CO1 ... 135 E7
St Mary's Ave
Billericay CM12 ... 297 A2
Brentwood CM15 ... 295 A4
Wanstead E11 ... 332 B4
St Mary's Bglws CM1 ... 177 B2
St Mary's Cath* CM1 ... 232 B2
St Mary's CE Foundation Prim Sch CM24 ... 119 E7
St Mary's CE Prim Sch
Ardleigh CO7 ... 111 E7
Burnham-on-C CM0 ... 306 C6
Hatfield Broad Oak CM22 ... 174 F6
Saffron Walden CB10 ... 22 D2
Shenfield CM15 ... 294 F3
Woodham Ferrers CM3 ... 279 B4
St Marys Cl
South Benfleet SS7 ... 344 D1
Southend-on-S SS3 ... 349 D1
St Mary's Cl Grays RM17 ... 378 D8
Great Baddow CM2 ... 254 F6
Panfield CM7 ... 127 B7
St Mary's Cotts CO10 ... 2 C5
St Mary's Cres
Basildon SS13 ... 343 C7
Felixstowe IP11 ... 381 D6
St Mary's Ct CO15 ... 195 E3
St Mary's Ct CM9 ... 237 B2
St Mary's Ct SS2 ... 347 F2
St Mary's Dr
South Benfleet SS7 ... 344 E1
Stansted Mountfitchet CM24 ... 119 F5
St Marys Fields CO3 ... 135 E7
St Mary's Hare Park Sch RM2 ... 336 C8
St Mary's Ho 6 CM0 ... 306 C4
St Mary's La Maldon CM9 ... 237 B2
Upminster RM14 ... 338 D3
West Horndon CM13 ... 339 B4
St Mary's Lodge E11 ... 332 B5
St Marys Mead CM1 ... 208 A1
St Marys Mews
Frinton-on-S CO13 ... 171 A5
Tollesbury CM9 ... 216 D2
St Mary's Path SS13 ... 343 C7
St Mary's Pl CM6 ... 151 D7
St Mary's Prittlewell CE Prim Sch SS2 ... 347 F1
St Mary's RC Prim Sch
Chingford E4 ... 287 D1
Hornchurch RM12 ... 336 A3
Ipswich IP4 ... 17 F7
Tilbury RM18 ... 378 F5
St Mary's RC Sch CM23 ... 145 E7
St Marys Rd Ilford IG1 ... 333 D2
Wickford SS12 ... 321 B5
St Mary's Rd Braintree CM7 128 B3
Burnham-on-C CM0 ... 306 B6
Clacton-on-S CO15 ... 195 E4
Frinton-on-S CO13 ... 171 A5
Grays RM16 ... 374 B2
Great Bentley CO7 ... 166 F6
Greenhithe DA9 ... 376 E2
Ipswich IP4 ... 17 F7
Kelvedon CO5 ... 158 C2
Rivenhall CM8 ... 184 B7
South Benfleet SS7 ... 363 E8
Southend-on-S SS2 ... 347 F2
St Mary's Sch
Colchester CO3 ... 135 C7
Copford CO3 ... 133 F5
St Mary's Sq CO5 ... 158 B1
St Marys Terr CO3 ... 135 D6
St Marys View CB10 ... 22 E4
St Mary's Villas CM7 ... 72 B1
St Marys Way IG7 ... 311 A5
St Mary's Wlk CB9 ... 27 B6
St Mathew's Ho 4 IP1 ... 17 B6
St Matthew's CE Prim Sch IP1 ... 17 B6
St Matthew's Cl RM13 ... 355 A5
St Matthew's St IP1 ... 17 B6
St Michaels Ave SS13 ... 343 C4
St Michaels CE Prep Sch SS9 ... 346 C1
St Michael's CE Prim Sch
Bishop's Stortford CM23 ... 145 F7
Braintree CM7 ... 127 D2
St Michaels Cl
Aveley RM15 ... 371 C6
Harlow CM20 ... 199 E1
Latchingdon CM3 ... 282 A5
St Michaels Ct 6 CO11 ... 86 D4
St Michael's Ct 11 CM7 ... 127 F2
St Michael's Dr CM1 ... 230 A5
St Michael's Hospl CM7 ... 127 E3
St Michael's La 2 CM7 ... 127 F2
ST MICHAEL'S MEAD ... 145 C5
St Michaels Mews 5 CM7 127 F2
St Michael's Mews CM6 ... 204 C7
St Michael's Prim Sch CO2 ... 135 C1
St Michaels Rd
Canvey Island SS8 ... 363 D4
Colchester CO2 ... 135 D1
Grays RM16 ... 374 B1
St Michael's Rd
Braintree CM7 ... 127 F2
Chelmsford CM2 ... 254 B8
Hadleigh SS7 ... 345 F6
Harwich CO12 ... 91 B2
Hoddesdon EN10 ... 221 A3
Thorpe-le-S CO16 ... 141 F2
St Michaels Wlk CM2 ... 254 C2
St Mildreds Rd CM2 ... 254 B8
St Monance Way CO4 ... 110 D2
St Nazaire Rd CM1 ... 231 E6
St Neots Cl CO4 ... 110 D2
St Neot's Rd RM3 ... 314 F4
St Nicholas Ave RM12 ... 336 A1
St Nicholas CE Prim Sch CM0 ... 263 E4
St Nicholas CE Sch SS6 ... 323 B5
St Nicholas Cl CM8 ... 183 F4
St Nicholas Ct
Chingford E4 ... 309 C4
Harwich CO12 ... 91 D6
15 Ipswich IP1 ... 17 C5
St Nicholas Field CM23 ... 92 B8
St Nicholas' Gdns CM7 ... 127 F8
St Nicholas Gn 1 CM17 ... 200 D1
St Nicholas Gr CM13 ... 317 C5
St Nicholas La SS15 ... 341 D7
St Nicholas Pas 16 CO1 ... 135 F7
St Nicholas Pl IG10 ... 289 A5
St Nicholas Rd
Tillingham CM0 ... 263 E4
Witham CM8 ... 183 F4
St Nicholas Rdbt CO12 ... 91 A4
St Nicholas Sch
Harlow CM17 ... 200 F3
Southend-on-S SS2 ... 348 E2
St Nicholas St
22 Colchester CO1 ... 135 F7
Ipswich IP1 ... 17 C5
St Nicholas Way CO6 ... 131 A3
St Olave's Rd E6 ... 352 A4
St Omar Cl SS12 ... 321 E6
ST OSYTH ... 194 B4
St Osyth CE Prim Sch
Clacton-on-S CO15 ... 195 E3
St Osyth CO16 ... 194 B4
St Osyth Cl IP2 ... 36 F8
ST OSYTH HEATH ... 167 D1
St Osyth Priory* CO16 ... 194 A4
St Osyth Rd Alresford CO7 . 165 D7
Clacton-on-S CO15 ... 195 D3
Little Clacton CO16 ... 168 B1
St Osyth Rd E CO16 ... 168 C2
St Osyth Rd W CO16 ... 168 C1
St Patrick's Ct E3 ... 309 E3
St Patrick's Pl RM16 ... 374 C2
St Patrick's RC Prim Sch RM7 ... 313 B2
St Paul's Cl RM15 ... 371 C6
St Paul's Ct SS0 ... 366 E8
St Pauls Gdns CM12 ... 297 A4
St Paul's Pl RM15 ... 371 C6
St Pauls Rd Barking IG11 ... 352 C4
Canvey Island SS8 ... 363 D4
St Paul's Rd
Clacton-on-S CO15 ... 196 A3
Colchester CO1 ... 135 E8
St Pauls Way EN9 ... 265 D6
St Peter's Ave
Chipping Ongar CM5 ... 249 A5
Maldon CM9 ... 236 F2
St Peters CE Prim Sch CM2 ... 276 F4
St Peter's CE Prim Sch
Brentwood CM14 ... 315 E8
Coggeshall CO6 ... 131 B2
Sible Hedingham CO9 ... 75 D8
St Peters Cl
Goldhanger CM9 ... 238 E6
Ilford IG2 ... 333 F7
St Peter's Cl CM7 ... 127 F4
St Peters Ct
Clacton-on-S CO15 ... 196 B5
Clare CO10 ... 12 B7
Colchester CO1 ... 135 E8
Southend-on-S SS3 ... 368 G7
10 Sudbury CO10 ... 33 E7
St Peter's Ct CM0 ... 263 E8
St Peters Field CM0 ... 306 A7
St Peter's High Sch CM0 ... 306 B6
St Peter's Hospl CM9 ... 236 F2
St Peter's-In-the-Fields CM7 ... 127 F4
St Peter's Pavement SS14 320 F1
St Peters RC Prim Sch CM11 ... 319 E6
St Peter's RC Prim Sch
Dagenham RM9 ... 353 F4
Romford RM1 ... 335 E8
St Peters Rd
Canvey Island SS8 ... 363 D4
Grays RM16 ... 374 B2
Hockley SS5 ... 324 B7
St Peter's Rd
Braintree CM7 ... 127 F4
Brentwood CM14 ... 316 B6
Chelmsford CM1 ... 231 E2
Coggeshall CO6 ... 131 B2
West Mersea CO5 ... 218 B6
St Peter's St
Colchester CO1 ... 135 F8
Ipswich IP1 ... 17 C5
St Peter's Terr SS12 ... 321 C7
St Peters View CO9 ... 51 D1
St Peters Wlk
Billericay CM12 ... 296 F4
Great Totham CM9 ... 213 B3
St Peter's Wlk CM7 ... 127 F3
St Philip's Priory Sch CM2 ... 254 A8
St Philomena's Sch CO13 170 F5
St Pius X RC Prim Sch CM1 ... 231 F6
St Raphaels Pl CM14 ... 316 B5
St Ronans Cres IG8 ... 310 A3
St Runwalds St 9 CO1 ... 135 F7
St Saviour Cl CO4 ... 110 D2
St Stephens Cres CM13 ... 317 A6
St Stephens Ct CM3 ... 283 A8
St Stephens La 13 IP1 ... 17 C6
St Stephens Rd CM3 ... 281 A4
St Swithins Cotts CM2 ... 255 C3
Saint's Wlk RM16 ... 374 C2
St Teresa RC Prim Sch The RM8 ... 353 C8
St Teresas Cl SS14 ... 342 F5
St Teresa's RC Prim Sch
Basildon SS14 ... 342 F6
Colchester CO3 ... 134 E5
Rochford SS4 ... 325 E3
St Teresa Wlk RM16 ... 374 B3
St Theresa Ct E4 ... 287 D2
St Thomas Cl CO4 ... 110 E2
St Thomas' Ct CM14 ... 316 D8
St Thomas Gdns IG1 ... 352 C6
St Thomas More High Sch for Boys SS0 ... 347 A3
St Thomas More RC Prim Sch CB11 ... 43 E8
St Thomas More's RC Prim Sch CO1 ... 136 A7
St Thomas of Canterbury CE Inf Sch CM15 ... 294 D2
St Thomas of Canterbury CE Jun Sch CM15 ... 294 D2
St Thomas of Canterbury RC Prim Sch RM17 ... 373 B2
St Thomas Rd
Belvedere DA17 ... 369 C4
Brentwood CM14 ... 316 D8
Rochford SS4 ... 303 B4
St Thomas's Cl EN9 ... 266 B6
St Thomas's Pl 4 RM17 ... 378 C8
St Thomas's Row CM0 ... 242 B2
St Ursula's RC Jun & Inf Schs RM3 ... 314 B4
St Valery CM22 ... 148 C7
St Vincent Chase CM7 ... 128 B5
St Vincent Rd CO15 ... 195 E1
St Vincents Ave DA1 ... 376 A2
ST VINCENT'S HAMLET ... 293 B1
St Vincent's RC Prim Sch RM8 ... 334 C2
St Vincents Rd
Chelmsford CM2 ... 254 B8
Dartford DA1 ... 376 A1
St Vincent's Rd SS0 ... 366 E7
St Winifred's Cl IG7 ... 311 C5
Sainty Cl CO7 ... 164 C8
Sairard Cl SS9 ... 346 D7
Sairard Gdns SS9 ... 346 D7
Sakins Croft CM18 ... 223 F5
Saladin Dr RM19 ... 371 A2
Salamanca Way CO2 ... 135 C2
Salamons Way RM13 ... 369 E7
Salary Cl CO4 ... 110 F1
Salcombe Dr RM6 ... 334 F5
Salcombe Pk IG10 ... 288 D4
Salcombe Rd CM7 ... 128 C1
Salcott Creek Ct CM7 ... 128 D1
Salcott Cres SS12 ... 321 F6
SALCOTT-CUM-VIRLEY ... 216 B7
Salcott Mews SS12 ... 321 F6
Salcott St CM9 ... 216 C8
Salehurst Rd IP3 ... 18 E3
Salem Wlk SS6 ... 323 B4
Salerno Cres CO2 ... 135 C2
Salerno Way CM1 ... 231 E6
Salesbury Dr CM11 ... 297 D2
Salforal Cl CM3 ... 278 B1
Saling Gn SS15 ... 319 F2
Saling Hall Gardens* CM7 ... 126 A8
Salisbury Ave Barking IG11 352 E5
Colchester CO3 ... 135 E6
Southend-on-S SS0 ... 347 E1
Stanford-le-H SS17 ... 360 D1
Salisbury Cl
Bishop's Stortford CM23 ... 145 F5
Rayleigh SS6 ... 323 C5
Upminster RM14 ... 337 F2
Salisbury Ct
Clacton-on-S CO15 ... 196 D5
2 Haverhill CB9 ... 8 F7
Southend-on-S SS9 ... 346 D2
Salisbury Gdns 4 IG9 ... 310 D8
Salisbury Hall Gdns E4 ... 309 A4
Salisbury Rd Chingford E4 ... 309 A7
Clacton-on-S CO15 ... 196 D5
Dagenham RM10 ... 354 B6
Grays RM17 ... 373 C1
Hoddesdon EN11 ... 221 C8
Ilford IG3 ... 333 E2
Ipswich IP3 ... 18 A4
Romford RM2 ... 336 B6
Southend-on-S SS9 ... 346 D1
Salisbury Terr 1 CO10 ... 33 E8
Salix Rd RM17 ... 378 E8
Sallows Cl IP1 ... 16 F7
Sally Murray Cl E12 ... 352 A8
Salmet Cl IP2 ... 17 A3
Salmon Cl CO3 ... 134 F4
Salmond's Gr CM13 ... 317 C5
Salmon Par CM1 ... 232 B3
Salmon Rd DA17 ... 369 A1
Salmons Cl CM6 ... 151 A5
Salmon's Cnr CO6 ... 132 A3
Salmon's La CO6 ... 132 A4
Saltash Rd IG6 ... 311 D3
Saltcoats CM3 ... 301 D8
Saltcoats Pk & Compass Gdns* CM3 ... 301 F7
Saltcote Maltings CM9 ... 237 E4
Salter Ct CO3 ... 135 E7
Saltern Ct 3 IG11 ... 353 B2
Salter Pl CM2 ... 232 B1
Salters CM23 ... 145 C4
Salters Hall Mews CO10 ... 33 D7
Salter's Mdw CM9 ... 215 D4
Saltford Cl DA8 ... 369 E1
Salthouse St 16 IP4 ... 17 D5
Saltings Cres CO5 ... 218 E7
Saltings The
Greenhithe DA9 ... 377 C3
Hadleigh SS7 ... 345 D3
Salt's Gn CM1 ... 205 D2
Salvia Cl CO16 ... 195 C4
Salway Cl IG8 ... 310 A3
Samantha Mews RM4 ... 313 E7
Samford Cl IP9 ... 62 D7
Samford Ct IP9 ... 61 D7
Samford Pl IP8 ... 16 B6
Samian Cl CM9 ... 236 F5
Samphire Cl CM8 ... 183 D3
Samphire Ct RM17 ... 378 E8
Sampson Dr CO10 ... 15 D8
Sampson's La CO5 ... 189 F3
Samson Ct 5 DA17 ... 369 A2
Samson Ho SS15 ... 319 B1
Samsons Cl CO7 ... 192 E8
Samson's Cnr CO7 ... 165 D1
Samson's Rd CO7 ... 165 E1
Samuel Ct IP4 ... 17 D6
Samuel Manor CM2 ... 232 F3
Samuel Rd SS16 ... 341 B4
Samuel's Cnr SS3 ... 350 D3
Samuels Dr SS1 ... 368 B8
Sanctuary Gdn SS17 ... 360 E2
Sanctuary Rd SS9 ... 346 A3
Sandbanks SS7 ... 345 D2
Sandcliff Rd DA8 ... 369 D1
Sanderling Gdns CM9 ... 237 C5
Sanderlings SS7 ... 344 C2
Sanderling Way DA9 ... 377 A1
Sanders Cl CM24 ... 119 D7
Sanders Dr CO3 ... 135 B7
Sanders Draper Sch & Specialist Science Coll The RM12 ... 355 D8
Sanderson Cl CM13 ... 339 C5
Sanderson Ct SS7 ... 344 C5
Sanderson Mews CO5 ... 163 F8
Sanders Rd SS8 ... 364 A6
Sandford Ave IG10 ... 289 C6
Sandford Cl CO7 ... 164 C8
Sandford Mill Rd
Chelmsford CM2 ... 232 F2
Chelmsford CM2 ... 233 B2
Great Baddow CM2 ... 255 C8
Sandford Rd CM2 ... 232 E3
Sandgate Cl RM7 ... 335 C4
Sandhill Rd SS9 ... 346 C8
Sandhills Cotts CM7 ... 73 D1
Sandhurst SS8 ... 363 C3
Sandhurst Ave IP3 ... 17 F4
Sandhurst Cl SS9 ... 346 F4
Sandhurst Cres SS9 ... 346 F4
Sandhurst Dr IG3 ... 352 F8
Sandhurst Rd RM18 ... 379 C5
Sand Island Ctr CM0 ... 306 A5
Sandleigh Rd SS9 ... 347 A1
Sandle Rd CM23 ... 146 A7
Sandling Cres IP4 ... 18 E5
Sandlings The IP3 ... 18 D1
Sandmartin Cres CO3 ... 134 C4
SANDON ... 255 D6
Sandon Brook Pl CM2 ... 255 E8
Sandon Cl Basildon SS14 ... 342 F5
Great Horkesley CO6 ... 109 C7
Rochford SS4 ... 325 D3
Sandon Ct Basildon SS14 ... 342 F5
Ilford IG3 ... 334 A1
SANDON GREEN ... 255 C6
Sandon Hall Bridleway CM2 ... 255 D4
Sandon Hill CM3 ... 179 A6
Sandon Pl CM5 ... 249 A1
Sandon Rd SS14 ... 342 F5
Sandon Sch The CM2 ... 255 B6
Sandown Ave
Dagenham RM10 ... 354 C6
Hornchurch RM12 ... 336 D2
Southend-on-S SS0 ... 347 B2
Sandown Cl
Clacton-on-S CO15 ... 196 A8
Wickford SS11 ... 322 A7
Sandown Ct RM10 ... 354 C6
Sandown Rd Orsett RM16 ... 374 E7
Thundersley SS7 ... 345 B7
Wickford SS11 ... 322 A7
Sandpiper Cl
Colchester CO4 ... 137 A8
Greenhithe DA9 ... 377 A1
Haverhill CB9 ... 9 C8
Heybridge CM9 ... 237 C5
Southend-on-S SS3 ... 368 E8
Sandpiper Ct 16 CM23 ... 145 F6
Sandpiper Rd IP2 ... 16 E2
Sandpipers SS3 ... 368 G6
Sandpiper Terr IG5 ... 333 B8
Sandpiper Wlk CM2 ... 254 C6
Sandpit Cl IP4 ... 18 F5
Sandpit La
9 Braintree CM7 ... 127 F3
Burnham-on-C CM0 ... 306 C5
Pilgrims Hatch CM14 ... 293 F2
Sandpit Rd SS3 ... 368 H8
Sandra Ct 5 CO2 ... 135 E6
Sandringham Ave
Harlow CM19 ... 222 E8
Hockley SS5 ... 324 D6
Sandringham Cl Ilford IG6 333 C8
Ipswich IP2 ... 16 F2
Stanford-le-H SS17 ... 360 E3
Sandringham Ct
Hadleigh SS7 ... 345 E2
Sudbury CO10 ... 34 A7
Sandringham Dr CO2 ... 136 A4
Sandringham Gdns
6 Bishop's Stortford CM23 ... 145 E5
Ilford IG6 ... 333 C8
Sandringham Lodge 7 EN11 ... 221 A6
Sandringham Pl CM2 ... 232 C2
Sandringham Rd
Barking IG11 ... 352 F6
Basildon SS15 ... 341 E8
Pilgrims Hatch CM15 ... 294 B3
Southend-on-S SS1 ... 367 D7
Sands Way IG8 ... 310 F4
Sandwich Cl CM7 ... 127 E6
Sandwich Rd
Brightlingsea CO7 ... 192 F8
Clacton-on-S CO15 ... 220 J8
Sandy Hill CO6 ... 80 D5
Sandyhill La IP3 ... 17 E1
Sandyhill Rd IG1 ... 352 B8
Sandy La Aveley RM15 ... 371 A6
Bulmer CO10 ... 32 F5
Grays, Chadwell St M RM16 374 C1
Grays, West Thurrock RM20 ... 377 B8
Sudbury CO10 ... 33 B5
Sangster Ct SS6 ... 323 F2
San Juan Dr RM16 ... 372 C2
San Luis Dr RM16 ... 372 C2
San Marcos Dr RM16 ... 372 C2
San Remo Mans SS0 ... 366 E7
San Remo Par SS0 ... 366 E7
San Remo Rd SS8 ... 364 D3
Sans Souci SS9 ... 365 D8
Santiago Cotts CO7 ... 192 E6
Santiago Way RM16 ... 372 D1
Sapling Pl IP4 ... 18 E5
Sappers Cl CM21 ... 172 F2
Sapphire Cl
Dagenham RM8 ... 334 C3
Ipswich IP1 ... 16 D8
Sapphire Ct SS1 ... 367 D6
Sapphire Ho 4 RM13 ... 355 A1
Sara Cres DA9 ... 377 B3
Sarah's Wlk CM22 ... 148 B7
Saran Ct CO7 ... 137 A2
Sarbir Ind Pk CM17 ... 200 C5
Sarcel CM77 ... 129 C6
Sargeant Cl CO2 ... 136 B3
Sark Gr SS12 ... 321 F5
Sarre Ave RM12 ... 355 C6
Sarre Way CO7 ... 192 E8
Sassoon Way 3 CM9 ... 237 A1
Satanita Rd SS0 ... 366 D8
Saturn Rd IP1 ... 16 D8
Saul's Ave CM8 ... 212 A8
Sauls Bridge Cl CM8 ... 212 A8
Saunders Ave CM7 ... 127 E3
Saunders Cl Elsenham CM22 94 C1
Ilford IG1 ... 333 D3
Saunton Rd RM12 ... 336 A2
Savannah Hts SS9 ... 347 A1
Savernake Rd CM1 ... 231 E1
Savill Ct IG8 ... 309 F4
Saville Cl CB11 ... 65 C4
Saville Rd RM6 ... 334 F4
Saville St CO14 ... 144 C1
Savill Rd CO2 ... 136 C2
Savill Row IG8 ... 309 F4
Savoy Cl SS16 ... 341 A5
Savoy Wood CM19 ... 223 B2
SAWBRIDGEWORTH ... 172 C3
Sawbridgeworth Rd
Hatfield Heath CM22 ... 173 D3
Little Hallingbury CM22 ... 173 B6
Sawbridgeworth Sta CM21 ... 173 A3
Sawkins Ave CM2 ... 254 D6
Sawkins Cl Abberton CO5 . 163 B2
Chelmsford CM2 ... 254 D6
Sawkins Gdns CM2 ... 254 D6
Sawney Brook CM1 ... 231 A1
Sawpit La CM23 ... 92 D7
Sawston Cl IP2 ... 17 A2
Sawston Ct 10 RM19 ... 371 B1
Sawyer's Chase RM4 ... 290 B6
Sawyers Cl 3 IP9 ... 35 A1
Sawyers Ct CM15 ... 294 F3
Sawyers Gr CM15 ... 294 D1
Sawyers Hall Coll of Science & Tech CM15 ... 294 C2
Sawyer's Hall La CM15 ... 294 D1
Sawyer's Rd CM9 ... 214 C5
Saxham Rd IG11 ... 352 E3
Saxlingham Rd E4 ... 309 D7
Saxmundham Way CO16 ... 195 A3
Saxon Bank CM7 ... 128 B2
Saxon Cl Brentwood CM13 ... 317 A7
Colchester CO3 ... 134 F4
Halstead CO9 ... 76 F2
Rayleigh SS6 ... 323 E5
Romford RM3 ... 314 F1
Wickford SS11 ... 299 E1
Saxon Ct Maldon CM9 ... 237 A3
South Benfleet SS7 ... 344 C5
Saxon Dr CM8 ... 183 E3
Saxon Gdns SS3 ... 368 D7
Saxon Ho RM14 ... 338 D4
Saxon La IP8 ... 35 D7
Saxon Pl SS4 ... 325 F2
Saxon Rd IG1 ... 352 B7
Saxonville SS7 ... 344 B4
Saxon Way
Chelmsford CM1 ... 232 B7
Holland-on-S CO15 ... 196 F6
Maldon CM9 ... 237 B1
Point Clear B CO16 ... 192 F3
Saffron Walden CB11 ... 22 C1
South Benfleet SS7 ... 344 C2
Waltham Abbey EN9 ... 265 C6
Saxstead Dr CO16 ... 195 A4
Sayer Cl DA9 ... 377 A2
Sayers SS7 ... 345 A7
Sayers Ho CO7 ... 192 F6
Sayesbury Ave CM21 ... 172 E3
Sayesbury Rd CM21 ... 172 E2
Sayes Gdns CM21 ... 172 F2
Saywell Brook CM2 ... 233 A2
Scalby Rd CM0 ... 284 A3
Scaldhurst SS13 ... 343 C8
Scarborough Dr SS9 ... 346 E2
Scarborough Rd CM0 ... 284 A3
Scarfe's Cnr CO6 ... 82 B4
Scarfe Way CO4 ... 136 E6
Scargill Jun & Inf Sch RM13 ... 355 A6
Scarles Croft CM3 ... 278 C7
Scarletts SS14 ... 342 C8
Scarletts Chase CO6 ... 108 E6
Scarletts Cl CM8 ... 212 A7
Scarletts Rd CO1 ... 136 C4
Sceptre Cl CM9 ... 216 D2
Scholars Ct 2 RM2 ... 336 B6
Scholars Ho 6 E4 ... 287 D1
Scholars Mews CM9 ... 213 B3
Scholars Rd E4 ... 287 D1
Scholars Way 4 RM2 ... 336 B6
School Barn Cotts CO10 ... 13 E7
School Bglws CM1 ... 230 A5
School Chase CO9 ... 103 E8
School Cl IP9 ... 35 A1
School Ct CO12 ... 91 D4
Schoolfield Birdbrook CO9 . 28 A6
Glemsford CO10 ... 2 B5
Schoolfield Rd RM20 ... 377 A8
SCHOOL GREEN ... 74 A3
School Green La CM16 ... 247 C6
School Hill Birch CO2 ... 161 A4
Washbrook IP8 ... 35 F8
School Ho
13 Colchester CO1 ... 136 A6
Shalford CM7 ... 100 E5
Schoolhouse Gdns IG10 ... 289 B5
School La
Abbess Roding CM5 ... 203 F3

Silcock Cl CO4 110 C2
Silcott St CO7 192 E6
Silent St IP1 17 C5
Silk Factory Row CO10 2 B6
Silk St IP4 17 D6
Silks Way CM7 127 F2
Sillett Cl CO16 195 D6
Siloam Pl IP3 17 E4
Silva Island Way SS12 321 F5
Silvanus Cl CO3 135 D6
Silver Birch Ave CM16 246 E4
Silver Birches CM13 295 A1
Silver Birch Lodge SS4 325 E2
Silver Birch Mews IG6 311 C4
Silverdale Rayleigh SS6 345 E8
Stanford-le-H SS17 360 D4
Thundersley SS7 344 F7
Silverdale Ave Ilford IG3 333 F6
Southend-on-S SS0 347 E2
Silverdale Ct CO15 196 B5
Silverdale Dr RM12 355 B7
Silverdale E SS17 360 D4
Silverdale Par IG3 333 F6
Silverdale Rd E4 309 D4
Silver Dawn Touring Pk CO16 195 A4
SILVER END 156 E4
Silver End Prim Sch CM8 156 E3
Silver La CM5 229 A2
Silver Leys IP9 60 E6
Silverlink Ct SS8 363 F5
Silverlocke Rd RM17 378 D8
Silvermead 7 E18 310 A2
Silvermere SS16 341 A5
Silvermere Ave RM5 313 B4
Silverpoint Marine SS8 365 A3
Silver Rd CM0 306 C4
Silver Row CB11 42 F5
Silvers IG9 288 C1
Silversea Dr SS0 347 B2
Silver Spring Cl DA8 369 B1
Silver St Abridge RM4 290 B6
Maldon CM9 236 F3
Silver End CM8 156 D4
Stansted Mountfitchet CM24 119 D6
Waltham Abbey EN9 265 C6
Wethersfield CM7 73 B3
Silverthorn Cl
Rochford SS4 325 D4
Tiptree CO5 186 F5
Silverthorne SS8 363 F3
Silverthorne Cl CO2 136 A3
Silverthorn Gdns E4 309 A8
Silvertown Ave SS17 360 D2
Silvertree Cl SS5 324 B6
Silver Way Romford RM7 335 B8
1 Wickford SS11 321 C8
Silverwood Cl Grays RM16 373 A6
Harlow EN9 222 E3
Silvester Way CM2 233 B4
Simmonds La CM9 259 A1
Simmonds Way CM3 256 F8
Simmons Dr RM8 334 E1
Simmons La E4 309 D8
Simmons Pl RM16 373 A5
Simon Campion Ct CM16 246 A1
Simon Ho IP4 17 F6
Simons Flats CO5 186 C7
Simons La CO1 136 B6
Simplicity La 6 CM17 200 D1
Simpson Cl IP3 17 F1
Simpson Rd RM13 354 F6
Simpsons La CO5 186 A3
Sims Cl Earls Colne CO6 105 B7
Romford RM1 335 F7
Sinclair Cl CO4 109 F2
Sinclair Dr IP2 17 C3
Sinclair Rd E4 309 A5
Sinclair Wlk SS12 321 D5
Singer Ave CO15 220 E7
Singleton Cl RM12 354 F8
Singleton Ct CO10 34 A5
Singleton Rd RM9 353 F7
Sinnington End CO4 110 C4
Sioux Cl CO4 110 C4
Sippetts Ct IG1 333 D3
Sir Alf Ramsey Way IP1 17 B5
Sir Charles Lucas Arts Coll CO4 136 E8
Sirdar Rd Ipswich IP1 17 A7
Rayleigh SS6 345 D8
Sir Francis Way CM14 316 B8
Sir George Monoux Sixth Form Coll E17 309 B1
Sir Isaac's Wlk CO1 135 F7
Sir Walter Raleigh Dr SS6 323 C4
Sir W Petre Almshouses CM4 274 B3
Siskin Cl CO4 136 F8
Sisley Rd IG11 352 F4
Sittang Cl CO2 135 C1
Sitwell Cl CO11 86 B4
Siviter Way RM10 354 B5
Siward Rd CM8 211 D8
Six Bells Ct CM7 127 F5
Sixpenny Ct 6 IG11 352 C6
Sixth Ave
Canvey Island SS8 363 E4
Chelmsford CM1 232 B6
Stansted Mountfitchet CM24 120 C3
Thundersley SS7 345 A5
Sixth Form Coll The CO1 135 E7
Skarnings Ct EN9 266 A6
Skate's Hill CO10 2 B2
Skeale's Ct RM12 336 C1
Skeins Way CB11 65 C4
Skelmersdale Rd CO15 195 F3
Skelter Stps 9 SS1 367 C7
Skelton Cl CO11 86 C4
Skerry Rise CM1 232 B7
Skiddaw Cl CM77 154 D7
Skighaugh CO12 141 C8
Skinner's La CM2 254 B3
Skinners St CM23 145 C4
Skipper Ct 6 Barking IG11 352 C4
Braintree CM7 154 F8
Skipper Rd IP8 36 E8
Skippers Cl 4 DA9 377 B2
Skipsey Ave E6 352 A1
Skitts Hill CM7 128 A1
Skitts Hill Ind Est CM7 128 B1
Skreens Ct CM1 231 D4
SKYE GREEN 131 E1
Sky Hall Hill CO4 83 D7
Skylark Cl CM11 297 C1
Skylark La IP8 16 C2
Skylark Wlk CM2 254 B5
Sky Peals Rd IG8 309 D3
Skyrmans Fee CO13 170 E6
Slacksbury Hatch CM19 223 B8
Sladburys La CO15 196 D8
Sladbury's La CO15 196 C6
Slade End CM16 267 F3
Slade Rd CO15 196 C6
Slades Cl CO10 2 C5
Slade's La CM2 254 A3
Slade St 14 IP4 17 D5
Slades The SS16 342 E3
Slade The CB10 22 F7
Slaney Rd RM1 335 E6
Slate CO9 76 F1
Slaters Cl CO13 170 E6
Sleaford Cl IP2 17 A3
Sleepers Farm Rd RM16 374 B4
Slewins Cl RM11 336 C6
Slewins La RM11 336 C6
Slipe La EN10 243 A7
Slipes Cnr CO11 87 C1
Sloane Mews CM12 296 F5
Sloan Ho RM10 354 B5
Sloeberry Rd IP3 38 C7
Sloe Hill CO9 76 C2
Slough Farm Rd CO9 76 D2
Slough House Cl CM7 128 D1
Slough La Ardleigh CO7 111 D4
Cock Clarks CM3 257 D3
Elmstead Market CO7 137 B6
Slough Rd
Brantham CO7, CO11 60 D2
Danbury CM3 257 C3
High Easter CM1 177 B2
Slushy La IP9 63 B3
Smaley La CO10 15 C8
Smallbridge Entry CO8 80 D8
Smallgains Ave SS8 364 E4
Small Gains La CM4 297 E8
Smallholdings SS2 347 D6
Smallwood Rd CO2 135 B3
Smarden Cl DA17 369 A1
Smart Cl RM3 314 B2
Smart's La IG10 288 E5
Smart St 11 IP4 17 D5
Smartt Ave SS8 364 A4
Smeaton Cl Colchester CO4 110 C6
Waltham Abbey EN9 265 E7
Smeaton Rd Chigwell IG8 310 F5
Holdbrook EN3 265 A2
Smeetham Hall La CO10 32 E6
Smither's Chase SS2 348 B5
Smithers Cl IP9 35 A1
Smithers Dr CM2 255 A6
Smiths Ave CM3 283 A8
Smiths Cotts CM22 93 E4
Smiths Ct CM16 246 C6
SMITH'S END 39 A8
Smith's End La SG8 39 A8
Smiths Field
Colchester CO1 136 C5
Rayne CM77 126 F2
Smiths Gn CB11 68 C6
SMITH'S GREEN
Steeple Bumpstead 26 F4
Takeley 148 D7
Smith's Green Cotts CB9 27 A5
Smith St SS3 368 F6
Smithy The CM21 172 E3
Smollett Pl SS12 321 D4
Smugglers Wlk 3 DA9 377 B2
Smyatts Cl CM0 284 D3
Smythe Cl Billericay CM11 297 D5
Clacton-on-S CO16 195 C6
Smythe Rd CM11 297 D5
Smythe Row CM3 280 C4
SMYTHE'S GREEN 160 C2
Smythies Ave CO1 136 A7
Snakes Hill CM14 293 C6
Snakes La
Southend-on-S SS2 347 A6
Stansted Mountfitchet CM24 93 F2
Ugley CM22 94 A2
Snakes La E IG8 310 C4
Snakes La W IG8 310 B4
Snape Cl CO16 195 A4
Snape Way CO13 170 F7
SNARESBROOK 332 A6
Snaresbrook Hall 12 E18 332 A8
Snaresbrook Prim Sch E18 332 A7
Snaresbrook Sta E11 332 A6
Sneating Hall La CO13 169 E8
Sneezor Way CM8 211 E7
Snelling Gr CM2 254 F6
Sniveller's La CO5 157 D3
Snoreham Gdns CM3 282 B5
Snowberry Ct CM7 128 D4
Snowberry Gr CO2 136 A3
Snowcroft IP9 35 A1
Snowden Hill DA11 378 A2
Snowdon Ct 5 Haverhill CB9 8 E6
5 Romford RM2 336 C7
Snowdonia Cl SS13 343 C8
Snowdon Rd IP2 17 B2
Snowdrop Cl
Bishop's Stortford CM23 145 C6
Chelmsford CM1 232 E7
Witham CM8 183 E4
Snowdrop Path RM3 314 D3
Snow Hill La CO6 57 D5
Snowley Par CM23 119 B1
Snows Way CO11 86 D8
Soames Mead CM15 272 A6
Soane St Basildon SS13 321 B1
Ipswich IP4 17 D6
Sodbury Ho CO15 195 F5
Soft Rd CO10 31 F5
Softwater La SS7 345 E3
Soils The CO12 116 E5
Solar Ct RM12 336 C2
Solid La CM15 293 F8
Solway RM18 375 C3
Solway Ct 3 CO4 136 E8
Somerby Cl EN10 221 A2
Somerby Rd IG11 352 D5
Somercotes SS15 341 C5
Somercotes Ct SS15 341 C5
Somerdean 2 SS13 343 C6
Somersby Gdns IG4 332 F6
Somerset Ave
Rochford SS4 325 E3
Southend-on-S SS0 347 B4
Somerset Cl
Colchester CO2 135 B3
Woodford IG8 310 A2
Somerset Cres SS0 347 B4
Somerset Ct
9 Buckhurst Hill IG9 310 C8
9 Haverhill CB9 8 E7
Somerset Gdns
Basildon SS13 343 B6
Hornchurch RM11 337 A3
Somerset Pl CM1 232 A7
Somerset Rd
Basildon SS15 341 B6
Holdbrook EN3 265 A1
Ipswich IP4 17 F8
Linford SS17 375 A4
Somerset Way CO15 194 F1
Somers Heath Prim Sch RM15 372 A6
Somers Rd CO3 135 A4
Somerton Ave SS0 347 A6
Somerton Ct IP11 381 F4
Somerville Gdns SS9 365 F8
Somerville Rd RM6 334 C6
Somnes Ave SS8 363 E6
Sonell Ct CO7 137 B2
Songers Cotts CO4 83 B6
Sonning Way SS3 349 D1
Sonters Down CM3 300 C5
Soper Mews 6 EN3 265 A1
Soper Sq 2 CM17 200 C1
Sopwith Cres SS11 322 B5
Sorrel Cl Colchester CO4 109 C2
Ipswich IP2 16 F3
Sorrel Ct RM17 378 D8
Sorrel Gr CM77 154 B7
Sorrel Horse Mews 22 IP4 17 D5
Sorrell Cl Goldhanger CM9 238 E7
Little Waltham CM3 208 B6
Sorrells The SS17 360 F3
Sorrels The SS7 344 D7
Sorrel Wlk Haverhill CB9 8 D8
Romford RM1 335 F8
Southall Ho 4 RM3 314 E4
Southall Way CM14 315 F6
South Area IP1 16 C7
South Ave Basildon SS16 360 B7
Chingford E4 287 C2
Hullbridge SS5 301 E1
Southend-on-S SS2 348 C1
South Beech Ave SS12 321 D7
SOUTH BENFLEET 344 E3
South Benfleet Foundation Prim Sch SS7 344 D2
South Block CM21 172 F2
Southborough Dr SS0 347 B2
Southborough Rd CM2 254 A8
South Boundary Rd E12 332 F1
Southbourne Gdns
Ilford IG1 352 C7
Southend-on-S SS0 347 B4
Southbourne Gr
Hockley SS5 325 A6
Southend-on-S SS0 347 B3
Wickford SS12 321 A8
Southbrook CM21 172 E1
Southbury Cl RM12 355 D7
Southbury Ct 8 RM1 335 E5
South Charlton Mead La EN11 221 D5
SOUTHCHURCH 367 E8
Southchurch Ave
Southend-on-S, Shoeburyness SS3 368 G7
Southend-on-S SS1 367 B8
Southchurch Bvd SS2 348 F1
Southchurch Hall Cl SS1 367 C8
Southchurch Hall Mus★ SS1 367 C8
Southchurch Rd SS1 367 C8
South Cl Dagenham RM10 354 A4
Halstead CO9 103 E8
Ipswich IP4 17 E8
St Osyth CO16 194 B4
Southcliff
South Benfleet SS7 344 C4
Walton-on-t-N CO14 171 C7
Southcliff Ct
Clacton-on-S CO15 196 B4
Walton-on-t-N CO14 171 C7
Southcliff Hall CO15 195 F2
Southcliff Pk CO15 196 A4
Southcliff Prom CO14 171 C7
South Colne SS16 342 D4
Southcote Cres SS14 342 F8
Southcote Rd CM8 183 F4
Southcote Row 2 SS14 342 F8
Southcote Sq SS14 342 F8
South Cres SS2 347 D5
South Crockerford SS16 342 E4
Southcroft Cl CO13 170 C6
South Cross Rd IG6 333 C6
Southdale IG7 311 D4
Southdown Cres IG2 333 E6
Southdown Rd RM11 336 B4
South Dr Brentwood CM14 316 D6
Romford RM2 336 C8
Wanstead E12 332 E1
South East Essex Coll of Arts & Tech
Southend-on-S SS1 366 F8
Southend-on-S SS2 347 F1
South East Essex Sixth Form Coll SS7 345 A5
Southend Arterial Rd
Basildon SS12, SS6, SS7 322 B2
Southend Arterial Rd *continued*
Basildon, Steeple View CM12, SS15 319 D1
Great Warley CM13, RM14 338 C6
Rayleigh SS6 345 E8
Romford RM2 314 D1
Upminster RM14, RM11 337 C7
West Horndon CM13 339 D7
Southend Central Sta SS1 367 A8
Southend East (Southchurch Village)Sta SS1 367 C8
Southend High Sch for Boys SS0 347 D3
Southend High Sch for Girls SS2 348 F1
Southend Ho SS17 360 E3
Southend La EN9 266 C5
SOUTHEND-ON-S 366 E6
Southend-on-Sea Central Mus & Planetarium★ SS2 348 A1
Southend-on-Sea Sea Life Ctr★ SS1 367 C6
Southend-on-Sea (Victoria) Sta SS2 348 A1
Southend Pier Mus★ SS1 367 B7
Southend Pier Rlwy★ SS1 367 B5
Southend Rd
Billericay CM11 319 D7
Grays RM17 373 C2
Great Baddow CM2 255 B4
Great Wakering SS3 349 C3
Hockley SS5 324 E5
Howe Green CM2 255 D2
Rochford SS4 347 F7
Stanford-le-H SS17 360 E4
Wallend E6 352 A6
Wickford SS11 322 B7
Woodford IG8 310 D1
Woodham Mortimer CM9 257 C5
South End Rd RM12, RM13 355 B5
Southend Rd (North Circular Rd) E17, E18 309 F1
Souther Cross CM1 205 E5
Souther Cross Cotts CM1 205 D5
Souther Cross Rd CM1 205 D5
Southern Dr Loughton IG10 288 F3
South Woodham Ferrers CM3 301 C7
Southernhay Basildon SS14 342 B5
Basildon SS14 342 B6
Loughton IG10 288 D4
Southend-on-S SS9 346 E5
Southern Lodge CM19 223 C5
Southern Terr 2 EN11 197 B1
Southern Way
Harlow CM18 223 D5
Romford RM7 335 A5
Southey Cl CM9 237 C4
SOUTHEY GREEN 75 D5
Southey Wlk RM18 379 B6
Southfalls Rd SS8 364 F3
SOUTH FAMBRIDGE 303 B4
Southfield CB10 3 A3
Southfield Chase CM12 318 E1
Southfield Cl SS7 345 E5
Southfield Dr SS7 345 E5
Southfield Rd EN11 221 A7
SOUTHFIELDS Basildon 340 F7
Chadwell St Mary 374 D7
Southfields CO7 84 F6
Southfields Way CM0 284 C4
Southfleet Rd DA10 377 F1
South Gate Harlow CM20 223 D8
Purfleet RM19 371 C2
Southgate Cres CO5 186 E5
Southgate Gdns CO10 15 C6
Southgate Ho 1 SS14 342 A6
Southgate Mews SS3 350 B3
Southgate Rd IP8 16 B1
South Gate Rd E12 332 E1
Southgates Ind Pk CB10 43 F7
Southgate St CO10 15 C6
South Gn CB11 67 D4
SOUTH GREEN 164 A3
319 D7
Southgreen Gdns CO16 195 C4
South Green Jun & Inf Schs CM11 319 C7
South Green Rd CO5 163 F3
South Gunnels 1 SS14 342 B6
South Hall Dr RM13 370 B8
SOUTH HANNINGFIELD 299 C8
South Hanningfield Rd CM3, SS11, CM11 299 C8
South Hanningfield Way SS11 299 D3
SOUTH HEATH 167 A3
South Heath Rd CO7 166 F3
South Hill
Basildon SS16, SS17 360 A7
Felixstowe IP11 381 D3
Horndon on t H SS17 360 A3
South Hill Cl CM3 256 D6
South Hill Cres SS17 360 A8
South Ho CO13 170 F4
SOUTH HORNCHURCH 354 F3
South House Chase CM9 259 C7
South Kent Ave DA11 378 C1
Southland Cl CO4 110 C1
Southlands Chase CM2 255 E2
Southlands Rd CM11 320 E6
Southland Terr 3 RM19 371 B1
South Mayne SS14 343 A5
South Mews SS2 348 C1
Southmill Ct CM23 146 A6
Southmill Rd CM23 146 A5
Southmill Trad Ctr CM23 146 A6
SOUTHMINSTER 284 E4
Southminster CE Prim Sch CM0 284 D4
Southminster Rd
Althorne CM3 283 C4
Asheldham CM0 285 A7
Burnham-on-C CM0 306 B8
St Lawrence CM0 262 F3
Southminster Sta CM0 284 E4
SOUTH OCKENDON 372 C7
South Ordnance Rd EN3 265 A2
South Par
Canvey Island SS8 364 E2
South Ockendon RM15 372 C8
South Park Bsns Ctr IG3 333 E2
South Park Cres IG1 333 E2
South Park Dr
Barking IG11 352 E8
Ilford IG3 333 E1
South Park Prim Sch IG1 333 E1
South Park Rd IG1 333 D1
South Park Terr IG1 333 E1
South Park Villas IG3 352 E8
South Pl Harlow CM20 200 A4
Waltham Abbey EN9 265 C6
South Point SS0 347 C4
South Primrose Hill CM1 231 F3
South Rd
Basildon, Vange SS17 342 C1
Bishop's Stortford CM23 146 A5
Crays Hill CM11 320 D5
Dagenham RM6 334 E5
Harlow CM20 200 A4
Ilford RM6 334 C6
Saffron Walden CB11 22 E1
South Ockendon RM15 372 C7
Takeley CM22 148 C8
South Residence IG3 334 B6
South Ridge CM11 297 C2
South Riding SS14 342 E6
South St Commercial Ctr 1 CM23 145 F6
Southsea Ave SS9 346 D1
Southsea Ho 13 RM3 314 D5
South St
Bishop's Stortford CM23 145 F6
Bradwell on S CM0 242 A2
Braintree CM7 127 F2
Brentwood CM14 316 C8
Colchester CO2 135 E6
Great Chesterford CB10 3 D2
Great Waltham CM3 207 E7
Ipswich IP1 17 B7
Manningtree CO11 86 D4
Rainham RM13 354 D3
Rochford SS4 325 F1
Romford RM1 335 E6
Romford RM1 335 F5
Stanstead Abbotts SG12 197 C4
Tillingham CM0 263 E3
Tolleshunt D'arcy CM9 215 D4
South Sta★ SS1 367 B3
SOUTH STIFFORD 372 E1
South Strand CO11 86 C5
South Suffolk Bsns Ctr CO10 34 A7
Southview 10 CM7 128 A2
South View
Great Dunmow CM6 150 C8
Orsett RM16 374 B8
Southview Ave RM18 379 A6
Southview Cl CM3 301 D8
South View Cl SS6 345 F8
South View Cres IG2 333 B5
Southview Dr
Holland-on-S CO15 196 F6
Southend-on-S SS0 347 C2
Walton-on-t-N CO14 171 C7
Wanstead E18 332 B8
South View Dr RM14 337 B1
South View Gn IP9 60 E6
Southview Hts RM20 377 C8
Southview Rd
Basildon SS16 342 E5
Danbury CM3 256 D6
Hockley SS5 324 F7
South View Rd
Grays RM20 377 C8
Loughton IG10 288 F3
Rettendon CM3 300 C5
South Benfleet SS7 344 C3
Southview Sch CM8 183 F6
Southview Terr CM3 256 D6
Southwalters SS8 363 F4
Southwark Path SS14 342 F7
South Wash Rd SS15 319 E1
Southway Basildon SS16 341 D2
Brightlingsea CO7 192 F7
Colchester CO1, CO3 135 E6
South Way RM19 371 E3
SOUTH WEALD 315 E8
South Weald Dr EN9 265 D6
South Weald Rd CM14 316 A7
Southwell Cl RM16 372 C1
Southwell Link SS15 341 D5
Southwell Rd SS7 344 E4
Southwick Gdns SS8 363 F3
Southwick Rd SS8 363 F3
South Wlk SS14 342 B5
Southwold Cres SS7 344 C5
Southwold Dr IG11 353 A7
Southwold Way CO16 195 A5
Southwood Chase CM3 257 A4
Southwood Ct
Basildon SS14 342 D8
Billericay CM11 319 D7
South Woodford Sta E18 310 B1
Southwood Gdns
Ilford IG2 333 B7
Rayleigh SS9 346 B8
SOUTH WOODHAM FERRERS 301 E8
South Woodham Ferrers Sta CM3 301 C8
Southwood Prim Sch RM9 353 E8
Sovereign Cl
Braintree CM7 128 D4
Rochford SS4 325 E2
Sovereign Cres CO3 135 C6
Sovereign Ct
7 Brentwood CM14 316 C7
Harlow CM19 223 B5
Southend-on-S, Leigh-on-S SS9 346 E2
Southend-on-S, Shoeburyness SS3 368 E7
Southend-on-S, Southchurch SS1 367 E6
Sovereign Ctr IP1 16 C7
Sovereign Ho RM13 355 B2
Sovereign Hts 5 SS4 325 F2
Sovereign Mews SS0 366 E8
Sovereign Pk SS14 320 E1
Sovereign Rd IG11 353 C2
Sowerberry Cl CM1 231 F7
Sowrey Ave RM13 355 A6
Spa Cl SS5 324 E6
Spa Ct SS5 324 E6
Spa Dr CM0 240 B1
SPAIN'S END 47 E6
Spains Hall Pl SS16 342 C5
Spains Hall Rd
Finchingfield CM7 72 C8
Willingale CM5 228 E2
Spalding Ave CM1 231 E5
Spalding Cl CM7 127 E4
Spalding Ct CM1 232 A3
Spalding Way CM2 254 F8
Spalt Cl CM13 317 B8
Spanbeek Rd SS8 364 B5
Spanbies Rd CO7 58 D2
Spanbrook IG7 311 B7
Spansey Ct 1 CO9 76 D1
Spa Rd Feering CO5 158 E4
Hockley SS5 324 E6
Witham CM8 183 E2
Spareleaze Hill IG10 288 F5
Sparepenny La N CB10 47 A4
Sparepenny La S CB10 47 A3
Sparkbridge 8 SS15 341 A6
Sparkey Cl CM8 212 A7
Sparks Cl RM8 334 D2
Sparks La CO9 29 A6
Spar La CM3 258 C3
Sparling Cl CO2 135 C2
Sparlings The CO13 170 C8
Sparrow Cl CO9 75 D8
Sparrow Ct E4 309 C4
Sparrow Gn RM10 335 B1
Sparrow Rd CO10 34 B6
Sparrows Cl CM1 252 A5
Sparrows Cnr CO12 116 E5
Sparrowsend Cotts CB11 43 A4
Sparrowsend Hill CB11 43 A5
Sparrows Herne
Basildon SS16 342 B4
Clacton-on-S CO15 195 F6
Sparrows Ho CO7 192 E6
Sparrow's La
Hatfield Heath CM22 174 F1
White Roothing or White Roding CM17, CM22 202 E6
Sparsholt Rd IG11 352 E4
Spartan Cl CB9 8 C8
Spearpoint Gdns IG2 333 F7
Speckled Wood Cl IP8 36 D8
Speckled Wood Ct CM7 154 E8
Spectrum Twr 1 IG1 333 C2
Speedwell Cl CM8 183 D4
Speedwell Ct RM17 378 E7
Speedwell Rd
Colchester CO2 136 D2
Ipswich IP2 16 F4
SPELLBROOK 172 F8
Spellbrook Cl SS12 321 F6
Spellbrook La E CM22 172 F8
Spellbrook La W CM23 172 E7
Spellbrook Prim Sch CM23 172 F7
Spells Cl CM0 284 D4
Spencer Cl Billericay CM12 296 F5
Elsenham CM22 94 C3
Epping CM16 246 B2
Maldon CM9 259 A8
Stansted Mountfitchet CM24 119 E6
Woodford IG8 310 C5
Spencer Ct
Hornchurch RM12 336 A1
South Woodham Ferrers CM3 301 E7
Spencer Gdns SS4 325 E5
Spencer Ho
Southend-on-S SS0 347 A1
Stansted Mountfitchet CM24 119 D7
Spencer Rd Chingford E17 309 C1
Great Chesterford CB10 3 D3
Ilford IG3 333 F3
Rainham RM13 354 D3
South Benfleet SS7 344 D6
Thorpe-le-S CO16 142 A2
Spencers SS5 324 F4
Spencers Croft CM18 224 B6
Spencers Ct SS12 321 C7
Spencers Piece CO4 83 E4
Spencer Sq CM7 127 F8
Spencer Wlk RM18 379 B6
Spendells Cl CO14 144 D2
Spendells Ho CO14 144 E2
Spenders Cl SS14 342 D8
Spenlow Dr CM1 231 D7
Spennells The CO16 142 A2
Spenser Cres RM14 337 C4
Spenser Way CO15 194 F1
Speyside Wlk 2 SS12 321 E5
Spey Way RM1 313 E3
Spicers La CO10 15 C8
Spike The 7 CB10 22 F2
Spillbutters CM15 272 B3
Spilsby Rd RM3 314 E3
Spindle Beams SS4 325 F1
Spindle Rd CB9 8 D8
Spindles RM18 379 A7
Spindle Wood CO4 110 B4
Spindrift Way CO7 164 B8
Spingate Cl RM12 355 D7
Spinks La CM8 183 F1
Spinnaker Cl Barking IG11 353 B2
Clacton-on-S CO15 220 J8
Spinnaker Dr CM9 237 E3
Spinnakers The SS7 344 B4
Spinnaker The CM3 301 E5
Spinnel's Hill CO11 88 B1
Spinnel's La Wix CO11 115 D7
Wrabness CO11 88 C1

Spinner Cl IP1 16 D8
Spinney Cl Rainham RM13 354 E3
 Wickford SS11 321 F7
Spinney Ct CM21 172 E2
Spinneyfields CO5 186 D6
Spinney Gdns RM9 353 E7
Spinney Jun & Inf Schs
 CM20 200 A1
Spinneys The Hockley SS5 324 D5
 Rayleigh SS6 324 A1
 Southend-on-S SS9 346 F7
Spinney The
 Billericay CM12 297 B4
 Braintree CM7 128 C1
 Brentwood CM13 295 C3
 Chipping Ongar CM5 248 F1
 Earls Colne CO6 105 A6
 1 Harlow CM20 200 A1
 Hatfield Peverel CM3 211 B3
 Jaywick CO16 195 A2
 Long Melford CO10 15 C7
 Loughton IG10 289 B5
 Newport CB11 67 A7
 Orsett RM16 359 A1
 Rushmere St A IP4 18 F4
 Stansted Mountfitchet
 CM24 119 E6
Spinneywood SS15 341 A8
Spinning Wheel Mead
 CM18 224 A5
Spire Green Ctr CM19 222 E7
Spire Rd SS15 341 C7
Spires The
 Bishop's Stortford CM23 145 D7
 Brentwood CM14 316 D8
 Great Baddow CM2 254 F6
Spiritus Ho CO2 136 D5
SPITALBROOK 221 B4
Spital La CM14 315 F6
Spital Rd Maldon CM9 236 F2
 Maldon CM9 258 D7
Spitfire Cl IP3 18 B1
Sporehams La
 Danbury CM3 256 C4
 Howe Green CM2, CM3 255 F4
Sporhams SS16 341 F4
Sportsmans La CM3 211 A2
Sportsway CO1 135 F8
Spots Wlk CM2 254 D3
Spout La CO10 55 D7
Spratt Hall Rd E11 332 A5
Spratts La CO11 113 B4
Spread Eagle Pl 2 CM4 274 C4
Spriggs Ct CM16 246 A2
Spriggs La CM4 251 A2
Spriggs Oak CM16 246 A2
Springbank Ave
 Hornchurch RM12 355 C7
 Lawford CO11 86 B3
Springbok Ho CM2 254 F5
Spring Chase
 Brightlingsea CO7 192 E7
 Wivenhoe CO7 137 B2
Spring Cl
 Clacton-on-S CO16 195 C5
 Colchester CO4 110 C3
 Dagenham RM8 334 D3
 Little Baddow CM3 234 D5
Spring Cotts CB9 9 C6
Spring Ct
 Southend-on-S SS0 347 D2
 10 Wanstead E18 332 B8
Spring Elms La CM3 234 F3
Springett Pl CM77 155 E6
Springett's Hill CO8 55 D2
Springfarm Cl RM13 355 D2
SPRINGFIELD 232 E6
Springfield
 Brentwood CM15 294 C1
 Epping CM16 267 F7
 Hadleigh SS7 345 D4
Springfield Ave
 Brentwood CM13 295 E2
 Felixstowe IP11 381 E5
Springfield Basin CM2 232 C2
Springfield Cl CM5 248 F5
Springfield Cotts CM9 237 B5
Springfield Ct
 Bishop's Stortford CM23 145 E8
 Clacton-on-S CO15 195 C3
 2 Ilford IG1 352 B7
 Rayleigh SS6 323 A4
 Upminster RM14 337 B1
Springfield Dr Ilford IG2 333 C5
 Southend-on-S SS0 347 D3
Springfield Gdns
 Upminster RM14 337 C1
 Woodford IG8 310 C3
Springfield Gn CM1 232 E4
Springfield Ind Est CM0 306 A5
Springfield Inf Sch IP1 16 F8
Springfield Jun Sch IP1 16 F8
Springfield La IP1 16 F8
Springfield Lyons App
 CM2 233 A5
Springfield Mdws CO16 168 C4
Springfield Nursery Est
 CM0 306 A6
Springfield Park Ave CM2 232 E2
Springfield Park Hill CM2 232 D2
Springfield Park La CM2 232 E2
Springfield Park Par CM2 232 D2
Springfield Park Rd CM2 232 E2
Springfield Pl CM1 232 E5
Springfield Rd
 Billericay CM12 297 B5
 Burnham-on-C CM0 306 A6
 Canvey Island SS8 364 F3
 Chelmsford CM1 232 E4
 Chingford E4 287 E2
 Grays RM16 373 E4
 Sudbury CO10 15 E1
 Wickford SS11 321 B8
Springfields Basildon SS16 342 F4
 Braintree CM77 127 C2
 Brightlingsea CO7 192 F7
 Great Dunmow CM6 150 D8
Springfields *continued*
 Waltham Abbey EN9 265 E5
Springfields Dr CO2 135 A3
Springfield Terr 2 CO10 33 F8
Spring Gardens Ind Est
 RM7 335 C5
Spring Gardens Rd CO6 106 E6
Spring Gdns
 Hornchurch RM12 355 B8
 Long Melford CO10 15 C8
 Rayleigh SS6 323 C2
 Romford RM7 335 C5
 Woodford IG8 310 C3
Spring Gr IG10 288 D3
Springhall Ct CM21 172 E2
Springhall La CM21 172 E1
Springhall Rd CM21 172 E2
Springham Dr CO4 110 A6
Springhead Rd DA11 378 D1
Spring Hill CB11 22 A1
Springhill Cl CO7 138 E8
Springhill Rd CB11 43 D8
Spring Hills CM20 199 B1
Spring Hills Twr CM20 199 A1
Springhouse La SS17 361 A2
Springhouse Rd SS17 360 F4
Springhurst Cl IP4 17 F6
Spring La Colchester CO3 135 A7
 Colchester, Lexden CO3 135 A8
 Eight Ash G CO3 108 B1
 Great Totham CM9 213 D7
 Hatfield Peverel CM3, CM9 211 F2
 Maldon CM9 237 B4
 West Bergholt CO6 108 E3
 Wivenhoe CO7 137 B2
Springland Cl IP4 18 A6
Springlands Way CO10 15 F2
Spring Lane Rdbt CO3 135 A7
Springleigh Pl SS0 347 D2
Spring Mdw CO10 2 B6
Springmead CM77 154 D7
Spring Meadow Prim Sch
 CO12 91 A3
Spring Mews CM21 172 E2
Spring Pl 2 IG11 352 C3
Spring Pond Cl CM2 254 E8
Spring Pond Mdw CM15 272 C4
Springpond Rd RM9 353 E7
Spring Rd
 Brightlingsea CO7 192 F7
 Ipswich IP4 18 A6
 St Osyth CO16 194 A3
 Tiptree CO5 186 C4
Spring Rise
 Galleywood CM2 254 C2
 Haverhill CB9 9 C6
Spring Sedge Cl CO3 134 C7
Springtail Rd IP8 36 E8
Spring Vale DA9 377 C1
Springvalley La CO7 111 C4
Springwater Cl SS9 346 C7
Springwater Gr SS9 346 C7
Springwater Rd SS9 346 C8
Spring Way CO9 51 E1
SPRINGWELL 22 A7
Springwell Ct SG12 197 C3
Springwell Rd CB10, CB11 22 A5
Springwood Ct CM7 127 D3
Springwood Dr CM7 127 C4
Springwood Ind Est CM7 127 D3
Springwood Way RM1 336 A6
Sprites End IP11 381 B7
Spriteshall La IP11 381 B7
Sprites La IP8, IP2 16 C2
Sprites Prim Sch IP2 16 C2
SPROUGHTON 16 A6
Sproughton Bsns Pk IP1 16 C8
Sproughton CE Prim Sch
 IP8 16 B6
Sproughton Ct IP8 16 A6
Sproughton Rd IP1 16 D7
Spruce Ave Colchester CO4 136 E8
 Great Dunmow CM6 123 B1
Spruce Cl Basildon SS15 319 C1
 West Mersea CO5 218 B7
 Witham CM8 184 A4
Spruce Hill CM18 223 E3
Spruce Hills Rd E17 309 C1
Sprundel Ave SS8 364 D2
Spur Cl RM4 290 B6
Spurgate CM13 295 B1
Spurgeon Cl
 11 Grays RM17 378 C8
 Sible Hedingham CO9 51 E1
Spurgeon Pl CO5 158 C2
Spurgeon St CO1 136 C6
Spurling Rd RM9 353 F6
Spurling Wks EN11 221 C7
Spur Rd IG11 352 C2
Spurway Par 2 IG2 332 F6
Squadrons App RM12 355 D6
Square St 3 CM17 200 C1
Square The
 10 Brentwood CM14 316 C8
 Colchester CO2 135 B3
 Heybridge CM9 237 A5
 Horndon on t H SS17 359 F3
 Ilford IG1 333 A4
 Sawbridgeworth CM21 172 E2
 Stansted Mountfitchet CM22 93 F3
 Stock CM4 275 E2
 Tillingham CM0 263 E4
 West Mersea CO5 218 B6
 Widdington CB11 67 D4
 Woodford IG8 310 A5
Squires Cl CM23 145 C8
Squires Ct Earls Colne CO6 105 B6
 Hoddesdon EN11 221 A5
Squire's Ct 1 CB9 8 E7
Squire St CM3 301 E7
Squires The RM7 335 B5
Squirrells Ct CM1 231 F5
Squirrels SS16 341 B3
Squirrel's Chase RM16 374 A4
Squirrels Cl 2 CM23 145 F8
Squirrels Ct RM2 336 C7
Squirrels Field CO4 109 F5
Squirrel's Heath Ave RM2 336 B8
Squirrels Heath Inf Sch
 RM2 336 B6
Squirrels Heath Jun Sch
 RM2 336 B6
Squirrels Heath La RM11,
 RM2 336 D7
Squirrels Heath Rd RM3 314 F1
Squirrel's La IG9 310 D7
Squirrels The IP9 35 A2
Stable Cl Colchester CO3 134 E6
 West Mersea CO5 218 E7
Stablecroft CM1 232 E8
Stablefield Rd CO14 171 A7
Stable Mews
 Southend-on-S SS2 347 F2
 West Mersea CO5 218 E8
Stables The
 Buckhurst Hill IG9 288 C2
 Sawbridgeworth CM21 173 B3
Stable Yard Cotts CM6 122 C4
Stacey Ct 9 CM23 145 F6
Stacey Dr SS16 341 C2
Stacey's Mount CM11 320 C5
Stackfield CM20 200 A3
Stackyard The CB10 3 A3
Stacy Ct CM6 123 C1
Staddles CM22 173 B8
Stadium Rd SS2 348 A1
Stadium Trad Est SS7 345 C7
Stadium Way Harlow CM19 198 F1
 Thundersley SS7 345 C7
Staffa Cl SS12 321 F5
Stafford Ave RM11 336 D8
Stafford Cl Grays RM16 372 C2
 Greenhithe DA9 376 F2
 Kirby Cross CO13 170 E6
 Linford SS17 375 A3
 Southend-on-S SS9 347 A6
Stafford Cres CM7 128 D4
Stafford Ct EN10 221 A3
Stafford Dr EN10 221 A3
Stafford Gn SS16 340 F4
Stafford Ho
 Bishop's Stortford CM23 145 F5
 Hoddesdon EN10 221 A3
Stafford Ind Est RM11 336 D8
Staffords CM17 200 E4
STAFFORD'S CORNER 188 E5
Stafford Wlk SS8 364 A5
Stagden Cross SS14 342 F5
Stagden Cross Villas CM1 177 E2
Staggart Gn IG7 311 F4
Stag Hts IG9 310 B8
Stag La IG9 310 B8
Stainer Cl 1 CM8 211 F7
Stainers CM23 145 C5
Staines Rd IG1 352 D8
Stainforth Rd IG2 333 D5
Stairs Rd SS3 350 F4
Stalham Way IG6 311 B2
Stalin Rd CO2 136 B4
Stallards Cres CO13 170 E6
STAMBOURNE 28 D3
STAMBOURNE GREEN 28 A1
Stambourne Rd
 Great Yeldham CO9 29 D3
 Ridgewell CO9 28 F5
 Toppesfield CO9 50 B8
Stambridge Prim Sch
 SS4 326 C2
Stambridge Rd
 Clacton-on-S CO15 195 C4
 Rochford SS4 326 C2
Stamford Cl IP2 36 F8
Stamford Gdns RM9 353 C5
Stamford Rd RM9 353 C5
Stammers Ct CM0 284 D4
Stammers Rd CO4 109 F4
STANBROOK 96 E7
Standard Ave CO15 220 D6
Standard Rd
 Belvedere DA17 369 A1
 9 Colchester CO1 136 C6
Standen Ave
 Hornchurch RM12 336 E1
 South Woodham Ferrers
 CM3 301 C5
Standfield Gdns RM10 354 A6
Standfield Rd RM10 354 A7
Standingford CM19 223 B3
Standley Rd CO14 144 D1
Standrums CM6 150 D8
Stane Cl CM23 118 F1
Stane Field CO6 132 E3
Stanes Rd CM7 127 F6
Stanetta Ct 3 RM6 334 B4
Staneway SS16 341 D3
Stanfield Cl CO3 134 E3
Stanfield Mdw CM8 155 F1
Stanfield Rd SS2 348 A1
Stanfields Ct CM20 199 E1
Stanford Cl Romford RM7 335 B5
 Woodford IG8 310 E5
Stanford Ct EN9 266 A6
Stanford Gdns RM15 371 E5
Stanford Hall 1 SS17 360 F3
Stanford Ho
 3 Barking IG11 353 B3
 East Tilbury RM18 375 B2
STANFORD-LE-H 360 E1
Stanford-Le-Hope By-Pass
 Basildon SS16, SS17 342 B1
 Orsett RM16 374 D8
 Stanford-le-H SS17 360 D4
Stanford-le-Hope Prim Sch
 SS17 360 D1
Stanford-le-Hope Sta
 SS17 360 C1
Stanford Marshes Nature
 Reserve* SS17 375 E7
Stanford Rd
 Canvey Island SS8 364 A3
 Grays RM16 373 E4
 Orsett SS17, RM16 374 E8
 Stanford-le-H SS17 360 B1
STANFORD RIVERS 270 C6
Stanford Rivers Rd CM5 271 A8
Stanhope Gdns
 1 Dagenham RM8 334 F1
 Redbridge IG1 332 F3
Stanhope Rd
 Dagenham RM8 334 F1
Stanhope Rd *continued*
 Rainham RM13 355 A3
 Swanscombe DA10 377 F1
Stanier Cl SS1 367 C8
Stanley Ave Barking IG11 352 F3
 Brightlingsea CO7 193 A7
 Dagenham RM8 334 F3
 Ipswich IP3 18 A4
 Romford RM2 336 A7
Stanley Cl Greenhithe DA9 376 E2
 Hornchurch RM12 336 C2
 Romford RM2 336 A7
Stanley Drapkin Prim Sch
 CB9 27 B6
Stanley Pl CM5 249 A2
Stanley Rd Bulphan RM14 358 F8
 Canvey Island SS8 364 D4
 Chingford E4 287 D1
 Clacton-on-S CO15 195 C2
 Felixstowe IP11 381 E3
 Grays RM17 378 B8
 Great Chesterford CB10 3 E3
 Halstead CO9 76 D2
 Hornchurch RM12 336 D2
 Ilford IG1 333 D2
 Rochford SS4 325 C7
 South Benfleet SS7 344 D6
 Southend-on-S SS1 367 B7
 Sudbury CO10 33 E8
 Swanscombe DA10 377 F1
 Wivenhoe CO7 137 C1
 Woodford E18 309 F2
Stanley Rd N RM13 354 E4
Stanley Rd S RM13 354 F3
Stanley Rise CM2 232 F3
Stanleys Farm Rd CB11 43 F8
Stanley Terr CM12 297 A1
Stanley Wood Ave CO10 15 F1
Stanley Wooster Way
 CO4 136 E7
Stanmore Cl CO16 195 D5
Stanmore Rd
 Belvedere DA17 369 C2
 Wickford SS11 322 B6
Stanmore Way
 Loughton IG10 289 A8
 St Osyth CO16 194 B4
Stannard Way CO10 34 A6
Stannetts SS15 341 B8
Stansfield Ct SS7 344 B7
Stansfield Rd SS7 344 B7
Stansgate Rd
 Dagenham RM10 335 A1
 Steeple CM0 261 F5
STANSTEAD 2 F7
STANSTEAD ABBOTTS 197 E4
Stanstead Dr EN11 221 B8
Stanstead Pl CO9 103 F8
Stanstead Rd Halstead CO9 103 F8
 Hoddesdon EN11 197 B1
 Wanstead E11 332 B6
Stansted Airport Sta
 CM24 121 B4
Stansted Cl Billericay CM11 297 D2
 Chelmsford CM1 231 E1
 Hornchurch RM12 355 B6
Stansted Ctyd CM24 121 B1
STANSTED
 MOUNTFITCHET 119 C8
Stansted Mountfitchet Sta
 CM24 119 E6
Stansted Rd
 Birchanger CM23 119 C4
 Bishop's Stortford CM23 119 B2
 Colchester CO2 136 A1
 Elsenham CM22 94 C1
Stansted Way CO13 171 A6
Stanstrete Field CM77 154 B5
Stanton Ct 4 RM10 354 A6
Stanton Gate RM7 335 D6
Stanton Pl 9 CB9 9 B8
Stantons CM20 199 B1
STANWAY 134 C5
Stanway Cl 2 Chigwell IG7 311 E5
 Glemsford CO10 2 C5
Stanway Ctr The CO3 134 E4
Stanway Fiveways Prim Sch
 CO3 134 D5
STANWAY GREEN 134 D3
Stanway Prim Sch CO3 134 C6
Stanway Rd
 South Benfleet SS7 344 C5
 Waltham Abbey EN9 266 A6
Stanway Sch The CO3 134 D5
Stanwell St 9 CO2 135 F6
Stanwyck Dr IG7 311 C5
Stanwyck Gdns RM3 314 B5
Stanwyn Ave CO15 195 E3
STAPLEFORD ABBOTTS 291 C3
Stapleford Abbotts Prim Sch
 RM4 291 C4
Stapleford Ave IG2 333 E6
Stapleford Cl
 Chelmsford CM2 232 A1
 Chingford E4 309 C7
Stapleford End SS11 322 B5
Stapleford Gdns RM5 313 A4
Stapleford Rd RM4 291 B5
STAPLEFORD TAWNEY 269 C3
Stapleford Way IG11 353 B2
Staplegrove SS3 368 D8
Staplers Cl CM9 213 B4
Staplers Heath CM9 213 B4
Staplers Wlk CM9 213 B4
Staples Rd IG10 288 E6
Staples Road Jun & Inf Sch
 IG10 288 E6
Stapleton Cres RM13 355 A6
Staple Tye CM18 223 D5
Staple Tye Sh Mews
 CM18 223 C5
Stapley Rd DA17 369 A1
Starboard Ave DA9 377 B1
Starboard View CM3 301 E6
Star Bsns Ctr RM13 369 D8
Starch House La IG6 311 D1
Starfield Cl IP4 18 B6
Star La Epping CM16 246 A1
 Great Dunmow CM6 123 D1
 Great Wakering SS3 349 E3
Star La *continued*
 Ingatestone CM4 274 C4
 Ipswich IP4 17 D5
Star Lane Ind Est SS3 349 E3
Starling Cl
 Buckhurst Hill IG9 288 A1
 Thundersley SS7 345 B7
Starling Ct 17 CM23 145 F6
STARLING'S GREEN 64 F3
Starling's Hill CO9 75 E4
Starmans Cl RM9 353 E4
Star Mead CM6 70 A2
Starr Rd CM22 94 F5
START HILL 147 A7
State Mans IG6 311 C1
State Par IG6 311 C1
Station App
 Basildon, Laindon SS15 341 C5
 Basildon, Pitsea SS16 343 B4
 Braintree CM7 128 A2
 Buckhurst Hill IG9 310 D6
 Burnham-on-C CM0 306 B5
 Canvey Island SS8 363 F6
 Frinton-on-S CO13 170 F5
 Grays RM17 378 A8
 Harlow CM20 200 C5
 Hockley SS5 324 E6
 North Fambridge CM3 303 B8
 Southend-on-S, Prittlewell
 SS2 347 F2
 Southend-on-S SS1 367 A8
 South Woodham Ferrers
 CM3 301 C8
 Theydon Bois CM16 267 E3
 Upminster RM14 337 C2
 Wanstead E11 332 A6
 Wickford SS11 321 D8
 Woodford IG8 310 B4
 2 Woodford, Snaresbrook
 E18 310 B1
Station Ave Rayleigh SS6 323 C3
 Southend-on-S SS2 348 A3
 Wickford SS11 321 D8
Station Cres
 Cold Norton CM3 280 F5
 Rayleigh SS6 323 D3
Station Ct
 Chipping Ongar CM5 249 A3
 Wickford SS11 321 D8
Station Est 1 E18 310 B1
Station Gate SS15 341 C5
Station Hill CO8 79 E8
Station Ind Est CM0 306 B5
Station La Basildon SS13 343 B5
 Harwich CO12 91 C4
 Hornchurch RM12 336 E2
 Ingatestone CM4 274 B3
Station Par Barking IG11 352 C5
 Dagenham RM10 354 A6
 Hornchurch RM12 355 B8
 3 Romford RM1 335 E5
 2 Wanstead E11 332 A6
 Woodford IG9 310 D6
Station Pas E18 310 B1
Station Rd Alresford CO7 165 A8
 Althorne CM3 282 F1
 Ardleigh CO7 111 E7
 Belvedere DA17 369 A3
 Bentley IP9 60 E6
 Billericay CM12 296 F2
 Birdbrook CO9 10 D1
 Bishop's Stortford CM23 146 A7
 Bradfield CO11 87 E3
 Braintree CM7 127 F2
 Brightlingsea CO7 192 E6
 Burnham-on-C CM0 306 B5
 Canvey Island SS8 364 E2
 Chigwell IG7 311 B7
 Chingford E4 287 D1
 Clacton-on-S CO15 195 F3
 Clare CO10 12 C7
 Cold Norton CM3 281 A5
 Colne Engaine CO6 77 F1
 Cressing CM8 156 A3
 Earls Colne CO6 105 A7
 East Tilbury RM18 380 B7
 Elsenham CM22 94 C2
 Epping CM16 268 A8
 Felsted CM6 151 F6
 Great Bentley CO7 166 E8
 Great Dunmow CM6 150 E8
 Greenhithe DA9 377 A2
 Greenhithe DA9 377 A3
 Harlow CM17 200 C4
 Harwich, Bath Side CO12 91 E5
 Harwich CO12 90 F5
 Harwich, Dovercourt CO12 91 D4
 Hatfield Peverel CM3 210 F5
 Haverhill CB9 9 A8
 Hockley SS5 324 E6
 Hoddesdon EN10 221 A3
 Holdbrook EN9 265 A5
 Ilford, Barkingside IG6 333 D8
 Ilford IG1 333 B1
 Kelvedon CO5 158 C3
 Kirby Cross CO13 170 B6
 Long Melford CO10 15 C5
 Loughton IG10 288 E4
 Maldon CM9 237 A3
 Manningtree CO11 86 C5
 Marks Tey CO6 133 B4
 Newport CB11 67 A8
 Northfleet DA11 378 B1
 North Weald Bassett CM16 247 B4
 Rayleigh SS6 323 C3
 Rayne CM77 126 F1
 Romford, Chadwell Heath RM6,
 RM8 334 D4
 Romford, Harold Wood RM3 314 F2
 Romford RM2 336 C7
 Saffron Walden CB11 22 D1
 Sawbridgeworth CM21 172 F3
 Sible Hedingham CO9 51 E2
 South Benfleet SS7 363 D8
 Southend-on-S, Eastwood
 SS9 346 E3
 Southend-on-S, Leigh-on-S
 SS9 346 E1
 Southend-on-S, Thorpe Bay
 SS1 368 B8
Station Rd *continued*
 Southend-on-S, Westcliff-on-S
 SS0 366 D7
 Southminster CM0 284 E4
 Stanstead Abbotts SG12 197 C4
 Stansted Mountfitchet
 CM24 119 E6
 Sudbury CO10 33 E7
 Takeley CM22 148 C7
 Thorpe-le-S CO16 168 F8
 Thorrington CO7 166 A6
 Tiptree CO5 186 C4
 Tollesbury CM9 216 D2
 Tolleshunt D'arcy CM9 215 E5
 Trimley St M IP11 381 A7
 Upminster RM14 337 C2
 Wakes Colne CO6 106 D6
 Wendens Ambo CB11 42 F5
 West Horndon CM13 339 D5
 White Notley CM8 155 F2
 Wickford SS11 299 C2
 Wickham Bishops CM8 212 C4
 Witham CM8 184 A3
 Wivenhoe CO7 164 B8
 Wrabness CO11 88 F3
Station Rd N DA17 369 B3
Station Road Ind Est
 Great Dunmow CM6 150 E7
 Tolleshunt D'arcy CM9 215 E5
Station Sq RM2 336 B7
Station St Ipswich IP2 17 C3
 Saffron Walden CB11 22 D1
 Walton-on-t-N CO14 171 C8
Station Terr CM3 210 F5
Station Way
 Basildon SS14, SS16 342 A5
 Buckhurst Hill IG9 310 D6
Station Yd IP2 17 B4
Staveley Ct 4 E11 332 A6
Staverton Rd RM11 336 D5
Stays La CM5 229 A3
Steadman Ho 4 RM10 335 A1
Steamer Terr 2 CM1 232 A3
Steam Mill Rd CO11 114 B8
STEBBING 124 E5
STEBBING GREEN 125 C3
Stebbing Prim Sch CM6 124 E5
Stebbing Rd CM6 152 B7
Stebbings SS16 341 C4
Stebbings Ct 5 CM0 306 C4
Stebbing Way IG11 353 A3
Stedman Ct CO15 220 D6
Steed Cl RM11 336 B2
Steed Cres CO2 136 A5
Steeds Mdw CO10 15 C8
Steeds Way IG10 288 E6
Steel App IG11 353 B3
Steele Ave DA9 377 A2
Steele Cl CO6 132 F3
Steen Cl CM4 274 B4
STEEPLE 261 E3
STEEPLE BUMPSTEAD 27 B8
Steeple Bumpstead Rd
 CB9 26 E7
Steeple Cl Heybridge CM9 237 D5
 Rochford SS4 325 D3
Steeplefield SS9 346 E6
Steeple Gate SS7 345 E2
Steeplehall SS13 343 A5
Steeple Hts SS7 344 B6
Steeple Mdws CM0 284 B4
Steeple Rd
 Latchingdon CM3 282 D7
 Steeple CM0 262 C4
 Steeple CM0 284 B7
STEEPLE VIEW 319 B1
Steeple View
 Bishop's Stortford CM23 145 F8
 Grays RM17 373 A1
Steeple Way CM15 272 B2
Steerforth Cl CM1 231 D7
Steli Ave SS8 363 F5
Stella Maris IP2 16 D5
Stella Maris Cl SS8 364 F3
Sten Cl EN3 265 A2
Stenning Ave SS17 375 B2
Stepfield CM8 184 B2
Stephen Ave RM13 355 A6
Stephen Cl Haverhill CB9 8 F8
 Long Melford CO10 15 B5
Stephen Cranfield Cl CO5 164 A7
Stephen Marshall Ave CM7 72 C6
Stephen Neville Ct CB11 43 D8
Stephens Cl RM3 314 C5
Stephens Cres SS17 359 F3
Stephen's Ct IP4 18 B6
Stephenson Ave RM18 379 A6
Stephenson Cl
 Hoddesdon EN11 221 C6
 Hoddesdon EN11 221 D6
Stephenson Rd
 Braintree CM7 128 A1
 Clacton-on-S CO15 196 B8
 Colchester CO4 110 D6
 North Fambridge CM3 303 A8
 Southend-on-S SS9 346 C6
Stephenson Rd W CO15 169 A1
Sterling Cl CO3 134 E5
Sterling Complex IP1 16 D7
Sterling Ind Est RM10 354 B8
Stern Cl IG11 353 C3
Sterry Cres RM10 354 A7
Sterry Gdns RM10 354 A6
Sterry Ho RM13 355 B2
Sterry Rd Barking IG11 352 F4
 Dagenham RM10 354 A7
Stevanne Ct 1 DA17 369 A1
Stevenage Rd E6 352 A6
Stevens Cl
 Canvey Island SS8 364 D4
 Colchester CO4 109 E3
Stevens La CM6 152 F6
Stevenson Rd IP1 17 B6
Stevenson Way SS12 321 C5
Stevens Rd Dagenham RM8 334 C1
 Witham CM8 183 E1
Stevens Way IG7 311 E6
Stevens Wlk CO4 136 F7
STEVENTON END 6 C2
STEWARDS 223 E3

Vineyards The★ CM7 .....153 D6
Vineyards The CM2 ....254 F7
Vinnicombe Ct 3 IP2 .....16 E1
Vintage Mews E4 ....309 A6
Vint Cres CO3 ....135 C6
Vintners The SS2 ....347 F5
Viola Cl Basildon SS15 .....341 C5
South Ockendon RM15 .....357 C2
Viola Wlk CO4 ....136 E7
Violet Cl Chelmsford CM1 ...232 E7
Ipswich IP2 ....16 F4
Violet Rd E18 ....310 B1
Virgil Rd CM8 ....183 F5
Virginia Cl Jaywick CO15 ...195 A1
Romford RM5 ....313 C3
South Benfleet SS7 ....344 B7
Virginia Gdns IG6 ....311 D1
Virley Cl CM9 ....237 D4
Viscount Dr CO4 ....110 C5
Visitor Ctr & Country Wlk★
CB9 ....9 C6
Vista Ave CO13 ....143 D1
Vista Ct IP2 ....17 B4
Vista Dr IG4 ....332 D6
Vista Rd Clacton-on-S CO15 .196 A3
Wickford SS11 ....321 F7
Vista The E4 ....287 D2
Vitllus Cl CO4 ....110 B6
Vitoria Mews CO2 ....135 C2
Vivian Ct CO14 ....171 C8
Voluntary Pl E11 ....332 A5
Volwycke Ave CM9 ....258 F8
Voorburg Rd SS8 ....364 D4
Vowler Rd SS16 ....341 B4
Voysey Gdns SS13 ....321 B1
Vyntoner Ho CO16 ....194 A4

W

Waalwyk Dr SS8 ....364 C4
Waarden Rd SS8 ....364 B4
Waarem Ave SS8 ....364 B4
Waddesdon Rd CO12 ......91 D4
Wade Rd CO15 ....196 B8
Wade Reach CO14 ....171 B8
Wadeville Ave RM6 ....334 F4
Wadeville Cl DA17 ....369 A1
Wadgate Rd IP11 ....381 C4
Wadham Ave E17 ....309 B3
Wadham Cl CM4 ....274 B4
Wadham Park Ave SS5 ...302 A1
Wadham Rd E17 ....309 B2
Wadhurst Ct E6 ....352 A3
Wadhurst Rd IP3 ....18 D3
Wadley Cl CO5 ....186 E5
Wagon Mead CM22 ....174 A3
Wagstaff Gdns RM9 ......353 C5
Wagtail Dr CM9 ....237 C5
Wagtail Pl CO5 ....158 C2
Waikato Lodge IG9 ....288 C1
Wainfleet Ave RM5 ....313 C1
Wainsfield Villas CM6 .....70 B2
Wainwright Ave
Brentwood CM13 ....295 D3
Great Notley CM77 ....154 D8
Wainwright St CM23 ......145 C5
Wake Arms Rdbt IG10 ....266 F3
Wakefield Ave CM12 ......297 A2
Wakefield Cl
Colchester CO1 ....136 A8
Great Chesterford CB10 .....3 D3
Wakefield Gdns IG1 ......332 E5
Wakefield Rd DA9 ....377 C2
Wakelin Chase CM4 ......274 A3
Wakelin Way CM8 ....184 B2
Wakerfield Cl RM11 ......336 F6
Wakering Ave SS3 ....368 G7
Wakering Rd Barking IG11 .352 C5
Great Wakering SS3 ......350 B1
Southend-on-S SS1, SS3 ...349 A2
WAKES COLNE 106 C6
Wakescolne SS11 ....322 A6
WAKES COLNE GREEN 79 C1
Wakes Hall Bsns Ctr CO6 .106 B6
Wakeshall La C10 ....30 C8
Wakes St CO6 ....106 C6
Walace Ct EN3 ....265 A2
Walbrook 10 E18 ....332 A8
Waldeck Ct CB11 ....43 D7
Waldeck Rd DA1 ....376 A1
Waldegrave SS16 ....342 B4
Waldegrave Cl CO11 ......86 B3
Waldegrave Ct
11 Barking IG11 ....352 D4
Upminster RM14 ....337 B3
Waldegrave Gdns RM14 ...337 B2
Waldegrave Rd
Dagenham RM8 ....334 C2
Lawford CO11 ....86 C3
Waldegraves Farm Cvn Site
CO5 ....218 G6
Waldegraves La CO5 ......218 G7
Waldegraves The CO8 .....79 F8
Waldegrave Way CO11 .....86 B3
Walden Ave
Elder Street CB10 ....44 E2
Rainham RM13 ....354 D3
Walden Castle★ CB10 .....22 D2
Walden Cl CM9 ....213 A4
Walden Ho CO13 ....170 F4
Walden House Rd CM8,
CM9 ....213 A4
Walden Pl CB10 ....22 D2
Walden Rd Ashdon CB10 ....23 E6
Great Chesterford CB10 .....3 E3
Hadstock CB1 ....5 B6
Hornchurch RM11 ....336 D5
Littlebury CB10 ....21 F4
Radwinter CB10 ....45 D7
Sewards End CB10 ....23 D1
Thaxted CM6 ....69 F5
Wendens Ambo CB11 ....42 F6
Wendens Ambo CB11 ....43 A6
Walden Way
Frinton-on-S CO13 ....171 A6
Hornchurch RM11 ....336 D5
Redbridge IG6 ....311 E3
Waldgrooms CM6 ....123 C1
Waldingfield Rd CO10 .....33 F8
Waldon RM18 ....375 C3
Waldringfield SS14 ....342 B7
WALES END 1 A7
Walford Cl CO6 ....131 A2
Walford Pl CM2 ....232 F2
Walfords Cl CM17 ....200 C3
Walford Way CO6 ....131 A2
Walfrey Gdns RM9 ....353 E5
Walker Ave CM5 ....227 D2
Walker Cl IP3 ....18 C5
Walker Dr SS9 ....346 A2
Walkers Cl CM1 ....232 D7
Walkers Sq SS17 ....360 D1
Walkey Way SS3 ....368 H7
Walk The Billericay CM12 ..297 A1
Great Ash G CO6 ....134 A8
Felixstowe IP11 ....381 C5
Hornchurch RM11 ....336 F2
Hullbridge SS5 ....301 D3
10 Ipswich IP1 ....17 C6
Walkways SS8 ....363 F5
Wallace Binder Cl CM9 ...236 F1
Wallace Cl SS5 ....301 D3
Wallace Cres CM2 ....254 D8
Wallace Dr SS12 ....321 E5
Wallace Gdns DA10 ....377 E1
Wallace La CM3 ....179 B7
Wallace Rd
1 Colchester CO4 ....109 E2
Grays RM17 ....373 A2
Ipswich IP1 ....16 E8
Wallace's La CM3 ....209 F4
Wallace St SS3 ....368 F7
Wallace Way RM1 ....313 D2
Wallasea Gdns CM1 ......232 F5
WALLASEA ISLAND 305 F2
Wall Chase CM6 ....178 F7
Wall Ct 6 CM7 ....127 F1
WALLEND 352 A4
Wall End Ct E6 ....352 A4
Wall End Rd E6 ....352 A5
Wallenger Ave RM2 ......336 B8
Wallers Cl Dagenham RM9 .353 E4
Woodford IG8 ....310 F4
Waller's Gr IP2 ....16 F4
Waller's Hoppet IG10 .....288 F7
Wallers Way EN11 ....197 B1
Wallflower Ct 11 CM1 ....232 F6
Wallingford Ho 2 RM3 ...314 E4
Wallington Rd IG3 ....333 F4
Wallis Ave SS2 ....347 F2
Wallis Cl RM11 ....336 B3
Wallis Ct Colchester CO3 ..134 E3
Waltham Abbey EN9 ......265 B4
Wallis Pk DA11 ....378 B2
Wall La CO11 ....88 D4
Wall Rd SS8 ....364 F3
WALL'S GREEN 229 B2
Wall St CO16 ....219 D6
Walls The CO11 ....86 E4
Walmer Cl
Brightlingsea CO7 ....192 F7
Chingford E4 ....309 B8
Romford RM7 ....313 B1
Walnut Cl Basildon SS15 ...319 C1
Ilford IG6 ....333 C7
Walnut Cotts CM21 ....172 E3
Walnut Ct SS5 ....324 E7
Walnut Dr
Bishop's Stortford CM23 ...145 D3
Colchester CO4 ....109 D5
Witham CM8 ....184 A4
Walnut Gr Braintree CM7 ...127 E2
Harlow CM20 ....199 B1
Hornchurch RM12 ....336 D3
Walnut Tree Ave CM21 ....172 E4
Walnut Tree Cl EN11 ......221 A6
Walnut Tree Cotts CM3 ...207 E5
Walnut Tree Cres CM21 ...172 E3
Walnut Tree Ho CO3 ......135 B4
Walnuttree Hospl CO10 ....33 D7
Walnut Tree La
Harkstead IP9 ....63 B2
Sudbury CO10 ....33 D7
Walnut Tree Rd
Dagenham RM8 ....334 E2
Erith DA8 ....369 E1
Walnut Tree Way
Colchester CO2 ....135 B3
Tiptree CO5 ....186 C7
Walnut Way
Brightlingsea CO7 ....192 E7
Buckhurst Hill IG9 ....310 D7
Clacton-on-S CO15 ....195 C2
Walnut Wlk CM6 ....123 B1
Walpole Cl RM17 ....373 C2
Walpole Rd E18 ....309 F2
Walpole Wlk SS6 ....324 A2
Walsham Ent Ctr RM17 ...373 C1
Walsingham Cl
7 Basildon SS15 ....341 C7
Great Cornard CO10 ....34 C5
Walsingham Ct IP2 ....37 A8
Walsingham Ho E4 ....287 D2
Walsingham Rd
Colchester CO2 ....135 F6
Southend-on-S SS2 ....348 B2
Walsingham Way CM12 ...297 B5
Walter Hurford Par 5
E12 ....352 A8
Walter Mead Cl CM5 .....249 A4
Walter Porter Ct CO4 .....110 D1
Walter Radcliffe Way
CO7 ....164 C7
Walters Cl Galleywood CM2 254 C3
Southend-on-S SS9 ....346 E6
Walters Yd 6 CO1 ....135 F7
Walter Way CM8 ....156 D4
WALTHAM ABBEY 265 D7
Waltham Abbey★ EN9 .....265 C6
Waltham Cl
1 Brentwood CM13 ......295 C3
Ipswich IP2 ....17 A2
Waltham Cres SS2 ....348 B3
Waltham Ct E17 ....309 C2
Waltham Forest Coll E17 .309 B1
Waltham Glen CM2 ....254 C7
Waltham Holy Cross Inf Sch
EN9 ....265 D6
Waltham Holy Cross Jun Sch
EN9 ....265 D6
Waltham Park Way E17 ...309 A3
Waltham Pk E17 ....309 A2
Waltham Rd Boreham CM3 210 A3
Lower Nazeing EN9 ....244 A6
Rayleigh SS6 ....323 B3
Terling CM3 ....182 A2
Woodford IG8 ....310 E4
Walthams SS13 ....343 B7
Walthams Pl SS13 ....343 B7
Walthamstow Acad E17 ...309 A2
Walthamstow Ave E4 .....309 A3
Walthamstow Ave (North
Circular Rd) E4 ....309 A3
Walthamstow Bsns Ctr
E17 ....309 C1
Waltham Way
Chingford E4 ....287 A1
Frinton-on-S CO13 ....171 A5
WALTON 381 D6
Walton Ave IP11 ....381 A2
Walton Ct Basildon SS15 ...341 C8
Colchester CO4 ....136 F4
Felixstowe IP11 ....381 D6
Hoddesdon EN11 ....221 C8
Walton Gdns
Brentwood CM13 ....295 C4
Waltham Abbey EN9 ......265 B6
Walton Hall Farm Mus★
SS17 ....375 B5
Walton Hall La CM3 ......258 B1
Walton Ho 4 Ipswich IP1 ...17 A6
Walton-on-t-N CO14 .....171 B8
Walton Maritime Mus★
CO14 ....144 D1
Walton-On-Naze Sta
CO14 ....171 C7
WALTON-ON-THE-NAZE 171 D8
Walton-on-the-Naze Prim
Sch CO14 ....144 D1
Walton Rd
Clacton-on-S CO15 ....196 A3
Frinton-on-S CO13 ....170 F6
Hoddesdon EN11 ....221 C8
Kirby-le-S CO13 ....170 E8
Little Ilford E12 ....352 A8
Romford RM5 ....312 F3
Southend-on-S SS1 ....367 F6
Thorpe-le-S CO13, CO16 ...142 D2
Walton-on-t-N CO13, CO14 .171 B7
Walton's Hall Rd SS17 ....375 B5
Wambrook SS3 ....349 D1
Wambrook Cl CM13 ......295 C1
Wamburg Rd SS8 ....364 E4
Wanderer Dr IG11 ....353 C2
Wangey Rd RM6 ....334 D4
Wannock Gdns IG6 ....311 B3
Wansfell Coll CM16 ......267 D4
Wansfell Gdns SS1 ....367 F8
Wansford Cl CM14 ....315 F7
Wansford Rd IG8 ....310 C2
WANSTEAD 332 C5
Wanstead Church Sch
E11 ....332 A6
Wanstead High Sch E11 ..332 C5
Wanstead Hospl E11 ......332 B7
Wanstead Hts 8 E11 .....332 A6
Wanstead La IG1 ....332 E5
Wanstead Park Ave E12 ..332 D2
Wanstead Park Rd
Ilford IG1 ....333 A2
Redbridge IG1 ....332 E3
Wanstead Pl E11 ....332 A6
Wanstead Sta E11 ....332 B5
Wantage Ho 10 RM3 .....314 D4
Wantfield Cotts CM4 .....274 F8
Wantz Chase CM9 ....237 A2
Wantz Cnr CM2 ....276 E5
Wantz Haven CM9 ....237 A2
Wantz La RM13 ....355 B1
Wantz Rd Dagenham RM10 .354 B7
Maldon CM9 ....237 A2
Margaretting CM4 ....275 A8
Wapping La CO7 ....165 B2
Warboys Cres E4 ....309 C5
Warburton Ave CO9 ....75 D8
Warburtons SS17 ....361 A2
Warburton Terr E17 ......309 B1
Ward Ave RM17 ....373 B2
Ward Cl SS15 ....341 D5
Ward Cres CM23 ....145 E6
Warde Chase CO14 ....171 B8
Warden Ave RM5 ....313 C5
Warder Cl CM6 ....123 E1
Ward Gdns RM3 ....314 E1
Ward Hatch CM20 ....200 A3
Wardle Way CM1 ....231 E7
Wardley Cl IP2 ....16 D1
Wardona Ct
Northfleet DA11 ....378 B2
Swanscombe DA10 ....377 F1
Wardour Ct 9 DA2 ....376 B1
Ward Path CM2 ....233 B4
Ward Rd IP8 ....16 B2
Wards Croft CB11 ....43 D7
Wards Rd IG2 ....333 D4
Wareham Ave IP3 ....18 D3
Warehouse Rd CM6 ....124 F4
Warehouse Villas CM6 ....125 A4
Waremead Rd IG2 ....333 B6
Ware Rd EN11 ....197 A1
Warescot Cl CM15 ....294 B2
Warescot Rd CM15 ....294 B2
Wares Rd
Margaret Roding CM1 .....205 E5
Mashbury CM1 ....206 A4
Wargrave Rd CO15 ....195 D4
Warham Rd CO12 ....90 F1
Warish Hall Farm CM24 ...121 D1
WARLEY 316 D5
Warley Ave RM8 ....334 F4
Warley Cl CM7 ....128 C4
Warley Gap CM13 ....316 C3
Warley Hall La RM14 .....338 F4
Warley Hill CM13, CM14 ...316 C5
Warley Hill Bsns Pk The
CM13 ....316 C4
Warley Hospl CM14 ....316 B5
Warley Mount CM14 ......316 C6
Warley Prim Sch CM14 ...316 C5
Warley Rd
Great Warley CM13 ....316 B3
Redbridge IG5 ....311 A2
Romford CM13 ....315 E1
Woodford IG8 ....310 B3
Warley St CM13, RM14 ....338 C5
Warley Way CO13 ....171 B6
Warleywoods Cres CM14 .316 B6
Warlow Cl EN3 ....265 A2
Warminster Ho RM3 ......314 F5
Warner Cl Billericay CM11 ..297 D1
Rayne CM77 ....126 F1
Warner Dr CM7 ....127 D4
Warners CM6 ....150 D8
Warners Bridge Chase
SS4 ....347 F6
Warners Cl IG8 ....310 A5
Warners Gdns SS4 ....347 E6
Warners Mill 13 CM7 .....127 F2
Warner Textile Archive
(Mus)★ CM7 ....127 F2
Warner Way CO10 ....34 A8
Warnham Cl CO16 ....195 B6
Warren Chase SS7 ....345 A4
Warren Cl Broomfield CM1 ..208 B3
Rayleigh SS6 ....345 C8
Stanford-le-H SS17 ....360 D1
Takeley CM22 ....148 D7
Warren Comp Sch The
RM6 ....334 F6
Warren Ct Chigwell IG7 ...311 D6
12 Haverhill CB9 ....8 E7
Warren Dr Basildon SS14 ...342 E6
Hornchurch RM12 ....336 B1
Wickford SS11 ....322 A8
Warren Dr The E11 ....332 C4
Warren Farm Cotts RM6 ..334 F7
Warren Field CM16 ....268 A7
Warren Hastings Ct DA11 .378 F1
WARREN HEATH 18 F1
Warren Heath Ave IP3 .....18 D2
Warren Heath Rd IP3 ......18 D2
Warren Hill IG10 ....288 C4
Warren Hts Grays RM16 ...372 E2
Loughton IG10 ....288 C4
Warren Jun Sch RM6 ......334 F6
Warren La Colchester CO3 ..134 C2
Doddinghurst CM15 ......294 A8
Grays RM16 ....372 D2
Warren Lingley Way CO5 .186 E6
Warren Pond Rd E4 ......287 F2
Warren Prim Sch RM16 ...372 C3
Warren Rd Braintree CM7 ..128 C2
Chingford E4 ....309 C8
Halstead CO9 ....76 D1
Ilford IG6 ....333 D6
Southend-on-S SS9 ....346 A3
South Hanningfield CM3 ...299 D7
Wanstead E11 ....332 C4
Warrenside CM7 ....155 A8
Warrens The
Kirby Cross CO13 ....170 E6
Wickham Bishops CM8 .....212 F5
Warren Terr Grays RM16 ..372 D4
Ilford RM6 ....334 D7
Warren The CM12 ....296 E4
Warriner Ave RM12 ....336 D2
Warrington Gdns RM11 ...336 D5
Warrington Rd
Dagenham RM8 ....334 E2
Ipswich IP1 ....17 B7
Warrington Sq
Billericay CM12 ....296 F3
Dagenham RM8 ....334 D2
Warrior Ho 7 SS1 ....367 A8
Warrior Sq Little Ilford E12 .352 A8
Southend-on-S SS1 ....367 A8
Warrior Sq E SS1 ....367 A8
Warrior Sq N SS1 ....367 A8
Warrior Square Rd SS3 ...368 F5
Warwick Bailey Cl CO4 ...109 D2
Warwick Cl Braintree CM7 .128 B4
Canvey Island SS8 ....364 A5
Hornchurch RM11 ....336 F7
Little Easton CM6 ....122 F5
Maldon CM9 ....237 A1
Rayleigh SS6 ....323 F1
South Benfleet SS7 ....344 D7
Warwick Cres
Clacton-on-S CO15 ....195 E3
Maldon CM9 ....237 A1
Warwick Ct
Brentwood CM13 ....317 B7
Burnham-on-C CM0 ......306 B4
2 Haverhill CB9 ....8 E8
Warwick Dr Maldon CM9 ...237 A1
Rochford SS4 ....347 F7
Warwick Gdns Ilford IG1 ..333 B3
Rayleigh SS6 ....323 F1
Romford RM2 ....336 C8
Warwick Gn SS6 ....324 A1
Warwick La RM13, RM14 ..356 B3
Warwick Par CM3 ....301 D8
Warwick Pl Basildon SS16 .340 F4
Northfleet DA11 ....378 B2
Pilgrims Hatch CM14 ......293 C5
Warwick Rd
Bishop's Stortford CM23 ...146 B6
Chingford E4 ....309 A5
Clacton-on-S CO15 ....195 E3
Ipswich IP4 ....17 E6
Rainham RM13 ....355 D2
Rayleigh SS6 ....323 F1
Rayleigh SS6 ....346 B8
Southend-on-S SS1 ....367 F6
Takeley CM6 ....148 E7
Wanstead E11 ....332 B6
Warwick Sq CM1 ....231 F4
Washall Dr CM77 ....154 D8
WASHBROOK 35 E8
Wash Cnr Aldham CO6 ....107 C3
Ramsey CO12 ....89 E1
Washford Gdns CO15 .....195 D2
Washington Ave SS15 .....341 A6
Washington Cl CM9 ....236 E1
Washington Ct
Colchester CO3 ....134 E5
Maldon CM9 ....236 E1
Washington Rd
Harwich CO12 ....91 A2
Maldon CM9 ....236 F1
2 Woodford E18 ....309 F1
Wash La Clacton-on-S CO15 .195 D1
Goldhanger CM9 ....238 B7
Wash Rd Basildon SS15 ....319 E2
Brentwood CM13 ....295 E4
Wasses Cnr CO16 ....141 D5
Watchfield La SS6 ....323 C1
WATCH HOUSE GREEN 152 E7
Watch House Rd CM6 .....124 F5
Watch House Villas CM6 ..152 D7
Watchouse Rd CM2 ....254 C3
Waterbeach Rd RM9 ......353 C6
Waterdene SS8 ....363 F5
WATER END 24 B6
Waterfall 20 SS1 ....367 C7
Waterfalls The SS16 ......341 B3
Waterfield Cl DA17 ....369 A3
Waterford Rd SS3 ....368 D5
Waterfront Terr CO14 .....144 D1
Waterfront Wlk SS14 .....320 B1
Watergardens The IG8 ...310 A5
Waterglade Ind Pk RM20 ..376 F8
Waterglade Ret Pk CO15 ..195 E2
Waterhale SS1 ....349 A1
Waterhall Ave E4 ....309 E6
Water Hall La CM7 ....100 F6
Waterhouse La
Ardleigh CO7 ....112 B5
Chelmsford CM1 ....231 F1
Waterhouse Moor CM18 ...223 F7
Waterhouse St CM1 ......231 F1
Water La
Bishop's Stortford CM23 ...145 F8
Bures CO8 ....55 E1
Cavendish CO10 ....1 D2
Colchester CO3 ....135 D8
Debden CB11 ....44 B1
Great Easton CM6 ....122 C7
Harlow CM19 ....223 A5
Helions Bumpstead CB9 ....26 D7
Ilford IG3 ....333 F1
Little Horkesley CO6 ....81 E6
Newport CB11 ....43 A1
Pebmarsh CO9 ....78 A7
Purfleet RM19 ....371 A2
Radwinter CB10 ....45 E8
Roydon CM19 ....222 E4
Shalford CM7 ....100 F3
Stansted Mountfitchet
CM24 ....119 E6
Steeple Bumpstead CB9 ....27 B6
Stisted CM77 ....129 C5
Stoke-by-N CO6 ....56 E8
Sturmer CB9 ....9 F5
Water Lane Prim Sch
CM19 ....223 A4
Waterloo Gdns RM7 ......335 E5
Waterloo La CM1 ....232 C2
Waterloo Rd
Brentwood CM14 ....294 C1
Ipswich IP1 ....17 A7
Redbridge IG6 ....311 C1
Romford RM7 ....335 E5
Southend-on-S SS3 ....368 D7
Watermans RM1 ....335 F6
Watermans Way
Greenhithe DA9 ....377 B3
North Weald Bassett CM16 247 A4
Watermark Ct 4 RM6 .....334 B5
Water Mdws Basildon SS13 343 A4
Linford SS17 ....375 A3
Watermill La CM23, CM24 ..119 B5
Watermill Rd CO5 ....158 E4
Waters Edge SS0 ....366 D7
Waters Edge Ct DA8 ......369 F1
Waters Gdns RM10 ....354 A7
Waterside
Brightlingsea CO7 ....192 F5
Southend-on-S SS1 ....367 D6
Stansted Mountfitchet
CM24 ....119 E6
Waterside Bsns Pk CM8 ...184 B4
Waterside Cl Barking IG11 .353 A8
Romford RM3 ....315 A3
Waterside Ind Est EN11 ...221 D5
Waterside La CO2 ....136 D4
Waterside Mead SS8 .....363 F6
Waterside Pl CM22 ....173 A2
Waterside Rd
Bradwell Waterside CM0 ...241 F3
Paglesham Eastend SS4 ...328 A5
Waters Mead SS1 ....368 A6
Watersmeet CM19 ....223 B4
Waterson Rd RM16 ....374 C2
Waterson Vale CM2 ......254 C8
Waters Villas CM22 ....175 A6
Water Tower Rd CM14 ....316 C5
Water Tower Site CM5 ....203 B2
Waterville Dr SS16 ....343 A4
Waterville Mews CO2 .....136 B3
Waterways Bsns Ctr 11
EN3 ....265 A1
Waterwick Hill CB11 ....40 B1
Waterworks Cl CO2 ....161 E3
Waterworks Cotts CO5 ....186 A6
Waterworks Dr CO16 .....195 B5
Waterworks La SS17 ......361 D5
Waterworks Rd CM9 ......216 D2
Waterworks St 6 IP4 ......17 D5
Watery La
Battlesbridge SS11 ....301 C1
Coggeshall CO6 ....130 A1
Great Dunmow CM6 ......150 A2
Manuden CM23 ....92 C1
Matching Green CM17 .....226 D8
Wates Way CM15 ....294 D1
Watford Ho RM3 ....314 F5
Watkin Mews EN3 ....265 A2
Watkins Cl SS13 ....321 D1
Watkins Way SS3 ....349 F1
Watling La CM6 ....69 F3
Watling St CM6 ....70 A3
Watlington Rd
Harlow CM17 ....200 D4
South Benfleet SS7 ....344 B2
Watsham Pl CO7 ....137 C2
Watson Ave E6 ....352 A5
Watson Cl Grays RM20 ....377 A6
Southend-on-S SS3 ....368 D7
Watson Ct 18 CM14 ....316 C7
Watson Gdns RM3 ....314 D1
Watson Rd CO15 ....195 E3
Watson's Cl CB10 ....47 B4
Watsons Lodge 9 RM10 ..354 B6
Watsons Yd 9 CM23 ......145 F8
WATTON'S GREEN 292 B3
Watts Cl CM6 ....151 B4
Watts Cres RM19 ....371 C2
Watts Ct IP4 ....17 D5
Watt's La SS4 ....325 F1
Watts Rd CO2 ....135 B2
Watts Yd CM23 ....93 A2
Wat Tyler Ctry Pk★ SS16 .343 B2
Wat Tyler Way SS16 ......362 B8
Wat Tyler Wlk 1 CO1 .....135 F7
Wavell Ave CO2 ....135 C4
Wavell Cl CM1 ....232 D8
Waveney Dr CM1 ....232 C6
Waveney Rd
Felixstowe IP11 ....381 C3
Ipswich IP1 ....16 E8
Waveney Terr CB9 ....9 A7
Waverley Bridge Ct CM9 ..237 B5
Waverley Cl E18 ....310 C1
Waverley Cres
Romford RM3 ....314 C3
Wickford SS11 ....299 C3
Waverley Gdns
Barking IG11 ....352 E3
Grays RM16 ....373 A4
Ilford IG6 ....311 C1
Redbridge IG6 ....311 C1
Waverley Rd Basildon SS15 319 E1
Rainham RM13 ....355 B2
South Benfleet SS7 ....344 C6
Woodford E18 ....310 C2
Wavertree Rd
South Benfleet SS7 ....344 B4
Woodford E18 ....310 A1
Waving Ave CO13 ....170 E7
Waxwell Rd SS5 ....301 E2
Wayback The CM6 ....22 E2
Way Bank La CO10 ....10 E7
Waycross Rd RM14 ....337 E5
Wayfarer Gdns CM0 ......306 A5
Wayfaring Gn RM17 ......372 F1
Waylands Ct IG1 ....352 D8
Waylands Dr CO16 ....140 E1
Wayletts Basildon SS15 ....341 A8
Southend-on-S SS9 ....346 B6
Wayletts Dr CM23 ....146 B7
Waymans RM15 ....371 D7
Wayre St CM17 ....200 C4
Wayre The CM17 ....200 C4
Wayside CM3 ....256 E8
Wayside Ave RM12 ....336 D2
Wayside Cl RM1 ....335 F8
Wayside Commercial Est
IG11 ....353 A3
Wayside Gdns RM10 .....354 A7
Wayside Mews IG2 ....333 A6
Waytemore Castle★
CM23 ....146 A7
Waytemore Rd CM23 .....145 E6
Weald Bridge Rd CM16 ...225 E2
Weald Cl CM14 ....316 A7
Weald Ctry Pk★ CM14 ....293 E2
Weald Ctry Pk Visitor Ctr★
CM14 ....293 D1
Wealden Ho CM15 ....294 B3
Weald Hall La CM16 ......246 E6
Weald Hall Lane Ind Est
CM16 ....246 C6
Weald Park Way CM14 ....315 F7
Weald Pl CM14 ....316 C8
Weald Rd
South Weald CM14 ....293 C1
South Weald CM14 ....293 F1
Weald The SS8 ....363 E4
Weald Way RM7 ....335 B5
Weale Rd E4 ....309 D7
Wear Dr CM1 ....232 D6
Weare Gifford SS3 ....368 C8
Weathervane Cotts CM7 ...72 B1
Weaver Cl IP1 ....16 D8
Weaverdale SS3 ....349 E1
Weaverhead Cl CM6 ....70 A3
Weaverhead La CM6 ....70 A3
Weavers SS16 ....343 A4
Weavers Cl
2 Billericay CM11 ....297 B2
Braintree CM7 ....127 F3
Colchester CO3 ....134 F5
Weavers Ct Halstead CO9 ...76 E1
Harwich CO12 ....91 D4
6 Sudbury CO10 ....33 E7
Weavers Dr CO10 ....2 B4
Weaversfield CM8 ....156 C5
Weavers Gn CO6 ....107 D6
Weavers Ho 5 E11 ......332 A5
Weavers La CO10 ....33 E7
Weavers Row CO9 ....76 F1
Weaver St CM23 ....145 C4
Weavers Terr 7 CO10 .....33 E7
Webb Cl CM2 ....233 B3
Webber Ho 6 IG11 ....352 B5
Webb Ho 2 RM10 ....335 A1
Webb Rd CM6 ....151 E6
Webbscroft Rd RM10 .....354 B8
Webb St IP2 ....17 C3
Webley Ct EN3 ....265 A2
Webster Cl
Hornchurch RM12 ....336 D1
Sible Hedingham CO9 .....75 D8
Waltham Abbey EN9 ......266 A6
Webster Ct SS6 ....323 D2
Webster Pl CM4 ....275 E2
Webster Rd SS17 ....360 E2
Websters Way SS6 ....323 D2
Weddell Rd CB9 ....9 C6
Wedderburn Rd IG11 .....352 E4
Wedds Way SS3 ....350 B4
Wedgewood Cl CM16 .....246 A1

Wedgewood Dr
4 Colchester CO4 109 E2
Harlow CM17 224 E7
Wedgewood End CM7 72 B2
Wedgwood Ct SS4 325 D6
Wedgwood Way SS4 325 C6
Wedhey CM19 223 C8
Wedlake Cl RM11 336 E3
Wedmore Ave IG5 311 A2
Wednesbury Gdns RM3 314 F3
Wednesbury Gn RM3 314 F3
Wednesbury Rd RM3 314 F3
Wedow Rd CM6 70 A3
WEELEY 140 E1
Weeley By-Pass Rd CO16 140 E1
WEELEY HEATH 168 A5
Weeley Rd
Great Bentley, Aingers Green CO7 166 F5
Great Bentley CO7 166 F8
Little Clacton CO16 168 C4
Weeley Sta CO16 167 F8
Weelkes Cl SS17 360 C3
Weel Rd SS8 364 D2
Weetmans Dr CO4 110 A5
Weggs Willow CO4 136 C7
Weighbridge Ct CB11 43 D8
Weight Rd CM2 232 C2
Weind The CM16 267 E3
WEIR 345 C8
Weirbrook SS7 345 B8
Weir Farm Rd SS6 345 C8
Weir Gdns SS6 323 C1
Weir La CO2, CO5 163 C7
Weir Pond Rd SS4 325 F2
Weir Wynd CM12 297 B1
Welbeck Cl Hockley SS5 324 F5
Trimley St M IP11 381 A7
Welbeck Dr SS16 341 A4
Welbeck Rd SS8 364 B3
Welbeck Rise SS16 341 A4
Welch Cl SS2 348 E2
Welhams Way CO11 86 D8
Welland RM18 375 C2
Welland Ave CM1 231 C5
Welland Rd CM0 306 A6
Wellands CM8 212 E5
Wellands Cl CM8 212 D5
Well Cottage Cl E11 332 C4
Weller Gr CM1 231 E7
Wellesley CM19 223 A3
Wellesley Ho 7 CO3 135 E6
Wellesley Hospl SS2 348 C3
Wellesley Rd
Brentwood CM14 294 C1
Clacton-on-S CO15 195 E4
Colchester CO3 135 E6
Ilford IG1 333 B3
Ipswich IP4 17 F5
Wanstead E11 332 A6
Well Field Halstead CO9 103 F8
Writtle CM1 231 A1
Wellfields IG10 289 A6
Wellfield Way CO13 170 D7
Well-Green Cl CB11 43 E7
Wellhouse Ave CO5 218 E7
Wellingborough Ho RM3 314 F5
Wellingbury SS7 344 C5
Welling Rd RM16 374 D7
Wellington Ave
Chingford E4 309 B8
Hullbridge SS5 323 D8
Southend-on-S SS0 347 B1
Wellington Cl
Braintree CM7 128 C4
Chelmsford CM1 231 D5
Dagenham RM10 354 C5
Wellington Ct Grays RM16 373 B5
5 Ipswich IP1 17 A7
Wellington Dr RM10 354 C5
Wellington Hill IG10 266 B1
Wellington Ho RM2 336 C7
Wellingtonia Ave RM4 313 E7
Wellington Mews CM12 297 A5
Wellington Pas 7 E11 332 A6
Wellington Pl CM14 316 C5
Wellington Prim Sch E4 309 B8
Wellington Rd
Harwich CO12 91 E6
Hockley SS5 302 F1
Maldon CM9 236 F2
North Weald Bassett CM16 247 A4
Rayleigh SS6 323 F4
Tilbury RM18 379 A5
Wanstead E11 332 A6
Wellington St
Brightlingsea CO7 192 F6
4 Colchester CO2 135 E6
Ipswich IP1 17 A7
Wellingtons The CM0 284 D3
Wellington Terr 7 CB9 8 E7
Well La Clare CO10 12 B7
Danbury CM3 256 C7
Easthorpe CO5 160 A6
Galleywood CM2 254 B2
Harlow CM19 199 A1
Harlow CM20 223 A8
Pilgrims Hatch CM15 293 F6
South Ockendon RM16 372 E5
Stock CM4 275 E1
Wellmead IG3 334 A4
Well Mead CM12 319 C7
Wellmeads CM2 254 B8
Wells Ave SS2 347 D6
Wells Cl 4 IP4 17 E6
Wells Ct Chelmsford CM1 232 D5
Great Dunmow CM6 123 C1
6 Romford RM1 335 E5
Wellsfield SS6 323 E4
Wells Gdns
7 Basildon SS14 342 F8
Dagenham RM10 354 B7
Rainham RM13 354 F6
Redbridge IG1 332 E4
Wells Hall Com Prim Sch CO10 34 B4
Wells Hall Rd CO10 34 C4
Wells Ho 4 IG11 353 A5
Well Side CO6 132 E3
Wells Mead CB11 67 D4
Wells Park Sch IG7 311 F6
Wells Prim Sch IG8 310 A6
Wells Rd CO1 136 B8
Well's St 3 CM1 232 A3
Well St CO7 192 E7
Wellstead Gdns SS0 347 B3
Wellstead Rd E6 352 A3
Wellstye Gn SS14 342 E8
Well Terr CM9 237 B5
Wellum Cl 8 CB9 8 E7
Wellwood Rd IG3 334 A4
WELSHWOOD PARK 110 F2
Welshwood Park Rd CO4 110 F2
Welton Way SS4 326 A1
Welwyn Ct CO15 195 D1
Wembley Ave CM3 283 A8
Wendene SS16 342 F4
Wenden Rd CB11 43 B7
WENDENS AMBO 42 E5
Wendon Cl SS4 325 C4
Wendover Ct SS17 360 D1
Wendover Gdns CM13 317 B7
Wendover Way RM12 355 C7
Wendy Cl IP9 63 F7
Wenham Dr SS0 347 E2
Wenham Gdns CM13 295 C3
Wenham La CO7 59 D6
Wenham Rd IP8 35 C7
Wenlock Rd CO16 167 F6
Wenlocks La CM4 272 E6
WENNINGTON 370 E6
Wennington Rd RM13 370 C7
Wensley Ave IG8 310 A3
Wensley Cl RM5 313 A5
Wensleydale Ave IG5 310 E1
Wensley Rd SS7 345 B5
Wentford Ct CB9 8 C8
Wents Cl CO7 139 E1
Wentworth Cl CM3 211 B4
Wentworth Cres CM7 127 F5
Wentworth Ct 5 E4 309 D5
Wentworth Dr
Bishop's Stortford CM23 145 D6
Ipswich IP8 16 C2
Wentworth Ho 6 IG8 311 A3
Wentworth Mdws CM9 236 F2
Wentworth Pl RM16 373 D3
Wentworth Prim Sch CM9 236 F1
Wentworth Rd SS2 348 B3
Wentworth Terr 5 CB9 8 E8
Wentworth Way RM13 355 B2
Werneth Hall Rd
Ilford IG5 333 A8
Redbridge IG5 332 F8
Wesel Ave IP11 381 B3
Wesley Ave CO4 136 C8
Wesley Ct SS1 367 B8
WESLEY END 28 E4
Wesley End Rd CO9 28 D4
Wesley Gdns CM12 296 F5
Wesley Rd SS1 367 B7
Wesley Way IP1 16 F8
Wessem Rd SS8 364 B5
Wessex Cl IG3 333 E5
Wessley Cl CM0 263 E4
West Acre Ct CO3 135 B7
Westall Rd IG10 289 C6
West Area IP1 16 C7
West Ave Althorne CM3 282 E2
Basildon SS16 340 E4
Chelmsford CM1 231 F5
Clacton-on-S CO15 195 E2
Hullbridge SS5 301 C3
Mayland CM3 260 E1
West Bank IG11 352 B4
West Bank Ferry Terminal IP2 17 C2
West Beech Ave SS11 321 E7
West Beech Cl SS11 321 E7
West Beech Mews SS12 321 D7
West Belvedere CM3 256 F7
WEST BERGHOLT 108 D4
Westborough Prim Sch The SS0 347 E2
Westborough Rd SS0 347 D2
WESTBOURNE 16 F7
Westbourne Cl
Hadleigh SS7 345 D5
Hockley SS5 325 A7
Westbourne Ct
1 Haverhill CB9 9 A8
Southend-on-S SS0 347 B2
Westbourne Dr CM14 315 F6
Westbourne Gdns CM12 297 B5
Westbourne Gr
Chelmsford CM2 254 D7
Southend-on-S SS0 347 B3
Westbourne Rd IP1 16 F8
West Bowers Rd CM9 235 C4
Westbury SS4 325 D4
Westbury Cl CO6 133 D5
Westbury Ct
3 Barking IG11 352 D4
1 Buckhurst Hill IG9 310 C8
Frinton-on-S CO13 170 F4
Westbury Dr CM14 316 C8
Westbury Ho SS2 348 C2
Westbury La IG9 310 C8
Westbury Rd Barking IG11 352 D4
Brentwood CM14 316 C8
Buckhurst Hill IG9 288 C1
Great Holland CO13 170 A5
Ilford IG1 333 C2
Ipswich IP4 18 B8
Redbridge IG1 333 A2
Southend-on-S SS2 348 C2
Westbury Rise CM17 224 D7
Westbury Terr RM14 337 E2
West Chase Maldon CM9 236 F3
Mundon CM9 259 E1
West Cl Hoddesdon EN11 221 A8
Rainham RM13 355 B1
Westcliff Ave SS0 366 E7
Westcliff Ct CO15 195 E1
Westcliff Dr SS9 346 D1
Westcliff Gdns SS8 364 E2
Westcliff High Sch for Boys SS0 347 A3
Westcliff High Sch for Girls SS0 347 A3
WESTCLIFF-ON-SEA 366 D8
Westcliff Par SS0 366 E7
Westcliff Park Dr SS0 347 D2
Westcliff Prep Day Sch SS0 366 C8
Westcliff Sta SS0 366 D8
West Cloister CM11 297 B2
Westcott Cl CO16 195 D6
West Cres SS8 363 F4
West Crescent Rd 1 DA12 379 C1
West Croft CM11 297 B1
Westcroft Ct EN10 221 A4
West Ct CM21 172 E3
West Dene Dr RM3 314 D5
West Dock Rd CO12 90 E5
West Dr CM7 73 C3
West End La CO12 91 B1
West End Mews CO3 135 B7
West End Rd Ipswich IP1 17 A5
Tiptree CO5 186 A3
Westerdale CM1 232 D7
Westerfield Ct IP4 17 D7
Westerfield Rd IP4 17 D8
Westergreen Meadow CM7 127 E1
Westerings Bicknacre CM3 256 F2
Purleigh CM3 258 D1
Westerings Prim Sch The SS5 324 E4
Westerings The
Great Baddow CM2 254 F5
Hockley SS5 324 E5
Westerland Ave SS8 364 D3
Westerlings The CM77 155 E6
Western Approaches SS2 347 A7
Western Ave
Brentwood CM14 294 C1
Dagenham RM10 354 D6
Epping CM16 267 F7
Romford RM2 314 C1
Western Cl
Rushmere St A IP4 18 F4
Silver End CM8 156 E3
Western Cross Cl DA9 377 C1
Western Ct 10 RM1 335 E6
Western Espl
Canvey Island SS8 364 B1
Southend-on-S SS0, SS1 366 E7
Western Gdns 3 CM14 316 C8
Western Ho CO5 158 C2
Western La CM8 156 E3
Western Mews CM12 297 A2
Western Prom
Brightlingsea CO7 192 D5
Point Clear B CO16 192 E4
Western Rd
Billericay CM12 297 A2
Brentwood CM14 316 C8
Brightlingsea CO7 192 E6
Burnham-on-C CM0 306 C4
Hadleigh SS7 345 E6
Lower Nazeing EN9 221 E1
Rayleigh SS6 323 B1
Romford RM1 335 F6
Silver End CM8 156 F3
Southend-on-S SS9 346 B1
Western's End CO11 86 D8
Western Terr 1 EN11 197 B1
Western View CM12 296 F1
Westernville Gdns IG2 333 C4
Westfield Basildon SS15 341 A8
Clare CO10 12 A6
Harlow CM18 223 E7
Loughton IG10 288 C4
Westfield Ave CM1 232 A4
Westfield Bglws CM9 259 E1
Westfield Cl
Bishop's Stortford CM23 145 E8
Rayleigh SS6 323 B5
Wickford SS11 321 F8
Westfield Com Prim Sch CB9 9 B7
Westfield Dr CO6 131 A3
Westfield Gdns RM6 334 C5
Westfield Park Dr IG8 310 E4
Westfield Rd
Bishop's Stortford CM23 145 E8
Dagenham RM9 353 F8
3 Hoddesdon EN11 221 A7
West Fields CB11 43 E8
Westfleet Trad Est SS11 321 F6
Westgate Basildon SS14 342 A6
Southend-on-S SS3 368 E6
West Gate 1 Harlow CM20 199 C1
Harlow CM20 223 C8
Westgate Ho 6 SS4 325 F2
Westgate Pk SS14 342 A5
Westgate St IP1 17 C6
West Gn SS7 344 B5
West Gr IG8 310 C5
West Green Cotts CO11 86 A7
WEST HANNINGFIELD 277 B4
West Hanningfield Rd
Great Baddow CM2 255 A3
West Hanningfield CM2 276 E7
West Hatch High Sch IG7 310 F5
West Hayes CM22 174 A3
West Ho IG11 352 B6
Westholme Rd IP1 17 A8
West Hook SS16 340 F4
WEST HORNDON 339 C5
West Horndon Prim Sch CM13 339 D6
West Horndon Sta CM13 339 C5
West House Est CM0 284 D4
West Kent Ave DA11 378 C1
Westlake Ave SS13 343 E6
Westlake Cres CO7 137 A2
Westland Ave RM11 336 E3
Westlands Com Prim Sch CM1 231 E2
Westland View RM16 373 A5
West Lawn
Galleywood CM2 254 C2
Ipswich IP4 18 C8
Westleigh Ave SS9 346 D1
Westleigh Ct
Southend-on-S SS9 346 D1
10 Wanstead E11 332 A6
West Leigh Jun & Inf Schs SS9 346 D2
Westleton Way IP11 381 B5
West Ley CM0 306 C5
West Mill DA11 378 F1
West Mill Gn IP9 60 E6
Westminster Cl IP4 18 B5
Westminster Ct
Clacton-on-S CO15 196 B3
Colchester CO2 136 C4
4 Wanstead E11 332 B5
Westminster Dr
Hockley SS5 324 D6
Southend-on-S SS0 347 B2
Westminster Gdns
Barking IG11 352 E3
Braintree CM7 128 B4
Chingford E4 287 E1
Redbridge IG6 311 D1
Westminster Mans SS0 347 B2
Westmoreland Ave RM11 336 C6
Westmorland Cl
New Mistley CO11 87 B3
Wanstead E12 332 D2
Weston Ave RM20 371 F1
Weston Cl CM13 295 C2
Westone Mans 6 IG11 352 F5
Weston Gn RM9 353 F8
Weston Rd Colchester CO2 136 B4
Dagenham RM9 353 E8
Southend-on-S SS1 367 A7
West Park Ave CM12 297 A3
West Park Cl RM6 334 E6
West Park Cres CM12 297 A2
West Park Dr CM12 297 A2
West Park Hill CM14 316 A7
West Pl CM20 200 A3
West Point Pl SS8 363 C3
West Quay CO7 164 B7
Westray Wlk SS12 322 A5
West Rd
Bishop's Stortford CM23 145 E6
Clacton-on-S CO15 220 H8
Dagenham RM6 334 E5
Halstead CO9 76 E1
Harlow CM20 200 A4
Ipswich IP3 38 E8
Romford RM7 335 D4
Saffron Walden CB11 43 D8
Sawbridgeworth CM21 172 C3
Southend-on-S, Cambridge Town SS3 368 D6
Southend-on-S SS0 347 E1
South Ockendon RM15 357 B2
Stansted Mountfitchet CM24 119 E6
West Ridge CM12 319 A8
Westridge Way CO15 196 A6
Westropps CO10 15 C5
Westrow Dr IG11 353 A7
Westrow Gdns IG3 333 F1
Westside Apartments 7 E12 333 A1
Westside Bsns Ctr CM19 222 F7
Westside Ctr CO3 134 A5
West Sq 2 Harlow CM20 199 C1
Maldon CM9 236 F3
West St Coggeshall CO6 130 E1
Colchester CO2 135 E6
Erith DA8 369 E1
Gravesend DA11 379 B1
Grays RM17 378 A8
Harwich CO12 91 D6
Rochford SS4 325 E2
Rowhedge CO5 163 F8
Southend-on-S, Chalkwell SS9 365 E8
Southend-on-S SS0, SS2 347 E2
Tollesbury CM9 216 C1
Walton-on-t-N CO14 171 C8
Wivenhoe CO7 164 B8
West Station Ind Est CM9 236 E1
West Station Rd CM9 236 E1
West Stockwell St CO1 135 F7
West Thorpe SS16 342 B6
WEST THURROCK 377 D8
West Thurrock Prim Sch RM20 377 A8
West Thurrock Way
Grays RM20 372 B2
Purfleet RM20 371 F2
WEST TILBURY 379 E8
West View Ilford RM6 334 C6
Loughton IG10 288 F6
Takeley CM22 148 C8
West View Cl
Colchester CO4 110 B3
Rainham RM13 355 C2
Westview Dr IG8 310 D1
West View Dr SS6 323 B1
Westward Ho SS1 366 F7
Westward Rd E4 309 A5
Westwater SS7 344 B4
Westway Chelmsford CM1 253 E8
Colchester CO1, CO3 135 E8
South Woodham Ferrers CM3 301 C7
West Way CM14 316 A7
West Wlk CM20 223 C8
Westwood Ave
Brentwood CM14 316 A6
Ipswich IP1 17 A8
West Wood Cl SS7 345 C4
Westwood Ct IP1 17 A7
Westwood Dr CO5 218 E6
Westwood Gdns SS7 345 D5
West Wood Hill CO4 109 B3
Westwood Lodge SS7 345 C5
Westwood Prim Sch SS7 345 D4
Westwood Rd
Canvey Island SS8 364 B3
Ilford IG3 334 A4
West Yd CO9 103 E8
Wetherfield CM24 119 D7
Wetherland SS16 341 F5
Wetherly Cl CM17 200 F4
WETHERSFIELD 73 C3
Wethersfield CE Prim Sch CM7 73 C3
Wethersfield Cl SS6 323 A3
Wethersfield Rd
Blackheath CO2 163 A8
Shalford CM7 100 E8
Sible Hedingham CO9 51 C1
Wethersfield Way SS11 322 B5
Wet La CO4 82 E5
Wetzlar Ct CO2 136 B4
Weybourne Cl SS2 348 B3
Weybourne Gdns SS2 348 B3
Weybridge Wlk SS3 349 E1
Weydale SS17 361 B4
Weyland Dr CO3 134 D4
Weylond Rd RM8 334 F1
Weymarks SS15 341 D7
Weymouth Cl CO15 220 J8
Weymouth Dr RM20 372 D1
Weymouth Rd
Chelmsford CM1 232 E6
Ipswich IP4 17 F6
Whadden Chase CM4 274 A3
Whalebone Ave RM6 334 F5
Whalebone Cnr CO4 83 F7
Whalebone Gr RM6 334 F5
Whalebone La N RM6 334 E8
Whalebone La S RM6, RM8 334 F4
Whaley Rd CO4 136 C7
Wharf Cl SS17 360 D1
Wharfe Cl CM8 183 E2
Wharf Ho DA8 369 E1
Wharf La CO8 79 F8
Wharf Pl CM23 146 A6
Wharf Rd
12 Bishop's Stortford CM23 145 F6
Brentwood CM14 316 C7
Chelmsford CM2 232 C2
Fobbing SS17 361 D3
Gravesend DA12 379 E1
Grays RM17 377 F8
Heybridge Basin CM9 237 F4
Hoddesdon EN10 243 A7
Stanford-le-H SS17 375 E7
Wharf Rd S RM17 377 F8
Wharfside Cl DA8 369 F1
Wharley Hook CM18 224 A5
Wharncliffe Ho 3 DA9 377 B1
Wharton Dr CM1 233 A7
Wheat Croft CM23 145 E4
Wheatear Pl CM11 297 C1
Wheater Ind Est CM8 184 B1
Wheatfield Rd CO3 134 D5
Wheatfields
3 Brentwood CM14 316 C6
Harlow CM17 200 D6
Rochford SS4 326 D4
Wheatfield Way
Basildon SS16 341 A4
Chelmsford CM1 231 F3
Wheatlands Ardleigh CO7 111 E7
Elmstead Market CO7 137 F6
Wheatley Ave CM7 128 C3
Wheatley Cl
Greenhithe DA9 377 A2
Hornchurch RM11 336 D6
Rochford SS4 325 D4
Sawbridgeworth CM21 172 C1
Wheatley Mans 8 IG11 353 A5
Wheatley Rd SS17 361 B4
Wheaton Rd CM8 184 B2
Wheatsheaf Cl CO11 88 D3
Wheatsheaf Ct 14 CO1 136 A6
Wheatsheaf La CO11 88 D3
Wheatsheaf Rd RM1 335 F5
Wheatstone Rd DA8 369 D1
Wheeler Cl Colchester CO4 136 E6
Woodford IG8 310 F5
Wheelers CM16 246 A2
Wheelers Cl EN9 221 F1
Wheelers Cross IG11 352 D3
Wheelers Farm Gdns CM16 247 B5
Wheeler's Hill CM3 208 D6
Wheelers La Fobbing SS17 361 D4
Pilgrims Hatch CM14 293 B6
Wheel Farm Dr RM10 335 C1
Wheelwrights Cl CM23 145 C4
Wheelwrights The
Southend-on-S SS2 348 A5
Trimley St M IP11 381 A8
Whernside Ave SS8 364 C5
Wherry La 15 IP4 17 D5
Wherry Quay IP2 17 D5
WHERSTEAD 37 B6
Wherstead Rd IP2 17 C2
Whieldon Grange CM17 224 E7
Whinchat Cl IP2 16 D3
Whinfield Ave CO12 90 F1
Whinhams Way CM12 296 F3
Whist Ave SS11 299 F1
Whistler Mews 1 RM8 353 B7
Whistler Rise SS3 368 G8
Whitakers Way IG10 288 F8
Whitbread Pl 11 CM14 316 C7
Whitbreads Farm La CM3 180 D4
Whitby Ave CM13 317 D4
Whitby Cl DA9 377 A2
Whitby Rd Ipswich IP4 17 F8
Southminster CM0 284 B2
Whitchurch Rd RM3 314 E6
Whitcroft SS16 341 C3
White Arch Pl CO4 83 B6
WHITEASH GREEN 76 B2
Whitebarn La RM10 354 A4
White Barns CM3 179 B6
Whitebeam Cl
Chelmsford CM2 253 F7
Colchester CO6 109 D5
Whitebeam Dr RM15 357 C2
White Bear CM24 119 E8
White Bridge Jun & Inf Schs The IG10 288 F2
White Caville CB9 8 C8
WHITE COLNE 105 E6
White Cotts CM3 181 E5
White Court Prim Sch CM77 154 C6
White Cross CO11 89 A2
Whiteditch La CB11 42 F2
White Elm Rd CM3 257 A2
White Elm St IP3 17 E4
Whitefield Ct CM3 283 A8
Whitefield Schs E17 309 D1
Whitefriars Cres SS0 366 C8
Whitefriars Way CO3 135 A5
Whitegate Rd
Brightlingsea CO7 193 A6
Southend-on-S SS1 367 A8
Whitegates CM6 97 F4
White Gates RM12 336 C3
Whitegates Cl CM77 154 C6
White Gdns RM10 354 A6
White Hall RM4 290 B6
Whitehall Cl Chigwell IG7 312 A7
Colchester CO2 136 C4
Lower Nazeing EN9 221 E1
Whitehall Cotts SG12 198 D8
Whitehall Ct CM8 184 A2
Whitehall Est CM19 222 E7
Whitehall Gdns E4 287 E1
Whitehall Ind Est CO2 136 D4
Whitehall La
Bishop's Stortford CM23 118 F1
Corringham SS17 361 C6
Grays RM17 373 C1
Thorpe-le-S CO16 141 C3
Woodford IG9 310 A8
Whitehall Lodge IG8 310 A7
Whitehall Prim Sch E4 309 E8
Whitehall Rd
Bishop's Stortford CM23 118 E1
Chingford E4 309 E8
Colchester CO2 136 D4
Grays RM17 373 C2
Woodford IG8 310 A7
White Hall Rd SS3 350 B4
White Hart Cotts CM2 233 A6
Whitehart Ct CO12 91 D6
White Hart La
Brentwood CM14 316 C8
Chelmsford CM1 232 F8
Hockley SS5 324 F5
Romford RM7 313 A1
West Bergholt CO6 108 E5
White Hart Yd DA11 379 B1
Whitehead Cl CM1 253 B8
Whitehills Rd IG10 289 A6
White Horse Ave CO9 103 D8
White Horse Cotts IP9 36 D1
White Horse Hill IP9 36 D1
White Horse La
Maldon CM9 236 F2
Newport CB11 43 A1
Witham CM8 183 F3
White Horse Rd
Capel St M IP9 35 B1
East Bergholt CO7 59 E1
White Ho The IG3 334 A3
White House Chase 1 SS6 323 E1
Whitehouse Cl CO4 83 D4
Whitehouse Cres CM2 254 D8
White House Ct 3 SS6 323 E1
Whitehouse Hill CM9 216 A7
Whitehouse La
Belchamp St P CO10 13 B2
West Bergholt CO6 108 D3
Whitehouse Meadows SS9 347 A6
Whitehouse Mews 2 SS6 323 E1
Whitehouse Rd
Southend-on-S SS9 347 A6
South Woodham Ferrers CM3 301 D8
Stebbing CM6 124 F5
Whitelands CM15 272 D4
Whitelands Cl SS11 299 E1
Whitelands Way RM3 314 D2
White Lodge Cres CO16 142 C1
White Lyons Rd CM14 316 C7
White Mead CM1 208 B2
WHITE NOTLEY 155 E1
White Notley CE Prim Sch CM8 155 F1
White Notley Sta CM8 155 F2
Whitepost Ct CM23 146 A5
White Post Field
Great Dunmow CM6 150 E8
Sawbridgeworth CM21 172 D2
White Rd SS8 363 C3
WHITE ROOTHING OR WHITE RODING 203 C8
Whites Ave IG2 333 E5
Whitesbridge La CM4 253 D1
Whites Cl DA9 377 C1
Whites Field CO7 59 B3
White's Hill CM4 275 F1
Whiteshott SS16 342 A4
Whiteshot Way CB10 22 F2
Whites La CM3 180 E6
Whitesmith Dr CM12 296 E3
White St CM6 150 D8
Whitethorn Cl CO4 136 D6
Whitethorn Gdns
Chelmsford CM2 254 C7
Hornchurch RM11 336 C5
Whitethorn Rd IP3 18 F1
White Tree Ct CM3 301 B6
Whitewaits CM20 199 E1
Whiteways Billericay CM11 297 E3
Canvey Island SS8 364 D2

Whiteways continued
Great Chesterford CB10 3 C2
Southend-on-S SS9 346 F6
Whiteways Ct CM8 183 E3
Whitewell Rd 10 CO2 135 F5
Whitfield Ct IG1 332 F4
Whitfield Link CM2 254 D7
Whitfields SS17 360 F2
Whiting Ave IG11 352 B5
Whitings The IG2 333 E6
Whitland Cl IP2 37 A8
Whitlands CO10 2 B6
Whitley Ct EN11 221 B8
Whitley Rd EN11 221 B8
Whitley's Chase CM7 48 D5
Whitlock Dr CO9 29 F1
Whitmore Ave Grays RM16 373 B6
Romford RM3 314 E1
Whitmore Cl RM16 374 E7
Whitmore Cres CM2 233 B4
Whitmore Ct SS14 342 E8
Whitmore Jun & Inf Sch
SS14 320 E1
Whitmore Way SS14 342 D8
Whitney Ave IG4 332 D7
Whittaker Way CO5 218 B7
Whittingham Ave SS2 348 E2
Whittingstall Rd EN11 221 C8
Whittington Rd CM13 295 D4
Whittington Way CM23 145 F3
Whittle Rd IP2 16 F6
Whitwell Ct SS17 375 C8
Whitworth Cl IP2 16 D2
Whitworth Cres EN3 265 A2
Whybrews
4 Colchester CO4 136 C8
Stanford-le-H SS17 360 F2
Whybridge Cl RM13 354 F4
Whybridge Inf Sch RM13 355 A4
Whybridge Jun Sch RM13 354 F4
Whytes Cotts CO6 133 B8
Whytewaters SS16 342 F4
Whyverne Cl CM1 232 E6
Wick Beech Ave SS11 321 E7
Wick Chase SS2 348 F1
Wick Cres SS12 321 E5
Wick Dr
Wickford, Nevendon
SS12 321 E5
Wickford SS12 321 D7
WICKEN BONHUNT 66 C7
Wicken Rd Arkesden CB11 41 F1
Newport CB11 66 F8
Wickets Way IG6 311 F4
Wick Farm Rd CM0 262 C8
Wickfield Ash CM1 231 D6
Wickfields IG7 311 D4
WICKFORD 321 A5
Wickford Ave SS13 343 B5
Wickford Bsns Pk 6
SS11 322 A5
Wickford CE Inf Sch SS11 321 E8
Wickford Cl RM3 314 F5
Wickford Ct 9 SS13 343 A6
Wickford Dr RM3 314 F5
Wickford Hall SS11 321 F8
Wickford Inf Sch The
SS12 321 C7
Wickford Jun Sch SS12 321 C8
Wickford Mews 7 SS13 343 A6
Wickford Pl 8 SS13 343 A6
Wickford Rd
Southend-on-S SS0 366 E7
South Woodham Ferrers
CM3 301 B8
Wickford Sta SS12 321 C8
Wick Glen CM12 296 F4
Wickham Bishop Rd CM3 211 D4
WICKHAM BISHOPS 212 D5
Wickhambrook Ct IP11 381 A4
Wickham Bsns Pk SS14 320 F2
Wickham Cres
Braintree CM7 128 A2
Chelmsford CM1 231 F6
Wickham Hall La CM8 212 D3
Wickham Pl SS16 342 C5
Wickham Rd Chingford E4 309 C3
Colchester CO3 135 D6
Grays RM16 374 C4
Witham CM8 211 F8
WICKHAM ST PAUL 53 C6
Wickham's Chase CM3 257 C2
Wickhay SS15 341 F5
Wickhay Cotts CM3 234 D5
Wick La Ardleigh CO7 111 B8
Fingringhoe CO5 164 C3
Harwich CO12 91 B2
St Osyth Heath CO7, CO16 167 C3
Wickford SS11 321 E7
Wicklands Rd SG12 198 D8
Wicklow Ave CM1 231 D6
Wicklow Wlk SS3 368 C7
Wickmead Cl SS2 348 E2
Wick Place Farm RM14 359 A8
Wick Rd
Burnham-on-C CM0 306 D4
Colchester CO2 136 D2
Great Bentley CO7 167 B5
Langham CO4 83 F3
Thorington Street CO4, CO6 57 C2
Wicks Cl CM7 127 C4
Wick Terr CO4 83 F3
Widbrook CM15 272 C3
Wid Cl CM13 295 D4
WIDDINGTON 67 E4
Widecombe Cl RM3 314 D2
Widecombe Gdns IG4 332 E7
WIDFORD 253 E6
Widford Chase CM2 253 F7
Widford Cl CM2 253 F7
Widford Gr CM2 253 F7
Widford Ind Est CM1 253 E8
Widford Lodge Sch CM2 253 F7
Widford Park Pl CM2 253 F7
Widford Rd CM2 253 F7
Widgeon Cl IP2 16 F3
Widgeon Pl CO5 158 C2
Widgeons SS13 343 C6
Widleybrook La
Blackmore End CM7 74 A2
Widleybrook La continued
Wethersfield CM7 73 F3
Wid Terr CM15 272 C3
Widworthy Hayes CM13 295 B1
Wigborough Rd
Layer de la H CO2 161 E2
Peldon CO5 189 C5
Wigboro Wick La CO16 193 F2
Wigeon Cl CM77 154 C5
WIGGENS GREEN 8 E1
Wiggins La CM12 318 E6
Wiggin's La CM12 318 E7
Wiggins View CM2 233 B4
Wigham Ho IG11 352 C5
Wigley Bush La CM14 315 E7
Wigmore Cl IP2 16 F1
Wignall St CO11 85 F3
Wigram Rd E11 332 C5
Wigton Rd RM3 314 E6
Wigton Way RM3 314 E6
Wilberforce St IP1 17 A6
Wilbye Cl CO2 135 B4
Wilbye Ho CO3 135 A7
Wild Boar Field CM7 128 D3
Wilde Cl RM18 379 C5
Wilding Rd IP8 16 B1
Wilfred Ave RM13 370 A8
Wilfred St 13 DA11 379 B1
Wilkes Rd CM13 295 D4
Wilkes Way CM6 151 E6
Wilkin Ct Colchester CO3 135 A4
Southend-on-S SS9 346 D2
Wilkin Dr CO5 186 E5
Wilkinson Cl DA1 376 A3
Wilkinson Drop SS7 345 E2
Wilkinson Gr CM77 155 B5
Wilkinson Pl CM3 211 A3
Wilkinsons Mead CM2 233 A4
Willets Pond CO7 59 E1
Willett Rd CO2 135 B3
Willetts Field CB10 47 A3
Willetts Mews EN11 221 A7
William Ash Cl RM9 353 B6
William Bellamy Inf Sch
RM10 335 A2
William Bellamy Jun Sch
RM10 335 A2
William Booth Way IP11 381 B5
William Boys Cl 1 CO4 136 D8
William Cl Romford RM5 313 D2
Wivenhoe CO7 137 C4
William Ct
4 Belvedere DA17 369 A2
Ilford IG6 333 D7
William de Ferrers Sch
CM3 301 E7
William Dr CO15 195 D2
William Edwards Sch & Sports Coll RM16 373 B6
William Ford CE Jun Sch
RM10 354 A5
William Groom Ave CO12 91 A2
William Harris Way
Beerchurch CO2 162 F8
Colchester CO2 135 F1
William Ho 7 IP4 17 D6
William Hunter Way
CM14 316 C8
William Julien Courtauld Hospl CM7 127 E2
William Martin CE Jun & Inf Schs CM18 223 F6
William Paul Housing Trust 3
IP2 17 C4
William Pike Ho 4 RM7 335 D5
William Rd SS13 343 F6
William Read Prim Sch
SS8 363 F3
Williams Dr CM7 127 F4
Williams Gn SS5 301 E3
William Smith Ho 10
DA17 369 A3
Williamson Ho 2 CO1 136 A6
Williamsons Way SS17 360 F5
William Sparrow Ct CO7 137 C2
Williams Rd CM1 208 B1
William St Barking IG11 352 C5
Grays RM17 378 C8
3 Ipswich IP1 17 C6
William's Wlk 8 CO1 135 F7
William Tansley Smith Ho
RM12 336 F2
William Torbitt Prim Sch
IG2 333 F6
William Wood Ho 16 CO10 33 E7
WILLINGALE 228 D3
Willingale Ave SS6 323 A3
Willingale Cl
Brentwood CM13 295 E3
Loughton IG10 289 C7
Woodford IG8 310 C4
Willingale Ct CM16 267 E3
Willingale Rd
Braintree CM7 128 D4
Fyfield CM5 227 F2
Loughton IG10 289 D7
Willingale CM4, CM5 250 E6
Willingales The 9 SS15 341 A6
Willingale Way SS1 349 A1
Willinghall Cl EN9 265 D7
Willingham Way CO4 136 E7
Willis Almshouses CM9 213 B3
Willis Ho 2 E12 333 A1
Willis Rd DA8 369 D2
Willmott Rd SS2 347 D6
Willoughby Ave CO5 218 D6
Willoughby Dr
Chelmsford CM2 232 F2
Rainham RM13 354 E5
Willoughby Rd IP2 17 B4
Willoughby's La CM7 128 C8
Willow Ave
Kirby Cross CO13 170 D6
Seawick CO16 220 B6
Willowbank CM2 254 B3
Willowbrook Prim Sch
CM13 295 D3
Willow Brook Prim Sch
CO4 110 C1
Willow Cl Ardleigh CO7 110 D6
Willow Cl continued
Bishop's Stortford CM23 145 E8
Brentwood CM13 295 B3
Brightlingsea CO7 192 D6
Broomfield CM1 208 B1
Buckhurst Hill IG9 310 D7
Burnham-on-C CM0 306 B6
Canvey Island SS8 363 F3
Doddinghurst CM15 272 D1
Hockley SS5 324 F6
Hornchurch RM12 336 B1
Rayleigh SS6 323 D4
Southend-on-S SS9 346 F6
Sudbury CO10 33 E6
Willow Cotts CM3 279 A6
Willow Cres CM3 211 A3
Willow Ct
8 Dagenham RM8 334 D4
Ilford IG1 352 C7
Willowdale Ctr SS12 321 D8
Willowdene CM15 293 F4
Willow Dene CO9 51 D2
Willowdene Ct CM14 316 C6
Willow Dr SS6 323 C4
Willowfield Basildon SS15 319 C1
Harlow CM18 223 D6
Willow Gn CM4 274 B4
Willow Gr CM3 279 A1
Willow Hall La CO11 115 D8
Willowherb Wlk RM3 314 C3
Willowhill SS17 360 E5
Willow Ho 1 SS13 343 B8
Willow Lo SS7 344 F6
Willow Lodge SS3 368 F8
Willow Mdws CO9 75 E8
Willowmead IG7 312 A7
Willow Mead CM21 172 E2
Willowmeade CM11 298 C5
Willowmere Cvn Pk CO10 34 B2
Willow Par RM14 337 E3
Willow Path EN9 265 E5
Willow Pk Copford CO6 133 E5
Ingatestone CM4 274 D4
Weeley Heath CO16 168 A6
Willow Pl CM17 225 A4
Willow Rd Dagenham RM6 334 E5
Great Dunmow CM6 123 C1
Willow Rise CM8 184 A5
WILLOWS GREEN 153 E4
Willows Prim Sch SS14 342 C8
Willows Prim Sch The IP2 16 F2
Willow St Chingford E4 287 D2
Romford RM7 335 C7
Willows The
13 Basildon SS13 343 C6
Billericay CM11 319 D7
Boreham CM3 233 F8
Chelmsford CM1 232 A2
Colchester CO2 136 A3
Frinton-on-S CO13 170 F5
Grays RM17 378 E8
Great Chesterford CB10 3 D3
1 Loughton IG10 288 D4
South Benfleet SS7 344 B4
Southend-on-S SS1 349 A1
Wallend E12 352 A5
Willow Tree Cl RM4 290 B6
Willow Tree Ct 1 CO4 136 E8
Willow Tree Way CO6 105 B6
Willow Way
Clacton-on-S CO15 220 G7
Halstead CO9 76 D1
Harwich CO12 90 F2
Romford RM3 315 B4
Willow Wlk Canewdon SS4 304 D1
Hadleigh SS7 345 D3
Heybridge CM9 237 C6
Hockley SS5 324 F6
Tiptree CO5 186 C7
Upminster RM14 337 E3
Weeley CO16 167 F8
Will Perrin Ct RM13 355 A4
Will's Ayley La CB10 23 F2
Wills Gn CO5 158 F6
Wills Hill SS17 360 D3
Willum Ho CB10 22 D1
Wilmington Gdns IG11 352 E5
Wilmington Rd CO4 110 C2
Wilmot Gn CM13 316 C4
Wilmot Ho CM13 316 C4
Wilmslow Dr IP2 16 C2
Wilmslowe SS8 364 E5
Wilmslowe Ho 3 RM3 314 E6
Wilnett Ct 4 RM6 334 B4
Wilnett Villas 5 RM6 334 B4
Wilrich Ave SS8 364 D3
Wilshire Ave CM2 232 F3
Wilsman Rd RM15 357 C3
Wilsner SS13 343 C7
Wilson Cl
Bishop's Stortford CM23 145 F5
Stanford-le-H SS17 375 C8
Wivenhoe CO7 137 A2
Wilson Ct
Clacton-on-S CO15 196 B8
Wickford SS12 321 C6
Wilson Marriage Rd CO4 110 C1
Wilson Rd Ipswich IP8 16 B1
Redbridge IG1 332 F4
Southend-on-S SS1 366 F7
Wilson's Cnr CM14, CM15 316 D8
Wilson's Ct CM9 237 B2
Wilson's La CO6 132 E3
Wilthorne Gdns RM10 354 B5
Wilton Cl CM23 146 B7
Wilton Ct 7 IG8 310 A4
Wilton Dr RM5 313 D3
Wilton Ho CO16 195 C5
Wiltshire Ave RM11 336 F7
Wiltshire Ct IG1 352 C6
Wimarc Cres SS6 323 B4
WIMBISH 45 C6
Wimbish Ct SS13 343 B6
Wimbish End SS13 343 B6
WIMBISH GREEN 45 E3
Wimbish Mews SS13 343 B6
Wimbish Prim Sch CB10 45 C4
Wimbish Wlk CB10 44 E2
Wimborne Ave IP3 18 E4
Wimborne Cl
Buckhurst Hill IG9 310 C8
Sawbridgeworth CM21 172 D2
Wimborne Rd SS2 348 B1
Wimbourne SS15 341 A7
Wimbourne Gdns CO13 170 F7
Wimbourne Ho CO12 91 D3
Wimhurst Cl SS5 324 E7
Wimpole Cl IP5 18 F6
Wimpole Rd CO1 136 B5
Wimsey Ct CM8 184 A5
Winbrook Cl SS6 345 E8
Winbrook Rd SS6 345 E8
Wincanton Gdns
Ilford IG6 333 B8
Redbridge IG6 311 B1
Wincanton Rd RM3 314 D7
Wincelow Hall Rd CB10 25 E2
Winchcombe Cl SS9 346 E3
Winchelsea Dr CM2 254 E7
Winchelsea Pl CO7 192 F8
Winchester Ave RM14 337 F2
Winchester Cl
Bishop's Stortford CM23 145 D4
Southend-on-S SS9 346 F7
8 Waltham Abbey EN9 265 B6
Winchester Ct
9 Belvedere DA17 369 A1
Frinton-on-S CO13 171 A5
Winchester Dr SS6 323 B6
Winchester Gdns SS15 319 C1
Winchester Ho 5 IG11 353 A5
Winchester Rd
Chingford E4 309 C3
Colchester CO2 136 B5
Frinton-on-S CO13 171 A5
Ilford IG1 333 D1
Winchester Way IP2 36 F8
Winckford Cl CM3 208 B6
Wincoat Cl SS7 344 C3
Wincoat Dr SS7 344 C3
Windermere Ave
Hornchurch RM12 355 A8
Hullbridge SS5 301 D2
Windermere Cl IP3 38 B8
Windermere Ct CO15 196 A3
Windermere Dr CM77 154 C6
Windermere Gdns IG4 332 E6
Windermere Rd
Clacton-on-S CO15 196 C6
Great Notley CM77 154 C7
South Benfleet SS7 344 E7
Southend-on-S SS1 367 C8
Sudbury CO10 34 A8
Windham Rd CO10 34 B8
Windhill CM23 145 E7
Wind Hill CM5 226 A4
Windhill Old Rd CM23 145 E7
Windhill Prim Sch CM23 145 E6
Winding Piece IP9 35 A1
Winding Way RM8 334 C1
Windley Tye CM1 231 E3
Windmill Cl Boxted CO4 82 F4
Great Dunmow CM6 123 E1
Ramsey CO12 89 F1
Stansted Mountfitchet
CM24 119 E7
Upminster RM14 337 A2
Waltham Abbey EN9 265 E5
Windmill Ct
Clacton-on-S CO15 195 F5
Colchester CO4 109 E4
Copford CO6 133 D4
Windmill Fields
Coggeshall CO6 130 F3
Harlow CM17 200 F4
Windmill Gdns CM7 128 A8
Windmill Hill CB10, CB11 22 B3
Windmill Hts CM12 319 B8
Windmill Mdws CM6 176 C2
Windmill Pk CO15 195 F5
Windmill Pl CO10 2 E7
Windmill Rd Bradfield CO11 87 C1
Halstead CO9 76 D1
Windmill Row CO10 2 C5
Windmills CO6 106 C1
Windmill St DA12 379 B1
Windmills The CM1 208 B3
Windmill Stps 6 SS1 367 C7
Windmill The CM24 119 D6
Windmill View CO5 186 C6
Windmill Way CM15 271 E2
Windrush Ct DA8 369 E1
Windrush Dr CM1 232 C6
Windsor Ave
Clacton-on-S CO15 195 D3
Corringham SS17 361 A4
Grays RM16 373 B4
Windsor Cl
Canvey Island SS8 364 B3
Colchester CO2 136 A2
Southend-on-S SS9 346 E3
Witham CM8 211 F8
Windsor Ct
1 Braintree CM7 128 B2
Brightlingsea CO7 192 F6
6 Colchester CO1 136 C6
Windsor Gdns
Bishop's Stortford CM23 145 C7
Braintree CM7 128 B4
Hadleigh SS7 345 C4
Hockley SS5 325 B4
Wickford SS11 299 D1
Windsor Ho CO5 218 D7
Windsor Mews SS6 323 C1
Windsor Pl CO10 34 A7
Windsor Rd
Basildon SS13, CM11 343 E8
Chingford E4 309 B6
Clacton-on-S CO15 195 D3
Dagenham RM8 334 E1
Felixstowe IP11 381 C3
Hornchurch RM11 336 C4
Ilford IG1 352 C8
Ipswich IP1 16 F7
Pilgrims Hatch CM15 294 B3
Ramsden Heath CM11 298 D4
Southend-on-S SS0 347 E1
Wanstead E11 332 A2
West Mersea CO5 218 D7
Windsors The IG9 310 E8
Windsor Terr CB9 8 E8
Windsor Trad Est CM11 298 D4
Windsor View CO9 53 C6
Windsor Way
Chelmsford CM1 231 E1
Rayleigh SS6 323 E1
Windsor Wood EN9 265 F6
Windward Way CM3 301 F6
Windy Hill CM13 295 C1
Winfields SS13 343 C7
Winfield Terr CO14 144 D2
Winford Dr EN10 221 A1
Winfrith Rd IP3 18 D4
Wingate Cl CM7 127 E5
Wingate Ho 6 IP1 17 A7
Wingate Rd IG1 352 B7
Wingfield RM17 372 F1
Wingfield Cl CM13 317 A7
Wingfield Dr RM16 374 A8
Wingfield Gdns RM14 337 E5
Wingfield St IP4 17 D5
Wingletye La RM11 337 A5
Wingrave Cres CM14 315 E6
Wingrave Ct CM14 315 E6
Wingrove Ct CM1 232 A6
Wingrove Dr 6 RM19 371 B1
Wingrove Ho E4 287 B2
Wingway CM14 294 C1
Winifred Ave RM12 355 E8
Winifred Rd Basildon SS13 343 B6
Dagenham RM8 334 E3
Erith DA8 369 E1
Winmill Rd RM8 334 F1
Winn Bridge Cl IG8 310 D2
Winningales Ct IG5 332 E8
Winnock Rd CO1 136 A6
Winnocks 5 CO1 136 A6
Winnock's Almshouses 4
CO1 136 A6
Winnowers Ct 1 SS4 325 F1
Winns Ave E17 309 A1
Winns Terr E17 309 A1
Winsbeach E17 309 D1
Winsey Chase CM7 72 C6
Winsford Gdns SS0 347 A4
Winsford Way CM2 233 C6
Winsgate Ho 6 IP1 17 A7
Winsley Rd CO1 136 B6
Winsley Sq CO1 136 B4
Winslow Gr E4 309 E8
Winstanley Rd CB11 43 E7
Winstanley Way SS14 342 A8
Winstead Gdns RM10 354 C7
Winston Ave
Colchester CO3 135 B4
Ipswich IP4 18 C8
Tiptree CO5 186 E5
Winston Cl Braintree CM7 127 E6
Felixstowe IP11 381 B5
Greenhithe DA9 376 F1
Romford RM7 335 B7
Winston Ct CO13 170 F4
Winston Way Halstead CO9 77 A3
Ilford IG1 333 B1
Winstree SS13 343 B8
Winstree Cl CO2 161 F5
Winstree Ct CO3 134 C4
Winstree Rd
Burnham-on-C CM0 306 B5
Colchester CO3 134 D5
Winterbourne Rd RM8 334 C2
Winterbournes CO14 171 A7
Winter Folly SS15 341 E5
WINTER GARDENS 363 E6
Winter Gardens Jun & Inf Schs SS8 364 A5
Winter Gardens Path SS8 363 E7
Winterscroft Rd 5 EN11 221 A7
Winter's Ct E4 309 B7
Winter's Hill CO2 160 F1
Winter's Rd CO5 160 E1
Winters Way EN9 266 A6
Winterswyk Ave SS8 364 E3
Winton Ave
Southend-on-S SS0 366 E7
Wickford SS12 321 A8
Winton Lodge SS0 347 C1
Wiscombe Hill SS16 341 C3
Wisdoms Gn CO6 131 B3
Wisdons Cl RM10 335 B3
Wisemans Gdns CM21 172 C1
Wissants CM19 223 C4
WISSINGTON 81 D7
Wistaria Cl CM15 294 B4
Wistaria Pl CO16 195 C5
Wisteria Cl IG1 352 B7
Wisteria Ct 3 CO4 136 E7
Wisteria Lodge 7 CM1 232 F6
Wiston Rd CO6 81 D8
Witchards SS16 342 B5
Witch Elm CO12 90 F2
Witch La CO6 131 B8
Witchtree La CB10 25 F3
WITHAM 183 E4
Witham Cl IG10 288 E3
Witham Gdns CM13 339 D5
Witham Lodge CM8 211 D7
Witham Rd
Black Notley CM77, CM8 155 B5
Cressing CM77 156 B3
Dagenham RM10 354 A7
Langford CM9 236 D7
Romford RM2 336 B6
Terling CM3 182 E2
Tolleshunt Major CM9 214 D5
Wickham Bishops CM8 212 E6
Witham Sta CM8 184 A3
Witherings The RM11 336 F6
WITHERMARSH GREEN 57 C7
Withersfield Rd CB9 8 F8
Withipoll St IP4 17 D6
Withrick Wlk CO16 194 A5
Withy Mead E4 309 D7
Withypool SS3 349 D1
Withywindle The CM3 301 C6
Witney Cl IP3 38 D8
Witney Rd CM0 306 C4
Wittem Rd SS8 364 B5
Wittenham Way E4 309 D7
Witterings The SS8 364 A5
Wittering Wlk RM12 355 C6
Witting Cl CO16 195 D5
Witton Wood Rd CO13 170 E5
WIVENHOE 137 C2
Wivenhoe Bsns Ctr CO7 164 C8
Wivenhoe Cross CO7 137 C2
WIVENHOE PARK 137 A4
Wivenhoe Rd
Alresford CO7 165 B7
Barking IG11 353 B3
Colchester CO7 111 C1
Wivenhoe Sta CO7 164 B8
WIX 115 C5
Wix and Wrabness Prim Sch
CO11 115 B5
Wix By-Pass CO11 115 C6
WIX GREEN 115 D5
Wix Rd Beaumont CO16 141 E8
Bradfield CO11 87 E1
Dagenham RM9 353 D4
Great Oakley CO12 116 B3
Ramsey CO12 89 F1
Tendring CO11 114 F8
Wix CO11 115 C3
Woburn Ave
Bishop's Stortford CM23 145 C7
Hornchurch RM12 355 A8
Kirby Cross CO13 170 D7
Theydon Bois CM16 267 E2
Woburn Ct
Chelmsford CM2 232 A1
Hornchurch RM12 355 A8
8 Woodford E18 310 A1
Woburn Ho CM16 267 E2
Woburn Pl CM12 296 F5
Wodehouse Rd DA1 376 A3
Woden Ave CO3 134 D4
Wokindon Rd RM16 374 B3
Wolfe Ave CO1, CO2 136 A5
Wollaston Cres SS13 321 D2
Wollaston Way SS13 321 D2
Wolmers Hey CM3 207 F7
Wolseley Ave CO15 220 E6
Wolseley Rd
Chelmsford CM2 232 A1
Romford RM7 335 D4
Wolsey Art Gall* IP4 17 D6
Wolsey Ave E6 352 A2
Wolsey Ct IP11 381 E3
Wolsey Gdns
Felixstowe IP11 381 E3
Redbridge IG6 311 C4
Wolsey St 9 IP1 17 C5
Wolton Rd CO2 135 B2
Wolverton Ho 1 RM3 314 E5
Wolves Hall La CO16 114 F1
Wonston Rd CM0 284 C4
Wood Ave Hockley SS5 324 E8
Purfleet RM19 371 C2
Wood Barn La CO11 85 D1
Woodberry Cl
Canvey Island SS8 364 A6
Southend-on-S SS9 346 C5
Woodberry Down CM16 246 A3
Woodberry Rd SS11 322 A6
Woodberry Way
Chingford E4 287 C2
Walton-on-t-N CO14 171 C7
Woodbine Cl CM19 223 C6
Woodbine Close Pk EN9 266 C4
Woodbine Pl E11 332 A5
Woodbridge Cl RM3 314 D6
Woodbridge Ct IG8 310 E3
Woodbridge Gr CO16 195 A4
Woodbridge High Sch
IG8 310 B3
Woodbridge La RM3 314 D6
Woodbridge Rd
Barking IG11 352 F7
Ipswich, California IP5 18 B7
Ipswich IP4 17 E6
Rushmere St A IP5 18 E7
Woodbridge Rd E IP4 18 D7
Woodbrook Cres CM12 296 F3
Woodbrooke Way SS17 361 B4
Woodbrook Gdns EN9 265 E6
Woodburn Cl SS7 345 B4
Woodbury Cl E11 332 B7
Woodbury Hill IG10 288 E7
Wood Cnr
Fordham Heath CO6 107 F1
Maldon CM9 236 B2
Woodcock Cl
Colchester CO4 136 E6
Haverhill CB9 9 C7
Woodcock Rd IP2 16 E2
Woodcote App SS7 344 B7
Woodcote Ave RM12 355 A8
Woodcote Cres 7 SS13 343 C6
Woodcote Mews IG10 288 D2
Woodcote Rd
Southend-on-S SS9 347 A2
Wanstead E11 332 A4
Woodcotes SS3 349 E1
Woodcote Way SS7 344 B7
Woodcroft CM18 223 D6
Woodcroft Ave SG12 197 E4
Woodcroft Cl SS7 345 C4
Woodcutters CM0 306 B8
Woodcutters Ave
Grays RM16 373 C4
Southend-on-S SS9 346 D5
Woodcutters Cl RM11 336 D7
Wood Dale CM2 254 E6
Woodedge Cl E4 287 F1
WOODEND 203 D1
Wood End Hockley SS5 324 D5
Widdington CB11 67 D3
Woodend Cl SS7 345 C4
WOODEND GREEN 95 A6
Woodend Rd E17 309 C1
Wood Farm Cl SS9 346 D4
Woodfield 5 SS12 321 D6
Woodfield Cl
Stansted Mountfitchet
CM24 119 E6